PC
5365
E48
1982

Y0-AVX-819

3 0000 001 247 232

DATE DUE

Demco, Inc. 38-293

WITHDRAWN

Encyclopedic
Handbook
of
Alcoholism

E. MANSELL PATTISON and EDWARD KAUFMAN

Editors

Encyclopedic Handbook of ALCOHOLISM

GARDNER PRESS, NEW YORK

ENCYCLOPEDIC HANDBOOK OF ALCOHOLISM

Copyright © 1982 by Gardner Press, Inc.

All rights reserved

No part of this book may be reproduced in any form,
by photostat, microform, retrieval system,
or by any means now known or later devised,
without prior written permission of the publisher.

Gardner Press, Inc.
19 Union Square West
New York 10003

LIBRARY OF CONGRESS CATALOGING IN PUBLICATION DATA

Main entry under title:

Encyclopedic handbook of alcoholism.

   Includes bibliographies and index.
   1. Alcoholism. I. Pattison, E. Mansell,
1933–   II. Kaufman, Edward. [DNLM:
1. Alcoholism. WM 274 E56]
RC565.E48   362.2'92   81-24196
ISBN 0-89867-017-8   AACR2

Printed in the United States of America

Design by Publishers Creative Services, New York

Photocomposition by Bytheway Typesetting Services, Norwich, New York

Printing by Noble Offset Printers, New York 10003

PREFACE

THIS BOOK DEVELOPED out of our attempts to organize the field of alcoholism into a coherent perspective. But the field is so unwieldy that this volume is less comprehensive than representative. We have tried to fit the main components of the field into an admittedly Procrustean bed of limitations of one volume with a breadth and depth of detail that can sustain reasonably general relevance to the wide diversity of alcoholism personnel.

The field is too fluid and inchoate to warrant the certainty of consensus needed for a textbook. A pure encyclopedia that would be comprehensive would either be so vast that many volumes would be required, or contain such summary information as to be cursory. A handbook of detailed, in-depth review and analysis would be impossible in one volume, would be too specialized to be generally useful, and would be highly uneven in quality even as the field is uneven.

Therefore, we arrived at our Procrustean bed of compromise — an encyclopedic handbook in one volume. We have constructed neither fish nor fowl, but some type of elephant book. All the parts belong to the animal, but it may be a genre sui generis. We have projected an encyclopedic sense of the field, and presented in a limited version of handbook the precision of analysis. We have sacrificed both depth and breadth, but we hope to have gained a reasonable perspective on the field as a whole.

We wish to acknowledge our profound appreciation to our many helpers: to Gardner Spungin, our publisher, whose unflagging support made the project possible, to Barbara Krohn, our project assistant, who graciously coped with the massive detail, to Jean Blackburn our production editor, who brought style and precision to our rough efforts, to our faithful administrative assistants, Kathryn Anderson and Leo Mailman, and finally, to our 117 authors, whose qualities are self-evident.

To all we simply say thank you for the opportunity and pleasure to work with you.

E. Mansell Pattison, MD
Edward Kaufman, MD

CONTENTS

Preface v
Alphabetical Guide to Chapters by Subject xix
Contributors xxiii
Prologue: Purpose, Concept, and Plan xxvii

SECTION I: THE DEFINITION AND DIAGNOSIS OF ALCOHOLISM

1. **The Alcoholism Syndrome: Definitions and Models** 3
   E. Mansell Pattison and Edward Kaufman

   The goals of diagnosis • The focus of diagnosis • Types of diagnosis • Methods of diagnosis • 'Definitions and diagnosis • Conclusions • Toward a model of the multivariate alcoholism syndrome • Summary • References

2. **The Concept of Alcoholism: Assumptions and Issues** 31
   William P. Rohan

   The concept of the "ghost in the machine" • Focus on objective description of drinking and consequences • Differences among drinkers • Connection of drinking and consequences • Variety in drinking sequences • Role of environment • Detailed analysis of drinking behavior • Causes and explanations of drinking behavior • The diagnosis of alcoholism • Unnecessary distinctions • Alcoholisms: Multiplying an error • Summary • References

3. **The Diagnosis of Alcoholism after DSM-III** 40
   Lee N. Robins

   General scheme of DSM-III regarding alcohol abuse and dependence • Diagnostic criteria • Roots of DSM-III diagnosis of alcohol dependence • How DSM-III diagnostic criteria were constructed • Remaining problems • Reliability and scalability of alcohol diagnoses • References

Contents

4. **Diagnostic Psychological Testing** 55
   Wilma J. Knox

   Rationale for standardized psychological tests • Detoxification prior to testing • Psychological tests • Concomitant diagnostic problems • Populations including alcoholics • Institutional contacts • Summary • References

5. **Blood Alcohol Level Discrimination and Diagnosis** ... 64
   Peter E. Nathan

   BAL discrimination by alcoholics • BAL discrimination by social drinkers • BAL discrimination: Comparisons • The role of tolerance • Summary • References

6. **Measurement of Alcohol Consumption** 72
   David J. Armor and J. Michael Polich

   Approach • Using consumption measures • References

SECTION II: THE BIOLOGY OF ALCOHOLISM

7. **Biochemistry of Alcohol and Alcohol Metabolism** 83
   Sujata Tewari and Virginia G. Carson

   Metabolism of ethanol • Tolerance and physical dependence • Perinatal effects of ethanol • Ethanol and cancer • References

8. **Neurophysiological Effects of Alcohol** 105
   Kenneth Blum

   Membrane-receptor effects of alcohol • Brain-neurotransmitter receptor-effector coupling effects of ethanol • The cyclic nucleotide model of alcohol tolerance and dependence • Neuropathological actions of alcohol • Addiction: A unified concept • Involvement of peptidyl opiates in the actions of alcohol • The psychogenetic theory of alcohol-seeking behavior • Effects of neuropharmacologic agents on acute and chronic actions of ethanol and opiates • Unified theory: Interpretations and speculations • Conclusion • References

9. **Genetic Factors in Alcoholism Predisposition** 135
   Robin M. Murray and James R. Stabenau

   Family studies • How might such an influence be transmitted? • Pharmacogenetics • Conclusions • References

SECTION III: MEDICAL ASPECTS OF ALCOHOLISM

10. **Alcohol Withdrawal and Delirium Tremens** 147
    Edward M. Sellers and Harold Kalant

    Pathophysiology • Major and minor withdrawal • Protracted alcohol withdrawal reaction • Treatment • Conclusions • References

11. **The Chronic Neuropsychiatric Disorders Associated with Alcoholism** 167
    Joseph P. McEvoy

    The direct effects of alcohol on the brain • The effects of malnutrition accompanying alcoholism • The effects of medical/surgical disorders associated with alcoholism • Overview • References

12. **Alcohol and the Sleep Disorders** 180
    Ernest L. Hartmann

    Effect of alcohol on sleep in nonalcoholics • The sleep of alcoholics • The sleep disorders • Effect of alcohol on the sleep disorders • References

13. **Peripheral and Autonomic Nervous System** 194
    Richard F. Mayer and Ramesh K. Khurana

Peripheral nervous system • Autonomic nervous system • References

14. **Myopathy in the Chronic Alcoholic** 204
    Evan R. Ferguson and James P. Knochel

    Possible causes of alcoholic myopathy • Conclusions • References

15. **The Skeletal System: Alcohol as a Factor** 215
    Floyd E. Bliven, Jr.

    Injury and fractures • Limb compression syndrome • Osteopenia • Nontraumatic idiopathic osteonecrosis of the femoral head • References

16. **Liver and Pancreas** 225
    Mark A. Korsten and Charles S. Lieber

    Liver • Pancreas • References

17. **Effects of Alcohol on the Gastrointestinal Tract** 245
    Esteban Mezey

    Absorption and metabolism of ethanol by the gastrointestinal tract • Alcohol and the esophagus • Alcohol and the stomach • Alcoholism and the small intestine • Summary • References

18. **Malnutrition in the Alcoholic and Related Nutritional Deficiencies** 255
    Elaine B. Feldman

    Etiology • Manifestations • Nutritional management of the alcoholic • Summary and conclusions • References

19. **Infectious Diseases and the Alcoholic** 263
    William H. Chew, Jr. and J. Peter Rissing

    Effects of acute alcohol ingestion/intoxication • Effects of alcoholic life style • Effects of alcoholic liver disease • References

20. **Skin Diseases Associated with Alcoholism** 275
    Charles L. Whitfield

    Conditions often peculiar to alcoholics • Conditions not peculiar to alcoholics • Rare skin conditions in alcoholics • References

21. **Effects of Alcohol on the Hematopoietic System** 281
    I. Chanarin

    The macrocytosis of alcoholism • The bone marrow in alcoholics • White blood cells in alcoholics • Megaloblastic anemia in alcoholics • Sideroblastic anemia in alcoholics • Hemolytic anemia in alcoholics • Some relevant metabolic disorders in alcoholics • Effect of alcohol in volunteers and effect of its withdrawal • Alcohol and hemostasis • References

22. **Alcohol Effects on the Reproductive Function** 293
    Hossam E. Fadel and Hamid A. Hadi

    Effect of ethanol on male gonads and hormones • Effect of alcohol on female reproduction • References

23. **Effects of Alcohol on the Fetus** .. 301
    Henry L. Rosett and Lyn Weiner

    Diagnosis of the fetal alcohol syndrome • Animal models • The maternal-placental-fetal system • Associated risk factors • Prospective studies • Prevention of adverse effects • References

24. **Endocrine Disturbances Associated with Alcohol and Alcoholism** 311
    Peter E. Stokes

    Hypothalamic-pituitary-adrenocortical activity • Summary of animal and human studies: Adrenal cortex • Thyroid function • Growth hormone • Prolactin • Gonadotrophins and sex steroids • Vasopressin • Summary • References

25. **The Respiratory System and Specifics of Alcoholism** 325
   Harold A. Lyons

   Alterations in systemic and pulmonary circulation • Respiratory infections • Other respiratory consequences of alcohol abuse • Summary • References

26. **Effects of Alcohol Ingestion on the Cardiovascular System** ... 332
   David H. Knott and James D. Beard

   Alcohol and circulatory disease: Morbidity and mortality • Effect of alcohol on the central circulation: Physiological considerations • Effect of alcohol on the central circulation: Pathophysiological considerations • Effect of alcohol on the peripheral circulation: Physiological considerations • Effect of alcohol on the peripheral circulation: Pathophysiological considerations • References

27. **Trauma, Surgery, and Anesthesia** 343
   Albert B. Lowenfels

   Alcoholism and trauma • Surgery and the alcoholic patient • Anesthesia • References

28. **The Clinical Pharmacology and Drug Interactions of Ethanol** 354
   Stanley E. Gitlow

   Ethanol and comparative drugs: Physiologic effects • The withdrawal syndrome: Ethanol-specific physiologic responses • Tolerance as a function of age • Ethanol and brain injury • Alcoholism and hypertension • References

SECTION IV: SOCIAL DIMENSIONS OF ALCOHOLISM

29. **Sociological Models for Understanding Deviant Drinking Behavior** 367
   Paul M. Roman

   Sociologists' influence on alcoholism definitions • Theoretical approaches • Impediments to a theoretical model • Toward a role theory of episodic drinking • References

30. **Alcohol and Criminality** 383
   M. Douglas Anglin

   Definitions • Alcohol-crime research • Theoretical models of the alcohol-crime relationship • Conclusions • References

31. **Alcohol and Highway Safety** 395
   Patricia F. Waller

   The drinking driver • Countermeasures • Conclusion • References

32. **Legal Issues of Alcoholism** 406
   Jonas R. Rappeport and Nicholas V. Conti

   Insanity versus voluntary and involuntary intoxication • Alcoholism as a disease • Legal ramifications of intoxication and criminal behavior • Summary • References

33. **Alcohol and Economics** 415
   Esa Osterberg

   Consumption of alcoholic beverages • Production and trade • Alcohol problems • Alcohol control • Summary • References

34. **Sociocultural Variants in Alcoholism** 426
   Dwight B. Heath

   Introduction • Why sociocultural variants are important • The nature and rate of drinking problems • Implications for diagnosis and treatment • Prospects for education and prevention • Conclusions • References

35. **The Epidemiology of Alcoholism and Its Implications** 441
   Harold A. Mulford

   The state of the art • A different approach • Official versus valid knowledge • Discussion • References

Contents

36. Alcoholism: Perspectives on Prevention Strategies 458
David Robinson

The problem is alcoholics • The problem is society • The problem is alcohol • A coordinated approach • References

37. Preventing Alcohol-Related Problems and Dependencies through Information and Education Programs 468
Wallace Mandell

Goals for information and education programs • Current state of public knowledge and attitudes about alcohol use, problems, and dependence • Classroom education • Public information campaigns • Advertising counteracting information efforts • Summary • References

38. Safe and Healthy Drinking 483
Morris E. Chafetz

Caveat • Physical factors • Psychological factors • Social factors • Alcohol education • Summary • References

39. Alcohol Use: Social Policy 490
E. Mansell Pattison

Definitions and classifications • Implications of definitions and classifications for social policy • Social perceptions as determinants of public policy • Implications of social perceptions for social policy • Relevance of biological determinants to social policy • Implications of biological determinants for social policy • Relevance of psychological determinants to social policy • Implications of psychological determinants for social policy • Relevance of sociocultural determinants to social policy • Distribution patterns of alcohol use • implications of distribution patterns for social policy • Toward social policy • Conclusions and summary • References

SECTION V: PSYCHOLOGICAL PERSPECTIVES ON ALCOHOLISM

40. Alcoholic Addiction: Psychological Tests and Measurements 517
Charles Neuringer

A note of caution • Major psychological tests • Diagnostic identification of the alcoholic • Personality characteristics • Future research strategies • References

41. A Psychological Perspective on Development of Alcoholism 529
Herbert Barry III

Predrinking social environment • Predrinking behavior • Early drinking behavior • Progression to alcoholism • Three types of alcoholism • Conclusions • References

42. Experimental Psychology and Alcoholism: Assessment, Contribution, and Impact 540
Ralph E. Tarter

The causes of alcoholism • The consequences of alcoholism • Toward an integrative approach • Summary • References

43. Behavioral Psychology Approaches to Alcoholism 560
G. Alan Marlatt and Dennis M. Donovan

Nonmediational behavioral approaches • Mediational behavioral approaches • References

SECTION VI: PSYCHIATRIC DISORDERS AND ALCOHOLISM

44. **Psychopathology, Psychodynamics, and Alcoholism** 581
    Edward J. Khantzian

    Psychopathology • Psychodynamics • Conclusion: Alcoholism, a spectrum disorder • References

45. **Neurotic Behavior and the Alcoholic** 598
    David W. Krueger

    Transference-countertransference • Drinking as attempted adaptation • References

46. **Character Disorders: Characterological Specificity and the Alcoholic** 607
    Henry Krystal

    Problems and the cause of alcoholism • References

47. **Alcoholism and Affective Disorder** 618
    Martin H. Keeler

    Alcoholism and affective disorders • The clinical problems: Examples • Bipolar disorder and alcoholism • Unipolar affective disorder and alcoholism • Methodological problems in studies of alcoholism and affective disorder • Alcohol intoxication and affect • Conclusion • References

48. **Borderline Syndrome and Alcoholism** 628
    Peter Hartocollis

    The borderline syndrome • Alcoholism and borderline pathology • Borderline pathology and pathological narcissism • Affect tolerance and structural deficit • References

49. **Alcoholism and Schizophrenia** .. 636
    Edward Gottheil and Howard M. Waxman

    Prevalence • Etiologic considerations • Diagnosis • Treatment considerations • References

50. **Alcoholism and Sociopathy: Diagnostic and Treatment Implications** 647
    Richard T. Rada

    The association between sociopathy and alcoholism • The diagnostic confusion between sociopathy and alcoholism • Treatment of the alcoholic sociopath • Conclusion • References

51. **Alcoholism and Suicide: Association Factors** 655
    Donald W. Goodwin

    Alcoholism and suicide • Alcoholism and suicide attempts • Demographic aspects of alcoholism and suicide • The racial difference: A theory • Summary • References

52. **The Family and Alcoholism** 663
    Edward Kaufman and E. Mansell Pattison

    Typical family dynamics • The family as a determinant of rehabilitation • References

53. **Marital Dysfunction: Alcoholism and Marriage** 673
    Barbara S. McCrady

    Statistics • Models of alcoholic marriages • Current issues and conclusions • References

54. **The Effects of Alcohol Relative to Sexual Dysfunction** 686
    Ismet Karacan and Terry L. Hanusa

    Theories of alcohol and sexual mechanism interaction • Limitations of laboratory research • Alcohol and sexual dysfunction in women • Alcohol and sexual dysfunction in men • Sexual attitudes and psychosocial characteristics of male alcoholics • Diagnosis and treatment of alcohol-associated impotence • Conclusion • References

Contents

55. **Alcoholism and the Use of Other Drugs** 696
    Edward Kaufman

    Extent of the problem • Treatment implications • References

SECTION VII: DISTINCTIVE TREATMENT POPULATIONS

56. **Alcoholism and Services for Ethnic Populations** 709
    Joseph Westermeyer

    Demographic variations • Clinical variations • Access to treatment • Treatment methods • Treatment outcome • Conclusions • References

57. **Alcohol Abuse and Alcoholism in Women** 718
    Sharon C. Wilsnack

    Drinking and drinking problems in women • Gender differences in alcoholism patterns and symptoms • Etiologic theories and risk factors • Consequences of alcoholism for women • Alcoholism treatment in women • Prevention of alcohol problems in women • Summary and conclusions • References

58. **Homosexuality and Alcoholism** . 736
    Jeffrey M. Brandsma and E. Mansell Pattison

    The incidence of alcoholism among homosexuals • Treatment of homosexual alcoholics • Attempts at solution to treatment problems • Summary • References

59. **Mixed Drug and Alcohol Populations** 742
    Jerome F. X. Carroll and Sidney H. Schnoll

    Multiple substance abuse • The generic perspective • Admission and diagnostic criteria • Does combined treatment work? • Special considerations in implementing combined treatment programming • Implementing a withdrawal program for mixed drug and alcohol populations • Implications of combined treatment for the substance abuse fields • References

60. **Alcohol Use and Abuse in Children** 759
    Matilda M. Rice

    Contributing factors • Elementary grade children • Junior high school children • High school children • References

61. **Adolescence and Alcohol** 769
    William J. Filstead

    Key assumptions and conceptual considerations • Etiology and prevalence of adolescent alcohol use and misuse • Treatment intervention strategies • Range of services • Future Directions • References

62. **Alcoholism and the Aged** 779
    Gabe J. Maletta

    The problem of alcohol abuse in the elderly • Treatment of the elderly alcohol abuser • References

SECTION VIII: ALCOHOLISM TREATMENT PERSONNEL

63. **The Professionals: The Issue of Alcoholism** 795
    Wilma J. Knox

    The disease concept • Psychiatrists and psychologists • Social workers and nurses • Administrative personnel • Younger professionals • Research tools • References

64. **The Paraprofessionals in Alcoholism Treatment** 802
    Chaim M. Rosenberg

    Alcoholism counselors • Conflict in the field • Treatment • The role of the paraprofessional • The present, the future • References

Contents

65. **Recovered Alcoholic Counselors** 810
    LeClair Bissell

    Attitudes and beliefs • Treatment strengths • Contacts with other professions • Competence • Counselor credentialing • Employment settings • Problems in the use of counselors • References

SECTION IX: ALCOHOLISM TREATMENT FACILITIES

66. **Information and Referral Centers** 821
    Eileen M. Corrigan

    Alcohol information and referral centers • Function of information and referral centers • Effectiveness of referrals • Conclusions • References

67. **General Hospitals in the Alcoholism Treatment System** .. 828
    Marc Galanter and Jacob Sperber

    Scope of the problem • Attitudes and the search for a solution • A system approach • References

68. **Emergency Room Treatment of Alcohol Abuse and Alcoholism** 837
    Kim A. Keeley

    References

69. **Mental Hospitals: Hospitalization and Treatment of the Alcoholic** 848
    Earl X. Freed

    The course of psychiatric hospitalization of alcohol-dependent persons • Utilization of psychiatric hospitals by persons with alcohol problems • Treatment of alcoholic patients in psychiatric hospitals • References

70. **The Involvement of Private Psychiatric Hospitals in Alcoholism Treatment** 856
    Robert A. Moore

    Treatment programs • The present and future role of the private psychiatric hospital • Summary • References

71. **The Alcoholism Rehabilitation Center** 865
    Robert F. Stuckey and Joseph S. Harrison

    Historical development • Essential components • The key to rehabilitation • The family component • Employer involvement • Some key ingredients in the rehabilitation process • References

72. **Treatment of Alcoholism in Aversion Conditioning Hospitals** 874
    James W. Smith

    Aversion conditioning • Shick Shadel Hospital treatment • Raleigh Hills Hospital • Treatment results • Ethical considerations • Conclusions • References

73. **Alcoholism Outpatient Treatment** 885
    Jeffrey M. Brandsma and Richard J. Welsh

    Criteria • Contexts • Treatment goals • Modal treatment • Other issues • References

74. **The Role of Shelter Facilities in the Treatment of Alcoholics** ... 894
    George R. Jacobson

    The present nature of shelters • Characteristics of the clientele • Outcomes, conflicts, abuses • The future of shelters • References

75. **Alcoholism Halfway Houses** 907
    Jim Orford and Richard Velleman

    Varieties of halfway houses • The outcome following halfway house residence • Issues requiring resolution • Conclusion • References

Contents

76. **Community Human Service Agencies and Alcoholism** *923*
    Harold W. Demone, Jr.

    Contrasting views • Definition • Component classification systems • Alcoholism and other problems • References

77. **Multidimensional Rehabilitation of the Alcoholic** *930*
    Larry S. Hart

    The interrelationship of rehabilitation and the multidimensional model of alcoholism • Research relevant to the rehabilitation of the alcoholic • The multidimensional model of rehabilitation assessment in clinical alcoholism • Summary • References

78. **The Police Court System and the Public Intoxication Offender** . *938*
    David J. Pittman

    Public drunkenness: A criminal offense • The magnitude of the problem • The traditional police court system • Innovations in handling public inebriates • The future of the police court system • References

79. **Skid Row Alcoholics: Treatment, Survival, and Escape** .. *946*
    Jacqueline P. Wiseman

    Skid row: Changing and yet constant • Treatment of skid row alcoholics • Skid row alcoholics as a community resource • Survival on skid row • Escape from skid row • References

80. **Job-Based Alcoholism Programs: Motivating Problem Drinkers to Rehabilitation** *954*
    Harrison M. Trice and Janice M. Beyer

    Intervention strategies underlying job-based alcoholism policies • Employee-assistance programs as a social movement • Evaluation of job-based programs • Summary • References

81. **The Fellowship of Alcoholics Anonymous** *979*
    Lucinda A. Alibrandi

    Service to others • Group process • Alcoholics Anonymous literature • Sponsorship as folk therapy • References

82. **Support System Dynamics of Al-Anon and Alateen** *987*
    Joan Ablon

    Al-Anon meetings • The dynamics of Al-Anon • Al-Anon as a supportive community • The Alateen program • For information • References

SECTION X: ALCOHOLISM TREATMENT METHODS

83. **Psychotherapy in the Treatment of Alcoholism** *999*
    Sheldon Zimberg

    Psychodynamics of alcoholism • Psychotherapeutic techniques • Principles of alcoholism psychotherapy • Summary • References

84. **Alcoholism and Group Psychotherapy** *1011*
    Nick Kanas

    Effectiveness of group psychotherapy for alcoholics • Psychological considerations • Therapeutic considerations • Other therapeutic groups • References

85. **Family and Network Therapy in Alcoholism** *1022*
    Edward Kaufman and E. Mansell Pattison

    Family therapy methods • Modifications of family therapy for alcoholism • Summary • References

86. **Disulfiram and Other Deterrent Drugs** *1033*
    John A. Ewing

    References

87. **The Role of Drug Therapies in the Context of Alcoholism** *1043*
    Joel Solomon

Antianxiety agents, minor tranquilizers, sedative-hypnotics • Antidepressants • Lithium • Major tranquilizers • Conclusion • References

88. **Current Behavioral Therapies in the Treatment of Alcoholism** . . 1054
    Ovide F. Pomerleau

    Techniques for abstinence • Techniques for moderation • Techniques for sustaining improvement • Conclusion • References

89. **The Alcohol Withdrawal Syndrome and Medical Detoxification** 1068
    Armando R. Favazza

    Characteristics of patients in need of detoxification • Alcohol withdrawal syndrome • Medical management of alcohol withdrawal syndrome • Conclusion • References

90. **Nonmedical Alcohol Detoxification** 1076
    David J. Huberty and James C. Brandon

    Hospital emergency rooms and alcoholics • Detoxification centers—An emergency room for the alcoholic • Summary • References

SECTION XI: ORGANIZATION AND EVALUATION OF ALCOHOLISM TREATMENT SYSTEMS

91. **A Systems Approach to Alcoholism Treatment** 1089
    E. Mansell Pattison

    Methods of analysis of treatment • Selection and matching of treatment • A pathway model of the treatment system • Block variables • Summary • References

92. **Community Epidemiology and Treatment Planning** 1109
    Allan Beigel and Barbara Reed Hartmann

    Epidemiologic investigation of alcoholism • A generic framework for treatment service planning decisions • Community epidemiology: Pima County, Arizona • Summary • References

93. **A Conceptual Framework for Alcoholism Treatment Evaluation** 1120
    Rudolf H. Moos, Ruth C. Cronkite, and John W. Finney

    The pretreatment domains • The treatment domain • The posttreatment domains • Issues in treatment evaluation • Conclusions • References

94. **Differential Treatment Planning for Alcohol Abusers** 1140
    Linda C. Sobell, Mark B. Sobell, and Ted D. Nirenberg

    Treatment planning • Assessment, a precursor to treatment planning • Identifying treatment needs • Developing treatment goals and strategies • Monitoring treatment progress • Summary • References

95. **Evaluation of Alcoholism Psychotherapy Methods** 1152
    Chad D. Emrick

    Results • Conclusion • References

96. **Evaluation of Behavioral Methods in the Study of Alcoholism** 1170
    Glenn R. Caddy

    Chemical aversion therapies • Electrical aversion techniques • Covert sensitization • Social skills training • Progressive relaxation and systematic desensitization • Operant methods and contingency contracting • Behavioral self-control training and cognitive therapies • Broad-spectrum behavioral approaches

• Behavioral treatment in perspective • Conclusions • References

97. **Evaluation of Alcoholism Treatment Programs** *1197*
Raymond M. Costello

Definition of treatment program • Evaluation strategies • References

98. **Management and Administration of Alcoholism Programs** *1211*
Marvin D. Feit

The use and meaning of management • Different management activities by organizational position • Conclusion • References

Epilogue   *1221*

Index   *1225*

ALPHABETICAL GUIDE TO CHAPTERS BY SUBJECT

Addiction, Alcoholic: Psychological Tests and Measurements	517	Biochemistry of Alcohol and Alcohol Metabolism	83
Adolescence and Alcohol	769	Blood Alcohol Level Discrimination and Diagnosis	64
Affective Disorder, Alcoholism and	618	Borderline Syndrome and Alcoholism	628
The Aged, Alcoholism and	779		
Al-Anon and Alateen, Support System Dynamics of	987	The Cardiovascular System, Effects of Alcohol Ingestion on	332
Alcohol Consumption, measurement of	72	Character Disorders: Characterological Specificity and the Alcoholic	607
Alcoholics Anonymous, The Fellowship of	979	Children, Alcohol Use and Abuse in	759
Alcoholism, The Concept of: Assumptions and Issues	31	Community Epidemiology and Treatment Planning	1109
The Alcoholism Syndrome: Definitions and Models	3	Community Human Service Agencies and Alcoholism	923
Alcohol Withdrawal and Delirium Tremens	147	Counselors, Recovered Alcoholic	810
The Alcohol Withdrawal Syndrome and Medical Detoxification	1068	Criminality, Alcohol and	383
Anesthesia, Trauma, Surgery, and	343	Delirium Tremens, Alcohol Withdrawal and	147
Behavioral Methods in the Study of Alcoholism, Evaluation of	1170	Detoxification, Medical, The Alcohol Withdrawal Syndrome and	1068
Behavioral Psychology Approaches to Alcoholism	560	Detoxification, Nonmedical Alcohol	1076
Behavioral Therapies, Current, in the Treatment of Alcoholism	1054	The Diagnosis of Alcoholism after DSM-III	40
		Disulfiram and Other Deterrent Drugs	1033

*This list begins with the major title word first as a quick reference for subjects. See table of contents for exact titles of chapters.

Alphabetical Guide to Chapters by Subject

Drinking, Safe and Healthy	483	tivating Problem Drinkers to Rehabilitation	954
Drug and Alcohol Populations, Mixed	742	Legal Issues of Alcoholism	406
Drug Interactions, The Clinical Pharmacology of Ethanol and	354	Liver and Pancreas	225
Drugs, Alcoholism and the Use of Other	696	Malnutrition in the Alcoholic and Related Nutritional Deficiencies	255
Drugs, Disulfiram and Other Deterrent	1033	Marital Dysfunction: Alcoholism and Marriage	673
Drug Therapies, The Role of, in the Context of Alcoholism	1043	Measurement of Alcohol Consumption	72
Economics, Alcohol and	415	Metabolism, Alcohol, Biochemistry of Alcohol and	83
Education Programs, Preventing Alcohol-Related Problems and Dependencies through Information and	468	Myopathy in the Chronic Alcoholic	204
Emergency Room Treatment of Alcohol Abuse and Alcoholism	837	Nervous System, Peripheral and Autonomic	194
Endocrine Disturbances Associated with Alcohol and Alcoholism	311	Neurophysiological Effects of Alcohol	105
The Epidemiology of Alcoholism and Its Implications	441	Neuropsychiatric Disorders, Chronic, Associated with Alcoholism	167
Epidemiology, Community, and Treatment Planning	1109	Neurotic Behavior and the Alcoholic	598
Ethnic Populations, Alcoholism and Services for	709	Nutritional Deficiencies, Malnutrition in the Alcoholic and Related	255
Experimental Psychology and Alcoholism: Assessment, Contribution, and Impact	540	Outpatient Treatment, Alcoholism	885
		Pancreas, Liver and	225
The Family and Alcoholism	663	The Paraprofessionals in Alcoholism Treatment	802
Family and Network Therapy in Alcoholism	1022	Pharmacology, the Clinical, of Ethanol, Drug Interactions and	354
The Fetus, Effects of Alcohol on	301	The Police Court System and the Public Intoxication Offender	938
The Gastrointestinal Tract, Effects of Alcohol on	245	Prevention Strategies, Alcoholism: Perspectives on	458
Genetic Factors in Alcoholism Predisposition	135	The Professionals: The Issue of Alcoholism	795
Group Psychotherapy, Alcoholism and	1011	A Psychological Perspective on Development of Alcoholism	529
Halfway Houses, Alcoholism	907	Psychological Testing, Diagnostic	55
The Hematopoietic System, Effects of Alcohol on	281	Psychological Tests and Measurements, Alcoholic Addiction:	517
Highway Safety, Alcohol and	395	Psychopathology, Psychodynamics, and Alcoholism	581
Homosexuality and Alcoholism	736	Psychotherapy Methods, Alcoholism, Evaluation of	1152
Hospital, Private Psychiatric, The Involvement of, in Alcoholism Treatment	856	Psychotherapy in the Treatment of Alcoholism	999
Hospitals, Aversion Conditioning, Treatment of Alcoholism in	874	The Public Intoxication Offender, The Police Court System and	938
Hospitals, General, in the Alcoholism Treatment System	828		
Hospitals, Mental: Hospitalization and Treatment of the Alcoholic	848	Recovered Alcoholic Counselors	810
Human Service Agencies, Community, and Alcoholism	923	Rehabilitation Center, The Alcoholism	865
		Rehabilitation, Job-Based Alcoholism Programs: Motivating Problem Drinkers to	954
Infectious Diseases and the Alcoholic	263	Rehabilitation, Multidimensional, of the Alcoholic	930
Information and Referral Centers	821	The Reproductive Function, Alcohol Effects on	293
Job-Based Alcoholism Programs: Mo-			

Alphabetical Guide to Chapters by Subject

The Respiratory System and Specifics of Alcoholism	325
Schizophrenia, Alcoholism and	636
Sexual Dysfunction, The Effects of Alcohol Relative to	686
Shelter Facilities, The Role of, in the Treatment of Alcoholics	894
The Skeletal System: Alcohol as a Factor	215
Skid Row Alcoholics: Treatment, Survival, and Escape	946
Skin Diseases Associated with Alcoholism	275
The Sleep Disorders, Alcohol and	180
Social Policy, Alcohol Use:	490
Sociocultural Variants in Alcoholism	426
Sociological Models for Understanding Deviant Drinking Behavior	367
Sociopathy, Alcoholism and: Diagnostic and Treatment Implications	647
Suicide, Alcoholism and: Association Factors	655
Surgery, Anesthesia, Trauma, and	343
A Systems Approach to Alcoholism Treatment	1089
Trauma, Surgery, and Anesthesia	343
Treatment, Alcoholism, A Systems Approach to	1089
Treatment Evaluation, Alcoholism, A Conceptual Framework for	1120
Treatment Planning, Community Epidemiology and	1109
Treatment Planning, Differential, for Alcohol Abusers	1140
Treatment Programs, Alcoholism, Evaluation of	1197
Women, Alcohol Abuse and Alcoholism in	718

CONTRIBUTORS

EDITORS

E. MANSELL PATTISON, MD, Professor and Chairman, Department of Psychiatry, Medical College of Georgia, Augusta, Georgia

EDWARD KAUFMAN, MD, Associate Professor in Residence, Department of Psychiatry and Human Behavior, University of California, Irvine Medical Center, Orange, California

AUTHORS

JOAN ABLON, PhD, Professor, Medical Anthropology Program, Departments of Epidemiology and International Health, and Psychiatry, School of Medicine, University of California, San Francisco, San Francisco, California

LUCINDA A. ALIBRANDI, PhD, Assistant Professor, Addiction Studies, University of Arizona, Tucson, Arizona

M. DOUGLAS ANGLIN, PhD, Adjunct Assistant Professor of Psychology, Department of Psychology, University of California at Los Angeles, Los Angeles, California

DAVID J. ARMOR, PhD, The Rand Corporation, Santa Monica, California

HERBERT BARRY III, PhD, Professor of Pharmacology, University of Pittsburgh School of Pharmacy, Pittsburgh, Pennsylvania

JAMES D. BEARD, PhD, Director, Alcohol Research Center, Memphis Mental Health Institute, and Associate Professor of Physiology in Psychiatry, University of Tennessee Center for the Health Sciences, Memphis, Tennessee

ALLAN BEIGEL, MD, Professor of Psychiatry, University of Arizona College of Medicine, and Director, Southern Arizona Mental Health Center, Tucson, Arizona

JANICE M. BEYER, PhD, Professor, School of Management, State University of New York at Buffalo, Buffalo, New York

LECLAIR BISSELL, MD, CAC, Clinical Associate Professor of Psychiatry and Human Behavior, Brown University, Providence, Rhode Island

FLOYD E. BLIVEN, JR., MD, Professor of Surgery (Orthopedics), Medical College of Georgia, Augusta, Georgia

KENNETH BLUM, PhD, Chief, Division of Substance and Alcohol Misuse, Department of Pharmacology, University of Texas, Health Science Center, San Antonio, Texas

JAMES C. BRANDON, Chemical Dependency Family Therapist, Northern Pines Mental Health Center, Brainerd, Minnesota

JEFFREY M. BRANDSMA, PhD, Professor of Psychiatry, Medical College of Georgia, Augusta, Georgia

GLENN R. CADDY, PhD, Professor and Director of Clinical Training, Nova University, Ft. Lauderdale, Florida

JEROME F. X. CARROLL, PhD, Director of Psychological Services, Eagleville Hospital and Rehabilitation Center, Eagleville, Pennsylvania

VIRGINIA G. CARSON, PhD, Associate Professor of Biology, Chapman College, Orange, California, and National Alcohol Research Center, Department of Psychiatry and Human Behavior, University of California, Irvine, Irvine, California

MORRIS E. CHAFETZ, MD, President, Health Education Foundation, Washington, D.C., and Senior

Psychiatrist, Fenwick Hall, Johns Island, Charleston, South Carolina

I. CHANARIN, MD, Head, Section of Hematology, Medical Research Council, Clinical Research Centre, Northwick Park Hospital, Harrow, United Kingdom

WILLIAM H. CHEW, JR., MD, Professor of Medicine, Department of Medicine, Section of Infectious Diseases, Medical College of Georgia, Augusta, Georgia

NICHOLAS V. CONTI, MSW, ACSW, Medical Administrator, Supreme Bench of Baltimore, and Field Instructor, University of Maryland School of Social Work and Community Planning, Baltimore, Maryland

EILEEN M. CORRIGAN, DSW, Professor, Graduate School of Social Work, Rutgers–The State University, New Brunswick, New Jersey

RAYMOND M. COSTELLO, PhD, Associate Professor of Psychiatry (Psychology), The University of Texas Health Science Center at San Antonio, and Assistant Director, Alcohol Treatment Unit, Audie Murphy Memorial Veterans Administration Hospital, San Antonio, Texas

RUTH C. CRONKITE, PhD, Social Ecology Laboratory, Department of Psychiatry and Behavioral Sciences, Stanford University, Stanford, California, and Veterans Administration Medical Center, Palo Alto, California

HAROLD W. DEMONE, JR., PhD, Dean, Graduate School of Social Work, Professor, Social Work, Sociology, and the Center for Alcohol Studies, Rutgers–The State University, New Brunswick, New Jersey

DENNIS M. DONOVAN, PhD, Alcohol Dependence Treatment Program, Veterans Administration Medical Center, and Department of Psychiatry and Behavioral Sciences, University of Washington, Seattle, Washington

CHAD D. EMRICK, PhD, Psychologist, Veterans Administration Medical Center, Mental Health and Behavioral Sciences, and Assistant Clinical Professor in Psychiatry, University of Colorado, Health Sciences Center, Denver, Colorado

JOHN A. EWING, MD, Director, Center for Alcohol Studies, and Professor of Psychiatry, School of Medicine, University of North Carolina at Chapel Hill, Chapel Hill, North Carolina

HOSSAM E. FADEL, MD, Professor and Chief of Maternal-Fetal Medicine, Department of Obstetrics and Gynecology, Medical College of Georgia, Augusta, Georgia

ARMANDO R. FAVAZZA, MD, Professor and Chief, Section of General Psychiatry, University of Missouri–Columbia School of Medicine, Columbia, Missouri

MARVIN D. FEIT, PhD, Associate Professor, University of Tennessee School of Social Work, and Assistant Clinical Professor, Department of Psychiatry, University of Tennessee Center for the Health Sciences, Memphis, Tennessee

ELAINE B. FELDMAN, MD, Professor of Medicine, Chief, Section of Nutrition, and Director, Clinical Nutrition Research Unit, Medical College of Georgia, Augusta, Georgia

EVAN R. FERGUSON, PhD, Research Assistant Professor of Medicine, Southwestern Medical School, and Veterans Administration Medical Center, Dallas, Texas

WILLIAM J. FILSTEAD, PhD, Lutheran Center for Substance Abuse, and Parkside Medical Services Corporation, Lutheran General Medical Center, Park Ridge, Illinois

JOHN W. FINNEY, PhD, Social Ecology Laboratory, Department of Psychiatry and Behavioral Sciences, Stanford University, Stanford, California, and Veterans Administration Medical Center, Palo Alto, California

EARL X. FREED, PhD, Deputy Assistant Chief Medical Director for Research and Development, Veterans Administration, Washington, D.C.

MARC GALANTER, MD, Associate Professor and Director, Division of Alcoholism and Drug Abuse, Department of Psychiatry, Albert Einstein College of Medicine, Bronx, New York

STANLEY E. GITLOW, MD, Clinical Professor of Medicine, Mount Sinai School of Medicine, New York, New York

DONALD W. GOODWIN, MD, Professor and Chairman, Department of Psychiatry, University of Kansas Medical Center, Kansas City, Kansas

EDWARD GOTTHEIL, MD, PhD, Professor, Department of Psychiatry and Human Behavior, Thomas Jefferson University, Philadelphia, Pennsylvania

HAMID A. HADI, MD, Instructor and Fellow in Maternal-Fetal Medicine, Department of Obstetrics and Gynecology, Medical College of Georgia, Augusta, Georgia

TERRY L. HANUSA, MD, Loyola University of Chicago, Stritch School of Medicine, Chicago, Illinois

JOSEPH S. HARRISON, MDiv, CAC, Program Director, Alcoholism Rehabilitation Unit, Fair Oaks Hospital, Summit, New Jersey

LARRY S. HART, PhD, Licensed Psychologist and Director, Center for Behavioral Consultation, Madison, Wisconsin

BARBARA REED HARTMANN, PhD, Assistant Professor, University of Arizona College of Medicine, Department of Family and Community Medicine, Tucson, Arizona

ERNEST L. HARTMANN, MD, Professor of Psychiatry, Tufts University School of Medicine, Director, Sleep Laboratory, Boston State Hospital, and Medical Director, Sleep Research Foundation, Boston, Massachusetts

PETER HARTOCOLLIS, MD, PhD, Professor and Chairman, Department of Psychiatry, The University of Patras, School of Medicine, Patras, Greece

DWIGHT B. HEATH, PhD, Professor of Anthropology, Brown University, Providence, Rhode Island

DAVID J. HUBERTY, MSW, Coordinator of Detoxification Services, Central Minnesota Mental Health Center, St. Cloud, Minnesota

GEORGE R. JACOBSON, PhD, Director, Research and Training, De Paul Rehabilitation Hospital, Assistant Professor, Department of Psychiatry and Mental Health Sciences, Medical College of Wisconsin, and Clinical Associate Professor, Department of Psychology, University of Wisconsin–Milwaukee, Milwaukee, Wisconsin

HAROLD KALANT, MD, PhD, Associate Director, Biological and Social Studies Division, Addiction Research Foundation, and Professor of Pharmacology, University of Toronto, Toronto, Canada

NICK KANAS, MD, Assistant Professor of Psychiatry, University of California, San Francisco, School of Medicine, and Assistant Chief, Psychiatry Serv-

Contributors

ice, Veterans Administration Medical Center, San Francisco, California

ISMET KARACAN, MD, DSc(Med), Professor of Psychiatry and Director, Sleep Disorders and Research Center, Baylor College of Medicine, and Associate Chief of Staff for Research, Veterans Administration Hospital, Houston, Texas

MARTIN H. KEELER, MD, Professor of Psychiatry, College of Medicine, Baylor University, Houston, Texas

KIM A. KEELEY, MD, MSH, Director for Inpatient Services, Kingsboro Psychiatric Center, and Clinical Associate Professor of Psychiatry, State University of New York Downstate Medical Center, Brooklyn, New York

EDWARD J. KHANTZIAN, MD, Associate Professor of Psychiatry, Department of Psychiatry, Harvard Medical School at The Cambridge Hospital, Cambridge, Massachusetts

RAMESH K. KHURANA, MD, Assistant Professor of Neurology, Department of Neurology, University of Maryland School of Medicine, Baltimore, Maryland

JAMES P. KNOCHEL, MD, Professor of Internal Medicine, Southwestern Medical School, and Veterans Administration Medical Center, Dallas, Texas

DAVID H. KNOTT, MD, PhD, Assistant Superintendent, Clinical/Residential Services, Memphis Mental Health Institute, and Clinical Associate Professor of Psychiatry, University of Tennessee Center for the Health Sciences, Memphis, Tennessee

WILMA J. KNOX, PhD, Staff Psychologist, Veterans Administration Medical Center, Biloxi, Mississippi, and Associate Professor, University of Southern Mississippi, Hattiesburg, Mississippi

MARK A. KORSTEN, MD, Assistant Professor of Medicine, Mount Sinai School of Medicine, New York, New York, and Staff Physician, Veterans Administration Medical Center, Bronx, New York

DAVID W. KRUEGER, MD, Department of Psychiatry, Baylor College of Medicine, Houston, Texas

HENRY KRYSTAL, MD, Professor of Psychiatry, Michigan State University, East Lansing, Michigan

CHARLES S. LIEBER, MD, Professor of Medicine and Pathology, Mount Sinai School of Medicine, New York, New York, and Director, Alcohol Research and Treatment Center and GI Liver Training Program, Veterans Administration Medical Center, Bronx, New York

ALBERT B. LOWENFELS, MD, Professor of Surgery, New York Medical College, New York, New York

HAROLD A. LYONS, MD, Professor of Medicine, State University of New York Downstate Medical Center, Brooklyn, New York

GABE J. MALETTA, PhD, MD, Director, Geriatric Research, Education and Clinical Center, Minneapolis Veterans Administration Medical Center, and Assistant Professor, Departments of Psychiatry and Neurology, University of Minnesota School of Medicine, Minneapolis, Minnesota

WALLACE MANDELL, PhD, MPH, Professor, Department of Mental Hygiene, School of Hygiene and Public Health, The Johns Hopkins University, Baltimore, Maryland

G. ALAN MARLATT, PhD, Professor, Department of Psychology, University of Washington, Seattle, Washington

RICHARD F. MAYER, MD, Professor of Neurology, Department of Neurology, University of Maryland School of Medicine, Baltimore, Maryland

BARBARA S. MCCRADY, PhD, Associate Professor, Section of Psychiatry and Human Behavior, Brown University and Butler Hospital, Providence, Rhode Island

JOSEPH P. MCEVOY, MD, Assistant Professor of Psychiatry, University of Pittsburgh School of Medicine, Western Psychiatric Institute and Clinic, Pittsburgh, Pennsylvania

ESTEBAN MEZEY, MD, Associate Professor of Medicine, Johns Hopkins University School of Medicine, and Chief of Hepatology, Baltimore City Hospitals, Baltimore, Maryland

ROBERT A. MOORE, MD, Clinical Professor of Psychiatry, University of California, San Diego, School of Medicine, and Medical Director, Mesa Vista Hospital, San Diego, California

RUDOLF H. MOOS, PhD, Social Ecology Laboratory, and Professor, Department of Psychiatry and Behavioral Sciences, Stanford University, Stanford, California, and Veterans Administration Medical Center, Palo Alto, California

HAROLD A. MULFORD, PhD, Professor of Psychiatry and Director of Alcohol Studies, University of Iowa, Iowa City, Iowa

ROBIN M. MURRAY, MD, Senior Lecturer, Genetics Section, Institute of Psychiatry, London, England

PETER E. NATHAN, PhD, Alcohol Behavior Research Laboratory, Rutgers–The State University, New Brunswick, New Jersey

CHARLES NEURINGER, PhD, Professor of Psychology, Psychology Department, University of Kansas, Lawrence, Kansas

TED D. NIRENBERG, PhD, Sea Pines Behavioral Institute, Hilton Head Island, South Carolina, and Georgia Southern University, Statesboro, Georgia

JIM ORFORD, PhD, Senior Lecturer in Clinical Psychology, University of Exeter, and Principal Clinical Psychologist, Exe Vale Hospital, Exeter, Devon, England

ESA OSTERBERG, MPolSc, The State Alcohol Monopoly, Social Research Institute of Alcohol Studies, Helsinki, Finland

DAVID J. PITTMAN, PhD, Chairman and Professor of Sociology, Washington University, St. Louis, Missouri

J. MICHAEL POLICH, PhD, The Rand Corporation, Santa Monica, California

OVIDE F. POMERLEAU, PhD, Professor of Psychiatry (Psychology), University of Connecticut School of Medicine, Farmington, Connecticut

RICHARD T. RADA, MD, Medical Director, College Hospital, Cerritos, California, and Clinical Professor of Psychiatry, Department of Psychiatry, University of New Mexico School of Medicine, Albuquerque, New Mexico

JONAS R. RAPPEPORT, MD, Chief Medical Officer, Supreme Bench of Baltimore, Assistant Professor, The Johns Hopkins School of Medicine, and Clinical Professor Psychiatry, University of Maryland School of Medicine, Baltimore, Maryland

MATILDA M. RICE, MD, Nassau County Department of Drug and Alcoholic Addiction, Nassau, New York

J. PETER RISSING, MD, Associate Professor of Medicine and Chief, Section of Infectious Diseases, Department of Medicine, Medical College of Georgia, Augusta, Georgia

LEE N. ROBINS, PhD, Professor of Psychiatry, School of Medicine, Washington University, St. Louis, Missouri

Contributors

DAVID ROBINSON, PhD, Senior Lecturer in Health Studies, Institute for Health Studies, University of Hull, Hull, England

WILLIAM P. ROHAN, PhD, Veterans Administration Hospital, Northampton, Massachusetts

PAUL M. ROMAN, PhD, Charles A. and Leo M. Favrot Professor of Human Relations, Department of Sociology, and Professor of Epidemiology, School of Public Health and Tropical Medicine, Tulane University, New Orleans, Louisiana

CHAIM M. ROSENBERG, MD, PhD, Associate Professor of Psychiatry, Boston University School of Medicine, Boston, Massachusetts

HENRY L. ROSETT, MD, Associate Professor of Psychiatry and Obstetrics and Gynecology, Boston University School of Medicine, Boston, Massachusetts

SIDNEY H. SCHNOLL, MD, PhD, Northwestern Institute of Psychiatry, Northwestern University School of Medicine, Chicago, Illinois

EDWARD M. SELLERS, MD, PhD, Director and Head of Medicine, Clinical Institute, Addiction Research Foundation, and Professor of Pharmacology and Medicine, University of Toronto, Toronto, Canada

JAMES W. SMITH, MD, Executive Director, Schick Shadel Hospital, Seattle, Washington

LINDA C. SOBELL, PhD, Clinical Institute, Addiction Research Foundation, and University of Toronto, Toronto, Canada

MARK B. SOBELL, PhD, Clinical Institute, Addiction Research Foundation, and University of Toronto, Toronto, Canada

JOEL SOLOMON, MD, Clinical Associate Professor, and Director, Division of Alcoholism and Drug Dependence, State University of New York Downstate Medical Center, Brooklyn, New York

JACOB SPERBER, MD, Clinical Instructor and Outpatient Director, Division of Alcoholism and Drug Abuse, Department of Psychiatry, Albert Einstein College of Medicine, Bronx, New York

JAMES R. STABENAU, MD, Professor of Psychiatry, University of Connecticut, Farmington, Connecticut

PETER E. STOKES, MD, Associate Professor of Medicine (Endocrinology), Associate Professor of Psychiatry, and Chief, Division of Psychobiology, Payne Whitney Clinic, New York Hospital–Cornell University Medical Center, New York, New York

ROBERT F. STUCKEY, MD, Medical Director, Alcohol Rehabilitation Unit, Fair Oaks Hospital, and Fair Oaks–South, Summit, New Jersey

RALPH E. TARTER, PhD, Chief, Clinical Neuropsychology, and Associate Professor of Psychiatry and Neurology, Department of Psychiatry, University of Pittsburgh School of Medicine, Pittsburgh, Pennsylvania

SUJATA TEWARI, PhD, Associate Professor and Scientific Director, National Alcohol Research Center, Department of Psychiatry and Human Behavior, College of Medicine, University of California, Irvine, Irvine, California

HARRISON M. TRICE, PhD, Professor, New York State School of Industrial and Labor Relations, Cornell University, Ithaca, New York, and Research Consultant, The Christopher D. Smithers Foundation, Mill Neck, New York

RICHARD VELLEMAN, MSc, Research Psychologist, University of Exeter, and Clinical Psychologist, Exe Vale Hospital, Exeter, Devon, England

PATRICIA F. WALLER, PhD, Associate Director for Driver Studies, and Research Professor, Department of Health Administration, School of Public Health, University of North Carolina at Chapel Hill, Chapel Hill, North Carolina

HOWARD M. WAXMAN, PhD, Assistant Professor, Department of Psychiatry and Human Behavior, Thomas Jefferson University, Philadelphia, Pennsylvania

LYN WEINER, MPH, Instructor in Psychiatry, Boston University School of Medicine, Boston, Massachusetts

RICHARD J. WELSH, MSW, Associate Professor of Clinical Social Work, University of Kentucky College of Medicine, Lexington, Kentucky

JOSEPH WESTERMEYER, MD, PhD, Professor, Department of Psychiatry, University of Minnesota, Minneapolis, Minnesota

CHARLES L. WHITFIELD, MD, Associate Professor of Medicine and Family Medicine, Assistant Professor of Psychiatry, and Director, Alcoholism and Drug Abuse Education, University of Maryland at Baltimore, Baltimore, Maryland

SHARON C. WILSNACK, PhD, Associate Professor of Psychology, Department of Neuroscience, University of North Dakota School of Medicine, Grand Forks, North Dakota

JACQUELINE P. WISEMAN, PhD, Professor of Sociology, University of California, San Diego, San Diego, California

SHELDON ZIMBERG, MD, Associate Professor of Psychiatry, Mount Sinai School of Medicine, and Director of Psychiatry, Joint Diseases North General Hospital, New York, New York

PROLOGUE: PURPOSE, CONCEPT, AND PLAN

THE FIELD OF ALCOHOLism is vast, ranging from the microprocesses of intracellular biology to issues of national and international social policy. The problems associated with alcoholism involve biological, psychological, social, and cultural processes. Sir William Osler observed at the turn of the 20th century that to understand syphilis was to know medicine. His comment referred to the protean and ubiquitous manifestations of syphilis in all aspects of health care. Syphilis has all but disappeared in modern society. But today we can apply the Oslerian aphorism to alcoholism, for the problems associated with alcohol involve virtually every aspect of health care.

It is virtually impossible for any one scientist, health professional, scholar, or clinician to keep abreast of the details of development in the wide spectrum of disciplines involved in alcoholism research. Yet for the field to advance, it is necessary that specialists in each area maintain a working knowledge of the field as a whole. Further, it is critical to move toward synthesis and integration of the discrete and disparate data from the various disciplinary domains. Finally, it is imperative to proceed with application of the scientific data base to the clinical and social problems of alcoholism.

Therefore we have prepared this volume with the following purposes in mind:

1. To present in one volume an overview of the major aspects of the field of alcoholism

2. To collate brief "state of the art" assessments of the major research and clinical issues

3. To offer the researcher a comprehensive perspective on the field as a whole

4. To provide the clinician with a scientific framework within which to view clinical treatment interventions

5. To offer an integration and synthesis of the alcoholism syndrome as a major health problem

The concept upon which this book is constructed is that alcoholism is best construed as a multivariate syndrome representing a major public health problem. Therefore, we present alcoholism from multiple perspectives.

The plan of the book follows from our purposes and basic concept. In Section I, we examine the problems of definition and diagnosis of the alcoholism syndrome. Our intent here is to demonstrate and illustrate the multivariate nature of alcoholism. Chapter 1 sets out the basic problems and various strategies now employed and concludes with a model for a multivariate alcoholism syndrome, which is described in a set of 11 postulates and their corollaries. This model establishes a linkage between current scientific data on the nature of the alcoholism syndrome and clinical applications of the model. The subsequent chapters in this first section examine in detail several methodological approaches to diagnosis and assessment.

Section II discusses the biological mechanisms of action of alcohol. It concludes with a review of possible genetic factors in the development of alcoholism.

Section III considers the effects of acute and chronic alcohol use on the many organ systems of the body. Included are the acute and chronic alcoholism medical syndromes, as well as the special medical conditions produced by alcoholism or medical treatment complicated by the presence of alcoholism. These are the medical consequences of alcoholism.

Section IV shifts focus to the social consequences of alcoholism. Here the relationships between alcohol use, misuse, and abuse and the generation, association, or correlation with a variety of social problems are presented. This includes the relationships between alcohol use and deviancy, criminality, and accidents. These are immediate adverse consequences of alcohol use, although not necessarily associated with alcoholism per se. Section IV continues with larger social issues of legal process, economics, sociocultural variations, and epidemiology. Finally, issues of prevention and social policy about the sanctions surrounding the use of alcohol are discussed.

Section V considers the psychology of alcoholism and the individual. This perspective rests on traditional lines of psychological inquiry and analysis. A similar theme follows in Section VI, in which the relationship between alcoholism and various psychiatric disorders is examined.

We have presented the syndrome of alcoholism as the interaction of biological, psychological, social, and cultural factors. The particular combinations of these factors give rise to different types of alcoholism syndromes. In turn, we have also presented biological, psychological, social, and cultural consequences of different patterns of alcohol use, misuse, and abuse.

The conclusions we wish to present at this point are the following:

1. Alcoholism is best construed as a syndrome.
2. The alcoholism syndrome is multivariate; that is, there are multiple variations of the syndrome that may be construed as alcoholism.
3. The use, misuse, and abuse of alcohol may produce multiple adverse consequences, not all of which are necessarily to be construed as an alcoholism syndrome, but all are public health problems associated with alcohol use.

In the latter part of the book we address the clinical issues of treatment intervention. Our approach is derived from the traditional public health epidemiologic model of inquiry, which asks the following general question: "What alcoholism syndromes, at which stage of their development, in what patients, will respond in what short- and long-range ways, to what measures, administered by whom?"

We can conveniently consider each major variable of this epidemiologic model. In Sections I through IV, we examine a wide variety of alcoholism syndromes at various stages of development. In Section VII, we examine distinctive patient populations; in Section VIII, treatment personnel; in Section IX, treatment facilities; and in Section X, treatment methods. Overall, we present a comprehensive survey of each major variable that makes up the epidemiologic model of a public health approach to treatment.

It finally remains to consider how to assemble each of these variables into a comprehensive treatment system. This is presented in Section XI. In Chapter 91, which opens the section, Pattison presents a systems approach to treatment that incorporates the public health model in a clinical system. He dissects the system of treatment into 16 separate blocks of treatment variables for more clinical and research precision. The next chapters move logically from community systems to individual systems of treatment. These are followed by reviews of treatment evaluation and the section concludes with program management and administration. Thus, this section presents a model for synthesis and integration of a clinical approach to the multivariate alcoholism syndrome.

As the editors of this text, we acknowledge the considerable disparity of viewpoint, ideology, and interpretation among the many outstanding workers in the field of alcoholism. Although we have organized this book in accordance with our explicit assumptions, we have deliberately not solicited participation from authorities from only one perspective. In fact, the "state of the art" is one of disparity rather than consensus. Rather than mask this state of affairs, we have chosen to provide each author autonomy to develop his or her topics with his or her own intellectual and scientific integrity. The result is a book without a uniform perspective on alcoholism, but rather variations in perspective—perhaps at times even opposing perspectives.

Nevertheless, we trust that this volume achieves some overarching sense of coherence about the field of alcoholism. We believe that the basic concept of alcoholism as a multivariate syndrome provides a meaningful base to initiate synthesis and integration of the field. And we propose that a systems approach to alcoholism treatment will afford an inclusive perspective on treatment.

E. Mansell Pattison, MD
Edward Kaufman, MD

Encyclopedic
Handbook
of
Alcoholism

Section I

The Definition and Diagnosis of Alcoholism

1

E. MANSELL PATTISON, MD, Medical College of Georgia, Augusta, Georgia
EDWARD KAUFMAN, MD, University of California, Irvine Medical Center, Orange, California

THE ALCOHOLISM SYNDROME: DEFINITIONS AND MODELS

THE USE, MISUSE, AND ABUSE of alcohol is one of the major health problems in the United States. Alcoholism ranks as the third most prevalent public health problem in this society. But the problems associated with alcohol are not limited to the health problems of alcoholic persons, because their alcoholismic behavior leads to familial, social, vocational, and legal problems. Thus alcoholism contaminates many persons associated with the target alcoholic.

Next one must consider the fact that people use, misuse, and abuse alcohol, yet may never become alcohol dependent nor defined as alcoholic. Yet these patterns of alcohol utilization contribute to health impairment, vehicular and pedestrian accidents, criminal behavior, destructive social behavior, and other adverse community consequences. Alcohol problems are therefore not limited to just alcoholics.

Alcohol is part of this overmedicated society, in which the use of psychoactive substances of many kinds is viewed as personally desirable and socially acceptable

---

E. Mansell Pattison, MD, Professor and Chairman, Department of Psychiatry, Medical College of Georgia, Augusta, Georgia.

Edward Kaufman, MD, Associate Professor in Residence, Department of Psychiatry and Human Behavior, University of California, Irvine Medical Center, Orange, California.

[53]. The current widespread use of alcohol is supported by legal, personal, professional, social, and cultural sanctions — or perhaps more accurately the lack of either positive or negative sanctions. There are few social rules or guidelines about the safe and proper use of alcohol, or the avoidance and deterrence of adverse consequences of use. Thus the problems of alcohol use are no respecter of age, sex, ethnicity, geography, or legality. Everyone encounters the use, misuse, and abuse of alcohol in daily life.

For these reasons the use, misuse, and abuse of alcohol are intertwined with current problems in constructing adequate definitions and diagnostic procedures to identify alcoholics and define alcoholism. One might hope for a simple definition of alcoholism, and a simple method to diagnose the alcoholic. Unfortunately, simple definitions and simple methods are not feasible without sacrificing important scientific and clinical distinctions.

The rationale for the diagnosis of alcoholism includes social, political, legal, and medical goals — each of which involves somewhat different definitions of alcoholism. The purposes for which one makes a diagnosis of alcoholism are multiple: to screen populations, to make legal decisions, to make medical referrals, to determine need for treatment, to select treatment facilities, to select treatment methods, to predict treatment outcome, and to assess etiologic factors. Again, each of the above purposes involves different diagnostic strategies.

This chapter reviews the issues of definition and diagnosis from the point of view that alcoholism is most prudently construed as a multivariate syndrome. This chapter focuses primarily on conceptual, methodological, and scientific aspects of the multivariate syndrome, concluding with a detailed discussion of the clinical implications and clinical applications of the multivariate syndrome.

THE GOALS OF DIAGNOSIS

The term "diagnosis" comes from the Greek root "diagignosko," which literally means to distinguish or discriminate. To diagnose thus means to identify a substance, event, behavior, or person. The diagnosis of alcoholism is the identification of alcoholism. What is it? There are several equally valid answers, dependent upon purpose. Therefore, four perspectives on the goals of diagnosis are examined.

The Legal-Political Perspective

Deviant human behavior may be considered in two major classifications: deviancy defined as immoral, sinful, or deviancy defined as nonmoral, a sickness. In turn, deviant behavior is addressed either through the social institutions of the political-legal system or the social institutions of the health care system. The major purpose of diagnosis of alcoholism in this perspective is to determine whether the nature of alcoholism is to be considered as sinful deviant behavior or sick deviant behavior, to discriminate between those persons whose deviancy should be addressed through the political-legal system and those who should be addressed through the health care system.

Cross-cultural research has demonstrated that societies vary widely in their definition of alcoholism, ranging from those societies in countries that prohibit alcohol use, such as certain Moslem nations, to preliterate societies that have widespread use of alcohol without intoxication or deviant behavior, to Western industrialized societies that have heavy alcohol consumption with various degrees of major social problems associated with drinking behavior [26, 50].

Alcoholism might be considered a legal problem in an abstinent nation, a social problem in a preliterate society, and both a legal and a medical problem in industrialized states. How drinking itself, drinking behavior, and the consequences of drinking behavior are defined will vary with the amount of drinking, the type of drinking behavior, and the consequences of drinking behavior exhibited in a given society [48].

In the United States, the cultural diagnosis of alcoholism still varies widely, including the diagnosis of alcoholism as a biological, moral, personality, emotional, or chemical phenomenon. In turn, effective treatment is perceived in terms of medical, psychological, will power, religious, or legal remedies [45].

The three main American cultural perspectives view alcoholism as a medical, social, or legal problem. The major thrust of the legal-political movement in the United States in this century has been to change the cultural diagnosis of alcoholism from that of a sinful, immoral behavior (legal diagnosis) to that of nonmoral, personal sickness (medical diagnosis).

In sum, the legal-political perspective is concerned with the definition of alcoholism within the moral domain or the medical domain. In this view, the diagnostic assertion that alcoholism is a disease is a cultural diagnosis of alcoholismic behavior as a nonmoral deviancy, to be dealt with through the health care institutions of the society. This is a generic and nonspecific diagnosis.

The Social Perspective

The social perspective is concerned with alcoholism as a social problem. From this perspective the diagnosis of alcoholism is viewed as a social process. At issue is how a specific society, or subsegment of society, creates and uses social rules to define certain behavior as alcoholic behavior, as differentiated from other drinking behaviors that are not to be classified as alcoholic. The range of drinking behavior that is diagnosed as alcoholism may be narrow or broad, depending on such social conventions [74]. In American culture there is a relatively common pattern of repetitive heavy drinking with obvious deterioration of the person that almost every common man on the street, using conventional wisdom, would surely diagnose as alcoholism. But with wider variations on this modal pattern of alcoholism the social rules for the diagnosis of alcoholism become more imprecise. Much social drinking has been called a myth, because alcoholic drinking in social settings is often not labeled as alcoholism [25]. Similarly, various patterns of erratic drinking, binge drinking, or high-volume drinking might be variously labeled "normal drinking," "heavy drinking," or "alcoholism," depending on the social rules of diagnosis. It is clear that different social processes result in very different diagnoses of what constitutes alcoholism. This problem has been referred to as "losing control over the concept of alcoholism" [73]. In fact, from the social perspective there are many social definitions of alcoholism.

Another major issue from the social perspective concerns the labeling of a person as alcoholic—or placing a person in the social role of an alcoholic. This is a diagnosis of a social label and a social role.

The social role of diagnosis of an alcoholic can be useful. It legitimates treatment of the person within the health care system, while at the same time the alcoholic person will be treated as a sick person in his or her social relationships. This can be salutary to all concerned. However, a person may resist being labeled as alcoholic and refuse treatment under that label, although he or she might accept treatment without the label and role [58]. A person may use the label and role of "alcoholic" to obtain social or legal exoneration for behavior. Or a person may find a type of negative identity as an alcoholic, and find it difficult to assume a nonalcoholic role [76].

The social perspective on diagnosis, then, focuses upon how social process discriminates a person as falling into the classification of alcoholic, and the possible positive or negative social consequences that may accrue.

The Treatment Perspective

The clinical view, the treatment perspective of alcoholism, is essentially a pragmatic one. First, one seeks to make a diagnosis that alcoholism is present, so that health care treatment can be legitimated. This is termed a "screening diagnosis." The intent is not to determine all types of drinking behavior that might be diagnosed as alcoholism, but rather to identify persons for whom there is reasonable certainty that treatment for alcoholism is indicated. Second, precise detail of diagnosis is closely related to precision of treatment. Where treatment is general and imprecise, there is little clinical need for detailed diagnosis. This has been the general state of clinical diagnosis of alcoholism, because until recently most treatment has been global and imprecise. Therefore, the detailed diagnosis of alcoholism was not a clinically useful exercise. However, as significantly different treatment methods and treatment goals have been developed in the past two decades, a need exists now for more detailed and precise diagnostic methods [61, 62, 63].

The Research Perspective

This approach to diagnosis aims to differentiate diagnostic criteria that will clarify etiology, prognosis, treatment prescription, prediction of response to various treatment methods, and evaluation of treatment effectiveness. These multiple goals of diagnosis are intertwined in complex fashion. Such complex diagnostic studies have been undertaken for the most part in just the last decade. Therefore, only the most preliminary and tentative conclusions can be drawn from these research efforts. However, advances in effective treatment methods are highly dependent upon the development of such sophisticated diagnostic research [3, 4, 51, 64, 65, 66].

THE FOCUS OF DIAGNOSIS

It is clear that alcoholics (persons with problems due to alcohol use) exist in the real world. Alcoholics are a consensual observed social reality. On the other hand, alcoholism is not a statement of social reality, but is a theoretical, conceptual, or hypothetical statement that refers to an assumed condition.

In his highly influential book, *The Disease Concept of Alcoholism*, Jellinek [36] proposed that the problems associated with alcohol use could be reasonably collated together in the concept of alcoholism. He further noted that there were many forms, patterns, and types of alcohol use subsumed under the concept of alcoholism, only some of which might properly be further defined as a disease. In fact, Jellinek referred to the concept in the plural, as "alcoholisms." Thus, for Jellinek, not all patterns of alcohol use were to be considered under the concept of alcoholism, and, indeed, not all types were to be considered a disease. Unfortunately, this circumspect and felicitous formulation of the problem of diagnosis was subsequently overlooked in much public rhetoric, in which the concept of alcoholism as a set of variable patterns was turned into a concrete entity — a specific illness. Technically, this is a logical process of reification of a concept into a thing.

A more accurate approach is to consider alcoholism as a hypothetical construct. Theory and hypothesis can be construed in two ways: (1) to intuit an explanation or formulation of a problem, which can then be tested; (2) to collect research data from which an explanatory theory or hypothesis can be formulated. Intermediate between these methods is the hypothetical construct, which MacCorquodale and Meehl [49] have described as a method to denote a set of heterogeneous observations, data, behavior. Thus, to say that alcoholism is a hypothetical construct is to say that one should denote a heterogeneous group of observations about people who use alcohol in a destructive fashion as alcoholism. The construct of alcoholism as a disease can legitimately be relabeled without logically implying that alcoholism is a specific thing or entity. And one can proceed to empirically determine various useful limits for behaviors that may be included under the construct of alcoholism.

Here the focus of diagnosis shifts from the concrete diagnosis of whether a person has "it" — namely, alcoholism — to a construct diagnosis, where the objective is to determine what patterns and types of alcohol use may be appropriately included in the construct of alcoholism for specific purposes.

Use, Misuse, and Abuse

The construct approach to diagnosis is clearly revealed in this consideration of patterns of use, misuse, and abuse.

The use of alcohol may be problematic for various reasons. In France it was long the custom to give young children diluted wine with their meals. As a result of such use, many French schoolchildren developed cirrhosis. In a similar vein, the high per capita consumption of alcohol by adult Frenchmen has resulted in an extraordinarily high level of medical illnesses as complications of chronic high alcohol consumption — it is estimated that perhaps 50% of medical hospitalizations in France are the direct consequence of chronic alcohol consumption (not just alcoholic admissions). Here use produces physical abuse. A second use pattern leads to psychotic reactions, or chronic psychological disorganization, or acute disorganization, creating panic states, suicidal ideation, and so forth. Here use produces psychological and physical abuse. Third, the illicit sale or use of alcohol can bring arrest, jail, and major social losses. Fourth, the use of alcohol in a social setting of prohibition may produce ostracism or other social sanctions, while at the same time provoking personal guilt, shame, anguish, or conflict. For example, social and psychological abuse might occur when a religious teetotaler adolescent starts drinking beer. In all such cases, the use per se would not construed as problematic, but physical, psychological, or social complications ensue. Thus use constitutes misuse and abuse.

The misuse of alcohol is construed in terms of adverse consequences directly consequent to alcohol use. For example, many people misuse alcohol at parties and other social occasions, in that there is reasonable expectation that such use may well result in arguments, fights, inappropriate behavior, sexual misconduct, and accidents. Here alsohol use may be claimed as social exoneration for the consequences; or, in another vein, alcohol may be used to prime oneself for deviant behavior. As a result, one finds a high incidence of drinking prior to criminal actions [68].

In abuse patterns, there is chronic recurrent use of alcohol, with both acute and chronic adverse consequences. Physiological and/or psychological dependence on alcohol is established. Such abuse can be socially acceptable, as in heavy social drinking; the use may be acceptable, as in drinking alcohol per se, but the consequent behavior may be unacceptable; or both use and consequences may be socially unacceptable.

Addiction, Habituation, and Dependence

Various terms have been used to denote alcohol dependence. In the first half of the century, many efforts were made to define a specific disease or state of addiction that was thought to be different from more moderate states of dependence, and was variously termed "alcohol habituation," "alcohol dependence," "alcohol misuse," or "problematic alcohol usage." These levels are ambiguous and clinically meaningless, for the patterns vary widely in symptomatology and severity. Such labels should be discarded.

It is more appropriate to discuss the syndrome of psychic dependence and physical dependence. The differences are clearly stated in the *World Health Organization Bulletin* [17].

> Drug dependence is a state of psychic or physical dependence, or both, on a drug, arising in a person following administration of that drug on a periodic or continuous basis.... All these drugs have one effect in common: they are capable of creating, in certain individuals, a particular state of mind that is termed "psychic dependence."
> ... This mental state may be the only factor involved, even in the case of the most intense craving and perpetuation of compulsive abuse ... psychic dependence can and does develop ... without any evidence of physical dependence.... Physical dependence, too, can be induced without notable psychic dependence, indeed, physical dependence is an inevitable result of the pharmacological action of some drugs with sufficient amount and time of administration. Psychic dependence, while also related to pharmacological action, is more particularly a manifestation of the individual's reaction to the effects of a specific drug and varies with the individual as well as the drug. [17]

The phenomenon of psychic dependence results from the fact that alcohol is psychoactive. It changes the conscious state of the consumer in one way or another. It does not matter much what change in consciousness is produced. The alcohol-dependent person relies on a change in consciousness to cope more effectively with self and to experience reality. Thus, alcohol-dependent people commonly also switch to other types of drugs, and develop mixed drug-alcohol dependence [59]. The alcohol-dependent person has a psychological reliance on the psychic effect of the drug to produce an altered state of consciousness.

As noted, physical dependence is not necessary for a person to acquire psychological dependence. Anyone can be made physically dependent, without necessarily acquiring a psychic dependence. In fact, most persons who drink a moderate quantity develop a mild tolerance to alcohol. Commonly this is termed "learning how to carry a drink."

The development of physical dependence lies in the pharmacologic properties of alcohol, which allow it to become incorporated into the metabolic cycles of cellular physiology. This is the pharmacologic addictive property. As a result of this metabolic incorporation, two clinical features emerge. The first is the development of tolerance. That is, the body can tolerate more alcohol biologically without manifesting the pharmacologic effects of the alcohol. As a result, one must consume more alcohol to produce a consciousness-changing effect. The second clinical feature is the production of withdrawal symptoms when alcohol is withheld. Withdrawal is a manifestation of altered organ function as a result of deprivation of the required alcohol as an essential metabolite.

In sum, physical dependence is a consequence of drinking. The primary roots of alcoholic behavior are rooted in psychic dependence. However, physical dependence can become a secondary reinforcer of drinking behavior.

Patterns of Alcohol Utilization

There are multiple patterns of alcohol utilization, comprising use, misuse, and abuse. People vary in vulnerability, their social milieu of prescriptions and proscriptions, and personal rewarding or adverse use experience, all of which influence patterns of actual alcohol use. One may consider actual alcohol use patterns as the consequence of a personal cost-benefit analysis.

Many people derive some psychic pleasure or reward, some social benefit, from alcohol use. At the same time there are personal and social controls and limits. These include legal constraints, moral and religious constraints, social expectations and sanctions about alcohol use, cultural norms, and personal values. As a result, most people establish a personal cost-benefit limit on how much they are willing to pay in a legal, social, moral, fiscal, and personal sense in exchange for the psychic and social rewards of alcohol use. Most people establish a reasonable cost-benefit ratio, and therefore avoid abuse of alcohol and use alcohol within low-cost limits [83].

On the other hand, under certain psychological or social conditions a person may be unable to set such limits, may be unable to behave in accordance with personal limits, may believe that the benefits outweigh the costs, or may develop distorted perspectives in which the individual believes that he or she is paying much less than is actually the case in use of alcohol. In all these different circumstances, alcohol misuse or dependence may develop.

Persons who might otherwise be highly vulnerable to developing alcohol dependence may avoid such a possibility through total avoidance of alcohol use. This alcohol avoidance may be for legal, moral, religious, psychological, or social reasons. Former alcoholics learn that for the most part an alcohol-free existence is a major and necessary step to maintain a life style that is devoid of dependence on alcohol.

The alcohol experimenter typically does not start out seeking or expecting to develop alcohol dependence.

1. If the drug experience is not rewarding, or if it produces adverse effects, the person may then become a nonalcohol user and an alcohol avoider.

2. Some people will experience nothing or will experience adverse alcohol effects, but will use alcohol occasionally as they participate in socially desirable or expected behavior.

3. Some, including a large number of average people, experience some positive, rewarding effects and engage in occasional legal use of alcohol. Here experimentation leads to degrees of use. Frequency and amount are well controlled, without adverse consequences.

4. A small number of people, who experience positive effects but who are not susceptible psychologically, will engage in more frequent use of alcohol in larger amounts. They may not experience loss of control over alcohol use, or develop any sense of psychic dependence, yet the amount of alcohol use may produce adverse effects physically, psychologically, or socially. This pattern typifies well-compensated, functional heavy drinkers, or habit drinkers.

5. There are those who are vulnerable psychologically and who engage in heavy alcohol use in a socially acceptable manner. They have a significant degree of alcohol dependence. Unlike the heavy drinkers above, these persons suffer degradation of function.

The prescribed-alcohol users present yet another developmental pattern. This category includes self-prescription and physician-prescription users.

1. Patients with primary neurotic symptoms, such as anxiety, depression, or hypochondriasis, may find that alcohol has symptom-relieving effects. Such patients may become dependent on alcohol to allay their symptoms, and they may develop psychological and physical dependence on alcohol secondary to their neurotic symptoms. This is a common pattern.

2. An uncommon pattern, but one that is nevertheless seen occasionally, is that of psychologically vulnerable patients who have some significant medical problem for which alcohol is prescribed (e.g., acute pain from an injury). When introduced to the psychic effects of alcohol, such patients rapidly develop alcohol dependence. Even more common is the prescription of alcohol as a tranquilizer [7].

3. Occurring with intermediate frequency is the pattern of patients with chronic pain, a chronic illness, or a fatal deteriorating illness. Here the use of alcohol may provide some realistic relief of pain and misery. A secondary psychic and physical dependence may ensue. For the dying patient such a situation may realistically be accepted. However, with chronic disease and pain problems, the complications of alcohol dependence rapidly outweigh the palliative value.

Finally, there is the group of alcohol seekers who can be divided into the self-medication group, the life style group, and the cultural crisis group. Those in the self-medication group typically face a life crisis, and turn to alcohol deliberately to provide symptom relief. Anxious and depressed persons may turn to alcohol deliberately to assuage their psychic state. In a sense, they do not care about becoming alcohol dependent because they seek relief at any cost. Another category is that of psychotic patients, who may find that alcohol causes their psychosis to remit. Such persons are usually very resistant to initial treatment, because alcohol is already their treatment.

The life style group represents those who start out in life without major maladjustments. They typically turn to alcohol early in life deliberately to escape from their unhappy existence. The rewards of living in an altered state of consciousness outweigh all the costs of a destructive, alcohol-dependent life style. For these people, an alcohol-free existence is no existence at all. Therefore, the development of a new life style is critical to any rehabilitation program.

The cultural crisis group involves primarily indigenous ethnic groups in the midst of major cultural change, changing norms of alcohol use, and severe cultural conflict. Here individual personality variables are not of major significance. Rather, many people in the cultural group misuse alcohol as a reflection of cultural disorganization. Intervention here is not primarily in terms of personal clinical treatment, but must address fundamental social disorganization. For example, Bacon [2], in a cross-cultural analysis of preliterate societies where Western patterns of alcohol use have been introduced in the past 100 years, reports that only about 8% have achieved cultural integration of alcohol use, whereas 92% have major alcoholism problems. Closer to home, in a recent study of the impact of the North Shore Alaskan oil development, Klausner et al. [41] report that 72% of the native villagers under study have symptomatic alcoholism!

In summary, there are multiple patterns of use, misuse, and abuse of alcohol, which in different contexts become the focus of diagnosis. However, such different alcoholisms vary widely in severity, prognosis, and type of societal intervention required. Therefore, the objective of diagnosis is to develop typological patterns that may have utility for different purposes: to determine etiology, to select treatment, to determine prognosis, to evaluate treatment, or to determine different methods of social intervention.

TYPES OF DIAGNOSIS

There are two major types of diagnosis: (1) binary diagnosis, and (2) multivariate diagnosis. Each has important conceptual and practical implications.

Binary Diagnosis

The binary type of diagnoses is an either/or method. One either is alcoholic or is not alcoholic. The binary approach may be based on either a unitary or a multivariate frame of reference.

First, a binary diagnosis may be based on the assumption that there is a discrete unitary entity termed "alcoholism." The diagnostic goal is simply to find an effective means to discriminate between those who suffer from alcoholism and those who do not. As indicated previously, this theoretical assumption has little utility, and the search for an unequivocal method of accurate binary diagnosis has failed because the term "alcoholism" does not refer to a concrete entity, but rather to a diverse set of behaviors and problems. As Pattison et al. [67] have outlined in detail, the unitary concept assumes that there is a distinct class of persons who have the specific disease of alcoholism, who are substantively different from problem drinkers, heavy drinkers, prodromal alcoholics, and prealcoholics. However, the research data of the past 20 years clearly demonstrate that the unitary concept of alcoholism is incorrect. There is no one entity to which a binary diagnostic method can be applied. As Rohan [75] has commented, "The results show that the label 'alcoholic' subsumes great quantitative diversity and that the present dichotomy of normal versus abnormal drinker, or social drinker versus alcoholic should be replaced with a concept of a continuum. The adverse effects of drinking are not linearly dependent on the quantity of drinking but depend on many other factors as well."

Second, the binary method of diagnosis may be based on a multivariate construct. Here one a priori sets limits on a binary diagnostic decision, to either include or exclude persons to be diagnosed as alcoholic. For example, the diagnostic limits of alcoholism might vary in a criminal trial, in screening drunken drivers, in assessing patients in an emergency room, in evaluating medical and surgical patients, and in cross-cultural, ethnic, or epidemiologic studies.

Multivariate Diagnosis

Most scientific authorities in the field of alcoholism now concur that the construct of alcoholism is most accurately construed as a multivariate syndrome. That is, there are multiple patterns of dysfunctional alcohol use that occur in multiple types of personalities, with multiple combinations of adverse consequences, with multiple prognoses, that may require different types of treatment interventions [5, 9, 13, 14, 28, 40, 44, 60, 69, 70, 84]. In brief, this construct of alcoholism implies the following:

1. There are multiple patterns of use, misuse, and abuse that may be denoted as a pattern of alcoholism.
2. There are multiple interactive etiological variables that may combine to produce a pattern of alcoholism.
3. All persons are vulnerable to the development of some type of alcoholism problem.
4. Treatment interventions must be multimodal to correspond to the particular pattern of alcoholism in a specific person.

5. Treatment outcomes will vary in accord with specific alcoholism patterns, persons, and social contexts.

6. Preventive interventions must be multiple and diverse to address diverse etiologic factors.

The utility of the multivariate diagnostic method, according to Miller [52], lies in the description of consistently intercorrelated sets of symptoms with implications for etiology, prognosis, treatment, and prevention. In contrast, the binary diagnostic method is limited, because, according to Miller, "A large amount of information is lost when the data regarding various aspects of the problem are reduced to a binary nomenclature. Certainly this reduction cannot improve our prediction of such complex events as treatment outcome."

The Concept of Alcoholism as a Syndrome

The multivariate approach to diagnosis leads one to consider alcoholism as a syndrome [18, 19, 20, 21]. Medical dictionaries define "syndrome" as a group or set of concurrent symptoms that together can be considered a disease. Note that considering alcoholism as a syndrome does not vitiate labeling alcoholism as a disease, for medical practice in general deals with many syndromes that are not specific diseases.

In medicine there are lists of signs and symptoms of many diseases and syndromes. However, signs and symptoms are not necessarily the same as definitive and obligatory diagnostic criteria. In medicine, there are signs and symptoms for most diseases. Yet the signs and symptoms may be identical for diseases of different etiology. For example, the signs and symptoms of pneumonia may be identical, even though there are different definitive diagnostic criteria in terms of etiology, such as pneumonia due to bacteria, or a virus, or a parasite, or congestive heart failure. Binary diagnosis of the condition of pneumonia is satisfactory to legitimate the diagnosis of the person as sick and in need of treatment. However, the binary diagnosis based on the signs of pneumonia is inadequate and insufficient to provide necessary and appropriate treatment. On the other hand, there are many syndromes in medicine for which signs and symptoms are the only available diagnosis, because specific etiologies have not been determined, or cannot easily be determined. In some such instances, as with a common cold or influenza, generic treatment methods may suffice, and the search for definitive diagnostic criteria are of no practical import. Or, in a syndrome such a senile dementia, multiple factors interplay to produce a clinical syndrome. Here specific diagnostic criteria cannot yet be provided. However, treatment of senile dementia can be effectively instituted to rectify known factors that may contribute to the syndrome, such as nutrition, perceptual deprivation, social deprivation, and physical complications. Thus, one can have a diagnostic set of criteria for treatment.

Returning to the case of pneumonia, the set of signs and symptoms provides justification for the diagnosis of the syndrome of pneumonia, which legitimates the person as ill with pneumonia, and justifies the treatment. This is the binary diagnosis of presence or absence of pneumonia. The utility of making the diagnosis of pneumonia is neither therapeutic nor scientific. It is social, legal, political, and economic. But a multivariate diagnosis must be used to achieve scientific and therapeutic diagnosis of pneumonia.

In summary, one may appropriately use a binary or a multivariate diagnosis of alcoholism, dependent upon the purpose of the diagnostic process.

METHODS OF DIAGNOSIS

There are a wide variety of methodological approaches to diagnosis. These are not reviewed in detail, for no one approach is definitive. Rather, the diagnostic results that given methods provide are examined.

Biological Methods

The basic assumption of biological methods is that there is some unitary biological phenomenon that underlies the clinical syndrome of alcoholism. Therefore, biological methods seek to find a specific biological marker unique to those persons demonstrating the clinical manifestations of alcoholism. There is no question but that there are substantial biological and physiological system alterations consequent to the acute and chronic use of alcohol. These may be considered the biological consequences of use or abuse. However, precedent biologic differences that might predict a general or specific alcoholism syndrome, or that might be considered to be an etiologic biological factor, have not been scientifically established [24, 46, 72]. This does not mean that biological correlates of alcoholism do not exist. Indeed, in severe chronic alcohol intake there are numerous classical biological consequences, such as liver, brain, heart, and nerve damage. Biological measures of such physical consequences will have a high correlation with an alcoholism syndrome.

There are two problems with such biological diagnostic methods. First, the biological measures are an indirect diagnosis, since they reflect the consequences of alcohol use. Second, many persons may have alcoholism syndromes without biological damage and will not be diagnosed by these methods [6].

Psychological Methods

Just as there have been attempts to diagnose a specific biological basis for alcoholism, there have been repetitive attempts to diagnose an alcoholic personality. As with the biology, the psychology has similarly failed. There are frequent and common patterns of psychological reactions found in persons with chronic, severe alcohol abuse, such as high levels of dependency, extensive use of denial, guilt, shame, anxiety, and significant depression. However, there is no unique personality or character structure common to all patterns of alcoholism [51, 56].

However, a variety of psychometric methods have been devised to achieve binary diagnoses of alcoholism. These methods may be subdivided into indirect psychometric methods and direct psychometric methods.

Indirect psychometric methods. Indirect psychometric methods rely on some test or measure of traits, attitudes, or behaviors that have a high correlation with a major and significant alcoholism syndrome. The prototype of this method is the MacAndrew alcoholism scale derived from the Minnesota Multiphasic Personality Inventory (MMPI) [47]. The scale does not assess alcoholic behavior, but is a collation of MMPI items that correlate significantly with clinical alcoholism. For diagnostic screening purposes, such indirect measures have some utility, although the validity and discrimination of less typical alcoholism syndromes are probably low [42, 55].

Direct psychometric methods. Direct psychometric methods have the same binary diagnostic intent and screening utility. These simple paper and pencil tests are composed of items directly referable to alcoholic behavior [29, 30]. The prototype for direct psychometric methods is the Michigan Alcoholism Screening Test (MAST), which has relatively high validity and reliability for screening [78]. Such tests might be termed "self-identification" tests [39]. For binary diagnostic screening, a number of short, simple, inexpensive forms have been developed [79, 87]. Their disadvantage is that atypical and less severe types of alcoholism are not likely to be identified.

Multivariate Methods

In contrast to the above methods, which might be termed "single-method and single-decision" diagnosis, the multivariate method employs multiple types of data collection, which may be subjected to several types of data analysis, yielding different diagnostic decision sets. The conceptual assumptions of this approach have been developed over the past 20 years to deal with measurement and assessment of social-behavioral phenomena. The problem of measurement is threefold. First, the target problem is usually a complex set of social behaviors that are construed together as a social construct; examples include all social problems like criminality, poverty, or alcoholism. There is no one thing to be measured or evaluated—rather, the construct itself is the target of evaluation. Second, there is no effective way to control all variables in actual social behaviors, so that a direct experimental design cannot be employed. Third, different specific pieces of the construct may require different types of measurement instruments—measures of personality, of attitude, of relationships, of behavior [57, 80].

Therefore, the diagnosis of social constructs assumes that fully controlled experiments cannot be conducted. Rather, one must use quasi experiments, in which uncontrolled variables are clearly defined and specified [12]. Further, one must collect data in combinations of sequential steps. This produces multimethod and multitrait matrices of data, which are not additive but multiplicative [10, 11]. Data analysis employs multivariate statistical techniques, which yield probability statements about the relationships between variables. The most recent of such methods is termed "causal pathway analysis." This approach provides a series of diagnoses rather than a single diagnosis.

DEFINITIONS AND DIAGNOSIS

As indicated, the diagnosis of alcoholism is problematic because there are many different conditions that can be diagnosed as alcoholism. The attempt to reach agreement on a core definition of alcoholism continues to be difficult and confusin. This is aptly reflected in the report of a special committee of the Royal College of Psychiatrists, Alcohol and Alcoholism:

> The word "alcoholism" is in common use, but at the same time there is general uncertainty about its meaning. Where is the dividing line between heavy drinking and this "illness"? It is a matter of quantity drunk or damage sustained, or of what else besides? This confusion is not limited to the layman, for final clarification has eluded the many experts and expert committees that have grappled with the terms to be used about drinking problems. [77]

The underlying problems center upon a delineation of the critical elements to be included in a definition of alcoholism. As Mendelson and Mello [51] observe, "Criteria for the diagnosis of alcohol abuse are imprecise and ambiguous."

The attempt to define critical elements has a long and checkered history among various official bodies; this history is briefly reviewed.

The Jellinek Classification

Jellinek [35] attempted to provide a set of provisional diagnostic categories of alcoholism, which he labeled in order simply alpha, beta, gamma, delta, epsilon. These are descriptive patterns of drinking. Jellinek did not consider these five types as all forms of alcoholism, but five types of alcohol use and abuse. Subsequent research has demonstrated that the five types are not useful for prescription of treatment or prediction of prognosis, because they are too vague and generalized.

Jellinek himself was well aware of the limitations of his descriptive approach to diagnosis and even expressed dire concerns over the simplistic application of his typologies.

The lay public uses the term "alcoholism" as designation for any form of excessive drinking, instead of as a label for a limited and well-defined area of excessive drinking behavior. Automatically, the disease conception of alcoholism becomes extended to all excessive drinking, irrespective of whether or not there is any physical or psychological pathology involved in the drinking behavior. Such an unwarranted extension of the disease conception can only be harmful because, sooner or later, the misapplication will reflect on the legitimate use too and, more importantly, will tend to weaken the ethical basis of social sanctions against drunkenness. [35]

In a very real sense, Jellinek anticipated the diagnostic work of the next 20 years, with his emphasis on differentiation between different patterns of alcohol abuse, the difference between dependence on alcohol and the consequences of alcohol use, and the importance of sociocultural variations in patterns of alcohol use, misuse, and abuse.

The World Health Organization

Through the work of a series of expert committees, the World Health Organization (WHO) has grappled with producing a universally and cross-culturally valid definition of alcoholism, for which diagnostic criteria could be developed.

The first salient report, in 1952 [85], already quoted in a 1965 revision, focused on the quality of psychic dependence, with secondary physical dependence, as the critical elements of alcoholism.

But what constituted dependence? In another WHO report [86] the term "dependence" was defined as, "A state, psychic, and sometimes also physical, resulting from the interaction between a living organism and a drug, characterized by behavioral and other responses that always include a compulsion to take a drug on a continuous or periodic basis in order to experience its psychic effects, and sometimes avoid the discomfort of its absence. Tolerance may or may not be present."

These reports gave rise to the ensuing formulation of alcoholism as a syndrome, termed the "alcohol dependence syndrome," with the following cardinal elements [20, 21]:

Narrowing of drinking repertoire
Salience of drink-seeking behavior
Increased tolerance to alcohol
Repeated withdrawal symptoms
Relief-avoidance of withdrawal
Subjective awareness of compulsion to drink
Reinstatement of syndrome after abstinence

However, the definition of the syndrome did not resolve matters. Further research revealed that many persons with some degree of the alcohol dependence syndrome were quite socially functional, while other persons, with little if any evidence of the syndrome, engaged in severe abuse of alcohol in terms of disordered behavior and adverse consequences of drinking. To address this situation the 1977 WHO report [22] and the Royal College of Psychiatrists' report [77] recommend that two basic classifications be employed: (1) the alcohol dependence syndrome, and (2) the alcohol-related disabilities. Both reports suggest an overlap between the two sets, yet they define two distinct types of alcohol problems.

In brief, the WHO reports present a substantial attempt to clarify the definition or definitions of alcoholism. Yet the current flux reflects the unresolved conceptual issues of definition [13].

The Diagnostic and Statistical Manual of the American Psychiatric Association

The new 1980 diagnostic criteria of American psychiatry [1] are explicitly atheoretical, in that they do not attempt to infer how a disorder develops. Rather, diagnosis is based on the description of clinical features. In this sense, the *Diagnostic and Statistical Manual of Mental Disorders*, third edition (DSM-III), approaches the definition of alcoholism in terms of observed typologies like Jellinek's. The WHO definitions are built upon etiologic assumptions.

DSM-III classifies alcohol intoxication, alcohol withdrawal, and alcohol organic mental disorders, as well as alcohol abuse and alcohol dependence. "Alcohol abuse" is defined as pathological use for at least 1 month that causes impairment in social or occupational functioning, while alcohol dependence in addition includes either tolerance or withdrawal.

As with the other definitions, the DSM-III categories are too general and imprecise for the purposes of treatment prescription or prognosis.

The National Council on Alcoholism Diagnostic Criteria

In 1972 the Criteria Committee of the National Council on Alcoholism (NCA) [54] published a diagnostic criteria instrument to meet the then-pressing social need to present a definitional set of criteria that would represent a consensus of medical opinion. Although widely publicized, the NCA criteria in their original form have been little used [23].

The diagnostic instrument consists of 86 items of information that are commonly associated with alcoholism, ranging from autopsy findings, to laboratory tests, to drinking behaviors, to information from family or friends. It is a "laundry list" of items that may help the physician review the overall status of the patient, and provide salient information upon which to base a diagnosis of alcoholism. It produces a binary diagnosis only.

The problems with this set of 86 criterion items are manifold and illustrate the problems of diagnosis based just on common signs or symptoms associated with alcoholism.

1. Emphasis on late adverse consequences of drinking in the items skews the diagnosis toward late stages of alcoholism, and fails to provide diagnostic markers of early or prodromal stages.
2. Item emphases on indirect consequences of drinking (e.g., marital fighting) are nonspecific, not unique or diagnostic of alcoholism.
3. Major emphasis on physical consequences of drinking minimizes diagnostic detection of alcoholics without such physical signs and symptoms.
4. Lack of discriminant validity of items (e.g., odor of alcohol on breath) weakens diagnosis, since an alcoholic may not have been drinking at an interview while a nonalcoholic may have.

Again, the general problem of developing accurate criteria items that are valid, reliable, and discriminatory is revealed in various diagnostic studies related to the NCA criteria items.

Item reliability was tested by Holland et al. [27], who found that items such as causes of drinking, psychological reasons for drinking, decreased tolerance reports, welfare or disability status, and usual times for drinking are diagnostically unreliable. Similarly, Stein and Bowman [81] found that measures of escape or symptomatic drinking were insignificantly related to drinking patterns or consequent behavior.

The issue of item validity is raised in a study by Justin [38] on routine breath analysis for alcohol. In 535 consecutive outpatients, Justin found six positives: one due to mouthwash, four nonalcoholics, and one alcoholic. Meanwhile, he clinically diagnosed 22 alcoholics in the series, none with positive breath analysis.

The problem of the heavy emphasis given to physical criteria in the NCA schemata is illustrated by two different types of investigations. First, Breitenbucher [8] examined 70 identified alcoholics. Only 27 were identified by clinical medical examination and 43 were identified by the MAST self-report, but only five of 70 had physical criteria matching the NCA diagnostic criteria. The second investigation is a series of papers by Drum and Jankowski [15, 16, 33, 34]. The only consistent physical and laboratory NCA items that were present in the majority of alcoholics were two laboratory findings: liver histopathology and erythrocyte macrocytosis. These were found only in severe chronic alcoholics. Although these researchers could increase their positive identification of alcoholics to 99% through an extensive battery of tests, such cases were only hospitalized severe cases of alcoholism. More important, this battery also produced up to 40% false positives. These studies illustrate the limitations of undue dependence on physical criteria items.

The problem of lack of item precision is illustrated in a study of eight different measures of alcohol consumption by Streissguth et al. [82]. They report low intercorrelations between the eight scales, while each scale tends to detect different types of alcoholism consumption. Thus, even with sophisticated scaling methods, one still does not have an acceptable diagnostic measure based on alcohol consumption.

The problems of item reliability and discriminant validity were specifically assessed on the NCA criteria by Ringer et al. [71]. They found that only 38 of the 86 items were discriminatory. While they did identify their alcoholic sample correctly at 99% accuracy, they also had 47.5% false positive identification of controls.

Although a physician sample has provided face validity concurrence with the NCA criteria items [23], it does not meet more precise psychometric requirements. An attempt to operationalize and quantify the NCA criteria items is reported by Landeen et al. [43]. They clustered nine major and 27 minor criteria. Their experimental sample consisted of severe chronic alcoholics. Given this population, they were able to use either major or minor criteria to discriminate alcoholics at a high level of statistical significance. However, in comparison, the simple self-report brief MAST (BMAST) test was just as effective a diagnostic instrument. Further, in a sample of 60 alcoholic patients, the BMAST produced only four diagnostic errors (6%), which were four false negatives. Using the major criteria produced 11 diagnostic errors (18%), which were 10 false negatives and one false positive; and using the minor criteria resulted in 20 diagnostic errors (33%), including 15 false negatives and five false positives. This study is particularly instructive, for it demonstrates that the NCA criteria can be quantified. But it produces high rates of false negative and false positive diagnoses and, more important, a simple quick test like the BMAST is much more accurate.

Other attempts are underway to modify the NCA criteria. Researchers at Brown University are devising sequential decision tracks for the differential use of criteria items. This project is in a preliminary stage of development [37]. A more advanced project under Jacobson [31, 32] has revised many of the NCA items to meet the psychometric problems identified. The last revision, called "MODCRIT II," has acceptable psychometric construction with very good binary screening validity.

CONCLUSIONS

In retrospect one can observe that there are multiple definitions of alcoholism. This is not necessarily undesirable, as long as one specifies the context, goals, and purposes for which a specific definition of alcoholism is employed. Admittedly this is a clumsy and imprecise solution. But at present that is considered a more desirable strategy than attempting to ignore the major definitional distinctions that are actually used in everyday life.

Similarly, it is currently necessary to employ different diagnostic tactics and methods, dependent upon the purposes of diagnosis within context. Binary diagnostic methods have utility for screening, triage referral, and limited epidemiologic research. However, multivariate diagnostic methods are required for treatment selection, evaluation, and research.

It is clear that this arena of alcoholism is still ambiguous and controversial, despite major advances in sophisticated new approaches to diagnosis.

TOWARD A MODEL OF THE MULTIVARIATE ALCOHOLISM SYNDROME

The past history of alcoholism research and treatment has generally been based on a set of assumptions about the nature of alcoholism; for convenience this has been called the "unitary model" of alcoholism. The assumptions of the unitary model were widely accepted until about 15 years ago, when new research directed specifically at each of several assumptions began to be conducted. This research has called into question the whole unitary model of alcoholism, because each of the assumptions have failed to be confirmed or are directly contradicted by extant research evidence.

In a recent book devoted primarily to this research evidence, Pattison et al. [67] collated the various assumptions of the unitary model in order to review the pertinent research data relevant to these assumptions. They presented the following assumptions of the unitary model:

1. There is a unitary phenomenon that can be identified as alcoholism. Despite variations, there is a distinct entity.

2. Alcoholics or prealcoholics are essentially different from nonalcoholics.

3. Alcoholics experience an irresistable physical craving for alcohol, or an overwhelming psychological compulsion to drink.

4. Alcoholics develop a process of loss of control over initiation of drinking and/or inability to stop drinking.

5. Alcoholism is a permanent and irreversible condition.

6. Alcoholism is a progressive disease that follows an inexorable development through a series of more or less distinctive phases.

Pattison et al. [67] examined the empirical scientific research on each of these assumptions of the conventional model. To sum up a whole book, they find substantial and serious contravening evidence against all six assumptions. They report that to various degrees each assumption is not supported by the scientific data, and requires significant reformulation. Therefore, they proposed a model of alcoholism based on the current scientific evidence. This model is presented here as a current working formulation of alcoholism.

Proposition 1. Alcoholism dependence subsumes a variety of syndromes defined by drinking patterns and the adverse consequences of such drinking.

Corollary A. These syndromes are defined as any combination of deleterious physical, psychological, or social consequences that follow the use of alcohol by an individual.

Corollary B. These syndromes can vary along a continuum from minimal consequences to severe and even fatal consequences.

Corollary C. These syndromes, jointly denoted as alcohol dependence, are best considered as serious health problems.

Corollary D. In specific circumstances it may be desirable for sociocultural, legal, political, and therapeutic goals to label alcohol dependence as a "disease," perhaps especially at the time of acute physical symptomatology. At the same time the alcohol-dependent person may appropriately be labeled as "sick." Such circumstances should be carefully delineated and limited in application to specific situations.

Proposition 2. An individual's use of alcohol can be considered as a point on a continuum from nonuse, to nonproblem drinking, to various degrees of deleterious drinking.

Corollary A. There may be preexisting differences between individual reactions to alcohol or vulnerability to adverse consequences of alcohol use, as a function of genetic, biological, psychological, and sociocultural factors. Such factors may increase or decrease the possibility that one may encounter problems in the use of alcohol.

Corollary B. Differing susceptibility to alcohol does not in and of itself produce alcohol dependence. Any person who uses alcohol can develop a syndrome of alcohol dependence.

Corollary C. There is no natural dichotomy between alcoholics and nonalcoholics but rather a continuous spectrum of drinking patterns that may result in different combinations of deleterious consequences.

Proposition 3. The development of alcohol problems follows variable patterns over time.

Corollary A. Alcohol problems may develop gradually over time, leading to increasingly severe consequences, or such problems may develop rapidly.

Corollary B. Alcohol problems do not necessarily proceed inexorably to severe fatal stages but may remain static at any level of severity.

Corollary C. Alcohol problems may be partially or completely reversed through either a natural process or a treatment program.

Proposition 4. Abstinence bears no necessary relation to rehabilitation.

Corollary A. A person may be totally abstinent without improvement in other areas of life function that are related to deleterious use of alcohol.

Corollary B. A person may demonstrate little change in his or her patterns of alcohol use yet make major improvements in other areas of life function that are related to his or her use of alcohol.

Corollary C. A person may change his or her patterns of alcohol use so that drinking no longer constitutes a problem in and of itself.

Proposition 5. Psychological dependence and physical dependence on alcohol are separate and not necessarily related phenomena.

Corollary A. Psychological dependence on alcohol is a syndrome of learned patterns of alcohol use.

Corollary B. Genetic, biological, psychological, and sociocultural factors may increase or decrease a person's vulnerability to develop a pattern of psychological dependence. None of these factors in isolation is necessarily sufficient to cause psychological dependence.

Corollary C. The consumption of a small amount of alcohol by a person once labeled "alcoholic" does not necessarily initiate a physical need that in turn causes further drinking.

Corollary D. An individual may experience a strongly felt need to drink in certain situations and not in others, which may be exacerbated by the consumption of small amounts of alcohol.

Proposition 6. Continued drinking of large doses of alcohol over an extended period of time is likely to initiate a process of physical dependence.

Corollary A. The state of physical dependence is marked by increased tolerance to alcohol, and may be manifest by the symptoms of an alcohol withdrawal syndrome of varying severity.

Corollary B. Any person who consumes a sufficient amount of alcohol over time will eventually develop some degree of physical dependence. This varies on a wide continuum: from the increased tolerance of the nonproblem light drinker, to the hangover of the occasionally intoxicated drinker, to severe withdrawal symptoms of the chronic heavy drinker.

Corollary C. The development of physical dependence is related primarily to amount and frequency of alcohol intake, not to a unique metabolic processing of alcohol.

Corollary D. A state of physical dependence may exist without any other adverse consequences of drinking, except the physiological sequelae.

Corollary E. There may be individual differences in biological sensitivity to the effects of alcohol, but such differences are neither necessary nor sufficient to establish physical dependence.

Corollary F. The state of physical dependence does not appear to be a permanent state but may vary with subsequent patterns of drinking after physical dependence is established. The degree of physical dependence appears to be reversible.

Proposition 7. The population of individuals with alcohol problems is multivariate.

Corollary A. While the range of types of problems and severity of problems may be arbitrarily defined into categories for research or clinical utility, such typologies must be recognized as relatively arbitrary heuristic classifications.

Corollary B. Treatment intervention must be multivariate. Individual treatment plans need to address: (1) the severity of the person's alcohol use; (2) the particular problems and consequences associated with the individual drinking pattern; and (3) the person's ability to achieve specific treatment goals.

Corollary C. Comprehensive rehabilitation requires a variety of services that range from information and education to intensive long-term care. Available services, methods, and goals should be flexible enough to meet individual needs and abilities to participate.

Proposition 8. Alcohol problems are typically interrelated with other life problems, especially when alcohol dependence is long established.

Corollary A. Rehabilitation should aim at specific changes in drinking behavior suitable to each individual.

Corollary B. Rehabilitation should aim at specific changes in problem areas of life function, in addition to efforts aimed at drinking behavior per se.

Corollary C. Rehabilitation must take into account individual preferences, goals, choices of treatment, degrees of disability, and abilities to attain goals.

Proposition 9. Because of the documented strong relationship between drinking behavior and environmental influences, emphasis should be placed on treatment procedures that relate to the drinking environment of the person.

Corollary A. The alcohol-dependent individual may require temporary removal from his or her environment (i.e., hospital, supportive residential facility, etc.), with a planned return to the natural environment.

Corollary B. To avoid further problems and achieve some stable level of existence, some alcohol-dependent individuals may require a quasi-permanent, sheltered living environment.

Corollary C. Rehabilitation is likely to require direct involvement in the environment. This should begin with an analysis of the alcohol-dependent person's interactions with his or her environment and proceed to planned environmental interventions with family, relatives, friends, and others in the social network.

Proposition 10. Treatment and rehabilitation services should be designed to provide for continuity of care over an extended period of time. This continuum of services should begin with effective identification, triage, and referral mechanisms, extend through acute and chronic phases of treatment, and provide follow-up aftercare.

Proposition 11. Evaluative studies of treatment of alcohol dependence must take into account the initial degree of disability, the potential for change, and an inventory of individual dysfunction in diverse life areas, in addition to drinking behavior. Assessment of improvement should include both drinking behavior and behavior in other areas of life function, consistent with presenting problems. Degrees of improvement must also be recognized. Change in all areas of life function should be assessed on an individual basis. This necessitates using pretreatment and posttreatment comparison measures of treatment outcome.

SUMMARY

This chapter reviews the different goals of diagnosis of alcoholism: legal-political, social, and treatment goals. Similarly, there are different purposes for which a diagnostic method can be appropriately employed. At present, there is no uniform diagnostic and classificatory system that appropriately encompasses the widely divergent contexts where diagnosis must be employed. The importance of defining the target construct of alcoholism to be used in a specific diagnostic setting is emphasized.

The reasons for construing alcoholisms as a multivariate syndrome are delineated. In accord with this construct a multivariate model of the alcohol syndrome as a set of postulates and corollaries is set forth. This model of alcoholism links current empirical research evidence on the nature of alcoholism to corollary implications for treatment interventions.

REFERENCES

1. American Psychiatric Association. *Diagnostic and Statistical Manual of Mental Disorders* (3rd ed.) (DSM-III). Author: Washington, D.C., 1980.
2. Bacon, M. K. Alcohol use in tribal societies. In: *Biology of Alcoholism: Social Aspects*

of Alcoholism (Vol. 4): Kissin, B. and Begleiter, H. (eds.). Plenum: New York, 1976.

3. Baekeland, F. Evaluation of treatment methods in chronic alcoholism. In: *Biology of Alcoholism: Treatment and Rehabilitation of the Chronic Alcoholic* (Vol. 5), Plenum: New York, 1977.

4. Baekeland, F., Ludwall, L. K., and Kissin, B. Methods for the treatment of chronic alcoholism: A critical appraisal. In: *Research Advances in Alcohol and Drug Problems* (Vol. 2), Israel, Y. (ed.). Wiley: New York, 1975.

5. Belasco, J. A. The criterion question revisited. *Br. J. Addict.* 66(1):39–44, 1971.

6. Berglund, M., Leijonquist, H., and Horlen, M. Prognostic significance and reversibility of cerebral dysfunction in alcoholism. *J. Stud. Alcohol* 38(9):1761–1770, 1977.

7. Blume, S. Iatrogenic alcoholism. *Q. J. Stud. Alcohol* 34:1348–1352, 1973.

8. Breitenbucher, R. B. The routine administration of the Michigan Alcoholic Screening Test to ambulatory patients. *Minn. Med.* 59(6):425–429, 1976.

9. Caddy, G. R. Toward a multivariate analysis of alcohol abuse. In *Alcoholism: New Directions in Behavior Research and Treatment*, Nathan, P. E., Marlatt, G. A. and Lorberg, T. (eds.). Plenum: New York, 1978.

10. Campbell, D. T., and Fiske, D. W. Convergent and discriminant validation by the multitrait multimethod matrix. *Psychol. Bull.* 56:81–105, 1959.

11. Campbell, D. T., and O'Connell, E. J. Method factors in multitrait multimethod matrices: Multiplicative rather than addictive? *Multivar. Behav. Res.* 2:409–426, 1967.

12. Campbell, D. T., and Stanley, J. C. *Experimental and Quasiexperimental Designs for Research.* Rand McNally: Chicago, 1966.

13. Davies, D. L. Defining alcoholism. In: *Alcoholism in Perspective*, Grant, M. and Gwinner, P. (eds.). University Park Press: Baltimore, 1979.

14. Davis, C. S., and Schmidt, M. R. (eds.). *Differential Treatment of Drug and Alcohol Abuses.* ETC: Palm Springs, Calif., 1977.

15. Drum, D. E., and Jankowski, D. Diagnostic algorithms for detection of alcoholism in general hospitals. In: *Currents in Alcoholism* (Vol. 1), Seixas, F. A. (ed.). Grune & Stratton: New York, 1977.

16. Drum, D. E., and Jankowski, C. Algorithms for alcoholism detection: Reduction of false positive diagnoses. In: *Currents in Alcoholism* (Vol. 3), Seixas, F. A. (ed.). Grune & Stratton: New York, 1978.

17. Eddy, N. B., Halbach, H., Isbell, H., and Seevers, M. H. Drug dependence: Its significance and characteristics. *WHO Bull.* 32(5):721–733, 1965.

18. Edwards, G. Drugs, drug dependence and the concept of plasticity. *Q. J. Stud. Alcohol* 35(1A):176–195, 1974.

19. Edwards, G. The alcohol dependence syndrome: Usefulness of an idea. In: *Alcoholism: New Knowledge and New Responses*, Edwards, G. and Grant, M. (eds.). University Park Press: Baltimore, 1977.

20. Edwards, G., and Gross, M. M. Alcohol dependence: Provisional description of a clinical syndrome. *Br. Med. J.* 1(6017):1058–1066, 1976.

21. Edwards, G., Gross, M. M., Keller, M., and Moser, J. Alcohol-related problems in the disability perspective: A summary of the consensus of the WHO group of investigators on criteria for identifying and classifying disabilities related to alcohol consumption. *J. Stud. Alcohol* 37(9):1360–1382, 1976.

22. Edwards, G., Gross, M. M., Keller, J., Moser, J., and Room, R. *Alcohol-Related Disabilities* (offset publication No. 32). World Health Organization: Geneva, 1977.

23. Filstead, W. J., Goby, M. J., and Bradley, N. J. Critical elements in the diagnosis of alcoholism: A national survey of physicians. *J.A.M.A.* 236(24):2767–2769, 1976.

24. Frances, R. J., Timm, S., and Bucky, S. Studies of familial and nonfamilial alcoholism. *Arch. Gen. Psychiatry* 37(5):564–570, 1980.

25. Hayman, M. The myth of social drinking. *Am. J. Psychiatry* 124(5):585–594, 1967.

26. Heath, D. B. A critical review of ethnographic studies of alcohol use. In: *Research Advances in Alcohol and Drug Problems* (Vol. 2), Gibbons, R. J. et al. (eds.). Wiley: New York, 1975.

27. Holland, R., Datta, K., Izadi, B., and Evenson, R. C. Reliability of an alcohol self-report instrument. *J. Stud. Alcohol* 40(1):142–144, 1979.

28. Horn, J. L. Comments on the many faces of alcoholism. In: *Alcoholism: New Directions in Behavioral Research and Treatment*, Marlatt, G. A. and Lorberg, T. (eds.). Plenum: New York, 1978.

29. Jacobson, G. R. *Diagnosis and Assessment of Alcohol Abuse and Alcoholism* (DHEW Pub. No. ADM 76-228). U.S. Government Printing Office: Washington, D.C., 1976.

30. Jacobson, G. R. *The Alcoholisms: Detection, Diagnosis, and Assessment*. Human Sciences Press: New York, 1976.

31. Jacobson, G. R., and Lindsay, D. Screening for alcohol problems among the unemployed. In: *Currents in Alcoholism* (Vol. 8), Galanter, M. (ed.). Grune & Stratton: New York, 1980.

32. Jacobson, G. R., Niles, D. H., Moberg, D. P., Mandehr, E., and Dusso, L. N. Identifying alcoholic and problem-drinking drivers: Wisconsin's field test of a modified NCA criteria for the diagnosis of alcoholism. In: *Currents in Alcoholism* (Vol. 6), Galanter, M. (ed.). Grune & Stratton, New York, 1979.

33. Jankowski, C., and Drum, D. E. Criteria for the diagnosis of alcoholism: Occurrence and limitations in general hospital patients. In: *Currents in Alcoholism* (Vol. 1), Seixas, F. A. (ed.). Grune & Stratton: New York, 1977.

34. Jankowski, C., and Drum, D. E. Algorithms for alcoholism detection: Initial prospective studies. In: *Currents in Alcoholism* (Vol. 3), Seixas, F. A. (ed.). Grune & Stratton: New York, 1978.

35. Jellinek, E. M. Phases of alcohol addiction. *Q. J. Stud. Alcohol* 13:673–684, 1952.

36. Jellinek, E. M. *The Disease Concept of Alcoholism*. Hillhouse Press: New Haven, Conn., 1960.

37. Johnston, R. G. M., Mayfield, D. G., and Lex, B. W. Reliable interpretation of the NCA criteria in an estimate of the prevalence of alcoholism in a general hospital. *Am. J. Drug. Alcohol Abuse* 7:25–31, 1980.

38. Justin, R. G. Use of routine breath alcohol tests in the diagnosis of alcoholism in a primary care practice. *J. Stud. Alcohol* 40(1):145–147, 1979.

39. Kaplan, H. B., Kansas, T., Pokorny, A. D., and Lively, G. Screening tests and self-identification in the detection of alcoholism. *J. Health Soc. Behav.* 15:51–56, 1974.

40. Kissin, B. Theory and practice in the treatment of alcoholism. In: *Biology of Alcoholism: Treatment and Rehabilitation of the Chronic Alcoholic* (Vol. 5), Kissin, B. and Begleiter, H. (eds.). Plenum: New York, 1977.

41. Klausner, S. Z., Foulkes, E. F., and Moore, M. H. *Social Change and the Alcohol Problem on the Alaskan North Slope*. Center for Research on the Acts of Man: Philadelphia, 1980.

42. Knox, W. J. Objective psychological measurements and alcoholism: Review of the literature 1971–72. *Psychol. Rep.* 35(3, part 2):1023–1050, 1976.

43. Landeen, R. H., Aaron, A. J., and Breer, P. E. A multipurpose self-administered drinking problem questionnaire. In: *Currents in Alcoholism* (Vol. 1), Seixas, F. A. (ed.). Grune & Stratton: New York, 1977.

44. Larkin, E. J. *The Treatment of Alcoholism: Theory, Practice, Evaluation*. Addiction Research Foundation: Toronto, 1974.

45. Linsky, A. S. Theories of behavior and the social control of alcoholism. *Soc. Psychiatry* 7:47–52, 1972.

46. Lipscomb, T. R., and Nathan, P. E. Blood alcohol level discrimination: The effect of family history of alcoholism, drinking pattern, and tolerance. *Arch. Gen. Psychiatry* 37(5): 571–576, 1980.
47. MacAndrew, C. The differentiation of male alcoholic outpatients from nonalcoholic psychiatric outpatients by means of the MMPI. *Q. J. Stud. Alcohol* 26(2):238–246, 1965.
48. MacAndrew, C., and Edgerton, R. B. *Drunken Comportment: A Social Explanation.* Aldine: Chicago, 1969.
49. MacCorquodale, K., and Meehl, P. E. On a distinction between hypothetical constructs and intervening variables. *Psychol. Rev.* 55:95–107, 1948.
50. Marshall, M. *Beliefs, Behaviors, and Alcoholic Beverages: A Cross-cultural Survey.* University of Michigan Press: Ann Arbor, 1979.
51. Mendelson, J. H., and Mello, N. K. (eds.). *The Diagnosis and Treatment of Alcoholism.* McGraw-Hill: New York, 1979.
52. Miller, W. R. Alcoholism scales and objective assessment methods: A review. *Psychol. Bull.* 83:649–674, 1976.
53. Muller, C. The over-medicated society. *Science* 176:488–492, 1972.
54. National Council on Alcoholism, Criteria Committee. Criteria for the diagnosis of alcoholism. *Ann. Intern. Med.* 77(2):249–258, 1972.
55. Neuringer, C., and Clopton, J. R. The use of psychological tests in the study of the identification, prediction, and treatment of alcoholism. In: *Empirical Studies of Alcoholism*, Goldstein, G. and Neuringer, C. (eds.). Ballinger: Cambridge, Mass., 1976.
56. Ogborne, A. C. Patient characteristics as predictors of treatment outcome for alcohol and drug abuse. In: *Research Advances in Alcohol and Drug Abuse Problems* (Vol. 4), Israel, Y. (ed.). Plenum: New York, 1978.
57. O'Leary, M. R., Rohsenow, D. J., and Chaney, E. F. The use of multivariate personality strategies in predicting attrition from alcoholism treatment. *J. Clin. Psychiatry* 40:190–193, 1979.
58. Orford, J. A comparison of alcoholics whose drinking is totally uncontrolled and those whose drinking is mainly controlled. *Behav. Res. Ther.* 11(4):565–576, 1973.
59. Ottenberg, D. J., Carroll, J. F. X., and Bolognese, C. *Treating Mixed Psychiatric-Drug Addicted and Alcoholic Patients.* Eagleville Hospital Proceedings 11th Conference, Eagleville, Pa., 1979.
60. Pattison, E. M. Rehabilitation of the chronic alcoholic. In: *The Biology of Alcoholism: Clinical Pathology* (Vol. 3), Kissin, B. and Begleiter, H. (eds.). Plenum: New York, 1974.
61. Pattison, E. M. A conceptual approach to alcoholism treatment goals. *Addict. Behav.* 1(3):177–192, 1976.
62. Pattison, E. M. Nonabstinent drinking goals in the treatment of alcoholism: A clinical typology. *Arch. Gen. Psychiatry* 33(8):923–930, 1976.
63. Pattison, E. M. Ten years of change in alcoholism treatment and delivery systems. *Am. J. Psychiatry* 134(3):261–266, 1977.
64. Pattison, E. M. The Jack Donovan Memorial Lecture, 1978: Differential approaches to multiple problems associated with alcoholism. *Contemp. Drug. Prob.* 9:265–309, 1979.
65. Pattison, E. M. The selection of treatment modalities for the alcoholic patient. In: *The Diagnosis and Treatment of Alcoholism*, Mendelson, J. H., and Mello, N. K. (eds.). McGraw-Hill: New York, 1979.
66. Pattison, E. M., and Kaufman, E. Alcoholism and drug dependence. In: *Psychiatry in General Medical Practice*, Usdin, G. and Lewis, J. M. (eds.). McGraw-Hill: New York, 1979.
67. Pattison, E. M., Sobell, M. B., and Sobell, L. C. *Emerging Concepts of Alcohol Dependence.* Springer: New York, 1977.

68. Pernanen, K. Alcohol and crimes of violence. In: *Biology of Alcoholism: Social Aspects of Alcoholism* (Vol. 4), Kissin, B. and Begleiter, H. (eds.). Plenum: New York, 1976.

69. Pomerleau, O., Pertschuk, M., and Stinnett, J. A critical examination of some current assumptions in the treatment of alcoholics. *J. Stud. Alcohol* 37(7):849–867, 1976.

70. Replogle, W. H., and Haim, J. F. Multivariate approaches to profiling alcoholism subtypes. *Multiv. Exp. Clin. Res.* 3:157–164, 1977.

71. Ringer, C., Kufner, H., Antons, K., and Feuerlein, W. The NCA criteria for the diagnosis of alcoholism: An empirical evaluation study. *J. Stud. Alcohol* 38(7):1259–1273, 1977.

72. Rix, K. J. B. *Alcohol and Alcoholism.* Eden Press: Montreal, 1977.

73. Robinson, D. The alcohologist's addiction—some implications of having lost control over the disease concept of alcoholism. *Q. J. Stud. Alcohol* 33(4A):1028–1042, 1972.

74. Robinson, D. *From Drinking to Alcoholism: A Sociological Commentary.* Wiley: New York, 1976.

75. Rohan, W. P. Quantitative dimensions of alcohol use for hospitalized problem drinkers. *Dis. Nerv. Syst.* 37(3):154–159, 1976.

76. Roman, P. M., and Trice, H. M. The sick role, labelling theory and the deviant drinker. *Int. J. Soc. Psychiatry* 14:245–251, 1978.

77. Royal College of Psychiatrists. *Alcohol and Alcoholism.* Free Press: New York, 1979.

78. Selzer, M. L. The Michigan Alcoholism Screening Test: The quest for a new diagnostic instrument. *Am. J. Psychiatry* 127:89–94, 1971.

79. Skinner, H. A. A multivariate evaluation of the MAST. *J. Stud. Alcohol* 40(9):831–844, 1979.

80. Sobell, L. C., and Sobell, M. B. Convergent validity: An approach to increasing confidence in treatment outcome conclusions with alcohol and drug abuse. In: *Evaluating Alcohol and Drug Abuse Treatment Effectiveness: Recent Advances,* Sobell, L. C., Sobell, M. B. and Ward, E. (eds.). Pergamon: New York, 1978.

81. Stein, L. I., and Bowman, R. S. Reasons for drinking: Relationship to social functioning and drinking behavior. In: *Currents in Alcoholism* (Vol. 2), Seixas, F. A. (ed.). Grune & Stratton: New York, 1977.

82. Streissguth, A. P., Martin D. C., and Buffington, V. E. Identifying heavy drinkers: A comparison of eight alcohol scores obtained on the same sample. In: *Currents in Alcoholism* (Vol. 2). Seixas, F. A. (ed.). Grune & Stratton: New York, 1977.

83. Vaillant, G. E. Natural history of male psychological health: VIII. Antecedent of alcoholism and "orality." *Am. J. Psychiatry* 137(2):181–186, 1980.

84. Willems, P. J. A., Letemendia, F. J. J., and Arroyave, F. A categorization for the assessment of prognosis and outcome in the treatment of alcoholism. *Br. J. Psychiatry* 122(571):649–654, 1973.

85. World Health Organization. *Expert Committee Report No. 48.* Author: Geneva, 1952.

86. World Health Organization. *Expert Committee Report on Mental Health.* (Technical Report Series, No. 273). Author: Geneva, 1964.

87. Zung, B. J. Psychometric properties of the MAST and two briefer versions. *J. Stud. Alcohol* 40(9):845–859, 1979.

2

WILLIAM P. ROHAN, PhD, Veterans Administration Hospital, Northampton, Massachusetts

THE CONCEPT OF ALCOHOLISM: ASSUMPTIONS AND ISSUES

Over a decade ago, Christie and Bruun [2] characterized the outcome of efforts to define alcoholism as a "conceptual mess." This chapter presents an analysis of some of the most salient conceptual problems encountered in the attempt to construct a definition of alcoholism. The thesis is that the attempt clearly to define the meaning of alcoholism has failed simply because there is no specific entity to be defined. The term "alcoholism" is merely a convenient shorthand label for selected events involving alcohol use and damage, not the name of an actual entity.

This thesis is based on the proposition that alcoholism is a conceptual "construct," as discussed in Chapter 1. How the construct has been misused and can be appropriately used is elaborated upon. The emphasis is on the inadequacy of using the construct to "explain" drinking behavior, and on its use as a descriptive term denoting a class of behaviors involving harmful alcohol use. This approach shares a similar emphasis to that found in Section IV on the social dimensions of alcoholism, and in particular to the behavioral analyses of alcohol use discussed in Chapters 5, 6, 43, 88, 94, and 96. Finally, this approach shares the same theoretical and descriptive approach to defining alcoholism as that discussed in Chapter 3. But the frame of reference here is different from the DSM-III diagnostic strate-

---

William P. Rohan, PhD, Veterans Administration Hospital, Northampton, Massachusetts.

The opinions expressed in this chapter do not necessarily represent those of the Veterans Administration.

gies presented in Chapter 3 in that DSM-III basically attempts to provide a binary diagnosis of alcoholism, whereas this chapter is concerned with a description of a diagnostic continuum of alcohol use [12].

THE CONCEPT OF THE "GHOST IN THE MACHINE"

One of the major issues in our attempt to understand human behavior is the relationship between the "seen" behavior and the "unseen" operations of the mind. A common solution has been to name some innate unseen force of the mind (and/or body) as the explanatory agent of the behavior. This has been commonly called the "ghost in the machine" explanation. The problem is that it is no explanation, but only a pseudo-explanation. The construct of alcoholism is an example of using a word or name in this manner to explain a set of behaviors.

The destructiveness of some drinking schedules and their persistence, despite horrendous consequences, makes it seem that some terrible power is operating that victimizes the individual. It leads to a search for unseen forces [13]. This has fostered the concept of "alcoholism" as an imputed "ghost" accounting for observable events. The difficulty in defining alcoholism is related to this attempt to decribe the personality of an invisible ghost that somehow controls a person's behavior. This ghost never leaves, although it may remain quiet for long periods of time, meanwhile increasing its strength. When a drink is taken, it usurps normal controls, and impels excessive drinking. The ghost in the machine represents a projection and transformation of our words and ideas into a thing of power disguised in the sophisticated and respectable language of medicine. This assumes a solution and assurance that something is there soon to be discovered and controlled. But the error of this assumption finds essence where only acts exist. To go beyond the observable activity of harmful alcohol ingestion in search of essences obscures the fact that a crucial aspect of the problem is no more mysterious than the particular kind of drinking behavior that occurs. Explanation of this behavior is not promoted by appeal to an assumed essence.

FOCUS ON OBJECTIVE DESCRIPTION OF DRINKING AND CONSEQUENCES

To resolve this difficulty it is necessary to shift the focus away from an assumed underlying essence and to observe the activity of drinking. The central problem is not to be construed as incidental to a mysterious process that is separate from the actual behavior of drinking. Rather, the focus is on observation and description of drinking behavior and how it becomes problematic. The term "alcoholism," if used at all, should be limited to being a convenient reference label for selected sequences of harmful ingestion activity. No assumption need be made that what is studied is a sign of a unique condition. Alcoholism may be defined in terms of patterns of behavior.

The need for an objective description of the characteristics of ingestion sequences is evident. Knowledge of how quantities are ingested over time forms a basis for the explanatory structure of problem drinking. It is critical to know in specific ways how drinking schedules occur, how they are alike and different, and how they change. This knowledge serves to determine the salient and, it is hoped, modifiable antecedents of positive and negative changes in drinking behavior. It is also the touchstone for relating the various physical, psychological, and social consequences of drinking to these consumption characteristics.

DIFFERENCES AMONG DRINKERS

The crucial difference among drinkers is in the way they drink—how much and in what way alcohol is processed over a given period of time. These differences can be assessed in terms of quantities consumed, the length of time taken for consumption, the frequency of episodes, the variation of intake patterns over time, and even more detailed analyses of drinking behaviors, such as those described by Pomerleau et al. [14]. These variables could be used for differentiating users of alcohol, identifying antecedents of drinking, and for predicting consequences. Although other factors might be important, such as the health habits and genetic susceptibility to damage from alcohol, a major thrust could be in relating consumption characteristics to antecedents and probable consequences.

CONNECTION OF DRINKING AND CONSEQUENCES

Mäkelä [9] states that there is a plethora of research to show that drinking or heavy drinking is associated with a wide array of pernicious consequences, and that the frequency of consequences is related to the overall level of drinking. But if more detailed questions are asked about such variables as the amount and pattern of intake on the probability of different types of consequences, the evidence is fragmentary. What is needed, then, is an objective look at drinking behavior and a connecting of this behavior to both antecedents and consequences. Within this frame of reference each drinker could be seen as differing in degree rather than kind from other drinkers. Those having similar ingestion histories might generally have similar damage probabilities. The greater the amount consumed and the longer the period of time over which it was consumed, the higher the probability of the various types and severity of negative consequences.

VARIETY IN DRINKING SEQUENCES

When drinking is considered as an observable and measurable activity, severely harmed drinkers and those engaged in faulty drinking practices are no longer seen as inexorably tracked through preordained stages of an unspecified disease. Fillmore [4] has indicated that many alcoholics to not conform to the postulated sequences of alcoholism. Alcohol ingestion schedules, severely damaging and otherwise, can be seen as varying in the possible direction of change, depending on the interplay of the complex variables that influence such behavior. The increases and decreases in drinking quantities over time could be a product of both past and present contingencies. Ingestion activity could be recognized as relatively open-ended, able to change in direction at any point in time on the dimensions of consumption. Here it becomes more feasible to conceptually apprehend the research-supported hypothesis that controlled drinking by alcoholics is possible.

ROLE OF ENVIRONMENT

As has been pointed out by Mello and Mendelson [11] and others (Gottheil et al. [5]; Marlatt et al. [10]), direct observation of alcoholics during periods when they could drink any amount has indicated that perpetuation of drinking behavior is controlled by a variety of complex social and environmental factors, rather than alcohol dosage per se.

Some alcoholics immediately and completely stop drinking with changes in environment, such as hospital entry, or after some dramatic constructive pressure in the work place. Also, there is evidence of controlled drinking in certain environments (Gottheil et al. [5]). This emphasizes that ingestion activity is susceptible to external factors and the compelling internal events that are thought of as primary accommodate environmental contingencies. Bruun et al. [1] have pointed out that external or social factors are determinants of the role of alcohol consumption even in the population labeled "alcoholics."

DETAILED ANALYSIS OF DRINKING BEHAVIOR

A careful and detailed analysis of drinking behavior could lead to a description of the varieties and variability of drinking sequences. Study of profiles of drinking histories could confirm the notion that the distribution of ingested quantities over time does not conform to the stereotype of the alcoholic, even in those who are eventually labeled as alcoholics (Rohan [16]; Fillmore [4]). Profiles might well include erratic as well as gradual increases and decreases in both normal and abnormal drinkers, either early or late in a drinking career. Extreme drinking does not always predict extreme drinking in all circumstances. Low-level consumption might be followed by periodic increases or intense sporadic intake. The probability of various sequences could be computed, and patterns could be differentiated and described. A drinker with a characteristic pattern might engage in atypical drinking with changing environmental events.

CAUSES AND EXPLANATIONS OF DRINKING BEHAVIOR

To answer the question of what causes such drinking or why individuals differ in their drinking habits is equivalent to trying to answer basic questions about behavior. To understand a subclass of behaviors involving repeated and harmful ingestion of alcohol over long periods of time is part of the larger issue of why people act as they do. It is a large question that cannot be reduced to simplistic notions that make the problem seem easier to handle. The science of accounting for behavioral events is only beginning. The major point is that we need to study drinking activity itself, since we have not done that yet, and allow our assumptions to be suspended; this is the scientific demand of carefully observing objective events without prematurely constructing assumption-ridden explanatory schemes.

If it were known how individuals conduct their drinking and how they differ from one another, explanations could then be elaborated that are more closely connected to observable and measured events, and lead toward the extermination of "fat words" (Christie and Bruun [2]). Problem-solving steps could more likely occur to help relieve the physical, psychological, and social consequences as the contingencies of drinking increases became apparent.

THE DIAGNOSIS OF ALCOHOLISM

It is likely that negative-consequence drinking occurs throughout the drinking population, to different degrees and at different times, and that there is no clear demarcation among drinkers. This emphasizes the necessity of describing the types and severity of damage that can occur among users of alcohol, without postulating essential differences. Why individuals exceed these safe limits of drinking, periodically or continuously and some to such an extreme, is not illuminated by the concept of alcoholism. The answer to this question is integrally connected to how a person drinks, and leads to further concern about how much to drink, how often, to what extremes, and in what ways could such drinking be changed to reduce the probability of risk. Some determination of the likely future consequence of continued drinking for a given schedule should be possible.

To establish a diagnosis of alcoholism does not increase our understanding of what has or is happening to an individual or add to the obvious conclusion that such a person has been ingesting enough alcohol for a sufficient period of time to do serious damage.

Diagnostic criteria should be seen, not as symptoms of an underlying disease, but as signs of faulty drinking practices. The types and degree of physical, psychological, and social problems can then be related to the kinds of drinking schedules that have been maintained. It becomes feasible to predict the likely outcome of various ingestion patterns at any point in time, based on the distribution of ingested quantities over time. Diagnosis must come from a careful analysis of the reality of drinking as it actually occurs among users of alcohol.

UNNECESSARY DISTINCTIONS

"Alcoholic" and "social drinker" are obfuscating terms that serve to differentiate certain segments of the drinking population on dubious assumptions. Those who suffer extreme and obvious damage are labeled alcoholics, while those suffering acceptable damage are not so labeled. By making a certain percentage of alcohol users essentially different and victims of a mysterious malady, the importance of the quantitative differences recedes, and distinct classes of drinkers are formed.

Bruun et al. [1] have criticized the widely entertained concept of alcoholism as a clear-cut disease entity, because it has encouraged the view that "normal drinkers" and "alcoholics" form two quite separate groups within the population. Alcoholism is seen as an essentially imminent condition that is immune to environmental manipulations or controls. The adverse implications of this view are detailed by Pattison in Chapter 39.

Once it is realized that alcoholism is not an actual entity, there is no need to postulate the characteristics of alcoholism, including the alleged stages, an inevitable progression, irreversibility, and the trigger mechanisms of the single drink. The interpretation of an "inevitable characteristic" is an assumption based on frequent observation of contiguous events. Frequently occurring events within the drinking population have, through repeated association, become causal necessities. Because one event often follows another, it is thought that it must follow — such as a binge following a single drink. Since many individuals do persist in drinking despite severely negative consequences, it is concluded they must do so, and that some internal ghost has captured their future. Those who do not persist are either unnoticed or disqualified as not being "real" alcoholics. Again, this conclusion is only justified if there is the a priori assumption of an entity termed "alcoholism."

It may be difficult to accept the notion that alcoholism is simply a construct that may misconstrue reality. But a more accommodating explanatory scheme becomes possible. It is not necessary or desirable to assume that a large group of alcohol users share a mysterious and permanent affliction. The assumed attributes of alcoholism can be re-examined. The circular reasoning involved in the statements, "I know that this persom is an alcoholic because he drinks too much," and "I know that this person drinks too much because he is an alcoholic" can be identified as tautological.

This frame of reference does not presume a special disposition toward misuse of alcohol; anyone can become involved in a destructive drinking sequence either periodically or continuously. Each user of alcohol is susceptible to increased ingestion when the circumstances occur that encourage ingestion beyond safe limits.

ALCOHOLISMS: MULTIPLYING AN ERROR

Such a shift in thinking comes very slowly, and rather than discarding the concept of alcoholism, some have suggested multiplying it, since it is increasingly obvious that the simple concept does not fit the problem. Hoff [6] and Jellinek [7] represent this position and have suggested that there are types of alcoholism, or alcoholisms. This compounds an already serious error and indicates the strength of the addiction to essences. A fundamental shift is needed to help recognize that our present conceptual scheme is a blind alley, and that viable alternatives are possible. Otherwise, we will continue the equivalent of trying to account for falling objects by the concept of "fallism," or worse, "fallisms," and remain immersed in a conceptual mess. "Alcohol-ism" is no more viable than "cigarette-ism," "food-ism," or other reified abstract nouns.

Madden [8] has already indicated that "the search for the essence of alcoholism has not been terminated by agreement in debate, and is incapable of settlement by scientific observation of sense data and experiment." He suggests that definitions should not ascribe an essential value to alcoholism, but should follow the scientific convention in which the defined term is simply a working label for a designated group of phenomena. The present conception of alcoholism is not understood as merely a convenient label and an arbitrary shorthand term for a class of events related to alcohol use and associated damage, but has come to signify an actual entity.

More persons are beginning to agree with the opinion expressed in *Lancet*

[17] that "Some people would indeed today question whether there is any sort of concrete 'it' to be defined. . . . Alcoholism, it can be argued, is more a label than a diagnosis. One view of the matter is therefore that the hunt for a definition of alcoholism should be abandoned as the pursuit of what was never more than an imagined animal: a medical diagnosis was being falsely imposed on behaviors and events of great variability."

SUMMARY

In summary, alcohol ingestion is an objective event, and, ultimately, quantifiable. Recognition of the fact that dosage and damage are related makes the goal of specifying this relationship a primary concern in the understanding of harmful drinking. This recognition serves as the basis for relating drinking conduct to the antecedents that determine it, and the consequences resulting from it. It is the beginning of clearly establishing the safe limits of drinking, thus permitting the elimination of the explanatory fiction, alcoholism.

REFERENCES

1. Bruun, K., Edwards, G., Lumio, M., Mäkelä, K., Pan, L., Popham, R. E., Room, R., Schmidt, W., Skog, O. J., , Sulkunen, P., and Österberg, E. Alcohol control policies in public health perspective. In: *Finnish Foundation for Alcohol Studies* (Vol. 25). Ahateeminen Kirjakauppa: Helsinki, 1976.
2. Christie, N., and Bruun, K. Alcohol problems: The conceptual framework. *Int. Congr. Alcohol Alcoholism, Lect.* 28th, 65-73, 1969.
3. DeLint, J., and Schmidt, W. The distribution of alcohol consumption in Ontario. *J. Stud. Alcohol* 29:968-973, 1968.
4. Fillmore, K. M. Drinking and problem drinking in early adulthood and middle age: An exploratory 20-year follow-up study. *J. Stud. Alcohol* 35:819-840, 1974.
5. Gottheil, E., Corbett, L. O., Grasberger, J. C., and Cornelison, F. S. Treating the alcoholic in the presence of alcohol. *Amer. J. Psychiatry* 128:475-480, 1971.
6. Hoff, E. C. The alcoholisms. *Int. Congr. Alcohol Alcoholism, Lect.* 28th, 84-90, 1969.
7. Jellinek, E. M. *The Disease Concept of Alcoholism*. Highland Park, N.J.: Hillhouse, 1960.
8. Madden, J. S. On defining alcoholism. *Brit. J. Addict.* 71:145-148, 1977.
9. Mäkelä, K. Level of consumption and social consequences of drinking. In: *Research Advances in Alcohol and Drug Problems* (Vol. 4), Israel, Y. et al. (eds.). Plenum: New York, 1978.
10. Marlatt, G. A., Demming, B., and Reid, J. B. Loss of control drinking in alcoholics: An experimental analogue. *J. Abnorm. Psychol.* 81:233-241, 1973.

11. Mello, N. K., and Mendelson, J. H. A quantitative analysis of drinking patterns in alcoholics. *Arch. Gen. Psychiatry* 25:527-539, 1971.

12. Miller, W. R. Alcoholism scales and objective assessment methods: A review. *Psychol. Bull.* 83:649-674, 1976.

13. Pemberton, W. H. A semanticist looks at alcoholism programs. In: *The First Step: A Conference on Drinking Problems*, U.S. Civil Service Commission, Bureau of Retirement and Insurance (ed.). U.S. Government Printing Office: Washington, D.C., 1967.

14. Pomerleau, O., Pertshuk, M., and Stinneit, J. A. A critical examination of some current assumptions in the treatment of alcoholism. *J. Stud. Alcohol* 37:849-867, 1976.

15. Rohan, W. P. Quantitative dimensions of alcohol use for hospitalized problem drinkers. *Dis. Nerv. Syst.* 37:154-159, 1976.

16. WHO and a new perspective on alcoholism. *Lancet* 1:1087-1088, 1977.

LEE N. ROBINS, PhD, Washington University

THE DIAGNOSIS OF ALCOHOLISM AFTER DSM-III

DIAGNOSES RELATED TO the use or abuse of alcohol appear in two sections of the third edition of the *Diagnostic and Statistical Manual* (DSM-III) [1], under "Organic Mental Disorders" and also under "Substance Abuse Disorders." Under "Organic Mental Disorders," as Table 1 shows, are seven diagnoses attributed to the use of alcohol: alcohol intoxication, alcohol idiosyncratic intoxication, alcohol amnestic disorder, dementia associated with alcoholism, alcohol withdrawal, alcohol withdrawal delirium, and alcohol hallucinosis. The first two diagnoses do not imply either chronic or prolonged alcohol intake. The other five, however, occur only after excessive alcohol consumption over some period of time.

The diagnoses under "Substance Abuse Disorders" are listed under the major topic, "Alcohol Dependence," and subdivided into abuse and dependence. The words "abuse" and "dependence" are used, rather than "probable" and "definite" alcoholism, to emphasize that alcohol is a drug, and that the disorders associated with its excessive use are to be described in terms similar to those used for disorders arising from the intake of other drugs. Alcohol dependence corresponds to what used to be called "alcoholism," and alcohol abuse corresponds to what used to be called "probable alcoholism."

This chapter concentrates on the diagnoses under substance abuse. It ex-

---

Lee N. Robins, PhD, Professor of Psychiatry, School of Medicine, Washington University, St. Louis, Missouri.

Table 1
Diagnoses Related to Alcohol in DSM-III

Alcohol Organic Mental Disorders
303.00 Alcohol Intoxication
291.40 Alcohol Idiosyncratic Intoxication
291.10 Alcohol Amnestic Disorder
291.2x Dementia Associated with Alcoholism
291.80 Alcohol Withdrawal
291.00 Alcohol Withdrawal Delirium
291.30 Alcohol Hallucinosis
Substance Abuse Disorders
303.9x Alcohol Dependence
   Alcohol Abuse
   Alcohol Dependence

plains how to make a diagnosis according to DSM-III, how the selection of criteria developed, and what problems in alcohol diagnosis remain. Finally, the accuracy and consistency of alcohol diagnoses are compared with those of other psychiatric diagnoses.

GENERAL SCHEME OF DSM-III REGARDING ALCOHOL ABUSE AND DEPENDENCE

In DSM-III, the descriptions of alcohol abuse and dependence follow the same general pattern as those of other diagnoses in the volume. First, each diagnosis is assigned a number corresponding to the number of the same syndrome as listed in the *International Classification of Diseases* (ICD), so that the two documents will be compatible. Next, each diagnosis is assigned to an axis. DSM-III allows coding a subject on five different axes. Alcohol abuse and alcohol dependence fall on axis I, "Clinical Psychiatric Syndromes and Other Conditions." Someone assigned a diagnosis of alcohol dependence or abuse can be simultaneously coded on axis II for a personality disorder, on axis III for a physical disorder, on axis IV for psychosocial stress, and on axis V for adaptive functioning in the last year. DSM-III also permits an individual to be assigned more than one diagnosis on axis I, although some diagnostic combinations are not allowed. However, no other diagnoses on axis I preclude diagnoses of alcohol abuse or dependence.

    The text of DSM-III initially describes the symptoms, subclassifications, associated features, age of onset, complications, predisposing factors, prevalence, sex ratio, and differential diagnosis of substance abuse disorders as a whole. Under alcohol dependence are sections on course, family patterns, and diagnostic criteria; this chapter focuses on those criteria.

DIAGNOSTIC CRITERIA

Throughout DSM-III, diagnostic criteria are listed as groups of symptoms, each group designated by a capital letter. To receive a positive diagnosis, an individual must present at least one symptom from each lettered group: Table 2 shows the titles under which alcohol symptoms are grouped. For alcohol abuse, group A is pattern of pathological alcohol use, B is impairment in social or occupational functioning due to alcohol use, and C is duration of disturbance for at least 1 month. The C criterion thus distinguishes alcohol abuse from alcohol intoxication, which can arise from a single drinking bout and which can also impair social and occupational function. The C group thus exempts those who merely taste and experiment from receiving a diagnosis of abuser.

For alcohol dependence, group A combines the criteria of groups A and B in alcohol abuse, and category B is either tolerance or withdrawal. Combining A and B of alcohol abuse into a single category in alcohol dependence permits application of the rule that there must be at least one positive symptom in each lettered group of symptoms. Thus, for alcohol dependence, one must have tolerance or withdrawal, and, in addition, either a pattern of pathological alcohol use or impairment of social or occupational function. A patient need not have both.

ROOTS OF DSM-III DIAGNOSIS OF ALCOHOL DEPENDENCE

The DSM-III diagnostic system grew out of the Research Diagnostic Criteria or RDC [9], which, in turn, developed from the Feighner criteria [3]. The RDC were originally developed for the National Institute of Mental Health's ongoing collaborative depression study. During the planning years, two of the members of the discussion group were Eli Robins and Robert Spitzer. Dr. Spitzer had been interested in systematic diagnostic methods [8] for a long time. While participat-

Table 2
The DSM-III Criteria for the Diagnoses of Alcohol Abuse and Dependence

Alcohol Abuse
A. Pattern of pathological alcohol use
B. Impairment in social or occupational functioning due to alcohol use
C. Duration of disturbance at least 1 month

Alcohol Dependence
A. Either A or B above
B. Either tolerance or withdrawal

ing in the United States–United Kingdom study of depression and schizophrenia, he had developed a systematic interview known as the Psychiatric Status Schedule. During the discussion about instruments to be used in the collaborative study, he became enthusiastic about the Feighner criteria. He, Jean Endicott, and Eli Robins worked together to modify the Feighner criteria, and their revision was called the "Research Diagnostic Criteria" [9].

A number of years ago, Dr. Spitzer was given the job of leading the task force to create DSM-III. His work with the RDC inspired him to try to give DSM-III the same kind of rigor the RDC provided, so that diagnoses across medical centers would be more comparable than had previously been the case. Not surprisingly, he invited some of the Washington University group responsible for the Feighner criteria to help him. This author served on the substance abuse panel, which had as one of its jobs writing the section on alcohol. Other members of that group were Drs. Henry Rosett, Robert Morse, Sheldon Zimberg, and Milton Gross, who had worked with a World Health Organization (WHO) steering group on alcoholism, led by Griffith Edwards, in 1975.

Tables 3–6 show the extent to which DSM-III evolved from RDC and Feighner criteria. On the left of the tables are the DSM-III criteria. The center column shows similar criteria as they appeared in RDC, and, at the right, the same items in Feighner. A number of new symptoms appear in DSM-III, representing input from a variety of persons. Symptoms that appeared in RDC and Feighner, but are not included in DSM-III, are italicized.

Criteria for Pathological Patterns of Use

One DSM-III criterion is the need for daily use of alcohol to function adequately. This particular item has been the subject of considerable discussion because of the vagueness of "adequate function." Some researchers have been concerned that the term might be extended to include individuals who are upset if they can't have their daily drink before dinner, even though they functioned perfectly well that day without alcohol and will function well again the next day. The difficulty here is in distinguishing between a desire to preserve pleasant habits and signs of pathology.

All three systems include as one of the criteria the inability to control one's drinking. DSM-III, however, omits the person's own opinion as to whether he or she drinks too much, which in fact is the most common symptom found among alcoholics. Only DSM-III includes a person's efforts to control drinking by "going on the wagon." Restricting drinking to certain times of day is found both in DSM-III and in the Feighner criteria; Feighner also includes control by rules against drinking alone.

Binge drinking appears in all three systems, although the binge must be of somewhat longer duration in RDC than in the other two. The RDC requirement

Table 3
The DSM-III Criteria for the Diagnosis of Alcohol Abuse and Dependence and Their Source: I. Pattern of Pathological Alcohol Use

DSM-III	Research Diagnostic Criteria	Feighner
Need for daily use for adequate functioning		
Inability to cut down or stop	(3) Admits often can't stop	Group 2. (1) Not able to stop
	(1) *Says he drinks too much*	Group 4. (1) *Thinks he drinks too much*
Repeated efforts to control by going on wagon or restriction to certain times of day		Group 2. (2) Allowing himself to drink . . . only after 5 P.M., only on weekends, *only with others*
Binges (at least 2 days)	(9) Three occasions of 3 days drinking more than one fifth per day	Group 1. (4) Binges. 2 days *with default of obligations*
Drinks more than one fifth per day		
Blackouts	(13) *Frequent* blackouts	Group 1. (3) Blackouts
Drinking exacerbates serious physical disorder		
Drinks nonbeverage alcohol		Group 2. (4) Nonbeverage alcohol

Note. Italicized phrases are not specifically covered in DSM-III; DSM-III criteria do not appear in other systems.

that the binge drinker consume more than one fifth a day guarantees that the individual will be intoxicated during these binges. DSM-III also uses drinking more than a fifth a day as an indicator of pathological drinking, but the quantity consumed need not be associated with a binge. Thus people who drink a great deal every day and whose consumption varies little from day to day are not excluded.

Blackouts are accepted in all three systems as a sign of pathological drinking. DSM-III includes as well drinking that exacerbates a serious physical disorder. This criterion was added to include persons whose drinking, if they were healthy, would not be pathological, but who, because of their physical state, should not drink at all. Their drinking is pathological for them, even though their consumption patterns are well within the social norms of the group in which they live. The difficulty with this criterion is in defining the severity of the physical illness. Clearly, many people who would like to lose weight drink, even though alcohol provides them with excess calories. Weight problems, however,

Table 4
The DSM-III Criteria for the Diagnoses of Alcohol Abuse and Dependence and Their Source: II. Impairment in Social or Occupational Functioning

DSM-III	Research Diagnostic Criteria	Feighner
Violence while intoxicated	(10) Physical violence	Group 3. (4) Fighting
Absence from work	(5) Missed work, impaired job performance, unable to take care of household responsibilities	(3) Trouble at work
Loss of job	(6) Job loss	
Arrest for intoxicated behavior	(12) Picked up by police due to behavior	(1) Arrests for drinking
Traffic accidents while intoxicated	(11) Traffic difficulties due to drinking, reckless driving, accidents, speeding	(2) Traffic difficulties
Arguments or difficulties with family or friends	(2) Others complain	Group 4. (4) Others object
	(7) Frequent difficulties with family members, friends, or associates	(2) Family objects
		(3) Lost friends
	(8) Divorce or separation where drinking is primary reason	

Note. Italicized phrases are not specifically covered in DSM-III; DSM-III criteria do not appear in other systems.

generally are not classified as serious medical disorders and do not qualify individuals under this criterion.

Criteria for Impairment of Social or Occupational Functioning

Table 4 shows the items included under social and occupational functioning, group B in alcohol abuse. Alcohol-related violence appears in all three systems, although it is more broadly defined in RDC and DSM-III than in Feighner. Absence from work and job loss because of drinking are the only occupational im-

Table 5
The DSM-III Criteria for the Diagnoses of Alcohol Abuse and Dependence and Their Source: III. Tolerance to Alcohol or Withdrawal Symptoms

DSM-III	Research Diagnostic Criteria	Feighner
Tolerance Need for increased amounts to achieve desired effect or diminished effect with same amount	—	—
Withdrawal Morning shakes and malaise after cessation or reduction relieved by drinking	(14) Tremors (4) Drinking before breakfast	Group 1. (1) Tremulousness Group 2. (3) Drinking before breakfast

Table 6
The DSM-III Criteria for the Diagnoses of Alcohol Abuse and Dependence and Their Source: IV. Medical Complications of Dependence

DSM-III	Research Diagnostic Criteria	Feighner
Not used in diagnosis	Used in Diagnosis	Used in diagnosis
Hepatitis, cirrhosis	(18) Cirrhosis	Group 1. (2) Cirrhosis
Peripheral neuropathy	(19) Polyneuropathy	(2) Polyneuropathy
Gastritis	—	(2) Gastritis
Alcohol withdrawal delirium	(15) DTs	(1) Delirium
Alcohol hallucinosis	(16) Hallucinations	(1) Hallucinations
Alcohol amnestic syndrome	(20) Korsakoff's psychosis	(2) Korsakoff's psychosis
Dementia associated with alcoholism	—	—
Other disorders Neurological	(17) Withdrawal seizures	(1) Convulsions
—	—	(2) *Myopathy*
—	—	(2) *Pancreatitis*

pairments listed in DSM-III; RDC and Feighner define work troubles more generally. Arrests for intoxication also are listed in all three systems, as are traffic accidents while intoxicated; again both RDC and Feighner include broader definitions of traffic difficulties. Interpersonal difficulties are mentioned in all three systems; DSM-III globally describes these as difficulties with family and friends. RDC generally includes more detail; only Feighner includes losing friends because of drinking. Losing friends is actually a rare occurrence because people tend to choose friends with drinking patterns similar to their own.

Criteria for Tolerance and Withdrawal

Table 5 shows criteria to gauge tolerance and withdrawal, which serve only for alcohol dependence, not for abuse. Tolerance does not appear in RDC or Feighner at all; it was added to alcohol dependence in DSM-III so that alcohol problems could be measured comparably with other drugs.

Determining personal tolerance to alcohol is something of a problem. People vary enormously in the amounts they can drink even when the individuals are inexperienced drinkers. Clearly, they develop tolerance to alcohol (alcoholics regularly drink amounts no inexperienced drinker can), but it is hard to obtain evidence of this tolerance. One can ask alcoholics whether they have had to increase their intake to get a desired effect or whether they have experienced diminished effect from the same intake. But by the time alcoholics see a physician to discuss drinking, most have been tolerant at about the same level for many years. They may not remember how much less they used to drink to achieve the same effect.

DSM-III restricts evidence of withdrawal to shakes and malaise relieved by drinking. These also appear in the RDC and Feighner criteria as tremors or tremulousness and drinking before breakfast.

Medical Complications as Criteria

Table 6 shows the medical complications of dependence. These are not used as diagnostic criteria in DSM-III, although they are used in the other two systems. DSM-III lists them as complications of dependence in the text preceding the diagnostic criteria. Their omission as diagnostic criteria is, no doubt, because of their separate enumeration under "Organic Brain Syndromes." Pancreatitis and myopathy appear in the Feighner criteria, but not in DSM-III. The authors' experience in a current study of frequency of moderate drinking in patients who were seen for an alcohol-related problem 5 to 10 years ago suggests that this omission is wise. When records were checked of medical and surgical patients with diagnoses of pancreatitis in the hospital, no elevated rates of problem drinking in their histories were found. Myopathy was too rare a diagnosis to be subjected to this kind of analysis.

HOW DSM-III DIAGNOSTIC CRITERIA WERE CONSTRUCTED

The history of the DSM-III criteria may explain some of the differences between DSM-III and the systems from which it originated. The first draft of the DSM-III section on alcohol abuse and dependence was written in 1975. There was little criticism of the specific criteria then, but reviewers did argue with the natural history of the disorder.

It said that alcoholics tend to have early onset and a history of antisocial behavior. Some of the reviewers treated only private patients and thought that alcoholism tended to be of much later onset and to occur frequently in people of middle-class origin. They were not impressed with its association with antisocial personality. Data from the literature were produced to convince them that their patients were somewhat atypical.

In 1976, Dr. Frank Seixas, president of the National Council on Alcoholism (NCA), reviewed the proposed criteria. He asked that the NCA definition be used instead of the one in the draft and objected to DSM-III's dropping the word "alcoholism." The term "alcoholism" now appears, but only in a statement that says, "Alcohol dependence has also been called alcoholism," and in the title of one of the alcohol organic mental disorders, "Dementia Associated with Alcoholism." Seixas particularly wanted to see psychological criteria omitted from the criteria for alcohol dependence and discussed only under alcohol abuse. Psychological dependence, disguised under the title "Pathological Use," is still part of criteria A for alcohol dependence, however.

One of the reasons the DSM-III task force resisted adopting the NCA definition was that it implied that any drinking at all after the occurrence of alcohol problems is associated with progression of the disorder. This viewpoint has been one part of NCA's battle against the findings reported in the Rand study [2]. The task force felt that the NCA statement would be better if limited to heavy drinking.

The panel also agreed not to include prognosis as part of the criteria. In the first place, criteria for diagnosis should be applicable early in the course of an illness, before the prognosis is known. Therefore, prognosis is often not a helpful criterion. Second, there is considerable evidence that at least a few persons who have been dependent on alcohol eventually drink moderately without problems, although the number who can do so is still very much in dispute. Finally, if one included prognosis among the criteria for a diagnosis, the diagnostic criteria would have to be changed as improvement in treatment brought about changes in prognosis.

In 1976, the criterion of 1 month's duration was adopted. Initially, it was stated as 1 month's continuous or episodic use, because those working on early drafts of DSM-III were still considering using the same criteria for licit and illicit drugs. Use of a drug for at least 1 month was intended to eliminate the person who was only an experimenter. But this criterion did not prove very useful when related to alcohol use, because almost everyone who drinks at all has been exposed to alcohol, at least episodically, for more than 1 month. Thus, the criterion has recently been changed to make the month's duration refer to "disturbance," that is, alcohol-related problems, not just exposure to alcohol.

The author's research group has been devising an interview schedule to be used in the general population to make diagnoses according to DSM-III criteria [6]. While writing computer programs to make DSM-III diagnoses, the group noticed recently that the criteria for alcohol dependence required tolerance or withdrawal and social complications, but did not mention pathological drinking. Therefore, if someone were tolerant, had withdrawal symptoms, and said that drinking could not be controlled, that person still would not qualify as dependent on alcohol. As a result, the panel temporarily changed the criteria by dropping social complications as a requirement. Then, however, people could be scored as positive for dependence if they had no symptoms other than tolerance. Since tolerance is probably an invariable consequence of considerable experience with alcohol, a large proportion of the population would have been diagnosable as dependent, making the diagnosis trivial. Finally, the current pattern was chosen: Tolerance alone is not enough; there must be at least some evidence of either pathological drinking or social problems as well. This saga illustrates the difficulty of writing criteria. One has to consider both the maximum case that could be missed and the minimum case that could be included, then strike some compromise between the two.

REMAINING PROBLEMS

The DSM-III criteria for alcohol dependence and abuse represent the input of a great many people trying to produce a system that reasonably reflects both research and clinical experience. But many problems with diagnosing alcohol-related disorders remain. One that comes up frequently is a consequence of the WHO idea that an alcohol disorder represents drinking in a way that is not acceptable in one's own subculture. The difficulty comes in defining exactly what the norms are for the subculture in which a particular person lives. Furthermore, what if the norms of that subculture are not compatible with good functioning? In some subcultures, such as in some fraternity houses or on some Native American reservations, the drinking norms are incompatible with optimal functioning.

Another difficulty that pertains to all drug disorders is deciding when the intake of the drug is responsible for the behavioral difficulties. Arrests, traffic accidents, suicide, or death for unexplained reasons, in someone who has ingested drugs, may or may not be the result of the drug consumption. The persons who tend to have high arrest rates, high suicide rates, and high rates of impulsive behavior also tend to use drugs and alcohol heavily. Thus, the drug or alcohol use and the event may both be caused by some preexisting factors.

RELIABILITY AND SCALABILITY OF ALCOHOL DIAGNOSES

Although problems in diagnosing alcohol abuse and dependence remain, it would be a mistake to be pessimistic about the potential research and clinical value of the DSM-III criteria. It is too early to have studied the efficacy of the DSM-III criteria themselves, but the RDC and Feighner criteria from which they grew have been studied extensively.

Reliability

The author's research group performed a test-retest study [5] of the reliability of all the Feighner diagnoses in 99 inpatients given the same interview on successive days by two psychiatrists, two lay interviewers, or one psychiatrist and one lay interviewer. Alcohol had the highest kappa of any diagnosis tested (0.77 out of a possible 1.00). Depression had a kappa value of 0.58; phobia, a value of 0.53; and mania, 0.52. These results show that psychiatrists agree with each other when they diagnose "alcoholism," as it was called in the Feighner diagnoses, and that lay interviewers can make the same diagnoses with considerable accuracy if they use the kinds of diagnostic criteria listed in DSM-III.

Scalability

The author in another study [7] also found that the symptoms typically used to diagnose alcoholism tend to form a Gutman-type scale in which the rarer symptoms are those that require the longest period of drinking, as shown in Table 7. The results come from a study of older white and black men in St. Louis. The subjects were patients of a public hospital and members of the Teamsters Union. Those who admitted to ever having been heavy drinkers (defined as drinking at least seven drinks on one occasion at least once a week for some period) were asked which alcohol symptoms they had had and over how many years they had been heavy drinkers. The more frequent the alcohol symptoms, the shorter the average history of drinking of men suffering from that symptom; the rarer the symptom, the longer the average drinking history. Men with delirium tremens, the rarest symptom, averaged 30 years of heavy drinking, while men concerned about drinking too much, which was the most common symptom, had been heavy drinkers for an average of only 17 years.

The Diagnosis of Alcoholism after DSM-III

Table 7
Symptoms and Duration of Heavy Drinking in Heavy Drinkers, Aged 45–64

Symptom	Percentage with This Symptom	Median Years of Heavy Drinking with This Symptom
DTs	7	30
Hospitalization for drinking problem	15	27
Lost job because of drinking	16	26
Drinking led to arrest	19	26
Trouble on job from drinking	21	25
Benders (more than 2 days without sobering up)	25	22
Trouble with wife over drink	28	22
Family objected on his drinking	38	21
Felt guilty about his drinking	41	20
Felt he drank too much	53	17

Generally, alcohol symptoms rank similarly by frequency. The most common symptoms are those of personal and family concern; the rarest are loss of employment, hospitalization, and delirium tremens. A study of alcoholics in the Veterans Administration [4] shows exactly the same pattern. Symptoms of other disorders are not known to occur in such a regular pattern nor to be so well predicted by the duration of the illness. Thus, the diagnosis of alcoholism or alcohol dependence may be more reliable and valid than other common psychiatric diagnoses.

Finally, it is important to note that the DSM-III diagnostic system allows multiple diagnoses. The author's research group at Washington University is currently applying the DSM-III diagnosis of alcoholism to their data bank of studies to see what additional diagnoses persons with a diagnosis of alcohol dependence would qualify for. The data bank now includes almost 3,000 protocols, listing psychiatric symptoms in a variety of subjects including emergency room cases, inpatients, clinic patients, and relatives of patients. As shown in Table 8, the emergency room cases produced the highest proportion of alcoholism diagnoses, with inpatients and clinic patients following, in that order. Relatives of patients had the lowest rate, 10%. This rate is probably somewhat above that of the general population, as one would expect, because many are relatives of alcoholic patients.

Table 9 lists other disorders diagnosed in alcoholics and compares their diagnostic patterns with those of other members of the same study. Among patients who were not alcoholics, there had to be at least one diagnosis, just to explain their presence in treatment. Consequently, emergency room patients and inpa-

Table 8
Diagnoses From a Data Bank (Percentage of Patients)

	Type of Study			
Disorders	Emergency Room Patients	Inpatients	Clinic Patients	Relatives of Patients
Total n	314	221	500	1,357
Alcoholism	33	28	13	10
Depression	37	75	50	7
Panic	10	23	21	5
Somatization	5	18	8	2
Antisocial personality	15	11	6	3

Table 9
Data Bank Studies: What Other Disorders Do Alcoholics Have?
(Percentage of Patients)

Type of Patients	Number of Patients	Depression	Panic	Somatization	Antisocial Personality
Emergency room patients					
Alcoholics	105	31	8	3	27
Others	209	40	12	7	10
Difference	—	−9	−4	−4	+17
Inpatients					
Alcoholics	61	69	32	13	20
Others	160	77	19	19	8
Difference	—	−8	+13	−6	+13
Clinic Patients					
Alcoholics	65	54	32	8	17
Others	435	49	20	8	4
Difference	—	+5	+12	0	+13
Relatives of patients					
Alcoholics	135	17	7	6	11
Others	1,222	6	5	1	3
Difference	—	+11	+2	+5	+8

tients who were not alcoholics tended to have somewhat higher rates for other diagnoses than did the alcoholics. What is interesting is that despite this other diagnosis, they were less likely to have antisocial personality than were the alcoholics. These results support the DSM-III text, which notes the association between alcoholism and antisocial personality.

It is also of interest that both inpatients and clinic patients who are alcoholics had more panic disorder (what used to be called "anxiety neurosis") than did other patients. And in nonpatients, that is, in the relatives of patients, alcoholism was associated with an increased rate of every other disorder, suggesting that the presence of any psychiatric disorder may make it more likely that one will also have at least one other problem.

Alcoholics as inpatients or clinic patients tend to be depressed. Alcoholics generally don't seek care in psychiatric facilities unless they have concurrent depression. Depression is less frequent in cases brought to the emergency room because of public inebriation.

In conclusion, the story of the development of the DSM-III diagnoses relating to alcohol intake reveals the logical complexities of describing the mixture of physical, social, and psychological correlates of using alcohol that constitute this diagnostic criteria. Some of these correlates are clearly effects of alcohol intake, while others, particularly the antisocial acts seen in heavy drinkers, may often be what DSM-III calls "associated features"—as often indicators of personality types predisposed to heavy drinking as consequences of the drinking itself. Some of these correlates, such as auto accidents, can occur in response to a single ingestion of large amounts, while others, like DTs and cirrhosis, require years of exposure.

It is remarkable, given these logical difficulties, the assembling of symptoms from grossly different conceptual realms, and the reported unreliability of alcoholics as historians, that the diagnosis of alcoholism by symptom self-report is repeatedly found to be one of the most valid and reliable of the psychiatric diagnoses. There seem little doubt that crude as these methods remain, despite the efforts of the DSM-III task force, a sturdy entity is being tapped with counting social, medical, and psychological alcohol problems.

ACKNOWLEDGMENTS

This work is supported by grants DA 00013, AA 03539, and AA 03852 from the U.S. Public Health Service. It originally appeared in *Evaluation of the Alcoholic*, Research Monograph 5, D.H.H.S. publication ADM 81-1033, U.S. Government Printing Office, Washington, D.C., 1981.

REFERENCES

1. American Psychiatric Association. *Diagnostic and Statistical Manual of Mental Disorders* (3rd ed.). Author: Washington, D.C., 1980.
2. Armor, D. J., Polich, J. M., and Stambul, H. B. *Alcoholism and Treatment.* Wiley: New York, 1978.
3. Feighner, J., Robins, E., Guze, S., Woodruff, R., Winokur, G., and Munoz, R. Diagnostic criteria for use in psychiatric research. *Arch. Gen. Psychiatry* 26:57-63, 1972.
4. Gomberg, E. S. Prevalence of alcoholism among ward patients in a Veterans Administration hospital. *J. Stud. Alcohol* 36:1458-1467, 1975.
5. Helzer, J. E., Robins, L. N., Croughan, J., and Welner, A. Reliability and validity of the Renard Diagnostic Interview as used by physicians and nonphysicians. In press, 1980.
6. Robins, L. N., Helzer, J., Croughan, J., Williams, J., and Spitzer, R. *The National Institute of Mental Health Diagnostic Interview (DIS, Version II).* National Institute of Mental Health: Washington, D.C., 1979.
7. Robins, L. N., West, P. A., and Murphy, G. E. The high rate of suicide in older white men: A study testing ten hypotheses. *Soc. Psychiatry* 12:1-20, 1977.
8. Spitzer, R., Endicott, J., Fleiss, J., and Cohen, J. The Psychiatric Status Schedule: A technique for evaluating psychopathology and impairment in role functioning. *Arch. Gen. Psychiatry* 23:41-55, 1970.
9. Spitzer, R., Endicott, J., and Robins, E. Clinical criteria for psychiatric diagnosis and DSM-III. *Am. J. Psychiatry* 132(11):1187-1192, 1975.

4

WILMA J. KNOX, PhD, Veterans Administration Medical Center, Biloxi, Mississippi

DIAGNOSTIC PSYCHOLOGICAL TESTING

THIS CHAPTER BRIEFLY considers the why, when, what, who, and where of diagnostic psychological testing. The rationale for using standardized psychological tests is followed by a discussion of detoxification prior to test administration, the cornerstone of accurate evaluation for alcoholism. Discussion of specific tests is limited to selected instruments frequently employed in published research identifying alcoholics. Names of additional tests can be readily obtained from references cited. Further discussions of validity and reliability of specific tests can be found in Buros [3].

Testing for problems of immediate concern concomitant with a diagnosis of alcoholism is considered briefly. In addition, certain subgroups have been identified that contain appreciable numbers of alcoholics and may be located within specific institutional settings. Fewer research replications are available pertaining to subgroups and institutional settings, but practical considerations in testing programs to diagnose alcoholism merit their inclusion.

RATIONALE FOR STANDARDIZED PSYCHOLOGICAL TESTS

In contacts with social institutions many people will respond to direct questions about drinking habits when they do not volunteer information. For the profes-

---

Wilma J. Knox, PhD, Staff Psychologist, Veterans Administration Medical Center, Biloxi, Mississippi, and Associate Professor, University of Southern Mississippi, Hattiesburg, Mississippi.

sional to overlook the problem of alcoholism invites disaster to the client through social chaos, exacerbation of physical symptomatology, or morbidity. Testing can be a relatively accurate method of detecting the problem in a variety of situations without an undue expenditure of costly professional interviewing time.

For example, computer-based interviews of 36 alcoholics took longer for each interview (26 minutes), but objective testing had considerable time-saving potential for two interviewers who averaged 12 and 17 minutes, respectively [14]. The computerized questions resulted in admissions of significantly higher liquor consumption in comparison to the two interviews with qualified psychiatrists.

The urge to draw on one's own experience and construct a casual list of alcoholism-eliciting questions should be checked firmly. In general, the needs of the field are proper utilization of available tests and published research providing comparable data to advance scientific understanding. In two samples of objective studies on alcoholism (usually reporting results from more than one test), the ratio was 55 different tests to 55 articles in one sample and 44 tests to 31 articles in the other [10]. The refinement of existing tests or development of new tests should be left to specialists in test construction.

Problems in reliability of test responses were demonstrated by Wilkins [22]. A Spare Time Activity Questionnaire was used to diagnose alcoholism at a general health center. Of 41 patients who were retested at intervals of 1 to 12 months, 6 out of 9 who were diagnosed alcoholic on the first test obtained scores in the non-alcoholic range upon retesting. The authors considered the initial testing valid, but such unreliable findings make the test impractical to use.

Every psychological test successfully employed to diagnose alcoholism conveys to the examinee that his or her personality is under scrutiny, and in many instances the tester's interest in drinking habits is evident. Although all tests have limitations in validity and reliability, these problems may be reduced somewhat by the use of a test battery. In settings or with groups that consistently contain only a small percentage of alcoholics, demographic or symptom information may be used to select those from the population who should be tested.

DETOXIFICATION PRIOR TO TESTING

The most dramatic illustration of the need for detoxification was provided by Libb and Taulbee [10]. Using the Minnesota Multiphasic Personality Inventory (MMPI), 20 alcoholics were selected who initially had elevated scores on psychotic scales. They were compared with a control group of schizophrenic patients. Twenty-one days after the initial testing, alcoholics showed significant decreases in scales considered diagnostic of psychosis. Other performance deficiencies during the detoxification period have been found in later studies.

Sharp, Rosenbaum, Goldman, and Whitman [19] employed the Synonym

Learning Test with alcoholics and administered the test to three matched groups at varying intervals (5, 15, and 25 days) following cessation of drinking. Acquisition of new verbal learning was impaired on 5-day testing, but returned to normal levels by the 15th day of testing. Vocabulary level was unaffected by drinking. This specific procedure has not been used widely, but impairment of verbal learning has been demonstrated in other studies [10]. These findings are considered noteworthy because diagnostic testing generally precedes treatment, and ability to assimilate verbal information is crucial in didactic programs.

PSYCHOLOGICAL TESTS

Representative tests of two types are briefly described. Personality tests contain questions that are not directly related to alcohol or alcoholic consumption, whereas alcohol-related questionnaires are based primarily on such items.

Personality Tests

Attempts to diagnose alcoholism by searching for an alcoholic personality type or types have met with little success. Personality tests have generally been included in diagnostic test batteries because collateral information is frequently desired in treatment settings. The MMPI is such a generalized personality test, and the MacAndrews Alcoholism Scale has been derived from it.

Among other personality tests frequently used in research with alcoholics is the Eysenck Personality Inventory, which has parallel forms of 57 items. It affords three scores: extroversion, neuroticism, and lie. The 16-item Personality Factor Questionnaire has two parallel forms, plus a short form and a special form for minimally literate adults. The Multiple Affect Adjective Check List is representative of tests used to assess current or general emotional stress. Anxiety, depression, and hostility are assessed in 132 items.

MMPI. The MMPI has many characteristics useful in diagnostic testing of alcoholics. This test was the most frequently used in research studies during a 1-year sample of publications [10]. The test has 566 items, is frequently scored by computer, and may be administered using automated techniques. The test affords 3 validity scales and 10 diagnostic scales developed by empirical methods. The profile of diagnostic scales provides considerable information about the severity of personality pathology, its type, and concomitant symptomatology.

Because of its length, considerable time is required to complete the MMPI, and administration becomes cumbersome if the testee cannot read. Several abbreviated forms of the test have been devised that show significant scale correlations with a full MMPI, but the high-point scale of the personality profile is not the same in about half the cases [5]. Hence, evaluation of individuals cannot be recommended through use of abbreviated MMPIs; these instruments may have a place in research.

MacAndrews Alcoholism Scale. The MacAndrews scale is made up of 49 selected MMPI items, has been widely used, and has compared favorably to other MMPI-derived alcoholism scales in research studies [10]. It has been successfully employed in longitudinal studies and has differentiated a group of college-tested students (hospitalized for alcoholism later in life) from a random sample of college classmates [12]. One problem noted has been the scale's inability to differentiate alcoholics from drug addicts [2]. This problem may be alleviated through use of tests that inquire into drinking habits.

Alcohol-Related Scales

The Michigan Alcoholism Screening Test (MAST) and the Alcadd Test described below have been used frequently to make diagnoses of alcoholism. In addition, several scales are available that inquire specifically as to the amount of alcohol used. These tests may be needed to separate alcoholics from drug addicts or to discern dual addiction; they include Mulford and Miller's Definition of Alcohol Scale and Calahan's Quantity-Frequency-Variability Index.

MAST. The MAST is a relatively short screening test that asks direct questions about alcohol consumption. Initial validation efforts in developing the scale were impressive, and objective confirmation of MAST diagnoses was obtained from a variety of institutional and public records [10]. It has been employed in a variety of settings with a variety of populations [10, 11, 12].

Criticism of the test has been conflicting because complaints of excessive false-positives have been accompanied by concern that only testees who already acknowledge an alcohol problem will score in the alcoholic range [16]. One factor analysis showed that alcoholics' MAST responses were related to several factors, but primary loading was on self-acceptance of an alcoholic problem [23]. Another factor analysis located the same factor, but it accounted for only 7.3% of the total variance [6]. The test does seem acceptable as a screening device.

Alcadd Test. The Alcadd Test, developed in 1949, is the oldest test still in use to diagnose alcoholism. The 1965 revision contains 65 items and has five scales to measure drinking in terms of regularity, preference over other activities, loss of control, rationalization, and emotionality [17]. While various criticisms of the instrument have been made, no test is without its detractors.

CONCOMITANT DIAGNOSTIC PROBLEMS

Several other problems may become of immediate importance when alcoholism is initially diagnosed: prognosis for treatment, suicide potential, aggressive potential, cerebral impairment (see Section III), and Korsakoff's syndrome.

Prognosis for Treatment

Withholding treatment does not appear to be justified on the basis of predicted success or failure. Gibbs and Flanagan [7] reviewed 45 experimental studies, utilizing 55 treatment groups and reporting on 208 different indicators. They concluded that highly stable predictors for successful treatment were not available. Of 29 test variables considered, a low psychopathic deviate scale score on the MMPI predicted successful outcome in four studies and was of no predictive value in one; a high Wechsler arithmetic score predicted success in four and was of no value in two studies. Of 15 outcome studies that appeared in the literature during 1974, all reported some degree of success with a variety of treatment programs and alcoholic populations [12].

Suicide Potential

Miles [15] estimates that 15% of alcoholics die of suicide. Surprisingly little direct information is available on testing alcoholics for suicide potential. Beck's Depression Inventory has been widely utilized in assessing depression, and the MMPI affords an assessment of depression, hostility, and acting-out potential in its 10 basic scales.

After matching subjects on age and sex, Leonard [13] compared MMPIs from 36 patients who did commit suicide with MMPIs of 36 suicidal patients and 36 nonsuicidal patients. Different test patterns emerged for 20 males and 16 females. Female suicides differed significantly from all other groups, and male suicides differed from all groups but the male suicidal patients. Stable predictors have by no means been established for this important diagnostic problem.

Aggressive Potential

Renson, Adams, and Tinkelberg [18] compared 26 alcoholics with documented violence while intoxicated with 25 matched nonviolent alcoholics. They used the Buss-Durkee Inventory to assess aggression, which includes eight subtests. Total hostility scores were higher for the violent group and essentially unrelated to age. The assaultiveness subtest and verbal aggressiveness subtest were positively related. Further study is needed in this socially relevant area.

Korsakoff's Syndrome

Articles dealing with this syndrome have compared types of memory and visual perceptive deficits in patients with alcoholic Korsakoff's syndrome as compared with other alcoholics. Interestingly, reports focus on theoretical problems related to type of damage and possible etiology rather than on making the diagnosis of Korsakoff's syndrome based on testing. Data are available, however, that document performance differences between the two groups [4].

POPULATIONS INCLUDING ALCOHOLICS

Sex, Age, Race Factors

Objective studies consistently show considerably more male alcoholics than females in adult populations considered. Research findings are needed concerning homosexual and preadolescent alcoholics. More problem drinkers are being found in adolescent populations. Studies of elderly populations have cited estimates of 10% problem drinkers [21]. Morbidity studies suggest that young black males should be carefully screened for alcoholism [12]. Available information about Spanish-speaking populations [21] and some American Indian tribes [20] suggest alcoholism should also be considered in these groups.

Psychiatric Problems

Repeated findings have linked alcoholism with neurotic and psychopathic personality problems. Several authors have pointed out that patients who present for psychiatric treatment with depressive or anxiety symptoms should also have concomitant alcoholism ruled out. Alcohol may be a contributing factor in suicide attempts. Numerous studies have demonstrated dual addictions so that alcoholism should be considered in those patients presenting as drug addicts. One study found untreated and clear-cut symptoms of alcoholism in half of a group hospitalized for manic-depressive reactions, but no such evidence was found in manic-depressive patients treated on an outpatient basis [12].

Physical Problems

The association between cirrhosis of the liver and alcoholism is well known and other relationships between alcoholism and physical problems have been demonstrated. For example, Brody [1] has noted that morbidity from cardiovascular disease occurred in alcoholics about 10 years earlier than in the general population. An objective study of patients with acute pancreatitis found 14 of 16 consecutive patients to be alcoholic; none had been referred for alcoholic treatment [12].

Occupations at Risk

Little work has been done in the United States to correlate occupation with alcoholism rate. Jones [9] found that 5% of physicians hospitalized as psychiatric patients were diagnosed as alcoholic. The armed services have made some attempts to identify subpopulations at risk on the basis of duties performed [12]. Occupational risk definitions could be extremely useful in increasing efficient screening for alcoholism.

INSTITUTIONAL CONTACTS

The numerous contacts alcoholics make with social service agencies and with psychiatric inpatient and outpatient facilities is widely recognized. General medical hospitals also have considerable unrealized potential for identifying alcoholics who enter with certain types of medical problems. Emergency rooms frequently handle suicide attempters and also receive accident victims of all types; the link between alcohol use and violent events has been well documented [21]. Jankowski and Drum [8] have found that patients leaving against medical advice from a general medical hospital included a noteworthy proportion of alcoholics.

The highest rate of treatment success has been in business settings [11, 12]. Employee-assistance programs have been supported increasingly by both management and unions, and have found many needing assistance with alcoholism. Psychological testing has not been reported in the literature in relation to these programs, but might be feasible on a selected basis with informed employee consent.

Many studies have documented drinking problems in adolescent and college populations, but the response of student health centers has appeared to be limited. Minimal response has also apparently characterized agencies assisting the aged.

The legal system has made extensive use of psychological testing to identify alcoholics, particularly in processing driving-while-intoxicated offenders. Long-term residents of prisons and jails list alcoholism among their many social problems [21].

SUMMARY

Psychological testing offers an efficient and standardized approach to case finding in alcoholism. The MacAndrews Alcoholism Scale and Michigan Alcoholism Screening Test merit widespread use, since they have proven effective with various populations tested in a variety of settings. These tests may be supplemented by other psychological tests for specific problems or to overcome specific test deficiencies. Examination of populations at risk in appropriate institutional settings seems justified in view of the increased availability of programs offering treatment for alcoholics.

ACKNOWLEDGMENTS

The author wishes to acknowledge the support of the Medical Research Service of the Veterans Administration.

REFERENCES

1. Brody, J. A. Medical surveillance program of the new epidemiological and special studies branch of NIAAA: An approach to an epidemiologic program on alcohol abuse and alcoholism. *Alcoholism: Clin. Exp. Res.* 1:349-354, 1977.
2. Burke, H. R., and Marcus, R. MacAndrews MMPI Alcoholism Scale: Alcoholism and drug addictiveness. *J. Psychol.* 96:141-148, 1977.
3. Buros, O. K. *The Seventh Mental Measurements Yearbook.* Gryphon: Highland Park, N.J., 1972.
4. Butters, N., Cermak, L. S., Montgomery, K., and Adinolfi, A. Some comparisons of the memory and visuoperceptive deficits of chronic alcoholics and patients with Korsakoff's disease. *Alcoholism: Clin. Exp. Res.* 1:73-80, 1977.
5. Freeman, C. W., O'Leary, M. R., and Calsyn, D. Application of the Faschingbauer abbreviated MMPI with alcoholic patients. *J. Clin. Psychol.* 33:303-306, 1977.
6. Friedrich, W. N., Boriskin, J. A., and Nelson, O. A factor analytic study of the Michigan Alcoholism Screening Test. *Psychol. Rep.* 42:865-866, 1978.
7. Gibbs, L., and Flanagan, J. Prognostic indicators of alcoholism treatment outcome. *Int. J. Addict.* 12:1097-1141, 1977.
8. Jankowski, C. B., and Drum, D. E. Diagnostic correlates of discharge against medical advice. *Arch. Gen. Psychiatry* 34:153-155, 1977.
9. Jones, R. E. A study of 100 physician psychiatric inpatients. *Am. J. Psychiatry* 134:119-123, 1977.
10. Knox, W. J. Objective psychological measurement and alcoholism: Review of literature, 1971-72. *Psychol. Rep.* 38:1023-1050, 1976. (Monograph Suppl. 1-V38)
11. Knox, W. J. Objective psychological measurement and alcoholism: Survey of the literature, 1973. *Psychol. Rep.* 42:439-480, 1978. (Monograph Suppl. 1-V38)
12. Knox, W. J. Objective psychological measurement and alcoholism: Survey of the literature, 1974. *Psychol. Rep.* 47:51-68, 1980. (Monograph Suppl. 1-V47)
13. Leonard, C. V. The MMPI as a suicide predictor. *J. Consult. Clin. Psychol.* 45:367-377, 1977.
14. Lucas, R. W., Mullin, P. J., Luna, C. B. X., and McInroy, D. C. Psychiatrists and a computer as interrogators of patients with alcohol-related illnesses: A comparison. *Brit. J. Psychiatry* 131:160-167, 1977.
15. Miles, C. P. Conditions predisposing to suicide: A review. *J. Nerv. Ment. Dis.* 164:231-246, 1977.
16. Miller, W. R. Alcoholism scales and objective assessment methods: A review. *Psychol. Bull.* 83:649-674, 1976.
17. Orstein, P. The Alcadd Test as a predictor of post-hospital drinking behavior. *Psychol. Rep.* 43:611-617, 1976.
18. Renson, G. J., Adams, J. C., and Tinkelberg, J. R. Buss-Durkee assessment and validation with violent versus nonviolent chronic alcohol abusers. *J. Consult. Clin. Psychol.* 46:360-361, 1978.
19. Sharp, J. R., Rosenbaum, G., Goldman, M. S., and Whitman, R. D. Recoverability of psychological functioning following alcohol abuse: Acquisition of meaningful synonyms. *J. Consult. Clin. Psychol.* 45:1023-1028, 1977.
20. Stratton, R., Zeiner, A., and Pardes, A. Tribal affiliation and prevalence of alcohol problems. *J. Stud. Alcohol* 39:1166-1177, 1978.
21. Summary of third report on alcohol and health. *NIAAA Inf. and Feat. Serv.* 53:3-7, 1978.

22. Wilkins, R. H. Denial of the hidden alcoholic in general practice. In: *Alcoholism and Drug Dependence: A Multidisciplinary Approach,* Madden, J. S., Walker, R., and Kenyon, W. H. (eds.). Plenum: New York, 1977.

23. Zung, B. J. Factor structure of the Michigan Alcoholism Screening Test. *J. Stud. Alcohol* 39:56–67, 1978.

5

PETER E. NATHAN, PhD, Rutgers University

BLOOD ALCOHOL LEVEL DISCRIMINATION AND DIAGNOSIS

THIS CHAPTER REVIEWS a program of research that now strongly suggests a reliable difference between alcoholics and nonalcoholics in blood alcohol level (BAL) discrimination accuracy. This difference in the capacity of alcoholics and nonalcoholics to inform themselves on their level of intoxication is marked enough to render it of diagnostic value. As well, since BAL discrimination ability relates directly to tolerance to alcohol's behavioral effects, which may in turn affect pattern of alcohol consumption, research on estimation accuracy may have significance not only for diagnosis but also for a fuller understanding of the etiology of alcoholism.

BAL DISCRIMINATION BY ALCOHOLICS

The first study of blood alcohol level discrimination, by Australians Lovibond and Caddy [7], investigated discrimination training as a therapeutic tool. Of 44 alcoholic subjects accepted into a treatment program, 31 were assigned to an experi-

---

Peter E. Nathan, PhD, Alcohol Behavior Research Laboratory, Rutgers–The State University, New Brunswick, New Jersey.

mental group, 13 to a control group. Experimental subjects were trained in BAL discrimination during a single 90- to 120-minute session, during which they (1) were shown a scale describing some typical behavioral effects of different BALs, (2) ingested an alcohol-fruit juice mixture that raised their BALs to about 65 mg/%, (3) examined their subjective experiences as a basis for estimating BALs, and (4) were given Breathalyzer tests every 15 to 20 minutes, estimated their own BAL, then were told their actual BAL. An aversive conditioning procedure to inhibit alcohol consumption at BALs above 65 mg/% was then implemented. This treatment, which consisted of painful electric shocks when subjects drank at BALs above 65 mg/%, lasted 6 to 12 sessions; subjects received between 30 to 70 shocks in all. Control subjects underwent BAL discrimination training but received random, rather than contingent, shock during three treatment sessions. A 4-month follow-up of subjects indicated that experimental subjects were maintaining greater control over their drinking than control subjects. The authors of the study attributed responsibility for this outcome to enhanced BAL discrimination accuracy, which led, in turn, to acquisition of a discriminated aversion to consumption at other than moderate BALs. Direct assessment of discrimination skill or learning was never carried out, however.

In an effort to replicate and extend Lovibond and Caddy's study, Silverstein, Nathan, and Taylor [9] designed a study initially including four male "gamma" alcoholics who participated as inpatients in both phases of a two-part, 36-day study. The goal of the first phase of the study (which lasted 10 days) was to examine some of the factors involved in training alcoholics to estimate their BAL accurately. Drinking was programmed in five 2-day cycles such that BALs rose on the first day of a cycle to 150 mg/%, then fell overnight and over the next day to zero. During the first (baseline) 2-day cycle, subjects estimated BALs approximately 10 times each day without receiving feedback on accuracy. During the following three 2-day cycles, subjects were continuously alerted to the emotional and physical correlates of changing levels of blood alcohol while receiving feedback after each BAL estimate, then after 50% of their estimates, and then after 50% of their estimates, with positive reinforcement delivered contingent on accurate BAL estimation. During the final 2-day cycle of this phase of the study, which represented a return to baseline conditions, subjects were again required to make their BAL estimates in the absence of training, feedback, or contingent reinforcement.

During the second phase of the study (which lasted 26 days), three of the four subjects who had participated in the study's first phase were trained to drink to reach, then to maintain, a prescribed BAL (80 mg/%). Three converging behavioral shaping procedures were utilized for this purpose: (1) responsibility for control over drinking was gradually shifted from the experimenter to the subject; (2) the range of positively reinforced BALs was successively narrowed closer and closer to the target BAL of 80 mg/%; (3) all reinforcement and feedback were gradually faded out over the nearly 4 weeks of this phase of the study.

Data from the first phase of the study showed that the most powerful factor influencing BAL estimation accuracy was the presence or absence of accurate feedback on blood alcohol level. Whether this feedback was continuous or intermittent, or accompanied or unaccompanied by reinforcement for accuracy, was unimportant; estimation error scores during the three training cycles were uniformly lower than those during the initial pretraining or concluding posttraining baseline periods of this phase of the study. During the second, control-training phase of the study, subjects were able to control their drinking effectively — to maintain their BAL within the prescribed range — but only as long as feedback on their BAL was provided. The degree of control decreased significantly when feedback was removed (during the postexperimental baseline assessment period).

These data by Silverstein and his colleagues called into question Lovibond and Caddy's presumption that subjects maintained the ability to discriminate BALs from internal cues through the follow-up period. Though the Silverstein study affirmed that alcoholics can learn to discriminate BALs with considerable accuracy and, following acquisition of that skill, to confine their drinking behavior to narrowly defined limits, both abilities were significantly attenuated once external feedback of accurate BALs was removed.

BAL DISCRIMINATION BY SOCIAL DRINKERS

In a study similar in intent to that of Silverstein, Nathan, and Taylor [9], Bois and Vogel-Sprott [1] reported some success in training social drinkers to estimate BALs and, subsequently, to use these estimates to self-titrate alcohol intake. Nine males participated in each of six daily sessions. During the first three sessions, all subjects consumed an amount of ethanol, mixed with an equal volume of 7-Up, equivalent to 135 ml of alcohol for a 150 lb individual. During the first session, subjects consumed four equal portions of the drink at 20-minute intervals, estimating BALs 10 times during that time. Accompanying each estimate, subjects provided symptom reports describing their immediate subjective experiences. The feedback on actual BALs was delivered only once during this session — when the BAL had reached its peak. The second session was identical to the first, except that accurate feedback was provided subjects following each BAL estimate. The third session was identical to the first session; it was designed to tap posttraining discrimination accuracy. Estimation accuracy improved significantly from the first session to the second session. A nonsignificant decrease in accuracy from the second session to the third session was also reported. These data suggest that these subjects, who were social drinkers, acquired — and maintained — BAL estimation accuracy on the basis of internal cues. However, BAL feedback was provided during the first and third sessions, and the amount and rate of drink consumption were identical all three sessions. As a result, subjects may have linked these external cues to the feedback provided in the second session and, in that way, learned to formulate subsequent estimates on this basis, rather than on the basis of internal cues.

The next study in the Rutgers BAL discrimination sequence addressed the same issue: Can nonalcoholics discriminate blood alcohol level via internal cues, or must they depend solely on external cues, as did the alcoholics studied earlier by Silverstein and his colleagues? The principal finding of the study by Huber, Karlin, and Nathan [2] was that nonalcoholics can acquire and maintain accurate BAL discriminations whether provided internal or external cue training. Thirty-six nonalcoholic college students participated in three day-long experimental sessions. In each, subjects consumed a total of 7 oz of vodka mixed with tomato juice and randomly distributed across six drinks. In the initial session, measures of pretraining estimation accuracy were obtained. In the second, subjects were assigned to one of three training groups on the basis of pretraining accuracy scores: internal training only (I); external training only (E); or both internal and external training (I + E). Internal training was designed to teach subjects to focus on changes in mood and body sensations as a basis for identifying changes in BAL. External training relied on a programmed booklet designed to teach subjects relationships between amount and frequency of alcohol intake and changes in BAL.

In order to disguise the alcoholic content of drinks during the second and third sessions, subjects were required to gargle before every drink with an anesthetic mouthwash. In both of these sessions, subjects also estimated the alcoholic content of their drinks to assess discriminability of drink strength. During training, BAL estimates, made seven times, were immediately followed by feedback. Subjects who received external training were told immediately prior to each estimate what the actual alcoholic content of the immediately preceding drink was; they were to use this information and the formulae taught them in the programmed learning booklet to estimate their BAL. Subjects who received internal training were not told the alcoholic content of their drinks during training; they were to formulate BAL estimates on the basis of internal sensations. Subjects in the I + E group made two sets of estimates, one based on external cues, the other on internal cues.

In the third (test) session of this study, subjects made four BAL estimates; no feedback was given following any of the estimates. Prior to the estimates, half the subjects in each group were told the actual alcoholic content of their drinks; the other half were not. An analysis of variance revealed that all subjects significantly improved BAL estimation accuracy during training, then maintained this improved accuracy in the third session. This improvement was independent of the kind of training provided and whether or not subjects had been told the alcoholic content of their drinks in the third session. These results suggested that these nonalcoholic subjects could use internal and external cues equally well to estimate their BAL. However, a word of caution is in order. Despite the elaborate procedures employed to disguise the strength of drinks, subjects were able to discriminate the various drink dosages to a limited extent; as a consequence, discriminability of drink doses may have played some role in subjects' improved posttraining BAL estimation accuracy.

Given that these data suggested that nonalcoholics can, in fact, learn to discriminate BALs on the basis of changes in mood and body sensations, it was still an open question whether alcoholics could learn to make BAL discriminations on the basis of the same cues. The question remained an open one because the design of the study by Silverstein and his colleagues [9], which suggested that alcoholics cannot utilize internal cues, did not include essential controls over other sources of information on intoxication level that the study of nonalcoholics by Huber and his coworkers possessed [2].

BAL DISCRIMINATION: COMPARISONS

To answer this important question, Lansky, Nathan, and Lawson [4] designed a study of BAL discrimination by alcoholic subjects identical in its essential features to that of Huber, Karlin, and Nathan [2]. Two separate groups of four chronic alcoholic subjects lived in the Alcohol Behavior Research Laboratory for 2-week periods. During those periods, one group of four was given training in BAL discrimination via internal cues, while the other received external cue training. All subjects participated in three experimental sessions, each separated by a day during which no experimental activities took place.

Prior to training both groups of alcoholics were unable to estimate BALs with accuracy. During training (the second session), when verdical BAL feedback was available, estimation accuracy increased significantly and equally for both groups: both groups of alcoholics acquired the ability to estimate actual BALs and to follow the changes that took place in their BALs over the course of the session. Results of the third (test) session revealed, however, that once the feedback of actual BALs was removed, only the externally trained alcoholics maintained the ability to accurately estimate BALs and to follow changes in the actual BALs.

Unlike the nonalcoholic subjects Huber, Nathan, and Karlin [2] had studied, the alcoholic subjects in this study by Lansky, Nathan, and Lawson [4] were not able to learn to discriminate BALs effectively on the basis of internal feelings and sensations, although they could do so when taught to use external cues. On analyzing data from 36 nonalcoholic social drinkers and 20 alcoholic subjects studied at the Alcohol Behavior Research Laboratory, Lansky, Nathan, Ersner-Hershfield, and Lipscomb [3] reported as well that before BAL discrimination training—before being trained to use either internal or external cues—the social drinkers were significantly better able to discriminate blood alcohol levels, suggesting again to these researchers that the alcoholic's deficit in discrimination ability is a pervasive and characteristic one.

Both studies by Lansky and his colleagues, then, support the hypothesis first put forth by Silverstein, Nathan, and Taylor [9], subsequently refined by Huber, Karlin, and Nathan [2], that alcoholics have a fundamental deficit in the ability to discriminate blood alcohol levels on the basis of internal cues. Huber and his colleagues suggested, in addition, that the relative inability of alcoholics to monitor internal cues may be a function, at least in part, of shifting levels of tolerance experienced during their lengthy drinking histories. As a result of these varying tolerance levels sets of internal cues had likely become associated with several BALs, not just one (as with most social drinkers). Other hypotheses to account for alcoholics' apparent inability to discriminate BALs on the basis of internal cues include inherited dysfunction of the internal receptors and the effects of sustained high levels of alcohol in the blood on the sensitivity of receptors.

THE ROLE OF TOLERANCE

The hypotheses of Huber and his colleagues [2] were tested in two recent studies [5, 6]. In the first of these studies [5] 24 male Rutgers University undergraduates were selected to fall into four experimental groups on the basis of their usual drinking pattern (heavy vs. light) and familial alcoholism (present vs. absent in close biological relatives). Subjects were also tested on a standing steadiness measure before and after consuming alcohol, then divided into high- and low-tolerance groups based on changes in standing stability. Because standing steadiness is an extremely sensitive measure of intoxication, it has also been suggested as a potentially valuable measure of tolerance (Moskowitz, Daily, and Henderson [8]).

Subjects participated in a three-session blood alcohol level discrimination training program that utilized only internal cue training. During the first session, the baseline session, subjects consumed alcohol in six programmed doses and made eight estimates of intoxication without training or feedback on actual BALs. Accurate BAL feedback following each estimate and internal cue training were provided in the second session. Subjects made BAL estimates without training or feedback during the third session, the test session. A week separated each of the three sessions.

Groups differing in drinking patterns and familial alcoholism did not differ in ultimate BAL estimation accuracy following internal training. By contrast, when subjects were grouped according to tolerance, low-tolerant subjects (those whose body sway sober and drunk differed markedly) were found to have been significantly more accurate in their third session estimates than high-tolerant subjects (those whose body sway sober and drunk differed very little). An analysis of covariance indicated that this effect could not be accounted for by pretraining differences alone, suggesting that low-tolerant subjects were better able to use internal training.

These results suggest that previously observed differences between alcoholics and nonalcoholics in the ability to monitor changes in intoxication level probably relate, at least in part, to the development of tolerance by alcoholics. Because inability to monitor the internal consequences of intoxication in turn may lead to more excessive drinking (the absence of negative consequences of consumption may well promote overconsumption), and interrelationship among blood alcohol level discrimination deficits, tolerances, and abusive drinking is hypothesized. This interrelationship becomes even more compelling when data from a related study by Lipscomb, Nathan, Wilson, and Abrams [6] are considered.

In that study, 32 male social drinkers were divided into high- and low-tolerance groups [6]. Subjects consumed either a high (1.0 g/kg) or a low (0.5 g/kg) dose of ethanol. On finishing their drinks, subjects interacted with a female confederate whose continued silence was designed to induce anxiety. Heart rate and skin conductance measures and behavioral and self-report indices were taken. Heart rate increased more in subjects at the low dose, a finding consistent with the tension-reduction hypothesis of alcohol's effect. In support of the presumed importance of the interrelationship among BAL discrimination deficits, tolerances, and abusive drinking, the heart rates of high-tolerant subjects, regardless of alcohol dose, and skin conductances of high-tolerant subjects at the low alcohol dose increased significantly more than heart rates and skin conductances of low-tolerant subjects. In other words, tolerance makes it necessary for the high-tolerant individual to consume larger quantities of alcohol than low-tolerant persons to dampen autonomic arousal in the face of stressors. In so doing, tolerance also increases the likelihood that the tolerant individual will consume larger quantities of ethanol than the nontolerant individual. Or, ethanol controls or reduces anxiety and the effects of stress less effectively in individuals higher in tolerance, requiring them to consume more alcohol to achieve the desired anxiety-reduction effect. As a consequence, the highly tolerant drinker, a person who has likely learned to drink before or during interpersonally stressful experiences, must consume more ethanol to achieve the desired effect. Increased consumption, in turn, as with the effect of tolerance on sensitivity to changing intoxication levels, leads to even higher tolerance, further increasing the dose of ethanol required to alleviate anxiety. In other words, tolerance and ethanol interact in a mutually perpetuating vicious cycle.

Taken together, these two studies by Lipscomb and his colleagues [5, 6] reinforce the view that tolerance to the behavioral effects of alcohol may be an important contributor to drinking.

SUMMARY

To summarize:

1. Alcoholics differ from nonalcoholics in the ability to discriminate blood alcohol level in the absence of training in this skill; this difference is of diagnostic import.

2. On being trained to discriminate among blood alcohol levels, nonalcohol-

ics can use both internal and external cues for this function, while alcoholics can use only external cues; this difference may also be of diagnostic significance;

3. High tolerance to the behavioral effects of alcohol appears responsible for alcoholics' relative inability to utilize internal cues for the purposes of BAL discrimination;

4. Two possible mechanisms could account for an hypothesized role of tolerance in the etiology of alcoholism: By freeing alcoholics from alcohol's negative effects, tolerance permits them to drink with relative impunity; by lessening alcohol's capacity to dampen autonomic arousal in the face of stressors, tolerance increases consumption to levels at which arousal is reduced. In both cases, tolerance both initiates and follows overconsumption.

ACKNOWLEDGMENTS

Preparation of this manuscript and support for most of the research reviewed in it were facilitated by National Institute on Alcohol Abuse and Alcoholism Grant No. AA00259.

REFERENCES

1. Bois, C., and Vogel-Sprott, M. Discrimination of low blood alcohol level and self-titration skills in social drinkers. *Q. J. Stud. Alcohol* 37:86–97, 1974.
2. Huber, H., Karlin, R., and Nathan, P. E. Blood alcohol level discrimination by nonalcoholics: The role of internal and external cues. *J. Stud. Alcohol* 37:27–39, 1976.
3. Lansky, D., Nathan, P. E., Ersner-Hershfield, S. M., and Lipscomb, T. R. Blood alcohol level discrimination: Pretraining monitoring accuracy of alcoholics and nonalcoholics. *Addict. Behav.* 3:209–214, 1978.
4. Lansky, D., Nathan, P. E., and Lawson, D. Blood alcohol level discrimination by alcoholics: The role of internal and external cues. *J. Consult. Clin. Psychol.* 46:953–960, 1978.
5. Lipscomb, T. R., and Nathan, P. E. Effect of family history of alcoholism, drinking pattern, and tolerance on blood alcohol level discrimination. *Arch. Gen. Psychiatry* 37:571–576, 1980.
6. Lipscomb, T. R., Nathan, P. E., Wilson, G. T., and Abrams, D. B. Effects of tolerance on the anxiety-reducing function of alcohol. *Arch. Gen. Psychiatry* 37:577–582, 1980.
7. Lovibond, S. H., and Caddy, G. R. Discriminated aversive control in the moderation of alcoholics' drinking behavior. *Behav. Ther.* 1:437–444, 1970.
8. Moscowitz, H., Daily, J., and Henderson, R. *Acute Tolerance to Behavioral Impairment by Alcohol in Moderate and Heavy Drinkers* (Report to the Highway Research Institute, National Highway Traffic Safety Administration, Department of Transportation). Washington, D.C., April 1974.
9. Silverstein, S. J., Nathan, P. E., and Taylor, H. A. Blood alcohol level estimation and controlled drinking by chronic alcoholics. *Behav. Ther.* 5:1–15, 1974.

6

DAVID J. ARMOR, PhD, The Rand Corporation
J. MICHAEL POLICH, PhD, The Rand Corporation

MEASUREMENT OF ALCOHOL CONSUMPTION

PERHAPS THE MOST DIFficult measure in the alcohol field is alcohol consumption itself. The difficulty arises from the inherent complexity of drinking behavior, which can vary from day to day or month to month in terms of amounts, frequency, and types of beverages consumed.

The purpose of this chapter is to describe a self-report measure of alcohol consumption that attempts to maximize reliability and validity while preserving simplicity and ease of administration. Specifically, this chapter outlines a measure of alcohol consumption recommended by a special advisory panel to the National Institute on Alcohol Abuse and Alcoholism (NIAAA).* The method represents a consensus among persons with diverse experience in self-report techniques; it is also similar to a method used successfully in a recent Air Force study to capture approximately 80% of consumption as measured by alcoholic beverage sales [5, 8].

David J. Armor, PhD, The Rand Corporation, Santa Monica, California.

J. Michael Polich, PhD, The Rand Corporation, Santa Monica, California.

The views expressed herein are the authors' own and do not necessarily reflect the opinions of The Rand Corporation or its research sponsors.

*The advisory panel includes David Armor, The Rand Corporation; Walter Clark, University of California, Berkeley; Harold Mulford, University of Iowa; Marcia Russell, Research Institute on Alcoholism, Buffalo; and Linda Sobell, Addiction Research Foundation, Toronto.

APPROACH

The approach taken herein combines the strategies of two differing but widely used techniques. The first, the quantity-frequency (QF) technique, has been used by NIAAA and many researchers to estimate the total volume of consumption in interview settings, particularly among alcoholic samples [1]. The QF technique measures the frequency of consumption of a particular beverage over some time period (usually 30 days), and the typical quantity of that beverage consumed on a drinking day. Estimated total volume is obtained by adding together the QFs for each beverage. As such, the measure is more properly called "typical quantity-frequency" (or "typical volume"), because respondents are in effect asked about the average quantities they consume on drinking days, thereby possibly missing atypical days of heavier drinking.

The second method, the quantity-variability (QV) technique, was introduced in general population surveys to assess episodic heavy drinking [2]. The technique measures the number of days in some time period (usually 1 year) a person consumed large quantities of a beverage (e.g., 12 or more cans of beer). By asking about a full range of quantities, one can expand this method to construct a total volume estimate.

Each of these methods has difficulties. In national surveys the QF method underestimates total beverage sales by about 50%, which might be due in part to reliance on typical drinking quantities [1]. The QV technique is a more direct method for assessing episodic heavy drinking, but in the Air Force study it appeared less valid than the QF method. The full QV method also has some internal consistency problems arising from the tendency of some respondents to account for more than 365 days in a year. A promising new approach combines these techniques into a total volume measure, the QFA (quantity-frequency, adjusted), which may give a more valid estimate of total consumption. In the Air Force study [8] the QFA measure produced a value that was considerably higher than other measures and much closer to the amount of total beverage sales. The QF measure yielded a per-capita estimate of 0.74 oz. of ethanol per day, QV yielded 0.67 oz. per day, while the QFA method yielded 1.01 oz. of ethanol per day.

The remainder of this chapter consists of three sections. The first section describes standardized alcohol consumption questions, the second section describes how to convert these questions into QF, QFA, and various alternate indices, and the third section presents recommendations for using alcohol consumption indices in research and evaluation.

Alcohol Consumption Questions

The questions described in this section are intended for structured questionnaire use, either in face-to-face interviews or in self-administrations. The particular format adopted presupposes an interview setting, but the questions can easily be converted to a self-administration format. Questions and instructions to be read to subjects are italicized; instructions to the interviewer are capitalized. Questions are followed by brief clarifying comments where necessary.

Now I would like to ask some questions about your alcohol consumption.

1. *What was the approximate date of your last drink of beer, wine, or liquor?* (IF EXACT DATE IS NOT REMEMBERED, RECORD MONTH AND/OR YEAR.)

   _____ / _____ / _____
   DAY   MONTH   YEAR

   IF SUBJECT NEVER DRANK, CODE 0 IN YEAR AND SKIP TO NEXT SECTION.

   Let's talk about the 30 days before your last drink, including that day. That would be from _____ to _____. (USE CALENDAR).

2. *About how many days altogether did you drink beer, wine, or liquor during that 30-day period?*

   Number of days _____
   (30 maximum)

By focusing consumption questions on the 30 days before one's last drink, length of abstention can be determined without impairing the 30-day window for observing consumption. This is especially important for alcoholic samples, since some alcoholics intersperse heavy drinking with significant periods of abstention. Depending on one's analysis objectives, consumption amounts can be tabulated only for those who drank in the past month, or past 6 months, or so forth. A calendar showing days and months over the past 2 years should be used to pinpoint the precise drinking period.

The next seven questions elicit the information needed for the QF index.

The next several questions are about that 30-day period before your last drink, that is, the period from _____ to _____.

3. *During that 30-day period, how many days did you drink beer?*

   Number of days _____
   (IF 0, SKIP TO QUESTION 5.)

4. *On a typical day when you drank beer, how much beer did you drink?*

   12 oz. cans _____   16 oz. cans _____   Quarts _____
   Other _____ (Specify: _____ oz.)

5. *During that 30-day period, how many days did you drink wine?*

   Number of days _____
   (IF 0, SKIP TO QUESTION 7.)

6. On a typical day when you drank wine, how much wine did you drink?

4 oz. glasses _____ Half-bottles _____ Fifths _____
Quarts   _____ Other   _____ (Specify: _____ oz.)

7. During that 30-day period, how many days did you drink hard liquor, such as whiskey, vodka, or gin?

Number of days _____
(IF 0, SKIP TO QUESTION 10.)

8. On a typical day when you drank hard liquor, how much liquor did you drink?

Drinks _____ Shots _____ Half-pints _____ Pints _____
Fifths _____ Quarts _____ Other _____ (Specify: _____ oz.)
(Note: Pint = 16 oz., fifth = 26 oz., quart = 32 oz.)

9. IF ANSWERED IN DRINKS: About how many ounces of hard liquor are in your typical drink?

Number of oz. _____
(Shot = 1 oz.; jigger or finger = 1.5 oz.)

The response categories can be expanded to include a larger variety of containers, although the ones listed are the most common. One can also have a box in question 6 to check for fortified wines, such as vermouth, sherry, and so forth, which might be important for some alcoholic samples but less important for general population samples. Finally, it is extremely important to include question 9 for persons who answer the hard liquor question in terms of drinks. Many persons will answer question 9 with 2 or 3 oz. of liquor (e.g., martini drinkers).

The final six questions are used for constructing the QFA Index.

Now think back over the past 12 months from today.

10. During that 12 months, on how many days did you drink 11 or more cans of beer [4 quarts or more]?

Number of days _____

11. During that 12 months, on how many days did you drink at least 5 cans of beer, but not more than 10 cans?

Number of days _____

12. During that 12 months, on how many days did you drink 11 or more glasses of wine [2 fifths or more] [1 wine glass = 4 oz.]?

Number of days _____

13. During that 12 months, on how many days did you drink at least 5 glasses of wine, but not more than 10 glasses [a fifth or so]?

Number of days _____

14. During that 12 months, on how many days did you drink 11 oz. or more of hard liquor [11 shots, 7 jiggers, or 3/4 of a pint]?

Number of days _____

15. During that 12 months, on how many days did you have at least 5 oz. of hard liquor [5 shots, 3 jiggers, or 1/4 of a pint], but not more than 10 oz.?

Number of days _____

From the preceding group of questions one can calculate quantities of atypical heavy drinking, but not a total volume index. To do so one would have to ask about a full range of quantities. The primary purpose of these questions is to calculate the QFA index, which is described in the next section. To help capture frequent heavy drinking more accurately, one can insert such response categories as "every day," "once or twice a week," or "once or twice a month"; if such categories are not explicitly stated, the interviewer should be prepared to translate such responses as "once a week" to 52 days per year, "three times a month" to 36 days per year, and so on.

Calculating Consumption Indices

The questions listed in the previous section can be used to compute several indices of alcohol consumption, including typical quantity (Q) and the total volume measures, QF and QFA. All measures descirbed here assume that the ethanol content of beer is 4%, wine 12%, and hard liquor 43%; these assumptions are used in most NIAAA studies of alcohol consumption.

Basic definitions. The symbols QB, QW, and QL represent the ounces of ethanol on a typical drinking day for beer (B), wine (W), and liquor (L), respectively. These are calculated as follows:

$QB = 0.04 \times$ ounces of beer in question 4
$QW = 0.12 \times$ ounces of wine in question 6
$QL = 0.43 \times$ ounces of liquor in question 8*

Next, F represents the total number of days in the past 30 days on which any alcohol was consumed, and FB, FW, and FL represents the number of days of consumption for beer, wine, and liquor.

$F =$ number of days from question 2†
$FB =$ number of days from question 3

---

*If question 8 is answered by drinks, ounces of liquor is calculated as number of drinks times number of ounces in a typical drink, as indicated.

†Note that F does not necessarily equal the sum of FB, FW, and FL, since different beverages can be consumed on the same days.

FW = number of days from question 5
FL = number of days from question 7

Typical quantity. The first index described is "typical quantity on drinking days" during the 30-day window of observation. This measure is a weighted average of typical quantities, where the weights are the fraction of drinking days on which a particular beverage was consumed. It is defined as

$$Q = (FB \times QB + FW \times QW + FL \times QL)/F$$

For persons drinking only one beverage, this index is simply the typical quantity for that beverage. The Q index may be preferred over QF for alcoholic samples where some subjects may intersperse a few very heavy drinking days with periods of total abstention.

Quantity-frequency index. The next index described is QF, the total volume index for the 30-day window. It is defined as follows:

$$QF = (FB \times QB + FW \times QW + FL \times QL)/30$$

The QF index is ounces of ethanol consumed per day, which is one of the more common ways of expressing total volume measures. Alternatively, one can express it as total ethanol per 30-day period by simply computing the numerator without dividing by 30.

Quantity-frequency, adjusted index. The QF index underestimates the total volume of alcohol consumption over longer periods by ignoring atypical days of heavy drinking. The QFA index corrects for this problem by incorporating information on heavy drinking days and estimating total volume over a 12-month period. The basic logic of the QFA index is to adjust the typical 30-day volume for a given beverage to include atypical volumes based on heavy drinking days as indicated by questions 10 to 15.

In questions 10 to 15, the subject is asked the frequency with which he or she drank a high (H) amount (11 drinks or more, estimated as 7 oz. of ethanol on the average), and a medium (M) amount (5 to 10 drinks, estimated as 4 oz. of ethanol). These frequencies are denoted as follows:

Frequencies, High Amounts　　*Frequencies, Medium Amounts*

FHB = days from question 10　　FMB = days from question 11
FHW = days from question 12　　FMW = days from question 13
FHL = days from question 14　　FML = days from question 15

Then, the frequencies with which the subject drank a typical amount are estimated as follows:

Frequencies, Typical Amounts

FTB = FB × (365/30) − FHB − FMB
FTW = FW × (365/30) − FHW − FMW
FTL = FL × (365/30) − FHL − FML

Finally, the separate beverage volumes are computed as follows, by formulas that multiply quantity times frequency for each type of drinking (high, medium, and typical):

QFB = (7 × FHB + 4 × FMB + QB × FTB)/365
QFW = (7 × FHW + 4 × FMW + QW × FTW)/365
QFL = (7 × FHL + 4 × FML + QL × FTL)/365

and the total index of quantity-frequency, adjusted is

QFA = QFB + QFW + QFL.

Note that questions 10 to 15 cannot be used to compute the Cahalan quantity-variability measure, because the range of quantities is not complete. To do so, one would minimally have to add a question for each beverage that asks the number of days on which 1 to 4 drinks are consumed.

The QFA index is not without methodological limitations; in particular, it will overstate the total 12-month volume for persons who drank heavily only during the 30-day window. More complex questions and computations could be developed to improve the measures. One refinement in the calculation of FTB (and FTW, FTL) would be to multiply FTB by (365 minus days since last drink)/30 rather than 365/30. This would have the effect of adjusting for recent abstention. However, overestimation is not a serious problem for any of these indices, and data from the Air Force alcohol abuse prevalence study show that QFA is a reasonably valid aggregate estimate of total consumption.

USING CONSUMPTION MEASURES

Alcohol consumption measures have an extremely varied history in the alcoholism field. Some investigators, fearing such measures might be invalid, have ignored them altogether except for crude distinctions between drinking versus abstaining. In fact, consumption measures have been shown to suffer more validity problems than other measures of alcohol abuse [6, 10, 11]. Nevertheless, the degree of invalidity is often exaggerated, and there is evidence that alcoholics in follow-up interviews give self-reports of 30-day consumption that are not inconsistent with blood alcohol concentration tests about 80% of the time [7].

Perhaps a more important problem is the proper theoretical place of alcohol consumption in the field of alcoholism and alcohol abuse. While neither of these disorders can exist in the absence of consumption, there are serious questions about whether the actual amount of consumption is or should be a determining factor in the definition of either disorder. There is little doubt that alcohol consumption is strongly correlated with other signs and symptoms of alcohol abuse and alcoholism, and heavier consumers may have a higher risk of developing certain types of alcohol problems [8]. The causal sequences themselves, however, and the precise quantities where heavy drinking becomes risky are not clearly worked out in the existing research literature.

Several researchers who have studied national alcohol statistics have focused on amount of alcohol consumption as the major defining attribute of alcoholism [9]. The amount of 5 oz. of ethanol per day is frequently cited as the threshold for determining alcoholism [3]. In contrast, other research groups have tended to deemphasize alcohol consumption in favor of dependence symptoms in the definition of alcoholism [4]. The emphasis on dependence has received some empirical support in a recent long-term national follow-up of treated alcoholics. This study found that existence of even a few dependence symptoms, for either lighter or heavier drinkers, strongly predicted alcoholic relapse, while amount of consumption — in the absence of dependence symptoms — did not [7].

Although these conceptual and methodological issues are unresolved, alcohol consumption measures will continue to be used to help improve the understanding of the course of alcoholism. For samples of alcoholics, a measure such as Q is probably the most meaningful, since it represents the amount of consumption on drinking days. For general population surveys, especially where one desires an aggregate estimate of total volume of consumption, a measure such as QFA might be preferable. Finally, studies of the behavioral consequences of alcohol use — such as fighting or incidents with the law — may find a measure of episodic heavy drinking most useful.

REFERENCES

1. Armor, D. J., Polich, J. M., and Stambul, H. B. *Alcoholism and Treatment.* Wiley: New York, 1978.
2. Cahalan, D., Cisin, I. H., and Crossley, H. M. Measuring massed versus spaced drinking. In: *American Drinking Practices.* Rutgers Center of Alcohol Studies: New Brunswick, N.J., 1969.
3. De Lint, J., and Schmidt, W. The epidemiology of alcoholism. In: *The Biological Basis of Alcoholism,* Israel, Y. and Mardones, J. (eds.), Wiley: New York, 1971.

4. Edwards, G., Gross, M. M., Keller, M., Moser, J., and Room, R. *Alcohol-Related Disabilities*. World Health Organization: Geneva, 1977.

5. Polich, J. M. Epidemiology of alcohol abuse in military and civilian populations. *Am. J. Public Health* 71:1125–1132, 1981.

6. Polich, J. M. The validity of self-reports in alcoholism research. *Addict. Behav.* 7:81–90, 1982.

7. Polich, J. M., Armor, D. J., and Braiker, H. B. *The Course of Alcoholism: Four Years After Treatment*. Wiley: New York, 1981.

8. Polich, J. M., and Orvis, B. R. *Alcohol Problems: Patterns and Prevalence in the U.S. Air Force*. Santa Monica: The Rand Corporation, 1979.

9. Schmidt, W., and Popham, R. E. The single distribution theory of alcohol consumption. *J. Stud. Alcohol* 39:400–419, 1978.

10. Sobell, L. C., and Sobell, M. B. Out-patient alcoholics give valid self-reports. *J. Nerv. Ment. Dis.* 161:32–42, 1975.

11. Sobell, M. B., Sobell, L. C., and VanderSpek, R. Relationship among clinical judgment, self-report, and breath analysis measures of intoxication in alcoholics. *J. Consult. Clin. Psychol.* 47:204–206, 1979.

Section II

The Biology
of Alcoholism

7

SUJATA TEWARI, PhD, National Alcohol Research Center, Irvine, California
VIRGINIA G. CARSON, PhD, Chapman College, Orange, California

BIOCHEMISTRY OF ALCOHOL AND ALCOHOL METABOLISM

THE CONSUMPTION OF ethanol (alcohol) results in a wide variety of biochemical changes in the body. Although the principal target organs of ethanol in the body are the cerebral and the hepatic tissue, other organs are also affected to some extent. Ethanol is the primary component of all alcoholic beverages and is a short-chain alcohol. Pharmacologically, it is a central nervous system (CNS) depressant and produces effects similar to the general anesthetics, which have dissimilar structures. What gives ethanol this potency is its lipid solubility and extremely rapid penetration of the blood-brain barrier.

In chronic alcoholics, ethanol has been shown to produce the severely deleterious effects observed on the CNS. Furthermore, in certain predisposed individuals chronic ethanol ingestion can lead to brain dysfunction even after ethanol's use has been discontinued. Also documented are the clinical manifestations of alcoholism, with effects ranging from increased tolerance and physical dependence, to affective disorders, encephalopathies, and complicated hepatic effects

---

Sujata Tewari, PhD, Associate Professor and Scientific Director, National Alcohol Research Center, Department of Psychiatry and Human Behavior, College of Medicine, University of California, Irvine, Irvine, California.

Virginia G. Carson, PhD, Associate Professor of Biology, Chapman College, Orange, California, and National Alcohol Research Center, Department of Psychiatry and Human Behavior, University of California, Irvine, Irvine, California.

[17]. Additional CNS dysfunctions, such as deficits in learning, memory, and conceptual abilities, have been connected with prolonged ethanol usage. Animal studies also have shown irreversible impairments in brain functions even after significant periods of abstinence following chronic ethanol consumption [8]. In addition, experimental studies have reported changes in a variety of biochemical processes, including the neurotransmitter and macromolecular metabolism. Moreover, ethanol usage for significant periods of time causes a rapid development of physical dependence that is manifested by heightened CNS excitability following the withdrawal of ethanol.

It is considered that the primary effect of ethanol is exerted on the CNS. In the liver, ethanol's effects are related to changes in the metabolic processes. In the brain ethanol metabolism is minimal; that is not to say that ethanol is not metabolized at all in this tissue. Some metabolism does occur; however, unlike liver, the metabolites of ethanol in conjunction with ethanol produce the major consequences in the metabolic processes and the phenomenon of development of tolerance and drug dependence. Additional clinical consequences of alcohol use are the teratogenic effects of alcohol. The estimates of the incidence of the fetal alcohol syndrome (FAS) range from one in 300 live births, to one in 5,000 live births [22]. In addition, in women who drink heavily, increased risks of spontaneous abortion, prematurity, and stillbirth have sometimes been reported. Also recognized is the lowered fertility in male alcoholics and interference with the female reproductive and lactation systems. Finally, there is increasing evidence that associates certain types of cancer with alcohol use. Ethanol has been considered in recent years both as a cocarcinogen and as a promoter. By virtue of its chemical properties, many substances are soluble in ethanol and these can quickly reach stances are soluble in ethanol and these can quickly reach the major tissues, blood, and brain in the body. In view of the above observation, there are four major consequences from the effects of ethanol on the body. These are (1) metabolism and metabolites; (2) the development of processes of tolerance and physical dependence; (3) the role of ethanol as a teratogen, or the perinatal effects of ethanol; and (4) the role of ethanol as a cocarinogen or promoter of cancer.

Biochemical correlates of these manifestations, although still incompletely understood, have recently contributed to a fuller understanding of the effects of alcohol on the body. Evidence presented in this chapter illustrates the intricate involvement of the metabolic pathway, or metabolism and metabolites of alcohol, in producing critical changes in biochemical processes in the body leading to the development of tolerance and physical dependence, to diseases of the nervous system and other organs, and, finally, in the maternal physiology. A relationship is shown between ethanol and other factors that influence and alter the dynamics of the body, resulting in a variety of clinical syndromes. The purpose of this chapter is to identify and report on the progress made in the past decade in clarifying the metabolic and toxic effects of ethanol on the body. Furthermore, it is important to identify the neurobiological concomitants of the basic nature of alcoholism in order to facilitate the detection, prevention, and treatment of this disease and its consequences. Consequently, the basic studies on the CNS, specifically on the initial molecular events leading to overt clinical manifestations, are of prime importance and, therefore, are prerequisite in the clinical treatment of alcoholism.

METABOLISM OF ETHANOL

Enzymes

In the body, alcohol is metabolized to CO_2 and water, thereby resulting in calories, which are produced primarily due to the preferential oxidation of ethanol over other nutrients by the hepatic tissue, which is the major site of ethanol metabolism. In the presence of alcohol, the oxidation of substances such as fatty acids virtually comes to a standstill. The major enzyme responsible for the removal of alcohol is alcohol dehydrogenase (ADH), which has been crystallized and obtained in the pure form. The reaction catalyzed by the ADH is

$$C_2H_5OH + NAD^+ \rightarrow CH_3CHO + NADH + H^+$$

The acetaldehyde is further oxidized to acetate and water by acetaldehyde dehydrogenase.

The oxidation of ethanol is an effective source of energy because it is coupled with synthesis of adenosine triphosphate (ATP). This subject of ethanol metabolism has been reviewed recently [2, 12]. The rate of removal of ethanol from the body is the sum of the rate of ethanol oxidation, plus the rates of excretion of ethanol in urine, breath, and sweat. The excretion process follows first-order kinetics, and at any given time, the rate of excretion is directly proportional to the alcohol concentration in the blood. It is important to note at this point that the amount of ethanol excreted, which is unmetabolized in the body, depends upon the actual dose of ethanol administered. The total excretion of ethanol, in general, accounts for 5 to 6% of ethanol elimination. However, this value will change if a very high blood alcohol level is maintained. Because ethanol can diffuse readily from the blood to the alveolar air, a close correlation can be seen between blood ethanol concentration and the amount of ethanol in the breath. Since alcohol can be considered both a drug and a nutrient, the metabolic processes play an important part in the body.

In ethanol-dependent persons, the rate of ethanol metabolism is the most important determinant of the actual amount of ethanol consumed during the time when high blood alcohol levels are maintained over 24-hour periods for a prolonged period of time. Such individuals can ingest over 300 g of ethanol a day (26 oz. of 50% v/v beverage) [12, 14]. This volume amounts to 2,100 calories a day, 7 cal/g ethanol. Chronic ethanol ingestion leads to increased rates of ethanol oxidation on the order of 30 to 100% in a variety of species, including man. The metabolism of ethanol leads to the formation of acetaldehyde, a very toxic substance that may be related to organic pathology in the alcoholic. Acetaldehyde is a very reactive compound and can undergo many reactions in the liver. However, it is mostly converted to acetate by metabolizing enzymes. Acetaldehyde can be oxidized by liver aldehyde dehydrogenases, aldehyde oxidase, and xanthine oxidases. The latter two enzymes have broad substrate specificities and low affinities for acetaldehyde ($K_m < 1$ mM), and are probably not involved in the metabolism of acetaldehyde [7]. The main enzyme primarily responsible for the oxidation of acetaldehyde is acetaldehyde dehydrogenase. Several studies have dealt with this enzymatic activity in the liver of the rat, human, horse, and sheep. Liver aldehyde dehydrogenase catalyzes oxidation of aldehydes in the presence of nicotinamide-adenine dinucleotide (NAD) as follows:

$$CH_3CHO + NAD^+ \rightarrow CH_3COO^- + NADH + H^+$$

The enzyme has been isolated from various subcellular fractions, such as the mitochondrial matrix, mitochondrial outer membrane, microsomes, and cytosol. Among all enzymes, the enzyme from the mitochrondrial matrix has a low K_m for acetaldehyde and appears to be responsible for the oxidation of most of the ethanol-derived acetaldehyde. Inhibition by disulfiram of the low K_m mitochondrial matrix enzyme in rats results in acetaldehyde accumulation in the blood. Additional support for this was obtained in animal studies using isolated liver cells, perfused liver, and labeled ethanol in liver slices; these studies indicated that, at low levels, acetaldehyde is oxidized mainly in mitochondria.

Alcohol metabolism is very low in the brain (1/4,000th of the activity in liver). The presence of ADH has been demonstrated in this organ, and the contribution of the cerebral tissue to total ethanol metabolism in the body is extremely small. The brain response to ethanol is different from the response of hepatic tissue, and since behavioral effects are also an important component, separate functions of the CNS that can be affected by ethanol must be considered.

The large increase in the NAD–NADH ratio by ethanol in the liver is not seen in the brain and, even in the presence of high concentrations of administered ethanol, brain CH_3CHO levels have been found to be small. This may be due to the efficient operation of brain aldehyde dehydrogenase, or due to interaction with or rapid binding of acetaldehyde to several membranes.

Metabolites

Acetaldehyde. The primary metabolite of ethanol, acetaldehyde, is a colorless, volatile liquid, with a boiling point of 20° C. It is readily soluble in water and in many organic solvents, and more soluble in liquids than is ethanol. Acetaldehyde is very reactive compound because of the presence of the carbonyl group. After acetaldehyde is formed by the oxidation of ethanol, it is rapidly converted to acetate in the liver, and it has also been shown that the elimination of acetaldehyde given by intraperitoneal, intravenous, or oral routes follows first-order kinetics. The rate of acetaldehyde elimination suggests that this reaction does not limit the rate of ethanol metabolism in vivo. Acetaldehyde forms additional compounds with alcohols to form hemiacetals and, with thiol reagents, to form mercaptohemiacetals. Acetaldehyde condenses with primary amines, forming Schiff bases, and condensation reactions involving naturally occurring amines in the body, such as catecholamines and serotonin, could result in the formation of tetrahydroisoquinolines (TIQs) and —carbolines, respectively. These neuroamine derived alkaloids have been speculated to play a role in alcohol addiction [12]. Recent studies have shown that, following the administration of large doses of penicillamine, a dimethyl analogue of cysteine, a condensation product with acetaldehyde is formed and is excreted in the urine both in rats and in humans.

Morphinelike Alkaloids. Ethanol and morphine share some physiological effects, such as hypothermia, and cross-tolerance has been shown between ethanol and morphine. The possible ethanol-induced formation of morphinelike alkaloids involved in the development of cross-tolerance was proposed independently by Davis and Cohen in 1970 [4]. Acetaldehyde can participate in the formation of morphinelike alkaloids by (1) reacting with the biogenic amines, and (2) by inhibiting the oxidative steps in the metabolism of the biogenic amines, resulting in condensation of the biogenic amines with their own aldehydes. The two compounds that have received the most attention are (1) the TIQ, salsolinol—the condensation product of dopamine and acetaldehyde—and (2) tetrahydropapaveroline (THP), the condensation product of dopamine with its aldehyde, 3,4-dihydroxyphenylacetaldehyde.

In the metabolism of the various biogenic amines, it is possible for the aldehydes to be acted upon by aldehyde reductase instead of aldehyde dehydrogenase (see Figure 1). In man, alcohol shifts metabolism to the reductive pathway, particularly for norepinephrine (forming 3-methoxy-4-hydroxyphenylglycol) and serotonin (forming 5-hydroxytryptophol). Salsolinol has been detected in the urine and lumber cerebrospinal fluid of human alcoholic patients; however, no significant difference in salsolinol levels were found in samples taken during intoxication and after detoxification. Detectable amounts of O-methylated salsolinol have been found in the brains of ethanol-treated rats. Failure of some investigators to detect salsolinol or THP in ethanol-treated animals may be due to the difficulty in detecting the small (possibly picogram) quantities present.

Salsolinol has been shown to have some opiatelike actions. It, like opiates, can deplete brain calcium levels, augment morphine analgesia, and compete with naloxone for binding sites [4]. Recently, it has been demonstrated that the infusion of THP or salsolinol into Sprague-Dawley or Long-Evans rats (strains that

1. NOREPINEPHRINE $\xrightarrow{\text{MONOAMINE OXIDASE (MAO)}}$ 3,4 DIHYDROXYPHENYLGLYCOLALDEHYDE

↓ CATECHOL-O-METHYLTRANSFERASE (COMT)   ↓ ALDEHYDE DEHYDROGENASE

NORMETANEPHRINE   3,4 DIHYDROXYMANDELIC ACID

↓ MAO   ↓ COMT

3 METHOXY-4-HYDROXYPHENYLGLYCOLALDEHYDE $\xrightarrow{\text{ALDEHYDE DEHYDROGENASE}}$ 3 METHOXY, 4 HYDROXY MANDELIC ACID

2. DOPAMINE $\xrightarrow{\text{MAO}}$ 3,4 DIHYDORXYPHENYLACETALDEHYDE

↓ COMT   ↓ ALDEHYDE DEHYDROGENASE

3-METHOXYTYRAMINE   3,4-DIHYDROXYPHENYLACETIC ACID

↓ MAO   ↓ COMT

3-METHOXY-4 HYDROXYPHENYLACETALDEHYDE $\xrightarrow{\text{ALDEHYDE DEHYDROGENASE}}$ HOMOVANILLIC ACID

3. SEROTONIN $\xrightarrow{\text{MAO}}$ INDOLACETALDEHYDE $\xrightarrow{\text{ALDEHYDE DEHYDROGENASE}}$ 5-HYDROXYINDOL-ACETIC ACID (5 HIAA)

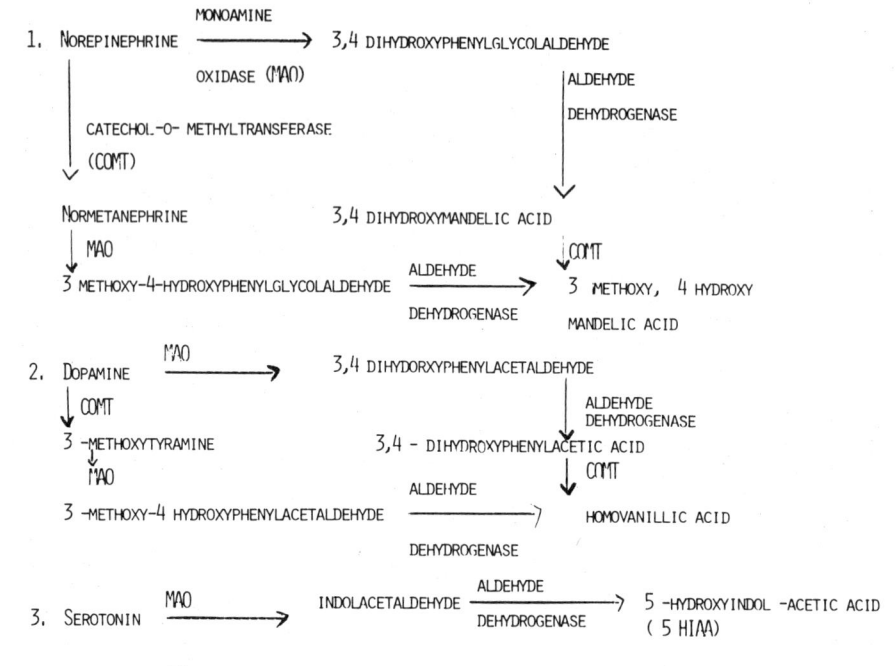

Figure 1. Metabolic Pathways for the Biogenic Amines

have a low preference for alcohol) induces increased alcohol intake, which is maintained for at least 10 months after the last infusion. The Wister rats (a strain having a high preference for ethanol), on the other hand, do not respond to THP infusion.

TOLERANCE AND PHYSICAL DEPENDENCE

In the brain, major effects of ethanol are intricately related to the phenomenon of tolerance and dependence, and the consequences resulting from excessive consumption. The continual drinking of ethanol causes the regular drinker to be able to tolerate larger amounts of ethanol. This is also true for barbiturates, for other hypnotics, and for minor tranquilizers. The fundamental biological mechanism of tolerance and dependence have been the subject of much investigation in recent years. Data demonstrate significant alterations in a number of physiological and biochemical processes in the brain and other tissues. These alterations were found to parallel or coincide in time and magnitude with alterations in the tolerance and physical dependence and have been designated as "the biochemical correlates of tolerance" [11]. To date, it remains unclear which of the changes are causally related to the development of tolerance and dependence, or are the consequence or concomitant result of the same basic mechanisms. Related to this line of thought is another aspect of the inquiries that relates to the considerable clinical problems arising due to the combined use of alcohol with other drugs — most frequently barbiturates, or prescription and over-the-counter drugs. Similar to alcohol, usage of these drugs has been found to produce clinical pictures of varying degrees of severity, characterized by manifestations of hyperexcitability of the CNS during reduction or withdrawal periods following sustained intoxication. As a general rule, drugs of the same class (e.g., CNS depressants such as alcohol, antianxiety drugs, and prescription hypnotics) will demonstrate cross-tolerance. Following the development of tolerance to one type of drug, an individual is likely to develop similar tolerances to the same class of drugs as long as the two drugs are not taken together. Then it is most likely that they will interfere with each other's metabolism, with the net result that their combined effects on the CNS become potentiated. Furthermore, a high risk exists for overdose death when alcohol is mixed with other drugs of a class. The clinical symptoms resulting from the alcohol-drug interaction are the toxic or overdose syndrome and depression of cardiac and respiratory functions.

Both the neural mechanisms and the neurochemical correlates that determine the development of tolerance to and dependence upon ethanol are still unclear. Currently, it is believed that the development of physical dependence upon ethanol is possibly accompanied by the acquisition of the CNS tolerance to the depressant action of ethanol. It has been suggested that similar neurochemical alterations that underlie the mechanisms of the development of tolerance may also explain the development of physical dependence upon this drug. Two lines of thought that predominate in this field are that (1) the development of tolerance and of physical dependence are equivalent, and (2) the development of tolerance to certain effects of ethanol and barbiturates can be prevented without halting the development of physical dependence. This second notion is supported by the appearance of the withdrawal syndrome upon discontinuation of chronic drug ingestion [28].

In the work reported by Ritzmann and Tabakoff [19], the dissociation of tolerance and physical dependence were shown in animals treated with 6-OHDA (6-hydroxydopamine) and fed ethanol-containing diets. These animals became physically ethanol-dependent (as evidenced by the appearance and presence of the withdrawal syndrome), but not tolerant to three of the major physiological effects of ethanol administration, that is, the hypnotic effect, sedation, and hypothermia. If the 6-OHDA was administered before chronic ethanol exposure, the cross-tolerance to barbiturates was also prevented under these conditions. However, if 6-OHDA was administered after tolerance to ethanol was established, the destruction of noradrenergic neurons had little effect in disrupting tolerance. These experiments provide valuable information and understanding of the addiction process. Complementing the above neurophysiological and pharmacologic studies are recent findings from this laboratory, and elsewhere, on the involvement of protein synthesis in the process of physical dependence and tolerance to ethanol and barbiturates.

Neural Membranes

The plasma membrane separates each cell from its extracellular environment and is the mechanism through which all substances enter and leave the cell. Transmission of the neural impulse from one neuron to another is one of the major activities of the nervous system, with the neural membrane being the chief regulator of this activity. The action potential relies on the flow of Na^+ and K^+ ions, which is, in turn, regulated by Na^+, K^+-ATPase embedded in the membrane. Interactions of the lipids, proteins, and polysaccharides making up the fluid mosaic membrane give it various functional activities. Any change in membrane structure due to ethanol would affect important membrane bound enzymes such as Na^+, K^+-ATPase, Ca^{++} content and binding capacity, neurotransmitter receptors, and cyclic nucleotides. The latter two aspects are described later.

Release of the neurotransmitter from the presynaptic membrane is triggered by Ca^{++} ions, which are controlled by the membrane. The neurotransmitters must cross the synaptic cleft and interact with receptors in the postsynaptic membrane. It is widely believed that after a neurotransmitter interacts with its receptor, a cyclic nucleotide is formed to act as a "second messenger" and causes varying responses in the postsynaptic cell. Thus, it is of interest to see how ethanol affects the membrane structure, Na^+, K^+-ATPase, Ca^{++} content and binding capacity, neurotransmitter receptors, and cyclic nucleotides.

Membrane structure. Ethanol's interaction with membranes has been studied by a variety of physiochemical methods—electron paramagnetic resonance, differential scanning colorimetry, nuclear magnetic resonance, fluorescent probes, and optical rotatory dispersion [25].

Ethanol's effects vary according to the type of ethanol exposure; that is, acute and chronic effects differ. In analyzing chronic effects of ethanol, a further distinction must be made as to whether or not the effects seen are due to tolerance or dependence.

Acute exposure of erythrocyte membranes to ethanol has been reported to increase the volume of the membrane. The fluidities of erythrocyte, mitochondrial, and synapsomal membranes are increased with in vitro exposure to ethanol, but there is no effect on myelin's fluidity [3]. Membranes from mice maintained on ethanol for 8 days were resistant to the in vitro fluidizing effect of ethanol. Chin et al. [3] have correlated this tolerance development with an increase in the cholesterol content of the membrane.

Conflicting data exist as to the effect of chronic ethanol administration on various brain lipids. Most of the differences are probably due to the varying lengths of time that investigators administer ethanol, the amount of ethanol given, the route of administration, and the animals used.

Na^+, K^+-ATPase. Changes in the cell membranes would be expected to affect sodium-potassium-activated adenosine triphosphatase (Na^+, K^+-ATPase) since it is closely associated with the plasma membrane and requires phospholipids for activity. This enzyme is considered one of the brain's key enzymes because it regulates membrane polarization and utilizes approximately 70% of the brain's total energy.

In vitro addition of rather large amounts of ethanol (0.22 M or more) has been shown to inhibit Na^+, K^+-ATPase. It has been hypothesized that this inhibition is due to a combination of ethanol's affecting Na^+, K^+-ATPase's essential lipid (phosphatidyl serine), and thereby the conformation of Na^+, K^+-ATPase and ethanol's interaction with the enzyme's protein moiety.

Data about the acute in vivo effect of ethanol on Na^+, K^+-ATPase is inconclusive. Sun [25] observed an increase in Na^+, K^+-ATPase activity after an acute dose of 6 to 8 g ethanol/kg by intragastric intubation and no change in activity after smaller, acute doses. The lack of evidence for in vivo inhibition of Na^+, K^+-ATPase activity, however, may not represent the true in vivo conditions for the preparation of subcellular fractions, and are such that ethanol is removed from the membranes, thereby erasing possible inhibition.

Chronic administration has been shown to have little effect on Na^+, K^+-ATPase in animals withdrawn from ethanol for 12 to 24 hours. Roach [20] summarizes these studies and concludes that if Na^+, K^+-ATPase activity is not inhibited after an acute administration of ethanol, then the increase in activity seen after chronic ethanol administration could not be an adaptive mechanism of tolerance. The increased activity might simply be due to the enhanced CNS activity seen with withdrawal.

Ca^{++} content and binding capacity. Ross [21] has found that acute treatment of rats with ethanol (2 g/kg intraperitoneally) decreased the Ca^{++} content of brain synaptic membranes while increasing the Ca^{++} binding capacity of these membranes. Chronic administration of ethanol has the opposite effect—increasing the Ca^{++} content of brain synaptic membranes while decreasing the Ca^{++} binding capacity of the membranes.

Neurotransmitters and Receptors

Since drugs that influence behavior and emotion have effects on brain levels of neurotransmitters, many investigators have been interested in the effects of ethanol on the various neurotransmitters. There are three general classes of purported neurotransmitters—monoamines, amino acids, and peptides. Monoamines are sometimes divided into biogenic amines (norepinephrine, dopamine, and serotonin) and acetylcholine. The biogenic amines are metabolized by monoamine oxidase (MAO). Monoamines have been studied the most even though they are only about one 1/1,000th as plentiful in the brain as the amino acids — existing in nM/g. Amino acids such as gamma-aminobutyric acid (GABA), glycine, and glutamic acid tend to be present in the brain in relatively large amounts — μM/g. Only the interactions of GABA and ethanol are discussed in this chapter. Pepties (such as enkephalins, endorphins, substance P, and somatostatin) exist in pM/g of brain tissue. Enkephalins and endorphins are described in this chapter.

The amount of a given neurotransmitter is dependent upon its rate of synthesis and its rate of metabolism. Figure 2 lists the substances that must be taken up by the CNS to start synthesis and the synthetic pathways for the major neurotransmitters. Since dopamine is a precursor for norepinephrine, its synthesis is part of the synthesis for norepinephrine. The synthetic pathways for enkaphalins and endorphins have not been determined. Figure 1 lists the metabolic pathways for the biogenic amines. Acetylcholine (ACh) is metabolized by acetyl cholinesterase (AChE) to choline and acetic acid. GABA is first metabolized by GABA-transaminase (GABA-T) to succinic semialdehyde, which can be further metabolized by the tricarboxylic acid cycle. The enkephalins and endorphins are believed to be metabolized by brain peptidases.

The small sizes and vast numbers of neurons in the CNS make it difficult to use pharmacologic criteria to identify each neurotransmitter. There are many purported neurotransmitters, but the major ones, whose receptors can be identified, are the monoamines and γ-aminobutyric acid. The receptors for norepinephrine are referred to as "adrenergic receptors." They, in turn, are divided into α and β adrenergic receptors. Different drugs have been found to bind selectively with receptors; ^{3}H-WB-4101 binds to α-adrenergic receptors, ^{125}I-iodohydroxybenzylpindolol binds to β-adrenergic receptors, and ^{3}H-spiroperidol and ^{3}H-haloperidol bind to dopamine receptors. ^{3}H-Serotonin is used to monitor serotonin receptors.

Norepinephrine. In studying the effects of ethanol on norepinephrine (NE), not only does one have to consider possible strain and sex differences, different techniques and lengths of ethanol administration, and different analytical procedures, but one also must be aware of the age of the animals. Acute administration of ethanol to adult rats did not appear to affect the steady state level of NE, but did have a biphasic effect on the turnover of NE and the uptake of NE. No change in the number of brain α or β receptors has been reported after acute administration of ethanol.

Chronic administration of ethanol to adult rats caused an increase or no change in their endogenous brain levels of NE and an increase in NE turnover. In contrast, rat pups chronically exposed to ethanol pre- or postnatally had a significantly lower NE level in the hypothalamus and reduced NE turnover due to a decreased rate of NE synthesis [5].

Chronic ethanol treatment produced no change in the binding of ^{3}H-WB-4101 on α-adrenergic receptors in a number of adult rat brain areas [15].

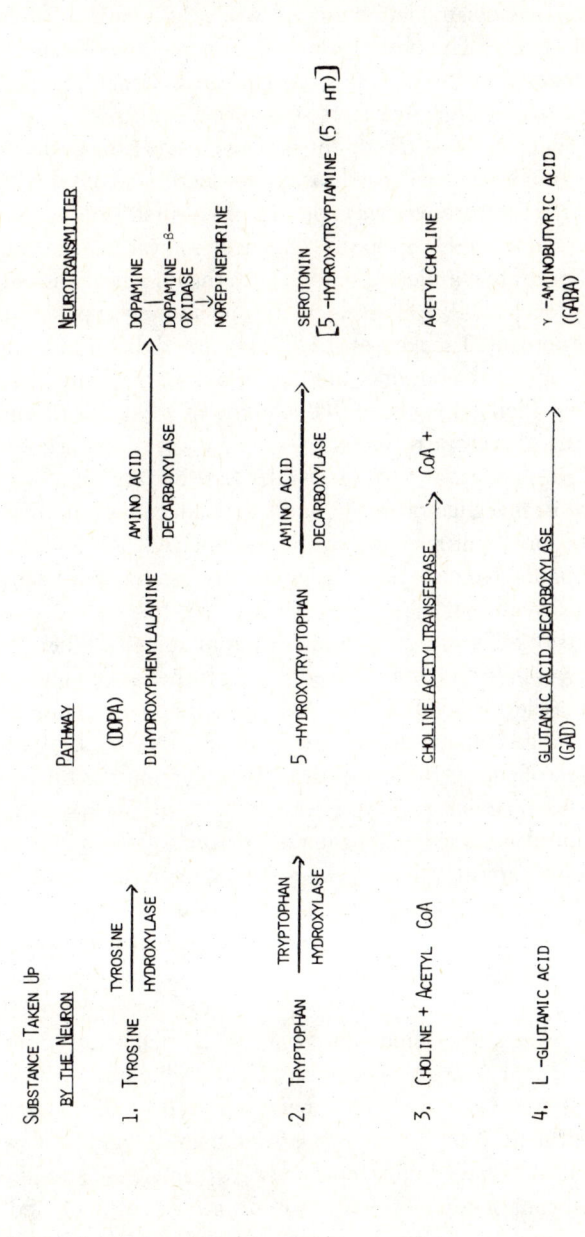

Substance Taken Up by the Neuron	Pathway	Neurotransmitter
1. Tyrosine $\xrightarrow{\text{TYROSINE HYDROXYLASE}}$	(DOPA) Dihydroxyphenylalanine $\xrightarrow{\text{AMINO ACID DECARBOXYLASE}}$	Dopamine $\xrightarrow{\text{DOPAMINE-}\beta\text{-OXIDASE}}$ Norepinephrine
2. Tryptophan $\xrightarrow{\text{TRYPTOPHAN HYDROXYLASE}}$	5-Hydroxytryptophan $\xrightarrow{\text{AMINO ACID DECARBOXYLASE}}$	Serotonin [5-hydroxytryptamine (5-HT)]
3. Choline + Acetyl CoA	$\xrightarrow{\text{CHOLINE ACETYLTRANSFERASE}}$ CoA +	Acetylcholine
4. L-Glutamic Acid	$\xrightarrow{\text{GLUTAMIC ACID DECARBOXYLASE}}$ (GAD)	γ-Aminobutyric Acid (GABA)

Figure 2. Synthetic Pathways for the Major Neurotransmitters

Male $C_{57}Bl/6$ mice fed on ethanol diet for 7 days and then withdrawn for 24 hours had a 10 to 15% decrease in the density of β-adrenergic receptors in the cerebral cortex. (β-receptors can be divided into β_1 and β_2. It has been postulated that the β_1 subtype is associated with neurons, while the β_2 subtype is associated with glia or blood vessels.) The observed decrease in β-adrenergic receptors was restricted to a change in β_2 subtype. Thus, chronic ethanol treatment does not appear to affect α- or β-adrenergic receptors on neurons in the brain.

Dopamine. Acute ethanol treatment resulted in no change in dopamine (DA) levels, but an increase in 3-4 dihydroxyphenylacetic acid (DOPAC), a metabolic product of DA. DA turnover was not affected at first, but then decreased. No change in the binding of ^{3}H-spiroperidol has been seen after acute administration of ethanol. There are conflicting reports as to the effects of chronic ethanol treatment on DA levels; DOPAC levels in chronic animals appeared to be the same as in control animals. Tabakoff et al. [27] have found that there is no change in ^{3}H-spiroperidol and ^{3}H-haloperidol binding in brain areas, but there is a decreased response of adenylate cyclase to dopamine in ethanol-withdrawn mice. They postulated that this is due to decreased efficiency of coupling between dopamine "receptor" sites and catalytic units of adenylate cyclase.

Serotonin. Most investigators have found no change in serotonin (5-hydroxytryptamine; 5-HT) or 5-hydroxyindole acetic acid (5-HIAA) levels after acute administration of ethanol. No change in the amount of binding has been reported after acute ethanol treatment.

Chronic effects of ethanol may differ in different animals. When Wistar rats were used, there were reports of enhanced 5-HT synthesis secondary to the increase in tryptophan levels due to ethanol's inhibition of liver tryptophan pyrro lase [1]. Many investigators have reported elevated 5-HIAA levels may be due to ethanol's inhibition of the active transport of 5-HIAA from the brain. After administering 4 g EtOH/kg per os every 12 hours for 11 to 15 days to Wistar rats, Muller et al. [15] found increased binding in the striatum and brain stem, decreased binding in the hippocampus, and no change in the cortex, hypothalamus, or mesolimbic areas. Hunt and Dalton [10] did not see any changes in ^{3}H-serotonin binding in the above areas of Sprague-Dawley rat brains after 4 days of administering 9 to 13 g EtOH/kg per os. Wistar rats differ from Sprague-Dawley rats in their ethanol intake.

Acetylcholine. The authors and others have found that acute administration of ethanol results in an increase of total brain ACh and choline (Ch) levels. Acetyl coenzyme A (CoA) and CoA levels have been reported to be unchanged after acute ethanol treatment. A biphasic change in ACh levels was found, with a significant increase of ACh in the brain stem and caudate nucleus 2 and 7 hours after treatment, a significant decrease in ACh 18 hours after treatment, and finally, a return to control levels 24 hours after the acute dose [10]. The initial increase is probably due to ethanol's inhibition of ACh release. Acute ethanol has been reported to reduce the rate of synthesis and turnover of ACh. These findings may explain the later depression of ACh levels.

^{3}H-Quinuclidinyl benzilate (QNB) binds specifically to muscarinic acetylcholine receptors. No changes have been reported in the density of muscarinic ACh receptors after acute ethanol treatment.

Chronically treated animals, sacrificed while intoxicated, had significantly depressed ACh levels. If the animals were in withdrawal when sacrificed, their ACh and Ch levels did not differ from those of control animals. Reductions in brain choline acetyltransferase have been reported after chronic alcohol treatment. The change in ACh levels from depressed to control values when the animal goes from a chronically intoxicated to a withdrawal state coincides with the observed increase and subsequent return to control level in the number of ACh receptors.

Tabakoff et al. [27] postulated that the changes in cholinergic receptor number in certain brain areas may be responsible for some signs of physical dependence during ethanol withdrawal.

Amino acids. GABA levels are subject to significant postmortem increases. Unfortunately there are no reports of the effects of ethanol on GABA levels from brains of animals sacrificed by focused microwave irradiation. GABA also is unique among the neurotransmitters in that it is synthesized from glutamate and is metabolized by undergoing transamination with $-$oxoglutarate to regenerate glutamate and yield succinate, which can enter the Krebs cycle. The metabolism of GABA is referred to as the "GABA shunt." The shunt may serve as an energy source for the brain when the glucose level is low.

Interest in GABA has been stimulated by reports that drugs that increase GABA by inhibiting GABA-T or that mimic GABA inhibit the locomotor hyperactivity seen after acute ethanol administration and the seizures observed during withdrawal.

There are contradictory reports about the affect of acute ethanol administration on GABA levels in brain of animals killed by decapitation or freezing. The differing data may be due to biphasic affects of ethanol. Syntinsky et al. [26] found that low (2 g/kg) doses of ethanol caused an increase in GABA levels, while high (6 g/kg) doses of ethanol caused a decrease in GABA levels. No study has yet been reported showing that ethanol has a biphasic effect on GABA levels over time.

Investigators using a variety of techniques, such as the binding of ^{3}H-GABA or ^{3}H-muscinol to GABA receptors in the brains of mice, seem to agree on the acute effects of ethanol. Acute ethanol treatment resulted in an increase in GABA receptors.

Contradictory reports also exist about the effects of chronic ethanol treatment on brain GABA levels. If the animals are dependent on ethanol, most recent investigators report a decrease in GABA levels while the animals are intoxicated. Increased, decreased, or control levels of GABA have all been reported when the animals are sacrificed during withdrawal. Further studies using focused microwave irradiation for sacrificing dependent animals during withdrawal are needed to resolve the present contradictions.

There may be significant species differences in ethanol's effect on GABA receptors. Investigators working with mice report a decrease in GABA receptors, while Hunt and Dalton [10] saw no changes in various sections of rat brains. There are reports of an increase in GABA receptors in postmortem brain samples from chronic alcoholics.

Peptides: Enkephalins and endorphins. In 1974 and 1975, three groups independently isolated pentapeptides with opiatelike properties. These peptides have similar amino acid sequences except for the fifth amino acid and have been named "methionine enkephalin" (met-enkephalin) and "leucine enkephalin" (leu-enkephalin). Shortly thereafter, a 91 amino acid pituitary peptide, β-lipotropin (β-LPH), was identified as the probable precursor for met-enkephalin because segment 61 through 65 was the same as met-enkephalin. An untriakontapeptide, β-endorphin, was also found that had optiate activity and was identical to residue 61 to 91 of β-LPH. Other endorphins have been identified that have structures similar to part of β-LPH, but β-endorphin is the most potent. (Since "endorphin" is a generic name for opiate peptides, there are also endorphins that are not derived from β-LPH.) The precursor for leu-endorphin has not yet been identified, nor have the synthetic pathways for met-enkephalin or β-endorphin been determined.

Research is just beginning to be reported about the interaction of ethanol with the enkephalins and endorphins. Schulz et al. [24] reported that acute ethanol treatment resulted in an increase in both met-enkephalin and β-endorphin in various areas of rat brain. They found that chronic ethanol treatment caused a decrease in met-enkephalin and β-endorphin, with the levels reverting to control values after 2 weeks of withdrawal. The rats studied by Schultz et al. [24] did not have signs of physical dependence. Other investigators that sacrificed their animals while they were dependent reported elevated met-enkephalin levels in the striatum and an elevated β-endorphin level in the pituitary. Obviously, more work needs to be done to understand the interaction of ethanol with enkephalins and endorphins.

Macromolecular Metabolism

At the macromolecular level, ethanol's effects have been studied regarding changes in (1) cyclic nucleotide, (2) protein, and (3) nucleic acid metabolism. The role of brain protein synthesis and nucleic acid synthesis in the learning and memory processes are well established. Clinical evidence shows that chronic alcoholics suffer from memory dysfunction and blackouts. In recent years these results have triggered investigations on the effects of alcohol on this group of macromolecules. The role of cyclic nucleotides as the "second messengers" or modulators has been considered in the regulation of neuronal function, either by affecting the release of neurotransmitters or by altering the activity of enzymes responsible for cerebral metabolic and/or neurophysiological activity.

Cyclic nucleotides. Cyclic nucleotides are believed to be important "secondary messengers" at synapses. Adenosine-3', 5'-cyclic monophosphate (cAMP) is formed when norepinephrine, dopamine, or serotonin interact with their receptors, releasing adenylate cyclase, which concerts ATP to cAMP. Guanosine-3'5'-cyclic monophosphate (cGMP) is formed when ACh or GABA act with their receptors, releasing guanylate cyclase, which converts guanosine triphosphate (GTP) to cGMP. The cyclic nucleotides, in turn, increase the activities of their respective cyclic nucleotide-dependent protein kinases, which catalyze the phosphorylation of proteins located in the synaptosomal membranes and, thereby, change the membrane permeability to ions. Changing the permeability of the membrane alters the membrane potential.

Measurement of cAMP, like ACh and GABA, can be difficult due to rapid postmortem changes. Rapid inactivation of brain enzymes is very important. The best method of inactivating enzymes is by using high-intensity microwave irradiation to sacrifice the animals.

The acute effects of ethanol on cAMP are unclear. Most investigators found decreased cAMP levels in the cerebellum and cerebral cortex regions of mouse and rat brains up to 3 hours after an acute dose of ethanol given per os or intraperitoneally. Other investigators, however, found no changes. Unlike cAMP, cGMP is not as prone to postmorten changes. Since neither guanylate cyclase nor cGMP's phosphodiesterase appear to be affected by ethanol, the reason for the depletion of cGMP must lie in ethanol's effects upon the neurotransmitters.

High doses of ethanol are thought to selectively and reversibly depress cyclic AMP levels in the cerebellum. Although the mechanism and functional effects of this change are still unclear, the target cells may be the Purkinje cells. Cyclic AMP inhibits the activity of Purkinje cells and cerebellar dysfunction is one important side effect of ethanol intoxication. Investigators seem to be in agreement that acute ethanol treatment depresses cGMP levels in the cerebellum, cerebral cortex, pons, and medulla oblongata. While increased cAMP levels in the cerebral cortex are observed during the early phase of alcohol withdrawal, there is less increase in the cGMP levels, and only late, during withdrawal. Similarly, increased sensitivity of cerebral cortical adenylcyclase to norepinephrine has been reported at 72 hours after withdrawal of rats from ethanol [9]. But, using shorter periods of alcohol administration, no changes in cerebral cyclic nucleotides were observed.

Investigators using microwave irradiation to sacrifice chronically treated rats found no change in cAMP levels. However, on cortical slices from rats or mice given ethanol over several days, investigators saw no changes in cAMP levels at first, but longer treatment resulted in an increase in basal adenylate cyclase-dependent accumulation of cAMP. By 24 hours after ethanol removal, cAMP reduction returned to control value. Tabakoff et al. [27] found that adenylate cyclase activity was less responsive to dopamine simulation in mice fed ethanol for 7 days. The adenylate cyclase activity returned to normal 3 days after withdrawal.

When microwave irradiation was used to study cGMP levels in rats chronically fed ethanol cGMP, cGMP was depressed in many brain areas during the treatment, but became elevated 8 to 72 hours after withdrawal.

Protein and nucleic acid metabolism. Many laboratories are involved now in determining ethanol's effects on the protein and nucleic acid metabolism. Several pertinent studies are available on ethanol's effects on hepatic protein metabolism [30]. These studies showed decreased protein synthesis by rat liver ribosomes under acute (4 g/kg) conditions, but not under chronic conditions. Other studies showed a time-dependent reduction of hepatic protein synthesis following long-term ethanol treatment and damage to the endoplasmic reticulum (ER) in human subjects receiving ethanol on a chronic basis. In addition, a definite disruption of the ER under these conditions and a reduction of albumin and transferrin synthesis 3 hours after ethanol intubation was observed. It was concluded that, since albumin is an exportable protein and not a liver tissue protein (a nonexportable protein), its synthesis is dependent on the integrity of the ER. Other ethanol studies on liver protein synthesis include effects on specific proteins, such as induction of cytochrome P-450, and also proliferation of smooth ER. Disaggregation of the ER-bound polysome, a loss of hepatic ribonucleic acid (RNA), and a low level of (^{3}H)uridine incorporation into RNA. Since the addition of ethanol to liver perfusate decreased both the synthesis of albumin and the labeling of 28S RNA by 60%, it was suggested that a slower rate of translation might be the underlying mechanism.

Studies of ethanol on brain protein metabolism include both in vivo and in vitro effects of ethanol [31]. Amino acids labeled both in vivo and in vitro have been found to be significantly diminished under conditions of acute ethanol administration. Similarly, reduced protein synthesis was found in the various brain regions—specifically in the glial cell fraction—and not in the neuronal fraction. Acute ethanol conditions caused in vitro (^{3}H)leucine incorporation into protein to be decreased in the microsomal fraction, but not in the mitochondria.

Chronic depression of in vivo protein synthesis has been observed in various regions of the brain, with an increased incorporation following 24 hours of withdrawal. Another study reported a stimulation of in vitro brain protein synthesis by the ribosomes and an increased activity of brain tryptophan hydroxylase. A liquid diet containing 5% ethanol depressed the activity of another enzyme, tyrosine hydroxylase, but only when ingested for up to 100 days and only following 3 to 15 days of ethanol ingestion.

Additional studies have shown disaggregation of brain polysomes and depression of protein synthesis in cerebellar and cerebral hemispheres and in cells grown in culture, following long-term ethanol ingestion and development of physical dependence and withdrawal. The two regions of the brain differed in their protein synthetic activity during the 24-hour withdrawal period. While the protein synthetic activity returned to normal in the cerebellum following alcohol withdrawal, the activity continued to be depressed in the cerebral hemispheres. Recent in-depth studies support the view that the ribosomes may be functionally altered following alcohol ingestion.

Similar to the adult brain, young brains are also highly susceptible to the effects of alcohol, especially following maternal consumption both during pregnancy and during lactation [29]. In studies on the immature brain, ethanol ingestion led to large decreases in the protein synthetic activity. In these studies, the sensitive period in the pregnancy was the third trimester and the postnatal period. In this respect, the immature or the developing brain appears to be more sensitive to the onslaught of ethanol than the adult, requiring a very short exposure period. Work carried out in the author's laboratory showed significant deficits in the brain protein synthetic activity of youngsters nursed by mothers ingesting ethanol. Ethanol is known to reduce lactation and passes through the mother's milk freely. In this regard, it should be mentioned that the placenta is an important tissue whose protein synthetic activity is also found to be reduced.

The involvement of protein synthesis could have many different implications, such as the alteration by ethanol at the cellular transcription level by effective RNA metabolism or by delaying or reducing the induction period of specific proteins or enzymes, or simply by increasing or decreasing the turnover of these proteins.

Investigations of RNA metabolism in brains of rodents showed that chronic ethanol ingestion depressed incorporation of the precursor label into tRNA, rRNA, polysomal RNA, mitochrondrial RNA, and nRNA [31]. These alterations occurred without changes in the labeling pattern and pool sizes of nucleotide triphosphates, suggesting that an altered availability of nucleotides was not a factor in the observed ethanol-induced changes in RNA metabolism. In a separate study, data revealed a defect in the processing and transport system of mRNA at the ribosomal level.

In conclusion, ethanol significantly affects brain protein and RNA metabolism following long-term ingestion. Since these macromolecules have wide and diverse structural as well as functional significance in the brain, it would not be too surprising that ethanol-induced changes in behavior might partly be ascribed to changes in brain protein and RNA metabolism. For example, impaired learning, observed in animal behavior experiments as well as psychological evaluation of FAS children, may be related to altered RNA and protein metabolism since, in addition to their function as cellular constituents in cellular regulations, RNA and proteins have been implicated in learning and in many other neural processes.

Some biochemical data are also available on the combined effects of alcohol and drugs on the brain protein synthesizing system.

It is well established that the continual ingestion of sedatives and hypnotics, such as barbiturates and ethanol, results in the development of CNS tolerance to and physical dependence upon these drugs. Usually the ethanol-tolerant subjects will show increased tolerance to barbiturates, anesthetics, and a variety of other drugs with more or less similar action and characteristics. Cross-tolerance is another consequence of the drug-drug interaction. Ethanol and barbiturates are the two most prevalently abused drugs. Experimental studies have shown changes in the brain protein synthetic activity following ethanol or barbiturate administration. An especially significant inhibition was demonstrated 60 minutes after sodium barbital (100 mg/kg) was administered intragastrically to control and chronic ethanol-dependent rats. On the other hand, lithium carbonate, presently used to treat alcohol withdrawal, unlike the barbital or chronic ethanol administration, increase the in vitro protein synthesis. Data suggest that ribosomes may have multiple sites of action for CNS-acting drugs. Since an intraventricular injection of cycloheximide can block functional barbiturate tolerance, data suggest that in the CNS the interaction of ethanol and sodium barbital involves the ribosomes.

PERINATAL EFFECTS OF ETHANOL

It is well recognized that ethanol exposure has a special significance when the exposure period is during the prenatal or early developmental period in the organism's life. The FAS is a well-established entity. Equally significant are the consequences of transplacental exposure of the fetus to other drugs, especially when they relate to maternal consumption of ethanol.

In addition to the well-established role of ethanol in teratogenesis, the involvement of acetaldehyde, the primary metabolite of ethanol, has also received considerable attention.

Both ethanol and acetaldehyde have been demonstrated to produce teratogenic effects in experimental animals, and evidence suggests that these compounds affect nucleic acid and protein synthesis and induce DNA damage and chromosomal aberrations [6]. One recent study showed a large inhibition of DNA synthesis in cells by ethanol and acetaldehyde.

One of the most recent studies in the present author's laboratory produced observations that there are long-lasting effects on brain ribosomal responses to sodium barbital following postnatal exposure of neonates to ethanol for 8 days. These data are consistent with the observation of Yanai and Tabakoff [33], who also demonstrated long-lasting effects to ethanol on brain responses following prenatal phenobarbital administration. Thus, postnatal treatment of ethanol changed the response of the brain protein synthetic activity to sodium barbital in the adult.

As described, offspring can be exposed either transplacentally or through their mother's milk to ethanol. Some data are now available on the effects of ethanol and acetaldehyde on protein synthetic activity of human and rat placenta. Using human placenta, large inhibitions were obtained in the presence of acetaldehyde. These data are consistent with those reported by O'Shea and Kaufman on neural tube defects and embryonic death in 10-day-old mouse embryos following a single injection of acetaldehyde [16]. Thus, the present evidence supports a strong role for the placenta and the metabolite acetaldehyde in the perinatal effects of ethanol. These studies on the placenta are exciting, as ethanol is known to cross the placental barrier freely and reach the fetus. Therefore, a dynamic relationship exists between the mother and the fetus; when ethanol is ingested, fetal alcohol levels are comparable to the maternal levels. However, due to immaturity of the fetal liver ADH, the alcohol level drops at a slower rate than in the mother. The ADH reaches its adult level of activity only at 5 years of age. In conclusion, the role of the placenta in metabolism, in addition to ethanol, must be considered in studying the teratogenic effects of ethanol.

ETHANOL AND CANCER

Recent investigations in the field of transplacental carcinogenesis have shown that cancer can be caused by certain exogenous chemical compounds acting on the fetus after resorption of them through the placenta. Certain types of cancer in progeny occur postnatally as a result of prenatal exposure to certain chemicals; the CNS seems to be the preferred tumor target site. This could be due to marked sensitivity of the nervous system to chemical compounds or other factors that can induce changes in the intrauterine environment.

Thus, the current belief that most human cancers are caused by environmental chemical carcinogens is well justified, and effective cancer prevention and prophylasis must consider exposure to chemicals, including ethanol, during pre- and postnatal life.

There is now strong experimental evidence that a chemical administered during pregnancy can reach the fetus, interact with the fetal cells, and cause tumors in progeny.

Clinical and experimental studies on chronic alcoholism have reported severe neuropathies resulting in memory dysfunction and altered brain protein metabolism. Now there is growing evidence from both prospective and retrospective epidemiologic studies that alcohol consumption is a cancer hazard [32]. Prospective studies on heavy drinkers have shown an increased risk of cancer of the mouth, pharynx, larynx, esophagus, liver, and lungs. Retrospective studies have confirmed this excess risk. Primary liver cancer is also associated with alcohol consumption, while data on the relationship between breast cancer and alcohol ingestion is almost nonexistent. Data are now available showing abnormal endocrine function caused by ethanol under both acute and chronic conditions. Some of these hormonal changes due to ethanol include reduction of luteinizing hormone (LH) secretion, as well as direct testicular and ovarian suppression [18].

How does ethanol increase the risk of cancer? Nutritional deficiencies could be one of the major contributing factors, with alcohol consumption leading to impaired absorption of nutrients and vitamins. Ethanol is known to decrease vitamin A level, which is essential to the regulation of epithelial cell differentiation [13].

It is also thought that heavily drinking women with chronic liver disease might endogenously produce hormones that alter fetal cardiovascular and genital development.

Another study has demonstrated that the in vitro metabolism of the hepatocarcinogen N-nitrosophrolidine is increased in microsomal fractions isolated from ethanol-ingesting rats, and that postmitochondrial supernatants isolated from these ethanol-treated animals are capable of greater conversions of nitrosopyrralidine to a mutagen than are control preparations. Other reports link development of breast, skin (melanoma), and thyroid cancer with alcohol use. Schrauzer et al. [23] studied the highly inbred strain of C3H/St mice, which develops spontaneous mammary adenocarcinoma at a 80 to 100% incidence under normal ethanol-maintenance conditions. The oncogenic agent in this animal tumor system is viral in nature (Bittner virus), and is transmitted vertically during breastfeeding of the young. This study demonstrated that long-term ethanol exposure could significantly reduce the latency period in genesis of spontaneous mammary adenocarcinoma in C3H/St mice. In addition, this study showed that serum prolactin levels were significantly lower in the alcohol-exposed mice than in the controls.

Recently, another important question that has concerned researchers in the alcoholism field is the role of other chemicals present in alcoholic beverages in addition to ethanol. Recent studies have indicated the presence of trace quantities of carcinogenic agents, such as nitrosamines, in certain alcoholic beverages, which raises the possibility that this class of carcinogens may play a role in the etiology of alcohol-related cancers [13]. Therefore, the carcinogenic property of an alcoholic beverage can be due to the action of ethanol, other chemicals, or constituents alone or in combination, acting synergistically in eliciting the cancer. The current belief is that alcohol acts primarily as a cocarcinogen, or as a promoter.

ACKNOWLEDGMENTS

This work was supported in part by research grants AA00252 and AA3506-04 (The National Alcohol Research Center Program) from the National Institute on Alcohol Abuse and Alcoholism, Alcohol, Drug Abuse and Mental Health Administration. Author Tewari was recipient of a Research Scientist Development Award, type II (AA70899).

REFERENCES

1. Badawy, A. A., Punjani, N. F., and Evans, M. Enhancement of rat brain tryptophan metabolism by chronic ethanol administration and possible involvement of decreased liver tryptophan pyrrolase activity. *Biochem. J.* 178:575–580, 1979.
2. Bode, J. C. Factors influencing alcohol metabolism in man: Alcohol and the gastrointestinal tract. *INSERM* 95:65–92, 1980.
3. Chin, J. H., Parsons, L. M., and Goldstein, D. B. Increased cholesterol content: Erythrocyte and brain membranes in ethanol-tolerant mice. *Biochem. Biophys. Acta* 513: 358–363, 1978.
4. Davis, V. E., Cashaw, J. L., and McMurtrey, K. D. Catecholamine-derived alkaloids in dependence. In: *Addiction and Brain Damage*, Richter, D. (ed.). University Park Press: Baltimore, 1980; Cohen, G., and Collins, M. Alkaloids from catecholamines in adrenal tissue: Possible role in alcoholism. *Science* 67:1749–1751, 1970.
5. Detering, N., Collins, R. M., Hawkins, R. L. Ozand, P. T., and Karahasan, A. Comparative effects of ethanol and malnutrition on the development of catecholamine neurons: Changes in norepinephrine turnover. *J. Neurochem.* 34:1788–1791, 1980.
6. Dreosti, I. E., Ballard, F. J., Belling, B. G., and Hetzel, B. S. Ethanol, DNA synthesis, and fetal development. *Alcoholism: Clin. Exp. Res.* 5:357–362, 1981.
7. Eriksson, C. I. P., and Sippel, H. The distribution and metabolism of acetaldehyde in rats during ethanol oxidation: I. The distribution of acetaldehyde in liver, brain, blood, and breath. *Biochem. Pharmacol.* 26:241–247, 1977.
8. Freund, G. Impairment of memory after prolonged alcohol consumption in mice. In: *Advances in Experimental Medicine and Biology*, Gross, M. M. (ed.). Plenum: New York, 1975.
9. Hunt, W. A. Effects of acute and chronic administration of ethanol on cyclic nucleotides and related systems. In: *Biochemistry and Pharmacology of Ethanol* (Vol. 2), Majchrowicz, E. and Noble, E. P. (eds.). Plenum: New York, 1979.
10. Hunt, W. A., and Dalton, T. K. Neurotransmitter-receptor binding in various brain regions in ethanol-dependent rats. *Pharmacol. Biochem. Behav.* 14:733–739, 1981.
11. Kalant, H., Leblanc, A. E., and Gribbins, R. J. Nonopiate psychotropic drugs. *Pharmacol. Rev.* 23:135–184, 1971.
12. Khanna, J. M., and Israel, Y. Ethanol metabolism: Liver and biliary tract physiology 1. *Int. Rev. Physiol.* 2:275–325, 1980.
13. Lowenfels, A. B. Alcohol and cancer. *Br. J. Alcohol Alcoholism* 14(3):148–163, 1979.
14. Mendelson, J. H. Biochemical mechanisms of alcohol addiction. In: *The Biology of Alcoholism*, Kissin, B. and Begleiter, H. (eds.). Plenum: New York, 1981.
15. Muller, P., Britton, R. S., and Seeman, P. The effects of long-term ethanol on brain receptors for dopamine, acetylcholine, serotonin and noradrenaline. *Eur. J. Pharmacol.* 65: 31–37, 1980.
16. O'Shea, K. S., and Kaufman, M. H. The teratogenic effect of acetaldehyde: Implications for the study of the fetal alcohol syndrome. *J. Anat.* 128:65–76, 1979.
17. Parsons, O. A. Brain damage in alcoholics: Altered states of unconsciousness. In: *Advances in Experimental Medicine and Biology*, Gross, M. M. (ed.). Plenum: New York, 1975.
18. Redmond, G. P. Effects of ethanol on endogenous synthesis of growth hormone secretions. *Alcoholism: Clin. Exp. Res.* 4(1):50–56, 1980.
19. Ritzmann, R. F. J., and Tabakoff, B. Dissociation of alcohol tolerance and dependence. *Nature* 263:418–419, 1976.

20. Roach, M. K. Changes in the activity of Na$^+$, K$^+$-ATPase during acute and chronic administration of ethanol. In: *Biochemistry and Pharmacology of Ethanol* (Vol. 2), Majchrowicz, E. and Noble, E. P. (eds.). Plenum: New York, 1979.

21. Ross, D. H. Adaptive changes in Ca^{++} membrane interactions following chronic ethanol exposure. In: *Advances in Experimental Medicine and Biology* (Vol. 85A), Gross, M. (ed.). Plenum: New York, 1977.

22. Russell, M. The impact of alcohol-related birth defects (ARBD) on New York State. *Neurobehav. Toxicol.* 2(3):277–283, 1980.

23. Schrauzer, G. N., McGinness, S. E., Ishmael, D., and Bell, L. J. Alcoholism and cancer: l. Effects of long-term exposure to alcohol on spontaneous mammary adenocarcinoma and prolactin levels in C3H/St mice. *J. Stud. Alcohol* 40(3):240–246, 1979.

24. Schulz, R., Wuster, M., Duka, T., and Herz, A. Acute and chronic ethanol treatment changes endorphin levels in brain and pituitary. *Psychopharmacol.* 68:221–227, 1980.

25. Sun, A. Y. Biochemical and biophysical approaches in the study of ethanol-membrane interaction. In: *Biochemistry and Pharmacology of Ethanol* (Vol. 2), Majchrowicz, E. and Noble, E. P. (eds.). Plenum: New York, 1979.

26. Syntinsky, I. A., Guzikov, M., Gomanko, M. V., Eremin, V. P., and Konovalova, N. N. The gamma-aminobutyric acid (GABA) system in brain during acute and chronic ethanol intoxication. *J. Neurochem.* 25:43–48, 1975.

27. Tabakoff, B., Melchior, C., Urwyler, S., and Hoffman, P. L. Alterations in neurotransmitter function during the development of ethanol tolerance and dependence. In: *Alcohol and Brain Research* (Vol. 62), Idestrom, C. M. (ed.). Acta Psychiatrica Scandinavica: Copenhagen, 1981.

28. Tabakoff, B., and Ritzmann, R. F. J. Body temperature in mice: A quantitative measure of alcohol tolerance and physical dependence. *J. Pharmacol. Exp. Ther.* 203:319–331, 1977.

29. Tewari, S., and Crain, S. Ethanol-induced changes on in vitro protein synthesis during the development and maturation of brain tissue. In: *Advances in Experimental Medicine and Biology*, Thurman, R. J. (ed.). Plenum: New York, 1980.

30. Tewari, S., and Noble, E. P. Chronic ethanol ingestion by rodents: Effects on brain RNA. In: *Alcohol and Abnormal Protein Biosynthesis*, Rothschild, M. A., Oratz, M., and Schreiber, S. S. (eds.). Pergamon: New York, 1975.

31. Tewari, S., and Noble, E. P. Effects of ethanol on cerebral protein and ribonucleic acid synthesis. In: *Biochemistry and Pharmacology of Ethanol* (Vol. 1), Majchrowicz, E. and Noble, E. P. (eds.). Plenum: New York, 1979.

32. Tuyns, A. J. Epidemiology of alcohol and cancer. *Cancer Res.* 39:2840–2843, 1979.

33. Yanai, J., and Tabakoff, B. Increased tolerance in mice following prenatal exposure to barbiturate. *Psychopharmacol.* 64:325–327, 1979.

8

KENNETH BLUM, PhD, University of Texas, San Antonio

NEUROPHYSIOLOGICAL EFFECTS OF ALCOHOL

THE USE OF ALCOHOLIC beverages can be traced back to the dawn of history. The oldest alcoholic drinks were fermented beverages of low alcohol content. In the Middle Ages, the alchemists believed that alcohol was the long-sought elixer of life. In fact, alcohol was held to be a remedy for almost all diseases, as indicated by the term "whiskey" (Gaelic, *usequebaugh*, meaning "water of life"). It now has very limited medical value, but its use and abuse is widespread.

This chapter explores the basic neurophysiological effects of ethanol on various central phenomena. It is known that the central nervous system (CNS) is more markedly affected by alcohol than is any other system of the body. However, not all areas of the brain are affected equally by ethanol. In fact, the cortex does not seem to be the part of the brain that is most sensitive to the action of alcohol. Electrophysiological studies [71] suggest that alcohol, like other general anesthetics, exerts its first depressant action upon a more primitive part of the brain, namely, the reticular activating system. There are basic neurological and physiological effects of alcohol, which have been reviewed by Kalant [71] and Mardones [85], and more recently, Majchrowicz and Noble [84].

Discussion of the neurophysiology of ethanol is presented as it relates to

---

Kenneth Blum, PhD, Chief, Division of Substance and Alcohol Misuse, Department of Pharmacology, University of Texas, Health Science Center, San Antonio, Texas.

1. Membrane-receptor effects
2. Brain-neurotransmitter receptor-effector coupling effects
3. The cyclic nucleotide model of alcohol tolerance and dependence
4. Neuropathological actions
5. Addiction – a unified concept
6. Involvement of peptidyl opiates in the action of alcohol
7. The psychogenetic theory of alcohol-seeking behavior
8. Effects of neuropharmacologic agents on acute and chronic actions

Space limitations do not allow for a complete review of all the neurophysiological actions of alcohol, and thus, only a select discussion is presented in the hope that it will provide a rationale for understanding better the chemical and biological mechanisms in response to the addictive agent, alcohol.

MEMBRANE-RECEPTOR EFFECTS OF ALCOHOL

At high concentrations, ethanol is capable of disorganizing neuronal membrane structure [104]. Chronic ethanol administration to animals has been found to produce changes in the conformation of membrane-bound proteins [53]. Chin and Goldstein [23] showed, by a sensitive electron paramagnetic resonance (EPR) technique, that low concentrations of ethanol increased the fluidity of mouse erythrocyte and synaptosomal plasma membranes. Additionally, in other studies, the same authors reported that tolerance to ethanol developed to this effect [23]. Of great interest was the finding that ethanol altered the lipid composition of neuronal membranes [24, 80]. Although ethanol could directly modify the characteristics of activities of membrane-bound proteins, it has also been demonstrated that membrane microenvironment is a critical regulator of the function of enzymes embedded in cell membranes [21, 33, 41]. In this regard, it has been suggested by Hoffman et al. [61] that adaptive modifications of neuronal membrane lipids after ethanol treatment could be expected to result in the observed conformational changes of the membrane-bound proteins.

Numerous studies [116] on the effects of ethanol on neurotransmitter function have already been reviewed. According to the consensus of the literature, the interaction of ethanol with neuronal membranes may also account in part for its diverse effects on neurotransmitter turnover and release. Since neurotransmitter receptors in the CNS have been demonstrated to respond to decreases or increases in the availability of their particular transmitters with adaptive changes that lead to altered sensitivity to these transmitters [29, 115], it might be postulated that ethanol exposure would secondarily alter receptor function. In this regard, it is plausible that a direct correlation between receptor interaction and alcohol membrane partition coefficients should occur. There are studies that either support [57] or refute [32] the above view.

Work by Tabakoff and coresearchers showed that ethanol could alter receptor microenvironment. Chronic administration of ethanol to mice, for example, resulted in abnormal function of striated dopamine (DA) receptors, possibly as a result of ethanol-induced modification of neuronal membrane structure [117, 119]. Specifically, Hoffman et al. [61] reported that the membrane-bound enzyme (Na^+-K^+) ATPase (adenosinetriphosphatase), obtained from ethanol-withdrawn animals, displays an altered transition temperature and resistance to the effects of ethanol on enzyme activity. These changes also suggest compensatory alterations in neuronal membrane properties. Additional support is derived from the work of Rangaraj and Kalant [95], similarly demonstrating that norepinephrine can alter the inhibitory effects of ethanol on (Na^+-K^+) ATPase activity of rat neuronal membranes. These findings, therefore, suggest that the norepinephrine-ethanol interaction is a direct effect on the membrane, probably mediated by an alpha receptor-modified pertubation of the membrane microenvironment of the enzyme.

BRAIN–NEUROTRANSMITTER RECEPTOR–EFFECTOR COUPLING EFFECTS OF ETHANOL

Central nervous system actions of ethanol may reflect alterations in the properties of one or more neurotransmitter receptor-effector systems. Prolonged treatment of rats with ethanol has been reported to result in changes in the cortical sensitivity to norepinephrine as measured by cyclic amp accumulation [44]. Banerjee et al. [2] reported that administration of ethanol for 60 days resulted in a decrease in the density of beta-adrenergic receptors in whole rat brain tissue, while receptor density was increased after 48 and 72 hours of withdrawal. It is of great interest that these changes were not associated with changes in the affinity of the receptor for the radioligand [^{3}H]-dihydroalprenolol.

Early studies from the author's laboratory [13] revealed that dopamine, when administered in conjunction with ethanol, prolonged ethanol-induced narcosis in mice. In 1974, Hunt and Majchrowicz [65] demonstrated that both acute and chronic administration of ethanol have a biphasic effect on dopamine turnover with no alterations in dopamine content. Along these lines, Blum et al. [14] demonstrated that ethanol-induced withdrawal convulsions in mice could be significantly suppressed by low concentrations of dopamine injections. Tabakoff et al. [119] reported a reduction in the effect of dopaminergic agonists on locomotor activity and body temperature during withdrawal following chronic ethanol treatment. These investigators also demonstrated that dopamine-stimulated adenylate cyclase activity in the striatum was reduced in mice withdrawn from ethanol for 24 hours [62, 118]. Conversely, Engel and Liljequist [37] and Liljequist [79], showed that rats treated with ethanol for 5 to 9 months displayed an increase in locomotor activity after the bilateral application of dopamine into the nucleus accumbers or striatum, suggesting that an increased sensitivity to dopamine occurs following ethanol administration.

Although Rabin and Molinoff [94] found altered norepinephrine sensitivity in animals chronically treated and withdrawn from ethanol, no change in cyclic amp accumulation in cortical slices was observed with either alpha-adrenergic receptor stimulation or beta-adrenergic receptor stimulation. Furthermore, no difference in dopamine-stimulated adenylate cyclase activity was observed in either ethanol-treated mice or in animals withdrawn from ethanol for 24 hours [94]. It is possible, however, that a decrease in dopamine-stimulated adenylate cyclase occurs only in severely withdrawing mice, as suggested by Tabakoff [Tabakoff, B., personal communication].

It is known that ethanol administration also induces changes in central cholinergic systems. The acute administration of ethanol depresses both the in vivo [40, 90] and in vitro release of acetylcholine [73].

Chronic ethanol administration reduces the content of acetylcholine in the hippocampus [64] and cortex [96] and eliminates the depressant action of ethanol on the in vitro release of acetylcholine [73]. In addition, both ethanol-induced electroencephalographic synchrony [39] and ethanol-induced sleep time [38] are antagonized by the acetylcholinesterase inhibitor, physostigmine.

Although neurotransmitter turnover may change with acute and chronic ethanol administration, and neurotransmitter precursor amines may influence ethanol intoxication, dependence, and withdrawal, studies designed to determine direct effects on numerous receptor sites reveal no apparent significant alterations [66].

In the Hunt et al. [66] investigations, ethanol did not alter [^{3}H]-haloperidol binding to study dopaminergic receptors, or [^{3}H]-3-guinuclidinyl benzilate (QWB) binding to study muscurinic cholinergic receptors.

In spite of these negative observations, recently Davis and Ticku [32] exquisitely demonstrated that ethanol enhances [^{3}H]-diazepam binding at the benzodiazepine-gamma-aminobutyric acid receptor-ionophore complex. The rank order of enhancement of [^{3}H]-diazepam binding with various alcohols (ethanol < methanol < isopropyl alcohol < propanol-1 or t-butyl alcohol) did not agree with their partition coefficients. These results suggest that ethanol, like pentobarbital, enhances [^{3}H]-diazepam binding at the benzodiazepine-gamma-aminobutyric acid (GABA) receptor-ionophore complex. This interaction will result in facilitation of GABAergic transmission and may be responsible for some of the central effects of alcohol, such as antianxiety, muscle relaxation, and sedation. In addition, these results by Davis and Ticku [32] may also explain the synergistic effects observed with alcohol and diazepam in vivo and the use of antianxiety drugs as agents of choice during alcohol withdrawal.

The cited literature reveals that acute and chronic administration of ethanol can effect neurotransmitter function, but this author would like to emphasize that neurotransmitter systems should not be examined in isolation. Studies on the neurophysiology and biochemistry of brain neurotransmitter receptor-coupling mechanisms is necessary to understand adequately the mechanisms that mediate ethanol-induced neurological and behavioral decrements.

THE CYCLIC NUCLEOTIDE MODEL OF ALCOHOL TOLERANCE AND DEPENDENCE

Cyclic nucleotides seem to function in the brain as mediators or second messengers of first messages communicated by agents such as neurotransmitters, hormones, or local modulators [5, 30, 108, 111]. Recently, Siggins [109] commented on cyclic nucleotides in the development of alcohol tolerance and dependence and the interested reader is strongly urged to review this paper.

According to Siggins, the homeostatic modulations of the norepinephrine-adenylate cyclase systems with alterations of functional norepinephrine levels, suggested by biochemical [43] and electrophysiological experiments, presents a hypothetical model for alcohol tolerance and dependence. Siggins proposes an interaction between the neurotransmitters norepinephrine and acetylcholine and alcohol.

It is known that norepinephrine normally inhibits and acetylcholine excites pyramidal neurons, to the extent that norepinephrine can prevent and acetylcholine augment or even trigger epileptiform activity [106]. These responses are thought to be mediated by cyclic adenosine monophosphate (AMP) and cyclic AMP, respectively [60].

Alcohol in this system could cause an increased release of norepinephrine [76, 124]. With continued alcohol administration, the norepinephrine-receptor-adenylate cyclase system would respond by down regulation to adjust to the increased local norepinephrine, while converse changes might occur in the acetylcholine-guanylate cyclase system. Abrupt removal of alcohol treatment would then find the diminished norepinephrine-adenylate cyclase system incapable of dampening the enhanced excitatory acetylchole system, with the result that seizures would develop. Similar sequelae could apply to the cerebral cortex, with the production of motor convulsions.

The Siggins model seems to agree with pharmacologic studies indicating that decreases in brain norepinephrine exacerbate the convulsions following alcohol withdrawal [17]. Furthermore, intraventricular administration of dibutyryl cyclic GMP increases the severity of alcohol withdrawal symptoms in mice, while dibutyryl cyclic AMP administration decreases the symptoms [109].

Although this proposal seems logical, it may be an oversimplification in that it does not involve other systems such as the peptidyl opiates, substance P, and other biologically active brain-endogenous substances.

NEUROPATHOLOGICAL ACTIONS OF ALCOHOL

Certainly, ethanol produces alterations of the electrophysiological pattern in the brain [110]. The response is complex, for example, using extracellular recordings of single neurons and iontophoretic and micropressure application of ethanol, which depressed cerebellar Purkinge cells in a concentration-dependent manner. However, the depressions appear to be nonspecific, and local anestheticlike in nature, since they are often accompanied by reduction in spike size with broadening of the spike duration. In accord with this interpretation, and in contrast to previous reports [77], Siggins and French [110] found that the inhibitions of activity produced by either iontophoretic GABA or norepinephrine were antagonized nonspecifically by direct application of alcohol to Purkinge cells.

In spite of the complex nature of the electrophysiological properties of ethanol, a variety of neuropathological [28, 127] and neuropsychological [20] alterations have been observed and delineated in chronic alcoholics. Initially, this observed brain damage and the resulting impairment in learning and memory were attributed to malnutrition, especially thiamine deficiency [126], rather than to the direct neurotoxic effects of ethanol. Nevertheless, both neuropathological [45] and neuropsychological [70] deficits have been observed in long-term alcoholic patients with no history of malnutrition. Furthermore, Walker and Hunter [130] reported that long-term ethanol exposure results in a residual impairment in the acquisition of a variety of behavioral tasks. Other works by Riley and Walker [98] demonstrated that 4 months of ethanol consumption by mature mice resulted in a 50 to 60% loss of dendritic spines on hippocampal pyramidal cells and dentate gyrus granule cells. Interpretation of this study strongly suggests that long-term ethanol consumption, in the absence of malnutrition, produces neuronal loss in the central nervous system. Additionally, it is plausible that the residual learning and memory deficits induced by long-term ethanol consumption in animals [129] and humans [120] may be related in part to hippocampal damage, or, as suggested by Victor et al. [127] for alcoholic Korsakoff patients, the dorsomedial thalamus is correlated with impaired memory.

Although it is clear that prolonged ethanol consumption can have neuropathological consequences, despite good nutrition, the exact mechanism by which it does remains unclear. Speculations include: (1) ethanol or a metabolite could be directly neurotoxic; or (2) ethanol could exert its effect by inhibiting neuronal protein synthesis (see Chapter 7, this volume); or (3) ethanol produces its effects by altering cerebral blood flow, resulting in chronic ischemia [48]. Further research in which quantitative behavioral neurohistological, neurophysiological data are obtained in ethanol-dependent and nutritionally controlled animals and humans should help clarify the relationship between the behavioral neuropathological consequences of alcohol abuse.

ADDICTION: A UNIFIED CONCEPT

A decade ago a review dealing with the subject matter of possible similarities or common interactions and mechanisms between alcohol and other drugs such as opiates would have contributed little to a volume concerned with the nature of alcoholism.

The widespread use of opiates and ethanol in modern society has led to intensive scientific investigation into the mechanisms of action of these two diverse classes of drugs. Although it is well known that excessive use of one drug is often associated with concurrent use of the other [16], only recently has there been effort devoted to establishing common underlying biochemical mechanisms between the two. This is not surprising, as it is difficult to envision the biochemical, physiological, or metabolic pathways that complex phenanthrene-type alkaloids would have in common with a simple 2-carbon molecule. Nevertheless, scrutiny of the literature points toward possible common mechanisms for certain actions of these two classes of addictive substances.

The basis for this research was an hypothesis proposed by Davis and Walsh in a provocative 1970 paper [31] in which they suggested that tetrahydroisoquinolines, alkaloid condensation products formed as a consequence of ethanol metabolism, might be involved in alcoholism. Davis and Walsh pointed out that benzylisoquinoline alkaloids are requisite intermediates in the biosynthesis of morphine in the poppy plant, *Papver somniferum* [3]. The possible biogenesis of these alkaloids in mammalian tissues stimulated the speculation that common biochemical mechanisms might exist between opiates and ethanol. In the same year, Cohen and Collins [25] proposed that simple tetrahydroisoquinolines (TIQs), such as those produced by condensation of catecholamines with acetaldehyde, may contribute to the acute and chronic effects of ethanol intoxication. This author subsequently suggested the link hypothesis (see Figure 1), which states that TIQs formed following ethanol ingestion can function as opiates and thus serve as the biochemical link between alcohol and opiates [15].

```
        /TIQS\
       /      \
      / ARE THERE COMMON MECHANISMS \
     /                                \
    /   BETWEEN ALCOHOL AND OPIATES ?  \
   /_____\
   ALCOHOL                        OPIATES
```

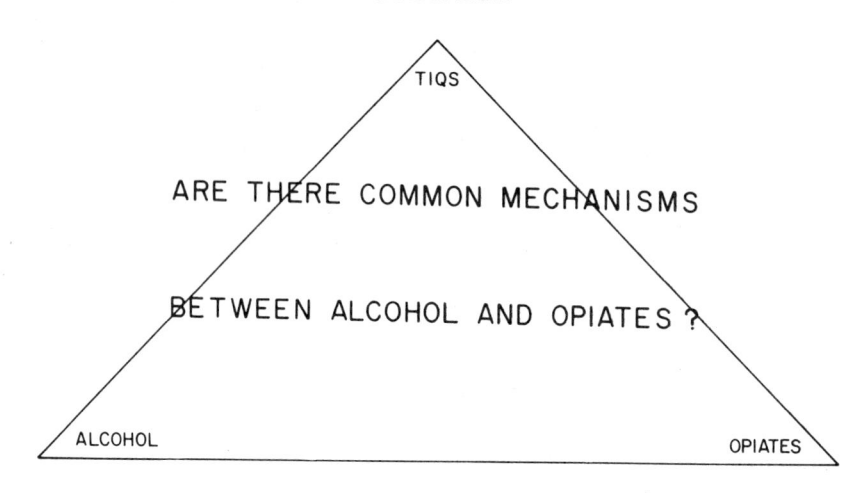

Figure 1. Link Hypothesis Schematic. (From Blum, K., Briggs, A. H., Hirst, M., Hamilton, M. G., Elston, S. F. A., and Verebey, K., in *Alcohol Tolerance and Dependence*, Ritger, H. and Crabbe, J. (eds.), Elsevier/North-Holland Biomedical Press, Amsterdam, 1980, p. 372.)

An acceptable link hypothesis would require that certain pharmacologic criteria be satisfied. Among these would be (1) the necessary identification of TIQs in biological tissues following acute and/or chronic exposure to ethanol; (2) evidence that the isoquinolines contribute to, or share, ethanollike and opiatelike properties, such as the production of tolerance and physical dependence, and that such pharmacologic actions be enhanced by common potentiators and reduced by appropriate antagonists. (See Table 1.)

These theories have met with severe criticism [51, 105], on the basis that the acute effects of opiates and ethanol are dissimilar, the dependence phenomena are different, narcotic antagonists do not antagonize ethanol or precipitate withdrawal symptoms in animals dependent on ethanol, the withdrawal symptoms of morphine are unlike those of ethanol, and there is no experimental evidence to link the isoquinolines with ethanol.

Although the isoquinoline question has not been resolved, numerous experiments in the past decade have substantiated the contention that common mechanisms exist between ethanol and opiates. Naloxone has been found to diminish ethanol narcosis [6] and dependence development [18]. Blum et al. [19] observed that morphine can inhibit ethanol withdrawal convulsions in mice. Ross et al. [101] have reported a decrease in voluntary ethanol consumption following naloxone administration in the hamster. Altshuler et al. [1] have observed that naloxone alters ethanol consumption in monkeys trained to auto-administer ethanol, resulting in an extinction curve. Ho et al. [58] have reported a decrease in voluntary ethanol consumption in alcohol-preferring mice following morphine,

Table 1
Alcohol/Opiate-Like Interaction Effects of Isoquinolines

Parameter Tested	General Finding	Authors
Identification	1. Evidence for the endogenous formation of the TIQ alkaloid salsolinol in alcoholics and normal humans.	Collins et al. 1979; Nijm et al. 1977
	2. Identification of an 0-methyl derivative of salsolinol in striata of mice exposed to ethanol vapor without any monoamine manipulation.	Hamilton et al. 1978, 1979
	3. Discovery that the 7-0-methoxy salsolinol is the principal 0-methylated product formed in vivo in both rat brain and heart following central and peripheral administration of salsolinol.	Bail et al. 1979
Ethanol-like actions	1. Salsolinol and 3-carboxy salsolinol enhanced the duration of ethanol-incuded narcosis in mice.	Marshall and Hirst 1976
	2. Salsolinol selectively decreased the activity of mice bred for differential alcohol sensitivities and a hypnotic dose of salsolinol induced significantly longer sleep times on the LS line than on the SS line.	Church et al. 1976
	3. Similar to ethanol, salsolinol induced depletion of regional brain calcium and inhibition of calcium binding to synaptic membranes.	Ross 1978; Ross et al. 1974
	4. Similar electrophysiological changes observed for ethanol and salsolinol.	Siggins et al. 1979
Opiate-like actions	1. 3-Carboxy salsolinol and salsolinol produced analgesia by themselves and also potentiated morphine analgesia. This effect was blocked by naloxone.	Marshall et al. 1977; Blum et al. 1976
	2. Partial agonist effect of salsolinol on the opiate-sensitive sites of the guinea pig ileum, which was blocked but not reversed by naloxone.	Hamilton et al. 1979; Blum et al 1979
	3. Naloxone reversal of salsolinol induced inhibition of calcium binding to synaptic membranes.	Ross et al. 1978
	4. Additive effects of salsolinol and D-Ala-[2]-Met-[5]-enkephalin on guinea pig ileum and vas deferens.	Blum et al. 1979; Blum 1980
	5. Salsolinol-induced attenuation of morphine response on the guinea pig ileum.	Hamilton et al. 1979
	6. Weak direct stereospecific binding of salsolinol and THP to opiate receptors in rat brain and guinea pig brain.	Greenwald et al. 1979; Goldstein (personal communication)
Preference studies	1. Beta carboline was found to produce a precipitous fall in alcohol intake in rats.	Messiha and Geller 1976

(continued)

Table 1 (continued)

Parameter tested	General Finding	Authors
	2. Isoquinolines (THP, salsolinol, and others) stimulated chronic volitional alcohol drinking in rats.	Myers 1978; Myers and Melchior 1977; Oblinger and Myers 1977
Tolerance and physical dependence production	1. Production of typical opiate-like abstinence signs following infusion of tetrahydropapaveroline (THP).	Myers and Melchior 1977; Myers 1978

Source: From Blum, K., Briggs, A. H., Hirst, M., Hamilton, M. G., Elston, S. F. A., and Verebey, K., in *Alcohol Tolerance and Dependence*, Ritger, H. and Crabbe, J. (eds.), Elsevier/North-Holland Biomedical Press, Amsterdam, 1980, p. 375.

methadone, or levorphanol administration, but no change in alcohol consumption after treatment with dextrophan, the inactive isomer of levorphanol. Acutely, morphine, ethanol, and salsolinol have been found to cause a decrease in brain calcium in specific regions [99, 102]. Interestingly, naloxone blocks the calcium-depleting action of these agents, which would further support the possibility of similar or associated sites of action for both ethanol and opiates.

More surprisingly is that, in humans, there are reports of naloxone-induced antagonism of acute ethanol intoxication [68] and reversal of ethanol-induced coma [83].

In addition to the number of reports that link the effect of ethanol action with opioids [12], ethanol has been shown to alter neuronal functions such as synthesis, release, or degradation of certain neurotransmitters [72, 79].

In consideration of the possible involvement of the peptidal opiate system in the actions of ethanol and possibly in alcohol-seeking behavior, in general, certain pertinent facts are presented herein.

INVOLVEMENT OF PEPTIDYL OPIATES IN THE ACTIONS OF ALCOHOL

Ethanol has been described as effectively interfering with the synthesis of brain peptides [35]. The peptidyl opiates, beta-endorphin and enkephalins, being putative neurotransmitters, neuromodulators, or hormones [4], have been shown to have altered concentrations upon acute and chronic treatment with various drugs [63, 93].

In terms of opiate receptor physiology, Pinsky et al. [91] have observed a shift in opiate receptor affinity utilizing a radioreceptor assay with rat brain homogenates after the addition of ethanol or acetaldehyde. These researchers found that these substances increased [^{3}H]-morphine binding, but decreased naloxone binding. Interestingly, salsolinol and tetrahydropaperoline, by-products of ethanol metabolism [54, 113], as previously mentioned, have been found to have a weak but stereospecific interaction at opiate receptors [52].

Since the discovery of endogenous opiates, it has become apparent that exogenous opiates such as morphine, codeine, or heroin simply mimic the actions of compounds found in the body. This situation is comparable to that of exogenous substances like nicotine or muscarine, which both stimulate the receptors of acetylcholine. As with other receptor populations, it is suspected that multiple types of opiate (beta-endorphine and/or enkephalin) receptors exist and that a wide range of functions may be mediated by their stimulation [49]. Accordingly, those actions of ethanol that are blocked by narcotic antagonists and may therefore be common or associated with exogenous opiates may include

1. Competition for opiate receptors by tetrahydroisoquinolines
2. The stimulation of enkephalin release by ethanol, similar to the proposed actions of general anesthetics
3. Postsynaptic membrane perturbation due to membrane fluidization induced by ethanol, which results in increased opiate receptor stimulation.

Since opiates occupy the receptor sites for endogenous ligands, the question of whether chronic treatment with opiates will alter enkephalin content in the brain has been raised. Kosterlitz and Hughes [75] have proposed that a reduction in enkephalin release might be involved in the development of tolerance and dependence to opiates. Using radioimmunoassay, a number of labs have studied the effects of chronic morphine treatment on enkaphalin levels in either the whole brain or brain regions known to be high in enkephalins [22, 42, 107, 131]. The consensus of opinion is that chronic morphine treatment does not change levels of metenkephalin or leuenkephalin. Shani et al. [107], however, did observe a fall in brain enkephalin in rats that received a single morphine pellet implant and were sacrificed 3 days later. In five other morphine regimens, they saw no change, which is in agreement with other investigators. Hollt et al. [63] have found a decrease in pituitary beta-endorphin in animals treated chronically with morphine for 1 month and an increase in plasma beta-endorphin with a precipitatory dose of naloxone on rats that were morphine tolerant and/or dependent. Interestingly, they observed a rise in plasma beta-endorphin coupled with a decrease in anterior pituitary lobe beta-endorphin in morphine-dependent rats acutely withdrawn with naloxone. It should be noted that in rats made dependent on a shorter 10-day morphine regimen, Hollt et al. [63] saw no significant changes in beta-endorphin levels. Ungar et al. [123] have reported an interesting experiment with rats injected with progressively decreasing doses of morphine. Brain extracts from these animals were subjected to electrophoretic fractionation and found to exhibit either opiate agonist or antagonist properties. Antagonist properties were assayed in vivo against morphine in mice, and in vitro against normorphine or synthetic endorphins in the mouse vas deferens. They found that fractions containing agonistlike activity had increased by 137% on day 12 of morphine treatment, but had fallen to 27% of the normal level on the 18th day. Antagonist activity was undetectable in untreated rat brains, but increased gradually during the first 12 days of morphine treatment and declined thereafter.

The agonistlike activity observed by Ungar et al. [123] was presumably due to endogenous opiates; the identity of those substances with antagonist properties is not known. Whatever interpretation is placed on Ungar's work, it is obvious that chronic morphine receptor stimulation may have a marked effect on the physiology of enkephalinergic systems. Pinsky et al. [91] have studied the effects of chronic alcohol treatment on enkephalin binding in rats. In rats treated with ethanol for 15 days, they observed a decrease in enkephalin activity. It should be noted, however, that they measured enkephalins directly via an opiate receptor-binding technique. A report by Schulz [103] indicates that chronic treatment with ethanol decreases methionine-enkephalin levels in striatum, medulla, pons, midbrain, or beta-endorphin in the intermediate posterior lobe of the rat pituitary. Certainly, these studies suggest possible involvement of the peptidyl opiate system in the actions of ethanol.

THE PSYCHOGENETIC THEORY OF ALCOHOL-SEEKING BEHAVIOR

The question of genetic versus environmental factors in the development of alcoholism has long been debated. McClearn and Rodgers [87] observed a substantial difference in preference for voluntary alcohol consumption among various mouse strains. Among the strains studied were the C57 strain, which was found to prefer alcohol over water, and the DBA strain, which prefers water over alcohol. The present author has observed differences between the two strains with respect to vas deferens responsibility to alcohol [8] and the induction of psychomotor impairment by alcohol [36]. Differences between the two strains can also be seen with respect to responses to morphine analgesia and running activity [27]. Since these differences are genetically determined, it is possible that a genetic marker reflecting an individual's preference and susceptibility to ethanol may be identified.

There is increasing evidence from both animals and man that seems to support the possibility that both ethanol and narcotic drugs may induce euphoria via the endorphinergic system [125]. Based on the evidence that ethanol or a byproduct of alcohol ingestion (i.e., isoquinolines) interact at opiate-mediated sites [52] and the possibility that alcohol- and opiate-seeking behavior is a function of endogenous peptidyl opiate levels [59] the author's laboratory proposed the psychogenetic theory of drug-seeking behavior [11]. In terms of alcohol- and opiate-seeking behavior, the psychogenetic theory proposes that individuals prone to such behavior possess a genetic deficiency of the peptidyl opiate system. In addition, continued utilization of either alcohol or opiates may, in part, be due to the possibility that long-term exposure of these drugs results in significant reduction of endogenous peptidyl opiates.

A simple mathematical representation of the components of the theory is as follows:

$$DSB = G_{DIO} + E$$

where DSB represents drug-seeking behavior, G_{DIO} equals genetic deficiency of the internal opiate, and E represents environment.

This laboratory has devoted considerable energies to the study of ethanol, and based on some experimental evidence, a model for typing alcoholics has been proposed and is depicted in Figure 2.

Preliminary evidence for support of type I is derived from the findings that a negative correlation (.909) exists between mouse whole brain methionine-enkephalin levels and genotype-linked ethanol preference [7, 10]. Currently, there is even some experimental support for the type II alcoholic [86]; however, more sociological data is warranted.

Since opiates occupy or alter the receptor sites for endogenous ligands, the question of whether chronic treatment with opiates, or as suggested in type III, ethanol as well, will alter enkephalin content in the brain has been raised. In this regard, the author's finding of a marked reduction of basal ganglia leucine-enkephalin in hamsters drinking ethanol for a 12-month period is in full agreement with the cited studies by Pinsky et al. [91] and Schulz [103], and further suggests possible opiate occupancy by ethanol as a metabolite. Interpretation of these results tends to support, in part, the negative feedback theory for agonist (opiate-like)-induced inhibition of neuronal enkephalin synthesis as proposed by Goldstein [50] and is certainly supportive for type III alcoholics as proposed. Alternatively, the ethanol-induced reduction of basal ganglia enkephalinlike material may simply be due to the direct neurotoxic effects of ethanol [47] and warrants further investigations.

At least the psychogenetic theory of alcohol-seeking behavior serves as a useful model for research directions in pursuit of the underlying mechanisms involved in the phenomenology of alcohol-seeking behavior. Certainly, future re-

ALCOHOLISM—RECLASSIFICATION

TYPE I

$$AD = G_{DIO} + E$$

TYPE II

$$AD = G_{NIO} + E$$

TYPE III

$$AD = G_{NIO} + E + A_{DIO}$$

AD = ALCOHOL DESIRE
DIO = DEFICIENCY OF INTERNAL OPIATE
A = ALCOHOL
G = GENETIC
E = ENVIRONMENT
NIO = NORMAL INTERNAL OPIATE

Figure 2. Schematic of Psychogenetic Theory of Alcohol-Seeking Behavior. (From Blum, K., Briggs, A. H., Elston, S. F. A., and DeLallo, L., Psychogenetics of drug-seeking behavior, *Subs. Alcohol Act./Mis.*, 1(3):225, 1980.)

search may ultimately include clinical development of nontoxic agents that will enhance the functional activity of brain peptidyl opiates via alteration of synthesis, release, turnover, or receptor interaction [34] and the utilization of a heterogeneous strain (HS) mice to allow for more accurate genetic correlation of peptidyl opiates and alcohol preference.

EFFECTS OF NEUROPHARMACOLOGIC AGENTS ON ACUTE AND CHRONIC ACTIONS OF ETHANOL AND OPIATES

Tables 2 and 3 illustrate a selected representation of the state-of-the-art review of the effects of alcohol (ethanol) and narcotics (morphine, etc.) on brain neurochemicals. Interested scientists should refer to the works of Blum [16], Loh and Ross [82], and Majchrowicz and Noble [84] for additional information.

Table 2
Effect(s) of Alcohol (Ethanol) and Narcotics (Morphine, etc.) on Brain Neurochemicals

Neurochemical	Narcotics (Morphine, etc.) Acute		Chronic		Withdrawal		Alcohol (Ethanol) Acute		Chronic		Withdrawal	
	L	T	L	T	L	T	L	T	L	T	L	T
NE	① ↑ ② ↓ ③ ↔	⑮ ↑ ⑯ ↔	⑱ ↑ ⑲ ↓ ⑱ ↔	㉗ ↑ ⑲ ↔	⑱ ↔ ㉚ ↓ ↔	① ↑	㉞ ↑ ㉟ ↓ ㊱ ↔	㊳ ↑↓		㊴ ↑ ㊴ ↔		(52) ↑
DA	② ↓ ④ ↔	⑰ ↑	⑱ ↑ ⑳ ↓ ㉑ ↔	③ ↑ ㉘ ↔	㉛ ↑ ㉜ ↓		㊲ ↓ ㊳ ↔	㊲ ↑ ㊳ ↓ ㊲ ↔	㊳ ↔	㊳ ↑ ㊳ ↓ (51) ↔		
5-HT	⑤ ↑ ⑥ ↓ ⑦ ↔		㉒ ↔	㉙ ↑	⑥ ↔		㊴ ↑ ㉟ ↓ ㊵ ↔	㊳ ↓ ㊵ ↔	㊴ ↑ ㊳ ↔	㊺ ↑ ㊳ ↓ ㊳ ↔	(52) ↑ (53) ↓ (53) ↔	
GABA	⑧ ↔		㉓ ↑				㊶ ↑ ㊷ ↓ ↔		㊶ ↑ ㊻ ↓ ㊼ ↔			
ACH	⑨ ↑ ⑩ ↓↑						㊸ ↑		㊽ ↓ ㊾ ↔			
CAMP	⑪ ↑ ⑫ ↓ ⑬ ↔		㉔ ↑ ㉕ ↔		㉝ ↑		㊹ ↓↑ ㊺ ↔					
Ca++	⑭ ↓	㉖ ↓	㉖ ↑				⑭ ↓		㊿ ↔	(54) ↑ (55) ↑		

Key: Level = L
Turnover = T
Increase = ↑
Decrease = ↓
No change = ↔

Author reference:

1. Way and Shen, 1971; 2. Takagi, and Nakamo, 1968; 3. Clouet and Ratner, 1970; 4. Sharman, 1966; 5. Maynert, and co-workers, 1962; 6. Bonneycastle and co-workers, 1962; 7. Brodie and co-workers, 1956; 8. Yoneda and co-workers, 1976; 9. Richter and Goldstein, 1970; 10. Crosslands, 1973; 11. Puri and co-workers, 1973; 12. Chou and co-workers, 1971; 13. Naito and Kuriyoma, 1973; 14. Ross and co-workers, 1974; 15. Roffman and co-workers, 1976; 16. Papeschi and co-workers, 1975; 17. Clouet and Ratner, 1970; 18. Gunne, 1963; 19. Neal, 1968; 20. Merali, 1975; 21. Simon and co-workers, 1975; 22. Cochin and Axelrod, 1959; 23. Clouet, 1977; 24. Bonnet, 1975; 25. Traber and co-workers, 1975; 26. Ross, 1977; 27. Akera and Brady, 1968; 28. Gunne and co-workers, 1968; 29. Shen and co-workers, 1975; 30. Sloan and co-workers, 1963; 31. Segal and Deneau, 1962; 32. Weil-Malherbe and co-workers, 1965; 33. Mehta and Johnson, 1975; 34. Reichle and co-workers, 1971; 35. Gursey and Olsen, 1960; 36. Efron and Gessa, 1963; 37. Carlsson and co-workers, 1973; 38. Hunt and Majchrowicz, 1974; 39. Poherecky and co-workers, 1974; 40. Tabakoff and co-workers, 1976; 41. Rawat, 1974; 42. Hakkinen and Kulonen, 1963; 43. Berry and Stolz, 1954; 44. Volicer and Gold, 1975; 45. Kuriyama and Israel, 1973; 46. Sytinsky and co-workers, 1975; 47. Patel and Lal, 1973; 48. Moss and co-workers, 1967; 49. Kalant, 1962; 50. Blum and co-workers, 1977; 51. Ahtee and Svartstrom-Fraser, 1975; 52. Griffiths and co-workers, 1974; 53. Kissin and co-workers, 1973; 54. Ross and co-workers, 1977; 55. Michaelis and co-workers, 1979.

Source: From Blum, K. in *Neurotoxicology*, L. Manzo (ed.), Pergamon, Oxford, 1980, p. 78.

Table 3
Effects of Manipulation of Neurochemicals on the Expression of Chronic Actions of Alcohol (Ethanol) and Narcotics (Morphine, etc.)

DRUG TREATMENT	TOLERANCE N	TOLERANCE A	DEPENDENCE N	DEPENDENCE A	WITHDRAWAL N	WITHDRAWAL A
1. Protein synthesis inhibitors	①↓	②↓	③↓	④↓		
2. Noradrenergic drugs						
6-OH Dopamine	⑤—	⑦↓	⑥—	⑦↓, ⑪↑	⑥↕	⑦—
L-Dopa			⑧↓	⑨↓	⑩↑	⑳↓
α-Blockers					⑫↓	⑮↑
β-Blockers				⑬↑	⑫↓, ⑭	⑮↑
α-methy-p-tyrosine	⑯↓		⑯↓	⑪↑	⑰↓, ⑥	⑮↓
Reserpine						⑮↑
Clonidine					⑱↑, ⑲↓	⑬↑
Norepinephrine						⑳↓, ⑬↑
Amphetamine						⑳↓
1-phenyl-2-(thiazolyl)-2 thiourea	㉑↓		㉑↓			
Disulfiram						㉒↑
Pargyline						㉓↑
Desipramine						⑩↑
3. Dopaminergic Drugs						
L-DOPA			⑧↓	⑨↓	⑩↑	⑳↓
6-OH dopamine	⑥—	⑦↓	⑥—	⑦↓, ⑪↑	⑥↕	⑦—
Dopamine						⑳↓
Apomorphine	⑫—		⑫—		⑩↑, ㉔	⑳↓
Haloperidol	㉕↑				㊳↓	㉖↑
Disulfiram					㉒↑	
Pargyline					㉗↓	
4. Gabaminergic drugs						
GABA	㉘↑		㉘↑			⑮↓
Amino-oxyacetic acid	㉘↑		㉘↑			⑮↓
Bicuculline	㉘↓		㉘↓			
Picrotoxin						⑮↑
5. Serotonergic drugs						
Serotonin				㉖—	⑧—	㉖↑↓—
Tryptophan	㉙↑		㉙↑		⑧↓	
5-OH Tryptophan				㉖—		⑳↑
5,6 di-OH-tryptamine	㉚↓		㉚↓		㉛↓	
p-chlorophenylalanine	㉙↓		㉙↓	⑬—, ⑳↓	㉛↓	⑮↓
Methysergide				⑬—		㉖↓ ⑳
Methergolin						⑳↓
MA1420						⑳↓

120

Table 3 *(continued)*

6. Cholinergic drugs					
Acetylcholine					(20)↑
Carbachol					(20)↑
Nicotine					(20)↓
Physostigmine	(32)—		(32)—	(33)↓ (34)	(20)↑, (15)
Hyoscine					(20)↓
Atropine				(33)↑ (34)	(15)—
Dihydro-β-erythroidine					(15)—
7. Drugs affecting cyclic AMP					
Cyclic AMP (cAMP)	(30)↑		(30)↑		
Cycloheximide+cAMP	(30)—		(30)—		
db-cyclic AMP					(20)↓
db-cyclic GMP					(20)↑
ATP					(20)↓
GTP					(20)↑
Theophylline				(35)—	(20)↑
Imidazole					(20)—
8. Prostaglandins					
PGE₁					(20)↑
PGE₂					(20)↑
PGF₂					(20)—
9. Calcium					
Ca++	(36)↓		(36)↓	(36)↓	(37)↓

Key:

N = Narcotics

A = Alcohol

↑ = increases

↓ = decreases

↔ = no change

Author reference:

1. Cochin, 1973; 2. LeBlanc and co-workers, 1976; 3. Loh and co-workers, 1969; 4. Blum, 1976; 5. Friedler and co-workers, 1972; 6. Blasig and co-workers, 1975; 7. Ritzman and Tabakoff, 1976; 8. Ruidobro and co-workers, 1963; 9. Blum and co-workers, 1975; 10. Herz and coworkers, 1974; 11. Blum and Wallace, 1974; 12. Blasig, 1978; 13. Blum and co-workers, 1977; 14. Martin and co-workers, 1974; 15. Goldstein, 1973; 16. Floresz and co-workers, 1973; 17. Glick and co-workers, 1973; 18. Schulz and Hertz, 1977; 19. Fielding and co-workers, 1977; 20. Collier and co-workers, 1976; 21. Bhargava and co-workers, 1974; 22. Mattila and coworkers, 1968; 23. Iwamoto and co-workers, 1976; 24. Ary and Lomax, 1976; 25. Zidleberg and Espamer, 1975; 26. Blum and co-workers, 1976; 27. Way and co-workers, 1976; 28. Way, 1973; 29. Ho and co-workers, 1972; 30. Ho and co-workers, 1973; 31. Shen and co-workers, 1970; 32. Barghava and Way, 1972; 33. Grumbach, 1969; 34. Croeslands, 1971; 35. Blum, unpublished; 36. Sanghvi and Gershan, 1976; 37. Hamilton and co-workers, 1977.

Source: From Blum, K. in *Neurotoxicology*, L. Manzo (Ed.), Pergamon, Oxford, 1980, p. 81.

Information presented herein leads to the following conclusions. First, both opiates and ethanol produce alterations in neuroamine metabolism and concentrations. These effects occur after acute administration, during chronic administration, and also during the withdrawal phase.

Second, from the results reported in Tables 2 and 3, there is little agreement concerning the effect that ethanol or opiates can produce on neurochemical mechanisms. The conflicting results obtained are most likely related to a combination of factors in the experimental protocols, including different routes of administration, different monoamine-measuring techniques and/or the timing of the measurements, or the difference in the utilized doses to produce the desired effect (acute intoxication or dependence). While this list is by no means exclusive, it does point out several reasons why there is no general agreement concerning the neurochemical alterations elicited by either ethanol or opiates. The lack of agreement in this area with either of these substances above obviously precludes a definite conclusion concerning similarities, or differences, in the neurochemical alterations induced by acute or chronic treatment.

Third, further evidence for a common mechanism of action has been obtained through pharmacologic manipulation of central monoaminergic function. Considerable research has implicated changes in brain biogenic amines, induced by opiates and ethanol administration, as mediating at least some of the effects of acute or chronic drug intoxication. Although the exact mechanism and direction of changes in biogenic amines induced by ethanol and opiates remains controversial, that changes occur is generally accepted. This has prompted several investigators to examine the effects of biogenic amines on behavioral changes induced by these two drugs.

As with the effects of administration of opiates or ethanol on endogenous neurochemical mechanisms, the effects of prior manipulation of these neurochemicals on subsequent tolerance to, dependence on, and withdrawal from these agents is similarly confusing.

It is apparent from the evidence presented that there is still considerable controversy surrounding the neurochemical effects and determinants of both opiates and ethanol. A definitive case cannot yet be made for any single biogenic amine, ion, or other endogenous substance as the initiator of dependence-producing properties of either agent.

Fourth, there are certain similarities between opiates and ethanol that became evident on inspection of the results presented in the summarized Table 3.

There are also some distinct differences that are evident in some reports. For instance, while dopamine has been reported to ameliorate ethanol-induced withdrawal [14], exacerbation of morphine withdrawal has been suggested to occur with stimulation of dopamine receptors [67]. However, this exacerbation of withdrawal pertained primarily to dominate withdrawal signs (e.g., jumping), while recessive signs (e.g., diarrhea) decreased [56, 78].

Thus the definition of exacerbation or amelioration depends on the importance ascribed to particular withdrawal signs, and a conclusion concerning the effects of a drug on abstinence from either opiates or ethanol rests on this definition.

UNIFIED THEORY: INTERPRETATIONS AND SPECULATIONS

A common denominator theory of addiction has been raised in the author's laboratory [16] and by others [31], especially with regard to alcohol and opiate common links [15]. As previously mentioned, when alcohol is ingested, it has been found that a new class of compounds, termed "isoquinolines," are subsequently formed. These isoquinolines, because of their ability to act on similar or associated sites in the brain (opiate receptors) may function as the link between alcohol and opiates. The isoquinolines have been found to induce long-term drinking of alcohol in rodents [88]. This may be important, when it is considered that certain mice (C57), which are genetically bred to drink alcohol, also tend to drink more morphine compared to other mice (DBA), which do not drink alcohol or morphine. This finding, although supportive of a common mechanism for preference, has been argued by the work of Whitney and Horowitz [132], who showed differential preference of morphine and ethanol in sublines of C57 mice.

This might suggest that more than one mechanism might be responsible for drug preference in animals. It is tempting to speculate that the delineation of preference might include the elucidation of more than one mechanism ($M_1 + M_2 + M_3$) and that any one mechanism might contribute a certain percentage to the overall picture. For example, M_1 might be a common site for both opiates and ethanol (endorphinergic), whereas M_2 is solely for alcohol (unknown site), and M_3 is solely for morphine (unknown site). For example, the common mechanism site might account for mediating only a third of preference response, whereas M_2 and M_3 could account for the rest. Research is urgently required to define the relative importance of each mechanism.

Since endorphins interact at opiate receptors and have been shown (1) to produce profound analgesia, (2) to produce dependence when administered to rodents, (3) to be euphogenic, and (4) to alter opiate abstinence in animals and humans, they are strong candidates for being biological markers to explain the genetic propensity for substance addiction. In addition, since opiates are primary reinforcers in operant self-administration paradigms, the endorphins may play a significant role in the central "reward system."

Goldstein [49] and Loh and Law [81] have speculated that a common pathway of all drugs could involve beta-endorphin and opiate receptors. In simpler terms, it is possible that a preexisting genetic deficiency of endorphins in the brain could lead to drug dependence.

Opiate effects are not uniquely related to any of the known neurotransmitters [49, 50], although changes in content and turnover of several transmitters are associated with opiate actions and with tolerance and dependence. Accordingly, Goldstein [49] points out that the "opiate receptors seem to subserve a general inhibitory function in various neuronal pathways—and that administration of an exogenous opiate might result in suppression of synthesis of endogenous opioids, by analogy to the effects of administering a hormone." This would suggest that administration of an opiate would produce a negative feedback due to saturation of the opiate (beta-endorphin) receptor, which could cause a shutdown of beta-endorphin production. (See Figure 3.) In this regard [7], a significant reduction in basal ganglia amounts of enkephalin measured by an immunocytochemical method in hamsters was observed following presentation of a 10% ethanol solution as a free-choice for over 12 months. It is tempting to speculate that the ethanol or possibly a metabolite (isoquinoline) saturated opiate (beta-endorphin) receptor sites and produced a negative feedback inhibition of enkephalin production. This is just a beginning and future research may lead to a clearer understanding of tolerance, physical dependence, and withdrawal from alcohol and opiates, as well as from other addictive agents. Other models that have clinical importance to test this hypothesis of common mechanisms are being developed and actively researched.

If it is true that ethanol's reinforcing effects are exerted through interactions with endorphinergic systems, it is not surprising that numerous investigators found similarities in certain opiate and ethanol effects [9, 55, 74, 97]. These similarities in their reinforcing properties may be the explanation why animals are willing to substitute opiates for alcohol [112] and vice versa [114], and naloxone alters self-administration of ethanol in primates [1] and rodents [58, 102]. Both opiates and alcohol directly or indirectly interact with the opiate receptors [52, 89]. If this is correct, then in chronic alcoholism or opiate dependence, the frequent occupation of the opiate receptors by exogenous opioid causes contact desensitization of the receptors (pharmacologic tolerance), and their reinforcing effects are lost unless the dose is increased. Chronic excessive use of both alcohol and opiates will result in the abolition of stimulation of the reward centers in the limbic system, for which effect both drugs were initially consumed. In order to preserve the reinforcing effects of both drugs, moderate and temporally well-spaced use of these drugs are necessary. The literature indicates that numerous opiate abusers are "chipping" or taking opiates sporadically; they do not develop the street addict personality [46, 92]. The parallel character in the alcohol scene is the light-to-moderate social drinker. Consensus of the literature would argue that an alternative explanation exists for alcohol, which is not similar to opiates with regard to tolerance. Tolerance for alcohol may be due to a membrane

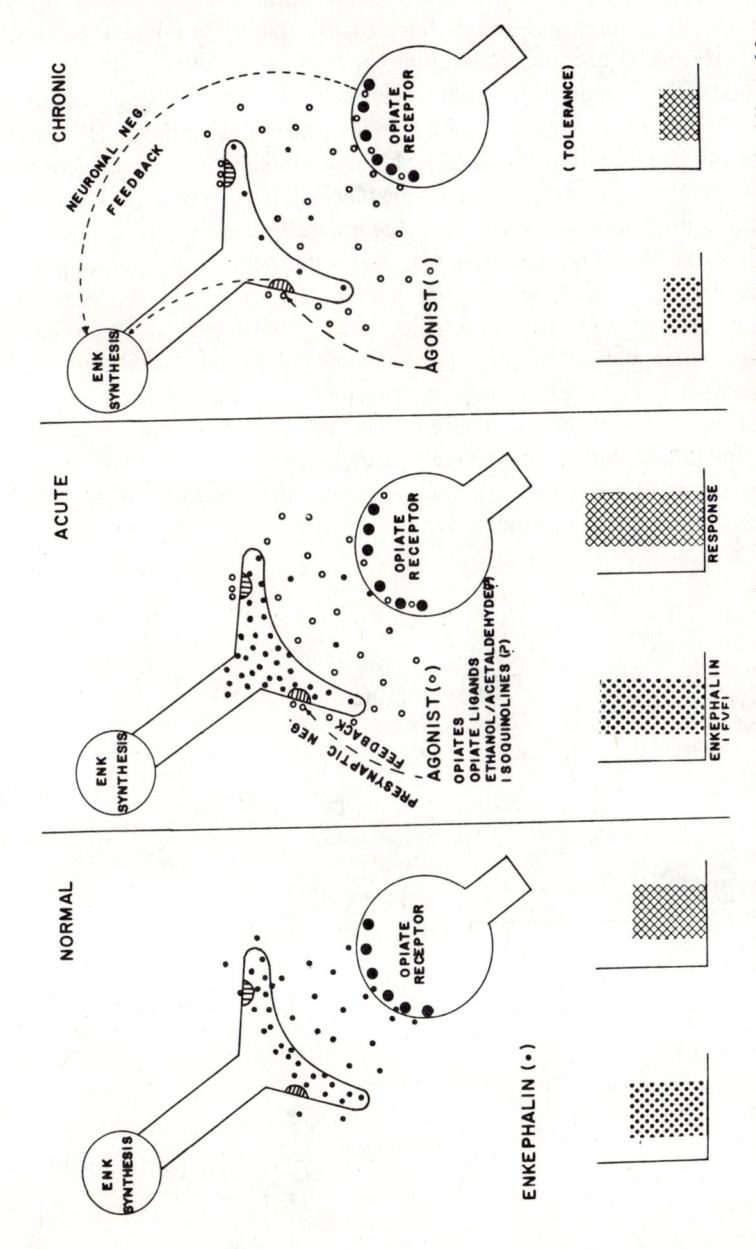

Figure 3. Proposed Model for Agonist-Opiate Ligand Interaction. (From Blum, K., Briggs, A. H., Hirst, M., Hamilton, M.G., Elston, S. F. A., and Verebey, K., in *Alcohol Tolerance and Dependence*, Rigter, H. and Crabbe, J. (eds.), Elsevier/North-Holland Biomedical Press, Amsterdam, 1980, p. 387.)

fluidization and alteration of membrane fatty acids not at all linked to morphine-induced neuronal adaptation. Thus, tolerances to alcohol and narcotic-like compounds probably are due to distinct mechanisms.

A tentative proposal of a common denominator theory for ethanol, opiates, and even barbiturates and benzodiazepines is depicted in Figure 4. Basically, this proposed central model is derived from available data and indicates that opiates can interact with the opiate receptor [89], and/or a calcium site [102] and the actions can be blocked by the narcotic antagonist naloxone; ethanol can also interact as a calcium site and this can also be blocked, but not reversed by naloxone [100]; isoquinolines can interact with the opiate receptor [52] and naloxone could partially block but not reverse opiate interaction effects [9]; and isoquinolines could interact with the calcium site and can be partially blocked by naloxone but not reversed [100]; ethanol interacts with a nonspecific site (membrane fluidization), which may not be altered by naloxone [69, 80]; and barbiturates and benzodiazepines interact with receptors associated with GABA [26, 122], which may not be blocked by naloxone. There may be an association between ethanol responses and GABA, but exact mechanisms are being actively investigated [121, 128]. Work on naloxone barbiturate and benzodiazepine receptor interactions have not as yet been accomplished.

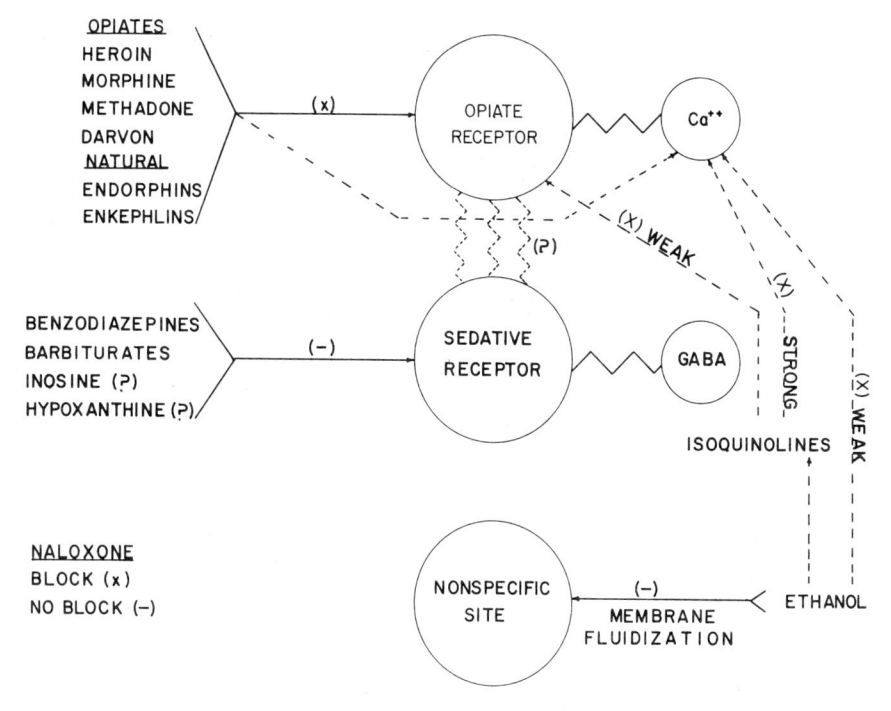

Figure 4. Unified Theory of Drug Dependence. (From Blum, K., in *Neurotoxicology*, L. Manzo (ed.), Pergamon, Oxford, 1980, p. 90.)

At its best, the psychogenetic theory of alcohol-seeking behavior is an interesting working hypothesis, which could serve as a model for future clinical directions. A prime significance would be that via this research, rational drug therapy may result, which could significantly improve both the preventive and treatment modalities of alcoholism.

CONCLUSION

This chapter explores numerous neurophysiological actions of alcohol, but focuses primarily on the possible chemical and biological mechanisms in response to this toxic agent. Inspection of the results of those studies reviewed reveals that alcohol is a very complex agent, having a multitude of central nervous system actions. It appears that alcohol is not simply a local anesthetic agent; nor is it a simple protein denaturant; nor is it a toxic pathogen; nor is it a false neurotransmitter (via the isoquinoline metabolite); nor is it an opiate receptor agonist or an antagonist; nor is it a releaser of biogenic amines and other neuropeptides like the enkephalins or endorphins; nor is it an intoxicant; nor is it an addictive agent leading to total devastation of the individual and his or her family. It is all of the above; and that is why society is compelled to continue to understand its biological activity. Thus, the basic and clinical scientist, through research, may someday provide information that will ultimately lead to the prevention and amelioration of the disease known as alcoholism.

ACKNOWLEDGMENTS

The author is grateful for the enthusiastic support of his staff, Leo DeLallo, Robert Ochoa, Stephen F. A. Elston, and Carolann Gerescher, and of Dr. Arthur H. Briggs, Chairman of the Department of Pharmacology, The University of Texas Health Science Center at San Antonio, San Antonio, Texas.

REFERENCES

1. Altshuler, H. L., Feinhandler, D., and Aitken, C. The effects of opiate antagonist compounds on fixed-ratio operant responding in rats. *Fed Proc.* 38, 424, 1979.
2. Banerjee, S. P., Sharma, V. K., and Khanna, J. M. Alterations in β-adrenergic receptor binding during ethanol withdrawal. *Nature* 276(5686):407–409, 1978.
3. Battersby, A. R. Alkaloid biosynthesis. *Q. Rev.* 25:255–286, 1961.

4. Beaumont, A., and Hughes, J. Biology of opioid peptides. *Ann. Rev. Pharmacol. Toxicol.* 19:245–267, 1979.

5. Bloom, F. E. The role of cyclic nucleotides in central synaptic function. *Pharmacol. Rev.* 74:1–103, 1975.

6. Blum, K. Neurochemical and behavioral considerations on the relationship between ethanol and opiate dependence. In: *Proceedings of the National Drug Abuse Conference*, Lowinson, J. H. (ed.). Marcel Dekker: New York, 1976.

7. Blum, K. Effects of ethanol on protein synthesis. *Proc. Internat. Symp.* (NIAAA Res. Monograph, Series 4). In Press.

8. Blum, K., Briggs, A. H., DeLallo, L., and Elston, S. F. A. Genotype-dependent responses to ethanol and normorphine on vas deferens of inbred strains of mice. *Subs. Alcohol Act./Mis.* 1(5):459–465, 1980.

9. Blum, K., Briggs, A. H., DeLallo, L., Elston, S. F. A., and Hirst, M. Naloxone antagonizes the action of low ethanol concentrations on mouse vas deferens. *Subs. Alcohol Act./Mis.* 1(4):327–334, 1980.

10. Blum, K., Briggs, A. H., DeLallo, L., Ochoa, R., and Elston, S. F. A. Whole brain methionine-enkephalin of ethanol-avoiding and ethanol-preferring C57BL mice. Manuscript submitted for publication, 1982.

11. Blum, K., Briggs, A. H., Elston, S. F. A., and DeLallo, L. Psychogenetics of drug-seeking behavior. *Subs. Alcohol Act./Mis.* 1(3):255–257, 1980.

12. Blum, K., Briggs, A. H., Hirst, M., Hamilton, M. G., Elston, S. F. A., and Verebey, K. In: *Alcohol Tolerance and Dependence*, Rigter, H. and Crabbe, J. (eds.). Elsevier–North Holland Biomedical Press: Amsterdam, 1980.

13. Blum, K., Calhoun, W., Merritt, J. H., and Wallace, J. E. L-DOPA: Effect on ethanol narcosis and brain biogenic amines in mice. *Nature* 242:407–409, 1973.

14. Blum, K., Eubanks, J. D., Wallace, J. E., and Schwertner, H. A. Suppression of ethanol withdrawal by dopamine. *Experientia* 32:493–495, 1976.

15. Blum, K., Hamilton, M. G., Hirst, M., and Wallace, J. E. Putative role of isoquinoline alkaloids in alcoholism: A link to opiates. *Alcoholism: Clin. Exp. Res.* 2:113–120, 1978.

16. Blum, K., Hamilton, M. G., and Wallace, J. E. Alcohol and opiates: A review of common neurochemical and behavioral mechanisms. In: *Alcohol and Opiates: Neurochemical and Behavioral Mechanisms*, Blum, K. (ed.). Academic Press: New York, 1977.

17. Blum, K., and Wallace, J. E. Effects of catecholamine synthesis inhibition on ethanol-induced withdrawal symptoms in mice. *Br. J. Pharmacol.* 51:109–111, 1974.

18. Blum, K., Wallace, J. E., and Futterman, S. L. Naloxone-induced inhibition of ethanol dependence in mice. *Nature* 265:49–51, 1977.

19. Blum, K., Wallace, J. E., Schwertner, H. A., and Eubanks, J. D. Morphine suppression of ethanol withdrawal in mice. *Experientia* 32:79–82, 1976.

20. Butters, N., and Cermak, L. S. Some analyses of amnesic syndromes in brain-damaged patients. In: *The Hippocampus*, Pribam, K. H. and Isaacson, R. L. (eds.). Plenum: New York, 1975.

21. Charnock, J. S., Cook, D. A., Almeida, A. F., and To, R. Activation energy and phospholipid requirements of membrane-bound aeenosine triphosphatases. *Arch. Biochim. Biophys.* 159:393–399, 1973.

22. Childers, S. R., Simantov, R., and Snyder, S. H. Enkephalin: Radioimmunoassay and radioreceptor assay in morphine-dependent rats. *Eur. J. Pharmacol.* 46(3):289–293, 1977.

23. Chin, J. H., and Goldstein, D. B. Drug tolerance in biomembranes: A spinlabel study of the effects of ethanol. *Science* 196:684–685, 1977.

24. Chin, J. H., Parsons, L. M., and Goldstein, D. B. Increased cholesterol content of erythrocyte and brain membranes in ethanol-treated mice. *Biochem. Biophys. Acta* 513: 358–363, 1978.

25. Cohen, G., and Collins, M. Alkaloids from catecholamines in adrenal tissue: Possible role in alcoholism. *Science* 167:1749–1751, 1970.

26. Costa, E., Rodbard, D., and Pert, C. B. Is the benzodiazepine receptor coupled to a chloride anion channel? *Nature* 277:315–317, 1979.

27. Costellano, C., and Oliverio, A. A genetic analysis of morphine-induced running and analgesia in the mouse. *Psychopharmacol.* 41:197–200, 1975.

28. Courville, C. B. *Effects of Alcohol on the Nervous System of Man.* San Lucas Press: Los Angeles, 1966.

29. Creese, I., Burt, D. P., and Snyder, S. H. Dopamine receptor binding enhancement accompanies lesion-induced behavioral supersensitivity. *Science* 197:596–598, 1977.

30. Daly, J. *Cyclic Nucleotides in the Nervous System.* Plenum Press: New York, 1977.

31. Davis, V. E., and Walsh, M. J. Alcohol, amines and alkaloids: A possible basis for alcohol addiction. *Science* 167:1005–1007, 1970.

32. Davis, W. C., and Ticku, M. J. Ethanol enhances [^{3}H]-diazepam binding at the benzodiazepine-γ-aminobutyric acid receptor-ionophore complex. *Mole. Pharmacol.* 20:287–294, 1981.

33. DeKruyff, B., Van Dijek, P. W. M., Goldback, R. W., Demel, R. A., and Van Deenen, L. L. M. Influence of fatty acid and sterol composition on the lipid phase transition and activity of membrane-bound enzymes. In: *Acholeplasma Laidlawii. Biochim. Biophys. Acta* 330:269–282, 1973.

34. Ehrenpreis, S., Balagot, R. C., Myles, S., Advocate, C., and Comaty, J. E. In: *Endogenous and Exogenous Opiate Agonists and Antagonists*, Leongway, E. (ed.). Pergamon Press: New York, 1980.

35. Ellingboe, J. Effects of alcohol on neurochemical processes. In: *Psychopharmacology: A Generation of Progress*, Lipton, M. A., DiMascio, A., and Killam, R. F. (eds.). Raven Press: New York, 1978.

36. Elston, S. F. A., Blum, K., Briggs, A. H., and DeLallo, L. Evaluation of ethanol intoxication as a function of genotype-dependent responses in three inbred strains of mice. *Biochem. Pharmacol. Behav.*, in Press.

37. Engel, J., and Liljequist, S. The effect of long-term ethanol treatment on the sensitivity of the dopamine receptors in the nucleus accumbens. *Psychopharmacol.* 49:253–257, 1976.

38. Erikson, C. K., and Burnam, W. L. Cholinergic alteration of ethanol-induced sleep and death in mice. *Agents Actions* 2:8–13, 1971.

39. Erikson, C. K., and Chai, K. J. Cholinergic modification of ethanol-induced electroencephalograph synchrony in the rat. *Neuropharmacol.* 15:39–43, 1976.

40. Erikson, C. K., and Graham, D. T. Alterations of cortical and reticular acetylcholine release by ethanol in vivo. *J. Pharmacol. Exp. Ther.* 185:583–593, 1973.

41. Farias, R. N., Bloj, B., Morers, R. D., Sineriz, F., and Trucco, R. E. Regulation of allostearic membrane-bound enzymes through changes in membrane lipid composition. *Biochim. Biophys. Acta* 415:231–251, 1975.

42. Fratta, W., Yan, H.-Y. T., Hong, J., and Costa, E. Stability of metenkephalin content in brain structures of morphine-dependent or foot shock-stressed rats. *Nature* 268 (5619):452–453, 1977.

43. French, S. W., Reid, P. E., Palmer, D. S., Narod, M. E., and Ramey, C. W. Adrenergic subsensitivity of the rat brain during chronic ethanol ingestion. *Res. Commun. Chem. Pathol. Pharmacol.* 9:575–578, 1974.

44. French, S. W., Palmer, D. S., Narod, M. E., Reid, P. E., and Ramey, C. W. Noradrenergic sensitivity of the cerebral cortex after chronic ethanol ingestion and withdrawal. *J. Pharmacol. Exp. Ther.* 194:319-326, 1975.

45. Freund, G. Chronic central nervous system toxicity of alcohol. *Ann. Rev. Pharmacol.* 13:217-227, 1973.

46. Gay, G. R., Winkler, J. J., and Neumeyer, J. A. Emerging trends of heroin abuse in the San Francisco Bay Area. *J. Psychedelic Drugs* 4:53-64, 1971.

47. Golden, C. J., Graber, B., Blose, I., Berg, R., Coffman, J., and Bloch, S. Difference in brain densities between chronic alcoholics and normal control patients. *Science* 211:508-510, 1981.

48. Goldman, H., Sapirstein, L. A., Murphy, S., and Moore, J. Alcohol and regional blood flow in brains of rats. *Proc. Soc. Exp. Biol. Med.* 144:983-988, 1973.

49. Goldstein, A. Future research on opioid peptides (endorphins): A preview. In: *Alcohol and Opiates: Neurochemical and Behavioral Mechanisms*, Blum, K. (ed.). Academic Press: New York, 1977.

50. Goldstein, A. Endorphins: Physiology and clinical implications. *Ann. N.Y. Acad. Sci.* 311:49-58, 1978.

51. Goldstein, A., and Judson, B. A. Alcohol dependence and opiate dependence: Lack of relationship in mice. *Science* 172:290-292, 1971.

52. Greenwald, J. E., Fertel, R. H., Wong, L. K., Schwarz, R. D., and Bianchine, J. R. Salsolinol and tetrahydropapaveroline bind opiate receptors in the rat brain. *Fed. Proc.* 38:379, 1979.

53. Gruber, B., Denavo, E. C., Noble, E. P., and Tewari, S. Ethanol-induced conformational changes in rat brain microsomal membrains. *Biochem. Pharmacol.* 26:2181-2185, 1977.

54. Hamilton, M. G., Blum, K., and Hirst, M. Identification of an isoquinoline alkaloid after chronic exposure to ethanol. *Alcoholism: Clin. Exp. Res.* 2(2):133-137, 1978.

55. Hamilton, M. G., and Hirst, M. Alcohol-related tetrahydroisoquinolines: Pharmacology and identification. *Subs. Alcohol Act./Mis.* 1(2):121-144, 1980.

56. Herz, A., Blasig, J., and Papeschu, R. Role of catecholaminergic mechanisms in the expression of the morphine abstinence syndrome in rats. *Psychopharmacol.* 39:121-143, 1974.

57. Hiller, J. M., Angel, L. M., and Simon, E. J. Multiple opiate receptors: Alcohol selectively inhibits binding to delta receptors. *Science* 214:468-469, 1981.

58. Ho, A. K. S., Chen, R. C. A., and Morrison, J. M. Opiate-ethanol interaction studies. In: *Alcohol and Opiates: Neurochemical and Behavioral Mechanisms*, Blum, K. (ed.). Academic Press: New York, 1977.

59. Ho, W. K. K., Wen, H. L., and Ling, N. β-endorphin-like immunoreactivity in the plasma of heroin addicts and normal subjects. *Neuropharmacol.* 19:117-120, 1980.

60. Hoffer, B., Seiger, Å., Freidman, R., Olson, L., and Taylor, D. Electrophysiology and cytalogy of hippocampal formation transplants in the anterior chamber of the Ege II cholinergic mechanism. *Brain Res.* 119:107-132, 1977.

61. Hoffman, P. L., Levental, M., Fields, J. Z., and Tabakoff, B. Receptor and membrane function in the alcohol tolerant/dependent animal. *Adv. Exp. Med. Biol.* 132:761-770, 1980.

62. Hoffman, P., and Tabakoff, B. Alterations in dopamine receptor sensitivity by chronic ethanol treatment. *Nature* 268:551-553, 1977.

63. Hollt, V., Przewlocki, R., and Herz, A. β-endorphin-like immunoreactivity in plasma, pituitaries, and hypothalamus of rats following treatment with opiates. *Life Sci.* 23:1057-1066, 1978.

64. Hunt, W. A., and Dalton, T. K. Regional brain acetylcholine levels in rats acutely treated with ethanol or rendered ethanol-dependent. *Brain Res.* 109:628–668, 1976.

65. Hunt, W. A., and Majchrowicz, E. Alterations in the turnover of brain norepinephrine and dopamine in alcohol-dependent rats. *J. Neurochem.* 23:549–552, 1974.

66. Hunt, W. A., Majchrowicz, E., Dalton, T. K., Swartzwelder, H. S., and Wixon, H. Alterations in neurotransmitter activity after acute and chronic ethanol treatment studies of transmitter interactions. *Alcoholism: Clin. Exp. Res.* 3(4):359–363, 1979.

67. Iwamoto, E. T., Ho, I. K., and Way, E. L. Sudden elevation of brain dopamine after naloxone-precipitated withdrawal in morphine-dependent mice and rats. *J. Pharm. Exp. Ther.* 187:567–588, 1973.

68. Jeffcoate, W., Herbert, M., Cullen, M., Hastings, A., and Walder, C. Prevention of effects of alcohol intoxication by naloxone. *Lancet* 1157–1159, 1979.

69. Johnson, D. A., Lee, N. M., Cook, R., and Ellman, G. Ethanol tolerance in reconstituted and intact neuromembranes: A fluorescence study. *Fed. Proc.* 38:1027, 1979.

70. Jones, B., and Parsons, D. A. Impaired abstracting ability in chronic alcoholics. *Arch. Gen. Psychiatry* 24:71–75, 1971.

71. Kalant, H. Some recent physiological and biochemical investigations on alcohol and alcoholism. *Q. J. Stud. Alcohol* 23:52–93, 1962.

72. Kalant, H. Biochemical aspects of tolerance to and physical dependence on control depressants. In: *Proc. Eur. Soc. Neurochem.*, Neuhoff, V. (ed.). Verlag Chemie, Weinheim: New York, 1978.

73. Kalant, H., and Grose, W. Effects of ethanol and pentobarbital on release of acetylcholine from cerebral cortex slices. *J. Pharmacol. Exp. Ther.* 158:386–393, 1969.

74. Koob, G. F., Strecker, R. E., and Bloom, F. E. Effects of naloxone on the anticonflict properties of alcohol and chlordiazepoxide. *Subs. Alcohol Act./Mis.* 1(5):447–457, 1980.

75. Kosterlitz, H. W., and Hughes, J. Some thoughts on the significance of enkephalin, the endogenous ligand. *Life Sci.* 17(1):91–96, 1975.

76. Kuriyama, K., Nakagawa, K., Muromatsu, M., and Kakita, K. Alterations of cerebral protein kinase activity following ethanol administration. *Biochem. Pharmacol.* 25:2541–2542, 1976.

77. Lake, N. J., Garbrough, G. G., and Phillis, J. W. Effects of ethanol on cerebral cortical neurons: Interactions with some putative transmitters. *J. Pharm. Pharmacol.* 25:582–584, 1973.

78. Liljequist, S. Changes in the sensitivity of dopamine receptors in the nucleus accumbens and in the striatum induced by chronic ethanol administration. *Acta Pharmacol. Toxicol.* (Copen.) 43(1):19–28, 1978.

79. Liljequist, S. Effects of dependence-producing drugs on neurotransmitters and neuronal excitability. In: *Proceedings of the European Society for Neurochemistry*, Neuhoff, V. (ed.). Verlag Chemie, Weinheim: New York, 1978.

80. Littleton, J. M., Joh, G. R., and Grieve, S. J. Alterations in phospholipid composition in ethanol tolerance and dependence. *Alcholism: Clin. Exp. Res.* 3:50–56, 1979.

81. Loh, H. H., and Law, P. Y. Pharmacology of endogenous opiate-like peptides. In: *Alcohol and Opiates: Neurochemical and Behavioral Mechanisms*, Blum, K. (ed.). Academic Press: New York, 1977.

82. Loh, H., and Ross, D. H. *Neurochemical Mechanisms for Opiate Drug Action.* Raven Press: New York, 1980.

83. Mackenzie, A. I. Naloxone in alcohol intoxication [letter]. *Lancet* 1(818):733–734, 1979.

84. Majchrowicz, E., and Noble, E. P. *Biochemistry and Pharmacology of Ethanol.* Plenum Press: New York, 1979.

85. Mardones, J. The alcohols. In: *Physiological Pharmacology* (Vol. 1), Root, W. S. and Hoffman, F. G. (eds.). Academic Press: New York, 1963.

86. Masserman, H. J., and Yum, K. S. An analysis of the influence of alcohol on experimental neurosis in cats. *Psychosom. Med.* 8:36-52, 1946.

87. McClearn, G. E., and Rodgers, D. A. Differences in alcohol preference among inbred strains of mice. *Q. J. Stud. Alcohol* 20:691, 1959.

88. Myers, R. D. Tetrahydroisoquinolines in the brain: The basis of an animal model of alcoholism. *Alcoholism: Clin. Exp. Res.* 2(2):145-154, 1978.

89. Pert, C. B., and Snyder, S. H. Opiate receptor: Demonstration in nervous tissue. *Science* 179:1011-1014, 1973.

90. Phillis, J. W., and Thamandas, K. The effects of chlorpromazine and ethanol on in vivo release of acetylcholine from the cerebral cortex. *Comp. Gen. Pharmacol.* 2:306-310, 1971.

91. Pinsky, C., LaBella, F. S., and Leybin, L. Alcohol and opiate narcotic dependencies: Possible interrelatedness via central endorphin opiate receptor system. In: *A Multicultural View of Drug Abuse*, Smith, D. E., Anderson, S. M., Buxton, M., Gottlieb, N., Harvey, W., and Chung, T. (eds.). B. K. Hill: Boston, 1979.

92. Powell, D. H. A pilot study of occasional heroin isers. *Arch. Gen. Psychiatry* 28:586-594, 1973.

93. Przewlocki, R., Hollt, V., Duka, T., Kleber, A., Gramsch, C., Haarmann, I., and Herz, A. Long-term morphine treatment decreases endorphin levels in rat brain and pituitary. *Brain Res.* 174(2):357-361, 1979.

94. Rabin, R., and Molinoff, P. B. Brain neurotransmitter receptor systems in alcohol-treated mice and in mice genetically selected for differences in sensitivity to alcohol. *Adv. Exp. Med. Biol.* 132:787-795, 1980.

95. Rangaraj, N., and Kalant, H. α-adrenoreceptor-mediated alteration of ethanol effects on (Na^+-K^+) ATPase of rat neuronal membranes. *Can. J. Physiol. Pharmacol.* 58(11):1342-1346, 1980.

96. Rawat, A. K. Developmental changes in the brain levels of neurotransmitters as influenced by maternal ethanol consumption in the rat. *J. Neurochem.* 28:1175-1182, 1977.

97. Reggiani, A., Barbaccia, M. L., Spano, P. F., and Trabucchi, M. Role of dopaminergic-enkephalinergic interactions in the neurochemical effects of ethanol. *Subs. Alcohol Act./Mis.* 1(2):151-158, 1980.

98. Riley, J. N., and Walker, D. W. Morphological alteration in hippocampus after long-term alcohol consumption in mice. *Science* 201:646-648, 1978.

99. Ross, D. H. Selective action of alcohols on cerebral calcium levels. *Ann. N.Y. Acad. Sci.* 273:280-294, 1975.

100. Ross, D. H. Inhibition of high affinity calcium binding by salsolinol. *Alcoholism: Clin. Exp. Res.* 2:139-143, 1978.

101. Ross, D. H., Hartmann, R. J., and Geller, I. Ethanol preference in the hamster: Effects of morphine sulfate and naltrexone, a long-acting morphine antagonist. *Proc. West. Pharmacol. Soc.* 19:326-330, 1976.

102. Ross, D. H., Medina, M. A., and Cardenas, H. L. Morphine and ethanol: Selective depletion of regional brain calcium. *Science* 186:63-65, 1974.

103. Schulz, R. Control of endorphin/receptor-interaction. *Naunyn-Schmiedeberg's Arch. Pharmacol.* 308:R4, 1979.

104. Seeman, P. The membrane actions of anesthetics and tranquilizers. *Pharmacol. Rev.* 24:583-645, 1972.

105. Seevers, M. H. Morphine and ethanol dependence: A critique of a hypothesis. *Science* 170:1113-1115, 1970.

106. Segal, M., and Bloom, F. E. The action of norepinephrine in the rat hippocampus: II. Activation of the input pathway. *Brain Res.* 72:99-114, 1974.

107. Shani, J., Azov, R., and Weissman, B. A. Enkephalin levels in rat brain after various regimens of morphine administration. *Neurosci. Let.* 12:319-322, 1979.

108. Siggins, G. R. Electrophysiolic assessment of mononucleotides and nucleosides as first and second messengers in the neurol system. In: *Neuronal Information Transfer*, Karlin, A., Tweeyson, V. M. and Vogel, H. J. (eds.). Academic Press: New York, 1978.

109. Siggins, G. R. Cyclic nucleotides in the development of alcohol tolerance and dependence: A commentary. *Drug Alc. Depend.* 4:307-319, 1979.

110. Siggins, G. R., and French, E. Central neurons are depressed by iontophoretic and micropressure application of ethanol and tetrahydropaveroline. *Drug Alc. Depend.* 4:239-243, 1979.

111. Siggins, G. R., Gruol, D. L., Padjen, A. L., and Formans, D. S. Purine and pyrimidine-mononucleotides depolarize neurons of explanted amphibian sympathetic ganglion. *Nature* 270(5634):263-265, 1977.

112. Sinclair, J. D., Adkins, J., and Walker, S. Morphine-induced suppression of voluntary alcohol drinking in rats. *Nature* 246:425-427, 1974.

113. Sjoquist, B., Borg, S., and Kvande, H. Catecholamine derived compounds in urine and cerebrospinal fluid from alcoholics during and after long-standing intoxication. *Subs. Alcohol Act./Mis.* 2(1):63-72, 1981.

114. Smith, S. G., Werner, T. E., and Davis, W. M. Intravenous drug self-administration in rats: Substitution of ethyl alcohol for morphine. *Psychol. Rec.* 25:17-20, 1975.

115. Spoon, J. R., Harden, T. K., Wolfe, B. B., and Molinoff, P. B. β-adrenergic receptor involvement in 6-hydroxydopamine-induced supersensitivity in rat cerebral cortex. *Science* 194:624-626, 1976.

116. Tabakoff, B. Neurochemical aspects of ethanol dependence. In: *Alcohol and Opiates: Neurochemical and Behavioral Mechanisms*, Blum, K. (ed.). Academic Press: New York, 1977.

117. Tabakoff, B., and Hoffman, P. L. Alterations in receptors controlling dopamine synthesis after chronic ethanol ingestion. *J. Neurochem.* 31:1223-1229, 1978.

118. Tabakoff, B., and Hoffman, P. L. Development of functional dependence on ethanol in dopaminergic systems. *J. Pharmacol. Exp. Ther.* 208:216-222, 1979.

119. Tabakoff, B., Hoffman, P. L., and Ritzmann, R. F. Dopamine receptor function after chronic ingestion of ethanol. *Life Sci.* 23:643-648, 1978.

120. Thalland, G. A. *Deranged Memory*. Academic Press: New York, 1965.

121. Ticku, M. K. The effects of acute and chronic ethanol administration and its withdrawal on γ-aminobutyric acid receptor binding in rat brain. *Br. J. Pharmacol.* 70:403-410, 1980.

122. Ticku, M. K., and Olsen, R. W. Interaction of barbiturates with dehydropicrotoxinin binding sites related to the GABA receptor-ionophore systems. *Life Sci.* 22:1643-1652, 1978.

123. Ungar, G., Ungar, A. L., Malin, D. H., and Sarantakis, D. Brain peptides with operate antagonist action: Their possible role in tolerance and dependence. *Psychoneuroendocrinology* 2(1):1-10, 1977.

124. Ungerstedt, U. Postsynaptic supersensitivity after 6-hydroxydopamine-induced degeneration of the nigro-striatal dopamine system. *Act Physiol. Scand. Suppl.* 367:69-93, 1971.

125. Verebey, K., and Blum, K. Alcohol euphoria: Possible mediation via endophinergic mechanisms. *J. Psychedel. Drugs* 11:305-311, 1979.

126. Victor, M., and Adams, R. D. On the etiology of the alcoholic neurologic diseases with special reference to the role of nutrition. *Ann. J. Nutri.* 9:379-397, 1961.

127. Victor, M., Adams, R. D., and Collins, G. H. *The Wernicke-Korsakoff Syndrome.* Davis: Philadelphia, 1971.

128. Volicer, L. GABA levels and receptor binding after acute and chronic ethanol administration. *Brain Res. Bull.* 5(Suppl. 2):809–813, 1980.

129. Walker, D. W., Barnes, D. E., Zornetzer, S. F., Hunter, B. E., and Kubanis, P. Neuronal loss in hippocampus induced by prolonged ethanol consumption in rats. *Science* 209:711–713, 1980.

130. Walker, D. W., and Hunter, B. E. Short-term memory impairment following chronic alcohol consumption in rats. *Neuropsychol.* 15:545–553, 1978.

131. Wesche, D., Hollt, V., and Herz, A. Radioimmunoassy of enkephalins' regional distribution in rat brain after morphine treatment and hypophysectomy. *Naunyn-Schmeideberg's Arch. Pharmacol.* 301:79, 1977.

132. Whitney, G., and Horowitz, G. P. Morphine preference of alcohol-avoiding and alcohol-preferring C57BL mice. *Behav. Genetics* 8:177–182, 1978.

9

ROBIN M. MURRAY, MD, Institute of Psychiatry, London, England
JAMES R. STABENAU, MD, University of Connecticut, Farmington, Connecticut

GENETIC FACTORS IN ALCOHOLISM PREDISPOSITION

RECENTLY THERE HAS been a great deal of interest in the possibility that heredity may contribute to alcoholism. This is not, of course, a new idea. Over a century ago Morel believed that parental drunkenness produced depravity and alcoholic excess in the first generation, with progressively more severe symptoms in subsequent children, until the fourth generation became sterile and the line ceased. By the turn of the century these Lamarckian notions of the inheritance of acquired characteristics had themselves died out, but Clifford Allbutt expressed the general view when he stated, "Drunkenness is most distinctly hereditary. It seems to me to be a very strong hereditary tendency to a special craving" [1].

Such views continued to hold sway and 40 years later Jellinek [12] complained, "The majority of discussions on alcoholism state, without any examination of the evidence, that alcoholism is a product of 'nonspecific heredity.'" Jellinke's searching analysis went to the heart of the matter when he posed the following three questions: (1) Does parental alcoholism cause such damage to the germ cells as to

---

Robin M. Murray, MD, Senior Lecturer, Genetics Section, Institute of Psychiatry, London, England.

James R. Stabenau, MD, Professor of Psychiatry, University of Connecticut, Farmington, Connecticut.

produce defects in the first generation? (2) Does parental alcoholism bring about a true mutation in the offspring? (3) Is there a hereditary liability factor involved in alcoholism?

But even as Jellinek asked these questions the intellectual climate began to change; the answers no longer seemed so pressing and soon genetic theories of alcholism seemed simplistic and old-fashioned. However, a quarter of a century later it is now known that maternal drinking can cause defects in the offspring, and the fetal alcohol syndrome is discussed elsewhere in this volume.

FAMILY STUDIES

The resurgence of interest in Jellinek's third question has its origins in the indisputable evidence that alcoholism is a family disorder. Without exception every study, irrespective of country, has shown higher rates among relatives of alcoholics than occur in the general population. Cotton [6], for instance, evaluated the best of 140 estimates of the familial incidence of alcoholism in the literature. She restricted her analysis to the 39 of the 90 studies in English in which definition of alcoholism, relationship of the family member, sample size, and sex of the subjects were clear. Cotton's review is summarized in Table 1, and it can be seen that on the average 27% of fathers and 5% of mothers of alcoholic probands were themselves alcoholic, rates considerably higher than those of the parents of medical and surgical control subjects. The percentage of brothers of alcoholics who were also alcoholic ranged from 12% to 50%, and that of sisters from 2% to 13%, but this information is less reliable than that for parents because in the majority of cases the siblings had not passed through the age of risk and age correction was not employed.

Among relatives the offspring of alcoholics have been subject to the most intensive scrutiny. The most complete example of this type of study is the work of Rhydelius and his mentor, Nylander. In 1960 Nylander studied 229 children of al-

Table 1
Frequency of Paternal and Maternal Alcoholism in Alcoholics and Controls

	Paternal %	Maternal %
Alcoholics	27.0	4.9
Other psychiatric patients	9.9	1.8
Nonpsychiatric patients	5.2	1.2

Source: Modified from "The Familia Incidence of Alcoholism" by N. S. Cotton, *J. Stud. Alcohol,* 1979, 40:89–115 (a summary of 39 studies).

coholic parents and 163 control children when both groups were aged between 4 and 12 years of age, and 20 years later Rhydelius followed up both groups [16]. The index children had required more social assistance. Furthermore, 35% of the proband boys were registered with the Temperance Board as alcohol abusers compared with only 20% of control boys; the comparable figures for the girls were 6% and 1% respectively. Similarly 42% of the proband boys had a criminal record compared with 25% of the control boys; 6% of both groups of girls had criminal records. The data collected in childhood had, in fact, little predictive power, but boys with aggressive acting-out behavior were more likely to later be registered as having an alcohol problem as were those whose father had had particularly severe alcoholism.

Assortive mating. Of course, the familial aggregation of alcoholism does not imply that any genetic mechanism is operating. It has been pointed out that speaking Chinese also runs in families and this behavior is obviously not inherited. One reason for favoring a similar theory of transmission of alcoholism via family culture is that although the risk for first-degree relatives (e.g., parents and siblings) is over 20%, the risk for grandsons and half-brothers is almost equally high. Most genetic theories would predict that these second-degree relatives should have a lower risk than parents and siblings. Such high risks are only compatible with genetic laws if alcoholics tend to marry individuals who also have a drinking problem. There is, of course, evidence that this occurs. Various studies have suggested that up to 33% of the spouses of alcoholics may also be alcoholic, and perhaps 25% of women married to alcoholics are themselves alcoholic. However, even this degree of assortive mating could not totally explain the high rates in second-degree relatives, so it is likely that familial environmental pressures toward drinking are also operating.

But is this the whole story or is heredity also operating? The two main ways in which researchers may tease apart these factors are via the study of twins and of adoptees. These will now be reviewed.

The Twin Method

The twin method of genetic determination depends on the fact that identical or monozygotic (MZ) twins share their family upbringing and all of their genes whereas familial or dizygotic (DZ) twins share their upbringing but on average only 50% of their genes. If MZ twins are found to be more alike for any given characteristic (e.g., blue eyes) than DZ twins then it is assumed that this is due to their greater genetic similarity.

Alcohol abuse. For a long time the only twin study directed specifically toward abnormal drinking was that of Kaij [13], who studied 174 male twin pairs born in southern Sweden and in whom one or both had been reported to the Temperance Board for alcohol abuse. Kaij classified his twins into five drinking categories, ranging from abstinence to chronic alcoholism, and found that monozygotic (MZ) twin pairs were more likely to fall into the same drinking category than dizygotiz (DZ) pairs. Most interestingly, the MZ concordance increased from 53.5% when all MZ probands were included to 71.4% when only strict concordance for the 14 MZ probands with chronic alcoholism was considered, whereas the DZ concordance rates stayed at roughly the same level (28.3 to 32.3%). On the face of it, therefore, Kaij's findings suggest a considerable genetic contribution to alcohol abuse and particularly to chronic alcoholism.

A second twin study of alcoholism is now underway in London. There, 78 twin probands have been identified who presented to the Maudsley Hospital and so far reliable information has been obtained on 56 of their cotwins. The preliminary pairwise concordance rates are 21% for monozygotic and 25% for dizygotic twins [11]. It is, of course, still possible that eventual findings for all 78 pairs will show slightly higher concordance rates for the MZ twins, but so far these results are clearly at variance with those of Kaij.

Normal drinking. The drinking habits of normal twins have also been examined. Partanen et al. [15] interviewed 902 male twins in Finland, and reported that symptoms that might have been thought to be related to problem drinking — loss of control, drunkenness arrests, and social complications — did not seem to be subject to any genetic predisposition. However, the heritability value for frequency and regularity of drinking was 0.39 and that for amount drunk at a session was 0.36, both figures suggesting a considerable genetic influence.

Similar results have emerged from 494 pairs of normal twins studied at the Institute of Psychiatry in London [4]. Among males genetic factors were of considerable importance in overall consumption levels and in escape and social drinking. Common family environment had its greatest influence on problem drinking and specific environmental factors on the psychological effects of alcohol; this latter is compatible with the observation that the immediate effects of alcohol are to a large extent dependent on the circumstances.

The Adoption Strategy

American studies. The first study of the adopted-away offspring of abnormal drinkers was that of Roe and Burks [17], who compared 36 fostered children whose biological fathers were alcoholics with 25 fostered controls whose biological parents were well adjusted without known history of psychiatric disorder or alcoholism. Data indicated that 10 of the former and only two of the latter got into serious difficulties in adolescence; two of the children with a father who was a heavy drinker and one of the children of normal biological parentage had a drinking problem themselves in adolescence. However, by adulthood these small differences had disappeared.

Roe consequently concluded that "the reported high incidence of inebriety and psychosis in the offspring of alcoholics is not explicable in terms of any hereditary factor" [17]. But, although the study design was far ahead of its time, the execution of that design left a lot to be desired, thus raising questions about how valid Roe's conclusions were.

In a smaller but more recent study from Iowa, Cadoret and Gath [3] compared six adult adoptees who had a biological parent with a drinking problem with 78 adult adoptees whose biological parents had no such history. Two of the former but only one of the latter were blindly diagnosed as definite primary alcoholics. When the criteria were broadened to encompass probable primary alcoholism then the figures were three out of six, and one out of 78. The difference between the two groups for definite alcoholism was significant at about the .03 level, and that for probable alcoholism at the .01 level.

However, the picture changes considerably when one considers secondary alcoholism. Seven adoptees received a secondary diagnosis of definite or probable alcoholism, but all of them came from the group without a biological parent with a drinking problem. Cadoret and Gath [3] interpret their findings as supporting an important genetic contribution to primary but not to secondary alcoholism. These results clearly contradict those of Roe and Burks [17], but can one put any more credence on their positive results than on Roe's negative ones? Probably not, for their sample was very small.

Scandinavian studies. It was, of course, Goodwin and his colleagues [7, 8, 9, 10] who reinvigorated the whole debate about a possible genetic contribution to alcoholism. In their initial investigation these authors reported on 55 Danish male adoptees with an alcoholic biological parent, and on 78 control adoptees without such a history. The former were nearly four times more likely themselves to become alcoholic in adult life (Table 2). Adopted-away sons of alcoholics were then compared with their own brothers who had been raised by the alcoholic biological parent; alcoholism rates were similar in the two groups. Length of exposure to the alcoholic parent was not associated with the development of alcoholism, but the severity of parental alcoholism was positively related to alcoholism in the offspring.

Table 2
Adoptive Study by Goodwin and His Colleagues (in percentages)

	Sons			Daughters		
	Adoptees without a biological parent with alcoholism	Biological parent hospitalized for alcoholism		Adoptees without a biological parent with alcoholism	Biological parent hospitalized for alcoholism	
Diagnosis ($n = 78$)		Adopted ($n = 55$)	Not adopted ($n = 30$)	($n = 47$)	Adopted ($n = 49$)	Not adopted ($n = 81$)
Alcoholism	5	18	17	4	2	3
Depression	20	15	20	15	14	27

Note: Data are based on information from References 6–9.

Adopted-away daughters of alcoholics (49) were then similarly compared to 47 control adoptees. This time 2% of the index adoptees were diagnosed as alcoholic as opposed to 4%, a difference that, although in the opposite direction to that expected, did not reach significance; 3% of nonadopted daughters of alcoholics became alcoholic in later life.

This series of studies is clearly very impressive and obviously points strongly toward a major genetic component toward alcoholism in males though not in females. Indeed Goodwin et al. [10] go so far as to state, "environmental factors contributed little, if anything, to the development of alcoholism in the sons of severe alcoholics in this sample." This statement is, of course, somewhat implausible given that the availability of alcohol is itself an environmental factor.

In 1978 Bohman [2] reported on a large adoption study of alcohol abuse that depended on data from the Swedish Temperance Board. The sample consisted of all 2,324 illegitimate children born in Stockholm between 1930 and 1949 who were later placed in adoptive homes before the age of 3 years. Male adoptees whose mothers or fathers had been registered as alcohol abusers were more likely to themselves be similarly registered.

Then Bohman and his colleagues selected 50 male adoptees whose fathers had been repeatedly registered for alcohol abuse (i.e., they were probably alcoholics) and very carefully matched them with adoptees whose parents had no such history. Bohman found 20% of the former but only 6% of the latter were similarly registered.

Thus this study also suggests a genetic contribution to alcoholism in men, but as in the Goodwin study, when similar analyses were made for female adoptees no evidence in favor of a genetic transmission was apparent. Of course, since alcohol abuse was uncommon among women at the time this study was carried out in Scandinavia, it may have been that the sample was too small to show any significant effect.

HOW MIGHT SUCH AN INFLUENCE BE TRANSMITTED?

One hypothesis suggests the inheritance of a predisposing personality or psychiatric disorder, while a second suggests that some pharmacogenetic mechanism may operate. Antisocial personality and criminality have been repeatedly noted to occur with greater than chance frequency in both alcoholics and their families, and there has been much speculation over whether antisocial personality might be the primary disorder transmitted. This hypothesis has been further elaborated by those who propose that what is inherited is an underlying neurophysiological abnormality that manifests itself as hyperactivity in children and alcoholism and sociopathy in later life. Such a mechanism could at best account for only a small proportion of alcoholism, since only a minority have antisocial personalities or were hyperactive as children. Furthermore, the relatives of probands who have only alcoholism or antisocial personality are at increased risk only for the same illness as the probands. Thus, it seems likely that the genetic contributions to drinking behavior and antisocial traits are independent, but they may interact synergistically with antisocial personality, increasing both the frequency of heavy drinking and the proportion of heavy drinkers who become alcoholic.

Alcoholism and depression also occur more frequently than expected in the same individual and in different members of the same family. There are various ways of explaining this association, but Winokur et al. [19] observed that, regradless of the sex, or primary diagnosis of the proband, alcoholism occurred predominantly in the male relatives, and depression in the female relatives. Furthermore, when alcoholism and depression were considered together, the morbidity in the two sexes was approximately equal. Winokur and his colleagues, therefore, postulated that there exists a hereditary disorder, depressive spectrum disease, that tends to express itself as early-onset depression in women but as alcoholism or antisocial personality in men. However, not only is there a paucity of evidence that antisocial personality and depression are genetically linked, but there is other evidence to suggest that the family association between alcoholism and depression in women is environmentally induced [5]. For instance, Goodwin et al. [9] found that the daughters of alcoholics reared by the alcoholic parent were more prone to depression than daughters fostered-away (Table 2), and suggested that this increase was the consequence of their disadvantaged upbringing.

PHARMACOGENETICS

Pharmacogenetic mechanisms could provide another avenue whereby a predisposition to alcoholism might be transmitted. This subject is reviewed in greater detail elsewhere [14]. The rate at which alcohol is eliminated from the blood shows a surprisingly high degree of heritability and electroencephalographic responses to similar blood alcohol concentrations are strikingly similar in identical twins.

Ethnic Differences

Another approach stems from the wide variations in the frequency of alcoholism in different ethnic groups. These variations could, of course, be a result of cultural differences. However, the fact that over 80% of Orientals exhibit a facial flush and negative feelings after first drinking alcohol has been attributed by some researchers to the possession by a high proportion of Asians of an atypically active variant of alcohol dehydrogenase (ADH). It has been suggested that this atypical ADH produces raised acetaldehyde levels, which cause an Antabuse-like reaction.

Acetaldehyde

Paradoxically, a tendency to produce high levels of acetaldehyde has also been said to predispose toward the development of alcoholism. Schuckit and Rayses [18] gave a challenge dose of alcohol to 20 normal young men with an alcoholic first-degree relative and to 20 control men without such a family history; the experimental subjects developed significantly higher blood acetaldehyde levels than the control subjects. Such high levels could serve as a substrate for condensation with monoamines for the production of potentially addictive tetrahydroisoquinolines.

Numerous attempts have also been made to find a marker gene for alcoholism. Color-blindness, blood group A, salivary secretor status, and low platelet monoamine oxidase have all been associated with alcoholism at one time or another but seem unlikely to be of any major importance. However, the HL-A antigen B-8 has been found to be present with increased frequency in patients with alcoholic cirrhosis, thus suggesting that the livers of certain individuals may be especially sensitive to alcohol-induced damage. Similarly, a minority of those drinking heavily may be especially at risk for the Wernicke-Korsakoff syndrome because of a defect in transketolase. However, all these postulated pharmacogenetic mechanisms remain very provisional.

CONCLUSIONS

In summary, the better of the studies of normal drinking have suggested a modest but significant genetic influence. They cannot by definition throw much light on pathological drinking because of the very normality of their samples. Kaij's work [13] does imply a considerable predisposition to both alcohol abuse and alcoholism, though the latter has not yet been confirmed in the Maudsley twin study. Three of the four adoption studies also implicate genetic factors in male alcoholics. That of Bohman [2] also suggests a hereditary influence on alcohol abuse while that of Goodwin et al. [7] do not. The family, twin, and adoptive studies concur in finding more evidence for male drinking being under genetic influence than female drinking.

One of the reasons why researchers have been slow to elucidate the exact nature of the genetic predisposition is that they have been looking for simple answers. The present evidence is incompatible with simple Mendelian inheritance through a single dominant or recessive gene, and sex-linked inheritance has also been excluded. Any successful etiologic model must obviously take into account environmental factors such as price and availability of alcohol, plus the effects of occupation and family attitudes to alcohol. It is, furthermore, unwise to assume that the same genetic factors contribute to an individual's likelihood of becoming dependent on alcohol as influence, for example, the same individual's chances of committing a crime while drunk. For these reasons polygenic models have been suggested in which multiple genetic factors interact with powerful environmental influences at several different levels [5, 14].

REFERENCES

1. Allbutt, C. A., quoted in Horsley, V., and Sturge, M. D. *Alcohol and the Human Body.* Macmillan: London, 1909.
2. Bohman, M. Some genetic aspects of alcoholism and criminality. *Arch. Gen. Psychiatry* 35:269-276, 1978.
3. Cadoret, R. J., and Gath, A. Inheritance of alcoholism in adoptees. *Br. J. Psychiatry* 132:252-258, 1978.
4. Clifford, C. A., Fulker, D. W., Gurling, H. M. D., and Murray, R. M. Preliminary findings from a twin study of alcohol use. In: *Advances in Twin Research* (Vol. 3), Parisi, P. (ed.). Alan Liss: New York, 1981.
5. Cloninger, C. R., Christiansen, K. O., Reich, T., and Gottesman, I. Implications of sex differences in the prevalences of antisocial personality, alcoholism, and criminality for familial transmission. *Arch. Gen. Psychiatry* 35:941-951, 1978.
6. Cotton, N. S. The familial incidence of alcoholism. *J. Stud. Alcohol* 40:89-115, 1979.
7. Goodwin, D. W., Schulsinger, F., Hermansen, L., Guze, S. B., and Winokur, G. Alcohol problems in adoptees raised apart from alcoholic biological parents. *Arch. Gen. Psychiatry* 28:238-243, 1973.
8. Goodwin, D. W., Schulsinger, F., Knop, J., Mednick, S., and Guze, S. B. Alcoholism and depression in adopted-out daughters of alcoholics. *Arch. Gen. Psychiatry* 34:751-755, 1977.
9. Goodwin, D. W., Schulsinger, F., Knop, J., Mednick, S., and Guze, S. B. Psychopathology in adopted and nonadopted daughters of alcoholics. *Arch. Gen. Psychiatry* 34: 1005-1009, 1977.
10. Goodwin, D. W., Schulsinger, F., Møller, N., Hermansen, L., Winokur, G., and Guze, S. B. Drinking problems in adopted and nonadopted sons of alcoholics. *Arch. Gen. Psychiatry* 31:164-169, 1974.
11. Gurling, H. M. D., Clifford, C. A., and Murray, R. M. Investigations into the genetics of alcohol dependence. In: *Advances in Twin Research* (Vol. 2), Parisi, P. (ed.). Alan Liss: New York, 1981.
12. Jellinek, E. M. Heredity of the alcoholic. In: *Alcohol, Science, and Society* (Yale Summer School on Alcohol Lectures, 1945). Reprinted by Greenwood Press: Westport, Conn., 1972.
13. Kaij, L. *Alcoholism in Twins.* Almqvist & Wiksell: Stockholm, 1960.
14. Murray, R. M., and Gurling, H. M. D. Genetic contributions to normal and abnormal drinking. In: *Psychopharmacology of Alcohol,* Sandler, M. (ed.). Raven Press: New York, 1980.
15. Partanen, J., Bruun, K., and Markkanen, T. *Inheritance of Drinking Behavior.* Finnish Foundation for Alcohol Studies: Helsinki, 1966.
16. Rhydelius, P. A. Children of alcoholic fathers. *Acta Paed. Scand.* (Suppl. 286) 1981.
17. Roe, A., and Burks, B. Adult adjustment of foster children of alcoholic and psychotic

parentage and the influence of the foster home. *Q. J. Stud. Alcohol* 6:127–141, 1945.

18. Schuckit, M. A., and Rayses, V. Ethanol ingestion: Differences in blood acetaldehyde concentrations in relatives of alcoholics and controls. *Science* 203:54–55, 1979.

19. Winokur, G., Rimmer, J., and Reich, T. Alcoholism: IV. Is there more than one type of alcoholism? *Br. J. Psychiatry* 118:525–531, 1970.

Section III

Medical Aspects of Alcoholism

10

EDWARD M. SELLERS, MD, PhD, Addiction Research Foundation and University of Toronto, Toronto, Canada

HAROLD KALANT, MD, PhD, Addiction Research Foundation and University of Toronto, Toronto, Canada

ALCOHOL WITHDRAWAL AND DELIRIUM TREMENS

DEATHS AND SERIOUS morbidity during alcohol withdrawal should be rare. The emphasis on early recognition of the problem, the methods of assessing the patient, and the optimal tactics for drug administration have both simplified and improved treatment to the point where a treatment failure is almost certainly due to delay in therapy, an error of omission or commission, or the severity of the concurrent illness and not alcohol withdrawal per se.

In contrast to the simplification and relative clarity of the clinical management, basic pharmacologic advances concerning the pathophysiology of the syndrome are emphasizing the complexity of the etiology and the empirical basis of clinical treatment. Advances in understanding do, however, suggest new, more specific treatments of alcohol withdrawal may exist.

Edward M. Sellers, MD, PhD, Director and Head of Medicine, Clinical Institute, Addiction Research Foundation, and Professor of Pharmacology and Medicine, University of Toronto, Toronto, Canada.

Harold Kalant, MD, PhD, Associate Director, Biological and Social Studies Division, Addiction Research Foundation, and Professor of Pharmacology, University of Toronto, Toronto, Canada.

In this chapter the pathophysiology and clinical aspects of alcohol withdrawal are reviewed with an emphasis on developments in the past 5 years. Other review articles provide more depth in selected areas [1, 8, 12]. The literature reviewed for the chapter includes citations up to June 30, 1981.

PATHOPHYSIOLOGY

Chronic exposure of excitable cells and tissues to ethanol results in a number of adaptive changes that are temporally correlated with, and, it is presumed, responsible for, the development of tolerance to the continued action of ethanol. Abrupt cessation of ethanol intake leaves these adaptive changes unopposed by the ethanol effect, so that they are maladaptive, giving rise to functional disturbances opposite in direction to those originally produced by intoxication [13]. Thus, physical dependence (as revealed by the withdrawal reaction) is probably another expression of the same cellular alterations that are responsible for tolerance. Acute intoxication produces alterations in various basic functions of neuronal membranes, including excitability, impulse conduction, and neurotransmitter release, as well as in such underlying biochemical properties as lipid structure, Ca^{++} binding, ion fluxes, and membrane-bound enzyme activities. It is not surprising, therefore, that changes have been found in all of these functions and properties of neuronal membranes from tolerant-dependent animals.

The clinical picture of the patient undergoing an alcohol withdrawal reaction is not limited to these changes. A major withdrawal reaction constitutes a severe physical stress, and the stress response may add to, or complicate, the primary withdrawal process. In addition, reduction or cessation of alcohol intake by an alcoholic is often the result of injury, intercurrent illness, or alcohol-related diseases such as gastritis or hepatitis. These factors may also modify or complicate the withdrawal response [1, 2, 5, 8, 12, 14].

Alterations of Neuronal Function

Changes in neuronal membranes. In vivo electrophysiological studies have revealed that ethanol causes both increases and decreases of excitability, spontaneous activity, and neurotransmitter release. The variety of responses probably depends on differences in dose, rate and route of administration, concurrent use of anesthetics and other drugs, and the interplay of direct and indirect effects of ethanol. Single-unit studies, however, suggest that most neurons, regardless of their type, show decreased excitability, impulse conduction, and transmitter release, especially at the high alcohol concentrations that would be produced in alcoholics. This decrease may be due, in part, to alcohol potentiation of the inhibitory effect of gamma-amino-butyric acid (GABA) on many neurons, but it also reflects direct effects of ethanol on the neuronal membrane, including fluidization of the lipid layers, blockage of Na^+ conductance channels, and displacement of membrane-bound Ca^{++}.

As might be anticipated, adaptive changes provoked by chronic ethanol exposure include changes in lipid composition, which make the membrane more resistant to fluidization; facilitation of ion flux in relation to the action potential; increased Ca^{++} binding sites and more bound calcium. These changes in membrane structure also alter the activity of various membrane-bound enzymes that play major roles in the regulation of neuronal function.

The activity of $(Na^+ + K^+)$-activated adenosinetriphosphatase (ATPase), the enzyme essential for active transport of Na^+ and K^+, catecholamines, various amino acids, and other important cellular constituents, is inhibited acutely by ethanol, and is increased in the alcohol withdrawal reaction. As a result corresponding changes occur in cation transport. Adenylate cyclase and guanylate cyclase are also affected similarly. Since cyclic-AMP (c-AMP) appears to be necessary for neurotransmitter release, changes in cyclic nucleotide levels may explain, in part, the increased release during the withdrawal reaction.

The consequences of these membrane changes are increased neuronal excitability, increased spontaneous and evoked activity, and the ability to sustain this markedly increased activity for long periods. The alcohol withdrawal reaction is therefore characterized by hyperacuity of all sensory modalities, hyperactivity of reflexes, muscular tension and tremor, overalertness, anxiety, insomnia, and reduced seizure threshold.

Possible role of aldehyde-amine condensation products. Ethanol is oxidized to acetaldehyde, which at sufficiently high concentration can inhibit the oxidation of aldehydes formed by deamination of serotonin, noradrenaline, and dopamine. Acetaldehyde itself, as well as these "biogenic aldehydes," can condense with the parent amines to form Schiff bases, which can undergo further modification to yield a variety of alkaloid materials. Some of these have significant pharmacologic activity, and it has been suggested that they may mediate the production of physical dependence by ethanol. However, there is virtually no evidence to support this suggestion.

Possible roles of other neurotransmitters. Decreased release of various neurotransmitters, as in denervation, may lead to compensatory increases in number or binding affinity of the postsynaptic receptors for those transmitters. There is some evidence that ethanol decreases the synaptic release of catecholamines at various sites in the central nervous system (CNS), and that chronic ethanol exposure results in a compensatory increase in postsynaptic binding of noradrenaline and dopamine. When catecholamine release returns to, or above, normal levels during alcohol withdrawal, the increased binding to their receptors could explain some of the physiological signs or exaggerated central autonomic activity seen in the later phase of severe withdrawal reactions. These signs include tachycardia, sweating, and elevation of body temperature, which may be so severe as to resemble thyroid storm.

Relation of withdrawal severity to preceding alcohol intake. Animal studies have shown a clear relation between the severity of the withdrawal reaction and both the intensity and duration of the preceding alcohol exposure. It is more difficult to establish this relationship clinically, but experiments with human volunteers have given results that are generally consistent with those of the animal studies. Ingestion of 442 g ethanol a day for about 2 months results in a major withdrawal syndrome in all subjects whereas ingestion of between 280 g to 377 g a day for 5 to 10 days results in a mild syndrome of anxiety and tremor. Such a relationship is to be expected if the severity of the withdrawal reaction is an expression of the degree of adaptive change to the preceding alcohol-induced functional disturbance.

Stress Factors in the Withdrawal Reaction

A second component of the alcohol withdrawal reaction is the physiological response to the nonspecific stress of the primary hyperexcitability phenomena resulting from neuronal adaptive changes. Plasma and urinary catecholamine and corticosteroid levels are increased during severe intoxication, but return toward normal as tolerance develops. After withdrawal of the alcohol, however, a second rise in levels occurs. While this rise is due to the stress of the withdrawal response, it may actually aggravate some of the withdrawal symptoms such as tremor, tachycardia, sweating, and elevation of temperature. Such an effect would be synergistic with that of induction of central catecholamine receptors (see above).

In human subjects undergoing alcohol withdrawal, there is usually a loss of previously accumulated excess body fluid, and this is generally accompanied by excessive renal loss of Mg^{++}, Zn^{++}, and other electrolytes. The Mg^{++} loss may be exaggerated by elevation of plasma pH, produced by hyperventilation and consequent reduction of pCO_2. The hyperventilation may represent a rebound reaction from ethanol-induced suppression of respiratory depth and frequency (i.e., a part of the primary hyperexcitability pattern) or it may constitute part of the nonspecific stress response to withdrawal. In either case, the resulting hypomagnesemia and fall in ionized Ca^{++} have been implicated in the muscular twitching and seizure activity seen in severe withdrawal reactions.

Role of Precipitating Disease

Since the withdrawal reaction may be precipitated by interruption of alcohol intake because of disease or injury, it is not surprising that the withdrawal picture may include elements of the precipitating disease. For example, patients with pneumonia may well have a much higher fever than would be expected from the withdrawal reaction alone. Similarly, a patient who has stopped drinking because of persistent vomiting is at greater risk of systemic alkalosis, because of the combination of vomiting and withdrawal hyperventilation, and may therefore show a greater incidence of myoclonus or seizures.

MAJOR AND MINOR WITHDRAWAL

Usual Clinical Presentations

Early minor withdrawal. The severity of the early alcohol withdrawal reaction (see Table 1) varies with both the intensity and duration of the preceding alcohol exposure; hence, it is quite variable among patients. The earliest symptoms reported by patients are insomnia, early morning waking, vivid dreaming, and of course hangover. This symptomatology appears to coincide with the rapid elimination of ethanol. The mild reaction is characterized by anxiety, mild agitation, anorexia, tremor, sleeplessness, mild tachycardia (< 100) and hypertension (< 150/90). It can appear within a few hours after cessation of drinking and is usually gone after 48 hours. Most such withdrawal requires no specific pharmacotherapy. The occurrence of such symptoms indicates persistent ethanol consumption in excess of 150 to 200 g a day.

Late major withdrawal (delirium tremens). In severe reactions, however, these initial symptoms are gradually followed by increasing psychomotor, speech,

Table 1
Clinical Features of Minor and Major Alcohol Withdrawal

	Early or Minor Withdrawal	Late or Major Withdrawal or Delirium Tremens
Symptoms	Mild agitation Anxiety Restlessness Tremor Anorexia Insomnia	Extreme overactivity (speech, psychomotor, autonomic) Disorientation Confusion Disordered sensory perception
Timing Postethanol	0–48 hours	24–150 hours
Peak	24–36 hours	72–96 hours
Severity	Mild	Potentially life-threatening
Seizures	Yes, 12–60 hours	No

and autonomic overactivity, disorientation, confusion, and disordered auditory or visual sensory perception. Disorientation and confusion are the essential hallmarks of delirium tremens (DTs). Seizures may occur in patients who do not progress to a major withdrawal reaction, but they precede such a reaction in 97% of cases. The severity and risk of the syndrome are increased by delay in recognition, and the presence of concurrent medical or surgical illnesses (e.g., fever, infection, malnutrition, dehydration, or hypovolemia, acid-base and electrolyte abnormalities, trauma, hemorrhage, cardiac disease, etc.). Fever over 104°F (40°C), malnutrition, and fluid and electrolyte disturbances are associated with a risk of developing major withdrawal signs (DTs).

Less than 5% of hospitalized patients in alcohol withdrawal develop a major reaction. Early reports estimated the mortality of such a reaction at above 40%. More recently, estimates of 5 to 15% and 18.5% have been suggested. However, the mortality rate is now much lower in most centers, probably because of improved supportive therapy of the coexisting medical complications of alcohol withdrawal. The patients at greatest risk of severe or fatal withdrawal reactions are those over 45 years of age and those with serious medical complications. In the few deaths that still do occur, delayed diagnosis, inadequate initial therapy, uncertainty about drug dose adjustment, and unrecognized concurrent disease are often apparent. Since these problems are amenable to careful clinical monitoring and standardization of pharmacotherapy, the mortality should be reducible to that of any coexistent medical or surgical problem.

Atypical Presentations

While typically several components of the mild or severe reaction are present, occasional patients may present with only a single prominent clinical finding (e.g., seizure, severe tremor, cardiac arrhythmia, hallucination, internuclear opthalmoplegia, confusion, etc.). Since some symptomatology may be delayed for 7 to 14 days, accurate diagnosis may be further confounded. Occurrence of these clinical features in isolation should always raise the possibility of alcohol as a primary or comorbid factor.

PROTRACTED ALCOHOL WITHDRAWAL REACTION

It has been suggested that physical dependence on ethanol takes considerably longer to disappear than might be expected from the rather short duration of the overt withdrawal reaction. According to this suggestion, subclinical degrees of dependence might persist for periods of months or longer, and constitute a source of discomfort that could lead the patient to resume drinking. This concept actually is derived from opiate research in which naloxone has been shown to be able to evoke an aversive state in rats for up to 30 days or more after the disappearance of other signs of morphine withdrawal. Unfortunately there is no pharmacologic tool analogous to naloxone that permits one to provoke an alcohol withdrawal reaction, and there is no method of demonstrating physical dependence on alcohol other than the spontaneous occurrence of a withdrawal reaction.

There are several types of evidence for a protracted alcohol abstinence syndrome. In human subjects, sleep electroencephalograph studies have demonstrated continued disturbance of sleep phases in alcoholics for 30 days or longer after the last ingestion of alcohol. In rats, studies of auditory-evoked brain stem potentials and visually evoked cortical potentials have indicated persistence of hyperexcitability of the CNS for as long as 4 to 8 weeks after withdrawal of chronic ethanol intubation. These changes are suggestive of slow disappearance of physical dependence but they do not prove it conclusively. Since they are rather nonspecific, they might be produced by other factors: In humans, for example, sleep disturbances might reflect emotional and other problems related to drug-free existence, rather than physical dependence on ethanol. Therefore, the existence of a protracted alcohol withdrawal reaction remains uncertain.

Probably the main reason for clinical interest in the concept of a protracted alcohol withdrawal reaction is the risk of relapse of drinking because of the occurrence of withdrawal-like symptoms (dry shakes), in the absence of preceding drinking bouts. Animal studies have shown that some components of the withdrawal reaction, such as hyperthermia, can become conditioned responses to stimuli previously associated with the administration of ethanol. Therefore it would be quite possible for these conditioned responses to be evoked by the same stimuli in the absence of ethanol, long after the physical dependence has disappeared.

TREATMENT

The objectives of therapy in minor and major alcohol withdrawal reactions are relief of subjective symptoms, prevention or treatment of the more serious complications, such as seizures and arrhythmias, and preparation for long-term rehabilitation with minimal hazard of new dependence problems or direct toxicity related to the drug therapy. These conditions apply to both hospital and outpatient management. To these considerations might also be added the therapeutic objectives that optimal treatment should be standardized, humane, as simple and economic as possible, and that it have a pharmacokinetic and pharmacodynamic rationale. (See Figure 1.)

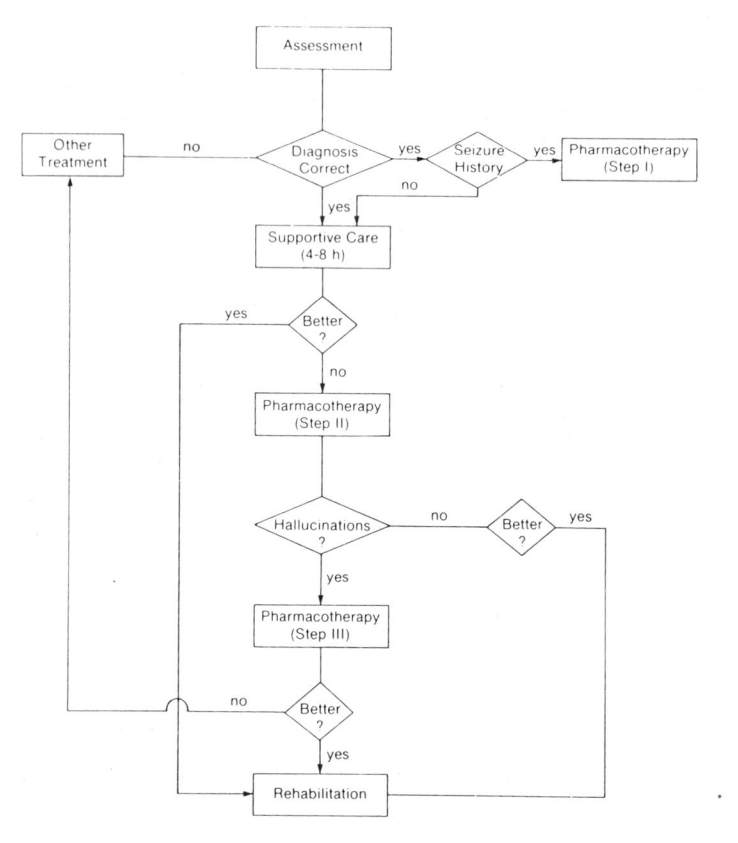

Figure 1. Step Care Plan of Alcohol Withdrawal (see also Tables 5 and 6)

A recent chart audit has confirmed a widely held impression that patients in withdrawal have many changes in pharmacotherapy (with respect to drug, dose, interval, route, etc.) regardless of the severity of the withdrawal reaction [9].

Assessment

All patients with severe withdrawal reactions, or with medical or surgical complications, should be hospitalized. Table 2 summarizes other criteria for hospitalization. Irrespective of whether the patient will be admitted or not, an appropriate history and physical and laboratory examination are mandatory because of the multisystem effects of alcohol.

Gross developed a 32-item Total Severity Assessment Scale to quantitate the severity of withdrawal. Eleven items found to be those most highly correlated with clinical judgment of withdrawal severity made up a subscale called the Selected Severity Assessment Scale (SSA). In the SSA, a numeric value was assigned to the signs and symptoms of heart rate, body temperature, convulsions, tremor, sweating, agitation, eating disturbances, clouding of sensorium, hallucinations, and quality of contact. This scale has been further modified so that it can be applied every 30 minutes and can be used to follow the clinical course of the withdrawal reaction. This modified scale is referred to as the Clinical Institute Withdrawal Assessment for Alcohol (CIWA-A). This modification has been extensively tested for reliability (interrater reliability linear $r = 0.94$), validity (comparison to physician global scores of severity $F = 4.6, p < 0.025$), and objective measure of tremor (linear $r = 0.92$) and has been successfully used in experimental research studies and the management of inpatient and emergency room patients. The CIWA-A is used to quantify the initial severity of patient symptoms and subsequent changes associated with treatment [8, 9].

Once nurses are familiar with its use they become aware of the symptoms that make up the alcohol withdrawal syndrome. With this clear delineation of symptoms, rather than global identification of the syndrome or unawareness of the

Table 2
Indications for Hospitalization of Withdrawing Alcoholic

Presence of medical or surgical condition requiring immediate investigation or treatment
    Hepatic decompensation
    Infection
    Dehydration
    Malnutrition
    Fever > 38.5 °C
    Ataxia
    Nystagmus
    Internuclear opthalmoplegia (Wernicke's encephalopathy)

Evidence of moderate-severe withdrawal
    Hallucinations
    Tachycardia > 110 per minute
    Severe tremor
    Extreme agitation
    History of severe withdrawal symptoms
    Confusion or delirium
    Recent seizure or past history of seizure during withdrawal
    Recent history of head injury with loss of consciousness
    Concurrent abuse of barbiturates
    Failure to respond to emergency room supportive care and/or chlordiazepoxide 100 mg per os or diazepam 20 mg per os
    Social factors (e.g., isolation)

syndrome, nurses are better able to plan nursing care for their patients and to evaluate the effect of their care.

Supportive Care

Reassurance, reality orientation, frequent monitoring of signs and symptoms, personal attention, and general supportive care have been found by Whitfield et al. [13] (in outpatients) and Toshney [11] to be effective in over 66% of patients in a mild alcohol withdrawal reaction. A recent study [9] examining moderate to severe withdrawal in hospitalized chronic alcoholics without serious concurrent medical problems found that standardized and systematized supportive nursing care was effective in symptom reduction and prevention of progression to a major reaction in 56% of patients within 4 hours and 74% of patients within 8 hours [9, 10]. In the emergency room, in excess of 85% of patients respond to supportive care [4]. Supportive care can reduce symptoms rapidly and often dramatically. Undoubtedly this component of care accounts for the success of acupuncture and many other maneuvers in withdrawal treatment. The response of patients to nonpharmacologic management raises major problems in the interpretation of most studies of drug treatment of alcohol withdrawal since patients in such studies never undergo a preliminary period of supportive care and always receive such care concurrent with drugs. Incorporation of this treatment procedure into studies would ensure that only patients requiring pharmacotherapy actually participate in a drug trial. The identification of patients not responding to supportive care would remove the need to include a placebo comparison group, but would substitute another problem — only 25% of patients in withdrawal would be eligible for such pharmacotherapy trials!

For ethical reasons, no proof that supportive care prevents progression to delirium tremens is possible. Unfortunately, no patient characteristics predict responsiveness to supportive care [10].

General Pharmacotherapy

Multivitamin preparations are commonly given, although their value is unproven. However, sixth cranial nerve paresis can be reversed dramatically by as little as 2 mg of thiamine given intravenously. Typically, doses of 50 to 100 mg are given intramuscularly or slowly intravenously. There is no evidence to justify the routine daily administration of thiamine, but it is harmless to give at least a single dose to all hospitalized alcoholics. In patients receiving intravenous glucose, thiamine should be given to avoid unmasking a relative thiamine deficiency.

Hydration may be required, although overhydration is more typically present in milder cases of withdrawal. Replacement of potassium is indicated in hypokalemic patients with weakness or cardiac arrhythmias, and those receiving digitalis glycosides. Total body magnesium is usually decreased in alcoholics in withdrawal. Although intravenous or intramuscular administration of magnesium may suppress withdrawal seizures, cardiac arrhythmias, and tremor, other drugs also are effective in these respects and probably less toxic.

Specific Pharmacotherapy

In the past 25 years, over 140 different drugs and drug combinations have been described for the treatment of alcohol withdrawal. This topic has been reviewed in detail in the past 5 years [1, 8]. Undoubtedly the most widely used "treatment" for withdrawal symptoms is more alcohol, but this is inappropriate because alcohol has direct toxicity to heart, liver, and brain, has a short duration of action, inhibits drug biotransformation, and perpetuates the many existing metabolic disturbances. Other time-honored remedies include various barbiturates, paraldehyde, and chloral hydrate; however, there are very few controlled trials of their efficacy in comparison with placebo or supportive therapy, or with each other. The rationale for their use (cross-tolerance with alcohol) is scientifically sound and there can be no doubt of their effectiveness. Nevertheless, they have been largely replaced by the benzodiazepines (see Tables 3 and 4).

Effective doses of benzodiazepines cause unwanted drowsiness less frequently than equivalent doses of barbiturates or meprobamate. Benzodiazepines do not cause enzyme induction and have a lower potential to produce physical dependence and tolerance. All proprietary benzodiazepines are relatively expensive.

Table 3
Pharmacokinetic Characterization of Benzodiazepines

Type I
　Prodrug (i.e., active metabolites)
　Long half-life
　Biotransformation susceptible to inhibitors (e.g., ethanol, disulfiram, oral contraceptives) and inducers (e.g., smoking) of mixed function oxidase enzymes; impaired by severe liver disease
　a. Slow conversion to active metabolites
　b. Fast conversion to active metabolites

Type II
　Inactive metabolites
　Shorter half-life
　Biotransformation not as susceptible to inhibitors, inducers, or liver disease

Type III
　Inactive metabolites
　Very short half-life

Table 4
Pharmacokinetics of Benzodiazepines

Type	Pharmacokinetic Features
I. A. Slow conversion to active metabolite	
chlordiazepoxide	parent compound t½, 12 to 20 hours, active metabolite 20 to 30 hours; slow systemic bioavailability after I.M. injection; peak blood level 2 hours after oral administration
diazepam	parent compound t½ 20 to 200 hours, active metabolite 50 hours; good I.M. absorption; peak blood level 1 hour after per os administration
B. Rapid conversion to active metabolite	
desmethyldiazepam (in prodrug form as chlorazepate, prazepam, fosazepam)	t½, 50 hours; no parenteral form; peak blood levels 2 to 3 hours after per os administration
desalkylflurazepam (in prodrug form as flurazepam)	t½, 50 hours; no parenteral form; peak blood levels 2 to 4 hours after per os administration
II. Slow conversion to inactive metabolite	
lorazepam	t½, 12 to 20 hours; good intramuscular bioavailability; peak blood levels 1 hour after per os administration
oxazepam; also in rapid conversion (prodrug form as temazepam)	t½, 6 to 10 hours; no parenteral form; peak blood levels 2 to 4 hours after per os administration
III. Triazolam	t½, 2 to 3 hours; rapid absorption; peak blood levels 0.5–1.0 hour after per os administration

The search for an ideal agent for the treatment of alcohol withdrawal is pointless since all agents can be ineffective or toxic in some circumstances. The benzodiazepines combine at least equal efficacy to other agents in treatment of most of the symptoms, with superior anticonvulsant activity and lesser toxicity than phenothiazines, barbiturates, and paraldehyde.

Antihistamines. Most antihistamines (e.g., diphenhydramine, hydroxyzine) have CNS depressant properties. Therefore they have occasionally been used for the treatment of anxiety, insominia, and alcohol withdrawal syndrome. A review of all studies with hydroxyzine suggests that treatment with the drug may be associated with increased numbers of seizures, more symptoms in withdrawal, and progression to delirium tremens. Other studies suggest that hydroxyzine is as efficacious as chlordiazepoxide, chlorpromazine, and mesoridazine but less than haloperidol. The efficacy of hydroxyzine as an anxiolytic is not established. Furthermore, particularly in older patients, higher dosage may cause anticholinergic toxicity, similar to atropine and scopolamine poisoning (i.e., dry mouth, urinary retention, constipation, confusion, delirium, hallucinations, tachycardia). The central anticholinergic effects may be indistinguishable from the confusion of severe alcohol withdrawal reactions. There is no evidence to justify use of antihistamines in alcohol withdrawal.

Barbiturates. Animal studies and a limited number of human studies indicate that barbital, amobarbital, and other barbiturates can control the alcohol withdrawal reaction. However, the abuse and dependence liability and narrow margin of safety of the shorter acting barbiturates preclude their use. On the other hand, further study with phenobarbital seems warranted since a very similar clinical condition, barbiturate withdrawal, is treated very effectively and safely with this drug [3, 6].

Benzodiazepines. Numerous benzodiazepine derivatives, including alprazolam, bromazepam, chlordiazepoxide, chlorazepate, clobazam, diazepam, lorazepam, oxazepam, and flurazepam have been used in the treatment of alcohol withdrawal reactions. There is no evidence of superiority of any one benzodiazepine over the others for this purpose. Approximate equivalent doses for the benzodiazepines relative to chlordiazepoxide 100 mg are diazepam 20 mg, oxazepam 120 mg, and lorazepam 5 mg. Most studies have been done with chlordiazepoxide. It is more effective than a placebo or no drug therapy in decreasing anxiety, restlessness, tremor, seizure frequency, and development of DTs. In effective dosages chlordiazepoxide is at least as effective as promazine, chlorpromazine, perphenazine, and paraldehyde chloral hydrate in controlling various system manifestations of withdrawal. Benzodiazepines are superior to phenothiazines in the prevention of seizure activity during withdrawal. Intravenous diazepam is effective in the control of continuous seizure activity during withdrawal.

Both chlordiazepoxide and diazepam are long-acting drugs with pharmacologically active metabolites. Repeated daily administration at constant dosage results in cumulation of the parent compound and/or metabolites in the body. Desired therapeutic and unwanted toxic effects therefore may not appear until after several days of continuous therapy [8]. Similar cumulation will occur with prazepam or chlorazepate, which are biotransformed to desmethyldiazepam, the same pharmacologically active long half-life metabolite formed after diazepam administration.

Some drowsiness may be a desirable therapeutic goal, but if dosages are not adjusted carefully excessive drowsiness, lethargy, ataxia, diplopia, and confusion may occur. Respiratory depression and increased risk of aspiration are hazards to be avoided. Excessive CNS depression is usually preventable by individual adjustment of dosage to the clinical state of the patient. To circumvent the consequences of cumulation kinetics, doses should be reduced progressively. Larger doses of diazepam or chlordiazepoxide should be given on the first day of treatment. Typically, multiple doses of diazepam 20 to 40 mg or chlordiazepoxide 100 to 400 mg are given until the patient has settled. Occasionally initial doses of chlordiazepoxide as high as 1,600 mg may be required. Lower dosages are given daily thereafter and can be tapered at a rate of about 25% of the initial dose a day. Because of important variability both in the severity of withdrawal symptoms and in metabolic disposition of the therapeutic agents, it is unwise to adhere strictly to standard or routine dosage schedules. These are likely to cause toxicity or ineffective treatment in many cases.

Chlordiazepoxide is slowly absorbed from intramuscular injection sites. When a rapid and consistent clinical effect is required the per os or intravenous routes of administration are preferred. Alternately, diazepam or lorazepam could be given intramuscularly. Interestingly, lorazepam is rapidly absorbed after sublingual administration and this route may be considered in the nauseated patient. A recent study has shown that lorazepam given sublingually can increase only slightly the rate of clinical improvement of nonhospitalized patients in withdrawal compared to placebo [4]. Higher doses of benzodiazepines may be required in patients who smoke heavily. Lower dosages might be anticipated in patients with severe liver disease (e.g., biopsy-proven cirrhosis) since chlordiazepoxide and diazepam are metabolized more slowly in cirrhotics. In contrast, the metabolism of oxazepam and lorazepam is not affected. With careful clinical titration of dose, unrecognized changes in biotransformation should not pose a problem.

The usual tapering dose approach to treating alcohol withdrawal has been further simplified in several recent studies [9, 10]. The tactic of this simplification consists of a loading dose of drug and taking advantage of the pharmacokinetic tapering afforded by diazepam's long half-life (40 hours) and active metabolites. The clinical course of 10 patients in severe withdrawal failing to respond to supportive care was documented by the CIWA-A. Eight patients, six men and two women, were treated with single intravenous loading doses of diazepam, and two patients with oral diazepam 20 mg q.l.h. Diazepam was infused at the rate of 0.34 mg/min (20 mg/hr.) until the patient was clinically asymptomatic. The mean duration of the infusion was 2.9 hr. (range 0.75-4.7 hr.) and the range of diazepam does was 15 to 94 mg (0.8-1.6 mg/kg). The median terminal phase elimination half-life, $t_{1/2}(\beta)$, for total diazepam was 26.7 hr. (range 14.7-69.5 hr.). All patients responded and none required additional drug. A subsequent controlled study indicated that 20 mg q.2.h. per os is also effective [10]. Typically 40 to 60 mg of diazepam is needed. Both of the noted studies were characterized by extremely careful and systematic patient assessment and monitoring using standardized clinical assessment instruments.

Diazepam, because of its pharmacokinetic properties, is one of the best drugs for treatment of alcohol withdrawal. Peak blood levels are reached quickly, ensuring a large amount of the drug is available when the target symptoms are more severe. Additionally, because of the drug's long half-life, a continued high blood level of the drug is maintained, making additional doses unnecessary when a large enough initial loading dose has been given. Thus this single loading dose treatment reduces the uncertainty of further pharmacotherapy. Patients do not have drug-seeking behavior reinforced, as is the case when a drug is given on a p.r.n. basis in divided doses over several days (see Table 5).

Beta-blockers. The hyperadrenergic manifestations of withdrawal reactions suggest that nonselective beta-blockers (e.g., propranolol) might be a useful therapeutic agent in withdrawal. Intravenous (0.5 mg) and per os (40 mg/day) propranolol decrease alcoholic withdrawal tremor. In a randomized double-blind controlled trial propranolol 10 mg q.6.h. and mg. q.6.h. decreased symptoms of tremor and urinary and plasma catecholamine levels during alcohol withdrawal to an extent equal to chlordiazepoxide 25 mg. q.6.h. and significantly more than placebo. Another study showed that propranolol 40 mg. q.6.h. decreased arrhythmias in alcohol withdrawal. It is important to note in this study that 5 of 15 patients receiving propranolol developed parahallucinatory side effects.

While propranolol can be used in patients with severe withdrawal tremor or cardiac arrhythmias associated with withdrawal, the limitation of the drug's use to patients without a history of bronchospasm, cardiomyopathy, or congestive failure, coupled with an apparent enhancement of the risk of hallucinations, limits the usefulness of the drug. Selective beta-blockers that do not enter the central nervous system are worthy of study.

Chlormethiazole. Chlormethiazole has been widely used in Europe and elsewhere for treatment of the alcohol withdrawal syndrome, but is not marketed in North America. Controlled studies have shown it to be superior to placebo, chlordiazepoxide, trifluoperazine, and piracetam and equal in efficacy to amobarbital. It clearly has sedative-hypnotic properties of the alcohol-barbiturate type. The chemical similarity of the drug to thiamine (vitamin B) seems unrelated to its clinical efficacy.

Table 5
Benzodiazepine Drug-Dosing Options

Four-day dosing tapering	Day 1	Day 2	Day 3	Day 4
Diazepam	20 mg q.6.h.	20 mg q.8.h.	20 mg q.12.h.	20 mg h.s.
Chlordiazepoxide	100 mg q.6.h.	100 mg q.8.h.	100 mg q.12.h.	100 mg h.s.

Multiple loading dose
   Unit dose, Chlordiazepoxide, 100 mg q.h.2 until mildly sedated; Diazepam, 20 mg q.h.1-2 until mildly sedated

Constant intravenous infusion
   Diazepam 20 mg intravenously; constant infusion until mildly sedated

Other observations of concern include reports of several deaths, addiction, and of marked changes in pharmacokinetics in liver disease and by alcohol. The drug may be given by intravenous infusion, which can be associated with phlebitis and, in large doses, hemolysis. Notwithstanding the popularity of this drug, its superiority on pharmacokinetic and safety grounds is not clearly established.

Lithium. Lithium carbonate, 0.3 g every 8 hours, significantly diminishes subjective symptoms of mild withdrawal and normalizes performance on a motor tracking task. Patients who had started lithium while drinking ethanol improved most, probably because it takes more than 3 days for lithium concentrations to plateau in the blood. These observations are of interest from a pathophysiologic point of view since lithium may be an inhibitor of the ethanol-induced increases of Na^+-K^+ ATPase observed in ethanol dependent animals. In clinical use, however, lithium has a narrow margin of safety and its use should be confined to chronic alcoholics with a proven manic-depressive illness.

Paraldehyde. Formerly a mainstay for the treatment of alcohol withdrawal, paraldehyde has been largely eclipsed by newer agents with wider margins of safety and better known pharmacokinetics.

Paraldehyde is a short-acting sedative-hypnotic that shows cross-tolerance with alcohol and is more effective alone or when combined with chloral hydrate than placebo in the treatment of alcohol withdrawal, but it is not more effective than barbiturates, phenothiazines, or benzodiazepine derivatives.

Paraldehyde is less effective and more toxic than diazepam. Despite its effectiveness, paraladehyde has important disadvantages that should discourage its use. Paraldehyde is available only as a liquid of which 10 to 15 ml constitute an effective dose. Intramuscular injection of this volume is painful and may be associated with severe local reaction or the formation of sterile abscesses after repeated use. Intravenous administration is dangerous if given too rapidly. Oral or rectal administration of paraldehyde is effective but is often impractical in the agitated alcoholic. Rectal administration may be unpleasant for the patient, and may result in severe proctitis or in an unacceptable delay in onset of pharmacologic effect. Despite the strong odor of paraldehyde on the breath of patients, little of the drug is eliminated by this route; most is biotransformed by the liver. The drug may be hepatotoxic, and its elimination may be slowed in severe hepatic disease.

The combination of chloral hydrate-paraldehyde has been advocated and is effective against seizures, but it cannot be compared with chlordiazepoxide or diazepam in patients requiring parenteral since chloral hydrate cannot be given parenterally.

Phenothiazines. Results from studies comparing phenothiazines to each other or to other drugs are conflicting and no clear superiority of any particular phenothiazine emerges. While the phenothiazines appear to be as effective as chlordiazepoxide, paraldehyde, hydroxyzine, and chlormethiazole for control of selected symptoms and signs of withdrawal, they do not appear to prevent the progression to DTs, and in general their potential for serious side effects far outweighs their therapeutic benefit in alcohol withdrawal reactions. Aliphatic side chain phenothiazines (e.g., promazine, chlorpromazine) are potent sedatives, but all have alpha-adrenergic blocking activity resulting occasionally in profound or even fatal hypotension and are associated with an increased frequency of seizures in withdrawal. Piperazine phenothiazines (e.g., trifluoperazine) and butyrophenones (e.g., haloperidol) cause less hypotension but also are less effective sedatives and may produce extrapyramidal motor disturbances (acute dystonic reactions such as oculogyric crises). All these agents impair thermoregulation. Several well-done studies and numerous less well-controlled ones indicate an increased number of seizures in patients receiving promazine or chlorpromazine and an increased risk of postural hypotension in patients receiving promazine. These observations are predictable since phenothiazines lower the seizure threshold and reversibly block peripheral alpha-receptors. The vast array of neuroendocrine, dermatological, and hematological side effects are additional reasons why these drugs should not be used, since equally efficacious and less toxic agents are available.

The butyrophenone antipsychotic drugs (e.g., haloperidol) cause less sedation or hypotension and are preferred for control of hallucinations in withdrawal. Benzodiazepines are not effective in this respect. Haloperidol (2 to 5 mg intramuscularly) is dramatically effective in controlling severe agitation, thought disorders, and hallucinatory and parahallucinatory problems in alcohol withdrawal. Since haloperidol decreases seizure threshold in animals, it is not unexpected that in mice made physically dependent on alcohol haloperidol significantly enhanced convulsive scores. Patients who receive haloperidol should also receive chlordiazepoxide or diazepam concurrently, in part to offset any increased risk of seizures. Newer drugs (e.g., trazodone), despite some specificity of action with respect to blockage of serotonin uptake, also cause postural hypotension and hence are not likely to be therapeutic advances in the context of withdrawal.

Seizures in Alcohol Withdrawal

Seizures during alcohol withdrawal reactions are typically grand mal, nonfocal, one or two in number, and are most likely to occur between 31 and 48 hours after cessation of drinking. They clearly require treatment if they are repeated, continuous, or life-threatening. The therapeutic and prophylactic value of diphenylhydantoin in alcohol withdrawal seizures is uncertain.

In most patients without a previous history of seizures, benzodiazepines alone probably have sufficient anticonvulsant activity to prevent withdrawal seizures. However, in patients with a previous history of withdrawal seizures a better result may be obtained when a benzodiazepine (e.g., chlordiazepoxide up to 400 mg daily) is combined with diphenylhydantoin 100 mg t.i.d. than with a placebo. Some studies, including some in laboratory animals, however, have indicated that phenytoin is relatively ineffective against alcohol withdrawal seizures. The contradictory findings possibly arise from the indiscriminate inclusion in the reported studies of patients with preexisting convulsive disease, those with a previous history of withdrawal seizures only, and those with no previous seizures.

Phenytoin. Since diphenylhydantoin is poorly absorbed after intramuscular injection, it should be given per os or intravenously. It is more effective when a loading dose of 10 mg/kg is infused intravenously at a rate of 50 mg a minute and followed by maintenance doses of 300 to 400 mg daily. For simplicity, a total loading dose of 1.0 g can be given and will be effective and safe in most patients except those whose weight is less than 50 kg.

Phenytoin seems to be effective at serum concentrations of only 3 to 5 mg/l in alcohol withdrawal, whereas concentrations of 10 to 20 mg/l are required for optimal control of idiopathic epilepsy. Phenytoin disposition is highly variable in chronic alcoholics. Steady state blood levels vary ninefold and are low because drug clearance is increased in these patients. The estimated drug half-life is only 7.4 hours (cf. normals 20 hr.). Therefore, to achieve drug concentrations of 10 to 20 mg/l the daily maintenance dose may need to be as high as 1,000 mg [6].

Sodium valproate. Dipropylacetate is an eight-carbon branch chain fatty acid that increases brain gamma aminobutyric acid levels. In animal studies, valproic acid decreased convulsions in dependent rats. Anecdotal and uncontrolled studies suggest the drug may be effective in decreasing withdrawal symptomatology, seizure frequency, and progression to DTs. Hepatotoxicity has been reported. More studies are needed.

CONCLUSIONS

Most patients with mild withdrawal symptoms need not be hospitalized. Full assessment of the patient to detect other medical complications and then early initiation of treatment with supportive nursing care and, if necessary, benzodiazepines usually will prevent progression to serious withdrawal reactions and provide the patient with considerable symptomatic relief. (See Table 6.) Pharmacotherapy can be considerably simplified by giving diazepam every 1 to 2 hours initially until the clinical withdrawal reaction is fully controlled. If long half-life drugs are used further therapy is rarely needed. Short-acting benzodiazepines can also be given in a similar fashion in the milder clinical syndrome. Phenytoin should be given to patients with a preexisting seizure disorder. Phenothiazines, barbiturates, paraldehyde, and antihistamines have no role in the treatment of withdrawal because of their toxicity. The exception to this would be

Table 6
Guidelines for Drug Therapy of Patients in Alcohol Withdrawal

Clinical Problem	Drug	Route	Dose	Interval	Comment
Seizures: Step I[a]					
History of seizure disorder of previous withdrawal seizures	Phenytoin	P.O.[b]	Diphenylhydantoin detected in blood: maintenance dose, 100 mg	q.8.h.	
			No diphenylhydantoin detected in blood: loading dose, 200 to 300 mg; maintenance dose, 100 mg	q.8.h.	
Repeated seizures requiring acute therapy	Phenytoin	I.V.	Loading dose, 1 g	infuse at 50 mg/min	Exact loading dose is 10 mg/kg (see text); do not dilute in saline or dextrose solution
		P.O.[b]	Maintenance dose, 100 mg	q.8.h.	Diazepam should be used in the treatment of status epilepticus
Withdrawal: Step II[a]					
Mild to severe	Diazepam	P.O.[b]	20 mg	q.6.h.	The initial dose can be repeated every 2 hours until a satisfactory effect is observed
	Chlordiazepoxide	P.O.[b]	100 mg		
	Diazepam	I.V.[c]	20 mg		
Extreme[a]	Chlordiazepoxide	I.V.[c]	12.5 mg/min	slow infusion	Give until patient is calm (Subsequent dosages must be individualized on the basis of the clinical picture)
	Diazepam	I.V.[c]	2.5 mg/min		
Hallucinations: Step III[a]					
	Haloperidol	I.M.[d]	0.5–5.0 mg	q.2.h.	Until controlled or to maximum of five doses

[a]Admitted patients only; see Figure 1. [b]Per os. [c]Intravenous. [d]Intramuscular.

the use of haloperidol for the specific control of hallucinations in patients also treated with a benzodiazepine.

The treatment of alcoholic intoxication and withdrawal is only the first step toward offering an opportunity for full rehabilitation.

REFERENCES

1. Gessner, P. K. Drug therapy of the alcohol withdrawal syndrome. In: *Biochemistry and Pharmacology of Ethanol* (Vol. 2), Majchrowicz, E. and Noble, E. (eds.). Plenum: New York, 1979.

2. Gross, M. M., Lewis, E., and Hastey, J. Acute alcohol withdrawal syndrome: The biology of alcoholism. *Clinical Pathology* (Vol. 3). Kissin, B. and Begleiter, H. (eds.). Plenum: New York, 1974.

3. Martin, P., Kapur, B., Whiteside, E., and Sellers, E. M. Intravenous phenobarbital therapy in barbiturate and other hypnosedative withdrawal reactions: A kinetic approach. *Clin. Pharmacol. Ther.* 26(2): 256–264, 1979.

4. Naranjo, C. A., Chater, K., Iversen, P., Roach, C., Sykora, K., and Sellers, E. M. Importance of nonpharmacologic factors in the treatment of acute alcohol withdrawal. *Clin. Pharmacol. Ther.*, in press.

5. Ogata, M., Mendelson, J. H., Mello, N. K., et al. Adrenal function and alcoholism: II. Catecholamines. *Psychosom. Med.* 33: 159–180, 1971.

6. Robinson, G. M., Sellers, E. M., and Janecek, E. Treatment of barbiturate and hypnosedative withdrawal by a multiple oral phenobarbital loading dose technique. *Clin. Pharmacol. Ther.* 30(1): 71–76, 1981.

7. Sandor, P., Sellers, E. M., Dumbrell, M., Khouw, V. Effect of short- and long-term alcohol use on phenytoin kinetics in chronic alcoholics. *Clin. Pharmacol. Ther.* 30(3):390–397, 1981.

8. Sellers, E. M., and Kalant, H. Drug therapy: Alcohol intoxication and withdrawal. *N. Eng. J. Med.* 294: 757–762, 1976.

9. Sellers, E. M., Sandor, P., Giles, G., and Shaw, J. Diazepam loading dose treatment of alcohol withdrawal. *Clin. Invest. Med.* 4(2):8B, 1981. (abstract)

10. Shaw, J. M., Kolesar, G. S., Sellers, E. M., Kaplan, H. L., and Sandor, P. Development of optimal treatment tactics for alcohol withdrawal: I. Assessment and effectiveness of supportive care. *J. Clin. Psychopharmacol.*, in press.

11. Toshney, J. An alcoholism and detoxication centre. *Nurs. Times,* 74: 573–576, 1978.

12. Victor, M. Treatment of alcoholic intoxication and the withdrawal syndrome: A critical analysis of the use of drugs and other forms of therapy. *Psychosom. Med.* 28: 636–650, 1966.

13. Whitfield, E. L., Thompson, G., Lamb, A., Spencer, U., Pferfer, M., Browning-Ferrando, M. Detoxication of 1,024 alcohol patients without psychoactive drugs. *J.A.M.A.* 293: 1409–1410, 1978.

14. Wolfe, S. M., and Victor, M. The Physiological Basis of the Alcohol Withdrawal Syndrome, Recent Advances in Studies of Alcoholism: An Interdisciplinary Symposium (NIH Publication No. HSM 71-9045). Mello, N. K. and Mendelson, J. H. (eds.). United States Government Printing Office: Washington, D.C., 1971.

11

JOSEPH P. MCEVOY, MD, University of Pittsburgh School of Medicine

THE CHRONIC NEUROPSYCHIATRIC DISORDERS ASSOCIATED WITH ALCOHOLISM

THIS CHAPTER DESCRIBES the distinctive patterns of chronic alteration in neuropsychiatric functioning that develop over years of persistent, excessive alcohol drinking; reviews the proposed direct or indirect relationships of these neuropsychiatric disorders to alcohol addiction; and provides information, where available, on the frequency, course, outcome, pathophysiological mechanisms, and treatment of these neuropsychiatric disorders. The direct effects of alcohol on the brain, the effects of malnutrition accompanying alcoholism, and the effects of medical/surgical illnesses associated with alcoholism are reviewed.

THE DIRECT EFFECTS OF ALCOHOL ON THE BRAIN

Generalized Neuropsychiatric Deterioraton (Alcoholic Dementia)

Bergman et al. [5, 6] compared a sample ($n = 130$) of consecutive, unselected male patients entering an alcohol treatment unit with a randomly selected sample ($n = 200$) from the general male population on neuropsychological test and com-

---

Joseph P. McEvoy, MD, Assistant Professor of Psychiatry, University of Pittsburgh School of Medicine, Western Psychiatric Institute and Clinic, Pittsburgh, Pennsylvania.

puterized tomography measures to obtain relative estimates of the frequencies of neuropsychiatric abnormalities in chronic alcoholics (see Table 1). Because this alcoholic population was unselected, the occurrence of neuropsychiatric impairment due to causes other than alcohol could not always be ruled out; although no patients were diagnosed as having the Wernicke-Korsakoff syndrome (WKS), 35% had a history of delirious episodes, 20% of epileptic seizures, 18% of head trauma, and 10% of concomitant sedative/hypnotic abuse. Still, a number of postulates may be proposed on the basis of these data: (1) neuropsychological impairment and brain shrinkage are common in chronic alcoholics; (2) evidence of deterioration is present as early as the third decade of life; and (3) chronic alcoholism accelerates the accretion of neuropsychiatric impairment that occurs with normal aging. Wells [33] notes alcoholism to be the named cause of dementia in 5.9% of cases in reported series of dementia patients, but he does not separate out those cases directly due to alcohol versus those due to malnutrition or the other epiphenomena of alcoholism.

Those computerized tomography (CT) studies of chronic alcoholics that utilize control groups and attempt to exclude patients with other potential causes of

Table 1
Abnormalities on Neuropsychological Assessment and Computed Tomography in a Consecutive Series of Male Alcoholic Patients and a Random Sample from the General Male Population [5, 6]

Measures	Age Range	General Population Sample (% Abnormal)	Alcoholic Sample (% Abnormal)
Neuropsychological			
Halstead-Reitan Category Test	20–29	8	38
(> 51 errors)	40–49	33	69
	60–65	62	86
Halstead-Reitan Average	20–29	0	25
Impairment Index (> 0.5)	40–49	27	68
	60–65	66	66
Psychologists' overall assess-	20–29	0	0
ment of definite impairment	40–49	10	22
	60–65	18	45
Computerized Tomography			
Anterior horn index (> .31)	20–29	3	15
	40–49	8	41
	60–65	23	67
Width of third ventricle	20–29	9	31
(> 6 mm)	40–49	8	58
	60–65	23	66
Cortical changes (atrophy)	20–29	5	46
	40–49	13	56
	60–65	31	89

brain disease have generally reported significant differences between alcoholic and control groups in group mean measures of brain shrinkage and in the distribution of individuals with abnormal brain measures [5, 6, 7, 9, 19]. Chronic alcoholics show a more rapid rae of brain shrinkage with advancing age than controls [9], and differences are often demonstrable between the groups as early as the third decade [5, 6, 9]. Brain shrinkage is common even among heavy social drinkers [7]. Hill and Mikhael [15] did not find CT scan differences between the alcoholic and control groups they studied, despite the facts that their alcoholic patients had long (mean 14.3 years) and heavy (a fifth of liquor daily when drinking heavily) drinking histories, and were judged impaired on the Halstead-Reitan neuropsychological battery (HRB) in 75% of cases. However, 8 of their 15 alcoholics had been abstinent for more than 1 month, 4 for more than 6 months. As is noted herein, evidence exists that brain shrinkage may at least partially resolve with abstinence.

Berglund [4] states that the normal decline in cerebral blood flow with age is probably accelerated in chronic alcoholics, with flow in the anterior brain regions relatively more reduced than in other areas. Porjesz and Begleiter [23] report delayed conduction of evoked potential early components in basic sensory (visual and auditory) pathways in chronic alcoholics, even after months of abstinence. The later components of the evoked potential (N1-P2 and P3), which are more related to the individual's evaluation and processing of the sensory input, are also frequently abnormal in chronic alcoholics. The normal variations in N1-P2 with relevancy of stimulus do not occur in chronic alcoholics, especially over right frontal and central brain regions. The P3 component, another measure of the significance of the stimulus to the subject, is of lower voltage in alcoholics than in normals, and alcoholics with enlarged cortical sulci on a CT scan have lower P3 amplitudes than alcoholics without cortical atrophy [2].

Parsons and Farr [22] propose that chronic alcoholics tend to show a relatively consistent, though nonspecific, pattern of deficits on neuropsychological testing: relatively impaired performance on tests of visual-spatial and tactual-spatial constructional abilities, nonverbal abstracting, set flexibility, and visual-motor speed on the Wechsler Adult Intelligence Scale (WAIS) and the Halstead-Reitan battery (HRB), with normal performance on tests of language function. These authors further note that, although the tests showing impairment are considered to address nondominant hemisphere function, this pattern of deficits may be found in certain diffusely brain-damaged patients and in aging normals. Tarter [28] reports that some alcoholics show impairments similar to patients with anterior basal brain damage on tasks such as the Wisconsin Card Sorting Test; that is, they have difficulties in sustaining a cognitive set that is producing correct responses, difficulties in discontinuing cognitive sets that no longer produce correct responses, and difficulties in utilizing mistakes to find a new cognitive set that will result in correct responses. Tarter found that the duration of heavy drinking is related to the severity of these cognitive problems [27]. Goldstein and Shelly [13] criticized this frontal lobe hypothesis, noting that much of the evidence for a frontal lobe deficit in chronic alcoholics comes from studies of patients with Korsakoff's psychosis (see below), a distinct subgroup of the alcoholic population frequently having destructive lesions of the dorsal medial nucleus of the thalamus, which has extensive connections with the frontal lobes [13]. Goldstein and Shelly [13] reported a pattern of neuropsychological deficits in the non-Korsakoff's alcoholics studied, a pattern that suggests diffuse dysfunction of the cerebral hemispheres. Those studies that have attempted to correlate CT measures of brain shrinkage with neuropsychologic test measures of impaired performance have generally demonstrated a relationship that is not powerful, explaining only about 50% of the variance [5, 6, 9].

Clinicians have noted that certain impaired alcoholics can improve their cerebral function remarkably with prolonged abstinence [33]. Tarter [28] reviewed 11 neuropsychologic test studies following alcoholics for 3 weeks to 1 year of abstinence and concluded that "alcoholics do demonstrate some recovery of capacities with sobriety." Carlen and Wilkinson [8] report diminished brain shrinkage measured on repeat CT scans of alcoholic patients obtained 2 to 9 months after an initial hospitalization and CT scan. They noted a trend, which did not reach statistical significance, toward smaller totals of interim alcohol consumption correlating with greater improvement on the CT scans. Within several weeks of abstinence improvements on mental status examinations and electroencephalograms (EEGs), and a normalization of cerebrospinal fluid acidosis occurred.

Lishman et al. [19] examined 23 patients, nine of whom had remained abstinent or nearly so for 31 to 91 weeks after an initial CT scan. In the abstinent group the ventricles to brain ratio decreased (again not to a degree reaching statistical significance), whereas no change occurred in the group who continued drinking. Of the nine abstinent patients, four were judged improved on measures of cortical atrophy. All patients in whom the cortical measures worsened belonged to the group that continued drinking. The improvements noted in these studies did not return to the normal range. Porjesz and Begleiter [23] note that delays in transmission time of early evoked potential activity (auditory and visual) diminished toward normal after 5 months of abstinence. Williams and Rundell [35] report that with 9 or more months of abstinence, some of the changes in sleep induced by chronic alcohol abuse (excessive stage 1 and rapid eye movement sleep, and markedly reduced high-voltage, slow-wave sleep) tend to return toward normal. However, some disruption of the sleep pattern (brief arousals — an index of sleep instability) persists even after 21 months of abstinence.

In summary, a more or less global and progressive decline in mental function, occurring gradually over many years, may affect some chronic alcoholics. Dysfunction at first demonstrable only on neuropsychological test batteries is later apparent on routine mental status examination; in some older alcoholics there may be progression to dementia [11]. Accompanying brain changes may be demonstrated on anatomical (computerized tomography) and functional (neuropsychological testing; evoked potential; possibly cerebral blood flow in advanced cases) measures. This decline may be halted and even partially reversed with continued abstinence from alcoholism.

Personality Alterations in Chronic Alcoholics

Jellinek [18] proposed that serially ordered changes in drinking patterns, subjective states, and behaviors occur in temporal progression with chronic, heavy alcohol consumption. The patients he surveyed reported that after 5 to 10 years of heavy drinking they often began to experience physical demand for alcohol accompanied by increased impulsivity (aggressive outbursts, suicide attempts). Later in this progression emotionality increases and grandiosity and unreasonable resentment may alternate with remorse and self-pity. Sexual drive diminishes and pathological jealousy may appear. Ultimately, after 15 to 20 years of heavy drinking the irruptive aggressivity and emotionality wane, and the patient is left in a dulled, defective state characterized by an inability to think clearly, numerous obsessional and undefinable fears, worries, and somatic complaints, and psychomotor inhibition. Other authors [21, 29] have corroborated and furthur clarified this pattern of personality deterioration, although all agree with Jellinek [18] that "not all symptoms ... occur necessarily in all addicts, nor do they occur in every addict in the same sequence." Ballenger and Post [1] suggest that this personality deterioration is linked to the progressive severity of withdrawal (tremulousness, to seizures, to delirium tremens) concurrently experienced by the patients. They suggest that the daily cycle of drinking and withdrawal during sleep at first kindles irritative foci in limbic system structures, and ultimately leads to destructive changes. They note similar behavioral changes in animals subjected to limbic kindling, and a similar progression of personality changes and ultimate deterioration occurring in poorly controlled temporal lobe epileptics. These hypotheses, though interesting, are based entirely on retrospective patient reports or chart reviews and have not been validated as yet by prospective study or clinicopathologic correlation.

THE EFFECTS OF MALNUTRITION ACCOMPANYING ALCOHOLISM

The Wernicke-Korsakoff Syndrome

The triad of Wernicke's encephalopathy (including confusion, ocular abnormalities, and ataxia) occurs acutely in alcoholics who often have obtained essentially all of their calories from alcohol for a period of months. There is usually a long drinking history, but more important is drinking to the exclusion of eating. Thiamine is the critically deficient nutrient. Upon recovery from Wernicke's encephalopathy, the vast majority of patients are left with a residual deficit, the most prominent feature of which is a disorder of learning and memory (Korsakoff's psychosis) [32].

Victor et al. [32] reports the WKS to be present clinically in 3% of all alcoholics admitted to the Boston City Hospital during a 2-year period (1950–51). However, 2.7% of 1,459 adult patients coming to autopsy between the years 1968 and 1973 at the Cleveland Metropolitan General Hospital showed pathologic evidence of the WKS. The onset of the disease is most common between 40 and 60 years of age.

The majority of patients with acute Wernicke's encephalopathy show a global confusional state: "This disorder seems to be compounded of several elements — apathy and an incapacity to sustain physical or mental activity, impairment of awareness and responsiveness, disorientation, inattention and failure of concentration and derangement of perceptual function" [32]. No mental abnormalities may be evident in 10% of patients and 15% develop concomitant signs of alcohol withdrawal.

Ocular abnormalities occur in over 95% of patients; the most common, in order of descending frequency, are nystagmus, abducens palsies, and palsies of conjugate gaze. Ataxia primarily affecting stance and gait is present in over 85% of patients, and is of such severity in 20% that they cannot stand or walk without support. There is usually little alteration of individual movements of the extremities.

Almost 20% of patients die during the acute phase of Wernicke's encephalopathy, usually from some nonneurological cause (over 75% from infection). In the remaining patients, treatment with thiamine results in rapid improvement of the ocular findings (hours to days), though in 60% of patients a fine horizontal nystagmus may persist chronically. Improvement of the ataxia occurs more slowly (1 to 3 weeks) and is complete in only 40% of patients. The remainder are left with a wide-based gait and are unable to walk tandem.

Approximately 15% of those patients treated with thiamine have rapid (1 to 2 weeks) and complete clearing of their mental state. However, in the remainder, as the global confusional state dissipates, a more or less pure disorder of memory (Korsakoff's psychosis) becomes apparent. Korsakoff's psychosis is characterized by: (1) profound impairment in the ability to learn (anterograde amnesia); the patient is lost in new surroundings and unable to benefit from experience; (2) a retrograde amnesia extending back in patchy fashion for several years prior to the onset of the syndrome; (3) apathy, indifference, and inertia; the patients have little insight into, or concern, about their illness; (4) the patients are, however, alert and responsive, and aware of their surroundings; they reason adequately within the limits imposed by their memory deficits; grooming, housekeeping skills, and social amenities are usually well preserved [3, 32].

Over months to years, perhaps 20% of patients with Korsakoff's psychosis have an essentially complete recovery. Incomplete improvement is shown in 60%, and 20% show no improvement in their condition and require chronic institutionalization.

Confabulation is not commonly found in uncomplicated WKS. During the acute phase, delirious misperceptions may result in the patient giving false answers to queries. As memory function begins to improve, the patient may mix together recent events with things that happened years ago, giving an unbelievable and jumbled character to his stories. If, however, spontaneous, self-propagating production of spectacular, fantastic stories occurs, severe bifrontal cerebral disease should be suspected and neurosurgical evaluation undertaken [26]. Flagrant confabulation occurs in amnesia complicated by a loss of ability to monitor responses and be self-corrective, secondary to frontal lobe damage [3].

The WKS is caused by thiamine deficiency [30]. Clinical features and pathological findings identical to those found in chronic alcoholics with WKS may be seen in nonalcoholic individuals subjected to grossly inadequate nutrition (e.g., prisoners of war, comatose or postsurgical patients, or women with hyperemesis gravidarum). The pathological lesions of WKS surround the ventricular system of the diencephalon, mesencephalon, and rhombencephalon, and consist of varying degrees of tissue necrosis, with reactive glial infiltration. Hemorrhage may rarely be present; inflammation is never prominent. In the classical clinicopathological studies of Victor, Adams, and Collins [32], lesions of the dorsal medial nucleus of the thalamus correlated best with the memory deficits, although the mammillary bodies were also frequently involved. Vertical nystagmus was related to lesions involving the third nerve nuclei and periaqueductal region of the midbrain. Horizontal nystagmus correlated best with lesions of the medial vestibular nuclei. The marked unsteadiness of stance and gait seen during the acute phase of the disorder was correlated with involvement of the vestibular nuclei (and abnormalities of calorics testing clinically), but the persistent central ataxia was related to atrophy of the superior cerebellar vermis.

Brain shrinkage on a CT scan may be found in patients with the WKS [5, 6, 9], but need not be present [13]. If present, brain shrinkage may merely signify the occurrence of two distinct processes concurrent in the same alcoholic patient [11]. Peripheral neuropathy with decreased ankle reflexes, diminished sensation, and wasting of distal musculature may be found in 80% of patients with the WKS; occasionally there is associated dysesthesia or hyperpathy and any touch will provoke intense pain. Some alcoholic patients present with a relatively localized lesion of the cerebellar vermis indistinguishable from that found in many patients with the WKS, accompanied by marked ataxia involving the trunk and lower extremities much more than the upper extremities (alcoholic cerebellar degeneration).

Acute Wernicke's encephalopathy is an emergency. Thiamine 50 mg given intravenously, followed by the same dose intramuscularly daily until nutrition is adequate, may result in rapid improvement of many of the clinical features, and may prevent or limit irreversible brain damage. A convincing argument has been made that the cost to society of supplementing all alcoholic beverages with thiamine would be far less than the cost of caring for patients developing the acute syndrome and chronic sequelae of WKS [10].

Pellagra

Pellagra, caused by niacin deficiency, is characterized by a triad of: (1) dermatitis—erythema and vesiculation, which develops into chronic, irregular, brown, hyperpigmented areas on the sun-exposed portions of the body; (2) gastrointestinal abnormalities—anorexia, nausea, vomiting, diarrhea or constipation (usually not responsive to standard remedies); and (3) neuropsychiatric abnormalities— psychiatric syndromes ranging from dysphoria, anxiety, and irritability to delirium, and spastic weakness of the extremities with abnormalities of gait, incontinence of bladder and bowel, and increased deep tendon reflexes.

Pellagra is felt to be very rare in developed countries (except among chronic alcoholics) because breads are fortified with niacin. However, in 20 of 74 chronic alcoholics autopsied at a hospital in Japan between 1965 and 1979, the neuropathological changes of pellagra were found: central chromatolysis (swollen and rounded neurons with displacement of the nuclei and Nissl substance to the periphery) in the large cells of the cortex (Betz cells) and basal ganglia, the cells of the cranial motor nuclei and of the dentate nuclei, and in the anterior horn cells of the spinal cord [17, 30].

Dermatitis may not be prominent in pallagra, especially if there has been little sun exposure. The presence of persistent and nonresponsive gastrointestinal abnormalities or of spastic motor weakness in a malnourished alcoholic should alert the clinician to the diagnosis. Untreated patients with pellagra may die of inanition and infection.

Disorders Suspected to Have a Nutritional Basis

Nutritionally based disorders have been reported to occur in debilitated, malnourished individuals, whether chronic alcoholics or not. More than one of these disorders may occur simultaneously in the same individual, and, at postmortem, the pathological changes in the nervous system, though different in location for each disorder, are very similar in character (degeneration of myelin sheaths with relative preservation, at least initially, of axons, nerve cells, and support tissues) [14, 32].

Central pontive myelinosis. In central pontive myelinosis the site of demyelination is the center of the pons. Depending on the size of the lesion, there may be no recognizable symptoms during life, or progressive spastic bulbar weakness and quadriparesis. This lesion was found at postmortem in 7.3% of the WKS patients of Victor et al. [32].

Deficiency amblyopia. A progressive loss of vision evolving gradually over several weeks, often with an oval relative blind spot extending between the macula and optic disc (centrocecal scotoma), deficiency amblyopia is characterized by demyelination in the central portions of the optic nerves, chiasm, and tracts (papillomacular bundles). This disorder was found in 2.6% of the WKS patients of Victor et al [32].

Marchiafava-Bignamini disease. A very rare disorder, the clinical picture of which is not well defined, Marchiafava-Bignamini disease may somewhat resemble a progressive dementing illness. At postmortem, demyelination involves the anterior central portions of the corpus callosum, and occasionally other major bundles of myelinated fibers. No case of this disorder was present in the sample of WKS of Victor et al [32].

THE EFFECTS OF MEDICAL/SURGICAL DISORDERS ASSOCIATED WITH ALCOHOLISM

The Hepatic Encephalopathies

The hepatic encephalopathies (HE) are a group of related brain dysfunctions that occur when severe hepatocellular disease and/or portal systemic shunting results in high levels of nitrogenous substances gaining access to the brain. These encephalopathies are characterized by: (1) alterations in mental function ranging from mild cognitive dysfunction through delirium to coma and death; (2) variable neurological signs frequently including disorders of movement — fluctuating hypertonicity of the trunk and limbs, grimacing, asterixis, or tremor; (3) EEG abnormalities characterized by high amplitude, slow waves [25]. Victor reports that in postmortem series of 3,548 adults, evidence for HE was found in 7.7%, 70% of whom had liver disease of the alcoholic type [31].

The alcoholic patient who develops HE usually has a long drinking history, Laennec's cirrhosis, and varices shunting blood around the damaged liver. The initial attack of HE may be precipitated by excessive intake of dietary protein or gastrointestinal bleeding with the resultant production of large amounts of nitrogenous products by urea-splitting organisms in the gut; these substances bypass their normal breakdown site in the liver and exert a toxic effect upon the brain.

Cirrhosis and portal systemic shunting are often chronic problems, resulting in persistent, fluctuating alterations in the patient's level of consciousness. Much of the time, mental status examination will show no clear evidence of cerebral dysfunction, but careful neuropsychological testing may show abnormalities (especially in performance tasks) [24], and slowing may be present on EEGs. Any increase in protein in the gut due to dietary indiscretion, gastrointestinal bleeding, or constipation will lead to a deterioration in mental status. Other incidental factors such as infection, azotemia, or sedative drugs may also cause deterioration. Vigorous treatment (see below) at this stage may result in a reversal of clinical, neuropsychological, and EEG changes to normal.

Some patients who survive an episode of acute HE are left with permanent residual deficits in cognition or motor function (choreoathetosis, ataxia, tremor, dysarthria). Repeated acute deteriorations in a chronic HE may result in an accretion of permanent deficits, including a progressive dementia. A portion of chronic HE patients develop this progressive deterioration associated with portal systemic shunting without fulminant episodes of acute HE.

Signs and symptoms of acute HE can be induced in cirrhotic patients by administering ammonium or other substances that can be degraded to ammonium by intestinal microorganisms. However, elevated blood ammonium levels have not been found in every case of HE, and other shunted substances not adequately metabolized by the liver (fatty acids, amino acids, mercaptans) have been suggested as alternative "toxins" [25].

Postmortem examination of the brains of patients who died during an episode of acute HE reveals an increased number of hypertrophied protoplasmic astrocytes in the deep layers of the cerebral cortex, the basal ganglia, thalamus, and certain brain stem nuclei, but no loss of neural or supportive elements. In contrast, examination of the brains of those patients who developed progressive neuropsychiatric deterioration and fixed neurological deficits with chronic HE reveals destruction of neural and supportive elements in a distribution identical to that marked only by astrocytic change during acute HE [31].

The treatment for HE should include limitation of dietary protein intake, preventing constipation, and lactulose (an inert sugar that acidifies the colonic contents, diminishing the production and absorption of ammonium). During exacerbations of HE oral neomycin may eliminate urease-producing microorganisms from the bowel. Bromocriptine given to patients with chronic HE in doses up to 15 mg daily may not only produce clinical improvement, but may also result in normalization of the EEG, cerebral blood flow, and cerebral oxygen consumption [20]. Although it has not been conclusively proven that attention to minimizing exposure of the brain to excessive levels of nitrogenous substances will prevent irreversible deterioration, this would seem a reasonable treatment recommendation until conclusive evidence is forthcoming [34].

The Sequelae of Head Trauma

Because of their disease and life styles, chronic alcoholics are more susceptible to falls, physical assaults, motor vehicle accidents, and other mechanisms of head trauma. The occurrence of seizures in a chronic alcoholic should not be ascribed automatically to withdrawal; even in patients with a previous history of alcohol withdrawal seizures, new treatable problems, especially traumatic injuries, may be encountered [16]. Focal signs accompanying seizures particularly require neurologic evaluation, including CT scans [12]. Even mild trauma, especially in an alcoholic with coagulopathy due to hepatic disorder, may lead to subdural hematoma with resultant persistent alteration of consciousness and deterioration of intellectual functioning.

OVERVIEW

A chronic alcoholic patient presenting with neuropsychiatric signs and symptoms requires: (1) neurological evaluation for evidence of traumatic brain injury; (2) attention to the manifestations of nutritional deficiency, and parenteral repletion of vitamins and other essential nutrients until oral intake is adequate; (3) assessment of severity of hepatic disease, especially regarding the presence of cirrhosis, portal systemic shunting, and sources of nitrogenous substances in the gut; (4) prevention or treatment of withdrawal phenomena. Only after the acute effects of neurological injury, nutritional deficiency, hepatic decompensation, and withdrawal have dissipated (which may require weeks or months) can some preliminary assessment of persistent brain injury be made. However, even at this point, further improvement in neuropsychiatric function over months and even years may be expected if abstinence is maintained.

REFERENCES

1. Ballenger, J. C., and Post, R. M. Kindling as a model for alcohol withdrawal syndromes. *Brit. J. Psychiatry* 133:1-14, 1978.
2. Begleiter, H., and Porjesz, B. Neuroradiological and neurophysiological evidence of brain deficits in chronic alcoholics. *Acta Psychiatr. Scand.* 62 (Suppl. 286):3-14, 1980.
3. Benson, D. F. Amnesia. *Southern Med. J.* 71:1221-1231, 1978.
4. Berglund, M. Cerebral blood flow in chronic alcoholics. *Alcoholism: Clin. Exp. Res.* 5:295-302, 1981.
5. Bergman, H., Borg, S., Hindmarsh, T., Idestrom, C-M, and Mutzell, S. Computed tomography of the brain and neuropsychological assessment of male alcoholic patients. In: *Addiction and Brain Damage*, Richter, D. (ed.). University Park Press: Baltimore, 1980.
6. Bergman, H., Borg, S., Hindmarsh, T., Idestrom, C-M., and Mutzell, S. Computed tomography of the brain and nueropsychological assessment of male alcoholic patients and a random sample from the general male population. *Acta Psychiatr. Scand.* 62 (Suppl. 286):77-88, 1980.
7. Cala, L. A., and Mastaglia, F. L. Computerized tomography in chronic alcoholics. *Alcoholism: Clin. Exp. Res.* 5:283-293, 1981.
8. Carlen, P. L., and Wilkinson, D. A. Alcoholic brain damage and reversible deficits. *Acta Psychiatr. Scand.* 62 (Suppl. 286):103-118, 1980.
9. Carlen, P. L., Wilkinson, D. A., Wortzman, G., et al. Cerebral atrophy and func-

tional deficits in alcoholics without clinically apparent liver disease. *Neurol.* 31:377-385, 1981.

10. Centerwell, B. S., and Criqui, J. H. Prevention of the Wernicke-Korsakoff syndrome—A cost-benefit analysis. *N. Eng. J. Med.* 299:285-288, 1978.

11. Cutting, J. The relationship between Korsakoff's syndrome and "alcoholic dementia." *Brit. J. Psychiatry* 132:240-251, 1978.

12. Fuessner, J. R., Linfors, E. W., Blessing, C. L., and Stariner, C. F. Computed tomography brain scanning in alcohol withdrawal seizures. *Ann. Intern. Med.* 94:519-522, 1981.

13. Goldstein, G., and Shelly, C. Neuropsychological investigation of brain lesion localization in alcoholism. *Adv. Exp. Med. Biol.* 126:731-743, 1980.

14. Haller, R. G. Alcoholism and neurologic disorders. In: *Neurology*, Rosenberg, R. N. (ed.). Grune & Stratton: New York, 1980.

15. Hill, S. Y., and Mikhael, M. A. Computerized transaxial tomographic and neuropsychological evaluations in chronic alcoholics and heroin abusers. *Am. J. Psychiatry* 136: 598-602, 1979.

16. Hillbom, M. E. Occurrence of cerebral seizures provoked by alcohol abuse. *Epilepsia* 21:459-466, 1980.

17. Ishii, N., and Nishihara, Y. Pellagra among chronic alcoholics: Clinical and pathological study of 20 necropsy cases. *J. Neurol. Neurosurg. Psychiatry* 44:209-215, 1981.

18. Jellinek, E. M. Phases of alcohol addiction. *J. Stud. Alcohol* 13:673-684, 1952.

19. Lishman, W. A., Ron, M., Acker, W. Computed tomography of the brain and psychometric assessment of alcoholic patients—A British study. In: *Addiction and Brain Damage*, Richter, D. (ed.). University Park Press: Baltimore, 1980.

20. Morgan, M. Y., Jakobovits, A. W., James, I. M., and Sherlock, S. Successful use of bromocriptine in the treatment of chronic hepatic encephalopathy. *Gastroenterology* 78: 663-670, 1980.

21. Park, P. Developmental ordering of experiences in alcoholism. *J. Stud. Alcohol* 34: 473-488, 1973.

22. Parsons, O. A., and Farr, S. P. The neuropsychology of alcohol and drug use. In: *Handbook of Clinical Neuropsychology*, Filskov, S. B. and Boll, T. J. (eds.). Wiley: New York, 1981.

23. Porjesz, B., and Begleiter, H. Human evoked brain potentials and alcohol. *Alcoholism: Clin. Exp. Res.* 5:304-314, 1981.

24. Rehnstrom, C., Simert, G., Hansson, J. A., Johnson, G., and Vang, J. Chronic hepatic encephalopathy. A psychometrical study. *Scand. J. Gastroenterol.* 12:305-311, 1977.

25. Schencker, S., Henderson, G. I., Hoyumpa, A. M., and McCandless, D. W. Hepatic and Wernicke's encephalopathies: Current concepts to pathogenesis. *Am. J. Clin. Nutr.* 33:2719-2726, 1980.

26. Stuss, D. T., Alexander, M. P., Lieberman, A., and Levine, H. An extraordinary form of confabulation. *Neurology* 28:1166-1172, 1978.

27. Tarter, R. E. Analysis of cognitive deficits in chronic alcoholics. *J. Nerv. Ment. Dis.* 157:138-147, 1973.

28. Tarter, R. E. Brain damage in chronic alcoholics: A review of the psychological evidence. In: *Addiction and Brain Damage*, Richter, D. (ed.). Unviersity Park Press: Baltimore, 1980.

29. Trice, H. M., and Wahl, J. R. A rank order analysis of the symptoms of alcoholism. *J. Stud. Alcohol* 19:636-648, 1958.

30. Victor, M. Nutrition and diseases of the nervous system. *Prog. Food Nutr. Sci.* 1: 145-172, 1975.

31. Victor, M. Neurologic disorders due to alcoholism and malnutrition. In: *Clinical Neurology*, Baker, A. B. and Baker, L. H. (eds.). 1979.

32. Victor, M., Adams, R. D., and Collins, G. H. *The Wernicke-Korsakoff Syndrome.* F. A. Davis: Philadelphia, 1971.

33. Wells, C. E. Diagnostic evaluation and treatment in dementia. In: *Dementia*, Wells, C. E. (ed.). F. A. Davis: Philadelphia, 1977.

34. Wells, C. E. Treatable forms of dementia. In: *Update II: Harrisan's Principles of Internal Medicine*, Isselbacher, K. J., Adams, R. D., Braunwald, E., Martin, J. B., Petersdorf, R. J., and Wilson, J. D. (eds.). McGraw-Hill: New York. In press.

35. Williams, H. L., and Rundell, O. H. Altered sleep physiology in chronic alcoholics: Reversal with abstinence. *Alcoholism: Clin. Exp. Res.* 5:318–325, 1981.

12

ERNEST L. HARTMANN, MD, Tufts University School of Medicine, Boston, Massachusetts

ALCOHOL AND THE SLEEP DISORDERS

THE RELATIONSHIP OF alcohol to sleep problems or sleep disorders is intriguing and even paradoxical: A drink of alcohol at bedtime has probably been the most widely used hypnotic medication in history, yet it is now clear that alcohol produces a great variety of sleep disturbances, including insomnia.

The interaction of alcohol and sleep could theoretically be considered in a number of separate ways. Thus one can study the effects of a single dose of alcohol (at many levels), a short episode (approximating an evening) of drinking, a prolonged period of drinking (days, weeks, etc.), a period of withdrawal, a period of stable abstinence; one can study each of these episodes in persons previously unacquainted with alcohol, in light, moderate, or heavy drinkers, or in known alcoholics. See Pokorny [23] for a detailed discussion of these possibilities.

To make this brief chapter of clinical use, the effects of alcohol on laboratory-recorded sleep are discussed, but not all the details of all the possibilities are covered. Animal studies are not included at all. Some current concepts and knowledge relating to classification and diagnosis of sleep problems and sleep disorders are summarized, and the relationship of alcohol and alcoholism to these sleep disorders is discussed.

Ernest L. Hartmann, MD, Professor of Psychiatry, Tufts University School of Medicine, Director, Sleep Laboratory, Boston State Hospital, and Medical Director, Sleep Research Foundation, Boston, Massachusetts.

EFFECT OF ALCOHOL ON SLEEP IN NONALCOHOLICS

A single dose of alcohol, in the range of about 1 g/k of body weight of ethanol at bedtime, produces an immediate reduction in desynchronized (D) sleep (rapid eye movement sleep), without much effect on waking time, sleep time, or other aspects of sleep [4, 31]. If alcohol administration at bedtime is continued over five nights D sleep gradually returns to baseline levels [31]. The initial reduction of D time has been repeatedly confirmed, although at some doses the decrease in D time may be found only in the first half of the night, with a rebound increase in the second half [18]. Several studies do report effects on other aspects of sleep: Rundell et al. [26] report rapid onset of sleep (reduced sleep latency) and rapid onset of slow-wave sleep. Williams et al. [29] studied young women at several doses of alcohol within the usual range; their most prominent findings were a reduction of D sleep in the first hours of the night and an increase in slow-wave sleep in the same period.

Most authors do not report any great effect of alcohol on qualitative aspects of sleep, such as number of rapid eye movements within D periods, or spindles during stage 2 sleep. There are reports of reduced galvanic skin response (GSR) activity in slow-wave sleep and increased pulse and respiratory rates [22, 31].

In general the effects of one or a few doses of alcohol in normals are quite similar to the effect of barbiturates; there is little here that can be called a specific alcohol effect [28].

It may be surprising that the sleep laboratory literature has found effects on D sleep and slow-wave sleep much more consistently than overall sleep effects such as reduction in sleep latency — the effect noted informally by so many informed experimenters. This author believes the accepted and expected facts are entirely right. The failure to find sleep latency in lab studies is in great part artifactual. Sleep researchers interested in the states and stages of sleep generally choose young, healthy subjects willing to sleep repeatedly in the laboratory, who have stable baseline measures and no sleep problems. These subjects often have sleep latencies of under 8 to 10 minutes when taking placebos, and it is difficult or impossible to find a reduction with alcohol. The same problem frequently arises in the study of hypnotic medication [9]. Normal subjects must be studied to determine pharmacologic effects on sleep, but then a different population — insomniacs of some kind — are necessary to establish clinical effects.

Alcohol can also have special effects on sleep in important situations that have not yet been widely studied. Thus, maternal drinking can have definite effects on the sleep organization of a newborn child, and this is not true only in women who are clear alcoholics. Children who were born of mothers who drank heavily throughout pregnancy had quite different sleep-wake organizations and sleep polygraphic patterns than normal when recorded 4 days after birth. It is not yet certain whether this can be considered an aspect of withdrawal from alcohol, or whether it is an indication of a more lasting disturbance in brain function. This is discussed further in Chapter 23 by Henry L. Rosett and Lyn Weiner regarding the fetal alcohol syndrome.

Also, there is no question clinically that alcohol substantially augments the sleep-inducing properties of many hypnotics and tranquilizers, though this has not been examined systematically in the laboratory.

THE SLEEP OF ALCOHOLICS

Sleep patterns in alcoholic persons, during alcohol intake, during withdrawal, and during long periods of abstinence, have been investigated in detail and well reviewed [8, 23, 28]. Only a few of the individual studies can be mentioned here; the accepted findings, derived from many experiments, are then summarized.

Laboratory studies agree that alcoholics have disturbed sleep in some way, but there is considerable variation: Johnson et al. [17] studied 14 alcoholics intensively with and without alcohol intake. They found a great deal of overall sleep disturbance. D sleep was reduced early in the drinking period. Slow-wave sleep became gradually reduced and fragmented during the drinking period [17].

Zarcone and Hoddes [32] studied 28 alcoholic subjects not on alcohol. He found that some had reduced time spent in D sleep and slow-wave sleep (stage 3-4). Those with these low D sleep and slow-wave sleep patterns also had low scores on intelligence tests [32]. This group suggested that abnormal regulation of sleep by serotonergic neurons results from chronic alcohol use. They were able to reverse it to some extent by giving 5-hydroxytryptophan (5-HTP).

Lester et al. [19] and Zarcone and Hoddes [32] found that alcoholics without alcohol had more arousals during the night and more changes in stages of sleep.

Our laboratory examined 14 male subjects with Korsakoff's syndrome and long histories of alcoholism, studied at a time when they had not had alcohol for a considerable period [2]; sleep was disturbed in some of the severe cases. There were differences in D time — older cases had significantly lower D time than recent cases, tending to be lower or higher respectively than controlled values for their ages.

Wolin and Mello [30] found that alcoholics had somewhat disturbed sleep, and a large amount of stage 1 (very light sleep) even when not drinking.

Long-term drinking in alcoholic subjects provides a number of laboratory-recorded sleep changes, including an initial increase in slow-wave sleep [27] and a reduction of D sleep, followed by later increases in D sleep and decreases in slow-wave sleep while alcohol intake continues [7, 27].

Withdrawal of alcohol is usually followed by a great increase in D time, especially prominent at the time when delirium tremens appears, and perhaps even related to the mechanism of delirium tremens [3, 5]. Withdrawal is almost inevitably associated with insomnia for a few days, but this sometimes lasts for weeks or even months.

Gross et al. [6] have reported on a group of alcoholics followed carefully through various phases of alcohol intake, withdrawal, and abstinence. The subjects gave histories on profound sleep disturbance—usually an initial insomnia associated with an onset of drinking episode; some patients attribute their increase of drinking to an attempt to cure the insomnia. During early periods of heavy drinking there is no clear sleep disturbance except for an increasingly felt need for alcohol in order to sleep. Then, after a time, the patients develop increasingly disturbing nightmares and other sorts of awakenings. Sometimes this leads to states where the patients are uncertain as to whether they were asleep or awake and hallucinating. Then, when the patients terminate an episode of drinking and begin to withdraw from alcohol, they have hallucinations followed sometimes by a period of terminal sleep—a night experienced as very deep, good sleep in which the patient awakes refreshed and without recollection of dreams.

From the laboratory studies as well as the clinical studies, there is some consensus as to the effects of alcohol, well summarized by Pokorny [23] and others: Single small or moderate doses of alcohol can cause reduction in sleep latency but increase wakefulness later in the night. D sleep will decrease during acute alcohol intake but increases on withdrawal. Slow-wave sleep increases early during intoxication and then decreases. Total sleep time sometimes increases during pronounced intoxication and decreases during withdrawal when insomnia is common.

Withdrawal is associated with insomnia, delayed sleep onset, and multiple awakenings, as well as frightening dreams and hallucinations. Withdrawal often ends with a prolonged terminal sleep. However, insomnia may persist for many months after withdrawal. Even long after withdrawal many previous alcoholics have decreased slow-wave sleep and some alterations in normal cyclic sleep patterns.

THE SLEEP DISORDERS

There is now fairly general agreement [12, 15, 25] that sleep disorders can be systematically organized clinically according to the chief complaint or symptom and that there are three (or, in one classification, four) major symptoms to be considered: insomnia, hypersomnolence (including hypersomnia and excessive daytime sleepiness), and episodic nocturnal events. We shall see that alcohol intake, especially continued alcohol intake in alcoholics, can produce or aggravate disorders in each of these three major symptom groups.

Table 1 presents an attempt to classify sleep problems [12]. The classification emphasizes that there is not a true pathophysiology of the sleep disorders and

Table I
The Sleep Disorders

A. Causes of Insomnia[a]

	Insomnias Secondary to Medical Conditions	Insomnias Secondary to Psychiatric or Environmental Conditions
Difficulty in falling asleep	Any painful or uncomfortable condition Brain stem lesions Conditions listed below, at times	Anxiety Anxiety, chronic neurotic Anxiety, prepsychotic Tension anxiety, muscular Environmental changes Conditioned (habit) insomnia Phase shift Non-24-hour cycles
Difficulty in remaining asleep	Sleep apnea Nocturnal myoclonus and restless legs syndrome Dietary factors Episodic events Direct drug effects (including alcohol) Drug withdrawal effects (including alcohol) Drug interactions Endocrine abnormalities Metabolic abnormalities Brain stem or hypothalmic lesions Aging	Depression, especially primary depression Environmental changes Phase shift Non-24-hour cycles Dream interruption insomnia

B. Causes of Hypersomnolence[b]

	Chiefly Medical	Chiefly psychiatric or Environmental
Principal symptom: excessive sleep (hypersomnia)	Kleine-Levin syndrome Menstrual associated Metabolic or toxic conditions Trypansomiasis or other encephalitic conditions	Depression (some) Alcohol Other depressant medications Withdrawal from amphetamines and other stimulants
Principal symptom: excessive daytime sleepiness	Narcolepsy Sleep apnea Hypoventilation syndrome Hyperthyroidism Other metabolic and toxic conditions	Depression (some) Medication and medication withdrawal (as above) Phase shift Non-24-hour cycles

Excessive daytime sleepiness is sometimes a secondary symptom of any of the causes of insomnia (see "Causes of Insomnia," above); in other words; insufficient sleep at night sometimes produces excessive daytime sleepiness.

(continued)

Table 1 (continued)

C. Episodic Nocturnal Events (Parasomnias)

Stage 4–related	Other Disorders
Sleepwalking (somnambulism) Night terrors (pavor nocturnus) Bed-wetting (enuresis)	D nightmares Bruxism Sleep talking Jactatio capitus nocturnus Painful erections Familial sleep paralysis Hyperactive gag reflex Paroxysmal nocturnal hemoglobinuria Nocturnal epileptic seizures Cluster headaches and chronic paroxysmal hemicrania Nocturnal cardiovascular symptoms Nocturnal asthma Nocturnal gastroesophageal reflex D nocturnal angina Nocturnal episodes of other illnesses

[a]The boundaries between the columns are not entirely distinct. In the column "Insomnias Secondary to Psychiatric or Environmental Conditions" are listed the illnesses and syndromes that are currently classified as psychiatric and that are most frequently seen by psychiatrists and conditions that, in the present state of knowledge, are best conceptualized by using psychiatric terms. However, all or most of those psychiatric illnesses will probably be understood eventually in terms of brain biological mechanisms and interactions with the social and physical environment, so that the distinction between the two columns may no longer be necessary in the future.
[b]The items listed in the two columns are not entirely separable (see note above).
Source: Reprinted with permission from E. Hartmann, "Sleep Disorders." In: *Comprehensive Textbook of Psychiatry III*, Kaplan, H., Freedman, A., and Sadock, B. (eds.). Williams & Wilkins: Baltimore, 1980.

thus at this stage it is best to classify using the principal or presenting symptom and then attempting to find a cause for the symptom. The symptoms, again, are difficulty in getting to sleep or remaining asleep (insomnia), sleepiness or sleep attacks during the day (hypersomnolence), and unusual occurrences during the night (episodic events or parasomnias).

Table 2 presents the latest classification of sleep disorders by the Association of Sleep Disorders Centers and the Association for the Psychophysiological Study of Sleep [25].

The two classifications are quite similar. Although the list in Table 2 speaks of disorders and dysfunctions, the introductory material makes it clear that what is meant is basically symptoms whose causes are known or must be sought. The only difference is that this classification includes a major section, "Disorders of the Sleep-Wake Schedule." There is no question that such disorders exist and have definite clinical importance. However, since they manifest themselves clinically — as do the other causes — either in the symptom of insomnia or the symptom of hypersomnolence, it seems more reasonable that these schedule disorders should be listed among the causes of these two symptoms, and in fact they do occur in this way in Table 1.

Table 2
Outline of Diagnostic Classification of Sleep and Arousal Disorders

A. DIMS: Disorders of Initiating and Maintaining Sleep (Insomnias)
   1. Psychophysiological
      a. Transient and situational
      b. Persistent
   2. *associated with*
      Psychiatric disorders
      a. Symptom and personality disorders
      b. Affective disorders
      c. Other functional psychoses
   3. *associated with*
      Use of drugs and alcohol
      a. Tolerance to or withdrawal from central nervous system (CNS) depressants
      b. Sustained use of CNS Stimulants
      c. Sustained use of or withdrawal from other drugs
      d. Chronic alcoholism
   4. *associated with*
      Sleep-Induced respiratory impairment
      a. Sleep apnea DIMS syndrome
      b. Alveolar hypoventilation DIMS syndrome
   5. *associated with*
      Sleep-Related (nocturnal) myoclonus and restless legs
      a. Sleep-Related (nocturnal) myoclonus DIMS syndrome
      b. Restless Legs DIMS syndrome
   6. *associated with*
      Other medical, toxic, and environmental conditions
   7. Childhood-onset DIMS
   8. *associated with*
      Other DIMS conditions
      a. Repeated REM sleep interruptions
      b. Atypical polysomnographic features
      c. Not otherwise specified[a]
   9. No DIMS abnormality
      a. Short sleeper
      b. Subjective DIMS complaint without objective findings
      c. Not otherwise specified[a]

B. DOES: Disorders of excessive somnolence
   1. Psychophysiological
      a. Transient and situational
      b. Persistent
   2. *associated with*
      Psychiatric disorders
      a. Affective disorders
      b. Other functional disorders
   3. *associated with*
      Use of drugs and alcohol
      a. Tolerance to or withdrawal from CNS stimulants
      b. Sustained use of CNS depressants
   4. *associated with*
      Sleep-induced respiratory impairment
      a. Sleep apnea DOES syndrome
      b. Alveolar hypoventilation DOES syndrome
   5. *associated with*
      Sleep-related (nocturnal) myoclonus and restless legs

(continued)

Table 2 *(continued)*

      a. Sleep-related (nocturnal) myoclonus DOES syndrome
      b. Restless legs DOES syndrome
  6. Narcolepsy
  7. Idiopathic CNS hypersomnolence
  8. *associated with*
    Other medical, toxic, and environmental conditions
  9. *associated with*
    Other DOES conditions
      a. Intermittent DOES (periodic) syndromes
         (1) Kleine-Levin syndrome
         (2) Menstrual-associated syndrome
      b. Insufficient sleep
      c. Sleep drunkenness
      d. Not otherwise specified[a]
  10. No DOES Abnormality
      a. Long sleeper
      b. Subjective DOES complaint without objective findings
      c. Not otherwise specified[a]
C. Disorders of the sleep-wake schedule
  1. Transient
      a. Rapid time zone change (jet lag) syndrome
      b. Work shift change in conventional sleep-wake schedule
  2. Persistent
      a. Frequently changing sleep-wake schedule
      b. Delayed sleep phase syndrome
      c. Advanced sleep phase syndrome
      d. Non-24-hour sleep-wake syndrome
      e. Irregular sleep-wake pattern
      f. Not otherwise specified[a]
D. Dysfunctions Associated with sleep, sleep stages, or partial arousals (parasomnias)
  1. Sleepwalking (somnambulism)
  2. Sleep terrors (pavor nocturnus, incubus)
  3. Sleep-related enuresis
  4. Other dysfunctions
      a. Dream anxiety attacks (nightmares)
      b. Sleep-related epileptic seizures
      c. Sleep-related bruxism
      d. Sleep-related headbanging (jactatio capitis nocturnus)
      e. Familial sleep paralysis
      f. Impaired sleep-related penile tumescence
      g. Sleep-related painful erections
      h. Sleep-related cluster headaches and chronic paroxysmal hemicrania
      i. Sleep-related abnormal swallowing syndrome
      j. Sleep-related asthma
      k. Sleep-related cardiovascular symptoms
      l. Sleep-related gastroesophageal reflux
      m. Sleep-related hemoylsis (paroxysmal nocturnal hemoglobinuria)
      n. Asymptomatic polysomnographic finding
      o. Not otherwise specified[a]

[a]This entry is intended to leave place in the classification for both undiagnosed ("don't know") conditions and additional (as yet undocumented) conditions that may be described in the future.

Source: Reprinted with permission from "Classification of the Sleep Disorders" by H. Roffwarg, *Sleep,* 2:17–19, 1979.

Space does not permit a fuller discussion of the diagnosis and treatment of the sleep disorders; this has been covered elsewhere [9, 12]. However, it should be clear that the clinical approach—taking as an example insomnia, the most common complaint—is first to recognize that insomnia is a symptom, and not an illness to be cured by administering a sleeping pill. Next the cause of the symptom must be sought through history, physical exam, and laboratory studies. Treatment then, wherever possible, is directed at the cause.

EFFECT OF ALCOHOL ON THE SLEEP DISORDERS

Although conclusive studies are not available in all situations, the impression from the research literature as well as case reports and personal clinical experience is that alcohol and alcoholism can play a serious initiating or aggravating role in all three of the major groups of sleep symptoms or sleep problems. Certainly there is enough evidence so that alcohol intake should be carefully evaluated and taken into account in the differentiation diagnosis of any patient with a sleep disorder.

The interaction of alcohol with the three major groups—insomnia, hypersomnolence, and episodic events—is examined and each group discussed in terms of general effects and also in terms of effects on some of the subgroups and causes.

Insomnia

Taken in large quantities there is no question that alcohol can actually produce insomnia. Early during the course of alcohol intake, drinkers often state that alcohol make them fall asleep sooner, and provided a deep or long sleep. However, even after a few weeks, although sleep may still feel deep and long, it no longer feels especially restful. This often becomes more prominent with continued periods of drinking; though sleep onset may still be rapid one begins to notice increasing brief awakenings during the night and restless sleep. In some cases the restless and disturbed quality of the sleep is much more obvious to the bed partner or roommate than to the drinker; memory of brief awakenings and sleep disturbances is often poor in any case, and is perhaps worsened by alcohol intake. Sleep laboratory studies confirm that sleep is disturbed and fragmented during long periods of continued drinking.

Alcohol withdrawal is also associated with insomnia in most cases. The first few nights of withdrawal, as discussed above, are associated with specific sleep changes, including large amounts of D time, and very fragmented sleep. This period is often characterized by vivid dreams, nightmares, and waking hallucinosis (delirium tremens). Following the acute period, sleep is often then reported as poor or disturbed for a period of weeks and sometimes months after withdrawal of alcohol [8, 23]. This is quite similar to the situation after withdrawal of opiates.

This insomnia is not always easy to treat. There is a justified reluctance in giving such a patient a possibly addicting sleeping medication. A great deal of support is required, and it is important for both the physician and patient to be aware that this insomnia is probably a result of the body's gradual withdrawal from alcohol. When insomnia persists for long periods after alcohol has stopped, it is, of course, appropriate to look for other conditions that may be producing or aggravating it (see above).

If no specific treatable cause can be found, nonpharmacological treatments such as exercise, regularization of life patterns, relaxation, or biofeedback [9, 15] may be worth trying in preference to central nervous system depressants. Another possibility is administration of the amino acid l-tryptophan, which has been shown to reduce sleep latency and usually decrease waking in a number of populations studied [10], including alcoholics suffering insomnia after withdrawal [21]. However, these studies involved only a few days of administration; long-term effects have not been investigated.

Hypersomnolence

There is no question that alcohol intake can produce excessive sleep. Several laboratory studies have demonstrated periods of increased sleep during alcohol intake in groups of alcoholics drinking for periods of several weeks [16, 20]. In one study alcoholics allowed to choose their own drinking patterns often drank heavily for periods of 6 to 8 days (during which there was often moderately increased sleep), and then stopped drinking for a day or so, during which time they slept for almost the entire 24 hours before resuming their drinking.

Withdrawal from alcohol, as mentioned, is associated with severe insomnia, but in some patients this is followed after a week or so by one night of deep and subjectively very restorative sleep [8]. This could be considered another sort of hypersomnolence.

In terms of the differential diagnosis of hypersomnolence, it is worth remembering that alcohol consumption can of course produce tiredness and excessive sleep in the daytime. This may seem entirely obvious; in a situation where an accurate history of heavy alcohol intake is obtained for certain days, there is nothing surprising in the fact that a patient may have slept for 12 or even 16 or 20 hours. However, there are times when a history of alcohol intake is not clear, or when it is denied entirely and a patient is referred for excessive sleepiness or hypersomnolence.

A careful history, taken separately from the patient and family members, as well as other signs of alcoholism, should make this diagnosis clear once it is suspected. But there are times when even an experienced clinician at one of the sleep disorder centers becomes intrigued by a question of possible narcolepsy or Kleine-

Levin syndrome or an unusual depressive reaction to explain extended periods of sleep, and a cause as simple as excessive alcohol intake is overlooked.

Hypersomnolence can sometimes be produced by relatively small amounts of alcohol in a person also ingesting other chemicals, such as tranquilizers or any central nervous system depressants. This also should be clear when, and if, an accurate history of drug intake is obtained.

Episodic Sleep Disorders

Alcohol can have quite profound effects on the episodic sleep disorders listed in Table 1. Reviews mention that alcoholics sometimes have night terrors and also episodes of sleepwalking or sleep talking while drinking [8]. However, there have been no studies directly examining these phenomena. The Sleep Laboratory at Boston State Hospital is initiating studies on this question; some relevant observations in groups of research subjects with these episodic disorders have been made, as well as in sleep-disorder patients specifically complaining of episodic sleep disorders.

Some data in support of three hypotheses covering the relationship of alcohol to the episodic disorders is available. First, alcohol may exacerbate the stage 4 disturbances (night terrors and sleepwalking). Several cases have been observed in which alcohol increased both the frequency and severity of night terrors and somnambulism. This is not simply of academic interest. One recent patient had been in an automobile accident in which four persons had been killed. The accident resulted when the patient, who had pulled over the side of the highway to rest, got up 1 hour later, drove onto the highway going in the wrong direction, and had a head-on collision. He had absolutely no recollection of the event. Subsequently, his history revealed that he had a long history of sleepwalking and night terror episodes, and on careful questioning it appeared that these episodes definitely tended to occur with greater severity at times of stress and times of alcohol intake. In fact, on the evening of the accident, 2 to 3 hours before the episode in question, he had consumed a considerable amount of alcohol and his blood alcohol levels were elevated. This man was a moderate drinker, definitely not an alcoholic. He had never passed out nor had he had a blackout episode due to drinking. Standard sleep laboratory recordings revealed no particular abnormality, but on one of two nights when alcohol (equivalent of about four drinks) was administered before bedtime he did have an episode of sleepwalking arising from stage 4 sleep. This case was unusually dramatic and laboratory recordings were obtained; there have been others in which alcohol appeared to increase episodes of this kind as well. Enuresis is another member of this stage 4 disorder group, but no evidence about effects of alcohol on it are available.

Another group of disturbances are those related to D sleep (rapid eye movement sleep). At present the D nightmare, or dream anxiety attack, is the only well-known disturbance in this group. The effect of alcohol on these phenomena has not been studied specifically, but the Sleep Laboratory has recently studied 50 adults who had frequent D nightmares (at least one a week at home) [13, 14]. Lengthy interviews included questions about the use of alcohol and other drugs and whether these had any effect on the nightmares.

Many of the subjects who suffered from frequent D nightmares reported that alcohol reduced the incidence of these nightmares; some reported an increase of nightmares a day or two after a night of large alcohol intake. In other words, the nightmares tended to be reduced on the night of alcohol intake and if anything they increased the night after. This would be consistent with the effects of alcohol on D time discussed earlier, and consistent with the severe nightmares experienced by alcoholics several days after withdrawal.

There are other episodic sleep disturbances, such as awakenings with nocturnal angina and with ulcer pain, which may be related to D sleep, but nothing is known about alcohol effects in these situations.

There is a third group of episodic disorders whose occurrence is temporally related neither to stage 4 sleep nor to D sleep. The best known members of this class are sleep talking, and bruxism (teeth grinding). Both appear to occur throughout the night [1, 24].

There is some evidence that alcohol intake may exacerbate these disturbances. Four cases have been studied in which the incidence and severity of bruxism was definitely increased by alcohol intake. The etiology of bruxism is complicated; there are probably familial factors, malocclusion of the jaws appears to play a role in some cases, and the condition is exacerbated by stress and anger. Nonetheless, in these four persons who increased their alcohol intake for a few weeks and then decreased it to zero on several occasions over a 6-month period, there was a clear correlation between alcohol intake and the amount of bruxism [11].

In several cases it appears that alcohol intake is related to amount of sleep talking in persons prone to this problem. Gross and Hastey [8], as mentioned above, have also made this observation. Other miscellaneous episodic sleep disorders are also in need of study.

Thus, alcohol has clinically significant effects on the episodic sleep disturbances. Alcohol intake increases the incidence and severity of the stage 4 disorders (night terrors, sleepwalking, possibly enuresis) and probably of the episodic disorders occurring throughout the night (bruxism, sleep talking). It decreased the incidence of D sleep related disturbances (nightmares), but these may increase during withdrawal. Of course the precise relationship of blood and brain alcohol levels to the episodes is entirely unknown; it is possible that some of the effects noted during alcohol intake might occur during periods of falling blood alcohol levels and might perhaps represent short-term withdrawal effects rather than direct alcohol effects.

In conclusion, alcohol can initiate or aggravate a number of sleep disorders. Dosage has not been discussed in detail. Most of the studies mentioned have dealt with doses within the normal range of intake: the equivalent of one to four drinks in single administration, and doses ranging as high as the equivalent of a quart of hard liquor a day in studies of alcoholics determining their own drinking patterns. Only a few of the studies in which sleep patterns were studied involved a wide dose-response curve, so one can only say that the effects on sleep are those of doses within the usual range of alcohol consumption.

Within this range it is striking that alcohol, frequently used informally to induce sleep, actually produces or greatly exacerbates a number of sleep disturbances, including insomnia, both during chronic intake and after withdrawal, hypersomnolence, and a number of episodic sleep disorders.

REFERENCES

1. Arkin, A. Sleeptalking. In: *The Mind in Sleep. Psychology and Psychophysiology*, Arkin, A., Antrobus, J., and Ellman, S. (eds.). Erlbaum: Hillsdale, N.J., 1978.
2. Greenberg, R. Mayer, R., Brook, R., Pearlman, C., and Hartmann, E. Sleep and dreaming in patients with postalcoholic Korsakoff's disease. *Arch. Gen. Psychiatry* 18:203-209, 1968.
3. Greenberg, R., and Pearlman, C. Delirium tremens and dreaming. *Am. J. Psychiatry* 124:37-46, 1967.
4. Gresham, S. C., Webb, W. B., and William, R. L. Alcohol and caffeine: Effect on inferred visual dreaming. *Science* 140:1226-1227, 1963.
5. Gross, M. M., and Goodenough, D. E. Sleep disturbances in the acute alcoholic psychoses. *Am. Psychiatr. Ann.* 23:132-147, 1968.
6. Gross, M. M., Goodenough, D., Tobin, M., Halpert, E., Lepore, D., Perlstein, A., Sirota, M., Dibianco, J., Fuller, R., and Kishner, I. Sleep disturbances and hallucinations in the acute alcoholic psychoses. *J. Nerv. Ment. Dis.* 142:493-514, 1966.
7. Gross, M. M., and Hastey, J. M. The relation between baseline slow-wave sleep and the slow-wave sleep response to alcohol in alcoholics. In: *Alcohol Intoxication and Withdrawal: Experimental Studies::*, Gross, M. M. (ed.). Plenum: New York, 1975.
8. Gross, M. M., and Hastey, J. M. Sleep disturbances in alcoholism. In: *Alcoholism*, Tarter, R. and Sugerman, A. (eds.). Addison-Wesley: New York, 1976.
9. Hartmann, E. *The Sleeping Pill*. Yale University Press: New Haven, 1978.
10. Hartmann, E. L-tryptophan: A rational hypnotic with clinical potential. *Am. J. Psychiatry* 134:366-370, 1977.
11. Hartmann, E. Alcohol and bruxism. *N. Eng. J. Med.* 301:334, 1979.
12. Hartmann, E. Sleep disorders. In: *Comprehensive Textbook of Psychiatry III*, Kaplan, H., Freedman, A., and Sadock, B. (eds.). Williams & Wilkins: Baltimore, 1980.
13. Hartmann, E., and Russ, D. Frequent nightmares and the vulnerability to schizophrenia. The personality of the nightmare sufferer. *Psychopharmacol. Bull.* 15:10-12, 1979.
14. Hartmann, E., Russ, D., van der Kolk, B. Lifelong nightmares: A possible indicator of vulnerability to schizophrenia. *Sleep Res.* 8:163, 1979.
15. Hauri, P. *The Sleep Disorders: Current Concepts*. Upjohn: Kalamazoo, 1977.
16. Isbell, H., Fraser, H., Wikler, A., Belleville, R., and Eiseman, A. An experimental study of the etiology of "rum-fits" and delirium tremens. *Q. J. Stud. Alcohol* 16:1-33, 1955.
17. Johnson, L. C., Burdick, J. A., and Smith, J. Sleep during alcohol intake and with-

drawal in the chronic alcoholic. *Arch. Gen. Psychiatry* 22:406-418, 1970.

18. Knowles, J. B., Laverty, S. G., and Kuechler, H. A. Effects of alcohol on REM sleep. *Q. J. Stud. Alcohol* 29:342-349, 1968.

19. Lester, B. K., Rundell, O. H., Cowden, L. C., and Williams, H. L. Chronic alcoholism: Alcohol and sleep. In: *Alcohol Intoxication and Withdrawal: Experimental Studies*, Gross, M. M. (ed.). Plenum: New York, 1973.

20. Mello, N. K., and Mendelson, J. H. Experimentally induced intoxication in alcoholics: A comparison between programmed and spontaneous drinking. *J. Pharmacol. Exp. Ther.* 173:271-298, 1970.

21. Makipour, H., Iber, F. L., and Hartmann, E. Effects of l-tryptophan on sleep in hospitalized insomniac patients. *Sleep Res. Abs.* 1:65, 1972.

22. Marbach, G., and Schwertz, M. T. Effects of physiologiques de l'alcohol et de la caffeine au cours du sommeil chez l'homme. *Arch. Sci. Physiol.* 18:163, 1964.

23. Pokorny, A. Sleep disturbances, alcohol, and alcoholism: A review. In: *Sleep Disorders: Diagnosis and Treatment*. Williams, R. and Karacan, I. (eds.). Wiley: New York, 1978.

24. Reding, G., Sepelin, H., Robinson, J. E., Jr., Zimmerman, S. O., and Smith, V. H. Nocturnal teeth-grinding: All night psychophysiology studies. *J. Dent. Res.* 47:786-797, 1968.

25. Roffwarg, H. et al. Classification of the sleep disorders. *Sleep* 2:1-137, 1979.

26. Rundell, O. H., Lester, B. K., Griffiths, W. J., and Williams, H. L.: Alcohol and sleep in young adults. *Psychopharmacol.* 26:201-218, 1972.

27. Wagman, A. M., and Allen, R. P. Effects of alcohol ingestion and abstinence on slow-wave sleep of alcoholics. In: *Alcohol Intoxication and Withdrawal: Experimental Studies II*, Gross, M. M. (ed.). Plenum: New York, 1975.

28. Williams, H. L., and Salamy, A. Alcohol and sleep. In: *The Biology of Alcoholism*, Kissin, B. and Begleites, H. (eds.). Plenum: New York, 1972.

29. Williams, L., MacLean, A. W., Cairns, J. Dose-response relationships between ethanol and the sleep of young women. *Sleep Res.* 4:122, 1975.

30. Wolin, S. J., and Mello, N. K. The effects of alcohol on dreams and hallucinations in alcohol addicts. *Ann. N.Y. Acad. Sci.* 215:266-302, 1973.

31. Yules, R. B., Lippman, M. E., and Freedman, D. X. Alcohol administration prior to sleep. *Arch. Gen. Psychiatry* 16:94-97, 1967.

32. Zarcone, V. P., and Hoddes, E. Effects of 5-hydroxytryptophan on fragmentation of REM sleep in alcoholics. *Am. J. Psychiatry* 132:74-76, 1975.

13

RICHARD F. MAYER, MD, University of Maryland School of Medicine
RAMESH K. KHURANA, MD, University of Maryland School of Medicine

PERIPHERAL AND AUTONOMIC NERVOUS SYSTEM

OCCURRENCE OF PEripheral neuropathy in patients with chronic alcoholism is well known. However, it remains unclear as to how peripheral nerves are damaged in patients who consume large amounts of alcohol for prolonged periods. A number of extensive reviews have summarized both data and opinions concerning the effects of alcohol on the peripheral nervous system [32, 40]. This chapter updates the subject of alcoholic polyneuropathy. In addition, the effects of alcoholism on function and structure of the peripheral autonomic nervous system are discussed.

PERIPHERAL NERVOUS SYSTEM

Clinical Studies

In patients with alcoholic polyneuropathy reflex, sensory, and motor functions are affected to varying degrees. The dysfunction is usually bilateral, symmetrical, and distal more than proximal and involves lower extremities more than

---

Richard F. Mayer, MD, Professor of Neurology, Department of Neurology, University of Maryland School of Medicine, Baltimore, Maryland.

Ramesh K. Khurana, MD, Assistant Professor of Neurology, Department of Neurology, University of Maryland School of Medicine, Baltimore, Maryland.

others. The clinical manifestations of polyneuropathy, which occur in chronic alcoholic patients, are well described and are not discussed further here [32, 40].

Electrophysiological studies in chronic alcoholic patients have revealed reduced conduction velocities in peripheral nerves both in the subclinical [29] as well as clinical stages of polyneuropathy [28]. Changes in distal segments precede proximal [10, 28] changes and distal sensory conduction may be reduced more than motor [8]. In some patients with severe polyneuropathy, there may be a complete block of nerve conduction [28]. Associated with the reduced nerve conduction velocity are reduced amplitudes of the compound muscle action potential, prolonged H-reflex latency, and reduced amplitudes of sensory nerve action potentials [8, 28, 42]. These physiological studies suggest loss both of sensory and motor nerve fibers, distally before proximally, as well as slowed conduction in some nerve fibers [7, 21, 28, 42].

Pathophysiology

Pathological studies of sural nerves biopsied from patients with alcoholic polyneuropathy have shown prominent axonal degeneration of myelinated and unmyelinated fibers [7, 32, 39, 42]. The pathological findings, taken with the physiological evidence of greater involvement of distal segments of nerves, suggest a primary neuronal process with distal axonal (dying back) degeneration. Axonal degeneration of nerve fibers can account for the slight decreases in conduction velocity, reduced amplitudes of nerve action potentials, and complete block of nerve conduction. This process, however, does not explain the slow conduction velocities recorded in some nerve fibers. It is likely that this change in conduction results from demyelination of nerve fibers [7, 32, 37, 42] and that paranodal and segmental demyelination observed in some patients with alcoholic polyneuropathy represents a secondary type of demyelination as observed in uremic polyneuropathy [14] and Friedreich's ataxia [15]. The initial pathologic event in alcoholic polyneuropathy may occur in the nerve cell with distal axonal degeneration and more proximal secondary paranodal demyelination. Slow nerve conduction velocities in some patients with long-term alcoholic polyneuropathy may result also from the repair process, either incomplete regeneration or remyelination of the peripheral nerves.

Pathogenesis

Although the pathophysiology of alcoholic polyneuropathy is more completely understood now, it remains unclear as to why and how the distal nerve fibers undergo axonal degeneration. A number of possible etiologies of alcoholic polyneuropathy have been suggested. These include a direct toxic effect of alcohol [7, 13], nutritional and vitamin deficiencies, especially thiamine lack [16, 40, 44], and other associated metabolic dysfunctions, such as gastrointestinal malabsorption [11] and liver failure [24].

Most of the data accumulated over the past 50 years have suggested that the polyneuropathy results from the nutritional deficiencies associated with chronic alcoholism (see recent review by Victor [40]). Of the nutritional deficiencies, whether lack of thiamine alone [16, 40, 44] is the causative factor in man remains unknown. Experimentally, thiamine deficiency produces distal axonal degeneration in the rat [34]. However, other B vitamin deficiencies are also known to produce polyneuropathy in man [6, 40, 41], and these deficiencies may be responsible in part for the varied clinical presentations of polyneuropathy in chronic alcoholics.

Possible metabolic causes of polyneuropathy in chronic alcoholism are the associated gastrointestinal malabsorption and liver dysfunction. The polyneuropathy observed in patients with adult coeliac disease [11] or following gastrectomy with malnutrition [7] may be similar clinically to alcoholic polyneuropathy. However, peripheral nerves do show demyelination in these conditions and experimentally induced protein deficiency in a subhuman primate may result in myelin degeneration [35].

Although liver disease occurs in many patients with chronic alcoholism, its role in the production of polyneuropathy is doubtful [38]. The effects of acute and chronic hepatic dysfunction on peripheral nerves have been studied in the developing and adult mouse [43]. Acute liver disease was produced by the mouse hepatitis virus. Chronic hepatitis was produced by biweekly injections of carbon tetrachloride (CCl_4) for periods up to 6 months. No signs of peripheral neuropathy were seen in these animals even though there was biochemical and histological evidence of acute or chronic hepatitis. Serial motor conduction velocities in the posterior tibial nerves remained normal in adult animals throughout the 6-month period of study. Peripheral nerves showed no evidence of axonal degeneration or segmental demyelination. The ratio of the internodal distance to fiber diameter in teased posterior tibial nerve fibers from mice with the chronic hepatitis model was the same as age-matched controls [Williams, I., and Mayer, R. F., unpublished observations]. In the developing mouse, maturation of peripheral nerve fibers, assessed by conduction velocities, was impeded during infection by the mouse hepatitis virus. This study in the mouse supports those observations in man that liver disease per se does not produce polyneuropathy. Moreover, neither malabsorption nor liver disease occurs in all patients with alcoholic polyneuropathy and hence both are unlikely to represent the basic etiology.

For many years alcohol (ethanol) has been considered toxic to the nervous system and it has been suggested that it is this effect that produces the polyneuropathy. In a recent physiological-morphological study, Behse and Buchthal [7] compared 37 patients with alcoholic polyneuropathy and six nonalcoholic patients with postgastrectomy neuropathy. Most of the alcoholic patients (23 of 37 patients) had no clinical evidence of nutritional deficiency, while those with neuropathy after gastrectomy had marked weight loss and malabsorption. Sensory and motor conductions were reduced in both groups of patients but somewhat more in the nonalcoholic group. Sural nerve biopsies from the alcoholic group revealed loss (axonal degeneration) both of large and small fibers but segmental and paranodal demyelination was rare. In the postgastrectomy group with malnutrition, however, many large fibers were preserved in the sural nerves and there was evidence of segmental and paranodal demyelination as well as remyelination. From these observations it was concluded that alcoholic polyneuropathy with axonal degeneration results from a toxic action of alcohol on peripheral nerves and that malnutrition results in segmental demyelination of peripheral nerves. Thus malnutrition could account for demyelination and consequently slow nerve conduction velocities observed in some patients with alcoholic polyneuropathy [21, 28, 37]. It is possible, therefore, that the etiology of alcoholic polyneuropathy is not the same in all patients and the varied nutritional and metabolic abnormalities may alter the pathological reactions of the peripheral nervous system.

A number of studies have been carried out in experimental animals to determine the effects of long-term alcohol consumption. In the rat, long-term consumption of a liquid diet nutritionally adequate but containing ethanol (36% of the calories replaced isocalorically) produced a fatty liver [12]. This change was attributed to the toxic effect of alcohol consumed in an amount comparable to a moderate intake in man [25]. Using this diet, rats were fed ethanol for periods up to 36 weeks as researchers looked for evidence of neuromuscular dysfunction [30]. No signs of neuropathy were detected by observing gait and motor function; also, peripheral (sciatic) nerves stained for axons and myelin showed neither axonal degeneration nor demyelination. Muscle fibers (anterior tibial and extensor digitorum longus—EDL—muscles) also failed to show histological or histochemical changes suggestive of neurogenic or myogenic pathology. The mean resting membrane potentials recorded in the EDL muscles were significantly less than controls only in animals maintained on alcohol for long periods of time (30 to 36 weeks). This partial depolarization of the muscle membrane may be the first sign of denervation [1] and suggests that long-term consumption of large amounts of ethanol may be toxic to the peripheral nervous system in the rat. However, on this alcoholic diet for 36 weeks, a frank neuropathy did not develop.

In a more recent study, rats were chronically fed alcohol either by the schedule-induced polydipsia technique or by liquid diets for 16 to 18 weeks [9]. These animals did not show signs of peripheral neuropathy and motor conduction velocities remained normal in the caudal nerve. However, there was morphologic evidence of a mild axonal neuropathy, but only in distal nerve fibers (the ventral caudal nerve but not in the posterior tibial nerve). No evidence of malnutrition or thiamine deficiency was apparent. These investigators concluded that the distal axonal degeneration was due to the toxic effects of alcohol itself. Another group of investigators concluded that ethanol produced changes in the Schwann cells in the more proximal sciatic nerve and that there was a greater tendency for the rats consuming alcohol to have nerve lesions if they were also deficient in thiamine [19, 20].

In a subhuman primate, Rubin and Lieber [36] demonstrated that the entire spectrum of alcoholic liver injury could be produced by chronic alcohol consumption with a nutritionally adequate diet. The changes produced in the liver were similar to those in patients with alcoholic cirrhosis. Clinical and postmortem examination of these same animals did not reveal gross evidence of neuropathy, although detailed physiologic and morphologic studies of peripheral nerves were not reported.

It has been reported that young adults, who consumed large amounts of alcohol for periods of 5 to 10 years and maintained a good diet, did not show clinical evidence of neuropathy [29]. Although these patients had a decrease in mean nerve conduction velocity, it was not clear whether this subclinical neuropathy resulted from the alcohol itself or from other factors related either to the withdrawal syndrome or nutrition.

Thus, in none of the animal models did a frank nueropathy develop. However, the amount and duration of alcohol consumption in man may exceed that studied in animals and recent studies have shown that chronic alcohol consumption can result in organ damage (e.g., liver cirrhosis) previously thought to be nutritional in origin. It is likely that factors other than alcohol or species differences are necessary for the production of the severe alcoholic polyneuropathy. Nutritional deficiencies remain the likely primary defect and must be corrected in the treatment of this disorder.

Because of the variability of signs and symptoms as well as the severity of the neuropathy, it is possible that the etiology of the polyneuropathy is not the same in all patients with chronic alcoholism. Thus it is possible that patients with greater slowing of nerve conduction and with more evidence of segmental or paranodal demyelination may have additional factors (e.g., protein and vitamin deficiencies) producing neuropathy. However, it is also possible that these differences in physiology and pathology represent the spectrum of nerve involvement in patients with alcoholic polyneuropathy.

In some patients with chronic alcoholism and polyneuropathy there is clinical or subclinical (determined by electrophysiological studies) evidence of focal nerve involvement [28]. This is especially prominent in the elbow segment of the ulnar nerve [27] and fibular segment of the peroneal nerve. However, any nerve or plexus that is superficial or adjacent to a firm structure may be compressed and damaged by pressure, ischemia, or both. This focal compressive neuropathy, which may be acute or subacute and progressive, is characterized by reduced conduction velocity and paranodal demyelination [31]. Occasionally multiple nerves are involved in patients who suffer from chronic alcoholism, marked weight loss, and nutritional deficiency. This clinical condition must be separated from the generalized neuropathy, since multifocal neuropathy does not result from the effects of either alcohol or nutritional deficiency alone, but from compression. This type of neuropathy may produce slow conduction and demyelination in some nerve fibers.

Treatment and Prognosis

The treatment of alcoholic polyneuropathy includes both cessation of alcohol consumption and improvement in nutritional status. In patients with mild signs of neuropathy, treatment with a high-calorie, high-protein, and high-carbohydrate diet and supplemental B vitamins is usually adequate. However, in patients with severe neuropathy, intravenous B vitamins in large doses should be used because of possible problems with absorption and metabolism. Active physical therapy is also important to prevent muscle shortening (e.g., permanent foot drop because of unopposed shortening of the calf muscles) and contractures. This therapeutic regimen is now routine in hospitals and clinics.

Since axonal degeneration is the major pathological reaction in alcoholic polyneuropathy, recovery will depend on the extent of peripheral nerve regeneration. This is a slow process and, therefore, clinical recovery will be slow. Although peripheral nerves readily regenerate both in man and experimental animals, ultrastructural studies of sural nerves from patients with alcoholic polyneuropathy have revealed limited nerve regeneration [7, 39]. This supports many clinical observations that alcoholic neuropathy with prominent clinical dysfunction does not improve completely but leaves the patient with reflex and sensory abnormalities. Additional studies are still needed to better understand the mechanisms of nerve degeneration and regeneration and how to restore nerve function completely to normal.

In patients with focal compressive neuropathies, measures should be taken to decrease pressure at the sites of nerve compression. This includes the use of foam rubber applied to the areas such as elbows and knees. In patients with severe nerve dysfunction, surgical decompression or nerve translocation may be necessary before function returns.

AUTONOMIC NERVOUS SYSTEM

Symptoms

Symptoms of autonomic dysfunction are stated to occur with variable frequency in severely affected alcoholic patients. Anhidrosis occurs frequently and approximates the area of sensory loss because postganglionic sympathetic fibers, in their distal distribution, travel with the somatic peripheral nerves [26]. Impotence is a common complaint among chronic alcoholics [2]. Orthostatic hypotension and hypothermia, frequent in a patient with Wernicke's encephalopathy, are not common in uncomplicated alcoholic polyneuropathy [18, 26, 33]. Barraclough and Sharpey-Schafer [5] noted hypotension in one of their seven patients, and Low et al. [26] found hypotension in none of their 12 patients. Symptoms of hoarseness, weak voice, dysphagia, urinary retention and incontinence, and fecal incontinence [33] have been rarely reported.

Clinical Assessment

Although tests for the assessment of autonomic functions are available [22], studies that document autonomic dysfunction in alcoholic patients using even a select number of these tests are few [5, 18, 26]. These tests are useful not only in establishing the presence of autonomic disturbance in clinically affected patients but may also help in detecting subclinical involvement of the autonomic nervous system.

The presence of postural hypotension, lack of systolic blood pressure overshoot in response to the Valsalva's maneuver [5], greater than normal fall in blood pressure following the administration of trinitroglycerine [26], absence of a blood pressure rise in response to noise and mental arithmetic, and anhidrosis [18] provide evidence of sympathetic insufficiency. Johnson and Spalding noted the involvement of the efferent pathway on the basis of impaired sweating and an absence of a blood pressure rise in response to noise and mental arithmetic [18]. On the other hand, Barraclough and Sharpey-Schafer [5] observed normal changes in hand blood flow in response to Valsalva's maneuver. These authors suggested that the efferent vasomotor nerves were intact and impairment of circulatory reflexes was due to an afferent block [5]. It is probable that lesions interrupting circulatory reflexes affect the afferent as well as efferent pathways.

Vocal cord paralysis in patients with dysphonia has been described [33]. Esophageal manometric studies in 10 alcoholic patients with polyneuropathy and without dysphagia have been reported to show selective deterioration of primary peristalsis, most prominent in the distal esophagus, with normal functions of the lower esophageal sphincter [45]. An abnormally low Valsalva ratio and absent or minimal bradycardia in response to simulated diving reflex have been found in patients with chronic alcoholism [Khurana, R. K., unpublished observations]. Simulated diving reflex, produced by an apnoeic facial immersion in cold water, tests the integrity of the vagus nerves provided the trigeminal nerves and brainstem functions are intact; bradycardia of approximately $37 \pm 15\%$ is considered within normal limits [23]. Lower values suggest vagal involvement. Reports of urinary retention, urinary and fecal incontinence, and patulous anal sphincter suggest involvement of the parasympathetic sacral outflow [33].

Pathology

Pathologic involvement of the sympathetic and the parasympathetic nervous system has been reported, but clinical significance of these studies is difficult to assess. Histopathology of intermediolateral column cells was normal [33]. A quantitative study of white rami communicantes in alcoholic patients with no evidence of peripheral or autonomic nerve dysfunction revealed uniformly short internodes, suggesting regeneration following wallerian degeneration [3]. Novak and Victor found active myelin degeneration in the paravertebral sympathetic chain of one patient with hepatic encephalopathy, Wernicke's disease, and severe polyneuropathy [33]. A recent study of the greater splanic nerve in patients with alcoholic polyneuropathy did not show any significant change [26]. Postmortem histopathology in three of the four patients with alcoholic polyneuropathy, without any autonomic evaluation, showed giant sympathetic neurons. The cytoplasm of these neurons contained abnormal accumulation of periodic acid Schiff-positive material and nuclei showed various stages of degeneration from pyknosis to complete disappearance. Large sympathetic neurons, however, have been reported in a variety of other disorders without known autonomic disturbances [4]. Ferriera and colleagues studied the effects of prolonged alcohol consumption on the adrenergic nerve endings of rat atrioventricular valves by the Falck-Hillarp method and observed reduction in catecholamine-containing fibers and terminals [17]. A histopathologic study of the vagus nerves and nuclei in four patients demonstrated extensive degeneration of myelin sheaths and axis cylinders of the cervical, recurrent, and distal portions of the vagus nerves; vagal neurons showed minimal involvement [33].

Treatment and Prognosis

The effect of autonomic involvement on the prognosis of patients has not been well studied and it may be that some aspects of dysautonomia threaten the patient's life. A recovery from hoarseness in one patient and improvement in systolic blood pressure overshoot in response to the Valsalva maneuver in a few patients over a period of few months have been described [33, 5]. A quantitative study of white rami communicantes demonstrating uniformly short internodes and increased numbers of small fibers suggest regeneration.

It is recommended that one should not wait for the onset of hypotension, hypothermia, cardiac arrythmias, dysphagia, or dysphonia to suspect autonomic involvement. Patients, particularly with severe alcoholic polyneuropathy, should be studied for dysautonomia in a thorough and systematic manner. Such investigation is likely to show that the incidence of disorders in autonomic nervous system function is greater than generally appreciated in these patients and may be of practical significance in their clinical care and prognosis.

REFERENCES

1. Albuquerque, E., Warnick, J., Tasse, J., and Sansone, F. Effects of vinblastine and colchicine on neural regulation of the fast and slow skeletal muscles of the rat. *Exp. Neurol.* 37:607-634, 1972.
2. Appenzeller, O. Reflex control of copulatory behavior and neurogenic disorders of sexual function. In: *The Autonomic Nervous System* (2nd ed.), Appenzeller, O. (ed.). North Holland Pub.: Amsterdam, 1976.

3. Appenzeller, O., and Ogin, G. Myelinated fibres in human paravertebral sympathetic chain: White rami communicantes in alcoholic and diabetic patients. *J. Neurol. Neurosurg. Psychiatry* 37:1155-1161, 1974.

4. Appenzeller, O., and Richardson, E., Jr. The sympathetic chain in patients with diabetic and alcoholic polyneuropathy. *Neurology (Minneap.)* 16:1205-1209, 1966.

5. Barraclough, M., and Sharpey-Schafer, E. Hypotension from absent circulatory refelxes: Effects of alcohol, barbiturates, psychotherapeutic drugs and other mechanisms. *Lancet* 1:1121-1126, 1963.

6. Bean, W., Hodges, R., and Daum, K. Pantothenic acid deficiency induced in human subjects. *J. Clin. Invest.* 34:1073-1084, 1955.

7. Behse, F., and Buchthal, F. Alcoholic neuropathy: Clinical, electrophysiological and biopsy findings. *Ann. Neurol.* 2:95-110, 1977.

8. Blackstock, E., Rushworth, G., and Cath, D. Electrophysiological studies in alcoholism. *J. Neurol. Neurosurg. Psychiatry* 35:326-334, 1972.

9. Bosch, E., Pelham, R., Rasool, C., Chatterjee, A., Lark, R., Brown, L., Munsat, T., and Bradley, W. Animal models of alcoholic neuropathy: Morphologic, electrophysiologic and biochemical findings. *Muscle Nerv.* 2:133-144, 1979.

10. Casey, E., and LeQuesne, P. Electrophysiological evidence for a distal lesion in alcoholic neuropathy. *J. Neurol. Neurosurg. Psychiatry* 35:624-630, 1970.

11. Cooke, W., and Smith, W. Neurological disorders associated with adult coeliac disease. *Brain* 89:683-723, 1966.

12. DeCarli, L., and Lieber, C. Fatty liver in the rat after prolonged intake of ethanol with a nutritionally adequate new liquid diet. *J. Nutr.* 91:331-336, 1967.

13. Denny-Brown, D. The neurologic aspects of thiamine deficiency. *Fed. Proc.* 17 (Suppl.2):35-39, 1958.

14. Dyck, P., Johnson, W., Lambert, E., and O'Brien, P. Segmental demyelination secondary to axonal degeneration in uremic neuropathy. *Mayo Clin. Proc.* 46:400-431, 1971.

15. Dyck, P., and Lais, A. Evidence for segmental demyelination secondary to axonal degeneration in Friedreich's ataxia. In: *Clinical Studies in Myology*, Kakulas, B. (ed.). Excerpta Medica: Amsterdam, 1973.

16. Fennelly, J., Frank, O., Baker, H., and Lewy, C. Red blood cell-transketolase activity in malnourished alcoholics with cirrhosis. *Am. J. Clin. Nutr.* 20:946-949, 1967.

17. Ferriera, A., Santos, J., and Rossi, M. Effects of alcohol ingestion on adrenergic nerve endings of rat atrioventricular valves. *Experientia* 31:82-83, 1975.

18. Johnson, R., and Spalding, J. Arterial hypotension. In: *Disorders of the Autonomic Nervous System*, Johnson, R. and Spalding, J. (eds.). Blackwell Scientific Publ: Oxford, 1974.

19. Juntunen, J., Teravainen, H., Eriksson, K., Larsen, A., and Hillborn, M. Peripheral neuropathy and myopathy: An experimental study of rats on alcohol and variable dietary thiamine. *Virchows Arch. (Pathol. Anat.)* 383:241-252, 1979.

20. Juntunen, J., Teravainen, H., Eriksson, K., Panula, P., and Larsen, A. Experimental alcoholic neuropathy in the rat: Histological and electrophysiological study on the myoneural junctions and the peripheral nerves. *Acta Neuropath. (Berl.)* 41:131-137, 1978.

21. Juul-Jensen, P., and Mayer, R. Threshold stimulation for nerve conduction studies in man. *Arch. Neurol.* 15:410-419, 1966.

22. Khurana, R. Clinical assessment of the autonomic nervous system. In: *Human Health and Disease*, Altman, P. and Katz, D. (eds.). Federation of American Societies for Experimental Biology: Bethesda, Md., 1977.

23. Khurana, R., Watabiki, S., Hebel, J., Toro, R., and Nelson, E. Cold face test in the assessment of trigeminal-brainstem-vagal function in humans. *Ann. Neurol.* 7:144-149, 1980.

24. Knill-Jones, R., Goodwill, C., Dayan, A., and Williams, R. Peripheral neuropathy in chronic liver disease: Clinical, electrodiagnostic and nerve biopsy findings. *J. Neurol. Neurosurg. Psychiatry* 35:22-30, 1972.

25. Lieber, C., and Rubin, E. Alcoholic fatty liver. *N. Eng. J. Med.* 280:705-708, 1969.

26. Low, P., Walsh, J., Huang, C., and McLeod, J. Sympathetic nervous system in alcoholic neuropathy: A clinical and pathological study. *Brain* 98:357-364, 1975.

27. Lugnegard, H., Walbreim, G., and Wennberg, A. Operative treatment of ulnar nerve neuropathy in the elbow region: A clinical and electrophysiological study. *Acta Orthop. Scand.* 48:168-176, 1977.

28. Mawdsley, C., and Mayer, R. Nerve conduction in alcoholic polyneuropathy. *Brain* 88:335-356, 1965.

29. Mayer, R. Peripheral nerve conduction in alcoholics: Studies of the effects of acute and chronic intoxication. *Psychosom. Med.* 28 (Part 2):475-483, 1966.

30. Mayer, R. Recent studies in man and animal of peripheral nerve and muscle dysfunction associated with chronic alcoholism. *Ann. N.Y. Acad. Sci.* 215:370-372, 1973.

31. Mayer, R., and Denny-Brown, D. Conduction velocity in peripheral nerve during experimental demyelination in the cat. *Neurology (Minneap.)* 14:714-726, 1964.

32. Mayer, R., and Garcia-Mullin, R. Peripheral nerve and muscle disorders associated with alcoholism. In *The Biology of Alcoholism* (Vol. 2), Kassin, B. and Begleiter, H. (eds.). Plenum Press: New York, 1972.

33. Novak, D., and Victor, M. The vagus and sympathetic nerves in alcoholic polyneuropathy. *Arch. Neurol.* 30:273-284, 1974.

34. Prineas, J. Peripheral nerve changes in thiamine deficient rats. *Arch. Neurol.* 23:541-548, 1970.

35. Roy, S., Singh, N., Deo, M., and Ramalingsaswami, V. Ultrastructure of skeletal muscle and peripheral nerve in experimental protein deficiency and its correlation with nerve conduction studies. *J. Neurol. Sci.* 17:399-409, 1972.

36. Rubin, E., and Lieber, C. Fatty liver, alcoholic hepatitis and cirrhosis produced by alcohol in primates. *N. Eng. J. Med.* 290:128-135, 1974.

37. Tackmann, W., Menkenberg, R., and Strenge, H. Correlation of electrophysiological and quantitative histological findings in the sural nerve of man: Studies on alcoholic neuropathy. *J. Neurol.* 216:289-299, 1977.

38. Thomas, P. Peripheral neuropathy. In: *Recent Advances in Clinical Neurology*, Matthews, W. (ed.). Churchill, Livingstone: Edinburgh, 1975.

39. Tredici, G., and Minazzi, M. Alcoholic neuropathy: An electron microscopic study. *J. Neurol. Sci.* 25:333-346, 1975.

40. Victor, M. Polyneuropathy due to nutritional deficiency and alcoholism. In: *Peripheral Neuropathy*, Dyck, P., Thomas, P. and Lambert, E., (eds.). Saunders: Philadelphia, 1975.

41. Vilter, R., Mueller, J., Glazer, H., Jarrold, T., Abraham, J., Thompson, C., and Hawkins, V. The effect of Vitamin B_6 deficiency induced by desoxypyridoxine in human beings. *J. Lab. Clin. Med.* 42:335-357, 1953.

42. Walsh, J., and McLeod, J. Alcoholic neuropathy: An electrophysiological and histological study. *J. Neurol. Sci.* 10:457-469, 1970.

43. Williams, I., and Mayer, R. Peripheral nerve in acute and chronic liver disease. *Electroencephalogr. Clin. Neurophysiol.* 34:808, 1973.

44. Williams, R., Mason, H., Power, M., and Wilder, R. Induced thiamine (Vitamin B_1) deficiency in man: Relation of depletion of thiamine to development of biochemical defect and of polneuropathy. *Arch. Intern. Med.* 71:38-53, 1943.

45. Winship, D., Caflisch, C., Zboralska, F., and Hogan, W. Deterioration of esophageal peristalsis in patients with alcoholic neuropathy. *Gastroenterology* 55:173-178, 1968.

14

EVAN R. FERGUSON, PhD, Southwestern Medical School, Dallas, Texas
JAMES P. KNOCHEL, MD, Southwestern Medical School, Dallas, Texas

MYOPATHY IN THE CHRONIC ALCOHOLIC

STRUCTURAL AND ELECtrochemical abnormalities of skeletal muscle cells are exceptionally common findings in patients with severe, chronic alcoholism. Indeed, electromyography shows that most chronic alcoholics have some abnormalities of skeletal muscle and nearly half have histological changes, including myofibrillar necrosis, inflammation and interstitial fibrosis, and abnormal mitochondria [16, 19]. The fact that ethanol and not malnutrition is the determinant in these changes is indicated by morphological studies that have shown intracellular edema, lipid droplets, excessive glycogen, and deranged myofibrillar elements in the skeletal muscle of well-nourished patients ingesting alcohol for a 1-month period [17]. In addition, muscle composition appears to be deranged in nearly all severe alcoholics. These changes include muscle cell phosphorus deficiency, low magnesium content, depressed intracellular potassium, and increased contents of intracellular sodium, chloride, and calcium [1].

Due to the wide variety of clinical manifestations seen in alcoholic myopathy,

---

Evan R. Ferguson, PhD, Research Assistant Professor of Medicine, Southwestern Medical School, and Veterans Administration Medical Center, Dallas, Texas.

James P. Knochel, MD, Professor of Internal Medicine, Southwestern Medical School, and Veterans Administration Medical Center, Dallas, Texas.

for the sake of convenience they have been classified into three types by Perkoff [15]. Type I alcoholic myopathy is subclinical in that recognizable symptoms and findings are usually lacking. Type II alcoholic myopathy is an acute disease with swelling and tenderness of affected muscles and classical findings of flank muscle necrosis (rhabdomyolysis), including hyperkalemia, hyperphosphatemia, myoglobinuria, acute renal failure, and paralysis. Type III alcoholic myopathy is a chronic disease, characterized by weakness and proximal muscle wasting with histoligical findings of atrophic muscle fibers, inflammation, and interstitial fibrosis. The subclinical and acute forms of alcoholic myopathy are usually reversible when alcohol abuse is discontinued except in cases of congestive heart failure or acute rhabdomyolysis and fatal myoglobinuria. The chronic form may also be arrested or improved with discontinued use of alcohol. It should be noted, however, that these improvements are based on abatement of clinical symptoms and to date experimental evidence is lacking to support these claims at a cellular or subcellular level.

Because of the wide variety of clinical manifestations, laboratory findings, and compositional alterations of skeletal muscle in alcoholic myopathy, numerous factors have been considered to play a role. Undoubtedly, part of the variety of experimental and clinical findings may be due to differences in quantity of alcohol consumed, length of alcohol abuse, and the nutritional status of the patient or experimental animal. In addition, the lack of adequate experimental models in which the clinical symptoms of alcoholic myopathy are reproduced has resulted in numerous factors that either alone or in some combination have been suggested to play an etiologic role in alcoholic myopathy. Whether any one or a combination of these factors results in the primary lesion of alcoholic myopathy or plays a pivotal role in the transition to acute alcoholic myopathy has yet to be ascertained.

POSSIBLE CAUSES OF ALCOHOLIC MYOPATHY

Phosphorus Deficiency

Studies on patients with clinical and laboratory evidence of alcoholic myopathy have shown abnormally low total phosphorus content of skeletal muscle [1]. In spite of low muscle phosphorus content, many patients on admission display normal or only moderately depressed values for serum phosphate and normal creatine phosphokinase (CPK) activity. However, when they are given nutrients, usually in the form of carbohydrates, their serum phosphorus concentration falls rapidly and when it has remained at values below 1.5 mg% for a 24- to 28-hour period, there may appear a sudden rise in CPK activity, myoglobinuria, and findings compatible with acute rhabdomyolysis. Although hypophosphatemia does not always occur, nearly all severe alcoholics have low muscle phosphorus content.

The role of phosphorus deficiency in alcoholic myopathy has been examined utilizing dogs with isolated phosphorus deficiency. Based on these studies, it appears that certain harmful consequences of severe hypophosphatemia depend on the condition of the muscle cell before hypophosphatemia. Thus, if hypophosphatemia is produced by feeding a high caloric, phosphate-free diet to underweight but otherwise healthy dogs, the muscle cells show little, if any, evidence of biochemical injury [12]. In contrast, if a dog is underfed and simultaneously deprived of phosphorus so as to produce an underweight phosphorus-deficient animal, muscle cells show low phosphorus content and an electrochemical disturbance that closely resembles skeletal muscle findings in patients with alcoholic myopathy (i.e., elevated intracellular concentrations of sodium, chloride, and water). When hyperalimentation-induced hypophosphatemia is superimposed on the phosphate-deficient animal, frank rhabdomyolysis ensues. Of importance, supplementation with adequate phosphorus to prevent hypophosphatemia during hyperalimentation prevents rhabdomyolysis [12]. These clinical and experimental observations suggest that phosphorus deficiency may induce a subtle, subclinical injury to the muscle cell and that an additional stress may result in frank rhabdomyolysis. Also, it appears that phosphorus deficiency per se cannot induce acute rhabdomyolysis and that other factors are required to precipitate rhabdomyolytic episodes.

Recent evidence indicates that ethanol per se may cause loss of muscle cell phosphorus [4]. In nutritionally adequate dogs consuming 6.2 gm ethanol/kg/day, a significant loss of muscle cell phosphorus is detectable after 28 days. This depression of muscle cell phosphorus remains for at least 7 months of alcohol intake despite the fact that the dogs gained weight throughout the study and serum phosphorus remained normal. These results are particularly encouraging since they mimic the clinical findings in subclinical alcoholic myopathy and occur in spite of adequate nutrition. The reasons underlying the losses of muscle cell phosphorus remain unexplained but may be related to the simultaneous loss of muscle cell magnesium seen in these and other studies, including clinical findings in chronic alcoholism [1]. Some evidence indicates that the loss of muscle cell phosphorus is linked to alcohol-induced phosphaturia, possibly coupled with simultaneous alcohol-induced magnesuria [18]. However, it has yet to be determined whether changes in muscle cell phosphorus are instrumental in precipitating alcoholic myopathy or are secondary to other changes induced by chronic ethanol intake.

Magnesium Deficiency

Magnesium deficiency has been cited as a possible factor underlying alcoholic myopathy since many alcoholics commonly show magnesium deficiency and hypomagnesmia. However, serum magnesium levels may be normal despite magnesium deficiency and it appears that serum magnesium levels are poor indicators of magnesium deficiency. Nonetheless, magnesium content of skeletal muscle is reduced in those who are severely alcoholic [1]. The underlying cause of alcoholic magnesium deficiency appears to be excessive losses of magnesium from the kidney and gastrointestinal tract. In fact, the administration of ethanol to both normal and alcoholic subjects has been shown to induce an acute urinary diuresis of magnesium [10].

Recently these authors have addressed the role of magnesium depletion in alcoholic myopathy by studying the effects of isolated magnesium deficiency in canine skeletal muscle. In brief, a slight but significant depression in skeletal muscle magnesium was seen at 7 weeks in dogs receiving a magensium-deficient diet. At 10 weeks, however, skeletal muscle magnesium content was normal. The most surprising finding in these studies was significant elevations of muscle calcium, sodium, and chloride contents and depression of skeletal muscle phosphorus in spite of only slight depression of muscle cell magnesium content. In other studies, a significant depression of muscle cell magnesium content was observed in dogs receiving a normal diet supplemented with alcohol over a 7-month period [4]. The alcoholic dog skeletal muscle also showed significant increases in muscle cell sodium, chloride, and calcium and significant depletions of potassium and phosphorus. Thus, in dogs receiving either alcohol- or magnesium-deficient diets, similar patterns of skeletal muscle ionic composition were seen. These studies, however, did not answer the critical question of whether magnesium depletion results in myopathy or whether myopathy is secondary to other ionic changes induced by magnesium depletion.

Potassium Deficiency

Martin et al. [14], noting that hypokalemia frequently occurs in alcoholics, examined the muscle content of potassium in patients with alcoholic myopathy. Since potassium content was subnormal, they proposed that potassium deficiency may have been responsible for the myopathy. Indeed, studies from the laboratory of the present authors have confirmed earlier reports that potassium deficiency can cause rhabdomyolysis and myoglobinuria [11]. Similar observations have been made in chronically alcoholic dogs. Skeletal muscle potassium content declines during early phases of alcohol intake to levels comparable with those seen in alcoholic patients. This decline is accompanied by increases in intracellular sodium and chloride and hyperpolarization of the resting transmembrane potential [4]. However, unlike the situation with continued potassium depletion, with continued ethanol intake electrolyte concentrations and the transmembrane potential return to normal. This suggests some adaptive mechanism to correct electrolyte imbalance in skeletal muscle of nutritionally adequate alcoholic dogs. This adaptive response may not occur, however, in situations where nutrition is inadequate or where extrarenal losses of potassium result in severe potassium depletion.

Despite the fact that potassium depletion and alcoholism bear resemblances in their effects in skeletal muscle, two lines of evidence indicate that potassium depletion per se may not be the single underlying cause of alcoholic myopathy. First, in about 50% of the patients examined thus far, skeletal muscle potassium content has been normal in spite of overt clinical findings of alcoholic myopathy. Secondly, in experimental dogs and rats in which the effects of malnutrition have been eliminated, skeletal muscle potassium content has been either normal or abnormal but subsequently returns to normal with continued alcohol intake. Thus, it appears that the effects of potassium depletion in the development of alcoholic myopathy may not become apparent unless either malnutrition and/or extrarenal losses of potassium induce severe potassium depletion. In the latter instance, potassium deficiency may certainly contribute toward the development of a myopathy in the alcoholic.

Alteration of Muscle Enzymes

Perkoff was among the first to suggest that alcohol might alter the characteristics or structure of enzymes in the muscle cell and thereby disturb metabolism sufficiently to result in myopathy [15]. Presumably, interference with intermediary metabolism would result in decreased energy stores available for muscle contraction, ion transport, and other energy-requiring processes of the muscle cell. Perkoff's findings were based upon evidence that ischemic exercise in patients with acute alcoholic myopathy was associated with abnormally low muscle phosphorylase activity and was not associated with release of lactate into the circulation, thereby enforcing impairment of glycolysis. Such effects did not occur in all patients with alcoholic myopathy. More recent studies have shown that pyridoxine, a vitamin necessary for phosphorylase activity, may, under the influence of acetaldehyde, become displaced from its apoprotein and thereby impair activity of phosphorylase. Based upon such evidence it would appear that impaired phosphorylase activity might play a role in alcoholic myopathy induced during exercise. However, the splitting of glycogen to provide energy is usually not a dominant pathway in resting or moderately working skeletal muscle. Thus, while phosphorylase abnormalities might contribute toward alcoholic myopathy, particularly during heavy exercise, they would not seem to be a likely candidate for a single underlying cause.

Interference with Muscle Blood Flow

Prolonged ischemia has been considered as a possible mechanism underlying alcoholic myopathy based upon evidence that intraarterial administration of ethanol results in vasoconstriction and decreased muscle perfusion. Therefore, muscle ischemia during exercise or rest could result in anoxic injury to the muscle cell [5]. This proposal was based upon plethysmographic measurements that were suggestive of cutaneous vasodilatation and simultaneously, decreased blood flow to skeletal muscle. Unfortunately, the plethysmographic technique is beset with technical difficulties and hemodynamic responsiveness to experimentally induced perturbations is difficult to assess. Recently the authors have examined this issue, employing the isolated gracilis muscle of the dog, which is very suitable for examination of hemodynamic responsiveness [2]. The effect of ethanol was examined at rest and during electrically stimulated contractions to simulate muscular work. Infusion of ethanol had no effect on resting blood flow. During subsequent electrically stimulated contractions both saline- and ethanol-infused muscles showed similar increases in muscle blood flow. In fact, the 1-minute flow rate for ethanol-infused animals was higher than that observed in saline controls. Potassium release from both ethanol- and saline-infused muscles was normal. Thus, the suggestion that ethanol induces myopathy via ischemia has little substantiating evidence.

Interference with Sodium Transport

Two lines of evidence implicate an ethanol inhibition of active sodium transport in skeletal muscle. First, results from compositional studies of human alcoholic skeletal muscle indicate that intracellular sodium and chloride are elevated, while potassium is depressed. These results would be expected if one assumes that ethanol inhibits the membrane-bound, Na, K-ATPase (sodium, potassium-adenosinetriphosphate), the enzymatic equivalent of the sodium pump. Secondly, in studies involving ethanol effects on Na, K-ATPase activity in tissue other than skeletal muscle (liver, brain, erythrocytes, and cardiac plasma membranes), acute exposure to ethanol appears to inhibit sodium transport [8]. Unfortunately, in many of these studies, nonphysiological levels of ethanol were utilized in vitro.

The effects of alcohol on sodium transport appear to be related to the length of alcohol intake. For example, in experimental animals, acute exposure to ethanol appears to inhibit Na, K-ATPase activity, while chronic exposure appears to result in increased enzyme activity [9]. Unfortunately, in none of these studies were the changes in transport activity closely correlated with changes in tissue electrolytes. Recent studies, however, have addressed the temporal effects of ethanol on skeletal muscle ionic composition and sodium transport activity in alcoholic dogs [4]. Intracellular muscle cell sodium and chloride were significantly elevated and potassium depressed after 1, 2, and 3 months, duplicating the results seen in human alcoholic skeletal muscle. However, after 4 and 7 months of alcohol intake, skeletal muscle sodium, potassium, and chloride concentrations were normal. Throughout the 7-month study period, Na, K-ATPase activity was significantly elevated, as was sodium-dependent respiration. These results indicate that increased Na, K-ATPase activity may correct an electrolyte imbalance in the skeletal muscle of nutritionally adequate experimental animals. Alternatively, since intracellular sodium and potassium concentrations are a result of their respective permeabilities through the plasma membrane and the relative activity of sodium transport, a decrease in sodium permeability as a result of changes in plasma membrane lipid concentration also would eventually result in decreased intracellular sodium concentrations. However, the continued increases in Na, K-ATPase activities seen in these studies indicates that sodium permeability is not appreciably altered with continued alcohol intake and thus forms a central role for Na, K-ATPase in regulating muscle electrolyte concentrations in alcoholic skeletal muscle.

Nutritional Disturbances

The role of nutritional disturbances in the development of alcoholic myopathy clearly has not been established. It is well appreciated that starvation and/or protein-calorie malnutrition in children may be associated with advanced depression of glycolytic enzymes in muscle tissue and abnormalities of muscle electrolyte composition. Whether these events occur in adults has not been elucidated. Even in experimental animals such changes are difficult to identify but can be readily reproduced in the growing animal. The repeated demonstration that alcoholic myopathy may exist in the absence of apparent nutritional deficiency and that damage of skeletal muscle occurs in normal human volunteers after consumption of ethanol despite a very adequate dietary intake suggests that nutrition per se does not play a major role in the development of alcoholic myopathy [17]. In addition, studies involving experimental animals with an adequate dietary intake also suggest that a demonstrable subclinical myopathy may be induced by ethanol per se. However, the fact remains that nutrition may play a major contributory role in the development of alcoholic myopathy. Recent studies involving the induction of alcoholic myopathy in the rat have shown that prolonged exposure (2 to 4 weeks) to ethanol and a brief period of food deprivation results in frank rhabdomyolysis [7]. The effects of fasting may be due to increased blood alcohol concentrations due to reduced alcohol clearance and/or by a fasting-induced potentiation of the toxic effect of high alcohol concentrations on skeletal muscle. Similar mechanisms may be operable in rhabdomyolytic episodes in chronic alcoholics. In these instances, if skeletal muscle can adapt to an alcohol-induced subclinical myopathy, then nutritional deprivation may precipitate the development of a subclinical myopathy into frank rhabdomyolysis. Thus, although nutritional disturbances may not induce alcoholic myopathy per se, they may play a pivotal role in the development of rhabdomyolytic episodes.

Interference with Calcium Transport

In human alcoholic skeletal muscle, increased calcium content is a consistent finding [1]. Likewise, in experimental animals receiving ethanol, increased skeletal muscle calcium content is demonstrable both in the acute and chronic phases of alcohol ingestion [4]. In conjunction with increased calcium content, intracellular sodium and chloride contents also increase while potassium, magnesium, and phosphorus decline. Therefore it has been difficult to determine if increased intracellular calcium is a true causative agent of cellular injury or is merely one of many ionic changes that occurs following muscle cell damage.

The mechanisms resulting in increased intracellular calcium during ethanol intake have not been explained. However, recent advances in the understanding of intracellular calcium regulation indicate that several possible points exist for ethanol inhibition of calcium content. Inhibition of one or more of the following mechanisms by ethanol would result in increased intracellular calcium:

1. Calcium uptake by the sarcoplasmic reticulum and/or the mitochondria
2. Sodium-calcium exchange in the plasma membrane, which passively exchanges intracellular calcium for extracellular sodium
3. Ca^{++}-ATPase in the plasma membrane, which actively extrudes intracellular calcium
4. Calcium binding to calmodulin
5. Regulation of Ca^{++} = ATPase by calmodulin
6. Calcium permeability of the plasma membrane

Unfortunately, little experimental evidence indicates the effects of ethanol on these mechanisms in skeletal muscle. One interesting speculation is the role of increased intracellular sodium and calcium in regulating intracellular calcium [3]. With increased intracellular sodium (either by increasing sodium permeability or inhibiting Na, K-ATPase) the sodium gradient across the cell membrane is decreased and the rate of sodium-calcium exchange, driven by the sodium gradient, is likewise decreased. Intracellular calcium would then temporarily increase and remain elevated, depending on the rate of sodium entry and inhibition of Na, K-ATPase. Similar results would occur if ethanol increased sodium permeability slightly but also inhibited calcium uptake by the mitochondria and sarcoplasmic reticulum or inhibited calmodulin regulation of Ca^{++}-ATPase for calcium extrusion.

The mechanisms whereby increased intracellular calcium interferes with skeletal muscle function have been addressed in only a few isolated studies. Both ethanol and acetaldehyde, in concentrations that occur in patients, inhibit the association of actin and myosin in vitro, possibly because both ethanol and acetaldehyde apparently inhibit the binding of calcium to troponin. Also, when actomyosin is isolated from baboons or volunteers chronically fed alcohol or from chronically alcoholic patients, the association of actin and myosin is impaired in vitro, even in the absence of ethanol or acetaldehyde [16]. These latter results indicate that chronic exposure of the muscle cell to ethanol or acetaldehyde may result in alteration of protein molecules necessary for muscle contraction.

Direct Damage to the Cell by Ethanol

Direct structural damage to the muscle cell by ethanol was proposed as a mechanism of injury by Rubin et al. [17]. Studying the effects of alcohol ingestion over a 1-month period in human nonalcoholic volunteers receiving a nutritious diet, these investigators found increased serum creatine phosphokinase in about 50% of the volunteers. Electron micrographs of skeletal muscle biopsies revealed intracellular edema, lipid droplets, excessive glycogen, abnormal mitochondria, and deranged elements of the sarcoplasmic reticulum. Since the diet was rigorously controlled in these studies, the effects of ethanol per se were proposed to be the underlying cause of alcoholic myopathy.

In addition to dietary-controlled studies using alcohol, numerous in vitro and in vivo experiments have shown that ethanol affects the structure and fluidity of biological membranes. Initially these experiments utilized pharmacologic concentrations of ethanol to demonstrate the effects on lipid composition of membranes in vivo and upon the physical-chemical parameters of cell membranes in vitro. Recently, using techniques such as electron paramagnetic resonance (EPR) or fluorescent probes, a large body of evidence indicates that acute intoxicating doses of ethanol may disrupt the structure of cell membranes. In general, several interesting effects of acute and chronic ethanol exposure appear to emerge. In vitro, ethanol appears to disorder cell membranes, making the lipid matrix more fluid [6]. Similar results are obtained using model membranes made of egg lecithin and cholesterol, implying that these effects may be universal for all cell membranes.

Several studies have focused on the effects of chronic ethanol exposure upon cell membrane composition. There appears to be an increased ratio of saturated to polyunsaturated fatty acids in phospholipids and an increased cholesterol content of cell membranes following chronic exposure to ethanol [13]. These observations are particularly relevant, since phospholipids and cholesterol are the major lipids of mammalian cell membranes. In addition, both of these effects would tend to make membranes more structured or less fluid. Thus, the increases in saturated fatty acids and cholesterol observed with chronic alcoholism may represent adaptation of cell membranes to the fluidizing effects of ethanol, possibly resulting in the development of tolerance.

These observations may ultimately supply clues to the underlying effects of ethanol on skeletal muscle cells and the development of alcoholic myopathy. It seems possible that changes in muscle cell membrane fluidity induced by ethanol may result in changes in membrane channels and/or transport proteins, which subsequently affect movement of ions or metabolic substrates necessary for the functional integrity of muscle cells. This implies that many of the observed effects of alcohol on skeletal muscle may be secondary effects resulting from subtle but significant changes in membrane structure or function induced by ethanol. In fact many of the possibilities discussed previously as causes of alcoholic myopathy may be secondary to alterations in membrane integrity induced by alcohol. The subsequent increases in membrane-saturated fatty acids and cholesterol seen with continued alcohol intake may be attempts by the muscle cell to adapt to the changes induced by alcohol. Failure to adapt adequately to these stresses would result in cell disintegration.

CONCLUSIONS

Several factors have been discussed as possible underlying causes of myopathy in the chronic alcoholic. Most of the proposals involving ionic deficiencies suffer from the fact that experimental studies using isolated ion deficiencies do not induce a myopathy identical to that seen in chronic alcoholism. Nonetheless, deficiencies of magnesium, phosphorus, and potassium and nutritional disturbances may be involved in the transition from a subclinical to an acute myopathy. The proposals involving etharol-induced changes in sodium or calcium transport are extremely interesting and are supported by both clinical and experimental data. However, they may reflect only secondary changes induced by ethanol. At the present time, the most logical candidate for an underlying cause of alcoholic myopathy is the effect of alcohol on the structure and/or function of cell membranes. These effects may involve not only the plasma membrane but mitochondrial and sarcoplasmic reticulum membranes as well. Thus, the physical changes induced by alcohol may lead to changes in the milieu of the normal cell, the end result of which is either adaptation by the cell itself or with the imposition of additional stress or stresses, acute myopathy and cell destruction.

REFERENCES

1. Anderson, R., Cohen, M., Haller, R., Elms, J., Carter, N. W., and Knochel, J. P. Skeletal muscle phosphorus and magnesium deficiency in alcoholic myopathy. *Min. Elect. Metab.* 4:106–112, 1980.
2. Blachley, J. D., Ferguson, E. R., Long, J. T., and Knochel, J. P. Normal resting and exercising muscle blood flow during acute ethanol infusion. *Clin. Toxicol.* 17:413–419, 1980.
3. Blaustein, M. P. Sodium ions, calcium ions, blood pressure regulation, and hypertension: A reassessment and a hypothesis. *Am. J. Physiol.* 232:C165–C173, 1977.
4. Ferguson, E. R., Blachley, J. D., and Knochel, J. P. Skeletal muscle ionic composition and sodium transport activity in chronic alcoholism. *Trans. Assoc. Am. Phys.* in press.
5. Fewings, J. D., Hanna, M. J. D., Walsh, J. A., and Whelan, R. F. The effects of ethyl

alcohol in the blood vessels of the hands and forearm in man. *Br. J. Pharmacol. Chemother.* 27:93-106, 1966.

6. Goldstein, D. B., and Chin, J. H. Interaction of ethanol with biological membranes. *Fed. Proc.* 40:2073-2076, 1981.

7. Haller, R. G., and Drochman, D. B. Alcoholic rhabdomyolysis: An experimental model in the rat. *Science* 208:412-415, 1980.

8. Israel, Y., Kalant, H., and Laufer, I. Effects of ethanol on Na, K, Mg-stimulated micromal ATPase activity. *Biochem. Pharmacol.* 14:1803-1814, 1965.

9. Israel, Y., Kalant, H., LeBlanc, E., Bernstein, J. C., and Salazar, I. Changes in cation transport and Na+K-activated adenosine triphosphatase produced by chronic administration of ethanol. *J. Pharmacol. Exp. Ther.* 174:330-336, 1970.

10. Kalbfleisch, J. M., Lindeman, R. D., Ginn, H. F., and Smith, W. O. Effects of ethanol administration on urinary excretion of magnesium and other electrolytes in alcoholic and normal subjects. *J. Clin. Invest.* 42:1471-1475, 1963.

11. Knochel, J. P. Rhabdomyolysis and effects of potassium deficiency on muscle structure and function. *Cardiovasc. Med.* 3:247-261, 1978.

12. Knochel, J. P., Haller, R., and Ferguson, E. R. Selective phosphorus deficiency in the hyperalimented hypophosphatemic dog and phosphorylation potentials in the muscle cell. *Adv. Exp. Biol. Med.* 128:323-334, 1980.

13. Littleton, J. M., and John, G. Synaptosomal membrane lipids of mice during continuous exposure to ethanol. *J. Pharm. Pharmacol.* 29:579-580, 1977.

14. Martin, J. B., Craig, J. W., Eckel, R. E., and Munger, J. Hypokalemic myopathy in chronic alcoholism. *Neurology* 21:1160-1168, 1971.

15. Perkoff, G. T., Hardy, P., Velez-Garcia, E. Reversible acute muscular syndrome in chronic alcoholism. *N. Eng. J. Med.* 274:1277-1285, 1966.

16. Rubin, E. Alcoholic myopathy in heart and muscle. *N. Engl. J. Med.* 301:28-33, 1979.

17. Rubin, E., Katz, A. M., and Lieber, C. S. Muscle damage produced by chronic alcohol consumption. *Ann. J. Pathol.* 83:499-575, 1976.

18. Sargent, W. Q., Simpson, J. R., and Beard, J. D. 7-day ethanol administration and sodium, magnesium and phosphate excretion. *Min. Elect. Metab.* 6:262, 1981.

19. Worden, R. E. Pattern of muscle and nerve pathology in alcoholism. *Ann. N. Y. Acad. Sci.* 273:351-359, 1976.

# 15

FLOYD E. BLIVEN, Jr., MD, Medical College of Georgia, Augusta, Georgia

THE SKELETAL SYSTEM: ALCOHOL AS A FACTOR

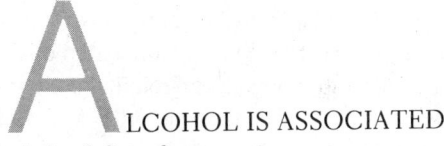

ALCOHOL IS ASSOCIATED as a significant factor in many musculoskeletal disturbances.

1. It is a major factor in injury—fractures and other injuries of the extremity that are incurred in falls, automobile accidents, gunshot wounds, and assault.
2. An injury of alcohol and drug abuse unconsciousness more frequently recognized today is the limb compression syndrome.
3. Bone weakness or osteopenia results from the acceleration of bone loss with alcohol and is the cause of the unusual frequency of fracture of the neck of the femur in the adult under 50.
4. Alcohol is the chief cause of idiopathic osteonecrosis of the hip, an uncommon but catastrophic disease and disability involving both hips.

INJURY AND FRACTURES

Injuries are more common in the alcoholic population [42]. Because of the alcoholic's impaired judgment, aggressive and irresponsible behavior, and neurological disturbances of balance and pain sensation, he or she is more frequently in-

---

Floyd E. Bliven, Jr., MD, Professor of Surgery (Orthopedics), Medical College of Georgia, Augusta, Georgia.

volved in violence, vehicular accidents, and falls. Because of physiological tissue changes the injuries are more severe and recovery is prolonged [37]. An early observation is recorded in an Egyptian papyrus more than 3,000 years ago: "Make not thyself helpless, drinking in the beer shop. . . . Falling down, thy limbs will be broken and no one will give thee a hand to help thee up" [42]. Today motor vehicle accidents are the major cause of violent death and serious injury in the United States and alcohol is consistently the most important related factor [2, 14, 15, 42]. Most injuries are head injuries and fractures. Repeatedly, reviews of fatal accidents show a majority of victims to have high blood alcohol levels. In one consecutive fatality study, 70% of males (age 16 to 35) who died were impaired by alcohol [5, 12]. The prevention of accidents appears to be the greatest need since severity of injury rather than treatment is the determinant of survival where trauma care has been organized [12].

Fractures are a very common problem in chronic alcoholics (those with a daily intake of 180 ml or more of alcohol or interval intoxication) even when those patients who are injured by large external forces are not included, such as in automobile accidents where the patient is an occupant or pedestrian. The fractures are more severe, the care is complicated by management of alcoholic disease, convalescence is prolonged, and reinjury common [37]. Patients are most often male; the average age is 50; there is often the appearance of nutritional depletion and changes usually attributed to aging are noted. Accident proneness is evident in a history of other fractures. The occurrence of more than one fracture within a 2-year interval was reported as 20% at one medical center [37]. The battered alcoholic syndrome is a designation introduced to mark the presence of three or more fractures in different stages of healing in the same individual. One report indicated only 17% of fracture patients were diagnosed as alcoholic at the first fracture episode, but with the second and third concomitant fractures, alcoholism was identified in 33% and 62% of the group [30].

The common association of alcohol as a factor in injury should be emphasized. The initial care of fractures in alcoholics is often delayed, the average time between injury and diagnosis being 42 hours [37]. This delay often coincides with onset of delirium tremens, which may involve 33% of patients, adding difficulty to effective management [20]. As many physicians with hospital accident experience know, alcoholics are a burden to staff and medical care. If the physician can recognize the alcoholic when treating fractures, he or she can anticipate and reduce some of these complications.

Tibial fractures, as an example, require extended protection of several months before union [20]. The alcoholic patient not only seems unaware of his or her responsibility for protection of healing by the use of crutches, follow-up examinations, and maintaining general good health, but may also lack some of the usual signals of pain that limit and protect the nonalcoholic patient. Abuse leads to refracture and the risk of additional injury. Too early weight bearing is the usual case of delayed union in alcoholics, which may be as high as 50% of cases; twice the expected time may be required for resumption of normal activity (10 months instead of 5 months). Infection is also a greater problem, even in closed fractures, and the rate may be as high as 20%. Several factors relate to this complication. Bleeding and the development of large hematomas at the injury and operative site may be due to blood coagulation deficits as a consequence of liver disease; it is noted in 33% of cases. Also, bacteremia is more common from skin, respiratory, urinary, and dental origins and leads to later infection of the inflammatory area. One aspect of prolonged immobilization is joint stiffness after the bone has healed. In an effort to reduce the complications of unprotected stress on a fracture, intramedullary fixation may be preferable to using a plate. Frequent examination and the newer plastic-plaster materials can be recommended for cast immobilization instead of plaster-of-Paris [20].

Higher fracture rates in the alcoholic patient group are also associated with a higher prevalence of patients with a history of delirium tremens, admissions for alcoholic treatment, liver disease or cirrhosis, low hematocrit, and peptic ulcer and gastric surgery [16, 27, 37]. Fracture distribution in the alcoholic population is different. It has much the pattern characteristics of a geriatric group with a high rate of fractures associated with intrinsic weakness of bone rather than external force. Particularly noteworthy is fracture of the hip, an injury that is uncommon before the eighth decade except after heavy trauma and severe falls. Hip fractures are equally divided between intertrochanteric (extracapsular) and cervical (intracapsular) fractures [29]. The healing time of this fracture is 3 to 6 months, and reinjury or delayed union is common because of the long requirement for crutch or walker protection of ambulation after reduction and internal fixation. Fractures of the neck have a poor prognosis. Approximately 50% develop osteonecrosis of the femoral head due to inadequate restoration of the circulation to the head; however, in alcoholics, osteonecrosis occurs in 80% and femoral prosthesis or total hip replacement is always a better choice of treatment than internal fixation of the fracture. Other sites of osteopenic fracture are the head of the humerus, vertebra, and calcaneous.

A physical rehabilitation program can reduce the extended disability of continued pain and a slow return to activity. Disability is often complex, reflecting socioeconomic factors and depression as much as structural limitations. An experience of a physical training program 2 to 3 hours a day for 8 to 12 weeks combined with a workshop has returned 60% of patients with back injury to work activity [26]. Similar programs are essential to prepare fracture patients for return to work.

LIMB COMPRESSION SYNDROME

A serious complication of alcohol and drug abuse is the limb compression syndrome [5]. The common pressure contact areas are face, chest, or extremity. The limb compression syndrome results from ischemia of soft tissue following prolonged pressure in a position assumed by an intoxicated individual [6, 7, 34, 41]. Because there are no wounds or fractures, and the patient is obtunded and unable to cooperate in the initial examination, the presence and extent of this injury is often not recognized. Further, the physician who does not see the patient in the position of pressure contact is often unaware of the possibility of this injury. The first sign of the compression tissue necrosis is erythema of the skin in the contact area. It may look like a burn; blebs and blisters often appear. The underlying and adjacent area becomes swollen and hard as deeper tissues are involved. The earliest reliable sign of muscle damage is compartment swelling. The anoxic muscles contained in a fascial compartment become swollen and necrosis develops. Only relief of pressure in the first few hours by fasciotomy can save the muscle. The problem, however, is early recognition of the severity of the injury and immediately proceeding to decompression of the compartment. Observation of a peripheral pulse, which is usually felt, gives the false assurance of an intact circulation and coolness does not develop so a compartment syndrome is not suspected. Rest pain and pain when flexed muscles are passively stretched are the confirmatory signs of increased compartment pressure but pain can not be elicited in the unresponsive patient. The late and irreversible change is repalcement of the muscle infarct by a fibrous contracture. The thenar and interossei muscles of the hand, forearm flexors, and leg muscles are the most commonly involved. The disability is even greater if nerve ischemia has occurred, adding a peripheral nerve deficit.

Renal insufficiency has been reported even with localized muscle change due to proteins from necrotizing muscle, causing renal tubular nephrosis. Myoglobinuria should be suspected if urine is dark. The benzidine test is positive in myoglobinuria and the urine should be routinely tested in the first few days. The extent of muscle damage is difficult to assess and renal tubular disease can often be prevented or treated by attention to early fluid replacement [34].

OSTEOPENIA

Osteopenia is atrophy of bone; the bone is normal but reduced in amount. This reduction in bone mass can be identified by the reduced density of the radiograph, indicating loss of mineral. This loss of density may occur with either osteomalacia due to lack of calcification of an intact osteoid matrix or may be due to osteoporosis, in which case both the mineral and collagen matrix have been reduced. Only biopsy can differentiate the process. A qualitative assessment of bone mass is obtained by comparison of radiographs but progressive changes are not readily apparent unless bone loss is greater than 50%. A more sensitive and reliable measure can now be determined by isotope absorption using the distal radius reading as an index of bone density of an individual. Bone strength increases in the first two decades of life and then decreases gradually over a lifetime. The density of bone as seen in x-ray correlates with bone strength; thus osteopenia indicates intrinsic weakness. Longitudinal studies show bone density to decline in all individuals at a predictable rate from about the third decade. This gradual loss of bone mass is remarkably accelerated in the alcoholic population.

The data on bone loss in the alcoholic patient do not present mechanisms but they are correlated with deficient nutrition and inactivity. In one study [27] bone density was compared at different ages for three groups: a normally active nonpatient group, patients from an alcohol treatment program, and alcoholics seen in an orthopedic department for fracture or backache (alcholics with more severe bone changes). The slope of the graph displaying bone density of the distal radius for each of these groups showed faster loss over the years in the alcoholic group and greater continued increment of loss in the orthopedic injury group.

The same advanced loss of bone mass in alcoholics was demonstrated in data using the dry weights of standardized bone plugs taken from the iliac crest of subjects who had an accidental death and came to autopsy by a medical examiner. Individuals known to be alcoholic, all of whom were under 45 years of age, had bone density about that of men and women over athe age 70 [32, 33]. Others have shown the similar low bone density of alcoholics and patients with postmenopausal osteoporosis [8, 9]. The strongest clinical correlation of bone loss and alcoholism is the fracture rate in epidemiologic studies. In different geographical, socioeconomic, and racial surveys, fractures of the hip have been found to accurately index the extent of osteopenia. Many observations show the early risk of fracture in the alcoholic [8, 9, 16, 27, 28, 29].

NONTRAUMATIC IDIOPATHIC OSTEONECROSIS OF THE FEMORAL HEAD

A severe disease and disability associated with alcoholism is nontraumatic idiopathic osteonecrosis of the hip [25]. Also called "aseptic necrosis" or "avascular necrosis" of the femoral head, it is a poorly understood destructive hip disorder, the consequences of an ischemic episode causing infarction of the femoral head. Adequate blood supply to the hip is threatened by any mechanism interfering with the vessels that cross the neck of the femur within the joint capsule or the vessels that form the terminal cascades of the subchondral bone supporting the femoral cartilage. The ischemic pattern is the same as that resulting from trauma. A fracture of the femoral neck is associated with the slow healing consistent with the slow return of vascularity and it is also correlated with a 50% incidence of aseptic necrosis due to inadequate return of circulation. The sequel to ischemia is an infarct that changes most of the head and is demarcated radiographically as the healing process develops.

The infarct of the femoral head includes about 66% of the head, usually like an inverted cone, the base being the central weight-bearing surface. In the immediate postischemic interval the area of the infarct apparently maintains its strength. Gradually, however, the infarct becomes separated from the unaffected neck and head by a repair process with invasive growth of osteoblasts and osteoclasts simultaneously thickening and resorbing trabecular bone. As the balance toward resoption increases, microfractures occur at the same time other trabeculae are reinforced and necrotic marrow is filled by fibrous tissue. This repair process has been called "creeping substitution." Invasion and resorption, especially in the subchondral area and the edge of the infarct, lead to collapse and the destructive changes seen in x-ray and associated with clinical disability [38].

Infarction is now recognized in many nontraumatic situations. The largest group in each of several reports has been patients with a history of chronic alcohol intake [3, 18, 24, 31, 35]. Osteonecrosis of the hip occurs in patients who have received large amounts of corticosteroids [31], in renal transplants [21], in connective tissue disease, in sickle cell disease, and in caisson disease. The common factor is believed to be circulatory deficiency. Hip pain in an alcoholic should alert physicians to the diagnosis of nontraumatic osteonecrosis of the hip and is indication for a pelvis x-ray as the means of diagnosis. The diagnosis is very often made when very prominent destructive changes of the femoral head are seen, changes far more extensive than anticipated by clinical symptoms. The disparity is explained by the long interval between the ischemic episode and the later collapse of bone structure due to weakness that develops during the course of healing.

The nontraumatic disease is frequently bilateral with a later onset in the second hip. Recent studies of the opposite and silent hip with biopsy and radiographs have elucidated the course of the disease [1, 23]. Tomograms and computerized tomography scans are helpful in outlining the extent of the infarct but the early diagnosis is best demonstrated by technitium 99 m diphosphonate scintigraphy, which may identify ischemia and the early healing months before definite radiographic change. Initially the TC-99m-MDP bone scan registers no concentration, indicating a loss of the blood supply to the infarcted area. As bone repair ensues, creeping substitution, increased isotope concentration is seen; only in the hypertrophic and repair process do radiographic changes develop, and thus the bone scan anticipates ordinary procedures by several months.

An excellent descriptive classification of the disease has been provided from the studies of Marcus and Enneking correlating clinical, radiographic, and pathological data [21, 23]. See Table 1.

No explanation of the etiology or mechanism of the ischemia in nontraumatic disease is generally accepted [13, 19, 22, 31]. One theory suggests that osteoporosis combined with a diminution of the normal inflammatory and protective pain

Table 1.
Nontraumatic Idiopathic Osteonecrosis of the Femoral Head (Hip)

Stage	Clinical	X-Ray	Bone	Cartilage
One	No symptoms	Mottled densities in anterior and superior part of head	Antero-lateral infarct	Normal
Two	No symptoms	Sclerotic areas in head, intact subchondral plate; infarct demonstrated by dense rim.	Reactive bone and repair of infarct edge	Normal
Three	Mild, intermittent groin pain	Cresent sign (lucent line beneath subchondral bone)	New bone on necrotic trabeculae, calcification of marrow	Periphery of infarct outlined by wrinkle
Four	Sudden increased hip pain, reduced range of motion, abductor limp	Head flattened with step-off at edge of infarct	Central and subchondral necrosis, new bone replacement at edge of infarct	Lateral cleft in cartilage, osteochondral flap
Five	Activity causes hip pain, abductor limp	Asymmetric flattened dome, lucent V-shaped zone at separation of infarct, compression, narrowed joint space	Fibrocartilage in central area necrosis replaced by fibrosis and fat, erosion	Degenerative cartilage changes, loose osteochondral fragment, acetabular cartilage degeneration
Six	Hip pain at rest, muscle atrophy	Compression, severe destruction of head erosion, degenerative joint changes	Erosion, collapse, dense bone, scar, necrotic debris	Severe degenerative change in cartilage, loss of cartilage

responses in an individual can account for the destructive changes of the hip, somewhat like the Charcot neuropathy [38]. An alternative explanation implicates a metabolic lipid disorder. Fatty liver and pancreative disease, often present in the alcoholic patient, contribute fat emboli [19]. Hyperlipemia or fat emboli in the circulation reach the subchondral areas of the femoral head, producing ischemia. Another theory attributes ischemia to a vasculitis resulting from free fatty acids arising in liver or from microfractures in subchondral bone as a result of osteoporosis.

Treatment is unsuccessful in abating loss of bone and joint once clinical symptoms have become definite; progression to these stages require total hip replacement for relief of pain and disability. Some recent hope of preventing the destructive progress has been given by intervention in stages one and two as might be done for the second hip in established disease. One approach is surgical decompression of the femoral head and neck by excising a core of bone from trochanter to subchondral plate [17, 23]; another technique drills the head and neck but also inserts a bone graft [4, 39]. Both require an extended period of several months of protected weight bearing using crutches. In stage three endoprosthesis might be chosen. Recently an osteotomy [40] has been introduced that displaces the weight-bearing defect in cartilage by rotation in the trochanteric plane. Bone grafts and drilling have not been satisfactory at this stage. After collapse of the head (stages five and six) total hip replacement appears to be the most reliable and functional procedure.

The initial diagnosis of osteonecrosis is still difficult to make and confirm. Though alcoholics are the largest group of patients with osteonecrosis, the incidence of osteonecrosis is very low among alcoholics. No screening technique has been discovered. In a careful review of hip films of 700 alcoholics compared to a control series no statistical difference of early radiographic changes were found [36] and in another series [13] the incidence of osteonecrosis of the hip in alcoholics was only .3%. Scintigraphy [10, 11], observation of the contralateral hip, and surgery do encourage optimism for meeting the challenge in diagnosis and treatment of this major disabling complication associated with alcohol.

REFERENCES

1. Arlet, J. and Ficat, P. Diagnostic de l'osteonecrose femorocapitale primitive au stade I (stade pre-radiologic). *Rev. Chir. Orthop.* 54:637, 1968.
2. Baker, S. P., and Fisher, R. S. Alcohol and motorcycle fatalities. *Am. J. Public Health* 67:246, 1977.
3. Boettcher, W. G., Bonfiglio, M., Hamilton, H. R., Sheets, R. F., and Smith, K. Nontraumatic necrosis of the femoral head: Part I. Relation of altered homeostasis to etiology. *J. Bone Joint Surg.* 52A:312, 1970.
4. Bonfiglio, M. and Voke, E.M. Aseptic necrosis of the femoral head and non-union of the femoral neck. *J. Bone Joint Surg.* 50A:48, 1968.
5. Braunstein, P. W., Weinberg, S. W., and Dal Cortivo, L. The drunk and drugged driver versus the law. *J. Trauma* 8:83, 1968.
6. Bywaters, E. G. L. Ischemic muscle necrosis: Crushing injury, traumatic edema, the crush syndrome, traumatic anuria, compression syndrome: A type of injury seen in air raid casualties following burial beneath debris. *J. A. M. A.* 124:1103, 1944.
7. Conner, A. N. Prolonged external pressure as a cause of ischaemic contracture. *J. Bone Joint Surg.* 53B:118, 1971.
8. Dalen, N. and Feldreich, A.L. Osteopenia in alcoholism. *Clin. Orthop.* 99:201, 1974.
9. Dalen, N. and Lamke, B. Bone mineral losses in alcoholics. *Acta Orthop. Scand.* 47:469, 1976.

10. D'Ambrosia, R. D., Riggins, R. S., Stadalnik, R. C., and DeNardo, G. L. Vascularity of the femoral head, ^{99m}TC diphosphonate scintigraphy validated with tetracycline labeling. Clin. Orthop. 107:146, 1975.

11. D'Ambrosia, R. D., Shoji, H., Riggins, R. S., Stadalnik, R. C., and DeNardo, G. L. Scintigraphy in the diagnosis of osteonecrosis. Clin. Orthop. 130:139, 1978.

12. Friesen, G. Vancouver Island traffic fatalities, 1966–1970. J. Trauma 14:791, 1974.

13. Gold, E. W. and Cangemi, P. J. Incidence and pathogenesis of alcohol-induced osteonecrosis of the femoral head. Clin. Orthop. 143:22, 1979.

14. Haberman, P. W., and Baden, M. M. Alcohol, Other Drugs and Violent Death. Oxford University Press: New York, 1978.

15. Holczabek, W. The alcoholized pedestrian as a victim of fatal traffic accidents. Wien. Klin. Wochenschn 88:206, 1976.

16. Horak, J., and Nilsson, B. E. Epidemiology of fracture of the upper end of the humerus. Clin. Orthop. 112:250, 1975.

17. Hungerford, D. S., and Zisic, M. D. Alcoholism-associated ischemic necrosis of the femoral head: Early diagnosis and treatment. Clin. Orthop. 130:144, 1978.

18. Jacobs, B. Epidemiology of traumatic and nontraumatic osteonecrosis. Clin. Orthop. 130:51, 1978.

19. Jones, J. P., Jameson, R. M., and Engleman, E. P. Alocholism, fat embolism, and avascular necrosis. J. Bone Joint Surg. 50A:1065, 1968.

20. Karlstrom, G., and Olerud, S. The management of tibial fractures in alcoholics and mentally distrubed patients. J. Bone Joint Surg. 56B:730, 1974.

21. Kenzora, J. E., and Sledge, C. Hip arthroplasty and the renal transplant patient. In: The Hip (Proceedings of the Third Open Scientific Meeting). Mosby: St. Louis, 1975.

22. Leach, R. E., and Baskies, A. Alcoholism and its effect on the human hip. Clin. Orthop. 90:95, 1973.

23. Marcus, N. D., Enneking, W. F., and Massam, R. A. The silent hip in idiopathic aseptic necrosis treatment by bone grafting. J. Bone Joint Surg. 55A:1351, 1973.

24. McCollum, D. E., Clippinger, F. W., O'Neil, M. T., and Mathews, R. S. Aseptic necrosis of the femoral head: Associated diseases and evaluation of treatment. J. Bone Joint Surg. 49A:1019, 1967.

25. Merle d'Aubigne, M., Postel, M., Mazabraud, A., Massias, P., and Jueguen, J. Idiopathic necrosis of the femoral head in adults. J. Bone Joint Surg. 47B:612, 1965.

26. Natvig, H. Vocational rehabilitation of patients with chronic backache. Nor-tidsske Nor laegeforen 97:1330, 1977.

27. Nilsson, B. E. Conditions contributing to fracture of the femoral neck. Acta Chir. Scand. 136:383, 1970.

28. Nilsson, B. E., and Westlin, N. E. Femur density in alcoholism and after gastrectomy. Calcif. Tissue Res. 10:167, 1972.

29. Nilsson, B. E., and Westlin, N. E. Changes in bone mass in alcoholics. Clin. Orthop. 90:229, 1973.

30. Oppenheim, W. L. The battered alcoholic syndrome. J. Trauma 17:11, 1977.

31. Patterson, R. J., Bickel, W. H., and Dahlin, D. C. Idiopathic avascular necrosis of the head of the femur. J. Bone Joint Surg. 56A:267, 1964.

32. Saville, P. D. Changes in bone mass with age and alcoholism. J. Bone Joint Surg. 47A:492, 1965.

33. Saville, P. D. Alcohol-related skeletal disorders. Ann. N. Y. Acad. Sci. 252:287, 1975.

34. Schreiber, S. N., Liebowitz, M. R., and Bernstein, L. H. Limb compression and renal impairment (crush syndrome) following narcotic and sedative overdose. J. Bone Joint Surg. 54A:1683, 1972.

35. Serre, H., and Simon, L. L'osteonecrose primitive de la tete formal chez l'adulte: II. Etiologie et pathogenie. *Rev. Rheum. Mal Osteoartic* 29:563, 1962.

36. Smith, K., Bonfiglio, M., and Dolan, K. Roentgenographic search for avascular necrosis of the femur in alcoholics and normal adults. *J. Bone Joint Surg.* 59A:391, 1977.

37. Snell, W. The chronic alcoholic and his fractures. *J. Bone Joint Surg.* 53A:1655, 1971.

38. Solomon, L. Drug-induced arthropathy and necrosis of the femoral head. *J. Bone Joint Surg.* 55B:246, 1973.

39. Springfield, D. S., and Enneking, W. F. Role of bone grafting in idiopathic aseptic necrosis of the femoral head. In: *The Hip* (Proceedings of the Third Open Scientific Meeting). Mosby: St. Louis, 1975.

40. Sugioka, Y. Transtrochanteric anterior rotational esteotomy of the femoral head in the treatment of osteonecrosis affecting the hip: A new osteotomy operation. *Clin. Orthop.* 130:191, 1978.

41. Weeks, R. S. The crush syndrome. *Surg. Gynec. Obstet.* 127:369, 1968.

42. Zuska, J. J. Wounds without cause. *Bull. Am. College Surgeons* 66:5–10, 1981.

16

MARK A. KORSTEN, MD, Mount Sinai School of Medicine,
New York, New York

CHARLES S. LIEBER, MD, Mount Sinai School of Medicine,
New York, New York

LIVER AND PANCREAS

LIVER AND PANCREATIC disease are common and often intractable complications of chronic alcoholism. As a result, clinicians expend much of their time and resources dealing with these disorders. The purpose of this chapter is to summarize relevant aspects of alcoholic liver and pancreatic injury. In so doing, fresh insights and innovative investigation may be stimulated in these fields.

LIVER

Liver Disease, Malnutrition, and Alcoholism

Until relatively recently, it was believed that alcohol was not a hepatotoxin and that dietary deficiencies alone resulted in liver injury. In part, this concept was based on experimental studies in the rat. When alcohol was given in the drinking

---

Mark A. Korsten, MD, Assistant Professor of Medicine, Mount Sinai School of Medicine, New York, New York, and Staff Physician, Veterans Administration Medical Center, Bronx, New York.

Charles S. Lieber, MD, Professor of Medicine and Pathology, Mount Sinai School of Medicine, New York, New York, and Director, Alcohol Research and Treatment Center and GI Liver Training Program, Veterans Administration Medical Center, Bronx, New York.

water, liver damage failed to develop unless the rats were also administered a nutritionally deficient diet [8]. However, under these experimental conditions, alcohol intake is minimal and blood ethanol levels are negligible. To overcome the natural aversion of rats for alcohol, ethanol was subsequently incorporated in a totally liquid diet [37]. By so doing, ethanol consumption was increased to 36% of total calories and fatty liver developed despite otherwise nutritious diets [33]. Using the same approach in the baboon, the consumption of alcohol was increased to 50% of total calories and lesions more severe than steatosis, particularly cirrhosis, were produced [34]. Protein constituted 36% of total nonalcohol calories and the diet was liberally supplemented with choline, minerals, and vitamins. The baboon diet was calculated to mimic a situation in which the alcoholic was trying to achieve a high-protein diet while drinking. Since 33% of the baboons still progressed to cirrhosis after 2 to 5 years, it was concluded that, in addition to dietary factors, alcohol per se plays an important etiologic role in the development of liver injury. These data indicate that despite dietary supplementation, heavy drinkers may not prevent the development of cirrhosis.

The extent to which malnutrition may potentiate the toxic effects of alcohol is controversial. In primates, protein deficiency alone does not result in cirrhosis [42]. Cirrhosis does ensue in monkeys given a high-cholesterol, low-protein diet, but these conditions are not normally achieved with natural food. In conclusion, high-protein diets cannot be recommended to prevent the development of cirrhosis and are unlikely to benefit (and may precipitate encephalopathy) in those with established cirrhosis.

Mechanisms of Ethanol Hepatotoxicity

NADH generation. Alcohol dehydrogenase (ADH) is a cytosolic enzyme found predominantly in the liver; it converts ingested alcohol to acetaldehyde. (Figure 1). In this reaction, nicotinamide-adenine dinucleotide (NAD) is also reduced to nicotinamide-adenine dinucleotide alcohol dehydrogenase (NADH). The enhanced NADH to NAD ratio that results leads to a change in the ratio of other redox couples and is responsible for a variety of alterations in the intermediary metabolism of lipids, carbohydrates, and protein.

The enhanced NADH to NAD ratio results in an increased lactate-pyruvate ratio since these metabolites reflect and are linked to the redox state of the cell. If hyperlactacidemia ensues, it may reduce the capacity of the kidney to excrete uric acid, lead to secondary hyperuricemia, and precipitate gouty arthropathy [36]. Ethanol may also cause hypoglycemia by limiting the availability of gluconeogenic precursors linked to NADH-NAD. The increased NADH to NAD ratio has important effects on the citric acid cycle. The redox change inhibits reactions of the cycle that require NAD and diminishes the availability of important cycle

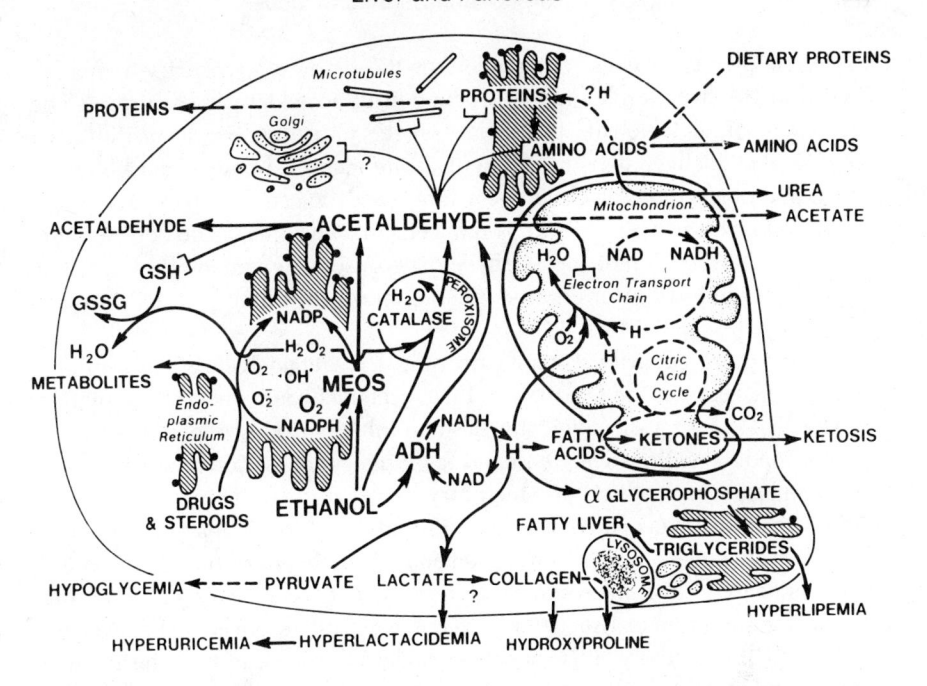

Figure 1. Oxidation of Ethanol in the Hepatocyte. NAD denotes nicotinamide adenine dinucleotide; NADH is reduced NAD; NADP denotes nicotinamide adenine dinucleotide phosphate; NADPH is reduced NADP; MEOS denotes the microsomal ethanol oxidizing system; and ADH denotes alcohol dehydrogenase. The broken lines indicate pathways that are depressed by ethanol. Acetaldehyde may interfere or bind to the Golgi apparatus, microtubules, proteins, and amino acids. (From "Metabolic Effects of Ethanol on the Liver and Other Digestive Organs" by C. S. Lieber, in *Clinics in Gastroenterology* (Vol. 10), C. M. Leevy, ed., Saunders: London, England, 1981. Reprinted by permission.)

substrates. The net effect of the slowing of citric acid cycle activity is that fatty acid oxidation is suppressed (see Figure 1) and lipids accumulate in the liver.

In addition, the abnormal redox state during ethanol oxidation may affect protein metabolism. Under in vitro conditions acute ethanol administration inhibits protein synthesis [50]. This action has been traced to a diversion of amino acids and their precursors from protein synthesis to the transport of reducing equivalents into the mitochondria [44]. However, both in vivo and in vitro after chronic ethanol feedings [51], redox changes are attenuated and alterations in protein synthesis are less apparent [5].

The attenuation of ethanol-induced redox changes may also explain why hepatic fat accumulation does not increase indefinitely. Indeed, other factors (*vide infra*) must be invoked to explain the progression of alcoholic liver injury beyond the steatotic stage.

Effects of acetaldehyde. Regardless of the pathway involved, ethanol oxidation in the liver results in the production of acetaldehyde (Figure 1). The breakdown of acetaldehyde takes place in the mitochondria, a reaction catalyzed by acetaldehyde dehydrogenase. Despite increased rates of acetaldehyde generation during chronic ethanol consumption, the capacity of rat liver mitochondria to oxidize acetaldehyde is reduced [20]. This imbalance between production and disposition of acetaldehyde may cause the elevated blood acetaldehyde levels observed after chronic ethanol intake in the rat [24], baboon [45], and man [27].

In view of its reactivity, it is not surprising that acetaldehyde exerts a number of adverse effects on the hepatocyte. First, acetaldehyde reduces the activity of various hydrogen translocation shuttles and inhibits oxidative phosphorylation [13]. Second, it may participate in and favor the condensation reactions of biogenic amines, the products of which may be hepatotoxic. Third, acetaldehyde binds to tubulin, alters polymerization of tubulin, and may impair protein secretion after ethanol. In addition, it has recently been demonstrated that acetaldehyde binds to rat liver microsomes, a property that was increased after chronic alcohol consumption in association with enhanced microsomal ethanol oxidizing system (MEOS) activity [40]. Fourth, acetaldehyde may lead to glutathione depletion and promote peroxidative damage of membranes [58]. To the extent that acetaldehydge has a deleterious effect on mitochondrial structure and function, the breakdown of acetaldehyde will be diminished and still higher levels of this substance will result. Such a vicious cycle might eventually result in levels of acetaldehyde high enough to cause clinically apparent liver injury.

Protein accumulation. As already noted, acetaldehyde binds to tubulin and may alter microtubular function. In part, this action may explain the increased concentration of export proteins (e.g., albumin and transferrin) that was observed after chronic ethanol consumption. Indeed, in animals fed alcohol-containing diets, lipids account for only half the increase in liver dry weight; the other half has been attributed to the retention of export proteins in the cytosol [4]. The delayed appearance of newly labeled albumin and transferrin in the serum of rats fed alcohol chronically is consistent with such a secretory defect [5].

Protein retention may contribute to alcoholic hepatomegaly, swelling of the hepatocyte, and perhaps promote hepatic injury. It has been proposed that ballooning of the hepatocyte may result in cellular disorganization and promote progressive liver damage in the alcoholic [32]. There is a precedent for such a pathogenic mechanism. It is well known that patients with homozygous alpha$_1$-antitrypsin deficiency may develop fibrosis and/or cirrhosis. The progression to cirrhosis in this disorder is associated with the accumulation of alpha$_1$trypsin.

In conclusion, it is likely that a variety of mechanisms result in necrosis of the hepatocyte. The relative importance of NADH generation, acetaldehyde toxicity, and protein retention in hepatocyte damage after alcohol remains to be established.

Clinical Aspects of Alcoholic Liver Injury

Alcoholic liver injury is an important cause of significant morbidity and mortality. Indeed, in large urban centers, alcoholic cirrhosis may be the third or fourth leading cause of death in young males.

Fatty liver. Despite adequate nutrition, alcohol induces the accumulation of intracytoplasmic fat in both alcoholic and nonalcoholic volunteers. These alterations cannot be prevented by supplementation of the diet with proteins or vitamins. Light microscopic examination reveals displacement of the nucleus by intracytoplasmic vacuoles; at the subcellular level, there are mitochondrial aberrations and dilation of the endoplasmic reticulum. Even at this early stage of liver injury, excess collagen (especially in the pericentral area) may be detected by chemical means [17, 43] or appropriate staining [67].

An increased number of myofibroblasts and fibroblasts have also been noted in the perivenular central areas of ethanol-fed baboons at the fatty liver stage [38]. Such cells may play an important role in the overabundant deposition of collagen that occurred in those animals who ultimately progressed to cirrhosis.

Alcoholic fatty liver usually presents as nontender hepatomegaly. Occasionally, pain (usually in the right upper quadrant), jaundice, dark urine, and acholic stools may be prominent symptoms of hepatic steatosis (*vide infra*). The diagnosis is established by liver biopsy, radionuclide scanning, and serum levels of liver enzymes, especially gamma glutamyl transpeptidase (GGTP) [59]. The serum glutamic-oxaloacetic transaminase (SGOT), serum glutamic-oxaloacetic transaminase (SGPT), alkaline phosphatase, and bilirubin correlate poorly with the degree of hepatic steatosis. Approximately 25% of patients with fatty liver will have no increase in any of these parameters. Rarely, hepatic steatosis is accompanied by hyperlipemia and hemolytic anemia (Zieve's syndrome).

In the unusual case of alcoholic fatty liver that presents with symptoms that mimic extrahepatic obstruction, abdominal ultrasonography is useful in visualizing the biliary tree. Depending upon its availability, either endoscopic retrograde cholangiopancreatography (ERCP) or percutaneous transhepatic cholangiography (PTC) will further clarify the nature of the cholestasis.

Therapeutic goals include abstinence from alcohol and improved nutritional status. The restriction of fat may be helpful but has not been studied in a randomized or controlled fashion. Similarly, anabolic steroids cannot be recommended and are potentially harmful given their androgenic and cholestatis sequelae.

Alcoholic hepatitis. In addition to the mechanisms reviewed, immunologic factors have been implicated in the development and progression of alcoholic hepatitis. To explain the progression of alcoholic hepatitis despite abstinence, it has been proposed that alcoholic hyalin is a neoantigen that engenders an autoimmune, cytotoxic process. A variety of studies seem to support this concept. For example, sensitized lymphocytes from patients with alcoholic hepatitis when stimulated with alcoholic hyalin elaborate transfer factor and migration-inhibition factor and are cytotoxic when added to cultured chang liver cells [29].

The pathogenic importance of these interesting findings remains to be established since the presence of alcoholic hyaline has not been shown to have prognostic value in either retrospective or prospective studies [19]. In addition, the prevailing view that alcoholic cirrhosis invariably develops in response to alcoholic hepatitis has been questioned. In both human and animals studies [35] it appears that florid alcoholic hepatitis may not be a necessary intermediate step in the development of cirrhosis.

The pathological criteria for diagnosing alcoholic hepatitis include parenchymal and portal infiltration with polymorphonuclear cells and varying degrees of necrosis, sclerosis, steatosis, and cholestasis. The presence of Mallory's bodies supports the diagnosis but this is not a histologic prequisite.

At times, alcoholic hepatitis may be present as a relatively mild illness with right upper quadrant pain and jaundice being the sole complaints. The diagnosis is suggested by a disproportionate increase in the level of SGOT (compared to the SGPT), an elevated serum bilirubin level, leukocytosis, and a prolonged prothrombin time. Unfortunately, there is a considerable overlap between these values in patients with and without hepatitis [68], and the correlation between the severity of clinical symptoms and histologic lesions is poor.

It has recently been reported that measurements of plasma glutamate dehydrogenase (GDH) early in the clinical course may correlate more closely with the severity of the histologic lesion [71]. In a subgroup of patients, the clinical syndrome may be more fulminant. These individuals present with jaundice, fever, right upper quadrant pain, and chemistries suggesting extrahepatic obstruction. These patients may rapidly succumb to hepatic encephalopathy and renal failure despite intensive medical care. The value of corticosteroid or propylthiouracil therapy [23] in this situation remains controversial, but may benefit a subgroup of patients.

The differentiation of alcoholic hepatitis, a medical condition, and extrahepatic obstruction, a surgical entity, is important and is usually possible with a combination of ultrasonography, PTC, and ERCP. The latter approach is especially indicated in the presence of a coagulopathy.

Cirrhosis. The cirrhotic patient exhibits a nodular and hard liver that is often enlarged at an early stage when fat is abundant; at later stages it may be shrunken in size. Other signs of cirrhosis include spider angiomata, palmar erythema, Dupuytren's contracture, splenomegaly, and a caput medusa (venous collaterals of the anterior abdominal wall). Biochemically, there may be a striking increase in immunoglobins (IgG, IgM, and IgA) in addition to alterations in conventional liver tests. The prognosis of the cirrhotic patient improves with cessation of drinking [47], but remains extremely guarded in those with ascites, encephalopathy, or gastrointestinal bleeding. In one series, 5-year survival in patients with uncomplicated cirrhosis was 75% and only 40% in cases with ascites. Although nutritional support of the cirrhotic patient is indicated, overzealous supplement of protein and vitamins (especially vitamin A) may be hazardous [30].

PANCREAS

Epidemiology of Alcoholic Pancreatitis

Pancreatitis is linked to alcoholism in as few as 5% and as many as 90% of cases. Statistics also vary considerably from one country to another in this respect. There are at least two reasons for the wide range of these estimates. First, the diagnosis of alcoholism is not always obvious on clinical grounds and the prevalence of alcoholism in a study population may be greatly underestimated. Second, studies based on postmortem material introduce a bias in the selection of pancreatic cases. In such studies severe cases of acute pancreatitis tend to be overrepresented. Death in such patients is often due to necrotizing hemorrhagic pancreatitis, a sequela much more common in patients with biliary tract disease.

Nevertheless, true variations in the geographical incidence of alcoholic pancreatitis probably do exist. Thus, in England it appeared to be rare up until 1950 and has been diagnosed with increasing frequency since then. The extent to which increased recognition accounts for this increased incidence is an important but unsettled issue.

Apart from possible geographical variations in the incidence of alcohol-related pancreatic disease, there may be variations among countries in the clinical presentations. In France, patients with alcoholic pancreatitis present mainly with features of pancreatic insufficiency, whereas in the United States, Australia, and South Africa, the predominant features are those of chronic relapsing pancreatitis (i.e., pain and hyperamylasemia). These apparent differences may be important in assessing the claims for pathogenic mechanisms from different centers.

It appears that the type of beverage consumed does not affect the likelihood of pancreatitis [53]. However, drinking patterns do influence the frequency of acute attacks. A common finding in several studies is that binges in chronic alcoholics often precipitate relapses of pancreatitis. In contrast, intermittent overindulgence by nonalcoholics (e.g., college students) rarely results in symptomatic pancreatitis [63].

Constitutional factors may favor the development of chronic pancreatitis, such as anomalies of the pancreatic duct or sphincter of Oddi, familial hyperlipemia, and the presence of H-LA antigen B-40 [16]. The frequency of H-LA antigen B-40 is also elevated in various forms of alcoholic liver injury [7]. Together, these last two observations indicate that a genetic locus closely linked to the histocompatibility complex may enhance one's susceptibility to alcohol-induced organ damage. Nutritional factors may be important, as discussed subsequently in connection with pathogenesis.

Pathology of Alcoholic Pancreatitis

The pathological features of alcoholic pancreatitis are nonspecific. Even calcification, a finding that strongly suggests an alcoholic etiology, is not pathognomonic.

In the mild forms of alcoholic pancreatitis, interstitial edema is common. Recently, Bordalo et al. [9] demonstrated that subcellular pancreatic injury is common in asymptomatic alcoholics. Although the pancreas was normal on routine histologic sections and its lobular architecture was intact, there was a high frequency of ultrastructural changes: an increase in intracellular fat vacuoles, a dilatation of the endoplasmic reticulum, autophagic vacuoles, and mitochondrial alterations. Similar ultrastructural damage was noted in patients with established pancreatitis.

Fibrosis, necrosis, inflammation, and atrophy are characteristic features of more severe alcoholic pancreatitis. These lesions are distributed in a patchy fashion throughout the pancreas, with often striking variation in the degree of lobular injury. The irregular distribution of the injury has been attributed to obstruction of peripheral pancreatic ducts by calcified proteinaceous plugs [55]. Acinar cells within involved lobules may be replaced by fibrous tissue or goblet cells and the epithelial cells around the central lumen of the acinus may be flattened (so-called canalicular dedifferentiation). The number of islet cells within the pancreatic parenchyma have been variably reported to be unchanged, decreased, or increased.

Abnormalities of the ductular epithelium are especially common in chronic pancreatitis. Squamous metaplasia of the normally cuboid duct-lining cells is frequently observed or the epithelium may be transformed to a more columnar mucin-producing cell. These changes in the duct epithelium are often associated with ductular dilatation and irregularity. Within the ducts, gellike eosinophic plugs have described and may become calcified [55]. Indeed, as already noted, intraductal calcification is considered a typical feature of alcoholic pancreatitis. Pancreatic lithiasis is most pronounced in advanced cases and appears to commence in the peripheral ducts [55].

Pseudocysts often develop after an episode of acute inflammation. Unlike true cysts they lack a lining epithelium and are surrounded by inflammatory exudate or granulation tissue. Such pseudocysts may or may not communicate with the pancreatic duct.

Pathogenesis of Alcoholic Pancreatitis

Pancreatitis is an autodigestive process with secondary inflammatory phenomena. Thus, in studying the pathogenesis of pancreatitis, much emphasis has been placed on investigating the synthesis, transport, activation, and inhibition of pancreatic enzymes.

Clinical aspects that require explanation are the presence of recurrent acute attacks and the chronic course of the illness. Most theories ignore the dual nature of the disease. Thus, hypotheses implicating dysfunction of the sphincter of Oddi overlook the chronic nature of alcoholic pancreatitis. Similarly, the theory of small duct obstruction by protein plugs fails to explain the abrupt onset of relapses.

As in studies related to alcoholic liver injury (*vide supra*), the role of diet in the pathogenesis of pancreatitis is unsettled. The traditional view is that malnutrition favors the development of pancreatitis in the alcoholic. This is supported by the occurrence of calfifying pancreatitis in regions of the world where severe malnutrition is prevalent and the observations of Pitchumoni et al. [46] of American patients with alcoholic pancreatitis. Furthermore, patients hospitalized after episodes of severe alcoholism and malnutrition have impaired pancreatic secretion with return to normal secretion after dietary restitution, even with continued alcohol intake [39].

The possibility that a high nutritional intake favors pancreatitis is raised by the finding that administration of high-fat diets predisposes dogs to experimental pancreatitis [18]. Furthermore, Sarles et al. [55] documented an increased intake of dietary fat and protein in French patients with chronic alcoholic pancreatitis. However, in a subsequent study, the Marseille group presented evidence that both an increase and a decrease in the intake of fat and protein appeared to predispose to alcoholic pancreatitis.

Acute effects of ethanol. After decades of intense controversy, the various "sphincter theories" have received less attention in recent years. As mentioned above, they all fail to satisfactorily explain the chronic nature of the disorder.

1. *Biliary-pancreatic reflux.* It has been proposed that dysfunction of the sphincter of Oddi favors diversion of bile into pancreatic ducts and that the composition of the bile (notably its lysolecithin content) is altered by ethanol, by previous pancreatic-biliary reflux, or by other factors. This theory is unsatisfactory since a common channel is absent in many patients and biliary-pancreatic diversion does not result in a reproducible animal model of pancreatitis.

2. *Obstruction-hypersecretion.* Pancreatic stimulation by alcohol might cause abnormal rises in pancreatic duct pressure if there was coincidental contraction of the sphincter of Oddi. Originally, it was thought that the local irritant effect of ethanol could cause such contraction, but recent studies indicate that it results from a systemic effect of ethanol.

3. *Duodeno-pancreatic reflux.* This theory proposes that alcohol-induced sphincteric dysfunction causes duodeno-pancreatic reflux and that this allows enterokinase to initiate the intrapancreatic activation of digestive enzymes. No convincing animal model has been developed that supports this theory.

The oral or intragastric administration of alcohol stimulates the exocrine pancreas in the dog [69] and rat [12, 25]. The mechanism, however, is no longer certain. It was previously accepted that the pancreatic response to alcohol was mediated by increased gastric acid (and secondary release of secretin from the duodenum). This view has been challenged in recent years. For example, when the isolated gastric antrum of the dog is perfused with alcohol, the pancreatic response precedes any increase in gastric acid [57]. In man, within 5 minutes of oral ethanol intake, there is a prompt elevation of serum secretin levels. Finally, the pancreatic stimulation after intragastric ethanol is not significantly different in control and achlorhydric (cimetidine-treated) rats [25]. These studies suggest that ethanol releases secretin or other polypeptides directly from the duodenum by an acid-independent mechanism.

The direct effects of ethanol on the exocrine pancreas are also controversial. The effects of parenteral alcohol appear to depend on several experimental conditions: the state of consciousness, the dose of alcohol given, the way in which juice is collected, and the use of exogenous stimulation. When intravenous ethanol was given to a conscious patient with a freely draining pancreatic fistula, there was a clear-cut increase in volume and protein output. Moreover, when intravenous alcohol is given to basally secreting rats, there is also a stimulatory effect [28]. On the other hand, when the pancreas is stimulated exogenously using secretin or secretin-cholecystokinin (CCK), depression of pancreatic secretion by alcohol is observed in dogs [6, 65], and rats [28]. In human studies, intravenous ethanol alone has been reported to have no effect on duodenal aspirate volume, but when given after secretin stimulation, there is a reduction. However, these experiments are difficult to assess in view of the possible effects of ethanol on the sphincter of Oddi. In the dog, vagotomy diminished the inhibitory action of intravenous ethanol [65] and the authors suggested that intravenous alcohol stimulated putative inhibitory vagal fibers.

The effects of ethanol in vitro are also conflicting. There have been reports of a reduction in secretion [60] and significant increases [62]. The latter study attributed this disparity to the calcium-free conditions of the incubation in the former study since Ca+ may mediate, at least in part, the pancreatic response to stimuli.

Little is known about the acute metabolic changes produced by ethanol in the pancreas. Rat pancreatic triglyceride synthesis is stimulated at the expense of phospholipid synthesis by ethanol in vitro as well as by acute ethanol administration in vivo [61]. Orrego-Matte et al. [41] demonstrated a decreased appearance of injected ^{32}P into rat pancreas phospholipid after acute (and chronic) ethanol administration. However, because of their experimental design and the rapid exchangeability of phospholipids, one cannot be certain that the labeled phospholipid in these experiments was actually synthesized in the pancreas and not elsewhere. Solomon et al. [60] found that ethanol given to rabbits acutely in vivo or added to pancreas in vitro caused a reduction in pancreatic adenosine triphosphate (ATP) levels. They related this to similar reductions in secretion. There was no associated change in cyclic adenosine monophosphate (AMP) concentrations.

Chronic effects of ethanol. Lesions comparable to those found in the human pancreas have been produced in dogs and rats after chronic ethanol administration. Pathological features resembling those seen in patients with chronic calcific pancreatitis were reproduced by Sarles and his colleagues in over half of the rats fed alcohol *ad libitum* (mean 4 g/day/rat) for up to 30 months. As in the human condition, the lesions were patchy and were characterized by atrophic acini, dustular proliferation, intraductal protein precipitates, and fibrosis.

The most widely accepted theory of the pathogenesis of alcoholic pancreatitis is that proposed by Sarles [53]. Sarles and his colleagues postulate that ethanol favors the precipitation of protein in peripheral pancreatic ducts and that these protein plugs cause obstructive changes, become calcified, and spread to involve larger ducts. The precipitation of protein might be favored by an increased concentration of protein in pancreatic juice [49], or by ionic changes such as a change in bicarbonate concentration. Alternatively, the intraductal activation of zymogens rather than their increased concentration might lead to these protein precipitates [1]. The attraction of this theory is its almost universal applicability to all forms of chronic pancreatitis. Its weakness is the absence of convincing evidence to date that the protein precipitates are the cause and not the result of metabolic derangements in the pancreas.

The effects of chronic ethanol administration on the concentration of secretory protein in rat pancreatic juice are variable with reports of increase [54], no change [12], and decreases [22]. In the dog, the pancreatic response to exogenous cholecystokinin was enhanced after 3 months of alcohol feeding but not after 2 years. However, in the latter situation, the pancreatic response to a standard dose of secretin was increased [56]. This enhanced sensitivity to secretin may have been due to changes in the ductular ephitelium (reduplication and hyperplasia). The failure to observe an enhanced response to CCK after 2 years of alcohol feeding may reflect damage to acinar cells.

Chronic ethanol consumption also alters the pancreatic response to intravenous alcohol. As discussed, intravenous alcohol markedly suppresses secretin-stimulated exocrine secretion in animals and nonalcoholic human subjects. After chronic ethanol ingestion, an acute infusion has the opposite effect (an increase in flow rate and in the outputs of bicarbonate and protein).

Variable changes in the tissue concentrations of pancreatic enzymes in animals after chronic ethanol intake have been reported by a number of authors. However, these studies are difficult to assess in view of the absence of pair feeding in some studies or the apparently small amount of ethanol consumed in others.

Clinical Aspects of Alcoholic Pancreatitis

Acute attack. Abdominal pain and vomiting are the most common symptoms of acute alcoholic pancreatitis. Typically, the pain is severe, constant, poorly localized to the upper abdomen with radiation to the back, and often relieved by leaning forward. A mild attack may last 2 to 3 days. Severe attacks may persist for 2 to 4 weeks and are associated with a mortality rate of up to 30%. Mild fever commonly develops in the first few days. A high swinging fever indicates the development of a pancreatic abscess. Other complications that may develop within the first week include renal dysfunction, mild jaundice, disturbances of coagulation, hypocalcemia, and local spread of inflammation to involve nearby organs.

Clinical course. The first attack of acute alcoholic pancreatitis most often occurs after 10 to 15 years of heavy drinking and is thus most often seen in males in the fourth decade of life. Recurrent attacks, precipitated by alcohol abuse, and recurring at intervals of weeks or months, are typical. With the passage of time, these attacks tend to become more frequent but less severe, and the complications of chronic pancreatitis then become more prominent, notably diabetes and malabsorption. Drug addiction is a common association, possibly because of the relentless pain or because of associated personality disorders. Malabsorption, diabetes, and self-neglect combine to produce a weakened, emaciated state commonly leading to death in middle age.

As discussed before, in some patients the illness is characterized by the insidious onset and steady progression of pancreatic insufficiency with very little in the way of acute inflammatory episodes. In still others, the dominant feature is relentless pain.

Diagnosis. In clinical practice, unequivocal proof of the existence of pancreatitis is unusual. The single most useful diagnostic test of pancreatitis is that of the serum amylase activity, especially one with a resulting value in excess of 1,100 IU/l. However the serum amylase level can fluctuate markedly within the space of hours, shows poor correlation with clinical severity, is normal in 10 to 20% of patients during an acute attack, and may be elevated by many other conditions [52]. Furthermore, it represents the sum of the activities of isoenzymes of salivary and pancreatic origin and the isoenzymes of the salivary type may originate from a variety of organs, including the pancreas [52]. The urinary clearance of amylase (Ca) is increased even more than the urinary output of creatinine (Ccr) in pancreatitis, but the measurement of the ratio of amylase clearance to creatinine clearance is not uniformly reliable in the diagnosis of pancreatitis and probably increases the diagnostic accuracy only marginally. Nonspecificity of the Ca-Ccr has been noted by several groups and has been attributed to the renal tubular dysfunction of acute illness [14].

The diagnosis of pancreatitis is strengthened by plain X rays of the abdomen showing the radiological features of inflammation in the vicinity of the pancreas. These features include a sentinel loop (localized small bowel ileus), a cut-off sign (constant constriction of the mild transverse colon with air proximally), pleural effusions (usually left-sided), and basal pulmonary atelectasis. A barium study of the upper GI tract may give further indirect evidence by showing widening of the duodenal loop, occasionally with distortion of the mucosa that may resemble that seen in malignant infiltration. The presence of chronic pancreatic disease is confirmed in a minority of patients by the demonstration of pancreatic calcification (best seen in an oblique or lateral view). The presence of gallstones should be sought, using oral cholecystography and/or ultrasonography.

More sophisticated tests may be used to assess the extent and severity of disease and the presence of complications. Ultrasonography is a noninvasive procedure involving no irradiation. It is of particular value in demonstrating the presence of pseudocysts and in assessing the size of the pancreas and may also be used to diagnose biliary tract disease (gallstones, dilated bile ducts). It does not consistently distinguish between the various causes of pancreatic enlargement (malignancy and acute or chronic inflammation). Computerized axial tomography is also noninvasive but does involve irradiation. Like ultrasonography, it is useful in showing the size, shape, and position of the pancreas, especially in obese patients, but does not reliably indicate the underlying pathology. ERCP is the procedure of choice for demonstrating the pancreatic duct system and assessing the presence of obstruction, dilatation, and strictures. Its main value is in providing structural information for planning surgery rather than in assessing etiology. The main complications of this procedure are pancreatitis and abscess formation and these occur more readily in the presence of acute inflammation and a pseudocyst respectively.

Complications. Some degree of cholestasis is common in pancreatitis and occasionally causes diagnostic confusion. It may present in three main forms. First, mild jaundice (bilirubin 3 mg/100 ml), with tapered narrowing of the common bile duct as it passes through the pancreas, is very common in all forms of acute pancreatic inflammation and requires no treatment. Second, elevation of the serum alkaline phosphatase is common. It is usually mild but occasionally very high levels are encountered in the absence of primary hepatobiliary disease. Third, severe jaundice occasionally develops because of significant biliary tract obstruction from a pancreatic stricture or pseudocyst. It is important in such cases to perform cholangiography (percutaneously or endoscopically) to exclude the presence of biliary tract calculis or malignancy and to assess the type and severity of the stricture. When the pancreatitis has an alcoholic etiology, the possibility always exists that the jaundice is due to alcoholic liver disease.

Pancreatic exocrine insufficiency is a complication of chronic relapsing pancreatitis that has important nutritional consequences. The diagnosis is established by simple nonintubative tests. The simplest is the examination of feces with Sudan III, which stains globules of neutral triglyceride with an orange color. The presence of these globules in a patient with steatorrhea suggests that the excess lipid has a pancreatic etiology. Quantitation of the fecal fat under controlled conditions (72-hour collection, 100 g dietary fat per day) gives a crude indication of progress of the disease or of response to therapy. A more rapid test of pancreatic function is the estimation of the urinary excretion of para-aminobenzoic acid (PABA) after an oral dose of N-benzoyl-L-tryrosyl-p-amino-benzoic acid

[3]. PABA excretion reflects the level of chymotrypsin in the pancreatic juice as well as factors influencing renal clearance, such as hydration, the presence of ascites, and renal function. Intubative tests provide a more detailed quantitation of pancreatic exocrine function. A standard stimulus, such as secretin and/or cholecystokinin, is given, followed by duodenal aspiration using a double-lumen tube or direct cannulation of the pancreatic duct. Direct aspiration of the pancreatic juice is much more cumbersome, has not as yet been shown to be more informative, and alters the flow and compositions of pancreatic juice.

Probably the best indicators of pancreatic insufficiency are a reduction in flow rate and in bicarbonate concentrations. However, at an early stage of alcoholic pancreatitis, there may be an increased flow rate. An alternative intubative method is the Ludh test, in which the duodenum is aspirated with a single-lumen tube after a standard meal. This method is often suited to less specialized units because the aspiration and the biochemical techniques are simple and no intravenous injections are required.

Medical therapy: acute attacks. Treatment is directed at relief of pain, avoidance of pancreatic stimulation, and maintenance of fluid balance and nutrition.

1. *Analgesia.* Pentazocine is the agent of choice because it has relatively little effect on the tone of the sphincter of Oddi. For the same reason, meperidine is preferable to morphine.

2. *Avoidance of pancreatic stimulation.* The value of nasogastric aspiration has not been supported by clinical trials [31]. However, the results of these studies may be applicable only to certain selected patients and it would be premature to abandon this form of treatment. Nasogastric suction often relieves pain in patients with pancreatitis, but this might be due to relief from gaseous distention and ileus.

3. *Fluid and nutritional replacement.* Intravenous fluids (dextrose and electrolytes) are given until pain subsides and oral feeding is then cautiously and progressively introduced. To combat shock and to replace the large volumes of fluid that may be lost retroperitoneally, infusion of plasma, low molecular weight dextrans, or blood may be required. Severe cases require monitoring of urinary output and central venous pressure. In prolonged cases, especially if surgery for a pseudocyst or abscess is contemplated, total parenteral nutrition will be needed.

4. *Miscellaneous.* Therapeutic agents that have not been shown to be of routine value in controlled clinical studies include antibiotics, Trasylol, glucagon, calcitonin, and cimetidine. Somatostatin, an inhibitor of pancreatic exocrime secretion, did not reduce the mortality of experimental pancreatitis in rats.

Medical therapy: chronic complications.

1. *Chronic pancreatic insufficiency.* Steatorrhea is usually improved but not completely corrected by the use of pancreatic extracts. The stability of the preparation is enhanced by administrations that reduce gastric acidity, such as bicarbonate and cimetidine; the usual regimen is 1 to 3 tablets with each meal. The dose can be increased to 6 to 8 tablets each meal but this may result in hyperuricosuria. A reduction in dietary fat intake may help symptomatically. It is uncommon to find a deficiency of fat-soluble vitamins and their supplementation is rarely indicated in chronic pancreatitis [15]. This may be because the affinity of triglycerides for fat-soluble vitamines is relatively limited. Vitamin B_{12} deficiency is rare in patients with pancreatitis [64] despite the fact that tests of vitamin B_{12} absorption frequently give abnormal results [66]. There may be enhanced absorption of iron and of folic acid. Thus, routine vitamin supplementation is not needed for chronic pancreatitis itself, but of course is commonly indicated for the patient who continues to drink [26].

Diabetes mellitus is usually mild but brittle, possibly because of glucagon deficiency. The usual dietary principles of the treatment of diabetes still apply, but reduction of obesity is less of a problem than in most diabetics. Although insulin may be needed, oral agents are less apt to precipitate hypoglycemia.

2. *Pseudocysts.* Pseudocysts may involve any part of the pancreas and often extend along tissue planes into adjacent abdominal structures, the pelvis, and, rarely, the mediastinum. Even in the absence of a palpable mass, this complication of alcoholic pancreatitis should be suspected in patients with abdominal pain and persistent increases in the serum amylase. Ultrasonic examination is the primary modality for confirming the diagnosis, since it is noninvasive and has reasonable sensitivity and specificity. ERCP is not generally required and may occasionally convert a pseudocyst into an abscess. Serious complications of untreated pseudocysts include rupture into the free peritoneal cavity or adjacent organs, intracystic hemorrhage, abscess formation, and obstructive jaundice. The timing of operative intervention in patients with pancreatic pseudocysts is undergoing revision. As a result of a study that demonstrated that about 25% of pseudocysts will undergo spontaneous resolution during serial ultrasonic examinations, a 3-week period of nonoperative treatment is advised [10]. In addition to allowing resolution, the delay of surgery should improve the encapsulation of the pseudocyst by fibrous tissue. After 4 to 6 weeks of observation spontaneous resolution of a pseudocyst is unlikely and the risk of serious complications exceeds that of elective drainage [11].

3. *Pancreatic ascites.* The clinical features of pancreatic ascites are relatively nonspecific: an increase in abdominal girth, abdominal pain, and weight loss. These symptoms, in the context of known chronic alcoholism, usually suggest cirrhosis with portal hypertension, peritoneal metastases, or tuberculous peritonitis. These diagnostic possibilities are readily distinguished by paracente-

sis. Typically, the fluid in pancreatic ascites contains a high amylase concentration and is exudative (the protein concentration greater than 2.5 g/100 ml).

Initial management of pancreatic ascites is medical. Nonoperative therapy usually involves a trial (4 to 6 weeks) of parenteral nutrition. If this approach fails to prevent fluid reaccumulation, low-dose pancreatic irradiation may be utilized. Ascites resistant to these conservative measures require surgical intervention. If preoperative ERCP demonstrates a pseudocyst, internal drainage (cystogastrostomy or Roux-en-Y cystojejunostomy) is employed. Roux-en-Y pancreatojejunostomy is performed if there is a documented ductal rupture.

Surgical therapy. In the acute attack, surgery is generally contraindicated. Occasionally the risks are outweighed by the advantages of exluding other abdominal emergencies and providing emergency treatment of biliary and pancreatic complications [70].

Chronic disabling pain is occasionally treated surgically. It has not been possible to perform controlled trials and reduced pain may represent progression of the disease and loss of functioning tissue rather than the effects of surgery [2].

The main surgical possibilities are pancreatic ductal decompression, pancreatic resection, and pancreatic denervation. The rational for ductal decompression is questionable since pain ofter persists despite proven patency of decompressive shunts [70]. Sphincteroplasty has generally been disappointing, possibly because of restricturing or because of areas of obstruction at other levels in the duct system apart from the sphincter of Oddi.

An alternative approach is a subtotal resection of the pancreas on the grounds that it is easier to treat malabsorption and mild diabetes than it is to manage continuing pancreatic inflammation. Various types of nerve blocks have been tried but are not uniformly successful. An old form of therapy, namely total pancreatic duct obstruction by ligation, has recently been revived in modified form by the introduction into the pancreatic duct system of an acrylate glue. The rationale is that total obstruction causes atrophy of exocrine tissue and thus prevents inflammation.

Prognosis. For the acute relapse of chronic pancreatitis a survival rate of greater than 90% can be expected. Poor prognostic signs include an age over 55 years, a blood glucose level greater than 200 mg/100 ml, a white cell count over 16,000/ml, signs of hemoconcentration, and a serum calcium level of less than 8 mg/100 ml [48].

Chronic pancreatic disease is already present at the time of the first detectable inflammatory episode. Unfortunately, most patients continue to drink heavily and further episodes, sometimes precipitated by quite small amounts of alcohol, tend to result in severe complications and death in about 10 years [21]. Abstinence from alcohol may be the most important determinant of prognosis. Among patients treated surgically for pancreatic pain, the 10-year survival is 80% in those who stop drinking and 25% to 60% in those who continue to drink.

REFERENCES

1. Allan, B. J., and White, T. T. An alternate mechanism for the formation of protein plugs in chronic calcifying pancreatitis. *Digestion* 11:428-431, 1974.
2. Ammann, R. W., Largiandèr, F., and Akovbiantz, A. Pain relief by surgery in chronic pancreatitis. *Scand. J. Gastroenterol.* 14:209-215, 1979.
3. Arvanitakis, C., and Greenberger, N. J. Diagnosis of pancreatic disease by a synthetic peptide: A new test of exocrine pancreatic function. *Lancet* 1:663-666, 1976.
4. Baraona, E., Leo, M. A., Borowsky, S. A., et al. Alcoholic hepatomegaly: Accumulation of protein in the liver. *Science* 190:794-795, 1975.
5. Baraona, E., Leo, M. A., Borowsky, S. A., et al. Pathogenesis of alcohol-induced accumulation of protein in the liver. *J. Clin. Invest.* 60:546-554, 1977.
6. Bayer, M., Rudick, J., Lieber, C. S., and Janowitz, D. H. Inhibitory effect of ethanol on canine exocrine pancreatic secretion. *Gastroenterol.* 63:619-626, 1972.
7. Bell, H., and Nordhagen, R. Association between HL-A B-40 and alcoholic liver disease with corrhosis. *Br. Med. J.* 1:822, 1978.
8. Best, C. H., Hartcroft, W. S., Lucas, C. C., and Ridout, J. H. Liver damage produced by feeding alcohol or sugar and its prevention by choline. *Br. Med. J.* ii:1001-1003, 1949.
9. Bordalo, O., Noronha, M., and Dreiling, D. A. Functional and morhologic studies of the effect of alcohol on the pancreatic parenchyma. *Mount Sinai J. Med.* 44:481-484, 1977.
10. Bradley, E. L., III, and Clements, J. L., Jr. Implications of diagnostic ultrasound in the surgical management of pancreatic pseudocysts. *Am. J. Surg.* 127:163-173, 1974.
11. Bradley, E. L., III, Clements, J. L., Jr., and Gonzalez, A. C. The natural history of pancreatic pseudocysts: A unified concept of management. *Am. J. Surgery* 137:135-141, 1979.
12. Cavarzan, A., Teixeira, A. S., Sarles, H., Palasciano, G., and Tiscornia, O. Action of intragastric ethanol on the pancreatic secretion of conscious rats. *Digestion* 13:145-152, 1975.
13. Cederbaum, A. L., Lieber, C. S., and Rubin, E. The effect of acetaldehyde on mitochondrial function. *Arch. Biochem. Biophys.* 161:26-39, 1974.
14. DiMagno, E. P., and Go, V. L. W. The exocrine pancreas. In: *Current Gastroenterology and Hepatology*, Gitnick, G. L. (ed.). Houghton Mifflin: Boston, 1979.
15. Evans, W. B., and Wollaeger, E. E. Incidence and severity of nutritional deficiency rates on chronic exocrine pancreatic insufficiency: Comparison with nontropical sprue. *Am. J. Dig. Dis.* 11:594-606, 1966.
16. Fauchet, R., Genetet, B., Gosselin, J., and Gastrad, J. HLA antigens in chronic alcoholic pancreatitis. *Tissue Antigens* 13:163-166, 1979.
17. Feinman, L., and Lieber, C. S. Hepatic collagen metabolism: Effect of alcohol consumption in rats and baboons. *Science* 176:795, 1972.
18. Haig, T. H. B. Experimental pancreatitis intensified by high-fat diet. *Surg. Gyn. Obst.* 131:914-918, 1970.
19. Harinasuta, U., and Zimmerman, H. J. Alcoholic steatonecrosis: I. Relationship between severity of hepatic disease and presence of Mallory bodies in the liver. *Gastroenterol.* 60:1036-1046, 1971.
20. Hasumura, Y., Teschke, R., and Lieber, C. S. Acetaldehyde oxidation by hepatic mitochondria: Decrease after chronic ethanol consumption. *Science* 189:727-729, 1975.
21. Howard, J. M., and Jordan, G. L. *Surgical Diseases of the Pancreas*. Lippincott: Philadelphia, 1960.

22. Huttunen, R., Huttunen, P., and Jalovaara, P. The effect of chronic intragastric alcohol ingestion on the pancreatic secretion of the rat. *Scan. J. Gastroenterol.* 11:103–106, 1976.

23. Israel, Y., and Orrego, H. Hepatocyte demand and substrate supply as factors in the susceptibility to alcoholic liver injury: Pathogenesis and prevention. *Clin. Gastroenterol.* 10:355–373, 1981.

24. Koivula, T., and Lindros, K. O. Effects of long-term ethanol treatment on aldehyde and alcohol dehydrogenase activities in rat liver. *Biochem. Pharmacol.* 24:1937–1942, 1975.

25. Korsten, M. A., Hodes, S. E., Saeli, J. F., Seitz, H. K., and Lieber, C. S. Effects of ethanol on pancreatic secretion: Roles of gastric acid and exogenous secretin. *Gastroenterol.* 76:1175, 1979.

26. Korsten, M. A., and Lieber, C. S. Nutrition in the alcoholic. *Med. Clin. N. Am.* 63:963–972, 1979.

27. Korsten, M. A., Matsuzaki, S., Feinman, L., et al. High blood acetaldehyde levels after ethanol administration in alcoholics. *N. Eng. J. Med.* 292:386–389, 1975.

28. Korsten, M. A., Seitz, H., Hodes, S. F., Klingenstein, J., and Lieber, C. S. The effect of intravenous ethanol on pancreatic secretion in the conscious rat. *Dig. Dis. Sci.* 26:760–765, 1981.

29. Leevy, C. M., Kanagasundaram, N., Matsumoto, K., et al. Alcoholic hyalin and immunologic reactivity. In: *Immune Reaction in Liver Disease,* Eddleston, A. L. W. F., Weber, J. C. P., and Williams, R. (eds.). Pitman Medical Publishing: Kent, England, 1979.

30. Leo, M., Sato, M., and Lieber C. S. Hepatotoxicity of moderate vitamin A supplementation: Potention by ethanol. *Hepatol.* 1:527, 1981.

31. Levant, J. A., Secrist, D. M., Resein, H., Sturdevant, R. A. L., and Guth, P. H. Nasogastric suction in the treatment of alcoholic pancreatitis: A controlled study. *J.A.M.A.* 229:51–53, 1974.

32. Lieber, C. S. Metabolic effects of ethanol on the liver and other digestive organs. In: *Clinics in Gastroenterology* (Vol. 10), Leevy, C. M. (ed.). Saunders: London, England, 1981.

33. Lieber, C. S., and DeCarli, L. M. Quantitative relationship between the amount of dietary fat and the severity of the alcoholic fatty liver. *Am. J. Clin. Nutr.* 23:474, 1970.

34. Lieber, C. S., and DeCarli, L. M. An experimental model of alcohol feeding and liver injury in the baboon. *J. Med. Primatol.* 3:153–163, 1974.

35. Lieber, C. S., DeCarli, L. M., and Rubin, E. Sequential production of fatty liver, hepatitis and cirrhosis in subhuman primates fed ethanol with adequate diets. *Proc. Nat. Acad. Sci.* 72:437–441, 1975.

36. Lieber, C. S., Jones, D. P., Losowsky, M. S., et al. Interrelation of uric acid and ethanol metabolism in man. *J. Clin. Invest.* 41:1863–1870, 1962.

37. Lieber, C. S., Jones, D. P., Mendelson, J., et al. Fatty liver, hyperlipemia and hyperuricemia produced by prolonged alcohol consumption, despite adequate dietary intake. *Trans. Assoc. Am. Phys.* 76:289–300, 1963.

38. Lieber, C. S., Nakano, M., and Worner, T. M. Ultrastructure of the initial stages of hepatic perivenular fibrosis after alcohol. *Trans. Assoc. Am. Phys.* in press.

39. Mezey, E., Jow, E., Slavin, R. E., and Tobin, F. Pancreatic function and intestinal absorption in chronic alcoholism. *Gastroenterol.* 56:657–664, 1970.

40. Nomura, E., and Lieber, C. S. Binding of acetaldehyde to rat liver microsomes: Enhancement after chronic alcohol consumption. *Biochem. Biophys. Res. Comm.* 100:131–137, 1981.

41. Orrego-Matte, H., Navia, E., Feres, A., and Costamaillere, L. Ethanol ingestion and

incorporation of ^{32}P into phospholipids of pancreas in the rat. *Gastroenterol.* 56:280–285, 1969.

42. Patek, A. J., Jr., Bowry, S., and Hayes, K. C. Cirrhosis of choline deficiency in the rhesus monkey: Possible role of dietary cholesterol. *Proc. Soc. Exp. Biol. Med.* 148:370, 1975.

43. Patek, A. J., Bowry, S. C., and Sabesin, S. M. Minimal hepatic changes in rats fed alcohol and high casein diet. *Arch. Pathol. Lab. Med.* 100:19–24, 1976.

44. Perin, A., and Sessa, A. In vitro effects of ethanol and acetaldehyde on tissue protein synthesis. In: *The Role of Acetaldehyde in the Action of Ethanol*, Lindros, K. O. and Eriksson, C. J. P. (eds.). Finnish Foundation for Alcohol Studies: Helsinki, 1975.

45. Pikkarainen, P. H., Gordon, E. R., Lebsack, M. E., and Lieber, C. S. Determinants of plasma-free acetaldehyde levels during the oxidation of ethanol. *Biochem. Pharmacol.* 30:799–802, 1981.

46. Pitchumoni, C. S., Sonnenshein, M., Candido, F. M., Panchackaram, P., and Cooperman, J. M. Nutrition in the pathogenesis of alcoholic pancreatitis. *Am. J. Clin. Nutr.* 33:631–636, 1980.

47. Powell, W. J., and Klatskin, G. Duration of survival in patients with Laennec's cirrhosis. *Am. J. Med.* 44:406–420, 1968.

48. Ranson, J. H. C., Rifkind, K. M., Roses, D. F., Fink, S. D., Eng, K., and Spencer, F. C. Prognostic signs and the role of operative management in acute pancreatitis. *Surg. Gyn. Obst.* 139:69–81, 1974.

49. Renner, I. G., Rinderknecht, H., and Doublas, A. P. Profiles of pure pancreatic secretions in patients with acute pancreatitis: The possible role of proteolytic enzyme in pathogenesis. *Gastroenterol.* 15:1090–1098, 1978.

50. Rothschild, M., Oratz, M., Mongelli, J., and Schreiber, S. S. Alcohol-induced depression of albumin synthesis: Reversal by tryptophan. *J. Clin. Invest.* 50:1812–1818, 1971.

51. Salaspuro, M. P., Shaw, S., Jayatilleke, E., Ross, W. A., and Lieber, C. S. Attenuation of the ethanol-induced hepatic redox change after chronic alcohol consumption in baboons: Metabolic consequences in vivo and in vitro. *Hepatol.* 1:33–38, 1981.

52. Salt, W. B., II, and Schenker, S. Amylase—Its clinical significance: A review of the literature. *Medicine* 55:269–289, 1976.

53. Sarles, H. Chronic calcifying pancreatitis—Chronic alcohol pancreatitis. *Gastroenterol.* 66:604–616, 1974.

54. Sarles, H., Figarella, C., and Clemente, F. The interaction of ethanol, dietary lipids and proteins on the rat pancreas: I. Digestive enzymes. *Digestion* 4:13–22, 1971.

55. Sarles, H., Sarles, J. G., Camatte, R., Muratore, R., Faini, M., Gulen, C., Pastro, J., and LeRoy, F. Observations of 205 confirmed cases of acute pancreatitis, recurring pancreatitis, and chronic pancreatitis. *Gut* 6:545–559, 1965.

56. Sarles, H., Tiscornia, O., and Palasciano, G. Chronic alcoholism and canine exocrine pancreas secretion. *Gastroenterol.* 72:238–243, 1977.

57. Schapiro, H., Wruble, L. D., Estes, J. W., and Britt, L. G. Pancreatic secretion stimulated by the action of alcohol on the gastric antrum. *Am. J. Dig. Dis.* 13:536–539, 1968.

58. Shaw, S., Jayatilleke, E., Ross, W. A., and Lieber, C. S. Hepatic lipid peroxidation and glutathione depression after alcohol. *Gastroenterol.* 77:41, 1979.

59. Shaw, S., and Lieber, C. S. Mechanism of increased gamma glutamyl transpeptidase after chronic alcohol consumption: Hepatic microsomal induction rather than dietary imbalance. *Substance Alcohol Actions/Misuse* 1:423–428, 1980.

60. Solomon, N., Solomon, T. E., Jacobson, E. D., and Shanbour, L. L. Direct effects of alcohol on in vivo and in vitro exocrine pancreatic secretion and metabolism. *Am. J. Dig. Dis.* 19:253–260, 1974.

61. Sommer, J. B., Thompson, G., and Pirola, R. C. Influence of ethanol on pancreatic lipid metabolism. *Alcohol. Clin. Exp. Res.* 4:341–345, 1980.

62. Steer, M. L., Glazer, G., and Manbe, T. Direct effects of ethanol on exocrine secretion from the in vitro rabbit pancreas. *Dig. Dis. Sci.* 24:769–774, 1979.

63. Strum, W. B., and Spiro, H. M. Chronic pancreatitis. *Ann. Int. Med.* 74:264–277, 1971.

64. Taubin, H. L., and Spiro, H. M. Nutritional aspects of chronic pancreatitis. *Am. J. Clin. Nutr.* 26:367–373, 1973.

65. Tiscornia, O. M., Hage, G., Palasciano, G., Brasca, A. P., and Sarles, H. The effects of pentolinium and vagotomy on the inhibition of canine exocrine pancreatic secretion by intravenous ethanol. *Biomed.* 18:159–163, 1973.

66. Toskes, P., and Smith, G. Isolation of low molecular weight vitamin B_{12} promoting protein from preparations of trypsin and chymotrypsin. *Gastroenterol.* 74:1106, 1978.

76. Van Waes, L., and Lieber, C. S. Glutamate dehydrogenase, a reliable marker of liver cell necrosis in the alcoholic. *Br. Med. J.* 2:1508–1510, 1977a.

68. Van Waes, L., and Lieber, C. S. Early perivenular sclerosis in alcoholic fatty liver: An index of progressive liver injury. *Gastroenterol.* 73:646–650, 1977.

69. Walton, B., Schapiro, H., and Woodward, E. R. The effect of alcohol on pancreatic secretion. *Surg. Forum* 11:365–367, 1960.

70. Warshaw, A. L., Popp, J. W., and Schapiro, R. H. Long-term potency, pancreatic function and pain relief after lateral pancreatico jejunostomy for chronic pancreatitis. *Gastroenterol.* 79:289–293, 1980.

71. Worner, T. M., and Lieber, C. S. Plasma glutamate dehydrogenase: A marker of alcoholic liver injury. *Pharmacol. Biochem. Behav. (Suppl 1)* 13:107–110, 1980.

17

ESTEBAN MEZEY, MD, Johns Hopkins University School of Medicine

EFFECTS OF ALCOHOL ON THE GASTROINTESTINAL TRACT

ALCOHOLISM IS A FREquent cause of gastrointestinal symptoms, and alcohol-related diseases of the gastrointestinal tract often are the cause of morbidity and mortality of alcoholic patients. Most of the changes in gastrointestinal function occur after the ingestion or administration of excessive amounts of ethanol. Both a direct toxic effect of ethanol and malnutrition are causes of gastrointestinal dysfunction in alcoholism. Gastrointestinal dysfunction in turn may contribute to the malnutrition in alcoholism. This chapter deals with the effects of ethanol on the gastrointestinal tract and with the pathogenesis of gastrointestinal dysfunction in alcoholism.

ABSORPTION AND METABOLISM OF ETHANOL BY THE GASTROINTESTINAL TRACT

Ethanol is rapidly absorbed by the gastrointestinal tract. The absorption starts in the stomach and continues in the upper small intestine. Immediately after the oral ingestion of ethanol, high concentrations of ethanol, similar to those of alco-

---

Esteban Mezey, MD, Associate Professor of Medicine, Johns Hopkins University School of Medicine, and Chief of Hepatology, Baltimore City Hospitals, Baltimore, Maryland.

holic beverages, are reached in the stomach and jejunum (see Figure 1); thereafter, as ethanol is absorbed its concentration in the upper gastrointestinal tract decreases rapidly, reaching levels that are in equilibrium with the vascular space [5]. Ethanol is detected in the blood as early as 5 minutes after ingestion and maximum concentrations are reached in 30 to 90 minutes. The concentrations of ethanol reached in the ileum following alcohol ingestion parallel the levels in the vascular space, suggesting that ethanol enters the ileum from the vascular space rather than traveling down the length of the intestine. The rate of ethanol absorption is decreased by delayed gastric emptying and by the presence of food in the stomach, and is increased after gastric surgery with gastroenterostomies.

Ethanol has been shown to be metabolized by rat stomach and small intestine *in vitro*. Alcohol dehydrogenase, the principal enzyme, which catalyzes the oxida-

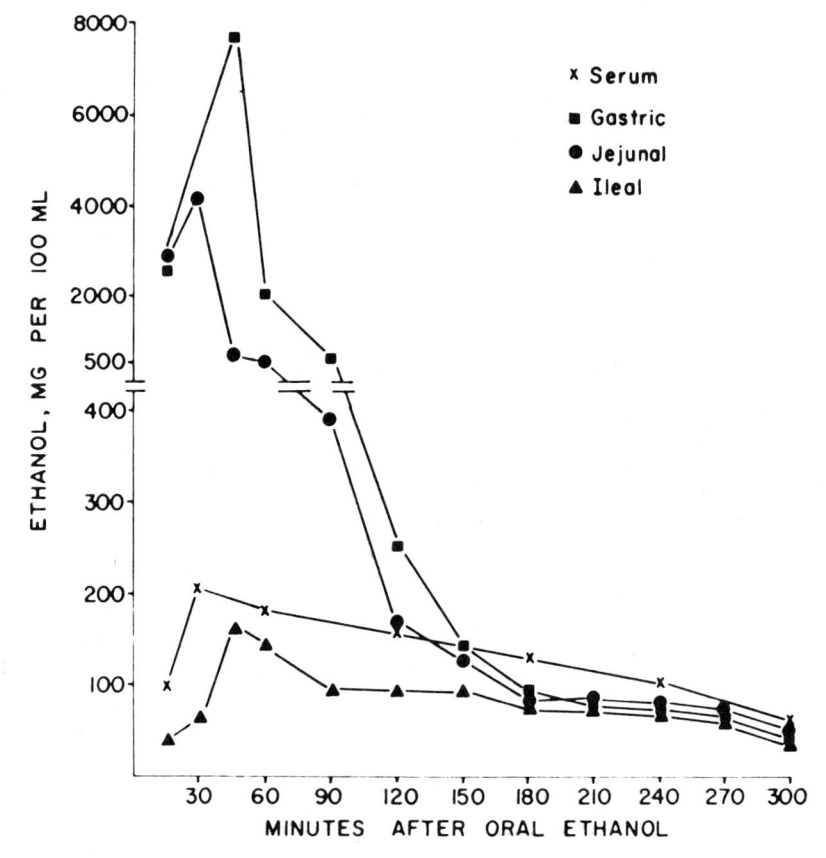

Figure 1. Concentrations of ethanol in the blood, stomach, jejunum, and ileum after the oral administration of ethanol, 0.8 g/kg body weight, on one patient. (*Source:* "Distribution of Ethanol in the Human Gastrointestinal Tract," by C. H. Halsted, A. Robles and E. Mezey. *Am. J. Clin. Nutr.* 26:831–834, 1973. Reprinted by permission of the American Journal of Clinical Nutrition.)

tion of ethanol, is present in the mucosa of the stomach, jejunum, and ileum. The amount of ethanol metabolized by the mucosa of the gastrointestinal tract is probably minimal because the amount of alcohol dehydrogenase enzyme present in the gastrointestinal mucosa is small and its affinity for ethanol lower (Km higher for ethanol) than is the case for the enzyme in the liver. However, some of the effects of ethanol in the intestine, such as its effect on enhancing triglyceride synthesis, may be linked to its metabolism in the intestinal mucosa.

ALCOHOL AND THE ESOPHAGUS

Alcoholism is associated with an increased incidence of reflux esophagitis and carcinoma of the esophagus. The acute ingestion of alcohol depresses the normal increase of lower gastroesophageal sphincter pressure in response to pentagastrin or a meal and increases gastroesophageal reflux, the latter demonstrated by esophageal pH recording [7]. The action of ethanol on delaying gastric emptying may contribute to reflux esophagitis. In chronic alcoholic patients with peripheral neuropathy who were sober, abnormalities consisting of both diminished esophageal peristasis and nonperistaltic contractions after deglutition have been found in the distal third of the esophagus. Inferior esophageal sphincter relaxation, however, was not affected. These abnormalities were not associated with any symptoms and their cause is unknown. A significant association has been found between alcohol intake alone and squamous cell carcinoma of the esophagus in various studies. In addition, a cooperative role between tobacco and alcohol has been demonstrated for carcinoma of the esophagus [11]. As many as 30 to 65% of patients who have carcinoma of the esophagus have been categorized as alcoholic in various reports.

ALCOHOL AND THE STOMACH

Alcoholics have an increased incidence of acute and chronic gastritis, and of upper gastrointestinal bleeding. No clear association has been demonstrated between alcohol consumption and either peptic ulcer disease or gastric carcinoma.

A prominent cause of gastrointestinal bleeding in alcoholics is acute hemorrhagic gastritis, accounting for 25% of the bleeding episodes in alcoholics as compared with 5% in nonalcoholic populations [2]. Another, more common cause of bleeding among alcoholics, is laceration of the gastric mucosa at the gastroesophageal junction, a condition known as the Mallory-Weiss syndrome. This syndrome accounts for 5 to 14% of episodes of gastrointestinal bleeding in hospital populations, of which 60 to 73% reported heavy alcohol intake prior to their episode [3]. The laceration of the gastric mucosa appears to be caused by a marked increase in the intragastric pressure produced by retching and vomiting. Peptic ulcer accounts for 25 to 50% of upper gastrointestinal hemorrhage in both alcoholic and nonalcoholic populations.

Gastric Emptying

The effect of ethanol on gastric emptying is dependent on the concentration of ethanol in the stomach. Concentrations of ethanol of 6% or less either accelerate or have no effect on gastric emptying. Concentrations greater than 10% delay gastric emptying. The most likely mechanism for the delay of gastric emptying is hyperosmolarity of the ethanol solution ingested; however, the effect of ethanol may also be mediated by hormonal or central nervous system mechanisms.

Gastric Secretion

There is no good evidence that oral administration of alcohol affects acid secretion of the stomach. The oral administration of ethanol in concentrations of 8, 12, and 16% in 350 ml of water had no effect on gastric acid output. By contrast, intravenously administered ethanol has been observed to result in increased gastric acid output in man and dogs. In dogs the stimulatory effect of intravenously administered alcohol on acid secretion in Heidenhain pouches is prevented by antral acidification, suggesting that the mechanism of ethanol stimulation is release of gastrin. Increases in serum gastrin have been demonstrated after oral and intravenous administration of ethanol.

Gastric Mucosa

The acute oral administration of ethanol in concentrations greater than 25% disrupts the gastric mucosal barrier, resulting in back diffusion of hydrogen ion into the mucosa. This is accompanied by histological changes consisting of decreases in both the mucus lining and the epithelial mucin granules, and in edema and cellular exfoliation. All these changes are rapidly reversible to normal. However, repeated instillations of acid, after the administration of one dose of ethanol, results in more severe changes in the histology of the mucosa, including necrosis and hemorrhage. The postulated mechanism for these changes is that increased back diffusion of hydrogen ion causes local histamine release and increased capillary permeability, with resulting interstitial hemorrhage and necrosis. In a clinical study 30 of 34 men who had gastroscopy within 6 hours of cessation of heavy alcohol intake were found to have gastric hyperemia, erosions, and petechial hemorrhages. Ethanol appears to increase significantly the effect of aspirin in breaking the gastric mucosa barrier and increasing blood loss. In rats administration of prostaglandin PGE_2 was shown to prevent gastric necrosis induced by oral administration of absolute alcohol by a mechanism that was independent of its effect in inhibiting gastric secretion.

Chronic atrophic gastritis is more common in alcoholics. Sobriety results in recovery of the mucosa to normal within 6 to 9 months in many of these patients [4]. Alcoholic patients with atrophic gastritis are more susceptible to gastric bleeding on the ingestion of ethanol. In addition, ingestion of ethanol in a concentration of 40% resulted in increased gastric loss of plasma albumin in patients with superficial and chronic atrophic gastritis as compared with subjects with a normal mucosa.

ALCOHOLISM AND THE SMALL INTESTINE

Disturbances in the digestion and absorption of nutrients are common in alcoholic patients [9]. The substances that have been found to be malabsorbed are D-xylose, thiamine, folic acid, vitamin B_{12}, and vitamin A. The alcoholic patients in whom these abnormalities were detected did not have overt clinical evidence of malabsorption. However, a history of vague abdominal pain, diarrhea, and weight loss is obtained in some of the patients. The malabsorption is detected after alcohol binges and in most cases is corrected to normal after a few weeks of hospitalization. A direct toxic effect of ethanol and malnutrition appear to be causes of the absorption abnormalities.

The steatorrhea, which is usually mild (stood fat > 15 g per day), is found in 33 to 50% of patients. Its cause is decreased pancreatic function rather than decreased intestinal absorption of fat. The presence of steatorrhea correlates best with low lipase output of the pancreas, measured following pancreatic stimulation by cholecystokinin (pacreozymin) or by a test meal.

Intestinal morphology in alcoholic patients with malabsorption is normal by light microscopy unless the patient has severe folate deficiency, in which case the intestinal cells show megalocytic changes and the villi are shortened. Chronic administration of ethanol with an adequate diet in man did not result in any changes in the intestinal mucosa by light microscopy, but resulted in ultrastructural changes consisting of abnormalities of the mitochondria, endoplasmic reticulum, and Golgi apparatus. In rats the acute administration of ethanol results in hemorrhagic erosion of intestinal villi, decreases in enzymatic activities of lactase and thimidine kinase, located principally in the villus and crypt cells respectively, and decreased oxygen consumption [1]. Chronic administration of ethanol with an adequate diet in rats resulted in decreases in the number of epithelial cells lining the villi and in shortening of the villi, as well as in decreases in the activity of lactase, sucrase, and alkaline phosphatase, but increases in the crypt enzyme, thimidine kinase, and in the incorporation of thimidine into deoxyribonucleic acid (DNA).

Intestinal Motility

Ethanol given either orally or intravenously in a dose of 0.8 g/kg of body weight was shown to alter the motility of the small intestine. In the jejunum ethanol inhibited type I waves, which impede the forward progress of intestinal contents, while in the ileum there was an enhancement of type III waves, which are associated with propulsion of the intestinal contents. These effects of ethanol on the intestine could result in increased transit of intestinal contents and contribute to the diarrhea seen in chronic alcholoics.

Intestinal Metabolism

Carbohydrates. The feeding of 48 g of ethanol per day for 6 days to normal volunteers resulted in decreases in the glycolytic enzymes hexokinase, fructose 1-phosphate aldolase, and fructose 1,6-diphosphate aldolase, and in the gluconeogenetic enzyme fructose 1,6-diphosphatase in the jejunum. The addition of folic acid, a known inducer of these enzymes, reversed the inhibitory effect of ethanol; however, the enzyme levels reached were not as high as those found with the administration of folate alone. Both ethanol and folate alone increased the activity of pyruvate kinase, and their combination resulted in a maximal activity consistent with a synergistic effect.

Lipids. The acute oral administration of ethanol increases triglyceride and cholesterol synthesis by intestinal slices, enhances activities of jejunal lipid–esterifying enzymes, and increases the triglyceride content of the small intestinal mucosa, and the lymphatic output of triglycerides, cholesterol, and phospholipids. In one study the acute administration of ethanol, or its addition *in vitro* to intestinal slices, decreased fatty acid oxidation and triglyceride formation, enhancing instead esterification of fatty acids with ethanol; however, in the same study chronic ethanol administration increased both fatty acid oxidation and triglyceride synthesis. The increases in intestinal lipid synthesis and lipid output by the lymph may contribute to the hyperlipemia and fatty infiltration of the liver induced by alcohol.

Intestinal Enzymes

Disaccharidases. Decreases in lactase activity were found in all of 11 black alcoholic patients studied following heavy alcohol ingestion, but in only 5 of the 10 black nonalcoholic controls. Of the patients who were lactase deficient 70% had abnormal lactose tolerance tests, most of them associated with symptoms of abdominal colic and diarrhea. No differences in lactase activity or lactose tolerance tests were found between white alcoholic and nonalcoholic subjects. Sucrase activity was decreased in 33% of alcoholics of both races. The abnormal activities of both disaccharidases rose after 2 weeks of abstinence from alcohol in five alcoholics of both races who had repeat intestinal biopsies.

Enzymes involved in intestinal transport. Effects of alcohol have been demonstrated *in vitro* in rat jejunum on enzymes that regulate water and electrolyte absorption and secretion. Ethanol in concentrations ranging from 0.5 to 4.6% inhibits Na$^+$-K$^+$-ATPase (adenosinetriphosphatase) activity, the sodium pump necessary for absorption of sodium and water, in basolateral membrane preparations of the rat jejunum [6]. Ethanol in concentrations of 11 to 13%, which are higher than concentrations found *in vivo* in the intestine after the ingestion of alcoholic beverages, stimulates adenylcyclase. This enzyme catalyzes the conversion ATP to cyclic AMP (adenosine monophosphate), a compound that mediates intestinal secretion. The ATP content of the intestine has been found to be decreased after the acute and chronic administration of ethanol in the rat [12]. The effect of ethanol in decreasing ATP concentration was also demonstrated *in vitro* with guinea pig small intestine, although it was not found after chronic ethanol consumption in this species.

Microsomal enzymes. Chronic ethanol feeding results in increases in the smooth reticulum in cytochrome P-450 and in the activity of benzo[α]pyrene hydroxylase. In addition, increased metabolic activation of benzo(α)pyrene to a mutagen was demonstrated by microsomes of ethanol-fed rats [10]. These studies suggest that increased activation of procarcinogens to carcinogens by the intestinal mucosa after ethanol consumption may contribute to carcinogenesis in alcoholism. Regarding the intestine, an association between intake of alcoholic beverages and cancer of the colon has been found [11].

Alcoholism and Intestinal Absorption

In studies of the effect of ethanol on intestinal absorption, it is important to distinguish the effects of acute ethanol administration from those of chronic feeding. In addition, dietary deficiencies often contribute and in some cases are the principal cause of the abnormalities of absorption observed. In this section of the effects of ethanol on the intestinal absorption of amino acids, carbohydrates, vitamins, and electrolytes are discussed.

Amino acids. In man, the direct addition of ethanol to intestinal perfusates in a concentration of 2% resulted on 55% reduction of the uptake of L-methionine. In animal experiments performed *in vivo* and *in vitro* the acute and chronic administration of ethanol was shown to inhibit the absorption of various amino acids and glucose.

Water and sodium transport. A decrease in water and sodium transport by the jejunum has been observed using the triple lumen perfusion technique in alcoholic patients studied a few days after an acute alcohol binge. Also the feeding of ethanol as 36% of the calories for 2 weeks to normal human volunteers resulted in similar decreases in water and sodium transport. These changes, which represent either decreased absorption, increased secretion, or both processes, were more pronounced when the subjects were given ethanol combined with a folate-deficient diet. The acute perfusion of ethanol in concentrations ranging from 2 to

10% in a glucose-free electrolyte solution in man did not result in any changes in water and sodium absorption. This latter observation differs from the findings in acute experiments in animals. Ethanol in a concentration of 2% decreased the net transport of water and glucose and the net mucosal to serosal transport of sodium by everted segments of hamster jejunum. In another study, using isolated jujunal mucosa from the rabbit in a chamber preparation, ethanol in a concentration of 3% inhibited transport of sodium, 3-0-methylglucose, and alanine. The effect of ethanol on these animal experiments was only found when it was added to the mucosal, but not when added to the serosal side, suggesting that it is due to an inhibition of uptake across the brush border, and not related to the effect of ethanol in depressing Na^+-K^+-ATPase activity in the basolateral membrane. In studies of perfusion of the hamster jejunum *in vivo*, glucose transport was reduced by ethanol concentrations of 2%, while water transport was only found depressed in concentrations of 4.8%. The difference in results of the acute effects of ethanol between animals and man may be related to the difficulty in maintaining a high intestinal ethanol concentration in the perfusion studies and the absence of glucose in the perfusion solution in the human studies [12].

D-xylose. D-xylose malabsorption, which is found in 18 to 74% of alcoholic patients on admission to the hospital, is rapidly reversible to normal after 2 weeks on a normal diet despite continuation of alcohol intake. The acute administration of ethanol (0.8 g/kg) results in decreased D-xylose absorption, while the chronic feeding of ethanol results in no change or enhances D-xylose absorption [9]. Malabsorption of D-xylose has been induced in man by the combination of ethanol and a folate-deficient diet, and in rats by the combination of ethanol and protein-deficient diet.

Thiamine. The actual oral or intravenous administration of ethanol in a dose of 1.5 g/kg has been shown to decrease the absorption of thiamine in one-third of patients studied. Rat investigations using isolated duodenal loops or everted jejunal sacs demonstrated that ethanol decreases active thiamine absorption that occurs at low concentrations of thiamine (0.06–2.0 μM) but does not affect passive transport at higher concentrations of thiamine. Further studies reveal that ethanol does not block uptake of thiamine into the mucosa, but rather blocks the exit of small concentrations of thiamine from the cell to the serosal compartment. This inhibitory effect of ethanol is similar to that obtained with ouabain, a known inhibitor of Na^+-K^+-ATPase (the sodium pump). Recent studies showing that ethanol inhibits the activity of intestinal basolateral membrane Na^+-K^+-ATPase suggest that the inhibitory effect of ethanol on thiamine transport is related to its inhibition of this enzyme [6]. Folate deficiency induced in rats resulting in megalocytosis of intestinal epithelial cells was also shown to result in decreased absorption of low, but not of high, concentrations of thiamine.

Folate. Malabsorption of folic acid has been demonstrated only in malnourished chronic alcoholic patients. The acute administration of ethanol did not have any consistent effects on folate absorption in normal volunteers, and the chronic administration of ethanol in a dose of 250 g for 2 weeks with an adequate diet had no effect on folate absorption. Decreased absorption of folate was induced by the administration of a folate-deficient diet and ethanol but not by either alone, and the abnormal absorption was corrected to normal by the administration of folic acid despite the continuation of ethanol. In the monkey decreased absorption of folic acid has been found after 12 months of ethanol feeding with an adequate diet.

Vitamin B_{12}. The absorption of vitamin B_{12} measured by the Schilling test was shown to be decreased in six of eight well-nourished alcoholics who received ethanol in daily doses ranging from 158–253 g for 11 to 38 days. The concomitant administration to one patient of pancreatic extract, which has been shown to correct vitamin B_{12} absorption in pancreatic insufficiency, did not prevent the effect of ethanol in decreasing vitamin B_{12} absorption.

Calcium. The acute and chronic administration of ethanol results in a decrease in calcium transport by the rat intestine. The acute effect that was demonstrated with a high dose of ethanol is associated with necrosis of the intestinal epithelium. No decrease in calcium absorption was demonstrated after intraperitoneal administration of ethanol, which did not alter intestinal morphology. The effect of chronic ethanol feeding in decreasing calcium could not be reversed by the administration of vitamin D or 25-hydroxyvitamin D, suggesting that ethanol interferes with calcium transport by a mechanism independent of vitamin D [8]. Recent studies show that pyrazole partially blocked the inhibitory effect of ethanol on calcium transport, and that on a molar basis, acetaldehyde is a more potent inhibitor of intestinal calcium transport than ethanol.

Iron. Increased hepatic iron stores are common in alcoholics. Possible causes for this increased iron disposition are ingestion of alcoholic beverages, such as wine, that have a high iron content, and pancreatic insufficiency, which is known to be associated with increased iron absorption. In one study of normal subjects, the administration of 60 ml of whiskey or brandy increased the absorption of ferric chloride, but did not affect the absorption of ferrous ascorbate or hemoglobin iron. In animals, the acute administration of ethanol inhibits intestinal ferrous absorption, while the chronic feeding of ethanol has no effect.

SUMMARY

Alcoholism is associated with abnormalities of the gastric mucosa, gastrointestinal motility, and intestinal absorption, most of which are reversible after the discontinuation of alcohol intake. A direct effect of ethanol is responsible for the changes in the gastric mucosa and gastrointestinal motility, while both nutritional deficiencies, in particular folate deficiency, and ethanol contribute to intestinal malabsorption. Alcoholics have an increased incidence of upper gastrointestinal bleeding. Prominent causes of bleeding in alcoholics as compared to nonalcoholic patients are hemorrhagic gastritis and the Mallory-Weiss syndrome. A positive association between the consumption of alcoholic beverages and cancer of the esophagus and colon has been demonstrated.

REFERENCES

1. Baraona, E., Pirola, R. C., and Lieber, C. S. Small intestinal damage and changes in cell population produced by ethanol ingestion in the rat. *Gastroenterology* 66:226-234, 1974.
2. Belber, J. P. Gastroscopy and duodenoscopy. In: *Gastrointestinal Disease*, Sleisenger, M. H. and Fordtran, J. S. (eds.). W. B. Sanders: Philadelphia, 1979.
3. Dagradi, A. E., Broderick, J. T., Juler, G., Wolinsky, S., and Stempien, S. J. The Mallory-Weiss syndrome and lesion. A study of 30 cases. *Am. J. Dig. Dis.* 11:710-721, 1966.
4. Dinoso, V. P., Jr., Chey, W. Y., Braverman, S. P., Rosen, A. P., Ottenberg, D., and Lorber, S. H. Gastric secretion and gastric mucosal morphology in chronic alcoholics. *Arch. Intern. Med.* 130:715-719, 1972.
5. Halsted, C. H., Robles, A., and Mezey, E. Distribution of ethanol in the human gastrointestinal tract. *Am. J. Clin. Nutr.* 26:831-834, 1973.
6. Hoyumpa, A. H., Jr., Nichols, S. G., Wilson, F. A., and Schenker, S. Effect of ethanol on intestinal (Na, K) ATPase and intestinal thiamine transport in rats. *J. Lab. Clin. Med.* 90:1086-1095, 1977.
7. Kaufman, S. E., and Kaye, M. D. Induction of gastro-esophageal reflux by alcohol. *Gut* 19:336-338, 1978.
8. Kravitt, E. L. Effect of ethanol ingestion on duodenal calcium transport. *J. Lab. Clin. Med.* 85:665-671, 1975.
9. Mezey, E. Intestinal function in chronic alcoholism. *Ann. N.Y. Acad. Sci.* 252:215-227, 1975.
10. Seitz, H. K., Garro, A. J., and Lieber, C. S. Effect of chronic ethanol ingestion on intestinal metabolism and mutagenicity of benzo(α)pyrene. *Biochem. Biophys. Res. Commun.* 85:1001-1006, 1978.
11. Williams, R. R., and Horm, J. W. Association of cancer sites with tobacco and alcohol consumption and socioeconomic status of patients: Interview study from the third national cancer survey. *J. Natl. Cancer Inst.* 58:525-547, 1977.
12. Wilson, F. A., and Hoyumpa, A. M., Jr. Ethanol and small intestinal transport. *Gastroenterology* 76:388-403, 1979.

18

ELAINE B. FELDMAN, MD, Medical College of Georgia, Augusta, Georgia

MALNUTRITION IN THE ALCOHOLIC AND RELATED NUTRITIONAL DEFICIENCIES

MALNUTRITION IS AN important result of chronic alcohol consumption. Indeed, specific nutrient deficiency syndromes, now uncommon in the United States due to enrichment and fortification of foods, are found almost exclusively in alcoholics. Alcohol may influence appetite adversely, replace other nutrients in the diet as a source of empty calories, and affect absorption, utilization, metabolism, and excretion of nutrients. Some deficiency states are life-threatening. Therefore, an awareness of the manifestations of these disorders is important in the medical evaluation of the alcoholic. As a rule, although treatment of specific deficiencies obviously requires repletion of the nutrient involved, only by cessation of drinking can the alcoholic's predisposition to malnutrition ultimately be treated.

ETIOLOGY

Because alcohol has high caloric value it displaces other foods in the diet. Alcohol is not, however, a source of essential nutrients (vitamins, minerals, protein). Limited available funds are often used by the alcoholic to purchase booze rather than food.

Elaine B. Feldman, MD, Professor of Medicine, Chief, Section of Nutrition, and Director, Clinical Nutrition Research Unit, Medical College of Georgia, Augusta, Georgia.

Food Intake: Appetite

For the nonalcoholic, consumption of alcoholic beverages such as wine may enhance the flavor and palatability of a meal. The use of tonics or a glass of sherry to stimulate appetite is a time-honored approach in nonalcoholics. The pleasant effects of alcohol are observed with small quantities, whereas larger intake of alcohol may depress the sensation of hunger. A decreased desire for food in alcoholics may be due not only to the alcohol calories taken in but to associated habits that may reduce hunger, including cigarette smoking and coffee drinking. Gastrointestinal effects of alcohol (such as gastritis and enteritis) may cause anorexia. Malnutrition itself, especially with specific deficiencies of B vitamins, results in anorexia [9]. The most constant cause of poor appetite is thiamin deficiency, one of the most common specific nutritional deficiencies of alcoholics [11]. At times specific nutrient deficiencies of B vitamins may cause glossitis, which makes food intake painful. With zinc deficiency anorexia and diminished taste may reduce food intake [8]. Since food taken along with alcohol may delay gastric emptying and decrease alcohol absorption, alcoholics who wish to get drunk quickly may willfully not eat.

Mechanisms of Malnutrition

In addition to the factors of decreased food intake and empty calories, alcoholism can interfere with digestion and absorption [5]. Alcohol has direct effects on the gastrointestinal tract and pancreas. Digestive enzymes may be reduced by specific effects of alcohol on these enzymes, which are necessary to digest food. Alcohol may also impair transport of amino acids, electrolytes, water, and fatty acids. Specifically, absorption of thiamin and B_{12} may be impaired; folate absorption may also be abnormal. Thus, alcohol may induce a malabsorption syndrome. This may be difficult to differentiate from the malabsorption due to specific nutrient deficiencies. In addition, there may be renal hyperexcretion of zinc or magnesium. Nutrients that require transformation to some other active metabolite to be effective may be influenced by abnormal liver function (e.g., activation of pyridoxine or hydroxylation of D). Alcohol may actually increase the cellular and tissue requirements for some nutrients.

MANIFESTATIONS

Nutritional disorders in the alcoholic may range from protein and calorie malnutrition, obesity, specific deficiency syndromes, and defects of one or another vitamin or mineral, to involve one or another organ system in an interaction of direct effects of alcohol with the end results of nutrient deficiencies [3, 6, 8, 9, 11].

Calorie Deficit or Excess

Calorie excess can result from consumption of snack foods with drinks, where wine is culturally an accompaniment of meals, or under social or business situations where eating and drinking are combined. The amount of body fat in drinkers may be related to age, sex, and socioeconomic status. According to Roe [8], body weight of the occasional drinker did not differ from that of the nondrinker for males of high or low socioeconomic status; among women of low income, nondrinkers were heavier. Alcoholic women were undernourished compared to nondrinkers or occasional drinkers; this was also true for men of low socioeconomic status, but, for men of high socioeconomic status, alcoholics were fatter than the non- or occasional drinker. The energy-wasting oxidation of ethanol may be a significant contributor to a defect in energy balance. There is no evidence that alcohol increases energy losses. It is probable that weight loss in alcoholics is determined by poor intake and the associated alcohol-induced diseases.

Specific Deficiency Syndromes

The most common deficiency syndromes in alcoholics are attributable to thiamin deficiency, among these specifically the Wernicke-Korsakoff syndrome [4]. Pellagra is uncommon nowadays; when seen it is almost exclusively in alcoholics. Scurvy, although rare, is also likely to occur in alcoholics. These deficiencies are more prone to occur if there are contributing factors such as old age or subtotal gastrectomy.

Wernicke-Korsakoff syndrome. The Wernicke-Korsakoff syndrome results from a lack of dietary thiamin. Interestingly, it develops in only a small minority of alcoholics. The syndrome can also be seen with thiamin deficiency resulting from voluntary reduction of calories without vitamin supplements in an attempt to lose weight, or in patients receiving total parenteral nutrition with increased demands for thiamine. The syndrome is of abrupt onset and occurs in certain chronic alcoholics who have not eaten or who have eatern irregularly for long periods of time. It may be precipitated by infusing glucose without added thiamine. At least half of the patients with Wernicke-Korsakoff syndrome have associated polyneuropathy.

Wernicke's encephalopathy is characterized by confusion, ataxia, and ocular manifestations, which include paralysis of eye muscles and nystagmus. The patient's state of consciousness is depressed, with stupor common. Korsakoff's psychosis is characterized by amnesia and confabulation. Hypothermia may be present. A deficiency in thiamin metabolism may also exist. Cultured fibroblasts from patients with the Wernicke-Korsakoff syndrome bind the thiamin-dependent enzyme transketolase less strongly than controls do [1]. Investigators proposed that a genetic defect is responsible; if thiamin intake is low and there is decreased activity of brain transketolase, Wernicke-Korsakoff syndrome results [1].

Wernicke's syndrome is reversed by administration of therapeutic doses of thiamin. Thiamin should be given intravenously, initially 100 mg. The abnormal ocular findings may revert to normal within 6 to 8 hours. If untreated the syndrome may be lethal. Even with treatment recovery occurs in less than one-third of reported cases.

Although the assay of red blood cell transketolase activity is not generally available, this biochemical functional test is a good index of thiamin status and may be available in some medical centers with nutrition laboratories.

Pellagra. Pellagra is characterized by the four Ds: dermatitis, diarrhea, dementia, and death [9]. The classical skin lesions are pigmented and occur at the neckline (Casal's necklace), over the dorsa of the hands and forearms, and over the shins — areas exposed to the sun. Exposure to sunlight, heavy exercise, coupled with an excessive intake of corn with a deficiency of niacin in the diet lead to this disease. Patients also have glossitis and stomatitis. The glossitis in pellagra is extremely severe and leads to a serious curtailment in food intake. Patients should be given large doses (100–500 mg) of nicotinic acid intravenously, with similar doses continued for a week to 10 days. Of epidemic proportions in the South during the earlier part of the century, pellagra is now rare.

Scurvy. Scurvy is a specific deficiency disease due to lack of ascorbic acid. The disease in alcoholics is attributable to a diet deficient in vitamin C. Ascorbic acid is mainly found in fresh fruits and vegetables, which may not be components of the alcoholic's diet. In addition, processing of food by steaming or exposure to light may destroy vitamin C when it is present. The manifestations of scurvy, namely, bleeding gums (when teeth are present), perifollicular hemorrhages, subperiosteal hemorrhages and bleeding, are no different in the alcoholic than in nondrinkers. Levels of ascorbic acid in white blood cells may be determined in some centers and nutritional laboratories. Scurvy should be treated by administration of large doses (500 mg) of ascorbic acid. This should be continued until there is repletion of tissue stores.

Other Nutrient Deficiencies

Not uncommonly the alcoholic is deficient in multiple B vitamins. The presence of Wernicke-Korsakoff syndrome, pellagra, or calorie deficit should lead one to suspect, particularly, concomitant deficiency of folate or pyridoxine. The most common mineral deficiencies may be those of magnesium and zinc [8].

Folate. Folate deficiency [5, 6] is another common nutritional problem in alcoholics. This may result from dietary deficiency, malabsorption, impaired utilization or hyperexcretion of folate. Consumption of alcohol causes plasma folate to fall. Dietary folate deficiency may develop more rapidly in alcoholics than in normals. Folic acid deficiency is the most common vitamin deficiency in cirrhotic patients. Hyperexcretion of folate contributes to the vitamin deficiency in chronic liver disease.

Clinical signs include glossitis, peripheral neuropathy, and macrocytic anemia. Folate deficiency is accompanied by a megaloblastic bone marrow. Levels of folate in serum and red blood cells are low. Folate deficiency itself may cause a malabsorption syndrome with specific pathologic changes of the small intestine. Alcohol when combined with limited dietary folate could produce the intestinal malabsorption syndrome.

Pyridoxine. Sideroblastic anemia may be attributable to deficiency of vitamin B_6. Serum levels of pyridoxal phosphate are reduced by alcohol. Alcohol blocks the conversion of vitamin B_6 metabolites. There is a reduction in pyridoxal kinase activity and in conversion of pyridoxine to pyridoxal phosphate. There may also be an increase in the B_6 phosphate phosphatase to accelerate breakdown of phosphorylated B_6 isomers. These defects may result in defective iron utilization for heme synthesis. Riboflavin deficiency may play a role in that this vitamin is required for conversion of pyridoxine phosphate to pyridoxal phosphate. Vitamin B_6 deficiency may contribute to peripheral neuropathy in alcoholics. A majority of patients with advanced liver disease have vitamin B_6 deficiencies. These patients may have an increased rate of degradation of pyridoxal phosphate or impaired conversion of pyridoxine to pyridoxal phosphate [12].

Magnesium. Magnesium deficiency [8] may be seen in alcoholics with low serum levels during withdrawal from alcohol and especially during delirium tremens. While magnesium deficiency may be associated with tremor, convulsions, and delirium, it is not clear that magnesium deficiency and delirium tremens (DTs) are identical. Magnesium levels may not be low during the DTs and administration of magnesium may not ameliorate the disorder. Magnesium deficiency, however, is prevalent in alcoholics. Causes include decrease in food intake and inadequate magnesium intake and negative magnesium balance with excess urinary excretion resulting from toxic effects of alcohol on the kidney. Magnesium deficiency in turn is associated with hypocalcemia and hypokalemia.

Zinc. Serum zinc concentrations are decreased in alcoholics, a condition associated with an increased renal clearance of zinc with increased zinc excretion [8]. Symptomatic zinc deficiency manifestations in alcoholics include a scaling dermatitis and poor wound healing as well as impaired taste. Zinc deficiency responds to administration of zinc sulfate. Alcohol dehydrogenase is a zinc-dependent enzyme; it is responsible for the conversion of retinol to retinal, a reaction necessary for normal dark adaptation. Symptomatic vitamin A deficiency with night blindness may respond to administration of zinc. Thus a nutritional rehabilitation program should include vitamin A as well as zinc supplementation. Measurement of serum zinc is recommended in nutritional assessment of alcoholics, especially those with liver disease or pancreatitis, those who undergo surgery with interruption of food intake, and those with clinical signs of zinc deficiency.

Other Disorders

Since multiple nutritional deficiencies are so common in alcoholics it is not surprising that some disorders occur that are not necessarily explainable by deficiency of a single nutrient. Examples are bone disease and cardiomyopathy.

Bone disease. Alcoholics may develop osteopenia [10] with pathologic fractures. Bone disease may be accelerated in alcoholics who undergo subtotal gastrectomy. Absorption of vitamin D and calcium is reduced. Steatorrhea may occur in alcoholics and result in malabsorption of vitamin D; thus, alcoholics may have osteomalacia. The 25-hydroxylation of vitamin D in the liver may be impaired in cirrhotics; metabolic bone disease may be related to this defect. Degradation of D metabolites may be accelerated in alcoholics [4]. The bone disease may also be associated with ascorbic acid deficiency, which may be related to iron overload accelerating breakdown of ascorbic acid.

Cardiomyopathy. The most prevalent form of primary alcoholic heart disease, cardiomyopathy [7], is probably a direct toxic effect of alcohol. Nonetheless there are some nutritional deficiencies in alcoholics that can cause heart disease. In particular, thiamin deficiency can be associated with wet beriberi, which results in a high output heart failure. Anemia, protein deficiency, hypokalemia, and hypomagnesemia can all be associated with cardiac fibrosis and cardiomyopathy. The relatively low incidence of alcoholic heart disease due to nutritional deficiency is due to fortification of flour and cereals with thiamin. Hypokalemia may in part explain the arrthythmias in alcoholic heart disease. Cardiomyopathy is characterized by cardiac arrhythmias, cardiomegaly, and heart failure.

NUTRITIONAL MANAGEMENT OF THE ALCOHOLIC

Nutritional assessment must be carried out prior to dietary counseling and should be a part of the evaluation of any hospitalized alcoholic [2, 8]. Assessment includes medical and dietary history, physical examination, including anthropometric measurements, and appropriate laboratory tests of nutritional status. The complete assessment requires the assistance of the dietitian or nutritionist. The diet history should include a minimum of 3 days or several 24-hour recalls. The nutritional history should include the details of alcohol intake. The treatment plan must be modified in accordance with the patient's medical status. Symptoms relevant to malnutrition include anorexia, loss of taste, abdominal pain, weight loss, weakness or paralysis of muscles, diarrhea, skin rash, shortness of breath, memory loss. The anthropometric measurements include weight, height, mid-upper arm circumference, tricep skin fold thickness. From the latter two measurements one can calculate mid-arm muscle circumference. These data should be compared with tables of normal values so that an estimate of percentage of ideal body weight can be made. Physical signs of skin, mucous membranes, and mouth are specific for nutritional deficiency when associated with depressed laboratory values of nutrients, preferably in tissue. If this evaluation is not possible it may be necessary to perform a therapeutic test in which the abnormal sign disappears in response to nutritional therapy. Where there is a gross calorie deficit or other indicator of malnutrition it may be useful to develop a biochemical profile. At the present time such tests are not generally available, with some exceptions, namely, serum proteins, transferrin, zinc, vitamin A, vitamin B_{12}, possibly vitamins B_6 and ascorbic acid, and some minerals, such as iron, magnesium, and zinc.

SUMMARY AND CONCLUSIONS

Alcoholism is an important contributor to malnutrition in the United States. Subclinical malnutrition should be recognized along with diseases due to deficiency of specific nutrients. These disorders are more prevalent in the presence of alcoholic liver disease. Alcohol has specific effects on the gastrointestinal tract leading to decreases of food intake and absorption. Nutrient deficiencies in turn also adversely affect appetite and absorption. Syndromes of B vitamin deficiencies are most common with alcohol interacting with genetic predisposition. Mineral deficiencies of zinc and magnesium are also important. Bone disease and cardiomyopathy may be determined by complex factors related to alcohol. No program of repletion will be successful unless alcohol abuse is curtailed.

REFERENCES

1. Blass, J. P., and Gibson, G. E. Abnormality of a thiamine-requiring enzyme in patients with Wernicke-Korsakoff syndrome. *N. Engl. J. Med.* 297:1367–1370, 1977.
2. Felig, P. Nutritional maintenance and diet therapy in acute and chronic disease. In: *Cecil Textbook of Medicine* (15th ed.), Beeson, P. B., McDermott, W. and Wyngaarden, J. B. (eds.). W. B. Saunders: Philadelphia, 1979.
3. Hillman, R. W. Alcoholism and malnutrition. In: *The Biology of Alcoholism: Clinical Pathology* (Vol. 3), Kissen, B. and Begleiter, H. (eds.). Plenum Press: New York, 1974.
4. Korsten, M. A., and Lieber, C. S. Nutrition in the alcoholic. In: *The Medical Clinics of North America* (Vol. 63, No. 5), Margen, S. and Caan B. (eds.). W. B. Saunders: Philadelphia, 1979.
5. Lindenbaum, J., and Lieber, C. S. Effects of chronic ethanol administration on intestinal absorption in man in the absence of nutritional deficiency. *Ann. N. Y. Acad. Sci.* 252:228–234, 1975.
6. Neville, J. N., Eagles, J. A., Samson, G., and Olson, R. E. Nutritional status of alcoholics. *Am. J. Clin. Nutr.* 21:1329–1340, 1968.

7. Regan, T. J. Alcoholic cardiomyopathy. In: *Nutrition and Cardiovascular Disease*, Feldman, E. B. (ed.). Appleton-Century-Crofts: New York, 1976.

8. Roe, D. *Alcohol and the Diet*. AVI Publishing: Westport, Conn., 1979.

9. Sandstead, H. H. Clinical manifestations of certain classical deficiency diseases. In: *Modern Nutrition in Health and Disease* (6th ed.), Goodhart, R. S. and Shils, M. E. (eds.). Lea & Febiger: Philadelphia, 1980.

10. Saville, P. D. Alcohol-related skeletal disorders. *Ann. N. Y. Acad. Sci.* 252:286–291, 1975.

11. Shaw, S., and Lieber, C. S. Nutrition and alcoholism. In: *Modern Nutrition in Health and Disease* (6th ed.), Goodhart, R. S. and Shils, M. E. (eds.). Lea & Febiger: Philadelphia, 1980.

12. Veitch, R. L., Lumeng, L., and Li, T. K. Vitamin B_6 metabolism in chronic alcohol-abuse. The effect of ethanol oxidation on hepatic pyredoxal $5'$-phosphate metabolism. *J. Clin. Invest.* 55:1026–1031, 1975.

19

WILLIAM H. CHEW, JR., MD, Medical College of Georgia, Augusta, Georgia
J. PETER RISSING, MD, Medical College of Georgia, Augusta, Georgia

INFECTIOUS DISEASES AND THE ALCOHOLIC

INFECTIONS ARE THOUGHT to be more frequent in alcoholics than in the general population. Prospective study has shown this impression to be true only for bacterial pneumonia and for tuberculosis [32]. Nonetheless, infection was the cause of death in 25% of alcoholics in one series [33]. Whether infection is a direct consequence of alcohol use or indirectly mediated through alcoholic liver disease is an unresolved issue. This chapter reviews host defense abnormalities caused by alcohol, the alcoholic life style, and alcoholic liver disease. Also reviewed are infections known or thought to occur more frequently in the alcoholic.

EFFECTS OF ACUTE ALCOHOL INGESTION/INTOXICATION

Alcohol intoxication of rodents is associated with aspiration of pharyngeal contents, but similar studies have not been done in humans. Clinical experience suggests more frequent aspiration of pharyngeal contents into the lower airway dur-

---

William H. Chew, Jr., MD, Professor of Medicine, Department of Medicine, Section of Infectious Diseases, Medical College of Georgia, Augusta, Georgia.

J. Peter Rissing, MD, Associate Professor of Medicine and Chief, Section of Infectious Diseases, Department of Medicine, Medical College of Georgia, Augusta, Georgia.

ing ethanol intoxication than occurs in sleep and depressed consciousness [18]. Abnormal activity of the cilial escalator is suspected but not confirmed.

There is reduced pulmonary clearance of organisms during acute ethanol intoxication in animals. The reduction is apparently related to the effect of alcohol on mobility of both alveolar macrophages and segmented neutrophils [14, 27]. Studies by Green and Green [16] found greater reduction in clearance of a gram-negative rod (Proteus) than of a gram-positive coccus (Staphylococcus). Acute alcohol ingestion may also inhibit lymphocyte transformation and granulopoiesis in the absence of a nutritional deficiency [42]. Liu found delayed clearing of aggregated human serum albumin by the reticuloendothelial system in alcoholics admitted to an alcohol rehabilitation unit [24].

In animal models [27] and human studies [3] the most consistent peripheral blood neutrophil defect found has been impaired neutrophil mobility. Louria proposed the occurrence of both depressed neutrophil exit from capillaries to the extravascular space and depressed extracapillary motility. Reduced neutrophil adherence has been reported [29]. Studies of the effects of acute alcohol intoxication on complement and serum bactericidal activity yield variable, inconclusive results [28].

EFFECTS OF THE ALCOHOLIC LIFE STYLE

Inadequate nutrition is the major influence of the alcoholic's life style on potential infection. Protein malnutrition has many adverse effects [6, 15, 38]. Folic acid and vitamin B_{12} deficiency may reduce the number of functioning neutrophils. Intercurrent nausea and vomiting may deplete serum phosphate, an important nutrient for cellular energy metabolism, and host defense particularly, through granulocyte function [9]. Cigarette smoking adds another reason for an abnormal lower airway.

EFFECTS OF ALCOHOLIC LIVER DISEASE

Little information is available on the effects of alcoholic steatosis and alcoholic hepatitis on host defense systems. Most human studies are in patients with alcoholic cirrhosis. The abnormalities found are not unique to alcoholic cirrhosis.

Neutrophil chemotaxis is markedly impaired in patients with cirrhosis [43]. A serum inhibitor of chemotaxis is suggested by crossover studies of neutrophils and serum from cirrhotic patients and healthy controls. Neutrophils from cirrhotic patients migrate normally in normal serum and normal neutrophils migrate slowly in serum from patients with cirrhosis. Addition of serum from cirrhotic patients to normal serum leads to abnormal migration of normal neutrophils. The third component of complement is depressed in some patients with cirrhosis [17].

Serum concentrations of immunoglobulins are increased in cirrhosis [25]. No systematic study of the functional capacity of the immunoglobulins has been carried out, but increased agglutination of *Escherichia coli* and bacteriodes has been reported. Efforts to explain the elevated immunoglobulins have not yielded consistent results. Exaggerated responses to antigens with increased antibody formation have been found, as have normal responses. Reduced hepatic clearance of antigen by a defective hepatic reticuloendothelial system and continued antigen stimulation [41] is an alternative hypothesis. Decreased hepatic clearance of antigen antibody complexes and bacteria has been reported [2, 41].

Cell-mediated immunity, as measured by delayed hypersensitivity, may be depressed in patients with alcoholic liver disease. Protein malnutrition is thought to be the major reason [34]. Reduced reactivity to DNCB (dinitrochlorobenzene) similarly shown and may also be related to nutrition [37].

The animal and human studies cited support a multifactorial decrease in the host defense system of alcoholics. Not mentioned specifically are the risks of trauma, burns, and environmental exposure while intoxicated, as well as the risks of nosocomial infection when the cirrhotic patient is admitted because of gastrointestinal bleeding, hepatic encephalopathy, or increasing ascites. Altered consciousness, vascular access devices, indwelling bladder catheters, and surgery each carries a risk of nosocomial infection.

Pneumococcal Pneumonia

Streptococcus pneumoniae is the most common cause of bacterial pneumonia [40] except in special situations, such as nosocomial settings. It is a frequent cause of pneumonia in alcoholics. Pneumococcal pneumonia may present classically with a single shaking chill, productive cough, pleuritic chest pain, yellow or bloody sputum, fever, tachypnea, physical signs of consolidation, leukocytosis and lobar radiographic consolidation. This classic illness is not always present and the alcoholic patient may be unable to give an adequate history of onset. There may be no sputum, fever absent, no consolidation, leukopenia rather than leukocytosis, and radiographic evidence of multilobe involvement or only a patchy "bronchopneumonia." With such findings the diagnosis is more difficult.

A vigorous attempt to obtain material from the lower airway is essential and transtracheal aspiration may be required. Once appropriate material is obtained and Gram-stained, microscopic examination normally discloses typical lancet-shaped gram-positive diplococci and acute inflammatory cells. All such specimens should be carefully reviewed for the marks of a true alveolar exudate: many polymorphonuclear leukocytes with gram-negative nuclei, few (preferably none) large cuboidally shaped epithelial cells with centrally located small nuclei, and a predominant bacterium. Gram-stain examination of the sputum also permits assessment of other potential causes of bacterial pneumonias, including *Hemophilus influenzae, Klebsiella pneumonia, Staphylococcus aureus,* and mixed anaerobes. Blood cultures are positive in 20-30% of patients with pneumococcal pneumonia and should be obtained in any alcoholic with a pneumonia.

If there is altered consciousness in pneumonia patients with cerebrospinal fluid should be examined for evidence of simultaneous bacterial meningitis. Coexistant meningitis increases the amount of penicillin one must administer to achieve satisfactory entry into the spinal fluid and decreases the probability of the patient's recovery. Osler called attention to the frequency with which the pneumococcus causes meningitis, pneumonia, and endocarditis in the alcoholic host.

Penicillin G continues to be the preferred therapy for pneumococcal pneumonia. Procaine penicillin G 600,000 units intramuscularly every 12 hours is as effective as larger doses and the risk of superinfection is lower [4]. Erythromycin or cephalothin are effective alternative agents. Oral therapy can be substituted when the patient has clearly improved; normal duration of therapy is 7 days, though longer courses are given, particularly in patients who respond slowly. The rate of radiographic resolution of the pulmonary lesion may be very slow, particularly in alcoholics [20].

Alcoholics are not specifically listed among patients for whom pneumococcal vaccine is indicated. Many alcoholics, because of age above 50 years, presence of another chronic disease, or residence in a chronic care facility, are likely to receive vaccine for another indication.

Aspiration Pneumonia/Lung Abscess

Altered closure of the epiglottis with aspiration of normal oropharyngeal bacteria into the lower airway is thought to occur with increased frequency in patients intoxicated with alcohol. In like manner, patients with alcoholic liver disease and hepatic encephalopathy may aspirate into the lower respiratory tract. Aspiration has been found to occur in 70% of patients with depressed consciousness from cerebrovascular accidents or hepatic encephalopathy and 45% of normals [18]. Frequent aspiration, combined with reduced clearance of aspirated microorganisms, leads to pneumonia. Three sequential clinical patterns follow aspiration: (1) chemical injury, (2) bronchial obstruction by particles, and (3) bacterial pneumonia. The latter may progress to lung abscess and/or empyema before the patient seeks medical care.

The bacteriology of aspiration pneumonia varies depending on whether aspiration occurs in the community or in the hospital [26]. Community-acquired aspiration pneumonia is more frequently caused by anaerobic bacteria alone or in combination with facultative organisms (aerobes) [1]. In contrast, hospital-acquired aspiration pneumonia is often due to aerobic gram-negative bacilli [26]. Bacterial aspiration pneumonia acquired in a nursing home is more like hospital-acquired pneumonia with *K. pneumoniae* the single most common cause in one series [12].

Antibiotic management of aspiration pneumonia in an alcoholic requires assessment of the probable etiologic organism(s). Knowing the setting in which the aspiration occurred is helpful. Even more useful information can be obtained by examination of a Gram-stained specimen of sputum. If an adequate specimen cannot be produced by the patient's coughing, additional measures, such as nasotracheal suction, transtracheal aspiration, or bronchoscopy, may be required.

If the setting and Gram stain indicate a mixed flora, probably anaerobic, penicillin G is the preferred agent. In extremely ill patients and in those allergic to penicillin, clindamycin is an effective alternative. When the setting is hospital- or nursing home–acquired aspiration and the Gram stain shows predominantly gram-negative bacilli, the combination of a first generation cephalosporin and an aminoglycoside is conventional initial treatment. Unique local epidemiologic data might indicate more specific agents (e.g., if Serratia or Pseudomonas is common). While blood cultures are not often positive, it is advisable to collect them because a positive result adds confidence to both the etiologic organism and the treatment needed.

Pneumonias caused by anaerobes, staphylococci, Legionella, and Klebsiella may all lead to lung necrosis. However, when there is a single abscess with an air-fluid level and surrounding infiltrate in an alcoholic with an illness of 2 to 3 weeks, and particularly when the breath is foul, anaerobic bacteria are the usual cause [1]. Adequate drainage by the airway or bronchoscopy and penicillin G are the essential modes of treatment. The dose and duration of penicillin treatment is controversial. One approach has been to give penicillin G by the intravenous route in doses of 6 to 8 million units each day until there is subjective and objective improvement (e.g., decreased fever and leukocyte count), at which time the drug is given orally. Penicillin is continued for as long as there is radiographic evidence of improvement. This may be for several weeks or months. Poor compliance with medication is a frequent problem after the patient leaves the hospital and returns to alcohol use.

Hemophilus Influenzae Pneumonia

Hemophilus influenzae is recognized as a common cause of bacterial pneumonia, and alcoholism is a frequent predisposing factor [22, 44]. It is not clear whether the patients with alcoholism also had chronic lung disease or were cigarette smokers.

The clinical presentation of *H. influenzae* pneumonia may be similar to the presentation of pneumonia caused by *S. pneumoniae*. Chills, fever, pleuritic chest pain, dyspnea, purulent sputum, and leukocytosis are frequent; hemoptysis may occur. Not infrequently the disease may have a less distinct onset and slower evolution. The chest radiograph may disclose lobar consolidation or a bronchopneumonia pattern. Cavitation is uncommon. Positive cultures of blood are found in only 20% of patients, except in those studies where a positive blood culture was required for the diagnosis. Complications include empyema, bacteremia, meningitis, septic arthritis, purulent pericarditis, and cellulitis. In the alcoholic who also has chronic pulmonary disease, *H. influenzae* may cause acute purulent bronchitis and lead to acute worsening of respiratory symptoms.

A Gram stain of sputum or material obtained by transtracheal aspiration shows the typical very small coccobacillary gram-negative organism accompanied by many acute inflammatory cells. Many inexperienced microscopists have missed these organisms. To isolate Hemophilus the specimen should be streaked onto chocolate agar and incubated aerobically at increased CO_2 content at 37° C. Typical colonies are speciated by determining the requirement of X (hematin) and Y (nicotinamide adenine dinucleotide) factors for growth.

Susceptibility testing of *H. influenzae* by the Kirby-Bauer method or by broth dilution to determine minimum inhibitory concentrations of antibiotics is not well standardized. Of greater importance is determination of beta lactamase production as an indicator of ampicillin sensitivity or resistance.

Ampicillin remains the preferred treatment, but increased resistance to ampicillin has been observed in type b *H. influenzae*, causing meningitis and/or bacteremia in young children and in the untypeable *H. influenzae*, usually causing adult pneumonia. In adults, ampicillin resistance has not been as great. In one series, 8% of *H. influenzae* isolates from adults were ampicillin resistant by beta lactamase production [35]. In seriously ill patients with *H. influenzae* pneumonia one might justifiably begin cefamandole until beta lactamase production can be excluded.

In patients allergic to ampicillin, alternative agents are tetracycline, trimethoprim, sulfamethoxazole, cefamandole, and chloramphenicol. If simultaneous infection in the central nervous system is suspected, chloramphenicol is preferred because of its excellent entry into the cerebrospinal fluid.

Klebsiella Pneumonia

K. pneumoniae is an infrequent cause of pneumonia acquired in the community. It occurs more often in alcoholics, a fact probably explained by increased pharyngeal colonization in alcoholics [30]. This increased pharyngeal colonization occurs independently of hospitalization.

Community-acquired Klebsiella pneumonia is likely to take the typical course of an acute illness, with fever, cough, chest pain, and thick, tenacious sputum. A chest radiograph may show a bulging horizontal fissue due to lobar expansion. Radiograph evidence of necrosis may also be present. The sputum Gram stain discloses many polymorphonuclear leukocytes and large gram-negative rods.

More frequent is hospital-acquired Klebsiella pneumonia. When there is an alteration of consciousness and few subjective symptoms, the first clue to pneumonia may be new fever, tachypnea, tachycardia, or hypotension. The chest radiograph rarely discloses an enlarged lobe and evidence of necrosis is variable. A specimen of material from the lower airway contains acute inflammatory cells and gram-negative rods. Care must be taken to assure the specimen is suitable for study and does not contain an excess of pharyngeal squamous cells [31]. Transtracheal aspiration may be required to assure sample adequacy. Blood cultures are positive in approximately 30% of patients with Klebsiella pneumonia.

Antibiotic management is with both a first-generation cephalosporin and an aminoglycoside. When Klebsiella pneumonia is acquired in the hospital, attention should be paid to both local epidemiologic information about Klebsiella sensitivities and specific sensitivities of the isolate from the patient. This information may indicate the need for a second-generation cephalosporin or the superiority of one aminoglycoside over others.

Legionnaires' Disease

Legionnaires' disease, caused by *Legionella pneumophilia*, is not discussed in detail herein. A case control study [39] strongly suggests that heavy alcohol use is a risk factor for acquiring Legionnaires' disease. The diagnosis should be considered in patients with pneumonia who have recurrent chills, gastrointestinal symptoms, particularly diarrhea, encephalopathy, hematuria, abnormal liver function, absent organisms on Gram-stained sputum, or progression of disease while receiving a penicillin, a cephalosporin, or an aminoglycoside antibiotic. Erythromycin administered intravenously appears to be an effective agent.

Pulmonary Tuberculosis

Tuberculosis occurs more frequently in alcoholics [32]. As in any subset of the population, pulmonary tuberculosis is the most common form observed, though peritoneal, meningeal, pericardial, bone, joint, or genitourinary disease can be seen.

Fever, cough, weight loss, and/or hemoptysis are the usual presenting symptoms, but the patient may have few symptoms with disease recognition following a routine chest radiograph. Unilateral or bilateral upper lobe fibronodular or cavity disease are the usual radiographic abnormalities. Carcinoma of the lung, aspiration pneumonia, histoplasmosis, or other visceral fungal disease may present similar findings and require differentiation from tuberculosis. Tuberculosis should be considered in any lung lesion in an alcoholic. Tuberculosis and carcinoma of the lung may be present simultaneously [13].

Acid-fast stains of sputum are the initial diagnostic procedure. If positive they lend strong support to the diagnosis. Sputum should also be cultured for *Mycobacterium tuberculosis*. Culture is more sensitive than acid-fast staining of sputum and allows both differentiation from other mycobacteria (e.g., *M. intracellularis, M. kansasii, M. fortuitum*) and sensitivity testing. Speciation and sensitivity testing are highly desirable because they guide therapeutic decisions.

Acid-fast staining, when positive, is of great value because results are available quickly. Cultures require weeks. Multiple samples are usually submitted for both smear and culture. When cough specimens cannot be obtained, culture of morning gastric aspirates are useful. Smears of gastric content are not done because nonpathogenic acid-fast bacilli may be present in the stomach.

Skin testing with 5 international units of Tween-stabilized purified protein derivative (PPD) is a valuable aid to the diagnosis. Doubtful or negative reactions (less than 10 mm in duration) should be interpreted with caution because of the observation that 21% of active tuberculous patients had negative PPD skin tests at entry into a hospital. Negative reactions declined to 5% after 2 weeks of a hospital diet [34]. Protein malnutrition was offered as the probable explanation for the initial negative results.

In alcoholic patients with a suggestive history and chest radiograph, positive PPD, and positive acid-fast stains of sputum, the clinical diagnosis can be made, treatment started, and the diagnosis confirmed by culture. A more difficult situation is the patient with suggestive clinical signs and radiograph, and a positive PPD, but negative acid-fast stains. Once several sputa or gastric aspirates have been submitted for culture, these patients should be treated for the 6 to 8 weeks required for cultural confirmation. Positive cultures confirm the diagnosis. If cultures are negative it seems prudent to completely reevaluate the patient for evidence of other disorders, such as carcinoma of the lung, histoplasmosis, or a slowly resolving aspiration pneumonia.

Many drug programs have been used in alcoholics with tuberculosis, including the combination of isoniazid and rifampin [11].

Two frequent clinical problems in the alcoholic host are (1) reactivation tuberculosis in a patient with a history of previous antituberculous drug therapy, and (2) a positive PPD without chest radiograph evidence of tuberculosis. In patients with confirmed or highly suspected reactivation tuberculosis who have had prior chemotherapy it is advised that isoniazid plus two drugs the patient has never taken be used until sensitivity testing can be completed.

The alcoholic with a positive tuberculin skin test represents a special dilemma. Isoniazid preventive therapy is used in patients under 35 years of age regardless of their previous tuberculin skin test reactivity if they have never been treated before. The rationale for this therapy is based on the probability that young patients are more likely to have recently converted and less likely to develop isoniazid hepatotoxicity. In patients in whom a recent conversion in skin reactivity to PPD can be documented and those who have no evidence of active pulmonary disease, most authorities recommend 1 year of treatment with isoniazid. The risk of pulmonary tuberculosis in a skin converter is approximately 9–15% and potentially higher with the protein malnutrition often associated with alcoholism.

No prospective studies have examined the separate risk factor of alcoholism in isoniazid hepatotoxicity, but an increased incidence of hepatotoxicity has been seen in alcoholic patients treated with isoniazid. Isoniazid hepatotoxicity is age-related [7]. An additional problem is the potential for isoniazid resistance induced by haphazard compliance with preventive therapy.

In light of these observations, preventive therapy with isoniazid is recommended for alcoholics who have recently converted their skin test or who are less than 35 years of age and are skin test-positive of unknown duration. PPD-positive patients without pulmonary disease who are known to be unreliable probably should not be treated, but should be followed with serial chest x-rays.

Spontaneous Bacterial Peritonitis

Spontaneous bacterial peritonitis has been recognized and described in patients with alcoholic cirrhosis [8]. Findings that suggest the diagnosis and indicate the need for study of the ascitic fluid are abdominal pain or tenderness, increasing ascites, fever, increasing hepatic encephalopathy, and decreased or absent bowel sounds [45]. The ascitic fluid is likely to be cloudy and contain more than 300 white blood cells/mm^3 with more than 30% polymorphonuclear leukocytes. Ascitic fluid leukocyte counts as high as 65,000/mm^3 have been described.

Gram stains of ascitic fluid yield disappointingly low results. Only five of 23 (22%) were positive in one series [4], while Conn [8] found 39% positive. Cultures are positive in 84-100% of patients, depending on the criteria for inclusion in the series reported. *E. coli* is the most common isolate. *S. pneumoniae, K. pneumoniae,* and *Strepto coccus fecalis* are also seen with some frequency. Many other organisms, including anaerobic bacilli of the gastrointestinal flora, Clostridia, staphylococci, *Aeromonas hydrophilia,* and *Listeria monocytogenes,* are reported. Blood cultures are positive in up to 75% of patients [8].

There is uncertainty over the means by which the organisms reach the peritoneum. Direct extention from the gastrointestinal lumen or entry from the blood stream are the suspected means. Some patients may have the peritoneal space contaminated by previous paracentesis, endoscopy, or intraarterial administration of vasopressin.

The definitive diagnosis of spontaneous bacterial peritonitis depends on isolation of the organism from the ascitic fluid. In patients with alcoholic liver disease, fever, abdominal pain, and ascites, many clinical judgments must be made about treatment before culture results are known. In those instances when the Gram stain is positive a decision to treat can be made with greater confidence. In the majority with no organisms seen on Gram stain the guide followed is that patients with ascitic fluid cell counts above 300/mm^3 and polymorphonuclear leukocytes of 70% or greater are sufficiently likely to have bacterial peritonitis to treat on strong clinical suspicion. Ampicillin and tobramycin are used initially and new decisions on antibiotics made pending culture results.

Mortality is high in spontaneous bacterial peritonitis (57-97%). Bad prognostic factors include severe liver disease, increasing encephalopathy, ascitic fluid polymorphonuclear leukocytes above 85%, and failure of the patient's temperature to exceed 38° C.

Tuberculous Peritonitis

A high frequency of cirrhosis has been found in some reports of tuberculous peritonitis [5] but the disease is not limited to alcoholics and there is no conclusive evidence of increased incidence in patients with alcoholic liver disease. Tuberculous peritonitis can be insidious and easily missed. Fever, abdominal distention, and positive reactions to intermediate-strength PPD are the features occurring with greatest frequency. Studies by Burack and Hollister [5] have provided information to facilitate differentiation of the ascites of cirrhosis from tuberculous peritonitis plus cirrhosis. Alcoholic patients with and without alcoholic liver disease who have abdominal pain, fever, and increasing abdominal girth warrant study of the peritoneal fluid. If the fluid is exudative in character (protein $\geq$ 2.5 g/dl), the cell count elevated ($\geq$ 300/mm^3), and there is a mononuclear cell predominance, tuberculous peritonitis is one potential cause [5]. Tuberculous peritonitis may occur with lower protein or cell count, and other intraabdominal processes may give the same findings as tuberculous peritonitis.

Acid-fast stains of peritoneal fluid are positive for tubercle bacilli in only 5% or fewer cases [10] and cultures are positive in only 40–50% [21]. Singh reported an 83% recovery by culture if a liter of peritoneal fluid was centrifuged and the sediment cultured [36]. Peritoneal biopsy by percutaneous needle [23, 36], peritoneoscopy [19], or laparotomy provides a high yield in making the diagnosis. Which procedure to employ depends on local experience and individual patient assessment.

Treatment is with isoniazid plus another agent (generally ethambutol or rifampin) for 18 to 24 months. Rifampin has not been prospectively studied in peritoneal tuberculosis, but good results in pulmonary tuberculosis suggest its efficacy.

REFERENCES

1. Bartlett, J. D., Gorbach, S. L., and Finegold, S. M. The bacteriology of aspiration pneumonia. *Am. J. Med.* 56:202–207, 1974.
2. Beeson, P. B., Brannon, E. S., and Warren, J. V. Observations on the sites of removal of bacteria from the blood in patients with bacterial endocarditis. *J. Exp. Med.* 81:9–23, 1945.
3. Brayton, R. G., Stokes, P. E., Schwartz, M. S., and Louria, D. B. Effects of alcohol and various diseases on leukocyte and mobilization phagocytosis and intracellular killing. *N. Engl. J. Med.* 282:123–128, 1970.
4. Breuin, A., Arango, L., Hadley, K., and Murray, J. F. High-dose penicillin therapy and pneumococcal pneumonia. *J.A.M.A.* 230:409–413, 1974.
5. Burack, W. R., and Hollister, R. M. Tuberculous peritonitis. *Am. J. Med.* 28:510–523, 1960.
6. Chandra, R. K. Cell-mediated immunity in nutritional imbalance. *Fed. Proc.* 39:3088–3092, 1980.
7. Comstock, G. W., and Edwards, P. Q. The competing risks of tuberculosis and hepa-

titis for adult tuberculin reactors (editorial). *Am. Rev. Respir. Dis.* 111:573-577, 1975.

8. Conn, H. O., and Fessel, J. M. Spontaneous bacterial peritonitis in cirrhosis: Variations on a theme. *Medicine* 50:161-197, 1971.

9. Craddock, P. R., Yawata, Y., Van Santen, L., Gilberstadt, S., Silvis, S., and Jacob, H. S. Acquired phagocyte dysfunction in a complication of the hypophosphatemia of parenteral hyperalimentation. *N. Engl. J. Med.* 290:1403-1407, 1974.

10. Cromartie, R. S. Tuberculous peritonitis. *Surg. Gynecol. Obstet.* 144:876-878, 1977.

11. Cross, F. S., Long, M. W., Banner, A. S., Snider, D. E., Jr. Rifampin-isoniazid therapy of alcoholic and nonalcoholic tuberculous patients in a U.S. Public Health Service cooperative therapy trial. *Am. Rev. Respir. Dis.* 122:349-353, 1980.

12. Garb, J. L., Brown, R. B., Garb, J. R., and Tuthill, R. W. Differences in etiology of pneumonias in nursing home and community patients. *J.A.M.A.* 240:2169-2172, 1978.

13. Gebel, P., Fulkerson, L., Sparger, C., and Epstein, H. Concomitant bronchogenic carcinoma and tuberculosis of the lung. *Dis. Chest* 41:610-617, 1962.

14. Gee, J. B., Kaskin, J., Duncombe, M. P., and Vassalo, C. L. The effects of ethanol on some metabolic features of phagocytosis in the alveolar macrophage. *J. Reticuloendothel. Soc.* 15:61-68, 1974.

15. Good, R. A., West, A., and Fernandes, G. Nutritional modulation of immune responses. *Fed. Proc.* 39:3098-3104, 1980.

16. Green, L. H., and Green, G. M. Differential suppression of pulmonary antibacterial activity as the mechanism of selection of a pathogen in mixed bacterial infection of the lung. *Am. Rev. Respir. Dis.* 98:819-824, 1968.

17. Grieco, M. H., Capra, J. D., and Paderson, H. Reduced serum beta Ic/Ia globulin levels in extra renal disease. *Am. J. Med.* 51:340-345, 1971.

18. Huxley, E. J., Viroslav, J., Gray, W. R., Pierce, A. K. Pharyngeal aspiration in normal adults and patients with depressed consciousness. *Am. J. Med.* 64:564-568, 1978.

19. Hyman, S., Villa, F., Alvarez, S., and Steigmann, F. The enigma of tuberculous peritonitis. *Gastroenterology* 42:1-6, 1962.

20. Jay, S. J., Johanson, W. G., and Pierce, A. K. The radiographic resolution of *Streptococcus pneumoniae* pneumonia. *N. Engl. J. Med.* 293:798-801, 1975.

21. Karney, W. W., O'Donoghue, J. M., Ostrow, J. H., Homes, K. K., and Beaty, H. N. The spectrum of tuberculous-peritonitis. *Chest* 72:310-315, 1977.

22. Levin, D. C., Schwarz, M. I., Matthay, R. A., LaForce, F. M. Bacteremic *Hemophilus influenzae* pneumonia in adults. *Am. J. Med.* 62:219-224, 1977.

23. Levine, H. Needle biopsy diagnosis of tuberculous peritonitis. *Am. Rev. Respir. Dis.* 97:889-894, 1968.

24. Liu, Y. K. Phagocytic capacity of reticuloendothelial system in alcoholics. *J. Reticuloendothel. Soc.* 25:605-613, 1979.

25. LoGrippo, G., Anselm, K., and Hayashi, H. Serum immunoglobulins and five serum proteins in extrahepatic obstructive jaundice and alcoholic cirrhosis. *Am. J. Gastroenterol.* 56:357-363, 1971.

26. Lorber, B., and Swenson, R. M. Bacteriology of aspiration pneumonia: A prospective study of community and hospital-acquired cases. *Ann. Intern. Med.* 81:329-331, 1974.

27. Louria, D. B., Almy, T. P. Susceptibility to infection during experimental alcohol intoxication. *Trans. Assoc. Am. Physicians* 76:102-112, 1963.

28. MacGregor, R. R., Gluckman, S. J., and Senior, J. R. Granulocyte function and levels of immunoglobulins and complement in patients admitted for withdrawal from alcohol. *J. Infect. Dis.* 138:747-753, 1978.

29. MacGregor, R. R., Spagnuolo, P. J., and Lentek, A. L. Inhibition of granulocyte adherence by ethanol, prednisone, and aspirin, measured with an assay system. *N. Engl. J. Med.* 291:642-646, 1974.

30. Mackowiak, P. A., Martin, R. M., Jones, S. R., and Smith, J. W. Pharyngeal colonization by gram negative bacilli in aspiration-prone persons. *Arch. Intern. Med.* 138:1224–1227, 1978.

31. Murray, P. R., Washington, J. A., III. Microscopic and bacteriologic analysis of expectorated sputum. *Mayo Clin. Proc.* 50:339–344, 1975.

32. Nolan, J. P. Alcohol as a factor in the illness of university service patients. *Am. J. Med. Sci.* 249:135–142, 1965.

33. Ratnoff, O. D., and Patek, A. J. The natural history of Laennec's cirrhosis of the liver. *Medicine* 21:207–268, 1942.

34. Rooney, J. J., Crocco, J. A., Kramer, S., and Lyons, H. A. Further observations on tuberculin reactions in active tuberculosis. *Am. J. Med.* 60:517–522, 1976.

35. Simon, H. B., Southuick, R. S., Moellering, R. C., and Sherman, E. *Hemophilus influenzae* in hospitalized adults: Current perspectives. *Am. J. Med.* 69:219–226, 1980.

36. Singh, M. M., Bhargava, A. N., and Jain, K. P. Tuberculous peritonitis. *N. Engl. J. Med.* 281:1091–1094, 1969.

37. Sorrell, M. F., and Leevy, C. M. Lymphocyte transformation and alcoholic liver injury. *Gastroenterology* 63:1020–1025, 1972.

38. Stiehm, E. F. Humoral immunity in malnutrition. *Fed. Proc.* 39:3093–3097, 1980.

39. Storch, G., Baine, W. B., Fraser, D. W., et al. Sporadic community acquired Legionnaires' disease in United States: A case-control study. *Ann. Intern. Med.* 90:596–600, 1979.

40. Sullivan, R. J., Dowdle, W. R., Marine, W. M., and Hierholzer, J. C. Adult pneumonia in a general hospital. *Arch. Intern. Med.* 129:935–942, 1972.

41. Thomas, H. C., McSween, R. N., and White, R. G. Role of the liver in controlling the immunogenicity of commensal bacteria in the gut. *Lancet* 1:1288–1291, 1973.

42. Tisman, G., and Herbert, V. *In vitro* myelosuppression and immunosuppression by ethanol. *J. Clin. Invest.* 52:1410–1414, 1973.

43. Van Epps, D. E., Strickland, R. G., and Williams, R. C. Inhibitors of leukocyte chemotaxis in alcoholic liver disease. *Am. J. Med.* 59:200–207, 1975.

44. Wallace, R. J., Musher, D. M., and Martin, R. R. *Hemophilus influenzae* pneumonia in adults. *Am. J. Med.* 64:87–93, 1978.

45. Weinstein, M. P., Iannini, P. B., Stratton, C. W., and Eickhoff, T. C. Spontaneous bacterial peritonitis. *Am. J. Med.* 64:592–598, 1978.

20

CHARLES L. WHITFIELD, MD, University of Maryland at Baltimore

SKIN DISEASES ASSOCIATED WITH ALCOHOLISM

HEAVY OR ALCOHOLIC drinking can affect the skin in three ways. It can cause skin problems that tend to be specific to alcoholism, it can aggravate or worsen common skin diseases, and it can cause or be associated with rare skin diseases [12].

In a study of 355 consecutive admissions of alcoholic patients to a public hospital, about 44% had active skin lesions of one or more types [10]. Another survey of 351 heavy or alcoholic drinkers showed that 24% had a significant skin rash, compared with 9% of nondrinkers having a rash [8].

Abstinence from alcohol and regular participation in a treatment program for alcoholism for at least 2 years, combined with dermatologic treatment for the specific lesion, usually brings about improvement of most of these skin conditions. The dermatologist or primary care physician should refer the patient to a competent alcoholism treater and should provide follow-up visits to assure that the patient is participating in the treatment.

Charles L. Whitfield, MD, Associate Professor of Medicine and Family Medicine, Assistant Professor of Psychiatry, and Director, Alcoholism and Drug Abuse Education, University of Maryland at Baltimore, Baltimore, Maryland.

CONDITIONS OFTEN PECULIAR TO ALCOHOLICS

Facial edema. Facial edema (puffy facies) is commonly found in active alcoholism. It tends to resolve by 1 or 2 weeks after drinking stops. It is a useful sign to help detect active alcoholism or a relapse of drinking. It is often especially prominent around the eyes, with accentuation of the periorbital creases or wrinkles by the edematous tissue. Differential diagnosis includes other total body edematous states, such as renal failure, and myxedema and allergic reaction.

The retention of fluid in active alcoholism is complex, although it appears to be associated with a stimulation of excess vasopressin (antidiuretic hormone – ADH) secretion [2]. The secretion of ADH is decreased during a rising blood alcohol level (BAL) and increased during the plateau phase and the fall of the BAL curve.

Cigarette smoking, found in about 90% of alcoholics, also increases wrinkles of the skin, causing an appearance of premature aging. These excess wrinkles may cause the facial edema to be more easily recognized. However, the facial edema of active alcoholism may also be subtle, often observed only in retrospect after abstinence (or if photographs are available when the person was abstinent for comparison).

Tobacco smoke stains. Tobacco smoke stains are yellow-to-brown discolorations on the skin, occurring mostly on the distal parts of the fingers where the person holds the cigarette such that the skin is most exposed to its heat and smoke. In alcoholism so advanced as to cause peripheral neuropathy, the neuropathy may also be a contributing factor, since the person feels that heat less intensely. Although the presence of stains can indicate recent active alcoholic drinking, this observation may not be as strong an evidence for or as timely an indication of alcoholic drinking as is facial edema, since the stains may take from 3 to 8 weeks to clear. Also, depending on how heavy a smoker the person is and how he or she holds the cigarette, a slight staining may remain in some even after drinking stops. Differential diagnosis includes other causes of peripheral neuropathy, although here the tobacco staining may not be as marked or as common as it is in heavy cigarette smoking among active alcoholics.

Rosacea and skin redness. Acne rosacea may be absent, mild, or prominent, depending on the individual alcoholic [8, 10]. It tends to improve or clear when drinking ceases. It occurs uncommonly in the epigastric region [13]. Rhinophyma is a lobular hypertrophy of the nose, often with red coloration. It is rare among alcoholics.

Other pigmentation. Some alcoholics suntan in a splotchy distribution. Also, proportional to the severity of liver disease, there may be a generalized dark or grayish cast to the skin. This is frequently related to the presence of hemochromatosis (i.e., iron overload in the liver and other organs, including the skin) [7].

Skin flushing reactions. Cutaneous flushing reactions may occur in association with alcohol ingestion. These flushes have been associated with ethnic background, and appear to occur most often among Orientals [4, 5].

Generalized pruritus. Generalized puritus has been described as an invisible dermatitis, noticed only by itching and by scratch marks on the skin. It can be the only symptom of liver cirrhosis for up to 2 years before the cirrhosis otherwise becomes manifest. It has been postulated as being related to toxic substances in the blood or to autonomic nervous system abnormalities [10, 15].

Spider nevi (vascular spiders). Spider nevi are dilated arterioles that fan out centrifugally from a central arteriole; their size is usually about 1 cm in diameter, though it may vary. The firey red lesion blanches on point pressure of the central arteriole and refills from the center [10]. They are usually present as several to many lesions, most commonly located from the face to the umbilicus, more on the front than the back. Their presence tends to indicate the presence of liver disease or cirrhosis [1]. The lesions do not tend to improve or disappear with cessation of drinking. When they rarely do disappear, it is presumed that the cause is vasospasm or thrombosis [10]. At times, small areas of depigmentation may be visible, often in associaiton with vascular spiders.

Glossitis. In a glossitis condition an inflamed mouth and tongue may be seen, most often in association with the folate deficiency observed with active alcoholism [3]. These changes usually improve or disappear when alcohol is stopped and a nutritious diet ingested. A purple or cyanotic-appearing tongue may also be seen associated with alcoholic liver disease [10, 15].

Feminine hair pattern. In men with advanced alcoholism the hair often becomes sparse, taking on a more feminine distribution. This finding is said to be most common among alcoholics with liver disease.

Gynecomastia. Excessive development of the male mammary glands is also most commonly found among alcoholics with advanced liver disease. Testicular atrophy is commonly found accompanying the gynecomastia.

Skin pathology in advanced alcoholics. One study described the histologic features of skin biopsies of 55 advanced alcoholics who had been admitted to the hospital for medical complications of their alcoholism [6]. The lesions noted were atrophy of the epidermis and of the pilosebaceous appendages, with abnormal structure of the pilomotor muscles, and increase of the ground substance of collagen in the upper part of the dermis. These lesions were said to correspond to the clinical appearance of the skin, which was smooth and fatty-appearing, with a light vascular pattern simulating silken threads on paper (sometimes called "paper money" skin). No correlation with other skin diseases was noted except for vascular spiders and disturbance of nail and hair growth [6].

CONDITIONS NOT PECULIAR TO ALCOHOLICS

Some dermatologists have observed that patients with psoriasis, seborrheic dermatitis, rosacea, and some other conditions tend to worsen or have flare-ups associated with drinking binges [15]. Stopping drinking on a long-term basis, through alcoholism treatment mentioned above, improves many of these conditions. Others have observed that contact- and light-sensitive dermatitis and nummular eczemas often occur in alcoholics [6].

In a study of 351 heavy or alcoholic drinkers [8] the most common skin conditions observed were eczema, keratosis, drug erruption, psoriasis, seborrheic dermatitis, contact dermatitis, and onychomycosis [8].

RARE SKIN CONDITIONS IN ALCOHOLICS

Certain skin conditions are relatively rare in active alcoholics. Even so, alcoholism is common among people presenting with them. Some of these rare conditions are alcoholic ulcero-osteolytic neuropathy, pellagra, zinc deficiency, and porphyria.

Alcoholic ulcero-osterolytic neuropathy. This is a rare condition, found almost solely among black alcoholic men from South Africa [9]. The skin and bone lesions occur as a result of the peripheral neuropathy of active alcoholism. Pain perception is absent, and trauma, combined with the active alcoholic's impaired immune system, opens the way for infection. Trophic ulcers and infection are seen, with varying degrees of digital resorption and clawing of the toes. Bone changes are due to infection. If an arteriogram is performed, typical findings of numerous abnormal vessels with neovascularization are usually seen, but with no other evidence of vascular insufficiency [9]. The neuropathy and skin changes can be seen also in diabetes mellitus, frostbite, tabes dorsalis, and leprosy.

Pellagra. Pellagra is a systemic condition with skin abnormalities. It is caused by severe protein deficiency in the diet, with a concomitant niacin (nicotinic acid) deficiency. It is most often due to active alcoholism in an impoverished individual, and is thus most likely to occur among skid row alcoholics. In a recent study of 18 patients with pellagra, 15 (83%) were alcoholic and consumed a diet low in protein and calories and high in alcohol [11]. Among these patients, marked weight loss was common. Stomatitis and diarrhea were each seen in 40%, and peripheral neuropathy and edema were each seen in 56%. Dementia was seen in 50%.

Dermatitis was seen in all of the 18 patients. It may present in a spectrum of skin changes, ranging from an acute erythematous rash of early pellagra to a chronic phase of hyperpigmentation and hyperkeratosis and desquamation. The lesions are seen most often over the extremities. They may also be seen on the chest and back, in the axillae, and over pressure points. Alopecia may also occur, often associated with steatorrhea. Gastrointestinal and other changes are often present [11]. Other vitamins, such as folate, B_1, and B_6 are often deficient. Pellagra may rarely be associated with isoniazid, ethionamide, or 6-mercaptopurine administration, although other factors are often present in patients taking these drugs that tend to aggravate the condition, such as gastrointestinal disease, cancer, pregnancy, and inanition [11].

Zinc deficiency. Overt zinc deficiency dermatitis may occur in chronic alcoholics who are given total parenteral nutrition, for example, in those with pancreatitis. The rash usually develops within 3 weeks to 4 months after starting the parenteral nutrition [14]. It begins in the nasolabial folds and spreads to the perioral area. At first it is erythematous and desquamative, though it may become bullous and hemorrhagic. Untreated, it may spread to the axillae, the perineum, and the finger creases. In some patients alopecia, diarrhea, and mental abberation develop. Serum zinc levels are characteristically less than 20 µg/dl when the rash first appears [14].

Treatment is with one 220 mg zinc sulfate tablet taken orally daily. The rash usually improves within from 2 to 7 days, and clears within from 1 to 3 weeks of treatment. Predisposing factors to zinc deficiency are chronic alcoholism, a poor diet, and liver cirrhosis, which may be associated with an increased urinary excretion of zinc. Zinc deficiency may also be a factor among alcoholics with night blindness and testicular damage. Zinc appears to be important in wound healing and cell-mediated immunity [14].

Porphyria cutanea tarda. Probably less than 1% of alcoholics with liver disease have porphyria cutanea tarda (PCT) [7], a photocutaneous syndrome with bullous skin lesions, increased skin fragility, and sclerodermoid plaques. The lesions are due to excessive porphyrin disposition in the skin, which in turn causes photosensitivity from the ability to absorb radiant energy that damages cells.

Other kinds of porphyria are inherited, and when clinically active, are often associated with acute neurologic syndromes. PCT occurs with several possible disorders, the most common being alcoholism. From 25 to 75% of case reports are alcoholic [7]. Also, 80% or more of people with PCT have iron overload in the liver [7]. Why alcoholism is associated with PCT is unknown.

Urine testing shows a normal porphobilinogen, with occasional slight increases in delta amino levulenic acid. Finding a urobilinogen to coprophyrin ratio of greater than 5:1 differentiates PCT from varigate porphyria [7].

Treatment consists of supportive management of the acute episodes and abstinence-oriented treatment of alcoholism.

REFERENCES

1. Bean, W. B. *Vascular Spiders and Related Lesions of the Skin.* Springfield, Ill: Charles C Thomas, 1958.
2. Cicero, T. J. Neuroendocrinological effects of alcohol. *Ann. Rev. Med.* 32:123-142, 1981.

3. Eichner, E. R. Alcohol and the blood. In: *The Patient with Alcoholism and Other Drug Problems*, Whitfield, C. L. (ed.). Year Book Medical Pubs.: Chicago. In press.

4. Ewing, J. A., Rouse, B. A., and Aderhold, R. M. Studies of the mechanism of Oriental hypersensitivity to alcohol. In: *Currents in Alcoholism* (Vol. 5), Galanter, M. (ed.). Grune & Stratton: New York, 1979.

5. Ewing, J. A., Rouse, B. A., and Pellizzari, E. D. Alcohol sensitivity and ethnic background. *Am. J. Psychiatry* 131:206–210, 1974.

6. Grosshans, E. L. Skin dermatoses in alcoholics. *Arch. Dermatol.* 113:1734, 1977.

7. Hines, J. D. Effects of alochol on inborn errors of metabolism: Porphyria cutanea tarda and hemochronmatosis. *Semin. Hematol.* 17:113–118, 1980.

8. Margolis, J., and Robert, D. M. Frequency of skin lesions in chronic drinkers. *Arch. Dermatol.* 112:1326–1327, 1976.

9. Miller, R. M., and Hunt, J. A. The radiologic features of alcoholic ulcero-osteolytic neuropathy in blacks. *S. Afr. Med. J.* 54:159–161, 1978.

10. Rosset, M., and Oki, G. Skin diseases in alcoholics. *Q. J. Stud. Alcohol* 32:1017–1024, 1971.

11. Spivak, J. L., and Jackson, D. L. Pellagra: An analysis of 18 patients and a review of the literature. *Johns Hopkins Med. J.* 140:295–309, 1977.

12. Whitfield, C. L., and Severinghaus, J. Miscellaneous medical consequences of alcoholsim. In: *The Patient with Alcoholism and Other Drug Problems*, Whitfield, C. L. (ed.). Year Book Medical Pubs.: Chicago. In press.

13. Wilkin, J. K. Epigastric rosacea. *Arch. Dermatol.* 116:584, 1980.

14. Williams, R. B., Russell, R. M., Dutta, S. K. et al. Alcoholic pancreatitis: Patients at high risk of acute zinc deficiency. *Amer. J. Med.* 66:889–893, 1979.

15. Woeber, K. The skin in diagnosing alcoholism. *Ann. N.Y. Acad. Sci.* 252:292–295, 1975.

21

I. CHANARIN, MD, Northwick Park Hospital, Harrow, United Kingdom

EFFECTS OF ALCOHOL ON THE HEMATOPOIETIC SYSTEM

ALCOHOL IS A MAJOR cause of hematologic abnormality and one that is often overlooked in clinical practice. Some 30 years ago Hotz [31] and Movitt [44, 45] described patients taking large amounts of alcohol who had megaloblastic anemia and liver disease. Since then there have been many detailed studies of the blood in alcoholism and many of these have been reviewed recently [24].

THE MACROCYTOSIS OF ALCOHOLISM

In 1974 Wu et al. [60] reported that 89% of 63 patients taking more than 80 g ethanol daily had abnormally large red blood cells. This macrocytosis was unrelated to their folate status; that is, it was as common in those who had low serum, red cell, and liver folate levels as in those with normal amounts of folate in these three tissues [61]. Further, the mean corpuscular volume (MCV) was not changed by treatment with folic acid but fell over the next 3 months in those who stopped taking alcohol. The alcohol was exerting its effect on the developing erythroblast and a return of a normal MCV required the replacement of these large red blood

---

I. Chanarin, MD, Head, Section of Hematology, Medical Research Council, Clinical Research Centre, Northwick Park Hospital, Harrow, United Kingdom.

cells by a new population of normal-sized red cells produced after alcohol withdrawal. This time is related to the normal red cell life span of 120 days. This is quite unlike the disappearance of other toxic effects induced by alcohol in which reversal is much more rapid. The majority of the patients studied by Wu et al. [60] were not anemic and, indeed, macrocytosis was the only abnormality noted in the blood. The patients were generally well nourished and taking a reasonable diet.

At about the same time Unger and Johnson [53] found, during the course of health checks on the employees of a large insurance company, that 3% had macrocytosis in the absence of anemia. Seventeen employees were selected consecutively from a list of subjects with raised MCVs. All but one was found to take excessive amounts of alcohol. Their serum folates were normal and the MCV did not change following administration of folic acid.

Macrocytosis in liver disease, the latter often alcoholic in origin, is well documented. Wintrobe [58] found that one-third of 132 patients with liver disease had a macrocytic anemia. Jarrold and Vilter [33] found a raised MCV in 20 out of 30 consecutive patients with cirrhosis and three, who had been taking grossly deficient diets, had megaloblastic marrow changes. These three patients responded to folate or liver therapy but the macrocytosis in the other patients was not changed by oral folate. Sheehy and Berman [51] noted macrocytosis in 10 out of 24 patients with cirrhosis all being normoblastic. Deller et al. [13] found macrocytosis in 28 out of 46 patients with cirrhosis, nine showing various degrees of megaloblastosis.

Hall [22] measured the mean cell diameter and the MCV in patients with liver disease. There was a high incidence of macrocytosis in those with a history of long-standing alcoholism, but only one out of 29 had a raised red cell diameter. This would suggest that flattened or thin red cells (leptocytes, target cells) with an increased diameter are a feature of liver damage, whereas alcohol, by contrast, increased red cell size with only minor effect on the diameter of the cell.

The effect of alcohol intake on the MCV has been confirmed from many sources. Four studies have found the incidence of macrocytosis in alcoholics to be between 82–96% [6, 43, 53, 61]. Studies showing a significantly lower frequency in subjects taking comparable amounts of alcohol (in excess of 80 g daily) suggest incorrectly calibrated coulter counters or setting a too high upper limit in controls.

Chalmers et al. [7] noted a significant difference between the sexes in the United Kingdom: The mean MCV in women alcoholics was 101.3 fl as compared to 96.7 fl in men and both were higher than control values (86.4 fl in women and 86.0 fl in men). Of the women 94% had a raised MCV, as did 71% of the men. Although the women took smaller amounts of alcohol and duration of excessive intake was shorter than that in men, they tended to drink wine, fortified wine, or spirits rather than beer or cider. Beer contains significant amounts of folate, whereas wines and spirits have a very low folate content. Correspondingly, women had lower serum and red cell folate levels.

THE BONE MARROW IN ALCOHOLICS

Cellularity. Excess alcohol intake leads to loss of marrow cellularity and regeneration follows withdrawal of alcohol [10].

Megaloblastosis. There are two common reasons why hemopoiesis may be megaloblastic in an alcoholic. The first is that megaloblastosis may result from the direct toxic effect of alcohol on marrow cells. These marrow changes revert to normal within a few days of alcohol withdrawal and hence, if it is desired to assess such changes, marrow samples should be collected before the patient stops taking alcohol. The second common reason for megaloblastosis in an alcoholic is nutritional folate deficiency. Apart from these two major causes, an alcoholic may have associated pernicious anemia or other causative factors. These combinations are unusual, but they indicate that megaloblastic anemia in an alcoholic should be investigated in the same way that one would investigate any patient with a megaloblastic anemia.

Wu et al. [60] noted megaloblasts in the marrows of 20 out of 57 patients (35%) taking excess alcohol, but this was well marked in only 2 patients. Giant metamyelocytes were present in 11 marrows (19%). The higher the MCV, the greater the likelihood of megaloblastosis.

Chalmers et al. [7] found 29% of 87 male and 37% of 51 female alcoholics in the United Kingdom had megaloblastic marrows. Of the 39 megaloblastic patients, 12 had low red cell folate levels indicative of folate deficiency. The remaining 27 patients (69%) had normal red cell folate levels, indicating that in all these 27 patients the megaloblastic changes were due to the toxic effects of alcohol. In the other 12 both folate deficiency and alcohol toxicity were operative.

In the skid row population megaloblastosis was present in 26 out of 65 patients (40%) [15] and in another 75 patients 20 (27%) were megaloblastic [30]. Jarrold et al. [34] found megaloblastosis in 8 out of 26 male alcoholics (30%). Pierce et al. [48] in a further study found megaloblastosis in 18 of 29 skid row alcoholics (62%) and in 10 out of 22 binge drinkers (27%). The latter were generally better nourished.

Usually macrocytosis is the only abnormality in the peripheral blood accompanying megaloblastosis in marrow. Where the megaloblastosis is due to folate deficiency as well as alcohol toxicity, there may be hypersegmented neutrophils in the peripheral blood as well as other evidence of megaloblastic anemia.

Vacuolation. The appearance of vacuoles in developing hemopoietic cells in marrow is a common response to the administration of a variety of toxic substances, the best known being chloramphenicol. Similar changes were noted in marrows from alcoholic patients by McCurdy et al. [41]. Vacuolation, particularly of early granulocytes, is not uncommon in otherwise normal marrows obtained from patients with a variety of disorders. The vacuoles in alcoholism are more prominent and occur particularly in proerythroblasts, but also other cells of the red and white cell series. They may be located in the cytoplasm or nucleus. They are present in both normoblastic and megaloblastic marrows and independent of the presence of sideroblasts. These findings have been confirmed [34, 55]. Volunteers show vacuoles in hemopoietic precursors after 5 to 7 days of alcohol ingestion and the vacuoles largely disappear from the marrow 3 to 7 days after withdrawal of alcohol. A Seattle study showed vacuolation in 31% of chronic alcoholics and in 41% of binge drinkers [48].

It was suggested that alcohol caused cell membrane damage that was followed by invagination and formation of clear vacuoles [62].

Pathological sideroblasts. Marrow stained for iron normally shows the presence of a small number of iron-containing granules in normoblast cytoplasm. Excess iron may be present in marrows from alcoholics and iron, when bound to mitochondria, forms a ring around the nucleus. Such ringed sideroblasts were present in marrows of 24 out of 33 severe alcoholic patients with liver disease and folate deficiency [27]. These sideroblasts disappeared 7 days after alcohol withdrawal in 80% of the marrows and had disappeared in all the patients by the 14th day [15]. These changes were less frequent in well-nourished alcoholics and Wu et al. [61] found a few ringed sideroblasts in only four out of 57 patients.

Hines and Cowan [29] reported that the *in vivo* conversion of pyridoxine to pyridoxal phosphate was impaired during alcohol ingestion and that treatment with pyridoxal phosphate caused disappearance of the ringed sideroblasts in alcoholics.

In some patients these ringed sideroblasts are accompanied by the classical dimorphic peripheral blood changes, but in the majority this is not the case. Apart from the presence of a dimorphic blood picture, there are no clinical criteria on which those with and without sideroblasts can be separated. Those with sideroblasts are usually megaloblast- and folate-deficient [27].

WHITE BLOOD CELLS IN ALCOHOLICS

Alcoholics have an increased susceptibility to infection and recovery, particularly of lung infections, may be slow. As part of the depressive effect of alcohol on hemopoiesis, neutropenia occurs in a small number of patients, perhaps in about 5% [14, 15].

Alcohol appears to interfere with the mobilization of granulocytes into sites of infection both in experimental studies in rabbits [47] and mice [39] and in Rebuck skin window preparations in man [5]. Phagocytosis and intracellular killing remain intact. The impairment of chemotaxis in man after alcohol was confirmed in volunteers given alcohol for 6 to 8 days [19] and there was a further impairment of granulocyte adherence [20].

Macrophages too are affected by alcohol. In alcoholics there is impaired clearance, presumably by macrophages, of labeled aggregated serum albumin given intravenously, and this is restored to normal 5 days after withdrawal of alcohol [38].

A reduction in lymphocyte numbers usually accompanies neutropenia and there is a rise in the lymphocyte count a week after alcohol withdrawal [46]. A fall in the number of T-lymphocytes in alcoholics has been reported [40] and, in addition to impaired responses to mitogens, sera from alcoholics have been found to have an inhibitory effect on lymphocyte transformation [63]. Impaired cell-mediated immune responses, such as response to dinitrochlorobenzene or keyhole limpet hemocyanin, occur with continued alcoholic intake [19]. It has been suggested that alcohol, by an effect on the cell membrane, activates membrane adenylcyclase and hence raises the intracellular level of cyclic adenosine monophosphate (AMP) [2].

MEGALOBLASTIC ANEMIA IN ALCOHOLICS

Megaloblastic changes in erythroblasts occur in a substantial proportion of alcoholics, but a megaloblastic anemia occurs only in those who have nutritional folate deficiency. In these patients the peripheral blood shows macrocytosis and, in more anemic patients, anisocytosis, poikilocytosis, and hypersegmentation of neutrophil polymorphs, as well.

Folate status. Folate deficiency is commonly found in the down-and-out or skid row alcoholic, but is relatively uncommon in well-nourished alcoholics.

The serum folate level was found to be low in 188 out of 380 patients with liver disease, usually alcoholic in origin [8]. Most of the megaloblastic patients had low serum folates. In two studies of skid row alcoholics low serum folates were present in 89 out of 120 patients [30, 48].

By contrast, 50 alcoholics admitted to a treatment center in Scotland had serum folate levels that did not differ from a control group [57]. In the group studied by Wu et al. [60] in London 28% had low serum folates.

Red cell folate levels were measured in 70 skid row alcoholics and were low in 30 [30]. Chalmers et al. [7] measured the red cell folate level in 221 well-nourished alcoholics in London and this was low in 12.3% of the men and 20% of the women. Megaloblastosis was present in 36% of those with a low red cell folate but in only 14% of those with normal red cell folates. Thus tissue depletion of folate is far more common than the corresponding morphological changes and this relationship between the "disease" and the distribution of the underlying deficiency is the rule in all nutritional deficiencies. The naïve expectation that folate deficiency must always manifest itself in the blood and marrow is a constant theme in the literature and is a misconception.

There are two studies of liver folate levels in alcoholics. In New Jersey, Leevy et al. [35] found that 33% of 20 patients had liver folate levels below 2.5 µg/g and, in London, Wu et al. [61] found that 31% of 48 alcoholics undergoing liver biopsy had levels below 2.5 µg folate/g liver.

Two factors are significant in determining the development of folate deficiency, the diet and the type of drink consumed. There is very strong association between a poor folate intake and megaloblastic anemia [13, 14, 15, 25, 27]. Alcoholics who took one adequate meal a day had significantly higher serum and red cell folate levels than those who did not [61].

Beer contains some 10 µg folate/100 ml [8], but wine and spirits contain negligible amounts; megaloblastic anemia and folate deficiency is thus more common in wine and spirit drinkers. Wine and spirit drinkers have significantly lower serum, red cell, and liver folate levels than beer drinkers [61].

Vitamin B_{12} status. The serum vitamin B_{12} level is normal or even slightly elevated in alcoholics [27]. The rise in the serum B_{12} is probably due to liver damage.

The deoxyuridine (dU) suppression test. The dU suppression test assesses the synthesis of deoxythymidine from its precursor, deoxyuridine, by marrow cells. The pathway is abnormal if either vitamin B_{12} or folate is lacking. Wickramasinghe and Saunders [56] performed this test with marrow cells from 45 alcoholic patients. All had macrocytosis; 14 had early megaloblastic changes. Of these 14 patients 8 gave abnormal results in the dU suppression test indicating folate deficiency, but the results in the other 6 megaloblastic patients and in the 31 macrocytic ones were normal.

These data then confirm the pattern previously described. Macrocytosis and megaloblastosis both occur in alcoholics in the absence of any detectable derangement of folate function, some show evidence of folate deficiency without manifesting biochemical evidence of folate dysfunction, and many more have macrocytosis as the only abnormality.

SIDEROBLASTIC ANEMIA IN ALCOHOLICS

Sideroblastic anemia is a variant of severe megaloblastic anemia, occurring in some alcoholics with nutritional deficiency. The peripheral blood shows a well-marked dimorphic blood picture with macrocytes and hypochromic microcytes, as well as aniso- and poikilocytosis. The marrow, when stained for iron, shows the presence of striking ringed sideroblasts. Erythropoiesis is megaloblastic.

Clinically these patients are anemic with a high serum iron and low serum and red cell folate levels. They often have a smooth tongue, angular stomatitis, hepatomegaly, and splenomegaly. They may be jaundiced and have ascites. Muscle weakness and diminished reflexes may be the result of hypokalemia. They may have peripheral neuropathy [27]. Delirium tremens occurred in eight of 13 patients.

Even in these patients withdrawal of alcohol, correction of electrolyte balance, sedation, and a normal hospital diet led to a return of normoblastic hemopoiesis and disappearance of sideroblasts with return toward normal of serum and red cell folate levels [27].

HEMOLYTIC ANEMIA IN ALCOHOLICS

Alcoholic cirrhosis may be associated with a shortened survival of red cells in the circulation and mild anemia. The red cell life span is reduced to about half the normal and, with an inadequate response by the marrow, mild anemia ensues [32]. These events relate to cirrhosis rather than to alcohol. The peripheral blood often shows an excess of target cells because of the acquisition of excess cholesterol and phospholipids from plasma by erythrocytes. There may be excess splenic sequestration of red cells by an enlarged spleen.

More marked red cell distortions have been termed "spur cells." Zieve [64] described a syndrome that consists of transient hemolytic anemia, jaundice, hyperlipoproteinemia, and alcoholic liver disease. As an entity this has come under some criticism [11]. Nevertheless, there are a small group of patients with a sustained reticulocytosis following alcoholic liver damage that is not due to folate therapy, nor to response to blood loss, nor to alcohol withdrawal. The hemolysis may be attributed to active splenic sequestration despite absence of clinical splenomegaly. However, direct damage to red cell membranes by alcohol and metabolic derangements in the red cells has been suggested [21].

SOME RELEVANT METABOLIC DISORDERS IN ALCOHOLICS

Iron. Repeated blood loss from varices may lead to an iron deficiency anemia. By contrast other alcoholics have increased iron stores. Some beverages, such as some wines, may have a high iron content and absorption of ferric iron may be enhanced by alcohol [9]. Beer brewed in iron pots by the Bantu in South

Africa also has a very high iron content and is responsible for the iron overhead found in this population.

A high alcohol intake suppresses hemopoiesis and is accompanied by a high serum iron level. Withdrawal of alcohol allows marrow recovery and is accompanied by a sharp fall in the serum iron [52]. In some alcoholics the very high tissue iron stores may resemble hemochromatosis and distinction can be difficult. However, iron stores rarely exceed 10 g in alcoholics and invariably do so in symptomatic patients with hemochromatosis. Serum ferritin measurements in liver disease may be unreliable, but urinary iron excretion following a dose of deferoxamine exceeding 10 mg favors a diagnosis of hemochromatosis [4].

Folate metabolism. Alcohol ingestion by volunteers produces a fall in serum folate starting several hours after the peak alcohol blood level has been reached and lasting a few hours [15, 16, 28]. A very similar fall occurs after a dose of diphenylhydantoin in man [49] and both may be the result of induction of hepatic enzymes.

Hillman et al. [26] reported that alcohol given to rats reduced the amount of folate excreted into bile. This work awaits confirmation. An intact enterohepatic circulation of folate is important in maintaining the serum folate level and its interruption may contribute to a fall in serum folate.

Chronic alcoholics have impaired intestinal absorption of folates as well as cobalamin [3, 23] and this is reversed on alcohol withdrawal. This too may explain the fall in serum folate after large amounts of alcohol.

The activity of methionine synthetase, which requires folate and cobalamin coenzymes, in livers of rats given alcohol and a low-protein diet was decreased to 67% of control values and the activities of other enzymes, including betaine-methyltransferase and S-adenosylmethionine synthetase, were increased [17]. This mild impairment of methionine synthetase, if it occurred in man, would tend to raise the serum folate level.

Other enzymes involved in blood formation. Impairment of globin chain synthesis by alcohol has been demonstrated [1, 18]. There is impairment of delta-aminolevulinic acid dehydrase activity [42]. There is induction of heme-degrading enzymes as shown by an increased output of labeled stercobilin after ^{15}N-delta-aminolevulinic acid [50].

EFFECT OF ALCOHOL IN VOLUNTEERS AND EFFECT OF ITS WITHDRAWAL

Alcohol has been given to volunteers and to patients who have recovered from the initial effects of alcohol. Alcohol given to healthy volunteers depressed the reticulocyte and platelet counts and raised the serum iron level [37]. These effects are not prevented by giving folic acid. The serum folate level falls. The marrow shows vacuolation of pronormoblasts and, less consistently, of promyelocytes.

Somewhat different effects are seen when hospitalized chronic alcoholics are returned to a high alcohol intake. In these patients megaloblastosis and ringed-sideroblast formation are added to the changes already noted [29, 52]. Withdrawal of alcohol reverses these manifestations.

Alcoholics who are hospitalized show a rise in the reticulocyte count and hemoglobin level. The reticulocytes reach a peak at about 7 days after stopping alcohol [32, 59]. There is a rise in the total white cell count [46]. The platelets rise [37]. The marrow changes return toward normality, the megaloblastosis earliest and the other changes thereafter, all being gone within 2 weeks.

ALCOHOL AND HEMOSTASIS

Patients with alcoholic cirrhosis have decreased levels of vitamin K-dependent coagulation factors (VII, IX, X, prothrombin) and may have abnormal fibrinolysis, sometimes with disseminated intravascular coagulation. This is due to liver damage. Alcohol per se does not affect coagulation [54], but has a profound effect on platelets [12]. Thrombocytopenia is common in severe alcoholism [36, 52] in the absence of splenomegaly and recovers on alcohol withdrawal. Low platelet counts occur in 25% of patients with acute alcohol intoxication and in 3% of chronic alcoholics [12]. This is unrelated to anemia or to their folate status. The low platelet levels tend to persist in those with splenomegaly. In the others a rise in platelets occurs 2 to 3 days after alcohol withdrawal, reaching maximum levels about 10 to 14 days later. There is a tendency to overshoot so that platelets decline to a plateau after the peak is reached. Clinically, purpura may be present, and thrombocytopenia may be one of the factors leading to a major gastrointestinal bleed.

There is increased platelet consumption in alcoholism so that platelet survival is shortened. At the same time the effect of alcohol on the marrow depresses normal thrombopoiesis. There are also defects in platelet function, including failure of the platelets to aggregate in response to adenosine diphosphate (ADP), epinephrine, thrombin, and collagen in patients whose blood alcohol level has exceeded 300 mg/dl for 7 or more days.

Following platelet aggregation the platelets contract and squeeze various metabolites out of the platelet. This is termed the "release reaction." This phase is also curtailed or even absent in platelets from alcoholics. The intraplatelet concentration of ADP and adenasine triphosphate (ATP) storage pool nucleotides are reduced and may account for the impaired secondary aggregation. The availability of platelet factor 3, another release reagent, is also reduced in some alcoholics.

The ultimate effect of these platelet changes is to cause a prolongation of the bleeding time and increase the risk of hemorrhage.

REFERENCES

1. Ali, M. F., and Nolan, J. P. Alcohol-induced depression of reticuloendothelial function in rats. *J. Lab. Clin. Med.* 70:295-301, 1967.

2. Atkinson, J. P., Sullivan, T. J., Kelly, J. P., and Parker, C. W. Stimulation by alcohols of cyclic AMP metabolism in human leukocytes: Possible role of cyclic AMP in the antiinflammatory effects of ethanol. *J. Clin. Invest.* 60:284-294, 1977.

3. Baker, H., Frank, O., Zetterman, R. K., Rajan, K. S., Ten-Hove, W., and Leevy, C. M. Inability of chronic alcoholics with liver disease to use food as a source of folates, thiamin and vitamin B_6. *Am. J. Clin. Nutr.* 28:1377-1380, 1975.

4. Barry, M., Carter, G. C., and Sherlock, S. Differential ferrioxamine test in haemochromatosis and liver disease. *Gut* 10:697-704, 1969.

5. Brayton, R. G., Stokes, P. E., Schwartz, M. S., and Louria, D. B. Effect of alcohol and various diseases on leukocyte mobilization, phagocytosis and intracellular bacterial killing. *N. Engl. J. Med.* 282:123-128, 1970.

6. Buffet, C., Chaput, J-C., Albuisson, F., Subtil, E., and Etienne, J. P. La macrocytose dans l'hepatite alcoholique chronique histologiquement prouveé. *Arch. Fr. Med. App. Diag.* 64:309-315, 1975.

7. Chalmers, D. M., Chanarin, I., Macdermott, S., and Levi, A. J. Sex-related differences in the hematological effects of excessive alcohol consumption. *J. Clin. Path.* 33:3-7, 1980.

8. Chanarin, I. *The Megaloblastic Anaemias* (2nd ed.). Blackwell: Oxford, 1979.

9. Charlton, R. W., Jacobs, P., Seftel, H., and Bothwell, T. H. Effect of alcohol on iron absorption. *Br. Med. J.* 2:1427-1429, 1964.

10. Conrad, M. E., and Barton, J. C. Anemia and iron kinetics in alcoholism. *Semin. Hemat.* 17:149-163, 1980.

11. Cooper, R. A. Hemolytic syndromes and red cell membrane abnormalities in liver disease. *Semin. Hemat.* 17:103-112, 1980.

12. Cowan, D. H. Effect of alcoholism on hemostasis. *Semin. Hemat.* 17:137-147, 1980. 1980.

13. Deller, D. J., Kimber, C. L., and Ibbotson, R. N. Folic acid deficiency in cirrhosis of the liver. *Am. J. Dig. Dis.* 10:35-42, 1965.

14. Eichner, E. R., Buchanan, B., Smith, J. W., and Hillman, R. S. Variations in the hematologic and medical status of alcoholics. *Am. J. Med. Sci.* 263:35-42, 1972.

15. Eichner, E. R., and Hillman, R. S. The evolution of anemia in alcoholic patients. *Am. J. Med.* 50:218-232, 1971.

16. Eichner, E. R., and Hillman, R. S. Effect of alcohol on serum folate level. *J. Clin. Invest.* 52:584-590, 1973.

17. Finkelstein, J. D., Cello, J. P., and Kyle, W. E. Ethanol-induced changes in methionine metabolism in rat liver. *Biochem. Biophys. Res. Commun.* 61:525-531, 1974.

18. Freedman, M. L., Cohen, H. S., Rosman, J., and Forte, F. J. Ethanol inhibition of reticulocyte protein synthesis: The role of haem. *Br. J. Haematol.* 30:351-363, 1975.

19. Gluckman, S. J., Dvorak, V. C., and MacGregor, R. R. Host defense during prolonged alcohol consumption in a controlled environment. *Arch. Intern. Med.* 137:1539-1543, 1977.
20. Gluckman, S. J., and MacGregor, R. R. Effect of acute alcohol intoxication on granulocyte mobilization and kinetics. *Blood* 52:551-559, 1979.
21. Goebel, K. M., Goebel, F. D., Schubotz, R., and Schneider, J. Red cell metabolic and membrane features in haemolytic anaemia of alcoholic liver disease (Zieve's syndrome). *Br. J. Haematol.* 35:573-585, 1977.
22. Hall, C. A. The macrocytosis of liver disease. *J. Lab. Clin. Med.* 48:345-355, 1956.
23. Halsted, C. H., Robles, E. A., and Mezey, E. Intestinal malabsorption in folate-deficient alcoholics. *Gastroenterology* 64:526-532, 1973.
24. Herbert, V. Hematologic complications of alcoholism. *Semin. Hemat.* 17:83-164, 1980.
25. Herbert, V., Zalusky, R., and Davidson, C. S. Correlation of folate deficiency with alcoholism and associated macrocytosis, anemia and liver disease. *Ann. Intern. Med.* 58:977-988, 1963.
26. Hillman, R. S., McGuffin, R., and Campbell, C. Alcohol interference with the folate enterohepatic cycle. *Trans. Assoc. Am. Physicians* 91:145-156, 1978.
27. Hines, J. D. Reversible megaloblastic and sideroblastic marrow abnormalities in alcoholic patients. *Br. J. Haematol.* 16:87-101, 1969.
28. Hines, J. D. Hematologic abnormalities involving vitamin B_6 and folate metabolism in alcoholic subjects. *Ann. N.Y. Acad. Sci.* 252:316-327, 1975.
29. Hines, J. D., and Cowan, D. H. Studies on the pathogenesis of alcohol-induced sideroblastic bone-marrow abnormalities. *N. Engl. J. Med.* 283:441-446, 1970.
30. Hines, J. D., and Cowan, D. H. Anemia in alcoholism. In: *Drugs and Hematologic Reaction*, Dimitrov, N. V. and Nodine, J. H. (eds.). Grune & Stratton: New York, 1974.
31. Hotz, H. W. Lebercirrhose und hämatopoese. *Ergebn. Inn. Med. Kinderheilkd.* 64:198-286, 1944.
32. Jandl, J. H. The anemia of liver disease: Observations on its mechanism. *J. Clin. Invest.* 34:390-404, 1955.
33. Jarrold, T., and Vilter, R. W. Hematologic observations in patients with chronic hepatic insufficiency. *J. Clin. Invest.* 28:286-292, 1949.
34. Jarrold, T., Will, J. T., Davies, A. R., Duffey, P. H., and Bramschreiber, J. L. Bone marrow-erythroid morphology in alcoholic patients. *Am. J. Clin. Nutr.* 20:716-722, 1967.
35. Leevy, C. M., Baker, H., TenHove, W., Frank, O., and Cherrick, C. M. B-complex vitamins in liver disease of the alcoholic. *Am. J. Clin. Nutr.* 17:339-346, 1965.
36. Lindenbaum, J., and Hargrove, R. L. Thrombocytopenia in alcoholics. *Ann. Intern. Med.* 68:526-532, 1968.
37. Lindenbaum, J., and Lieber, C. S. Hematologic effects of alcohol in man in the absence of nutritional deficiency. *N. Engl. J. Med.* 281:333-338, 1969.
38. Liu, Y. K. Phagocytic capacity of reticuloendothelial system in alcoholics. *J. Reticuloendothel. Soc.* 25:605-613, 1979.
39. Louria, D. B. Susceptibility to infection during experimental alcohol intoxication. *Trans. Assoc. Am. Physicians* 76:102-110, 1963.
40. Lundy, J., Raaf, J. H., Deakins, S., Wanebo, H. J., Jacobs, D. A., Tsung-dao L., Jacobowitz, D., Spear, C., and Oettgen, H. F. The acute and chronic effects of alcohol on the human immune system. *Surg. Gynecol. Obstet.* 141:212-218, 1975.
41. McCurdy, P. R., Pierce, L. E., and Rath, C. E. Abnormal bone marrow morphology in acute alcoholism. *N. Engl. J. Med.* 266:505-507, 1962.
42. Moore, M. R., Beattie, A. D., Thompson, G. G., and Goldberg, A. Depression of

delta-aminolaevulinic acid dehydrase activity by ethanol in man and rat. *Clin. Sci.* 40: 81-88, 1971.

43. Morin, J., and Porte, P. Macrocytose erythrocytaire chez les ethyliques. *Nouv. Presse. Med.* 5:273, 1976.

44. Movitt, E. R. Megaloblastic bone marrow in liver disease. *Am. J. Med.* 7:145-194, 1949.

45. Movitt, E. R. Megaloblastic erythropoiesis in patients with cirrhosis of the liver. *Blood* 5:468-477, 1950.

46. Myrhed, M., Berglund, L., and Böttiger, L. E. Alcohol consumption and hematology. *Acta. Med. Scand.* 202:11-15, 1977.

47. Pickrell, K. L. The effect of alcohol intoxication and ether anesthesia in resistance to pneumococcal infection. *Bull. Johns Hopkins Hosp.* 63:238-260, 1938.

48. Pierce, H. I., McGuffin, R. G., and Hillman, R. S. Clinical studies in alcoholic sideroblastosis. *Arch. Intern. Med.* 136:283-289, 1976.

49. Richens, A., and Waters, A. H. Acute effect of phenytoin on serum folate concentration. *Proc. Brit. Pharmacol. Soc.* 136:283-289, 1971.

50. Samson, D., Halliday, D., and Chanarin, I. Enhancement of bilirubin clearance and hepatic haem turnover by ethanol. *Lancet* ii:256, 1976.

51. Sheehy, T. W., and Berman, A. The anemia of cirrhosis. *J. Lab. Clin. Med.* 56:72-82, 1960.

52. Sullivan, L. W., and Herbert, V. Suppression of hematopoiesis by ethanol. *J. Clin. Invest.* 43:2048-2062, 1964.

53. Unger, K. W., and Johnson, D., Jr. Red blood cell mean corpuscular volume: A potential indicator of alcohol usage in a working population. *Am. J. Med. Sci.* 267:281-289, 1974.

54. Wallerstedt, S., Cederblad, G., Korsan-bengtsen, K., and Olsson, R. Coagulation factors and other plasma proteins during abstinence after heavy alcohol consumption in chronic alcoholics. *Scand. J. Gastroenterol.* 12:649-655, 1977.

55. Waters, A. H., Morley, A. A., and Rankin, J. G. Effect of alcohol on haemopoiesis. *Br. Med. J.* 2:1565-1568, 1966.

56. Wickramasinghe, S. N., and Saunders, J. E. Results of three years' experience with the deoxyuridine suppression test. *Acta Haematol.* 58:193-206, 1977.

57. Williams, I. R., and Girdwood, R. H. The folate status of alcoholics. *Scott. Med. J.* 15:285-288, 1970.

58. Wintrobe, M. M. *Clinical Hematology* (2nd ed.). Lea & Febiger: Philadelphia, 1946.

59. Wintrobe, M. M., and Shumacker, H. S. The occurrence of macrocytic anemia in association with disorder of the liver together with a consideration of the relation of this anemia to pernicious anemia. *Bull. Johns Hopkins Hosp.* 52:387-404, 1933.

60. Wu, A., Chanarin, I., and Levi, A. J. Macrocyosis of chronic alcoholism. *Lancet* 1:829-831, 1974.

61. Wu, A., Chanarin, I., Slavin, G., and Levi, A. J. Folate deficiency in the alcoholic — Its relationship to clinical and haematological abnormalities, liver disease and folate status. *Br. J. Haematol.* 29:469-478, 1975.

62. Yeung, K. Y., Klug, P. P., Brower, M., and Lessin, L. S. Mechanism of alcohol-induced vacuolization in human bone marrow cells. *Blood* 42:998, 1973.

63. Young, G. P., van der Weyden, M. B., Rose, I. S., and Dudley, F. J. Lymphopenic and lymphocyte transformation in alcoholics. *Experientia* 35:268-269, 1979.

64. Zieve, L. Jaundice, hyperlipemia and hemolytic anemia: A heretofore unrecognized syndrome associated with alcoholic fatty liver and cirrhosis. *Ann. Intern. Med.* 48: 471-496, 1958.

22

HOSSAM E. FADEL, MD, Medical College of Georgia, Augusta, Georgia
HAMID A. HADI, MD, Medical College of Georgia, Augusta, Georgia

ALCOHOL EFFECTS ON THE REPRODUCTIVE FUNCTION

ALTHOUGH MANY PApers have been written about alcohol and its effect on various aspects of human organism, very little research has been conducted regarding the effects of alcohol on reproductive functions, especially in females. The only exception has been the numerous studies of ethanol effects in the pregnant myometrium that resulted in its use for the supression of preterm labor.

Old publications regarding the effect of alcohol on male and female reproductive functional capacity were speculative rather than factual. It is only in the last two decades that increasing attention has been directed to this subject and interesting papers appeared concerning the effect of alcohol on the gonads and hormones, which may directly or indirectly interfere with reproductive function. A brief review of the currently available information on this topic is presented.

Hossam E. Fadel, MD, Professor and Chief of Maternal-Fetal Medicine, Department of Obstetrics and Gynecology, Medical College of Georgia, Augusta, Georgia.

Hamid A. Hadi, MD, Instructor and Fellow in Maternal-Fetal Medicine, Department of Obstetrics and Gynecology, Medical College of Georgia, Augusta, Georgia.

EFFECT OF ETHANOL ON MALE GONADS AND HORMONES

Hypogonadism is a common feature in alcoholic men and is manifested by a high prevalence (70-80%) of decreased libido and/or impotence, and testicular atrophy and infertility (70-80%) [30].

Impotence is commonly observed in acute alcoholism, whereas hyperestrogenism is a relatively common manifestation of chronic alcoholism. Evidence of female escutcheon develops in about 50%, gynecomastia in 20%, and palmar erythema and spider angiomata in 40 to 50% of chronic alcoholic men, [30]. This hyperestrogenic state was thought to be the result of irreversible liver disease. However, sexual dysfunction does occur early in the course of chronic alcoholism both in men and experimental animals, in the absence of liver damage [30].

Acute or chronic alcohol consumption can interfere with spermatogenesis. There are significant effects on the number, morphology, and motility of the spermatozoa, and damage of testicular germinal epithelium, along with alterations in pituitary-gonad hormones and gonadal enzymes. These are discussed in the following sections.

Spermatogenesis

After acute ethanol consumption (0.4-0.8 g/kg) a variety of spermatozoal morphological abnormalities, such as breakage of the head, distention of the midsection, and curling of the tail, can be observed [30]. These changes may lead to sterility or to defective offspring. Observations both in humans and animals have shown that ethanol decreases sperm motility [3, 11]. This decrease in sperm motility is possibly caused by an increased amount of mucus in the semen as a result of alcohol irritation of the prostate gland [25].

Chronic consumption of alcohol results initially in a reduction of seminiferous tubular diameter and reduction and damage of tubular germinal epithelium, so that fewer completely developed spermatozoa are produced from spermatids [2, 20, 32]. Those that are produced usually lack normal tails. As a result, fewer spermatozoa are found in the tubules and the tubules become filled with spermatids. In the later stages those spermatids remaining in the narrowed tubules ultimately undergo degeneration and aspermia results. This alcohol-induced aspermia is observed in both men and animals [1, 21].

Vitamin A and zinc deficiency are known to occur in chronic alcoholics, and have been implicated in the hypogonadism observed in male alcoholics [22]. It seems that retinal is essential for normal testicular function. The conversion of retinol (the alcohol form of vitamin A) to retinal is mediated by the zinc metallenyzme alcohol dehydrogenase and its formation can be inhibited by vitamin A and/or zinc deficiency [22].

Hormonal Levels

Ethanol affects the hypothalamus-pituitary axis. There have been reports of inadequate secretion of both follicle-stimulating hormone (FSH) and luteinizing hormone (LH) in response to clomiphene in alcoholic individuals [30]. Further, LH response to leuteinizing hormone–releasing hormone (LH-RH) in these individuals was reported to be inadequate. These seem to be direct effects of ethanol on the hypothalamus-pituitary axis. More recently [36], using radioimmunoassay methods, the basal levels of pituitary hormones and the change in their concentration after administration of hypothalamic releasing hormones during periods of acute ethanol intoxication and withdrawal have been studied in a group of male and female volunteers. During acute ethanol intoxication (1.5 g of ethanol/kg body weight), there were no significant changes in the basal levels of plasma thyroid-stimulating hormone (TSH), prolactin (PRL), LH, and testosterone in both males and females. The secretion of growth hormone (GH) was suppressed in females but not in males. Moreover, there was no change in the response of TSH or LH to the injection of thyroid releasing hormone (TRH) and (LH-RH) respectively in either males or females. The response of PRL to TRH was exaggerated [36].

During the period of ethanol withdrawal (the hangover period), both the levels of TSH and LH and their responses to TRH and LH-RH remained unchanged. However, the response of PRL to TRH was completely blocked both in males and females. Levels of PRL and GH were also within normal limits in this period. In males, during the withdrawal period, unlike acute intoxication, plasma testosterone concentration was significantly decreased. Toward the end of the withdrawal period, testosterone levels increased significantly, but most of the values remained within the normal limits. Throughout the experimental period the plasma concentration of thyroid hormones was not changed. The most obvious endocrine finding during the hangover period, and the more severe alcohol withdrawal syndrome, was a decreased response of PRL secretion to TRH. Dopamine is known to inhibit the secretion of PRL. It is speculated that abnormal response of PRL to TRH reflects increased dopaminogenic activity in the hypothalamus during the ethanol withdrawal period.

Mendelson [24] studied the levels of plasma testosterone and LH in 16 adult males during acute ethanol intoxication and found decreased testosterone levels but an increased surge of LH. Furthermore, in chronic alcoholic men, and in animals chronically treated with ethanol, the gonads were reported to be less responsive to human chorionic gonadotropin (HCG), and the levels of plasma testosterone were found to be low. This reduction of plasma testosterone levels in chronic alcoholics along with the decreased responsiveness to HCG are consistent with Leydig cell damage [20, 30]. As a result of clinical observations and experiments on animals, it is suggested that ethanol exerts a dual effect on plasma testosterone levels both locally on the gonads and centrally on the hypothalamus-pituitary axis.

Testicular Steroidogenesis. The effects of ethanol on testosterone secretion in males have been investigated, yet a clear picture has not emerged. A decrease in testosterone levels during alcohol intoxication was reported in some studies [16, 30], but not in others [36]. On the other hand, testosterone levels were reported to decrease in the hangover period, and in chronic alcoholics [36]. In rats, a dose-dependent fall in plasma testosterone was shown, and perfusion of isolated rat testes with ethanol over a dose range of 50 to 300 mg/dl resulted in suppression of testosterone secretion by as much as 75% [30].

The specific mechanism by which ethanol adversely affects steroidogenesis is unknown. This could result from its central action on the hypothalamus-pituitary axis with decrease of the frequency and amplitude of gonadotropin secretory surge [30]. It could also be due to alteration in vitamin A metabolism, limiting the availability of retinal, as discussed. At present, many investigations are directed to finding out if ethanol effects are mediated through changes in the enzymes involved in steriodogenesis. Ethanol is known to induce microsomal enzymes that are involved in the synthesis of testosterone from pregnenolone [9]. More recently, the effects of ethanol on four testicular enzymes (17 alpha-hydroxylase; 17,20-lyase; 3 beta-hydroxysteroid dehydrogenase-isomerase; and 17 beta-hydroxysteroid dehydrogenase) have been studied in rats. Ethanol was shown to increase the activity of 17 alpha-hydroxylase and 17,20-lyase, to have no effect on the activity of 17 beta-hydroxysteriod dehydrogenase, and to cause reduction of 3 beta-hydroxysteroid dehydrogenase-isomerase activity, the rate-limiting step in testosterone production from pregnenolone [9]. It has been postulated that inhibition of this enzyme is caused by limiting the availability of the cofactor nicotinamide-adenine dinucleotide (NAD), since the oxidation of ethanol (to acetaldehyde) increases the ratio of NADH to NAD [9]. The increase in this ratio as a result of chronic ethanol administration might also promote the synthesis of metabolites of progesterone such as 20 alpha-reduced compounds, which have been reported to be inhibitors of some of the enzymes involved in testosterone synthesis [5]. Also it was found that acetaldehyde (the metabolic end product of ethanol) suppresses the conversion of androstenedione to testosterone by competetive inhibition of the enzyme 17 beta-hydroxysteroid oxidoreductase [10]. This also suggests that at least some of the ethanol effects might be due to metabolite acetaldehyde rather than the ethanol itself.

EFFECT OF ALCOHOL ON FEMALE REPRODUCTION

In spite of increasing alcohol abuse in women there have been very few studies on the effect of ethanol on female sexuality and reproductive function. With the recent development of vaginal photoplethysmography, a technique to measure the vaginal blood flow, it became possible to monitor female sexual responsiveness. Wilson and Lawson [34, 35] found a dose-related decrease in vaginal blood flow as ethanol levels in serum increased, although these women reported more sexual arousal. This suggests that subjective and objective measures of sexual arousal are not directly related in women.

Chronic use of alcohol in women has been related to menstrual disorders [4, 26], infertility [19, 33], and repeated miscarriages [33]. The mechanism by which ethanol causes these problems is unknown. Animal studies show that excessive exposure to alcohol can result in comparable effects. When female rats were placed on a 7-week alcohol diet, their ovaries, uteri, and fallopian tubes became atrophic. Histologic examination of the ovaries demonstrated the absence of well-developed follicles, corpora lutea, corpora hemorrhagica, and secretory granulosa cells [31]. Also, the plasma estradiol and progesterone levels were markedly reduced. Furthermore, inhibition of ovulation in rats was shown to occur as the result of alcohol administration [6]. The infusion of 95% alcohol inhibited the spontaneous release of LH but did not affect LH release in response to LH-RH, suggesting that alcohol inhibited ovulation by affecting the hypothalamic pituitary axis [6, 18]. However, inhibition of ovulation is not regularly seen in other animal species. Acute administration of ethanol (3.9 g/kg, 10% per os) to rabbits 30 minutes prior to mating, was reported to prevent conception, but not ovulation [7]. Furthermore, exposure of mice to an alcohol diet prior to and/or during pregnancy has been shown to increase resorption (the equivalent of abortion in humans) [8, 28].

McNamee [23] studied the effect of acute alcohol intake on the serum levels of FSH, LH, PRL, and gonadal steriods in 80 normal women whose mean age was 28 years. None of these women gave a history of alcohol abuse or oral contraceptive use and they were all in their early follicular phase of menstruation. Alcohol was given in the form of vodka (65.5% proof) at a dosage of 2.8 ml/kg body weight. Because of the episodic nature of gonadotropin secretion, blood samples were drawn every 20 minutes through an indwelling catheter. There was no change in serum FSH, LH, or PRL levels, and no consistent effects on serum progesterone, estradiol, or testosterone were observed.

Ethanol effects on ovarian function may be local. They might be mediated by a change in the enzymatic activity of gonadal cells. In a recent study, ovarian lactic dehydrogenase (LDH) content was reduced after intraperitoneal injection of ethanol in pregnant mice [27].

It is well known that alcohol can cause fetal malformations [17] (see Chapter 23). The mechanism by which these malformations occur are not yet clear. However, the complex actions of ethanol on all levels of reproductive function, hypothalamic, pituitary, and gonadal, raise the possibility that changes in the hormonal milieu before or during pregnancy, or damage to the spermatozoa of ova may be the cause of these malformations. It is clear from this brief review that little is actually known and that some of the earlier observations have not been substantiated in subsequent studies. This emphasizes the need for a much more detailed study of the effects of alcohol on the various reproductive functions, especially in the human female.

Effect on the Pregnant Uterus

Ethanol has been known for sometime to be capable of suppressing uterine contraction and hence was used for the inhibition of threatened preterm labor [12, 14]. This tocolytic effect is thought to be due to the inhibition of oxytocin release from the neurohypophysis. Suppression of oxytocin release in response to suckling has been shown to occur in lactating rabbits, rats, and women [13, 15]. Ethanol also inhibits the release of the antidiuretic hormone (ADH) from the posterior pituitary.

The mechanism by which ethanol exerts its action on neurohypophysial function is unknown. Possibly it inhibits hormonal release through a general CNS depression, by inhibition of the synaptic transmission of afferent impulses to the magnocellular neurones of the paraventricular and supraoptic nuclei of the hypothalamus, or by inhibition of the release mechanism at the nerve ending or the transmission of impulses along the axons from the nuclei to the nerve terminals in the hypophysis [37].

It has been shown that the fetus secretes a significant amount of oxytocin and ADH during labor, and that these hormones may have a role in the initiation of parturition [30]. It is likely that ethanol infused into the mother rapidly crosses the placenta and exerts the same inhibiting effect on the release of the fetal neurohypophysial hormones, thus interfering with labor [14].

In addition to its central actions, ethanol may suppress uterine contraction through any of several possibly peripheral mechanisms. Ethanol may interfere with the release of uterine stimulants such as prostaglandins or norepinephrine, may release inhibitory substances, or may have a direct action on the myometruim. Metabolic changes due to alcohol oxidation may alter the contractile potential of the myometruim [14].

Ethanol has been reported to be effective in the management of patients with threatened preterm labor. Postponement of delivery in two groups of patients treated with ethanol and placebo was 81% and 38% respectively [37]. Ethanol is recommended for suppression of preterm labor in the form of 10% solution (vol/vol) in 5% detrose in water and is given intravenously as a loading dose at a rate of 7.5 ml/kg body weight/h for 2 hours, followed by a maintenance dose of 1.5 ml/kg body weight/h for 10 hours or more. If premature labor recurs after ethanol infusion, up to two additional courses of intravenous ethanol is permitted.

Unfortunately the clinical use of ethanol under such circumstances has been associated with both maternal and fetal side effects. This resulted in a decline of its use in many centers as the beta-mimetics were introduced as tocolytic agents.

In 1980, the Food and Drug Administration approved the beta-mimetic ritodrine for the specific purpose of suppression of preterm labor, resulting in the almost complete abandonment of ethanol use for this indication.

REFERENCES

1. Anderson, R. A., Beyler, S. A., and Zanereld, L. J. D. Alterations of male reproductive induced by chronic ingestion of ethanol: Development of an animal model. *Fertil. Steril.* 30:103–105, 1978.
2. Arlit, A. A., and Wells, M. G. The effect of alcohol on the reproductive tissue. *J. Exp. Med.* 26:769–778, 1917.
3. Beckman, L. J. Reported effects of alcohol on the sexual feelings and behavior of alcoholic and nonalcoholic women. *J. Stud. Alcohol* 40:272–282, 1979.
4. Benedek, T. G. Food and drink as aphrodisiacs. *Sex. Behav.* 2:5–10, 1972.
5. Betz, G., Tsai, P., and Weakley, R. Heterogeneity of cytochrome P-450 in rat testes microsomes. *J. Bio. Chem.* 251:2839–2841, 1976.
6. Blake, C. A. Localization of inhibitory actions of ovulation-blocking drugs or release of luteinizing hormone in ovarictomized rats. *Endocrinology* 95:999–1004, 1974.
7. Chandhurry, R. R., and Mathews, M. Effect of alcohol in the fertility of female rabbits. *J. Endocrinol.* 34:275–276, 1966.
8. Chernoff, G. F. The fetal alcohol syndrome in mice: An animal model. *Teratology* 15:223–229, 1977.
9. Chiao, Y. B., Johnston, D. E., Judith, S., Gavaler, B. S., and Van Thiel, D. H. Effects on chronic alcohol feeding on testosterone content of enzymes required for testosteronogenesis. *Alcoholism: Clin. Exp. Res.* 5:230–236, 1981.
10. Cicero, T. J., Bell, R. D., and Meyer, E. Effects of ethanol on testicular steroidogenesis: Mechanism of action. *Drug Alcohol Depend.* 6:50–51, 1980.
11. Doepfmer, R., and Hinckers, H. J. Zur frage der keimschadigung im akuten rausch. *Z. Haut Geschleshtshr* 39:94–107, 1965.
12. Fadel, H. E. Preterm labor. In: *Obstetrics Emergencies for the Primary Physician,* Fadel, H. E. (ed.). Addison-Wesley: Menlo Park, Calif., 1982.
13. Fuchs, A. R., and Dawood, M. Y. Oxytocin levels and uterine activity during parturition and lactations in rabbits. *Program Endocr. Soc. Ann. Mtg. Abstract* 227: 188, 1978.
14. Fuchs, A. R., and Fuchs, F. Ethanol for prevention of preterm birth. *Seminars Perinatology* 3:236–251, 1981.
15. Fuchs, A. R., and Wagner, G. Effect of alcohol on the release of oxytocin. *Nature* 198:92, 1963.
16. Gorden, G. G., Altman, K., Southren, L. A., Rubin, E., and Lieber, C. Effect of alcohol (ethanol) administration on sex hormones in normal men. *N. Eng. J. Med.* 295-793, 1976.
17. Hill, M. R., and Tennyson, L. M. An historical review and longitudinal study of an infant with the fetal alcohol syndrome. In: *Alcoholism: A Prespective,* Fathy, M. and Tyner, S. (eds.). PJD Publications: New York, 1980.
18. Kieffer, J. D., and Ketchel, M. Blockage of ovulation in the rats by ethanol. *Acta Endocrinol.* 65:117–124, 1970.
19. Kinsey, B. A. Psychological factors in alcoholic women from a state hospital sample. *Am. J. Psychiatry,* 124:1463–1466, 1968.

20. Klaussen, R. W., and Persaud, T. V. N. Influence of alcohol on the reproductive system of male rat. *Int. J. Fertil.* 23:176-184, 1978.

21. Lester, R., and Van Thiel, D. H. Gonadol function in chronic alcoholism. *Adv. Exp. Med. Biol.* 85A: 399-414, 1977.

22. McClain, C. J., Van Thiel, D. H., Parker, S., Badzin, L. K., and Gilbert, H. Zinc, vitamin A and retinol-binding protein in chronic alcoholics: A possible mechanism for night blindness and hypogonadism. *Alcoholism: Clin. Exp. Res.* 3:135-141, 1979.

23. McNamee, B., Grant, J., Ratcliffe, J., et al. Lack of effect of alcohol on pituitary-gonadol hormones in women. *Bri. J. Addict.* 74:316-317, 1979.

24. Mendelson, J. H., Mello, N. K., and Ellingboe, J. Effect of acute alcohol intake on pituitary gonadol hormones in normal human males. *J. Pharm. Exp. Therapeut.* 202:676-682, 1977.

25. Molnar, J., and Papp, G. Alkohal als moglicher schleimforderner faktor in samen. *Andrologie* 5:105-106, 1973.

26. Podalsky, E. The alcoholic woman and premenstrual tension. *J. Am. Med. Women's Assoc.* 18:816-818, 1963.

27. Prasad, R., Kaufman, R. H., and Prasad, N. Effect of maternal alcohol exposure of fetal ovarian lactate dehydrogenase. *Obstet. Gynecol.* 52:318-320, 1978.

28. Randall, C. L., Taylor, W. J., and Walker, W. D. Ethanol-induced malformations in mice. *Alcoholism: Clin. Exp. Res.* 1:219-223, 1977.

29. Smith, S. Metabolic consequences of acute ethanol intoxication. In: *Alcoholism — A Prespective,* Fathy, M. and Tyner, S. (eds.). PJD Publications: New York, 1980.

30. Van Thiel, D. H., Gavaler, J. S., Eagon, P., and Lester, R. Effect of alcohol on gonadol function. *Drug Alcohol Depend.* 6:41-42, 1980.

31. Van Thiel, D. H., Gavaler, J. S., and Lester, R.: Alcohol-induced ovarian failure in the rat. *J. Clin. Inves.* 61:624-632, 1978.

32. Van Thiel, D. H., Gavaler, J. S., Lester, R., and Goodman, M. D. Alcohol-induced testicular atrophy: An experimental model for hypogonadism occurring in chronic alcoholic men. *Metabolism* 24:1015-1019, 1975.

33. Wilsnack, S. C. Sex role identity in female alcoholism. *J. Abnorm. Psychol.* 82:253-261, 1973.

34. Wilson, G. T., and Lawson, D. M. Effects of alcohol on sexual arousal in women. *J. Abnorm. Psychol.* 85:489-497, 1976.

35. Wilson, G. T., and Lawson, D. M. Expectancies, alcohol and sexual arousal in women. *J. Abnorm. Psychol.* 87:358-367, 1978.

36. Ylikahri, R. H. Hormonal changes during alcohol intoxication and withdrawal. *Drug Alcohol Depend.* 6:42-43, 1980.

37. Zlatnik, F., and Fuchs, F. A controlled study of ethanol in threatened premature labor. *Am. J. Obstet. Gynecol.* 112:610-612, 1972.

23

HENRY L. ROSETT, MD, Boston University School of Medicine
LYN WEINER, MPH, Boston University School of Medicine

EFFECTS OF ALCOHOL ON THE FETUS

SINCE CLASSICAL ANtiquity the relationship between heavy alcohol use during pregnancy and abnormal development of offspring has been suspected. Aristotle wrote that "foolish, drunken or harebrained women for the most part bring forth children like unto themselves, morose and languid." Observations during the Gin Epidemic in England 250 years ago caused the College of Physicians to petition Parliament for control of the distillation trade, calling gin a cause of "weak, feeble and distempered children." Writers on temperance in the 19th century attributed a wide range of pathology in children to their parents' drinking. The careful studies of this period were discredited, together with the exaggerated propaganda tracts, after the repeal of Prohibition [36].

In 1968, Lemoine et al. [18] described a pattern of malformations among 127 offspring from 69 French families in which there was chronic alcoholism. In America, awareness of this problem was stimulated by observations by Ulleland et al. [34] that six infants who failed to thrive all had mothers who were chronic alcoholics. Jones and Smith recognized a common pattern of malformations

---

Henry L. Rosett, MD, Associate Professor of Psychiatry and Obstetrics and Gynecology, Boston University School of Medicine, Boston, Massachusetts.

Lyn Weiner, MPH, Instructor in Psychiatry, Boston University School of Medicine, Boston, Massachusetts.

among infants comparable to that described by Lemoine. They called this pattern the Fetal Alcohol Syndrome (FAS) [13, 14].

DIAGNOSIS OF THE FETAL ALCOHOL SYNDROME

The Fetal Alcohol Study Group of the Research Society on Alcoholism has recommended that the diagnosis of FAS be made only when the patient has signs in each of the three following categories [29]:

1. Prenatal and/or postnatal growth retardation (weight, length, and/or head circumference below the 10th percentile when corrected for gestational age)
2. Central nervous system involvement (signs of neurological abnormality, developmental delay, or intellectual impairment)
3. Characteristic facial dysmorphology with at least two of these three signs: (a) microcephaly (head circumference below the 3rd percentile); (b) micropthalmia and/or short palpebral fissures; (c) poorly developed philtrum, thin upper lip, and flattening of the maxillary area

Clinical experience and epidemiologic findings suggest a wide range of effects of alcohol on the developing embryo and fetus with the FAS at the far end of the spectrum. In the absence of the full FAS, the most accurate descriptive term might be "possible fetal alcohol effects." Because of similarities in dysmorphology, a careful history is needed about use of other drugs, cigarette smoking, nutrition, and genetics before the abnormality can be attributed to maternal alcohol consumption. In some cases, the diagnosis of FAS can be made in the neonate; in others, postnatal growth retardation and developmental and intellectual delay may not be apparent before 1 or 2 years. Characteristic facial anomalies may be more easily discerned after the newborn period.

ANIMAL MODELS

Clinical and epidemiologic studies inherently are limited by the imprecision of self-reports of alcohol consumption due to impaired recall and day-to-day variability of drinking. Alcohol use may also potentiate adverse effects of associated behaviors (i.e., cigarette smoking, use of other drugs, poor eating habits). Animal models permit study of the sensitivity to ethanol of various organ systems at different stages of pregnancy in the absence of other risk factors [28].

Research has now been conducted in many different species, including the mouse [2, 23], rat [6, 24], beagle dog [8], swine [5], and monkey [12]. Each species has specific advantages for different aspects of FAS research: duration of gestation, cost, pharmacodynamics of alcohol, longevity, brain development, and behavioral capabilities.

A beagle dog model of the FAS, developed by Ellis and Pick [8], demonstrates a dose-response relationship when ethanol is administered by intragastric tube throughout gestation. At a daily dose of 5.66 g/kg, fertilization and implantation occurred but no fetal differentiation was observed. A daily dose of 4.71 g/kg resulted in spontaneous abortion of dead fetuses or uterine retention of immature fetuses. Bitches receiving a dose of 4.2 g/kg daily delivered 49 viable offspring with severe growth retardation and malformations (e.g., absence of one kidney or cleft palate). Growth retardation without anomalies was found when bitches were administered 3.0 and 3.6 g/kg daily. Bitches fed 2.4 g/kg daily delivered more stillbirths; however, their viable offspring were not smaller than those born to the controls.

Miniature swine, used in alcoholism research by Dexter et al. [5], consume ethanol voluntarily and continue heavy drinking for many years. Growth retardation, anomalie rates, and stillbirth rates were significantly higher among piglets born to ethanol-exposed dams as compared with controls. Second-litter piglets were more severely affected than those in the first litters.

Diaz and Samson [6] administered ethanol via intragastric cannulas to rat pups 4 to 7 days postpartum. Brain weight among pups fed alcohol was 19% smaller than control pups fed equicaloric sucrose, although total body weight was not different. The period of rapid brain growth that occurs in the rat pup during the first few days postpartum is comparable to that occurring during the third trimester in humans.

Behavioral changes and developmental delays in rat pups have been observed in the absence of morphological abnormalities when alcohol was administered at critical stages of pregnancy [24]. Changes in the organization of mossy fibers in the hippocampus of rats exposed to ethanol in utero [37] are consistent with observations of hyperactivity among rat offspring.

THE MATERNAL-PLACENTAL-FETAL SYSTEM

Ethanol has the capacity to cause a variety of metabolic and physiological disturbances with the potential for adversely affecting fetal development. While the mother, placenta, and fetus interact as a dynamic system, it is helpful to consider the effects of alcohol in terms of mechanisms that directly affect the fetus and those that have their primary effects on maternal metabolism and physiology. A detailed review of research on the effects on mother, placenta, and fetus has been published [25]; cited below are brief references to some of the studies.

Fetal Physiology and Metabolism

The effect of ethanol infusion on maternal and fetal acid-base balance was investigated in pregnant ewes by Mann et al. [19]. Fetal metabolic acidosis observed during the alcohol infusion worsened during the postinfusion period. The fetal electroencephalogram (EEG) showed a decrease in amplitude and a slowing of the dominant rhythm as the blood alcohol concentration increased and became isoelectric during the postinfusion period associated with severe fetal acidosis. Horiguchi et al. [11] reported similar findings with 13 pregnant rhesus monkeys.

Exposure of the fetal central nervous system (CNS) to moderate or high concentrations of ethanol probably has different effects at different gestational stages, with damage at the earliest stages of embryonic growth incompatible with life. Clarren et al. [3] presented neuropathological data on brains of four human neonates exposed during the first trimester to high peak concentrations of ethanol. The most frequent finding was leptomeningeal neuroglial heterotopia, a sheet of aberrant neural and glial tissue covering part of the brain surface.

Havlicek et al. [9] compared EEG frequency spectrum characteristics of sleep states in infants of alcoholic mothers with those of infants matched for postconceptual age born to healthy mothers. Two-hour sleep polygraphy sessions demonstrated that infants of alcoholic mothers had more difficulty reaching quiet sleep, were more restless, and were more easily disturbed. At Boston City Hospital 31 infants were studied to determine the extent to which high blood alcohol concentrations in early or late stages of gestation affect 24-hour distribution of sleep-awake states on the third day of life [27]. Pilot observations suggest that heavy maternal consumption of alcohol, when continued throughout pregnancy, is associated with a disturbance of sleep-awake state distribution. Cessation of heavy drinking during pregnancy improves the physiological competence of the newborn to regulate sleep-awake states and may facilitate interaction between mother and infant.

Maternal Physiology and Metabolism

Chronic heavy alcohol consumption can adversely affect almost every organ system in the body. Alcohol-induced metabolic disturbances in the mother, such as alcohol hypoglycemia, alcohol ketoacidosis, alterations in lactate, uric acid, and lipid metabolism, or changes in the metabolism of individual amino acids may all have effects on the fetus.

Seven episodes of severe ketoacidosis have been reported in six nondiabetic patients who indulged in heavy chronic alcohol use and in binges [4]. Fetal development may also be adversely affected by alterations in the maternal metabolism of minerals and vitamins [25]. Endocrine production by both the mother and the fetus can be affected [15, 35].

ASSOCIATED RISK FACTORS

Nutrition

Utilization of nutrients may be impaired by the effects of alcohol on intestinal absorption, liver function, urinary excretion of vitamins and trace minerals, disturbances of intermediate metabolism, and gastrointestinal disturbances such as vomiting and diarrhea. Naeye et al. [20] present evidence that undernutrition has its greatest effect on fetal growth in late gestation. Dobbing [7] reports that two growth spurts represent periods of critical vulnerability for the development of the human brain. The first period is between the 12th and 18th gestational week, the time of greatest neuronal multiplication. The second spurt of brain growth begins during the third trimester and continues during the first 18 months of life. During this time there is an explosive increase in dendritic complexity with establishment of synaptic connections. Restriction of brain growth due to malnutrition can be compensated following dietary improvement [20]. The possibility of rebound growth following cessation of intrauterine ethanol exposure may also exist.

Nicotine and Other Drugs

The use of cigarettes and other drugs, such as heroin, methadone, LSD, and barbiturates, has been associated with a higher incidence of low birth weight infants and increased perinatal mortality. There is a well-known association between heavy drinking and heavy smoking. In addition, heavier drinkers are more likely to have used other drugs. Prospective studies, currently underway, must investigate the impact of each of these substances separately and synergistically.

A pattern of congenital malformations, growth deficiency, and retarded mental development, which may resemble the Fetal Alcohol Syndrome, has been observed in neonates exposed in utero to antiepileptic drugs [10].

Disulfiram

Disulfiram (Antabuse), which may be useful as an adjunct to the treatment of alcoholism, should not be prescribed during pregnancy. A prospective cohort of five pregnancies in which there was maternal exposure to between 250 mg and 500 mg of disulfiram daily revealed one spontaneous abortion in the second month, two infants with club feet, and two normal babies [32]. A teratogen surveillance program identified two infants with severe limb-reduction anomalies whose mothers had been maintained on disulfiram during the first trimester of pregnancy [21]. Neither mother was exposed to alcohol or any other established teratogen during this trimester. One infant had multiple anomalies, including radial aplasia, vertebral fusion, and tracheoesophogeal fistula (Vacterl syndrome), while the other had phocomelia of the lower extremities. A cohort of 1,320 histories during the same time frame revealed no other exposures to disulfiram. Disulfiram inhibits several enzymes, including aldehyde dehydrogenase, needed for oxidation of acetaldehyde, and dopamine betahydroxylase, which catalyzes the conversion of dopamine to norepinephrine [33]. In addition, the three major metabolites of disulfiram, carbon disulfide, diethylamine, and diethyldithiocarbamate have been found to be neurotoxic [22].

Paternal Drinking

The possibility that heavy alcohol consumption by the male can cause genetic damage has been the subject of speculation for over 200 years. The mutagenic role of ethanol in male mice was studied by Badr and Badr [1], who administered ethanol in doses of 1.24 g/kg by gastric tube to male mice for 3 consecutive days. There was a two- to four-fold increase in the number of dead implants found in females mated to alcohol-fed mates. Klassen and Persaud [17] fed six male rats a 6% ethanol Metrecal diet for 1 week and a 10% ethanol Metrecal diet the next 4 weeks. Pups of alcohol-fed fathers demonstrated significantly lower weight, length, and placental index ($p < .01$) and lower growth index ($p < .5$).

PROSPECTIVE STUDIES

The FAS was described following clinical observation of abnormal infants and retrospective recognition of the role of maternal drinking. Prospective studies, necessary to identify the frequency, quantity, and variability of alcohol consumption by pregnant women as well as the wide range of effects on offspring, have now been conducted. A few are cited below.

Kaminski et al. [16] studied 9,236 pregnancies at 13 French maternity centers between 1963 and 1969. Offspring of women who drank more than the equivalent of 1.5 oz of absolute alcohol daily were compared with those born to mothers who consumed less. When possible confounding factors were taken into account statistically, an increased risk due to alcohol usage remained significant for perinatal mortality and reduced birth weight and placental weight.

More than 12,000 pregnancies were studied prospectively by Sokol et al. [31] to define the relative risk to offspring of heavy drinkers. Pregnancies of 204 alcohol abusers were marked by a higher risk of premature placental separation and infection, fetal distress during labor, growth retardation, and fetal anomalies. The estimate of risk due to alcohol abuse for adverse perinatal outcome was 50%, 20 times the 2.5% risk for the full FAS.

A program to study patterns of alcohol use prospectively by prenatal clinic patients and the effects on their offspring was initiated in May 1974, at the Boston City Hospital [26]. Heavy-drinking women were defined as those who consumed at least five drinks on some occasions and no less than 45 drinks a month. (A drink was defined as a volume of beverage containing 15 cc (0.5 oz) of absolute alcohol; for example, 360 cc (12 oz) of beer, 48 cc (4 oz) of wine, or 36 cc (1.2 oz) of 80 proof liquor.) Rare drinkers either abstained or used alcohol less than once a month and never consumed five drinks on any occasion. All women who drank more frequently than once a month but did not meet the criteria for heavy drinking were classified as moderate drinkers. The heavy drinkers drank an average of 174 ml (5.8 oz) of absolute alcohol each day; 31% of them drank between 240 and 480 ml (8 and 16 oz) of absolute alcohol a day; their mean dose was estimated at 2.2 g/k of absolute alcohol each day.

Offspring of the heavily drinking women, as compared with offsrping of the moderately and rarely drinking women, demonstrated significantly more congenital malformations, growth retardation, and functional abnormalities.

All women who reported heavy alcohol use were encouraged to participate in counseling sessions scheduled to coincide with their routine prenatal clinic appointments [30]. The 25 mothers who abstained from alcohol or markedly reduced consumption before the third trimester had fewer babies with weight, length, and/or head circumference measurements below the 10th percentile than did the 44 mothers who continued heavy drinking. When drinking patterns during the third trimester were held constant, a number of potential confounding variables were found to have little effect on fetal outcome, including age, parity, trimester of registration, and use of cigarettes.

PREVENTION OF ADVERSE EFFECTS

A theoretical understanding of the etiologic mechanisms of the fetal alcohol syndrome and of the psychological and environmental forces affecting the heavy-drinking woman must be incorporated in the design of programs for prevention. One theory of FAS etiology is that alcohol functions as a teratogen analagous to thalidomide. Exposure of the embryo or fetus at a critical developmental point can result in malformation. Since no safe level of such a teratogenic substance has been determined, total abstinence is the only safe strategy. Once the drug has been ingested during a vulnerable developmental period, the only option remaining for prevention is therapeutic termination of pregnancy.

An alternative theory considers the multiple effects of alcohol on biochemistry and physiology, as well as the implications for the mother-fetus system of the entire spectrum of pathophysiology of alcoholism. Alcohol's multiple effects depend on the variability of the blood alcohol concentration during different stages of pregnancy, as well as on changes in the biological susceptibility of the mother-fetus system. During the first trimester, the effects of alcohol on the cell membrane and cell migration can affect the embryonic organization of tissue. During the second trimester, alterations in the metabolism of carbohydrates, lipids, and proteins probably affect cell growth and division. The organ systems with the most rapid growth are most susceptible: at critical stages, this may be the cardiovascular, the urogenital, the musculoskeletal, or the central nervous system. During the third trimester, rapid brain growth continues and neurophysiological functioning organizes for regulation of the infant following birth.

Early damage may not be reversible; however, whenever heavy drinking ceases, an opportunity is created for physiological restitution and catch-up growth. There is spontaneous variability in drinking patterns throughout pregnancy. The primary goal of therapy to lower risks to the fetus is reduction of alcohol consumption. Modification of other risk factors, such as smoking and poor nutrition, will reduce hazards due to synergistic mechanisms.

Obstetricians and other health professionals working with pregnant women must become aware of the potential risks of maternal alcohol use and must develop new attitudes toward women who drink heavily. They must learn that they cannot recognize problem drinkers by appearance or socioeconomic characteristics. A systematic drinking history is essential and should be obtained from all patients during the initial history. A brief Ten-Question Drinking History has been developed for clinical use and has been shown to be utilized reliably by the obstetrical house staff at Boston City Hospital [29].

When heavy drinking is identified, an estimate of risk within the limitations of current knowledge should be presented to the patient. The possibility of reducing risk by abstaining for the remainder of the pregnancy should be presented supportively. Disulfiram should not be prescribed during pregnancy because of the possible teratogenic effects, as described above. Counseling should be initiated or referral made for appropriate treatment. Most professionals have sufficient skills to provide supportive counseling focused on reduction of alcohol use and to provide practical help in dealing with difficult life situations. Pregnant women who do not respond within 2 weeks should be referred to specialized treatment programs.

While the dangers of heavy drinking during pregnancy have been established, more research is needed to evaluate the effects of moderate or light alcohol consumption. The most conservative advice is to abstain from all alcohol from conception through delivery and lactation. However, the danger from light drinking (less than 1 oz of absolute alcohol a day) has not been demonstrated and should not be overstated. Exaggeration could decrease credibility about the adverse effects of heavy drinking. In addition, exaggeration may cause parents of abnormal children to feel guilt that small amounts of alcoholic beverages caused abnormalities that may actually be due to other factors.

Reduction of alcohol consumption during pregnancy will improve a woman's chances of having a healthier baby. This knowledge, together with the interest and concern of health care providers, is a powerful force for improving maternal health and that of the unborn child.

REFERENCES

1. Badr, F. M., and Badr, R. S. Induction of dominant lethal mutation in male mice by ethyl alcohol. *Nature* 253:134–136, 1975.
2. Chernoff, G. A. Mouse model of the fetal alcohol syndrome. *Teratology* 15:223–230, 1977.
3. Clarren, S. K., Alvord, E. C., Jr., Sumi, S. M., Streissguth, A. P., and Smith, D. W. Brain malformations related to prenatal exposure to ethanol. *J. Pediatr.* 92:64–67, 1978.
4. Cooperman, M. T., Davidoff, F., Spark, R., and Pallotta, J. Clinical studies of alcoholic ketoacidosis. *Diabetes* 23:433–439, 1974.
5. Dexter, J. D., Tumbleson, M. E., Decker, J. D., and Middleton, C. C. Fetal alcohol syndrome in sinclair (S-1) miniature swine. *Alcoholism: Clin. Exp. Res.* 4:146–151, 1980.
6. Diaz, J., and Samson, H. H. Impaired brain growth in neonatal rats exposed to ethanol. *Science* 208:751–753, 1980.
7. Dobbing, J. The later growth of the brain and its vulnerability. *Pediatrics* 53:2–6, 1974.
8. Ellis, F. W., and Pick, J. R. An animal model of the fetal alcohol syndrome in beagles. *Alcoholism: Clin. Exp. Res.* 4:123–134, 1980.
9. Havlicek, V., Childiaeva, R., and Chernick, V. EEG frequency spectrum characteristics of sleep states in infants of alcoholic mothers. *Neuropaediatrie* 8:360–373, 1977.
10. Hill, R. M. Fetal malformations and antiepileptic drugs. *Am. J. Dis. Child.* 130:923–925, 1976.
11. Horiguchi, T., Suzuki, K., Comas-Urrutia, A. C., Mueeler-Heubach, E., Boyer-Milic, A. M., Baratz, R. A., Morishima, H. O., James, L. S., and Adamsons, K. Effect of ethanol upon uterine activity and fetal acid-base state of the rhesus monkey. *Am. J. Obstet. Gynecol.* 122:910–917, 1975.
12. Jacobson, S., Seghal, P., Bronson, R., Dorr, B., Klepper-Kilgore, H., and Burnap, J. A non-human primate model to demonstrate the teratogenic effects of ethanol. *Teratology* 21:45A, 1980.
13. Jones, K. L., and Smith, D. W. Recognition of the fetal alcohol syndrome in early infancy. *Lancet* 2:999–1001, 1973.
14. Jones, K. L., Smith, D. W., Ulleland, C. N., and Streissguth, S. P. Pattern of malformation in offspring of chronic alcoholic mothers. *Lancet* 1:1267–1271, 1973.
15. Kakihana, R., Butte, J. C., and Moore, J. A. Endocrine effects of maternal alcoholization: Plasma and brain testosterone, dihydrotestosterone, estradiol and corticosterone. *Alcoholism: Clin. Exp. Res.* 4:57–61, 1980.
16. Kaminski, M., Rumeau-Rouquette, C., and Schwartz, D. Consommation d'alcool

chez les femmes enceintes et issue de la grossesse (Alcohol consumption among pregnant women and outcome of pregnancy). *Rev. Epidem. et Sante Publique* 24:27-40, 1976.

17. Klassen, R. W., and Persaud, T. V. N. Experimental studies on the influence of male alcoholism on pregnancy and progeny. *Exp. Pathol.* 12:38-45, 1976.

18. Lemoine, P., Haronsseau, H., Borteryu, J.-P., and Menuet, J.-P. Les enfants de parents alcoholiques: Anomalies observeés à propos de 127 cas (Children of alcoholic parents: Anomalies observed in 127 cases). *Quest Med.* 25:476-482, 1968.

19. Mann, L. I., Bhakthavathsalan, A., Lui, M., and Makowski, P. Placental transport of alcohol and its effect on maternal and fetal acid-base balance. *Am. J. Obstet. Gynecol.* 122:837-844, 1975.

20. Naeye, R. L., Blanc, W., and Paul, C. Effects of maternal nutrition on the human fetus. *Pediatrics* 52:494-503, 1973.

21. Nora, A. H., Nora, J. I., and Blu, J. Limb-reduction anomalies in infants born to disulfiram-treated alcoholic mothers. *Lancet* 2:664, 1977.

22. Rainey, J. M., Jr. Disulfiram toxicity and carbon disulfide poisoning. *Am. J. Psychiatry* 134:371-378, 1977.

23. Randall, C. L., Taylor, W. J., and Walker, D. W. Ethanol-induced malformations in mice. *Alcoholism: Clin. Exp. Res.* 1:219-224, 1977.

24. Riley, E. P., Shapiro, N. R., and Lochry, E. A. Nose-poking and head-dipping behaviors in rats prenatally exposed to alcohol. *Pharm. Biochem. Behav.* 11:513-519, 1979.

25. Rosett, H. L. The effects of alcohol on the fetus and offspring. In: *Alcohol and Drug Problems in Women*, Kalant, O. J. (ed.). Plenum Press: New York, 1980.

26. Rosett, H. L., Ouellette, E. M., Weiner, L., and Owens, E. Therapy of heavy drinking during pregnancy. *Obstet. Gynecol.* 51:41-46, 1978.

27. Rosett, H. L., Snyder, P., Sander, L. W., Lee, A., Cook, P., Weiner, L., and Gould, J. Effects of maternal drinking on neonate state regulation. *Develop. Med. Child Neurol.* 21:464-473, 1979.

28. Rosett, H. L., and Weiner, L. Clinical and experimental perspectives on prevention of the fetal alcohol syndrome. *Neurobehav. Toxicol.* 2:267-270, 1980.

29. Rosett, H. L., Weiner, L., and Edelin, K. C. Strategies for prevention of fetal alcohol effects. *Obstet. Gynecol.* 57:1-7, 1981.

30. Rosett, H. L., Weiner, L., Zuckerman, B., McKinlay, S., and Edelin, K. Reduction of alcohol consumption during pregnancy with benefits to newborn. *Alcoholism: Clin. Exp. Res.* 4:178-184, 1980.

31. Sokol, R. J., Miller, S. I., and Reed, G. Alcohol abuse during pregnancy: An epidemiological model. *Alcoholism: Clin. Exp. Res.* 4:135-145, 1980.

32. Tissot-Favre, M., and Delatour, P. Psychopharmacologic et teratogenese à propos du disulfirame: Essai experimental (Psychopharmacology and teratogenicity of disulfiram: An experimental study). *Ann. Med. Psychol. (Paris)* 1:735-740, 1965.

33. Truitt, E. B., and Walsh, M. J. The role of acetaldehyde in the actions of ethanol. In: *The Biology of Alcohol: Biochemistry* (Vol. 1), Kissin, B. and Begleiter, H. (eds.). Plenum: New York, 1971.

34. Ulleland, C., Wennberg, R. P., Igo, R. P., and Smith, N. J. The offspring of alcoholic mothers. *Pediatr. Res.* 4:474, 1970.

35. Van Thiel, D. H., Gavaler, J. S., and Lester, R. Ethanol: A gonadal toxin in the female. *Drug Alcohol Depend.* 2:373-380, 1977.

36. Warner, R., and Rosett, H. L. The effects of drinking on offspring: An historical survey of the American and British literature. *J. Stud. Alcohol* 36:1395-1420, 1975.

37. West, J. R., Hodges, C. A., and Black, A. C. Prenatal exposure to ethanol alters the organization of hippocampal mossy fibers in rats. *Science* 211:957-959, 1981.

24

PETER E. STOKES, MD, New York Hospital–Cornell University Medical Center

ENDOCRINE DISTURBANCES ASSOCIATED WITH ALCOHOL AND ALCOHOLISM

THE PURPOSE OF THIS chapter is to cover the major endocrine systems that have been studied sufficiently to date with regard to perturbations induced in those systems by alcohol and alcoholism. The references given are chosen to provide either particularly seminal or provocative studies, or to offer a recent reference, which, through its presentation and bibliography, provides a current entry into the appropriate literature.

HYPOTHALAMIC–PITUITARY–ADRENOCORTICAL ACTIVITY

In the past 15 years increasingly precise and extensive measurements of hypothalamic-pituitary-adrenocortical (HYPAC) activity have shown that alcohol administration to animals and humans is associated with HYPAC hyperactivity under some, but not all, circumstances. The most revealing measurements of

---

Peter E. Stokes, MD, Associate Professor of Medicine (Endocrinology), Associate Professor of Psychiatry, and Chief, Division of Psychobiology, Payne Whitney Clinic, New York Hospital–Cornell University Medical Center, New York, New York.

HYPAC activity have included plasma hydrocortisone (cortisol or 17-hydroxycorticosteroid—17-OCHS) levels, total urinary 17-OHCS excretion, 24-hour urinary free cortisol excretion (UFC), 24-hour estimated cortisol secretion or production rate (CSR), plasma cortisol half-life, suppressiblity of HYPAC function via the dexamethasone suppression test (DST), and measures of adrenocorticotrophic hormone (ACTH) levels.

Modern experimental investigation of the effects of alcohol on HYPAC function was ushered in by Smith [21]. His work 30 years ago suggested that alcohol administration to guinea pigs was associated with apparent adrenocortical activation as shown by adrenal ascorbic acid and cholesterol depletion. Smith's (and Forbes and Duncan's [5] essentially simultaneous observations of the lack of effect of alcohol on the adrenal cortex in hypophysectomized animals indicated the direction for further studies on the mechanism of the action of alcohol on the HYPAC system and demonstrated the essential nature of the intact pituitary for the HYPAC response to alcohol. However, it has been subsequently demonstrated that adrenal ascorbic acid depletion correlates poorly with the more precise measures of HYPAC function available more recently.

Ellis [3] made the first use of more direct measures of HYPAC activity in animals receiving alcohol and showed that plasma 17-OHCS (hydroxyl) levels increased in a dose-related manner to an amount of alcohol from 0.5 to 2.0 g/kg body weight. The smallest doses were reported as producing no perceptible depression of central nervous system (CNS) function, though inducing a significant (3.5 mcg/dl) increment in plasma 17-OHCS. He also showed that eliminating the stress of pain induced by intraperitoneal alcohol through prior administration of the local anethesia Xylocaine did not prevent the increase in plasma 17-OHCS. General anesthesia by pretreatment with pentobarbitol (50 mg/kg body weight) reduced by about 50% the 17-OHCS response to intraperitoneal alcohol. These data demonstrated that behavioral alterations associated with alcohol administration (intoxication, pain) were not essential to the induced HYPAC response. Ellis also reported complete blockade of the 17-OHCS response to alcohol with prior administration of pentobarbital and morphine, which was consistent with the known HYPAC-blocking action of these drugs in large doses in dogs [8]. These drugs are thought to block the stress activation of the HYPAC system by their action on neural elements in the hypothalamus. In summary, the studies above suggested that the acute effects of alcohol on adrenocortical function were via the hypothalamus (via an increased CRH release) and they demonstrated the necessity of an intact pituitary. They do not provide an answer as to whether the alcohol effect is the result of a direct action on the hypothalamic neurosecretory neurons elaborating corticotrophin-(ACTH) releasing hormone (CRH) or if they result from neural transients from higher CNS centers. These transients are perhaps themselves the result of alcohol-induced changes in biogenic amine levels in neural systems now known to influence CRH release (i.e., especially noradrenergic and serotonergic systems).

Precise studies in humans using currently accepted measures of the effects of alcohol on adrenocortical activity actually predate those done in animals. In 1960 Kissin [11] showed a small rise in urinary 17-OHCS in most but not all normals and chronic alcoholics during the initial 4 hours of mild diuresis (greater than 3 ml/min) after a moderate (1 ml/kg body weight) dose of alcohol diluted to 25% in water when compared to retest with water alone. Others found minimal or no increase in urinary 17-OHCS after about equal doses of ethanol (as whiskey) but without associated water loading. The differences in response probably reflected the difference in diuresis produced between alcohol alone versus alcohol-and water-loading, with the expected wash out of water-soluble glucuronides and sulfate conjugates of hydrocortisone more pronounced after water-loading. There was a good correlation between urinary 17-OHCS and urine volume. Plasma 17-OHCS increased slightly in some individuals during the first 2 hours after alcohol, but in others with marked diuresis plasma 17-OHCS levels fell slightly.

Fazekas [4] provided data in five normal men showing a clear correlation between alcohol dose (1.0–1.5 g/kg body weight), resultant blood level (BAL), and plasma 17-OHCS increment. Plasma 17-OHCSs were only minimally (but significantly) elevated at the end of the first hour after either alcohol dose when the BAL was .083 for the smaller and 118. mg/dl for the larger alcohol dose. The BAL and 17-OHCS peaks occurred almost simultaneously at 2 hours with the 1.0 g dose and 3 hours with the 1.5 g dose. Both increased magnitude and duration of 17-OHCS response resulted from the larger alcohol dose. This and subsequent data [10] suggests that BALs must approach .100 mg/dl to produce more than minimal HYPAC activation as measured by increased plasma steroid levels. Merry and Marks [17] reported that in five dried-out alcoholics, ingestion of whiskey equivalent to about 100 ml absolute alcohol produced no increase in plasma 17-OHCS levels, but equal doses in normal volunteers produced marked (greater than 15 mcg/dl) increments in plasma 17-OHCS with a maximum at 90 to 120 minutes after ingestion of alcohol. This difference between normals and dried-out chronic alcoholics may have been secondary, at least in part, to the intoxication, nausea, and vomiting in the normals, which did not occur in the dried-out chronic alcoholics. The author suggests that the latter showed no symptoms because the alcohol may have suppressed the potentially emerging alcohol withdrawal syndrome. A second explanation may be derived from the tolerance of the alcoholics to alcohol, with consequent minimal alcohol effect on the CNS higher centers (emotional-arousal). A direct effect of alcohol on brain stem and hypothalamic centers having to do with CRH-ACTH release cannot be ruled out.

Chronic administration of large amounts of alcohol (up to 4 g/kg body weight daily) was given in divided doses over the day for 11 to 29 days to four dried-out institutionalized chronic alcoholics who were otherwise in good health [16]. These subjects showed very significant and persistant elevations of plasma cortisol levels from their prealcohol normal ranges of 8 to 13 mcg/dl to levels of 20 to 30 mcg/dl, which are at or above the usually accepted upper limits of normal for their method [19]. Further, increases in plasma cortisol were observed during episodes of gastrointestinal distress during the period of ingestion of these large doses of alcohol. Plasma cortisol levels tended to parallel increases in blood alcohol and concomitant increases in levels of intoxication.

Perhaps not surprisingly, 9:00 A.M. plasma cortisol levels are increased in about 50% of chronic alcoholics who suddenly are withdrawn from alcohol for about 12 hours, while their BALs are falling or have reached zero [18]. Administration of alcohol at 9:00 A.M. to these alcoholics acutely withdrawn from alcohol was then associated with a fall in plasma cortisol levels in the five chronic alcoholics studied over the next 2 hours. The decrease was at least that which would be expected by the normal diurnal pattern of falling plasma cortisol at that time of day. In contrast, three normal subjects given the same large dose of alcohol (284 ml of whiskey) showed significant cortisol elevations (15-30%) from their 9:00 A.M. baseline level. Amounts of amylobarbitone (400-500 mg), sufficient to suppress withdrawal symptoms and produce a similar clinical response as compared to alcohol in the alcoholics, also produced gradual decrease in plasma cortisol similar to that observed after alcohol. Diazepam in similar clinically equivalent amounts (30-40 mg) was equally effective to alcohol and amylobarbitone in suppressing withdrawal symptoms and relieving anxiety but did not diminish plasma cortisol levels. This suggests that the mechanisms by which HYPAC activity is decreased are not the suppression of the anxiety and withdrawal symptoms that are common to all three drugs. Amylobarbitone may have an effect on hypothalamic centers controlling CRH-ACTH release that diazepam does not have. It is also possible that the more rapid and pronounced induction of hepatic microsomal enzymes expected after the administration of barbituates as compared to benzodiazepines would result in greater metabolism of circulating cortisol, and hence lower plasma levels in those patients with a centrally inhibited HYPAC system.

Plasma cortisol levels were elevated significantly above normal throughout the day (9:00 A.M. = 23.5, 4:00 P.M. = 14.3, 11:00 P.M. = 9.2 mcg/dl) during a period of constant and heavy (greater than 256 ml absolute alcohol a day in 10 divided doses) alcohol intake in 18 chronic alcoholics without cirrhosis studied by Stokes [22] (BAL mean = .092 mEq %). There was no evidence of adaptation of HYPAC function to continued alcohol ingestion since these elevated cortisol levels persisted for about 2 weeks after hospitalization and were obtained in patients with evidence of chronic drinking for at least 2 weeks before hospitalization. The elevated cortisol levels did not change significantly during a subsequent experimental period of mild intoxication in spite of the marked increase in BALs (group mean = .169 mg/dl) induced by increasing the alcohol intake, nor during a 5-to-10-day period of gradual alcohol withdrawal. Plasma cortisol levels did not correlate closely with BAL or ratings of depression, which were generally mild or absent in those patients devoid of primary affective illness. Plasma cortisol levels after patients were off alcohol approximately 1 week and without withdrawal symptoms were significantly lower, but still elevated above normal, especially in the 4:00 P.M. and 11:00 P.M. samples. This study suggests a direct effect of alcohol (not that via primary alterations in behavior) on HYPAC activity because of the lack of correlations between degree of intoxication and plasma cortisol level. The conditions of the study were such as to minimize a behaviorally mediated effect on HYPAC activity because of the use of chronic drinkers who were already ingesting large amounts of alcohol at the onset of the study and who were familiar with its behavioral affects. In addition, there was a low incidence of mild gastrointestinal distress noted during this study. The elevated cortisol levels noted must reflect increased HYPAC function, since in the absence of cirrhosis and liver failure plasma cortisol metabolism is normal or increased after chronic drinking.

The DST has been reported to be abnormal in detoxified alcoholics, though pretest dexamethasone cortisol levels were normal (9.25 mcg/dl at 9:00 A.M.). However, normal DST suppression has been observed in alcoholics during drinking and after withdrawal [author, unpublished]. Furthermore, in the last 4 years some 20 cases of alcohol-induced Cushing's syndrome have been reported. Only about 50% of these patients have been reported to have an abnormal DST during alcohol ingestion as well as elevated and flattened diurnal levels of plasma cortisol. All biochemical and clinical aspects of Cushing's syndrome disappeared in all reported cases within 1 to 2 weeks of hospitalization and withdrawal of alcohol. The cause of the alcohol-induced Cushing's syndrome is still obscure, but it is apparent that chronic drinking for approximately 1 month or more with associated persistant hypercortisolemia is not sufficient, by itself, to induce Cushing's syndrome. Most likely a considerable degree of liver failure with decreased corticosteroid-binding globulin (CBG) levels contributes, in at least some chronic alcoholic patients, to the development of Cushing's syndrome [6, 12].

SUMMARY OF ANIMAL AND HUMAN STUDIES: ADRENAL CORTEX

Alcohol administration under certain conditions, and in moderate to large doses, produces clear activation of the HYPAC system in naive animals, man, and in chronic alcoholics, (although larger doses are generally required for alcoholics). HYPAC activity requires an intact hypothalamus and anterior pituitary. BALs approaching 100 mg/dl are required to produce significant HYPAC activation in man. There is no evidence to suggest HYPAC exhaustion in chronic alcohol administration in animals or in chronic alcoholics. A few chronic alcoholics present with what appears to be an alcohol-induced Cushing's syndrome with clinical and biochemical hormonal findings typical of that disease, even to the point of abnormal DSTs. All clinical and laboratory findings regress after alcoholics are off alcohol for about 2 weeks. No evidence exists to suggest a causative role of abnormal HYPAC function in the genesis of alcoholism.

THYROID FUNCTION

Thyroid function has not been convincingly demonstrated to be altered by alcohol administration per se in animals or in humans. Many of the reported studies were obtained before the availability of precise and multiple measures of thyroid function, such as are now available by radioimmunoassay. In studies of chronic alcoholics, alterations in diet and/or the presence of liver disease can influence body and thyroidal iodide pools and alter hepatic and peripheral thyroid hormone metabolism, making interpretation of findings difficult. It is important to note that the incidence of clinical thyroid disease in alcoholics (hyper- or hypothyroidism) is very infrequent in this author's experience. Serum T-4 and thyroid-stimulating hormone (TSH) levels are almost universally in the normal range in alcoholics and strongly suggest normal thyroid function, even if serum T-3 levels (free T-3) or protein bindings are low. The hepatic and peripheral conversion of T-4 to T-3 is diminished in both hepatic disease or malnutrition. Recently a study [14] showed an elevated serum-free T-4 and total T-4 level during acute withdrawal with a subsequent return to normal in the post withdrawal state in 12 alcoholics without chemical evidence of cirrhosis or a history of thyroid disorder. A blunted TSH response to thyrotropin-releasing hormone (TRH) was reported in some alcoholics in the acute withdrawal and postwithdrawal state. These authors [14] suggest that their findings regarding thyroid hormone measures are compatible with a hyperdopaminergic state in the CNS since they also found a slight increase in resting growth hormone and a decrease in resting prolactin levels in these subjects, consistent with such a state. Increased dopamine turnover in the CNS has been reported in animals and is thought to be one factor responsible for the inhibition of TSH release. TSH response to TRH is known to be very variable and more work is needed to confirm or reject the possibility of abnormal TSH response in alcoholics. No evidence exists suggesting that thyroid dsysfunction plays a significant role in the development or persistence of alcoholism.

GROWTH HORMONE

Growth hormone (GH) response to intravenous arginine infusion has been reported to be reduced in normals after a overnight fast and an acute intravenous dose of alcohol. A reduced response after alcohol was also reported in acromegalics [23]. The natural fluctuations of growth hormone secretions in alcoholics make this conclusion tenuous pending further data.

A single acute oral dose of alcohol has been reported to diminish the subsequent mean GH response to insulin-induced hypoglycemia in 12-hour-plus fasted normal young male and female volunteers (n-9) when compared to growth hormone responses in insulin hypoglycemia without alcohol. The group mean blood sugar fall after alcohol plus insulin (50 % decrease) was greater than with alcohol alone (40 % decrease), though not statistically significant. No absolute sugar values were given. The growth hormone response to insulin hypoglycemia (0.1 units/kg body weight) was studied in seven male chronic alcoholics with at least a 5-year history of heavy, continuous alcohol intake, but without marked liver damage. Studies were performed after alcohol withdrawal in a hospital for 2 to 7 days. The growth hormone response was diminished in extent and/or late in onset in four of seven patients compared to 10 age-matched male and female normal controls in spite of equal and pronounced hypoglycemia (greater than 50% fall from fasting level). Plasma cortisol response was also significantly diminished in three subjects, two of which had shown deficient GH response. No data is provided on the behavioral state of these acutely withdrawn individuals, nor is mention made of what, if any, treatment medications were used during alcohol withdrawal [1].

A nonspecific and anomalous GH rise after TRH has been found in 33 of 48 patients with chronic liver disease, yet it was not correlated to degree of liver disease or to the origin (i.e., alcoholic or nonalcoholic). Many had clinical signs of hyperestrogenism, which may contribute to the GH rise. The GH elevation could be inhibited by somatostatin or GH-release inhibiting factor, suggesting normal hypothalamic and pituitary control of GH [20].

The mechanism of growth hormone inhibition by alcohol is certainly not clear in the relatively few studies and numbers of patients reported thus far. However, it may represent alcohol-induced alterations in catecholamine neurons in the hypothalamic centers (ventral median nucleus) controlling GH-releasing hormone (GH-RH) secretion and hence controlling pituitary release of growth hormone. Whether concomitant alteration in somatostatin could contribute to the suppression of growth hormone response has not been studied. Dopaminergic input is stimulatory to GH release. GH release in relation to hypoglycemia, at least insulin-induced hypoglycemia, appears to be the result of alpha-adrenergic receptor stimulation since it is blocked by phenotolamine. Beta-adrenergic receptor stimulation alone inhibits GH release. Clarification will be difficult and will depend on further studies in larger numbers of normals and well-nourished chronic alcoholics (during drinking vs. withdrawal from alcohol). This population should be devoid of severe liver disease so that the effects of prior diet and hepatic metabolism can be factored out of the results.

PROLACTIN

Gynecomastia is a frequent finding in alcoholic cirrhosis and is often associated with decreased libido and hypogonadism. Alcoholics without cirrhosis, but with fatty liver, have slightly decreased basal levels of prolactin (PRL), but show brisk increases in serum PRL levels after TRH administration and are even somewhat exaggerated in their response compared to normals. Patients with alcoholic cirrhosis and gynecomastia have, some reports suggest, a bimodal distribution for resting nonstimulated baseline prolactin levels correlated with the presence or absence of clinically palpable gynecomastia. Alcoholics with gynecomastia and cirrhosis have markedly increased basal PRL levels. Alcoholics without gynecomastia (and with cirrhosis) have normal baseline PRL levels. Those with fatty livers only have normal or perhaps decreased baseline PRL values in the small numbers thus far reported. TRH-stimulated PRL response is similar to normals in alcoholics with cirrhosis (with or without gynecomastia), but may be relatively diminished in view of the known increase in conversion of adrenal (weak) androgens to estrogens by peripheral tissues and the significantly increased serum estrogen levels reported in such patients [25]. Increased estrogen levels augment PRL secretion. Other reports find PRL levels approximately twice as elevated in the resting basal state in chronic alcoholics ($n = 10$) even without gynecomastia and the absence of advanced liver disease [15].

Studies in 22 chronically alcoholic men during withdrawal and again after complete withdrawal showed low baseline PRL levels (TSH was normal or low) during both conditions. The PRL response to TRH was not abnormal under either condition, but TSH response was slightly lower than that observed in normals. Thus, hyperprolactinemia is only an occasional associate of alcoholism and is perhaps most often present (though not exclusively) in those with gynecomastia.

The mechanism for development of gynecomastia in alcoholism probably results as a direct effect of prolactin on breast tissue in association with increased circulating estrogen. Perhaps there is in addition a prolactin-induced increased number of estrogen receptor sites on the breast tissue. Why the PRL levels are normal or low in alcoholic patients without gynecomastia is unclear. The data reveals adequate, even increased, anterior pituitary reserve and ability to release PRL to TRH stimulus. The cause of the reversal from low to high basal PRL levels as alcoholism progresses and gynecomastia develops is unclear, but may relate to the effect of progressive hepatic disease with resultant increases in circulating estrogens that finally reach a critical level and initiate chronic prolactin hypersecretion similar to that observed in estrogen-treated castrated males. The elevated basal PRL levels present in alcoholism with cirrhosis and gynecomastia may also reflect alcohol-induced hypothalamus-pituitary dysfunction, perhaps secondary to altered central biogenic amine levels, since alcohol is known to induce depletion in central amines similar to that observed with reserpine (another drug whose chronic administration is associated sometimes with gynecomastia). Dopamine infusion and antiserotonergic drugs have been reported to decrease the TRH-induced PRL rise as readily in alcoholics as in normals, supporting a dopamine inhibitory and serotonergic stimulatory control of PRL release.

A higher incidence of breast and thyroid cancer and malignant melanoma has been reported in association with alcohol ingestion in the Third National Cancer Survey data from the United States [2]. Williams has proposed a hypothesis that the increased incidence of certain malignancies in drinkers is associated with increased secretion of pituitary trophic hormones specific to those tissues: PRL, TSH, and melanocyte-stimulating hormone (MSH). Under excessive stimulation by these trophic hormones the target tissues show increased mitotic (possibly precancerous) activity. However, to date, only PRL secretion has been shown to be elevated, and then only in some alcoholics.

GONADOTROPHINS AND SEX STEROIDS

Chronic alcoholic men often show clinical evidence of hypoandrogenism (demasculinization) and simultaneous hyperestrogenism (feminization). The demasculinization is evident by hypogonadism, decreased libido, impotence, and infertility. The feminization is evident in female fat and hair distribution, gynecomastia, spider angiomata, and palmar erythema.

Evidence has accumulated for multiple effects of alcohol on gonadotrophins and sex steroids in humans and in animals. These effects, in a complex manner, probably account for the demasculinization and feminization.

Testicular histology on biopsy specimens from 30 chronic alcoholics off alcohol for 1 week, and in generally good physical condition aside from liver disease, showed changes in germinal cells only [13]. Only one patient had gynecomastia. There was no spermatogenesis in 40%, and severe reduction in 30%. Leydig cells and vasculature were normal. These findings confirmed earlier histologic studies on men with advanced liver disease, some without alcoholism. No correlation was found between spermatogenesis (or PRL levels) and liver disease. However, a highly significant inverse correlation occurred between spermatogenesis and serum PRL levels and, as expected, a similar negative correlation between spermatogenesis and follicle-stimulating hormone (FSH) levels since the latter has been shown to increase in other causes of oligospermia. The oligospermia is probably, at least in part, a result of diminished testosterone and luteinizing hormone (LH) levels in chronic alcoholics.

Reports in the literature in general are consistent in finding diminished plasma testosterone (T) and LH in chronic alcoholics, especially, perhaps not surprisingly, in those with clinical testicular atrophy or hypogonadism. Animal and human studies in normals also reveal decreased plasma LH and T in relation to acute and chronic alcohol administration, in moderate to large doses. Small single doses of alcohol have been reported to increase plasma LH and T levels. The exact dose at which these hormones decrease in nonalcoholic normals whose habit is daily ingestion of alcohol is not clear, but may be a little as 3 or 4 oz. of whisky or its equivalent each day.

The causes of the decreased plasma LH and testosterone and the associated hypogonadism are probably multiple. A hypothalamic effect of alcohol on LH-RH (releasing hormone) secretion is seen in the rat because the low LH levels observed after alcohol, even in castrates with expected elevated LH levels, are overcome by exogenous LH-RH administration. However, human volunteers given alcohol for 3 days showed less increase in plasma LH after LH-RH administration than during a prealcohol control period, suggesting a defect in pituitary release of LH. However, after chronic alcohol feeding for 12 days basal LH levels also diminished. Testosterone synthesis in animals after acute or chronic alcohol administration was reported to remain low even after human chorionic gonadotrophin administration in vivo and in vitro (testicular tissue), showing diminished Leydig cell response to trophic hormone stimulation.

There is evidence in men, not only of decreased production or secretion of gonadal T, but a modest increase in plasma clearance rate after alcohol [7]. Both of these factors contribute to decreased plasma T levels. These effects can be seen after acute, single, moderately large doses of alcohol (1.2 ml/kg body weight), but the plasma T changes are relatively small and remain within the normal range. In rats fed large amounts of alcohol chronically, there may be a direct effect on the production of T from gonadal Leydig cells because of altered enzymatic activity in the biosynthetic pathways for T. Increased hepatic clearance of T results from increased activity of the enzyme 5-alpha-ring-reductase that occurs after chronic alcohol feeding in man and in animals. Identical enzyme changes have been shown recently to occur in peripheral nonhepatic tissue also. Thus, the pathogenesis of hypogonadism associated with accessive alcohol ingestion is the result of multiple factors, including hypothalamic inhibition of LH-RH secretion, possibly diminished pituitary LH response, decreased gonadal T production (probably a direct result of alcohol and diminished Leydig cell response to LH), increased metabolic clearance, and perhaps other, not as yet clarified, factors such as altered plasma protein binding of T or disruption of androgen receptor function.

The feminization of chronic alcoholics also apparently results from multiple causes, perhaps less clearly defined than the cause of demasculinization described above.

There is good evidence for some increase in plasma estrogen in cirrotic men, though it is unusual in those alcoholics without liver disease and in patients with chronic liver disease of nonalcoholic origin. These observations suggest that the feminization relates to alcohol ingestion and abnormal liver disease.

The increased estrogen levels result mainly from increased estrone and perhaps to a lesser degree estradiol. Free (nonprotein-bound) estrogen levels may be increased, but the measurements of free estrogens, presumed to be the metabolically active fraction of total plasma estrogen, are fraught with great methodological difficulties and reported results are contradictory. Estrone, the main estrogen increased in these patients, is a biologically weak estrogen, normally accounting for little of the total estrogenic activity. Prolactin probably plays only a secondary role in producing the gynecomastia associated with the defeminization. Some investigators have suggested that the decrease in T together with increased estrogen (altered estrogen-testosterone ratio) is what accounts for the feminization. However, this appears to be too simple an explanation in light of more recent data. In addition, elderly men have increased estrogen-testosterone ratios but are not feminized. One current possibility is that there is an alteration in estrogen receptor activity in the liver. It is known that estrogen acts on the male and female liver as a target organ and can alter its metabolic activity. For example, estrogens increase the synthesis of various proteins secreted into the plasma from the livers including sex steroid and corticosteroid-binding protein. Normal males have an excess of a nonreceptor protein within their liver that binds estrogen and limits the availability of estrogen to the specific estrogen receptors present in the male liver. However, when hypogonadism occurs (low T), this hepatic low-affinity estrogen-removing protein diminishes since it is T dependent. More estrogen is then available to the hepatic-specific estrogen receptors even at the same or normal plasma estrogen level. Consequently the liver becomes estrogenized in its functions. An example of this is the remarkable elevation in sex steroid–binding globulin levels that can occur in chronic alcoholic. If these same characteristics of male rat livers occur in human liver and in other hepatic tissues, then a pathogenesis for estrogen stimulation in these tissues is apparent. Further work is needed to clarify this possibility.

Chronic alcohol ingestion as seen in chronic alcoholics is usually associated with adrenal cortical activation, as described. In addition to cortisol there is secretion of weak adrenal androgens, which, it has been shown, can be enzymatically aromatized to estrogens in peripheral tissues as well as in the liver. The conversion of these weak androgens (androstenedione and dehydroepiandrosterone) to estrone, and less so to estradiol, is increased in alcoholics. Rats with surgically ligated portal veins and hence portal hypertension and presumed portal systemic blood shunting have been shown to have increased peripheral estrone levels even without alcohol feeding. Van Thiel [24] postulates that in the alcoholic with portal to hypertension and portal systemic shunting, there is abnormal peripheral shunting of estrogens and weak androgens that are reabsorbed from the gut, after their normal hepatic secretion, via the bile into the gastrointestinal tract. These reabsorbed weak androgens are aromatized to estrogen in the periphery and add to the excessive estrogen levels shunted to the periphery.

Thus, it can be seen that multiple effects of chronic alcohol ingestion and liver disease probably contribute to the feminization syndrome frequently seen in these patients.

VASOPRESSIN

Alcohol-induced water diuresis and increased urine flow is well known even to lay persons. The effects of ethanol on vasopressin have been long and intensively studied. A rising BAL is associated with increased urine flow and increased free water clearance. The diuresis subsides when the BAL starts to fall. It can be initiated again by further increases in the BAL as long as extracellular fluid (ECF) does not become hyperosmolar and is augmented by water loading. Alcohol-induced diuresis gradually ceases even with repeated alcohol ingestion or administration after the first few hours, unless water replacement occurs simultaneously. Injections of vasopressin will counteract the alcohol-induced diuresis. In dogs with posterior pituitary insufficiency and secondary diabetes insipidus because of absent vasopressin, alcohol administration does not further increase the urine flow. Recently [9], actual measurement of plasma vasopressin and neurophysin were made for the first time and alcohol administration was shown to inhibit the expected release of vasopressin and neurophysin caused by the nicotine obtained from smoking two cigarettes. Ethanol will not induce diuresis when hypertonic saline is infused or ingestion of sodium chloride is taken concomitantly because the ECF becomes hyperosmolar and this stimulus to vasopressin release overrides the inhibitory effect of alcohol. These investigations have demonstrated that the diuretic effect of ethanol is dependent upon inhibition of vasopressin release and is apparent only in the normally hydrated animal or man during increasing BAL. Alcohol does not affect the renal response to vasopressin. The exact mechanism of ethanol action on inhibition of vasopressin release is not known and may be at the level of the posterior pituitary and its hypothalamic neurons or at higher CNS levels.

SUMMARY

A variety of endocrine disturbances have been found associated with acute and chronic alcohol ingestion. Most marked are the HYPAC, pituitary-gonad, and vasopressin-neurophysin systems. Alterations in secretion rates and metabolism of hormones has been identified. All abnormalities appear to revert to normal when alcohol is stopped if chronic and irreversible liver disease has not supervened. In the presence of chronic liver disease multiple abnormalities may persist, most notably those in the pituitary-gonad system.

No evidence is at hand suggesting that the identified endocrine disturbances are related to the pathogenesis of alcoholism. The ingestion of alcohol plus the multifactorial alcohol-induced alterations in secretion of hormones and their metabolism in the liver and peripheral tissues are what accounts for the endocrine disturbances recorded. At this time no hormonal therapy is of use or generally indicated in alcoholism or its secondary complications.

REFERENCES

1. Chalmers, R. J., Bennie, E. H., Johnson, R. H., and Kinnell, H. G. The growth hormone response to insulin-induced hypoglycaemia in alcoholics. *Psychol. Med.* 7:607, 1977.
2. Dixon, K., Exon, P. D., and Malins, J. M. Third National Cancer Survey: Data from the United States. *Q. J. Med.* 44:343, 1975.
3. Ellis, F. W. Effect of ethanol on plasma corticosterone levels. *J. Pharmacol. Exp. Ther.* 153:121, 1966.
4. Fazekas, I. G. Hudrocortisone content of human blood, and alcohol content of blood and urine, after wine consumption *Q. J. Stud. Alcohol* 27:439, 1966.
5. Forbes, J. C., and Duncan, G. M. The effect of acute alcohol intoxication on the adrenal glands of rats and guinea pigs. *Q. J. Stud. Alcohol* 12:355, 1951.
6. Frajria, R., and Angeli, A. Alcohol-induced pseudo-Cushing's syndrome [letter]. *Lancet* 1:1050, 1977.
7. Gordon, G. G., Altman, K., Southren, A. L., Rubin, E., and Lieber, C. S. Effect of alcohol (ethanol) administration on sex-hormone metabolism in normal men. *N. Eng. J. Med.* 295:793, 1976.
8. Hedge, G. A., Yates, M. B., Marcus, R., and Yates, F. E. Site of action of vasopressin causing corticotrophin release. *Endocrinology* 79:328, 1966.
9. Husain, M. K., Andrew, G. F., Ciarochi, F., and Robinson, A. G. Nicotine-stimulated release of neurophysin and vasopressin in humans. *J. Clin. Endocrin. Metab.* 41:1113, 1975.
10. Jenkins, J. S., and Connolly, J. Adrenocortical response to ethanol in man. *Br. Med. J.* 2:804, 1968.
11. Kissin, B., Schenker, V., and Schenker, A. C. The acute effect of ethanol ingestion on plasma and urinary 17-hydroxycorticoids in alcoholic subjects. *Am. J. Med. Sci.* 239:690, 1960.

12. Kley, H. K., Both, H., and Kruskemper, H. L. Hypercortisolism in patients with cirrhosis of the liver due to decreased binding of plasma cortisol. *Horm. Metab. Res.* 10:569, 1978.

13. Lindholm, J., Fabricius-Bjerre, N., Bahnsen, M., Boiesen, P., Bangstrup, L., Pedersen, M. L., and Hagen, C. Pituitary-testicular function in patients with chronic alcoholism. *Eur. J. Clin. Invest.* 8:269, 1978.

14. Loosen, P. T., Prange, J., and Wilson, I. C. TRH (Protirelin) in depressed alcoholic men: Behavioral changes and endocrine responses. *Arch. Gen. Psychiatry* 36:540, 1979.

15. Majumdar, S. K. Serum prolactin in chronic alcoholics. *Practitioner* 222:693, 1979.

16. Mendelson, J. H., Ogata, M., and Mello, K. Adrenal function and alcoholism: Serum cortisol. *Psychosom. Med.* 33:145, 1971.

17. Merry, J., and Marks, V. Plasma-hydrocortisone response to ethanol in chronic alcoholics. *Lancet* 1:921, 1969.

18. Merry, J. and Marks, V. The effect of alcohol, barbituate, and diazepam on hypothalmic-pituitary-adrenal function in chronic alcoholics. *Lancet* 2:990, 1972.

19. Murphy, B. P., Engelberg, W., and Pattee, C. J. Simple method for the determination of plasma corticoids. *J. Clin. Endocrin.* 23:293, 1963.

20. Salerno, F., Cocchi, D., Zanardi, P., Casaneuva, F., and Muller, E. E. Growth hormone and prolactin secretion in cirrhotic patients. In: *Metabolic Effects of Alcohol.* Avogaro, P., Sirtori, C. R., and Tremoli, E. (eds.). Elsevier-North-Holland Biomedical Press: Amsterdam, 1979.

21. Smith, J. J. Effect of alcohol on the adrenal ascorbic acid and cholesterol of the rat. *J. Clin. Endocrin.* 11:792, 1951.

22. Stokes, P. E. Adrenocortical activation in alcoholics during chronic drinking. *Ann. N.Y. Acad. Sci.* 215:77, 1973.

23. Tamburrano, G., Tamburrano, S., Gambardella, S., and Andreani, D. Effects of alcohol on growth hormone secretion in acromegaly. *J. Clin. Endocrin. Metab.* 42:193, 1976.

24. Van Thiel, D. H. Feminization of chronic alcoholic men: A formulation. *Yale J. Biol. Med.* 52:219, 1979.

25. Van Thiel, D. H., Gavaler, J. S., Lester, R., Loriaux, D. L., and Braunstein, G. D. Plasma estrone, prolactin, neurophysin, and sex steroid-binding globulin in chronic alcoholic men. *Metabolism* 24:1015–1019, 1975.

25

HAROLD A. LYONS, MD, State University of New York Downstate Medical Center, Brooklyn, New York

THE RESPIRATORY SYSTEM AND SPECIFICS OF ALCOHOLISM

ALCOHOL ABUSERS ARE especially vulnerable to lung diseases, lung infections, and lung damage. Identification of alcohol-related lesions is difficult, because these individuals are often smokers, and run the risk of repeated aspirations [4, 10, 19, 21, 25, 28].

The defense mechanisms of the respiratory tract are impaired by alcohol. Subsequently, gag reflexes are diminished, cough is depressed, and the motion of the respiratory cilia is stopped. These defects decrease the clearance mechanism of the respiratory tract and ease entry of organisms and material. Additional factors also seem to contribute to the alcoholic's decreased resistance to infections: (1) poor dentition leads to the predisposition for harboring anaerobic microorganisms, and (2) dietary deficiencies lead to nutritional effects on the lung.

There are three major mechanisms protecting the lung from damage: (1) the cough mechanisms, (2) the transport by the mucociliary stream, and (3) phagocytosis—the destruction of inhaled material by the leucocytes and alveolar macrophages.

The lung clearance mechanism is most important within the first hour after inhalation of foreign particles. Those particles, which settle below the respiratory bronchioles, are eliminated by phagocytosis [5, 15, 17]. Failure of this mechanism

---

Harold A. Lyons, MD, Professor of Medicine, State University of New York Downstate Medical Center, Brooklyn, New York.

causes lung infection and damage. Alcohol is known to interfere with and inhibit these defense mechanisms. As a result, the alcoholic is susceptible to infectious processes and other forms of pulmonary disease.

Resistance to infection is lowered by alcohol. Experiments with various species of bacteria have demonstrated an increase in morbidity and mortality with acute alcoholic intoxication [7, 30, 31, 34]. Not only is impaired phagocytosis observed, but also a fall in the opsonizing index, suggesting a decrease in antibody production by alcohol [23]. Inhibition migration of both polymorphonuclear leucocytes and alveolar macrophages is caused by alcohol. Evidence is present for alcohol to alter the peroxidase and catalase cellular reactions [8, 9, 13, 14, 32, 35]. Impaired bactericidal action and cellular damage are resultants induced by alcohol. The incorporation of the precursors of the phospholipid molecule is interrupted by ingestion of alcohol [1, 22]. It may be that surface lining material is limited in amount and that diminished surface activity can lead to irreversible structural lung changes in the lung parenchyma.

ALTERATIONS IN SYSTEMIC AND PULMONARY CIRCULATION

These defects in the basic mechanisms of defense and integrity of the lung are paramount for producing pulmonary disease. Several investigators have pointed to the higher incidence of chronic bronchitis, chronic obstructive airways disease, pneumonias, suppurative lung diseases, and pulmonary tuberculosis among alcoholics [16, 21, 24]. Studies of pulmonary function indicate that lung volumes and the subdivisions, and diffusing capacity, are all affected by excessive alcohol consumption [2, 10, 21, 26]. Maldistribution between ventilation and blood flow has been observed [12, 27].

The presence of cirrhosis of the liver is associated with the development of collateral circulation, which allows blood to bypass the pulmonary circulation [12]. Likewise, the splanchnic circulation develops collaterals that bypass the liver. The lung develops arteriovenous formations, spiders [3]. These collateral bypasses increase venous admixture and probably account in part for the hypoxemia often observed in the cirrhotic. Another interesting phenomenon is the lack of a vasoconstrictive response of the pulmonary arteries to hypoxia in the cirrhotic patient, unlike the normal. The conversion of angiotensin I to angiotensin II appears less evident in these patients and may account for the absence of systemic hypertension [29].

The high incidence of chronic pulmonary disease in the alcoholic may be accounted for by these defects. Burch and DePasquale produced histological changes in the lung after ingestion of alcohol [6]. Altered metabolic pathways and denaturing of proteins were considered responsible for the changes in the lung parenchyma.

Animal studies indicate that starvation or markedly reduced food consumption result in abnormal ultrastructural cellular patterns, changes in mechanical properties and metabolic activities. Because the alcoholic is often deficient in his dietary needs, this nutritional factor adds to the damage of lung parenchyma.

An interesting finding of increased superoxide dismutase in lysates of erythrocytes of black alcoholics suggests a response for delaying or preventing the pathological changes in the lung. As pointed out, O_2- interacts with DNA, lipids, and proteins, disrupting cellular metabolism [13, 14]. The increase in superoxide dismutase levels may protect against alcohol-induced pathology by quickly dismutasing O_2-. Of course, continued use of alcohol will cause this protection [11] to be lost.

The respiratory problems encountered among alcoholics are (1) aspiration pneumonia, (2) bronchiectasis, (3) chronic bronchitis, (4) lung abscess, (5) chronic obstructive airway disease, (6) tuberculosis, and (7) laryngeal carcinoma. Esophageal carcinoma is another type of neoplasm observed among alcoholics.

RESPIRATORY INFECTIONS

Aspiration Pneumonia

Alcoholism has all the conditions for predisposition to aspiration. If the aspiration is acid and from gastric juice, the onset of acute respiratory distress, wheezing, and dyspnea occurs. Frequently, shock is also present. The chest x-ray film has mottled densities present in one or both lower lobes, and at times, may be in the upper lobes. The radiographic changes resemble pulmonary edema, but the absence of pulmonary venous engorgement is a helpful differentiating sign. Mortality, ranging between 30 and 60%, even with intensive respiratory care, is due to the hypoxemia, edema, and bacterial infection. Additional therapy includes intravenous fluids, tracheal suction, and use of corticosteroids in massive dose within the first 12 hours. Steroid therapy should be maintained for 3 to 4 days, but its use later appears without effect. Antimicrobial drugs are given for the probable bacterial infection in the damaged areas of the lung.

Foreign bodies and particles of food are known aspirated material in alcoholics. When suspected, bronchoscopic aspiration should be performed. Foreign bodies can be suspected when there is atelectasis with mediastinal displacement, and/or obstructive emphysema as detected on expiratory chest films. A more severe problem is the aspiration of a bolus of food, which lodges in the larynx or trachea. Sudden dyspnea, aphonia cyanosis, and rapid death results. In such instances, rapid action using the Heimlich maneuver becomes imperative. The maneuver consists of forcible upward thrusts over the upper abdomen below the costal margin. This should be attempted until it is successful, with the bolus being expelled. In both forms of aspiration, attention to appropriate oxygenation, airway patency, and treatment of infection should be undertaken.

Bacterial Pneumonia

Pneumonia is frequent in alcoholics and attended with an increased mortality. Death rates are three times that for nonalcoholics [31]. *Diplococcus pneumoniae* is the infectious agent in 80% of cases. Frequent occurrence of pneumonia due to *Klebsiella* and *Hemophilus influenzae* is also observed. Staphylococcal and streptococcal pneumonias have been recorded. Appropriate antibiotic therapy and supportive therapy are the mainstays of therapy. In spite of the advances in antibiotic therapy and improved knowledge, mortality remains high. The resolution of pneumonias in alcoholics is very slow, often suggesting the presence of a lung cancer [20].

Lung Abscess

Lung abscess is another complication of the alcoholic with pneumonia, because frequently a necrotizing pneumonia is present. Breakdown of tissue results with the formation of an abscess. Cultures usually show mixed flora with anaerobic organisms. Conditions for the development of a lung abscess are favorable because of poor dentition and aspiration of this material in the alcoholic patient with depressed defense and clearing mechanisms. Carious teeth harbor anerobic organisms. The recommended management is early bronchoscopy for the removal of secretions and any foreign material, and high-dose penicillin administered intravenously. The penicillin is given until there is no further improvement in the abscess cavity or until complete resolution has occurred. If the cavity persists, then it should be decided whether resection is necessary or whether it can be observed dependent on continued good drainage because of its favorable location within the lung. At times, repeated bronchoscopies may be required for institution of drainage. Drainage is the principle for treatment of an abscess. Even with complete resolution, follow-up bronchographic studies often demonstrate residual cysts or bronchiectasis that are not detected on the plain chest film.

Bronchiectasis

The repeated aspirations and depressed cough reflex of the alcoholic lead to infection of the bronchial tree. Chronic bronchitis with persistent cough and sputum production is frequent among alcoholics. Often repeated pneumonias and retained secretions lead to obstruction and infection of the bronchial wall with eventual destruction. These chronically dilated bronchi with collections of infected secretions produce cough and purulent sputum with frequent exacerbations of symptoms due to surrounding pneumonias (peribronchiectatic pneumonitis). Dyspnea and wheezing are frequently observed. Hemoptysis is not uncommon.

The physical examination may disclose areas of wheezing, rales, and bronchial or bronchovesicular breath sounds. In advanced stages of the disease, clubbing of the digits and hypoxemia are present. Bronchography is the definitive procedure for establishing the diagnosis.

The treatment consists of promoting drainage by the use of postural drainage, and the administration of appropriate antibiotics for exacerbations associated with increase of symptoms and any increase in purulent sputum production when a peribronchiectatic pneumonitis is present. If localized unilateral saccular bronchiectasis is demonstrated by bronchography, surgical resection may be necessary if it is not responsive to conservative management.

Tuberculosis

Tuberculosis, as with other respiratory diseases, seems to be more frequent among alcoholics. Because the alcoholic is a noncompliant patient, treatment is a difficult problem. Resistant organisms are frequently present, often due to intermittent and inadequate therapy. The inadequate diet of the alcoholic adds to the propensity to develop tuberculosis. The difficulty in managing these patients leads to the spreading of disease in the community.

OTHER RESPIRATORY CONSEQUENCES OF ALCOHOL ABUSE

Laryngeal and Esophageal Carcinoma

Laryngeal and esophageal carcinoma continue to be a consequence of alcohol abuse. The combination of smoking and alcohol appears to be a significant factor in the etiology of these forms of carcinoma. Certainly, screening and suspicion should be held for the presence of either of these neoplasms in the alcoholic patient, even when another respiratory disease exists. Attention may be diverted by the symptoms and clinical features of current disease.

Pulmonary Vasculature

The rare pulmonary hypertension that occurs in alcoholic cirrhosis is another problem that can affect the lung. The factors responsible for the development of pulmonary arterial hypertension are not known. It is suspected that vasoactive substances or hormones may enter the pulmonary circulation and cause vasoconstriction. Eventually, structural changes of the vessels result in sustained pulmonary hypertension [20]. This is a very serious complication of cirrhosis of the liver.

SUMMARY

Alcoholics, by virtue of their indulgence, have depressed the defense and clearing actions of their respiratory tracts and have impaired certain immunologic mechanisms, making them prone to respiratory disease, not only producing a higher incidence of these diseases in alcoholic populations than in the general population, but also a higher mortality. Increase in the occurrence of neoplasms of the larynx and esophagus are other risks of alcohol abuse. Because alcoholics are difficult to treat and manage, they are a health risk to the community, especially when they have an infectious and contagious disease like tuberculosis.

REFERENCES

1. Askin, F. B., Kuhn, C. The cellular origin of pulmonary surfactant. Lab. Invest. 25: 260, 1971.
2. Banner, A. S. Pulmonary function in chronic alcoholism. Am. Rev. Respir. Dis. 108: 851, 1973.
3. Berthelot, P., Walker, J. G., and Sherlock, S. Arterial changes in the lungs in cirrhosis of the liver—lung spider nevi. N. Eng. J. Med. 274:291, 1966.
4. Besman, I. R., and Lyons, H. A. Aspiration pneumonia. Dis. Chest 35:6-10, 1959.
5. Brayton, R. G., Stokes, P. E., Schwartz, M. S., and Louria, D. B. Effect of alcohol and various diseases on leukocyte mobilization, phagocytosis and intracellular bacterial killing. N. Eng. J. Med. 282:123-128, 1970.
6. Burch, G. E., and DePasquale, N. P. Alcoholic lung disease—An hypothesis. Am. Heart J. 73:147, 1967.
7. Capps, J. A., and Coleman, G. H. Influence of alcohol on prognosis of pneumonia in Cook County Hospital, J.A.M.A. 80:750-752, 1923.
8. Chow, C. K., and Tuppel, A. L. An enzymatic protective mechanism against lipid peroxidation damage to lungs of ozone-exposed rats. Lipids 7:518, 1972.
9. Cross, C. E. The type II pneumocyte and lung antioxidant defense. Ann. Int. Med. 80:409, 1974.
10. Emergil, C., Sobol, B. J., and Heymann, B. Pulmonary function in alcoholics. Am. J. Med. 57:69, 1974.
11. Elevated superoxide dismutase in black alcoholics. Science 207:991-993, 1980.
12. Fritts, H. Systemic circulatory adjustments in hepatic disease. Med. Clin. N. Am. 47: 563, 1963.
13. Gee, B. L., Vassallo, C. L., and Bell, P. Catalase-dependent peroxidative metabolism in the alveolar macrophage during phagocytosis. J. Clin. Invest. 49:1260, 1970.
14. Gee, B. L., Vassallo, C. L., and Vogt, M. T. Peroxidative metabolism in alveolar macrophages. Arch. Int. Med. 127:1046, 1971.
15. Green, G. Pulmonary antibacterial mechanisms and the pathogenesis of pulmonary disease. Yale J. Biol. Med. 40:414-429, 1968.
16. Green, G. M. Pulmonary antibacterial mechanisms and pathogenesis of pulmonary disease. Aspen Emphysema Conf. 10:463-480, 1967.
17. Guarer, J. J., and Laurenzi, G. A. Effect of alcohol on mobilization of alveolar macrophages. J. Lab. Clin. Med. 72:40-45, 1968.

18. Heineman, H. O. Alcohol and the lung: A brief review. *Am. J. Med.* 63:81–85, 1977.

19. Jones, H. W., Roberts, J., and Brantner, J. Incidence of tuberculosis among homeless men. *J.A.M.A.* 155:1222–1223, 1934.

20. Kirby, W. M., Waddington, W. S., and Byron, F. Differentiation of right upper lobe pneumonia from bronchogenic carcinoma. *N. Eng. J. Med.* 256:828–833, 1957.

21. Lyons, H. A., and Saltzman, A. Diseases of the respiratory tract in alcoholics. *Biology of Alcohol: Clinical* (Vol. 3), Kissin, B. and Begleiter, H. (eds.). Plenum: New York, 1974.

22. Maimark, A. Cellular dynamics and lipid metabolism in the lung. *Fed. Proc.* 32, 1967, 1973.

23. Parkinson, P. R. The relationship of alcohol to immunity. *Lancet* 2:1580–1582, 1909.

24. Perlman, L. V., Lerner, E., and D'Esoppo, N. Clinical classification and analysis of 97 cases of lung abscess. *Am. Rev. Respir. Dis.* 99:390–398, 1969.

25. Ranking, J. G., Hale, G. S., Wilkinson, P., O'Day, D. M., Santamaria, J. M., and Babarczy, G. Relationship between smoking and pulmonary disease in alcoholism. *Med. J. Anat.* 1:730–733, 1969.

26. Rodman, T., Sobel, M., and Clone, H. P. Arterial oxygen unsaturation and the ventilation-perfusion defect of Laennec's cirrhosis. *N. Eng. J. Med.* 263:73, 1960.

27. Ruff, F., Hughes, J. M. B., Hiff, L. D., McCarthy, D., and Milic-Emili, J. Distribution of pulmonary blood flow and ventilation in patients with liver cirrhosis. *Thorax* 26:229, 1971.

28. Rush, B. An enquiry into the effects of ardent spirits upon the human body and mind with an account of preventing and of remedies for curing them. *J. Stud. Alcohol* 4: 321–341, 1943–1944. (Reprint of 1814)

29. Ryan, J. W., Smith, V., and Niemeyer, R. S. Angiotensin I: Metabolism by plasma membrane of lung. *Science* 176:64, 1972.

30. Schmidt, W., and DeLint, J. Mortality experiences of male and female alcoholics Q. *J. Stud. Alcohol* 30:112–118, 1969.

31. Shattuck, F. C., and Lawrence, C. H. Acute lobar pneumonia. *Boston Med. Surg. J.* 178:245–251, 1918.

32. Stossel, T. P. Phagocytosis. *N. Eng. J. Med.* 290:717–833, 1974.

33. Vane, J. R. The release and fate of vaso-active hormones in the circulation. *Br. J. Pharmacol.* 35:209, 1969.

34. Van Mettre, T. E., Jr. Pneumococcal pneumonia treated with antibiotics. *N. Eng. J. Med.* 251:1048–1052, 1954.

35. Vogt, M. T., Thomas, C., and Vassallo, C. L. Glutathione-dependent perioxidative metabolism in alveolar macrophages. *J. Clin. Invest.* 50:401, 1971.

26

DAVID H. KNOTT, MD, PhD, Memphis Mental Health Institute, Memphis, Tennessee

JAMES D. BEARD, PhD, Memphis Mental Health Institute, Memphis, Tennessee

EFFECTS OF ALCOHOL INGESTION ON THE CARDIOVASCULAR SYSTEM

THE DELETERIOUS EFfects of acute and chronic alcohol ingestion on the heart and blood vessels have long been recognized; however, research interest in and clinical appreciation of this area have only recently begun to flourish. Early reports that suggested the direct cardiotoxicity of alcohol were offset by the assumption that nutritional and vitamin deficiencies associated with heavy alcohol use were necessary ingredients to produce cardiovascular disease. The societal ambivalence toward the benefit-risk ratio of drinking alcohol was reflected in the endorsement of the discretionary use of alcohol in the treatment of various cardiovascular disorders such as angina pectoris, hypertension, and obliterative vascular disease. During the past decade this concept has not been widely accepted by clinicians; however, recent sugges-

---

David H. Knott, MD, PhD, Assistant Superintendent, Clinical/Residential Services, Memphis Mental Health Institute, and Clinical Associate Professor of Psychiatry, University of Tennessee Center for the Health Sciences, Memphis, Tennessee.

James D. Beard, PhD, Director, Alcohol Research Center, Memphis Mental Health Institute, and Associate Professor of Physiology in Psychiatry, University of Tennessee Center for the Health Sciences, Memphis, Tennessee.

tions that alcohol might exert a protective effect in the development of coronary atherogenesis is again causing confusion and controversy.

ALCOHOL AND CIRCULATORY DISEASE: MORBIDITY AND MORTALITY

The disease concept of alcoholism has prompted a number of mortality and morbidity studies of alcoholics and heavily drinking populations. The mortality in these populations exceeds the expected death rate, and cardiovascular mortality makes up more than 20% of the excess [1].

Although morbidity data are not extensive, studies do suggest that vocational dysfunction secondary to cardiovascular diseases was 1.9 times greater in an employed alcoholic population versus matched controls.

There is no reason to doubt the direct toxic effects of alcohol on the cardiovascular system; however, other factors certainly contribute to the enhanced circulatory disease mortality and morbidity in heavily drinking and alcoholic persons.

1. Heavy smoking. Most heavy drinkers are also heavy smokers; epidemiologically, cigarette smoking has been established as a major risk factor for ischemic heart disease and hypertension. Whether or not heavy smoking and heavy drinking act in concert additively or synergistically is not known. Studies do reveal that the consumption of three or more drinks a day results in higher systolic and diastolic pressures in both men and women independent of smoking, and hypertension is known to play a role in circulatory disease mortality and morbidity.

2. Nutritional-metabolic abnormalities. The chronic and prodigious use of alcohol adversely affects nutrition and metabolism, which can produce a negative impact on normal cardiovascular functioning. These effects include but certainly are not limited to (a) hyperlipidemia; (b) vitamin deficiencies, especially those involving thiamine and vitamin c; (c) protein deficiency; (d) carbohydrate intolerance; (e) hypoglycemia; (f) abnormalities in mineral metabolism (e.g., reduction in total exchangeable magnesium, Na^+ retention and increase in intracellular Na^+ in the myocardium, and possibly the intima of the peripheral vasculature), alterations in Ca^{++} metabolism, and deficiencies in and abnormal metabolism of zinc).

3. Life style patterns of alcoholics. Such factors as neglect of health, physical inactivity, and lack of compliance with prevention and treatment regimen could conceivably contribute to alcohol-related circulatory disease mortality and morbidity.

These factors, coupled with the direct cardiovascular toxicity of alcohol, mandate a continuing search for mechanisms and processes since cardiovascular disease per se leads all other causes of morbidity and mortality in this and many other countries.

EFFECT OF ALCOHOL ON THE CENTRAL CIRCULATION: PHYSIOLOGICAL CONSIDERATIONS

Cardiac Metabolism

The acute administration of ethanol to experimental animals and chronic alcoholic subjects results in an immediate increase in myocardial glyceride content. The initial response is an increase in triglyceride uptake by the heart in the absence of triglyceridemia. Secondarily, there appears to be an enhanced triglyceride production by cardiac tissue, utilizing as a substrate increased available amounts of acetate consequent to alcohol metabolism. Studies that focus on the chronic experimental administration of alcohol reveal that the glyceride content remains elevated but does return to normal following abstinence from alcohol. Accompanying the increase in myocardial triglyceride uptake and production, there is a concomitant decrease in free fatty acid uptake by the heart. With these changes in lipid metabolism, there is an increase in cardiac uptake of glucose, lactate, and acetate, the metabolism of which temporarily impairs the primary utilization of lipids for energy. It appears that both the acute and chronic ingestion of alcohol changes the formation and utilization of substrates to effect a more inefficient energy production [8, 10].

While there is a major effect on cardiac lipids, alcohol also exerts a profound effect on mineral metabolism. Potassium and phosphate egress from cardiac tissue occurs after an acute insult with alcohol and is similar to that seen in ischemic necrosis but appears to be rapidly reversible. Acute and chronic alcohol ingestion in the experimental situation (canine) leads to an increase in intracellular Na^+ content, which is reversible with abstinence from alcohol [8]. Recent advances in knowledge of excitation contraction coupling mechanisms and the effect that acute and chronic alcohol consumption exerts in this regard are pertinent to the impact that ethanol has on cardiac performance. Although direct alcohol-induced mitochondrial damage leads to metabolic defects, injury to the excitation contraction coupling mechanism and contractile proteins occurs as well. Excitation contraction coupling and relaxation in the myocardium results from interactions between myofibrillar proteins actin and myosin and an energy-dependent calcium movement. The functional anatomic site for this process is the sarcoplasmic reticulum, which alcohol damages both structurally and biochemically. Additionally, the direct and indirect impairment of adenosinetriphosphatase (ATPase) by alcohol may adversely affect the active uptake and transport of Ca^{++}.

Chronic alcohol use leads to a deficiency in myocardial protein synthesis obviously affecting the contractile elements. The effect on protein synthesis may be due to acetaldehyde rather than ethanol per se.

The observation that zinc deficiencies, which can be caused by experimental chronic alcohol use, are involved with cardiac dysfunction is stimulating further investigation into the role that alcohol-induced abnormalities in trace metal metabolism plays in cardiac disease associated with alcoholism.

Cardiac Morphology

Alcohol-induced metabolic changes are generally thought to precede structural alterations. Based on the above discussion one would expect these alterations to primarily involve the mitochondria, sarcoplasmic reticulum, and the contractile elements. The developmental progression of alcohol-induced morphological abnormalities in the heart appears to be as follows: mitochondrial swelling → increased mitochondrial lipid inclusions → degenerating mitochondrial cristae → intramyocardial accumulation of lipids → swelling and degeneration of the sarcoplasmic reticulum → changes in the myocytes with loss of cross-striation, pyknotic nuclei, vaculolization, and hydropic and fatty and hyaline degeneration → areas of degeneration, fibrosis, and endocardial thickening. Coronary vessels show little evidence of arteriosclerotic change. These pathological findings have been described in experimental and clinical situations involving alcoholic cardiomyopathy and are extremely similar to the picture seen in cases of cardiomyopathy from other causes. The metabolic and structural aberrations are consonant with the effect of alcohol on cardiac function [4].

Cardiac Function

Contractility and cardiac reserve. A number of experimental and clinical observations have suggested that alcohol causes a functional impairment on the heart even in the absence of clinical cardiac disease [9]. Acute and chronic studies using invasive and noninvasive techniques and involving isolated cardiac muscle fibers, anesthetized and unanesthetized experimental animals, alcoholic patients with and without heart disease, and normal, healthy subjects generally indicate that alcohol is a myocardial depressant that reduces contractility. This depressant activity is more pronounced if clinical heart disease (especially coronary artery disease) is coexistent [3].

Cardiovascular reflexes. Relatively little attention has been paid to the effect of alcohol on reflex activity of the cardiovascular system. A study that involved healthy, normal volunteers who ingested doses of alcohol characterized as "social drinking" indicated that acceleration of heart rate and peripheral vasoconstriction in response to stress were more pronounced than in the absence of alcohol and suggested that alcohol enhances cardiovascular reflex modulation. While this may be of little import in nonalcoholic, physiologically healthy subjects, it may be significant in persons with underlying cardiac disease [11].

Electrophysiology of the heart. The metabolic and structural effects of alcohol on the contractile tissue of the heart appear also in the conducting system;

thus, one would expect some electrophysiological consequences. Although there are a number of clinical reports describing electrocardiogram (EKG) changes associated with alcoholic heart disease, there is little experimental evidence derived from either in vitro or in vivo studies of the effect of alcohol on the cardiac conducting system. Extensive investigation of the influence that alcohol exerts on skeletal muscle suggests that acute exposure to ethanol results in an increase in membrane conductance, lowering of membrane resistance, and a decrease in resting membrane potential, all of which appear to be dose-dependent. An increase in intracellular Na^+ plus alterations in the availability and binding of Mg^{++} and Ca^{++} may be implicated. The overall result appears to be a heightened excitability, along with an increase in conduction time as reflected by a prolongation of both depolarization and repolarization intervals. The depression of alcohol of the cardiac conduction system is augmented in patients with organic heart disease.

Coronary circulation. The inconsistency and controversy involving the effect of acute and chronic alcohol exposure in animal (and a few human) studies result from varying investigative approaches (e.g., open chest vs. closed chest, anesthetized vs. unanesthetized animals, and the measurement of total coronary blood flow vs. regional cardiac blood flow). Since alcohol has been prescribed as a coronary vasodilator, further research is needed in this area. Even though studies have shown an increase or a decrease or no change in coronary flow during the acute administration of alcohol, there is general consensus that concomitant hemodynamic and metabolic consequences such as increased O_2 requirements, tachycardia, elevated systolic and diastolic blood pressure, and increased left ventricular end-diastolic pressure offer no cardiac benefits to persons with organic heart disease and probably not to normal, healthy individuals as well [4].

EFFECT OF ALCOHOL ON THE CENTRAL CIRCULATION: PATHOPHYSIOLOGICAL CONSIDERATIONS

Alcoholic Cardiomyopathy

Primary myocardial disease (PMD) that is not clearly secondary to congenital, hypertensive, or arteriosclerotic causes is attracting increasing etiologic, diagnostic, therapeutic, and prognostic consideration. The association between chronic heavy alcohol use and heart failure has been recognized for well over 100 years. Most clinicians now agree that while the combination of alcoholism and malnutrition are mutually exacerbating factors in the development of certain cases of PMD, alcohol itself can effect a cardiomyopathy [8, 10].

Etiology. The light and electron microscopic morphological abnormalities of alcoholic cardiomyopathy are generally indistinguishable from those associated with cardiomyopathies from other causes. An attractive postulate as to the pathogenesis of alcoholic heart disease involves pathology in the intramyocardial coronary arteries. A study that included a relatively young group of patients suffering from a chronic alcoholic state and in whom there was no clinical evidence of alcoholic cardiomyopathy or of pathology of the large coronary arteries revealed five basic vascular abnormalities in the intramyocardial small arteries: vascular wall edema, perivascular fibrosis, vascular sclerosis, subendothelial lumps, and vascular wall inflammation with primary endothelial cell damage as a common pathogenic mechanism for all the changes [6]. These changes in turn result in ischemia, which, if severe and prolonged enough, would lead to the clinical manifestation of alcoholic cardiomyopathy. The vascular changes occur at a later time than the appearance of structural damage to the mitochondria, sarcoplasmic reticulum, myofibrils, and so forth. Possible etiologic considerations in the development of the intramyocardial small vessel disease include a direct toxic effect of ethanol and/or acetaldehyde and alcohol-related indirect effects such as depletion of myocardial catecholamines and cardiac magnesium depletion.

Save levels of alcohol ingestion have not been established in regard to the cardiotoxicity of this drug; however, it has been estimated that 80 g of ethanol a day (equivalent to six standard drinks) over a period of several years are required to produce a clinically apparent cardiomyopathy in persons without underlying organic heart disease.

Diagnosis. Alcoholic cardiomyopathy covers a broad spectrum of signs and symptoms and exists to different degrees of severity; early diagnosis is critical for a favorable prognosis. The following are early manifestations of this disease:

1. Regular consumption of excessive amounts of alcohol for many years (possibly 10 to 15 years or more)
2. Complaints of shortness of breath with exertion, palpitations, paroxysmal nocturnal dyspnea
3. Persistent sinus tachycardia and an elevated resting systolic blood pressure
4. Alteration of systolic time intervals—that is, a prolonged preejection period (PEP) and an increased preejection period (PEP) relative to left ventricular ejection time (LVET) in the resting state and following exercise when compared to nonalcoholic controls.
5. Marked decrease in exercise tolerance
6. Although EKG changes may be absent in the earlier phases, the following (in association with the history and other signs and symptoms) are suggestive even though the person is asymptomatic: (a) sinus tachycardia; (b) nonspecific S-T-T wave changes; (c) multifocal extra systoles; (d) T-P phenomenon—that is, a prolongation of the S-T segment so that the P wave is inscribed before the T wave returns to the isoelectric line

7. Abnormal liver function tests
8. Prominent hilar vascular shadows on chest x-ray with little or no congestion in the peripheral lung fields

More advanced forms present with overall congestive heart failure often accompanied by atrial fibrillation, congestion of peripheral lung fields, S-T segment depression, bundle branch block, generalized (biventricular) cardiac enlargement, prominent venous distention and pulse in the neck, gallop rhythm, systolic murmur of either mitral or tricuspid insufficiency, significantly abnormal liver function tests, and hypesthesia and parethesia, particularly in the lower extremities.

Abstinence from alcohol is the foundation of treatment for all cases of alcoholic cardiomyopathy regardless of the extent of severity. Frequently this will interrupt the progression and even reverse the disease in its earlier forms. Frank congestive heart failure is managed conventionally; however, the prognosis is generally considered to be more grave than in cases of congestive failure from other causes.

Coronary Artery Disease

There is considerable historical and current documentation of the negative association between heavy drinking, alcoholism, and occlusion of the large coronary arteries [2]. Recent findings suggest a coronary obstruction and limiting effect of alcohol independent from other coronary risk factors such as hypertension, heavy smoking, and triglyceridemia, all of which are associated with heavy alcohol use. A popular speculation is that the apparently protective effect of alcohol on the development of coronary artery disease is due to the fact that alcohol use is associated with increased levels of high density lipoproteins that reportedly prevent and possibly reverse the coronary atherogenic process. It should be noted that there may be extensive intramyocardial small vessel pathology associated with heavy drinking even in the absence of large vessel pathology. In view of this, there is currently insufficient evidence to propose that alcohol is protective and thus beneficial to cardiac functioning and further to cardiac mortality and morbidity.

Cardiac Arrythmias

Clinical case reports indicate that the use and occasional overuse of alcohol can, in some instances, produce transient arrythmias, namely, paroxysmal atrial tachycardia, atrial fibrillation, atrial and ventricular ectopic beats, and sinus tachycardia in individuals who are not alcoholics and have no organic heart disease ("the holiday heart") [5]. If underlying heart disease is present, these conduction disturbances occur more regularly. The EKG changes of alcoholic cardiomyopathy are described above.

Angina and Myocardial Infarction

Recent studies have suggested an inverse relationship between alcohol use and myocardial infarction. This inverse relationship appears to be slightly progressive with drinking up to six or more drinks a day; however, the most striking difference in the risk for myocardial infarction is that between nondrinkers and those who consume two drinks or fewer a day, with the latter group showing a diminished incidence for major coronary events [7]. Extreme caution must be used in interpreting these data; while there may be agreement that moderate drinking is associated with reduced incidence of heart attacks, this does not prevail with problem drinkers and alcoholics. Necroscopic evidence has shown that among alcoholics who die a cardiac death there is frequently a transmural myocardial scar; however, there is no clinical history of a myocardial infarction and no significant coronary (large vessel) atherosclerosis. The intramyocardial small artery disease associated with cardiac myopathy described previously could conceivably compromise appropriate cardiac nutrition, especially in high blood flow requirement situations, so atypical and subclinical myocardial infarctions might occur more frequently than previously suspected. Another possible explanation of myocardial infarction without coronary atherosclerosis in heavy drinkers and alcoholics is external constriction of coronary vessels by scarring due to an underlying cardiomyopathy [10].

Classical angina is unusual with alcoholic cardiomyopathy and with the atypical myocardial infarction observed in alcoholics. The Prinzmetal variant of angina allegedly due to large vessel coronary vasospasm can be induced and exacerbated by alcohol. There appears to be no rationale for the prescription of alcohol in patients with angina.

EFFECT OF ALCOHOL ON THE PERIPHERAL CIRCULATION: PHYSIOLOGICAL CONSIDERATIONS

A limited number of studies on the hemodynamic impact of ethanol on the peripheral circulation (pressure-volume-flow relationships) suggest that ethanol exerts no effect—a hypodynamic effect or a hyperdynamic effect. The conflicting data result from a number of differences in methodology, doses of alcohol, choice of experimental subjects, level of anesthesia, presence or absence of cardiovascular disease, and such. It has been assumed that any acute or chronic drastic change in peripheral hemodynamics caused by alcohol is primarily a reflection of the action on the central circulation [8].

For many years a presumed effect of alcohol has been a vasodilatory action, particularly involving the circulation of the skin. There appears to be a distinct difference in this regrad depending on whether or nor alcohol is ingested orally or infused intravenously. Intravenous alcohol causes constriction of the arterioles of the skin and skeletal muscle; this vasoconstrictive action is not abolished by either sympathectomy or prior treatment with phenoxybenzamine. The data suggest that ethanol per se exerts a direct vasoconstrictive influence on the arteriolar beds of both skin and muscle. When alcohol is given orally, vasodilation of arterioles supplying the skin is observed, with a concomitant vasoconstriction of vessels supplying the corresponding muscle mass. Thus, the vasodilating properties of alcohol appear to be mediated through central reflex phenomena involving neural vasomotor regulatory centers; the vasoconstricting action may be due to a direct effect on arterioles. Another postulate is that alcohol's action is totally vasoconstrictive; the vasodilation occurs because of the peripheral and/or central effects of acetaldehyde.

There is a paucity of information concerning morphological changes in the peripheral vasculature due to acute and chronic exposure to alcohol. In view of the effect of alcohol on intramyocardial small vessels and of the secondary consequences of acute and chronic alcohol consumption such as hyperosmolality, intracellular metabolic changes, Na^+ retention, transcellular electrolyte shifts, and the central and possibly peripheral release and depletion of catecholamines, it is attractive to speculate that some structural changes do occur, particularly at the arteriolar and capillary levels. The growing awareness of the association of heavy drinking, alcoholism, and hypertension demands further research and clinical correlation.

EFFECT OF ALCOHOL ON THE PERIPHERAL CIRCULATION: PATHOPHYSIOLOGICAL CONSIDERATIONS

Cerebral Vascular Accident

There is currently a suspicion that a positive relationship exists between heavy alcohol use and cerebral vascular accident (stroke) — with the hemorrhagic type predominating over the thrombotic type [7]. This relationship appears to be, at least in part, independent from hypertension. The direct effect of alcohol on platelet function and the indirect hemostatic effects secondary to liver dysfunction may be of some importance.

Hypertension

For years alcohol use has either been prescribed or certainly not discouraged as a means of treating or even preventing hypertension. Early epidemiological studies failed to demonstrate an association between hypertension and alcohol use;

however, these studies were not designed with an appreciation of or sensitivity to different levels of alcohol use.

Hypertension is known to be associated with the alcohol abstinence syndrome. Frequently, blood pressures remain elevated and labile for 2 to 3 weeks after cessation of drinking, during which time clinically significant signs and symptoms of withdrawal are absent. Thereafter, with abstinence blood pressure returns to normal. Alcohol-induced hypertension could be due to a number of factors associated with heavy drinking, such as Na+ retention and an increase in circulating catecholamines. Reversible alcohol-induced hypertension should not be mistaken for essential hypertension (hypertensive vascular disease) since abstinence from alcohol or a dramatic change in the drinking pattern are curative, thus obviating the need for antihypertensive medication [8].

Recent, more sophisticated epidemiologic studies designed to assess the morbidity of alcohol consumption reveal increasingly convincing evidence that an association does exist between the regular and substantial use of alcohol and clinically significant elevations in blood pressure [7].

Data indicate that mean blood pressures in a drinking population that consumes two or fewer drinks a day were similar to the pressures of nondrinkers. However, persons consuming three or more drinks a day had higher systolic and diastolic pressures than nondrinkers or moderate drinkers (two or fewer drinks a day). This positive correlation continued to increase in Caucasian males and females up to the consumption of six to eight drinks a day. The pressures of black males and females showed a positive correlation from two up to three to five drinks a day, but not above this level. According to Klatsky et al. [7], the association between alcohol use and elevated blood pressure appears to be "independent of age, sex, race, cigarette smoking, coffee use, past heavy drinking, adiposity, educational attainment, or regular salt use." Thus, while unequivocal proof does not exist that alcohol use above two drinks daily causes hypertension, the current evidence certainly suggests a strong possibility. The diagnostic and management implications for hypertensive individuals who use alcohol should be carefully considered by the treating physician.

Considering recent information concerning cardiovascular mortality and morbidity associated with alcohol, it is difficult to avoid appreciating the direct and indirect toxicity of this drug on the central and peripheral circulatory systems. Future basic and clinical research in this area is certainly pertinent to the diagnosis, treatment, and prevention of both cardiovascular disease and alcoholism, which rank first and third respectively as the major causes of mortality and morbidity in this country.

REFERENCES

1. Ashley, M. J., and Rankin, J. Hazardous alcohol consumption and diseases of the circulatory system. *J. Stud. Alcohol* 41:1040-1069, 1980.
2. Barboriak, J. J., Anderson, A. J., Rimm, A. A., and Tristani, F. E. Alcohol and coronary arteries. *Alcoholism: Clin. Exp. Res.* 3:29-32, 1979.
3. Bing, R. J., and Tillmans, H. Metabolic effects of alcohol on the heart. *Ann. N.Y. Acad. Sci.* 252:243-249, 1975.
4. Bing, R. J., and Tillmans, H. The effect of alcohol on the heart. In: *Metabolic Aspects of Alcoholism*, Lieber, C. (ed.). MTP Press: Lancaster, 1977.
5. Ettinger, P. O., Lyons, M., Oldewurtel, H. A., and Regan, T. J. Cardiac conduction abnormalities produced by chronic alcoholism. *Am. Heart J.* 91:66-78, 1976.
6. Factor, S. M. Intramyocardial small vessel disease in chronic alcoholism. *Am. Heart J.* 92:561-575, 1976.
7. Klatsky, A. L., Friedman, G. D., and Siegelaub, A. B. Alcohol use, myocardial infarction, sudden cardiac death, and hypertension. *Alcoholism: Clin. Exp. Res.* 3(1):33-39, 1979.
8. Knott, D. H., and Beard, J. D. Changes in cardiovascular activity as a function of alcohol intake. In: *The Biology of Alcoholism* (Vol. 2), Kissin, B. and Begleiter, H. (eds.). Plenum: New York, 1972.
9. Liedtke, A. J., and DeMuth, W. E. Effects of alcohol on cardiovascular performance after experimental nonpenetrating chest trauma. *Am. J. Cardiol.* 35:243-250, 1975.
10. Regan, T. J., Ettinger, P. O., Haider, B., Ahmed, S., Oldewurtel, H. A., and Lyons, M. M. The role of ethanol in cardiac disease. *Ann. Rev. Med.* 28:393-409, 1977.
11. Zsoter, T. T., and Sellers, E. M. Effect of alcohol on cardiovascular reflexes. *J. Stud. Alcohol* 38:1-10, 1976.

27

ALBERT B. LOWENFELS, MD, New York Medical College

TRAUMA, SURGERY, AND ANESTHESIA

OF ALL THE CHRONIC illnesses, alcoholism is undoubtedly the most widespread, and for the surgeon, the alcoholic patient can be a most difficult diagnostic and therapeutic challenge. Some of the adverse results of alcoholism are as follows:

1. It can mask the symptoms of an unrelated but potentially life-threatening illness or injury. For example, the diagnosis of serious head injury is notoriously difficult in the acutely intoxicated individual.

2. Alcohol causes a large number of serious diseases often referred to the surgeon (Table 1).

3. Alcoholism frequently interferes with normal pre- and postoperative care so that even simple procedures become hazardous. For example, withdrawal syndromes in the immediate postoperative period can be particularly hazardous for the recently operated patient.

ALCOHOLISM AND TRAUMA

There is a close relationship between alcoholism and trauma — a linear increase in blood alcohol levels causes a geometric rise in the chance of being involved in an accident. This is why approximately 50% of fatal automobile accidents are alco-

---

Albert B. Lowenfels, MD, Professor of Surgery, New York Medical College, New York, New York.

Table 1
Common Surgical Problems in Alcoholic Patients

Head and Neck	Colon, Rectum
Laceration, skull fracture	Hemorrhoids (check for cirrhosis)
Subdural hematoma	
Cancer of oropharynx or larynx	Liver, Biliary
Rhinophyma (brandy nose)	Nonvisualization of gallbladder after spree drinking
Thorax	Hepatoma
Gallstones (frequent in cirrhosis)	
Aspiration pneumonia	
Lung abscess	Pancreas
Esophageal cancer	Acute, chronic pancreatitis
Esophageal varices	Pancreatic pseudocyst
Spontaneous rupture of esophagus	
Fractured ribs	
Stomach	Extremities
Gastritis	Dupuytren's contracture
Mallory-Weiss syndrome	Venous leg ulcers (wine sores)
Peptic ulcer	Fractures

hol-related. This worldwide problem of alcoholism and automobile fatalities can be only marginally improved by improvements in surgical diagnosis and therapy; it will require a change in attitudes so that driving after excessive drinking becomes socially and legally unacceptable.

Head Injury

All forms of trauma are common in alcoholics, but head injury is especially common [2]. About one-third of all patients hospitalized with head injury will be alcoholic. Fortunately, the simplest type of injury, a scalp laceration, is the most frequent, but serious intracranial injury often accompanies an apparently trivial external laceration. Deciding whether the patient's symptoms are caused by alcohol or by trauma can be vexing and whenever there is any doubt it is far safer to admit the patient for a few hours of observation. Indications for hospitalization of the head-injured alcoholic should be quite liberal (see Table 2).

Scalp lacerations, as mentioned, are the most frequent and the simplest type of injury to manage. Here the association with acute alcoholism does offer one benefit — these lacerations can often be sutured without additional anesthesia.

Skull x-rays are generally ordered in patients admitted after head injury. Little information can be obtained from poor quality films obtained when the patient is belligerent. It is far better to postpone x-rays until the patient is sober so that informative x-rays are possible. Proper timing is just as essential for other investigative procedures, such as computerized tomography (CT) scans — if possible, these should be postponed until the patient can cooperate. However, it is safe and informative to use the gloved finger to palpate the base of any scalp laceration because this maneuver will sometimes detect a linear or depressed skull fracture.

Fracture Problems

Severe, complicated fracture problems resulting from a fall or an auto accident are often encountered in the injured alcoholic [4]. In some instances the patient has been so inebriated that he or she remains unaware of the injury and doesn't even seek medical attention for several days after the accident. Generally, one should consider any painful, swollen, or deformed extremity in the alcoholic as a fracture until proven otherwise, even in the absence of a definite history of injury.

Acutely inebriated patients or patients undergoing withdrawal symptoms with extremity fractures do not tolerate traction and it is best simply to immobilize the injured limb in a sturdy, well-padded splint until the patient becomes cooperative.

Fat embolism is a special problem for the injured alcoholic because in addition to the fracture site, a fatty liver can also give rise to embolic droplets of fat. Fat embolism often mimics the withdrawal syndrome—both cause fever and restlessness. Fat droplets in the urine, a petechial skin rash, and a low arterial PO_2 favor the diagnosis of fat embolism.

Abdominal Injury

Serious internal bleeding or injury can occur in the injured alcoholic patient without any visible external signs. The spleen is the organ most frequently injured after a fall or an accident and when torn it can be the source of life-threatening hemorrhage. Many times there is an accompanying head injury and when an unconscious patient with an obvious head injury develops shock it is tempting to attribute the hypotension to the head injury. Since head injury by itself usually does not cause hypotension, one should search for internal bleeding. Does the abdomen seem tender to deep palpation? Is the pulse rapid? Abdominal paracente-

Table 2
Suggested Criteria for Hospitalizing Head-Injured Alcoholic Patients

Unconsciousness
History of loss of consciousness
Definite or suspected skull fracture
Confusion or amnesia
Multiple injuries, even if the head injury is considered minor
Unreliability of patient
Single living arrangement or distance from the hospital

sis (abdominal tap) is a safe, rapid, and reliable diagnostic procedure that can be used to make the diagnosis of concealed internal hemorrhage. By inserting a needle or catheter into the abdomen the physician withdraws a sample of fluid — the presence of significant amounts of blood is telltale evidence of internal bleeding. Furthermore, it is helpful to remember that although the injury usually immediately precedes the acute bleeding episode, there can be a 1- to 2-week delay between injury and hemorrhage. Again, the history of injury may be difficult to obtain in the alcoholic patient.

SURGERY AND THE ALCOHOLIC PATIENT

Every surgical patient must be questioned about alcohol consumption; failure to do so inevitably invites disaster. Surgery can be specially hazardous for any patient who admits to daily consumption of 500 ml or more of distilled spirits or its equivalent in wine or beer. These individuals may have contracted any of a large number of serious surgical problems associated with alcoholism, and, in addition, withdrawal syndromes are likely to develop in the postoperative period.

Pre- and Postoperative Care

Both acute and chronic alcoholic patients require careful attention if surgery is to be performed safely. The following points have been useful:

1. Since abrupt cessation of drinking often leads to withdrawal syndromes, it is wise to defer elective surgery in known heavy drinkers for a 48-hour detoxification period. This time can be profitably used to assess the extent of damage to the liver and other vital organ systems.

2. If the history or the physical examination suggests heavy drinking, the preoperative workup must include studies to define liver function and nutritional status. A needle biopsy of the liver gives the most accurate, objective information about the status of the liver.

3. If liver damage is detected, a careful evaluation of the coagulation mechanism must be included. The patient should be questioned about prior bleeding episodes. The abdomen should be examined with care to determine if there is splenomegaly, often associated with portal hypertension. A complete blood count, platelet count, partial thromboplastin time, and prothrombin time should be performed.

4. Operating on the acutely intoxicated individual should be avoided unless it is truly an emergency. When possible surgery should be postponed for a few hours

to allow time for proper preoperative assessment and to be sure the stomach will be empty.

5. Withdrawal syndromes occurring in the immediate postoperative period must be considered a major complication requiring prompt treatment. Intravenous alcohol is not a safe drug to use.

Acute Abdominal Pain and Alcoholism

Even the most experienced surgeon can be baffled by abdominal pain in the alcoholic patient. Table 3 lists the most frequent causes of pain encountered in 100 consecutive alcoholics. Diseases of the stomach, duodenum, and pancreas head the list, but small bowel obstruction from prior surgery was common and was a frequent cause of death. Inability to remember significant details greatly hampers proper history taking. As an example in six of the most recent alcoholics with torn spleens, only one remembered being injured.

If an alcoholic patient takes a few drinks to relieve abdominal pain, the ensuing delay in seeking help significantly increases morbidity and mortality. When the patient finally does arrive at the local emergency room, intoxicated and belligerent, it is predictable that the physician will assume the symptoms are caused by alcohol rather than by something as serious as a perforated ulcer.

Of all the nonoperative causes for abdominal pain in the alcoholic patient, acute pancreatitis is the most puzzling [3, 8, 10]. An elevated amylase usually identifies these patients, but one must remember that this test may be abnormal with several other conditions (see Table 4). When it is impossible to distinguish between pancreatitis and a life-threatening condition requiring surgery, it is generally wiser to operate because laparotomy does not seem to increase the mortality rate if the patient does have pancreatitis [9].

Finally, the physician must remember that any acute abdominal emergency can arise in alcoholic patients.

Table 3
Causes for Acute Abdominal Pain in Alcoholic Patients

Disease	Number of Patients
Lesions of pancreas	33
Gastroduodenal, esophageal lesions	24
Small bowel obstruction (adhesions)	10
Abdominal trauma	9
Liver, biliary tract disorders	8
Colorectal lesions	8
Miscellaneous	8
Total	100

Table 4
Nonpancreatic Causes of Elevated Serum Amylase

Perforation of upper GI tract	Salivary gland lesions
Small bowel obstruction or infarction	Afferent loop obstruction
	Acute appendicitis
Biliary tract disease	Cerebral trauma
Renal insufficiency	Burns
Pregnancy (ectopic or intrauterine)	Postoperative state
	Diabetic ketoacidosis
Macroamylasemia	Renal transplantation
	Tumors

Case Example

A 43-year-old man had been recently hospitalized with an attack of acute pancreatitis. One month after discharge he returned to the hospital with fever, generalized abdominal pain, and vomiting. He admitted to continued drinking in the interval since his first hospitalization. On examination most of the tenderness was located in the lower right quadrant of the abdomen. There was leukocytosis, but serum amylase was normal.

At surgery he was found to have an acutely inflamed appendix. It was tempting to assume that the pain was caused by another attack of pancreatitis. Unfortunately, alcoholism does not reduce the risk of any of the common causes of abdominal pain.

Gastrointestinal Bleeding

Upper gastrointestinal hemorrhage must always be regarded as an ominous event in the alcoholic patient. Even patients with apparently minor acute bleeding episodes should be hospitalized because it is impossible to predict whether the bleeding will cease spontaneously or whether there will be a subsequent massive hemorrhage.

If the patient states that black stools have been present for several days it implies that the bleeding has been slow and that the workup can be more leisurely. However in many individuals copious vomiting of large quantities of bright red blood may be the first manifestation of a serious upper gastrointestinal disorder. In the alcoholic patient the usual causes are gastritis, duodenal ulcer, gastric ulcer, bleeding varices, and the Mallory-Weiss syndrome (a mucosal tear at the gastroesophageal junction from forceful retching). Most centers now have the capability to perform endoscopy and selective angiography for patients with emergency upper gastrointestinal bleeding. In nearly every instance, these two procedures, followed when necessary by barium meal, will pinpoint the source of the bleeding.

Even when the alcoholic patient is known to have developed esophageal varices it is dangerous to assume that varices are the cause of the bleeding without further investigation because a large percentage of these individuals will be hemorrhaging from another source. Additionally, all alcoholic patients with upper gastrointestinal bleeding must be asked about recent aspirin ingestion, since the combination of aspirin and alcohol is especially likely to cause acute gastritis.

A surgeon should be available whenever an alcoholic patient is hospitalized with upper gastrointestinal bleeding. In the majority of cases the bleeding will cease spontaneously, but if surgery is necessary it may have to be performed urgently.

The role of surgery for patients with esophageal varices is still in a state of evolution. It is clear that surgery should not be performed prophylactically in asymptomatic patients with varices. It is also clear that surgery is of considerable value for certain patients with bleeding varices, although which patients and which operations are not as clear.

Operative mortality is high when emergency surgery is performed for bleeding varices and if surgery is required a rapidly performed portacaval shunt, or perhaps a procedure to divide the varices with one of the newer stapling devices, may be the best answer.

Alcohol and Cancer

By some poorly understood mechanism, alcohol is known to increase the risk of several human cancers [1, 5, 6], including cancers of the oropharynx, the larynx, the esophagus, and the liver (see Figure 1). All of these tumors tend to be aggressive and when diagnosed late (which is usually the case) they are difficult to eradicate. The combination of heavy drinking and heavy smoking is especially hazardous — indeed, these two self-destructive habits are known to be the major risk factors for head and neck cancer in most parts of the world.

Health professionals who treat alcoholics should be aware of the increased risk of cancer so that symptoms suggesting malignancy, such as a painful sore in the mouth, persistent sore throat, voice change, or difficulty swallowing, can be recognized and investigated promptly and accurately.

Extremity Problems

As mentioned, complicated fracture problems are extremely common in alcoholic patients. Proper triage is important; when an extremity fracture is accompanied by an abdominal or head injury, definitive treatment of the injured extremity must be postponed until more urgent problems have been managed.

Neglect, poor hygiene, and migrant habits in skid row alcoholics lead to large venous ulcers termed "wine sores." Sometimes these ulcers will completely encircle the leg before the patient seeks attention. Although they usually heal after bed rest and skin grafting, resumption of a neglectful life style will usually result in recurrence.

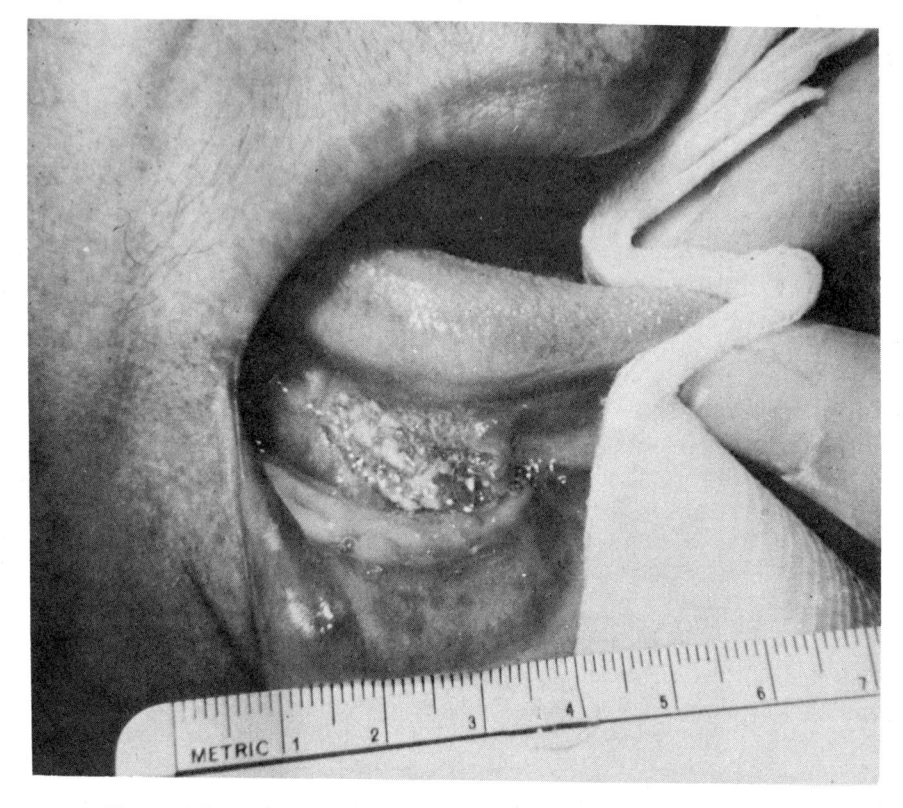

Figure 1. Cancer of the Mouth, a Common Tumor in Heavy Drinkers.

So far there is no evidence that alcoholism protects against ischemic disease of the extremities. Therefore, one encounters the same peripheral arterial lesions in drinkers as in abstinent individuals. Frostbite, a devastating extremity lesion, is most frequently seen in alcoholics (see Figure 2). Extreme cold is not a prerequisite, and indeed this injury is often seen at times when there is a combination of moderately cold temperatures and either rain or snow. The correct surgical approach is to be conservative until the exact extent of damage becomes evident. Loss of both feet severely limits any form of gainful employment.

ANESTHESIA

The presence of preexisting alcoholism markedly increases the risk of anesthesia for both the acutely intoxicated patient and for the chronic inebriate. In spite of notable advances in the field of anesthesia in recent years, these risks have not diminished [7, 11].

Anesthesia for the Acutely Intoxicated Patient

In all probability the acutely intoxicated individual will require urgent surgery for trauma, as, for example, following an automobile accident. Alcohol may act synergistically with certain anesthetic agents, such as barbiturates, so that the anesthesiologist must proceed cautiously to avoid significant central nervous system depression. Of particular concern is protection of the airway from the hazard of aspiration of gastric contents. It is safe to assume that every acutely intoxicated patient requiring anesthesia has a full stomach that will flood the lungs unless protective measures are taken prior to inducing anesthesia (see Figure 3). Undoubtedly the safest procedure is to empty the stomach with a large tube before starting anesthesia. This can be followed by a rapid intubation of the trachea with a cuffed tube administered with the patient's head and shoulders elevated. These measures will reduce the risk of aspiration, but whenever possible, it is far better to

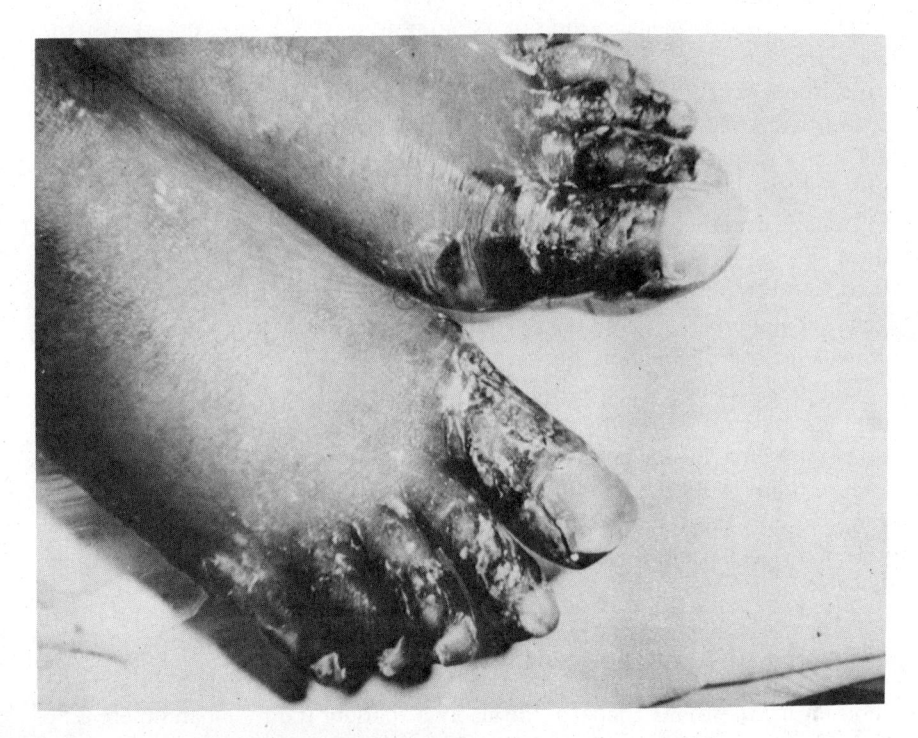

Figure 2. Bilateral Frostbite in an Alcoholic Patient.

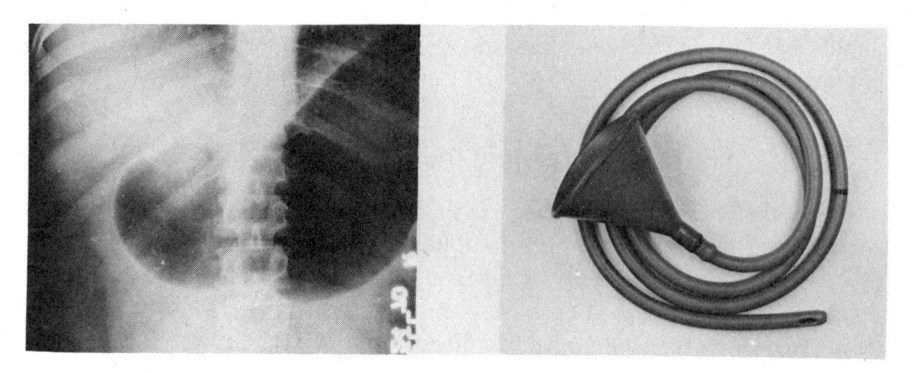

Figure 3. A Full Stomach, as Shown in This X-ray, Is a Serious Hazard for the Acutely Inebriated Patient Anesthetic. Use a Large Bore Tube To Aspirate the Stomach.

postpone surgery to allow the stomach to empty before the patient undergoes the operation.

The Chronic Alcoholic

Chronic alcoholism damages multiple organ systems; the changes observed in the heart, lungs, and liver are of particular concern to the anesthesiologist. Alcoholic myocardiopathy substantially reduces cardiac reserve, and may even predispose to cardiac failure when combined with the stress of anesthesia, injury, and blood loss. Alcoholic patients often exhibit bradycardia, arrhythmias, acidosis, hypotension, and left-heart failure.

Hepatic dysfunction may cause decreased detoxification of anesthetic drugs, thus prolonging the period required for the patient to recover from anesthesia. Also, hypotension, hypoxia, and acidosis are poorly tolerated by the alcohol-damaged liver and prolonged anesthesia combined with bleeding may be sufficient to produce hepatic decompensation.

Chronic alcoholics are nearly always heavy smokers, so it is hardly surprising that these patients frequently suffer from chronic lung disease such as bronchitis and emphysema. If time permits, pulmonary functions tests are well worthwhile because there is often a reduction in vital capacity and in expiratory flow rate. During surgery the patient's lungs should be ventilated with large tidal volumes to prevent atelectasis and blood gases should be monitored carefully in the postoperative period.

Choice of Anesthetic Agent

Choosing an anesthetic agent for the alcoholic patient is difficult and there is no single clearly superior drug that can be recommended for routine use. As pointed out previously, any general anesthetic agent is unsafe if the patient's stomach is full.

Certain choices are obviously unwise. For example, halothane would be a poor choice for an alcoholic patient with jaundice and liver cirrhosis. Barbiturates, if used, may have to be administered in greater than predicted amounts; probably alcoholics are tolerant to this drug as well as to other general anesthetic agents.

Some of these problems can be avoided by using regional anesthesia combined with judicious sedation. But in the final analysis, a skilled anesthesiologist must evaluate each patient individually to select the safest method.

REFERENCES

1. Alcohol and Cancer Workshop. *Cancer Res.* 39 (Part 2):2815-2908, 1979.
2. Gurdjian, E. S. Acute head injuries. *Surg. Gynecol. Obstet.* 146:805-820, 1978.
3. Kraft, A. R., and Saletta, J. D. Acute alcoholic pancreatitis: Current concepts and controversies. *Surgery Annu.* 8:145-171, 1976.
4. Lowenfels, A. B. The alcoholic patient. In: *Immediate Care of the Acutely Ill and Injured* (2nd ed.), Stephenson, H. E., Jr. (ed .). C. V. Mosby: St. Louis, 1978.
5. Lowenfels, A. B. Alcohol and cancer: A review and update. *Br. J. Alcohol Alcoholism* 14(3):148-163, 1979.
6. McMichael, A. J. Increases in laryngeal cancer in Britain and Australia in relation to alcohol and tobacco consumption trends. *Lancet* 1:1244-1247, 1978.
7. Orkin, L. R. Addiction, alcoholism, and anesthesia. *South. Med. J.* 70:1172-1174, 1977.
8. Paloyan, D., and Simonowitz, D. Diagnostic considerations in acute alcoholic and gallstone pancreatitis. *Am. J. Surg.* 132:329-331, 1976.
9. Ranson, J. H., Rifkind, K. M., Roses, D. F., Fink, S. D., Eng, K., and Spencer, F. C. Prognostic signs and the role of operative management in acute pancreatitis. *Surg. Gynecol. Obstet.* 139:69-81, 1974.
10. Sarles, H. Alcohol and the pancreas. *Adv. Exp. Med. Biol.* 85A:429-448, 1977.
11. Watson, T. D. and Lee, J. F. Preanesthetic care, intoxication and trauma. *Clin. Anesth.* 11:31-38, 1976.

28

STANLEY E. GITLOW, MD, Mount Sinai School of Medicine, New York, New York

THE CLINICAL PHARMACOLOGY AND DRUG INTERACTIONS OF ETHANOL

THE PRECEDING CHAPTERS offer the reader detailed insight into the effect of alcohol upon animal and even human tissues. This commentary redirects attention from the human organs to the organism. In deference to the pedantic, if one were forced to study but a single organ in order to develop clinical understanding of the use and effects of ethanol, the brain would surely be the organ of choice [6]. No one drinks alcohol for what it does to the liver. Rather, the drug is used for its ability to modify central nervous system (CNS) function. It shares this particular pharmacologic effect with numerous other chemical agents variously referred to as sedatives, hypnotics, soporifics, or somnifacients (Table 1). Although numerous drugs interact with alcohol in a myriad of ways, these particular agents mimic the quintessential action of alcohol upon the brain [12] to such an extent that were any to have appeared historically prior to alcohol, it is more than likely that the name of the illness, alcoholism, might instead have been barbism, chloralism, or paraldehydism.

Stanley E. Gitlow, MD, Clinical Professor of Medicine, Mount Sinai School of Medicine, New York, New York.

ETHANOL AND COMPARATIVE DRUGS: PHYSIOLOGIC EFFECTS

It is critical in an examination of the clinical pharmacology of ethanol to appreciate that it represents only a prototype of a group of drugs, any of which may replace it, and too often for the alcoholic, does. They are all irregular CNS depressants capable of modifying psychomotor activity. They differ from one another in route of administration, rate of absorption, dosage, distribution within the body, rate of turnover, degradation, and excretion. Their critical clinical act, however, they share. This is not to say that each modifies brain function by the same biochemical mechanism, though their intimate relationships in eliciting tolerance and dependence might suggest some common pathway.

Of all the ingested sedatives, ethanol represents one of the most rapidly acting. It is one of the few substances capable of absorption through the gastric lining, although the major portion of a dose may not be absorbed until passage into the jejunum. Only those agents administered parenterally or across the pulmonary (alveolar-capillary) membrane rival ethanol for rapidity of onset of action. Ethanol's rate of absorption may be diminished by food or other substances in the stomach. After absorption ethanol is broadly distributed, readily passing the blood-brain barrier. The sedative effect of the drug may therefore begin within 10 or 15 minutes of ingestion.

Within 12 to 24 hours of ethanol ingestion the body has essentially rid itself of this drug. The methods by which it does so play a role in its interrelationships with other drugs. When the blood alcohol concentration (BAC) exceeds 20%, its turnover follows zero-order kinetics. About 75% of the drug is catabolized in the liver. Less than 15% is excreted unchanged by the kidneys and lungs. The major catabolic system within the liver consists of alcohol dehydrogenase in the cytosol [5]. Secondary pathways include catalase in the peroxisomes and the microsomal ethanol oxidizing system (MEOS) in the smooth endoplasmic reticulum (SER). The initial step of ethanol oxidation results in the formation of large quantities of acetaldehyde, a toxic substance requiring aldehyde dehydrogenase for conversion. Although ubiquitous, this enzyme has its highest concentration in the mitochondria of the liver. These metabolic processes assume appropriate import when one realizes that of all the soporific drugs ethanol represents the only one supplying a major caloric load to the body. Indeed, its dosage is oftimes 1,000 times greater than those of the other sedative drugs.

As the BAC rises, the sedative effect increases. About 2 hours after ethanol ingestion, the BAC falls and agitation becomes apparent. Thus, at a singular BAC one may experience sedation (rising BAC) or agitation (falling BAC). These circumstances may be depicted graphically (Figure 1) by a short duration, large amplitude sedative action and a long duration, small amplitude agitative action. Clearly the duration of each of these will vary with dosage, rate of ingestion, and duration of drinking, but acute studies with ingestion of 30 to 100 gms. of ethanol

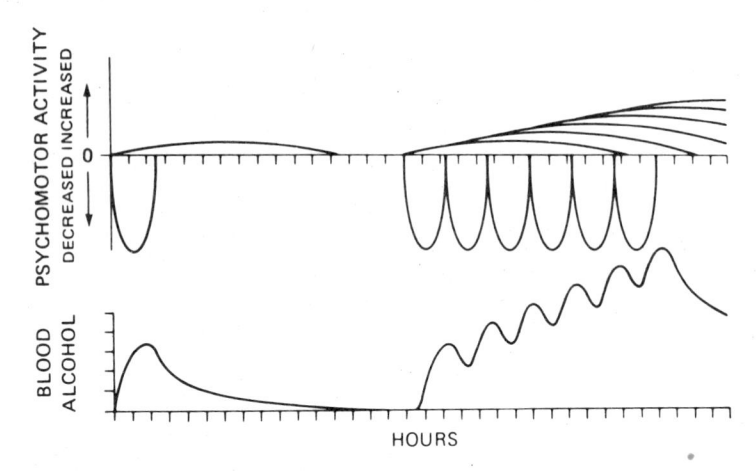

Figure 1. Schematic Representation of Asynchronous Relationship between Short-term, Large Amplitude Sedative Effect of Ethanol and Its Long-term, Low Amplitude Agitating Effect *(left)*. Repeated Doses of Ethanol Result in Summation of Its Agitating Effect *(right)*. (From "Alcoholism: A Disease" by S. E. Gitlow, in *Alcoholism: Progress in Research and Treatment*, P. G. Bourne and R. Fox, ed., Academic Press: New York, 1973. Reprinted by permission.)

usually result in 2 hours of obvious sedation followed by about 12 hours of subtle agitation. Repeated drinking of large quantities of ethanol gives rise to varying combinations of sedation from that most recently consumed and agitation resulting from that previously ingested. Under those circumstances, the resultant agitation may persist for considerably longer than 12 hours; in fact, it might be observed for many days [6].

THE WITHDRAWAL SYNDROME: ETHANOL–SPECIFIC PHYSIOLOGIC RESPONSES

The period of agitation has been labeled, somewhat erroneously, the "withdrawal syndrome." It is always associated with a decreased seizure threshold. When mild, it is characterized by no more than tremulousness, sweating, tachycardia, insomnia, and a general sense of foreboding; when severe, all the signs and symptoms of a severe toxic psychosis (acute alcoholic hallucinosis or delirium tremens) are exhibited. This asynchronous change in psychomotor activity represents the primary pharmacologic response; amplitude and duration of these changes in CNS function vary when one contrasts ethanol with the other soporifics. It is of more than casual interest to note that fully 50% of patients with alcoholism in a large urban community use or have used not only ethanol in a chemically dependent manner but one or more of its related sedatives as well. This figure is appreciably higher than one observes in a similar group when evaluating other psychotropic drugs, such as narcotics, antidepressants, (tricyclics or monoamine oxidase inhibitors), or major tranquilizers. In general, the alcoholic demonstrates preference for those pharmacologic agents possessing the peculiar ability to elicit the sequential change in psychomotor activity pathognomonic of ethanol use. In actuality, the biphasic change in psychomotor activity resulting from each of the soporifics may not represent that quality that attracts the alcoholic, but rather some characteristic of their shared sedative effect. Thus ethanol's sedation will diminish the augmented perceptual reactance of the alcoholic, whereas sedation resulting from chlorpromazine fails to accomplish this [18]. It is obvious that no one drinks for the effect observed the morning after, but rather for the almost immediate sedative action of the drug observed during the 2 hours following ingestion. It must be emphasized that this sedative period is not only translated clinically into a few hours of repose or sleep, although an appropriate dosage for any individual might elicit just that. Rather, a mild sedative effect might give another subject a feeling of vigor, strength, equanimity, or freedom and release. Whatever these subjective sensations during the first few hours after ethanol ingestion, their opposites are generated during the prolonged agitation phase. Thus the spree drinker is gratified upon entering bed that tomorrow is not a workday — only to awaken early and be unable to return to sleep the next morning. Despite the absence of an upset stomach or headache, the general irritability, sense of vague foreboding, and tremulousness persist until time is permitted to transpire (the agitation period wearing off during the afternoon of the night before), or unless the patient makes the poisonous discovery that the current sedation of recently ingested ethanol easily counteracts the agitation resulting from yesterday's drinking ("hair of the dog"). Unfortunately, each and every dose of alcohol results eventually in its own period of prolonged agitation. The game rapidly becomes one of borrowing from Peter to pay Paul, with the "interest" continually mounting: if sedation is equivalent to comfort, the soporific drugs always yield quantitatively less than the eventual discomfort resulting from the prolonged period of agitation. Studies of changes in sleep patterns following the use of barbiturates for short periods reveal this same disadvantageous ratio of immediate gratification versus prolonged discomfort ("Sleep now, pay later")[3].

Lack of a scientific understanding of this basic pharmacologic effect of ethanol has led to misunderstandings of social versus alcoholic drinking and even has led to such semantic difficulties as an attempt to euphemize alcoholism with the term "alcohol abuse." It should be obvious that each and every drink of alcohol results in the predictable asynchronous sequential change in psychomotor activity noted above. This is true whether the subject is an abstainer, a social drinker, an alcoholic, a dog, a cat, or a mouse. Moreover, the agitated state known as the withdrawal syndrome cannot only be produced in any mammal given enough ethanol for a long enough period but in its most subtle form begins with the first drink. In the human, one may require fairly low tolerance in order to perceive such modest effects, but in the rodent one can translate the psychomotor activity state into electroconvulsive or chemoconvulsive thresholds. A single dose of ethanol may then be noted to protect against seizure activity (sedation) for about 2 hours and then increase seizure activity (agitation) for some 12 hours prior to the return to normal [16]. This effect bears a striking temporal similarity to that which occurs in the human, despite the fact that the rodent metabolizes ethanol 10-fold faster than the human. Apparently all mammalian neural tissue possesses this specific pharmacologic response to ethanol and the rate of ethanol degradation or excretion bears no more relationship to this phenomenon than the rate with which one removes a hammer from the skull bears a relationship to the residual injury after head trauma. More importantly, such studies enable one to appreciate the fact that elevated psychomotor activity follows even a single modest dose of ethanol—or such rapid soporifics as the short-acting parenteral barbiturates [12]. This psychomotor hyperactivity is the precise reason for not only the withdrawal syndrome but it also explains why the soporific drug must be readministered in order to relieve the objective pathophysiology (i.e., current sedation is used in order to relieve the agitation resulting from previous sedation). Since the classical pharmacologic definition of the term "addiction" requires only that the drug in question result in objective evidence of pathophysiology that can be ameliorated in whole or part by its readministration, it is apparent that hard evidence exists for addiction to soporifics starting with the first dose. Even social drinkers experience such addictive phenomena (isomnia, agitation, elevated pulse and blood pressure, tremulousness, diaphoresis, and other evidence of autonomic instability). In fact, the increased tendency toward seizure activity can also be observed in the human. Patients with childhood onset of epilepsy occasionally reflect changes in their psychomotor activity state more modest than normal subjects may note. When they start to ingest ethanol, seizure activity diminishes (sedation), but for about 5 days thereafter seizure activity increases above their control level (agitation). Rodents given repeated doses of ethanol follow the same course, the 12-hour period of agitation after one dose of alcohol extending to 3 to 5 days. Interestingly, the most severe pathophysiologic aberrations associated with withdrawal occur to both the rodent and the human about 24 to 48 hours after the last drink.

To differentiate the three terms "social drinker," "alcohol abuser," and "alcoholic" on the basis of addiction to ethanol makes no scientific, not to say pharmacologic, sense whatever. Theoretically the alcoholic would drink more than others and hence be addicted more often and to a more severe degree. Even that belief falls before clinical experience, however. Some of the most severe alcoholic patients, those whose disease leads to death or severely maladapted lives, drink but periodically—some at only considerable intervals. Their total ethanol intake each year may be considerably less than that of many social drinkers. Thus, the volume of ethanol consumed is no more of an absolute criterion for differentiating the three groups noted above than is pharmacologic addiction.

One may produce addiction to alcohol in any volunteer, only the willingness to drink being required [11]. The severity of the addiction (physical dependence) will be proportional to many circumstances, not the least of which will be the daily dose and the duration of the experiment. Isbell et al. [11], in classical study of rum fits, demonstrated this ability to raise the psychomotor activity level (Figure 1) of nonalcoholic volunteers despite a more than adequate diet. What was missing from that study, however, was the request of a volunteer who had suffered an acute alcoholic hallucinosis with a grand mal seizure and a fractured spine to repeat the entire experiment. Isbell made (temporary) ethanol addicts, not alcoholics. What spells the difference is the willingness to reexperience the suffering by the alcoholic as opposed to the (volunteer) ethanol addict. The disease of alcoholism is not the drinking or the addiction but rather the need to return to the use of the soporific despite its cost.

This concept serves to reemphasize the importance of understanding the clinical pharmacology of alcohol only insofar as its CNS actions are concerned. How does this drug interface with the need of the alcoholic? Moreover, what pharmacologic actions upon the CNS does it share with the other soporifics? For the human organism, any action of ethanol unshared by chloral hydrate, phenobarbital, paraldehyde, and the host of other soporific drugs, is unlikely to shed much light upon the disease of alcoholism.

Not only do the soporific drugs demonstrate cross-addiction (when one is addicted severely and repeatedly to any one of them, there is increased likelihood to become dependent upon with any other), but the pathophysiology of the addiction to any one drug may be relieved by administration not only of that drug but any other of the group as well. The addictive phenomena may be held in abeyance by replacing the alcohol with a barbiturate, meprobamate, or diazepam. Indeed, when used within a controlled environment such substances are used to treat the withdrawal syndrome. But when used by the alcoholic as an outpatient, the temporary amelioration resulting from sedation is followed by increasing psychomotor hyperactivity, a deepened and more prolonged addictive state, and a patient whose illness is more difficult to treat.

Drug tolerance, that circumstance leading to increasing dosage in order to accomplish the same pharmacologic effect, is also characteristic of the soporific substances. In contrast to the narcotic group of drugs, wherein a 20-fold increase in tolerance may develop, the soporifics rarely attain more than a twofold tolerance. A daily quart of vodka might eventually be required to accomplish that which a pint did previously, but 20 pints could never be ingested in that time period. On the other hand, 5 mg of the narcotic methadon might eventually be replaced by 100 mg.

Tolerance that is attained during ethanol use falls into two broad categories, one related to CNS adaptation and the other resulting from changes in its metabolism. CNS adaptation may be conceptualized from Figure 1. Each drink leads to sedation of but short duration. The prolonged agitation becomes additive, however, and with continued drinking one eventually achieves a state of psychomotor hyperactivity. At this point, the subject can often tolerate a more considerable amount of sedation than normally. It is as though one were to give a sedative shortly after a stimulant. Under such circumstances, even the ascending limb of BAC may fail to witness a lethal sedative effect in the presence of 0.5 to 0.7% blood alcohol levels (levels which may result in death of subjects without elevated tolerance). The "hollow leg" is less a measure of machismo than it is a measure of how much and how consistently one has been drinking during recent yesterdays.

It is for this very reason that the BAC is such a meaningless measurement of sedation. At a singular alcohol level, the subject might be sedated or agitated, and at some high blood level one human might be near death and another driving a motor vehicle. All of this is the result of the single most important determinant of tolerance, CNS adaptation.

Despite the memory of possessing high tolerance when they first began to drink, alcoholic subjects appear to catabolize ethanol no faster than control subjects, as long as neither had ingested ethanol or other drugs in the recent past [17]. Moreover, prolonged abstinence by the middle-aged alcoholic commonly results in a clinically notable reduction in tolerance. Despite some studies of Native Americans and Orientals to the contrary, it does not appear that factors of tolerance have a great deal to do with the pathogenesis of alcoholism [17].

The second mechanism, metabolic tolerance, may well account for changes in the turnover rate of ethanol of up to 50%. Of great import to the understanding of the relationship of ethanol metabolism to the metabolism of various other drugs, this tolerance results from the ability of ethanol and many other compounds to induce the catabolic enzyme activity associated with SER [15, 19]. Thus, drinking induces increased MEOS activity, and a modest increase in tolerance results. Such a mechanism obviously fails to explain why a subject with a BAC of 0.5% continues to walk about (CNS adaptation does that), but it does assist in an understanding of the interrelationship of ethanol to oral anticoagulants, barbiturates, benzodiazepines, allopurinol, phenylbutazone, oral hypoglycemics, rifampin phenytoin (Dilantin), quinidine, and others [1, 13, 14, 20]. All of these drugs can induce enzyme activity such as to increase the turnover of any other such substance. Their effects persist for as long as a few weeks after enzyme induction. On the other hand, since each uses the common catabolic pathway, the simultaneous use of such agents may well result in the relative blockage of turnover of one of them. Thus, chronic ingestion of ethanol prior to administration of chlordiazepoxide (Librium) might result in rapid turnover of the latter and elevated (metabolic) tolerance. The subject might well conclude that Librium in the normal dose has little effect. On the next occasion, however, both agents may be used simultaneously. The turnover for the Librium quite expectedly would be slowed and the net result could be lethal. To attempt to balance the daily administration of an oral hypoglycemic or an anticoagulant with an intermittent dosage of ethanol might prove difficult or even disastrous. At any one

Table 1
Sedative-Hypnotic-Somnifacient-Soporific Drugs

Ethanol
Barbiturates
Benzodiazepines
Meprobamate
Chloral hydrate
Glutethimide
Paraldehyde
Ethchlorvynol
Methyprylon
Bromides
Methaqualone
Nitrous oxide and other anesthetic agents

moment the pharmacologic effect of the medication might be too great or not enough, based solely upon how much ethanol was ingested and its temporal relationship to the other drugs.

All of the drugs on the soporific list (Table 1) result not only in the development of tolerance, but in cross-tolerance as well. This term implies that the use of ethanol makes a subject tolerant to barbital despite the fact that the subject never ingested barbital. Although there is cross-tolerance among the soporific drugs as well as among the narcotics, there is no substantive cross-tolerance between the sedative and the narcotic groups. Moreover, cross-tolerance among sedatives is predominantly (though not solely) of the CNS adaptation type. For instance, paraldehyde demonstrates cross-tolerance with ethanol despite the fact that paraldehyde fails to elicit enzyme (SER) induction.

TOLERANCE AS A FUNCTION OF AGE

Another major determinant of tolerance to soporifics seems to be the state of health and especially the age of the brain [2]. Although the rate may vary individually, tolerance to alcohol diminishes with advancing age. This becomes clinically evident in the mid- to late 40s and explains, in part, patients seeking assistance at about that age. They find that they suffer more despite lesser drinking and a shorter period of relief. Not only does resistance to biochemical injury to the brain fail noticeably in the 40s, but that to other brain injury decreases as well. The boxer can maintain strength and stamina after age 40 but reflex speed and the tolerance of head trauma diminishes. What the young alcoholic can drink and can continue to perform changes radically with advancing years. This is one of the reasons why the disease of alcoholism presents a somewhat different clinical picture in the youth, the mature adult, and the aged. The differences are largely the result of this clinical pharmacologic phenomenon. Interestingly, many diseases present clinical pictures that vary with the resistance of the host. They are therefore dependent upon age, race, socioeconomic status, and the like.

ETHANOL AND BRAIN INJURY

Not only does tolerance to sedatives fall with aging, but ethanol in large quantities appears to injure the brain as well. There are biochemical, anatomical, and psychometric data to support such an observation. Such injury would be expected to aggravate the loss of tolerance resulting from aging alone. It is rare for alcoholic patients past their 40th birthday not to reveal such evidence of cognitive deficits as decreased ability to concentrate, diminished attention span, and loss of memory for recent events. These subtle suggestions of a presenile dementia are common in alcoholics beyond middle age (30 to 50 years).

Whether related to nonspecific brain injury resulting from ethanol ingestion or to some specific pharmacologic result of the drug itself, a number of more recent studies have demonstrated that chronic ethanol administration can induce a long-term, perhaps permanent, change in response to its readministration [8]. Moderate, daily ingestion of ethanol by rodents for 6 weeks resulted in abnormal tolerance to a test dose of this drug 6 months later. One cannot be too sanguine about such subtle long-term effects associated with a drug broadly believed capable of no more than brief and reversible pharmacologic actions. The specificity and dosage requirements for ethanol to induce chronic abnormalities in responsivity have not as yet been delineated.

ALCOHOLISM AND HYPERTENSION

There are certain pharmacologic results of ethanol administration that do not stem directly from its membership in the soporific group. Ethanol in modest doses (0.5 kg of body weight/day modifies catecholamine metabolism [21]. Not only does it competitively inhibit the oxidative pathway of the aldehyde products of monamine oxidation favoring their reduction to alcohol or glycol derivatives, but it stimulates synthesis of their adrenergic precursors as well [7]. In light of the vascular hypersensitivity of patients with essential hypertension to adrenergic substances, it is not surprising that the coincidence of alcoholism and hypertension is high. Similarly, ethanol ingestion results in marked fluctuations of blood pressure in patients receiving antihypertensive theapy. It is likely that many such patients would benefit considerably more from ethanol reduction rather than salt reduction in order to achieve normal blood pressure.

During World War II, it was noted that workers cleaning a ship's electrical equipment with carbon tetrachloride (CCl_4) often failed to suffer its toxicity, whereas their mates ingesting beer at the opposite end of the hold came down with subacute yellow atrophy shortly thereafter. Obviously ethanol ingestion can predispose one to CCl_4 injury to such an extent that the abstemious worker breathing the higher concentration failed to experience toxicity. More recently this has been ascribed to enzyme induction via the microsomal system [5, 15]. Facilitation of the formation of toxic metabolites may thereby explain the adverse effects of ethanol ingestion upon CCl_4, acetaminophen, and isoniazid toxicity [10].

Human liver alcohol dehydrogenase may be involved in the oxidation of the genins digitoxin, digoxin, and gitoxigenin to their 3-keto derivatives. Competitive metabolism of the cardiac sterols with alcohol might thereby lead to digitalis toxicity in a patient ingesting both drugs [4, 5].

Concern has been expressed about the use of an adrenergic B-blocker, such as propranolol, in the presence of a potential hypoglycemic reaction to ethanol ingestion [1, 13, 15]. Propranolol can mask the clinical signs of hypoglycemia in diabetics given excess insulin. On the other hand, a few such subjects with severely compromised hepatic glycogen who ingested large quantities of ethanol and suffered significant hypoglycemic reactions failed to demonstrate any diaphoresis whatever to this observer. It is therefore questioned whether the addition of B-blockade would make any difference in the clinical picture of such an event.

Drugs capable of inhibiting aldehyde dehydrogenase would pose another problem for the drinker. Ethanol, under those circumstances, would lead to a substantive acetaldehyde load. Acute acetaldehyde toxicity (flushing, change in blood pressure and pulse, headache, and vomiting) would result. The prototype of these drugs would be that used occasionally in the treatment of alcoholism, disulfiram (Antabuse) [9]. Quinacrine (Atabrine), metronidazole (Flagyl), oral hypoglycemics, and chloramphenicol (Chloromycetin) have been suspected of a similar though less marked propensity [1, 13].

Finally, there exists a clinical pharmacologic advantage to administration of ethanol. Rare though it may be, patients with methanol or ethylene glycol poisoning may, through the competitive metabolism of ethanol, inhibit the formation of their more toxic byproducts. Time may then permit their gradual excretion [5]. Sadly, such a therapeutic use of ethanol would hardly warrant including it in the pharmacopoeia today. Its pharmacologic utility would hardly support the burden of its toxicity. Yet over 100 million Americans use this drug, many in order to achieve the gratification associated with its brief sedative action. Fortunately the majority can tolerate both their psychomotor activity level before they drink and the modestly elevated one resulting from the drug. Ten million cannot. For them the brief surcease associated with the drug is traded for long-term discomfort, the hook of addiction.

REFERENCES

1. Abramovicz, M. (ed.). Interactions of drugs with alcohol. *Med. Letter* 23:33-34, 1981.
2. Casteldon, C. M., George, C. F., Marcer, D., and Hallett, C. Increased sensitivity to nitrazepam in old age. *Br. Med. J.* 1:10-12, 1977.
3. Editorial: Sleep now, pay later. *J.A.M.A.* 208:1485, 1969.
4. Fre, W. A., and Vallee, B. L. Digitalis metabolism and human liver alcohol dehydrogenase. *Proc. Natl. Acad. Sci. USA* 77:924-935, 1980.
5. Geokas, M. C., Lieber, C. S., French, S., and Halsted, C. H. Ethanol, the liver, and the gastrointestinal tract. *Ann. Int. Med.* 95:198-211, 1981.
6. Gitlow, S. E. Treatment of the reversible acute complications of alcoholism. *Mod. Treat.* 3:472-490, 1966.
7. Gitlow, S. E., Dziedzic, L. M., and Dziedzic, S. W. Influence of ethanol on human catecholamine metabolism. *Ann. N.Y. Acad. Sci.* 273:263-279, 1976.
8. Gitlow, S. E., Dziedzic, S. W., and Dziedzic, L. B. Persistent abnormalities in central nervous system function (long-term tolerance) after brief ethanol administration. *Drug Alcohol Depend.* 2:453-468, 1977.
9. Gitlow, S. E., and Peyser, H. S. *Alcoholism: A Practical Treatment Guide.* Grune & Stratton: New York, 1980.
10. Hasumura, Y., Teschke, R., and Lieber, C. S. Increased carbon tetrachloride hepatotoxicity and its mechanism after chronic ethanol consumption. *Gastroenterol.* 66: 415-422, 1974.
11. Isbell, H., Fraser, H. F., Wikler, A., Belleville, R. E., and Eisenman, A. J. An experimental study of the etiology of "rum fits" and delirium tremens. *Q. J. Stud. Alcohol* 16: 1-33, 1955.
12. Jaffe, J. H., and Sharpless, S. K. Rapid development of physical dependence on barbiturates. *J. Pharmacol. Exp. Ther.* 150:140-145, 1965.
13. Kennedy, D., and Editorial Board. Alcohol-drug interactions. *F.D.A. Drug Bull.* 9:10-12, 1979.
14. Khanna, J. M., Chung, S., Ho, G., and Shah, G. Acute metabolic interaction of ethanol and drugs. *Currents Alcoholism* 7:93-108, 1980.
15. Lieber, C. S. Interaction of ethanol and drug metabolism. *Adv. Alcoholism* 1(22), 1980.
16. McQuarrie, D. G., and Fingl, E. Effects of single doses and chronic administration of ethanol on experimental seizures in mice. *J. Pharmacol. Exp. Ther.* 124:264-271, 1958.
17. Mendelson, J. H., and Mello, N. K. Biologic concomitants of alcoholism. *N. Eng. J. Med.* 301:912-921, 1979.
18. Petrie, A. *Individuality in Pain and Suffering.* University of Chicago Press: Chicago, 1978.
19. Rubin, E., and Lieber, C. S. Hepatic microsomal enzymes in man and rat: Induction and inhibition by ethanol. *Science* 162:690-691, 1968.
20. Schuckit, M. A. Combined alcohol and drug abuse. *Adv. Alcoholism* 1(24), 1980.
21. Smith, A. A., Gitlow, S. E., Gall, E., Wortis, S. B., and Mendlowitz, M. Effect of disulfiram and ethanol on the metabolism of d,1-B-H^3-norepinephrine. *Clin. Res.* 8: 367, 1960.

Section IV

Social Dimensions of Alcoholism

29

PAUL M. ROMAN, PhD, Tulane University

SOCIOLOGICAL MODELS FOR UNDERSTANDING DEVIANT DRINKING BEHAVIOR

THE STUDY OF DRINKING, alcohol abuse, and alcoholism within sociological frameworks is one of the least developed specialty areas in the alcohol studies field. Some speculations have been offered to account for this limited development; Straus [21, 22] has suggested that social scientists have avoided alcohol studies because of the derived stigma that may accompany such a professional engagement. This is also referred to as "courtesy stigma" by sociologists who have commented on their colleagues' scholarly avoidance of various types of physically and mentally handicapped people. An empirical example mentioned by Straus is the repugnance with which many of the Yale University faculty regarded the Yale Center for Alcohol Studies during its early years, an observation that may have had continuing relevance at the time the center was disengaged from Yale. It may be that the focus of biomedical scientists on many of the nonsocial and nonhuman aspects of alcohol and alcoholism is a barrier to their being similarly stigmatized.

At least a partial assessment of the value, utility, and importance of sociological research in drinking, alcohol abuse, and alcoholism is reflected in the Reagan administration's 1981 curtailment of federal funding of social research on alcohol,

---

Paul M. Roman, PhD, Charles A. and Leo M. Favrot Professor of Human Relations, Department of Sociology, and Professor of Epidemiology, School of Public Health and Tropical Medicine, Tulane University, New Orleans, Louisiana.

drugs, and mental health. While the impact of this move remains to be seen, there is no question that alcohol studies have been dominated by both the theories and the methods of biomedical researchers.

Biomedical dominance has reduced the conceptual territory within which sociological theories of the etiology of alcoholism can be developed, tested, and diffused to the alcohol studies community. The receptivity to such theories of alcoholism is further impeded by the large-scale national efforts to move public thinking toward medical conceptions of alcohol problems.

There is no doubt, however, that the dominant biomedical orientation is preoccupied with attention to the problems manifest as alcohol abuse and alcoholism, together with other phenomena that are believed to be consequences of these problems. Sociologists' studies of the nature of norms, their sources, their enforcement, and their violations, offer the potential for a broad perspective on alcohol and its interrelations with social life and social organization. The call for such an alcohol sociology originated with Bacon [1] and has been recently updated and refined by Levine [10]. These authors argue that alcohol problems and alcoholism are only a small part of the entire matrix of relationships between alcohol and human society, and that social scientists are well equipped to study dimensions of this broader picture. In so doing, there are opportunities to cast new light on persistent research problems as well as to offer explanations for why the vast majority of human drinking events are not associated with adverse consequences.

It is the purpose of this chapter to review sociological perspectives on alcohol problems within the perspective of theories of deviance, and to offer an extension of some of these concepts in a tentative role theory of habitual drinking and heavy drinking. This review provides some insight into the utility of sociological concepts in organizing observations about drinking behavior, and should demonstrate some of the contrasts between sociological and biomedical approaches.

While much of the discussion herein is centered on problems associated with drinking, alcohol abuse (deviant drinking), and alcoholism as representing areas on a continuum. The discussion is not exclusively concerned with alcoholism, and it is noteworthy that sociologists, probably more than other specialists in the alcohol studies field, are generally uncomfortable with the concept of alcoholism as a disease entity with characteristics that are discontinuous with other drinking [14, 17]. Discomfort with the typical alcoholism concept stems from the general notion that alcoholic behavior, in most respects, represents more of the various components of nonalcoholic drinking behavior. It is difficult, within the continuous perspective, to distinguish milestones, points, or passages where these quantities exceed some limit and become alcoholism, other than the distinctive social passage of the formal administration of the alcoholic label.

In addition to these conceptual problems, many social scientists have difficulty in assigning an objective scientific reality to the disease concept of alcoholism separate from the organizational and political support systems within which that concept has emerged and flourished [3, 9, 25].

SOCIOLOGISTS' INFLUENCE ON ALCOHOLISM DEFINITIONS

A substantial amount of the sociological involvement in alcohol studies has been centered in epidemiologic research, attempting to establish the distribution and correlates of various types of drinking behavior in different populations. Due to the need to utilize research definitions that have meaning in nontreated populations, the conceptual and operational definition of problem drinking was developed, in part as a surrogate for attempting to locate various types or stages of alcoholism in field survey studies. This definition is eminently sociological in that it requires impaired role performance concomitant with drinking as the primary basis for defining the presence of a problem with alcohol; such an approach allows for examining impaired performance in a range of roles, and thus creates a quantitive dimension for the concept of problem drinking. Of considerable importance to the present discussion is the fact that nearly all of the role impairments rest upon the definitions of others that the drinker's role performance is beyond the bounds of acceptability [6, 7]. Such a definition, with its elegant simplicity and relative ease of quantification, has found its way into many areas of practice, and increasingly is utilized in research. A particularly influential example is employee alcoholism programming, wherein the sole basis for intervention with an employee is impaired job performance [16, 18].

THEORETICAL APPROACHES

Beyond the epidemiologic influences, there are several important theoretical approaches that have been developed by sociologists, and that illustrate the patterns of sociological reasoning.

These approaches, which are more or less concerned with the etiology of chronic heavy drinking or alcoholism, can be classified into four overlapping types: social deprivation, differential association, social personality, and social labeling. None of these theoretical perspectives is dominant among sociologists, and a detailed review of empirical literature would indicate that all have been partially verified in research studies.

The Social Deprivation Approach

The social deprivation approach is based in the work of Merton [13], further developed by Snyder [20]. The basic assumption of this approach can be traced to the work of Emile Durkheim, in which the strength of social normative structures is a fundamental predictor of the rates of deviant behavior in particular populations. The strength of normative controls is in turn a function of the support for these structures within the broader social environment, which includes the extent to which conformity to the norms is facilitated.

Merton attempted to develop a theory that accounted for the reported higher rates of deviant behavior among the lower social classes. He posited that the lower classes are exposed to societal norms on economic achievement and success, but are not provided with the means for achieving these prescribed goals. He described the disjunction between the prescribed norms and the means for achieving these prescriptions as anomie, a term earlier utilized by Durkheim in his analysis of differential rates of suicide in France. Merton argued that it was necessary for those facing this disjunction to make adaptations to it, and that those adaptations frequently constituted deviant behavior. While a nondeviant adaptation was described as "ritual conformity," the deviant adaptations include rebellion, innovation, and retreat. Rebellion is the effort to overthrow the existing normative structures, while innovation is the means of working within existing structures to achieve valued goals, usually through modes such as crime. Retreatism is rejection of both the goals and the means for achieving them, and alcoholism has been commonly described as an adaptation of this type. The long-term stereotype that tended to equate alcoholism with public inebriate status definitely fit the concept of anomic retreatism, since the skid row bum is a classic rejector of practically all societal norms as well as rejector of the occupancy of central life roles of worker and family member. The social deprivation theory thus could be utilized to account for the most prominent group of alcoholics, although the lifelong, lower class position of most skid row residents (as well as the assumption that most of them are chronic alcoholics) has been questioned by researchers who have intensively investigated these populations. More recent epidemiologic data [6, 7] does, however, indicate higher rates of problem drinking in the lower social classes, offering the possibility of continuing support for the social deprivation theory. Doubtless there are elements of the differential association approach embedded in this general scheme of the etiology of alcoholism, but its greatest significance lies in the posing of the alcoholic as a social loser who adapts to his or her fate by escapism into drink, which, in turn, supports the prominent American social imagery of alcoholism.

The Differential Association Approach

An examplar of the differential association approach is found in the work of Trice [23]. He proposes that repeated events of excessive drinking result in social exclusion (i.e., the drinker causes friction in social interaction such that others do not want association with him or her). This leads to the drinker seeking out other drinking companions whose behavior while drinking is more similar to that of the drinker's. The new companions are likely to frequent bars and taverns, and are thus openly available to the drinker; these available drinking settings do, however, vary in the extent to which deviant behaviors accompanying excessive drinking are tolerated. Trice proposes that some drinkers follow a path of changing associations with drinking companions as their own drinking behavior escalates, moving from setting to setting in the search of tolerance and acceptance for deviant behavior. The alcoholic behavior is thus a product of social supports that have been sought by the drinker; the drinker's changes in companions and settings results in continuing acceptance for his or her behavior. The drinker may eventually become a public inebriate, as is implicit throughout this approach. It is clear that this particular theory rests on the action of a somewhat independent disease or addiction process, whereas the drinker must drink more and thus seek out companions who will accept the rising levels of consumption and accompanying behaviors. It is also obvious that the proposed interplay between this addiction process and the pattern of changing associations is complex and difficult to specify in terms of cause and effect relationships.

The Social Personality Approach

A third approach is embedded in the work of a great many writers, both within and outside sociology, and it is summarily labeled here as "the social personality approach." It bears some structural similarity to the social deprivation approach in that it posits some form of inadequacy or unmet need. In this case the inadequacy is the product of previous life experience or inheritance that renders one's social personality in a state of readiness for alcoholism. This comes about through the unique service of psychological needs that are provided for some people by alcohol (i.e., alcohol provides for the filling of some gap in the individual's personality structure). Thus, certain individuals are faced with inadequate feelings of power of control in their everyday life, they suffer from chronic depression, they have a homosexual orientation that they desire to repress, they were brutally victimized by alcoholic parents and have developed an identification with the aggressor, or they are basically schizoid and are unable to relate to others in a manner that fulfills needs. This list can be considerably lengthened, but the basic proposition is that the consumption of alcohol serves to overcome or at least temporarily blunt these individually perceived inadequacies; the powerless feel more powerful, the depressed become less sad, preoccupation with homosexual feelings is lessened, one senses warm identify with the deceased parents and remembers some of the good times, or one loses interpersonal ambivalence and warms up to others. These rewarding experiences are repeated, and the course toward alcohol dependence and addiction is begun.

This theoretical approach is not wholly psychological in its cast, however. Trice [23], for example, poses a personality predisposition as a possibly necessary but clearly insufficient condition for the development of alcoholism. In the hands of the sociologist, the personality theory acquires its social ingredient by the posing of necessary environmental conditions in order for the personal inadequacies to be served by alcohol. Seemingly, role performance of some sort would have to improve in order for the individual to find alcohol consumption socially rewarding. Thus, as with the differential association approach, social and psycological elements are intertwined in ways that are neither simple nor obvious.

The Social Labeling Approach

The social labeling approach to explaining the development of alcohol abuse and alcoholism is part of a large and diffuse theoretical approach that developed in American and British sociology during the 1960s and 1970s. The fundamental hypothesis is that certain episodes of deviant behavior result in formal labeling events. These labels, in turn, have a dramatic impact on the individual's self-concept.

More specifically, certain individuals are identified by social control agents on the basis of their drinking or drinking-related behavior and subsequently receive the label of "alcoholic" from an official labeling agent. Since persons are socialized to believe that such agents possess substantial mandate and social authority, it is posited that this label will change the individual's self-image. This change in image will, in turn, lead to the individual engaging in behavior that is regarded as appropriate to the particular label, namely, inappropriate or uncontrolled drinking.

The social impact of the label is increased as information about the label extends to the individual's social audience. As with the focal individual, these persons are socialized to accept the validity of official labelers' judgment, with the consequence that they begin treating the individual as if he or she were an alcoholic. This offers further reinforcement for drinking behavior that is consistent with the social role of an alcoholic.

It should be obvious that there are myriad embellishments of this basic notion; the foregoing statement is a rather gross generalization intended to describe the flavor of the labeling approach. There is within the labeling school of thought a substantial degree of attention to the role of informal labeling events. Attention is focused on the possibility that an individual's significant others may effectively utilize labeling even though they do not possess a societal mandate to label; in other words, a lay person's verbalized judgment that certain acts are characteristic of placement in a deviant category may have an impact on the focal person, depending on the qualities of the relationship with this other. A further refinement centers on the chronological series of events wherein the individual's significant others play important roles in directing the individual to an official labeling agent; here are considered the contingency effects of different types of levels of screening, which includes the possibility of neutralizing or normalizing deviant acts.

Finally, it is obvious that significant others can serve to counteract a formal label administered by a mandated agent, through discreditation or counterlabeling that elevates the degraded behavior, and thus, through reverse social pressure, prevents the individual from adopting a label that has been administered by such an agent.

Some proponents of the labeling approach have taken strong issue with the social deprivation hypothesis presented herein. It is argued that the high rates of alcohol problems and other types of deviant behavior in low-class populations are an artifact of the vulnerability of low-status people to both social observations and labeling by official agencies [19]. Identical behavior among middle- and upper-class persons allegedly does not result in labeling. It is therefore concluded that statistics that indicate higher rates of alcoholism in lower social classes are simply an artifact of the dynamics of the social class system.

It should not be surprising that the labeling approach receives a generally negative reception among the clinical community and among those most committed to the disease concept of alcoholism [8]. The very processes that are advocated by most alcoholism clinicians, for example, the importance of having the individual accept the label of alcoholic as a prerequisite for entry into treatment and behaviorial change, are viewed by the labeling theory proponents as high-risk situations for permanent entry into a deviant drinking role [7]. The key issue separating labelists from mainline clinical thought seems to be the effectiveness of altering drinking behavior once a label of alcoholic has been administered. It appears that the individual must be restrained within a formal or informal network of social control to assure that the effect of the label is to motivate change away from the alcoholic behavior rather than motivating behavior in service of the label's expectations. The importance of accepting the alcoholic label is a principle adopted by clinicians directly from Alcoholics Anonymous (AA); without admission of a drinking problem, progress through the AA steps is impossible. Within AA, however, admission of a severe problem and acceptance of the potent label of "alcoholic" occurs within a context of social support for behaving like a recovering alcoholic. As long as the individual maintains a sincere desire to stop drinking, this support is, ideally, without conditions or contingencies. By contrast, a formal labeling agent's administration of a label need not include the presence of a support system that will move the individual away from alcoholic behavior. While superb support systems of this nature may be present in inpatient treatment settings, their availability is conditional upon being a patient. Thus, the risks of behaving like an alcoholic after labeling seem considerably greater when this labeling is done by an official agent who is separated from social support systems.

An excellent and detailed application of the labeling perspective in describing how an individual may become alcoholic through labeling and subsequently have labels removed by a reversal of the same process is provided in the work of Lofland [11]. A more recent review of research related to labeling does, however, strongly challenge the validity of portions of the approach [15], although the research evidence is far from complete.

IMPEDIMENTS TO A THEORETICAL MODEL

While the foregoing review does not do justice to the complexity of the various theoretical approaches, it should be obvious that the construction of a rigorous and thoroughly tested theoretical model of the development of alcohol abuse and alcoholism has not been achieved in the sociological community. A major impediment to this development has been a lack of clarity in the definitions of the subject matter at hand, with many scholars accepting the disease concept of alcoholism rather uncritically. Other barriers have been the apparent political and cultural barriers to an appreciative stance on drinking. A principal feature of the generally ambiguous norms about drinking in American society is the absence of detailed justification for drinking, including heavy drinking [5]. For example, most of the theoretical approaches that have emanated from the sociological community have failed to account for the cases in which individuals sustain patterns of heavy drinking over a long period of time without untoward consequences. Also lacking are explanatory accounts for numerous cases where the development of chronic, heavy drinking is apparently reversed without external intervention [6]. Failure to seriously consider these cases seems embedded in the latent assumptions of most writers, namely that there is a steplike process of alcoholic progression that eventuates in death unless intervention occurs; the progression notion implicitly supports the disease concept of alcoholism. Deviant types of cases, such as those mentioned, may be dismissed by the tautological reasoning that they are not really alcoholics.

What is almost completely missing from the literature is a phenomenology of drinking behavior. The work of Weil [24] is an approximation of such an approach in dealing with marijuana and psychedelics; he ironically refuses to apply his perspective to alcohol use, dismissing alcohol as a nonmeaningful drug early in his book. In approaching drinking in everyday life, a three-fold typology of normal drinking may be drawn as a basis for developing objective descriptions of drinking behavior.

1. Those events where drinking is a minor part of the setting, where little attention is given to drinking, and where there is no intoxication make up one category of alcohol drinking.

2. A second category, that of deviant drinking by normal people, can include all events of idiosyncratic intoxication, that is, intoxication that occurs in different places, at different times, and with different actors present.

3. A third category of alcohol drinking includes a vast range of repeated in-

stances of intoxication carried out by the same individual in a similar setting without the intrusion of formal agents of social control.

The attempts to prevent alcohol problems have resulted in defining a preoccupation with alcohol as problematic in intself. Therefore, a phenomenology is almost prevented by the implicit definition of normal drinking as including only the first category, those episodes where drinking is incidental to other events occurring in the situation. The difficulties in systematic understanding of other common drinking events are further highlighted by the fact that all intoxication is essentially defined as deviant in American culture, even though intoxication is commonly permitted as long as justification associated with the nature of the occasion or the nature of the individuals can be provided. While this patterned deviance from norms is recognized, it is poorly understood yet obviously essential in deriving the meanings of social drinking.

Most of the sociological work aimed at explaining different rates of alcohol abuse and alcoholism has been piecemeal. It is difficult to identify programs of research that have attracted multiple scholars to an ongoing process of theoretical development, testing, refinement, and further testing. There are several reasons for this.

First, as mentioned, the study of alcohol abuse and alcoholism becomes invariably intertwined in historical and political issues about alcohol consumption versus alcoholism as the key problem. Paralleling this issue are the social and organizational implications of conceptualizing alcoholism within medical frames of reference. These confusions seem to quickly squelch potential long-term research efforts that challenge cherished beliefs of one or another constituency group; research work on biological issues, work that is built upon a medical model, seems largely insulated from these problems and consequently may become programmatic and cumulative.

Second, most social and behavioral scientists working in this specialty appear genuinely ambivalent about the disease concept, with most giving at least minimal acceptance to the utility of the disease metaphor in intervention processes of both AA and professional treatment. Thus, there is scant commitment to an exclusively social-psychological etiology of alcohol abuse and alcoholism, given the inconsistency of such a perspective with even partial acceptance of the disease model or metaphor.

Third, the theoretical perspectives that have developed do not lend themselves readily to testing or refinement. In addition to the measurement difficulties associated with such constructs as personality needs and labeling, each of the perspectives is limited to after-the-fact reconstructions rather than being able to operate in predictive fashion. This dilemma is in part reflected in the pragmatic use of the impaired performance criterion for defining alcohol problems; rather than drawing from the total population of drinkers, this assumption limits the research sampling frame to people in trouble at the outset. It is this mind-set within the alcohol studies field that has largely precluded the development of a sociology of drinking behavior.

TOWARD A ROLE THEORY OF EPISODIC DRINKING

The remainder of this chapter presents an outline for a role theory of episodic drinking. This presentation is intended to serve three purposes. First, it should illustrate the nature and utility of sociological approaches to studying drinking behavior of all types and varieties. Second, the outline attempts a degree of integration of the four sociological perspectives that have already been described. Third, the outline is geared to a conceptualization that is explicitly sociological and is not intermingled with psychological and psychiatric theories, as is the tendency with the several other perspectives.

Role theory provides a framework for examining the development, maintenance, dynamics, and cessation of behavioral patterns; it is not a propositional inventory, but rather a set of interrelated concepts [4]. For some sociologists, the substance that fills in the role theory framework is included in a second set of concepts known as "symbolic interactionism" [12]. This is also not a rigid or highly specified theory; its fundamental ingredients are centered on the concept of self. Symbolic interactionism is concerned with the ongoing processes of social interaction wherein attributes of the self are in part molded by the reactions of others; these may in turn be manipulated by the focal person as he or she seeks reinforcement for a particular type of self-image. Beyond the effects of social interaction with others, the focal person is a reactor to his or her own behavior through the symbolic processes of thought that are made possible by language. Thus, the focal person comments, evaluates, reacts, and alters his or her own behavior on the basis of norms and values that have been learned or internalized through socialization processes beginning in infancy. These embodied norms and values may be viewed as the core self, which tempers the direction of behavior and determines choices among those behaviors that are or are not repeated.

The ongoing presentation, maintenance, and further development of the self occurs in behavior that may be objectively categorized into roles. Roles are sets of norms or expectations that are associated with occupying different social positions or statuses. Role performance is guided by the expectations of others. Role performance is at the same time guided by the expectations of the focal person about how his or her behavior should proceed in accordance with the development or maintenance of the desired self.

Obviously, different skills are necessary for different role performances. The acquisition of these skills is part of the lifelong processes of socialization, wherein people are more or less successful in learning the skills necessary to perform roles that are associated with changes in status that occur throughout the life cycle. Judgment of the adequacy of role performance rests with both the focal person and those with whom he or she interacts: the role senders or significant others.

The starting point for a role theory of episodic drinking is that drinking is intermingled with role performances. The relationship between drinking and role performance is subject to the judgments of the focal person and his or her significant others in a particular situation. Thus, in contrast to positing drinking as a role per se, it appears more accurate to view most drinking as adjunctive to other role performances.

Obviously, drinking can enhance the quality of some role performances and reduce the quality of others. It is very important to note that role performances are usually judged from multiple perspectives, those of the focal person and those of the significant others who are his or her role senders in a particular situation. Given the multiplicity of orientations among these people as they each strive to maintain a unique construction of self, it is unlikely that there would be exact consensus in the judgments rendered about a particular focal person's role performance. Even if judgments are in a similar direction (i.e., "Jack is not doing a good job of presenting the new marketing strategy because of the wine that we had at lunch" might be a shared judgment among several role senders) it is obvious these judgments can be individually embellished in almost an infinity of directions.

"Jack won't be getting the promotion he was hoping for."

"It's a good thing the boss was drinking too or Jack would really be in trouble."

"That lunchtime drinking is really going to ruin the business if none of us can work in the afternoon."

"Jack was so nervous about his presentation that he probably could not have done it without a few drinks under his belt."

The emergent point is that the impact of drinking on role performance cannot be subject to simple generalizations, or glib categorizations into "normal" versus "deviant" drinking episodes.

Each person performs some roles better than others and some roles more easily than others. Both the quality and the energy investment associated with a particular role performance are contingent upon the significant others who are present in a social situation. Thus, while people can directly acquire the skills necessary to change a tire on a 1981 Chevrolet, people cannot be so easily guaranteed of success in attempting to acquire the skills needed for repeatedly adequate social role performances (i.e., continuously successful episodes of dating the opposite sex or lecturing to different classes of students). One means of dealing with ambivalence or doubts about one's adequacy of skills to ever perform certain roles or to perform certain roles in certain situations is to use adjunctive aids, among which drinking alcohol is a prominent choice in contemporary American life.

This moves to the heart of this particular theoretical offering, the concepts of easing and pampering presented by Bacon in 1973 [2]. In a lengthy article in which he attempts to provide a generalized description of the social events that accompany the development of alcoholism, Bacon offers two brilliant concepts that have received practically no subsequent attention by behavioral scientists.

Bacon begins by pointing out that the consumption of alcohol alters the brain in several ways, but that these effects may be simply summarized as change in sensitivity to cues, in mood, in decision making, and in both social actions and reactions.

He then goes on to state that these change effects will be most profound on "those sets of attitudes and behaviors which were learned poorly, or with difficulty, or with pain or anxiety" [2, p. 11]. This statement can be slightly altered for present purposes by relabeling "attitudes and behavior" to "role skills." In other words, areas of marginal performance will be most affected by drinking.

It is thus argued that one experiences an easing of tension and fear if one uses alcohol to produce cognitive change prior to entering a social situation wherein one anticipates an inadequacy of role skills. Adding to Bacon's formulation within the symbolic interaction framework, alcohol obviously diminishes the sensitivity of the focal actor as a judge of his or her own behavior. This easing function of alcohol is of course best known in social settings where alcohol use tends to be very common: when social strangers are brought together. It can be added to Bacon's formulation that it is likely that the easing of social expectations is enhanced substantially when both role performers and role senders are drinking. This occurs in many settings where the functions of alcohol have been otherwise described as social lubricants and as aids to conviviality.

Bacon further describes the transition from alcohol's easing function to its pampering function. It is essentially argued that the easing experience may be rewarding such that it is repeated when the same anxiety-producing role demands occur again. When this repetition occurs, Bacon relabels the phenomenon as "pampering," and he rather quickly goes on to describe the possibilities of generalizing the easing experience into other adjacent areas of poorly developed role skills, and of trying to move situations where easing is needed to where drinking is available.

The almost moralistic essence that distinguishes pampering from easing for Bacon is that the pampered individual has abandoned attempts to improve his or her role skills. Since the pampered person adopts alcohol instead of improving skills, the poorly developed skills become even poorer, so that he or she may perceive that entry into a particular role performance is not possible without drinking.

After having briefly explicated this eminently sociological contribution, which fits directly into role theory, Bacon moves rather quickly to describe a series of other social processes that will interact with pampering and eventuate in alcohol addiction. It is ironic that Bacon employs the concepts of easing and pampering exclusively in the explanation of the development of alcoholism, seemingly overlooking the potential value of these two concepts in understanding social drinking in general; these essential concepts may be building blocks for the study of normal drinking that Bacon called for years earlier [1].

Bacon has thus offered the fundamentals of a role theory wherein people learn to use alcohol to augment their perceived skills in dealing with particular role demands: The mechanism that needs to be added to Bacon's scheme is the reduction of self-consciousness that is produced by alcohol's impact on the brain, with an alteration of one's judgment of one's own behavior. To elaborate further, it appears that the role performances that ensue under conditions of easing or pampering may be some mixture of

1. Adequate role performance by the standards of significant others or of the self, but this is not perceived as such by the focal person due to easing
2. Inadequate role performance by the standards of the significant others or of the self, but not perceived as such by the focal person due to easing
3. Nonperformance or partial performance of the role due to the easing of perceived pressures to perform from the self and others
4. Performance of a new role not played before, but possible with easing; one may become the life of the party, or a good buddy, or a sloppy drunk

It is obvious that the degree of easing and freedom from feedback is a function of the level of intoxication achieved. Thus, it is completely erroneous to assume easing effects are produced during all events of alcohol consumption. Bacon does, however, imply that anxiety relief may be the operating definition of a sociological high. When the individual consumes enough to get comfortable, it may be assumed that an easing process has begun; thus, the appropriate criterion may be a simple subjective report.

It is also erroneous to assume that all attempts at easing are successful. One may drink too much and be the object of highly negative feedback from the group. Drinking may have adverse effects on one's behavior in other ways, without intoxication occuring. Attempts at easing that fail may lead people away from alcohol, away from certain role demands, or toward better role skills.

For those who have positive experiences, easing may eventuate in pampering due to the individual's inability to discriminate between the facilitating effects of alcohol and the actual quality of the role performance. In other words, if the individual receives positive feedback while meeting strangers and drinking at a cocktail party, he or she may not know whether their role skills are indeed effective or if they needed the drinks in order to get through the situation. Thus, alcohol's effects could negate important information about the reactions of others if the focal person explains his or her successful performance on the basis of easing. If there is no information given that one can genuinely perform adequately in the situation without drinking then the preexisting anxiety will be present again when the particular role demands are repeated and drinking will likely ensue in pursuit of easing. The opportunity for the necessary controlled experiment in which alcohol's effects are compared to role skills may never arise.

A further extension of Bacon's basic formulation relates to new role expectations that emerge over the life course. If the new role demands create anxiety, anxiety itself may be the cue to seeking the easing comfort of alcohol. Equally pertinent are the generalizations whereby new role demands are easily classified with prior performances that required alcohol.

Bacon's presentation does, however, move too quickly in the translation of easing to pampering to pathology. The terms "easing" and "pampering" have pejorative tones. The potential value of this formulation lies in its application to everyday life rather than in the overprediction of pathology that is evident in most sociological etiologies of deviant behavior. A remarkable characteristic of Bacon's formulation is the anthropomorphic echo of King Alcohol as a being that can help, aid, ease, and pamper; of course, therein can be seen its seductive menace. Thus, in line with the earlier discussion, this approach also has the potential for being politicized.

A very important contribution of this formulation is the shedding of light on why people do not drink all the time. Even most alcoholics only drink some of the time, and it does not appear valid to account for all of their nondrinking time as recovery from the impacts of drinking time.

Most adults in American society drink, and most are not alcoholic. The patterning of social drinking in American society has been known for some time, but most accounts are simply tautologies that explain social drinking patterns on the basis of social drinking norms. The Bacon approach sets the stage for explaining drinking patterns on the basis of perceived inadequacies in role skills coupled with opportunities for drinking. The theory that can be built upon Bacon's basic formulation may be a predictive tool to assess different types of drinking in social settings, beyond the clearly important types involving easing and pampering. The formulation that some drinking occurs primarily to reduce role performance anxiety is considerably superior to vague and moralistic concepts such as escaping from reality and seeking relief from personal troubles.

Returning to the earlier typology of reasons for drinking, this formulation can, however, be easily overextended in attempting to account for all drinking episodes on the basis of instrumental efforts to achieve easing. Bacon's formulation applies to a category of deviant acts that Lofland [11] has labeled "defensive" in that the individual perceives a threat and reacts to it. In this case, the threat is to his or her self-esteem if a role performance is attempted when skills are perceived as inadequate. Protection against one's own judgment of one's own behavior through drinking is a defense.

Lofland also draws attention to what he calls "adventurous deviant acts." Somewhat parallel to Weil's [24] positing the innate drive to get high, Lofland argues that there are occasions in which one engages in dangerous and illegal acts, as well as substance use, for the sheer thrill or pleasure of the experience. As mentioned previously, the peculiar cultural attitude toward alcohol in American society prevents an appreciative stance toward alcohol's effects. Prevailing norms appear to allow use only if there are minimal or no effects in a highly controlled environment, with the residual category of purposeful mood-altering defined as deviant, and symptomatic of developing alcoholism if repeated on numerous occasions.

A final extension of the Bacon formulation is its potential explanation of nondrinking episodes among both alcoholic and nonalcoholic drinkers [26]. Just as there are occasions where one doubts one's role skills and seeks means for easing the anxiety for the performance, there are occasions where one is proud of one's role skills and thus desires to maximize feedback from both the social audience and the self. There are thus numerous occasions when otherwise heavy drinkers would not dream of taking a drink, and would even be hostile to the possibility if it were raised. Thus, one finds many adult male alcoholics will have adopted drinking patterns of nearly constant intoxication during their waking hours away from the job, but they maintain their self-concepts by regular presence on the job, where they never bring a bottle or take a drink.

The Bacon formulation and its extensions thus have substantial application to understanding drinking in everyday life as well as to understanding the relationship between role skill problems and the development of severe alcohol problems. The explication presented in this chapter is only an outline of the hypotheses that can be drawn from this formulation, which, it is hoped, is the forerunner of a program of empirical research. The formulation's grounding in sociological role theory and its linkages to symbolic interactionist mechanisms stand as evidence of the potential theoretical contributions of sociology to alcohol studies.

ACKNOWLEDGMENTS

Partial support during the preparation of this manuscript from the United States Public Health Service Grant No. AA-04165 from the National Institute on Alcohol Abuse and Alcoholism is gratefully acknowledged.

REFERENCES

1. Bacon, S. Sociology and the problems of alcohol. *Q. J. Stud. Alcohol* 4:1–25, 1943.
2. Bacon, S. The process of addiction to alcohol. *J. Stud. Alcohol* 34:1–27, 1973.
3. Beauchamp, D. *Beyond Alcoholism*. Temple University Press: Philadelphia, 1980.
4. Biddle, B. *Role Theory*. Wiley: New York, 1964.
5. Brissett, D. Toward and interactionist understanding of heavy drinking. *Pacific Sociol. Rev.* 21(1):3–20, 1978.
6. Cahalan, D. *Problem Drinkers*. Jossey-Bass: San Francisco, 1970.

7. Cahalan, D., and Room, R. *Problem Drinking among American Men.* Rutgers Center for Alcohol Studies: New Brunswick, N.J., 1974.

8. Keller, M. Current concepts of alcoholism. Paper presented at the annual meeting of the National Council on Alcoholism Forum, New Orleans, April 1981.

9. Levine, H. The discovery of addiction: Changing conceptions of habitual drunkenness in America. *J. Stud. Alcohol* 39(1):143–174, 1978.

10. Levine, H. *Sociology and Alcohol Studies: The Study of Alcohol in Modern Society.* Unpublished manuscript, Queens College of the City University of New York, 1981.

11. Lofland, J. *Deviance and Identity.* Prentice-Hall: Englewood Cliffs, N.J., 1966.

12. Manis, J., and Meltzer, B. (eds.). *Symbolic Interaction.* Allyn & Bacon: Boston, 1967.

13. Merton, R. *Social Theory and Social Structure.* Free Press: Glencoe, Ill., 1957.

14. Pattison, E. M., Sobell, M., and Sobell, L. *Emerging Concepts of Alcohol Dependence.* Springer: New York, 1977.

15. Robins, L. Alcoholism and social labelling. In: *The Labelling of Deviance* (2nd ed.), Gove, W. (ed.). Beverly Hills, CA: Sage: Beverly Hills, Calif., 1980.

16. Roman, P. From employee alcoholism to employee assistance: An analysis of the deemphasis on alcohol problems and prevention in work-based programs. *J. Stud. on Alcohol* 42:244–272, 1981.

17. Roman, P., and Trice, H. The sick role, labelling theory and the deviant drinker. *Int. J. Soc. Psychiatry* 14:245–251, 1968.

18. Roman, P., and Trice, H. Alcohol abuse and work organizations. In: *Social Aspects of Alcoholism*, Kissin, B. and Begleiter, H. (eds.). Plenum: New York, 1976.

19. Schur, E. *Labelling Deviant Behavior.* Harper & Row: New York, 1971.

20. Snyder, C. Inebriety, alcoholism and anomie. In: *Anomie and Deviant Behavior*, Clinard, M. (ed.). Free Press: New York, 1964.

21. Straus, R. Alcohol and society. *Psychiatr. Ann.* (whole number 10):1973.

22. Straus, R. Problem drinking in the perspective of social change, 1940–1973. In: *Alcohol and Alcohol Problems*, Filstead, W., Rossi, J., and Keller, M. (eds.). Ballinger: Cambridge, Mass., 1976.

23. Trice, H. *Alcoholism in America.* McGraw-Hill: New York, 1966.

24. Weil, A. *The Natural Mind.* Houghton Mifflin: Boston, 1972.

25. Wiener, C. *The Politics of Alcoholism.* Transaction Books: New Brunswick, N.J., 1981.

26. Wiseman, J. Sober comportment: Patterns and perspectives on alcohol addiction. *J. Stud. Alcohol* 42(1):106–126, 1981.

30

M. DOUGLAS ANGLIN, PhD, University of California at Los Angeles

ALCOHOL AND CRIMINALITY

ALCOHOL CONSUMPTION and criminal behavior have been associated in the public mind for centuries. Most people have observed or have been participants in verbal or physical aggression in the context of drinking. It is also a common experience to know or read of alcoholics who are repeatedly involved in violent or other crimes. However, such instances offer only casual, uncontrolled, and unreliable evidence of a relationship between alcohol and criminal behavior.

In Western societies there is a pronounced tendency to ascribe a pejorative influence to alcohol whenever it is present in circumstances resulting in undesirable outcomes. This inclination, which has been referred to as the "malevolence assumption" [7] is common not only within the general society, but within the social science literature as well. Thus, an examination of the alcohol-crime issue must eliminate this prejudicial aspect of public attitude, which presupposes an existing and negative relationship.

The basic question has been, "Are alcohol ingestion and criminal behavior related?" The basic answer has been, "Yes, the behaviors are commonly observed simultaneously." However, the relationship may not generally be a causal one. As attempts are made to understand the ways in which alcohol may be implicated in criminality, the questions become more complex. It becomes necessary to redirect attention from alcohol to people using alcohol and to specify frequency,

---

M. Douglas Anglin, PhD, Adjunct Assistant Professor of Psychology, Department of Psychology, University of California at Los Angeles, Los Angeles, California.

amount, and occasion. Additionally, crime must be specified as to type, offender and victim characteristics, pattern of occurrence, and the context in which it occurs.

This chapter (1) presents the definitions of alcohol use or alcoholism that most commonly appear in the literature and specifies the criminal behaviors of interest; (2) provides a brief literature summary of reviews covering research studies linking the two; (3) discusses the varied methodological problems that limit conclusions that can be drawn from the existing research; (4) lists questions of interest concerning the possible alcohol-crime relationships; and (5) enumerates current theories that attempt to determine the relationship between alcohol consumption and crime, with reference to research results offered in their support.

DEFINITIONS

Crime

The majority of research reports and reviews have concentrated on the relationship of alcohol to violent crime. Apparently because of the self-evident motivation of personal gain in property crimes, little attention has been directed to alcohol involvement in property crime. Crimes of violence in this discussion include homicide, robbery with injury, assault, forcible rape, and intrafamily violence. Excluded categories are those of premeditated murder and suicide. "Property crimes" are defined as robbery, burglary, all categories of theft, and forgery. Vandalism, arson, and the so-called victimless crimes are not discussed. It is important to specify the type of crime when discussing possible alcohol involvement. A deviant behavior sufficiently extreme to be called "criminal" results from the culmination of many contributions, and different crimes have different patterns of etiology. Although alcohol-defined crimes of negligence, such as drunken driving, have the greatest social and personal consequences and associated costs of any alcohol-crime relationship, this topic is discussed elsewhere in the volume (Chapter 40) and is not treated here.

Alcohol

Alcohol use has not been consistently defined in the context of crime. In some instances the mere presence of alcohol in the situation has been sufficient for crimes to have been specified as alcohol-related. In other cases the criminal file notation "had been drinking" is sufficient for inclusion as an alcohol-related crime, regardless of the amount, type, or duration of drinking. More sophisticated studies determine blood alcohol content (BAC) through blood, urine, or breath analysis. A distinction must also be made between acute alcohol intoxication, chronic alcoholism, and episodic alcoholism. The relationship between these types of alcohol involvement and crime may be very different.

Research Approaches

There are five basic approaches to the study of the alcohol-crime relationship [6]. The descriptive approach presents data on all crimes and delineates those that are alcohol-defined in contrast to other crimes. While the data accrued shows a larger proportion of all crime is alcohol-defined, of interest here are more serious offenses of violence or property crime.

The second approach is to determine what proportion of offenders, or their victims, had consumed alcohol prior to the reported crime. These data are commonly collected from police reports or at the time of booking.

A third approach is to study a population of incarcerated offenders, usually jail or prison inmates, and enumerate the proportion who had been drinking at the time of the offense and/or the proportion with alcohol-related problems. Institution files or self-reports provide the majority of data in this approach.

A fourth approach is to examine populations of chronic alcoholics or problem drinkers and determine their criminal histories, excluding alcohol offenses. Most of these populations are from alcohol treatment programs or are repeat offenders for alcohol charges.

A fifth approach has been defined by Blum [3] as a methodological-theoretical one. It critically examines the empirical data, consistencies in results across studies, the logic between data and conclusions, and the complexity of the possible relationships among what has been observed.

ALCOHOL-CRIME RESEARCH

Several excellent reviews discuss in detail the research findings relating alcohol and crime [2, 3, 4, 6, 12, 16, 19]. The discussion that follows is a synthesis of several reviews of the literature.

Acute Alcohol Use and Category of Crime

Literature review. Of the approaches mentioned, the second has been one of the most common. The study of Shupe [18] in the United States is representative and often cited. His findings on 882 offenders arrested during or immediately after the commission of a felony in Columbus, Ohio during 1951–53 are presented in Table 1. There is a constant rate of alcohol use in property crimes and a more

Table 1
Percentage of Arrestees with Various Urine Alcohol Concentrations (UAC) within Crime Categories

Offense	Cases Studied n	UAC 0%	UAC < .10%	UAC > .10–19%	UAC ≥ .20%
Violent Crime					
Murder	30	17	17	30	36
Shooting	33	18	3	27	51
Cutting	40	8	5	20	68
Felonious assault	64	52	5	9	35
Other assault	60	8	13	25	53
Rape	42	50	5	19	26
Concealed weapons	48	8	81	21	62
Property Crime					
Robbery	85	28	12	15	44
Burglary	181	29	7	24	40
Larceny	141	27	9	13	51
Auto theft	138	30	11	25	34
Forgery	20	40	0	20	40

Source: Adapted from "Alcohol and Crime" by L. Shupe, Journal of Criminal Law and Criminal Political Science, 44:661–664, 1953.

varied and usually higher rate in violent crime. No distinction is made, as in most studies of this type, between chronic abusers of alcohol and those merely intoxicated when apprehended.

The majority of studies focus on alcohol and violent crime, particularly homicide. Wolfgang [20] provides one of the most comprehensive analyses. In 588 cases of homicide in the city of Philadelphia between 1948 and 1952, alcohol was present in both offender and victim in 44% of the cases, in the offender only in 16%, in the victim only in 9%.

MacDonald [10] reviewed 10 studies of alcohol involvement in homicide offenders. The majority of the studies, including all with larger sample sizes (n 200), reported between 50% and 60% had been drinking. Studies from other Western developed nations show these results to be consistent in England, Canada, Australia, Sweden, Finland, the Soviet Union, Poland, and several other European nations. One Canadian study of 521 cases of homicide, assaults, rapes, and robberies in Montreal during 1964 related the amount of alcohol to the severity of injury [12].

Discussion. Although the majority of studies report a significant correlation between alcohol and crime, especially violent crime, it is premature to infer a causal relationship based on this data alone. There are several reasons for this reserve. First, methodological flaws can be specified for all such studies. The most serious of these is the lack of adequate knowledge of base rates of drinking in those populations represented in crime statistics. Most crime is committed by young males residing in highly urbanized areas [6]. These are also characteristics of populations with high alcohol consumption. Additionally, the periodicity of crime and alcohol use is similar; both are higher in the evenings and peaks occur on weekend evenings. Thus, if a defined group is drinking 75% of the time on Saturday night, then 75% of the arrests that night would be expected to show evidence of drinking in the offender. Other methodological problems include (1) the high probability that those engaged in criminality are more likely to be apprehended when drinking and thus be overrepresented in arrest data; (2) the independent variable of alcohol involvement is not always reported in records; it is rarely more than a subjective judgment by an official, not necessarily the arresting officer; and such indications are sometimes made on the self-report of an offender seeking to mitigate the charges filed; (3) the dependent variable of crime is also variously defined, making comparisons between studies difficult. Different jurisdictions follow varying procedures for processing offenders, some of which distort the actual offense with overbooking of the arrest charge, reduction to a lesser charge by the district attorney, and/or plea-bargaining in the courts.

Alcoholic Histories of Incarcerated Populations

Literature review. Studies of defined incarcerated populations, often selected for convenience, investigate, through records or self-reports, problem drinking or alcoholism. Both Blum [3] and Pernanen [12] review studies in which the proportion of problem drinkers among inmates is ascertained. Barnay's study of Sing-Sing prisoners for 1939–40 is cited as representative by Pernanen: Alcoholic criminals made up 25% of homicide offenders, 35% of assault offenders, 38% of sex-crime offenders, 29% of robbers, 33% of burglars, 29% of grand larceny offenders, and 15% of all other offenders. Numerous other studies corroborate this link between problem drinking and inmate populations. Collins [6] cites a 1978 United States Bureau of the Census survey of 10,000 inmates in state correctional institutions. The percentage of inmates reporting they had been drinking at the time of offense were robbery 39%, burglary 47%, larceny 38%, auto theft 46%, forgery 38%, and arson 67%. These percentages are less than those reported by Shupe (see Table 1) for the arrestee population whose alcohol involvement was measured by urinalysis. Considerable variation occurs in the proportion of problem drinkers in the offense categories and for different samples. The proportion of problem drinkers tends to be higher, for example, in psychiatric inmate populations and for recidivists as opposed to initial offenders.

Discussion. Again, although the link between alcohol abuse and inmate populations is clearly evident, problems arise in attributing causality. The most serious methodological flaw in these studies is the extreme selectivity of samples. For an individual to be included the selection criteria of incarceration excludes the majority of arrestees and the majority of those convicted who receive short jail terms or probation at sentencing. Thus these samples are weighted heavily toward criminals who received longer sentences [14]. A second problem is the validity of self-report data from persons wishing to disavow personal responsibility for their act by implicating alcohol. This reporting bias probably exaggerates the frequency and degree of alcohol use in these populations [11].

Criminal Histories of Alcoholic Populations

Literature review. Studies examining the criminal histories of samples defined as problem drinkers or alcoholics generally show a disproportionate number with records of crimes other than those associated with alcohol use. These samples are usually obtained from two sources: repeat alcohol offenders from inmate populations or clients of alcohol treatment programs. As might be expected, the characteristics of samples from the two sources are quite different. The former are more likely to be from lower socioeconomic levels and deviate in many ways other than alcohol abuse. Blum [3] cites a New York study of 187 chronic drunkenness offenders. Of this sample, 33% had been arrested only for alcohol use offenses, 12% for burglary, and 23% for larceny.

Criminal histories of alcoholics in treatment show results more consistent with the social class of the individual rather than with the selection factor of alcoholism. Lindelius and Salum [9] examined three groups of Swedish alcoholics in treatment and found that for volunteers, criminal histories did not differ from the general population. Data derived from two registers, one for nonalcohol-related criminal behaviors and one for alcohol-related offenses, showed that for two additional groups, of those who were identified on the criminal register 87% and 98% were also on the alcohol register. Conversely, of those identified on the alcohol register, 52% and 78% were also on the criminal register. The authors point out that, if one proceeds from samples defined by criminality, the role of alcoholism in crime appears overwhelming. If one proceeds from alcoholics, a relatively large number have not committed criminal offenses.

Discussion. Drinking does not lead to criminal acts for most individuals, nor do the majority of alcoholics become involved in crime. The data available show a disproportionate number of alcoholics involved in crime, although the extent to which this is an artifact of sampling bias is unknown [14]. The data from treatment samples moderate that from incarcerated samples, but replicate the findings. However, neither source represents the general drinking population.

THEORETICAL MODELS OF THE ALCOHOL–CRIME RELATIONSHIP

Theories as to the nature of a linking relationship were varied and often diametrically opposed. Blum's approach, the fifth discussed under "Research Approaches," is the theoretical level and is important not only as an attempt to find explanatory models for any alcohol-crime relationship, but also in that it suggests intervention strategies. Alcohol abuse and crime are significant social problems that appear to be increasing and becoming more costly to society. Accurate information and theory linking them may provide direction for efficient social efforts toward limiting their impact. The prominent theories are presented and discussed with respect to the degree of explanation of relevant data, supportive logic, and research implications.

Pernanen [12] describes four primary explanatory models that have been used to structure the empirical correlation found between alcohol consumption and crimes of violence. The most commonly offered model proposes the association of alcohol and violence to be a result of the direct pharmacologic effects of alcohol. The association is also explained by common-cause or third-factor theories (i.e., alcohol abuse and violence are both caused by the same factor or factors). A third approach examines interactive, conditional, or conjunctive models. That is, alcohol may increase violence, but many other factors also contribute and must be specified, as well as their relationship to alcohol use. A fourth model is called by Pernanen the "spuriousness model." Here, the empirical association is described as an artifact of nonrepresentative data collection, as discussed previously under problems of sample bias. This last approach falls within the area of methodological issues and is not discussed further.

Direct Effects Theories

The most common theory has postulated a direct physiological effect of alcohol in disinhibiting impulsive and aggressive behavior. The malevolence assumption discussed earlier seems to provide a basis for its popular acceptance. Its basic elements are that alcohol is assumed to have a pharmacologic effect, either causing the release of basic impulses or the suppression of higher cognitive functioning, including the censoring of unacceptable social behavior. Thus sexual or aggressive behavior is released when it would otherwise continue to be controlled. It is a common experience in situations involving alcohol for human behavior to appear disinhibited. The self-evident nature of this theory is illusory. Several underlying and unproven tenets must be accepted before even reaching the alcohol-crime connection: (1) that human beings are constantly suppressing unacceptable behavior; (2) that internal mechanisms for this suppression exist; and (3) that alcohol, in some unexplained manner, either directly increases the response strength of the former, or reduces control of the latter. Within the social science literature on alcohol, causality is often inferred from correlational data by explicitly or implicitly invoking the disinhibition theory. Pernanen has labeled this theory the "disinhibition" fallacy.

Attempts have been made to experimentally study the direct effects of alcohol on animal and human sexual and aggressive behavior. Results, thus far, have been equivocal. The experimental approach to the study of the direct effects of alcohol on aggression is more likely to be methodologically sound and relevant to the general population of alcohol users.

A review of the available literature indicates that in nonsocial situations where subjects were allowed to shock other participants, alcohol, in doses resulting in up to 0.09 blood alcohol concentration, did not affect the shock level delivered. In the small group context, experimental conditions involving semistructured social interaction, verbal aggression increased for alcohol groups. Interestingly, the amount of aggression was not different for BAC groups of 0.09 and 0.15%, but was different for the type of beverage consumed. Distilled beverages produced more aggression than beer, even though the BACs were equivalent. Further analyses showed that aggression increased only for some members of the groups [5].

In summary, experimental studies have not shown any consistent direct effect of alcohol on aggression. When effects are seen, the social context and the personalities of the individuals are involved to an as yet unspecified degree. One limitation of the experimental data is that studies rarely exceed BACs of 0.10%. This limits the possibility of generalization since, as Shupes data indicates, it is common for criminal offenders to have BACs well in excess of .20%.

Other theories of the direct action of alcohol in producing violent behavior are limited in applicable population or require the specification of mediating alcohol-induced conditions. For example, a clinical entity known as pathological intoxication has been described in which susceptible individuals may behave chaotically and violently after the ingestion of even small amounts of alcohol [1]. These outbursts have been compared to psychotic and epileptic episodes and the number of individuals affected is exceedingly small. Such individuals often display other physiological or behavioral abnormalities, which raises questions as to possible interactive effects rather than direct effects of alcohol. In terms of alcohol-induced mediating conditions, sleep deprivation, cerebral atrophy leading to temporal lobe epileptic seizures, and hypoglycemia have all been linked to increased violent behavior and all may result from chronic alcohol ingestion.

Common Cause Theories

The argument in favor of a common cause or third-factor theory is that nonnormative alcohol consumption, either acute or chronic, and nonnormative social behavior, either aggression or crime, both appear as symptoms of psychopathology or sociopathy in specific populations. Research results obtained by Robins [15] strongly support this explanatory model. In a 30-year longitudinal study of children seen in a child guidance center in St. Louis, disproportionate levels of both alcoholism and crime were observed in adults who were classified as having an antisocial behavior pattern in childhood as opposed to a control group of children. The percentages arrested by follow-up study were 94% and 17%, respectively. As adults 68% of the sociopathic group had serious alcohol problems, but only 7% of the controls had such problems. That antisocial behavior in childhood predicts adult alcohol consumption and criminal behavior implies a stable personality pathology.

Other studies cited by Pernanen consistently report disproportionate numbers of alcoholics involved in violent or other antisocial behavior years prior to their initiation of drinking. As with Robins' data, this implies that alcoholism and violent behavior can be seen as symptoms of a common developmental or genetic cause.

Interactive, Conditional, and Conjunctive Theories

Clearly no one theory could encompass all the relationships between the set of possible variables that may affect the alcohol-crime relationship. Theories at the interactive, conditional, and conjunctive level (often called theories of the middle range) are directed at explaining empirical results in specific rather than general terms. Thus questions regarding a possible effect of alcohol become more sophisticated, requiring specification of cultural milieu, population, drinking parameters, types of crime, and so on. The basic question becomes, "Does alcohol use in a particular context cause an increase in the commission of criminal acts beyond the rate that would occur under the same circumstances in the absence of alcohol?" For intervention purposes, corollary questions are, "To what extent does this effect occur in the presented context?" (i.e., how important a contributor is it in comparison to other factors), and "What is the underlying mechanism of action?" (i.e., at what point will intervention be possible and/or socially cost-effective).

It is important to note that in these approaches any effect of alcohol on crime is expected to vary considerably and across many levels. As previously discussed, these effects may be direct, as in pathological intoxication, or indirect, as in cerebral atrophy, hypoglycemia, or temporal lobe seizures. Variation is also expected across cultures, where alcohol use may take on different meanings and be regulated by different social norms. Within the anthropological literature reviewed by Heath [8], examples were provided by larger increases in aggression associated with alcohol use in some societies, and no increase in other societies. These data imply that it is not alcohol per se but rather the meaning ascribed to its use that may increase aggression.

Other interactive or conditional variation is seen in alcohol-crime comparisons across age, gender, and ethnic origin. Collins [6] discusses regularities in the empirical data in respect to these variables. Men commit more crime and consume more alcohol than women; young men are more involved with both crime and alcohol than older men; and, although an alcohol-crime association is generally characteristic of most modern Western societies, the strength of the association is variable by culture.

Individual personality characteristics clearly influence alcohol's effects on behavior. Regular personality traits or patterns of behavior have long been noted within certain populations of alcoholics and in subsets of criminally involved alcoholics. Alcohol use may then be simply associated with certain personality characteristics, which also produce criminal behavior. Its possible causal influence on the latter requires empirical and theoretical assessment, which has not yet been possible.

The final area of interaction-condition theories is the immediate situational conditions surrounding a criminal act where alcohol is involved. Most violent crimes occur among family members or social acquaintances. This is true for homicide, assault, and, of course, spouse and child abuse. Thus such events occur most often in a socially historical context and in an immediate situational context. Additionally, a process of interaction occurs, composed of reciprocal and escalating behaviors between offender and victim culminating in the violent act. It has been suggested that determination of the participant finally escalating to aggression is partly determined by the structure of the situation [17]. Given this perspective on the situational aspect, questions concerning contributory factors, such as alcohol and their relationship to the process become more easily specified.

Pernanen [13] has developed a sophisticated situational model based, in part, on alcohol's well-known pharmacologic effects on cognitive function. Alcohol impairs perception, judgment, and motor coordination. Pernanen suggests this disorganizing effect will increase the likelihood of violent behavior in interpersonal situations. He states, "A decrease in the conceptual and abstracting abilities can be used to construct a model to explain the extremeness and unpredictability of affect and behavior under the influence of alcohol" [12, p. 414]. The posited cognitive impairment narrows the perceptual field, causing the interacting participants to focus only on the most obvious cues (social and personal) to the exclusion of other moderating cues, and to often misinterpret their meaning. If the misconstruing initiates aggressive behavior, which is reciprocated by other participants (who are probably also drinking), successive exchanges may escalate and culminate in a violent act. The actual initiator of the act is more likely to be determined by preexisting personality characteristics or situational factors rather than alcohol use. Much of the previously discussed empirical results fit well within this model. It also provides numerous hypothesis subject to empirical testing.

CONCLUSIONS

Although a strong empirical correlation exists between alcohol use and crime, the preponderance of evidence indicates alcohol use and criminal behavior are not causally related for the majority of alcohol users or alcoholics. When they are either, the association is most likely to be through a common cause, or there is an influence in some categories of crimes, but only under certain circumstances of culture, person, place, and situation. The state of the art in alcohol crime research has barely specified qualitative relationships and is inadequate to attempt quantitative estimations. The research methodologies developed in studying alcohol and traffic safety need to be examined for applicability to specific hypotheses concerning alcohol and crime. The alcohol-crime relationship would be best approached by complex theoretical models within a multidisciplinary perspective. Simple questions, answers, or solutions do not exist.

REFERENCES

1. Bach-y-Rita, G., Lion, J., and Ervin, F. Pathological intoxication: Clinic and electroencephalographic studies. *Am. J. Psychiatry* 127:698–703, 1970.
2. Bartholomew, A. Alcoholism and crime. *Aust. N.Z. J. Criminol.* 2:71–99, 1968.
3. Blum, R. Mind-altering drugs and dangerous behavior: Alcohol. In: *Drunkeness, Annotations, Consultant's Papers and Related Materials* (The President's Commission on Law Enforcement and Administration of Justice Task Force Report). U.S. Government Printing Office: Washington, D.C., 1967.
4. Blum, R. Drugs and violence. In: *Crimes of Violence*. Mulvihill, D. and Tumin, D. (eds.). U.S. Government Printing Office: Washington, D.C., 1969.
5. Carpenter, J., and Armenti, N. Some effects of ethanol on human sexual and aggressive behavior. In: *The Biology of Alcoholism*, Kissin, B. and Begleiter, H. (eds.). Plenum: New York, 1972.
6. Collins, J. *Alcohol Use and Criminal Behavior: An Empirical, Theoretical and Methodological Overview*. Research Triangle Institute: Research Triangle Park, N.C., 1980.
7. Hamilton, C., and Collins, J. The role of alcohol in wife beating and child abuse: A review of the literature. In: *Drinking and Crime: Perspectives on the Relationship between Alcohol Consumption and Criminal Behavior*, Collins, J. (ed.). Guilford Press: New York, 1981.
8. Heath, D. A critical review of ethnographic studies of alcohol use. In: *Research Advances in Alcohol and Drug Problems* (Vol. 2), Gibbons, R., Israel, Y., Kalant, H., Popham, R., Schmidt, W., and Smart, R. G. (eds.). Wiley: New York, 1975.
9. Lindelius, R., and Salum, I. Alcoholism and crime: A comparative study of three groups of alcoholics. *J. Stud. Alcohol* 36:1452–1457, 1975.
10. MacDonald, J. *The Murderer and His Victim*. Charles C Thomas: Springfield, Ill., 1961.
11. McCaghy, C. Drinking and deviance disavowal: The case of child molesters. *Social Problems* 16:43–49, 1968.
12. Pernanen, K. Alcohol and crimes of violence. In: *The Biology of Alcoholism: Social Aspects of Alcoholism* (Vol. 4), Kissin, B. and Begleiter, H. (eds.). Plenum: New York, 1976.
13. Pernanen, K. Theoretical aspects of the relationship between alcohol use and crime. In: *Drinking and Crime: Perspectives on the Relationship between Alcohol Consumption and Assaultive Criminal Behavior*, Collins, J. (ed.). Guilford Press: New York, 1981.
14. Pottieger, A. Sample bias in drugs/crime research: An empirical study. In: *Annual Reviews of Drug and Alcohol Abuse: The Drugs-Crime Connection* (Vol. 5), Inciardi, J. (ed.). Sage: Beverly Hills, Calif., 1981.
15. Robins, L. *Deviant Children Grown Up*. Williams & Wilkins: Baltimore, Md., 1966.
16. Roizen, J., and Schneberk, D. Alcohol and crime. In: *Alcohol, Casualties, and Crime,*

Aarens, M., Cameron, T., Roizen, J., Room, R., Schneberk, D., and Wingard, D. (eds.). Social Research Group: Berkeley, Calif., 1978.

17. Shoham, S., Ben-David, S., and Rahav, G. Interaction in violence. *Hum. Rel.* 27: 417-430, 1974.

18. Shupe, L. Alcohol and crime. *J. Crim. Law Crimin. Pol. Sci.* 44:661-664, 1953.

19. Tinklenberg, J. Drugs and crime. In: *Drug Use in America: Problem in Perspective* (The Second Report of the National Commission on Marihuana and Drug Abuse, Appendix, Vol. 1, Patterns and Consequences of Drug Use). U.S. Government Printing Office: Washington, D.C., 1973.

20. Wolfgang, M. *Patterns in Criminal Homicide.* Wiley: New York, 1958.

31

PATRICIA F. WALLER, PhD, University of North Carolina at Chapel Hill

ALCOHOL AND HIGHWAY SAFETY

ALCOHOL IS THE SINGLE most important factor yet identified in serious and fatal motor vehicle crashes. It is estimated that approximately half of all fatal crashes involve excessive use of alcohol; that is, a blood alcohol concentration (BAC) of .10% or higher is involved. This is not to say that half of all drivers in fatal crashes are legally drunk. A significant portion of fatal motor vehicle crashes involve a pedestrian with a BAC at or above the legal limit.

To put the problem into perspective, it should be pointed out that in the United States traffic crashes are the fourth leading cause of death for all ages and the leading cause of death from age 6 months to about 40 years. When losses are measured in working years of life rather than number of lives lost, the role of traffic crashes is even greater because these accidents strike the young most heavily. Hence the heavy involvement of alcohol in fatal motor vehicle crashes is a significant health and economic problem in society today.

Unfortunately traffic injuries and deaths are too often considered accidents in the sense that they are chance events and hence cannot be avoided. Although there has been some change in this attitude and motor vehicle death rates per million vehicle miles traveled have decreased significantly, the alcohol-related crash remains stubbornly resistant to amelioration. It continues to account for roughly half of annual motor vehicle fatalities.

Patricia F. Waller, PhD, Associate Director for Driver Studies, and Research Professor, Department of Health Administration, School of Public Health, University of North Carolina at Chapel Hill, Chapel Hill, North Carolina.

The alcohol-related crash is not a new phenomenon. As early as 1904 an editorial in the *Quarterly Journal of Inebriety* reported on the involvement of alcohol in "fatal accidents to automobile wagons" and warned of the likelihood of an increase in the problem as the popularity of the automobile wagons grew [12]. However, scientific investigation of the role of alcohol in motor vehicle crashes could not proceed effectively until appropriate technology had been developed. Measures of the BAC of crash-involved drivers began in the 1930s but were originally confined to those drivers who had been fatally injured. To arrive at any meaningful estimates of risk it was necessary to get similar measures from drivers who were not in crashes. So long as measurement of the BAC required a blood sample, it was virtually impossible to discover the extent to which alcohol increased crash risk.

The development of methodology for measuring the BAC using a breath sample opened the door to epidemiologic studies, that is, studies of the population at risk of crash as well as those who were crash-involved. The first major study and still the most important such study ever conducted is that of Borkenstein et al. conducted in Grand Rapids, Michigan in 1962-63 [1]. Interviews and breath samples were obtained from almost 6,000 accident-invovled drivers and over 7,500 other drivers who were selected at accident sites at a time and day corresponding to the time and day at which a previous accident had occurred. The carefully trained interviewers succeeded in collecting information from almost 96% of the accident sample and almost 98% of the control drivers. The analyses considered driver age, sex, estimated annual mileage, education, race or nationality, marital status, occupation, average drinking frequency, and blood alcohol concentration. All these factors were found to be significantly related to alcohol-involved crashes. However, even when these factors were controlled, the results clearly underscored the importance of alcohol in crashes. Figure 1 shows the differences between accident and control groups by BAC. The drivers in accidents reached higher BACs than any found in the control group. Although the accident and control groups varied on the other driver variables considered, it was found that even when these variables were taken into account the higher BACs were associated with a higher accident experience.

In addition, judgments were made as to which drivers caused the accidents. Figure 2 illustrates the relationship between the BAC and the probability of being responsible for an accident. It can be seen that this probability increases as the BAC exceeds .05% and above .08% the probability of causing an accident rises dramatically.

There is a curious finding in the Borkenstein et al. study; namely, at low levels of alcohol (i.e., BACs of .01-.04%) the probability of crash not only does not appear to rise but actually appears to be slightly lower than when there is no alcohol present. This finding, confirmed in at least one subsequent study, led to speculation that a little alcohol may actually improve driving performance. However, a more careful analysis of driving groups that controlled for reported frequency of

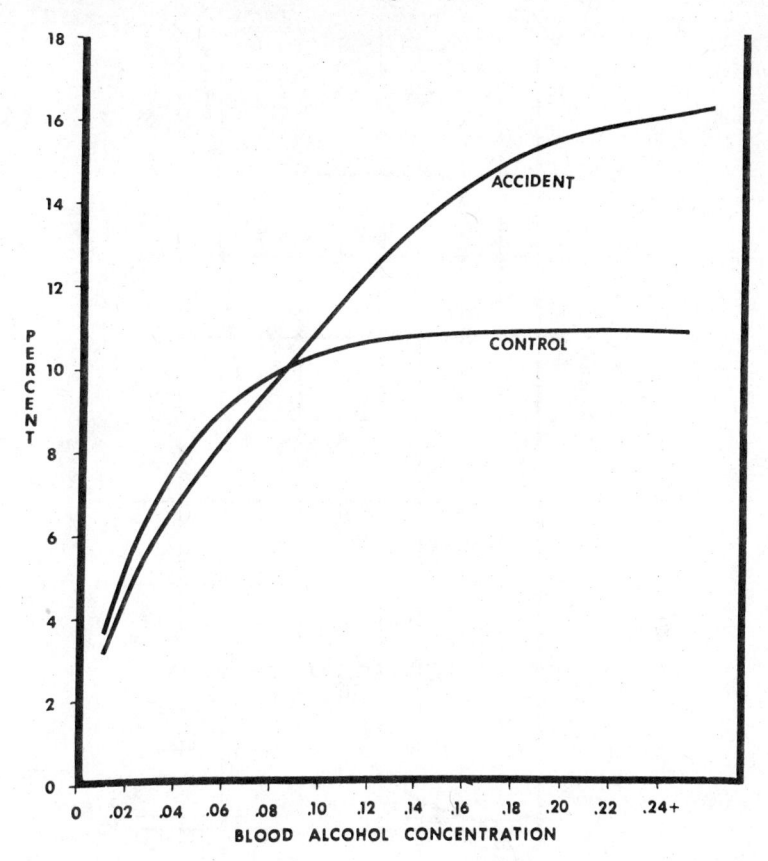

Figure 1. Cumulative Percentage at or below Specific Alcohol Concentrations for Accident and Control Groups. (From *The Role of the Drinking Driver in Traffic Accidents,* by R. F. Borkenstein, R. F. Crawther, R. P. Shumate, W. B. Ziel, and R. Zylman, Indiana University Department of Police Administration: Bloomington, 1964. Reprinted by permission.)

drinking has shown that this dip is actually an artifact [3]. Drivers who report drinking daily have much lower crash probabilities when there is no alcohol in their system than drivers who report drinking less frequently (i.e., three times a week, weekly, monthly, yearly, or less). At all BAC levels the more practiced drinker has a lower crash probability than the less practiced drinker. Yet every drinking group shows an increase in crash probability as the BAC increases. Because the more frequent drinker is more likely to be found on the road with some alcohol present, and because these drivers on the whole appear to be better drivers at any BAC, including .00%, it is likely that their better driving performance rather than their BAC is accounting for the apparent findings that lower BACs are associated with a somewhat lower crash probability than .00% BACs. Figure 3 illustrates this finding. It should be noted, however, that these results do not include any BACs

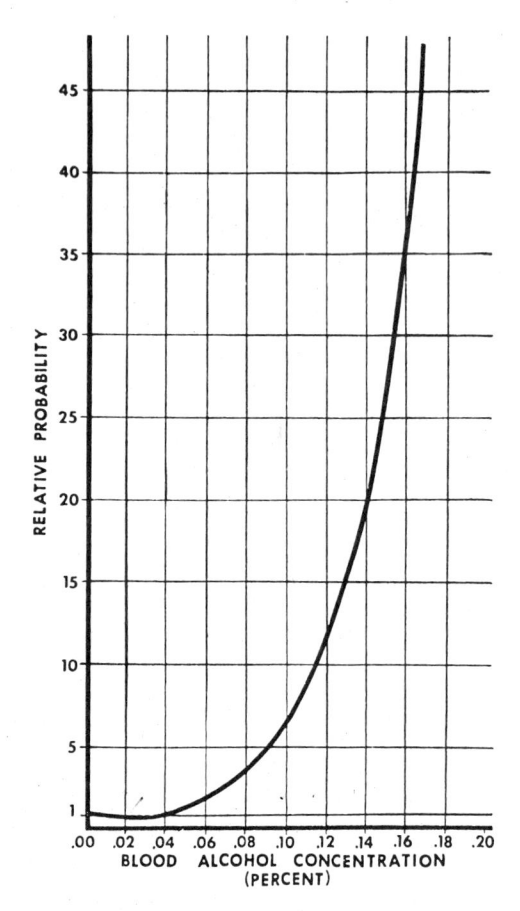

Figure 2. Relative Probability of Causing an Accident. (From *The Role of the Drinking Driver in Traffic Accidents,* by R. F. Borkenstein, R. F. Crawther, R. P. Shumate, W. B. Ziel, and R. Zylman, Indiana University Department of Police Administration: Bloomington, 1964. Reprinted by permission.)

above .09%. Drinking drivers in fatal crashes usually have BACs well beyond this level.

Although well-controlled studies of drinking behavior in drivers are difficult to conduct, the few studies that have been reported generally confirm the findings of Borkenstein et al. [1]. Interestingly, a large study conducted in Vermont and covering the entire state reports findings almost identical to those for Grand Rapids [8]. It appears that the relationship between alcohol and crash risk is similar whether the driving environment is urban or rural.

The Vermont findings showed that at .08% BAC the risk of being responsible for a fatal crash is about four times greater than when no alcohol is present. At .10% BAC the risk is about seven times greater, and at .15% it is about 25 times greater than when no alcohol is present. In light of such findings it is of interest that the average BAC of drivers arrested for driving under the influence (DUI) or driving while intoxicated (DWI) is ordinarily .15% or higher and BACs of .25% or above are not unusual.

It is important to understand that the relationship between alcohol and crash risk varies as a function of the seriousness of the crash. In those crashes involving property damage only, alcohol is present in about 16% of the drivers, but only about 5% are above .10% BAC. In personal injury crashes, the proportion of drivers with alcohol present increases to about 25%, with about 11% above .10% BAC. The data are less clear for fatal crashes because if there is more than one driver involved the BAC is not always obtained on surviving drivers. For all drivers who are fatally injured, between 40 and 55% have BACs at or above .10%. Many of these drivers (29 to 43%) are at levels of .15% BAC or higher. When only single vehicle crashes in which the driver is killed are considered, the alcohol involvement is even greater. Between 55 and 65% of these drivers have BACs at or above .10%, and between 34 and 53% are at .15% or higher. Thus it can be seen that the

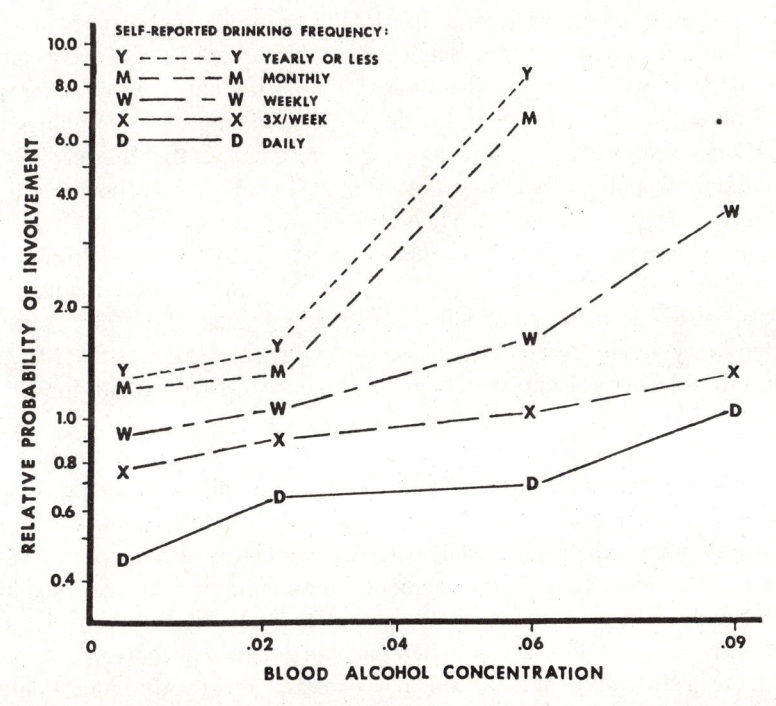

Figure 3. Relative Probability of Crash Involvement (by Drinking Frequency Group) as a Function of BAC where 1.0 = Relative Probability of Composite Group at Zero Alcohol. (From "Epidemiological Aspects of Alcohol in Driver Crashes and Citations" by P. M. Hurst, *Journal of Safety Research,* 1973, 5, 135. Reprinted by permission.)

more serious the crash, the greater the probability that a high level of alcohol concentration is present [4].

THE DRINKING DRIVER

In the United States today almost all adults drive and about 75% of the adult population drinks. Furthermore, at some time most adults drive after drinking. However, most people do not have drinking problems. What differentiates the driver who gets into difficulty from the rest of the driving population? Because most people at some time drive after drinking, they tend to identify with the driver who is being prosecuted for driving under the influence and believe, "There but for the grace of God go I." Yet the person arrested for drunk driving is not typical of most drivers. His or her BAC is usually much higher than that reached by the majority of drivers. To reach a BAC of .10% an average 150 lb. person would have to consume four to five drinks in 1 hour on an empty stomach. Most persons who drink combine their drinking with some eating and do not drink so rapidly. The average person who is arrested for drunk driving has probably consumed at least fifteen drinks. Clearly this is not characteristic of most adults who use alcohol.

Drinking drivers are predominantly male. Males not only report greater frequency of drinking but also report drinking more at one time. These findings are supported by epidemiologic studies as well as arrest data, so that they cannot be accounted for by police bias in who is arrested. It should be noted, however, that females run a higher risk of crash when they do drink.

Drinking drivers are more likely to be between ages 20 and 59, and drunk driving rates are particularly high in the 25- to 44-year range. These middle-aged drivers are also likely to have higher BACs. However, younger drivers are overrepresented in alcohol-related crashes and get into difficulty at lower BAC levels. Apparently combining alcohol with their inexperience in driving greatly increases their crash risk.

There is some evidence that drivers who are unmarried (single, widowed, separated, or divorced) may be more likely to get into difficulty with their drinking and driving. Persons who have recently experienced a divorce and persons recently released from prison are also at higher risk of being in an alcohol-related crash [6]. Also, drivers who report higher frequency of drinking are more likely to have alcohol present. Drivers with high BACs have more crashes and more convictions on their driver records than drivers with no alcohol present. Alcohol-related crashes are more likely to occur at night and on weekends, but of course a much higher proportion of the drivers on the road at those times have been drinking.

Of particular interest is the finding that drivers with high BACs are more likely to report a preference for beer. Many people do not recognize beer as being alcoholic in the same sense that hard liquor is. Yet the alcohol content of a 12 oz.

bottle of beer is about the same as that of one 3 oz. glass of wine or 1 oz. of liquor in a mixed drink or by itself. A driver can get just as drunk on beer as on whiskey. In fact, most drunk driving involves beer. This finding is especially important because policies for controlling beer are often different from those for liquor, and as a result erroneous information may be communicated to the public and especially to young drivers. For example, the sale of beer is often allowed to younger persons than is the sale of hard liquor. Likewise the advertising policies for beer and wine are much more lenient than those for hard liquor.

COUNTERMEASURES

There have been efforts to combat the drinking-driver problem for almost as long as the problem has existed. The traditional deterrent approaches may be classified into three major areas, namely, legal, public information and education, and, more recently, health. There are also several newer approaches that are gaining some favor, namely, the technological approach, the systems approach, and, the citizen action approach.

Legal

The oldest form of countermeasure is the legal approach. Although New Jersey passed a statute in 1913, it was the Scandinavian countries that were earliest to take a strong stand against drinking and driving. Norway passed legislation prohibiting drinking and driving as early as 1912, when there were only 730 vehicles registered in the country [10]. Initially laws prohibiting drunk driving relied upon a subjective judgment of the extent of impairment. In 1936 Norway passed the first per se law, that is, a law that prohibited operating a motor vehicle with a BAC of a specified level or higher. The per se law is analogous to speed laws. Speed limits apply to everyone regardless of one's capability to operate a vehicle at higher speeds. Likewise, the per se laws do not address whether the person is impaired at the specified level. However, the BACs generally used have been shown to result in impaired judgment even in the case of experienced drinkers.

There is considerable variation in the BAC level that defines drunk driving in different countries. In the United States states generally use a higher BAC, namely, .10%, than some countries use. Canada and England define drunk driving as occurring at .08% BAC or higher, while the Scandinavian countries and the state of Victoria in Australia define it as .05% BAC or above [11].

In Sweden a legal distinction is made between lower and higher BACs, corresponding to two levels of the drunk driving offense. The second-degree offense occurs at a BAC between .05 and .15% and is punishable by fines. The first-degree offense occurs at a BAC of .15% or higher and is punishable by imprisonment. Another interesting characteristic of the Swedish system is that fines are levied as a percentage of income so that variation in the socioeconomic status of the offender becomes less relevant. Furthermore, the fines may be quite high, running to as much as 10% of one's annual income [10].

The British Road Safety Act of 1967 represents a significant attempt to deter drunk driving through laws and enforcement. This act provided that when a driver was involved in a traffic violation or accident, the investigating officer could require a roadside screening breath test. If the test were refused or failed (i.e., if the BAC was found to be .08% or above), the officer could require a blood test. If this second test confirmed the earlier finding, the driver was considered guilty of a crime and punished accordingly, including mandatory license suspension for 1 year. The passage of the law was surrounded by considerable controversy and hence publicity. Ross [9] conducted a careful evaluation of the impact of the law, examining changes not only in alcohol-related highway crashes but also in other types of highway crashes, drunk driving charges, amount of driving, court sentences, liquor consumption, and a number of other factors. He concluded that neither drinking nor driving was significantly reduced, but British drivers were indeed reducing the amount of driving after drinking. Unfortunately, the effect was transitory. Ross argues that it was the public's belief that there was a high probability of detection and arrest that led to the law's impact. As it became clear that the probability of detection was actually quite low, the effect of the law diminished. The same phenomenon has been detected in similar publicized attempts to crack down on the drinking driver.

A major problem with the legal approach is that laws by themselves do not solve a problem. Similar laws can lead to very different results, depending upon the level of enforcement, the rate of conviction, and the severity of the penalty. Laws are most effective when the public views the probability of detection as high and the punishment as certain, swift, and severe. These conditions have simply not been maintained in most countries in the case of drinking-driving laws.

Public Information and Education

Laws are most effective when they have broad public support. In the past, educational approaches to drinking and driving have not proved to be particularly effective. Large sums of money have been spent on campaigns that admonish, "If you drink, don't drive." However, because most adults in the United States at some time drive after drinking and do not get into serious trouble, they fail to take the slogan seriously.

More recently educational efforts have been aimed at helping the public to understand the seriousness of the drinking-driving problem and what they can do to make a difference. There is some evidence that messages such as, "Friends don't let friends drive drunk," may make a difference in some instances. However, public education and information is most effective when it is combined with specific action programs. It is usually difficult to develop and implement countermeasures in the absence of sound public information and education. There is still considerable confusion and misunderstanding about drunk driving and it is only through public information and education that the true picture can be communicated.

The Health Approach

Historically drunk driving was considered a crime and handled accordingly. Although it is still a criminal act, there has been a major move toward determining whether the drunk driver has a drinking problem. This change stems from the view that problem drinking is a disease and that the person can no longer control his or her drinking behavior. Although experts differ on their definitions of problem drinking, there have been attempts to separate persons convicted of drunk driving into social drinkers and problem drinkers. Presumably social drinkers can respond more readily to information than problem drinkers.

Alcohol safety schools have been developed as a way of treating convicted drunk drivers. Evaluations of these schools have resulted in mixed verdicts. The most carefully controlled studies show the least promising results, although there is some support for the contention that the social drinker is more likely to benefit from the information given [7]. The more serious problem drinker remains difficult to reach. In fact, one study in California found that as far as highway safety is concerned, it is better to suspend the license of a convicted drunk driver than to send him or her to a rehabilitative program [2]. Nevertheless, the health approach represents an attempt to get at the cause of the drinking rather than simply to treat the symptom, namely, drunk driving. The limited success of such programs to date should not deter any further efforts along these lines. Rather, the findings to date should be used in developing different approaches to the problem.

Technological Approach

Some efforts have been made to make it more difficult for the convicted drunk driver to operate a vehicle while under the influence of alcohol. Devices have been developed that can be attached as an integral part of the ignition system in vehicles operated by these drivers. To be able to start the ignition the person first has to demonstrate fitness by performing a task. One device requires that the operator punch in a series of numbers that are displayed on the device. Several sequences of numbers are given with the person duplicating them each time. If the test is completed successfully the ignition can be turned on. Another device requires that the driver successfully track a moving target for a specified period of time. There have been many problems with this approach, both technological and legal [4]. Whether a feasible system can be developed that will be politically acceptable remains to be seen.

Systems Approach

In 1970 the United States federal government, working with local jurisdictions, launched a major countermeasure program that attempted to use a systems approach to reduce drinking and driving [5], that is, an approach that coordinated all major components of the drinking driver control system. Implementing the first of a total of 35 alcohol safety action programs (ASAPs), this effort coordinated five separate categories of countermeasure activities, namely, enforcement, judicial and legislative, presentence investigation and probation, rehabilitation, and public information and education. Although the early reports claimed considerable success, more careful evaluation showed less promising findings [7]. However, the length of time that the ASAPs were in operation was probably not great enough to afford a reasonable trial. Society's attitudes and behaviors toward alcohol are so deeply ingrained that it is unrealistic to expect major changes in the course of a demonstration project.

Ultimately if drinking and driving are to be reduced significantly this reduction will almost have to come from a systems approach.

Citizen Action Groups

In recent years in the United States a new phenomenon has developed in regard to drinking and driving, namely, citizen groups that assume responsibility for seeing that something is done to combat this problem. Ordinarily these groups are initiated as a result of a personal tragedy in which an innocent victim is killed or seriously injured by a drunk driver. The citizen actions groups are especially promising in that they are able to monitor the different components of the system. Many states have laws on the books that, if enforced, would lead to the conviction of many more drunk drivers. However, because of plea bargaining, repeated continuation of cases, suspended sentences, and other such maneuvers, many persons arrested for drunk driving and shown to have BACs well beyond the legal limit nevertheless do not suffer the penalties that the laws were enacted to impose. The citizen groups are not only working with legislators to enact appropriate laws but also monitoring courtrooms to see how judges and prosecutors handle cases. The voting records of legislators and the records of prosecutors and judges are widely publicized so that elective officials have to account for their behavior to their constituents.

The citizen groups are also working to overcome the many obstacles that have previously impeded control of the drinking driver, such as insufficient funding for adequate enforcement or prosecution. No matter how effective an approach may be on paper, if there is no effort to monitor how well the program is implemented, it is almost doomed to failure. The rise of the citizen action groups may prove to be the essential ingredient that has thus far been missing in attempts to make control of the drinking driver a reality.

CONCLUSION

The combination of alcohol with driving exacts an enormous toll in both lives and dollars. Significant progress has been made in identifying and apprehending the drinking driver, but these gains have not been accompanied by a meaningful decrease in the size of the drinking-driving problem. Because many countermeasures are costly and because some place serious restrictions and demands on the individual's freedom and rights, it is essential that countermeasures be subjected to careful evaluation to determine the extent of their effectiveness, if any.

The problem of excessive use of beverage alcohol and its relation to injury has been known since earliest recorded history. One should not anticipate rapid progress in this most difficult area, but should recognize the full import of the problem and the corresponding obligation to continue to explore possibilities for reducing the tragic consequences.

REFERENCES

1. Borkenstein, R. F., Crawther, R. F., Shumate, R. P., Ziel, W. B., and Zylman, R. *The Role of the Drinking Driver in Traffic Accidents.* Indiana University Department of Police Administration: Bloomington, 1964.
2. Hagen, R. E., Williams, R. L., McConnell, E. J., and Fleming, C. W. *An Evaluation of Alcohol Abuse Treatment as an Alternative to Drivers License Suspension or Revocation.* Department of Motor Vehicles: Sacramento, Calif., 1978.
3. Hurst, P. M. Epidemiological aspects of alcohol in driver crashes and citations. *J. Safety Res.* 5:130-148, 1973.
4. Jones, R. K., and Joscelyn, K. B. *Alcohol and Highway Safety 1978: A Review of the State of Knowledge* (Summary Vol.). National Highway Traffic Safety Administration: Washington, D.C., 1978.
5. Joscelyn, K. B., and Jones, R. K. *A Systems Approach to the Analysis of the Drinking Driver Control System.* National Highway Traffic Safety Administration: Washington, D.C., 1971.
6. Lacey, J. H., Council, F. M., and Stewart, J. R. *Techniques for Predicting High-Risk Drivers for Alcohol Countermeasures* (Vol. 1). University of North Carolina at Chapel Hill Highway Safety Research Center: Chapel Hill, 1979.
7. Nichols, J. L., Weinstein, E. B., Ellingstad, V. S., and Struckman-Johnson, D. L. *The Specific Deterrence Effect of ASAP Education and Rehabilitation Programs.* Paper presented at the National Safety Congress, Washington, D.C., October 1978.
8. Perrine, M. W., Waller, J. A., and Harris, L. S. *Alcohol and Highway Safety: Behavioral and Medical Aspects.* National Highway Traffic Administration: Washington, D.C., 1971.
9. Ross, H. L. Law, science, and accidents: The British Road Safety Act of 1967. *J. Legal Stud.* 2:1-78, 1973.
10. Ross, H. L. The Scandinavian myth: The effectiveness of drinking-and-driving legislation in Sweden and Norway. *J. Legal Stud.* 4:285-310, 1975.
11. Ross, H. L. *Deterrence of the Drinking Driver: An International Survey.* National Highway Traffic Safety Administration: Washington, D.C., 1981.
12. United States Department of Transportation. *The 1968 Alcohol and Highway Safety Report.* U.S. Government Printing Office: Washington, D.C., 1968.

32

JONAS R. RAPPEPORT, MD, Supreme Bench of Baltimore
NICHOLAS V. CONTI, MSW, ACSW, Supreme Bench of Baltimore

LEGAL ISSUES OF ALCOHOLISM

THIS CHAPTER FOCUSES on the issue of criminal responsibility as it relates to those who become involved in illegal behavior using alcohol. The intent is to provide for the reader an understanding of the basic issues underlying American jurisprudence regarding the use of alcohol and criminal behavior, along with an ample understanding of the doctrine of *mens rea* (criminal intent). As the chapter progresses, the need for accountability of one's actions, in spite of the use of alcohol, is presented, along with various legal cases that have dealt with the behavioral and social issues of those using alcohol who have committed crimes. An attempt is made to carefully separate the individual who suffers from alcoholism and the individual who is clearly not responsible for his or her behavior by virtue of a mental disorder. It is quite important for the reader at all times to be aware that in the federalistic form of democracy, case laws and laws created by legislatures differ from state to state. While there are federal statutes and case laws that deal with these issues, they are not always applicable at the local level. This concept was underscored by the Supreme Court

---

Jonas R. Rappeport, MD, Chief Medical Officer, Supreme Bench of Baltimore, Assistant Professor, The Johns Hopkins School of Medicine, and Clinical Professor of Psychiatry, University of Maryland School of Medicine, Baltimore Maryland.

Nicholas V. Conti, MSW, ACSW, Medical Administrator, Supreme Bench of Baltimore, and Field Instructor, University of Maryland School of Social Work and Community Planning, Baltimore, Maryland.

of the United States in *Powell* v. *Texas*, when Justice Marshall completed his opinion with the following paragraph:

> We cannot cast aside the centuries-long evolution of the collections of interlocking and overlapping concepts which the common law has utilized to assess the moral accountability of an individual for his antisocial deeds. The doctrine of *actus reus mens rea*, insanity, mistake, justification and duress have historically provided the tools for a constantly shifting adjustment of the tension between the evolving aims of the criminal law and changing religious, moral, philosophical, and medical views of the nature of man. This process of adjustment has always been thought to be the province of the states.
>
> It is simply not time to write the constitutional formula's case in terms whose meaning, let alone relevance, is not yet clear either to doctors or lawyers. [4, p. 596]

INSANITY VERSUS VOLUNTARY AND INVOLUNTARY INTOXICATION

Criminal Intent

The fabric of American jurisprudence was carefully woven from the traditions of English common law. This body of law gave to the American legal system certain specific concepts. The common law traditions require that a person within the greater society be held "personally accountable" [4, p. 596] for all behavior that he or she manifests while functioning in the greater society. An individual is therefore both morally and legally responsible for any behavior against individuals in society. Notably, the exception to this basic concept has been when the lack of *mens rea* can be established. Custom and tradition have held the individual who is not criminally responsible exempt from the usual channels of societal retribution. The law's emphasis in those matters has clearly been not only to find such an individual not guilty by reason of insanity but also to establish the need for psychiatric treatment as both remedial to the individual and protective of society. Laws pertaining to those found not guilty by reason of insanity (NGRI) also provide for inpatient treatment until such persons are able to function without harming themselves or those within society. Several tests to determine the need for exculpation by lack of *mens rea* exist. Briefly these are referred to as the M'Naughten tests and the American Law Institute tests (ALI). M'Naughten, while the simpler of the two, generally appears the harsher and requires only that the person be unable to distinguish right from wrong. The ALI test, on the other hand, is considerably clearer and, it is hoped, more objective. In this test, the individual must, by reason of a mental disorder, lack substantial capacity to either appreciate the criminality of his or her behavior or to conform his or her behavior to the requirements of the law. With either or both of these conditions existing, a person may be found insane at the time of the commission of a crime. A person found not guilty by reason of insanity may then be involuntarily committed to a hospital for psychiatric treatment. Usually this involuntary status continues until an administrative hearing occurs wherein the individual's psychiatric treatment and progress are reviewed along with the person's potential for further dangerous behavior. This hearing results in either a recommendation to the court of jurisdiction for release into the community or of retention for further inpatient care. Release into the community is usually done in a conditional manner for a specific period of time. This type of conditional release may be revoked if the patient violates a specific condition of release or becomes so psychiatrically disturbed that he or she cannot remain in the community.

An alternative to involuntary inpatient commitment can be direct return to the community with specific conditions that may or may not include psychiatric care.

Certain similarities in the individual who is legally insane and the individual who is intoxicated can be confusing vis-à-vis culpability. For instance, people who are legally insane may have the same erratic, unpredictable, and unpremeditated behavior that one sees in an alcoholic. An alcoholic may in turn exhibit both delusional and hallucinatory ideas, which one can also see in the person who is legally insane. The legally insane individual may not remember any or a vast portion of his or her criminal behavior, just as the intoxicated person who commits a crime may not remember anything.

Voluntary Intoxication

What then determines the alcoholic's responsibility for his or her behavior and the criminally insane person not responsible? In order to address this issue, one must distinguish between those who by reason of a mental disorder lacked *mens rea* and those who made a free will decision to initially consume alcohol.

Alexander D. Brooks clearly states, "It is generally agreed that a defendant will not be relieved of criminal responsibility because he was under the influence of intoxicating drugs voluntarily taken" [2, p. 250]. He goes on further to say

> This principle rests on public policy demanding that he who seeks the influence of liquor or narcotics should not be insulated from criminal liability because that influence impaired his judgment or control. The element of required badness can be found in the intentional use of stimulants or depressants. Moreover, to say that one who offended while under such influence was sick would suggest that his sickness disappeared when he sobered up and hence [he] should be released. Such a concept could hardly protect others from the prospect of repeated personal injury. [2, p. 250]

The intoxicated person who has used alcohol in such an irresponsible fashion, knowing that the drug by its nature can make one aggressive, hostile, and destructive, may well have previously entertained the behavior he or she exhibited and merely used alcohol as a vehicle to release inhibitions. The law mandates that the individual not be exculpated by virtue of the alcoholism problem he or she may possess, regardless of whether or not the alcoholic condition is chronic or episodic.

It is significant to note that the "required badness" that Brooks refers to is a central feature of the use of intoxicants in the commission of a crime. Such is not the case in the individual who is legally insane, as this behavior emanates from incapacitating mental health problems of such magnitude that they render the individual incapable of having criminal intent.

Involuntary Intoxication

There are several areas in which the person charged with a crime may not be responsible even though there may have been the use of alcohol, including: (1) commission of a crime in states in which the individual had a permanent and fixed insanity prior to the use of alcohol; (2) conditions wherein a person was voluntarily intoxicated but the crime was one in which the voluntary intoxication prevented the formation of a specific intent (a concept discussed later in the chapter); (3) conditions in which the intoxication was involuntary or an unexpected side effect from an alcohol-based medication prescribed by a physician. In addition, pathological intoxication and paradoxical reactions might also relieve an individual of criminal responsibility. Beyond this, however, the individual who is voluntarily intoxicated is responsible for all behavior, whether or not the individual is amnesic. Since alcoholism is so prevalent, it would seem irresponsible for society to move from this stance. Any other position would be tantamount to excusing individuals on a wholesale basis for their crimes and thereby allowing them to escape societal accountability. In addition, removal of responsibility might well affect the motivation for an individual to remain personally accountable. Marvin A. Block, MD, an early leader in the study and treatment of alcoholism, states, "Alcohol offers an escape from responsibility, which so many patients tend to need. Any agent which tends to diminish motivation for recovery would therefore tend to increase the severity of the illness and eventually contribute to the disintegration of the patient" [1, pp. 62–63]. Further implication for the need of personal accountability is suggested when excusing alcoholics would "discourage them from assessing the responsibility of caring for themselves" [1, pp. 62–63].

ALCOHOLISM AS A DISEASE

The concept of alcoholism as a disease is vital to the understanding of the manner in which the legal standards and the medical issues interact. As early as 1956 the World Health Organization officially viewed the disease of alcoholism as

> Any form of drinking which in its extent goes beyond the traditional and customary "dietary" use or the ordinary compliance with social drinking customs of the whole

community concerned, irrespective of the etiological factors leading to such behavior, and irrespective also of the extent to which such etiological factors are dependent upon heredity, constitutions, or acquired physiopathological and metabolic influences. [1, p. 22]

The disease pattern of alcoholism is one that goes beyond the socially accepted norm of drinking and results in behavior that violates the accepted norms of the community. It is characterized often by a compulsivity to drink and a loss of will to stop drinking. The law, however, is designed to maintain peace, harmony, and tranquility in the community. It must, therefore, hold the individual accountable for initiation of the compulsive aspect of drinking by in fact operating on the principle that an individual with such a disease must not take the first drink. If a person does take a first drink, then all subsequent behavior resulting from the compulsive aspects of the disease are the responsibility of the individual and not the disease or defect of alcoholism per se.

LEGAL RAMIFICATIONS OF INTOXICATION AND CRIMINAL BEHAVIOR

Alcoholism by Itself Is Not an Offense

In 1962, the Supreme Court of the United States in *Robinson v. California* made an historic decision when it eliminated the concept that one could be found guilty of being addicted to narcotics. This decision is most significant to the alcoholic in that it provided protection under the Fourteenth Amendment when the court stated

> It is unlikely that any state at this moment in history would attempt to make it a criminal offense for a person to be mentally ill or a leper or to be afflicted with venereal disease. A state might determine that the general health and welfare require that the victims of these and other human afflictions be dealt with by compulsory treatment, involving quarantine, confinement, or sequestration. But, in the light of contemporary human knowledge, a law which made a criminal offense of such a disease would doubtless be universally thought to be an affliction of cruel and unusual punishment in violation of the Eighth and Fourteenth Amendments. [4, p. 581]

In this particular case, the defendant, Leroy Robinson, had been found guilty of the misdemeanor of being addicted to narcotics by a municipal court jury. There was no requirement that the defendant had ever used or trafficked in narcotics within the court's jurisdiction (the county of Los Angeles) but simply the requirement to prove that he was addicted to a narcotic. The statute itself was not one specifically designed to either punish antisocial behavior or to help rehabilitate the defendant; rather, it was one that sought to make the "status of narcotic addiction a criminal offense, for which the offender [might] ... be prosecuted anytime before he reforms [4, p. 581]. This case has tremendous significance from a social policy standpoint regarding the alcoholic. For, indeed, while there are existing laws in numerous jurisdictions regarding drunk and disorderly behavior, there should not be, according to this decision, a law that punishes a person merely because he or she is in the status of being an alcoholic. Essentially, then, this decision provides and guarantees the choice, from a criminal law standpoint, for the individual to be an alcoholic as long as there is no accompanying antisocial behavior.

The law's position, expressed in *Robinson v. California,* guarantees the individual the freedom to continue the use of intoxicants if that person so desires. The decision eliminates the ability of the government to parternalistically dictate the individual choices one may have. In the light of the consequences of prohibition and its failure, the reaffirmation of the right to have the disease of alcoholism and to be free from societal control seems appropriate. As is shown later, it is only when that individual's alcohol problems conflict with society that there must be appropriate legal sanctions. The statute in California prior to the *Robinson v. California* decision stated that "a person could be continuously guilty of this offense [narcotic addiction], whether or not he has ever possessed any narcotics within the state and whether or not he has been guilty of any antisocial behavior there" [4, p. 581]. The court viewed the problem of drug addiction as a serious one, but found fault with the notion that a person could be sentenced for even 1 day for being an addict, comparing it with the common cold, saying that a sentence was cruel and unusual punishment [4, p. 582]. Therefore, from a common law standpoint, as long as the alcoholic or drug addict remains personally accountable for his or her actions, the law should not discriminate against that person or make provisions for that person to be sentenced under criminal law for his or her decisions, albeit harmful. *Robinson v. California* recognizes that legislative or judicial imposition of social norms rarely works, as was demonstrated when the Congress and states of the Union abolished alcohol in hopes of completely undoing the problem. Likewise, to threaten a person with conviction merely because of his or her status is not only meaningless but seriously intrusive upon that individual's right as a citizen in a free society.

Criminal Behavior and Alcohol Usage

Chronic alcoholism by itself is not a defense. Moving from this basic constitutional guarantee, the issue presented in the case of *Powell v. Texas* is pertinent. The decision regarding this case was rendered in 1968 and deals with the problem of being found intoxicated in a public place. At that time in Texas, one could be fined not in excess of $100 for being drunk in a public place or any private home except his or her own [4, p. 591]. This issue strays from the one presented in *Robinson v. California* in that now under consideration is that individual whose alcoholic state infringes upon the orderly functioning of a society. The trial judge ruled in this matter that "chronic alcoholism was not a defense" [4, p. 591]. The trial judge found the defendant guilty and fined him $50.

In the *Powell* v. *Texas* case on appeal to the United States Supreme Court there was extensive testimony regarding the chronic and episodic use of alcohol. The court focused on several issues: (1) the state of Mr. Powell when not intoxicated, and (2) the volition of Mr. Powell regarding his decision to take the first drink and not his compulsion to take his first drink [4, p. 595]. It became clear as the medical testimony proceeded that, while Mr. Powell had much difficulty in controlling his decision to drink, the decision to take the first drink was volitional and was not an overpowering one. Therefore, he did retain some level of free will when he decided to take the initial drink. Were Mr. Powell unable by reason of a mental disorder to decide whether or not he should take the first drink, the issue of *mens rea* might well have been significant.

Free will and alcohol usage. But even the psychiatrist testifying for the defense in the *Powell* v. *Texas* case could not unequivocally state that Mr. Powell did not have some level of free will regarding the issue of taking the first drink. The court pushed away the concept that this might be akin to *Robinson* v. *California* because, in the *Robinson* case, no demonstrable antisocial behavior had taken place. One of the concerns of the court was that, if this case were extended to include the concepts of the *Robinson* decision, the issue of "the doctrine of criminal responsibility might well be affected" [4, p. 595]. The court defined this even further when it said, "If Leroy Powell cannot be convicted of public intoxication, it is difficult to see how a state can convict an individual for murder, if that individual, while exhibiting normal behavior in all respects, suffers from a 'compulsion' to kill, which is 'an exceedingly strong influence' but 'not an overpowering one' " [4, p. 595]. Again, the basic issue of being personally accountable presents itself. As long as Leroy Powell remained in his own home or apartment and became intoxicated, there was no legal issue. However, when he left his home and was intoxicated in public, he then transgressed the societal boundary constructed by the penal code of Texas. It is important to emphasize that the issue of Mr. Powell's original state of sobriety, his free will, and choice to end that state of sobriety, left him criminally responsible for his behavior. This becomes increasingly more significant in considering the following review of a case in which the individual was intoxicated when a murder was committed.

The Maryland Court of Appeals (the highest court in that state) decided the matter of *Jackie C. Parker* v. *The State of Maryland* on June 6, 1969 [3, pp. 167–199]. It carefully delineated several issues regarding intoxication. Mr. Parker had been found guilty by a lower court for the commission of first-degree murder committed in the course of an armed robbery. He was sentenced to life imprisonment for the murder and 20 years for the armed robbery, the second sentence to run consecutively following the first sentence.

Mr. Parker appealed this decision, saying that he was intoxicated at the time of the commission of the crimes and was thereby insane. In the brief before the appellate court, Mr. Parker alleged

> [That he] completely lacked the mental ability and will power to abstain from taking the first drink on December 30, 1966 ... and further lacked the ability and will power to abstain from continued drinking until he reached a state of intoxication. ... His ultimate intoxication should be deemed involuntary ... and should be considered with all other evidence in determining his sanity or insanity. [3, p. 167-199]

Furthermore, Parker alleged that his mere state of intoxication left him unable to appreciate the criminality of his conduct or conform his behavior to the requirements of the law. The court was most explicit in its decision regarding these issues. It stated that Mr. Parker did have a free will and choice in deciding to become intoxicated. Because this was a voluntarily intoxicated state, Mr. Parker was responsible for his behavior. Voluntary drunkenness was not a defense for his crimes. The court did, however, state that in a crime of specific intent (i.e., "whenever the actual existence of any particular motive, purpose or intent is a necessary element to constitute any particular species or degree of crime" [3, p. 167]) the issue of intoxication may serve to lessen the degree of the crime, in the same manner that diminished capacity might.

The Maryland Court of Appeals further delineated that there was a difference between an alcoholic psychosis and voluntary intoxication that resulted from an episode or bout of drinking. It said that a person might be excused from criminal responsibility if his or her continued habits of excessive drinking resulted in an alcoholic psychosis [3, p. 167]. It was, furthermore, very clear that had there been a preexisting mental disease and Mr. Parker was unable to be seen as sane prior to the first drink, the issue of insanity might have been raised.

Loss of memory and intoxication. The importance of Mr. Parker being found criminally responsible cannot be overestimated in terms of the need for personal accountability within society. Even if Mr. Parker could not remember any of the events occurring during the crime, he would still be responsible because he was able to freely decide to take the first drink and, in his preexisting state, before voluntary intoxication, he was free of significant mental disease or defect. These issues then clearly support the English common law notion of individual accountability. They also support the basic tenets of the Alcoholic Anonymous program, which holds each of its members responsible for taking the first drink.

SUMMARY

The origins of the development of the American legal system are in English common law. Issues pertinent to alcoholism concern *mens rea* and the legal differentiations between an individual who is intoxicated versus an individual who is criminally insane. The case of *Robinson v. California,* which states that narcotics addicts and alcoholics cannot by their status be considered criminals, and the cases of *Powell v. Texas* and *Parker v. Maryland,* delineate the parameters that society imposes upon alcoholic intoxication. The issue of voluntary drunkenness and the offense of being drunk in a public place (*Powell v. Texas*) rests upon the free will choice of taking the first drink. Basically, if one freely chooses to take the first drink and is free of a substantial mental disorder, then he or she is criminally responsible for all behavior that occurs.

Some might say that, on the surface, legal strictures would appear to be very harsh. However, if society were to excuse the alcoholic for his or her behavior while intoxicated, then that individual would have a carte blanche to do anything he or she desired and claim intoxication as the excuse.

Alcohol has been traditionally used throughout recorded history. Its customary use in society presents no real problems as long as the individual's behavior remains within the context of the acceptable standards of that society. The disease of alcoholism presents a degree of alarm to those who must interact with the alcoholic. But, the law does not become involved until one transgresses societal limits. From the forensic psychiatric standpoint, alcohol can be seen not only as a drug that removes inhibitions but also as one that enables the individual to do things that he or she would not normally consider doing without the release of those inhibitions through drinking. Alcohol can provide the vehicle to permit violent, aggressive, antisocial fantasies to become reality. In this context, society must protect itself by laying aside the customary social acceptability of drinking and the concept of the disease of alcoholism to demand of each individual personal accountability when the initial drink is taken with a conscious, free will decision.

REFERENCES

1. Block, M. A. *Alcoholism: Its Facets and Phases.* John Day: St. Paul, 1978.
2. Brooks, A. D. *Law, Medicine and the Mental Health System.* Little, Brown: Boston, 1974.
3. *Parker v. Maryland.* 7 MD. App., 167, 254 A.2d. 323 (1969).
4. Sharpe, D., Fiscina, F., and Head, M. *Law and Medicine.* West Publ.: St. Paul, 1978.

33

ESA OSTERBERG, MPolSc, Social Research Institute of Alcohol Studies, Helsinki, Finland

ALCOHOL AND ECONOMICS

ECONOMICS, CONSIDERED as an academic discipline, is far from being a central aspect of alcohol research. Anthropology, biology, epidemiology, medicine, psychiatry and psychology, and sociology all play a more substantial role in research into alcohol and alcoholism. Those economists who have paid attention to the social liquor question have tended to concentrate on analyzing alcohol consumption and expenditures on alcohol. Some part of this contribution has been a spillover from work in other areas — consumer demand and public finance, in particular. Other topics that economists have dealt with include the production and distribution of alcoholic beverages, the cost to society of the adverse consequences of drinking, and the economic aspects of alcohol control.

CONSUMPTION OF ALCOHOLIC BEVERAGES

Consumer demand for alcoholic beverages has been studied quite extensively. The brunt of the empirical work has been addressed to estimating the price and income elasticity of the demand for alcoholic beverages. Indeed, the manner in

---

Esa Osterberg, MPolSc, The State Alcohol Monopoly, Social Research Institute of Alcohol Studies, Helsinki, Finland.

which price changes influence alcohol consumption has been studied more exhaustively than any other potential alcohol control measure.

Elasticity

In econometric studies of demand, "price elasticity" is customarily defined as the ratio of the proportionate change in the quantity demanded of a commodity to the proportionate change in its price, provided that the price alteration is very slight and that all other factors that might influence demand remain constant. The price elasticity of alcoholic beverages thus expresses the degree to which alcohol consumption responds to changes in the price of alcoholic beverages. Consequently, the income elasticity of alcoholic beverages constitutes a measurement of the responsiveness of the demand for alcoholic beverages to changes in consumer income.

A normal commodity will have a positive income elasticity; with respect to its own price, its elasticity will be negative. Simply stated, consumers will buy more of a given normal commodity as their income rises (or less as it falls), and consumer demand will fall off as prices go up (or grow if prices drop). A given commodity has an income elasticity value of 1.0 if, for instance, a 1% rise in consumer income generates a 1% rise in the commodity's consumption. If incomes are growing and demand for a given commodity rises at a greater rate, the economist will refer to the commodity as "income elastic." Correspondingly, demand for an income elastic commodity will drop more rapidly than incomes if a converse situation pertains. Inelasticity is characterized by demand failing to respond fully to income fluctuation. In absolute terms, therefore, a price-inelastic commodity will have a price elasticity value of less than 1.0; the elasticity value of a price-elastic commodity will be greater than 1.0.

A variety of methods have been employed to estimate price and income elasticity. Some investigators have estimated the elasticity of all alcoholic beverages; others have estimated the elasticity of distilled spirits, wines, and beers, considering each separately. The elasticities of off-premise and on-premise consumption also sometimes have been studied in isolation. Again, some analyses have relied on cross-section consumption data obtained from household expenditure survey statistics, and others on time series data obtained from sales records or tax statistics. On occasion, price series have been computed using the prices of the most popular brands; the weighted prices of all alcoholic beverages also have been employed. Various types of income have been used: gross income or disposable income, and personal income or family income. Whereas some studies have relied on static models, others have employed dynamic models. Finally, the wide assortment of econometric methodology and the differing estimation procedures used has resulted in the very results themselves being different, too [8, 15, 16].

The diversity of research procedures and methodology is not, however, the only reason why elasticity estimates are disparate. Drinkers do not behave uniformly: Changes in income and the price of alcoholic beverages will generate different consumer reactions according to time and place, because price and income elasticities reflect also prevailing drinking habits and the availability of alcoholic beverages. More generally, elasticity mirrors those fundamental biological, cultural, and social factors that explain why alcohol is consumed and dictate the manner in which people drink. For example, drinkers in countries where wines are customarily served with meals will, quite naturally, not react to price changes in the same way as their counterparts in countries where alcohol is either considered as a luxury commodity or primarily used as an intoxicant. Indeed, the great extent to which the price and income elasticity of wines varies from country to country would seem, in the main, to be an accurate reflection of differing circumstances [15].

Results of Econometric Studies

Elasticity is not an inherent quality of alcoholic beverages. For instance, it is not possible to give one elasticity value for beer that would hold good for all countries at all times. Nevertheless, the price elasticity of beer can be very similar in two different countries if the determinants of demand are alike in both. The United States and Canada are a case in point: They seem to have a uniform price elasticity of beer between -0.3 and -0.4 owing to their similar socioeconomic, cultural, and economic characteristics [15]. Price inelasticity would also appear to be a characteristic of the demand for beer at least in Finland, Ireland, and the United Kingdom [8]. Notwithstanding, the first lesson to be learned from econometric studies dealing with alcohol consumption is that elasticity has no universal or suprahistorical values. On the contrary, any interpretation of elasticity or move to employ elasticity in formulating alcohol control policy must take full account of all those social, cultural, and ecoonomic aspects that affect alcohol consumption.

Econometric analyses based on the theory of consumer demand demonstrate that, by and large, fluctuations in the demand for alcoholic beverages can be statistically explained by changes in price, income, and consumer preference. That is to say, the variables that affect fluctuation in the demand for alcoholic beverages are the same as those that apply to other consumer goods. The market behavior of alcoholic beverages is indistinguishable from that of other goods.

From an economic perspective, alcoholic beverages behave on the market like normal goods. In other words, provided that all other factors that might influence demand remain constant, a rise in the price of alcoholic beverages will tend to bring about a drop in consumption; an increase in consumer income will generally result in greater consumption [4]. But, as was observed, the intensity of the rise or fall in consumption will vary geographically and temporally. Price inelasticity is not synonymous with utter unresponsiveness to price changes. Therefore, even if the demand for alcoholic beverages is price inelastic, higher prices would still tend to bring consumption down and price increases would still be a viable instrument of alcohol control. Of course, price policies are more effective when demand is price elastic.

Some Special Observations

One must use caution when drawing generalizations on the basis of econometric analysis. However, there are a few points that deserve special mention. The first example is taken from studies of postwar Sweden, where it was found that the demand for alcoholic beverages became more price elastic after the Bratt rationing system was abolished [5]. (The system set an upper limit to the amount of distilled spirits that each person could buy off the premises in 1 month.) The assumption is that the more restricted the availability of alcoholic beverages, the less pronounced the influence of price and consumer income on consumption [4]. This has important implications. It would appear that pricing and taxation policies become more effective measures of control whenever alcohol is made more freely available — exactly the state of affairs that has characterized the industrialized countries of the West since World War II.

Economists have discussed the question of how price and income elasticities behave when consumption increases, and some amount of empirical evidence has been collected, too. Elasticity of demand has generally been thought to decline in absolute value whenever aggregate alcohol consumption increases; moreover, the income elasticities of both wines and beer have been found to vary inversely with income levels. It seems to be evident that increased alcohol consumption and greater prosperity reduce the effectiveness of economic alcohol control measures.

Econometric studies of the demand for alcoholic beverages have tended to focus on the way in which fluctuations in consumer income and alcohol prices affect the demand for alcoholic beverages. There are also some studies that have analyzed other socioeconomic factors influencing consumption. As a result, econometric analysis has incidentally strengthened the awareness of how other control measures operate. Increasing the number of on-premise licenses and off-premise licenses, for instance, or the introduction of new brands of alcoholic beverages and the abandonment of individual control measures have had a measurable effect on consumption [13, 14].

Economic Thinking

Economists have not only engaged in empirical analysis, they have also looked at the economic aspects of consumption from a theoretical point of view. Unfortunately, some of the views that have been advanced have been based purely on economic theory and have failed to take the particular characteristics of alcohol consumption into account. Again, some investigators have gone to the other extreme and drawn generalized, oversimplified economic conclusions about alcohol use. Alcohol has, for instance, been regarded as a luxury item — the sole ground for this conclusion being that man can exist without alcohol. The reverse view has been put forward, too — alcohol has been held to be a necessity, as drink constitutes a foodstuff in southern Europe and because it has been assumed that alcoholics cannot live without alcohol.

One of the major points of contention revolves around consumption and alcoholism. It is often argued that price increases will have no effect on the alcoholic, whose drinking is thought of as uncontrollable. The next stage is to say that higher prices will only result in alcoholics spending more because the demand of alcoholics is inelastic with respect to price. And if the incomes of alcoholics are constant, the proportion of the alcoholic's total income spent on drink will go up and both the alcoholic and the alcoholic's family, it is believed, will be likely to suffer from malnutrition.

There is, however, recent evidence to suggest that the alcoholic's drinking can be modified by environmental circumstance. There are also indications that alcohol control measures do affect alcoholics. The evidence is supported by the findings of both laboratory and social experiments [1, 4]. In addition, purely economic considerations back the hypothesis as well. One may, for example, hold that since alcoholics are not renowned for their prosperity, higher prices would mean that they will be unable to buy the quantities to which they are accustomed. At least the skid row alcoholic, in all likelihood, will have already sacrificed the very utmost to ensure a continued supply of drink. Moreover, heavy drinkers show a marked preference for the cheapest alternatives in each category of alcoholic beverages. Heavy consumers are also notably price conscious: They are strongly aware which brands they should buy in order to become intoxicated by using as little money as possible. This provides further evidence that alcoholics do adapt to external circumstance, and leads to the question of the extent to which different beverages can substitute for each other.

Many economists have eagerly assumed that any alcoholic beverage can easily be substituted for any other. But such views fail to take the particular characteristics of alcoholic beverages into account. Admittedly, all alcoholic beverages contain ethanol and are thus obviously interchangeable as sources of intoxication. But alcohol's addictive properties mean that in principle at least, the very act of drinking can be the cause of the next drinking act, and so on. In one sense, therefore, different types of alcoholic beverages can be complements of each other. And there is another fact that speaks against alcoholic beverages being readily interchangeable. Different beverages are used in different ways: Drinking wine with a meal, one would hesitate to switch over to distilled spirits. Similarly, beer and distilled spirits are not equally good thirst quenchers.

Cross-price elasticities form one indication of the extent to which various goods substitute for or complement each other. It has, however, proved difficult in the extreme to arrive at estimates of cross elasticity in econometric studies. The evidence that does exist seems to point to the tentative conclusion that some substitution takes place [4, 5, 14]. Nevertheless, the substitutability among beer, wine, and distilled spirits seems not to be very clear or strong. Furthermore, the findings of many studies have been inconsistent. In the United States, for instance, it has been found that beer is a substitute for wine but that wine is not a substitute for beer. Beer and distilled spirits, on the other hand, have been viewed as complements in one study and as substitutes in another [15].

The degree to which alcoholic beverages can be substituted by other goods is very important to alcohol control policy. It is not, however, an easy matter to study, being closely bound to the actual uses of alcohol and other goods. If the price of wine goes up, for instance, the consumption of nonalcoholic beverages may rise in consequence — as well as the consumption of homemade wine or illegally produced alcohol. The possibility that higher prices might prompt drinkers to switch to illicit alcohol or prescribed drugs has been cited to argue against raising prices. The possibility is a real one, but it would nevertheless appear that the control measures that bear upon the availability of substitutes are more decisive [4]. On the other hand, it is scarcely credible that cutting alcohol prices could ever prevent illicit traffic altogether — though it might serve to alleviate matters. And even were the virtually impossible to somehow become actual, lower prices would probably result in the harm wrought by legitimate alcohol use attaining greater proportions. Moreover, an increased availability of legitimate alcohol has, on occasion, actually caused illicit alcohol use to flourish rather than to wane.

PRODUCTION AND TRADE

The harm that excessive drinking brings about is the reason why there is virtually no country where the consumption of alcohol is not subject to regulation by the state. Indeed, the production and distribution of alcoholic beverages take place under special control in many countries. In other respects, however, alcohol would seem nowadays to be just one commodity among many. The production of alcoholic beverages is not, for instance, bound with great external effects. Distilling is no longer a good method for coping with excessive grain harvests and the weight-monetary value axis has relatively little importance in today's transportation and trade.

Trends in Production and Distribution

As one would expect, the world, and the industrialized countries in particular, now produces far larger quantities of alcoholic beverages than it used to. There has been a corresponding increase in international trade, too. Generally speaking, alcohol plays a relatively minor role in the national economies of most countries. Furthermore, its relative importance has, if anything, lessened since the 1940s, despite the increase in production and trade in absolute terms [11]. In some places, however, particularly in wine-producing areas, the production of alcohol and the employment that it provides are far from negligible factors. And there are also places where the production of the raw materials used in alcoholic beverages and similar auxillary industries make their weight felt.

In common with most other industries alcoholic beverages are now produced in great units. Distillation industries are highly concentrated and brewing has been transformed from a small-scale local activity into a capital-intensive branch of industry. The practice of brewing under license has become more widespread and brewing concerns frequently make international investments. Technological advances and the economics of scale—in production, transportation, and marketing—have all played their part. On the other hand, wine-making tends to be a different proposition: there is still a great deal of small-scale production. Even wine makers, however, have been affected by productivity growth and structural change; the problems of the wine-producing countries are clearly linked to the difficulties encountered by agriculture throughout the developed world.

As a rule, more people will be employed in the distribution of alcoholic beverages than in the production of alcohol. Consumption figures have risen and alcohol outlets have tended to proliferate since World War II and this has meant that many more people are employed in the distribution of alcoholic beverages than used to be the case in many countries. Moreover, this postwar development has come about despite the fact that the changed structure of the retail trade has resulted in a move toward self-service alcohol outlets and that the degree of concentration has increased [11].

Advertising

Many studies have pointed out that the alcoholic beverage industry is an important commercial advertiser. The mere fact that the alcohol industry advertises its wares has been held to prove that advertising affects both consumers and consumption. A great part of the alcohol industry itself would seem to think that there is a high correlation between advertising expenditure and sales figures, and this has been pointed out, too [13]. The subject, however, is a vexing one: Advertising is just one of a number of factors that affect consumption and it is difficult to ascertain the part that it plays in making people drink more [6, 17]. Moreover, research in this area, where conflicting interests will continue to generate controversy, is unlikely to be acceptable to all parties.

Alcohol advertising aims at promoting sales and therefore seeks to present alcoholic beverages in a favorable light. And it is quite easy to believe that advertising legitimizes and glamorizes drinking and thereby modifies the climate of policy making and ensures that restricting the availability of alcoholic beverages becomes a more difficult thing to do [3]. Advertising, then, probably does have an effect on alcohol consumption in the long run. Advertising affects the sales of specific brands in the short run, too—though the evidence for this is not as conclusive as is often believed. Finally, one should remember that one of the roles of advertising under oligopoly is to discourage would-be competitors. This certainly applies to alcoholic beverages, where advertising ensures that the costs of launching a new drink are very high.

ALCOHOL PROBLEMS

Alcoholism and alcohol abuse are, as is well known, harmful to the national economy in a variety of ways. This is reflected in alcohol-induced mortality, absenteeism, and diminished productivity, for instance. Similarly, alcohol compels society to deploy its limited resources to treat and control alcohol problems. On the other hand, alcohol's economic effects are not entirely detrimental— drinking also serves to facilitate sociality.

The interests of economists has tended to be directed toward computing the economic cost of alcohol abuse, rather than to alcohol problems as such. This trend is by no means a recent phenomenon: The social cost of the use of alcohol played a part in the general debate on prohibition that characterized the beginning of this century. The amount of attention paid to the costs of alcohol problems has, however, grown of late and studies have become more complex and more ambiguous [2, 9].

A good case in point is the work of Berry and Boland [2]. They estimate that the economic costs of alcohol abuse in the United States in 1971 ran to some 30 billion dollars. Roughly two-thirds of that figure was due to lost production. This is not the place to comment on the study in detail, nor to discuss the basic assumptions and questions of such studies in general [10, 12]. Nevertheless, it is one thing to believe that rational social policy demands that alcohol consumption be controlled; to convince policy makers of the truth of the assumption is another matter altogether. It is not at all certain that demonstrating that the social cost of drinking is high will make the claim for control more credible, especially if no attention has been paid to the beneficial aspects of drinking. Furthermore, it is by no means clear that state expenditures engendered by alcohol abuse and alcoholism exceeds the revenues that the state gains from taxing alcoholic beverages [18]. Virtually the only certainty at the moment is that the cost and benefit of alcohol use will be the subject of animated discussion in the near future.

ALCOHOL CONTROL

Cost-benefit analysts have paid some attention to assessing the efficaciousness of rehabilitation. They have also tried to ascertain which form of treatment is best from society's point of view. The extent to which cost-benefit analysis has affected actual policy is, however, difficult to judge.

Theoretically at least, the cost of alcohol use is tied with the way in which alcoholic beverages are taxed. This is because economists often maintain that the alcohol trade should pay the social costs of drinking. The other reason why alcoholic beverages are so eagerly taxed is that alcohol taxation helps to augment the national coffers. The state, however, tends to use tax revenues for general purposes; comparatively little goes toward alleviating alcohol problems.

Taxation of alcohol has traditionally been an important source of state revenue in many countries. Between 1911 and 1917, for example, in the United States the federal revenues from alcoholic beverages each year amounted to over one-third of the total receipts from taxes levied by the national government [7]. The relative importance of alcohol taxation has declined in most countries, particularly after the advent of modern income taxation. In many countries the share of alcohol taxes in state budgets has declined also, because of the decline in alcohol tax rates. Despite these trends, alcohol revenue is still in many countries of considerable fiscal significance [11].

The dilemma of policies that view taxation as a means of preventing alcohol problems is exacerbated when consumer demand for alcoholic beverages is inelastic—when higher prices result in only a small drop in alcohol consumption but a subtantial increase in alcohol expenditure. It has even been said that lowering the amount that a heavy drinker consumes will mean that the family will suffer greater financial hardship. This is not, however, necessarily the case. If people spend more money on alcohol, the state comes into more tax revenue. And, in principle, this should mean that other forms of taxation will fall or, conversely, that more public services will become available. The taxation question, then, is largely a matter of who pays alcohol taxes and how tax revenue is employed—if employed wisely, the outcome can be a greater measure of prosperity for all.

Raising alcohol prices or limiting availability in some other way will not only affect the drinker; the alcohol industry and its employees will also be hit. Understandably, those engaged in the production and distribution of alcoholic beverages therefore feel that they must have as big a say in alcohol control policy as possible. This is particularly true in countries where the alcohol industry is fettered by stringent control measures. But, even in such countries, there exists a difference between the short-term and the long-term controls. On the one hand, limiting availability may result in a number of brewery and distillery workers losing their jobs over the short term. On the other, those displaced can be given employment elsewhere and the long-term outcome may well be increased general prosperity.

SUMMARY

Even though economists have not paid a great deal of attention to the social liquor question, they have produced important conclusions. In particular, economic research has demonstrated that pricing has a marked effect on alcohol consumption. And, no matter whether taxation is directed toward improving public health or toward finding markets for an overproduction of alcoholic beverages, it is still efficacious.

Economists have also shown that alcohol consumption can be regarded as economic behavior. Alcohol control policy and alcohol problems have their economic aspects. Furthermore, research has stressed that all the various facets of the alcohol field are interconnected; they are actually part of one and the same process. The economic consequences of alcohol control measures have to be taken into account if alcohol control policy is to be successful. Economic considerations thus have a bearing on how alcohol policies are formulated.

REFERENCES

1. Ahlström-Laakso, S. *Drinking Habits among Alcoholics* (Vol. 21). The Finnish Foundation for Alcohol Studies: Forssa, Finland, 1975.
2. Berry, E. R., and Boland, J. P. *The Economic Cost of Alcohol Abuse.* Free Press: New York, 1977.
3. Breed, W., and De Foe, J. R. Themes in magazine alcohol advertisements: A critique. *J. Drug Issues* 9:511-522, 1979.
4. Bruun, K., Edwards, G., Lumio, M., Mäkelä, K., Pan, L., Popham, R. E., Room, R., Schmidt, W., Skog, O.-J., Sulkunen, P., and Österberg, E. *Alcohol Control Policies in Public Health Perspective* (Vol. 25). The Finnish Foundation for Alcohol Studies: Forssa, Finland, 1975.
5. Huitfeldt, B., and Jorner, U. *Efterfragan pa Rusdrycker i Sverige.* Statens Offentliga Utredningen: Stockholm, 1972.
6. Katzper, M., Ryback, R., and Hertzman, M. Alcohol beverage advertisement and consumption. *J. Drug Issues* 8:339-353, 1978.
7. Landis, B. Y. Some economic aspects of inebriety. In: *Alcohol, Science and Society.* Quarterly Journal of Studies on Alcohol: New Haven, 1952.
8. Lau, H.-H. Cost of alcoholic beverages as a determinant of alcohol consumption. In: *Research Advances in Alcohol and Drug Problems* (Vol. 2), Gibbins, R., Israel, Y., Kalant, H. et al. (eds.). Wiley: New York, 1975.
9. Leu, R., and Lutz, P. *Ökonomische Aspekte des Alkoholkonsums in der Schweiz.* Schulthess Polygraphischer Verlag: Zürich, 1977.
10. Light, D. Costs and benefits of alcohol consumption. *Society* 12:18.24, 1975.
11. Mäkelä, K., Room, R., Single, E., et al. *Alcohol, Society and the State. Vol. 1: A Comparative Study of Alcohol Control.* Addiction Research Foundation: Toronto. In press.
12. Mäkelä, K., and Österberg, E. Notes on analyzing economic costs of alcohol use. *Surveyor* 15:7-10, 1979.
13. McGuinness, T. An econometric analysis of total demand for alcoholic beverages in the U.K., 1956-75. *J. Indus. Ec.* 29:85-109, 1980.
14. Nyberg, A. *Alkoholijuomien Kulutus ja Hinnat* (Vol. 15). The Finnish Foundation for Alcohol Studies: Helsinki, 1967.
15. Ornstein, S. I. Control of alcohol consumption through price increases. *J. Stud. Alcohol* 41:807-818, 1980.

16. Österberg, E. *The Pricing of Alcoholic Beverages as an Instrument of Control Policy* (No. 83). Social Research Institute of Alcohol Studies: Helsinki, 1975.

17. Pittman, D. J., and Lambert, M. *Alcohol, Alcoholism and Advertising: A Preliminary Investigation of Asserter Associations.* St. Louis, 1978.

18. Walsh, B. M. The economic costs of alcohol abuse in Ireland: Approaches and problems. *Surveyor* 15:3–6, 1979.

34

DWIGHT B. HEATH, PhD, Brown University

SOCIOCULTURAL VARIANTS IN ALCOHOLISM

THIS CHAPTER BRIEFLY examines why sociocultural variants are important in alcoholism, how they affect both the nature and the rate of drinking problems, how they can be relevant factors in terms of diagnosis and treatment, how they might be useful in education and prevention efforts, and what other practical implications are currently under development by those who study sociocultural variants.

INTRODUCTION

In dealing with any drug, it is important to recognize that its effects are not merely the product of its chemical and pharmacological characteristics. By the same token, a basic understanding of the biochemical and physiological processes of the living organism is valuable — but not sufficient. To understand the interaction of alcohol and human behavior, it is necessary that a complex combination of factors be considered, including the beliefs, attitudes, values, and behaviors of people — frequent concerns of social and behavioral scientists — as well as those fundamental facts that dominate in what many people consider the hard sciences.

Dwight B. Heath, PhD, Professor of Anthropology, Brown University, Providence, Rhode Island.

Among those who deal with drinking and drinkers, the vast majority have said, at one time or another, something to the effect, "In order to understand the effects of alcohol, we have to pay attention to biological, psychological, and sociocultural variables." It is unfortunate that, having made such a nod in the direction of recognizing diverse influences, few go on to pay any systematic attention to the last category. This is especially ironic because the factor that most dramatically differentiates the species *Homo sapiens* from other animals is sociocultural variation—the overwhelming majority of human behavior is learned within a social group rather than being instinctive or inborn.

The patterns of belief and action that are learned vary from one society to another, and the systems made up of those patterns are the diverse cultures that have both fascinated and frustrated travelers throughout history. It may be helpful to think of culture as having the same kind of relation to behavior that grammar has to language—just as people learn to speak a language long before they systematically study grammar, most people learn to behave without ever paying special attention to the structure of their culture. Similarly, just as codified grammatical rules do not assure uniform patterns of speech, all members of a society do not conform strictly to all of the cultural norms.

With reference to alcohol use, significant sociocultural variants occur in both ideological and material features. Because fermentation is a natural process, subject to relatively simple and inexpensive refinement in various ways, there is enormous variation at the most elementary level of what different peoples drink. It is unquestionably significant when a society is encountered in which alcoholic beverages are not made, and may even be unknown, as was the case among Eskimos and most North American Indian groups in aboriginal times. It is also significant, in a very different way, when another society is encountered in which scores of beverages, both fermented and distilled, are made and are readily available, and where even a modestly equipped household may have a dozen differently shaped containers for different kinds of drinks.

Even more variable, and unquestionably more important, are the attitudes, norms, values, and other symbolic factors that are associated with alcohol. At the simplest level, a broad spectrum of views about alcoholic beverages is recognized ranging from abstinence and condemnation of any drinking, to enthusiastic connoisseurship, or frequent heavy consumption in drunken binges. For others, alcoholic beverages are a staple part of the diet, a nutritious and enjoyable complement to every meal. In some contexts, a particular drink may serve important medical functions, as a tonic or even as a medicine for specific ills. Sociability is unthinkable without drinking in some groups, for whom alcohol is a valuable social lubricant. Still others view drinking as a sacred act to be performed only in highly ritualized settings.

This is not an appropriate context in which to offer an encyclopedic inventory of beliefs and behaviors that are associated with alcoholic beverages throughout the world.* A few case examples are cited below in summary fashion to illustrate some of the major issues that behavioral scientists, clinicians, public health officials, and others have found to be important for various reasons. It is important to note, however, that the relevance of sociocultural variation in respect to alcohol is not simply an academic or theoretic proposition. It is widely accepted by people who have no special interest or competence in behavioral science or in the study of alcohol, and is even imbedded in some of the stereotypes that dominate popular thinking about various ethnic groups.†

Case Example

Whatever else one may think of in connection with a Polish wedding, it seems unlikely that heavy drinking would not be one of the images that come readily to mind. However many inaccurate depictions of Native Americans can be attributed to Hollywood, the idea of "the drunken Indian" was firmly set in the thinking of Anglo-Americans and Europeans long before movies were invented.

The fact that such stereotypes often diverse significantly from reality does not lessen their significance as widespread ideas that affect social relations.

WHY SOCIOCULTURAL VARIANTS ARE IMPORTANT

Among the many psychoactive drugs that have been used by humankind, alcohol is probably the oldest, usually the easiest to obtain, and certainly the most widespread. Ethanol is the active agent in that immensely broad category called "alcoholic beverages" (whether fermented or distilled, whether made from fruit, vegetable, sap, honey, grain, or other base, whether aged or not, and regardless of whatever other additives may be used). Much is known about the biochemistry of ethanol as it affects and is affected by the human body. Nevertheless, one cannot

---

*In recent years, a few sources have appeared that help to make the diverse and scattered literature on alcohol-related sociocultural variants more readily accessible. A comprehensive worldwide bibliography of anthropological sources [6] is well indexed; another on American Indians [11] is also annotated. Several specialists contributed interdisciplinary perspectives on sociocultural variants and their significance [3], and others tried to integrate research findings with the concerns of treatment [7]. An anthology of brief descriptive and analytic articles by various authors [12] provides a broad sampling of the range of diversity that marks beliefs and behaviors about alcoholic beverages throughout the world today, and an ambitious review article points out the conceptual and theoretic relevance of anthropological studies of drinking [4].

†The several inconsistent meanings with which "ethnic," "race," "minority," and related terms are used in nonscientific parlance are briefly discussed in Chapter 89; I agree with the reservations expressed there.

avoid noticing that different societies not only have different sets of beliefs and rules about drinking, but they also show very different outcomes when people do drink. In view of the toxicity of ethanol, it is also dramatic that different societies have different rates of pathology, somatic and other, in relation to drinking.

In simple terms, the widely varied patterns of belief and behavior with respect to ethanol provide a classic natural experiment — members of the same species deal with the same substance and do so in significantly different ways, and with significantly different outcomes resulting.

It is true that, even within a given population, there are often major differences among individual human beings in ways that make for different drinking patterns and different consequences from drinking. Such individual variation can be of crucial importance for certain kinds of analysis, for selecting among modalities of treatment, and so forth. But, when one attempts to arrive at meaningful generalizations about alcohol — similarities and differences that may be important in helping to understand the interactions of alcohol and human behavior — it is striking that most members of any society tend to share drinking customs just as they share other customs. For example, most people in one society may have wine with every meal but rarely drink enough alcohol to affect their ability to talk or walk normally; in another society, women and children are supposed never to drink and men drink only infrequently, but during those occasions drinking becomes a measure of manliness and stuporous intoxication is commonplace. In another society, a fermented home brew may be a nutritious staple of the diet from infancy, while another group considers wine a sacred substance, to be offered to the gods or shared in a ritual of social communion.

The fact that different expectations about drinking apply to people in different statuses within a society does not contradict this. Returning to the analogy between language and culture, although all who speak one language do so within the framework of a standard grammar, not only does every individual have considerable latitude in what can be said, but there are also recognizable patterns that are appropriate (or inappropriate) to various segments of the population, whether grouped by age, sex, occupation, or some other salient characteristics. Such rules about speech are often flexible in relation to specific contexts; the same is true of drinking.

It would be a serious mistake to think of sociocultural variants with respect to beliefs and behaviors about alcohol as simply quaint and curious customs that have little relevance except to a few anthropologists. On the contrary, they have major importance with relation to drinking problems and their outcomes. In fact, the nature of problems is in large part affected by the nature of drinking. A population that drinks daily may have a high rate of cirrhosis and other medical problems but few accidents, fights, homicides, or other violent alcohol-associated traumas; a population with predominantly binge drinking usually shows the opposite complex of drinking problems. The rate of occurrence of such problems within a society is also significantly affected by the patterns of belief and behavior that relate to alcohol. A group that views drinking as a ritually significant act is not likely to develop many alcohol-related problems of any sort, whereas another group, which sees it primarily as a way to escape from stress or to demonstrate one's strength, are at high risk of developing problems with drinking. With such differences in mind, it should be obvious that the diagnosis of problem drinking or alcoholism should be based on different attitudes, acts, and other symptoms depending on the sociocultural context in which an individual lives and works. For the same reason, a treatment modality that is effective in one population may not be in another, and the development of a strategy for prevention must take into consideration sociocultural variants in terms of the expectations about who should drink what, where drinking should take place, in the company of whom, for what purpose, and with what outcomes.

A brief but ambitious attempt to survey ethnographic and historical variations among patterns of drunken comportment emphasized that drinking often represents "time-out," in which some of the standard norms of behavior are suspended [10]. Such a view not only explains why people sometimes get drunk with the aim of committing some breach of etiquette, but it also underscores the fundamental importance of learned (i.e., sociocultural) factors in behavior, even while one is under the influence.

THE NATURE AND RATE OF DRINKING PROBLEMS

The idea that sociocultural variants are important in relation to what kinds of problems people have in connection with drinking, and how many members of a group will have problems, is not new, nor is it limited to social scientists. Like recognition of differences in the ways that different populations use alcohol, the problem implications are widely accepted.

Case Example

It has become common knowledge that the rural French pattern of drinking wine throughout the day, similar to Americans use of coffee or British use of tea, is associated with "liver trouble," and most who work in the alcohol field probably also are aware that such a constant low level of alcohol in the blood can result in addiction, with full-blown physiological dependence, withdrawal, and related symptoms, even among individuals who have never in their lives been visibly intoxicated.

In the early days of the United Nations, when there was a heady enthusiasm to solve some of the major problems of humankind, an Expert Committee on Mental Health was formed within the fledgling World Health Organization. The Subcommittee on Alcoholism encountered difficulty in defining its area of concern, because the French emphasized cirrhosis, while those from Scandinavian countries were more preoccupied with public safety, those from the United States looked more at economic costs, and so forth. Everyone agreed that misuse of alcohol, made for problems, but there was little agreement on the relative importance of various problems, as indicated in the broad definition of alcoholics that finally was agreed upon: "Alcoholics are those excessive drinkers whose dependence upon alcohol has attained such a degree that it shows a noticeable disturbance of or an interference with their bodily or mental health, their interpersonal relations, and their smooth social and economic functioning; or who show the prodromal signs of such developments" [15]. Although none of the members of that committee was a behavioral or social scientist, it is difficult to imagine a more culturally relativistic approach or one more open to the relevance of sociocultural variance.

Similarly today, different beliefs and behaviors with respect to alcohol are associated with different kinds of problems.

Case Example

The Navajo Indian Reservation sprawls over vast portions of Arizona, New Mexico, and Utah in the southwestern United States, and it completely surrounds the relatively small area set aside for Hopi Indians. Living in the same region, subject to similar ecological and interethnic pressures, the Hopis have an exceptionally high rate of alcoholic cirrhosis; the Navajos do not; instead, they suffer an exceptionally high rate of death in alcohol-related accidents.

A simplistic interpretation of the different kinds of alcohol-related problems that prevail in Navajo and Hopi life might be that Hopis normally drink much more than Navajos, but exactly the opposite seems to be true. Hopi culture is strongly opposed to any form of losing control, so the few individuals who do drink are virtually outcasts from that tightly integrated society. They gather in an unusual rural variant of the skid row pattern, and quietly drink their lives away. By contrast, most Navajo men drink, and they seem to relish drunkenness and the fact that it allows them to do things for which they might otherwise be censured. But Navajo drinking is sporadic, with heavy binges occurring only occasionally and with long periods of abstinence between them.

One need not seek out tribal or peasant communities in faraway places to encounter significant differences in the kinds of problems that people feel are important with respect to alcohol.

Case Example

In the course of only a few weeks, in a major city in the United States, dealing with English-speaking people, one could encounter groups whose assessments of drinkers and the problem implications of their drinking varied enormously. Such judgments might range from wariness about alcoholism and danger in connection with an employee's having drunk three highballs too fast and insulted the boss, to assurances that "Jack's okay. At least he never killed nobody when he was drunk."

Various other views encountered in the same context could be ranged along an approximate continuum of permissiveness. For example, the fact that a person is drunk "too many nights" each week and spends "too much" on liquor may be deplored but accepted because "at least she doesn't neglect her kids"; another person might be guilty of all of the above but still be deemed not to have a problem "because he was never arrested."

With such divergent views about what does or does not constitute a drinking problem, it is clear that early detection, referral, and diagnosis are likely to vary among different populations. Similarly, at least a portion of what is often labeled "denial" may be wholly appropriate from the point of view of the client whose ideas about the range of acceptable behavior may be far more permissive than those of a counselor or clinician. In short, the same kind of behavior can be seen as "normal" by some, and as clearly reflecting or even constituting a "drinking problem" by others.

Case Example

An Indian who had worked quietly and efficiently in the city for 3 months abruptly disappeared, without a word to his employer, and turned up in jail for aggravated assault and public inebriation on the reservation a few days later. As much as she liked the employee, the Anglo employer was hesitant to risk rehiring him for fear of alcoholism. An Indian view would have emphasized the loyalty of a person who had, on short notice, returned to contribute to a healing ceremony for a relative, the generosity of one who shared liquor freely with friends, and the honor of one who fought to avenge some supposed insult.

In the same way that the nature of drinking problems differs from one population to another, the frequency or rate of occurrence of problems also differs. In Yugoslavia, fully half of the adult males who use mental health services have a primary diagnosis of "alcoholism"; in Israel, "drug dependence" is commonplace, but only with reference to drugs other than alcohol.

Case Example

Although it may have been sociologists who most carefully analyzed the social and psychological dynamics involved, most laypersons have some awareness that, although virtually all Jews drink, only a small portion of them appear to have drinking problems, and that, by contrast, Irish-Americans have an exceptionally high rate of alcoholism, however it is defined or measured.

These cases are particularly pertinent because they also illustrate how systematic research goes far beyond the common knowledge that, when it is congenial, it is praised as folk wisdom, but when it seems inappropriate, is dismissed as stereotyping.

Jewish drinking patterns have been noted for centuries as both distinctly moderate and relatively unproblematic, and various interpretations have been offered by interested observers. In terms of socialization, Jews learn to drink at a young age, in the supportive context of the family, with an emphasis on both moderation and religious symbolism; Irish experience contrasts on virtually every point, with initiation often deferred to adolescence, in a boisterous male milieu, with an emphasis on heavy drinking in a decidedly secular environment. Ritual meanings and values for Jews contrast with Irish convivial "drnking like a man"; cooperation in consecration contrasts with competition expressed in verbal and physical aggression. Meanings, reasons, and outcomes all differ and there are similarly large differences in such measures as rates of admission to hospital for alcohol-related problems, participation in psychiatric or other counseling for alcoholism, and so forth. Whatever the combination of traits selected for emphasis, the striking fact is that lay and scientific observers consistently focus on sociocultural factors, even though they rarely use that term.

During recent years, it is noteworthy that both of these sociocultural examples are being viewed in a somewhat different light. The best known studies of Jewish and Irish drinking were written by American sociologists more than 25 years ago [1, 13], but there is increasing evidence that Jews are by no means immune to drinking problems, and Irish patterns persist in the United States, where the Old World traditions of late marriage and prolonged dependency on landholding parents no longer apply. A variety of interpretations have been put forth to account for the apparent rise in drinking problems among Jews, as follows: the diminution of orthodoxy has attenuated the sacred and ritual significance of drinking; progressive loosening of family cohesion weakens parental norms and models with respect to drinking and other behaviors that might be overdone in response to peer pressure; acculturation in the direction of adopting Gentile patterns of business and hospitality gives new secular meanings to alcohol; and so forth. Others suggest that Jewish problem drinkers were not necessarily any more rare a generation ago, but that people didn't talk about it, or the family took care of it, or alcoholics were given other, less stigmatized psychiatric labels. There is probably considerable truth and relevance in each of these explanations, and the extent to which many Jews are acknowledging the prevalence of drinking problems today is reflected in new sensitivity and readiness to counsel on the part of rabbis, the affiliation of Alcoholics Anonymous groups with synagogues [2], and so forth. A significant point that might easily be overlooked is the fact that these attempts to account for change — just like the earlier attempts to account for continuity — are, without exception, couched in terms of sociocultural factors.

Although it has had less publicity, sociological reappraisal of Irish-American drinking patterns in recent years — emphasizing continuity rather than change — has also stressed sociocultural factors. In a context where drinking problems are virtually expected among men, it is not surprising that they serve as a sort of badge of ethnicity [14].

For much the same reason, an anthropologist refers to the way some Native Americans willfully embrace the stereotyped behavior of "the drunken Indian" as "the world's oldest ongoing protest demonstration" [9]. There is a considerable amount of unfounded popular belief, and a small amount of inconsistent and controversial research evidence, that attributes differences in short-term effects of alcohol, degree of drunkenness, and various forms of drunken behavior, to racial differences. Probably the best known among such views is that American Indians, because of a greater constitutional susceptibility to alcohol, get drunk faster, stay drunk longer, and are mean drunks. Anecdotal evidence in support of this firewater myth abounds in literary and historical sources, but systematic studies, sometimes combining genetic and physiological methods as well as social science perspectives, do not support it [8]. In a broadly comparative study of drinking among Indian and other populations, it was found, "Over the course of socialization, people learn about drunkenness what their society 'knows' about drunkenness; and, accepting and acting upon the understandings thus imparted to them, they become the living confirmation of their society's teachings" (italicized in original) [10].

Particular kinds of problems are often thought to be unusually prevalent among various populations, as causes rather than results of heavy drinking. One of the most common of these among minority groups is that of "anomie," a term sometimes used to refer to one's loss of traditional norms, and at other times to refer to one's inability to achieve new norms, however enthusiastically they may have been embraced. This is sometimes explained as the dilemma of the marginal man, an individual supposedly caught between two worlds and not comfortable with either the dominant or the subordinate society's way of life.

Such problems are not only psychological, but often economic, political, or social in some other sense. For example, poverty is often glibly cited as a cause of problem drinking, with little recognition that the occurrence of alcohol-related problems is in direct proportion to wealth in many groups. The apparently increasing rate of drinking problems noted among American women in recent years is attributed by some to the greater freedom they enjoy to behave as men do, and by others to the stress engendered by status inconsistency and uncertainty about self-image. Another sociocultural factor that is often thought to contribute to problem drinking is ambivalence—not about oneself, but about alcoholic beverages. This is epitomized in the confusion encountered in mainstream American society, where children are not permitted to drink at all, but young men are then suddenly expected to hold their liquor and young women to accept social drinks. The absence of clear, unequivocal, and consistent guidelines for using alcohol can be problematic for many individuals.

Unfortunately, the presence of guidelines can also be problematic. Mention has been made of some societies in which the norm of heavy drinking and frequent drunkenness can be harmful. It was for a time considered an anomaly that members of some religious sects that prescribe abstinence were also at high risk in terms of developing drinking problems. Then systematic research revealed that, although few drink, any one who once broke the rule felt doomed or resigned and so the "fall of the drunkard" became a kind of self-fulfilling prophecy.

It is apparent that sociocultural variants are of major importance with respect to both the nature and the rate of occurrence of alcohol-related problems in various populations throughout the world, just as they have been throughout human history.

IMPLICATIONS FOR DIAGNOSIS AND TREATMENT

Drinking problems vary among populations as a direct result of variations in patterns of belief, behavior, attitudes, and values. The ways in which members of a group view drinking and its consequences obviously influence their willingness to seek various kinds of help for themselves or to recommend it for others. Similarly, even after an individual has eventually arrived at an appropriate context for securing help in relation to some sort of problem in terms of health or welfare, identification of drinking as an etiological factor will more readily be made for members of some groups than of others. It has been found that some Jews long denied having drinking problems until they were disabused of the idea that Jews can't become alcoholics.

The topic of ethnic variation in diagnosis and treatment is addressed in some detail elsewhere in this volume (Section VII). The increasing demand for culturally appropriate treatment and other specific facilities for minority populations reflects widespread recognition of the fact that, just as alcohol-related problems are not uniform, alcohol-related resolutions cannot be uniform either [7].

Case Example

Alcoholics Anonymous (AA) has achieved a remarkable international record of helping people who want to resolve drinking problems. But even the most ardent proponent of AA is presumably aware that it is not merely ineffective but positively objectionable to at least some of those who come sincerely seeking help. For many, the unofficial but commonplace religious emphasis (e.g., recitation of The Lord's Prayer at meetings), is a turnoff. One Latin American probably spoke for many when he complained, "I'm not about to admit that alcohol is stronger than I am. What kind of man would say that?" A widespread complaint among American Indians is that troubles in one's family should not be discussed with outsiders; another is that anonymity is a negative principle.

Alcoholics Anonymous is sufficiently flexible, however, that the core value of social support among problem drinkers can be achieved in many ways. Various Indian tribes in both Canada and the United States have developed AA groups that are congenial to them (e.g., incorporating various indigenous themes as well as involving friends and relatives together with self-styled alcoholics).

Other kinds of treatment are more or less culturally congenial, depending on a number of sensitive norms and values. Psychotherapy could not be efffective where one's dreams are viewed as so powerful a part of the self that one would be vulnerable revealing them. Group therapy would be difficult with people who have been socialized that it is in bad taste, or even dangerous, to discuss one's feelings with others. Participation in the Native American Church or in a tradition-oriented ceremonial or other activity is often remarkably therapeutic for members of some Indian groups, whereas signing a pledge or making a vow to a saint may be equally effective for a Scot or a Hispano who considers such an act significant and binding.

PROSPECTS FOR EDUCATION AND PREVENTION

The fundamental value of exploring sociocultural variants is the recognition that what we so often misconstrue as human nature has more to do with what one has learned growing up in a particular society than it does with inherent characteristics of the species. There are many different kinds of human nature, with an amazing array or variation in beliefs and behaviors about any given aspect of culture. One comes to realize that people who conform to different grammatical rules are not without language, although that ethnocentric view persisted until a century ago. Similarly, people who conform to different cultural rules are not without norms—although the relevance of alien norms is still not widely accepted.

It is important to realize that drinking problems are virtually unknown in most of the world's cultures, including many where drinking is commonplace and occasional drunkenness is accepted. This suggests that even a technologically advanced culture might have something to learn from other cultures, some of which are smaller, less diverse, but apparently more sophisticated in many respects. A major value of focusing on sociocultural variants is that of profiting from the experience of many other populations throughout time and space. To speak of adopting traits from other cultures is problematic, because each culture is itself a complex web of interrelationships in which the parts have more meaning to each other than in isolation. It would be fallacious to suppose that the ritual imbeddedness of a Jew's initial drinking experience could be wrenched out of all that went before and grafted onto a Gentile family's routine in the hope of immunizing children against alcoholism. Nevertheless, it is apparent that certain ways of thinking and acting with respect to alcohol, ways that are consistently associated with drinking problems, might fruitfully be rejected, while others, those that correlate with unproblematic drinking, might well be fostered.*

Consistency and continuity are generally recognized as important components of efficient learning. In this respect, the integral role that alcoholic beverages play, visibly and unequivocally, in the workday lives of many peoples may help shape wholesome expectations about drinking. By contrast, the mystique of drinking to escape from stress, or of alcohol as a tool for seduction, is incomprehensible to most people around the world. The special qualities attributed to drinking in this society put it in a category very similar to that other quintessentially natural but affectively powerful activity, sex. Young people are rarely told enough about either, and yet many of the consequences are plainly visible. Children are not supposed to indulge in either, and yet they are to achieve comfortable mastery of complex skills readily when they come of age. The forbidden fruit exerts an attraction that is too compelling for many, so that secretive experimentation, often based on gross misunderstandings, can have disastrous consequences. Early demystification of alcohol would presumably help many young people to avoid drinking problems.

But drinking is also like sex in the respect that ignorance and faulty knowledge remain commonplace among too many adults. Personal tastes become the focus not only of positive emotional commitment and negative prejudice, but also of cherished but inaccurate beliefs. For example, many beer drinkers feel confident that they cannot develop drinking problems, although the most elementary familiarity with the absolute alcohol contents of various beverages demonstrates how fallacious that view is. Similarly, the popular view that coffee or a cold shower will quickly sober a drunk must often result in traffic fatalities that could easily have been avoided. There is some distressing evidence to the effect that increased knowledge about alcohol and its effects does not always result in the abandonment of risky drinking practices, but less than total success is no reason to abandon education in any field.

It is perhaps as important to signal common pitfalls that should be avoided as well as to make positive recommendations.

Case Example

It seems useful to know that legal prohibition as a "noble experiment" failed to curtail the consumption of alcoholic beverages not only in the United States but also earlier in both Finland and Great Britain, and subsequently in some smaller countries, as well as in many counties and Indian reservations. Except where explicitly linked with religious precepts, it seems to have been effective nowhere in world history.

---

*This is not meant to imply that abstinence is not the most appropriate way for many people to avoid drinking problems. Rather, it recognizes the importance of a wide range of social and economic pressures that favor widespread continuing use of alcoholic beverages and are not likely to be countered in the foreseeable future.

On some occasions, unfortunately, a superficial concern for sociocultural variants can be counterproductive. Inappropriate generalization from one minority population to another can be not only ineffective but insulting and alienating, as when an advertising compaign designed to counter the association of drinking with machismo is addressed to any of the several Hispanic populations among whom assertive masculinity is not a preoccupation. By the same token, enormous local variation among Native American populations has too long been ignored in ways that do violence to significant differences that affect drinking and its consequences.

CONCLUSIONS

Sociocultural variants are at least as important as physiological and psychological variants when we are trying to understand the interrelations of alcohol and human behavior. Ways of drinking and of thinking about drinking are learned by individuals within the context in which they learn ways of doing other things and of thinking about them—that is, whatever else drinking may be, it is an aspect of culture about which patterns of belief and behavior are modeled by a combination of example, exhortation, rewards, punishments, and the many other means, both formal and informal, that societies use for communicating norms, attitudes, and values.

The variety of sociocultural patterns associated with alcohol use and its consequences have immediate and grave practical implications. Populations differ not only in terms of the way people drink but also in terms of the way people behave when drunk. They also differ in terms of what they consider appropriate or acceptable behavior, and, consequently, what they consider to be problems. Although most adults in most of the world's cultures customarily drink some alcoholic beverage, the concept of alcoholism is extremely rare and even the more general view that drinking may be related to any kind of problem is also unusual. For these reasons, attitudinal differences as well as differences in drinking practices affect both the nature and rate of occurrence of drinking problems in various populations. Attitudinal differences also influence decisions about whether or how to seek help once problems are identified, making for variation in both diagnosis and treatment. The fact that such sociocultural variants are learned means that, to a significant extent, deleterious patterns can also be unlearned and others can be learned, with culturally appropriate education holding significant promise as a means of preventing the progressive proliferation of alcohol-related problems among various drinking populations.*

---

*It is ironic that many people in the field of alcohol studies mistakenly think of the sociocultural model only in the limited sense of using education as a technique of prevention, whereas it clearly has relevance to epidemiology, diagnosis, treatment, and most other aspects of alcohol-related problems [5].

There are still important questions about sociocultural variants that have not been adequately analyzed, and about which clinicians and counselors can gain useful insights even before social scientists conduct systematic research. One crucial area of concern has to do with the actual process, in detail, by which young people learn what it is that they know about drinking. The general outline of the process is familiar, but evidence of increasingly early experimentation by young people raises questions about what they learn and how they learn it in peer groups before most families or educational institutions address alcohol in any coherent way.

Another topic that should be of obvious interest to those who are actively engaged in early identification of problem drinkers, and in counseling or treatment, is the process of seeking help on the part of those who do recognize that they have problems that stem from drinking. Elaborate procedures have been developed in some areas to monitor cross-referrals and multiple services that are offered once a client is engaged within the network of formal agencies that provide various support in terms of health delivery, welfare, and other assistance. But little attention has been paid to the informal channels through which individuals seek similar kinds of support before they arrive at an agency. In many instances, networks of friends and kin are crucial, while other individuals may resort readily to coworkers, clergy, hairdressers, bartenders, or other persons who are supportive and perhaps otherwise helpful in various ways. Although such community-based support systems are often helpful to individuals with problems, better equipped agencies might be more effective if people came to them sooner. Learning about such informal channels of help-seeking could be advantageous for both practitioners and clients inasmuch as it could facilitate outreach, make more early identification and intervention on behalf of problem drinkers, provide invaluable feedback about how the facility is viewed within the community, and so forth.

An English humorist is credited with having first recommended, "Don't do unto others as you would have them do unto you. They may have very different tastes." However comfortable one may be with the original Golden Rule, this latter-day revised version deserves consideration whenever one is dealing with sociocultural variants.

ACKNOWLEDGMENTS

This chapter was written while the author was program director of "Social Science Research Training on Alcohol," Grant 5 T32 AA 07131, awarded by the National Institute on Alcohol Abuse and Alcoholism.

REFERENCES

1. Bales, R. F. Cultural differences in rates of alcoholism. *Q. J. Stud. Alcohol* 6:480–499, 1946.
2. Blaine, A. (ed.). *Alcoholism in the Jewish Community*. Commission on Synagogue Relations: New York, 1980.
3. Everett, M. W., Waddell, J. O., and Heath, D. B. (eds.). *Cross-Cultural Approaches to the Study of Alcohol: An Interdisciplinary Perspective*. Mouton: The Hague, 1976.
4. Heath, D. B. A critical review of ethnographic studies of alcohol use. In: *Research Advances in Alcohol and Drug Problems* (Vol. 2), (Gibbins, R. J., Israel, Y., Kalant, H., Popham, R., Schmidt, W., and Smart, R. (eds). Wiley: New York, 1975.
5. Heath, D. B. A critical review of the sociocultural model of alcohol use. In: *Normative Approaches to the Prevention of Alcohol Abuse and Alcoholism* (Monograph 3): Harford, T. C., Parker, D. A., and Light, L. (eds.). National Institute on Alcohol Abuse and Alcoholism Research: Rockville, Md., 1980.
6. Heath, D. B., and Cooper, A. M. *Alcohol Use and World Cultures: A Comprehensive Bibliography of Anthropological Sources* (Bibliographic Series 15). Addiction Research Foundation: Toronto, 1981.
7. Heath, D. B., Waddell, J. O., and Topper, M. D. (eds.). *Cultural Factors in Alcohol Research and Treatment of Drinking Problems*. Smithsonian Institution: Washington, D.C., 1981.
8. Leland, J. *Firewater Myths: North American Indian Drinking and Alcohol Addiction* (Monograph 11). Rutgers Center of Alcohol Studies: New Brunswick, N.J., 1976.
9. Lurie, N. O. The world's oldest on-going protest demonstration: North American Indian drinking patterns. *Pacific Historical Rev.* 40:311–332, 1971.
10. MacAndrew, C., and Edgerton, R. B. *Drunken Comportment: A Social Explanation*. Aldine: Chicago, 1969.
11. Mail, P. D., and McDonald, D. R. *Tulapai to Tokay: A Bibliography of Alcohol Use and Abuse among Native Americans of North America*. HRAF Press: New Haven, Conn., 1980.
12. Marshall, M. (ed.). *Beliefs, Behaviors and Alcoholic Beverages: A Cross-Cultural Survey*. University of Michigan Press: Ann Arbor, 1979.
13. Snyder, C. R. *Alcohol and the Jews: A Cultural Study of Drinking and Sobriety*. Free Press: Glencoe, Ill., 1958.
14. Stivers, R. A. *A Hair of the Dog: Irish Drinking and American Stereotype*. Pennsylvania State University Press: University Park, Pa., 1976.
15. World Health Organization, Expert Committee on Mental Health. *Second Report of the Alcoholism Subcommittee* (WHO Technical Report Series 48). WHO: Geneva, 1952.

35

HAROLD A. MULFORD, PhD, University of Iowa

THE EPIDEMIOLOGY OF ALCOHOLISM AND ITS IMPLICATIONS

THE EPIDEMIOLOGY OF alcoholism, not unlike the balance of the field, is unsettled. Space constraints do not allow an exhaustive examination of all of the theoretical, substantive, and methodological issues affecting the current state of knowledge. Summaries and reviews are available elsewhere. Room's [21] excellent summary includes a comprehensive methodological critique. Bruun et al. [3] offer an international review, and Edwards [8] has reviewed substantive issues. Summaries of national data can be found in the reports to Congress by the National Institute on Alcohol Abuse and Alcoholism (NIAAA) [25].

Purpose

Here only some of the major issues of this evolving field of study are discussed, as well as why epidemiological conclusions do not yet deserve to be taken uncritically. The primary concentration herein is on problems of defining alcoholics and measuring prevalence rates. To illustrate some of the issues, and show how one study approached them, certain results of a recent general population survey of problem drinkers in the state of Iowa are presented. It is not the intent of this

---

Harold A. Mulford, PhD, Professor of Psychiatry and Director of Alcohol Studies, University of Iowa, Iowa City, Iowa.

chapter to discredit the epidemiological research that has been done, but to point to some basic challenges that must be met before epidemiological knowledge about alcoholics can, from a scientific viewpoint, legitimately be treated as more than a point of departure for further research. Nor is there any pretense that a definitive resolution of any of the issues is being offered.

Definition of Terms

Epidemiology. Epidemiology is the study of the distribution of a disease and the factors that might influence its distribution in a population. The distribution is described in terms of either prevalence — the number of active cases in a specified population at a given time — or incidence — the number of new cases occurring during a defined time period. The scant attention that epidemiologists have given to alcoholism has mainly involved prevalence rates, probably because prevalence data are easier to obtain.

The distribution of a disease is studied in search of causal clues that will lead to greater understanding and ultimately to more effective control. Being largely descriptive, epidemiological research cannot conclusively establish the cause of becoming alcoholic. Rather, the analysis of variations in prevalence or incidence rates is a search for clues that will generate specific causal hypotheses for experimental testing and guide further research. For example, the consistently observed higher rates of alcoholism for men than for women suggests, but does not prove, that there is something, perhaps many things, about being male that facilitates, and/or being female that constrains, the development of alcoholism. It also directs further research to analyze the two sexes separately. At the same time, the identification of one sex as being at greater risk has control policy implications.

Alcoholic/problem drinker. As students of disease, epidemiologists have, understandably, been reluctant to enter a field where the appropriateness of medical terms (including the terms "epidemiology" and "alcoholism") for discussing the subjects of interest is still being debated, and where there is not even agreement on what to call them. While the labels "alcoholic" and "problem drinker" are currently in vogue, laymen and experts alike are about evenly divided on their preference for these two terms [13]. When a distinction is made, the term "alcoholic" usually connotes a more advanced case, or one who is thought more likely to have the presumed disease. In this work, the two terms are used interchangeably. The definition herein of "alcoholic/problem drinker" is anyone who qualifies on the Iowa Alcoholic Stages Index (see Table 1), operationally defined in a later section.

Alcoholism. A universally accepted definition of the postulated disease (alcoholism) has so far defied scientific research. Despite many efforts to do so, alcoholics have not been fitted into the classical medical model. It remains to be demonstrated that alcoholism is anything more than a supposition, a concept, lying more in the head of the observer than in the body of the observed. Although alco-

Table 1
Iowa Alcoholic Stages Index

A. Trouble Due to Drinking

(Qualifying score, 2 or more "yes" responses)

During Past 12 Months:

1. Has your employer fired or threatened to fire you because of your drinking?
2. Has your spouse left or threatened to leave you because of your drinking?
3. Has a family member complained you spend too much money on alcohol?
4. Have you been picked up by the police because of your drinking?
5. Has a physician told you drinking was injuring your health?
6. Have you had any illness due to drinking?
7. Have you had difficulty meeting bills because too much money was spent on liquor?
8. Have you quit or changed jobs because you were in trouble or likely to get into difficulty due to drinking?
9. Have you had any accidents or injuries due to drinking?
10. Have you failed to do some of the things you should—keeping appointments, getting things done around the house, or attending to your job—because of drinking?

B. Personal Effects of Drinking

(Qualifying score, 3 or more "yes" responses)

Would You Say These Things about Your Drinking:

1. Drinking helps me forget I am not the kind of person I really want to be.
2. Drinking helps me get along better with other people.
3. Drinking helps me feel more satisfied with myself.
4. Drinking gives me more confidence in myself.
5. Drinking helps me overcome shyness.
6. Drinking makes me less self-conscious.

C. Preoccupied Drinking

(Qualifying score, 3 or more "frequently" or "sometimes" responses)

1. I stay intoxicated for several days at a time.
2. I worry about not being able to get a drink when I need one.
3. I sneak drinks when no one is looking.
4. Once I start drinking it is difficult for me to stop before I become completely intoxicated.
5. I get intoxicated on work days.
6. I take a drink the first thing when I get up in the morning.
7. I awaken next day not being able to remember some of the things I had done while I was drinking.
8. I take a few quick ones before going to a party to make sure I have enough.
9. I neglect my regular meals when I am drinking.

D. Uncontrolled Drinking Scale

(Qualifying score, "frequently" response to either item)

1. Without realizing it, I end up drinking more than I had planned to.
2. Once I start drinking it is difficult for me to stop before I become completely intoxicated.

Source: From "Stages in the Alcoholic Process: Toward a Cumulative Nonsequential Index" by H. Mulford, *J. Stud. Alcohol*, 38:565, 1977. Reprinted with permission.

holism is commonly thought to be a unitary entity and a physical property of the individual, independent of interaction with others, neither alcoholism, nor persons to whom it is attributed (by whatever name they are called) have been found to exist independent of the drinking and related behavior that those about them perceive and label. Viable though the disease hypothesis may still be, alcoholism as a disease entity remains a thing attributed to persons given the label "alcoholic" to explain their drinking and related behavior. However, such an explanation will remain a mere tautology until "alcoholism" is defined in terms independent of the drinking and related behavior it is supposed to explain.

Fortunately, the alcoholism disease issue has not prevented researchers from applying epidemiological methods to the study of alcoholics. While awaiting a scientific verdict on the disease hypothesis, many researchers have simply sidestepped the issue. Some even make the contrary assumption and pursue their research from another way of thinking about alcoholics and how they might have come to be. For example, alcoholics can be thought of as the product of a life-long process and as representing the cumulative effect of a multitude of weak interacting social, psychological, and physiological forces. From this viewpoint, the alcoholism disease concept loses much of its appeal. Instead of positing a mysterious "thing" merely awaiting discovery and analysis, the processes perspective dictates research that seeks to specify what drinking and related behavior occurs, and under what specified conditions.

Although alcoholism has no empirical referent, people with drinking-related problems can be pointed out. Their numbers have been estimated and their distribution in the population analyzed in order to better understand how they came to be alcoholics, how they can be helped out of that classification, and what needs be done to prevent drinkers from becoming alcoholics. This approach has contributed much of today's epidemiology knowledge.

THE STATE OF THE ART

Defining Prevalence Rates

No question is more frequently asked by alcoholism program policy makers and designers than the one that is also of primary concern to epidemiologists: "How many persons become alcoholic, under what conditions, and who are they?" Answers to this question not only establish the size of the problem and suggest possible causes, they also ultimately determine the nature, the effectiveness, and the efficiency of remedial policies and programs.

Unfortunately, today one can find an alcoholic prevalence rate for all occasions and purposes, and one to fit any of the theories and personal predilections that abound. For example, rate estimates for the United States range from around

2 or 3% and less to 50% and more of the drinkers. Hence, an alcoholic prevalence rate can easily be misinterpreted, and even misused. Before accepting a published prevalence rate on faith, one should determine how it was arrived at and what purpose it is intended to serve. It is not impertinent to assess the work for unstated biases. For example, is the work scientifically motivated or politically motivated? Does it have a "wet" or a "dry" bias?

Cases must be counted and rates established before their distribution in the population can be analyzed. The rate formula is simply the number of alcoholics divided by the population at risk. Before uncritically accepting a prevalence rate, one should learn how the denominator (the population at risk) of the rate formula, as well as its numerator (the number of alcoholics), is defined.

The Risk Population

Table 2 presents data from a recent Iowa general population survey demonstrating how both the prevalence rate, and its distribution in the population, can differ depending upon the population at risk. It is seen, for example, that when the total rate is based to the higher risk population composed of persons who have had a drink during the 30 days prior to being interviewed, it is nearly double the rate based to the entire sample of adult Iowans (17.2% vs. 9.6%).

Moreover, the distribution can reverse and causal clues can point in opposite directions, depending upon the risk population. That does not happen in Table 2, but clearly the observed extent of risk differs depending upon the risk population. For example, the table shows that when rates are based to the total sample, being reared in a home where alcohol is served increases the risk of becoming alcoholic nearly 2.5 times, but the risk is only 1.5 times greater when based to only persons who drank in the past 30 days.

Obviously, defining the risk population has its problems. Even determining who drinks, and who does not, is not as simple as it might appear. Nonetheless, a prevalence rate and its distribution is meaningful only to the extent that the risk population is clearly defined.

Who to Count and How

Determining who to count and how to count them is far more difficult than defining the risk population. A direct count of alcoholics is not feasible, but a variety of indirect methods have been used to make prevalence estimates.

Jellinek formula estimates. An early, systematic effort to determine prevalence rates was the Jellinek estimation formula, which is based on the observation that alcoholics have an abnormally high liver cirrhosis mortality rate. For several years, until the late 1950s, the Jellinek formula provided the official estimate of the number of alcoholics in the nation. However, criticisms of the formula eventually led Jellinek to recommend that it no longer be used.

Table 2
**Iowa Problem Drinker Prevalence Rates, by Risk Populations
and by Selected Early Socioenvironmental Factors**

	Drink Last 30 Days		All Drinkers		Total Sample	
	n	%	n	%	n	%
Childhood residence						
City (over 2,500)	318	19.8	426	14.8	531	11.9
Town (under 2,500)	181	18.8	228	14.9	319	10.7
Farm	351	13.4	476	9.9	661	7.1
Combination	11	27.3	13	23.1	22	13.6
Alcohol served in childhood home						
Yes	519	19.7	658	15.5	747	13.7
No	333	13.2	473	9.3	769	5.7
Age started drinking						
Under 14	10	20.0	13	15.4	13	15.4
14–15	46	50.0	47	48.9	47	48.9
16–17	131	30.5	148	27.0	148	27.0
18–19	235	14.0	274	12.0	274	12.0
20–21	208	10.1	241	8.7	241	8.7
22–29	132	13.6	155	11.6	157	11.5
30–39	35	8.6	51	5.9	51	5.9
40+	24	20.8	30	16.7	30	16.7
Early alcoholic role model						
Father alcoholic						
Yes	66	24.2	90	17.8	111	14.4
No	784	16.6	1038	12.5	1406	9.2
Mother alcoholic						
Yes	18	38.9	23	30.4	25	28.0
No	832	16.7	1105	12.6	1492	9.3
Sex						
Male	466	21.0	570	17.2	733	13.4
Female	396	12.6	574	8.7	802	6.2
Religious preference						
Catholic	244	20.1	298	16.4	343	14.3
Protestant	553	14.5	762	10.5	1082	7.4
None	48	33.3	59	27.1	69	23.2
Other	10	30.0	14	21.4	27	11.1
Total	862	17.2	1144	12.9	1535	9.6

The single distribution estimate. Currently, the most vigorously debated, but so far not widely used, prevalence estimation procedure is based on the so-called single distribution theory [22]. This approach does not directly estimate the number of alcoholics in a population. Rather, the number of excessive or heavy drinkers in the population is estimated from the distribution of all drinkers by their consumption levels. In theory, the distribution of drinkers is such that the mean consumption of a population inevitably determines the excessive drinker rate. While this hypothesis appears to have some empirical support, data are emerging that challenge its universal applicability [17]. Even if the distribution mean did invariably determine the excessive drinker rate, the relationship between excessive drinker rates and alcoholic rates (much less the prevalence of alcoholism), remains to be determined. Furthermore, since sales data are generally relied on in this approach and are rarely available for subpopulations, the single distribution estimate is of limited value for epidemiological research.

Generalizing from institutionalized alcoholics. Prior to the development of the Jellinek formula, epidemiological knowledge consisted of informal guesses about the prevalence and distribution of alcoholics in the general population, based on observations of persons institutionalized, mainly in hospitals and jails, for reasons apparently related to their drinking.

Later, a more systematic approach using institutionalized cases attempted to count the total number of alcoholics seen by the several agencies in the community at the points where alcoholics tend to concentrate—jails, hospitals, welfare offices, alcoholism treatment centers, AA meetings, and physicians' offices. This approach reveals only the tip of the iceberg—only a small, highly selected portion of all alcoholics who have been through the serial filtration that occurs in the social process by which persons arrive in those institutions as alcoholics.

Generalizing from clinical cases. A more focused version of the above approach concentrates on clinically diagnosed alcoholics. The assumption is that if alcoholics have been professionally diagnosed, usually in a medical setting, then surely they must represent real alcoholics, those who suffer the disease. Even granting this assumption, clinic alcoholics (and even all persons in the general population who look like them) constitute a very narrow, highly selected segment of the alcoholic population.

The clinicalization process. If all institutionalized alcoholics are a select sample of alcoholics at large, clinic cases are even more selected. Little is known about the selection process whereby certain persons end up being clinically diagnosed as alcoholic, but the diagnostic procedure itself is such that it virtually assures an unrepresentative sample of all alcoholics. As with mental illnesses generally [24, 26], the clinical diagnosis of alcoholism is unsystematic, unreliable, and not scientifically replicable. Actually, the widespread belief that clinicians make a differential diagnosis of alcoholism is largely a myth. In actual practice, the patient and his or her peers out in the community have been engaged in a diagnostic process for months, if not years, before the clinician ever sees the patient. Eventually, the person's peers conclude, usually after much indecision, vacillation, and frustration, that the person's drinking and related behavior has become intolerable and they tentatively label him or her "alcoholic," or "problem drinker," or whatever. The clinician is not likely to dispute this, and even if the patient disputes it, the clinician is likely to agree with the complainants that the patient drinks too much and is an alcoholic. Then, and for want of a better explanation of the perceived deviant drinking and related behavior, the patient is attributed the disease alcoholism, and becomes an officially certified alcoholic. The clinician's contribution to the process amounts to little more than confirming and legitimizing the community's diagnosis.

Clinic alcoholics versus general population alcoholics. Exactly how clinic alcoholics differ from alcoholics at large has been little researched. Descriptive profiles of the two populations have been compared, but with rare exceptions [20] it is not known to what extent the cases met the same identifying criteria.

In Table 3 a sample of general population alcoholics (GPAs) isolated in a representative sample of the general adult (18 + years) population of Iowa in 1979 is compared with a large population of professionally diagnosed alcoholics appearing in alcoholism clinics across the state, with both samples meeting a common operational definition of alcoholic; they all qualified as alcoholics on the Iowa Alcoholic Stages Index. To give more meaning to the comparisons, the two alcoholic populations can also be compared with normal drinkers (i.e., persons in the sample who had had a drink in the past 30 days but did not meet the qualifying criteria as alcoholics). Further methodological details are given below and elsewhere [9, 14, 17].

The data in Table 3 illustrate the hazards of supposing that clinically diagnosed alcoholics are representative of alcoholics at large. To begin with, since only about one in 10 of the clinic cases, but three out of 10 of the GPAs, were women, Table 3 is restricted to males. Observing only the clinic cases, the clinician might conclude that most alcoholics are middle age or older, males with little advanced formal education, unmarried, unemployed, and have little income. The all too familiar stereotype of the alcoholic would appear to be confirmed once again. The epidemiologist, however, looking at the general population of alcoholics who are from the same state and who met the same objective criteria as did the clinic cases, would challenge those conclusions, especially when the GPAs profile is compared with that of the normal drinkers. If there are these differences between clinic alcoholics and general population alcoholics on the basic sociodemographic attributes presented in Table 3, probably there are many other differences. As Room points out [21], for the epidemiologist to use clinic, or other institutionalized, cases to estimate the prevalence, and to study the distribution, of alcoholics, or even to count only cases in the general population who look like clinically diagnosed alcoholics, is very likely to lead to false conclusions. Such a method is likely to grossly underestimate the prevalence of alcoholics in the general population, produce distorted distributions, and yield sterile causal hypotheses.

Blane et al. [2] documented the influence that the long-standing stereotype of the alcoholic as a socially isolated and impoverished chronic inebriate has had on physicians' diagnosis of alcoholism. They found that physicians were more inclined to diagnose a patient alcoholic whose general appearance fit the social derelict stereotype. Hence, the stereotype was self-perpetuating until epidemiologists took a closer look.

Table 3
Comparison of Male Normal Drinkers, Iowa General Population Alcoholics, and Clinic Alcoholics, by Selected Socioenvironmental Attributes

	General Population Drinkers[a]		
	Normal (n = 354)	Alcoholic (n = 98)	Clinic Alcoholics (n = 7,122)
Age			
Under 25 years	8.2	26.5	15.2
25–29	13.8	18.4	12.3
30–39	25.1	14.3	22.2
40–49	15.0	6.1	23.4
50–59	17.8	15.3	18.1
60+	19.8	19.4	7.9
Education in years			
1–8	9.3	6.1	22.6
9–11	11.6	14.3	25.8
12	38.4	51.0	37.1
13+	40.4	27.6	12.9
Current family status			
Married, living with spouse	85.3	65.3	46.3
Single, never married	10.5	23.5	18.9
Other	4.0	11.2	34.1
Annual family income			
$0–4,999	4.0	10.2	40.6
$5,000–10,000	10.2	5.1	31.0
$10,000–14,999	15.5	16.3	15.8
$15,000–25,000	31.4	31.6	
Over $25,000	24.0	18.4	
Refused; missing data	15.0	18.4	3.1
Employment status			
Own business, self-employed	24.6	17.3	8.4
Permanent job, full-time	52.3	44.9	45.1
Part-time	4.0	10.2	6.1
Unemployed, in labor market	2.0	6.1	28.3
Not in labor market (student, retired, etc.)	16.9	21.4	10.4

[a] n = 100%; percentages do not always total 100 because of missing data.

General Population Surveys

Recognizing the need for a more representative sample of alcoholics at large, researchers have in recent years increasingly turned to survey studies of alcoholics/problem drinkers in the general population. This approach employs a little different terminology. Instead of dealing with alcoholics and alcoholism, it studies problem drinkers and drinking-related problems. However, survey researchers have generally been careful to specify the operations that identify the subjects of study. This not only helps reduce semantic confusion but also allows for scientific replication of the work. Unfortunately, replication has been rare and few precisely comparable studies have appeared.

Survey Identification Problems

Index biases. Although the issue has been little researched, it appears likely that most indices for diagnosing or identifying alcoholics tend to be as biased as the institutional populations on which they were developed. Room [21] has noted the remarkable degree to which the constituent items of most indices are traceable to Jellinek's [11] early analysis of a questionnaire study of AA members. There has also been a tendency to validate these indices against clinic and other institutionalized cases. Consequently, survey samples of alcoholics likely represent alcoholics in the AA image and also reflect the sex, age, and probably other biases of clinic cases more than is generally realized [17, 18].

Cut-off points. Another factor affecting survey-measured prevalence rates is the cut-off point setting the qualifying criterion for the index. In the absence of agreement on what a real alcoholic really is, setting the cut-off point is necessarily an arbitrary decision of the researcher. Since only a slight shift of the cutting point defining who to count can have a very great effect on the prevalence rate [6], an author may unconsciously express personal preference for a higher or lower rate.

Self-reports and recall. General population surveys, even more than clinical observations, depend upon self-reports of drinking and related behavior. Although it is unrealistic to expect absolute accuracy from self-reports, and in any event, it is unparsimonious for a researcher to seek any greater measurement precision than necessary for the task at hand, the fact remains that the accuracy of self-reports of drinking behavior is unsettled. The accuracy evidently decreases the farther in the past the individual is asked to recall. Test-retest reliability studies [10, 18, 23] indicate that efforts to make a lifetime diagnosis of alcoholism by asking whether specific drinking problems were ever experienced yield highly inconsistent results. Thus lifetime prevalence rates based on recall of drinking problems are especially suspect. Some reviews have concluded that self-reports of current (i.e., during the past year or so) drinking and related behaviors are usefully accurate, at least for certain purposes [1].

While these and other problems remain to be solved, survey indices do have certain advantages. Compared with clinical diagnosis, survey alcoholic indices have the scientific virtue of being operationally defined, permitting replication. Also, with self-reports obtained by an anonymous survey interviewer from a sample of the general population, there is at least the possibility of isolating a representative sample of alcoholics at large. Self-reports given to clinicians by individuals who have been through the selection process and who often have more to gain (such as avoiding institutionalization) by distorting the truth are more likely to lead to false conclusions. Want of an independent, objective validation criteria probably explains the dearth of validity tests of alcoholic indices. More common reliability studies have yielded mixed results [12].

Conceptual problems. The researcher's choice of who to count as an alcoholic is unavoidably influenced by his conceptual orientation, which all too often can only be inferred. As yet, there is no theory of alcoholism worthy of the name. Nonetheless, research, as well as policy making and implementation, of necessity reflects the author's notions about whether the phenomenon in question is a disease, a crime, moral degeneracy, drinking behavior, or something else. It would help advance the field if everyone would spell out their conceptual models. Thus, there is need for more work at the conceptual, as well as the methodological level — perhaps even a bold departure from conventional ways of thinking about, and identifying, the target population.

A DIFFERENT APPROACH

Another Way of Thinking

Given the failure of the alcoholism disease model to synthesize the rapidly accumulating research findings or to generate effective remedial action, there is need for an alternative way of thinking — one that would (1) make more sense of the research findings, and impose some discipline on further research; (2) generate a less biased index for identifying the target population; and (3) ultimately lead to more effective control of the alcohol problem. As an alternative to the common, static, unidimensional view of alcoholics as suffering a disease entity with a unitary cause, one can turn to a multifactored processes model. This way of thinking views every drinker as being at some stage of a dynamic, lifelong, alcoholic process influenced by a multitude of weak, interacting social, psychological, and physical forces with no single factor, except alcohol, being necessary, and none at all being sufficient, to cause advancement in the process to the point of being labeled "alcoholic" or "problem drinker" [14, 19]. From this viewpoint, the alcoholologist's task of identifying the forces influencing the alcoholic process and untangling their complex interrelationships is much like that of the meteorologist's attempts to understand the processes called "the weather."

Another Index

The above way of thinking led to the development of the Iowa Alcoholic Stages Index (Table 1). If, as is supposed, the system of forces influencing a person's progress in the alcoholic process changes with time and differs according to one's stage in the process, then there is need for an index that not merely identifies alcoholics, but one that also measures their stage in the process. Although many of the items in Table 1 are also traceable to Jellinek's phases study, an attempt has been made to validate it against the criteria used by the community at large, rather than against clinical diagnosis [14]. The rationale for the stages index, its development, and evidence of reliability and validity have been reported elsewhere [14, 15, 16]. Results of its use in a general population survey have also been reported [1] (see Table 1).

To qualify as an alcoholic on the index, a person must meet the qualifying criteria specified for at least one of the four subscales. For present purposes, the individual must, additionally, report having had a drink during the 30 days prior to interview in order to qualify as an alcoholic. A person's stage in the alcoholic process is indicated by the index score, which can range from 0 (nonalcoholic) to 4 (advanced alcoholic). The score is simply a count of the number of the four subscales on which the individual qualifies.

Some New Findings

Because of differences in methods, the Iowa findings are not precisely comparable with those of other surveys. Nevertheless, they lend further weight to the repeated observation that males, the younger age group, city residents, and persons with more income and more years of formal education have higher problem drinker rates than do their counterparts. However, the differences found are generally less than commonly reported. For example, the male to female ratio of only 2:1, revealed by the stages index, is significantly less than the more commonly reported ratio of around 4:1. This may mean that the stages index represents some progress toward reducing the sex bias, and perhaps other biases, inherent in most alcoholic index [17, 18].

Epidemiologists also study trends. Consistent with national findings [7, 25], it has been reported [17] that the overall problem drinker rates in Iowa in 1979 had increased little, if any, since 1961, when a baseline study was conducted. However, one segment of the population, farm residents, did have a notable increase. At the same time, the rate for city dwellers declined slightly. Thus, the rural-urban difference in problem drinker rates in Iowa in 1979 is less than it was in 1961, and less than it has generally been reported to be elsewhere. The epidemiological implication is, of course, that whatever there is about living in urban areas that increases, or living in rural areas that decreases, the risk of problem drinking, the effect is less today — at least in Iowa.

These Iowa findings also illustrate how prevalence rates differ depending upon the type of index used, and the sensitivity of alcoholic rates to slight shifts of qualifying cutting points. Had the trouble subscale of the stages index been used to identify alcoholics, with a criterion score set at the usual 2 or more, only 1.3% of the respondents reporting drinking in the past 30 days would have qualified as alcoholics. Lowering the cutting point to a criterion score of only 1 or more raises this rate nearly five-fold, to 6.1%. The rate is nearly tripled again to 17.2% when the stages index is used to measure the rate (as seen in Table 2).

Thinking of alcoholics as representing the cumulative effect of a lifetime of experiences also led to analyzing the distribution of alcoholics according to certain early life socioenvironmental factors. Table 2 shows that, as expected, the rates do vary with childhood experiences. These findings, of course, do not prove cause. But it may be hypothesized that these and probably other early life experiences somehow influence the alcoholic process for some people, under some conditions. It is reasonable to hypothesize that further analysis will reveal that they add something to the amount of variance in problem drinker rates that is explained by more contemporary environmental factors [4]. But there will undoubtedly still remain much to be explained, probably some of it by psychological and physiological factors.

OFFICIAL VERSUS VALID KNOWLEDGE

NIAAA's legislatively mandated reports to Congress contain the official prevalence and distribution data for the nation. They are the most publicized prevalence and distribution conclusions and the ones most often cited by politicians and program policy makers. Their official character, however, is not to be confused with scientific validity. Whether by design or not, the reports to Congress likely reflect a contemporary fact of life. The welfare, perhaps even the survival, of NIAAA, depends upon (1) the apparent magnitude of the alcohol problem, and (2) whether it is made to appear that a disease (rather than a moral or social problem) is being attacked. Before accepting the reports at face value, the primary sources of data should be consulted. For example, the reports draw heavily upon the seminal work of Cahalan and colleagues, namely their national drinking practices surveys conducted in the 1960s [4, 5], supplemented by more recent work. Cahalan [4] was careful to operationally define the problem drinker. He explicitly disclaimed any pretense of studying the prevalence and distribution of the disease alcoholism. He even cautioned that the problem drinker rate was not being measured very accurately. He deliberately defined "problem drinker" very broadly, casting a wide net designed to catch both problem drinkers and potential problem drinkers. The aim was to catch everyone who had experienced a drinking problem during the 3 years prior to the interview and also to identify all who were likely to have a problem.

Presenting Cahalan's problem drinker rate as the official rate for the nation, NIAAA, in effect, suddenly nearly doubled the apparent size of the nation's alcoholic population from around 5 million, as had been estimated by the Jellinek formula, to some 9 or 10 million. It is all too easy to conclude from the reports to Congress that there are 10 million Americans suffering a disease requiring medical treatment — a conclusion one might question after studying Cahalan's procedures for identifying problem drinkers.

DISCUSSION

In summary, the scientific study of alcoholism is in its infancy. Its methods are rudimentary. Its terminology is ambiguous, its findings are controversial, and its conclusions are unsettled. Even the alcoholism disease remains a mystery.

This has not, however, deterred researchers from applying epidemiological methods to the investigation of persons who are perceived to drink too much, by whatever name they are called, and regardless of whether they suffer the supposed disease. Their prevalence rates have been estimated and their distributions in the population analyzed. Although the results are unsettled and cannot be taken uncritically, still, policy makers and remedial program designers, if they are to act at all, have no choice but to act upon the available knowledge. The research challenge is to scientifically reassess, refine, and add to that knowledge.

Implications for Prevention

It is unlikely that alcohol abuse, much less the potential for it, will ever be entirely eliminated. On the other hand, there are reasons to believe that it can be reduced. Certainly it has long been largely contained by most societies. The epidemiological evidence is that alcoholic prevalence rates vary according to time and place, vary from society to society, vary for different segments of the same society, and vary through time for a given society. This, together with the self-evident truth that countless societies have for innumerable generations prevented the bulk of drinkers from abusing alcohol and somehow rehabilitated many abusers, plus the fact that some societies more successfully accomplish this than others, even to the point of virtually eliminating individual abuse, all strongly suggests that society somehow can, and does, influence drinking patterns, including the pattern perceived and labeled as "alcoholic."

Although no unique alcoholic physiology or personality has been identified, it is not unlikely that physical and psychological, as well as social, forces influence an individual's drinking. However, given today's epidemiological knowledge, it is difficult to conceive that there is an alcoholic germ, or virus, or gene, or biochemical or psychic defect, or personal disposition, or social force, or any single factor that would, by itself, explain the observed distribution of alcoholics in the population.

Epidemiological findings, such as the lower alcoholic rates for women than for men, and the trend for the traditionally lower rural rate to catch up with the urban rate, suggests that alcohol abuse is more of a people problem involving judgments, values, and so forth, and less of a technical problem amenable to a quick fix, as the disease concept and medical model lead us to suppose. If, as the findings to date suggest, more effective prevention lies in the development of more responsible drinking norms and informal controls, then epidemiologists might help communities do this by identifying the drinking attitudes and practices most highly associated with responsible drinking, as well as those associated with alcohol abuse.

Clinical Implications

Program policy makers and clinic directors striving to build remedial programs that have maximum penetration of, and overall impact on, the alcoholic population would be well advised to compare the distribution of their clinic populations with that of alcoholics at large in their community. Then they can ask themselves, for example, why, as is usually the case, younger alcoholics and women do not appear in clinics in the expected proportions, and what should, or can, be done about it?

If, as has been argued [14, 19], alcoholics enter treatment being not only at some stage of the alcoholic process, but also in some stage of a natural recovery process, then clinicians need be less concerned with diagnosing and treating an undefined disease and more concerned with helping the alcoholic to assess his or her relative status in the two processes and to identify, and more effectively manage, the social, as well as personal, forces influencing the patient's movement in the two processes. Probably no single set of forces would fit all cases; they would likely differ from community to community. Epidemiological knowledge of alcoholics in the community would help alert the clinicians to the most cogent forces affecting alcoholics in their communities.

Implications for Further Research

Given the unmet challenges and problems mentioned, plus the many not mentioned, it may seem premature to draw any conclusions at all about the prevalence and distribution of alcoholics. However, waiting for final answers is not the way science—or society—works. Instead, science cautiously, methodically tests and retests its findings and formulates and reformulates its way of thinking about an area of investigation. Constantly reminding oneself of the unsolved conceptual and methodological problems of research efforts to date, and the tentative nature of today's conclusions, is part of the process of furthering scientific knowledge of alcoholics. Meanwhile, society draws on available knowledge and procedes with the inexorable process of trying to fit alcohol into the culture as harmlessly as possible.

Although progress is being made, there remains a great deal of research to be done—at the conceptual level, no less than at the empirical level—before there is a definitive answer to the question, "How many people become alcoholic, under what conditions, and who are they?" Today, research analysis is greatly outpacing synthesis. There is need for a theory that would make sense of the rapidly emerging empirical findings and impose a modicum of discipline on further empirical research. If the reader has been challenged to do further research, with imagination and fresh thoughts, then this work will have achieved its purpose. Another step will have been taken toward a more useful way of thinking, more precise measures, more accurate epidemiological descriptions, and, ultimately, more effective control of the alcohol problem.

ACKNOWLEDGMENTS

Supported by NIAAA Grant AA03829, and by the Department of Psychiatry and the Office of Vice President for Educational Development and Research, University of Iowa. My thanks to Jerry Fitzgerald, Research Associate, and to Leroy Mullinnix, Computer Analyst, for assistance in the preparation of this work.

REFERENCES

1. Armor, D., Polich, J., and Stambul, H. *Alcoholism and Treatment* (Report prepared for National Institute on Alcohol Abuse and Alcoholism Contract No. 2 R01-AA-01203-03). Rand Corp.: Santa Monica, 1976.
2. Blane, H., Overton, W., and Chafetz, M. Social factors in the diagnosis of alcoholism. *J. Stud. Alcohol* 24:640–663, 1963.
3. Bruun, K., Edwards, G., Lumio, M., Makela, K., Pan, L., Popham, R., Room, R., Schmidt, W., Skog, O., Sulkunen, P., and Osterberg, E. *Alcohol Control Policies in Public Health Perspective*. Finnish Foundation for Alcohol Studies: Helsinki, 1975.
4. Cahalan, D. *Problem Drinkers*. Jossey-Bass: San Francisco, 1970.
5. Cahalan, D., and Room, R. *Problem Drinking among American Men* (Monograph No. 7). Rutgers Center of Alcohol Studies: New Brunswick, 1974.
6. Clark, W. Operational definitions of drinking problems and associated prevalence rates. *J. Stud. Alcohol* 27:648–668, 1966.
7. Clark, W., and Midanik, L. Alcohol use and alcohol problems among U.S. Adults. In: *National Institute on Alcohol Abuse and Alcoholism: Alcohol Consumption and Related Problems* (Alcohol and Health Monograph No. 1). NIAAA: Rockville, Md. In press.
8. Edwards, G. Epidemiology applied to alcoholism: A review and examination of purposes. *J. Stud. Alcohol* 34:28–56, 1973.
9. Fitzgerald, J., and Mulford, H. The prevalence and extent of drinking in Iowa revisited, 1979. *J. Stud. Alcohol* 42:38–47, 1981.
10. Guze, S., and Goodwin, D. Consistency of drinking history and diagnosis of alcoholism. *J. Stud. Alcohol* 33:111–116, 1972.
11. Jellinek, E. Phases in the drinking history of alcoholics: Analysis of a survey conducted by the official organ of Alcoholics Anonymous. *J. Stud. Alcohol* 7:1–87, 1946.

12. Jacobson, G. *The Alcoholisms: Detection, Diagnosis and Assessment.* Human Sciences Press: New York, 1976.

13. Mulford, H. *"Alcoholics," "Alcoholism" and "Problem Drinkers": Social Objects in the Making* (Report to the National Center for Health Statistics, Contract No. PH 86-65-91). Iowa City, 1969. (Mimeographed)

14. Mulford, H. Stages in the alcoholic process: Toward a cumulative nonsequential index. *J. Stud. Alcohol* 38:563-583, 1977.

15. Mulford, H. On the validity of the Iowa alcoholic stages index. *J. Stud. Alcohol* 41: 86-88, 1980.

16. Mulford, H., and Fitzgerald, J. On the reliability of the Iowa alcoholic stages index. *J. Stud. Alcohol* 38:2197-2198, 1977.

17. Mulford, H., and Fitzgerald, J. Changes in alcohol sales and drinking problems, Iowa, 1961-1979. Submitted for publication.

18. Mulford, H., and Fitzgerald, J. On the validity of the research diagnostic criteria and the feighner criteria for diagnosing alcoholism. *J. Nerv. Ment. Dis.*, 169(10), in press.

19. Mulford, H., and Moessner, H. Alcoholism. In: *Family Practice*, Rakel, R. and Conn, H. (eds.). W. B. Saunders: Philadelphia, 1978.

20. Mulford, H., and Wilson, R. *Identifying Problem Drinkers in a Household Health Survey.* U.S. Government Printing Office: Washington, D.C., 1966.

21. Room, R. Measurement and distribution of drinking patterns and problems in general populations. In: *Alcohol-Related Disabilities*, Edwards, G., Gross, M., Keller, M., Moser, J. and Room, R. (eds.). World Health Organization: Geneva, 1977.

22. Schmidt, W., and Popham, R. The single distribution theory of alcohol consumption. *J. Stud. Alcohol* 39:400-505, 1978.

23. Shanks, P. *Response Effects and Sample Bias in Longitudinal Surveys.* Social Research Group: University of California at Berkeley, 1975.

24. Spitzer, R., Endicott, J., and Robins, E. Research diagnostic criteria: Rationale and reliability. *Arch. Gen. Psychiatry* 35:773-782, 1978.

25. U.S. National Institute on Alcohol Abuse and Alcoholism. *Alcohol and Health: Fourth Special Report to the Congress.* U.S. Government Printing Office: Washington, D.C., 1981.

26. Weissman, M., and Klerman, G. Epidemiology of mental disorders, emerging trends in the United States. *Arch. Gen. Psychiatry*, 35:705-712, 1978.

36

DAVID ROBINSON, PhD, University of Hull, England

ALCOHOLISM: PERSPECTIVES ON PREVENTION STRATEGIES

OVER THE PAST DECADE there has been increasing recognition of the fact that treatment alone, however sophisticated and successful it may be, is unlikely to make much impression on the overall alcohol problem. In an increasing number of countries, therefore, the hitherto largely ignored question of how to prevent alcohol-related problems is assuming central and overwhelming importance.

Most of the effort put into actually doing something about the prevention of alcoholism has focused on individuals and their problems, with health education as the main preventive measure. Recently, however, with the significant stimulus of the World Health Organization and its consultants [3], there has been a great deal of interest in the role of policy manipulation in the attempt to prevent and cut down the number of alcohol problems of various kinds.

Although prevention is an easy word to introduce into any discussion of alcohol problems, the construction of a coordinated prevention program is extremely difficult. For if recent biomedical and sociopsychological research has done nothing else, it has made it quite clear that alcohol-related problems arise in all manner of situations, in association with all manner of drinking patterns, and with all manner of consequences for drinkers, their intimates, and the wider society.

Given this, it is not surprising that there should be so much controversy over

---

David Robinson, PhD, Senior Lecturer in Health Studies, Institute for Health Studies, University of Hull, Hull, England.

what is the best or most appropriate or most feasible preventive approach. At heart the disagreement has revolved around differences over the central focus of "the alcohol problem." Some see the alcoholic as the real problem, others see society and the nature of contemporary social life as the problem, while yet others see the problem as alcohol itself.

The aim of this chapter is to set out the three main foci of concern and the associated perspectives on prevention that underpin particular strategies, together with an indication of the main educational and control measures that are usually advocated. Detailed discussion of the nature and efficacy of specific alcohol education and societal control measures can be found elsewhere in this volume.

THE PROBLEM IS ALCOHOLICS

A familiar and widely held view of the alcohol problem is to see it as really a matter of alcoholics. This is a natural outcome of the traditional temperance position, that all alcohol problems are symptoms of a basic condition—alcohol addiction. During the 19th century it was felt that the addiction was inherent in the alcohol and so all drinkers were potential alcoholics. Prohibition was the obvious preventive policy for those who held this view.

During the postprohibition period the notion of alcohol addiction has been retained, but with an important difference. Instead of the addiction being something inherent in the alcohol it is now seen as something inherent in the alcoholic [9]. The view is that some people, for reasons as yet unknown, are susceptible or vulnerable to alcohol addiction. For these people, perhaps 2 or 3% of the population, alcohol causes a whole series of problems over which they have little or no control. They are alcoholics, with the disease of alcoholism, and the only remedy is an individual prohibition, known as abstinence. Alcoholics Anonymous, its philosophy, literature, and self-help process [12], typifies this view, which is widely held by laymen and professionals alike.

According to this perspective there are really two distinct drinking populations: alcoholics and normal drinkers. The former are unable to control their drinking, suffer all kinds of physical, mental, and social damage, and are in need of extensive help, while the latter are people who drink normally, are able to control consumption, and do not get into difficulties.

This way of seeing things is certainly commonsensical, comforting for those who take themselves to be normal drinkers, nicely circumscribed for government departments and helping professionals, and unthreatening to the producers, distributors, and sellers of alcoholic beverages. The Association of Canadian Distillers, for example, put it this way in 1973: "Alcohol and alcoholism are two entirely different subjects—while alcoholism is a major health problem, alcohol is not. Just as sugar is not the cause of diabetes, alcohol is not the cause of alcoholism" [15].

The "two populations" view of the alcohol problem has meant that almost all attention has focused on those people, called alcoholics, who develop over a period of time a collection of alcohol-related problems, such as physical damage of various kinds, trouble with the law, marital and job disharmony, injury, and mental stress. The major effort has been put into the treatment and support of this sick minority of drinkers, the alcohol addicts. As a corollary, the main preventive effort has been secondary prevention: devising ways of getting people to recognize the early signs of alcoholism in themselves and other people.

The most common way of attempting to get people to come forward for treatment or help is to encourage them to ask themselves a number of questions about their drinking and its effects. Alcoholics Anonymous, treatment agencies, newspapers, and other branches of the media have all developed checklists of varying degrees of complexity that are designed to help people to decide whether they have some particular alcohol problem or set of problems; these checklists, in addition, detail what to do, who to contact, or where to go in the event of having checked a sufficient number of warning signs.

The second target for secondary prevention is professionals and other helpers. The aim here is to encourage those who come across people with problems in the course of their work to be more aware of the possible role of alcohol in those problems and to be able to recognize the signs of a potentially harmful drinking pattern. There has been recently an increasing emphasis on the place of alcohol and alcoholism information in the training of many medical, nursing, and social work professionals. Guidelines have been designed to aid health and other helping professionals pick up potential alcoholics from their case loads.

The third target has been specific high-risk groups. Blane [2] suggested, for example, that particular attention should be given to children of alcoholics, delinquents, recurrent absentees, drinking drivers, and students who suffer accidental injury. To this list would be added members of particular occupations that show a consistently higher than average number of people with severe alcohol problems, such as people involved with the production, distribution, or sale of alcohol beverages, members of the armed forces, or commercial travelers.

The success of any kind of secondary prevention, however, depends on there being some facility that can deal with the problem once it is identified, and the willingness of the person with the problem to agree that he or she actually has a problem and to cooperate with those who are available to help.

To those who hold the view that alcoholics are the real problem, any proposal to limit overall alcohol consumption or change overall drinking patterns is likely to be seen as irrelevant, since it would not stop the alcoholic from being addicted and would merely inconvenience the overwhelming majority of the drinking public who are not the problem. Unfortunately, the assumption that there is some as yet unfound underlying disease or physical, biochemical, or personality predisposition that would explain why some people rather than others develop a syndrome of alcohol-related problems is not only unjustified in itself, but gives the unhelpful impression that the remainder, the normal population, is of no great interest because these individuals are not addicted to alcohol.

Much recent research, however, based on general population studies rather than on case studies of the clients of special alcoholism treatment units, has shown that almost any particular alcohol-related problem that alcoholics have is shared by very many people in the wider community. Not only that, but it is also clear that having some particular alcohol problem at one time is only moderately related to having it at another time or with having some other particular alcohol-related problem or set of problems [13].

So, instead of alcoholics constituting almost the sum total of the alcohol problem, the reality is that there are many major alcohol problems and many different populations, which themselves overlap only to a certain extent.

Developing appropriate treatments and methods for the early detection of those who have multiple problems, whether or not such people are called alcoholics or they are taken to be addicted to alcohol, is, of course, a necessary part of any humane response to the overall alcohol problem. But to do so at the expense of a coordinated approach to the prevention of the much greater number of different alcohol problems that affect the wider community is, at best, unsatisfactory.

THE PROBLEM IS SOCIETY

Many people feel that the real root of the alcohol problem lies in the way in which alcohol is used in a society and the meanings that are attached to its use. The focus is on unhealthy drinking and unhealthy attitudes.

The notion of unhealthy drinking covers such things as drinking for effect: to be tough, to solve problems, or to make bearable otherwise difficult relationships or situations. Unhealthy drinking is drinking in situations in which there is a weak system of informal social control, or in situations where the consumption of alcohol is the focal activity rather than the accompaniment to something else. Unhealthy drinking attitudes include the belief that all social occasions must be drinking occasions, that intoxication is something to be tolerated or even encouraged, or that drunkenness is an adequate excuse for otherwise unacceptable behavior.

The aim of prevention is to encourage a more healthy approach to the use and place of alcohol in everyday life. This sociocultural approach to the alcohol problem [16] has grown out of the large body of field research over the past 30 years that has focused on the everyday drinking habits and associated rates of alcohol problems of different national, cultural, ethnic, and religious communities. After reviewing a great deal of this literature, Blacker [1] concludes, "In any group or society in which drinking customs, values, and sanctions . . . are well established, known, and agreed upon by all, consistent with the rest of the culture, and are characterized by prescriptions for moderate drinking and proscriptions against excessive drinking, the rate of alcoholism will be low."

This was the kind of thinking that dominated the 1950s and clearly underpinned reports such as that of the Cooperative Commission on the Study of Alcoholism [10], which suggested that what was needed, in order to stem the rising tide of alcoholism, was a set of national drinking norms to replace the diverse, fragmented, and frequently contradictory set of norms that merely fostered ambiguity, anxiety, and confusion over what proper drinking practices ought to be.

It is certainly true that, in many countries, there is now an increased awareness of the seriousness of a wide range of alcohol problems. Not only that, but ideas about appropriate behavior in relation to drinking are changing too [7], with more and more people agreeing, for example, that alcohol is a drug or that hosts who push drinks on their guests are being irresponsible. This has encouraged those who see positive health education as the main answer to the alcohol problem.

Most school health education programs and mass media campaigns include information on the nature of alcohol and the harm that it can do. Many, in addition, give guidelines for healthy drinking and for encouraging responsibility in others. The second special report to the United States Congress on Alcohol and Health suggests four guidelines for the responsible use of alcohol, as follows:

> Make sure that the use of alcohol improves social relationships, rather than impairing or destroying them.
> Make sure the use of alcohol is an adjunct to an activity rather than being the primary focus of action.
> Make sure alcohol is used carefully in connection with other drugs.
> Make sure human dignity is served by the use of alcohol. [7]

and for encouraging responsible drinking in other people:

> Respect the person who chooses to abstain.
> Respect the person who chooses to drink in moderation; do not be insistent about "refreshing" his drinks or refilling his glass.
> Provide food with alcohol at all times, especially proteins such as dairy products, fish, and meats.
> Provide transportation or overnight accommodations for those unable to drive safely, recognizing that the host is just as responsible for preventing drunken driving as his guests. [7]

While the good sense of these suggestions is undeniable, there is little evidence that health education campaigns have played any significant part in establishing healthy drinking behavior [8].

Those who see society as the root of the alcohol problem have also argued that drinking problems can be reduced by encouraging people to develop healthy drinking practices, such as drinking wine with meals, and, in particular, by integrating the use of alcoholic beverages into a wide variety of social situations, such as sporting events, and by encouraging more congenial drinking places where people would go to meet their friends rather than simply to drink. To encourage all this, proponents also suggest that certain restrictions, such as those on advertising, age of legal consumption, and on the places and hours of sale, should be relaxed, because they are seen as impediments to the adoption of integrated, healthy drinking styles.

This integration philosophy is given support by research on young children, such as that by Davies and Stacey [6], which shows that children begin to learn about alcohol early in life, even before primary school. By the age of 6 a majority recognize the behavioral manifestations of drunkenness, and many are capable of identifying some alcoholic drinks by smell alone; they also perceive people in different roles to like alcohol in different degrees. By the age of 8 most children have attained a mastery of the concept of alcohol and in general the rate at which children acquire a broad understanding in this sphere was greater than researchers anticipated.

In the light of all this, it has become increasingly respectable to give drink to one's young children in order that, from an early age, they may grow up to see drinking as part of family or group activity, to be taken for granted rather than something special, and in general to demystify the whole drinking experience.

In an ideal world, this would be fine. Unfortunately many parents are far too confused and guilty about their own drinking, as the Davies and Stacey study [6] also showed, to transmit anything to their children beyond their own ambivalence. Those who understand this point and yet still put forward a sociocultural approach are forced back on some kind of education campaign outside the family setting. Chafetz [4], for example, who admitted that most campaigns and educational programs had been a complete failure, was forced, by the logic of his own sociocultural position, to propose an educational campaign: "I believe that by providing educational information within a didactic setting and by integrating drinking experience with family use, immunization against unhealthy, irresponsible drinking behavior can be provided as a bulwark against alcoholism."

THE PROBLEM IS ALCOHOL

Alcohol in the 19th century, as was pointed out, was seen to be inherently addictive and, therefore, since all drinkers were potential alcoholics, total prohibition was the obvious preventive measure. Alcohol as the problem has again become a major focus of attention in relation to prevention, particularly over the past decade, but not necessarily with a view to advocating a new prohibition.

The stimulus for this discussion of alcohol per se has been a body of research that has demonstrated that the popular, commensensical distinction between alcoholics and normal drinkers cannot be made on the basis of consumption alone since, graphically speaking, the distribution of alcohol consumption in a community does not produce a large number of people clustered at the low-consumption end of the distribution — normal drinkers — and a hiccup at the high end of the distribution curve caused by that minority of the population — alcoholics. In fact, the distribution of consumption curve appears to be unimodal, smooth and without discontinuities. Furthermore, the general character of the curve appears to be the same across various levels of overall consumption, and in communities with differing drinking patterns and practices [11].

It follows from this, runs the argument, that the proportion of heavy drinkers, at whatever consumption level that is defined, is directly related to the average per capita consumption in that community and factors that alter the latter may be expected to alter the former. In spite of heated debate about the precise mathematical properties of the curve of alcohol consumption [5] those who focus on the alcohol dimension of the alcohol problem conclude that there is, as yet, no way of significantly modifying the prevalence of heavy drinkers in a community without altering the average consumption of all drinkers.

There is increasing evidence, from many parts of the world, that any relaxation of the controls on the overall availability of alcohol consumption leads to an increase in consumption, and any increase in consumption leads to an increase in the number of alcohol-related problems of all kinds in that community. The implications of this are clear: Any realistic preventive policy must attempt to control the availability of alcohol itself [3].

Much attention is being given, therefore, to the regulation of the amount or character of alcohol consumption. Some would control the drinker or the setting in which he or she drinks, while others would control the alcohol itself. The principal regulation measures proposed are those that control the number of places in which alcoholic beverages may be bought, the type and location of outlets, the age at which people may buy and consume alcohol, the hours and days of sale, the alcoholic content of the drink, differential taxation and price control, and state control of production. Of these, the most frequently heard proposal is that of controlling the price of alcohol itself [11].

In the light of the Prohibition experience in the United States, and other examples of drastic controls on liquor availability, it is clear that highly restrictive controls on availability do lead to lower consumption and a reduction in certain major alcohol problems. However, tight control needs political clout and is only likely to be achieved if there is substantial public support — while the controls themselves are apt to involve costs that may be seen to outweigh their benefits. Such costs include resentment of the system by those who consider themselves normal drinkers, an increase in the production of illicit liquor, difficulties of law enforcement, the loss of tax revenues, and the reduction in the personal and social enjoyment that alcohol consumption so clearly provides for large sections of the population.

But, say the proponents of overall consumption control, the possibility of certain costs resulting from drastic controls, like Prohibition, is no reason for rejecting all forms of restraint on alcohol production, availability, or consumption. And certainly, in several countries, serious thought is being given to the possibility of a gradual reduction in overall consumption. The first major step in any such preventive strategy, it is argued, should be for governments to manipulate alcohol duties and taxes in order to ensure that the cost of alcoholic beverages does not continue to decline in real terms, as it has done over the past decade in so many parts of the world.

A COORDINATED APPROACH

Discussion of the prevention of alcohol-related problems has been dominated by arguments in favor of one or the other of the three perspectives presented. Informed debate, as opposed to bland assertion about the relative value or feasibility of alternative approaches, has been conspicuously absent. Evaluative research on particular proposals has been scanty, while comparative research on competing strategies has been nonexistent.

Parochialism, in fact, has been the distinguishing feature of the past 15 years. As Whitehead [16] points out, Wilkinson, who wrote one of the most influential works [18] on the importance of the sociocultural approach (the problem is society), did not make a single reference to the distribution of consumption approach (the problem is alcohol) or even acknowledge that it existed, in spite of having been on the staff of the Addiction Research Foundation, where most of the work along those lines had been conducted over the previous decade.

If any real progress is to be made during the 1980s, then every effort must be put into developing a coordinated approach to the prevention of alcohol problems. Whitehead [16] has taken a useful step along the right road by identifying preventive strategies that conform to the basic principles of one perspective without violating the principles of another. His aim was to identify strategies that increase the integration of drinking practices without significantly changing per capita consumption, or those that reduce per capita consumption without significantly changing the integration of drinking practices, or, ideally, those that simultaneously increase the integration of drinking practices and reduce per capita consumption.

So, instead of repeating the many tired arguments in favor of secondary prevention or the encouragement of healthy drinking practices or the control of overall availability, the real task is to begin the process of constructing an overall preventive strategy that takes into account and interrelates each of these major preventive goals. Once this is taken to be the prime task in the prevention field, the importance of coordination is obvious.

Since there are many alcohol problems with distinctive features and varying degrees of overlap, it is important that particular goals, aims, and strategies are consistent with each other. No problem can be ignored and none can be sloughed off as though it is unique or totally circumscribed. Just as problems overlap with each other, so do preventive strategies, and unless they are coordinated and compatible they will, at best, fail to reinforce and, at worst, undermine or negate one another.

A coordinated approach is not, of course, just a matter of the logic of particular strategies and the intelligent integration of ideas, although both are essential. It also demands the coordination of actions, and thus the cooperation of institutions. As the report of a Special Committee of the Royal College of Psychiatrists [14] put it, "Alcoholism is in many ways a test case for the ability of the administrative structure to tackle a complex problem which crosses orthodox boundaries." It would be difficult to find any major government department whose routine actions do not affect the nature and size of, or response to, the alcohol problem.

Constructing a coordinated approach to prevention, therefore, presents a significant administrative as well as intellectual challenge. Not only that, it presents a challenge to the political will of any community, since the prevention of alcohol problems is an inherently political matter, raising issues of individual freedom, civil and commercial rights, persuasion and coercion, paternalism, intervention, regulation, welfare, and much more besides [17]. As with the prevention of any major social problem, the prevention of the alcohol problem is everybody's business: the drinker, the guest, the host, the helper, and the state. No one is unaffected by the problem; no one is exempt from involvement in its prevention.

REFERENCES

1. Blacker, E. Socio-cultural factors in alcoholism. *Int. Psychiatry Clin.* 3(2):51-80, 1966.

2. Blane, H. T. Trends in the prevention of alcoholism. *Psychiatr. Res. Rep.* 24(1):1968.

3. Bruun, K., Edwards, G., Lumis, M., et al. *Alcohol Control Policies in Public Health Perspective.* Finnish Foundation for Alcohol Studies: Helsinki, 1975.

4. Chafetz, M. E. Prevention of alcoholism in the United States: Utilizing cultural and educational forces. *Prev. Med.* 3:5-10, 1974.

5. Davies, D. L. (ed.). *The Ledermann Curve.* Alcohol Education Centre: London, 1977.

6. Davies, J., and Stacey, B. *Teenagers and Alcohol.* Her Majesty's Stationery Office: London, 1972.

7. Department of Health, Education and Welfare. *Alcohol and Health* (Second special report to the United States Congress). U.S. Government Printing Office: Washington, D.C., 1974.

8. Goodstadt, M. S. Alcohol and drug education: Models and outcomes. In: *Prevention of Alcohol-Related problems*, Meser, J. (ed.). WHO Addiction Research Foundation: Toronto, 1980.

9. Levine, H. G. The discovery of addiction: Changing conceptions of habitual drunkenness in america. *J. Stud. Alcohol* 39(1):143–174, 1978.

10. Plaut, T. F. A. *Alcohol Problems: A Report to the Nation by the Cooperative Commission on the Study of Alcholism*. Oxford University Press: London, 1968.

11. Popham, R. E., Schmidt, W., and de Lint, J. The effects of legal restraint on drinking. In: *Social Aspects of Alcoholism*, Kissen, B. and Begleiter, H., (eds.). Plenum: New York, 1976.

12. Robinson, D. *Talking Out of Alcoholism: The Self-Help Process of Alcoholics Anonymous*. Groom Helm: London, 1979.

13. Room, R. Measurement and distribution of drinking patterns and problems in general populations. In: *Alcohol-Related Disabilities*, Edwards, G., Gross, M. M., Keller, M. et al. (eds.). World Health Organization: Geneva, 1977.

14. Royal College of Psychiatrists. *Alcohol and Alcoholism: Report of a Special Committee*. Tavistock: London, 1979.

15. Schmidt, W. Cirrhosis and alcohol consumption: An epidemiological perspective. In: *Alcoholism: New Knowledge and New Responses*, Edwards, G. and Grant, M. (eds.). Groom Helm: London, 1977.

16. Whitehead, P. C. The prevention of alcoholism: Divergence and convergences of two approaches. *Addict. Dis.* 1:431–443, 1975.

17. Wikler, D. I. Persuasion and coercion for health: Ethical issues in governmental efforts to change life styles. *Milbank Mem. Fund Q.* 56:303–338, 1978.

18. Wilkinson, R. *The Prevention of Drinking Problems: Legal Controls and Cultural Influences*. Oxford University Press: New York, 1970.

37

WALLACE MANDELL, PhD, MPH, The Johns Hopkins University

PREVENTING ALCOHOL-RELATED PROBLEMS AND DEPENDENCIES THROUGH INFORMATION AND EDUCATION PROGRAMS

THE CONTROL OF THE drinking of alcoholic beverages, related behaviors, and attendant illnesses has been a problem for various societies from the beginning of recorded history. Several authors [2, 16, 21, 25, 26, 27] have proposed schema for classifying the wide variety of actions taken by societies and governments to accomplish the control of alcohol-related problems.

All the models of control used by governments have as their goal minimizing the social and health costs of intoxication and drunkenness. Because of minimal investments in relevant research, there is very little evidence available with which to evaluate the effectiveness of most of the individual actions taken by governments to reduce the social costs associated with alcohol use. A few types of governmental actions, such as major price changes for alcoholic beverages, do produce an impact on levels of consumption. This effect seems to be time-limited, lasting only for several years. Extreme governmental actions, such as total prohibition of alcoholic beverages, are followed by major changes in alcohol consumption pat-

---

Wallace Mandell, PhD, MPH, Professor, Department of Mental Hygiene, School of Hygiene and Public Health, The Johns Hopkins University, Baltimore, Maryland.

terns and associated problems. However, prohibition produces a number of major social costs, including decreases in the economy, employment, and tax revenue, and increases in the costs of enforcement, costs that lead to the removal of total prohibition. Other major factors in removal of prohibition are cultural resistance to prohibition and political resistance to the increased police involvement in the control over personal behavior.

Many writers have suggested that governmental actions intended to control alcohol-related problems also reduce the number of individuals who become psychologically or physiologically dependent on alcohol. The physically dependent subset of the population generates disproportionate costs to society in terms of accidents, lost productivity, and health care. No substantial evidence has as yet been presented that governmental regulation of alcoholic beverages is effective in reducing the number of alcohol-dependent individuals in a country.

Polemical writers have polarized public opinion. One camp believes that the highest priority in public efforts should be to develop programs for early identification of alcohol-dependent individuals and to provide treatment. The other camp believes that changing patterns of consumption through education and limiting alcohol availability will decrease the level of societal costs since the bulk of problems are produced by nondependent individuals.

The presentation of these two positions as mutually exclusive has distracted attention from the fact that both the population using alcohol at high per capita levels and the alcohol-dependent population produce great societal costs. Both groups deserve priority in public attention, each requiring an independent plan for public action.

Five models for social control of alcohol-related costs in society are popular under a host of labels, such as the public health model, the social science model, and the like. The labels are not necessarily descriptive of the actions involved in the programs. For this reason in the present chapter these models are descriptively labeled as (1) the prohibition of alcohol model; (2) the regulation of alcohol consumption model; (3) the providing alternatives to alcohol model; (4) the deterrance and treatment model; (5) the information and education model. All of these models have been tried repeatedly and have had limited success because of factors that operate against them.

In the prohibition model, legal coercive controls are used to prohibit manufacture, distribution, and consumption of alcoholic beverages. Factors that operate against long-term maintenance of prohibition include high costs to the economy, costs of enforcement, the instability of ruling groups, the limitations of available means of enforcement, the historic growth of general resistance to coercion, and changes in values as the problems diminish over time.

The regulation model focuses on reducing per capita consumption of alcohol through regulating economic and physical availability of alcohol and the types of alcoholic beverages generally consumed. Factors that operate against this model include governmental incentives to increase tax revenue through sales and the economic benefit to farmers, producers, and distributors of increased consumption.

The alternative model for alcohol control focuses on offering alternative sources of satisfaction to groups or communities that have used alcohol to overcome the effects of social deprivation. Factors that operate against this model include its costliness and community forces that operate against redistribution of power and resources.

The deterrence treatment model for control of alcohol problems involves developing systems for the early identification of individuals who produce social costs, individuals who are then faced with sanctions and incentives to reduce problem behavior. This model has been expanded in recent years to include professionally directed treatment programs to facilitate behavior change. Factors operating against this model include cultural resistance to labeling individuals as alcoholic, the legal difficulties in applying sanctions, and the cost of operating a treatment system.

In the information and education model the information media and the public education system are used to disseminate information about the consequences of using alcohol with the intent of leading to moderate drinking or abstinence. In earlier versions of this model, it was proposed that information would lead to change in attitudes and values. More recent proponents of this general approach have incorporated techniques designed specifically to modify attitudes and behavior. These techniques, which were developed based on research initiated during World War II, include small face-to-face group meetings and other group involvement procedures. Factors operating against this model include the difficulty of accessing mass media and school systems, the high cost of such efforts, the presence of competing information, the lack of technical sophistication in the groups charged with changing behavior, and competing values, including those about the utility of alcohol in facilitating social participation and reducing stresses.

GOALS FOR INFORMATION AND EDUCATION PROGRAMS

An examination of information and education programs for the prevention of alcohol problems begins with an analysis of the goals to be achieved. The two most common goals set are either total abstinence or moderate drinking, sometimes called "responsible drinking." Most countries have difficulty in maintaining a consensus as to which goal is to be achieved. This instability weakens the effectiveness of educational programs.

Public health officials place priorities on prevention activities in terms of the relative amount of death (mortality) and illness (morbidity) produced by a condition. Mortality is produced by alcohol in several ways. Chronic consumption of large quantities of alcohol injures body organs, particularly the liver and the brain. Acute consumption of large quantities of alcohol leads to mortality by alcohol overdose. Acute consumption of a larger than accustomed amount of alcohol also leads to mortality by interfering with psychophysiological functions, resulting either in accidents or in aggressive outbursts.

Morbidity produced by alcohol occurs in several ways. Injuries are sustained by both chronic heavy drinkers and individuals who on a specific occasion consume more than their accustomed amount and more than the norms for safe consumption in this society.

Organ deterioration is produced by chronic consumption of large amounts of alcohol. Liver and gastrointestinal problems are well-known effects. Brain dysfunction at less than psychotic levels is less easily diagnosed and so its prevalence is not known. Disorders of memory and sleep resulting from periodic use have been well substantiated. Vulnerability to convulsive episodes is also increased by alcohol use.

Psychiatric disorders may be exacerbated by acute as well as chronic alcohol consumption. These disorders include outbursts of aggression leading to depression and homicide or suicide.

Dependence on alcohol may itself become a major factor in disrupting the ability to care for one's own health, thereby leading to dietary deficiencies and infectious processes.

Alcohol effects on morbidity and mortality have led to the suggestion that alcoholism and alcohol-related problems should be approached as a matter of public health control techniques.

The rising level of per capita consumption of alcohol and the concomitant increase in associated social and health problems and dependent individuals, particularly in younger age groups, has stimulated public and legislative pressure for prevention action. This has taken concrete form in legislative designation of tax funds for prevention activities. Unfortunately, both media techniques and school instructional techniques have not been developed enough to allow adequate assessment of their potential contribution to prevention programming.

One of the major obstacles to achieving effective prevention programs either at the local or national levels is the lack of a suitable social mechanism for developing policies and programs about alcohol-related problems. From time to time specific agencies may undertake prevention activities related to a specific problem. Some examples are the Federal Highway Traffic Safety Administration's attempt to reduce alcohol-related accidents, health maintenance organizations' attempts to reduce health service costs, or employer attempts to reduce absenteeism and losses in productivity. Only in a few countries [21] have policy-planning commissions been established, which deal with the continuous collection of data about the current situation, probable outcome of trends in consumption, and the assessment of prevention policies and programs as they produce impacts on health, social problems, the economy, and the values of the country.

In the United States, a Cooperative Commission on the Study of Alcoholism was formed in the early 1960s. The report [24] of the commission led to the formation of the National Center for Prevention and Control of Alcoholism within the National Institute of Mental Health. This was followed by the National Institute on Alcohol Abuse and Alcoholism (NIAAA), created in 1970 as part of the federal government's Department of Health, Education and Welfare; the NIAAA was charged with reviewing the impact of alcohol on health. This was a historic step in creating a center for the accumulation of policy-relevant information. However, the information available on the effects of this widely used chemical is still very fragmentary. Biannually a report has been issued, called *Alcohol and Health*, which summarizes the current state of knowledge about the effects of alcohol on physical health.

In practice, prevention activities within the United States rest on the public health model (although it is not always so named). Specific indicators of problems, defined either by health officials or political others, are selected as targets for prevention activities [1, 26, 27, 28]. Specific activities are undertaken to lower the indices of problems. These include three categories of activities: removal or weakening of the noxious agent, alchol; reduction of contact by the population with the agent through regulation of the environment; and increasing host immunity to the effects of contact with the agent through education.

Beginning with Lemmuel Shattuch in 1850, the public health field espoused the view that an educated citizenry would act in their own behalf to decrease the risk of ill health, where patterns of behavior are a significant factor, if they were informed about the consequences of particular actions. Thus from the very beginning the public health field has developed programs based on the notion that information and education could prevent illness by leading to healthy habits. Special educational programs are made necessary by the instability of American society. In more stable societies, alcohol use is strongly influenced by sociocultural factors such as drinking habits, attitudes toward alcoholic intoxication, acceptable levels of consumption, and the integration of minority group life styles within the larger society. In such circumstances cultural and religious institutions are believed to be adequate to keep alcohol consumption within acceptable bounds.

Currently the two most popular types of prevention activities related to alcohol are mass media efforts to improve public information about its effects and youth education efforts to change knowledge, attitudes, and particularly behavior.

CURRENT STATE OF PUBLIC KNOWLEDGE AND ATTITUDES ABOUT ALCOHOL USE, PROBLEMS, AND DEPENDENCE

In four nationwide surveys carried out by Louis Harris and Associates, Inc., 1971 to 1974, with cross-sections of adults 18 years and older, a picture of current American attitudes and knowledge about alcohol emerges [11]. About 66% of the population considers heavy drinking of alcoholic beverages as a serious national problem. Between 6% and 11% of the population spontaneously think of alcoholism as one of the "two or three major problems facing their community today." About 2% to 3% named drinking or alcoholism as a major personal problem. In 1974, 61% of respondents agreed that if a person needs a drink to be social, they have a drinking problem. Alcohol was perceived as a drug by 72% of the respondents. About 67% of the population can correctly select seven out of 11 knowledge items about the effects of alcohol and the causes of alcoholism. Though 66% of the American adult public believe that heavy drinking is a serious problem, significantly 33% does not. And in fact, this 33% may include the younger population, which has a high level of social problems associated with alcohol use, and a small segment of the older population that is experiencing health problems related to alcohol. This evidence suggests that there is room for substantial improvement in general knowledge about alcohol.

Beginning during World War II, an increased research effort was mounted to explore the factors that might make mass media campaigns and school instructional programs more effective in increasing individual and population resistance to problems associated with the use of legally controlled drugs, particularly dependency-addiction. Periods of official enthusiasm for such programatic efforts have alternated with despair about the possibility of producing change in drug use patterns.

Two approaches to improving knowledge and attitudes are currently in vogue, mass media announcements and school-based education. The value of widespread media campaigns to change alcohol consumption patterns has been questioned in recent years. This in part due to the recognition that alcohol consumption has continued to increase despite such efforts. This doubting of effectiveness has had a beneficial effect leading to evaluations of media efforts and to more realistic goal setting. Media and educational campaigns now are directed to specific goals, such as reducing alcohol-related traffic accidents, a short-range detectable effect.

CLASSROOM EDUCATION

Prior to 1970, prevention activities in the United States were directed toward teenagers, reflecting a focus of effort toward individuals beginning their use of alcohol. Currently the targeted age of the groups toward whom prevention is directed has been expanded to include 8- to 11-year-olds, the predrinking group. There are few programs targeted toward adult and elderly populations.

Every state government in the United States mandates education about alcohol in the public schools. Though this is often not carried out, there is a recent upsurge of public support for such efforts. Schapps et al. [29] evaluated the quality of evaluation studies of prevention programs. Their tabulation of 435 studies suggests that the methodologically more rigorous studies report about the same level of positive effect for any program type as do the less rigorous evaluations. However, the more rigorous studies were more likely to report higher levels of negative effects occurring along with positive effects.

The techniques used for changing knowledge about drugs produce effects well within the range of the technologies used by educators for other topics. However, knowledge about drugs is generally uncorrelated with changing attitudes or decreasing drug use [29]. By contrast, in 10 studies of programming techniques to influence affective development and school performance, only one failed to show some positive results in attitude change and behavior [29].

In recent years the NIAAA has placed emphasis on alcohol information in the curriculum, involvement of the target audience in activities designed to change attitudes, and the use of special learning settings to increase educational influence [22]. Illustrating the first approach, the Seattle, Washington, Education Service District 121 has developed an alcohol curriculum that matches alcohol information with the cognitive and affective development of students in various grades. Another approach is illustrated by the Cambridge-Somerville Program for Alcoholism Rehabilitation, which involves training teachers and peer leaders to transmit educational materials. Both programs provide information about the physiological and psychological effects of alcohol and explore beliefs as these may influence alcohol consumption with the goal of promoting responsible decisions about alcohol use. Various activities are also used to promote better management of self. A third model, supported by NIAAA at the University of Massachusetts, is the development of a special alcohol workshop, campus staff training, peer training, and media development tuned to the culture of the particular school.

The data suggest that the earlier classroom technology for influencing attitudes and behavior was inadequate, while newer technologies seem to be effective.

PUBLIC INFORMATION CAMPAIGNS

Public information campaigns designed to eventually reduce alcohol abuse and alcohol-related problems are conducted in the United States by federal and state governments, voluntary agencies, and alcohol-producing industry groups. The campaigns have focused on unacceptable use of alcohol, and problems of drunkenness, health, and safety. Several types of campaigns have been conducted. These include public information campaigns through media announcements, information campaigns in conjunction with community organizing efforts, and attempts to influence the content and portrayal of alcohol use in the entertainment media.

The NIAAA has conducted a campaign to increase responsible drinking and awareness of the consequences of levels of alcohol use, the symptoms of alcoholism, and the availability of successful treatment for the illness. The campaign has been conducted through advertisements. Each advertisement is designed to dispel a cultural stereotype about alcohol and alcoholics. The assumption is made that with more correct information people will be more likely to choose to not drink or to drink responsibly.

The National Highway Safety Administration (NHISA) has had a program, begun in 1970, to reduce highway fatalities by reducing excessive drinking by individuals before they drive. One group of frequently drinking drivers defined as problem drinkers is particularly targeted for efforts to decrease their involvement in accidents. This aspect of the campaign is intended to increase strict law enforcement to get the problem drinker off the road.

The National Council on Alcoholism has campaigned to heighten awareness of the nature of alcoholism and the availability of treatment. The National Congress of Parents and Teachers has focused on primary prevention with school-aged individuals. The liquor industry has fielded several campaigns that stress moderate and responsible use of alcohol.

There have been very few evaluations of public education campaigns carried out before 1975 and these findings are difficult to interpret. Haskins [12] pointed out that most research was of poor design, without control groups, and relied on verbal measures of effects. In addition, the range of media strategies examined was very limited, focusing mostly on fear-inducing or threatening messages. Most evaluations of media efforts occur within historical contexts in which confounding variables such as changes in law or law enforcement coincide with the campaign. This makes it impossible to evaluate the independent contribution of the mass media effort. Wilde [34] and Kinder [15] both conclude that it is not possible to evaluate mass media effects on behavior. Blane [2] found the available evidence up to that time not encouraging. Blane and Hewitt [3] report that most often the effects of general campaigns are to increase knowledge without producing change in attitudes or behavior.

Authors such as Room [27] propose that campaigns to reduce specific problems associated with alcohol use might be more effective. The National Highway Safety Administration has undertaken the largest effort working toward such a single objective. Zador [35] found that casualties declined during the Alcohol Safety Action Project carried out in more than 20 United States communities. However, this occured in control as well as experimental cities. Cameron [6] has found that information strategies have not been noticeably effective in reducing drunk driving or crashes.

Whitehead [33], in reviewing five media campaigns, found that they produced only a modest increase in public awareness of the campaign, ranging from 16% to 24%.

It is not clear whether the lack of effectiveness in alcohol campaigns is the result of technically inadequate campaigns, countervailing forces in society, or lack of effective institutional arrangements to support the development of public information-prevention programs. The most extensive research on the effects of such campaigns has been done on cigarette smoking. The use of cigarettes also involves a legally obtainable, dependency-producing substance. Governmental and voluntary organizations have carried out many campaigns intended to reduce cigarette use. The new approach taken to producing attitude and behavior change is the multipronged effort developed for anticigarette smoking campaigns.

Warner [32] has used a regression analysis model to estimate the effects of such campaigns on per capita cigarette smoking in the United States during the period 1947 to 1980. The method involves correlating the observed annual percapita cigarette consumption with variables that are proposed as potentially accounting for the observed trend. Using a least squares regression, a statistically significant equation was developed that could account for 97% of the variance using the following variables: the per capita consumption in the preceding year; the increase in smoking-age population; the antismoking campaigns as represented by the year in which they occured; the percentage of the population in states that restrict smoking in public places; and the relative real price of cigarettes indexed to the year 1967.

Warner projected the per capita consumption trend during this period, all influences taken into account, and then examined the observed decrease in per capita consumption from the projected use pattern.

There has been about 1% per year decrease in per capita consumption of cigarettes since 1973. This has occured in the context of two of the highest authorities, the Surgeon General and the Supreme Court, endorsing the position that cigarettes have ill effects, followed by local laws prohibiting smoking in public places. This occured in a context of declining real prices of cigarettes.

Relative real price of cigarettes and prohibition of public smoking each account for a small but statistically significant proportion of the per capita use. Most interesting is the fact that in five of each of the 6 years in which there was an antismoking educational campaign, there was a statistically significant decrease in per capita consumption.

Warner estimates that the smoking campaigns by 1978 were contributing to 36% of the annual reduction in smoking.

As in all post hoc correlational studies, the interpretation of causality is open to question. The observed associations may be the result of other factors. For instance, the decrease in per capita consumption occured during a period of change in composition of the population — for example, the proportion of older adults increased markedly and there was a general upsurge in interest in health. Warner attributes a large part of the decrease, 21%, to the prohibition of smoking in public places and to the campaigns, 36%, rather than to the influence of public health officials' actions, such as the Surgeon General's report of 1964. The action of the Supreme Court, which held that smoking in enclosed environments was a danger to others, also occurred during the period of decreasing per capita use.

If this model holds, it seems reasonable to expect that a campaign might produce between .3% to 1% annual reduction in per capita consumption. This may be a lot or too little, considering the urgency of the problem and alternative methods of producing the effect.

A second approach to improving educational campaigns involves linking them to face-to-face behavior change efforts. Maccoby et al. [19] reported on the test of a prevention program intended to reduce risk of disease by producing changes in behavior including cigarette smoking, intake of calories, salt, sugar, fat, and cholesterol. A multimedia campaign was directed at the Northern California community of Gilroy, while a similar city, Tracy, was used as the control, in part because of its media isolation. A systematic probability sample of adults aged 35 to 59 was surveyed in 1972 before the campaign and again in 1973 and 1974. The mass media were able to produce stable gains in knowledge measured by a 25-item test of 18% the first year and 25% the second. A sample from a third community, Watsonville, which had also received the media campaign, was provided with intensive face-to-face instruction for high-risk subjects. Individuals who received both the media and face-to-face interventions increased in knowledge by 54% the first year and remained at this level of improvement the second year. Within Watsonville a subsample of high-risk subjects who had only received the mass media campaign gained significantly more information than the high-risk group in Gilroy, where no part of the community received intensive instruction. The data indicated that the mass media campaign was effective and was made more effective where some part of the community was receiving face-to-face instruction. Those individuals receiving both interventions, of course, did best.

The findings on immediate behavioral change, such as diet and cigarette smoking, follows the pattern of change in knowledge. Particularly relevant is the 42% reduction in number of cigarettes smoked after the 2-year campaign with intensive instruction among both general and high-risk subjects in Watsonville. There was no significant difference in cigarette smoking in high-risk subjects with just the campaign in any of the other communities

These findings support the author's hypothesis that campaigns may be differentially effective for different segments of the population. Thus the high-risk individuals were more likely to change behavior with individualized attention, whereas such subjects did not change behavior with media-only campaigns even though their knowledge changed significantly.

The effects of the campaign were enduring, but not equally so for all targeted behaviors. The follow-up at 3 years [20] found that in dietary control (measured by blood tryglyceride levels) the media campaign was as successful as the intensive instruction. On the other hand, for cigarette smoking measured either by number of smokers or average number of cigarettes consumed, intensive intervention was able to sustain a 50% reduction during the 3-year period. It is not clear from this study which element, campaign or face-to-face education, produced the effect.

This study is of such significance that it has been subjected to a number of critiques. Leventhal et al. [17], reviewing the study, suggest that the measurement procedure may have produced some of the effect and that some of the observed difference may be due to differential loss from experimental and control groups. However, the observed difference is really much larger than could be accounted for by methodological artifacts.

The research evidence suggests that media campaigns, bolstered by public leaders and laws or by face-to-face activities, can produce an impact on levels of use of cigarettes. Such effects have not been demonstrated in relation to alcohol use.

ADVERTISING COUNTERACTING INFORMATION EFFORTS

Mass media information campaigns take place in a context of mass media advertising by alcohol producers and distributors to influence consumption patterns.

The goal of alcohol advertising is to gain the largest net profit [5]. The goal of advertising by any individual company is to increase its share of the market. This may be by motivating change in preference among established consumers or among new and potential consumers. The effect of advertising by an industry as a whole produces the appearance of public endorsement of the use of that category of product. Since 1955 in the United States [18] advertising expenditures for alcohol beverages have increased in parallel with per capita consumption.

From the advertising point of view, sales are encouraged more by capturing the loyalty of heavy consumers of alcohol [14], since a small portion of the total population of drinkers consume the most part of the alcohol sold in the United States [13, 27]. The small population of heavy drinkers, 15%, those who drink more than 2 drinks a day, consume approximately 74% of the alcohol sold. Actually 6% of drinkers consume 41% of all alcoholic beverages.

The overall effect of industry advertising in increasing the total market for liquor has been studied, but the evidence is inconclusive. Ogborne and Smart [23], evaluating the effects of restricting beer advertisements in Manitoba in 1974, using a time series analysis of per capita beer consumption between 1970 and 1978, showed no effect of restriction of advertising. Simon [30, 31] believes that it requires very large changes in advertising expenditures to produce a change in the total market. However, as Blane and Hewitt [4] point out, advertising may serve to maintain consumption levels.

Under current circumstances it is unlikely that the contribution of advertising to consumption levels will ever be assessed experimentally. Statistical studies comparable to those done in the cigarette smoking area have yet to be carried out. Important factors, such as the drinking population, the proportion of the population residing where it is legal to consume alcohol for relevant age groups, and the income available to age-specific segments of the population, have not been studied.

Some evidence of association between advertising and consumption is available. During 1978 the alcoholic beverage industry responded to declining profitability by a sharp increase in advertising expenditures averaging about 33% over the 1977 expenditures for the distilled spirits industry, 54% for the wine industry, and 29% for the beer industry. In 1978, the distilled spirits industry increased its sales by 0.02 gallons of ethanol per capita, the same as the year before; wine, 0.02 gallons per capita, twice the increase of the previous year; and beer, 0.04 gallons per capita, about the same as the year before. It is not possible to make definitive interpretations of a single year's data. However, taking into account the population base, there was an increase in per capita alcohol consumption with a considerable advantage for the wine industry associated with its proportional increase in expenditure.

A major factor previously not taken into account in evaluating information campaigns is that of countermessages delivered by the media. An important study by Hanneman and McEwan [10] selected 2-week-long periods in 1973 to examine mass media content in the Hartford, Connecticut metropolitan area for information related to drugs and alcohol. During the period of 1 week, about 1 minute of public service TV announcement time (compared to 80 hours of prime time) was devoted to alcohol, warning about driving after drinking alcoholic beverages. No message was delivered in print. In contrast, 20 minutes were devoted to alcohol-related advertising in the best broadcast time. In addition, 29 minutes of advertising for headache remedies and 29 minutes of advertising for other pharmaceutical agents appeared in prime time. In printed media, 34 pages of alcohol advertisements appeared.

In TV programming there was at least one depiction of alcohol in every 2 hours of comedy-variety shows and a bit more in drama shows. In over 50% of the depictions, alcohol was being accepted or used accompanied by some discussion of its use and its benefits. Thus the net effects of media communication is to support alcohol and drug use.

In 1975 Garlington [8] found an average of 3 occasions of use of alcohol an hour in 14 different soap operas. Drinking usually took place in drinking scenes. Dillin [7] reported in the *Christian Science Monitor* that in an analysis of 66 hours of prime time between 8 and 11 P.M., there were on an average 3 alcohol-use incidents an hour. Greenberg et al. [9] examined network-produced fictional shows for 1 week, sampling 80 different shows. In the 1976-77 season, there was an hourly rate of 2.19 alcohol incidents. In contrast, cigarette usage declined from 0.7 incidents an hour to 0.48 an hour. Using projected amounts from other studies, a child could observe 3,000 incidents of alcohol use a year.

It is plausible that information and education campaigns are counteracted by the large-scale advertising efforts of the alcohol production and distribution industry. One of the efforts to overcome advertising effects has been to require warning labels on beverage containers and in advertising. On November 17, 1977, Dr. Donald Kennedy, Commissioner of the Food and Drug Administration, requested that the Bureau of Alcohol, Tobacco, and Firearms (BATF) of the United

States Treasury Department require that all alcoholic beverage containers carry a warning label about the fetal alcohol syndrome. This action was necessary because a federal judge in Bourbon County, Kentucky, ruled that the BATF had exclusive jurisdiction over the matter.

In 1979, Senator Strom Thurmond (Republican, South Carolina), for the fifth time, introduced a bill to require warning labels on alcoholic beverages containing over 24% alcohol. The bill was passed by the Senate. To obtain House of Representative approval, the bill was revised to call for a study of the basis for labeling to be completed by June 1, 1980. No warning labels have as yet been required on alcoholic beverages.

The state of Utah has approved a bill mandating that each place dispensing alcoholic beverages post a sign warning of health hazards associated with alcohol use. No evaluation of the effects of the labeling approach has been carried out.

It seems reasonable to conclude that at this time advertising adds to the mass media's overwhelming communication of the acceptability of alcohol consumption.

SUMMARY

There are currently five models of how the prevention of alcohol-related problem costs to society should be undertaken. Of these, the information and education model has had continuing popular and political appeal. In the mid-1970s, about 33% of the American population was relatively uninformed about the effects of alcohol and the causes of alcoholism. Evaluative studies of the effects of traditional information and education programs have consistently shown little or no effect in producing attitude and behavior change in use of alcohol beverages. This may be because of ineffective technology. Analysis of mass media content indicates that the predominant message that reaches the public is that alcohol use is an acceptable part of American life. One study of large-scale efforts to reduce cigarette smoking indicates that modest but significant effects of 1 to 2% a year can be achieved when national leaders, the law, and information and education programs are operating in unison. Another important study indicated that cigarette smoking could be reduced by a combination of a media campaign with face-to-face supportive educational procedures. The NIAAA is supporting research on analogous approaches directed toward younger populations. At present there is no mechanism for achieving consensus on prevention goals. There is also a scarcity of evaluative research on which techniques of information and education are more effective in producing behavior change. These factors are major obstacles in developing effective information and education programs for the prevention of alcohol problems.

REFERENCES

1. Aarens, M., Cameron, T., Roizen, J., Roizen, R., Room, R., Schneberk, D., and Winegard, D. *Alcohol, casualties and crime* (Final report: NIAAA Contract ADM-281-76-0027). Social Research Group, University of California: Berkeley, 1977.
2. Blane, H. T. Education and the prevention of alcoholism. In: *The Biology of Alcoholism: Social Aspects of Alcohol* (Vol. 4), Kissen, B. and Begleiter, H. (eds.). Plenum: New York, 1976.
3. Blane, H. T., and Hewitt, L. E. *Mass Media, Public Education and Alcohol: A State of the Art Review*. National Institute on Alchol Abuse and Alcoholism: Rockville, Md., 1977.
4. Blane, H. T., and Hewitt, L. E. Alcohol public education and the mass media: An overview. *Alcohol Health Res. World* 5:2-14, 1980.
5. Bretzfield, H. *Liquor Marketing and Liquor Advertising*. Abelard-Schuman: New York, 1955.
6. Cameron, T. *The Impact of Drinking-Driving Countermeasures: A Review and Evaluation* (Working paper F-81). Social Research Group, Berkeley, Calif.: 1978.
7. Dillin, J. TV continues to emphasize liquor. *Christian Science Monitor* December 26, 1975.
8. Garlington, W. Drinking on television: A preliminary study with emphasis on method. *J. Stud. Alcohol* 38:2199-2205, 1977.
9. Greenberg, B. S. Fernande-Collado, Graef, D., Korzenny, F., and Atkin, C. K. Trends in the use of alcohol and other substances on television. *The Bottom Line* 3:11-16, 1979.
10. Hanneman, G. J., and McEwen, W. J. The use and abuse of drugs: An analysis of mass media content. In: *Communication Research and Drug Education*, Astman, R. (ed.). Sage Publications: Beverly Hills, Calif., 1976.
11. Harris, L. and Associates, Inc. *Public Awareness of the NIAAA Advertising Campaign and Public Attitudes toward Drinking and Alcohol Abuse* (Four studies, 1971-74); reports prepared for the National Institute on Alcohol Abuse and Alcoholism). Author: New York, 1974.
12. Haskins, J. B. Effects of safety communication campaigns: A review of the research evidence. *J. Safety Res.* 1:58, 1969.
13. Hyman, M. H. The Ledermann curve. *J. Stud. Alcohol* 40:339-347, 1979.
14. Key, W. B. *Media Sexploitation*. Prentice-Hall: Englewood Cliffs, N.J., 1976.
15. Kinder, B. N. Attitudes toward alcohol and drug abuse: II. Experimental data, mass media research and methodological considerations. *Int. J. Addict.* 10:1035, 1975.
16. Lemert, E. Alcohol, values and social control. In: *Society, Culture and Drinking Patterns*, Pittman, D. and Snyder, C. (eds.). Wiley: New York, 1962.
17. Leventhal, A., Safer, M. A., Cleary, P. B., and Gutman, M. Cardiovascular risk modification by the community-based programs for life style change: Comments on the Stanford study. *J. Consult. Clin. Psychol.* 48:152-158, 1980.
18. *The Liquor Handbook*. Gayin-Jobson: New York, 1975.
19. Maccoby, N., Farquhar, J. W., Wood, P. D., and Alexander, J. Reducing the risk of cardiovascular disease: Effects of community-based campaign on knowledge and behavior. *J. Commun. Health* 3:100-114, 1977.
20. Meyer, A. J., Nash, J. D., McAlister, A. L., Maccoby, N., and Farquhar, V. K. Skills training in a cardiovascular health education campaign. *J. Consult. Clin. Psychol.* 48:129-142, 1980.
21. Moser, J. *Prevention of Alcohol Related Problems: An International Review of Pre-*

ventive Measures, Policies and Programmes. Alcoholism and Drug Addiction Research Foundation: Toronto, 1981.

22. National Institute on Alcohol Abuse and Alcoholism. *Prevention X Three: Alcohol Education for Youth*. National Clearinghouse for Alcohol Information: Rockville, Md., 1980.

23. Ogborne, A. C., and Smart, R. Will restrictions on alcohol advertising reduce alcohol consumption? *Br. J. Addict.* 75:293-296, 1980.

24. Plaut, T. F. A. *Alcohol Problems: A Report on the Nation*. Oxford University Press: New York, 1967.

25. Popham, R. E., Schmidt, W., and Delint, J. Effects of legal restraint on drinking. In: *The Biology of Alcoholism: Social Aspects of Alcoholism* (Vol. 4), Kissen, B. and Begleiter, H. (eds.). Plenum: New York, 1976.

26. Room, R. *Areas for Development in NIAAA Prevention Programs*. Social Research Group, University of California: Berkeley, 1977.

27. Room, R. Measurement and distribution of drinking patterns and problems in general population. In: *Alcohol-related Disabilities* (Offset Publication No. 32), Edwards, G., Gross, M. M., Keller, J., Moser, J., and Room, R. (eds.). World Health Organization: Geneva, 1977.

28. Room, R. *The Prevention of Alcohol Problems*. Social Research Group, University of California: Berkeley, 1977.

29. Schaps, E., Churgin, S., and Palley, C. Primary prevention research: A preliminary review of program outcome studies. *Int. J. Addict.* 15(5):657-676, 1980.

30. Simon, J. L. *The Management of Advertising*. Prentice-Hall: Englewood Clitts, N.J., 1971.

31. Simon, J. L. *Issues on the Economics of Advertising*. University of Illinois: Urbana, 1979.

32. Warner, K. E., Cigarette smoking in the 1970s: The Impact of the anti-smoking campaign on consumption. *Science* 211:729-731, 1981.

33. Whitehead, P. *Public Policy and Alcohol-Related Damage: Media Campaigns or Social Controls*. Pergamon: New York, 1979.

34. Wilde, G. J. Evaluation of effectiveness of public education and information programmes related to alcohol, drugs, and traffic safety. In: *Alcohol, Drugs, and Traffic Safety*, Israelstam, S. and Lanbert, S. (eds.). Addiction Research Foundation: Toronto, 1975.

35. Zador, P. Statistical evaluation of the effectiveness of "alcohol safety action projects." *Accident Anal. Preven.* 8:51-66, 1976.

38

MORRIS E. CHAFETZ, MD, Health Education Foundation, Washington, D.C.

SAFE AND HEALTHY DRINKING

PEOPLE IN SOCIETIES troubled with alcohol problems are implicitly or explicitly uncomfortable about their use of alcohol. Feelings of ambivalence, conflict, guilt, and confusion usually coexist about the place of alcohol in one's life. Furthermore, there is ascribed to alcohol a special, magical quality that places it in a focus of undeserved prominence. The purpose of this chapter is to put into perspective a frame of reference for safe and healthy drinking.

CAVEAT

No chapter on safe and healthy drinking can be written without a caveat at its outset. Scientific steps examining safe drinking levels are discrete endeavors demanding duplication and repetition before conclusions are warranted. The conclusions of scientific findings require interpretation and judgment about the application of this knowledge. Science in whatever certainty it achieves respects the rights of people to add their own interpretations and decisions, and to accept their own risks. Ideally decisions about these risks will be based on the best avail-

---

Morris E. Chafetz, MD, President, Health Education Foundation, Washington, D.C., and Senior Psychiatrist, Fenwick Hall, Johns Island, Charleston, South Carolina.

able knowledge, and caution requires pointing out the limitations of applying broad findings (conclusions) from statistical populations to the process of decision making by an individual.

Not for Everyone

Although recent scientific evidence gathered from population samples confirms that moderate drinkers live longer and have fewer heart attacks than those who drink heavily or those who abstain, it would be a gross and perhaps fatal error to suggest that ex-drinkers or abstainers begin to drink again. The complexities of personal decision making are such that a scientific finding should not hold larger sway over individual experience, ethics, health values, and moral issues.

PHYSICAL FACTORS

The Drug

Most people do not know that alcohol is an anesthetic drug. The use of any pharmacologic agent without understanding its properties may result in unhealthy and unsafe practices. Although moderate amounts of alcohol produce the indirect effects of stimulation, the cause of these pseudoeffects is the alcohol-induced sedation of brain centers that control uninhibited behavior and feelings. Many other sources of stimuli, such as messages relating to exhaustion, are also depressed. For these reasons alcohol can make one feel stronger physically and freer emotionally. Heavy doses of alcohol put to sleep other centers affecting judgment and motor functions, and with enough alcohol those centers that regulate breathing and heartbeat can be put to sleep permanently.

Time, Place, and Circumstance

To drink safely and healthily, the time, place, and circumstance are important factors that must be chosen with care. An obvious, responsible question asks, "Will this activity be impaired by a given dose of an anesthetic drug?" Highly complex mental and physical activities are performed best with the highest acuity of mind and nervous system. If, on the other hand, the activity consists of a relaxed sharing of a meal or other human interchange, alcohol can be a gentle fellow traveler to the quintessential human experience of socializing.

The Amount

A second essential point regarding alcohol usage is the known safe level of amount. As was reported in the Second Report to the Congress on Alcohol and Health [1], the equivalent of 1.5 oz of absolute alcohol a day was determined as the safe or moderate use of alcohol. The 1.5 oz of absolute alcohol translates into everyday measurements of three 1 oz drinks of 100 proof whiskey (which should be drunk diluted), or four 8 oz glasses of beer, or one-half bottle of table wine.

Anstie's law. The safe limit supported by recent scientific corroboration as reported to the Congress of the United States was the reaffirmation of *Anstie's Law of Safe Drinking*, published in 1862 by Sir Francis Anstie, a British psychiatrist [2]. Anstie's limit is an upper limit, a statistical average not applicable to all individuals. For some people, one drop of alcohol is a drop too much. Furthermore, one day's unused ration cannot be added onto that for the next day.

Alcohol and driving. Statistical studies show that the driver who consumes a moderate amount of alcohol within Anstie's law is no more likely to suffer an automobile accident than a driver who takes no alcohol. Statistics reveal no difference in the incidence of traffic accidents between people who do not drink and moderate drinkers.

The Manner

Beyond amount, the manner of drinking is crucial. Alcohol should always be sipped slowly because of its highly unusual action in the body. In contrast to other materials ingested, 20% of alcohol is absorbed directly from the stomach into the blood stream without undergoing digestive processes. With gulping, for example, a sudden, marked rise of the blood alcohol level overwhelms the system, causing an exaggerated response to a given dose. This exaggerated response to a given dose. This exaggerated response can lead to fatalities when a person chugalugs a pint of whiskey.

Rate control. An individual's ability to control the amount of alcohol drunk can be exercised only by controlling the rate at which it goes into the blood stream. Alcohol in the blood stream cannot be cleared any faster than by the natural action of the body's own steady metabolic rate of .75 oz of absolute alcohol an hour. A healthy adult sipping an alcoholic drink (which usually contains .75 oz of absolute alcohol) can metabolize it in about an hour.

Food and rate. Along with sipping, food in the stomach will control the rate of absorption. Protein or fatty foods eaten before taking an alcoholic drink will help assure benefits without unpleasantness. Food delays alcohol's natural tendency to rush into the blood stream and brain. Any experienced drinker knows the difference, all things being equal, between the effects from a dose of alcohol taken with food in the stomach from a dose taken on an empty stomach.

PSYCHOLOGICAL FACTORS

Expectations

Regardless of how one drinks and where one drinks, what is expected from alcohol is what results. With alcohol, as with all drugs, expectation is strongly related to outcome.

Loneliness and Solace

Alcohol is better not taken when one is emotionally upset, lonely, or in need of solace. Alcohol solves no problems, nor is it a substitute for another person. Although it is true that alcohol's easy anesthetic effect will dull the pain of loneliness, it will not permit one to transcend the straitjacket of reality. Flights of fancy and enthusiasm are better experienced when shared with at least one other human being.

Meaning

Psychologically, the significance of taking alcohol has different meanings in different contexts. For example, Americans drink to celebrate their independence and individuality and to prove something. This pastime encourages a focus on prowess, on how much one can hold. The Chinese, on the other hand, drink to celebrate their mutual interdependence. As they sip alcohol, savoring each drop, they revel in the strength each person can lend to another. Alcohol used as an adjunct to social behavior and in celebration of human interdependence is a safe and healthy psychological practice.

Setting

The setting of the drinking experience is important. A setting of relaxation is desirable and conducive to safe drinking. Standing in a crush of people is not a particularly comfortable way to drink, nor is drinking in dark, secluded places that invite uncontrolled drinking.

The cocktail party. For example, the drinking done around a table laden with good food and drink in an atmosphere conducive to good talk and amiability is in contrast to the kind of drinking done at a cocktail party. The former is a way to share and celebrate the essence of human, social, and psychological intercourse, with alcohol an adjunct to the activity, whereas the latter is a pressured, unrelaxed setting that promotes a tendency to gulp drinks.* Even by its name and setting, the focus on drinking as a purpose of the cocktail party is generally assumed by those attending. As gibberish flows, so does the alcohol—often consumed in greater amounts than intended, unrelated to any substantial intake of food, unrelated to conversation, and unrelated to social intercourse.

The bar. The effects of setting can be reflected in the design of a drinking establishment. Dark, dingy bars with isolated booths are more likely to produce excessive drinking than a setting with a well-lit, circular bar where people have no choice but to face each other and talk with one another.

Business. The use of alcohol in order to function in business or professional

---

*This point and many other points in this chapter are discussed in greater detail in Chafetz [3].

life is a serious matter. Alcohol taken as a component necessary to accomplish one's work places it in an unsafe arena of importance. People who cannot manage their work without this anesthetic agent are courting addiction and its potential dangers.

SOCIAL FACTORS

There is no question that psychological factors overlap with social implications, and the dividing line between the two is hazy. For the purposes of this chapter, the term "social factors" refers to the environment of people surrounding the individual.

Expectation

Just as the individual's expectations are strongly related to outcome, so will the surrounding society's expectations and tolerance determine the response—irrespective of dose. If one is part of a group whose expectations are to act drunk, then even with small doses one will feel drunk. The code of safe drinking involves more than the response of an individual to a given dose. It requires the willingness of individuals who share the immediate environment to take responsibility for setting expectations that are socially useful and not destructive.

Limits

Most people behave in a socially acceptable fashion not because of rules, regulations, and laws, but because of the hunger for affection and respect from a few individuals in the personal milieu. The limits of what these individuals will or will not tolerate as acceptable behavior are quickly transmitted. If one cares to continue the relationship, the implied bounds are not transgressed. It becomes increasingly clear, therefore, in the development of a code of safe and healthy drinking, that if someone in their environment misuses alcohol, beyond offering compassion to the troubled person, individuals should ask themselves if they contributed in any way to that misuse.

Images

Four images about alcohol use are portrayed in story and advertisement: alcohol as a reward for a day's work; alcohol as a goal for which to aim in and of itself; alcohol as a proof of sophistication and worldliness; and alcohol as a cause of laughable behavior when misused.

Drunkenness. Laughing at someone who is drunk gives intoxication social sanction. But getting drunk means one has overdosed with a drug, lost control over physical and emotional facilities. In societies that use alcohol and have no major problems with it, drunkenness is not sanctioned. Therefore, a tangible guideline for safe drinking is offered: Take all caution to avoid circumstances conducive to excessive or irresponsible use of alcohol by drinking companions.

Test of Comfort

A simple test of one's own attitudes toward alcohol is exemplified by the response to people who choose not to drink. People who choose not to use the drug alcohol make an excellent guide for gauging a drinker's comfort with his or her personal use of alcohol: Is the drinker uptight around people who choose not to drink or more comfortable with people who are drinking? In the safe context of drinking people should not be uncomfortable in the presence of nondrinkers as they would not be discomforted by a person who chose not to eat spinach with them.

ALCOHOL EDUCATION

The importance of the role of education in safe and healthy drinking is obvious. But it is not the intent of this chapter to talk about educational institutions. Education here refers to what is taught to children about alcohol in everyday life. Even toddlers absorb knowledge about alcohol in varied and sundry ways. Their perceptive eyes note the different way their parents and other grownups behave after they drink alcohol. What makes this liquid even more special is the forbidden fruit aspect of its usage. Children imitate and identify with the adult world that surrounds and protects them, and when they naturally ask for a taste, a refusal implies that it is bad for them. The hypocrisy of this kind of educational exercise is reinforced in the way everyday items like clothing, events, parties, and songs relate to alcohol. Ad agencies closely identify sex and sophistication with the use of alcohol. It stands to reason that children quickly pick up these signals. This kind of education practiced in the public forum is an everyday part of children's learning experiences. Hence, a parent's sensible guidance and responsible behavior with alcohol is the best teacher.

SUMMARY

The safe and healthy use of alcohol does not relate to the amount alone — even though the expressed safe statistical limit is that amount in Anstie's law. For most people, observing this limit will preclude the health hazards common to the misuse of alcohol. People who go beyond this limit will not necessarily develop problems — though they will surely increase their risk. One must remember that anything that affects human beings has a potential for harm. Knowledge of safe parameters can help people in making decisions about risk-taking, such as choosing to drink or not to drink, how much, where, and with whom. Being sensitive to the vicissitudes of responses to alcohol in oneself and in those with whom one drinks — while applying a knowledge of alcohol's action — is a sure way to safe and healthy drinking.

REFERENCES

1. Alcohol and Health — New Knowledge (The Second Special Report to Congress). National Institute on Alcohol Abuse and Alcoholism: Washington, D. C., June 1974.
2. Anstie, F. *Stimulants and Narcotics, Their Mutual Relations; with Special Researches on the Action of Alcohol, Aether, and Chloroform on the Vital Organism.* Macmillan: London, 1864.
3. Chafetz, M. E. *Why Drinking Can Be Good for You.* Stein & Day: Briarcliff Manor, N.Y., 1976.

39

E. MANSELL PATTISON, MD, Medical College of Georgia, Augusta, Georgia

ALCOHOL USE: SOCIAL POLICY

THE USE OF ALCOHOL has been described in most societies since the beginning of written human history. Concomitant with such use have been implicit social codes that both prescribed and proscribed patterns of use and patterns of behavior. In preliterate societies, such social policy was written in the hearts of men, which was as strong and obdurate a social policy as any written on parchment and encoded in statutes. In fact, such unwritten social policies may be the most sensible, suasive, and effective social policies created. In literate societies, the development of written social policy increased commensurate with the complexity of social structure. With the advent of the Western Industrial Revolution, which created dense urban enclaves of socially disaffiliated people, the effectiveness of unwritten social policy was undermined. Social policy "writ in the heart" is dependent upon face-to-face affiliative social exchange. It is not surprising that the first major waves of written social policy to regulate alcohol use appeared in the 18th century, hard on the heels of Western industrialization and urbanization. The history of social policy since has been checkered by fear, failure, and futility. Social policy has wobbled wildly between stringent regulation to the point of total prohibition and laissez-faire permissiveness with utter laxity. Thus far, civilized man has failed to create effective social policy, whereas primitive man was relatively successful in doing so.

E. Mansell Pattison, MD, Professor and Chairman, Department of Psychiatry, Medical College of Georgia, Augusta, Georgia.

A simple comparison of preliterate versus literate societies will not do, however. First, preliterate societies had the advantage of effective social communication, social consensus, and social control embedded in multilinkages of relatively small face-to-face groups. In one sense, family was community, community was society, and society was culture, creating a compressed and intimate life space. In contrast, Western literate peoples live in nuclear families, loosely tied to vague and ambiguous communities, which are pluralistic segments of subsocietal units, which make up amorphous culture. These individuals live in a seemingly infinite space of thinly discerned loose connections. Second, preliterate societies often had one form of intoxicant, so that social policy addressed one substance and one form thereof, whereas literate technological society is producing myriad forms of alcohol. Thus no single social policy can pertain to all. Third, the adverse social consequences in preliterate society were limited in terms of technological additives to intoxication. In comparison, in modern technological society, the potential consequences of drinking are magnified by adding guns, cars, glass, and iron, which increase the potential lethality to self and others; at the same time complex living and working task, spatial and time arrangements can be easily disrupted by small aberrations consequent to drinking. Fourth, in preliterate societies there was relative integration of all spheres of life, so that work, play, family life, social relations, communal ceremony and ritual, and religious belief and practice were intertwined in a coherent matrix. Within this matrix the use of alcohol was fit into place; in modern Western societies the domains of life have been fragmented into isolated spheres. Work is not play; family life is not religious; and there are no compelling ceremonials and rituals to symbolically unite people in reaffirmation of common goals and commitments. In such anomic, compartmentalized, and fragmented life spheres, the use of alcohol is likely to become still another compartment isolated from all other life spheres, and hence highly impervious to social policy aimed at just the single social compartment of alcohol use.

One might rightly ask, "Why attempt to develop social policy at all, given such a set of improbable obstacles?" The answer would be negative if the production of alcohol were a trivial cost, and if the consequences of alcohol use were trivial. However, the raw materials cost of production is growing, the expenditure of gross national product dollars is growing, and the adverse consequences of use are growing—all at startling rates in Western modern society. Thus these societies cannot afford to ignore or disdain deliberate social policy in regard to alcohol that consumes major material resources, results in major gross national product expenditures, and produces enormous human costs, both economic and personal.

In addition to the above utilitarian reasons, there are moral reasons for the institution of social policy on alcohol use in the largest sense. That is, no society can long endure that fails to morally encode norms of behavior. To ignore moral codes for the use of alcohol is to allow the breeding of social anarchy. As the late Harvard anthropologist, Clyde Kluckhohn, noted,

> There is a need for a moral order. Human life is necessarily a moral life precisely because it is a social life, and in the case of the human animal the minimum requirements for predictability of social behavior that will insure some stability and continuity are not taken care of automatically by biologically inherited instincts, as is the case with the bees and the ants. Hence there must be generally accepted standards of conduct, and these values are more compelling if they are invested with divine authority and continually symbolized in rites that appeal to the senses. [9]

Similarly, sociologist Philip Rieff has observed the progressive secularization of society, which has impoverished this society's capacity to symbolize meanings and values that integrate people and evoke commitment to communal existence. To Rieff, the notion of an amoral life and an amoral society is antithetical to communal existence. He comments

> To speak of a moral culture would be redundant. Every culture has two main functions: (1) to organize the moral demands that make men intelligible and trustworthy to each other, thus rendering also the world intelligible and trustworthy; (2) to organize the expressive remissions by which men release themselves in some degree from the strain of conforming to the controlling symbolic, internalized readings of culture that constitute individual character. The process by which a culture changes at its profoundest levels may be traced in the shifting balance of controls and releases which constitute a system of moral demands. [21]

It is fashionable to rationalize and justify social policy solely in terms of utilitarian cost-benefit analyses for a society. Yet the present author submits that the most profound obligation of a society for itself is precisely in the moral domain, as outlined herein. Inasmuch as alcohol serves as a major vehicle for expressive remissions by which men release themselves one can ill ignore formulation of social policy to organize both the prescriptions and proscriptions for alcohol use.

At this point it should be clear that this author intends to address a much larger venue of concepts (termed "social policy") than mere legislation, for social policy adumbrates one's social beliefs, values, attitudes, expected behaviors, tolerance of deviance, and the social embeddedness of the use of alcohol.

Such an ambitious agenda for a social policy requires that definitions, models, and the best empirical evidence on the use, misuse, and abuse of alcohol be reviewed, for social policy emanates from the base of definitional understandings.

DEFINITIONS AND CLASSIFICATIONS

At the outset one must recognize that there is a subtle interplay between uses, misuses, and abuses of alcohol. As outlined in Chapter 1, this volume, there are a variety of patterns of alcohol use, misuse, and abuse. Users of alcohol can misuse or abuse alcohol, either occasionally, intermittently, or chronically. How a particular pattern of alcohol use is labeled as misuse or abuse depends upon social processes and ultimately reflects social assumptions and social policy.

Similarly, the patterns of alcohol utilization, again discussed in the Chapter 1, this volume, reflect different, variable, and consequential social processes. Patterns of alcohol utilization do not reflect merely personal processes, but are reflective of the society and its sanctions.

IMPLICATIONS OF DEFINITIONS AND CLASSIFICATIONS FOR SOCIAL POLICY

First, use, misuse, and abuse are intertwined with each other. Any member of society who uses alcohol is potentially vulnerable to develop drug or alcohol problems.

Second, different patterns of alcohol utilization carry different risks for both the person and the society.

Third, alcohol use is an equilibrium process of costs and benefits. There are many costs and many benefits. Each individual lives in both a personal and social equilibrium, which can be unbalanced by both personal and social variables. Thus the equilibrium can be varied to make more people vulnerable and at risk or less vulnerable and at less risk. Shifts in either direction can be accomplished through changes in individual people and changes in the social milieu.

SOCIAL PERCEPTIONS AS DETERMINANTS OF PUBLIC POLICY

Each person carries about a private psychic homunculus. That is, each has some notion, concept, or construct of what it means to be a human. Each has an answer to the question posed three millenia ago by the Psalmist who asked, "What then is man, that thou are mindful of him?" [Psalms 8:4]. For the most part, one's private image of man is acquired from and is congruent with the ambient public image of man held as the conventional wisdom of the culture in which one lives. Social attitudes and social behaviors emanate from this common image of man.

Several important issues stem from this commonly held public image of man. First, societies differ substantially in their conventional wisdom about the nature of man. Second, indigenous and ethnic subgroups within a larger dominant culture may hold to substantially different images of man from that held in the larger dominant culture. Third, public images of man change over time, thereby providing the ground justification for shifts in social policy. Fourth, changes in conventional wisdom lag considerably behind changes in scientific descriptions or scientific image of man. Fifth, since public officials, legislators, and administrators are part of the common society, they are most likely to frame social policy in terms of its conventional wisdom. Sixth, the current conventional wisdom that frames a public image of man gives rise to and supports a folk science. In contrast to empirical science, which appeals to the deduction of principles and applications from changeable sets of data under constant challenge and revision, folk science is based on an accretion of beliefs, values, ideologies, and experiences that are molded into a rather immutable image of man, concretized in personal experience, from which the person inducts applications to life, based on the sense that "I and everyone else knows this to be true" [8].

The differences between public images of man and scientific images of man, differences between folk science prescriptions for public policy and empirical science prescriptions for public policy, are nowhere seen more clearly than in the instance of drug and alcohol problems [10].

To illustrate these processes, some data are presented from one of the author's studies on changes in public images about drug and alcohol abuse [14]. Public opinion was measured from popular literature in the United States for seven decades between 1900 and 1970, on three separate dimensions: (1) the moral blame ascribed to the addict for his or her problem; (2) the moral blame ascribed to the drug supplier; (3) the locus of causal etiologic factors — between individual causal factors and social causal factors.

Before analysis of the data, it should be noted that social scientists such as Glock [4] have observed that in Western culture the public image of man has been changing from a free will, moral image of man to a deterministic, nonmoral image of man. Does the same hold true for public images of the alcohol and drug abuser?

Figure 1 shows the moral blame imputed to the addict each decade. In 1900 there was high moral blame, which decreases over three decades to a relatively low level of moral blame. This indicates a definite shift from high to low moral blame in accord with the predicted general shift. Thus the public viewed the addict as much more the product of impersonal determined forces that made the person drug dependent. Thus drug abuse shifted from being a moral problem to a sickness problem.

In Figure 2 the moral blame ascribed to drug suppliers is charted. For the first six decades there was high moral blame, but a remarkable shift to low moral blame in the last decade. This reflects the changes in the prior twenty years from control of drug traffic as social policy to emphasis on treatment of the drug user as social policy. The importance of controlling drug traffic and moral condemnation of it is deemphasized in such statements as, "The demand is so high there will always be a supply."

In Figure 3 the locus of causal factors is presented. Social etiology was given highest importance in 1900, rising to a peak in the 1920s. There was a gradual change to a mixture of social and individual factors, leading to a primary emphasis on individual factors in the last decade. The content of the items reveals an even

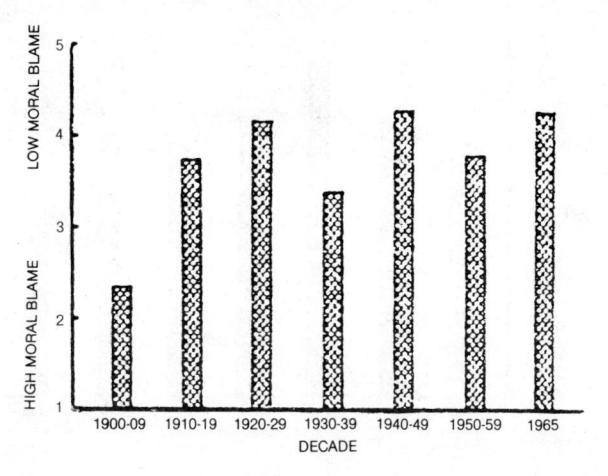

Figure 1. Moral Blame of the Addict. (From "Changes in Public Attitudes on Narcotic Addiction" by E. M. Pattison, L. A. Bishop and A. S. Linsky, *American Journal of Psychiatry*, 1968, *125*, 160-168. Reprinted by permission.)

more pronounced emphasis on individualism. In the early 1900s the social factors were predominantly bad living conditions such as slums, and bad suppliers who pushed drugs on unwilling victims, whereas the social factors of the 1960s were the association with fellow alcoholics, fellow addicts, and abuse-prone family associations.

The change in public images ascribes less moral blame to the drug abuser, even though the cause of drug abuse is atributed to and located in the individual.

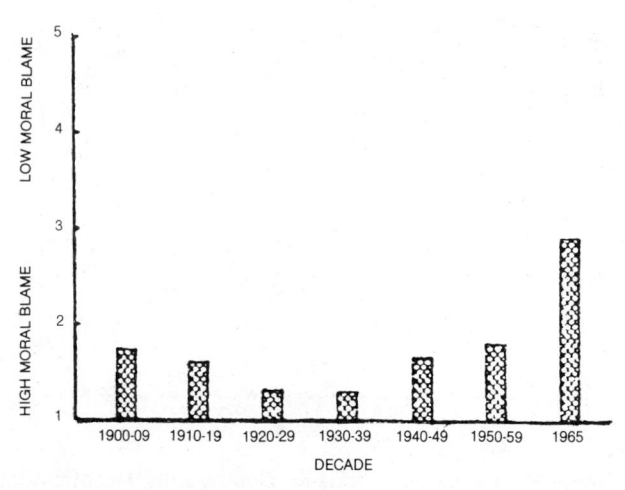

Figure 2. Moral Blame of Drug Suppliers. (From "Changes in Public Attitudes on Narcotic Addiction" by E. M. Pattison, L. A. Bishop and A. S. Linsky, *American Journal of Psychiatry*, 1968, *125*, 160-168. Reprinted by permission.)

496   E. Mansell Pattison

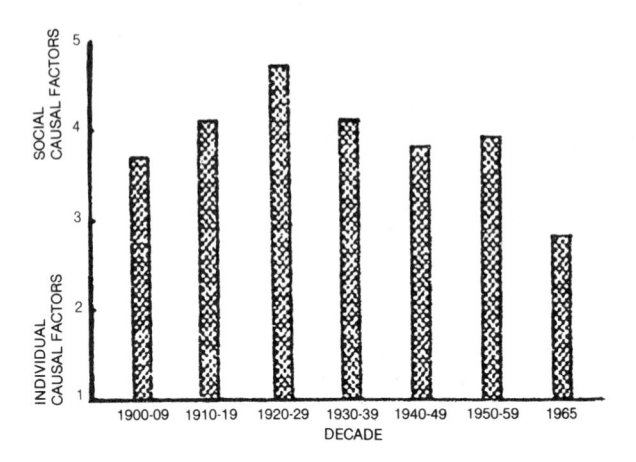

Figure 3. Locus of Causal Factors in Drug Addiction. (From "Changes in Public Attitudes on Narcotic Addiction" by E. M. Pattison, L. A. Bishop and A. S. Linsky, *American Journal of Psychiatry,* 1968, *125,* 160–168. Reprinted by permission.)

This reflects public acceptance of the concept of drug and alcohol problems as sick behavior. The person is seen as exercising free will in choosing deviant behavior, but is not held morally blameable, because the choice is the product of a sick mind.

In keeping with the public image, one finds corollary changes in public conventional wisdom about desired intervention methods. Recommendations for coping with narcotic addiction are presented in Figure 4. Again in 1900 social remedies lie with legal control, which drops off precipitously after 1950 with the

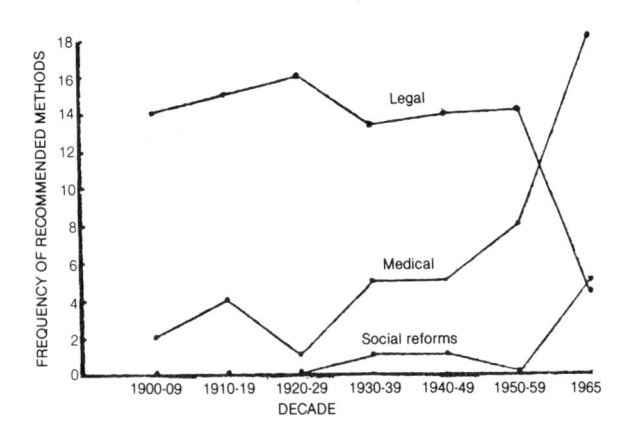

Figure 4. Trends in Recommendations for Coping with Narcotic Addiction. (From "Changes in Public Attitudes on Narcotic Addiction" by E. M. Pattison, L. A. Bishop and A. S. Linsky, *American Journal of Psychiatry,* 1968, *125,* 160–168. Reprinted by permission.)

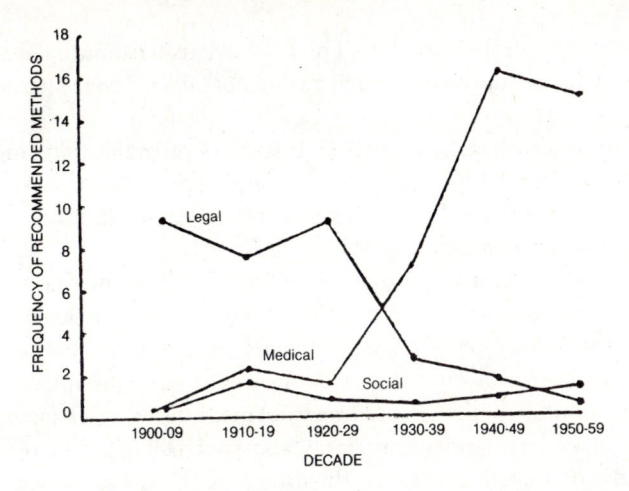

Figure 5. Trends in Recommendations for Coping with Alcoholism. (From "Changes in Public Attitudes on Narcotic Addiction" by E. M. Pattison, L. A. Bishop and A. S. Linsky, *American Journal of Psychiatry*, 1968, *125*, 160–168. Reprinted by permission.)

medicalization of drug problems. Concomitantly there is a sharp rise in individual medical treatment, with modest increase in social reform.

Similarly, in Figure 5 the recommendations for coping with alcoholism are presented. The general pattern is the same, with a more rapid decline in legal programs and a sharper rise in individual medical treatment. Social reform figures even less in coping with alcoholism.

IMPLICATIONS OF SOCIAL PERCEPTIONS FOR SOCIAL POLICY

The data in Figures 1 through 5 indicate the significant degree to which social policy has shifted along with changing views of the nature of the person. One might feel gratified that punitive attitudes have been replaced by therapeutic attitudes, as indicative of a more accurate assessment of the nature of the problem, a more realistic assessment of needed social interventions, and a more humane appreciation for the human dilemma.

Yet there are major problems produced by these shifts in public images. First, there has been a confusion between moral blame and moral responsibility. Too often, when the drug and/or alcohol abuser has been placed in the sick role to reduce moral blame, there has also been a reduction or even abolition of moral responsibility. The abuser qua patient says, "I am sick, I can't help it, you treat me, and cure my drug and/or alcohol abuse." Similarly, the professional therapist says, "You are sick, you don't know how to treat yourself. Be passive and acquiesce to my demands and you shall be well." This folie à deux (i.e., mutual distortion) between sick alcoholic and therapist has two major adverse consequences.

1. The professional fails to construct treatment programs that emphasize the necessity for patient action, patient choice, and patient assumption of responsibility. As a result the majority of professional treatment programs have been minimally successful in rehabilitation.

2. Public observation has often been more wise than professional opinion. People observe that a rigid medicalization of the drug and/or alcohol abuser fails to account for the degrees of personal choice, accountability, and responsibility that the drug and/or alcohol abuser does exercise. In consequence, there has been public counterreaction, rejecting a strict medicalization, challenging the value of medical model treatment programs, and even calling for the reconstitution of legal and moral sanctions against the drug and/or alcohol abuser.

Thus the mark has been overshot in the extent to which drug and alcohol abuse have been construed as solely or primarily the product of the sick mind of a sick individual. That model, which reached its apogee in the 1960s, has been under increasing attack in the 1970s from both public and professional ranks.

A second major problem is the shift in assumptions about the population at risk. In 1900 the drug and/or alcohol abuser was portrayed as the hapless victim of social circumstance. The faithful husband was seduced and waylaid by the siren call of the handy saloon; the innocent child was cozzened into surreptitious use of an evil drug, which magically captivated the body and mind of the child. Thus, in 1900, people were all at risk to evil social force. It is no wonder then that social policy was directed to abolition of the saloon and the drug traders. The policy was consistent with image.

By 1970, however, a radical, albeit subtle, shift in image had occurred. At this time the problem was perceived as being located in the individual. The majority of people were not perceived at risk. Only the socially and psychologically vulnerable and intrinsically sick person was at risk for alcohol abuse. Therefore, there were two populations: a majority who were not at risk, and a sick minority at high risk. In accord with this view, social policy was directed toward interventions aimed at just the high-risk sick minority—mainly individual medical treatment, whereas legal constraints, moral sanctions, and social reform and regulatory policies that would effect the nonrisk majority population were seen as irrelevant, unnecessary, and unimportant. In sum, it is necessary now not to have social policy for alcohol use for the majority, because the majority are not sick and not at risk for alcohol abuse.

The social consequence of this shift has been an ever increasing laxity of social policy toward alcohol use in society, while primary social attention is given to treatment programs for the sick alcoholic.

The inadequacies of this social perception and social image are several.

1. It averts attention from social policy for the prevention or reduction of alcohol abuse.

2. It ignores the data that demonstrate that all people are at risk to various degrees of alcohol misuse and abuse.

3. It ignores the data on effect of social policy on alcohol use and adverse consequences thereof.

4. It promotes a nihilistic attitude of futility of social policy, rather than exploration of limited but viable and valuable social policy.

5. It ignores and minimizes the extent to which treatment and rehabilitation are interdigitated with social attitudes, behaviors, sanctions, prescriptions, and proscriptions. Treatment and rehabilitation is not and cannot be effective apart from the social milieu in which treatment is embedded.

RELEVANCE OF BIOLOGICAL DETERMINANTS TO SOCIAL POLICY

The search for biological determinants of alcohol abuse has a long and checkered history. There is no question but that there are substantial biological and physiological system alterations consequent to the acute and chronic use of alcohol. These may be considered biological consequences of use and abuse. However, precedent biological differences that might predict abuse or be considered as etiologic have not been scientifically established. Many biological mechanisms have been proposed, but none to date are proven.

The most famous biological theory has been the allergy concept. Despite the well-recognized scientific lack of evidence—in fact, contrary scientific evidence—the belief is still strongly held in much current conventional wisdom. The reason is obvious. The allergy theory rationalizes and justifies the social definition of the alcoholic as a victim of a medical disease. Thus social moral blame is reduced and the person is morally exonerated. The allergy theory is also used to legitimate alcoholism as a medical disease.

A more credible variant of biological investigation has been genetic research. Here the data is inconsistent and even contradictory. However, it is entirely plausible that genetic characteristics may influence the development of personality traits and/or physiological traits that may make a person more or less psychologically or physiologically vulnerable if and when a person uses alcohol. Although such genetic vulnerabilities have not been established, this reasoning is logically and scientifically plausible [22].

However, the above cautious conclusions stand at far distance from the oversimplified, concrete popular declarations that alcoholism is a genetic disease. Such an overextension is neither logically nor scientifically justified. Given the suasive evidence of variation in patterns, personalities, and cultural configurations that constitute various syndromes of misuse and abuse, it would stretch credibility to assume that all widely variant alcoholims syndromes were specifically and solely genetic phenomena. Further, in particular regard to possible differences in ethanol metabolism in Mongoloid and Oriental people (given ambiguous and conflicting data), where such people may have lower rates of alcoholism, it is logically plausible to argue that such physiological differences actually protect against alcohol abuse, rather than promote it!

IMPLICATIONS OF BIOLOGICAL DETERMINANTS FOR SOCIAL POLICY

Although the search for biological determinants is scientifically credible, the interpretation and use of data about biological determinants has been problematic at best, unwarranted and unjustifiable often, and polemic at times. The search for biological determinants seems at times not grounded in scientific query, but rather the need to find a basis to legitimate medicalization of the problem, to justify labeling abuse as a disease, and to undergird social opinion about moral imputation. All three goals are worthy, but can be achieved without distorting the available data about biological determinants.

RELEVANCE OF PSYCHOLOGICAL DETERMINANTS TO SOCIAL POLICY

Similar to the biological arena, there have been arduous search forces out looking for the alcoholic personality. Sightings of the ephemeral object have been reported, but like a mirage in the desert, the object disappears as it is approached in reality. Personality variables, per se, are not predictive of alcohol use, misuse, or abuse.

This is not to say that different personality types and persons with specific attitudes, values, and beliefs may not be more vulnerable than others. But those personal traits are interactive with both an immediate social mileau and a larger cultural context. Thus Plaut observes

> A tentative model may be developed for understanding the causes of problem drinking, even though the precise factors have not yet been determined. An individual who (1) responds to beverage alcohol in a certain way, perhaps physiologically determined, by experiencing intense relief and relaxation, and who (2) has certain personality characteristics, such as difficulty in dealing with and overcoming depression, frustration, and anxiety, and who (3) is a member of a culture in which there is both pressure to drink and culturally induced guilt and confusion regarding what kinds of drinking behavior are appropriate, is more likely to develop trouble. [17]

The interaction is placed more precisely by Jessor et al.

> The likelihood of deviant behavior will vary directly with the degree of personal disjunction, alienation, belief in external control, tolerance of deviance, and tendencies toward short time perspective and immediate gratification characterizing an individual at a given moment in time. [6]

Both commentators link personal beliefs and attitudes about the management of life, the management of social stress, and the use and consequences of alcohol use to the ambient culture. Obviously people have different personalities, but the vulnerability of those personalities can only be assessed within a sociocultural context that either decreases or increases the vulnerability of the individuals if and when they use alcohol. A most cogent illustration of these principles is illustrated in the high incidence of heroin use and other psychoactive drug misuse and abuse among United States military personnel in Vietnam. Yet several years after return to civilian life, they had given up their drug use, and even the so-called addicts were no longer addicted (using control population comparisons) [2, 19].

One can proceed to an even more intimate interaction between the personality and his or her immediate social interactions. Cahalan and Cisin [3] report from their United States studies of drinking behavior that the immediate social context of drinking attitudes and drinking behavior as well as the immediate social matrix were the most significant determinants of problem drinking. Thus in Table 1 one can see the six most significant variables of 51 intervening variables determining problem drinking. Note that these are not personality variables, but rather psychosocial variables—that is, the self in interaction with significant others.

Further, Pattison et al. [15] have investigated the intimate psychosocial network structure and function of normals, alcoholics, addicts, and other psychiatric conditions. As shown in Table 2, the alcoholic has an impoverished social network

Table 1
Multiple Correlation of Six Most Significant of 51 Variables against Combined Drinking Problems Score

Intervening Variable	Multiple Correlation	Partial Correlation	Simple Correlation (Pearson r)
Drinking by significant others	0.26	0.15	.26
Tolerance of deviance	0.33	0.13	.22
Own attitude toward drinking	0.37	0.18	.26
Index of social position	0.41	0.11	.16
Black	0.42	0.09	.15
Nonhelpfulness of others	0.43	0.06	.16

Source. "Drinking Behavior and Drinking Problems in the United States" by D. Calahan and I. H. Cisin, in *Social Aspects of Alcoholism*, B. Kissin and H. Begleiter, eds., Plenum, New York, 1976.

Table 2
Intimate Psychosocial Network and Psychopathology

	Normals	Psychotic Thought Disorders	Psychotic Mood Disorders	Psychotics in Remission	Suicide Attempters	Heroin Addicts	Socio-paths	Personality Disorders	Active Alcoholics	Recovered Alcoholics	Marital Disorders
Total persons in network	22.4	13.7	16.47	13.44	13.95	14.61	12.58	15.57	16.35	21.95	19.51
Family sector	5.31	5.42	5.68	4.16	5.16	4.83	6.5	3.65	5.57	5.73	4.7
Relatives' sector	6.11	3.12	3.42	3.44	2.65	2.72	2.0	3.8	4.2	6.18	6.13
Friends' sector	5.37	3.42	5.26	5.12	4.3	4.78	3.5	4.57	4.78	5.27	4.55
Coworkers' sector	4.45	0.64	0.68	0.40	1.22	1.67	0.25	2.3	3.81	4.41	2.55

Source. From "Social Network Mediation of Anxiety" by E. M. Pattison, R. Llamas and G. Hurd, *Psychiatric Annals*, 1979, 9, 474–482. Reprinted by permission.

structure. Research data support the foregoing analysis of the critical influence of the immediate psychosocial milieu.

IMPLICATIONS OF PSYCHOLOGICAL DETERMINANTS FOR SOCIAL POLICY

Again, little support is found for the current conventional wisdom that alcohol abuse is primarily the product of a minority of sick people. The implication of the data presented here is again that all people can be at risk to various degrees. More importantly, the degree of vulnerability is directly related to both cultural attitudes, beliefs, and expectations, and directly related to significant others of the intimate psychosocial network of one's life. These data suggest the vital importance of social policy at a broad social level, as well as its implementation in the immediate mileau of everyday social transactions that involve all.

RELEVANCE OF SOCIOCULTURAL DETERMINANTS TO SOCIAL POLICY

As Heath [5] has noted, "There is no universal use, meaning, or function for alcohol." Alcohol is used for religious, ceremonial, hedonistic, and utilitarian purposes. How alcohol is used and the consequences of use are intimately tied to the cultural definitions of meaning, value, use, and consequent prescriptions and proscriptions of behavior. Recently, Marshall [13] has analyzed and summarized these cultural determinants, which this author has summarized as follows:

1. Solitary, addictive, pathological drinking behavior does not occur to a significant extent in small-scale, traditional, preindustrial societies; such behavior appears to be a concomitant of modern, industrialized societies.

2. Beverage alcohol use per se is not a problem in a society unless the society is ambivalent or overpermissive in it use of alcohol.

3. Where a society has a set of established and widely shared beliefs and values about drinking and drunkenness, the consequences of alcohol consumption are not usually disruptive for most persons of that society.

4. Where beverage alcohol has been recently introduced into a tribal society by a dominant external culture, the tribal society will likely not develop social and cultural mechanisms for integration of use of alcohol into the culture, but may adopt many of the disintegrative and adverse behavior of the dominant culture. Thus Bacon [1] reports that only 8.5% of such societies in the past 100 years have achieved cultural integration of alcohol.

5. The amount of pure ethanol content in the beverage consumed has little or

no direct relationship to the kind of consequent behavior. Thus the use of beer, wine, or spirits is, per se, unrelated to consequences.

6. All societies recognize permissible alterations in behavior from normal, sober comportment, but these alterations are always within normal limits. Thus in tribal societies where there is a high prevalence of drinking and even a high level of consumption, there are usually very low levels of adverse social behavior or consequences due to drinking. Further, in such societies where alcohol use is well integrated, there is little drunkenness per se (r = .05)[1]. That is, most people may drink, they may consume substantial amounts, but they do not get drunk, nor do they engage in adverse behavior. Here there are strong social expectations and social reinforcement that both prescribe and proscribe drinking behavior [11].

7. Beverage alcohol is usually described as a social facilitator, even if the use of alcohol is dysfunctional, antisocial, and socially disruptive. Here alcohol is used in a society for utilitarian reasons, to primarily relieve personal and social tensions, to rationalize or justify antisocial behavior. In sociological terms, the manifest use of alcohol is for social purposes, yet the latent social function is to serve personal or social conflict. This is often the meaning of alcohol use in social subgroups at the margin of social conflict.

8. Socially disruptive drinking occurs only in secular settings. When alcoholic beverages are used in sacred or religious contexts it is rarely disruptive.

9. Beverage alcohol is used for festive, ceremonial, or ritual celebrations the world over. Disruptive consequences depend upon the cultural prescriptions and proscriptions. Thus in the South American Andes, there are Indian tribes with annual ritualized festivals of drunkenness with no social disruption, whereas at the New Orleans Mardi Gras or the Munich Oktoberfest, there is the expectation of both getting drunk and indulging in a variety of antisocial behaviors without fear of social sanction.

10. Where opportunities for group or community recreation are few and alcoholic beverages are available, alcohol consumption will become a major form of recreational activity in a community. Particularly in Western industrialized societies where use of alcohol is no longer integrated, alcohol consumption tends to be compartmentalized as a separate function and human activity, rather than an integrated aspect of recreation, work, business, worship, or family and social life. Alcohol use becomes a behavior sui generis, apart and unto itself.

11. Typically, alcoholic beverages are used more by males than by females, and more by young adults than by preadolescents or older persons. Hence in any society the major consumers of beverage alcohol are most likely to be young men between their midteens and their mid-30s.

12. Not only do males usually drink more and more frequently than females, but the drunken comportment of males usually is more exaggerated and potentially more explosive than that of females, regardless of ethanol consumption.

13. The drinking of alcoholic beverages occurs usually with friends or relatives and not strangers. Where drinking among strangers does take place, violence is

much more likely to erupt. Thus with increasing compartmentalization of drinking in Western society, drinking among strangers increases, and there is less social control.

14. When alcoholic beverages are defined culturally as a food and/or medicine, drunkenness is seldom disruptive or antisocial.

15. Alcoholic beverages are the drug of choice for a majority of persons in any society, even if alternative drug substances are available.

16. Adverse drinking behavior is strongly linked to frequency of drunkenness, which in turn is linked to three major social customs: (1) limitations on indulgence of dependency in infancy, especially limitations on the diffusion of nurturance among many caretakers, (2) emphasis on and demands for achievement in childhood, and (3) limitations on dependent behavior between adults. Thus frequent drunkenness and adverse behavior is tied to social conditions that promote isolation, individualism, self-reliance, and at the same time demand high achievement.

DISTRIBUTION PATTERNS OF ALCOHOL USE

The strength of the aforementioned observations holds most clearly in tribal societies where alcoholism is not prevalent. Thus public policy derived just from that data may be quite misleading. Therefore, one must examine some more specific data in regard to the industrialized modern complex societies, where the use of alcohol is most problematic and where the vast bulk of so-called addictive drinkers live. This discussion owes much to the superb data synthesis and analysis by the Finnish econometrist Pekka Sulkunen [23].

First, there has been an ever-increasing rise in the prevalence and consumption of alcohol in modern societies since the Industrial Revolution. In fact, today about 25% of the world population consumes 80% of the beverage alcohol! As shown in Table 3, if one compares beer, wine, and spirits consumption worldwide, the disparity is even more striking. In brief, the modern industrialized societies produce most of beverage alcohol, consume proportionately even much more of the alcohol, and experience the most prevalent and serious adverse consequences of alcohol use.

Second, alcohol consumption in modern societies is currently rising faster than inflationary rates. For example, in the 20-year span 1950-70, there was a 40% rise in consumption in the aggregate of wine countries, and an 80% rise in the aggregate of beer countries, and a 175% rise in the aggregate of spirits countries. A similar pattern is revealed in alcohol beverage production between 1960 and 1968, in which there was an increase of over 100% in production, as shown in Table 4.

Table 3
Consumption Share of Top Five Consuming Countries of Total World Output, 1968

Type of Alcohol	Consumption Share of Total World Output (in Percentage)	Share of Total World Population (in Percentage)
Beer	30	4
Wine	67	5
Spirits	36	10

Source. "Drinking Patterns and the Level of Alcohol Consumption: An International Overview" by P. Sulkunen, in *Research Advances in Alcohol and Drug Problems* (Vol. 3), R. J. Gibbins, ed., Wiley, New York, 1976.

Third, although in the past there have been rather distinctive differences between patterns of alcohol consumption in beer, wine, and spirits countries, such patterns are being extinguished. There has been a general policy of increasing relaxation of beverage alcohol control in modern socieities in the past 25 years. In general this has been based on the sense of futility of public control policies, the shift of emphasis from public drinking policies to treatment of the problem drinker, and the assumption that relaxation of social control would "detoxify" public attitudes toward alcohol. It was supposed that with more alcohol available, and more readily available, people would tend to adopt more healthy patterns of drinking. This has been termed the "substitution" hypothesis.

In fact, the substitution hypothesis has not been proven in experience. What has happened is an additive process of drinking. With increased social and legal laxity, there is increased consumption. Further, new subpopulations of abstainers

Table 4
Alcohol Production for Beverages, 1960–68

	Alcohol in Millions of Hectoliters				Rate of Increase in Production of 100% Alcohol in Relation to Population
	Wine	Beer	Distilled Liquors	Total	
World					
1960	24.7	20.2	20.2	65.1	100
1968	28.3	28.4	28.2	84.9	109
Europe					
1960	18.7	9.6	6.1	34.4	100
1968	20.4	13.5	9.3	43.2	117

Source. Adapted from "Drinking Patterns and the Level of Alcohol Consumption: An International Overview" by P. Sulkunen, in *Research Advances in Alcohol and Drug Problems* (Vol. 3), R. J. Gibbins, ed., Wiley, New York, 1976.

or light drinkers have entered the class and/or shifted to heavier drinking, while the adverse consequences of drinking mount [12, 18].

Fourth, the concept that there was a bimodal distribution of drinkers in a society has been challenged. This distribution theory was based on the assumption that there was a large category of normal drinkers, and a small minority of pathological drinkers. Therefore, the drinking behavior of the normal drinking population was unrelated to the drinking of the pathological minority. Some data superficially appears to support a bimodal theory. For example, in 1968, 10% of the adult Finnish males drank 53% of all alcohol consumed by males, while 10% of the women drank 72% of all alcohol consumption by females. However, this comparison of the two extreme ends of the consumption curve fails to identify the actual distribution range. Recent population consumption surveys are strongly confirmatory of the so-called Ledermann curve. This curve describes a unimodal distribution theory; that is, increased per capita consumption increases the frequency and amount that everyone drinks. Consequently, rising per capita consumption results in more people who drink, and an overal increase in the amount each person drinks. The final result is that more people become at risk for the adverse consequences of drinking. The difference between a bimodal curve assumption and a unimodal Lederman curve assumption is shown in Figure 6. And as noted, the actual data supports the unimodal curve theory.

These findings have major significance in terms of alcohol abuse, because if

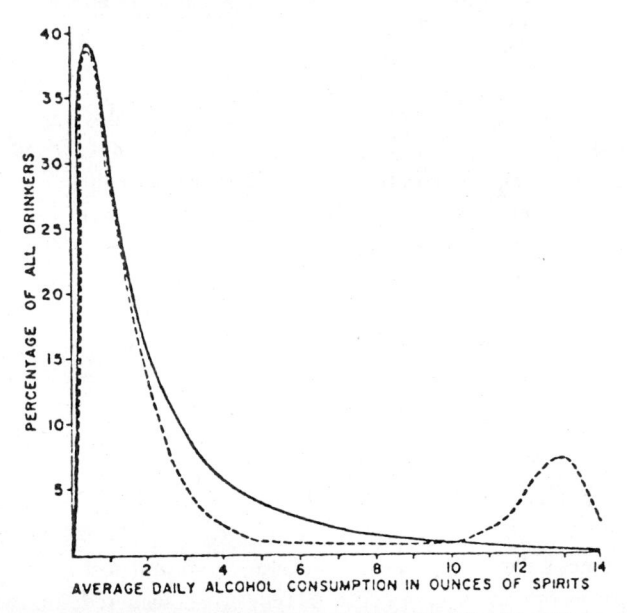

Figure 6. Bimodal versus Unimodal Consumption Distribution. (From *Drugs, Society, and Personal Choice* by H. Kalant and O. J. Kalant, Addiction Research Foundation, Toronto, 1971. Reprinted by permission.)

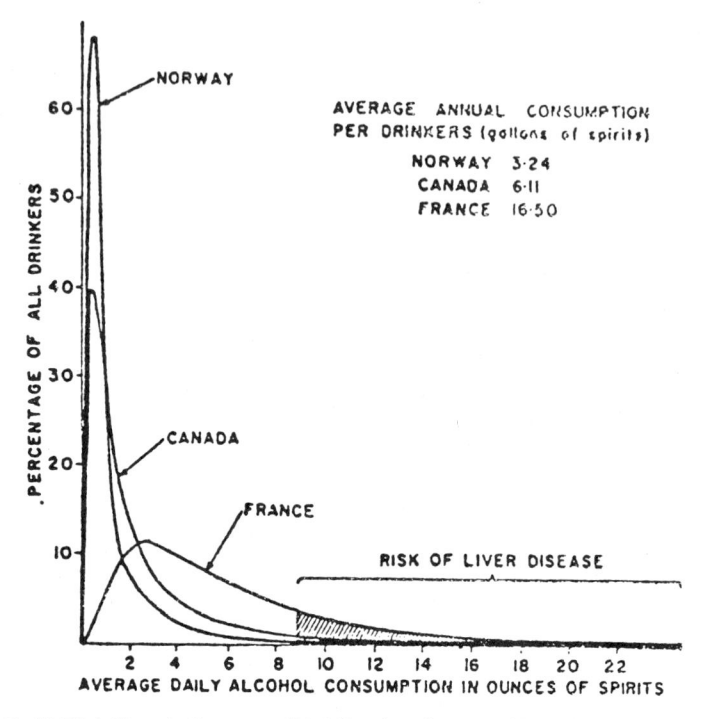

Figure 7. At-Risk Populations per Distribution Curves. (From *Drugs, Society, and Personal Choice* by H. Kalant and O. J. Kalant, Addiction Research Foundation, Toronto, 1971. Reprinted by permission.)

social policy allows increasing per capita assumption, then abstainers who are vulnerable will become drinkers at high risk. Further, light drinkers will tend to become heavier drinkers, which in turn increases the vulnerability to adverse drinking consequences. This process is shown in Figure 7, where different per capita consumption curves increase or decrease the population at risk for liver cirrhosis. One can similarly argue that increasing the number of drinkers, the frequency of drinking, and the quantity consumed will both place more people at risk and increase the risk of people who already drink.

IMPLICATIONS OF DISTRIBUTION PATTERNS FOR SOCIAL POLICY

Various schemes have been proposed to classify a cultural posture toward alcohol use [16, 20]. For convenience four cultural types are considered: the abstinent culture, the ambivalent culture, the integrated-structured culture, and the overpermissive culture, as shown in Table 5. The data reviewed here suggest that the

Table 5
Types of Cultural Orientations toward Alcohol Use

Orientation	Number of Countries	Type of Country	Sanctions about Alcohol Use	Populations at High Risk	Populations at Low Risk	Variations
Abstinent	Few	Tribal Moslem (erratic)	Strongly negative	Few deviant individuals	Most	Population at high risk if alcohol introduced
Ambivalent	Few	Ascetic, Christian	Conflictual (+) and (−)	Heavily drinking subgroups	Abstinent or light drinkers	Produces addicts
Integrated-Structured	Many	Tribal	Strong (+) and (−)	Few deviant individuals	Most	Disintegration with cultural change, loss of drinking norms
Overpermissive	Many	Modern industrial	Weak, vague, ambiguous	Many at all levels of drinking	Few	Diverse adverse problems (social, personal, physical)

abstinent culture is rare. Once a culture acquires alcohol use, it apparently never successfully restores abstinence. An abstinent culture that acquires alcohol without the accompanying integration is most likely to experience cultural disintegration due to alcohol use. The ambivalent culture, such as the prototype English and American traditions, does not achieve structured integration of alcohol use. As a result these cultures have large segments of the population who are abstinent or very light drinkers with minimal adverse consequences; yet these cultures also produce minority subgroups of very heavy drinkers who sustain very high adverse consequences for themselves and their culture. The integrated-structured cultures may have a high prevalence of the use of alcohol, but maintain low per capita consumption, with low frequency of drunkenness, and maintain strong sociocultural definitions and sanctions that both prescribe drinking behavior and proscribe adversive drinking behavior. These cultures are almost exclusively small tribal societies, and most have minimal alcoholism problems. The overpermissive cultures describe most of the modern industrial societies. These societies appear to be overpermissive in an attempt to emulate and recreate the integrated-structured cultures. The overpermissive societies only achieve high prevalence of drinking, without at the same time promoting low consumption, low frequency of drunkenness, and without widely accepted universal social prescriptions and proscriptions. As a result, the overpremissive cultures are producing diverse increased adverse consequences of drinking.

In sum, sociocultural determinantas are demonstrated to have high saliency in the etiology, treatment, and prevention of alcohol problems. Again, this evidence undergirds the importance one should give to social policy.

TOWARD SOCIAL POLICY

It would be foolhardy and presumptuous to attempt detailed recommendations for specific social policies, since data are lacking on the effectiveness of many social policies heretofore pursued. The lack of experiential or scientific guidelines is related to several factors [18].

1. Sufficient specificity is lacking in the stated objectives of most public policy measures.

2. The formidable complexity of the factors that may be involved in producing change after the introduction of social policy make evaluation difficult.

3. Those who enact legislation or promote social action normally are not influenced to develop rational policy through appropriate testing of alternatives, but by the probable reactions of their constituents — whether they be voters, parish members, students, or scientific peers.

4. The problem is overmedicalized, which separates social policy about alco-

hol use for the majority population from the social policy for the minority problem population.

With these caveates in mind, this author sets forth areas to which social policy should be addressed.

1. It is necessary to forthrightly assert that social policy in regard to alcohol use is not an elective option, but an imperative requirement for both utilitarian and social moral reasons.

2. Affirmation must come that social policy must emanate from and involve multiple sectors of the society. Social policy must emanate from the legislature, executive public officials, the churches, the school systems, the law enforcement and correctional systems, the treatment and rehabilitation systems, from the social clubs, community interest groups, fraternal and civic associations, and most ultimately from the informal social networks of personal affiliations.

3. One must distinguish between social policy that is formal in nature, such as laws, policies, and regulations, and social policy that is informal in nature, such as social values, social attitudes, and social sanctions enacted at a personal level of exchange. Either without the other is likely to be ineffectual.

4. It is imperative to examine and reformulate much of the conventional wisdom and folk science assumptions about the nature of alcohol problems. Most paramount here is the need to explicitly clarify that it is not just the problem of the pathological drinker but the collective alcohol use of the entire society that is the problem.

5. Professionals and lay persons alike must examine the reasons for alcohol use in the culture. It is remarkable that there has been almost no contemporary discussion of why a person should use alcohol. What use of alcohol should be prescribed in society? Is it for religious, ceremonial, hedonistic, or utilitarian purposes? How does one differentiate between prescriptions for positive use and proscriptions for misuse and abuse? Much focus has been upon what is misuse and abuse, and yet professionals have neglected to prescribe the healthy, moral, and beneficial ways to use alcohol.

6. Similarly, explicit behavioral proscriptions must be developed. It would seem prudent to proscribe drunkenness in general, and frequency of drunkenness in particular. It is imperative to decrease the social exoneration of dyssocial behavior due to drinking, and to increase social sanctions against adverse drinking behavior.

7. The integration of drinking into the everyday aspects of social life must be promoted, and the trend reversed toward the isolation of drinking into its own separate compartment, where drinking becomes an end unto itself.

8. Current efforts must be continued toward destigmatization of the person with an alcohol problem, but at the same time personal responsibility should be promoted.

9. It is necessary to address the problem of an overmedicated society. "Better living through chemistry" is an advertising slogan, not a fact of life. Physicians too freely resort to pills and drugs of every type. Tranquilizers and sedatives are prescribed, promoted, and purchased too easily, too quickly, too freely. People self-medicate themselves as a major modus operandi in society. People seek the answer in the bottle of whatever, rather than seeking answers with themselves, their families, and their friends. Drug switching becomes more common, and there is a trend toward a polymorphous perverse use of any drug readily available.

10. One should carefully pursue review, evaluation, and controlled experimentation with legal regulation of the distribution of alcohol, including number of sales outlets, location and hours of outlets, social settings of outlets, legal age of use, amounts sold, taxation control, and legal penalties. These are all controversial, no doubt, but that should not deter one from prudent consideration of alternatives.

11. The development of public information and public education should be vigorously pursued in regard to alcohol use; they should not be limited to just the issues of misuse and abuse. One must address both prescriptive and proscriptive norms for use that will be enforced by all.

12. The current trend toward ever higher per capita consumption appears to be a high-risk direction in which to move. Therefore, one should forthrightly address the advisability of proceeding with the current lax and overpermissive policy that promotes rising consumption. This will require explicit consultation and evaluation with economic interests, including agricultural interests, manufacturing interests, and supply, marketing, and advertising interests.

CONCLUSIONS AND SUMMARY

This author has cast a wide net to catch many fish in the net of social policy. Issues have been addressed that reach down to the very fundamental stratum of the constitution of a viable society. From a utilitarian standpoint, the issues of social policy are those of cost-benefit ratio, the balance of the beneficial uses versus the adverse consequences. There is balance of social protection versus social freedom. There is the balance of regulations versus the adverse effects and costs of regulation.

From a moral standpoint, it is often said, "You can't legislate morality." And indeed one cannot. For morality in its essence is the warp and woof of social structure. It is perhaps an ironic paradox that professionals have worked hard to affirm that alcohol abuse is not a moral problem. Yet now, this body must in turn work just as hard to affirm that alcohol use is a moral problem, the answer to which lies in the social commitment to define the good and the bad, the acceptable and the not allowable, the goals of life that shall be pursued and the adverse behavior that shall not be tolerated. In the end, then, social policy is matter of fundamental values, beliefs, and the actualization of a commitment to them.

REFERENCES

1. Bacon, M. K. Alcohol use in tribal societies. In: *Social Aspects of Alcoholism*, Kissin, B. and Begleiter, H. (eds.). Plenum: New York, 1976.
2. Boscarino, J. Current drug involvement among Vietnam and non-Vietnam veterans. *Am. J. Drug Alcohol Abuse* 6:301–307, 1979.
3. Cahalan, D., and Cisin, I. H. Drinking behavior and drinking problems in the United States. In: *Social Aspects of Alcoholism*, Kissin, B. and Begleiter, H. (eds.). Plenum: New York, 1976.
4. Glock, C. Y. Images of man and public opinion. *Public Opin. Q.* 28:539–542, 1964.
5. Heath, D. B. A critical review of ethnographi studies of alcohol use. In: *Research Advances in Alcohol and Drug Problems* (Vol. 2), Gibbins, R. J. (Ed.). Wiley: New York, 1975.
6. Jessor, R., Graves, T. D., Hanson, R. C., and Jessor, S. L. *Society, Personality, and Deviant Behavior: A Study of a Tri-Ethnic Community*. Holt, Rinehart & Winston: New York, 1968.
7. Kalant, H., and Kalant, O. J. *Drugs, Society, and Personal Choice*. Addiction Research Foundation: Toronto, 1971.
8. Kalb, M., and Propper, M. The future of alcohology: Craft or science? *Am. J. Psychiatry* 133:641–646, 1976.
9. Kluckhohn, C. Introduction. In: *Reader in Comparative Religion: An Anthropologic Approach*, Lessa, W. A. and Vogt, E. Z. (eds.). Harper & Row: New York, 1966.
10. Linsky, A. S. Theories of behavior and the social control of alcoholism. *Soc. Psychiatry* 7:47–51, 1972.
11. MacAndrew, C., and Edgerton, R. B. *Drunken Comportment: A Social Explanation*. Aldine: Chicago, 1969.
12. Makela, K. Consumption levels and cultural drinking patterns as determinants of alcohol problems. *J. Drug Issues* 5:344–350, 1975.
13. Marshall, M. *Beliefs, Behaviors, and Alcoholic Beverages: A Cross-Cultural Survey*. University of Michigan Press: Ann Arbor, 1979.
14. Pattison, E. M., Bishop, L. A., and Linsky, A. S. Changes in public attitudes on narcotic addiction. *Am. J. Psychiatry* 125:160–168, 1968.
15. Pattison, E. M., Llamas, R., and Hurd, G. Social network mediation of anxiety. *Psychiatr. Ann.* 9:474–482, 1979.
16. Pittman, D. J., and Snyder, C. R. (eds.). *Society, Culture and Drinking Patterns*. Wiley: New York, 1962.
17. Plaut, T. F. *Alcohol Problems: A Report to the Nation*. Oxford University Press: New York, 1967.
18. Popham, R. E., Schmidt, W., and de Lint, J. The effects of legal restraint on drinking. In: *Social Aspects of Alcoholism*, Kissin, B. and Begleiter, H. (eds.). Plenum: New York, 1976.
19. Robins, L. N. *The Vietnam Drug User Returns*, U.S. Government Printing Office: Washington, D.C., 1973.
20. Robinson, D. *From Drinking to Alcoholism: A Sociological Commentary*. Wiley: New York, 1976.

21. Rieff, P. *The Triumph of the Therapeutic: Uses of Faith after Freud*. Harper & Row: New York, 1976.

22. Shields, J. Genetics and alcoholism. In: *Alcoholism: New Knowledge and New Responses*, Edwards, G. and Grant, M. (eds.). University Park Press: Baltimore, 1976.

23. Sulkunen, P. Drinking patterns and the level of alcohol consumption: An international overview. In: *Research Advances in Alcohol and Drug Problems* (Vol. 3), Gibbins, R. J. (ed.). Wiley: New York, 1976.

Section V

Psychological Perspectives on Alcoholism

40

CHARLES NEURINGER, PhD, University of Kansas

ALCOHOLIC ADDICTION: PSYCHOLOGICAL TESTS AND MEASUREMENTS

PSYCHOLOGICAL TESTS and measurements have had a long and distinguished role to play in the understanding of the alcoholic addiction process. Their greatest contribution has been to stimulate research that cast doubt on the old cherished concept that all alcoholic behavior is identical and is caused by the same factors in all human beings. Psychological tests and measurements have also been of great utility in discovering the multiplicity of personality organizations underlying alcoholism.

Even the early users of psychological tests accepted the premise of a single alcoholism syndrome and attempted to use their measuring instruments to identify the unifying hallmarks of alcoholism (i.e., the behavior pattern that would reflect the universal manifestation of alcohol addiction). The earliest use of psychological tests was basically one of diagnostic identification of alcoholism. As is seen later in this chapter, the effort to find the single diagnostic indicator of alcoholism was doomed to meet with failure.

The diagnostic effort was concerned with the seemingly simple task of first identifying the alcoholic. Evaluation of the seriousness (or extent) of the alcoholic problem was a corollary area, developed to augment the diagnostic task.

Charles Neuringer, PhD, Professor of Psychology, Psychology Department, University of Kansas, Lawrence, Kansas.

Early researchers in the area of personality attributes of alcoholism failed to uncover a single reliable pathognomic sign, motivational drive, or personality characteristic in alcoholics. Attempts to validate the concept that all alcoholism was due to one psychological root cause also met with failure. Later investigators moved from conceptualizing alcoholism as a product of a single trait to a manifestation of a unique constellation of traits (i.e., the "alcoholic personality"). This constellation of traits was thought to be idiosyncratic to alcoholics.

It is a source of irony that it was the failures of psychological tests to support any of the above contentions that forced investigators to reject the single cause of alcoholism hypothesis. There began to develop a realization that alcoholism was a complicated disorder, having multiple roots and varied manifestations.

Since psychological tests have played such a widespread role in alcoholism studies, the literature of alcoholism measurements is enormous. Aside from their diagnostic and personality trait assessment roles, they have been used to measure the effects of alcohol on psychomotor and cognitive functions such as memory, reasoning, manual dexterity, reaction time, and so forth. They have also been used to assess the efficiency of various alcoholism treatment programs. They have been used to discover the diagnostic differentials between the cognitive changes associated with psychosis and those related to the effects of alcoholic toxicity on the brain. This chapter restricts itself, of necessity, to the areas of diagnostic identification and prediction, and the "teasing out" of personality variables associated with excessive drinking.

A NOTE OF CAUTION

One note of caution should be sounded at this point. Alcoholism is a topic that lends itself to emotional overeaction. Investigators are often, in spite of themselves, the victims of their own conscious or unconscious attitudes toward alcoholism. Marconi [24] pointed out that researchers' attitudes toward alcoholism lead them to either overemphasize or underemphasize various aspects of the disorder. These same attitudes have also influenced scientists in how they conceptualize alcoholism (i.e., either as a disease or as learned behavior). Their concept of alcoholism also determines their approach to alcoholic studies. If the researcher feels that excessive drinking is mediated by deep, unconscious personality dynamics, he or she is drawn to hypothesize the presence of an alcoholic personality and to ignore situational variables as determiners of alcoholic addiction. The researcher will then probably utilize projective personality measurements. If the investigator feels that alcoholism is just a learned behavior habit or even an isolated superficial symptom, the role of situation-determining variables will be emphasized and enduring developmental personality aspects will be ignored as contributors to the etiology of alcoholism. Such a researcher will probably utilize psychometric tests that deal with transitory behavioral responses to environmental stimuli. These conceptualizations of alcoholism, when compounded with moral approbation, leads to research designs and strategies that are geared to support the investigator's assumptions rather than to illuminate the problem of why some people become addicted to alcohol and others do not. This is an enduring problem in alcoholism research, as it is in all research into socially taboo behaviors. It is one of the reasons inconclusive and contradictory research results are found in such abundance in this area.

MAJOR PSYCHOLOGICAL TESTS

Almost every standard psychological test has been employed in some aspect of alcoholic research, diagnosis, and treatment evaluation. The range of psychological tests and measurements used by investigators interested in alcoholism has been enormous. Intelligence tests, projective personality tests, psychometric instruments, attitude surveys, and the like have all been utilized in attempts to elucidate the processes underlying the inception and course of alcohol addiction. A recent trend in alcoholism research is the development of alcoholism-specific measurement techniques. Because standard psychological tests were not developed to specifically study the alcoholic process, they have certain limitations that have proved to be a handicap to the discovery of valid and reliable data about excessive drinking. To remedy this situation, various investigators have developed specific alcoholism detection scales [27, 28]. These have proved to be very successful. (The reader who is interested in a review of the utilization of specific psychological tests and measurements in alcoholism studies should consult Neuringer and Clopton [32].

The two most commonly used psychological tests in alcoholism research are the Rorschach Inkblot test and the Minnesota Multiphasic Personality Inventory (MMPI). The Rorschach is a member of a family of instruments known as projective techniques. Projective tests are constructed so that there is no correct response. Usually the test stimuli are ambiguous and the individual being evaluated uses inner psychodynamics in order to make sense out of the test stimuli (i.e., he or she projects unconscious wishes, needs, motives, and such onto the ambiguous materials). It is thought that projective techniques measure the deep layers of personality. The Rorschach is composed of 10 vaguely formed, meaningless inkblots. The individual being evaluated is invited to tell the examiner what he or she sees (i.e., what these inkblots might represent).

The MMPI is a psychometric device. Psychometric measures are often called "paper and pencil" tests, since the individual being evaluated usually writes the answers to specific questions on some form. They are considered to be objective tests for two reasons: first, the test items are not ambiguous, and, second, the answers, which are usually given as yes or no, or as some numerical rating, can be counted and are therefore open to statistical analysis. The MMPI is composed of 566 questions. The questions are answered either true or false in terms of how they apply to the individual taking the test. The pattern of responses, called a profile, is matched against the known response profile patterns of various diagnostic groups. The MMPI has proved to be a particularly valid instrument. It has a special advantage over other psychometric tests in that it allows for the development of new diagnostic group response patterns (i.e., profiles). It is thought that the MMPI, and tests like it, tend to measure transitory effects on behavior.

DIAGNOSTIC IDENTIFICATION OF THE ALCOHOLIC

The identification of the absence or presence of alcoholism was historically the earliest task of psychological tests in alcoholism studies. The interest in the assessment of the extent or seriousness of the drinking problem developed as a supplement to the problem of diagnosing alcoholic dependency. The diagnostic yield from psychological tests has been meager and contradictory. Specific reasons for this failure are discussed later. The inability to find good diagnostic indicators of excessive drinking is in itself not as great a blow to alcoholism studies as it is for diagnostic efforts in other areas. It needs to be pointed out that the diagnostic task of identifying alcoholic dependency is probably the least important problem for alcoholism researchers. The establishing of whether a person has a serious drinking problem is better done by social history data (drinking habits and patterns, daily level of alcohol intake, disruptive interpersonal relationships, employment history, medical symptoms, etc.) than by psychological tests. There are many clinicians who feel that alcoholism can be adequately identified by simply asking an individual if he has a drinking problem. The answers to this question certainly yield results that are more reliable than that given by standard psychological tests.

Projective Tests

Since the Rorschach Inkblot test is the premier projective personality test, it has been used extensively in the identification and diagnosis of alcoholism. The test was thought by early investigators to be ideally suited for the diagnosis of excessive drinking. Roy Schafer [37], one of the early pioneers in Rorschach interpretation and heavily influenced by psychoanalytic theory, linked alcoholism to orality. He felt that the Rorschach was particularly well suited to identify orality and, therefore, to diagnose alcoholism. Other Rorschach experts [18] agreed with Schafer and added the dimension of an excessive perception of surface shading responses (e.g., "furry animal skins") to orality as the key to identifying the excessive drinker. This was an early example of the hypothesis that alcoholism could be identified by one single trait. This one hypothesis stimulated a great number of studies in which the Rorschach test was administered to all kinds of excessive drinkers. A large number of research reports using the Rorschach test for alcoholism diagnosis were published between 1940 and 1960. The results were disappointing in that they were contradictory and equivocal. Since that time, the usage of the Rorschach as an alcoholism diagnostic instrument has diminished. (The test still holds an important place in personality research into the psychodynamics of alcoholism.) Contemporary critics and reviewers of the Rorschach Test–alcoholism diagnostic literature have not surprisingly concluded that the test is insufficient for alcoholism diagnosis [8, 9, 30, 41, 42, 43, 48]. Other projective personality tests have fared no better than the Rorschach test in identifying alcoholics from nonalcoholics [2, 19, 29, 34, 38].

Psychometric Tests

Psychometric (i.e., objective) measuring instruments have fared only a little better in the diagnostic task than projective tests. However, the MMPI has proved to be the most efficient of the psychometric instruments.

Alcoholism identification and diagnosis from only the MMPI profiles were quickly found to be disappointing. This led various investigators to develop specific MMPI alcoholism detection scales [3, 13, 16, 21]. Unfortunately, the validity of these scales was brought into question by further research [23, 36, 44]. The equivocal validation results of MMPI alcoholism scales seems to be due to attempts to apply them in contexts different from those for which they were developed. MMPI alcoholism detection scales that were developed to differentiate hospitalized alcoholics from nonalcoholic neuropsychiatric patients cannot be used to differentiate nonhospitalized alcoholics from nonhospitalized nonalcoholics. Many of the MMPI alcoholism scale validation studies have used inappropriate comparison groups for the critical evaluation of these scales. There is legitimate cause for doubt about the validity of these scales, but their rejection may be premature.

Although the use of psychometric tests with alcoholism has been dominated by the MMPI, other objective measures have been utilized in the identification of alcoholism task. Significant differences in the test scores of alcoholics and nonalcoholics has been found by Hoffman and Nelson [15] on the Edwards Personal Preference Schedule [6], by Rosenberg [35] on the Eysenck Personality Inventory [7], and by Hoffman [14] on the Personality Research Form [17]. However, these latter findings need to be validated.

Methodological Problems

The failure of projective and psychometric psychological tests to reliably identify alcoholism can be attributed to various sources. The investigator's moral stance on alcoholism has already been discussed. Poor research methodologies also can be found in this area of investigation. Many of the studies used inadequate and inappropriate control groups. Some of the studies did not use any control groups. Naïve research designs comparing ill-defined groups were common. Not enough care was taken to define alcoholism and nonalcoholism. Age, length and amount of drinking, physical status, drug levels, and the like were ignored. Sociocultural backgrounds were rarely considered by the investigator. Validation studies misapplied various criteria and tried to validate on groups for which the test was not developed. There were some carefully designed and well-executed studies that failed to produce adequate validation results. However, it is felt that the greatest cause of difficulty in developing adequate identification criteria was the assumption that alcoholism is a single disorder. This belief led researchers to look for a single identifier for a multivariate disorder. The failure to discover diagnostic indicators can also be explained by the research discoveries to be described following. It was in the investigations of the alcoholic's personality that it was demonstrated that there was more than one kind of alcoholism. Since alcoholism cannot be related to any one personality or behavior pattern, no one identifying pathognomic characteristic can be expected to be discovered.

PERSONALITY CHARACTERISTICS

It is in the area of personality characteristics associated with alcoholic dependency that psychological tests have made their greatest contribution. It was mainly from research using these instruments that questions began to be raised about the hypothesis of a unitary, or single, motivational system mediating all alcoholism.

The movement away from the concept of alcoholism as a single unitary disorder has been one of the major conceptual steps taken by researchers and clinicians interested in alcoholic dependency. Early attempts at breaking down alcoholism into multiple types were somewhat tentative in the sense that they involved only two types of alcoholic configurations. Schafer [37], using a wide variety of psychological tests, deduced the existence of "essential" drinkers (individuals who drink in order to capture a heightening of experience) and of "reactive" drinkers (those who drink in order to diminish contact with the world around them). Jellnick's historically important hypothesis about gamma and delta alcoholics was investigated by Walton [46] using the Cattell Sixteen Personality Factor Questionnaire [4]. Walton was able to produce evidence that gamma alcoholics (the compulsive drinkers) were more self-punitive and frightened of their own drives than the delta drinkers, who were unable to control their impulses and tolerate frustration, and were, therefore, unable to abstain. Mortimor, Filkins, Kerlan, and Lower [28] produced evidence that there are differing constellations of characteristics associated with the problem drinker and the social drinker. These tentative dualistic characterizations were developed because of the failures of attempts to link alcoholism to a single personality characteristic.

Single Personality Variables

The following are illustrations of the ensuing contradictory results found for two oft-cited hypothesized univariate causes of alcoholism (dependency and negative self-concept). The research cited below is not exhaustive of work done with these variables, nor of other single variables, but is only illustrative of the morass that follows when alcoholism is conceptualized as being linked to a single personality variable.

Massive dependency in alcoholics was reported by Snibbe [40] and Hoffman [14] but not by Goldstein, Neuringer, Reiff and Shelly [10]. Some studies report that alcoholics see themselves as inadequate and lacking personal worth [5, 11, 45]. Contradictory results were reported by MacAndrew [22], Reinehr [33], and Gross and Carpenter [12].

Single Alcoholic Personality Constellations

Opposed to the hypothesis of a single personality variable as uniquely linked to alcoholism is the concept of a single personality constellation that is isotonically related to alcoholism. Such a particular constellation has been called "the alcoholic personality."

The possible existence of a cohesive constellation of traits and characteristics associated exclusively with alcoholism has been an idea that had attracted many investigators. It is a seductive concept and is basically only a small step beyond the earlier belief in alcoholism as a single unitary disorder. Psychological tests have been extensively used in the search for the alcoholic personality since it was thought that such tests had the capacity to simultaneously measure a broad range of personality structures and dynamics. Wittman [47], using the Chassell Inventory, concluded that alcoholism was the product of a personality configuration fostered by maternal indulgence. The hypothesis that alcoholism is a manifestation of an oral personality organization was investigated by Bertrand and Masling [1] using the Rorschach test.

The two studies cited above were basically attempts to validate already-existing theories about the alcoholic personality. Other attempts to discover the alcoholic personality have been empirical (i.e., atheoretical) in nature. A battery of psychological tests is usually administered to groups of drinkers and nondrinkers. Lists of differentiating responses are drawn up. Further analysis (either intuitive or using factorial statistical analysis techniques) leads to the construction of a set of personality characteristics that are considered to exist only in alcoholics. Over 60 such studies of this kind have been attempted. Unfortunately, the mass of results from such attempts has been so contradictory that it is impossible to accept the hypothesis that there is one personality constellation that exists in all alcoholics. Rather, the research supports the contention of multiple alcoholic personality types. For a close review of these studies, the reader is referred to Sutherland, Shroeder, and Tordella [41], Syme [42], and Zwerling and Rosenbaum [49].

Multiple Alcoholic Personality Constellations

Both projective and psychometric tests have yielded data to support the hypothesis of a wide variety of alcoholic personalities or types, and, therefore, the existence of a wide variety of personality traits that are associated with excessive alcoholic intake.

Projective tests, by their very nature, will produce more global results than will psychometric tests. However, even with projective measures the variety of alcoholic patterns is obvious. Six alcoholic constellations have emerged from projective test studies.

1. Individuals who have not developed the cognitive and intellectual skills to overcome frustrations and for whom such frustration is extremely painful. Drinking is thought to be an escape from the pain of frustration.

2. Individuals who have difficulty delaying gratification. They are generally infantile in development. Drinking is thought to be a childish dependency gratification behavior.

3. Individuals who are extremely guilt-ridden. They drink to diminish their intolerable feelings of guilt and anxiety.

4. Individuals who have unrealistically high levels of aspiration and grandiose plans. When coupled with limited cognitive capacities, failure is assured. They drink in order to escape from disappointment into fantasy.

5. Social isolates with extremely constricted thought processes. They drink in order to achieve mental stimulation. It is the glow or "buzz" effect of alcohol that is most important to them.

6. Individuals whose drinking behavior is determined by the social situation. These are individuals who have few inner-directed tendencies and will drink excessively when they find themselves in a social context that demands heavy drinking behavior. They do not miss alcohol when abstention is forced upon them by the environment.

The above is a summary developed by this author after reviewing the projective test literature in the area of alcoholic types. Since this literature is too vast to be reproduced here, the reader may wish to review the sources personally and is referred to Neuringer and Clopton [32] for bibliographic references.

The following is only a sample of the work done with psychometric tests. These tests have been able to yield more specific personality patterns associated with alcoholism than have the projective tests. Lawlis and Rubin [20], using the Sixteen Personality Factor Questionnaire, found three major general personality configurations among alcoholics. They were (1) an unsocial aggressive pattern, (2) a psychopathic pattern, and (3) an inhibited-conflicted pattern. Neale [31], using the MMPI, discovered six distinct alcoholic profiles. Mogar, Wilson, and Helm [26] were able to successfully sort alcoholic profiles into five female and four male profile patterns. Using a factor analytic approach, Skinner, Jackson, and Hoffman [39] found eight male inpatient alcoholic profiles. Other studies support the hypothesis of the existence of a variety of alcoholic types. There is no one character type or personality pattern that is owned by all alcoholics. Work in this area has been competently reviewed by Franks [8], Gibbon [9], Gross and Carpenter [12], and McCord and McCord [25].

FUTURE RESEARCH STRATEGIES

The fact that the alcoholic types discovered by the various investigators are somewhat different from each other is a matter of great concern to those interested in discovering the range of alcoholic personality patterns. The same set of multiple patterns are not found in all of the various research projects. This seems to be the outcome of methodological and research design differences to be found among the various studies.

The utilization of measuring instruments varied from study to study. Since different tests are developed to highlight certain variables, comparability is difficult from one measurement battery to another. If one investigator has a predilection for ego defense measuring instruments, the results associated with the use of these tests will tend to be oriented around describing the layers of self-protection employed by the alcoholic. If another investigator is partial to affect-stability assessment, his or her tests will tend to highlight the emotional reactivity of the excessive drinker. The first investigator's work will produce a set of several alcoholic defense patterns, and he or she will then conclude that these are the alcoholic personalities. The second investigator will probably find a set of affect types and feel that a panorama of alcoholic types has been discovered.

The subject populations have also varied from study to study. Hospitalized individuals in an alcoholic rehabilitation program served as subjects for some of the studies. Alcoholics Anonymous members were used in other studies. Patients suffering from delerium tremens or alcoholic hallucinosis were used in different investigations. Amount and length of drinking, intellectual deterioration, age, sex, and so forth, have been more carefully controlled in these researches than for the diagnostic identification investigations. However, there is still a great deal of noncomparability of subject populations among the various studies. The noncomparability leads to the emergence of differing alcoholic cluster types.

Nonalcoholic comparison groups also vary from investigation to investigation. In some studies moderate drinkers are compared to the alcoholics. In other studies abstainers are used as the control group. And in some cases nonalcoholic, but psychotic individuals, are used for comparison purposes. Different results will invariably emerge from different investigations, depending on who is being compared to whom.

Statistical evaluations also vary a great deal. Different kinds of factor analysis rotations will yield different factor clusters. Investigators tend to prefer certain rotation techniques over others and there may be a theoretical bias in the use of different factor rotations. If the researcher feels that each alcoholic type is composed of one particular pervasive personality trait, the tendency will be to use a rotation technique that searches for a main general factor. If alcoholism is conceptualized as being due to a set of multiple traits, rotation techniques that are guaranteed to find multiple factors will be used.

It is, at present, very difficult to estimate the number of possible alcoholic personality types. Because of the operational differences among the various research efforts, it is also difficult to assess which patterns are reliably reproduceable, and, therefore, which are the valid set of alcoholic personality patterns. It is imperative that efforts be directed toward standardization in terms of carefully defining and using all of the various alcoholic and comparative subject populations, submitting the data to all of the different statistical evaluations, and utilizing all of the available psychological tests and measurements. This is the next critical programmatic step for those interested in alcoholic personality typologies.

REFERENCES

1. Bertrand, S., and Masling, J. Oral imagery and alcoholism. *J. Abnorm. Psychol.* 74: 50-53, 1969.
2. Brown, R., and Lacey, O. L. The diagnostic value of the Rosenzweig Picture Frustration Test. *J. Clin. Psychol.* 10:72-75, 1954.
3. Button, A. D. A study of alcoholics with the Minnesota Multiphasic Personality Inventory. *Q. J. Stud. Alcohol* 17:263-281, 1956.
4. Cattell, R. B., Ebner, H. W., and Totsuoka, M. M. *Handbook for the Sixteen Personality Factor Questionnaire.* Institute for Personality and Ability Testing: Champaign, Ill., 1970.
5. Connor, R. G. *The Self-Concept of Alcoholics.* Unpublished doctoral dissertation, University of Washington, 1961.
6. Edwards, A. L. *Edwards Personal Preference Schedule.* Psychology Corporation: New York, 1959.
7. Eysenck, H. J., and Eysenck, S. B. G. *Manual of the Eysenck Personality Inventory.* University of London Press: London, 1964.
8. Franks, C. M. Alcoholism. In: *Symptoms of Psychopathology*, Costello, C. G. (ed.). Wiley: New York, 1970.
9. Gibbon, R. J. *Chronic Addiction.* Toronto University Press: Toronto, 1953.
10. Goldstein, G., Neuringer, C., Reiff, C., and Shelly, C. H. Generalizability of field dependency in alcoholics. *J. Consult. Clin. Psychol.* 32:560-564, 1968.
11. Gross, W. F., and Adler, L. O. Aspects of alcoholics' self-concept as measured by the Tennessee Self-Concept Scale. *Psychol. Rep.* 27:431-434, 1970.
12. Gross, W. F., and Carpenter, L. L. Alcoholic personality: Reality or fiction. *Psychol. Rep.* 28:375-378, 1971.

13. Hampton, P. J. The development of a personality questionnaire for drinkers. *Genet. Psychol. Mono.* 48:55-115, 1953.

14. Hoffmann, H. Personality characteristics of alcoholics in relation to age. *Psychol. Rep.* 27:167-171, 1970.

15. Hoffman, H., and Nelson, P. C. Personality characteristics of alcoholics in relation to age and intelligence. *Psychol. Rep.* 29:143-146, 1971.

16. Hoyt, D. P., and Sedlacek, G. M. Differentiating alcoholics from normals and abnormals with the MMPI. *J. Clin. Psych.* 14:69-74, 1958.

17. Jackson, D. N. *Personality Research Form Manual.* Goshen: New York, 1967.

18. Klopfer, B., and Spiegelman, M. Differential diagnosis. In: *Developments in the Rorschach Technique* (Vol. 2), Klopfer, B. (ed.). World: Yonkers, N.Y., 1956.

19. Knehr, C. A., Vickery, A., and Guy, M. Problem-action responses and emotions in TAT stories recounted by alcoholic patients. *J. Psychol.* 61:201-226, 1953.

20. Lawlis, G. F., and Rubin, S. E. 16PF study of personality patterns in alcoholics. *Q. J. Stud. Alcohol* 32:318-327, 1971.

21. MacAndrew, C. The differentiation of male alcoholic outpatients by means of the MMPI. *Q. J. Stud. Alcohol* 26:238-246, 1965.

22. MacAndrew, C. Self-reports of male alcoholics: A dimensional analysis of certain differences from male psychiatric outpatients. *Q. J. Stud. Alcohol* 28:43-51, 1967.

23. MacAndrew, C., and Geertsma, R. H. A critique of alcoholism scales derived from the MMPI. *Q. J. Stud. Alcohol* 25:68-76, 1964.

24. Marconi, J. Scientific theory and operational definitions in psychopathology with special references to alcoholism. *Q. J. Stud. Alcohol* 28:631-640, 1967.

25. McCord, W., and McCord, J. *Origins of Alcoholism.* Stanford University Press: Stanford, 1960.

26. Mogar, R. E., Wilson, W. M., and Helm, S. T. Personality subtypes of male and female alcoholic patients. *Int. J. Addictions* 5:99-113, 1970.

27. Moore, R. A. The diagnosis of alcoholism in a psychiatric hospital. *Am. J. Psychiatry* 128:1565-1569, 1972.

28. Mortimor, R. G., Filkins, L. D., Kerlan, M. W., and Lower, J. S. Psychometric identification of problem drinkers. *Q. J. Stud. Alcohol* 34:1132-1335, 1973.

29. Murphy, M. M. Social class differences in frustration patterns of alcoholics. *Q. J. Stud. Alcohol* 17:255-262, 1956.

30. Nathan, P. E., and Harris, S. L. *Psychopathology and Society.* McGraw-Hill: New York, 1975.

31. Neale, C. R. *An Investigation of Perception of Visual Space among Alcoholics.* Unpublished doctoral dissertation, University of Utah, 1963.

32. Neuringer, C., and Clopton, J. R. The use of psychological tests for the study of the identification, prediction, and treatment of alcoholism. In: *Empirical Studies of Alcoholism*, Goldstein, G., and Neuringer, C. (eds.). Ballinger: Cambridge, Mass., 1976.

33. Reinehr, R. C. Therapist and patient perceptions of hospitalized alcoholics. *J. Clin. Psychol.* 25:443-445, 1969.

34. Roe, A. Alcohol and creative work. Part I: Painters. *Q. J. Stud. Alcohol* 6:415-467, 1946.

35. Rosenberg, C. M. Young alcoholics. *Brit. J. Psychiatry* 115:181-188, 1969.

36. Rotman, S. R., and Vestre, N. D. The use of the MMPI in identifying problem drinkers among psychiatric hospital admissions. *J. Clin. Psychol.* 20:526-530, 1964.

37. Schafer, R. *The Clinical Application of Psychological Tests.* International Universities Press: New York, 1948.

38. Singer, E. Personality structure of chronic alcoholism. *Am. Psychologist* 5:323, 1950.

39. Skinner, H. A., Jackson, D. N., and Hoffmann, H. Alcoholic personality types: Identification and correlates. *J. Abnorm. Psychol.* 83:658–666, 1974.

40. Snibbe, J. R. *The Effects of Various Therapeutic Episodes on Dependency Feelings in Alcoholics as Measured by Four Tests.* Unpublished doctoral dissertation, University of Utah, 1970.

41. Sutherland, E. H., Schroeder, H. G., and Tordella, C. L. Personality traits and the alcoholic. *Q. J. Stud. Alcohol* 11:547–561, 1950.

42. Syme, L. Personality characteristics and the alcoholic. *Q. J. Stud. Alcohol* 18:288–302, 1957.

43. Tremper, M. Dependency in alcoholics: A sociological view. *Q. J. Stud. Alcohol* 33:186–190, 1972.

44. Uecker, A. E., Kish, G. B., and Ball, M. E. Differentiation of alcoholism from general psychopathology by means of two MMPI scales. *J. Clin. Psychol.* 5:287–289, 1969.

45. Vanderpool, J. A. Alcoholism and the self-concept. *Q. J. Stud. Alcohol* 30:59–77, 1969.

46. Walton, H. J. Personality as a determinant of the form of alcoholism. *Br. J. Psychiatry* 114:761–766, 1968.

47. Wittman, M. P. Developmental characteristics and personality of chronic alcoholics. *J. Abnor. Social Psychol.* 34:316–377, 1939.

48. Zucker, R. A., and Van Horn, H. Sibling social structure and oral behavior: Drinking and smoking in adolescence. *Q. J. Stud. Alcohol* 33:193–197, 1972.

49. Zwerling, I., and Rosenbaum, M. Alcoholic addiction and personality (nonpsychotic conditions). In: *American Handbook of Psychiatry* (Vol. 1), Arieti, S. (ed.). Basic Books: New York, 1956.

41

HERBERT BARRY III, PhD, University of Pittsburgh School of Pharmacy

A PSYCHOLOGICAL PERSPECTIVE ON DEVELOPMENT OF ALCOHOLISM

THE DEVELOPMENT OF alcoholism involves opposite behaviors. The self-destructive act of chronic, excessive drinking is counteracted by efforts to renounce and deny this pathological pattern. The competition between these opposing behaviors accounts for the slow, unsteady progression typical of the development of alcoholism.

A brief definition of "alcoholism" is chronic, heavy drinking that causes social or physical damage. An early indication of alcoholism is when the person continues drinking after the drunkenness threatens loss of job or spouse or health. This self-destructive urge is pathological, and accordingly it is associated with pathological conditions, such as disrupted development and an unfavorable social environment.

Alcoholism also constitutes the selection of a particular type of pathology. Drinking is usually a socially approved activity, and it has various pleasurable effects [7], including feelings of power [23]. Most alcoholics have a high degree of social skills and ambition. Impressive achievements and social attractiveness during sobriety alternate with the destructive consequences of drunkenness. Alcoholism is the tragedy of self-destruction by people with great potential and lofty aspirations.

Herbert Barry III, PhD, Professor of Pharmacology, University of Pittsburgh School of Pharmacy, Pittsburgh, Pennsylvania.

PREDRINKING SOCIAL ENVIRONMENT

Attributes of the early social environment may cause the child to be vulnerable to the later development of alcoholism. Experiences during infancy and early childhood occur many years prior to the first drink. Nevertheless, these experiences may be influential by orienting subsequent development in a pathological direction.

Table 1 summarizes pathological conditions during early childhood reported to increase the risk of alcoholism among males. These pathological conditions are not specific to alcoholism because they are also associated with other types of psychiatric illnesses.

The first two items in Table 1 are especially convincing because they are derived from studies in which male children were studied and subsequently classified according to whether they developed alcoholism [24, 26]. The conclusions by Cahalan and Room [12] are based on interviews with large numbers of men and comparisons of alcoholics with nonalcoholics. Retrospective accounts by alcoholics or by their relatives account for the general attributes of family and parents summarized by Barry [2].

Alienation of the young boy from his father might be a consistent consequence of the conditions shown in Table 1. Parental separation or loss involves the father much more often than the mother. Conflict over dependency feelings and antagonism toward masculine authority figures might give rise to the anger and alienation that are prominent in alcoholics.

The boys in the studies by McCord [24] and Robins [26] were seen because of behavior problems. This circumstance may be expected to increase the likelihood of a pathological childhood environment. The future alcoholics were compared with future nonalcoholics in the same sample, but the effects of pathological childhood environment on susceptibility to alcoholism might be limited to this

**Table 1
Pathological Conditions of Childhood Environment Increasing Risk of Alcoholism among Males**

Father is a criminal [24]
Inadequate parents [26]
Parental separation during childhood [12]
Early childhood loss of parent [14]
Lack of cohesion in the family [12]
Father is weak, distant, or absent [2]
Mother is dominant, overprotective, discourages assertiveness [2]

Note. The citations in brackets identify the principal report or review that describes the finding.

**Table 2
Attributes of Family Structure
Increasing Risk of Alcoholism
among Males**

Last born from large family [10]
Second-older sibling is sister [11]
No brothers or sisters [13]

Note. The citations in brackets identify the principal report or review that describes the finding.

type of sample. In a study of college men, Vaillant [28] concluded that subsequent development of alcoholism was not related to adverse conditions in childhood. The data showed a tendency, however, for the future alcoholics to have experienced a poor relationship with the mother and a relatively bad childhood.

Table 2 shows attributes of the social structure of the family that give evidence for increasing vulnerability to alcoholism. Since these ordinal birth positions and family sizes are not necessarily pathological, they may be useful indications of the reasons why the pathological influences shown in Table 1 result in the choice of alcoholism rather than an alternative form of deviant behavior. A further special value of the measures of ordinal birth position and family size is that they constitute simple, objective measures that are not likely to be distorted by forgetting or deception.

The increased probability of being last born in large families [10] is based on a summary of many separate studies. The tendency for the second-older sibling to be a sister rather than a brother was found in a sample of hospitalized alcoholics [11] and also in five of six cases among presidents of the United States and their brothers who were alcoholics [4]. Conley [13] found that the proportion of adults who had been the only child was reliably higher among a sample of alcoholics (11%) than a sample of the general population (8%).

The family positions shown in Table 2 indicate close relationships of the child with the mother or with an alternate female caretaker. An overprotected, indulged relationship with the parents, especially the mother, is likely to be characterize the last child in a large family [7]. In particular, the mother may be reluctant to relinquish her maternal function when her last child approaches maturity. This attitude may also tend to be directed toward the only child. These experiences may retard the child's development of independence and impulse control [13]. Further evidence for this type of influence is a report that alcoholics were more likely than the nonalcoholic comparison group to sleep in the same room with their parents after 1 year of age [15].

The early experiences summarized in Tables 1 and 2 may be expected to result in severe conflict over dependence. Overprotection develops dependent behavior, but this behavior conflicts with the need to express independence, especially in boys. Disruption of the family at an early age (Table 1) may intensify the conflict between dependence and independence. Expressions of alienation and antagonism may counteract a deep craving for dependence and security. This conflict was discussed by Blane [9], Barry [2], and Barry and Blane [7].

The smaller amount of information on girls who subsequently became alcoholics is consistent with the attributes for boys shown in Tables 1 and 2. A review [8] concluded that the mother of the future female alcoholic is typically cold, severe, and dominating, whereas the father is warm, gentle, and in many cases alcoholic. There is a tendency for female alcoholics to have been last born in large families [11].

PREDRINKING BEHAVIOR

Table 3 summarizes behavioral attributes that have been reported or observed in boys who subsequently developed alcoholism. They show a pattern of assertive, sociable behavior. The problems concern submission to authority rather than relationships with other boys.

McCord et al. [24] emphasized that in spite of the fact that their sample of boys were seen because of behavior problems, few signs of neurotic disorders or social withdrawal were observed. Jones [18], in common with McCord et al. [24], studied boys who were subsequently classified according to whether they developed alcoholism. In the study by Goodwin et al. [16], the assertive behavior was related to the syndrome of restless, hyperactive behavior. In addition, the majority of alcoholics reported that they felt shy, sensitive, and insecure. Zucker [29] has reviewed these and other childhood characteristics of future alcoholics.

The meager information on childhood of female alcoholics is consistent with this pattern of assertive behavior with underlying conflict. Jones [19] reported that three girls who became problem drinkers were convinced at the age of 12 that they were smart, attractive, and well-thought-of, but, at the age of 15, they were full of adolescent self-doubt and confusion, they were fearful and rejecting of life, and they distrusted people. Their religious beliefs emphasized judgment and punishment. They tended to escape into ultrafemininity.

Future alcoholics therefore do not usually show the severe social deficiencies seen in many children who subsequently become schizophrenic or neurotically withdrawn. The assertive, sociable behavior of future alcoholics may express antagonism toward authority figures and deficiency in controlling their impulses and appetites. These characteristics may result from the maternal overprotection and disrupted childhood families that are indicated in Tables 1 and 2.

Table 3
Behavioral Attributes Reported in Male Children Who Developed Alcoholism

Antisocial behavior [26]
Undercontrolled, impulsive, rebellious [18]
Aggressive and disobedient [12]
Aggressive, impulsive, hot-tempered [16]
Poor intellectual functioning in school [20]

Note. The citations in brackets identify the principal report or review that describes the finding.

EARLY DRINKING BEHAVIOR

Drinking behavior prior to the onset of social or physical problems constitutes part of the development of alcoholism. This stage provides useful information on the conditions and behaviors closely associated with the emergence of alcoholism. The initial exposure to alcoholic beverages may indicate whether the pathological drinking by alcoholics is based on pathological earlier development or involves an abnormal response to alcohol.

In a comparison of alcoholics with college students, Ullman [27] asked about memories of the first drink. The alcoholics were more likely to have remembered that occasion, which also was more likely to have occurred at a later age, to have resulted in drunkenness, and to have been separated by more than 1 year from the next drinking occasion. A later study [22] likewise reported that alcoholics showed better memory of the details of their first drinking experience.

These studies indicate for alcoholics a special importance of liquor on the initial drinking occasion. On the other hand, the development of problems is usually gradual rather than sudden. The overt drinking problems develop after several months or years rather than in the first few drinking experiences. Hesitation to repeat the attractive but pathological experience may be indicated by the report that the second drinking occasion for alcoholics is often more than 1 year after the first [27].

In spite of the typically later age of the first drink by alcoholics [27] and the gradual onset of chronic, heavy drinking, the problems often develop at a young age. Cahalan and Room [12] showed that the greatest occurrence of pathological heavy drinking is between the ages of 20 and 29.

The behavior of young people who are heavy drinkers is generally assertive and gregarious [3]. The experience of drinking at first apparently enhances the same behavioral attributes that Table 3 identifies in (male) children who subsequently develop alcoholism. The drinking itself at first does not alter the prior personality. Zucker [29] likewise emphasized the continuity of behavior during development of alcoholism.

An important indication of characteristics of alcoholics at an early stage was reported by Kammeier et al. [21]. Scores on the Minnesota Multiphasic Personality Inventory (MMPI) of alcoholic men at the time of their hospitalization were compared with their scores when they entered the University of Minnesota as freshmen, an average of 15 years earlier. It is a reasonable assumption that most of the freshmen were at an early stage of drinking. Their scores were high on a scale of psychopathic deviancy, which measures unrestrained, antisocial behavior, but low on a scale of depression. At the time of hospitalization, their scores were high on both scales, in accordance with the usual findings for alcoholic patients.

In a study of a different sample of college students [28] those who subsequently developed alcoholism showed a tendency for poorer integration in college. This predictor of future alcoholism was not statistically significant and applied only to a minority of the future alcoholics, but it was at least partly explainable by heavy drinking in college by some of the men who subsequently developed alcoholism.

Some differences between alcoholism and delinquency are indicated by a study of delinquent boys, 16 to 18 years old, with alcohol involvement [6]. Contrary to most samples of alcoholics, the delinquents were predominantly from large families and from the first rather than second half of the birth order. A subgroup of delinquents with the most severe alcohol involvement showed a slight tendency to be in the second rather than first half of the birth order. This tendency was contrary to the rest of the sample but consistent with the samples of alcoholics (Table 2).

PROGRESSION TO ALCOHOLISM

Various types of pathological influences may increase the likelihood that the self-destructive behavior of alcoholism will develop and become severe enough to be diagnosed. Therefore, several attributes of social disruption or alienation are associated with alcoholism.

A comparison of alcoholic men with their fathers and brothers [20] has shown a lower socioeconomic status of the alcoholics. This difference developed prior to the onset of heavy drinking. Alcoholism rates are higher in large cities, in occupations that require traveling or performing in public, and among single or divorced people. These conditions increase the likelihood of social alienation.

Impressive evidence for a genetic component in susceptibility to alcoholism [17] also gives evidence for an important role of social disruption during adulthood. Table 4 shows a combination of genetic and social factors. Males who had been adopted out of their biological families in early infancy were divided into two groups, on the basis of whether alcoholism was present or absent in a biological parent. Alcoholism developed in 33% of those who had an alcoholic biological parent (genetic factor) and had been divorced (social factor). Much lower inci-

Table 4
Relationship of Alcoholism to Divorce in Adopted Males with and without an Alcoholic Biological Parent

	Alcoholism in Son		
	Absent	Present	Percentage Present
Alcoholism present in biological parent			
Son has been divorced	10	5	33
Son never divorced	35	5	13
Alcoholism absent in biological parent			
Son has been divorced	7	0	0
Son never divorced	67	4	6

Source. This information, from data summarized by Goodwin et al. [17], was kindly provided by Dr. Donald W. Goodwin.

dences of alcoholism were found in those who did not have an alcoholic biological parent or who had not been divorced. Since their drinking behavior was studied at an average age of only 30 years, the high frequency of divorce among alcoholics in this sample probably indicates an early predisposing influences rather than a consequence of chronic alcoholism.

Some features of social integration may effectively prevent alcoholism in most people who are otherwise susceptible. This author [4] has summarized several such protective attributes. Very few monarchs have been described as alcoholics although they have ample opportunity for heavy drinking. Their elevated, hereditary social status may prevent feelings of alienation. Alcoholism seems to be more frequent among political leaders than kings, but only two of the presidents of the United States (approximately 5%) were alcoholic. Both of these (Pierce, Grant) tried persistently and sometimes successfully to abstain. The lower incidence of alcoholism among women than men may be attributable to a tendency for women to have more intense social relationships, especially with their immediate family. These social relationships may involve severe conflicts, and they do not protect women from susceptibility to other psychiatric illnesses, such as depression and schizophrenia. However, the frequent contacts with family and friends may protect most women from the alienation and social isolation that lead to alcoholism.

THREE TYPES OF ALCOHOLISM

Alcoholics have in common the behavior of chronic, excessive drinking, but diverse personality patterns are represented [2]. Zucker [29] has pointed out the multiple antecedents of alcoholism. Several types of alcoholism can be associated with other psychiatric illnesses, especially depression and sociopathy [5]. Figure 1 portrays three types of alcoholism: antisocial, dependent, and reclusive. This classification is based on whether feelings of anger are predominantly externalized against other people or internalized against oneself.

Antisocial alcoholism is associated with externalized anger. The pattern of aggressive, impulsive, rebellious behavior is typical of the childhood behavior of future alcoholics (Table 3). Violent alcoholism constitutes an intense expression of this behavior. Sociopathy is the psychiatric illness closely associated with this type of alcoholism.

This behavior pattern most often occurs at a young age, within the first few years after the onset of heavy drinking. Alcohol intake is typically limited to sporadic or periodic occasions, such as during weekends or holidays, alternating with days or weeks of sobriety.

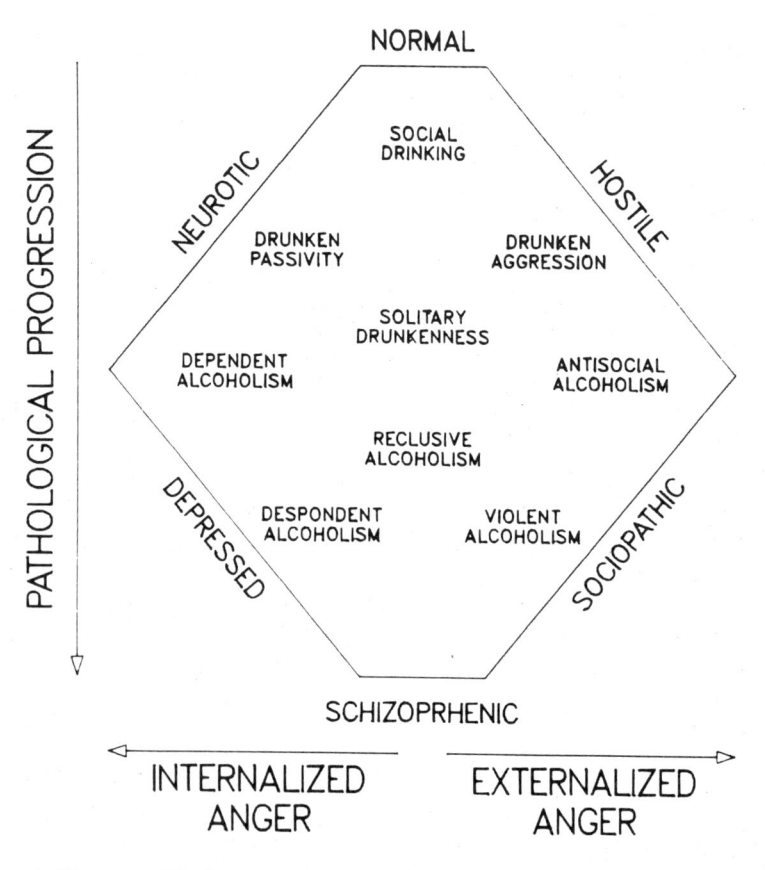

Figure 1. Diagram of Drinking Patterns Depending on Whether Anger Is Predominantly Internalized or Externalized and Degree of Pathological Progression.

Dependent alcoholism results from a preponderance of internalized rather than externalized anger. The self-destructive behavior is overtly directed against oneself and involves others only by frustrations of needs or making excessive dependent demands on others. Despondent alcoholism results from the dependent behavior together with the destructive effects of chronic drinking. Depression is a closely associated psychiatric illness, with the risk of the final self-destructive act of suicide.

This pattern of internalized anger is typically associated with drinking every day, without overt signs of intoxication. The detection or diagnosis of alcoholism may depend on the physical damage that results. The definitive diagnosis of alcoholism is when the person continues drinking after urgent warnings by the physician. This pattern is often seen in wine-drinking countries, notably France, but the type of alcoholic beverage does not matter. The person who drinks several cocktails each evening or several bottles of beer every day also may develop this type of alcoholism.

A preponderance of either externalized or internalized anger indicates a well-established distinction of one's personal identity from others. Deficiency of this distinction indicates that the sense of identity is confused and fragmented. Feelings of anger thus are not directed against the differentiated targets of other people or oneself. Figure 1 identifies schizophrenia as an expression of this type of psychopathology.

In common with schizophrenia, reclusive alcoholism is associated with an undifferentiated target of anger. This type of alcoholism appears to occur less frequently than antisocial or dependent alcoholism. Most alcoholics maintain intense, although ambivalent, social relationships. Solitary drinking occurs by necessity rather than by choice.

The number of reclusive alcoholics is probably underestimated. The diagnosis of schizophrenia may decrease the likelihood of identifying alcoholism as an additional type of psychopathology. Nevertheless, Barry [2, 5] has identified many reports indicating substantial frequency of alcoholism and schizophrenia in the same patients. Alterman et al. [1] reported that approximately 5% of a sample of hospitalized schizophrenics showed definite, concurrent drinking problems.

Many elderly people are socially isolated. A substantial proportion of them are alcoholics, but many more are probably not detected. Very few elderly alcoholics voluntarily seek treatment for their drinking problem [25].

CONCLUSIONS

Alcoholism develops throughout the years from infancy to the onset of the social or physical problems that indicate pathological effects of drinking. The self-destructive consequence of chronic, excessive drinking suggests that the dominant motive is self-destructive. Expressions of this self-destructive motive can be seen in the compulsive antisocial behavior and dangerously heavy intoxication during early stages and in the prominence of depressed, suicidal behavior at later stages and older ages. This self-destructive urge continually competes with efforts for self-preservation.

The childhood background of alcoholics shows a tendency for broken or disturbed families and assertive, impatient, antisocial behavior. The birth order patterns suggest a high frequency of parental indulgence, and may be interpreted as resulting in retarded development of independence and of impulse control. These experiences and responses may lead to the feeling of alienation expressed by alcoholics.

Alcohol provides a powerful agent for self-destruction while enabling the drinker to deny the existence of this motive. The first drink is typically a memorable experience for people who subsequently develop alcoholism, but it constitutes a continuation and extension rather than a reversal of prior tendencies. The pattern of assertive, sociable, antisocial behavior is enhanced by the drinking.

Three types of alcoholics are distinguished on the basis of whether anger is predominantly externalized or internalized. Externalized anger results in antisocial alcoholism, which is typical in the early stages. Internalized anger results in dependent alcoholism, which is typical in the later stages, leading to despondence, depression, and sometimes suicide. Inadequate differentiation of oneself from others, due to a disturbed sense of self-identity, results in reclusive alcoholism. This is associated with schizophrenia and with old age.

REFERENCES

1. Alterman, A. I., Erdlen, F. R., and McLellan, A. T. Problem drinking in a psychiatric hospital: Alcoholic schizophrenics. In: *Substance Abuse and Psychiatric Illness*, Gottheil, E., McLellan, A. T., and Druley, K. A. (eds.). Pergamon: New York, 1980.
2. Barry, H., III. Psychological factors in alcoholism. In: *The Biology of Alcoholism: Clinical Pathology* (Vol. 3), Kissin, B. and Begleiter, H. (eds.). Plenum: New York, 1974.
3. Barry, H., III. The correlation between personality and the risk of alcoholism. In: *Recent Advances in the Study of Alcoholism*, Idestrom, C.-M. (ed.). Amsterdam: Excerpta Medica, 1977.
4. Barry, H., III. Childhood family influences on risk of alcoholism. *Prog. Neuro-Psychopharmacol.* 3:601–612, 1979.
5. Barry, H., III. Psychiatric illnesses of alcoholics. In: *Substance Abuse and Psychiatric Illness*, Gottheil, E., McLellan, A. T., and Druley, K. A. (eds.). Pergamon: New York, 1980.
6. Barry, H., Jr., Barry, H., III, and Blane, H. T. Birth order of delinquent boys with alcohol involvement. *Q. J. Stud. Alcohol* 30:408–413, 1969.
7. Barry, H., III, and Blane, H. T. Birth positions of alcoholics. *J. Individual Psychol.* 33:62–69, 1977.

8. Beckman, L. J. Women alcoholics: A review of social and psychological studies. *J. Stud. Alcohol* 36:797–824, 1975.

9. Blane, H. T. *The Personality of the Alcoholic: Guises of Dependency.* Harper & Row: New York, 1968.

10. Blane, H. T., and Barry, H., III. Birth order and alcoholism: A review. *Q. J. Stud. Alcohol* 34:837–852, 1973.

11. Blane, H. T., and Barry, H., III. Sex of siblings of male alcoholics. *Arch. Gen. Psychiatry* 32:1403–1405, 1975.

12. Cahalan, D., and Room, R. *Problem Drinking among American Men.* Rutgers Center of Alcohol Studies: New Brunswick, N.J., 1974.

13. Conley, J. J. Family configuration as an etiological factor in alcoholism. *J. Abnorm. Psychol.* 88:670–673, 1980.

14. deLint, J., Blane, H. T., and Barry, H., III. Birth order and alcoholism. *Q. J. Stud. Alcohol* 35:292–295, 1974.

15. deSaugy, D. L'alcoholique et sa femme. *Hygiene Mentale* 51:81–105, 1962.

16. Goodwin, D. W., Schulsinger, F., Hermansen, L., Guze, S. B., and Winokur, G. Alcoholism and the hyperactive child syndrome. *J. Nerv. Ment. Dis.* 160:349–353, 1975.

17. Goodwin, D. W., Schulsinger, F., Hermansen, L., Guze, S. B., and Winokur, G. Alcohol problems in adoptees raised apart from alcoholic biological parents. *Arch. Gen. Psychiatry* 28:238–243, 1973.

18. Jones, M. C. Personality antecedents and correlates of drinking patterns in adult males. *J. Consult. Clin. Psychol.* 32:2–12, 1968.

19. Jones, M. C. Personality antecedents and correlates of drinking patterns in women. *J. Consult. Clin. Psychol.* 36:61–69, 1971.

20. Jones, M. B., and Borland, B. L. Social mobility and alcoholism: A comparison of alcoholics with their fathers and brothers. *J. Stud. Alcohol* 36:62–68, 1975.

21. Kammeier, M. L., Hoffman, H., and Loper, R. G. Personality characteristics of alcoholics as college freshmen and at time of treatment. *Q. J. Stud. Alcohol* 34:390–399, 1973.

22. Kuehnle, J. C., Anderson, W. H., and Chandler, E. First drinking experience in addictive and nonaddictive drinkers. *Arch. Gen. Psychiatry* 31:521–523, 1974.

23. McClelland, D. C., Davis, W. N., Kalin, R., and Wanner, E. *The Drinking Man.* Free Press: New York, 1972.

24. McCord, W., McCord, J., and Gudeman, J. *Origins of Alcoholism.* Stanford University Press: Stanford, Calif., 1960.

25. Mishara, B. L., and Kastenbaum, R. *Alcohol and Old Age.* Grune & Stratton: New York, 1980.

26. Robins, L. N. *Deviant Children Grown Up: A Sociological and Psychiatric Study of Sociopathic Personality.* Williams & Wilkins: Baltimore, 1966.

27. Ullman, A. D. The first drinking experience of addictive and of "normal" drinkers. *Q. J. Stud. Alcohol* 14:181–191, 1953.

28. Vaillant, G. E. Natural history of male psychological health: VIII. Antecedents of alcoholism and "orality." *Am. J. Psychiatry* 137:181–186, 1980.

29. Zucker, R. A. Developmental aspects of drinking through the young adult years. In: *Youth, Alcohol, and Social Policy,* Blane, H. T. and Chafetz, M. E. (eds.). Plenum: New York, 1979.

42

RALPH E. TARTER, PhD, University of Pittsburgh School of Medicine

EXPERIMENTAL PSYCHOLOGY AND ALCOHOLISM: ASSESSMENT, CONTRIBUTION, AND IMPACT

EXPERIMENTAL PSYCHOLogy, defined as the science of behavior analysis and control, has typically been concerned with two broad problems in the field of alcoholism. First, research has been devoted to elucidating the processes traditionally considered as psychological (e.g., learning, motivation, and personality) that could conceivably be responsible for the causes and maintenance of problem drinking. And secondly, experimental techniques have been utilized in an effort to bridge psychological observations with findings from the other levels of biological organization. Toward the latter objective, research has been aimed at investigating the anatomical, biochemical, and physiological correlates of disturbed behavioral functioning in persons identified as alcoholics.

At the outset, it is important to conceptualize how the multivariate organismic processes are interrelated and organized. In Figure 1 it can be seen that overt behavior (in this case, alcohol consumption) is the product of complex and diverse fac-

---

Ralph E. Tarter, PhD, Chief, Clinical Neuropsychology, and Associate Professor of Psychiatry and Neurology, Department of Psychiatry, University of Pittsburgh School of Medicine, Pittsburgh, Pennsylvania.

tors. Considering simply the number of processes involved, it is naïve to think of drinking behavior or alcoholism as a unidemensional phenomenon that is explicable as the symptom of a disease, a rigidly defined syndrome, or a global personality disorder. Nor can the invocation of singular constructs (e.g., tension reduction, power strivings, or dependency needs) be expected to adequately serve as universal explanations of alcohol abuse. Like the blind men, each one grappling with a different part of the elephant and making hypotheses about the nature of the beast from limited information, psychological experimentation has been characterized in the past by the accumulation of fragmented and often isolated observations that were inflated into general theories about the etiology of alcoholism.

More recently, the orientation of experimental psychologists has been to identify the multifaceted processes and their interrelationships that dispose the person to normal and/or abusive drinking practices. Within such a conceptual framework, the task before experimental psychology is thus not simply to discover differences between alcoholics and nonalcoholics, but also the impetus is directed toward revealing the functional relationships within the alcoholic individual that are integral to the initiation and persistence of excessive patterns of alcohol consumption [6].

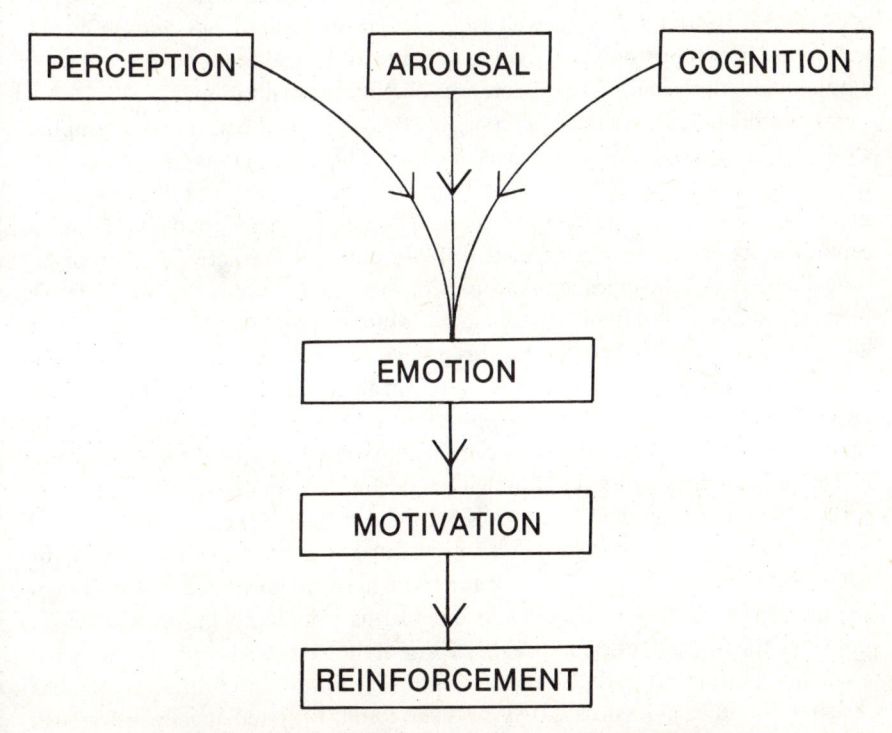

Figure 1. Psychological Determinants of Drinking Behavior

THE CAUSES OF ALCOHOLISM

Hypotheses about the etiology of alcoholism can be categorized into six areas of psychological functioning; these areas are perception, arousal, cognition, emotion, motivation, and reinforcement history.

Perception

A fundamental question concerns whether or not alcoholic individuals have a unique perceptual style, and thus process sensory input and view the world differently from nonalcoholics. One perceptual style that has been extensively studied is perceptual field orientation. Alcoholics, as a group, have repeatedly been found to be perceptually field dependent [47]. On a task that requires perceptual analysis, such as orienting a rod to the true vertical axis despite a distracting background frame and/or the body in various degrees of tilt, alcoholics are unable to make accurate perceptual judgments. Alcoholics, like the obese and brain-damaged, adjust the rod according to the orientation of the frame, and are thus field dependent; those who can adjust the rod despite the distractions are field independent. Field-dependent individuals tend to have a poorly articulated concept of corporeal awareness [55], as well as utilize less specialized ego defense mechanisms such as repression and denial, in contrast to field-independent persons, who employ more sophisticated defenses like intellectualization.

While alcoholics tend to be perceptually field dependent, it should be emphasized that they are all not so inclined. A number of investigators have identified field-independent alcoholics, illustrating the heterogeneity of the alcoholic population. Moreover, the cause of the field-dependent perceptual orientation is unknown. Whether it is antecedent to drinking onset, or alternatively a manifestation of a neuropsychological impairment consequent to chronic drinking, has yet to be determined. And finally, what exactly is measured by the rod and frame test and the underlying mechanism for this perceptual style remains unclear. Jacobson [20] has theorized that field dependency in alcoholics results from a deficient awareness of interoceptive cues. Support for this hypothesis was provided when, upon exposure of alcoholics to perceptual deprivation, at which time they were instructed to focus on internal stimuli, their performance subsequently improved when retested, in contrast to controls, who did not have the benefit of the interoceptive training experience. This is an intriguing finding and is congruent with results reported by other investigators who have demonstrated that alcoholics are unable to utilize internal cues in modulating drinking behavior. Generally, however, the research on perceptual field orientation has not been very fruitful in elucidating mechanisms that could be responsible for excessive drinking. Nor has research on other perceptual processes been found to systematically distinguish alcoholics from nonalcoholics.

Arousal

Initiation of goal-directed behavior requires the priming of the organism. Physiological arousal serves such a function and involves a number of interacting neurological systems. Autonomic arousal is critical for the occurrence of an emotional experience [44], while the thalamic, cortical, and reticular activating systems are primarily involved in attentional and motivational mechanisms [27]. The substrate of arousal thus comprises a number of integrated systems that mediate the ongoing moment-to-moment attentional, emotional, and motivational states of the organism.

It has been hypothesized that some alcoholics suffer from a fundamental defect in arousal modulating mechanisms. Tarter [50] has theorized that a subgroup of alcoholics manifest a hyperactivity disorder that stems from an underlying disturbance in sustaining optimal and stable states of arousal. These fluctuating states are hypothesized to be stabilized by the pharmacologic properties of alcohol. Supporting evidence for this notion is derived in part by the findings of Naitoh and Docter [36], who found that alcoholics who were administered a low dose of alcohol (0.5 mg/kg) experienced a primarily stimulant effect. Corresponding to positive subjective changes were electroencephalograph (EEG) correlates in the form of increased amounts of alpha activity and a slowing of its frequency, leading these investigators to hypothesize that alcoholics may drink to achieve a psychological state of calm alertness.

Psychophysiological studies of alcoholism have been conducted, but without promising results. Jones, Parsons, and Rundell [22] concluded that the evidence for disturbed autonomic functioning is inconclusive and contradictory, and that this area of study is beset with a host of methodological problems and poorly conducted research. Of the specific psychophysiological changes that alcohol has been hypothesized to exert is that of a normalizing effect upon disturbed premorbid autonomic function [24]. While this hypothesis is intriguing, there is unfortunately a dearth of supporting evidence. A hypothesis advanced by Garfield and McBrearthy [12] asserts that alcohol causes an increase in arousal in the alcoholic, with a simultaneous decrease in responsivity to external stimuli. There is, as yet, no direct support for this hypothesis, but the work of Nathan and associates [38], as well as Mendelson [34] and Mellor [33] is noteworthy in that they observed that alcoholics in a controlled laboratory setting, during a period of intoxication, became progressively more anxious over a period of several days. Thus, the effects of alcohol are not simply depressant, but may have arousal-augmenting effects as well. Russell and Mehrabian [42] have aptly concluded in their theoretical review that small doses of alcohol are arousal-enhancing, while continued consumption and larger doses of alcohol exert an attenuating effect on arousal. Could it be that alcoholics strive to maintain an optimal state of intoxication that induces both stimulating and tranquilizing effects? Why they drink to the point where they lapse into an aversive psychological and physiological state is a crucial issue, the answer to which so far has eluded experimental clarification. What these studies do serve to point out, however, is that the physiological effects of alcohol on the individual are more complex than is commonly appreciated, which not surprisingly is undoubtedly a major factor that has contributed to the failure to derive adequate explanations for problem drinking behavior. The fact that alcohol can exert both augmenting and attenuating effects upon arousal necessarily suggests at least two possible motive states that could trigger a drinking episode.

Cognition

Cognitive-appraisal of self. Self-concept and self-esteem have been investigated in male and female alcoholics. Wilsnack [53] has observed that female drinkers manifest a conflict over conformity to the culturally defined sex-role stereotype of femininity. Similar sex-role conflicts have been reported by Harrington [15] among heavily drinking male adolescents. In the latter study, overt masculinity was strong but lower scores were obtained on measures of covert masculinity. A lower level of self-esteem in alcoholics relative to nonalcoholics has also been describe [8], but it is unclear as to whether or not these reduced feelings of self-worth are the product of depression that is frequently found in conjunction with alcoholism. Thus, as a group, alcoholics exhibit lower self-esteem and a disturbed self-concept as it relates to sex-role stereotyping, but this may not be unique to alcoholism, and may instead be due to other concomitant factors, such as the presence of an affective disturbance in the overall clinical disorder.

Another area of interest concerns the degree to which self-esteem fluctuates according to the pharmacologic state of the individual. Alcoholics subjectively judge themselves much more differently in the sober than in the intoxicated state than do nonalcoholics. The alcoholic describes his or her sober self as feeling physically healthy, warm, and purposeful, but during inebriation sees himself or herself as dominant and less desirable than the sober self. Partington [42] theorized that alcoholics perceive themselves in dualistic terms, and that their self-concept depends greatly upon whether or not they are sober or intoxicated. Changes in self-concept have also been reported by Tamerin, Weiner, and Mendelson [48], who found that alcoholics during intoxication perceived themselves differently from when sober, and while in the former state typically saw themselves as being more aggressive, euphoric, sexy, and irresponsible.

In conclusion, it appears that self-esteem during the sober state is generally low in alcoholics. Alcoholics also evidence a greater disparity in self-concept between the sober and inebriated states as compared to a nonpathological population. The precise role that this dimension of self-appraisal plays in being causal to drinking onset or serving to maintain abusive drinking is, however, unknown.

Cognitive appraisal of internal states. Alcoholics are incapable of evaluating interoceptive stimuli of a volumetric nature concomitant to fluid intake. Moreover, they are impaired in assessing their blood alcohol level for quantity of alcohol consumed. These findings have led to the hypothesis that alcoholics cannot regulate the amount of alcohol ingested because they are unable to perceive or evaluate internal cues [37]. Moreover, individuals with a low tolerance for alcohol are better able to employ internal cues in monitoring blood alcohol level than persons with a high tolerance for alcohol. Thus, the large volume of alcohol consumed may be due to high tolerance that itself stems from a disturbance in internal cue perception. Whether this reflects a cognitive disturbance of normal physiological functioning, or is a neurophysiological feedback disorder, remains to be determined.

Cognitive set.   Expectancy factors greatly determine drinking patterns and response to alcohol. For example Marlatt, Demming, and Reid [29] observed that a single dose of alcohol administered to alcoholics does not inevitably lead to loss of control over further drinking. By manipulation of instructional set conditions, these authors observed that expectancy was a powerful determinant of drinking behavior. In another investigation, Asp [1] found that the expectation of alcohol in the beverage led alcoholics to a greater consumption of a nonalcoholic tonic than if they believed that they were drinking tonic only. Thus, one's belief about the contents of the beverage contributes to the amount consumed. Expectancy effects have also been demonstrated to play a role in aggression and sexual arousal in social drinkers [54].

Perceived control of reinforcement.   Whether or not alcoholics view their behavior and its consequences as outside of their control has received some attention by researchers. Perceived locus of control of reinforcement within a social learning theoretical context is an important area of inquiry, inasmuch as it may reflect striking differences between alcoholics and nonalcoholics in the attribution of responsibility for their drinking and other associated deviant behaviors. Individuals who assume responsibility for the outcome of their behavior are viewed as functioning under an internal locus of control. In contrast, individuals under an external locus of control perceive their behavior outcome as due to fate, chance, or environment. Administering the Rotter Locus of Control Scale has however, not revealed consistent differences between alcoholics and nonalcoholics [18].

Emotion

A potentially important factor in alcohol consumption concerns emotional disturbance. Emotion, as can be seen in Figure 1, is the product of both cognitive and physiological variables. Thus, emotion is neither simply a physiological response or a cognitive set, but rather the interaction of these two processes. Schacter [44] theorized that an emotional experience results from the undifferentiated arousal of the sympathetic nervous system combined with cognitive and social factors.

Numerous studies have identified three basic dimensions of an emotional experience. These dimensions, as described by Russell and Mehrabian [42], are pleasure-displeasure, level of arousal, and social context. The emotional components of alcoholic drinking behavior thus involve at least three constituent dimensions in need of analysis.

Pleasure-displeasure. It has long been held that alcohol has tension-reducing properties and thus can alleviate a state of displeasure. From initial animal studies conducted by Masserman and Yum [30] in which it was observed that alcohol reduced the fear of acquired punishment, and by Conger [9], who found that alcohol weakened the avoidance response in a conflict paradigm, numerous investigations have since been conducted, but with equivocal results. Cappell [7] concluded in a thorough review of the literature that the evidence in support of the tension-reduction hypothesis is still unconvincing. Apart from laboratory studies, however, there stands in contrast evidence, from naturalistic observations, that stress or tension is related to alcohol consumption. For example, Henderson and Moore [17] reported that individuals exposed to combat stress manifested increased rates of alcohol consumption. Horton [19] concluded that in societies where the constituent members live in a state of stress in attempting to meet basic biological needs, and are thus presumably more anxious, there are higher levels of alcohol consumption. Thus, from controlled laboratory experiments, of which the vast majority have been conducted with animals, there is no conclusive evidence that tension reduction is a mediating factor in alcoholism. However, there is some evidence in a general sense that stress and tension are related to increased rates of drinking. Whether or not the construct of tension is either heuristic or predictive of alcoholism and related problems still remains to be determined.

Arousal level. As previously discussed, small doses of alcohol exert an arousing effect on the organism, while larger doses tend to have a depressant effect. In addition, there is a biphasic effect whereby alcohol during the ascending (absorption) limb of the blood alcohol curve exerts a general euphoric and excitatory effect, while during the descending (excreting) limb, there ensues dysphoria and fatigue. In a study of alcoholics, Mayfield and Allen [31] observed that 3.3 oz of 50% alcohol relieved depression in affectively disturbed and alcoholic subjects. They attributed this effect to the temporary stimulating properties of the low dose of alcohol. However, a larger dose (6.6 oz of 50% alcohol) did not exert this effect. Thus, a small amount of alcohol has positive benefits in modifying certain aversive emotional states, whereas larger doses are ineffectual. Congruent with this finding, it has frequently been reported that individuals suffering from a bipolar manic-depressive condition drink mostly during the depressed phase of the cycle, which possibly reflects an attempt to alleviate affective distresses through the stimulant effect of alcohol.

A biphasic pattern seems to apply to alcoholic drinking as well. Initial positive feelings followed by aversive reactions seem to be common. This finding has been observed in a number of controlled laboratory studies where alcoholics were given access to alcohol over a period of several days. In the studies by Mendelson, Mello, and their colleagues [33], it was found that alcoholics receiving up to 40 oz of 43% alcohol beverage a day became increasingly depressed and anxious across sessions. Furthermore, they became more hostile, irritable, and demanding. Thus, while the initial reported expectation prior to drinking was to relieve anxiety and induce a pleasurable state, the eventual experience was quite aversive.

Social context. Brown and Cutter [5] found in a study of college students that solitary drinkers experienced greater pain relief after alcohol consumption than social drinkers. Moreover, it has been demonstrated that social drinkers describe the effects of alcohol in terms of emotional changes, in contrast to solitary drinkers, who identify the effects in terms of physical characteristics [41]. These studies demonstrate that the reactions to alcohol depend largely upon the social context in which it is consumed.

Another emotion that has been considered a cardinal feature of the addictions is craving. In controlled laboratory studies, craving for alcohol has generally not been observed. In situations where the manipulation of external cues is so structured as to become salient, then a craving emotion is more likely to be manifest. Since alcoholics are not as capable as nonalcoholics in tuning into interoceptive cues, they are consequently more sensitive to external stimuli in modulating behavior. Hence, social cues, pressure from peers, and signs and advertisements about liquor induce heightened states of arousal, which can elicit craving. The presence or absence of craving thus, to a great extent, depends upon the social context, in this case the laboratory or hospital ward, versus the natural setting in which the drinking typically occurs. Assuming that craving can occur during an organismic state of arousal and in a social context where the environment is ladened with drinking-inducing cues, it is still unclear as to what causal role, if any, this emotion plays in excessive alcohol consumption [28].

Motivation

Emotion by itself need not necessarily result in an overt response, and hence, invoking motivation is an essential additional construct to explain behavior. It is the task before researchers to identify the external and internal stimuli that arouse a motivational state in the alcoholic. From there, the scientific objective is to determine the neurobehavioral mechanisms underlying the particular motivation.

Motivation for alcohol by alcoholics can be inferred to be different from the motivation of nonalcoholics in that the former prefer straight drinks, tend to gulp the beverage, and consume it more rapidly than the latter [45]. These findings suggest that the intensity of the motivation for alcohol is greater in alcoholics than nonalcoholics. However, as Mello [33] has pointed out, alcoholics do not drink until they reach a state of oblivion. Furthermore, their motivation for alcohol is subject to a number of manipulations that can influence the pattern and effort the individual will expend toward acquiring an alcoholic beverage. Bandura [2] has similarly argued that drinking behavior is controlled by the laws of learning and is thus maintained by specific antecedent cues and consequent reinforcers. Keehn [23] has demonstrated that drinking behavior is an operant response that is under schedule control, and that alcohol is not distinctly different from other reinforcers.

Personality. A subcategory of motivation is personality. Personality organization, defined here as a set of dispositional traits that are generalized across specific situations and predispose the individual to characteristic and stable patterns of overt action, has been speculated to be unique in alcoholics. While most researchers reject the notion of a single personality type, there is evidence that alcoholics can be differentiated into several typologies, utilizing such measures as the Minnesota Multiphasic Personality Inventory. However, the causal relationships between personality typologies and drinking behavior remain to be elucidated.

One of the few personality constructs that has been subjected to detailed conceptualization and research concerns the notion of dependency [4]. Among the two personality dispositions relevant to alcoholism are dependency and counterdependency. This theory argues that alcoholism originates as a response to an independence-dependence conflict within the individual. Inebriation results in the person being able to be outwardly dependent, while simultaneously subjectively experiencing independence, accompanied by feelings of power. In contrast, the counterdependent person resolves conflict by overcompensating and behaving in an excessively assertive and even antisocial fashion (the two-fisted drinker) to cover up the underlying dependency. While the evidence is far from conclusive, this construct has proven useful in identifying some of the predrinking characteristics in adolescence that could place the individual at risk for adult alcoholism. As such, the construct appears to be quite heuristic and certainly worthy of more detailed investigation.

Overall, however, personality constructs have unfortunately not been able to accurately predict drinking behavior or who will eventually become alcoholic. Perhaps this is due to the vagueness of the concepts employed, or, alternatively, it may be a result of the fact that personality constructs are too molar to serve as explanatory constructs within the context of a functional behavioral analysis.

Intrapsychic factors. Intrapsychic factors have been largely ignored in alcoholism research apart from the use of various projective tests. Experimental psychologists have tended to shy away from such phenomena despite recent innovative techniques that have been developed. Recent work in experimental analyses of personality has yielded new information on the degree to which intrapsychic coping strategies can exert an effect on organismic functioning. Lazarus, Averill, and Opton [25] reported that the utilization of intrapsychic defenses (such as denial or intellectualization) has the effect of reducing physiological indicators of stress as inferred from autonomic indices of arousal. This intriguing study, as well as others that have been carried out by Lazarus and his colleagues, strongly indicates that intrapsychic mechanisms can actually be helpful in exerting some degree of control over physiological responsivity. Considering the central role that denial has been hypothesized to play in the drinking behavior of alcoholics, the possibility that such a defense by the abusive drinker may have very adaptive benefits in reducing physiological stress needs to be examined. While denial has typically been advanced to explain resistance in therapy, it is plausible that a more important psychological function is that it serves as a stress reducer, and thus reflects an attempt by the individual to adapt to a real or perceived state of duress.

The experimental application of projective techniques has yielded information abut the underlying motive states as revealed through fantasy elaboration. Employing the Thematic Apperception Test, McClelland, Davis, Kalin, and Wanner [32] found that alcohol induced feelings of power in male social drinkers. At lower doses the feelings related more to a social dimension of power, but higher doses resulted in a more personalized feeling of power. While intriguing in terms of the sociocultural implications of drinking behavior in this society, this research has failed to control for the expectancy effect that alcohol creates in the quality of the emotional experience and motivational states.

In conclusion, there is very little that is presently understood about the motivational substrate of alcoholic drinking. A variety of emotional and motivational constructs have been invoked as explanatory factors, but yet none have been convincingly demonstrated to be extant across all individuals or all situations. There are no known universal emotional or motivational correlates of drinking behavior in alcoholics. Mello [33], for example, has clearly demonstrated that the pattern of alcoholic drinking is quite idiosyncratic. While general conclusions cannot be offered, recent research has, nonetheless, yielded valuable information about the complexity and interaction of the factors that serve to initiate and sustain drinking behavior. Furthermore, psychological research has clarified some commonly held notions about the role of such factors as craving, loss of control, tension reduction, and personality constructs as causal precursors that have been presumed to be necessary to excessive drinking.

Reinforcement

Ultimately the reinforcement derived from drinking is what maintains the behavior. Caddy [6] delineated the reinforcement parameters that could sustain repetitive excessive alcohol consumption. First, alcohol is highly rewarding because of its pharmacologic properties as a relaxant and/or euphoriant. Second, alcohol consumption can become associated with a variety of positive social conditions that are conducive to drinking. Thus, peer group interaction, combined with drinking behavior, can enhance the affiliative-emotional needs of the individual. Third, alcohol is a reinforcer by dampening aversive environmental conditions such as boredom or domestic stress. Fourth, alcohol can be utilized to relieve negative physical states like pain, and thus be an analgesic. In addition, alcohol can relieve the aversive physiological state associated with detoxification. Fifth, as discussed, alcohol is a reinforcer by modifying the diverse psychological processes of emotion, motivation, and cognition. Thus, the reinforcing properties of alcohol are derived from an interaction of both pharmacologic and psychological processes. Within the multivariate framework, consumption of alcohol can be reinforcing for a number of reasons, casting further doubt on unidimensional theories of alcoholism.

THE CONSEQUENCES OF ALCOHOLISM

Chronic alcohol abuse exerts deleterious organismic changes across the various levels of biological organization. Referring to Figure 2, it can be seen that psychological and behavioral sequelae can be evaluated in relation to the anatomical, biochemical, and physiological disturbances induced directly or indirectly by a longstanding history of alcohol consumption. Research elucidating the consequences of long-standing abuse across levels of empirical analysis is crucial for a comprehensive understanding of the alcohol-organismic interaction.

Neuropsychological Investigation

Alcoholics perform poorly on a variety of tests that are sensitive to neuroanatomical integrity. Detoxified alcoholics exhibit impairments on abstracting tasks, particularly where the concept to be identified is visual-spatial in nature. Moreover, deficits in abstracting have been observed to be tied to difficulties in set persistence, set shifting, and inability to profit from feedback concerning erroneous responses so

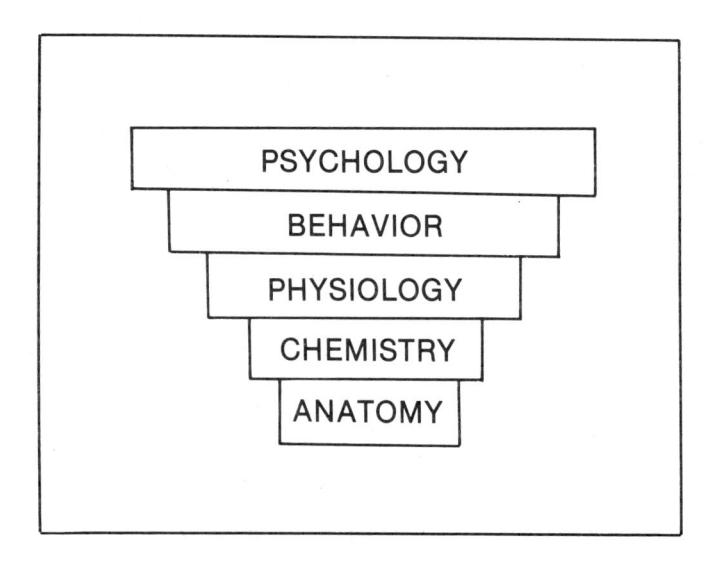

Figure 2. Levels of Empirical Analysis of Biological Organization

as to redirect cognitive processes toward a correct strategy of responding. While intellectual capacity of alcoholics is intact, as reflected by summary IQ scores on the Wechsler Adult Intelligent Scale (WAIS) and Wechsler-Bellevue, performance, on the other hand, is in the organic ranges on measures of biological intelligence, such as the Halstead-Reitan neuropsychological battery. The competency of alcoholics on the latter measures typically range between that of normals and acutely brain-damaged individuals. Tarter [51] reviewed the neuropsychological studies and concluded that impairments, in addition to those on abstraction, are most frequently found in tasks that require spatial integration, orientation, and visualization.

Disturbances have also been noted in short-term memory, with a greater propensity for a nonverbal than a verbal disorder. Disturbances in memory, however, appear to be transient in nature with recovery proceeding more quickly for verbal than nonverbal types of tasks. Where a verbal memory impairment is observed, it is more likely to be found on a serial learning, rather than a paired association, task.

Given the adverse effects of alcoholism on the peripheral nervous system, it is not surprising that muscle weakness has been frequently observed. Similarly, conduction velocity of peripheral nerves has also been found to be slower in alcoholics than nonalcoholics. Despite such pathology, the behavioral studies have not consistently revealed a perceptual-motor disturbance. Neither has motor speed nor reaction time been found to be disrupted. In one study [39] alcoholics were demonstrated to be deficient in modulating a manual motor response, which the authors concluded reflected a disturbance in motor control.

Four competing neuropsychological hypotheses have been advanced in an attempt to identify the neuroanatomical substrate for the observed impairments [49]. The anatomical disturbances have been theorized to be characterized as follows.

Diffused brain damage. The symptom pattern of generalized cerebral atrophy is poor judgment, reduced intellectual competence, memory impairment, reduced clarity of consciousness, and disorientation. The neuropsychological research has not confirmed the presence of a global dementia since no generalized impairment across all psychological functions has been found.

Lateralization of pathology. It has been observed that alcoholics are most impaired on those functions and capacities that are subserved by the right hemisphere. In addition, alcoholics perform relatively more poorly with the left hand than nonalcoholics on manual tasks. Moreover, alcoholics exhibit faster recovery of verbal capacities than nonverbal capacities with sobriety. It is still not clear, however, whether the manifest disturbances implicate a greater pathology of the right hemisphere, or whether these findings are artifactual inasmuch as verbal processes are very automatic and overlearned in the habits of everyday living and thus may be less susceptible to detection of impairment.

Acceleration of the aging process. The brain age quotient, an index derived from a battery of psychometric and neuropsychological tests, is lower in alcoholics than in controls. Young alcoholics perform as well as young normals on clinical neuropsychological tests, but older alcoholics perform significantly more poorly than age-matched controls, suggesting that youthful alcoholics may have a period of immunity before overt impairments are reflected on neuropsychological tests. Employing more sensitive experimental neuropsychological tests has revealed that even young alcoholics are deficient on learning and memory tasks [43]. While the age factor may descriptively aid an understanding of the rate of decline in neuropsychological competency, demonstrating parallel processes does not, however, enhance knowledge about the anatomical systems and substrate that are disturbed.

Anterior-basal pathology. Of the neuropsychological hypotheses that have been advanced, anterior-basal pathology is the only one that implicates a known neurophysiological system. It appears to be the most comprehensive, and supportive evidence has been marshalled from a number of sources. Considering the presence of diencephalic pathology in the Wernicke-Korsakoff syndrome, a similar but more subtle impairment may also exist in the alcoholic. Moreover, there is substantial congruence between the pattern of psychological impairment exhibited by alcoholics and other persons, as well as animals, that have suffered acute lesions in the frontal and basal regions of the brain. A third source of evidence for an anterior-basal disruption is derived from direct observation of the brains of alcoholics at autopsy. Atrophy of the anterior region, accompanied by a proliferation of neurolgia and ventricular enlargement, was first reported 25 years ago by Courville [10]. Studies with the pneumoencephalogram have also revealed ventricular enlargement, particularly with respect to the third ventricle. In one study [16] it was observed that the degree of ventricular enlargement was negatively correlated with abstracting ability. It has also been reported that alcoholics suffer from a reduction of blood flow to the anterior temporal and frontal regions of the brain. And finally, the technique of computerized tomography (CT) has, for the most part, confirmed the findings of ventricular enlargement, as well as cortical atrophy in alcoholics. Thus, the neuropsychological research suggests continuity of impairment between alcoholics and Korsakoff patients that resembles an accelerated aging process, and which seems to incorporate a substantial portion of brain mass that includes the frontal limbic-diencephalic regions of the brain.

Reversibility of impairment. Tarter [51] concluded that the manifest neuropsychological disturbances may be reversible, but recovery, if complete, probably involves a number of different mechanisms. Initial improvement is related to detoxification. The next stage of recovery has been linked to nutritional status and the reversing or halting of hepatic pathology. Deficits ameliorated after about 6 months seem to be tied to the long-lasting toxic effects of alcohol on nervous tissue, and thus improvement on test performance has been speculated to be due to a reorganization of psychological functions, accompanied by the learning of new cognitive strategies.

Studies of reversibility of the neuropsychological deficits have unfortunately not been systematically conducted or, for that matter, well designed. Given these limitations, the mechanisms hypothesized to underly the recovery process must be viewed as tenuous. In some studies improvement and sometimes complete recovery is observed after several months, while in other studies, residual deficits have been noted after a year of sobriety. The course of recovery is also related to the type of psychological function, as indicated by the finding that after detoxification verbal ability recovers more quickly than nonverbal ability. In light of the current evidence it apperas that neuropsychological recovery is a multistage process. The rate of improvement is theorized to depend both on the involved mechanisms (e.g., detoxification, nutrition, neurochemical) and the nature of the psychological function. What is not clear from the research conducted so far is whether or not continued abstinence from alcohol, that is, abstinence beyond 1 year, leads to a full recovery of psychological capacity.

Biochemical-Behavioral Integration

The degree to which alcohol-induced biochemical changes affect behavioral and psychological processes is not known. There are several biochemical systems, which are known to be influenced by alcohol consumption, that directly and indirectly have psychological ramifications. Goddard [13], for example, observed that an acute dose of alcohol prior to a stressful experience (a glider flight) had the effect of reducing norepinephrine levels measured in the urine relative to controls who did not receive a preflight drink. Thus, alcohol may exert an attenuating effect on the mechanisms of the stress reaction, which, when considered in light of the discussion in the first section of this chapter, could have both emotional and motivational sequelae.

Alcohol also interacts with the endocrinological systems. Jones and Jones [21] found, for example, that the rate of alcohol metabolism was slower in women who were receiving oral contraceptives. Such women also voluntarily, and without a conscious decision to do so, consumed less alcohol than those not on the pill. Furthermore, Belfer and Shader [3] reported that 67% of menstruating women related their drinking excesses to the menstrual cycle. Drinking is most frequent during the premenstruum when estrogen levels are lowest, which, in light of the findings by Jones and Jones [21], suggests that alcohol interacts with hormones to influence mood states and behavior.

There are some indications that individuals suffering from cirrhosis are impaired on psychological tests. Smith and Smith [46] found that cirrhotic alcoholics performed at a lower level of intellectual competency than noncirrhotic alcoholics who were matched for age and drinking history. These results were not confirmed, however, by Lee et al. [26], who did not observe a relationship between liver pathology and intellectual competence. These investigators also did not find an association between intellectual impairment and presence of cerebral atrophy as measured by the CT scan. The role of hepatic pathology as a contributor to the psychological deficits obviously needs to be clarified.

Nutritional status is another variable that may contribute to the psychological deficits of alcoholics. Fleming and Guthrie [11] found that EEG disturbances in detoxified alcoholics were correlated with indices of malnutrition, specifically folate deficiency. Reversal of the EEG abnormalities tended to occur with the restoration of nutrition. Psychometric capacity was observed to be correlated with the EEG as well. In another investigation Guthrie and Elliott [14] demonstrated that cerebral impairment, as inferred from neuropsychological measures, was correlated with malnutrition.

One factor that has largely been ignored concerns the role of congeners in the alcohol beverage. Impure substances, such as flavorings, and fermentation and distillation by-products in commercial beverages, may contribute to the psychological deficits. While acute effects of congeners on physiological functioning have been reported, it is unknown if there is a cumulative toxic effect of congeners concommitant to chronic alcohol consumption. There is some evidence that Marchiafava-Bignami disease, a syndrome characterized by central nervous system degeneration that is associated with alcoholism, may be in fact due to the congeners in certain types of wine.

In conclusion, there are biochemical, nutritional, and endocrinological correlates of drinking that may affect psychological processes and capacities.

Psychophysiology

One factor that is possibly responsible for the onset of excessive drinking is the nature of the psychophysiological reaction experienced by the individual. Integral to this notion is the ethnic sensitivity hypothesis, which asserts that certain racial groups have a lower incidence of alcoholism because they experience aversive physiological consequences after ethanol ingestion. Consequently, such individuals, would be inclined to drink less because of the aversive state induced by the ethanol. Oriental individuals have been observed to exhibit a larger magnitude of the flushing response after an acute dose of alcohol than Caucasians, which is also accompanied by a larger drop in blood pressure, increased heart rate, and enhanced state of discomfort. This flushing reaction is manifested by both infants and adults, indicating that it is due to biological differences between racial groups in autonomic nervous system responsivity that is independent of environmental or learning factors. The flushing response has also been reported in North American Indians, Americans of Mongolian extraction, and Eskimos. These findings are intriguing insofar as sensitivity to alcohol is concerned, but as Jones et al. [22] point out, alcohol, even though causing an aversive reaction in these individuals, does not explain the fact that there is a very high incidence of alcohol among such responders as North American Indians. Hence, ethnic sensitivity to alcohol cannot by itself adequately explain either drinking problems or the absence thereof in specific racial groups.

Psychological techniques can be useful in determining how and if tension reduction occurs after alcohol consumption. Psychophysiological reactions during the ascending and descending limbs after alcohol consumption need to be elucidated, since tension reduction could occur during either absorption or excretion but not necessarily in both metabolic phases. Similarly, the organ system most susceptible to modification by alcohol needs to be analyzed with psychophysiological techniques. Unfortunately, there has been no systematic research on these questions.

The long-term effects of ethanol on psychophysiological functioning has been succinctly reviewed by Naitoh [35]. If cortical and diencephalic lesions of the brain are the consequences of alcohol abuse, then one would expect concomitant visceral disturbances. The upsetting of these systems by chronic alcohol consumption may produce lasting psychophysiological changes, although whether in fact such does take place is unknown. Jones et al. [22] summarized the confusing and often contradictory array of findings that have been reported in the literature. They concluded that no organ system has been found to be consistently disturbed in sober alcoholics, nor do alcoholics exhibit a unique psychophysiological profile.

TOWARD AN INTEGRATIVE APPROACH

Experimental analysis ideally should proceed across all levels of biological organization in order to provide a comprehensive portrait of the clinical phenomenon under inquiry. Inasmuch as genetic, anatomical, biochemical, psychological, and sociocultural factors have all been invoked to explain the causes and/or effects of alcohol abuse, it is not surprising that an abundance of hypotheses and theories have been advanced. One etiologic feature that has been theorized to be extant in a subgroup of alcoholics is hyperactivity [52]. Many of the observed characteristics of the prealcoholic are also found in hyperactive children, such as impulsivity, rebelliousness, psychosocial immaturity, and disturbances in arousal regulatory mechanisms. These inherent or acquired characteristics may place the person at risk for alcohol abuse for the pharmacologic and psychological effects that could be accrued. Support for this notion is provided by the findings from adoption and family studies in which an association between alcoholism and hyperactivity has been reported. Thus, the phenotypic expression of the genetic endowment for one type of alcoholism may be hyperactivity in childhood. During a course of development that is marked by poor behavioral and interpersonal adjustment, along with a facilitating environment and role models, the person is predisposed to alcohol consumption as a coping strategy. Such a hypothesis is heuristic and also enables a conceptualization of drinking behavior that incorporates different levels of empirical analysis involving psychological and biological processes. Moreover, such an approach paves the way for the development of empirically derived typologies of problem drinkers. While this specific hypothesis may not withstand future experimental examination, it does nonetheless illustrate how to attack the complex problem of alcoholism, mainly by pulling together findings from different disciplines and levels of biological organization.

SUMMARY

Problem drinking is viewed by the experimental psychologist as existing along a continuum of severity, with manifold factors contributing to the etiology and maintenance of this complex behavior. The causes and maintenance of excessive drinking are not viewed as a unidimensional process or disease, but rather as a multivariate disorder. In this regard, a major contribution from experimental psychology has been the demonstration that the pharmacologic properties of ethanol cannot totally explain the diversity and patterns of excessive alcohol consumption. A second major contribution from experimental psychology has been the elucidation of psychological and behavioral sequelae of alcohol-induced changes at the anatomical, biochemical, and physiological levels of biological organization.

Considering the two concepts of multivariate description and levels of biological organization, future research ought to be directed toward integrating the diverse processes in order to derive an empirically established classification system of problem drinkers. With such an orientation, the field of experimental psychology can have a major impact in adding to knowledge of both the causes and consequences of alcohol use and abuse.

REFERENCES

1. Asp, D. Effects of alcoholics' expectation of a drink. *J. Stud. Alcohol* 38:1790–1795, 1977.
2. Bandura, A. *Principles of Behavior Modification*. Holt, Rinehart & Winston: New York, 1969.
3. Belfer, M., and Shader, R. Premenstrual factors as determinants of alcoholism in women. In: *Alcoholism Problems in Women and Children*, Greenblatt, M. and Schukit, M. (eds.). Grune & Stratton: New York, 1976.
4. Blane, H. *The Personality of the Alcoholic: Guises of Dependence*. Harper & Row: New York, 1968.
5. Brown, R., and Cutter, H. Alcohol, customary drinking behavior and pain. *J. Abnorm. Psychol.* 86:179–188, 1977.
6. Caddy, G. Toward a multivariate analysis of alcohol abuse. In: *Alcoholism: New Di-*

rections in Behavioral Research and Treatment, Nathan, P., Marlatt, G. and Loberg, T. (eds.). Plenum: New York, 1978.

7. Cappell, H. An evaluation of tension models of alcohol consumption. In: *Research Advances in Alcohol and Drug Problems* (Vol. 2), Gibbons, R., Israel, Y., Kalant, R., Popham, R., Schmidt, W. and Smart, R. (eds.). Wiley: New York, 1975.

8. Charalampous, K., Ford, K., and Skinner, T. Self-esteem in alcoholics and nonalcoholics. *J. Stud. Alcohol* 37:990-994, 1976.

9. Conger, J. The effect of alcohol on conflict behavior in the albino rat. *J. Stud. Alcohol* 12:1-29, 1951.

10. Courville, C. *Effects of Alcohol on the Central Nervous System.* San Lucas Press: Los Angeles, 1955.

11. Fleming, A., and Guthrie, A. The electroencephalogram, psychological testing and other investigations in abstinent alcoholics: A longitudinal study. In preparation.

12. Garfield, Z., and McBrearty, J. Arousal level and stimulus response in alcoholics after drinking. *J. Stud. Alcohol* 31:832-838, 1970.

13. Goddard, P. Effect of alcohol on excretion of catecholamines in conditions giving rise to anxiety. *J. Appl. Physiol.* 13:118-120, 1958.

14. Guthrie, A., and Elliott, W. *The Nature and Reversibility of Cerebral Impairment in Alcoholism: Treatment Implications.* Paper presented at NATO conference, Experimental and Behavioral Approaches to Alcoholism, Bergen, Norway, 1977.

15. Harrington, C. *Errors in Sex-Role Behavior in Teen-Age Boys.* Teachers College Press: New York, 1970.

16. Haug, J. Pneumoencephalographic evidence of brain damage in chronic alcoholics. *Acta Psychiat. Scand.* 203:135-143, 1968.

17. Henderson, J., and Moore, M. The psychoneuroses of war. *N. Eng. J. Med.* 230:273-278, 1944.

18. Hinrichsen, J. Locus of control among alcoholics: Some empirical findings and conceptual issues. *J. Stud. Alcohol* 37:908-916, 1976.

19. Horton, D. The functions of alcohol in primitive societies: A cross cultural study. *Q. J. Stud. Alcohol* 4:199-320, 1943.

20. Jacobson, G. *Sensory Deprivation and Field Dependence in Alcoholics.* Unpublished doctoral dissertation, Illinois Institute of Technology, 1971. (University Microfilms No. 72-22, 839)

21. Jones, B., and Jones, M. Women and alcohol intoxication, metabolism, and the menstrual cycle. In: *Alcoholism Problems in Women and Children,* Greenblatt, M. and Schukit, M. (eds.). Grune & Stratton: New York, 1976.

22. Jones, B., Parsons, O., and Rundell, O. Psychophysiological correlates of alcoholism. In: *Alcoholism: Interdisciplinary Approaches to an Enduring Problem,* Tarter, R. and Sugerman, A. (eds.). Addison-Wesley: Reading, Mass., 1976.

23. Keehn, J. Reinforcement of alcoholism: Schedule control of solitary drinking. *Q. J. Stud. Alcohol* 31:28-39, 1970.

24. Kissin, B., Schenker, V., and Schenker, A. The acute effects of ethyl alcohol and chlorpromazine on certain physiological functions in alcoholics. *Q. J. Stud. Alcohol* 20:480-492, 1959.

25. Lazarus, R., Averill, J., and Opton, E. The psychology of coping: Issues of research and assessment. In: *Coping and Adaptation,* Coleho, G., Hamburg, D. and Adams, J. (eds.). Basic Books: New York, 1974.

26. Lee, K., Moller, L., Hardt, F., Haubek, A., and Jensen, E. Alcohol-induced brain damage and liver damage in young males. *Lancet* 2:759-761, 1979.

27. Lindsley, D. Psychophysiology and motivation. In: *Nebraska Symposium on Motivation,* Jones, M. (ed.). University of Nebraska Press: Lincoln, 1957.

28. Ludwig, A., and Wilker, A. "Craving" and relapse to drink. *Q. J. Stud. Alcohol* 35: 108–130, 1974.
29. Marlatt, G., Demming, B., and Reid, J. Loss of control drinking in alcoholics: An experimental analogue. *J. Abnorm. Psychol.* 81:233–241, 1973.
30. Masserman, J., and Yum, K. An analysis of the influence of alcohol on experimental neuroses in cats. *Psychosom. Med.* 8:36–52, 1946.
31. Mayfield, D., and Allen, D. Alcohol and affect: A psychopharmacological study. *Am. J. Psychiatry* 123:1346–1351, 1967.
32. McClelland, D., Davis, W., Kalin, R., and Wanner, E. *The Drinking Man.* Free Press: New York, 1972.
33. Mello, N. Behavioral studies of alcoholism. In: *The Biology of Alcoholism* (Vol. 2), Kissin, B. and Begleiter, H. (eds.). Plenum: New York, 1972.
34. Mendelson, J. (ed.). Experimentally induced chronic intoxication and withdrawal in alcoholics. *Q. J. Stud. Alcohol* (Suppl No. 2), 1964.
35. Naitoh, P. The effect of alcohol on the autonomic nervous system of humans: Psychophysiological approach. In: *The Biology of Alcoholism* (Vol. 2), Kissin, B. and Begleiter, H. (eds.). Plenum: New York, 1972.
36. Naitoh, P., and Docter, R. Electroencephalographic and behavioral correlates of experimentally induced intoxication with alcoholic subjects. *Int. Congr. Alcoholism. Abst.*, 33, 1968.
37. Nathan, P. Studies in blood alcohol discrimination. In: *Alcoholism: New Directions in Behavioral Research and Treatment*, Nathan, P., Marlatt, G., and Loberg, T. (eds.). Plenum: New York, 1978.
38. Nathan, P., Titler, N., Lowenstein, L., Solomon, P., and Rossi, A. Behavioral analysis of chronic alcoholism: Interaction of alcohol and human contact. *Arch. Gen. Psychiatry* 22:419–430, 1970.
39. Parsons, O., Tarter, R., and Edelberg, R. Altered motor control in chronic alcoholics. *J. Abnorm. Psychol.* 72:308–314, 1972.
40. Partington, J. Dr. Jekyll and Mr. High: Multidimensional scaling of alcoholics' self-evaluations *J. Abnorm. Psychol.* 75:131–138, 1970.
41. Pliner, P., and Cappell, H. Modification of affective consequences of alcohol: A comparison of social and solitary drinking. *J. Abnorm. Psychol.* 83:418–425, 1974.
42. Russell, J., and Mehrabian, A. The mediating role of emotions in alcohol use. *J. Stud. Alcohol* 36:1508–1536, 1975.
43. Ryan, C., and Butters, N. *Accelerated Aging and Chronic Alcoholics: Evidence from Tests of Learning and Memory.* Paper presented at 10th Annual NCA Medical-Scientific Conference, Washington, D.C., 1979.
44. Schacter, S. *Emotion, Obesity and Crime.* Academic Press: New York, 1971.
45. Schaefer, H., Sobell, M., and Mills, K. Baseline drinking behaviors in alcoholics and social drinkers: Kinds of drinking and sip magnitude. *Behav. Res. Ther.* 9:23–27, 1971.
46. Smith, H., and Smith, L. WAIS functioning of cirrhotic and noncirrhotic alcoholics. *J. Clin. Psychol.* 33:309–313, 1977.
47. Sugerman, A., and Schneider, D. Cognitive styles in alcoholism. In: *Alcoholism: Interdisciplinary Approaches to an Enduring Problem*, Tarter, R. and Sugerman, A. (eds.). Addison-Wesley: Reading, Mass., 1976.
48. Tamerin, J., Weiner, S., and Mendelson, J. Alcoholics' expectancies and recall of experiences during intoxication. *Am. J. Psychiatry* 126:1697–1704, 1970.
49. Tarter, R. Empirical investigations of psychological deficit. In: *Alcoholism: Interdisciplinary Approaches to an Enduring Problem*, Tarter, R. and Sugerman, A. (eds.). Addison-Wesley: Reading, Mass., 1976.
50. Tarter, R. Etiology of alcoholism: Interdisciplinary integration. In: *Alcoholism: New*

Directions in Behavioral Research and Treatment, Nathan, P., Marlatt, G., and Loberg, T. (eds.). Plenum: New York, 1978.

51. Tarter, R. Brain damage in chronic alcoholics: A review of the psychological evidence. In: *Addiction: Biochemical Aspects of Dependence and Brain Damage,* Richter, D. (ed.). Groon Helen: London, 1980.

52. Tarter, R. Minimal brain dysfunction as an etiological predisposition to alcoholism. In press.

53. Wilsnack, S. The impact of sex roles and women's alcohol use and abuse. In: *Alcoholism Problems in Women and Children,* Greenblatt, M. and Schukit, M. (eds.) Grune & Stratton: New York, 1976.

54. Wilson, G. Booze, beliefs and behavior: Cognitive processes in alcohol use and abuse. In: *Alcoholism: New Directions in Behavioral Research and Treatment,* Nathan, P., Marlatt, G., and Loberg, T. (eds.). Plenum: New York, 1978.

55. Witkin, H., Dyk, H., Faterson, H., Goodenough, D., and Karp, S. *Psychological Differentiation.* Wiley: New York, 1962.

43

G. ALAN MARLATT, PhD, University of Washington
DENNIS M. DONOVAN, PhD, Veterans Administration Medical Center, Seattle, Washington

BEHAVIORAL PSYCHOLOGY APPROACHES TO ALCOHOLISM

RECENT YEARS HAVE witnessed a marked increase in behavioral psychological research concerning the development, maintenance, and treatment of alcoholism and problem drinking. A major impetus to this increase has been a growing body of findings questioning the validity of a number of assumptions that serve as cornerstones to the more traditional disease models of alcoholism [17]. It appears that such basic tenets of the disease model as the orderly progression of symptom manifestation, the concepts of physiologically based craving and loss of control, and the choice of abstinence as the only viable goal in treatment, have been challenged by recent empirical findings [46]. While the purpose and scope of the present chapter are not to debate the validity of the more traditional model, such challenges provide a foundation from which is emerging a relatively new, alternative perspective of alcoholism within a behavioral framework. This view is embodied in the context of cognitive social learning theory.

G. Alan Marlatt, PhD, Professor, Department of Psychology, University of Washington, Seattle, Washington.

Dennis M. Donovan, PhD, Alcohol Dependence Treatment Program, Veterans Administration Medical Center, and Department of Psychiatry and Behavioral Sciences, University of Washington, Seattle, Washington.

The cognitive social learning approach differs from more traditional models with respect to the assumptions made about the nature of drinking and the development of drinking problems [28, 42]. Problem drinking is viewed as a multiply determined, learned behavioral disorder. It can be understood best through the empirically derived principles of social learning, cognitive psychology, and behavior therapies. The focus of this approach is on the observable aspects of drinking behavior, including the frequency and duration of drinking episodes, amount of alcohol consumed, and the problems associated with excessive use. Particular interest is paid to the determinants of drinking behavior. These include situational and environmental antecedents, the individual's past learning history, prior experiences with alcohol, and cognitive processes and expectations about the effects of alcohol. Such factors serve as antecedent cues that often precipitate excessive alcohol use. An equal emphasis is placed on the consequences of drinking, which serve to maintain the behavior. Such factors provide information concerning the potential reinforcing effects of alcohol. Also included in this class of variables are the social and interpersonal reactions experienced by the drinker.

All drinking behavior, from social drinking to alcohol abuse, is assumed to be governed by similar principles of learning and reinforcement. Alcohol use and abuse are viewed as falling along a continuum. There does not appear to be a crucial difference with respect to the quantity and/or frequency of alcohol consumed or the principles governing drinking behavior that differentiates between the social drinker and the problem drinker [28, 42]. Within this context, an individual is considered to be a problem drinker in terms of the effects that alcohol has on his or her daily life functioning. An individual whose alcohol consumption consistently has a negative influence on his or her social, emotional, physiological, occupational, or mental functioning is considered to be a problem drinker. The frequency of the problems attendant to drinking is indicative of the seriousness of the problem [42].

A large body of data concerning the behavioral assessment and treatment of problem drinking is being amassed. Much of this information stems from carefully designed and controlled laboratory, analogue, and clinical evaluation studies. However, these empirical advances in knowledge have not yet led to the development of fully integrated theoretical models to account for the development or etiology of alcoholism [26]. While the theoretical underpinnings of behavioral psychological models are founded in general learning theory, particularly in classical and operant conditioning, it is more appropriate to speak of behavioral approaches. These represent varying methods of studying social drinking and alcoholism that focus on the observable parameters of drinking behavior.

The development of the behavioral approaches seems to have passed through a number of stages that parallel the evolution of general learning theory and behavior therapy. As in any evolutionary process, there is a progression in the level of sophistication and in the breadth of phenomena that are to be explained. Furthermore, the progression continues, with currently emerging trends suggesting areas of future importance. Cognitive social learning theory appears to be such an emergent approach to alcoholism and problem drinking, evolving from and building upon those behavioral principles that have survived empirical validation.

The purpose of this chapter is to provide a brief historical review of those early behavioral approaches that have provided a foundation for and have helped to shape the currently emerging conceptualization of problem drinking and alcoholism. For this purpose, it is useful to think of a major distinction in learning theory that is appropriate to the subsequent discussion. General psychological theories of learning and behavior may be viewed as falling along a continuum with respect to the extent to which nonobservable, "person" variables, such as beliefs, values, perceptions, expectations, and attributional processes, are involved in or mediate the explanation and prediction of behavior. Earlier behavioral approaches to alcoholism, in their classical interpretation, were nonmediational in nature. Drinking behavior was explained entirely in terms of the temporal relationship between certain stimuli cues and alcohol consumption or the reinforcing properties of alcohol. Little or no attention was paid to social or cognitive variables that might influence or mediate drinking. While such approaches initially appeared to be parsimonious, recent research suggests that such early models are not able to account for a wide range of phenomena related to drinking behavior.

The emerging behavioral approaches to problem drinking and alcoholism may be considered mediational in nature. These approaches extend beyond the pure stimulus-response focus of earlier behavioral models, while building on those principles that have been empirically validated. Current behavioral perspectives view drinking as a social behavior, acquired through the processes of vicarious learning, modeling, social reinforcement, and the anticipated effects of alcohol [2, 45]. A heavy emphasis is placed upon the individual's expectancies about alcohol and its anticipated effects as they influence drinking and a number of related behaviors. It has been demonstrated empirically that such cognitive expectancies appear to override the pharmacologic effects of alcohol for a variety of human behaviors in which one's beliefs about alcohol play an important role, including aggressive behavior, sexual arousal, anxiety reduction, craving for alcohol, and loss of control over drinking [27, 32, 50].

NONMEDIATIONAL BEHAVIORAL APPROACHES

Classical Conditioning Approaches

The earliest behavioral approach to alcoholism viewed it as a behavioral disorder in which alcohol acquired a positive valence through a classical conditioning process. Within such a paradigm, previously neutral stimuli (conditioning stimuli) are paired in time with another stimulus (unconditioned stimulus) that produces some quantifiable physiological response (unconditioned response) in the individual. After a number of such pairings, the previously neutral stimuli are capable of eliciting the response (conditioned response). However, it is unclear how such a paradigm, alone, accounts for the acquisition of problem drinking patterns. The preponderance of literature on classical conditioning in the area of alcoholism has focused on its treatment through aversive therapy techniques. Little emphasis has been directed toward the etiology of the disorder within this framework.

Ludwig and Wikler [23] have recently attempted to extend the classical conditioning paradigm to explain the phenomenon of craving among alcoholics. These authors consider craving for alcohol as the psychological or cognitive correlate of a subclinical conditioned withdrawal syndrome. The craving and related sensations that are assumed to occur during an alcoholic's withdrawal from the drug can become classically conditioned to stimuli that are related in time with the withdrawal experience. These stimuli include the physical environment, drug-using or drug-dispensing associates, and certain emotional states. If an abstinent alcoholic is exposed to these conditioned stimuli at a later date, he will experience symptoms of craving (conditioned response) that may predispose him to drink. It is felt that more frequent and severe prior withdrawal experiences will lead to stronger sensations of craving in response to the conditioned stimuli. However, the authors go far beyond limiting the stimuli capable of eliciting craving to those directly associated with instances of withdrawal. The conditioned or eliciting stimuli are expanded to include a variety of internal and external cues that have been associated with prior heavy drinking, such as passing a bar or being with other people who are drinking. General states of physiological and/or emotional arousal may also give rise to sensations of craving. Consumption of an initial drink after a period of abstinence acts to further increase the craving for alcohol, thus increasing the probability that continued drinking (loss of control) will occur. "The first drink, then, would act like an 'appetizer,' stimulating hunger (craving, as a conditioned withdrawal response) even further because it has become sequentially conditioned to the later consumption of the 'entree' (intoxication)" [23, p. 128]. The extension of eliciting power to such cues that have not been associated directly with the withdrawal episode represents a departure from a strict classical conditioning interpretation.

A further departure from the traditional model is found in the importance placed on cognitive factors by Ludwig and Wikler [23]. They suggest that the way in which the alcoholic cognitively labels the subclinical conditioned withdrawal syndrome will influence whether the attendant constellation of sensations and feelings will be interpreted consciously as craving. Those cues that have been associated with prior drinking (e.g., the presence of drinking companions, a bar or social gathering, or the solitary confines of a hotel room) would be likely to provide a cognitive set conducive to the interpretation of arousal as a powerful state of craving. Those stimuli that are directly associated with the withdrawal experience (e.g., the social and environmental cues found in detoxification and treatment settings), which theoretically should be prepotent, may in fact not lead to the interpretation of a craving state. The influence of such eliciting stimuli may be overridden by the demand characteristics both explicit and implicit in such settings that the alcoholic should not drink or crave alcohol.

What began as a relatively straightforward attempt to explain craving for alcohol by a simple classical conditioning paradigm has thus been expanded to a more complex cognitive interpretation. In the process, the model has become somewhat inconsistent, and it appears as though the cognitive labeling of arousal states has assumed a more dominant role than the conditioned elicitation of the subclinical withdrawal state. The results of an empirical test of the model [24] appear to further substantiate this assertion.

According to the proposed theory, craving should be maximal under the influence of small doses of alcohol consumed in the presence of drinking-related cues. As noted above, such cues, although not directly paired with physical withdrawal, provide a cognitive set appropriate to the labeling of sensations as craving. It was further hypothesized that the low dose of alcohol should produce a greater craving for alcohol than a high dose, because of the conditioned appetizer effect associated with small amounts. Presumably, higher doses would satisfy the craving for more alcohol.

To test this hypothesis, Ludwig, Wikler, and Stark [24] conducted a study in which 24 detoxified male alcoholics were administered alcohol under various conditions. Half of the subjects consumed their preferred drink in the presence of alcohol-related cues (the appropriate labeling condition), and half consumed alcohol with an artificially sweetened mixer in the absence of alcohol cues (the nonlabel condition). Subjects were also assigned to one of three alcohol dose conditions: high dose (1.2 ml/kg), low dose (0.6 ml/kg), or a placebo with a small amount of alcohol floating on the top of the mixer. Subjective reports of craving were obtained at four time intervals following the beverage administration (ranging from 20 to 200 minutes later). These estimates were assessed by means of a craving meter, a device that permitted the subject to indicate the degree of craving on a scale from 0 to 100.

While the results of the study are difficult to interpret because of a number of methodological and data analysis problems, in general they fail to support the authors' hypothesis. At the first assessment 20 minutes after beverage administration, the highest level of craving was reported by the placebo group in the appropriate labeling condition. At no time period was there a significant difference in the craving reported by subjects consuming beverages in the presence of appropriate alcohol-related cues, regardless of the actual dose. Furthermore, in all beverage groups (including the placebo), the appropriate labeling condition led to significantly higher levels of craving than did the nonlabel condition. In contrast to the author's original model, the overall pattern of findings seems to support the role of cognitive expectancy factors rather than the classically conditioned, physically appetizing effects of a low dose of alcohol.

While the traditional classical conditioning model as applied to alcoholism represented a nonmediational position, it appears that cognitive factors may play a more significant role than had been thought originally. The view that alcoholism and its related behaviors are acquired through a single process, while appearing parsimonious, does not adequately account for the disorder. It should also be noted that recent critiques have suggested that the effectiveness of aversive counterconditioning therapies, in which the sight, smell, and taste of alcohol are repeatedly paired with noxious stimuli, may be mediated primarily by cognitive factors [2, 37].

Hullian Learning Theory: Tension-Reduction Approaches

A second early behavioral formulation of the development of problem drinking was based upon the Hullian learning principles popular during the 1950s. The basic tenet of this position was that those behaviors that lead to a decrease in arousal are reinforced, and thus are more likely to occur under subsequent states of arousal. A focus was placed upon the apparent tension-reducing pharmacologic action of alcohol as an etiologic factor in the development of problem drinking. The tension-reduction hypothesis (TRH), as this approach was later called, assumed that alcohol serves to reduce tension, and that the relief of tension serves to reinforce the drinking response. A corollary of this hypothesis assumed that the experience of subsequent tension or stress will increase the probability of drinking [5, 25].

With the current emphasis on drive-reduction theories of general reinforcement and learning, combined with the commonsense notion that alcohol serves as a relaxing agent, the tension-reduction hypothesis was generalized from its infrahuman laboratory origins and readily accepted by proponents of a learning theory approach to drinking behavior. This acceptance was spurred by the publication of a number of influential theoretical papers extending Hullian principles to the analysis of alcoholism in humans [8, 18, 19]. Research with both humans and animals proliferated in an attempt to support the basic assumptions of the hypothesis. However, a review of this burgeoning literature suggested that the results were equivocal, at best, and often conflicting [4, 5]. No unequivocal results were found that directly supported the assumption that alcohol has an inherent tension-reducing property or that individuals consume alcohol for its tension-reducing effects.

While such findings question the validity of the tension-reduction hypothesis within a nonmediational framework, a large percentage of individuals expect alcohol to reduce tension and eliminate or minimize negative affective states [10, 51]. It also appears that negative emotional states, such as anger, tension, anxiety, and depression, represent frequently reported reasons given for drinking by both social drinkers and alcoholics [9, 22, 30]. How is it that such observations can be so discrepant from the research on the tension-reduction hypothesis?

Although the anticipated mood-altering effects of alcohol appear to motivate much drinking, how the person expects to feel under the influence of alcohol does not always correspond to the actual emotional states while intoxicated. Alcoholics, for example, who anticipated that they would feel less despressed and more relaxed and comfortable while drinking actually reported experiencing an increase in dysphoria and tension following prolonged periods of intoxication [34, 44]. This discrepancy may be related to the biphasic response to alcohol, as well as an opponent process underlying reaction to many other psychoactive drugs [48]. Recent reviews [27, 28] suggest that at low doses alcohol leads to increased physiological arousal. This aroused state is often subjectively experienced and cognitively labeled by the drinker as feelings of excitement, euphoria, increased energy, and perceptions of the self as more powerful. As time passes and the amount consumed increases, the initial feelings of euphoria are transformed to feelings of increasing dysphoria. Steffen, Nathan, and Taylor [49], for example, found that while alcoholics experienced a decreased level of muscle tension with increasing blood alcohol levels (a finding consistent with the TRH), they reported an increase in subjective tension and distress. The resultant negative affective states that occur during this second phase appear to exert a minimal impact on reducing subsequent drinking since their onset is delayed in time. Rather, such increases in subjectively experienced tension and dysphoria may actually increase the probability of drinking. This result would be predicted from the individual's belief that alcohol should reduce tension and/or the attempt to regain the previously experienced "high" associated with the low dose stimulant effects of alcohol. It appears to be the immediate pleasurable effects of the initial phase of alcohol's biphasic response curve that have the greatest influence on learning and on shaping the individual's expectations about alcohol as a tension-reducing agent. Furthermore, it appears that it is these anticipated positive effects of alcohol, rather than the actual effects, that mediate the reinforcement for drinking.

The nonmediational context of the tension-reduction hypothesis again appears to be unable to fully explain important aspects of drinking behavior. The way in which the individual interprets arousal and its alteration, his or her beliefs and expectancies about the effects of alcohol, and personal attributional processes play an important role in any hypothesis that focuses on alcohol as a tension-reducing agent.

Operant Learning Approaches

The mid-1960s witnessed a shift away from a reliance on a purely tension-reduction perspective of Hullian learning theory to a somewhat more comprehensive, functional analysis of drinking behavior based upon Skinnerian principles of operant conditioning. As in the TRH, a continued focus was placed upon the consequences that are contingent upon drinking and serve to maintain this behavior.

However, the reduction of tension represents only one of a variety of factors that may serve to reinforce drinking. Miller and Barlow [38] suggest that drinking behavior may be maintained by enabling the individual to avoid or escape anxiety-producing situations, exhibit more varied and spontaneous social behavior, gain increased social reinforcement from friends and relatives, or avoid withdrawal symptoms associated with the cessation of drinking. Thus, to the extent that drinking produces a positive consequence or allows the individual to escape from or avoid unpleasant or aversive situations, these consequences will be reinforcing and the probability of drinking will be increased.

As found in the classical conditioning approach to alcoholism, an emphasis is also placed upon the antecedents of drinking by proponents of an operant approach. However, these drinking-related cues are not assumed to operate by eliciting a conditioned response. Rather, Miller [37] suggests that such antecedents represent setting events, or environmental stimuli that set the occasion for drinking to occur. Cues, such as negative mood states, including depression, anxiety, loneliness, boredom, and perceived personal failure, as well as situational cues, such as the presence of drinking acquaintances and a barroom setting, have been associated so frequently with the reinforcement derived from excessive drinking that they have acquired secondary reinforcing properties. The mere presence of such cues serves to initiate drinking. The extent to which alcoholics' and social drinkers' alcohol consumption is controlled by such cues appears to differ. Miller, Hersen, Eisler, Epstein, and Wooten [40] engaged alcoholics and social drinkers, matched on age and education, in an operant lever-pressing task in order to obtain alcohol under two cue conditions. In the cue salience condition a variety of visual alcohol-related stimuli were prominently displayed on the response console; in the no cue condition these stimuli were absent from view. It was found that the alcoholics did not respond differentially across the two cue conditions. However, the social drinkers made significantly more operant responses in the presence of the alcohol cues than in their absence. The results suggest that social drinkers are more responsive to appropriate alcohol-related discriminative stimuli than are alcoholics. The social drinkers' consummatory behavior appeared to be more situation-specific, while the drinking of the alcoholics was more generalized and less controlled by situational variables.

The use of such operant tasks to investigate the antecedent and consequent events influencing drinking behavior in a systematic fashion was pioneered in the work of Mello and Mendelson [36]. In these tasks subjects are required to work by engaging in some quantifiable behavior, ranging from simple button-pressing to more complex social and/or interpersonal interactions. Alcohol was provided as a reinforcer for meeting certain levels of performance. The number of responses required to obtain alcohol was systematically varied to evaluate the influence of differing response costs on drinking. The amount of work done by the subjects, defined in terms of the frequency, rate, intensity, or patterning of responding, has been used to evaluate the relative reinforcement value of alcohol as compared to other sources of reinforcement, such as money or social interaction. Reviews of early operant studies [35, 37, 43] have indicated that such a functional analysis has provided a number of interesting and important findings concerning the topography of drinking and the variables that control it.

The operant approach to problem drinking represents an important advance over its predecessors. The classical conditioning paradigm placed a primary focus on the antecedents of drinking, while the tension-reduction hypothesis emphasized the reinforcing consequences. The operant approach integrates both of these classes of events as factors that exert control on drinking behavior. An assumption of this approach is that the reinforcement contingent on drinking serves directly (i.e., without mediation) to shape and maintain this behavior. However, recent conceptualizations of reinforcement theory as it applies to behavior in general [47] and specifically to drinking [10, 12] have questioned this assumption.

Rather than shaping behavior directly, reinforcement may serve instead to develop a set of generalized expectancies concerning the relationship between a particular behavior and its most probable outcome. These expectancies are strengthened with further experience as the behavior produces the desired outcome with greater frequency and predictability. These are generalized expectancies in that they are evoked by a variety of situations that are perceived by the individual as having similar stimulus properties. Also, as the individual gains a greater familiarity with the response-outcome contingencies within a particular situation or setting, a set of more influential, situationally specific expectancies develop. These generalized and specific expectancies and situational parameters operate interactively, along with the perceived value of the anticipated reinforcer, to determine behavior. Within this model, the probability of a particular behavior is high when the individual anticipates that an action will lead predictably to a highly valued outcome within a situational context previously associated with its occurrence. As it applies to drinking, this model suggests that the individual has developed a number of generalized and specific expectancies about alcohol and its effects. For the problem drinker, drinking appears to have acquired a high level of perceived value as a reinforcer relative to other behaviors that might produce comparable outcomes. When confronted by situations where drinking is anticipated to result in some desired instrumental outcome, the probability of consuming alcohol increases. Drinking-related cues, viewed as setting events have secondary reinforcing properties in the operant model, serve to evoke the situationally specific expectancies concerning alcohol's effects and to enhance the perceived reinforcing value of drinking.

MEDIATIONAL BEHAVIORAL APPROACHES

The previous sections have highlighted the contributions made by earlier behavioral models to the understanding of alcoholism and problem drinking. Each of these, in its more traditional formulation, was presented by its original proponents as nonmediational in nature. It was felt that cognitive factors played an important role. However, as noted, subsequent research and conceptualization have questioned such strict interpretations that do not take into account the individual's perceptions, beliefs, and expectations. It is felt that the inclusion of such cognitive factors with the general principles of learning previously discussed enhances the ability to more fully account for the phenomena associated with the acquisition and maintenance of problem drinking. It is this integration that has led to the emergence of the cognitive social learning approach.

Cognitive Social Learning Approaches

Acquisition of drinking behavior. Bandura [2] indicated that while the avoidance or escape from aversive situations and the other forms of positive reinforcement that accompany drinking may account in part for its maintenance, an adequate approach to alcoholism must include additional social learning variables to account for the initial acquisition of drinking behavior. A particularly relevant set of variables includes the cultural and subcultural norms and mores that define the reinforcement contingencies governing the use of alcohol. These norms are to a large extent transmitted through the modeling behavior of parents and peers. O'Leary, O'Leary, and Donovan [45] reviewed a large body of literature concerning the psychosocial development of individuals who were later defined as alcoholic. It was found that the parents of such individuals fail to present a model for moderate social drinking. They frequently are heavy drinkers or alcoholics themselves and tend to approve of their children's drinking. As Bandura [2] notes, such a familial situation, where alcohol is consumed extensively across a variety of circumstances and is often used as a means of coping, is likely to transmit a similar pattern of drinking to the children. This modeling influence may also represent the origin of the individual's expectations concerning alcohol's effects as a primary source of reinforcement. This pattern of drinking, along with its associated expectancies, appears to be furthered by peer relationships, in that adolescent problem drinkers tend to select heavy drinkers as friends [45].

The influence of the effects of modeling on alcohol consumption was demonstrated by Caudill and Marlatt [6]. Males who were heavily drinking social drinkers asked to participate in a taste-rating task in the presence of a peer partner. In this task, an unobtrusive measure of alcohol consumption, the subjects were asked to rate three varieties of wines along a variety of taste dimensions, consuming as much of each necessary to make accurate judgments. Both subjects were asked to work on the taste-rating task independently without talking to one another. Unknown to the real subject, the other person was a confederate subject acting as a drinking model. In two conditions of the experiment, the model played the role of either a heavy or a light social drinker. In the former condition, the model consumed 700 ml of wine (equivalent to a full bottle) during the 15-minute experimental task; in the latter condition, he consumed 100 ml of wine. A third group constituted a no model control condition. The results demonstrated the striking effects that peer modeling exerted on drinking behavior. Subjects who observed the heavily drinking model drank twice as much wine as subjects in the no model control group; the light drinking model produced a further drop of 22% relative to the control condition. This powerful modeling effect seems to be relatively specific to males who are heavy drinkers exposed to a heavily drinking model of the same sex. Lied and Marlatt [21] found that females and light drinking males did not show the same susceptibility to the modeling effect.

Influence of expectancies. Through the processes of peer and parental modeling, direct and indirect past experiences with drinking, and exposure to media and advertising, a number of specific expectancies concerning alcohol appear to develop. These cognitions, which appear to apply with differing degrees to social and problem drinkers, tend to have a marked influence on drinking-related phenomena in a manner consistent with self-fulfilling prophecies. These expectancies often serve to both initiate and maintain drinking behavior. The outcome of consuming alcohol, often perceived by the individual as being reinforcing and serving some instrumental function, serves to strengthen further the expectancies and their influence on drinking [10]. Furthermore, one's belief about what alcohol is expected to do often overrides the actual pharmacologic effects of the drug [27, 50].

Alcohol is expected to reduce tension, eliminate or minimize negative affective states, and enhance social interaction [10]. It is likely that the probability of drinking will increase in those situations that the individual perceives and personally defines as stressful and for which he or she expects alcohol to reduce the experience of tension or stress. This represents a reinterpretation of the traditional tension-reduction hypothesis within the context of a cognitive mediational approach. The application of these two assumptions is demonstrated in research on interpersonal anxiety resulting from anticipated or actual personal evaluation by members of the opposite sex. Higgins and Marlatt [16] found that heavily drinking males who anticipated that they would be rated along selected dimensions of personal attractiveness by a group of female peers drank significantly more alcohol than those in a low-interpersonal threat control group. Wilson and Abrams [51] extended this research by employing a balanced placebo design [32] to evaluate the relative contribution of cognitive expectancies and alcohol's pharmacologic effects to the reduction of such interpersonal anxiety. In this paradigm, as described by Marlatt, Demming, and Reid [29], half of the subjects are led to believe that they are consuming vodka in a tonic base, while the other half are told that they are receiving only tonic. Within each of these two conditions, half the subjects actually receive alcohol, while the others receive only tonic. In the Wilson and Abrams study [51], all subjects were told that they were participating in a study on the effects of alcohol on interpersonal communication patterns. The subjects' task was to make as favorable an impression on a female rater as possible. The findings indicated that subjects who believed that they had consumed alcohol, regardless of the actual alcoholic content of their beverage, evidenced significantly less increase in heart rate and a lower level of self-reported anxiety during the anxiety-induction phase than those who believed that they had drunk only tonic.

A second set of expectancies particularly relevant to problem drinkers is that the consumption of alcohol will result in sensations of craving and loss of control over drinking [10]. The results of research employing the balanced placebo design with alcoholics have challenged the physiologic underpinnings of these traditional assumptions. Engle and Williams [14] provided their alcoholic subjects with strongly flavored "vitamin mixtures" as a supplement to their treatment. Half of these mixtures contained 1 oz of 100 proof vodka. Half of the subjects were led to believe that they had been given alcohol, while the remainder were led to believe that they had received only the vitamin mixture. Approximately 40 minutes after consuming this beverage, the subjects completed a brief questionnaire with an embedded question about their immediate desire for a drink. The results indicated that those subjects who had been led to believe that they had been given vodka, regardless of the actual alcoholic content, reported significantly higher levels of subjective craving. Marlatt et al. [29] similarly found that both alcoholic and social drinker subjects who drank heavily consumed significantly more beverage in a taste-rating task when they believed it contained alcohol; the actual presence or absence of alcohol in the mixtures exerted no control over drinking.

Social skill deficits. An important component in the area of problem drinking is the availability of appropriate social skills and interpersonal competencies that can be employed to deal effectively with stress and negative emotional states as they arise. O'Leary, et al. [45] noted that individuals who are later identified as alcoholics have significant deficits in those social skills that might increase the accessibility to desired and reinforcing outcomes. It has been found that complex interpersonal situations requiring the use of well-developed social skills may provoke social anxiety that, in the absence of more adaptive responses, may precipitate drinking among heavily drinking social drinkers and alcoholics [15, 20]. Drinking serves as a means of coping with strong external pressures; its initiation is enhanced by the individual's expectation that alcohol will reduce tension. Furthermore, drinking for such individuals, deficient in social skills, appears to have a high level of perceived reinforcement value, since it is engaged in instead of a variety of other more appropriate behaviors that might produce comparable results.

The influence of social skill deficits on drinking behavior has been demonstrated in a number of analogue studies. Miller, Hersen, Eisler, and Hilsman [41] involved alcoholics and social drinkers in either socially stressful or nonstressful conditions. Interpersonal stress was induced by criticizing the individual's responses in a number of social situations requiring assertive behavior. The nonstressful condition consisted of a discussion of leisure-time activities. The subjects engaged in an operant task to earn alcohol after their participation in these conditions. Physiologic measures indicated that the anxiety-inducing condition was equally stressful to both the alcoholics and the nonalcoholics. However, while the two groups did not differ in their operant response rates under the nonstress condition, the alcoholics emitted significantly more responses to obtain alcohol under the stressful condition. The authors inferred from these findings that the alcoholics were deficient in adequate interpersonal coping skills relative to the nonalcoholics and thus responded to the stress by drinking. Miller and Eisler [39] similarly found that deficits in alcoholic subjects' ability to express negative feelings was significantly related to increased drinking on an operant task. Marlatt, Kosturn, and Lang [31] also found that heavily drinking social drinkers who were provoked to anger without the opportunity to express these feelings tended to significantly increase the amount they drank relative to subjects who were not angered. However, those subjects who were provoked but were allowed the opportunity to express their anger against the individual who had criticized them drank even less than the nonprovoked controls.

Issues of perceived control and self-efficacy. The previous findings suggest that the availability of appropriate coping skills tends to increase the individual's sense of control within stressful situations and reduces the need to rely upon alcohol as a means of reducing stress. The issue of control, both perceived and experienced, appears to assume an important role in the development and maintenance of problem drinking [11, 12, 13]. The problem drinker, in the absence of adaptive social skills, experiences a decrease in the amount of control experienced within a stressful situation. Bandura [3] has recently developed a cognitive formulation of behavior that relies heavily upon the notion of perceived self-efficacy. An efficacy expectancy represents the individual's belief that he or she either can or cannot successfully execute the behavior required in a particular situation in order to produce a desired outcome. The level of one's self-efficacy thus appears to be an interactive function of the individual's appraisal of the behavioral requirements of the situation and the perceived availability of appropriate, adaptive coping skills within his or her repertoire. A lowered level of personal efficacy or the lack of perceived and experienced control in a stressful situation will lead to a failure to attempt to exert control. The attribution of such deficits to personal inadequacies leads to increases in the level of perceived stress, dysphoria, and helplessness, decreases self-esteem, and a decreased likelihood to attempt to exert control in similar situations in the future [1].

The loss of perceived control and personal self-efficacy among individuals lacking adequate social skills is relevant to another predominant expectancy: Alcohol is expected to enhance one's perception of personal control or power. McClelland and his coworkers [33] have found that as the dosage of alcohol consumed by social drinkers increases there is an increase in the perception of personal control, suggesting that for some individuals drinking may be a response to needs for power and control. This finding is consistent with the results of a number of clinical and experimental analogue studies that demonstrate that alcohol consumption increases in situations where the individual perceives himself or herself as powerless or as having low levels of personal efficacy [31, 39, 41].

A Cognitive-Behavioral Model of Problem Drinking

The expectancies that one has about alcohol and its effects, the relative deficits in one's adaptive social skills, and the resulting decreased level of personal efficacy and perceived control represent factors that appear to operate interactively to influence drinking. The proposed model [25, 28] predicts that the probability of excessive drinking will vary in a particular situation as a function of the following factors:

1. The degree to which the drinker feels controlled by or helpless relative to the influence of another individual, or group (e.g., social pressure to conform, modeling, evaluation or criticism by others, being frustrated or angered by others), or external environmental events that are perceived by the individual as beyond his or her personal control. Such situations, which threaten the drinker's perception of control, represent high-risk situations.

2. The availability of an adequate coping response as an alternative to drinking in high-risk situations. If, due to deficits in one's repertoire of social skills, the individual fails to perform an appropriate coping response, the level of perceived self-efficacy is lowered. This results in a further reduction in perceived control, an increase in the perceived stressfulness of the situation, and an increased sense of personal helplessness.

3. The availability of alcohol and the constraints upon drinking in the particular situation.

4. The drinker's expectations about the effects of alcohol as one means of attempting to cope with the situation. If the individual has developed the belief that drinking will increase feelings of personal power or perceived control, as well as decrease stress, alcohol becomes a prepotent source of reinforcement. If the drinker is confronted by a situation that is personally defined as stressful and for which he or she has no adequate coping response available, thus resulting in a decreased perception of control and self-efficacy, and if he or she expects alcohol to be an effective means of both decreasing the perceived stress and enhancing a sense of control, the probability of drinking will be high.

A Cognitive-Behavioral Model of Alcoholic Relapse

The previous model appears to apply to both heavily drinking social drinkers and alcoholics. Marlatt [27] has recently extended these principles to a cognitive-behavioral model accounting for the apparent loss of control associated with alcoholic relapse. A number of specific, high-risk relapse situations have been identified for the alcoholic [7, 22, 30]. These include negative emotional states such as depression, anxiety, and boredom; becoming frustrated and angry without being able to express these feelings; an inability to resist social pressure from others to drink; and intrapersonal temptations analogous to craving. Again, it appears that the individual often is lacking in appropriate skills to deal effectively with these situations, with a resultant feeling of perceived helplessness [22]. The alcoholic may cognitively interpret and label the strong desire for the anticipated reinforcing effects of drinking as a state of craving. Within this situational context, along with the individual's beliefs about alcohol as a means of coping, the likelihood of drinking is enhanced. When an alcoholic takes an initial drink following a prolonged period of voluntary sobriety, the probability of continued drinking, or loss of control, is enhanced. This appears to be facilitated by the belief that even a single drink will trigger loss of control. On a cognitive level, the relapse results in an abstinence violation effect (AVE) [27]. The intensity of this effect and the magnitude of its resulting consequences are a function of the drinker's degree of commitment to abstinence and the length of sobriety achieved. It is hypothesized that the AVE is mediated by two primary cognitive processes. The first is a cognitive dissonance effect, in which the individual's drinking behavior is perceived as discrepant from the predrinking cognition of the self as abstinent. Such dissonance often results in a negative emotional drive state involving depression, guilt, and lowered self-esteem. Continued drinking would seem likely given the alcoholic's belief that alcohol minimizes such negative emotions as well as the expectancy that one drink leads to a drunk. Subsequent drinking would also serve to modify the person's cognitions and self-image to be consonant with no longer being abstinent. The second component process is a personal attribution effect, in which the individual attributes the return to drinking to internal weakness and personal failure rather than to external or situational factors. Such attributions concerning the failure to control important outcomes are associated with further feelings of dysphoria and helplessness, with a resultant decrease in one's motivation to exert control [1]. The attribution of failure to one's personal deficiencies also leads to a decrease in the individual's self-efficacy expectancies. Again, given the alcoholic's belief about alcohol as a means of coping and of enhancing the perception of control, such internal attributions concerning the causes of the initial relapse would be predicted to increase the probability of further drinking.

The previous discussion suggests that a cognitive social learning approach is capable of explaining a wide variety of aspects of drinking behavior, ranging from the acquisition of alcohol consumption as a means of coping to loss of control among alcoholics following relapse. This model represents an extension of previous behavioral approaches, building upon the basic principles derived from these predecessors. As in other areas of behavioral psychology, reconceptualization of a particular behavior disorder is paralleled by a change in orientation toward treatment and intervention. The presently emerging behavioral perspective of problem drinking and alcoholism has direct implications for treatment [28, 30, 37, 42]. The focus of such interventions should be directed toward the development of social skills, both generalized and specific, to high-risk drinking situations, perceived control and enhanced personal efficacy, and relapse-prevention techniques. Only future research will establish the usefulness and effectiveness of the cognitive social learning model of problem drinking and the treatment strategies that are as yet emerging from it.

REFERENCES

1. Abramson, L. Y., Seligman, M. E. P., and Teasdale, J. Learned helplessness in humans: Critique and reformulation. *J. Abnorm. Psychol.* 87:49-74, 1978.
2. Bandura, A. *Principles of Behavior Modification.* Holt, Rinehart & Winston: New York, 1969.
3. Bandura, A. Self-efficacy: Toward a unifying theory of behavioral change. *Psychol. Rev.* 84:191-215, 1977.
4. Cappell, H. An evaluation of tension models of alcohol consumption. In: *Research Advances in Alcohol and Drug Problems*, Gibbons, R. J., Israel, Y., Kalant, H., Popham, R. E., Schmidt, W. and Smart, R. G. (eds.). Wiley: New York, 1975.
5. Cappell, H., and Herman, C. P. Alcohol and tension reduction: A review. *Q. J. Stud. Alcohol* 33:33-64, 1972.
6. Caudill, B. D., and Marlatt, G. A. Modeling influences in social drinking: An experimental analogue. *J. Consult. Clin. Psychol.* 43:405-415, 1975.
7. Chaney, E. F., O'Leary, M. R., and Marlatt, G. A. Skill training with alcoholics. *J. Consult. Clin. Psychol.* 46:1092-1104, 1978.
8. Conger, J. J. Alcoholism: Theory, problem and challenge. II. Reinforcement theory and the dynamics of alcoholism. *Q. J. Stud. Alcohol* 17:291-324, 1956.
9. Deardorff, C. M., Melges, F. T., Hout, C. N., and Savage, D. J. Situations related to drinking alcohol: A factor analysis of questionnaire responses. *J. Stud. Alcohol* 36:1184-1195, 1975.
10. Donovan, D. M., and Marlatt, G. A. Behavioral assessment of social and problematic drinking: A cognitive social learning formulation. *J. Stud. Alcohol* 41:1153-1185, 1980.
11. Donovan, D. M., and O'Leary, M. R. Comparisons of perceived and experienced control among alcoholics and nonalcoholics. *J. Abnorm. Psychol.* 84:726-728, 1975.
12. Donovan, D. M., and O'Leary, M. R. The drinking-related locus of control scale: Reliability, factor structure and validity. *J. Stud. Alcohol* 39:759-784, 1978.
13. Donovan, D. M., and O'Leary, M. R. Control orientation among alcoholics: A cognitive social learning perspective. *Am. J. Drug Alcohol.* 6:487-499, 1979.
14. Engle, K. B., and Williams, T. K. Effect of an ounce of vodka on alcoholics' desire for alcohol. *Q. J. Stud. Alcohol* 33:1099-1105, 1972.
15. Hamburg, S. Behavior therapy in alcoholism: A critical review of broad-spectrum approaches. *J. Stud. Alcohol* 36:69-87, 1975.
16. Higgins, R. L., and Marlatt, G. A. Fear of interpersonal evaluation as a determinant of alcohol consumption in male social drinkers. *J. Abnorm. Psychol.* 84:644-651, 1975.

17. Jellinek, E. M. *The Disease Concept of Alcoholism*. Hillhouse: New Brunswick, N.J., 1960.
18. Kepner, E. Application of learning theory to the etiology and treatment of alcoholism. *Q. J. Stud. Alcohol* 25:279–291, 1964.
19. Kingham, R. J. Alcoholism and the reinforcement theory of learning. *Q. J. Stud. Alcohol* 19:320–330, 1958.
20. Kraft, T. Social anxiety model of alcoholism. *Percept. Mot. Skills* 33:797–798, 1971.
21. Lied, E. R., and Marlatt, G. A. Modeling as a determinant of alcohol consumption: Effects of subject sex and prior drinking history. *Addict. Behav.* 4:49–54, 1979.
22. Litman, G. K., Eiser, J. R., Rawson, N. S. B., and Oppenheim, A. N. Differences in relapse precipitants and coping behavior between alcohol relapsers and survivors. *Behav. Res. Ther.* 17:84–94, 1979.
23. Ludwig, A. M., and Wikler, A. "Craving" and relapse to drink. *Q. J. Stud. Alcohol* 35:108–130, 1974.
24. Ludwig, A. M., Wikler, A., and Stark, L. H. The first drink: Psychobiological aspects of craving. *Arch. Gen. Psychiatry* 30:539–547, 1974.
25. Marlatt, G. A. Alcohol, stress, and cognitive control. In: *Stress and Anxiety* (Vol. 3), Sarason, I. G. and Spielberger, C. D. (eds.). Hemisphere: Washington, D.C., 1976.
26. Marlatt, G. A. Behavioral approaches to alcoholism: A look to the future. In: *Behavioral Approaches to Alcoholism*, Marlatt, G. A. and Nathan, P. E. (eds.). Rutgers Center of Alcohol Studies: New Brunswick, N.J., 1978.
27. Marlatt, G. A. Craving for alcohol, loss of control, and relapse: A cognitive-behavioral analysis. In: *Alcoholism: New Directions in Behavioral Research and Treatment*, Nathan, P. E., Marlatt, G. A. and Løberg, T. (eds.). Plenum: New York, 1978.
28. Marlatt, G. A. Alcohol use and problem drinking: A cognitive-behavioral analysis. In: *Cognitive-Behavioral Interventions: Theory, Research, and Procedures*, Kendall, P. C. and Hollon, S. P. (eds.). Academic Press: New York, 1979.
29. Marlatt, G. A., Demming, B., and Reid, J. B. Loss of control drinking in alcoholics: An experimental analogue. *J. Abnorm. Psychol.* 81:223–241, 1973.
30. Marlatt, G. A., and Gordon, J. R. Determinants of relapse: Implications for the maintenance of behavior change. In: *Behavioral Medicine: Changing Health Lifestyles*, Davidson, P. (ed.). Brunner/Mazel: New York, 1979.
31. Marlatt, G. A., Kosturn, C. F., and Lang, A. R. Provocation to anger and opportunity for retaliation as determinants of alcohol consumption in social drinkers. *J. Abnorm. Psychol.* 84:652–659, 1975.
32. Marlatt, G. A., and Rohsenow, D. J. Cognitive processes in alcohol use: Expectancy and the balanced placebo design. In: *Advances in Substance Abuse: Behavioral and Biological Research*, Mello, N. K. (ed.). JAI Press: Greenwich, Conn., 1980.
33. McClelland, D. C., Davis, W. M., Kalin, R., and Wanner, E. *The Drinking Man*. Free Press: New York, 1972.
34. McGuire, M. T., Mendelson, J. H., and Stein, S. Comparative psychosocial studies of alcoholic and nonalcoholic subjects undergoing experimentally induced ethanol intoxication. *Psychosom. Med.* 28:13–25, 1966.
35. Mello, N. K. Behavioral studies of alcoholism. In: *The Biology of Alcoholism* (Vol. 2), Kissin, B. and Begleiter, H. (eds.). Plenum: New York, 1972.
36. Mello, N. K., and Mendelson, J. H. Operant analysis of drinking patterns of chronic alcoholics. *Nature* 206:43–46, 1965.
37. Miller, P. M. *Behavioral Treatment of Alcoholism*. Pergamon: New York, 1976.
38. Miller, P. M., and Barlow, D. H. Behavioral approaches to the treatment of alcoholism. *J. Nerv. Ment. Dis.* 178:10–20, 1973.

39. Miller, P. M., and Eisler, R. M. Assertive behavior in alcoholics: A descriptive analysis. *Behav. Ther.* 8:146-149, 1977.

40. Miller, P. M., Hersen, M., Eisler, R. M., Epstein, L. H., and Wooten, L. S. Relationship of alcohol cues to the drinking of alcoholics and social drinkers: An analogue study. *Psychol. Record* 24:61-66, 1974.

41. Miller, P. M., Hersen, M., Eisler, R. M., and Hilsman, G. Effects of social stress on operant drinking of alcoholics and social drinkers. *Behav. Res. Ther.* 12:67-72, 1974.

42. Miller, P. M., and Mastria, M. A. *Alternatives to Alcohol Abuse: A Social Learning Model.* Research Press: Champaign, Ill., 1977.

43. Nathan, P. E. Alcoholism. In: *Handbook of Behavior Modification and Behavior Therapy,* Lieitenberg, H. (ed.). Prentice-Hall: Englewood Cliffs, N.J., 1976.

44. Nathan, P. E., Titler, N. A., Lowenstein, L. M., Solomon, L., and Rossi, A. M. Behavioral analysis of chronic alcoholism. *Arch. Gen. Psychiatry* 22:419-430, 1970.

45. O'Leary, D. E., O'Leary, M. R., and Donovan, D. M. Social skill acquisition and psychosocial development of alcoholics: A review. *Addict. Behav.* 1:111-120, 1976.

46. Pattison, E. M., Sobell, M. B., and Sobell, L. C. (eds.). *Emerging Concepts of Alcohol Dependence.* Springer: New York, 1977.

47. Rotter, J. B. Generalized expectancies for internal versus external control of reinforcement. *Psychol. Monographs* 80: whole no. 609, 1966.

48. Solomon, R. L. An opponent-process theory of acquired motivation: IV. The effective dynamics of addiction. In: *Psychopathology: Experimental Models,* Maser, J. and Seligman, M. E. P. (eds.). W. H. Freeman: San Francisco, 1977.

49. Steffen, J. J., Nathan, P. E., and Taylor, H. A. Tension-reducing effects of alcohol: Further evidence and some methodological considerations. *J. Abnorm. Psychol.,* 83:542-547, 1974.

50. Wilson, G. T. Booze, beliefs, and behavior: Cognitive processes in alcohol use and abuse. In: *Alcoholism: New Directions in Behavioral Research and Treatment,* Nathan, P. E., Marlatt, G. A. and Løberg, T. (eds.). Plenum: New York, 1978.

51. Wilson, G. T., and Abrams, D. Effects of alcohol on social anxiety and physiological arousal: Cognitive versus pharmacological processes. *Cog. Ther. Res.* 1:195-210, 1977.

Section VI

Psychiatric Disorders and Alcoholism

44

EDWARD J. KHANTZIAN, MD, Harvard Medical School at The Cambridge Hospital

PSYCHOPATHOLOGY, PSYCHODYNAMICS, AND ALCOHOLISM

THIS CHAPTER REVIEWS some of the principal psychiatric and psychopathologic findings associated with alcoholism and considers how these findings are related psychodynamically to the subjective distress and behavioral disturbances, including drinking behavior, with which alcoholics suffer. Subsequent chapters in Section VI review in more detail specific psychiatric disorders and related conditions and situations associated with alcoholism. The psychopathology associated with alcoholism may be a cause or a consequence of the overuse or misuse of alcohol. Previous sections and chapters in this volume amply document the consequences of alcoholism; this chapter emphasizes psychiatric findings and psychodynamics that have appeared to predispose certain individuals to alcoholism.

Background and Early Psychodynamic Formulations

Early psychodynamic formulations of alcoholism were grounded in instinct theory and a topographic model that emphasized instinctual drives and the

---

Edward J. Khantzian, MD, Associate Professor of Psychiatry, Department of Psychiatry, Harvard Medical School at The Cambridge Hospital, Cambridge, Massachusetts.

unconscious symbolic meaning of alcohol to explain the compelling appeal of alcohol. Thus, early psychoanalytic formulations stressed unconscious self-destructive drives, oral regressive longings, and homosexual tendencies as major psychodynamic determinants of the alcoholism [1, 9, 27, 39, 47]. It should also be noted, however, that many of these early formulations also considered other contributing influences, such as depression, diminished self-esteem, faulty ego ideal formation, and other forms of narcissistic disturbances.

This chapter attempts to advance a contemporary psychoanalytic perspective that considers how the psychiatric disorders and psychopathology associated with alcoholism are psychodynamically related to and the result of vulnerabilities and disturbances in ego and self structures that leave alcoholics ill-suited to regulate and manage their behavior, feelings (affects), and inner states of well-being involving self-comfort and self-esteem. As a result, alcoholics resort to the use of alcohol both as manifestations of such disturbances and as attempts to cope with and compensate for them.

PSYCHOPATHOLOGY

Overview

An emphasis is placed here mainly on findings from the psychiatric literature that highlight some of the prominent psychopathology associated with alcoholism. To a lesser extent, evidence from the psychology literature is cited that seems to complement and support the findings from the psychiatric literature. However, before reporting on these diagnostic findings in association with alcoholism, it should be emphasized that trying to fathom the problem of psychiatric findings associated with alcoholism has been complex, controversial, and elusive. Several factors contribute to the difficulties in diagnosing psychiatric disorders in alcoholism: In part, the success of the disease concept, at first heuristically advanced by Jellinek [15] and later parochially advanced by others, has detracted from more careful evaluation of psychiatric and psychological factors that might underlie alcoholism [20, 36, 37]. Also, the cause and effect relationships between alcohol use and coexistent psychopathology are not specified in many studies, thus making comparison of different reports and populations difficult. In addition, until recently there have been major lacks in standardized diagnostic criteria as well as longitudinal studies, which are necessary for meaningful comparisons and for more objective bases for sorting out such issues as cause and effect relationships between alcohol and psychopathology. An attempt is made to circumvent these pitfalls in this chapter, but current approaches and knowledge make it impossible to escape entirely these difficulties. Accordingly, this chapter focuses selectively on studies and clinical reports that seem to avoid repeating and perpetuating the above-mentioned pitfalls.

In general, the most consistent psychiatric finding in various groups of alcoholics that have been studied has been the existence of depression and/or sociopathy. To a lesser extent there are a few, but important, reports that show an association of anxious-phobic (or panic) conditions associated with some cases of alcoholism. With a few exceptions, most diagnostic reports on alcoholics show a low incidence of neurosis or psychosis. However, a number of investigators have debated whether alcoholism might mask psychopathology involving depression, neurosis, and psychosis [4, 13, 20].

Sociopathic, Personality, and Behavioral Disturbances

The alcoholic's obvious behavioral problems have led investigators to concentrate on and emphasize the alcoholic's antisocial and personality disturbances as major determinants of the alcoholism. Many studies underscore preexisting juvenile delinquency, criminality, and other forms of impulsivity as major contributing factors in the background of alcoholics. Others have found important associations between problems of restlessness, hyperactivity, extroversion, and aggression in childhood and adolescence and the subsequent development of alcoholism. Although many of these studies are retrospective and fail to consider or account for children and adolescents who showed these features and did not become alcoholics, there does seem to be enough common denominators in these studies to review and consider how certain early behavioral disturbances and features might subsequently be contributory to and part of the alcoholism syndrome and alcohol problems.

The works of Woodruff, Guze, Robins, Goodwin, and their associates are notable in consistently documenting preexisting histories of troubling and delinquent behavior in alcoholics. Guze et al. [11, 12] and Goodwin et al. [10] reported that a high proportion of felons were alcoholics (43%) and that sociopathy was found to be much more frequently associated with alcoholic felons than nonalcoholic felons. Robins et al. [41] found that alcoholism among young, urban, black men was closely related to antisocial behavior in childhood and adolescence. Barry, who recently reviewed these trends [4], documented similar findings of a high incidence of alcohol problems among white, urban, delinquent adolescents in a separate study with his associates [5]. Along somewhat different lines, but supporting the evidence of sociopathy in relation to alcoholism, emergency room studies of alcoholics by Robins et al. [40] and more recently by Rund et al. [42] found that 25% and 28% respectively of individuals satisfying a criteria of alcoholism were also diagnosed as antisocial personality.

In an interesting study that supports a link between sociopathy and alcoholism, Woodruff et al. [53] set out to study the relationship between alcoholism and depression based on the assumption that successful treatment of the depression could alleviate the alcoholism. What they discovered instead was that alcoholics with depression were more like alcoholics without depression in their backgrounds and prealcoholic histories than they were like individuals with depression alone. That is, the alcoholism had preceded the depression, and, in the cases of depressed alcoholics and alcoholics without depression, both groups had backgrounds with significant evidence of sociopathy that began prior to the onset of clinical alcoholism (37% of all male and 22% of all female alcoholics—regardless of depression—were diagnosed as sociopaths). In 58% of the cases of nondepressed alcoholics and in 73% of the cases of depressed alcoholics there were background histories of major disruptions in the family life of these alcoholics, including illegitimacy, separations, divorces, cruelty, neglect, alcohol and/or drug experimentation, suicide, and employment difficulties. The past, prealcoholic histories of the alcoholics themselves revealed a high incidence of childhood and adolescent fighting and rageful outbursts, runaway behavior, school disciplinary problems, military misconduct, and arrests for a range of criminal activities.

Tarter et al. [48] undertook a study to differentiate alcoholics according to the degree of severity of alcohol abuse and specific childhood characteristics. They employed the concept of minimal brain dysfunction (MBD) to characterize the childhood backgrounds of certain alcoholics the way Woodruff and Guze and others employ the term "sociopathy," whereby features of impulsivity, restlessness, hyperactivity, and aggression of alcoholics in their youth predominated. Tarter and his associates designated this group of alcoholics as primary alcoholics. They were found to be a group who exhibited hyperactivity and other MBD symptoms in their youth, became addicted to alcohol at an earlier age, and manifested a more severe form of alcoholism, but otherwise were less disturbed psychiatrically than nonprimary alcoholics. Primary alcoholics were compared with secondary alcoholics, as well as psychiatric and normal controls. In Tarter et al.'s study [48] they were able to clearly identify a subpopulation of alcoholics who had early behavioral difficulties. Although they showed little evidence of psychiatric distress, behavioral measures and the MacAndrew Alcoholism scale derived from the Minnesota Multiphasic Personality Inventory (MMPI) clearly revealed this group as having had childhood MBD and/or sociopathic symptoms, as well as an earlier onset and a more severe form of alcoholism.

Owens and Butcher [35] and Barnes [3] have recently reviewed and reexamined the evidence for specific personality factors preceeding and/or contributing to the development of problem drinking and alcoholism. Principally drawing on results using the MMPI, their reports highlight certain themes and trends that are consistent with the previously cited literature that documents a preexistent history of sociopathy in association with alcoholism. Alcoholics are repeatedly noted in most of these studies to be elevated on scale 4 (psychopathic deviant, Pd), which reflects personality features that are sociopathic in nature. That is, these populations are unable to learn from past experiences, lack manifest anxiety, and have unstable interpersonal relations and problems with authority. With some success, attempts have been made in a number of studies using the MMPI to differentiate subgroups; two main subgroups have emerged, one characterized by anxiety and depression, the other characterized by psychopathy.

Of promising consequence, the MacAndrew Alcoholism scale (MAC), which has been derived from 49 MMPI items, has been shown to separate and differentiate more clearly features of alcoholics from psychiatric and normal controls. The characteristics that the MAC scale seem to identify appear to be persistent and immutable over time in contrast to the MMPI profile in general of alcoholics, which changes over time and progressively approaches normal profiles postdetoxification and with prolonged abstinence. The MAC scale thus makes more possible, comparable, and meaningful longitudinal studies of individuals who become alcoholics.

Both Barnes and Owens [35] and Butcher [3] single out the works of Kammeier, Hoffman, and Loper as significant contributions that documented MMPI and MAC findings in a group of college men studied longitudinally, some of whom subsequently became alcoholics. In their series of studies a group of 38 problem drinkers were compared to a control group of 148 of their male classmates, both groups having been administered the MMPI during their freshman year in college. In these studies, Kammeier and her associates [14, 16, 32] found the following:

1. Thirteen years before coming for treatment (i.e., when they were freshmen), the problem drinkers had significantly higher scale 4 (Pd) and scale 9 (Ma) scores, and even at that age these men gave evidence that they were more gregarious, impulsive, and less conforming than their peers, but psychological maladjustment was not evident.

2. Freshman MAC scores of the subjects who later developed drinking problems were significantly higher than those of the classmate controls.

3. While the overall MMPI scores of those individuals who later became alcoholics were within normal limits when they were freshman, most of their scales were elevated at the time of treatment.

Owens and Butcher [35] suggest that components and items of the MAC scale measure characterologic factors such as self-confidence, interpersonal competence, religiosity, risk taking, school maladjustment, impulsiveness, and inability to delay gratification. Barnes believes these findings might be singularly important in documenting evidence for a prealcoholic personality in which early problems with impulsiveness, nonconformity, controls, and lacks in ego strength might be related to subsequent problem drinking. Of particular consequence, and worth emphasizing here, is the similarity of the psychological findings in the studies by Kammeier and associates [14, 16, 32] and the observations and conclusions by Owens and Butcher [35] and Barnes [3] with the findings from the psychiatric literature that underscore the association between sociopathy and alcoholism. These findings are similar also to structural disturbances in self-care and self-regulation, described elsewhere in this chapter.

Depression and Other Affect Disturbances

There are many studies that document an association between alcoholism and depression. What is not clear in many of these studies is whether alcoholism causes depression or depression causes alcoholism. There is fairly reliable evidence that alcoholism leads to depressive syndromes, and that, as the alcoholic abstains, the depressive symptomatology lifts [35]. However, as previously indicated, it is the causal connection of depression leading to alcoholism with which this chapter is concerned. In this instance the evidence for such a connection is more scanty and inconsistent. Depending on the study, the incidence of depression in alcoholism has ranged between 3% and 98%. Nevertheless, two developments over the past 25 years have made it possible to tease out more carefully the part depression and other affect disturbances might play in the development of alcoholism, namely, the development of different classes of psychotropic drugs (especially the antidepressant drugs) and the adoption of explicit, standardized diagnostic criteria. A number of careful studies that have taken advantage of these developments have more consistently documented evidence that suggests depression predisposes to and may be causally linked to alcoholism. Although not exclusively so, this is especially the case with women alcoholics.

Schuckit et al. [43] evaluated psychiatrically a group of 70 female alcoholics. Although they found a majority of the women to be suffering from primary alcoholism, in which by definition the alcoholism predated any other psychiatric disorder, they also documented that 19 (27%) of these women had suffered severe depression prior to their alcoholism. In this group, Schuckit and associates considered the alcoholism to be secondary to the affective disorder.

Responsivity to various classes of psychotropic drugs in a number of carefully controlled studies suggests that depression in particular, and to a lesser extent, anxiety disorders, seem to significantly contribute to alcoholism problems. A number of these studies also suggest that the depression is actually an anxious depression that superficially or descriptively seems mild, but in many instances has the qualities of the more severe endogenous depressions with regard to responsiveness to the various classes of drugs (see Khantzian [20, 21] for reviews of these trends). Kissin and Gross [24] demonstrated the superiority of combining chlordiazepoxide with imipramine in controlling drinking and overall improvement compared to using either drug alone. Bliding [7] demonstrated the effectiveness of the benzodiazepine oxazepam to be effective in treating alcoholism. Belfer and Shader [6] concluded that certain patterns of excessive drinking in women were significantly related to anxiety associated with premenstrual tension and that Valium was effective in relieving the anxiety and reducing reliance on alcohol. Reports by Butterworth [8] and Overall et al. [35] demonstrated the efficacy of tricyclic antidepressants in relieving underlying symptoms of depression in alcoholics (to a lesser extent, the Overall study also showed phenothiazines to be effective). Overall et al. [35] in their study emphasized that despite a superficial resemblance to mild anxious depressions, alcoholics suffered with a depression more similar to an endogenous depression based on their responsivity to antidepressant drugs. Quitkin et al. [38] identified an alcoholic group (according to their study, about 10% of any cohort of alcoholics) that suffers with a phobic-anxious syndrome and responds positively in both their anxious-phobic and alcoholic symptomatology to the tricyclic antidepressant imipramine. Finally, reports by Wren et al. [54], Kline et al. [26], and Merry et al. [33] seem to indicate that lithium is effective in cases of alcoholism associated with depression.

Using standardized diagnostic criteria, and based on a large metropolitan survey, Weisman and associates [49, 50] have reported on the prevalence of depression in association with alcoholism. Of the 34 individuals who were diagnosed as ever having been alcoholic, 71% had at some time received at least one other psychiatric diagnosis. In the majority of the cases the other diagnosis was depression. Of those receiving a concomitant diagnosis of depression, the majority of the alcoholics satisfied a criteria for either major depression (44%) or minor depression (15%), with the remainder being individuals with bipolar depression (6%) or depressive personalities (18%). Of those receiving a diagnosis of depression, 60% were considered to have suffered a primary depression wherein the depression had preceeded the alcoholism.

Finally, Winokur and his associates [51, 52] reported on the prevalence of an entity designated as "depression spectrum disease." They have accumulated significant data to suggest there is a type of unipolar depression occurring predominantly in women 40 years old or younger in which first-degree male relatives have a significantly higher occurrence of sociopathy or alcoholism, and in which female relatives have a higher occurrence of depression. Winokur's work focuses on the intergenerational appearances of these disorders and emphasizes descriptive findings and the biological and/or hereditary basis of these disorders, but his findings might also have intriguing possibilities for suggesting the operation of psychodynamic relationships and influences intrafamilially among depression, sociopathy, and alcoholism. In "Psychodynamics," which follows, an attempt is made to demonstrate how psychic structures responsible for regulating behavior and affects develop and how vulnerabilities and disturbances in such structures might influence an individual's involvement with or appeal for alcohol. In addition to a biological predisposition, such vulnerabilities develop in a context of individual and family dynamics where patterns of managing or failures in managing behavior and feelings evolve and are established that may later contribute to the disturbances associated with the sociopathy, depression, and/or alcoholism that occurs in such families.

PSYCHODYNAMICS

Overview

As previously indicated, early psychodynamic formulations emphasized the centrality of instinctual drives and fixations, particularly oral dependency, to account for the alcoholic's compulsive involvement with alcohol. Paralleling developments in psychoanalytic theory in general, more recent formulations have attempted to account for the dynamics of alcoholism by considering the nature of the vulnerabilities and disturbances in psychic structure of such individuals. In this section the focus is on ego structures responsible for regulating behavior and feelings, and self structures that are important in maintaining self-esteem and inner states of comfort and well-being. Consideration is given to how vulnerabilities and disturbances in such structures of alcoholics leave them susceptible to hazardous and pathological dependency on alcohol.

Before proceeding with a more precise description of the structural disturbances associated with alcoholism, it is important to emphasize once again that cause and effect relationships between such disturbances and alcoholism are complex and often cannot be ascertained easily. It is likely that the degree and magnitude of the disturbances described are more on the order of tendencies or vulnerabilities early in the course of alcoholic disorders, and that the toxic effects of alcohol on cognitive structures and the destabilizing effects of the alcohol intoxication-withdrawal cycles worsen such a tendency and cause regression in ego functions. As a result of this regression, alcoholics then give the appearance of being more unstable and disturbed than they otherwise would. It is in this respect that an addiction is often said to have a life of its own and leads to the corollary observation that once alcoholics abstain, they feel and act better. However, it is just as likely that more severe structural disturbances could be at the root of alcoholism. That is, given that the natural course of the illness is not usually one of an unrelenting continuous use of alcohol, and that intervening periods of abstinence allow consideration of the dangers of alcohol, one could then argue that there must be significant pathological factors and forces at work that compel or drive a person to revert repeatedly to the excess use of alcohol despite the obvious devastating consequences of such reversions. Resolution of this debate cannot be resolved here, but this distinction between a vulnerability and more severe psychopathology should be kept in mind. Probably the most reasonable lesson can be drawn from observations based on clinical experience and the course of different patients who, in fact, demonstrate varying degrees of vulnerability and pathology over the course of their involvement with and recovery from their alcoholism.

In what follows, some of the distinctions between ego and self are arbitrary, but are adopted for purposes of emphasizing, explaining, and distinguishing the differences between structures and functions that regulate behavior and affects in the case of the former, and subjective attitudes and states of well-being about self in the case of the latter. Ego and self structures develop as a result of early internalization processes in which the caring, protective, comforting, admiring, and admired functions and qualities of the parents are internalized. If successful, the processes of internalization establish within the person adequate ego functions that serve purposes of defense and adaptation and a coherent sense of the self and appreciation of the separate existence of others [21]. In the case of the ego impairments in alcoholics, there is a tendency to overregulate, underregulate, or fail to regulate one's emotions and behavior; in the case of disturbances in the sense of self in alcoholics, there is a tendency to overestimate or underestimate one's worth or to inadequately provide and maintain cohesion and/or comfort of the self and an inner sense of well-being.

Disturbances in Ego Structures

The alcoholic's problems are not as compelled or driven by instinctual forces as the early psychoanalytic literature suggests, but are more often the result of failures in psychic structures responsible for containing regulating behavior and affects. An emphasis is placed herein on two areas of vulnerability in ego function that seem to predispose to an excess use of alcohol, namely, disturbances in self-care functions and affect regulation.

Self-care. Alcoholics give the appearance of being acutely and chronically self-destructive. What is this quality about? Early psychoanalytic formulations invoked mechanisms, such as unconscious self-destructive motives, counterphobia, or denial, to explain such trends. Although such mechanisms can and do play a part in the self-destructive aspects of alcoholism, such mechanisms are often invoked speculatively and to the exclusion of other considerations to explain the puzzling and recurrent tendency of alcoholics to bring harm to themselves with their excesses around alcohol and other troubling behaviors. The more recent attempt in psychoanalysis to consider the influence of disturbances in psychic structure to explain psychopathology is also helpful in understanding the alcoholic's seeming self-destructiveness. Such a perspective suggests that alcoholics are deficient or underdeveloped in their ego capacity for taking care of themselves. Khantzian and associates [18, 21, 22, 23] have referred to this ego function as "self-care." They emphasize the importance developmentally of optimal parental nurturance and protection early in children's development for the establishment of this function, and how extremes of deprivation or indulgence have devastating consequences for the development of this capacity.

Disturbances in self-care are the result of an impairment in the ego wherein the individual fails to be aware, cautious, worried, or frightened enough to avoid or desist in behavior that has damaging and/or dangerous consequences. Self-care functions are basic in that they are evident and may be observed in normal children, or, if absent and impaired, explain much of the reckless and impulsive behavior in children so affected [22]. In other respects, the capacity for self-care is complex and is related to other functions and processes, such as signal anxiety, reality testing, delay, judgment, and synthesis. When this capacity is impaired, defenses, such as denial phobias, counterphobias, projection, justification, and rationalization, are prominently evident—all of which are frequently observed in alcoholics. In short, individuals with self-care problems react differently than most people would when it comes to considering consequences of their actions and behavior. This is very evident in substance-dependent individuals who often reveal how little thought they have given to patterns of behavior leading to drug and/or alcohol involvement and how little fear or worry they show about the dangers and consequences of their alcoholic and other excesses. Self-care functions are deficient, impaired, or absent in most alcoholics, which accounts for much of their disastrous and destructive behavior. This deficiency also appears to be central to the prealcoholic histories of impulsivity, restlessness, and delinquent, aggressive and/or violent behavior so often associated with alcoholism. Individuals so affected also reveal past histories of preventable medical and dental problems as a result of such deficiencies [21, 22].

Affect regulation. Whereas self-care protects against external dangers and consequences of careless behavior, ego functions involved in regulation of feelings serve as guides and signals in managing and protecting against instability and chaos of one's internal emotional life. Establishment of ego functions responsible for affect regulation involves internalization processes developmentally similar to those involved in the establishment of self-care. Manifestations of alcoholics' disturbances in regulating affects include an inability to identify and verbalize feelings, an intolerance or incapacity for anxiety and depression, an inability to modulate feelings, activation and initiative problems, and extreme manifestations of affect, such as hypomania, phobic-anxious states, panic, and lability.

Many of the extreme patterns that alcoholics display in managing their feelings are the result of disturbances in the development of affects. Like so many other aspects of mental life, affects are subject to developmental fixations, distortions, and regression. Krystal [31], along lines pursued by Schur [44], has traced how anxiety and depression develop out of a common undifferentiated matrix and how affects at the outset of development are undifferentiated (i.e., anxiety and depression are fused), somatized, and not verbalized. With progression, affects or feelings become differentiated, desomatized, and verbalized, and lead to the development of the stimulus barrier. With the establishment of the stimulus barrier as an important part of the ego's capacity to regulate affects, feelings are kept minimally unpleasant through appropriate action and mechanisms of defense. If development is optimal, feelings act as guides or signals for regulating one's emotions and behaviors. Because of developmental arrest or traumatic regression, alcoholics fail to differentiate and progress in affect development such that they are unable to use feelings as signals or guides. That is, they suffer an ego defect in their stimulus barrier whereby they are either unable to identify affects, or their feelings are unbearable or overwhelming. As a result, denial or the effects of alcohol are used to ward off overwhelming feeling states in circumstances that would not be traumatic for other people [21, 31].

Kernberg [17] has linked borderline pathology to alcholism and Klein [25] has singled out dysphoric affect states as being common to so-called borderline conditions and alcoholism. Both investigators emphasize difficulties in affect management as being central to alcohol problems. Kernberg's emphases, in particular, on ego weakness, lack of anxiety tolerance, impulsivity, and primitive defenses in borderline conditions, seem to be germane to and consistent with the psychopathology frequently identified in alcoholics. Although there is little basis to conclude that borderline conditions are at the root of alcoholism, it is possible that similar processes and structural disturbances are operative in both conditions. Klein discounts ego defects in borderline conditions and instead emphasizes that such conditions are more related to affective disorders than to schizophrenia and character disorders. He advocates a descriptive approach that carefully identifies and categorizes a range of dysphoric affect states or conditions as being central to the problems of so-called borderline patients. He considers the compulsive use of alcohol and antianxiety agents to be related to such dysphoric states, and especially singles out hysteroid dysphoria, chronic anxiety-tension states, and phobic neurosis with panic attacks to predispose such individuals to the use of these substances. Although Klein eschews a structural model in explaining alcoholic and borderline conditions, his description of these problems as an "affective or activation disorder, or stereotyped affective overresponse" [25, p. 369] supports a notion of ego impairments in regulating affects.

In brief then, there is convincing evidence from several convergent lines of investigation to support a view that impairments in ego structure predispose to alcoholism. Disturbances in self-care leave individuals poorly prepared to properly evaluate and anticipate the consequences of risky and self-damaging behavior, especially in relation to the consequences of their alcohol involvement. The other area of ego disturbance in alcoholics involves problems in recognizing, regulating, and harnessing feeling states wherein states of immobilization or being overwhelmed with affects result, and alcohol is sought to overcome or relieve such conditions [21].

Disturbances in Self Structures

Alcoholics suffer not only because of impairments in their ego. They also suffer because of impairments and injury to their sense of self. The development of the sense of self involves processes and viscissitudes around the developing child acquiring qualities and attitudes from the caring parents. Previously the alcoholic's ego impairments in self-care and affect regulation were stressed. Here, the alcoholic's impairments in sense of self are explored, emphasizing how individuals with such problems are unable or poorly equipped to value, comfort, sooth, care about, or express themselves. Emphasis is placed on the nature of the alcoholic's dependency problems and related pathological self structures that are evident in alcoholics.

Dependency and the self. Alcoholics are desperately dependent people. However, formulations about the nature of this dependency have been reductionistic and simplistic and unduly stress regressive oral drives and attachments to the alcohol itself, or emphasize the infantile, clinging nature of the alcoholic's relationships. The dependency of alcoholics has less to do with oral cravings and infantile attachments; they are more the result of defects and vulnerabilities in ego and self structures that cause alcoholics to depend on the effects of alcohol, and to attach themselves to others to compensate for these defects and vulnerabilities. Such an appreciation of the alcoholic's structural problems has led Balint [2] to characterize the alcoholic's dependency as a basic fault, one in which the alcoholic resorts to the use of alcohol to establish a feeling of harmony that he or she cannot otherwise obtain—a problem that does not have the form or quality of an instinct or conflict. It has also led Kohut [28] to characterize individuals dependent on substances in general as seeking a "replacement for a defect in psychological structures" [28], and not as a loved or loving object.

The fault or defect is the result of failures in ego-ideal formation (Kohut refers to the idealized superego) whereby the admired and admiring, encouraging, valued, and idealized qualities of the parents have not been adequately internalized. As a result, alcoholics acutely and chronically suffer from a lack of self-worth. Self-esteem suffers given their faulty ego-ideal formation and they are forever unable to judge themselves and their relationships as adequate or satisfying. As a consequence of this inadequate measure of themselves, they greatly depend on other people and sources outside themselves for approval and thus constantly seek external reassurance, recognition, and solace. Alcohol, people, and activities are sought out, then, not so much for gratification of oral, infantile drives and wishes, but more as attempts by alcoholics to feel better or good about themselves, as they are almost totally unable to achieve this for themselves from within [19, 21].

Parallel to the disturbance in ego-ideal formation are disturbances related to capacities to comfort, sooth, and care for one's self [30]. Alcoholics evidence modes of polar extremes regarding such needs and functions. Their quest for external supplies, and dependency on alcohol and people is the result of a failure to internalize and develop adequately capacities for nurturance and comfort from within, thus causing such individuals to turn primarily outside themselves for comfort, searching for soothing and caring, or to defensively ward off and deny such needs or wants [21].

Pathological self formations. As a result of the ego and self disturbances, alcoholics develop and display troublesome and self-defeating compensatory defenses and pathological self structures. In some instances the defenses that are employed serve to compensate and counteract for the sense of incompleteness such people feel as a result of deficits in affect defense and self-esteem. In other instances the more rigid and primitive defenses that are adopted seem to be the result of pathological internalizations, identifications, and self structures. Whether such defenses are compensatory for deficits, or the result of pathological internalizations and distortions, the releasing effect of alcohol can overcome such rigid and overdrawn defenses and can facilitate and regulate the experiencing and expression of affectionate or aggressive feelings in the absence of ego and self structures that help to modulate such affects and drives [19, 21].

A number of contemporary psychoanalysts have provided useful insights to some of the pathological defenses and self structures employed by alcoholics and how the effects and patterns of alcohol use interact with such structures. Kernberg [17] stresses the rigid and primitive defenses of splitting, denial, and projection and how such defenses cause repression and dissociation of parts of the self; the effect of alcohol acts to refuel the grandiose self and to activate the all-good self and object images and to deny the all-bad internalized objects [17, p. 222]. Along similar lines Krystal and Raskin [31] and Krystal [30] have suggested that alcoholics rigidly wall off and are unable to experience their aggressive and loving feelings and that alcohol effects allow a brief and therefore tolerable enjoyment of such feelings. Although Kohut stresses deficits in ego and self structures, he emphasizes how substances act to release individuals from compensatory and/or defensive reactions such as massive repression, self-sufficiency, and disavowal, and allow self-soothing and resurgence of self-esteem [28, 29]. Silber [45, 46], along somewhat different lines, has focused on the pathological and destructive identifications of alcoholics with psychotic and/or very disturbed parents and how the self-damaging and destructive aspects of alcohol involvement parallel and represent internalizations of the self-neglecting, self-destructive aspects of the parents.

CONCLUSION: ALCOHOLISM, A SPECTRUM DISORDER

Alcoholics seem to be constantly caught in an interpersonal and intrapsychic web in which they are unable to judge or measure adequately their actions and behavior or to express, contain, or modulate their feelings. The use of alcohol becomes both an expression of these problems as well as an attempt to solve them. Rather than considering alcoholism as any one disorder, the condition of alcoholism and the problems that alcoholics display might more usefully be considered a spectrum disorder in which at one pole of the problem behavior disturbances are paramount, and at the other pole affect disturbances loom large. (The term "spectrum disorder" is in part derived from Winokur's term, "depression spectrum disease." It shares with Winokur the notion of a range of presentations, but in contrast to Winokur, emphasizes a psychodynamic, intragenerational perspective.) Patients might then be positioned or considered to be on a spectrum between these poles, with a tendency for either behavior problems or affect disturbances to predominate. However, in most cases, clinical experience would probably reveal elements of both to be present and influential in the alcoholism. A psychodynamic perspective could then allow both patient and clinician to understand better the relationships between troublesome feelings and behavior and to manage more effectively these problems associated with alcoholism.

Such a perspective might help in cutting through pejorative and alienating labels, such as "sociopath," "impulsive," or "antisocial," ascribed to alcoholics. The behavior to which such labels refer is related dynamically, as is the alcohol behavior, to the alcoholic's inability to contain or modulate his or her feelings and/or to otherwise comfort and sooth the self from within. Given that alcoholics have problems in recognizing, identifying, and verbalizing their feelings, repressed or vaguely perceived affect states are discharged through action and impulsive behavior. Also, as indicated, alcoholics tend to act upon and extract from the environment a sense of comfort and satisfaction that they cannot provide from within through self-comforting and self-soothing functions. Both of these outwardly directed behaviors and tendencies distract from the more painful underlying problems of affect regulation and subjective problems with self-worth and comfort.

Most of the other psychiatric findings and symptoms associated with alcoholism (reviewed in the beginning of the chapter), such as depression and anxiety, but including the sociopathy and impulsivity, are indicators and the result of more fundamental disturbances in the ego and self structures just reviewed. The evidence suggests that findings of a psychodynamic approach complement a descriptive approach that identifies psychiatric disorders and target symptomatology [21]. The alcoholic's behavior problems often combine with the alcoholic's disturbances in regulating affects and states of well-being to make excesses with alcohol malignantly compelling. Short-term relief is obtained from overwhelming and painful feelings, or rigid defenses are overcome and allow for the release of affection or anger that cannot otherwise be experienced or expressed. In still other instances alcohol helps to overcome states of immobilization and inertia and makes activity and action possible. However, all too often, unfortunately, the use of alcohol as a solution to such problems eventually becomes a devastating and destructive problem in and of itself. It is little wonder then that debate continues whether psychopathology causes alcoholism or alcoholism causes psychopathology. Both are true.

REFERENCES

1. Abraham, K. The psychological relation between sexuality and alcoholism. In: *Selected Papers on Psychoanalysis.* Basic Books: New York, 1960. (Originally published 1908)

2. Balint, M. *The Basic Fault.* Tavistock: London, 1968.
3. Barnes, G. E. The alcoholic personality: A reanalysis of the literature. *J. Stud. Alcohol* 40:571-634, 1979.
4. Barry, H. Psychological factors in alcoholism. In: *The Biology of Alcoholism,* Kissin, B. and Begleiter, H. (eds.). Plenum: New York, 1974.
5. Barry, H., Jr., Barry, H., III, and Blane, H. T. Birth order of delinquent boys with alcohol involvement. *Q. J. Stud. Alcohol* 30:408-413, 1969.
6. Belfer, M. L., and Shader, R. I. Premenstrual factors as determinants of alcoholism in women. In: *Alcoholism Problems in Women and Children,* Greenblatt, M. and Schuckit, M., (eds.). Grune & Stratton: New York, 1976.
7. Bliding, A. Efficacy of anti-anxiety drug therapy in alcoholic postintoxication symptoms: A double-blind study of chlorpromazine, oxazepam and placebo. *Br. J. Psychiatry* 122:465-468, 1973.
8. Butterworth, A. T. Depression associated with alcohol withdrawal: Imipramine therapy compared with placebo. *Q. J. Stud. Alcohol* 32:343-348, 1971.
9. Freud, S. Three essays on the theory of sexuality. In: *Standard Edition* (Vol. 7), Strachey, J. (ed.). Hogarth Press: London, 1955. (Originally published 1905).
10. Goodwin, D. W., Crane, J. B., and Guze, S. B. Felons who drink. *Q. J. Stud. Alcohol* 32:136-148, 1971.
11. Guze, S. B., Goodwin, D. W., and Crane, J. B. Criminality and psychiatric disorders. *Arch. Gen. Psychiatry* 20:583-591, 1969.
12. Guze, S. B., Tuason, V. B., Gatfield, P. D., Stewart, M. A., and Picken, B. Psychiatric illness and crime with particular reference to alcoholism: A study of 223 criminals. *J. Nerv. Ment. Dis.* 134:512-521, 1962.
13. Hayman, M. The relationship of depression to alcoholism. In: *Masked Depression,* Lesse, S. (ed.). Aronson: New York, 1974.
14. Hoffman, H., Loper, R. G., and Kammeier, M. L. Identifying future alcoholics with MMPI alcoholism scales. *Q. J. Stud. Alcohol* 35:490-498, 1974.
15. Jellinek, E. *The Disease Concept of Alcoholism.* Hillhouse: New Haven, Conn., 1960.
16. Kammeier, M. L., Hoffman, H., and Loper, R. G. Personality characteristics of alcoholics as college freshman and at time of treatment. *Q. J. Stud. Alcohol* 34:390-399, 1973.
17. Kernberg, O. F. *Borderline Conditions and Pathological Narcissism.* Aronson: New York, 1975.
18. Khantzian, E. J. The ego, the self and opiate addiction: Theoretical and treatment considerations. *Int. Rev. Psychoanal.* 5:189-198, 1978.
19. Khantzian, E. J. On the nature of the dependency and denial problems of alcoholics. *J. Geriatr. Psychiatry* 2(2):191-202, 1979.
20. Khantzian, E. J. The alcoholic patient: An overview and perspective. *Am. J. Psychother.* 34:4-19, 1980.
21. Khantzian, E. J. Some treatment implications of the ego and self disturbances in alcoholism. In: *Dynamic Approaches to the Understanding and Treatment of Alcoholism,* Zinberg, N. and Bean, M. (eds.). Free Press: New York, 1981.
22. Khantzian, E. J., and Mack, J. E. *Self-Preservation and the Care of the Self-Ego Instincts Revisited.* Unpublished manuscript, 1981.
23. Khantzian, E. J., Mack, J. E., and Schatzberg, A. F. Heroin use as an attempt to cope: Clinical observations. *Am. J. Psychiatry* 131:160-164, 1974.
24. Kissin, B., and Gross, M. M. Drug therapy in alcoholism. *Am. J. Psychiatry* 125:31-41, 1968.
25. Klein, D. F. Psychopharmacology and the borderline patient. In: *Borderline States in Psychiatry,* Hartocollis, P. (ed.). Grune & Stratton: New York, 1975.

26. Kline, N. S., Wren, J. C., Cooper, T. B., Varga, E., and Canal, O. Evaluation of lithium therapy in chronic and periodic alcoholism. *Am. J. Med. Sci.* 268:15–22, 1974.

27. Knight, R. P. The dynamics and treatment of chronic alcohol addiction. *Bull. Menninger Clin.* 1:233–250, 1937.

28. Kohut, H. *The Analysis of the Self.* International Universities Press: New York, 1971.

29. Kohut, H. Preface. In: *Psychodynamics of Drug Dependence* (Research Monograph 12, pp. vii–ix). National Institute on Drug Abuse: Rockville, Md., 1977.

30. Krystal, H. Self- and object-representation in alcoholism and other drug dependence: Implications for therapy. In: *Psychodynamics of Drug Dependence* (Research Monograph 12, pp. 88–100). National Institute on Drug Abuse: Rockville, Md., 1977.

31. Krystal, H., and Raskin, H. A. *Drug Dependence: Aspects of Ego Functions.* Wayne State University Press: Detroit, 1970.

32. Loper, R. G., Kammeier, M. L., and Hoffman, H. MMPI characteristics of college freshman males who later became alcoholics. *J. Abnorm. Psychol.* 82:159–162, 1973.

33. Merry, J., Reynolds, C. M., Bailey, J., and Coopen, A. Prophylactic treatment of alcoholism by lithium carbonate. *Lancet* 2:481–482, 1976.

34. Overall, J. E., Brown, D., Williams, J. D. et al. Drug treatment of anxiety and depression in detoxified alcoholic patients. *Arch. Gen. Psychiatry* 29:218–221, 1973.

35. Owens, P. L., and Butcher, J. N. Personality factors in problem drinking: A review of the evidence on some suggested directions. In: *Psychiatric Factors in Drug Abuse*, Pickens, R. and Heston, L. (eds.). Grune & Stratton: New York, 1979.

36. Pattison, E. M. Rehabilitation of the chronic alcoholic. In: *The Biology of Alcoholism Physiology and Behavior* (Vol. 2), Kissin, B. and Begleiter, H. (eds.). Plenum: New York, 1972.

37. Pattison, E. M., Sobell, M. B., and Sobell, L. C. *Emerging Concepts of Alcohol Dependence.* Springer: New York, 1977.

38. Quitkin, F. M., Rifkin, A., Kaplan, J., and Klein, D. F. Phobic anxiety syndrome complicated by drug dependence and addiction. *Arch. Gen. Psychiatry* 27:159–162, 1972.

39. Rado, S. The psychoanalysis of pharmacothymia. *Psychoanal. Q.* 2:1–23, 1933.

40. Robins, E., Gentry, K. A., Munoz, R. A., and Marten, S. A contrast of the three more common illnesses with the ten less common in a study and 18-month follow-up of 314 psychiatric room patients: II. Characteristics of patients with the three more common illnesses. *Arch. Gen. Psychiatry* 34:269–281, 1977.

41. Robins, L. N., Murphy, G. E., and Breckenridge, M. D. Drinking behavior of young urban Negro men. *Q. J. Stud. Alcohol* 29:657–684, 1968.

42. Rund, D. A., Summers, W. K., and Levin, M. Alcohol use and psychiatric illness in emergency patients. *J.A.M.A.* 245:1240–1241, 1981.

43. Schuckit, M., Pitts, F. N. Jr., Reich, T., King, L. J., and Winokur, G. Alcoholism: I. Two types of alcoholism in women. *Arch. Gen. Psychiatry* 20(3):301–306, 1969.

44. Schur, M. Comments on the metapsychology of somatization. *Psychoanal. Stud. Child* 10:119–164, 1955.

45. Silber, A. An addendum to the technique of psychotherapy with alcoholics. *J. Nerv. Ment. Dis.* 150:423–437, 1970.

46. Silber, A. Rationale for the technique of psychotherapy with alcoholics. *Int. J. Psychoanal. Psychother.* 28:47, 1974.

47. Simmel, E. Alcoholism and addiction. *Psychoanal. Q.* 17:6–31, 1948.

48. Tarter, R. E., McBride, H., Buonpane, N., and Schneider, D.U. Differentiation of alcoholics. *Arch. Gen. Psychiatry* 34:761–776, 1977.

49. Weisman, M. M., and Meyers, J. K. Clinical depression in alcoholism. *Am. J. Psychiatry* 137:372–373, 1980.

50. Weisman, M. M., Meyers, J. K., and Harding, P. S. The prevalence rates and psychiatric heterogeneity of alcoholism in a United States urban community. *Q. J. Stud. Alcohol* 41:672–681, 1980.

51. Winokur, G. Unipolar depression. *Arch. Gen. Psychiatry* 36:47–56, 1979.

52. Winokur, G., Reich, T., Rimmer, J., and Pitts, F. N. Alcoholism: III. Diagnosis and familial psychiatric illness in 259 alcoholic probands. *Arch. Gen. Psychiatry* 23:104–111, 1970.

53. Woodruff, R. A., Guze, S. B., Clayton, P. J., and Carr, D. Alcoholism and depression. *Arch. Gen. Psychiatry* 28:97–100, 1973.

54. Wren, J., Kline, N., and Cooper, T. Evaluation of lithium therapy in chronic alcoholism. *Clin. Med.* 81:33–36, 1974.

45

DAVID W. KRUEGER, MD, Baylor College of Medicine

NEUROTIC BEHAVIOR AND THE ALCOHOLIC

SUPPORTIVE THERAPIES, pharmacologic treatment, and insight-oriented treatment are encompassed by the basic issues and principles discussed herein regarding the relationships of neuroticism and alcoholism and the importance of recognizing neurotic mechanisms and behavior in treating alcoholic patients. Recognition of common, regularly occurring, neurotic defense mechanisms in the alcoholic patient requires careful observation, understanding, and a willingness to look beyond alcohol in identifying the operative factors in alcoholism.

Denial, a scenario of anger, guilt, and withdrawal from treatment, and assertions of omnipotence are commonly seen defense postures among alcoholics. Complementary and counterpart mechanisms in the therapist, called countertransference, are also discussed as they relate to the therapist's ability to reorganize these issues and utilize them in successful treatment. These mechanisms, in both patient and therapist, can be used as tools for understanding the patient's mental processes, including the content, mechanism, and intensity of his or her mental life and the role and function served by the alcoholic behavior.

A comprehensive evaluation of the patient, including developmental and descriptive diagnoses, assessment of the patient's neurotic and other conflicts, and consideration of the meaning and use of drinking behavior for the individual, is

---

David W. Krueger, MD, Department of Psychiatry, Baylor College of Medicine, Houston, Texas.

prerequisite to the appropriate prescription of a treatment plan, its type, scope, duration, and expected course [7].

While symptomatic behavior can vary markedly from person to person, the historical, dynamic, and adaptive meaning of drinking behavior has even broader diversity. A comprehensive evaluation and treatment prescription for each individual patient is essential to therapeutic success. Part of this individual assessment should be consideration of whether the particular patient can comply with the prescribed abstinence as a goal of treatment and as a condition of treatment.

Neurotic behavior within the context of alcoholic behavior has been discussed by Krystal [9], who believes that evaluation of both the patient's assets and the nature of the conflicts that lead him or her to drink would be facilitated by understanding the unconscious fantasies that underlie drinking, and overt fantasies that pertain to the meaning of alcohol and its intake. Krystal suggests that clues to these fantasies can be found in the patient's behavior related to the procurement of alcohol, the method of drinking, the handling of alcohol, the behavior while intoxicated, the nature of the affect sought from drinking, the reaction to drinking after the fact, and the social perspective of drinking.

TRANSFERENCE-COUNTERTRANSFERENCE

Alcoholic patients are difficult to treat. Alcohol-abusing patients are more likely than nonabusing patients to be critical, defiant, alienating of others, and resistant to cooperation when in treatment. The potential for countertransference by the therapist is readily apparent. The countertransference reactions may stem from reactions to (1) the drinking behavior; (2) the alienating, provoking, characterological features of the patient; and (3) the counterreactions to the patient's character pathology. Successful treatment of the alcoholic patient often requires special recognition by the therapist of his or her own countertransference reactions.

Comprehensive psychiatric therapy requires the therapist's freely working attention and empathic sensitivity to the patient's emotional movement and unconscious fantasies. Countertransference is, in a way, analogous to the function of controls in a scientific study, which emphasizes the counterpart and parallel processes of patient transference-therapist countertransference. The countertransference does not include all responses of the therapist to the patient, but those that are responses to the transference reaction of the patient in a therapeutic situation, which distinguishes it from attitudes of the therapist, the real relationship, and the working alliance [8]. The differentiation of the therapist's response ranges from (1) countertransference reactions to the alcoholic patient's specific developmental conflicts, character pathology, current neurotic behavior to drinking behavior; (2) transference reactions to the alcoholic patient due to preset or predetermined attitudes, expectations, and feelings; or (3) a lack of information or education about treatment of the alcoholic. For example, frustration and anger at patients may be created by insufficient information combined with unrealistic or even omnipotent expectations of permanent abstinence. Both patient and therapist may share reactions of guilt, anger, failure, and hopelessness when abstinence is considered the sole measure of successful treatment and the patient is not totally abstinent. This failure to recognize the chronic aspects of alcoholism is a problem of both education and dynamic misunderstanding.

There is a broad consensus that there are many types of alcoholics and many types of alcohol-related problems requiring a variety of treatments specific to the individual patient and his or her characteristic interactions with alcohol [1].

The attitude, skill, and countertransference behavior of the therapist has a significant effect on the course of treatment — perhaps at least as much as the particular modality of treatment chosen. An understanding of alcoholism as a human problem rather than as a physiological disease process is important in determining the meaning of alcohol to the patient and its integral use as an adjunct defense mechanism. In addition to its disease aspects, alcoholism is intertwined with the wide range of human psychic suffering and neurotic behavior associated with psychological conflict and disturbance in ego functions [6].

The reactions of the patient and counterreactions of the therapist can be viewed in three broad categories: (1) denial; (2) anger, guilt, and withdrawal; (3) omnipotence and/or threatened omnipotence.

Denial

Denial is often the chief defense mechanism operative in the personality and in the drinking behavior of the alcoholic. Denial may be specifically of the nature, extent, and affects of drinking behavior. The common countertransference reaction is the therapist's own unconscious denial colluding with that of the patient, especially if the patient is intelligent, well-to-do, and married.

The recognition by both patient and therapist of the patient's denial and rationalization, in a concomitant avoidance of confrontation of this denial to intervene and disrupt the life-threatening illness of alcoholism, is paramount to treatment. The feeling of helplessness in certain adaptive and coping problems, especially regarding ability to stop drinking, may be the result of attributing difficulties and projecting blame onto an external component of the patient's world. The patient's denial of responsibility may be reflected in a therapist's negative attitude, unconscious pessimistic expectation for treatment, or attempt to psychologically minimize the extent or impact of drinking on the patient's life.

The massive use of denial, along with obsessive defenses, provides alcoholics with an armour of self-deception. This is the same armour that will isolate them from close and involved relationships with others, compounding the internal experience of emptiness and anger. Drinking behavior may reflect a very low tolerance for any direct expression of anger, with the need to deny any hostile or aggressive impulses, displacing these impulses into drinking behavior with its anesthetic effect. Viewed in this way, drinking serves to enhance the defense mechanism of denial. There is then a secondary denial of the aspects of drinking and its consequences.

The alcoholic has a tendency to behave well and not complain, looking like an ideal patient. This behavior, driven by a need for and a difficulty in acknowledging dependency, may result in diminished vigilance or even diminished interest by those concerned with treatment. This superficial and fragile form of reaction formation and obsessiveness, which shields the patient from unpleasant affects of anger and narcissistic hurt, may envelop the therapist in the transference-countertransference issue; as a result the therapist may unconsciously allow or even subtly urge the patient to relax or stop treatment. A sense of inadequacy, of being misunderstood, and of being deprived of protection and care, to the extent that one ceases to seek care for fear of rejection, creates that which it fears: a rejection, subtle or overt, from treatment, driving the patient back to drinking and away from treatment. The anger, emptiness, and sense of alienation is then perpetuated in this patient, who may then be labeled "recividist" [3]. Hartocollis [2] recommends that in such cases, "Firmness and limit-setting should be combined with empathic attention, personal warmth, and encouraging comments, even active advice on occasion."

Anger, Guilt, Withdrawal

A psychodynamic characteristic that is consistently seen in alcoholic patients is an interweaving of passive-dependent wishes, a concomitant need to control a need-fulfilling object (self-object), and a manifestation of anger when this need is thwarted [11]. Certain alcoholic patients may lack the integrated ego function to soothe or calm themselves to insulate against anxiety and overstimulation. This inability to internally supply tension-reducing gratification results in turning to an external method: alcohol and/or (it is hoped) the therapist. An appropriate therapeutic approach will meet this need constructively.

The personality of the patient indulging excessively in alcohol may dynamically extend from frustration when demands are not met to overtly hostile acts for which he or she feels guilty and may punish the self masochistically. This cycles into an increased need for affection and indulgence to reassure the patient of self-worth and value. The patient is not able to understand, or even put into words, this rage of frustrated developmental gratification. He or she displaces this onto alcohol and/or the therapist to achieve both gratification and revenge, resulting in the need for punishment to alleviate guilt when sober. The patient who is convinced that he or she is bad, deserving the guilt and concomitant punishment experienced, concludes that rejection will ensue because of this badness if help is sought. The final act of this scenario may be played out if the physician acts on the patient's expectation by turning him or her away or becoming angry at the patient who resumes drinking.

Regression and at times archaic relationships with the therapist, which include blurring of the boundaries of self and others, can occur during treatment. When these regressive episodes are recognized, it becomes important for the therapist to provide the patient with the sort of comfort and support once received from a mothering figure in order to dissuade the patient from resorting to the maladaptive use of alcohol.

It should be recognized that the neurotic or other regressive behaviors of the alcoholic are attempts at adaptation, attempts at self-treatment. Recognition of the adaptive component and the negative internal experiences that the patient's behavior is unconsciously designed to combat is central to empathic understanding of the alcoholic and the alcoholic's neurotic features. This understanding must be communicated to the patient in both process and content for effective intervention to occur. It is not uncommon for a patient to project upon the therapist or others in the environment the active role of the superego, particularly the harsh and punitive aspects of the superego. The patient may then expect angry, critical remarks and attempt to control the inevitable occurrence of reprimands by behaving in ways that precipitate them. It is important for the therapist to recognize the possibility of a countertransference reaction manifesting itself in angry, critical, or judgmental responses to the patient's negative behavior. Patients are exquisitely sensitive to such responses and often extend themselves to misinterpret a therapist's neutral comments as critical, particularly when alcohol-related behavior is the topic. The vicious cycle of drinking, anxiety due to guilt, and further punitive retribution for this behavior will result if the therapist is not attentive to his or her own responses and to how heavily the patient weighs them. The therapist's withdrawal during periods of patient upheaval or exacerbated drinking behavior exemplifies how the unconscious of the patient and the unconscious of the therapist may respond to one another. The alcoholic's guilt, depression, isolation, and self-hatred are especially prominent at times of drinking and may be readily displaced onto the therapist.

The initial anger and denial that can follow a confrontation with an alcoholic patient may drive the therapist from therapy. A decision to cease intervention, rationalized by a belief that confrontation about alcoholism or drinking will result in a patient's insulation, anger, and avoidance of further therapeutic contact, can be seen as a countertransference avoidance of these issues in the patient.

Threatened Omnipotence

A frequent component of the alcoholic's personality is a controlling and omnipotent fantasy of being able to drink despite the best efforts of significant others, including the therapist. One patient angrily stated that neither her husband, nor lover, nor psychiatrist could keep her from drinking if she so decided. The threatened loss of the defensive, attempted adaptive, and omnipotence-enhancing aspects of drinking with its psychological and physiological effects can be terrifying to the patient. The narcissistic injury of an assault upon omnipotence can result in refusal to comply with treatment, and return to the use of alcohol.

Countertransferential anger at the patient can occur when the therapist's own sense of omnipotence is challenged verbally or indirectly by a refusal to comply with treatment. The alcoholic patient's resistance to treatment and return to the use of alcohol may represent a frustration for the therapist whose omnipotence is confronted, and who may at some level doubt his or her medical or therapeutic skill. This may be viewed by the therapist as a defeat of the therapeutic intent, or as an assault upon one's own narcissism.

Recognition of alcoholism as a treatable disease should be balanced by realistic expectations in treating a chronic and perhaps relapsing disease. Because the therapist has had the gratifying experience of successfully treating some alcoholics, he or she is at risk for development of a marked countertransference reaction and a failure of empathic understanding when other alcoholic patients display chronicity or exacerbations of their pathology. An empathic appreciation of the amount of change necessary for an alcoholic to abstain from alcohol is required; this change represents an extreme life crisis that threatens one of the patient's major ways of existing.

DRINKING AS ATTEMPTED ADAPTATION

Much recent psychodynamically oriented consideration of alcoholism focuses on alcohol use as a manifestation of ego deficit and difficulties of the impaired ego with impulse control. Excessive use of alcohol often parallels pathological excesses in other types of behavior, indicating the internal regulatory difficulty of an ego system and self structure that is deficient or pathological. The pathological aspects of the self-system, referred to as the narcissistic line of development, can be summarized by Kohut's [10] indication that drugs are not symbolic substitutes for absent love objects, but are replacements for psychological structure. The addictionlike intensity of many activities can be seen as a hunger for self-esteem–enhancing need to fill a structural defect [10]. The intake of alcohol, however, like eating for a person with gastric fistula, satiates the intense hunger only for a brief period of time, while providing no emotional nourishment.

With the conceptualization of the psychopathology predisposing to and intermingling with an alcoholic behavior, the essential therapeutic approach to the patient would be from an ego-oriented direction, focusing on mastery and understanding of feelings and needs. An id-oriented approach would probably worsen the condition of most patients with alcoholic behavior. Active participation by the therapist is important in gaining an empathic understanding of the desperately inadequate self-reliance of the alcoholic in dealing with his or her own affective, impulsive, and self-regulating inabilities. The ability to soothe oneself is not present, as it might be in an individual with an adequate internal self-structure, and the need and reliance on external objects and chemicals to perform the soothing and regulating function is critical. The therapist must become this function (i.e., a self-object), in assisting the regulatory function. This functioning may include ancillary regulatory aides, such as medication or hospitalization.

An understanding of the alcoholic's mental mechanisms involves the range of psychopathology and symptoms that contribute to the development of alcoholism, as well as the current meaning and function of the drinking behavior. For example, drinking in response to pathological grief may relieve the symptoms of reactive depression in one person, another may attempt to treat anxiety or panic attacks with drinking, while another may be chronically attempting to supplement a deficient ego's coping ability. Work with the alcoholic must discriminate drinking behavior from its affiliated and intermeshed underlying pathology. Drinking behavior must be analyzed from a positive, noncritical, and nonjudgmental ego-oriented consideration of its usefulness to the patient as an adaptive aide that can be understood and whose function can be fulfilled in a more effective way.

Many authors who work psychotherapeutically with alcoholic patients emphasize the need to understand, in addition to the biological and disease conceptualization of alcoholism, the psychopathology predisposing to and interacting with the alcohol problem. This psychopathology often involves difficulties with ego impairment, giving rise to affect intolerance, diminished self-esteem, impulsivity, and predominant symptomatology of anxieties, depression, and emptiness.

It is important that neither the therapist nor the patient attempts to postpone any activity aimed at better level of adaptation and functioning until the motivation for that behavior is discovered and resolved.

Drinking indicates on the one hand a weakening of the primary defenses of the patient, and on the other a strengthening of an attempt at adaptation. Drinking becomes, in one sense, an attempt at adaptive compensation for a person whose basic defensive and mental mechanisms have begun to lose their ability to adapt and cope. Drinking behavior is behavior aimed at providing some relief from internal pain. An alcoholic whose personality structure consists of denial, splitting, rationalization, and projection uses these defenses more intensively and extensively after becoming a heavy drinker than he or she does premorbidly [2]. A secondary line of defense supporting this premorbid character structure in an alcoholic often includes obsessiveness and reaction formation, often in a superficial and maladaptive form, which further serves to insulate the alcoholic from a primary dysphoria as well as from the dysphoria created by alcoholism and its emotional, physiological, and social consequences.

Khantzian [5], in reviewing the contemporary literature on addictive personality structure, concludes that work has evolved to understand the importance of ego functions and ego impairments, with attention concentrated on the areas of tolerance or intolerance of affect. Previous emphasis had been on the regressive acting-out aspects of behavior. Major steps forward in understanding the mechanisms utilized by the alcoholics include the focus on the adaptive function of alcohol and the dynamic interplay between the structural organization of the addicted individual vis-á-vis the pharmacologic effects of alcohol.

The developmentally mixed picture of ego defense mechanisms, predominantly denial, splitting, projection, and omnipotence, constitutes only a portion of the character pathology frequently displayed by alcoholics. Other aspects of character pathology include some disturbance in object relationships, with inadequate object constancy and identity diffusion, a pathological mix of genital and pregenital instinctual strivings with predominantly pregenital aggression, and a somewhat poorly integrated superego [4].

Drinking behavior must be distinguished as a symptom, as a defense in resistance to treatment, and as an autonomous problem with physiological sequelae. Drinking behavior may be used as a barrier to psychological treatment; it also requires direct symptomatic treatment of alcohol intake per se.

In more intensive treatment, the anxiety and other dysphoric feelings generated in the therapeutic situation may be dissipated and syphoned into drinking. At these points it must be dealt with as resistance to treatment that disallows intense affect from developing in treatment. An abiding question has to be whether or not drinking becomes an autonomous problem in itself, meriting autonomous treatment.

REFERENCES

1. Costello, R., Biever, P., and Baillargen, J. Alcoholism treatment programming: Historical trends and modern approaches. *Alcoholism: Clin. Exp. Res.* 4:311-318, 1978.
2. Hartocollis, P. A dynamic view of alcoholism. Drinking in the service of denial. *Dynam. Psychiatry* 2:173-182, 1969.
3. Hartocollis, P., and Hartocollis, C. Alcoholism, borderline and narcissistic disorder: A psychodynamic overview. In: *Phenomenology and Treatment of Alcoholism*, Fann, W., Pokorny, A., and Williams, R. (eds.). Spectrum: New York, 1980.

4. Kernberg, O. A psychoanalytic classification of character pathology. *J. Am. Psychoanal. Assoc.* 18:800–822, 1970.

5. Khantzian, E. The ego, the self, and opiate addiction: Theoretical and treatment considerations. In: *Psychodynamics of Drug Dependence* (NIDA Research Monograph 12), Blaine, J. and Julius, D. (eds.). U.S. Government Printing Office: Washington, D.C., 1977.

6. Khantzian, E. The alcoholic patient: An overview and perspective. *Am. J. Psychother.* 34:4–19, 1980.

7. Krueger, D. W. Clinical considerations in the prescription of group, brief, long-term and couples psychotherapy. *Psychiat. Q.* 51:92–105, 1979.

8. Krueger, D. W. Countertransference in the treatment of the alcoholic patient. In: *Alcoholism: Phenomenology and Treatment*, Fann, W., Pokorny, A., Karacan, I., and Williams, R. (eds.). Spectrum: New York, 1980.

9. Krystal, H. The problem of abstinence by the patient as a requisite for the psychotherapy of alcoholism. *J. Stud. Alcohol* 23:105, 1962.

10. Kohut, H. *The Search for the Self*. International Universities Press: New York, 1978.

11. Silber, A. Rationale for the technique of psychotherapy with the alcoholic. *Int. J. Psychoanal. Psychother.* 3:28–47, 1974.

46

HENRY KRYSTAL, MD, Michigan State University

CHARACTER DISORDERS: CHARACTEROLOGICAL SPECIFICITY AND THE ALCOHOLIC

THE SEARCH FOR A SPECIFIC character disorder in alcoholism has been a long and frustrating endeavor. Psychiatrists, psychoanalysts, and psychologists have for many years applied their special techniques trying to find specific personality disorders that predisposed an individual to alcoholism and/or could be used in the diagnosis of the problem. This search was doomed to failure because it overlooked the fact that, unlike specific emotional and disease states, alcoholism and other drug dependence states do not represent a single psychopathological state. A number of problems and difficulties can be handled by the use of alcohol. In fact, one of the most confusing aspects of alcohol is that it may be used for very opposite effects. Some people take alcohol to control their aggresion and prevent action, whereas others use it to work up "dutch courage" and proceed with violent action. Many people drink to remove sexual inhibition and enable themselves to act sexually, but others utilize the same drug to suppress their sexual needs. Most people use the substance for sedative purposes, facilitating regression and enabling them to endulge passivity, but some, as Glover [3] pointed out, use it to prevent regression and to enable themselves to keep working.

Henry Krystal, MD, Professor of Psychiatry, Michigan State University, East Lansing, Michigan.

Alcohol Use in Relation to Function

Despite a multitude of uses some commonalities can be expected among people dependent upon the use of the substance alcohol—both in terms of their underlying personality and the effect upon their character resulting from the "natural history" of the particular problem drinking pattern. It is useful to start consideration with the classification of the use of psychoactive substances suggested by Kaplan and Weider [6] into type I drug users, who use agents intermittently and optionally for the purpose of obtaining or enhancing pleasure, type II individuals, who use the drug to relieve the distress of particularly painful emotional states resulting from the unusual situations, and type III individuals, people who take the drug to manage the suffering and distress in their everyday condition and make it possible to get through an ordinary day.

Why Characterological Specificity?

A number of observations of a characterologically relevant type can be made on the basis of this classification. Even type I use of alcohol poses important questions regarding the need for such a "social lubricant." Is it used primarily to remove inhibitions? Does it have any direct effect upon the hedonic regulation (i.e., does it influence the anatomical and physiological, particularly endocrinological system, which is involved with the regulation of pleasure and pain experiences)? Is this a search for the "ultimate high"? If so, is this illusion also a factor in alcohol abuse?

Type II alcohol users are unable to handle intense affects resulting from stressful situations, and thus can be said to require the drug because of impaired affect tolerance. Of course, affect tolerance is an essential and complex function, referring to the reaction to "having" an emotion and the skill in utilizing it adaptively [10]. Type III behavior implies that there is some chronic distress for which the relief is needed, and/or the regulation of the pharmacotoxic gratification is impaired. One is inclined to think first that there is a weaker superego function and that the opposition to self-medication on the part of the sufferer's ideals and values is lesser. This expectation, however, is not confirmed by observation of alcoholics. On the contrary, the presence of a severe, punitive conscience and a social or familiar prohibition of the use of alcohol is a predisposition to addiction —provided that other factors make the use of alcohol imperative, and the superego is "corruptable." The common situation is that the conscience is one that can be bribed by self-punishment. Hence, many alcoholics suffer such unbearable guilt and self-castigation after they become sober that the need for relief by the use of more alcohol is enormous. Many of the same people have such terrible shame about drinking that they hardly drink socially, but sneak the drinks and eventually become solitary in their abuse patterns.

These commonplace observations show that certain characterological factors or habitual behaviors that favor the development of problem drinking may be identified. Also, one may expect to find other personality traits that are frequent in type III alcohol use as a result of the introduction of this powerful modification into one's life. For instance, one may expect that alcoholics share with other drug addicts the capacity to sacrifice their attachment to reality and settle for modification of their affective responses to what is going on in their lives, instead of trying to accomplish alloplastic modifications.

There is another area of psychiatric and psychoanalytic research that shares a number of personality disturbances with substance dependence and in which the question of characterological specificity has been the subject of much study for many years — the area of psychosomatic diseases. Pollock [16], who has continued the work of the Chicago school of psychoanalytic psychosomaticists initiated by Alexander, in 1979 proposed that the idea of specificity of characterological problems now has to involve so many predispositional, precipitating, and behavior- (or illness-) maintaining factors, that configurational or combinational specificity must be considered. In this broader view one ranges from genetic, even molecular, specificity considerations to the summation of all the many identifiable factors that influence the dynamic equilibrium, which becomes disturbed by the various stresses of living. Thus, in the research related to the combinational specificity one can hope to isolate factors that favor or predispose the use of certain response patterns, be they psychosomatic, addictive, or other, and at the same time identify the factors that make such responses unlikely — and thus glean information relative to primary prevention of alcoholism.

The reason some persist in the search for characterological traits relative to the problem of alcoholism is a therapeutic one. Characterological patterns represent a dramatization of some conflict and expose it for study, understanding, and interpretation to the patient. Of course, a number of practical reasons determine that only a small minority of alcoholics will be treated psychotherapeutically. However, this is the group from whom much is learned about the psychological aspects of the problem. This has been the reason why many contributions to the characterology of alcoholism have been made by analysts. However, there had been much disappointment in the past with the psychotherapeutic approaches to alcoholism, primarily because the early workers attempted to treat alcoholics with the same techniques as they developed for neurotics. The patients simply did not stay in treatment. The newer contributions regarding alexithymia, disturbances in affect tolerance, nature of self- and object representations, and the recognition that interpretation of the transference is often not an effective technique of treatment with these patients, will probably extend the applicability of psychotherapy somewhat. In regard to such considerations, the following views become relevant. By contrast, the Alcoholics Anonymous (AA) approach to alcoholism, as well as behavior modification and pharmacologic ones, do not concern themselves with the personality of the subject and some tend to be defensive and propagandist in their zeal to stress that anyone can become an alcoholic. What must be said however, is that barring very extraordinary circumstances, the occurrence of alcoholism in stable, normal, and certain other personality types is possible but not likely.

Psychoanalytic Contributions

The following brief review of psychoanalytic contributions depicts a few themes that, although they have undergone changes and permutations in the process of changes in psychoanalytic theory and practices, have retained some relevance to present approaches and concerns.

One such conception, which has been changing and yet keeps coming up, is the question of dependency, related to possibility and certain aspects of narcissistic personality traits. Abraham's early formulation of the oral character [1] gave a picture of an individual whose mental life is dominated by the passive-receptive view of one's self as dependent upon "external" supplies. While this view lost its central importance in dynamic psychiatry as such, it has been reemerging in a new form repeatedly. Rado's more sophisticated view of the character type underlying pharmacothymia stated, "There is a group of human beings who respond to frustrations in life with a special type of emotional alternation which might be designated 'tense depression'" [17, p. 5]. Because of the inability to bear the attending fall in narcissistic omnipotence, the individual is driven to seek a mood-altering magical substance, by which the state of elation is obtained. By so doing, the pharmacothymic regime is established, at the sacrifice of the realistic regime of the ego [17, p. 22], establishing dependence upon the drug. But, owing to the ambivalence toward the drug, and guilt derived from a variety of sources, the effect of the drug is always diminished and finally fails to give relief with the predictable onset of the pharmacogenic crisis [17, p. 22].

Similarly, Knight [7] stressed excessive needs for indulgence, which are doomed to frustration, resulting in a rage. The rage in turn results in hostile behavior and severe problems of guilt and potentially dangerous self-destructive masochism. The alcohol becomes the pacifier but also the tool of both hostile and self-debasing behavior.

Finally, Abraham's oral character traits may be recognized in Kohut's [8] formulations of the narcissistic character's predisposition to substance dependence. The narcissistic character is similarly dependent upon external supplementation in regard to a deficient function of self-respect regulation.

> The trauma which they suffered is most frequently the severe disappointment in a mother who, because of her defective empathy with the child's needs (or for some other reasons), did not appropriately fulfill the functions (as a stimulus barrier; as an optimal provider of needed stimuli; or a supplier of tension-relieving gratification, etc.) which the mature psychic apparatus should later be able to perform (or initiate) predominantly on its own. Traumatic disappointments suffered during these archaic

stages of the development of the idealized self object deprive the child of the gradual internalization of early experiences of being optimally soothed, or of being aided in going to sleep. Such individuals remain thus fixated on aspects of archaic objects and they find them, for example, in the form of drugs. The drug, however, serves not as a substitute for loved or loving objects, or for a relationship with them, but as a replacement for a defect in the psychological structure. [8, p. 46]

In Kohut's view the narcissistic character's inability to obtain self-soothing gratification is relieved by the use of the drug and may be "cured" by psychoanalysis through the process of "transmuting internalization" [8, p. 49] of the maternal functions. Recently, exception has been taken to this view [11], the argument being that alcoholics and other drug addicts do indeed show a severe impairment in their capacity to exercise a variety of self-caring functions, including self-soothing and self-comforting, but that this problem was not due to a personality deficiency but to an inhibition resulting from a mistaken attribution of these functions to the object rather than the self-representation. It was pointed out that the "deficiency" theory that Kohut and most analysts have embraced was in fact taken over from these patients' own theories of their problems. Many of these patients' lives are dominated by a deficiency theory in which they see themselves as victims of childhood deprivation. If the therapist can only supply them with the missing love, they will be good and all will be well. However, one of the reasons that this request cannot be fulfilled hinges upon their definition of love, which is, "If you love me, you will make me feel good; therefore, as long as everything is not perfect and I do not feel blissful, you do not love me." Besides, the patients also have terrible resentments about their past, and demand that the therapist "roll back the reel" of their lives and "fix everything" retroactively. Although Kohut's formulations confirm an old principle that some patients help themselves greatly through identification with their therapist, reservations must be retained regarding the narcissistic character explaining the alcoholic's predicament.

The passive-dependent attributes of alcoholics that result in masochistic rage were carried to their ultimate conclusion in the work of Menninger [14], who pictured the alcoholics as a "chronic suicide" based on the unleashing of the dominance by the death instinct. This view is pertinent, of course, to the exceedingly high suicide rate in this group (Chapter 51). However, it needs to be stressed that some alcoholics become involved in a particularly rapid self-destructive course, as if their problem took a malignant tack, and in these individuals the manifest drive toward bringing on their rapid destruction becomes the most conspicuous character trait. However, for the most part this development sets in late in the course of the addiction, and specific causes stemming from the patient's life circumstances or psychic reality should be investigated.

Two other characterological contributions stem from psychoanalytic investigations. A number of authors, particularly Weijl [21], emphasized the latent homosexual conflicts as a particularly important trait predisposing to alcoholism in men. Another group, particularly Simmel [20], stressed that alcoholics' tendencies to present themselves as schizoid characters were the result of their dealing in this way with their aggression. These issues are explored further in Chapter 44.

Psychological Contributions

While the many psychological testing studies failed to identify a single alcoholic character pattern, they did further highlight the problems of dependent yearnings. Rorschach studies by Billig and Sullivan [2] stressed the type of high expectations accompanied by low performance and vulnerability to severe disappointment and depression, which fits beautifully the oral character. The same explosive mixture of unrealistically grandious expectations, with poor frustration tolerance, poor techniques for alleviating feelings of discomfort, and refusal (or inability) to accept limitations was also found by Halpern [5].

PROBLEMS AND THE CAUSE OF ALCOHOLISM

Rather than being able to identify any personality type that predicts of accompanies alcoholism, one must be content with observing that certain personality characteristics occur more often among alcoholics, and in retrospect, one can understand how, with these particular handicaps or problems in the picture, an individual might be more likely to resort to the use of alcohol as a "problem solvent."

It cannot be said that these problems or weaknesses cause alcoholism, only perhaps that they increase the statistical probability that if such a person discovers alcohol and starts using it, he or she may tend to develop an increasing dependency upon it. It should not be concluded, however, that this refers to simple functions directly augmented by the drug alone. Such uses do take place. Krystal and Raskin [13] have pointed out, for instance, that it could be said that alcohol and sedative drugs bolster the stimulus barrier. But the situation is much more complicated. For instance, the problem of guilt related to the ingestion of alcohol, guilt that may be derived from a variety of sources, would also represent such a predisposition to addiction. For, after indulgence, the unbearably painful guilt crisis (hangover) requires more self-medication, thus contributing to the vicious circle formation. Thus a tragic-comic statement has been descriptive of an alcoholic as being two double shots behind the rest of the world. The schizoid attitude of the drinker has been aptly summed up by George Nathan: "I drink to make other people more interesting" [15].

Predisposition to Alcoholism

Increasingly, the picture of alcoholism and other substance-dependent individuals is correlated to severe infantile traumatization [13], particularly that resulting from alcoholism in the parents [4]. One is apt to find multiple disturbances in ego function, self-integration, and cohesion, and disturbances in the process of separation-individuation. Thus, a multitude of problems constitute a predisposition to alcoholism and an obstacle to its treatment. Selzer [18] has emphasized the role of dependency, egocentricity, depression, and hostility.

Wurmser's Heptad

Wurmser [22] has constructed a vicious-circle picture of the addiction process in which the personality of the addicted individual is such that upon suffering a significant acute narcissistic crisis, (e.g., disappointment in self and a love object) such an unbearable blow to self-respect is caused that he or she is plunged into a regressive spin. In it, in succession:

1. The addict encounters an affect regression wherein affects become primitive and mixed, mostly somatic, and not utilizable as signals to the self.
2. These "global" affect responses are unbearable and motivate various affect defenses that involve drug-augmented defense against affects — avoidance, dissociation, escape into action, boundary modifications, denial, and splitting of object representation, with a polarization into idealized and maligned object representations.
3. As a result of these losses in the integrative function there is an increasing dependence upon externalization (i.e., a failure to recognize and deal with interpsychic material and conflict as such.
4. This development permits the dealing with aggression (which has been a probelm to start with) by directing it to "external" objects in a way freeing it from intrapsychic restraints.
5. All of these developments represent such a severe impairment in integration that a split in the superego appears as illustrated by the sudden and radical changes in the behavior of the substance-dependent person.
6. With the regression there is a greater insistence on pleasure, gratification, or the pleasure-oriented regime of the ego [17].
7. Because of these regressions and increasing dependence upon the drug, it becomes a significant transference object of the yearning for the return-to-fantasy paradise wherein the unity with the ideal mother is restored. This demand for

the "restoration" of a blissful situation creates an extraordinary demanding, unrealistic, aggressively colored attitude on the part of the individual, which predisposes him or her to severe disappointment and thus to more narcissistic crises — returning to the starting point in the vicious circle.

Alexithymia

Wurmser brought together characteristic vulnerabilities that can be viewed as separate liabilities, as described above. For instance, the matter of affect regression has been considered a major problem in substance dependence, as well as a factor interfering seriously with the effectiveness of psychotherapy in alcoholics [9, 12]. The characteristic dedifferentiation, along with deverbalization and resomatization of affect responses, causes the alcoholic to be confronted with sensations rather than feelings. These physiological responses are not useful as signals, but are painful and overwhelming. They call attention to themselves, rather than to the "story behind them." Therefore the tendency is to block them with alcohol, rather than to attend to what they signal. This disturbance is viewed to be part of a characteristic pattern that Sifneos [19] has named "alexithymia." Along with the inability to name and use one's emotions, there is also a diminution in the capacity for drive-oriented fantasy. Thinking becomes "operative," mundane, and boring. The capacity for empathy with others and the development of utilizable transference is seriously diminished. It is noted that this regression in affect was what Rado [17] referred to when he talked about the anxious depression of the alcoholic as the affects return to their undifferentiated precursors. Similarly, in regard to the impairment in fantasy formation, Wurmser [23] stressed the importance of the problem of hyposymbolization [22, 23].

Self-Care Incapacity

Another serious problem to which reference has been made, is the inhibition in the capacity for self-care, which has a number of implications in terms of making an individual more vulnerable to problems of alcoholism and other depressive drugs. The problem has to do with a specific feeling that self-gratification, self-soothing, and any form of self-care, from babying one's self to taking care of one's affairs, is not possible. What is not known to the subject, unless psychotherapeutic exploration is possible, is that these functions are experienced as prohibited and reserved for the mother and her substitute (i.e., transference objects such as a spouse, doctor, AA group). Involved in this problem is a disturbance of self-representation wherein all the welfare and vital functions are attributed to the mother and reserved for her [11]. Because the alcoholic is often unable to tell whether he or she is feeling tired, angry, sick, hungry, or deprived when anxious and/or depressed, and because he or she does not feel free to soothe and comfort the self when distressed, he or she becomes dependent upon an external agent to do so. Alcohol soothes and gratifies a number of needs at the same time — including that of a placebo in permitting the exercise of functions otherwise blocked.

Anhedonia

Another characterological problem frequently found in alcoholics is anhedonia. This is a partial to severe impairment in the capacity to experience pleasure, joy, or happiness. This characteristic goes along with the previously mentioned history of severe psychic trauma, particularly in childhood. Krystal[11] has pointed out that the aftereffects of infantile traumatization consist in arrest in affective development, a "doomsday" orientation involving a dread expectation of the return of the unbearable traumatic state, and most of all, anhedonia. The early traumatization possibly causes an actual shift in the relative intensity of the experience of the pleasure center as opposed to the distress centers. While as yet the psychological aspects of these disturbances have not been worked out, the shifts in the hedonic capacity under certain conditions is well documented. Anhedonia is also a regularly occuring phenomenon accompanying depression.

As the alcoholic discovers that the drug is virtually the only way he or she can obtain gratification and simultaneous relief from distressful affective states, reliance on it increases. At the same time, the increasing depressive pressures and descending spiral of social maladjustment continue to dimish the hedonic capacity because of an increase in depressive reactions. Thus, in severe and advanced stages of alcoholism, the occurance of anhedonia is so frequent that it is taken for granted. Another reason for ignoring this important character trait is that there is hardly any knowledge about how to help the patients to cultivate their capacity for pleasure and joy. This problem is an especially serious one in dealing with the alcoholic professional, such as the alcoholic physician. These individuals tend to present a combination of severe compulsiveness, "work addiction," and anhedonia underlying their problem drinking. The drug is often used to maintain a severe machinelike self-control regime. Many of these patients maintain for a long time a very high degree of success in their professional and business careers. Their "superb" adjustment to reality is actually part of the "operative" life style mentioned above. Thus one should look out for the combination of anhedonia and alexithymia in the "pillar of the community" who has to depend upon alcohol to maintain a heroic function.

In these various defects and deficits lie the kinds of problems that make it difficult for an individual to function effectively. They thus compose not a specific personality type, rather they are traits that make it more probable that a person with these attributes, when exposed to alcohol under favorable conditions, will develop some form of alcohol abuse, some drinking problem.

The Natural History of Alcoholism

In addition, every syndrome has a natural history of its own. As Wurmser [22] pointed out, certain developments tend to perpetuate substance dependence. The type II use of alcohol for the purpose of being able to bear stressful affect diminishes the skills in affect tolerance and an individual's self-confidence about his or her own strength and resourcefulness. Similarly, the type III use of alcohol adds a factor shaping the personality in addition to the previous neurotic, borderline, or psychotic character structure.

Zinberg [23] has pointed out that the street culture attending the use of heroin produces practically the same type of junkie, regardless of the original personality. Similarly, there is little question about the similarities in the personalities of skid row alcoholics. But one should not need to wait until the picture becomes that obvious in order to appreciate that alcoholism promotes the deterioration of the alcoholic's sense of self-respect and self-reliance. It promotes a schizoid withdrawal from all actual and potention object relations, thus contributing to the alcoholic's loss of compunction to be honest, to be truthful, or to try to maintain contact with reality. Thus the schizoid tendencies and the unrealistic, grandiose demands promote externalization of rage and further accentuate the problems of aggression, with its suicidal aspects. Thus it happens that while there is no such thing as an alcoholic personality, alcoholics manage to appear quite similar in the most severe and self-destructive cases and stages of the problem.

REFERENCES

1. Abraham, K. The influence of oral erotism on character formation. In:*Selected Papers of Karl Abraham*. Bryan D. and Stachey, A. (trans.). New York: Basic Books, 1954. (Originally published 1924).

2. Billig, O., and Sullivan, T. D. personality structure and prognosis of alcohol addiction: A Rorschach study. *Q. J. Stud. Alcohol* 3:554-563, 1943.

3. Glover, E. The prevention and treatment of drug addiction. *Br. J. Inebriety* 29:13-18, 1931.

4. Guze, S., Tuason, V., Gatfield, P., Stewart, M., and Picken, B. Psychiatric illness and crime with particular reference to alcoholism: A study of 223 criminals. *J. Nerv. Ment. Dis.* 134:512-521, 1962.

5. Halpern, F. Studies of compulsive drinkers. *Q. J. Stud. Alcohol* 6:468-479, 1946.

6. Kaplan, E. H., and Wieder, H. *People Take Drugs*. Lyle Stuart: Seacaucus, N.J., 1974. Stuart 1974.

7. Knight, R. P. The psychodynamics of chronic alcoholism. *J. Nerv. Ment. Dis.* 86:538-548, 1937.

8. Kohut, H. *The Analysis of the Self*. International Universities Press: New York, 1971.

9. Krystal, H. The genetic development of affects and affect regression. In: *The Annual of Psychoanalysis* (Vol. 2). International Universities Press: New York, 1974.

10. Krystal, H. Affect tolerance. In: *The Annual of Psychoanalysis* (Vol. 3). International Universities Press: New York, 1975.

11. Krystal, H. Self-representation and the capacity for self-care. In: *The Annual of Psychoanalysis* (Vol. 6). International Universities Press: New York, 1978.

12. Krystal, H. Trauma and affect. In: *The Psychoanalytic Study of the Child* (Vol. 33). Yale University Press: New Haven, 1978.

13. Krystal, H., and Raskin, H. *Drug Dependence.* Wayne State University Press: Detroit, 1970.

14. Menninger, C. A. *Man Against Himself.* Harcourt Brace Jovanovich: New York, 1938.

15. Nathan, G. J. Statement attributed to G. J. Nathan by Krystal, H., Moore, R. A., and Dorsey, J. Alcoholism and the forces of education. *Pers. Guid. J.* 45:134-139.

16. Pollock, G. *Psychosomatic Specificity and the Life Cycle* Paper presented as part of the panel, Psychosomatic Hypotheses: Current Status, American Psychiatric Association 132nd annual meeting, Chicago, 1979.

17. Rado, S. The psychoanalysis of pharmacothymia. *Psychoan. Q.* 2:1-23, 1933.

18. Selzer, M. The periodicity of the alcoholic as an impediment to psychotherapy. *Psychiat. Q.* (no vol.):1-8, 1967.

19. Sifneos, P. E. Clinical observations on some patients suffering from a variety of psychosomatic diseases. *Acta Med. Psychosom.* 1-10, 1967.

20. Simmel, E. Alcoholism and addiction. *Psychoan. Q.* 17:6-31, 1948.

21. Weijl, S. Theoretical and practical aspects of psychoanalytic therapy of problem drinkers. *Q. J. Stud. Alcohol* 5:200-211, 1944.

22. Wurmser, L. *The Hidden Dimension:Psychodynamics in Compulsive Drug Use.* J. Aronson: New York, 1978.

23. Zinberg, N. W. Addiction and ego function. In: *The Psychoanalytic Study of the Child* (Vol. 30). 1975.

47

MARTIN H. KEELER, MD, Baylor University

ALCOHOLISM AND AFFECTIVE DISORDER

TWO ASPECTS OF THE relation of affective disorder and alcoholism are of importance to clinical practice and to research. The first is whether affective disorder precipitates, predisposes to, or aggravates alcoholism. This is relevant because there are better methods available to treat and prevent affective disorder than there are to treat or prevent alcoholism. If mood disorder and alcoholism are related, a treatment for the former may be of value for the latter. A second significant aspect is the relation of alcohol intoxication to mood disorder.

ALCOHOLISM AND AFFECTIVE DISORDERS

It is essential in attempting to evaluate the relation between mood disorder and alcoholism to be aware of the classification of mood disorder. Three distinct dimensions are used [3]: mania versus depression; a history of a single episode versus repeated episodes; and the severity of the disorder. Research is seldom precise as to the nature of the affective disturbance among alcoholics. At best patients who have ever had a manic episode are considered to constitute one group and all other patients are considered to constitute another group. From this point of view it could be argued that all studies of the relation of alcoholism and affective disorder are of uncertain value.

Martin H. Keeler, MD, Professor of Psychiatry, College of Medicine, Baylor University, Houston, Texas.

Another type of study classifies mood disorder among alcoholics on the basis of increased scores in one or more rating scales of depression or mania. Such methods include all depression in one category and do not exclude patients who have other conditions that might elevate the scales. Rating scales are of great use in measuring changes in mood if a mood disorder has been established using other methods, but they are not a substitute for clinical diagnoses.

THE CLINICAL PROBLEMS: EXAMPLES

A patient who has a severe depressive episode every year and a patient who has no history of disorder but becomes depressed following the death of a child are both depressed. A patient who cannot sleep and paces constantly and a patient who is motionless and sleeps 12 hours a night are both depressed. The distinction between single episode and repeated episode disease is difficult: If a patient has three episodes in his or her lifetime will the first one be considered a single episode?

The diagnosis of alcoholism requires only evidence of excessive use and resultant physical, social, or psychological harm. A person who drinks a fifth of whiskey every Saturday night and becames grossly intoxicated but does not drink at other times, a person who can abstain totally for years but drinks continuously after taking one drink, and a person who drinks moderately for months and then engages in binge drinking are all diagnosed as alcoholic for most research purposes.

Even if there is a powerful relation between a type of affective disorder and a type of alcoholism it is likely to be overlooked in a study that does not account for subtypes of each entity.

BIPOLAR DISORDER AND ALCOHOLISM

Some patients with affective disorder have manic episodes. In practice these individuals are considered as a homogeneous population whether they have had one episode or many of mania and/or depression and whether they have had a depressive episode or not. The group is usually called "bipolar"; the complete term should be "recurrent bipolar affective disorder."

Two strategies are used to determine whether there is a correlation between alcoholism and bipolar affective disorder. The first is an attempt to correlate the two clinical diagnoses. This can be done on the direct observation of both conditions or on the basis of the presence of one and a history of the other. The second method is to determine the rate of bipolar disorder among the relatives of alcoholics. Bipolar disease is familial, so if it is correlated with alcoholism the rate would be increased among the relatives of alcoholics.

Winokur, [34] reported that the use of alcohol is increased by patients during manic episodes. Mayfield and Coleman [16] described an increased rate of alcoholism among patients with manic episodes. Reich [23] reported a high rate of alcoholism among hospitalized manic-depressives but not among those never hospitalized. Morrison [20] reported a high rate of bipolar affective disorder among abstinent alcoholics. Cassidy [6] also reported a correlation between bipolar affective disorder and alcoholism. Morrison, in a more recent study [19], reported no correlation between bipolar affective disorder and alcoholism in a patient population. Woodruff [38] reported a low rate of bipolar disorder in a study of mood disturbance among alcoholics. Some (but not all clinical studies) report some correlation. Reich's [23] observation that this is true among inpatients but not outpatients indicates that severity of disturbance may be critical. It is difficult to design a study that would settle the question by direct study of patients.

Another strategy used to study correlation between bipolar mood disorder and alcoholism is to study the rate of bipolar illness among the relatives of alcoholics. Bipolar illness does have familial occurrence. If the rate of bipolar illness is not increased among the relatives of alcoholics it could not be maintained that bipolar illness predisposes to alcoholism. The advantage of this method of study is that direct clinical studies require two separate diagnoses to be made of the same patient, which is at best an uncertain procedure. Those studies that are most careful to identify instances of bipolar illness among the relatives of alcoholics indicate that the condition and alcoholism are independently distributed. Amark [2] found no correlation between the two processes. Winokur [36] reported that the rate of ever having had a manic episode was the same among the relatives of alcoholics as in the general population. The pool of subjects with verified bipolar disorder is so small that fewer studies have been conducted using only such patients. The question, therefore, despite negative results, is still open.

Clinical and genetic studies, taken together, at this time indicate that alcoholism and bipolar affective disorder are not related. It is possible that the combination of an episode of bipolar disorder and excessive drinking is apt to lead to hospitalization, whereas a mood disorder of the same severity would not do so. It could be argued that a mania might be missed in a retrospective diagnosis but this would be as true for alcoholics and their relatives as for others.

UNIPOLAR AFFECTIVE DISORDER AND ALCOHOLISM

For practical purposes all patients who have never had a manic episode are grouped in the category of unipolar disorder. The reality situation of an alcoholic after prolonged excessive drinking in itself might be a basis for situational depression. A person who is physically ill, has lost a spouse, and has lost a job would be depressed. Alcoholics are frequently in this situation. This is not unipolar depression affective disorder. It is not surprising that clinical studies that correlate diagnoses among patients are inconclusive and readily criticized. Research practice usually consists of using a score in a rating scale to verify depression. No study has utilized accepted clinical criteria to compare the correlation of alcoholism with specific categories of depressive illness in a randomly selected population. Winokur [37] did study patients using precise diagnostic criteria for depression and for alcoholism. Only three of 139 patients who met the criteria for unipolar depressive disorder were alcoholic. Another finding in the study was that patients with alcoholism and depression tend to resemble alcoholics without depression more than they resemble depressives without alcoholism using measures of behavior, personal history, and family history. Shaw [26] reported a 98% rate of depression among alcoholics by accepting an elevation in any of three rating scales as indicating depression. Weingold [31], using the Zung Depression Scale, and Rosen [25] using the Minnesota Multiphasic Personality Inventory, reported the rate of depression to be higher among alcoholics than it is the general population. Keeler [14] reported that the rate of depression among a group of alcoholics varied from 8.6% to 66%, depending on diagnostic criteria using tests employed in the reports of other investigators. Keeler concluded that the method of diagnosis was the critical variable in studies of the need for later diagnosis of depression among alcoholics.

It would be difficult to design an experiment that would definitely establish or refute a relation between alcoholism and any widely accepted depressive entity. The principal difficulty is that a precise diagnosis of depression can only be made when the patient is neither intoxicated nor experiencing alcohol withdrawal and many alcoholics cannot be studied in this condition. If the study is limited to patients who are hospitalized, only the more severely disturbed are included. In most instances retrospective diagnoses would be even less accurate than diagnoses based on direct observation of the patient.

The direct study of the relations between depressive entities and alcoholism has not proven useful. Studies of familial incidence provide most of the more convincing data. Such studies of unipolar disorder are more readily conducted than are studies of bipolar disorder because many more people are or have been depressed than are or have been manic. It is much easier to gather a significant sample when depressive illness, as compared to mixed illness, is investigated.

Winokur [33] reported that when the proband had depressive illness there was a 15.5% probability of depressive illness but only a 3.1% probability of alcoholism among first-degree relatives. If the proband is alcoholic there is a 15.1% chance of alcoholism and a 15.5% chance of depression among first-degree relatives. In this study Winokur reported that alcoholism was increased among the relatives of male probands provided that depression occurred before the proband was 40, but alcoholism was not increased if depression first occurred when the patient was over 40 and if the proband was female. This study is of particular significance because relatives of the probands were interviewed. Winokur [35] did not confirm these findings in a study in which only patients were interviewed. A study by Gershon [8] in which relatives were interviewed reported no increase of the rate of alcoholism among the relatives of probands with unipolar or bipolar disorder. This study was conducted in Israel, a country with a very low rate of alcoholism. This complete lack of correlation indicates that something other than a direct genetic linkage between alcoholism and affective disorder exacts even if there is a correlation. It is necessary to assume that some social or cultural factor prevents alcoholism or that some additional factor, genetic or otherwise, is necessary for alcoholism to express itself in the relatives of probands.

It is likely that the specific relation of increased alcoholism in the relatives of men who experience depression before they are 40 years old is, in effect, a way of studying a specific type of depression. As noted previously, the methodologies of the studies did not include differentiating among the several defined depressive entities. This situation is unfortunate in that clinical diagnoses and research findings cannot be directly compared. Clinical practice does not differentiate affective disorder using the age of onset.

Studies of familial occurrence of alcoholism and of affective disorder can be subjected to rather complex analysis. Winokur [37] categorized alcoholism as primary, alcoholism with affective disorder, and alcoholism with sociopathy and compared males and females within each subgroup. The first-degree relatives, but not other relatives, tended to have the same subtype of alcoholism as the proband. For each subgroup the sum of depression and alcoholism was the same among male and female relatives but female relatives had more depressions and male relatives had more alcoholism.

Analyses of a study by Winokur [36] cited that there was a familial tendency for male alcoholics to have female relatives with depressive disorder. This is an intriguing finding because alcoholism is more common among men and depression is more common among women. Goodwin [11] however, reported that if the daughters of alcoholics are raised by nonalcoholics they have no more depression than does the general population. This suggests that being raised by an alcoholic parent might make women prime to develop depression.

There is an extensive literature pertinent to the question of the relationship between affective disorder and alcoholism that is difficult to interpret because of lack of differentiation between unipolar and bipolar mood disorder and to change in diagnostic practice. Two extensive reviews are available, those of Winokur [37] and Gershon [9]. In particular Stendstedt [29] and Slater [27] reported no increase in alcoholism among relatives of depressive probands. Woodruff [38] reported that patients with alcoholism and depression are essentially similar to other alcoholic patients. Guze [12] considered alcoholism in terms of secondary affective disorder, which introduces a diagnostic system not in clinical use. Pitts and Winokur [22] reported an increase in affective disorder among the siblings of alcoholics. Winokur [32] introduced the concept of depressive spectrum disease in an attempt to resolve some of the methodological problems involved in the unipolar-bipolar categorization. An association of alcoholism and suicide has been reported [24].

The coexistence of alcoholism and sociopathic behavior has been studied because of the reported association of these entities and affective disorder in families. Sociopathy is not increased in families in which alcoholism and depression are increased.

METHODOLOGICAL PROBLEMS IN STUDIES OF ALCOHOLISM AND AFFECTIVE DISORDER

A comprehensive review of the problems involved in studies of the relation between alcoholism and affective disorder has been published by Cloninger [5]. There are many difficulties present in such research.

Whether a person who has had one condition during his or her lifetime will also have another condition can only be determined at the end of that lifetime. Obviously if a 20-year-old alcoholic has not had a depressive episode, one might well occur later. There are statistical methods to correct for this possible source of error.

Familial occurrence of one or two entities can reflect environment as well as heredity. No study of the coincidence of alcoholism and affective disorder either among patients or among their relatives can be assumed to represent genetic factors unless some special methods are used to determine this. Such determination can be accomplished by comparing rates of coincidence in monozygotic versus dizygotic twins and rates of coincidence in children raised by other than their biological parents. These are difficult methods because of the small number of suitable subjects. The inevitable errors in diagnoses, discussed below, necessitate large numbers of subjects, so sophisticated studies using twin or cross-adoption methodologies may not be possible [30].

The error factor in retrospective diagnoses when the subject is directly examined is high. The error rate when other than the subject is interviewed is enormous. What does "I heard that my aunt had a nervous breakdown" mean? In clinical practice clinicians often disagree as to whether a psychotic episode represents schizophrenia or affective disorder. The same difficulties exist for all patients, so diagnostic errors can be compensated by increasing the size of the study. Large numbers of patients who are twins or have been adopted are not available and only such patients can solve the question as to whether heredity or early environment is the critical factor.

Other problems, previously described, can be resolved by available but tedious and thus often neglected methods. Diagnosis requires exclusion as well as inclusion of criteria. If diagnoses are made in other than standard terms the criteria should be stated and diagnoses using standard methods also provided. The term "sociopathic alcoholism" does not mean that the patient or any relative so identified could be classified as a sociopath.

ALCOHOL INTOXICATION AND AFFECT

There is a seldom-stated but frequent assumption that alcoholics drink in an attempt to self-medicate themselves for some other problem. Anxiety or depression may be assumed to be such problems. The use of small amounts of alcohol does cause some elevation of mood among normal subjects [15, 28] but the extent of this is minor. Judd [13] reports that alcohol elevates only the confusion scale of the profile of mood states if given to alcoholics. Mendelson [18], McGuire [17], Goldman [10] and Allman [1] report that alcoholics become progressively dysphoric as they drink to excess over long periods of time. Mayfield [16], Pauleikhoff [21], and Campanella [4] reported clinical series that indicate that an increase in drinking does not accompany depression among patients who have both entities.

The situation with mania is quite different. Freed [7] and Reich [23] reported that the use of alcohol was increased during periods of mood elevation among patients with bipolar mood disorder.

There is a high degree of consistency in the clinical and experimental studies of the relation of drinking to excess and depression. Such drinking does not relieve depression and patients who are depressed do not increase their drinking. Patients with mood elevation accompanying bipolar mood disorder do increase their drinking.

CONCLUSION

Although there is apparently no correlation between bipolar affective disorder and alcoholism, several relationships exist. Patients increase their drinking during manic episodes. If the total severity of disturbance requires hospitalization the two conditions coexist more than would be expected by chance alone. The most economical hypothesis is that individuals drink more when they are manic. This also suggests that lithium prophylaxes of excessive drinking might have some value among patients with bipolar affective disorder. This might be trivial; such prophylaxis is often indicated whether a bipolar patients ever drinks to excess or not. In any event there does seem to be a clinical relation between mania and increased drinking that suggests further clinical and experimental studies.

The finding that there is a correlation among males between early onset of unipolar depressive illness and alcoholism is reasonably established. This suggests that further investigations of the subtype of depression are justified. It would be of particular interest to determine if drinking increases during depressive episodes among patients who have had an episode of depression early in life. The many negative studies of the relationship between affective disorder and alcoholism and unspecified depression do not refute this possibility. It is hoped that such a study would also attempt to classify depression using the accepted clinical standards.

The simple hypothesis that depression and alcoholism are related in that patients drink to relieve their depression has little experimental or clinical basis. Patients with periodic depression do not drink more when depressed and excessive drinking does not relieve depression.

Any conclusive study of the relationships between affective disorder and alcoholism will have to include a method to distinguish between genetic factors and the results of being raised by an alcoholic parent or a parent with affective disorder. If this is not done any relationship could reflect environment as well as heredity.

There is a possibility of a false negative result in studies of the familial correlations of affective disorder and alcoholism because of the error factor in retrospective diagnosis, or diagnosis made from a history given by other than the individual examined or interviewed.

It is possible that some noncontroversial subtyping of alcoholism and of affective disorder might locate relations heretofore undetected. This should be accompanied by analyses using conventional diagnostic procedures.

REFERENCES

1. Allman, L., Taylor, H., and Nathan, P. Group drinking during stress: Effects on drinking behavior, affect, psychopathology. Am. J. Psychiatry 129:669-678, 1972.
2. Amark, C. A study in alcoholism. Acta Psychia. Scand. (Suppl.) 70:283, 1951.
3. American Psychiatric Association. Diagnostic and Statistical Manual of Mental Disorders, (3rd ed.). Author: Washington, D. C., 1981.
4. Campanella, G., and Fossi, E. Considerazioni sui rapporti fra alcoolismo e manifestazioni depressive. Rass. Stud. Psichiatry 52:617-632, 1967.
5. Cloninger, C., Reich, T., and Westzel, R. Alcoholism and affective disorders: Familial associations and genetic models. In: Alcoholism and Affective Disorders, Goodwin, D. W. et al. (eds.). Spectrum: New York, 1979.
6. Feighner, J. P., Robins, E., Guze, S. B., et al. Diagnostic criteria for use in psychiatric research. Arch. Gen. Psychiatry 26:57-63, 1972.
7. Freed, E. Alcohol abuse by manic patients. Psychol. Rep. 25:280, 1969.
8. Gershon, E., Baron, M., and Leckman, J. Genetic models of the transmission of affective disorders. J. Psychiat. Res. 12:301-317, 1975.

9. Gershon, E., Bunney, W., Leckman, J., Van Eerdewegh, M., and DeBauche, B. The inheritance of affective disorders: A review of data and hypotheses. *Behav. Genet.* 6:227-261, 1976.

10. Goldman, M. To drink or not to drink: An experimental analysis of group drinking decisions by four alcoholics. *Am. J. Psychiatry* 131:1123-1130, 1974.

11. Goodwin, D., Schulsinger, F., Knop, J., Mednick, S., and Guze, S. Alcoholism and depression in adopted-out daughters of alcoholics. *Arch. Gen. Psychiatry* 34:176-184, 1977.

12. Guze, S., Goodwin, D., and Crane, J. Criminality and psychiatric illness. *Arch. Gen. Psychiatry* 20:583-591, 1969.

13. Judd, L., Hubbard, B., Janowsky, D., Huey, L., Abrams, A., Riney, W., and Pendery, M. Ethanol-lithium interaction in alcoholics. In: *Alcoholism and Affective Disorders*, Goodwin, D. W. et al. (eds.). Spectrum: New York, 1979.

14. Keeler, M., Taylor, C., and Miller, W. Are all recently detoxified alcoholics depressed? *Am. J. Psychiatry* 136:4B, 1979.

15. Mayfield, D., and Allen, D. Alcohol and affect: A psychopharmacological study. *Am. J. Psychiatry* 123:1346-1351, 1967.

16. Mayfield, D. C., and Coleman, L. L. Alcohol use and affective disorder. *Dis. Nerv. Syst.* 29:467-474, 1968.

17. McGuire, M., Mendelson, J., and Stein, S. Comparative psychosocial studies of alcholic and non-alcoholic subjects undergoing experimentally induced ethanol intoxication. *Psychosom. Med.* 28:13-26, 1966.

18. Mendelson, J. H. (ed.). Experimentally induced chronic intoxication and withdrawal in alcoholics *Q. J. Stud. Alcohol (Suppl.)* 2, 1964.

19. Morrison, J. R. Bipolar affective disorder and alcoholism. *Am. J. Psychiatry* 131:1130-1133, 1974.

20. Morrison, J. R. *Psychiatric Illness in Abstinent Alcoholics.* Unpublished paper.

21. Pauleikhoff, B. Uber die seltenheit von alkoholabusus bei zyklothym depressiven. *Nervenarzt* 24:445-448, 1953.

22. Pitts, F., and Winokur, G. Affective disorder: VII. Alcoholism and affective disorder. *J. Psychiat. Res.* 4:37-50, 1966.

23. Reich, L. H., Davies, R. K., and Himmelhoch, J. M. Excessive alcohol use in manic-depressive illness. *Am. J. Psychiatry* 131:83-86, 1974.

24. Robins, L., Bates, W., and O'Neal, P. Adult drinking patterns of former problem children. In: *Society, Culture and Drinking Patterns.* Pittman, D. J. and Snyder, C. R. (eds.). Wiley: New York, 1962.

25. Rosen, A. C. A comparative study of alcoholic and psychiatric patients with the MMPI. *Q. J. Stud. Alcohol* 21:253-266, 1960.

26. Shaw, J. A., Donley, P., Morgan, D. W., et al. Treatment of depression in alcoholics. *Am. J. Psychiatry* 132:641-644, 1975.

27. Slater, E., and Cowie, V. *The Genetics of Mental Disorders.* Oxford University Press: London, 1971.

28. Smith, R., Parker, E., and Noble, E. Alcohol and affect in a dyadic social interaction. *Psychosom. Med.* 37:25-40, 1975.

29. Stendstedt, A. A study of manic-depressive psychosis. *Acta Psychiatry Neurol. Scand. (Suppl.)* 79:1-111, 1952.

30. Tanna, V., Winokur, G., Elston, R., and Go, R. A linkage study of depressive spectrum disease: The use of the sib-pair method. *Neuropsychobiol.* 2:52-62, 1976.

31. Weingold, H. P., Lachin, J. M., Bell, A. H., et al. Depression as a symptom of alcoholism: Search for a phenomenon. *J. Abnorm. Psychol.* 73:195-197, 1968.

32. Winokur, G., Cadoret, R., Baker, M., and Dorzab, J. Depressive spectrum disease vs.

pure depressive disease: Some further data. *Br. J. Psychiatry* 127:75-77, 1975.

33. Winokur, G., Cadoret, R., Dorzab, J., and Baker, M. Depressive disease: A genetic study. *Arch. Gen. Psychiatry* 24:135-144, 1971.

34. Winokur, G., Clayton, P. J., and Reich, T. *Manic-Depressive Illness.* Mosby: St. Louis, 1969.

35. Winokur, G., Morrison, J., Clancy, J., and Crowe, R. The Iowa 500: Familial and clinical findings favor two kinds of depressive illness. *Comprehens. Psychiatry* 14:99-107, 1973.

36. Winokur, G., Reich, T., Rimmer, J., and Pitts, F. Alcoholism: III. Diagnosis and familial psychiatric illness in 259 alcoholic probands. *Arch. Gen. Psychiatry* 23:104-111, 1970.

37. Winokur, G., Rimmer, J., and Reich, T. Alcoholism: IV. Is there more than one type of alcoholism? *Br. J. Psychiatry* 118:525-531, 1971.

38. Woodruff, R., Guze, S., Clayton, P., and Carr, D. Alcoholism and depression. In: *Alcoholism and Affective Disorders*, Goodwin, D. W. et al. (eds.). Spectrum: New York, 1979.

48

PETER HARTOCOLLIS, MD, PhD, University of Patras School of Medicine, Patras, Greece

BORDERLINE SYNDROME AND ALCOHOLISM

THE DIAGNOSTIC AND *Statistical Manual* (DSM-III) [1] of the American Psychiatric Association, has adopted "borderline personality disorder" as a formal diagnostic category, thus giving the term official sanction for the first time in its long, controversial history. Even though limited in scope, the concept's formal recognition reflects its widespread popularity and, indeed, applicability in current clinical practice. This development is ironic in that the renewed interest in the term and its success are to be largely attributed to psychoanalysts at a time when the paradigm of their clinical theory, psychoneurosis, is all but abolished by the official representatives of American psychiatry. A concomitant development of note is the identification of the psychodynamics of alcoholism with those underlying borderline and narcissistic personality disorders. The present chapter traces these two lines of development and then focuses on that part of the borderline spectrum of disorders identifiable as alcoholism.

The first one to describe the borderline patient in modern literature was Stern [14], a psychoanalyst in private practice in New York. Stern's patient was different from the traditional neurotic in that he displayed a hypersensitivity to failure and rejection, a narcissistic vulnerability that made psychoanalytic treat-

---

Peter Hartocollis, MD, PhD, Professor and Chairman, Department of Psychiatry, The University of Patras, School of Medicine, Patras, Greece.

ment difficult, if at all possible. Stern speculated that such a patient had been subjected to sustained affect deprivation in his infancy and as a result he had developed a chronic affect hunger. Along with it went a denial of intrapsychic problems. The borderline patient that Stern described could be easily recognized in Deutsch's [3] description of the "as if" personality. Deutsch emphasized the superficiality as well as vulnerability of the interpersonal relations of such a patient. Behind the facade of amiable normality, there was a poverty of feeling, a lack of emotional investment, and a constant wish to please, prompting the patient to identify with the ideas and wishes of whoever happened to pay attention to him or to her. Hungry for approval, such a person felt empty and yielded readily to external influence. As with Stern's patient, a pleasant, passive facade concealed a great deal of hostility, anger, and, in general, aggressiveness.

On the other hand, a number of clinicians described a much more marginal patient, one whose social and psychological adjustment was even more precarious and behavior more deviant, associated with delinquency, perversion, or addiction. Even though ordinarily free from major psychotic symptoms such as delusions or hallucinations, this patient was thought to be basically psychotic, the condition being variously labeled as "ambulatory schizophrenia," "borderline schizophrenia," "latent psychosis," "prepsychotic schizophrenia," or "psychotic character." Grinker et al. [6] confirmed the existence of the borderline patient operationally, identifying four degrees of pathology within a conceptual space distinct from either neurosis or psychosis.

In a parallel way, Fairbairn [4] and a number of other analytic writers in Great Britain described in depth the schizoid personality, one of the most typical borderline disorders. Fairbairn felt self-conscious about the fact that his description bordered so much on the normal that it might be discarded as irrelevant. Indeed, the universality of such important aspects of the borderline condition as loneliness and narcissism could make the phenomenologically inclined clinician impatient with the borderline diagnosis, which is why Kernberg's [7] contribution, with its emphasis on the dynamic aspects of the condition, in particular defense mechanisms and superego function, was so crucial in establishing it conceptually as a self-sufficient psychiatric syndrome. Kernberg's conceptualization assumed a basic personality organization, stable and qualitatively different from the personality structure underlying neurotic or psychotic disorders.

THE BORDERLINE SYNDROME

Even though still controversial in that different authors describe it somewhat differently — a discrepancy attributed to the fact that different authors have reference to different patient populations — the borderline syndrome has been generally defined in terms of five aspects of human functioning: affective disposition, impulse control, reality testing, personal identity, and interpersonal relationships. In such a general framework, the borderline patient displays a number of specific, pathognomonic characteristics, symptom and behavior patterns, as well as psychodynamics, which, inferential as they may be, are not difficult to demonstrate in clinical practice. Anxiety, diffuse, free-floating, and chronic; obsessive-compulsive symptoms; phobias of all sorts; bizarre conversions; dissociative reactions; and hypochondriasis combine to form what looks like a polysymptomatic neurosis. The picture is colored by an affective, subjective disturbance that, dominated by anger, is seething under the surface of an otherwise impassive or even amiable individual. Manifested readily in hateful outbursts and nearly indiscriminate targets, the borderline's anger or rage is accompanied by a sense of frustration or disappointment, narcissistic hurt and feelings of rejection, injustice, and entitlement. Besides anger, the borderline person experiences an array of poorly defined, largely interchangeable affects or moods, such as boredom, disgust, emptiness, loneliness, alienation, and low-grade depression (what has been described as "affectless depression," or "anhedonia"), all of which may be experienced as free-floating anxiety and acted out in impulsive, seemingly purposeless, unpredictable behavior. Such affects betray a diffuse sense of identity, which leads to drinking sprees, sexually promiscuous or perverse behavior, suicidal gestures or brief psychotic episodes triggered by some identifiable external stress, usually abuse of alcohol or drugs.

The borderline's affective disturbance can be readily traced to primitive, maladaptive defense mechanisms, such as splitting, denial, projection, projective identification, primitive idealization, omnipotence, and devaluation, by means of which the borderline patient tries to defend himself or herself against a deeply ingrained sense of unworthiness, self-hatred, and persecutory fear. This extremely unhappy and vulnerable inner core of the self is presumably based on early traumatic relations with a mother object that has been experienced as malevolent and unreliable. As a consequence, the patient's current object relations tend to be intense but shallow and unstable. Even though eager for companionship and love, the borderline patient's poor sense of identity makes him or her feel chronically rejected, lonesome, and alienated. Ego-weakening and maladaptive as the affects and defense mechanisms are, however, they do not interfere with reality testing, at least as long as he or she is provided with external structure and does not find the self in a stressful, emotionally demanding situation. External structure is, indeed, of crucial importance in safeguarding the adequacy of performance and emotional stability of the borderline person, whose anxiety tolerance is short, and sublimatory channels limited or absent.

The borderline syndrome, or borderline pathology in general, has always been identified with character disturbance. In fact, that is how it appears in the new DSM-III classification—as a character (personality) disorder. Conceptually, however, character disturbance is independent of borderline pathology. Not all character disorders are borderline in nature, and some are more seriously borderline than others, involving a more severe pathology and a more problematic prognosis. Character disorders typically borderline are infantile, antisocial, and prepsychotic — the latter being subdivided into paranoid, schizoid, and hypomanic. Two new personality disorders in DSM-III — introverted and schizotypal — are variants of the schizoid character. Even though narcissism is an important feature in borderline pathology, not all narcissistic personality disorders are borderline. To the extent that character disturbance is ego-syntonic and neurotic symptomatology (implying inhibition) missing, borderline pathology tends to be more severe.

ALCOHOLISM AND BORDERLINE PATHOLOGY

Even before the borderline syndrome was recognized as such, a number of clinicians described alcoholism and its psychodynamics in terms strikingly similar to those used in identifying borderline pathology. Early psychoanalysts suggested that alcoholics are struggling against latent homosexual wishes and paranoia. Others described oral narcissistic and depressive personality traits. Glover [5] pointed out that, besides gratifying oral needs, drinking releases aggression; he suggested that such disorders as alcoholism and drug addiction represent transitional states, on the borderland between the neuroses and the psychoses. He specifically described a localized or transient disturbance in reality testing, object relations invested with pre-Oedipal aggression, frustration, and disappointment, and an archaic, severe, and inconsistent superego — all major features of the borderline syndrome. Simmel, [13] who treated alcoholics with psychoanalysis and hospitalization, saw in their condition a latent psychosis ("narcissistic neurosis") controlled by means of obsessional mechanisms. Simmel's ideas were adopted by The Menninger Clinic, where Knight [8, 9] provided alcoholics with the structure of a hospital setting and treated them analytically. Knight identified two types of alcoholism: a malignant one, polysymptomatic, with an early onset, serious behavioral problems, and poor response to treatment, which he called "essential," and a second type, prognostically more benign, that seemed to develop as a reaction to some recognizable external or internal stress, after a more or less successful social and family adjustment; for that reason he called it "reactive."

Knight [8] declared, "Alcohol addiction, along with other drug addiction, constitutes a borderline condition psychiatrically" [8 p. 235]. In agreement with Knight, Karl Menninger (as quoted in Knight) said, "I regard it as near a psychosis. . . . I think that addiction to alcohol is more serious than any neurosis and should be thought of along with psychosis" [9, p. 1447]. Knight's contribution to the theory and treatment of alcoholism has had considerable influence. But Knight [10] abandoned the field of alcoholism, turning instead his attention to borderline disorders, what he called "borderline states" or "borderline schizophrenia." In view of the fact that he described borderline patients and their treatment in terms similar, if not identical, to those he used for alcoholics indicates that he found the two conditions equivalent.

Assuming that the essential and reactive types constituted the majority of alcoholics, W. C. Menninger [12] identified two more groups of patients who habitually abuse drinking: neurotic characters, or borderline neurotics, and psychotic personalities, or borderline psychotics.

On the basis of genetic research, Winokur et al. [15] have more recently described two types of alcoholism: (1) sociopathic alcoholism, characterized by parental dysharmony, early onset, drug experimentation or drug addiction, reckless behavior, and social problems, including school and job failures (characteristics similar to those Knight attributes to essential alcoholism); and (2) primary alcoholism, which is later in development, with a longer history of alcohol abuse but better social and personal adjustment (this second type sounding very much like what Knight described as reactive alcoholism). Winokur and his group described a third type, depression-alcoholism, characterized by a serious suicidal potential, which they ascribed primarily to women.

Using as a model Kernberg's multifactorial method of diagnosing borderline patients, Wurmser [16] concluded that all drug addicts, with the probable exception of some alcoholics, share a borderline personality organization. Alcoholics are characterized by a severe disturbance in object relationships; identity diffusion; a pathological condensation of genital and pregenital drives with a predominence of oral aggression; a primitive, poorly integrated and largely insufficient superego; and a developmentally mixed picture of ego defenses, predominantly denial, splitting, projection, and omnipotence. Such structural characteristics, defining Kernberg's lower level of character pathology, are pathognomonic of borderline patients.

BORDERLINE PATHOLOGY AND PATHOLOGICAL NARCISSISM

Some alcoholics become publicly identified as sick relatively late in life, following what appears to be a successful personal and social adjustment. Such persons might still pass for normal except for their excessive drinking and its disorganizing effects. Indeed, some alcoholics may manage to function in an apparently normal way indefinitely. Narcissistic character traits, obsessive defenses, and a massive use of denial provide them with a protective shield of self-deception, isolating them from close personal contacts with people whom they depend on but can neither trust nor respect. They feel empty and angry inside, very much like patients with an "as if" personality; but, as far as anyone else is concerned, they are pleasant and function adequately. Gradually, however, as the cumulative impact of internal and external frustrations undermines the effectiveness of their defenses, their functioning begins to falter. In a desperate effort to maintain their precarious emotional equilibrium, they resort to increasing amounts of alcohol, which soothes their feelings and reinforces their denial but not their performance, which continues to deteriorate, exposing further their borderline pathology. Most patients of this kind may be classified as narcissistic.

As already pointed out, the two conditions cannot be distinguished very clearly. Compared to people whose borderline pathology manifests itself in terms of other personality disorders, narcissistic individuals are, as a rule, able to function better at work and to deal more effectively, even though unfeelingly, exploitively, or even ruthlessly, with others. They are often beautiful or talented, and know how to take advantage of their assets, but in a self-centered, often destructive, rather than creative or helpful, way. They find it difficult to regulate affects and self-esteem, vacillating between states of obsessional self-aborption and expansive, grandiose sociability, feeling worthless and special, envious of other people's success and contemptuous of others' worth or accomplishments — their sense of well-being, indeed, sense of identity, depending greatly on uncritical admiration and public acclaim. Sharing similar feelings and defenses, they differ from other borderline individuals in that their grandiose self compensates for an ever-present sense of oral (in origin) deprivation, making for a more coherent self and better all-around functioning. Kohut [11] has emphasized the reality of the narcissistic patient's emotional deprivation, tracing it to the patient's early childhood, specifically to the dysempathic nature of the mother and her tendency to treat the child as a narcissistic object.

AFFECT TOLERANCE AND STRUCTURAL DEFICIT

The ability of alcohol to relieve painful feelings has led to the hypothesis that problem drinking is an attempt at self-healing. According to this view, the compulsory nature of alcoholic drinking is a reflection of the intensity of the drinker's affects. Addiction to alcohol is presumably a defense against affects that, having lost the capacity to serve as signals of inner distress, revert to a primitive, massive, psychosomatic state normally experienced in a traumatic situation, specifically in early childhood before the establishment of a cohesive ego structure. Alcohol is not a symbolic representation of a missing love object, as Knight and other early analysts assumed, but a substitute for psychological structure. Indeed, there is evidence that the use of alcohol is an unsuccessful attempt at self-cure [2]. Alcoholics recall that long before they began abusing alcohol, they tended to lack self-confidence, to find it difficult to express anger, and to experience greater than average tension and sensitivity. Drinking tended to correct for these inadequacies.

In general, alcohol serves adoptive functions, its psychopharmacologic effect interacting dynamically with the personality organization of the addicted individual in the current environment. Wurmser's [16] formulation regarding the addictive process as such may be used to summarize the dynamics of alcoholism as well. There is a core pathogenic conflict, involving self-esteem, self-valuation, and meaning—a narcissistic conflict rendered into an acute crisis by developmental variables and personal, family, and social circumstances. Such a narcissistic crisis triggers affect regression, a totalization and radicalization of feelings, typically anger, shame, guilt, boredom, loneliness, and depression. The intensity of these feelings triggers, in turn, a defense operation dominated by primitive, aggressive mechanisms, such as denial, splitting, and externalization, which are predicated on action, excitement, risk, and euphoria, and lead to the final common pathway of drug abuse and dependence—one of the most available drugs to abuse and depend on being alcohol.

REFERENCES

1. American Psychiatric Association. *Diagnostic and Statistical Manual of Mental Disorders* (3rd ed.). Author: Washington, D.C., 1980.
2. Blume, S. B., and Sheppard, C. The changing effects of drinking on the changing personalities of alcoholics. *Q. J. Stud. Alcohol* 28:436–443, 1967.
3. Deutsch, H. Some forms of emotional disturbance and their relationship to schizophrenia. *Psychoanal. Q.* 11:301–321, 1942.
4. Fairbairn, W. R. D. Schizoid factors in the personality. In: *An Object-Relations Theory of the Personality*, Fairbairn, W. R. D. (ed.). Basic Books: New York, 1954. (Originally published 1940)
5. Glover, E. On the etiology of drug addiction. *Int. J. Psychoanal.* 13:298–328, 1932.
6. Grinker, R., Sr., Werble, B., and Drye, R. *The Borderline Syndrome.* Basic Books: New York, 1968.
7. Kernberg, O. *Borderline Conditions and Pathological Narcissism.* Jason Aronson: New York, 1975.
8. Knight, R. P. The dynamics and treatment of chronic alcoholism. *Bull. Menninger Clin.* 1:233–250, 1937.
9. Knight, R. P. The psychoanalytic treatment in sanatorium of chronic addiction to alcohol. *J.A.M.A.* 111:1443–1448, 1938.
10. Knight, R. P. Borderline states. *Bull. Menninger Clin.* 17:1–12, 1953.
11. Kohut, H. *The Analysis of the Self.* International Universities Press: New York, 1971.
12. Menninger, W. C. The treatment of chronic alcohol addiction. *Bull. Menninger Clin.* 1:101–112, 1937.
13. Simmel, E. Psychoanalytic treatment in a sanatorium. *Int. J. Psychoanal.* 10:70–89, 1929.
14. Stern, A. Psychoanalytic investigation of a therapy in the borderline group of neu-

roses. *Psychoanal. Q.* 7:467–489, 1938.

15. Winokur, G., Rimmer, J., and Reich, T. Alcoholism: IV. Is there more than one type of alcoholism? *Br. J. Psychiatry* 118:525–531, 1971.

16. Wurmser, L. *The Hidden Dimension: Psychodynamics in Compulsive Drug Use.* Jason Aronson: New York, 1978.

49

EDWARD GOTTHEIL, MD, PhD, Thomas Jefferson University, Philadelphia, Pennsylvania

HOWARD M. WAXMAN, PhD, Thomas Jefferson University, Philadelphia, Pennsylvania

ALCOHOLISM AND SCHIZOPHRENIA

AS NOTED THROUGHOUT this section, alcoholism can often be seen in combination with other psychiatric disorders. Generally, depression and sociopathy have been the disorders most frequently associated with alcoholism, and the numerous clinical and research reports on those combined problems attest to the importance of understanding the contributions of each disorder in order to properly diagnose and treat the other [17, 30, 43, 44]. Less attention, however, has been paid to the combined problems of alcoholism and schizophrenia. Not only have the combined diagnoses of alcoholism and schizophrenia been assigned sparingly to individuals entering general service hospitals, emergency rooms, psychiatric hospitals, and alcohol treatment programs [22], but there has been little written about the subject as well. Thus, an examination of some 28 general alcoholism texts on the shelves of a university library failed to reveal a single chapter where the terms "alcoholism" and "schizophrenia" shared a common heading. Freed [18], in the only truly comprehensive review of the area that has been done, did cite 186 references. However, most of the cited papers were primarily focused either on alcoholism or on schizophrenia,

---

Edward Gottheil, MD, PhD, Professor, Department of Psychiatry and Human Behavior, Thomas Jefferson University, Philadelphia, Pennsylvania.

Howard M. Waxman, PhD, Assistant Professor, Department of Psychiatry and Human Behavior, Thomas Jefferson University, Philadelphia, Pennsylvania.

mentioning the other disorder only incidentally. There were but 22 articles in which direct attempts were made to contrast or relate alcoholism and schizophrenia and, interestingly, only 11 were conducted in the United States.

In view of the many difficult problems in treating alcoholic patients with schizophrenia symptoms, or schizophrenic patients who drink [21], there appears to be little justification for this omission. In this chapter, therefore, several important questions are discussed concerning these disorders as they may exist in combination. First, what is known about the prevalence of the combined problems of alcohol abuse and schizophrenia among various populations? What are the similarities between these two disorders, and what are their differences? Are alcoholism and schizophrenia etiologically related, or are they independent? How should one diagnose alcoholic schizophrenic or schizophrenic alcoholics? Are these individuals being properly cared for through existing treatment approaches or should new treatments or new combinations of treatments be recommended? Finally, what additional knowledge will be required from future research in order to better understand and successfully treat individuals with these combined problems?

PREVALENCE

Barry [10] summarized the evidence concerning the association of alcoholism with schizophrenia and concluded that it was evident that an appreciable number of patients suffer from both disorders concurrently. Freed [18], on the basis of his review, suggested that "not an insignificant proportion of schizophrenics are intemperate and that many alcoholics suffer an underlying schizophrenia." Nevertheless, there is considerable variability in reports of the extent to which these disorders are found to be associated.

Gillis and Keet [19], in a study of 797 alcoholic inpatients, determined that only 1% were schizophrenic at follow-up. Rimmer et al. [42] provided an estimate of 2%. Sherfey [46] found an 8% prevalence of paranoid schizophrenia among 161 hospitalized alcoholics, while Bleuler [13] wrote that approximately 10% of the alcoholics he observed were also schizophrenics. Higher estimates were reported by Panepinto et al. [37], who indicated that 18% of 340 alcoholic patients assigned to supportive drug therapy fit the diagnostic criteria for schizophrenia; by Tomsovic [47], who found that 19% of 411 hospitalized alcoholic patients were schizophrenic; and by Tomsovic and Edwards [48], who concluded that among 258 hospitalized alcoholics, 49% had schizophrenia.

Estimates of the number of schizophrenic patients who evidence drinking problems are also variable. Parker et al. [38] found 22% of 150 hospitalized schizophrenics to be alcohol abusers, while Johanson [26] reported that 35% of 100 male schizophrenics were problem drinkers. Among 30 hospitalized Irish schizophrenics, Opler [34] found 63% to be alcohol abusers, while the same-sized sample of

Italian schizophrenics yielded an alcohol problem prevalence rate of but 3%. In a more recent study, Rimmer and Jacobsen [41] found that only 3% of 33 schizophrenic adoptees in Denmark showed a history of alcoholism, which was not significantly different from that found among the same number of matched nonschizophrenic adoptee controls.

On the average, about 10 to 15% of diagnosed inpatient and outpatient alcoholics have been described as also having schizophrenia, and about 10 to 15% of hospitalized schizophrenics have been described as also having serious drinking problems. Both of these proportions may represent underestimates [22, 32]. It would seem that, although the prevalence estimates are variable, most probably due to differences in criteria, timing of diagnosis, and patient populations, the number of individuals with the combined problem appears sizable enough in most studies to justify an exploration of possible common etiological factors.

ETIOLOGIC CONSIDERATIONS

Alcoholism and schizophrenia do have some characteristics that bear at least superficial resemblance. Both often evidence their onset in adolescence or early adulthood and are marked by a chronic and/or relapsing course, deterioration in social and occupational functioning, and shortened life span [3]. Similarity between two disorders may reflect a common etiology. There are more alcoholics who are schizophrenics than is found in the general population and the same is true of schizophrenics with drinking problems. This may possibly be the result of a common genetic predisposition, similar environmental precipitators, self-medication of anxious schizophrenics with alcohol, or one disorder may even cause the other.

Family studies have failed to convincingly demonstrate a genetic link between the two disorders [18]. Thus, while there is a suggestion that families of patients with alcoholic hallucinosis may be at increased risk for schizophrenia [33], other studies on families of chronic alcoholics have turned up negative results [6, 13, 46, 51]. Rimmer and Jacobsen [41] recently examined the biological families of Danish schizophrenic adoptees and found a low prevalence of alcohol problem histories, which did not significantly differ from that found among families of controls. Their study is notable in that adoptees were used, largely eliminating postnatal experience as a confounding factor, and comparisons were made with a matched group of nonschizophrenic adoptees. The unusually low prevalence (3%) of alcohol problems in the schizophrenic index group, however, suggests that this important study should be repeated with other populations.

The similarities between alcoholic hallucinosis and the hallucinations commonly experienced by many schizophrenics have prompted some to suggest that alcoholic hallucinosis may have an underlying schizophrenic basis [12, 25]. There is disagreement on this issue, however, and Gross [23, 24] believes that while resembling schizophrenic hallucinations, alcoholic hallucinosis does not necessarily depend upon an underlying psychotic disorder. Wolfensberger [52] reported that 10 (63%) of 16 patients hospitalized with alcoholic hallucinosis developed schizophrenia, whereas Vorontsova [49] found only one case of schizophrenia among 60 alcoholics with atypical hallucinatory-delerious psychoses. Benedetti [11] reported that there were no instances of schizophrenia occurring in 113 patients following acute episodes of alcoholic hallucinosis, but that 13 (57%) of 23 patients with chronic alcoholic hallucinosis developed typical schizophrenia patterns. According to the latest *Diagnostic and Statistical Manual of Mental Disorders* (DSM-III), [3], alcoholic hallucinosis is to be distinguished from schizophrenia on the basis of a temporal relationship of the hallucinations to drinking, later age of onset, and lack of a chronic course. Most frequently the disorder lasts less than a week; however, in about 10% of cases it may last weeks or months and be clinically indistinguishable from schizophrenia, with the development of vague and illogical thinking, tangential associations, and inappropriate affect. The chronic form is more likely to develop after repeated episodes of the disorder; however, it is stated that "contrary to previously held belief, there is no evidence that schizophrenia predisposes to the development of this disorder" [3]. It must be noted, nevertheless, that some cases develop into a chronic form that is clinically indistinguishable from and has often been diagnosed as schizophrenia.

Alcohol does suppress anxiety in some individuals in some circumstances and thus may be helpful for some schizophrenics who are experiencing social discomfort or frightening thoughts, or even hallucinations and delusions [18]. A small number of alcoholics, treated in a fixed interval drinking decisions program [20] where alcohol is available, look better and do better when drinking and show almost no signs of intoxication from consuming 26 oz of 80 proof alcohol daily. These patients generally had Minnesota Multiphasic Personality Inventory (MMPI) profiles that could be interpreted as schizophrenic and were quiet and withdrawn on or off alcohol, but appeared more apathetic and more withdrawn when not drinking. A number of clinical reports indicate that the consumption of alcohol may suppress overt psychotic manifestations and thus even serve to mask schizophrenia [4, 31, 46]. However, at the present time, there is actually little empirical evidence concerning this hypothesis, and Rimmer and Jacobsens' [41] failure to find an increased risk for alcohol problems among a group at high risk for schizophrenia is problematic. If the hypothesis that alcoholism serves to mask schizophrenia were true, however, one might expect there would be a greater number of alcoholics with underlying schizophrenia than has previously been indicated. It would also suggest that the detection of schizophrenia would be complicated in patients entering alcohol treatment facilities intoxicated and stress the need for the collection of a complete psychiatric history as well as psychiatric assessment of the patient after any withdrawal symptoms have subsided and the patient is in an alcohol-free state.

DIAGNOSIS

Many of the difficulties in establishing prevalence rates, etiological factors, and treatment results for individuals with a combination of alcoholism and schizophrenia are due in large measure to the lack of clarity of diagnostic formulations. That this should be so is hardly surprising when one considers the many and changing criteria for each of these disorders separately. Classification is further complicated by the variety of possible relationships that have been presumed to exist between the disorders. Thus, alcoholism has been said to mask schizophrenia or be a symptom of it, to precipitate it or be precipitated by it, to be an expression of a common predisposition or to co-exist as a distinct and separate disorder. Moreover, it would be remiss to neglect to indicate the possible influence of administrative and fiscal constraints in determining which of two coexisting disorders is the primary one when funding levels and bed allocations are tied to the number of patients in a specified category.

Medical and psychiatric facilities have most often been criticized for failing to recognize alcoholism among incoming patients, but individuals in many alcoholism facilities also fail to recognize, report, and refer psychiatric disorders. Gottheil and Weinstein [22], for example, found that among a number of large alcoholism facilities, some assigned secondary psychiatric disorders much more frequently than did others. The variability was not related to the particular treatment modality employed or to the age, sex, or minority status of the patient population, but was related to the proportion of professional staff. In those facilities with a greater proportion of professionals, more psychiatric diagnoses were made. It was suggested that these differences in staffing patterns and diagnostic procedures are likely to result from differences in program or institutional philosophy.

Certainly the question of whether a particular patient should be classified as an alcoholic schizophrenic, a schizophrenic alcoholic, or as having schizophrenia and alcoholism, will not be addressed unless the symptoms of both disorders are recognized and reported. The diagnostic issue is also unlikely to be addressed by those who espouse a problems in living rather than a disease model of alcoholism. Indeed, some even consider a psychiatric diagnosis as nonproductive, tending to overemphasize classification to the detriment of treatment [16]. Carroll [14], for example, writes, "In point of fact, the very process of deriving a psychiatric diagnosis/label, especially the more serious variety (e.g., schizophrenia), often induces a sense of insidious despair for both the treater and the patient." While this unfortunately may be a problem for some individuals, programs, or institutions, it is not an inherent or necessary problem. Diagnosis and treatment are, and should be, interdependent, not incompatible. A reasonable treatment plan incorporates the findings of a careful diagnostic evaluation. A reasonable classification system incorporates findings relevant to therapeutic responsiveness.

Alcoholism has not always been regarded as a medical disorder but in recent decades the disease concept has gained increasing prominence and acceptance

[9, 27]. As such, Seixas [45] notes that it can coexist with a variety of other psychiatric disorders and has argued cogently for the need to make separate diagnoses. The diagnostic and statistical manuals of the American Psychiatric Association have reflected this trend. In 1952 [1], alcoholism was listed as a subtype of addiction, which was considered a subtype of sociopathic personality disturbance under the general rubric of "Personality Disorders." Multiple diagnoses were not encouraged. By 1968, alcoholism was listed as a subtype of personality disorders and certain other nonpsychotic mental disorders [2]. It was stated that individuals may have more than one mental disorder and encouragement was given to "the recording of the diagnosis of alcoholism separately even when it begins as a symptomatic expression of another disorder." DSM-III [3] now lists "Alcohol Abuse" and "Alcohol Dependence" as major subtypes of the substance abuse disorders and strongly encourages multiple diagnoses.

DSM-III takes an atheoretical and descriptive approach to classification in order to enhance the reliability of clinical diagnoses and research data. Nowhere is such an approach needed more than to gain information about the coexistence of alcoholism and schizophrenia. If any progress is ever to be made in this area, it will require that every patient, regardless of the type of treatment facility, receive a careful and thorough diagnostic evaluation, and a separate diagnosis be recorded according to standard and accepted criteria for each disorder that is present. Issues concerning the proper diagnosis and defining criteria of alcoholism are treated in Section I of this volume. The emphasis herein is that the diagnosis be made, regardless of the type of facility, whether it is felt to be primary or secondary, and irrespective of the coexistence of another disorder.

TREATMENT CONSIDERATIONS

While there are some similarities in the methods used for treating alcoholism and schizophrenia, there are also important differences. Insight-oriented therapy, for example, has not proven especially successful and is seldom employed as the sole or primary treatment for either disorder. Group therapy, supportive counseling, and family therapy, on the other hand, have generally been found to be helpful and are commonly employed in treating these disorders. The approach to the schizophrenic patient, however, is typically supportive, intense emotional expressions and interpersonal interactions are not usually encouraged, and drugs, especially the neuroleptics, are often employed. In contrast, with alcoholic patients there is a tendency to avoid medication and to promote confrontation, emotional expression, and interpersonal sharing (see Section X for a discussion of the clinical aspects of treatment of alcoholism).

Liss [29] has pointed out that alcoholics may respond and schizophrenics withdraw in a treatment milieu that stresses collective responsibility. Panepinto et al.

[37], in an interesting study, reported that schizophrenic alcoholic patients did well in continuing to come to a program for brief visits with an internist, but were not likely to become more actively involved with other staff members. The visits were only 10 minutes long, symptom-oriented, involved only minimal exploration of thoughts and feelings, and required little active participation. Alcoholics with personality disorders became more involved with other staff members, but were quick to drop out of treatment with the internist.

Schizophrenic alcoholics may not only respond differently than alcoholics or schizophrenics to particular treatment programs, but they may present additional problems as well. Disulfiram therapy, for example, has been noted to uncover preexisting schizophrenic conditions and to precipitate relapses in schizophrenic patients in remission [7, 8]. In a study of 1,063 patients on the psychiatric wards of a Veterans Administration medical center, Alterman et al. [5] found that 101 had received both a primary diagnosis of schizophrenia and a secondary diagnosis of alcoholism. Of these patients, 55% continued to drink while in the hospital, 45% to the point of intoxication. The treatment and management problems resulting from their drinking included smoking in bed, missing roll calls, maintaining negative peer relationships, evidencing assaultiveness, and refusing medication. If such patients are difficult to manage on inpatient psychiatric wards, they are no less difficult to manage in alcoholism rehabilitation centers. Ottenberg [35] notes that the erratic and bizarre behavior of psychotic addicted patients may on occasion disrupt the entire program of a treatment unit.

Dichter and Eusanio [15] suggest that many alcoholism and mental health programs are now finding their therapeutic regimes inadequate to provide the comprehensive services necessary to meet the needs of increasing numbers of patients with chronic patterns of addiction as well as severe emotional dysfunction. Alcoholism programs refer such patients to mental health programs to manage their craziness, while mental health programs refer them to alcoholism programs to deal with their drunkenness. They may be shuttled back and forth and in the process drop out and be lost to treatment or they may continue receiving treatment in both programs, with conflicting methods and confusing effects.

It seems reasonable and prudent to suggest that these patients would be better treated in a single program and by one therapist rather than two [40]. The primary therapist should be capable of taking a thorough history, performing a careful diagnostic assessment, and feel competent and comfortable in treating either or both disorders. This could be accomplished by having primary therapists who are well versed in all aspects of alcoholism and other mental disorders, or by having a variety of consultants working with them in one of several service delivery models.

Zosa [53], working in an inpatient county mental health–mental retardation setting where patients with psychiatric, alcohol, and drug problems are all treated within an integrated unit, emphasizes the need for careful patient evaluation. Important factors requiring assessment include the degree of psychopathology, level of functioning in various areas, need for supervision, and ability to live independently; whether the patient requires potent psychotropic medications; whether medication effects interfere with daily functioning; the relationship between psychiatric symptoms and drug-taking behavior; and the patient's ability to deal with stress and social pressures, particularly in a therapeutic community setting. The clinical staff of the unit are all cross-trained in mental health and the addictions and, presumably as a result of the cross-training, appear to have little difficulty in treating their mixture of patients. According to Ottenberg et al. [36], approximately 20% of the addicted patients now admitted to the Eagleville Hospital and Rehabilitation Center have emotional disturbances serious enough to require psychiatric attention. Psychiatric consultation and services are available at the hospital and are provided, but in nearly all instances the addiction counselor remains as the patient's primary therapist. The relationship between the psychiatric and counseling staff in team discussions to reach shared decisions concerning appropriate treatment plans is considered critical. Weinstein and Gottheil [50] described what they term a coordinated, rather than a combined or integrated, outpatient program in which alcohol counselors are assigned to and work in mental health units. Patients with combined disorders are accepted and the counselors receive consultation from and are responsible to the administration of the local mental health unit and the central alcohol service.

The models above, developed to provide the necessary expertise and comprehensive services required for treating patients with combined addictive and other psychiatric disorders, are considered to be workable and helpful. However, no comparative outcome data have been provided. Moreover, there is little information of any kind about the treatment outcome of patients with both alcoholism and schizophrenia. Indeed, most systematic outcome studies of alcoholism treatment have specifically excluded patients with a history or an associated diagnosis of schizophrenia, and studies of the treatment outcome of schizophrenia have excluded patients with alcoholism.

The growing recognition of the existence of these combined disorders and of the difficulties in meeting their treatment needs is hopeful and should lead to an increase in interest and research in the area. At the present time, accumulated clinical experience [21, 28, 36, 39] suggests that patients with alcoholism and schizophrenia should be treated in facilities where comprehensive, multimodality services are available to avoid shuttling patients between facilities, where staff has been trained according to a generic model [50] to feel competent and comfortable in treating alcoholism, substance abuse, and other psychiatric disorders either separately or in combination, and where interdisciplinary consultation is readily available. The patient should have a primary therapist who can employ those treatment techniques that are commonly helpful across these conditions, is capable of assessing and evaluating the specific, special treatment needs of particular patients, and is prepared to request, discuss, and incorporate consultant recommendations in fashioning an appropriate treatment plan.

Clearly, the most pressing need is to be aware of the coexistence of these disorders, to make separate diagnoses according to standard criteria, and to record these diagnoses. Only then will one be able to arrive at more accurate prevalence data, obtain information about possible etiological factors and relationships, and conduct appropriate and systematic outcome studies.

REFERENCES

1. Alpert, M., and Silvers, K. N. Perceptual characteristics distinguishing auditory hallucinations in schizophrenia and acute alcoholic psychoses. *Am. J. Psychiatry* 127:198-302, 1970.
2. Alterman, A. I., Erdleis, F. R., and McLellan, A. T. Problem drinking in a psychiatric hospital: Alcoholic schizophrenics. In: *Substance Abuse and Psychiatric Illness*, Gottheil, E., McLellan, A. T., and Druley, K. A. (eds.). Pergamon: Elmsford, N.Y., 1980.
3. American Psychiatric Association. *Diagnostic and Statistical Manual* (1st ed.). Author: Washington, D.C., 1952.
4. American Psychiatric Association. *Diagnostic and Statistical Manual* (2nd ed.). Author: Washington, D.C., 1968.
5. American Psychiatric Association. *Diagnostic and Statistical Manual of Mental Disorders* (3rd ed.). Author: Washington, D.C., 1980.
6. Amark, C. A. A study in alcoholism: Clinical, social-psychiatric and genetic investigations. *Acta Psychiatry (Suppl.)* 70:1-28, 1951.
7. Andreyeva, V. A., Gavrilova, L. V., Levin, V. M., and Reshetnikova, Z. V. [The problem of acute psychotic conditions occurring during Antabuse treatment of patients with chronic alcoholism]. *Zh. Nevropatol. Psikhiatr.* 59:673-679, 1959.
8. Bann, T. A. Alcoholism and schizophrenia: Diagnostic and therapeutic considerations. *Alcohol. Clin. Exp. Res.* 1:113-117, 1977.
9. Barry, H., III. Psychological factors in alcoholism. In: *The Biology of Alcoholism: Clinical Pathology* (Vol. 3), Kissin, B., and Beglecter, H. (eds.). Plenum: New York, 1974.
10. Barry, H., III. Psychiatric illness of alcoholics. In: *Substance Abuse and Psychiatric Illness*, Gottheil, E., McClellan, A. T., and Druley, K. A. Elmsford, N.Y., 1980.
11. Benedetti, G. *Die Alkoholhalluzinosen*. Stuttgart: Thieme, 1952.
12. Bleuler, E. *Textbook of Psychiatry*. Dover: New York, 1951.
13. Bleuler, M. Familial and personal background of chronic alcoholics. In: *Etiology of Chronic Alcoholism*, Diethelm, D. (ed.). Charles C Thomas: Springfield, Ill., 1955.
14. Carroll, J. F. X. Mental illness and addiction: Perspectives which overemphasize differences and undervalue commonalities. In: *Treating Mixed Psychiatric—Drug Addicted and Alcohol Patients*. Eagleville Hospital and Rehabilitation Center: Eagleville, Pa., 1979.
15. Dichter, M., and Eusanio, A. Rationale for a generic-based training model for mixed substance abuse–psychiatric populations. In: *Treating Mixed Psychiatric–Drug Addicted and Alcohol Patients*, Ottenberg, D., Carroll, J. F. X., and Bolognese, C. (eds.). Eagleville Hospital and Rehabilitation Center: Eagleville, Pa., 1979.
16. Farnsworth, D. L. Medical perspectives on alcoholism and around-the-clock psychiatric services. *Am. J. Psychiatry* 124:1659-1663, 1968.
17. Fine, E. W. The syndrome of alcohol dependency and depression. In: *Substance*

Abuse and Psychiatric Illness, Gottheil, E., McClellan, A. T., and Druley, K. A. (eds.). Pergamon: Elmsford, N.Y., 1980.

18. Freed, E. X. Alcoholism and schizophrenia: The search for perspectives. *J. Stud. Alcohol* 36:853–881, 1975.

19. Gillis, L. S., and Keet, M. Prognostic factors and treatment results in hospitalized alcoholics. *Q. J. Stud. Alcohol* 30:426–437, 1969.

20. Gottheil, E., Corbett, L. O., Grasberger, J. C., and Cornelison, F. S., Jr. Treating the alcoholic in the presence of alcohol. *Am. J. Psychiatry* 128:475–480, 1971.

21. Gottheil, E., McLellan, A. T., and Druley, K. A. (eds.). *Substance Abuse and Psychiatric Illness.* Pergamon: Elmsford, N.Y., 1980.

22. Gottheil, E., and Weinstein, S. P. Staffing patterns, treatment setting, and percevied psychiatric problems in alcoholism services. In: *Substance Abuse and Psychiatric Illness,* Gottheil, E., McLellan, A. T. and Druley, K. A. (eds.). Pergamon: Elmsford, N.Y., 1980.

23. Gross, M. M. Management of acute alcohol withdrawal states. *Q. J. Stud. Alcohol* 28:655–666, 1967.

24. Gross, M. M., Halpert, E., and Sabot, L. Some comments on Bleuler's concept of acute alcoholic hallucinosis. *Q. J. Stud. Alcohol* 24:54–60, 1963.

25. Hudolin, V. Acute complications of alcoholism. In: *Alcohol and Alcoholism,* Popham, R. E. (ed.). University of Toronto Press: Toronto, 1970.

26. Johanson, E. A study of schizophrenia in the male: A psychiatric and social study based on 138 cases with follow-up. *Acta Psychiat. Neurol. Scand. (Suppl.)* 33(125):1958.

27. Keller, M. Should psychiatrists treat alcoholism? In *Substance Abuse and Psychiatric Illness,* Gottheil, E., McClellan, A. T., and Druley, K. A. (eds.). Pergamon: Elmsford, N.Y., 1980.

28. Kissin, B. Medical management of the alcoholic patient. In: *The Biology of Alcoholism: Treatment and Rehabilitation of the Chronic Alcoholic* (Vol. 5), Kissin, B. and Begleiter, H. (eds.). Plenum: New York, 1977.

29. Liss, R. A. The need for homogeneity and consistency. In: *Treating Mixed Psychiatric–Drug Addicted and Alcohol Patients,* Ottenberg, D. J., Carroll, J. F. X., and Bolognese, C. (eds.). Eagleville Hospital and Rehabilitation Center: Eagleville, Pa., 1979.

30. Mandell, W., and Scott, J. E. Sociopathic alcoholics: Matching treatment and patients. In: *Matching Patient Needs and Treatment Methods in Alcoholism and Drug Abuse,* Gottheil, E., McClellan, A. T., and Druley, K. A. (eds.). Charles C Thomas: Springfield, Ill., 1981.

31. Markham, J. Casework treatment of an alcoholic woman with severe underlying pathology. *Q. J. Stud. Alcohol* 18:475–491, 1957.

32. McLellan, A. T., Druley, K. A., and Carson, J. E. Evaluation of substance abuse problems in a psychiatric hospital. *J. Clin. Psychiatry* 39:425–430, 1978.

33. Nagao, S. [Clinic-genetic study of chronic alcoholism]. *Jinrui Idengaku Zasshi* 9:111–135, 1964.

34. Opler, M. K. Schizophrenia and culture. *Sci. Am.* 197 (2):103–110, 1957.

35. Ottenberg, D. J. Clinical and programmatic perspectives. In: *Substance Abuse and Psychiatric Illness,* Gottheil, E., McClellan, A. T., and Druley, K. A. (eds.). Pergamon: Elmsford, N.Y., 1980.

36. Ottenberg, D. J., Carroll, J. F. X., and Bolognese, C. *Treating Mixed Psychiatric–Drug Addicted and Alcohol Patients,* Ottenberg, D. J., Carroll, J. F. X., and Bolognese, C. (eds.). Eagleville Hospital and Rehabilitation Center: Eagleville, Pa., 1979.

37. Panepinto, W. C., Higgins, M. J., Keane-Dawes, W. Y., and Smith, D. Underlying psychiatric diagnoses as an indicator of participation in alcoholism therapy. *Q. J. Stud. Alcohol* 31:950–956, 1970.

38. Parker, J. B., Jr., Meiller, R. M., and Andrews, G. W. Major psychiatric disorders masquerading as alcoholism. *5th Med. J.* 53:560-564, 1960.

39. Pattison, E. M. The selection of treatment modalities for the alcoholic patient. In: *The Diagnosis and Treatment of Alcoholism*, Mendelson, J. and Mello, N. K. (eds.). McGraw-Hill: New York, 1977.

40. Pollak, O. One therapist or two? In: *Substance Abuse and Psychiatric Illness*, Gottheil, E., McClellan, A. T., and Druley, K. A. (eds.). Pergamon: Elmsford, N.Y., 1980.

41. Rimmer, J., and Jacobsen, B. Alcoholism and schizophrenics and their relatives. *J. Stud. Alcohol* 38:1781-1784, 1977.

42. Rimmer, J., Reich, T., and Winokur, G. Alcoholism, diagnosis and clinical variation among alcoholics. *Q. J. Stud. Alcohol* 33:658-666, 1972.

43. Schuckit, M. A. Alcoholism and sociopathy: Diagnostic confusion. *Q. J. Stud. Alcohol* 34:157-164, 1973.

44. Schuckit, M. A. Treatment of alcoholism in office and outpatient settings. In: *The Diagnosis and Treatment of Alcoholism*, Mendelsohn, J. and Mello, N. K. (eds.). McGraw-Hill: New York, 1979.

45. Seixas, F. A. A historical perspective on alcoholism. In: *Substance Abuse and Psychiatric Illness*. Gottheil, E., et al. (eds.). Pergamon: Elmsford, N. Y., 1980.

46. Sherfey, M. J. Psychopathology and character structure in chronic alcoholism. In: *Etiology of Chronic Alcoholism*, Diethelm, D. (ed.). Charles C Thomas: Springfield, Ill., 1955.

47. Tomsovic, M. Hospitalized alcoholic patients: I. A two-year study of medical, social, and psychological characteristics. *Hosp. Community Psychiatry* 19:197-203, 1968.

48. Tomsovic, M., and Edwards, R. V. Lysergide treatment of schizophrenic and nonschizophrenic alcoholics: A controlled evaluation. *Q. J. Stud. Alcohol* 31:932-949, 1970.

49. Vorontsova, G. S. [On atypical alcoholic psychoses]. *Zh. Nevropatol.* 59:657-667, 1959.

50. Weinstein, S. P., and Gottheil, E. A coordinated program for treating combined mental health and substance abuse problems. In: *Substance Abuse and Psychiatric Illness*, Gottheil, E., McLellan, A. T. and Druley, K. A. (eds.). Pergamon: Elmsford, N.Y., 1980.

51. Winokur, G., and Clayton, P. J. Family history studies: IV. Comparison of male and female alcoholics. *Q. J. Stud. Alcohol* 29:885-891, 1968.

52. Wolfensberger, M. Der alkoholwahnsinn (akute hallucinose der trinker) und seine beziehunger zu den schizophrenien (an Hand der kasuistik der Zurcher Psychiatrischen Klinik 1898-1921). *Z. ges. Neurol. Psychiat.* 82:385-418, 1923.

53. Zosa, A. "Psychiatric problems" can no longer be automatically used to screen patients out of drug and alcohol rehabilitation programs. In: *Treating Mixed Psychiatric-Drug Addicted and Alcohol Patients*, Ottenberg, D. J., Carroll, J. F. X., and Bolognese, C. (eds.). Eagleville Hospital and Rehabilitation Center: Eagleville, Pa., 1979.

50

RICHARD T. RADA, MD, College Hospital, Cerritos, California

ALCOHOLISM AND SOCIOPATHY: DIAGNOSTIC AND TREATMENT IMPLICATIONS

GROWING EVIDENCE indicates an association between alcoholism and sociopathy. Recognition of this association has important implications for diagnosis and treatment planning. The purpose of this chapter is to discuss the major ways in which sociopathy and alcoholism may be related. This presentation focuses on (1) the association between alcoholism and sociopathy; (2) the importance of clarifying the diagnostic confusion between the two; and (3) treatment implications when both conditions coexist in the same patient.

THE ASSOCIATION BETWEEN SOCIOPATHY AND ALCOHOLISM

A growing body of literature suggests an association between alcoholism and sociopathy based on genetic and familial patterning, criminal and antisocial acts, personality characteristics, and psychiatric diagnosis.

Richard T. Rada, MD, Medical Director, College Hospital, Cerritos, California, and Clinical Professor of Psychiatry, Department of Psychiatry, University of New Mexico School of Medicine, Albuquerque, New Mexico.

Genetic and Familial Patterning

The clustering of alcoholism in families is generally recognized; recent studies indicate that sociopathy and criminality tend to run in families. In addition, some studies suggest a hereditary component in alcoholism [7] and in sociopathy [3]. Whether the increased frequency of alcoholism and criminality in some families is due to a hereditary link between the two conditions remains to be determined.

Robins et al. [14] reported a 30-year follow-up study on 502 children who had been seen in a child guidance clinic and compared this group to untreated, matched controls. A significantly larger percentage of the ex-child guidance clinic patients eventually developed alcoholism. Factors in the childhood history of the clinic patients significantly related to alcoholism in later life included low familial social status, parental inadequacy (particularly antisocial behavior on the part of the father), and serious antisocial behavior in the patients themselves. A greater frequency of criminal behavior and sociopathy among first-degree relatives of alcoholics or male felons has also been reported in other studies [2, 8].

Recent studies suggest that alcoholism and sociopathy may be associated with a third condition, the hyperactive child syndrome. Some hyperactive children become sociopaths or alcoholics when adults, and it has been suggested that minimal brain dysfunction in childhood may persist into adulthood concealed by a number of different diagnostic labels. These preliminary studies must be viewed with caution, however, if for no other reason than that the diagnosis of hyperactive child syndrome may not be based on precise diagnostic criteria but rather may represent a label used for difficult-to-handle children. In sum, family pedigree studies indicate an association between sociopathy and alcoholism, but to what extent these conditions are genetically linked remains to be determined.

Criminal and Antisocial Acts

Studies of crime and offender populations suggest another possible link between alcoholism and sociopathy. Certain crimes (e.g., rape and murder) are frequently associated with alcoholism and with heavy drinking at the time of the commission of the offense [12]. Likewise, those committing the crimes are often diagnosed as sociopathic. Therefore it is tempting to link alcoholism and sociopathy based on their association with criminal behavior and violent antisocial acts. But the nature of these associations is confounded by many important methodologic considerations. Pernanen [10] has recently presented an excellent critical analysis of the relationship between drinking, alcoholism, and crimes of violence. Methodologic problems include sampling bias, use of different diagnostic criteria, and the frequently overlooked distinction between drinking at the time of the commission of the offense and history of alcoholism in the offender. Furthermore, although many criminals are sociopaths, not all of the crimes associated with heavy drinking and alcoholism are committed primarily by sociopaths. Although this appears to be a fruitful area for further research, a link between alcoholism and sociopathy based on their association with criminal behavior and acts of violence has not been clearly established.

Personality Characteristics and Psychiatric Diagnoses

Over the years a considerable body of literature has attempted to show an association between alcoholism and sociopathy of the basis of psychological tests purporting to measure personality profiles. Although statistically significant differences between alcoholics and others are frequently reported using traditional psychometric instruments, it appears there is no firm evidence to suggest that there is a typical alcoholic profile. As Keller [9] has stated, "The investigation of any trait in alcoholics will show that they have either more or less of it." However, many studies have shown an association between scale 4, the psychopathic deviate (Pd) scale of the Minnesota Multiphasic Personality Inventory (MMPI), and a history of alcoholism in the subject. It is true that an elevated Pd scale has been the most consistent psychological test finding differentiating alcoholics from normal and other clinic groups. Nevertheless, this may be an artifact of the MMPI and the association may be due to confounding or overlapping variables rather than to a specific psychopathic personality characteristic of alcoholics.

Robins et al. [13] have recently reported on the characteristics of 314 psychiatric emergency room patients. This study has practical importance for the diagnostician. The three most common conditions diagnosed were affective disorders, alcoholism, and antisocial personality. Among the antisocial personality patients, only 11% received a single diagnosis of antisocial personality, whereas 61% were found to have an additional diagnosis of alcoholism.

THE DIAGNOSTIC CONFUSION BETWEEN SOCIOPATHY AND ALCOHOLISM

Schuckit [15] has indicated the importance of adequately distinguishing between the diagnostic categories of alcoholism and sociopathy in order to avoid diagnostic confusion. Primary alcoholism is characterized by alcohol abuse with no prior history of major psychiatric problems. Secondary alcoholism is found as a complication of some other psychiatric illness (e.g., depression or sociopathy). Furthermore, the proper diagnosis of sociopathy requires the use of specific diagnostic criteria, with major emphasis on the early history of characteristic behavioral symptoms and not simply on subjective findings such as lack of conscience, irresponsibility, or impulsivity. The Feighner criteria [4] offer an effective tool for establishing primary and secondary diagnostic categories.

With the use of primary and secondary diagnostic categories, it is possible to classify drinking sociopaths and sociopathic alcoholics into certain subgroups.

Rada [11] has proposed one such classification system that separates sociopaths and alcoholics into four different types: the drinking sociopath, the alcoholic sociopath, the sociopathic alcoholic, and the primary alcoholic. The differences in the most common characteristics of the patients within each of these groups may be important in treatment planning.

In this regard, most studies dealing with alcoholics and sociopaths focus on male populations. Although it is now well recognized that alcoholism is a serious problem among women, it is not always fully appreciated that women too may have a primary diagnosis of sociopathic personality. Schuckit and Morrissey [16] have recently reported on 293 consecutive female admissions to a public detoxification facility. Of these women patients 14% had a primary diagnosis of antisocial personality.

TREATMENT OF THE ALCOHOLIC SOCIOPATH

At the present time there are not any controlled studies reporting the treatment of the alcoholic sociopath. This may be in large measure a definitional problem, since only recently has the separation of these conditions into primary and secondary diagnoses been emphasized. Furthermore, it is generally agreed that treatment of the sociopathic personality is difficult even when the condition is not complicated by alcohol abuse or alcoholism. This pessimistic belief is supported by reports that a combination of sociopathy and alcoholism indicates a poor prognosis or, conversely, that a low psychopathic deviate scale on the MMPI among alcoholic patients is one indicator of a greater likelihood of successful outcome of treatment.

A number of recent reports suggest that sociopathy in conjunction with alcoholism does not necessarily prevent a successful outcome [1, 5, 6]. For example, Goodwin et al. [6] have recently reported on an 8-year follow-up of felons who drink. Differences in the life histories and personality and familial factors between alcoholic and nonalcoholic felons, and between remitted and unremitted alcoholics, were reported. A majority of the convicted felons were diagnosed in prison as alcoholics, and 60% of felons interviewed at follow-up reported drinking problems. Nearly 75% of the alcoholics were also sociopaths. Criminal recidivism rates were significantly higher in the alcoholism group. However, at follow-up 38 of 93 unequivocal alcoholics reported no drinking problem, all but two without psychiatric treatment. The authors make an important point, also noted by others, that the natural history of both alcoholism and socipathy indicates some burning out of these disease processes with age. Furthermore, recent studied indicate that sociopathy per se did not seem to affect treatment outcome in a group of alcoholics, and conversely, that alcohol abuse was not associated with poor outcome of treatment in patients with deviant social conduct [1, 5, 17].

Since controlled studies are lacking, treatment suggestions and strategies must be based on the current state of the art in treatment of sociopaths or alcoholics, and those occasional studies that report treatment of patient populations where the two conditions are more likely to coexist (e.g., criminal offenders).

Verbal Therapy

In recent years the earlier emphasis on the importance of treatment of superego or conscience problems in the sociopath has been replaced by greater emphasis on ego dysfunctional aspects of psychopathic personalities. Most programs treating sociopaths emphasize that treatment must be long-term and must focus on a fundamental reorganization of the sociopath's values, thinking, and action patterns. A prerequisite to accomplishing these goals is the development of trust, which in these patients often takes a considerable period of time.

Therapists often emphasize the importance of helping sociopaths and alcoholics develop a sense of personal responsibility for their conduct. This may account for the increased recent interest in group therapy, since the no-nonsense peer confrontation technique frequently employed in these groups tends to undercut rationalization or denial by group members. Therapy dropouts and noncompliance with the treatment plan are constant problems. Although enforced therapy may appear contrary to many therapists' values and orientation, court-ordered therapy has been successful with some alcoholic offenders. Except in a controlled situation such as a penal institution, it is often difficult to establish the continuing type of relationship with the alcoholic sociopath that is necessary for effective treatment using standard verbal therapies. The need for more rapid therapeutic techniques may account in part for increased recent interest in behavior modification approaches.

Behavior Modification Therapy

Alcoholism may have been the first behavior disorder for which therapy derived exclusively from the principles of conditioning was used on a wide scale. Aversive conditioning based on Pavlovian principles has long been used with alcoholics. However, a confounding variable in aversive conditioning with psychopaths relates to recent findings from experiments measuring autonomic correlates of psychopaths. A consistent finding, as measured by galvanic skin response, is that psychopaths anticipating an aversive stimulus show a relatively small increase in electrodermal activity as compared to nonantisocial subjects. Implications of these data are that the psychopaths' apparent decreased fear of punishment and their inability to learn from previous experience may be, in part, physiologically induced. Therefore, it is not clear whether behavior modification techniques based on Pavlovian conditioning with sociopathic alcoholics may be less effective for physiological reasons.

A number of investigators have suggested operant techniques in the treatment of alcoholism (e.g., a community reinforcement method, and even the successful use of monetary rewards). Although operant techniques may offer significant treatment advantages for some alcoholics, it is not certain that these techniques will be successful with the alcoholic sociopath. At the very least, further development of behavior modification approaches with the alcoholic sociopath will require the following refinements: (1) precise identification of reinforcers for the sociopath's behavior, as even the skilled observer frequently has difficulty identifying what reinforces the behavior of the sociopath; and (2) the necessity for programming a high density of a wide variety of reinforcers into the patient's natural environment. This may be extremely difficult for sociopaths who have little positive contact with significant others and whose alcohol abuse has distanced them from major community support.

Drug Therapy

Although it is generally recognized that psychotropic drugs may be an important adjunct in the treatment of various symptoms associated with either alcoholism or sociopathy, there is at present no drug that is specific for the treatment of either of these conditions. It must be emphasized that the combination of alcoholism and sociopathy may present special considerations for the physician prescribing various types of medication. For example, certain minor tranquilizers like the benzodiazepines have been reported to increase the incidence of violent and aggressive behaviors in prisoners. Second, sociopaths and alcoholics appear to have increased risk for medication abuse, an important fact to consider in prescribing any drug with abuse potential. Third, overdose deaths from a combination of alcohol and minor tranquilizers have been reported.

The use of disulfiram (Antabuse) with the sociopathic alcoholic is controversial. Some authorities believe that inadequate, aggressive personalities with little or no ability to control sudden impulses are not suitable for Antabuse treatment. On the other hand, Antabuse is sometimes the most effective treatment with patients whose return to alcohol is prompted by sudden emotional flare-ups. The selection of patients for Antabuse should be individualized and based largely on the patient's wish to take the drug and the physician's judgment as to whether Antabuse is a suitable addition to the treatment program.

Finally, the following are general principles and suggestions regarding therapy with the alcoholic sociopath:

1. It is essential that the clinician carefully establish which diagnosis, alcoholism or sociopathy, is primary and construct treatment strategy accordingly. It is apparent that further research based on careful delineation of these diagnostic entities is necessary.

2. Regardless of the primary diagnosis, controlling the alcohol abuse is the first goal of therapy.

3. Sociopathic personalities can be extremely disruptive to an inpatient milieu program. Thus, when hospitalization of the sociopathic alcoholic is required, the course should be short-term and clearly goal-oriented.

4. The manipulative and exploitative features of many alcoholic sociopaths pose significant countertransference problems for the clinician. Before undertaking such therapy, the clinician must be scrupulously honest with himself or herself and in some instances should consider referral to those clinicians who have better tolerance for such behavior.

CONCLUSION

Current evidence indicates that alcoholism and sociopathy are associated in some major ways, but methodologic problems confound the nature of these associations. Not all sociopaths abuse alcohol and most alcoholics do not commit antisocial acts or have sociopathic personalities when stringent diagnostic criteria are used. Therefore, in order to avoid diagnostic confusion, clinicians should carefully establish primary and secondary diagnoses of these entities when working with alcoholic patients. Sociopathic behavior does complicate the treatment of the alcoholic and, conversely, heavy alcohol abuse complicates the treatment of a sociopathic personality. Nevertheless, alcoholism is a treatable condition and some recent studies indicate that alcoholism in association with sociopathy does not automatically indicate a poor prognosis.

REFERENCES

1. Caster, D. V., and Parsons, O. A. Relationship of depression, sociopathy, and locus of control to treatment outcome in alcoholics. *J. Consult. Clin. Psychol.* 45:751–756, 1977.
2. Cloninger, C. R., and Guze, S. B. Psychiatric illness in the families of female criminals: A study of 288 first-degree relatives. *Br. J. Psychiatry* 122:697–703, 1973.
3. Crowe, R. An adoption study of antisocial personality. *Arch. Gen. Psychiatry* 31:785–791, 1974.
4. Feighner, J. P., Robins, E., Guze, S. B., et al. Diagnostic criteria for use in psychiatric research. *Arch. Gen. Psychiatry* 26:57–63, 1972.
5. Gellens, H. K., Gottheil, E., and Alterman, A. I. Drinking outcome of specific alcoholic subgroups. *J. Stud. Alcohol* 37:986–989, 1976.
6. Goodwin, D. W., Crane, J. B., and Guze, S. B. Felons who drink: An 8-year follow-up. *Q. J. Stud. Alcohol* 32:136–147, 1971.
7. Goodwin, D., Schulsinger, F., and Hermansen, L., et al. Alcohol problems in adopt-

ees raised apart from alcoholic biological parents. *Arch. Gen. Psychiatry* 28:238-243, 1973.

8. Guze, S. B., Wolfgram, E. D., and McKinney, J. K., et al. Psychiatric illness in the families of convicted criminals: A study of 519 first-degree relatives. *Dis. Nerv. Syst.* 28:651-659, 1967.

9. Keller, M. The oddities of alcoholics. *Q. J. Stud. Alcohol* 33:1147-1148, 1972.

10. Pernanen, K. Alcohol and crimes of violence. In: *The Biology of Alcoholism: Social Aspects of Alcoholism* (Vol. 4). Kissin, B. and Begleiter, H. (eds.). Plenum: New York, 1976.

11. Rada, R. T. Sociopathy and alcohol abuse. In: *The Psychopath: A Comprehensive Study of Antisocial Disorders and Behaviors,* Reid, W. H. (ed.). Brunner/Mazel: New York, 1978.

12. Rada, R. T., Kellner, R., Laws, D. R., et al. Drinking, alcoholism, and the mentally disordered sex offender. *Bull. Am. Acad. Psychiatry Law* 6:296-300, 1978.

13. Robins, E., Gentry, K. A., Munoz, R. A., et al. A contrast of the three more common illnesses with the ten less common in a study and 18-month follow-up of 314 psychiatric emergency room patients: II. Characteristics of patients with the three more common illnesses. *Arch. Gen. Psychiatry* 34:269-281, 1977.

14. Robins, L. N., Bates, W., and O'Neal, P. Adult drinking patterns of former problem children. In: *Society, Culture, and Drinking Patterns,* Pittman, D. J. and Snyder, C. R. (eds.). Wiley: New York, 1962.

15. Schuckit, M. A. Alcoholism and sociopathy: Diagnostic confusion. *Q. J. Stud. Alcohol* 34:157-164, 1973.

16. Schuckit, M. A., and Morrissey, M. A. Psychiatric problems in women admitted to an alcoholic detoxification center. *Amer. J. Psychiatry* 136:611-617, 1979.

17. Watts, F. N., and Bennett, D. H. Social deviance in a day hospital. *Br. J. Psychiatry* 132:455-462, 1978.

51

DONALD W. GOODWIN, MD, University of Kansas Medical Center, Kansas City, Kansas

ALCOHOLISM AND SUICIDE: ASSOCIATION FACTORS

AN ASSOCIATION BETWEEN alcoholism and suicide can be studied in two ways, one of which is to study the drinking habits of suicide victims and suicide attempters; the other method is to determine how many alcoholics die by suicide or attempt suicide. This chapter reviews both kinds of studies and offers tentative explanations for differences in alcoholic suicides along lines of race, age, and sex.

ALCOHOLISM AND SUICIDE

In 1825 Casper [5], studying 218 suicides, found that 28% could be attributed to "alcoholism or debauchery." Numerous investigators have subsequently reported a connection between excessive drinking and suicide.

In 10 of 11 studies of the drinking histories of suicide victims [11], rates of alcoholism among suicides were substantially higher than the 5% rate often estimated to apply to the general adult population [8]; in four studies, about 10% of the suicides had been alcoholics or heavy drinkers; in six others, nearly 33% had been alcoholics.

Donald W. Goodwin, MD, Professor and Chairman, Department of Psychiatry, University of Kansas Medical Center, Kansas City, Kansas.

In other studies, groups of alcoholics were studied to determine how many die by suicide. Conducted in several different countries, these studies indicate that 6 to 29% of alcoholics commit suicide [19]. Only about 1% of the general population in the United States and United Kingdom do so. Kessel and Grossman [14] in a follow-up study of alcoholics in London found that 8% died by suicide within a 1- to 11-year period after hospitalization—a rate 75 to 85 times greater than expected for men of their age in London. Gabriel [10], in his 1935 study of mortality in a group of alcoholics, found that tuberculosis and suicide were the most common causes of death (23% and 20%, respectively). With the decline in mortality from tuberculosis in recent years, suicide has no doubt increased in relative importance as a cause of death.

Only two studies followed a large series of alcoholics to their death. One found that 27% died by suicide [17]. The other found that 11% had committed suicide [19].

ALCOHOLISM AND SUICIDE ATTEMPTS

Drinking habits of suicide attempters have also been studied. Among suicide attempters, alcoholism is even more common than among suicides: In seven studies, rates of alcoholism among attempters ranged from 13 to 50% [11]. In the most comprehensive of these studies, Dahlgren [6] found that nearly half of the male suicide attempters abused alcohol.

Studies of suicide indicate that suicides and suicide attempters represent overlapping but separate populations [21]. For example, attempters generally are younger, more likely to be women, and more likely to suffer personality disorders; among suicides, depression and alcoholism are the two most common diagnoses. A history of suicide attempt is of limited value in predicting suicide; although most suicides have made previous attempts, most people who attempt suicide do not later succeed. Within 1 or 2 years after an attempt, probably no more than 1 to 3% of attempters commit suicide [20], although the rate is somewhat higher in patients who have recently been hospitalized after a suicide attempt [24]. Over a period of many years, suicide attempters probably do represent a high-risk group for suicide, but the extent is unknown.

DEMOGRAPHIC ASPECTS OF ALCOHOLISM AND SUICIDE

In studies of suicide and alcoholism, men invariably outnumber women among both victims and attempters. Generally, the higher the rate of suicide among alcoholics, or of alcoholism among suicides, the higher the ratio of men to women.

Since alcoholism is more common in men than in women (by a ratio of 5:1, according to some estimates), the relevance of this sex difference is not clear.

Race is another variable affecting alcoholism-suicide rates. The interaction among race, sex, and age factors is a complex one. Blacks have lower rates of suicide than do whites, but the difference is much more striking between men and women, and the difference between white and black men only begins to emerge after age 35 [30]. After this age, the difference increases with increasing age, reaching a 5:1 ratio by age 75. Since blacks apparently have more drinking problems than whites [13, 15], their low suicide rate is curious. Robins [L. N. Robins, personal communication] has suggested that the difference may be related to the fact that black alcoholics apparently begin drinking excessively at a younger age than do white alcoholics.

There is evidence that alcoholism contributes to suicide chiefly in the middle years [11]. Two factors may explain this. First, alcoholics have an excess of deaths from causes (accidents, cirrhosis, etc.) other than suicide [27, 29] and alcoholics are, therefore, relatively unlikely to survive long enough to contribute many deaths by suicide in the aging population. Assuming that alcoholics' propensity to suicide is constant over the years, their excess mortality means that they should contribute more to younger suicides than to older ones, simply because they constitute a larger part of the younger population. Second, a sizable proportion of alcoholics apparently recover spontaneously or with treatment as they age, and recovered alcoholics are not replaced by new cases of the same age [7]. Amark [1] found that virtually no cases of alcoholism emerge for the first time after age 50. Recovery without replacement again leads to a lower proportion of alcoholics in the aged than in the younger population. Thus, recoveries and early deaths can explain a declining contribution to suicide by alcoholics in the later years.

Even among the remaining alcoholics, however, risk of suicide may decline with age. Attkisson [2] found that in San Francisco's skid row area, younger suicides tended to be alcoholics, while older suicides were not. Since it is unclear how many older skid row residents are alcoholics, interpretation of this finding is difficult.

While no study has reported suicide rates among alcoholics by age, Dahlgren [6] found excess mortality from all causes only in lower middle age (40 to 55) and his alcoholics showed, if anything, a low mortality rate in the later years. Schmidt and De Lint [27] reported excess mortality among alcoholics throughout life, but the excess was much greater before age 50 than after. Dahlgren showed that deaths by suicide and by accident (62%) were more heavily concentrated within the first 5 years of follow-up than were deaths by nonviolent means (35%).

This suggests that when alcoholics commit suicide they do so relatively early in the course of their alcoholism. Unfortunately, Dahlgren dealt with exits from his sample only by death, not by recovery, so it is not possible to tell what proportion continued in their alcoholism in later years without committing suicide.

Sundby [29] similarly showed that suicides accounted for 12% of all alcoholics' deaths in the first 5 years of follow-up but only 6% of all deaths during the total follow-up period. He also found a second high suicide risk late in the course of alcoholism, but only among alcoholics who had not lost their social standing early in their lives. Although Sundby attempted to confirm the persistence or recovery from alcoholism over the period of follow-up, he did not calculate suicide rates based only on subjects known still to be alcoholics.

Sundby's comment that late suicides differ from early suicides in not having lost their social standing early suggests that suicide in alcoholics is a response to actual or impending loss of status, occupational role, and/or interpersonal relationships. This hypothesis is consistent with the observation by Murphy and Robins [22] that, among suicides, alcoholics (but not depressives) had usually experienced or anticipated a major loss within the last 6 weeks of their lives. Such losses may well occur typically in the middle years of alcoholism. After an alcoholic hits bottom, he or she has little left to lose in the way of prestige or human relationships. The alcoholic therefore may be even less likely than persons in the general population to experience the losses that may precipitate suicide in the older population. Occasions for feeling hopeless — an emotion believed to motivate suicide by alcoholics [4] — may be fewer.

THE RACIAL DIFFERENCE: A THEORY

These observations prepare the way for a possible explanation of racial differences in alcoholic suicides.

A number of studies, as noted earlier, indicate that the onset of alcoholism is at an earlier age in blacks than in whites [25]. Bahr [3] reports that the age of loss of personal ties (disaffiliation) is related to the age of onset of heavy drinking. Alcoholics with histories of early heavy drinking showed more family breakups, unemployment, and lack of membership in voluntary associations than did alcoholics of the same age with later onsets. The early onset of alcoholism in blacks, together with their higher overall rate of alcoholism, leads to the hypothesis that older black men may commit suicide less frequently than older white men because a higher proportion of the older black population are late-stage alcoholics who have long since passed through the disaffiliation stage that precipitates suicide.

This hypothesis, however, requires one assumption for which there is no direct evidence: that late-stage alcoholics are not only less suicidal than early-stage alcoholics, but that they may also be less suicidal than the general population. At this point there is no evidence that late-stage alcoholism is protective against suicide, only that late-stage alcoholism does not seem to be a cause of suicide.

Robins [L. N. Robins, personal communication] further speculates that if late-stage alcoholism actually were protective against suicide, one reason might be that the later stages of alcoholism are associated with sufficient brain damage "to dull the experience of suffering and to prevent the preparation necessary for successful suicidal behavior."

It is not known how widespread brain damage may be in the general population of alcoholics, nor after how many years of drinking it usually appears. Schmidt, Smart, and Moss [28] have observed that the chronic brain syndromes of alcoholism are associated with both poverty and old age. The association with age suggests that brain damage occurs only after many years of drinking. The association with poverty could be explained in a number of ways, such as less protection from damage because of poor nutrition or an earlier onset of heavy drinking (and thus longer total exposure to alcohol). Whatever combination of these explanations may be correct, one would expect more brain damage among black than among white alcoholics of equal age, since they are poorer and begin drinking younger. Therefore, if brain damage does protect against suicide, black alcoholics should be protected disproportionately.

Thus, two hypotheses may help simultaneously to explain both the decrease in suicide with aging and the low rate of suicide among black men: Suicide becomes less probable (1) the less an alcoholic has to lose in the way of wealth, status, and interpersonal relationships, and (2) the more brain damage the alcoholic has suffered.

Neither hypothesis has been explored directly, and both require further study, but certainly the fact that suicide is rare among black alcoholics is one of the most challenging of demographic observations. It is particularly interesting because the suicide rate would be expected to be higher in blacks than in whites for a number of reasons: It is high among Protestants, divorced persons, agricultural workers, laborers, and the unemployed [30], and blacks have higher rates than whites on each of these predictors.

Rushing [26] has a different theory to account for the lower suicide rates among black than among white alcoholics. He believes that attitudes toward heavy drinking in the black culture are more permissive than in white groups of comparable socioeconomic status. If, as he suspects, suicide is a consequence of the disruptive effect of heavy drinking on interpersonal relations, then presumably less disruption would occur in the more permissive society and occasions for suicide would therefore be reduced.

In contrast with these processional explanations, some observers prefer to view alcoholism and suicide as different expressions of a single variable. Wallinga [31] has traced both alcoholism and suicide to "an underlying personality disturbance which finally was brought to medical attention through an attempt at self-destruction ... previously evidenced for a prolonged length of time by the refuge in alcohol." Menninger [18] viewed alcoholism and suicide as extreme expressions of a universal self-destructive instinct — Freud's famous Thanatos. According to this view, alcoholism is merely chronic suicide. As Kessel and Grossman [14] point out, the corollary of this proposition (i.e., because heavy drinking is a substitute for suicide, alcoholics rarely commit suicide) is inconsistent with the facts.

Related to but not synonymous with the above explanations is the possibility that at least certain types of alcoholism and suicide arise from the same predisposition to depression. Family history data tend to support such a possibility. Depression is overrepresented among the relatives of alcoholics—especially the women in the family—and alcoholism is common in the relatives of depressives—especially the men in the family [23]. This so-called depressive spectrum disorder, however, apparently does not exist when daughters of alcoholics are raised by nonalcoholic adoptive parents [12]. Moreover, only a minority of alcoholics have a clear-cut depressive illness independent of their alcoholism, and since alcoholism itself produces depressive symptoms, it is usually impossible to determine which comes first, the alcoholism or the depression. Like the other hypotheses, this one lacks substantiation.

SUMMARY

In conclusion, it appears clear that alcoholics, as a group, more often commit suicide than do nonalcoholics. The association may only apply to white male alcoholics, however, and studies suggest that alcoholism even in this group contributes to suicide mainly in the middle years.

Attempts to explain the association are made difficult by marked discrepancies in suicide-alcoholism findings. These discrepancies may arise for several reasons. Rarely is alcoholism or heavy drinking defined with any degree of rigor; the terms are often used interchangeably and the groups they represent are probably etiologically heterogeneous. Studies of suicide among alcoholics usually involve relatively short follow-ups, and identifying the alcoholics among suicide victims inevitably is *post factum*.

Finally, it is unclear in several studies whether suicide was associated with the alcoholism or merely with intoxication. Undoubtedly some victims drank before committing suicide, and intoxication may have helped to cause suicides that might not otherwise have occurred. It is unlikely, however, that this happens only in alcoholics. Little is known concerning the role of intoxication itself in suicide. Of suicides brought to autopsy, about 25% have alcohol in their blood or stomach contents [9, 32]. To conclude that drinking caused these deaths would be misleading, however; in no instance was the alcohol concentration at a lethal level, and it was impossible to tell *ex post facto* whether drinking contributed indirectly. Mayfield's finding [16] that nearly half of alcoholics attempting suicide do so during an alcoholic blackout may provide at least direction for further study.

REFERENCES

1. Amark, C. A study in alcoholism: Clinical, social-psychiatric and genetic investigations. *Acta Psychiat. Scand. (Suppl.)* No. 70: 1951.
2. Attkisson, C. C. Suicide in San Francisco's skid row. *Arch. Gen. Psychiatry* 23:149–157, 1970.

3. Bahr, H. M. Lifetime affiliation patterns of early- and late-onset heavy drinkers on skid row. *Q. J. Stud. Alcohol* 30:645-656, 1969.

4. Beck, A., Weissman, A., and Kovacs, M. Alcoholism, hopelessness and suicidal behavior. *J. Stud. Alcohol* 37:66-77, 1976.

5. Casper, J. L. Uber den Selbstmord und seine Zunahme in unserer. Zeit: Berlin, 1825.

6. Dahlgren, K. G. On suicide and attempted suicide: A psychiatrical and statistical investigation. Hakan Ohlssons: Lund, 1945.

7. Drew, L. R. H. Alcoholism as a self-limiting disease. *Q. J. Stud. Alcohol* 29:956-967, 1968.

8. Efron, V., Keller, M., and Gurioli, C. *Statistics on Consumption of Alcohol and on Alcoholism.* Rutgers University Center of Alcohol Studies: New Brunswick, N.J., 1972.

9. Elo, O. Uber Selbstmorde und Selbstmorder in Finnland. *Deutsch A. Ges. Gerichtl. Med.* 17:348, 1931.

10. Gabriel, E. Uber die Todesursachen bei Alkoholikern. Z. *Ges. Neurol. Psychiat.* 153:385-406, 1935.

11. Goodwin, D. W. Alcohol in suicide and homicide. *Q. J. Stud. Alcohol* 34:144-156, 1973.

12. Goodwin, D. W. Alcoholism and heredity: A review and hypothesis. *Arch. Gen. Psychiatry* 36:1, 57-61, 1979.

13. Hyman, M. M. Accident vulnerability and blood alcohol concentrations of drivers by demographic characteristics. *Q. J. Stud. Alcohol (Suppl.)* No. 4:34-57, 1968.

14. Kessel, N., and Grossman, G. Suicide in alcoholics. *Br. Med. J.* 2:1671-1672, 1961.

15. Malzberg, B. *The Mental Health of the Negro: A Study of First Admissions to Hospitals for Mental Diseases in New York State,* 1949-1951. Research Foundation for Mental Hygiene: Albany, N.Y., 1962.

16. Mayfield, D. G., and Montgomery, D. Alcoholism alcohol intoxication and suicide attempts. *Arch. Gen. Psychiatry* 27:349-353, 1972.

17. Mecir, J., Breyinova, V., and Vondracek, V. The causes of deaths in alcoholics. *Q. J. Stud. Alcohol* 17:633-642, 1956.

18. Menninger, K. A. *Man against Himself.* Harcourt Brace: New York, 1938.

19. Miles, C. P. Conditions predisposing to suicide: A review. *J. Nerv. Ment. Dis.* 164:231-246, 1977.

20. Munoz, R. A., Marten, S., Gentry, K. A., and Robins, E. Mortality following a psychiatric emergency room visit: An 18-month follow-up study. *Am. J. Psychiatry* 128:220-224, 1971.

21. Murphy, G. E. Recognition of suicidal risk: The physician's responsibility. *South. Med. J.* 62:723-728, 1969.

22. Murphy, G. E., and Robins, E. Social factors in suicide. *J.A.M.A.* 199:303-308, 1967.

23. Pitts, F. N., and Winokur, G. Affective disorders: III. Diagnostic correlates in incidence of suicide. *J. Nerv. Ment. Dis.* 139:176-181, 1964.

24. Pokorny, A. D. Human violence: A comparison of homicide, aggravated assault, suicide, and attempted suicide. *J. Crim. Law Criminol.* 56:488-497, 1965.

25. Robins, L. N., Murphy, G. E., and Breckenridge, M. B. Drinking behavior of young urban Negro men. *Q. J. Stud. Alcohol* 29:657-684, 1968.

26. Rushing, W. A. Suicide and the interaction of alcoholism (liver cirrhosis) with the social situation. *Q. J. Stud. Alcohol* 30:93-103, 1969.

27. Schmidt, W., and De Lint, J. Social class and the mortality of clinically treated alcoholics. *Br. J. Addict.* 64:327-331, 1970.

28. Schmidt, W., Smart, R. G., and Moss, M. K. *Social Class and the Treatment of Alcoholism: An Investigation of Social Class as a Determinant of Diagnosis, Prognosis, and Thera-*

py (Brookside Monograph No. 7). University of Toronto Press: Toronto, 1968.

29. Sundby, P. Alcoholism and Mortality (National Institute for Alcohol Research, Publ. No. 6). Universitetaforlaget: Oslo, 1967.

30. United States National Center for Health Statistics. *Suicide in the United States, 1950-1964* (U.S. Public Health Service Publ. No. 1000, Ser. 20, No. 5.). U.S. Government Printing Office: Washington, D.C., 1967.

31. Wallinga, J. V. Attempted suicide: A ten-year survey. *Dis. Nerv. Syst.* 10:15-20, 1949.

32. Wilentz, W. C., and Brady, J. P. The alcohol factor in violent deaths. *Am. Practit. Dig. Treat.* 12:829-835, 1961.

52

EDWARD KAUFMAN, MD, University of California, Irvine Medical Center, Orange, California

E. MANSELL PATTISON, MD, Medical College of Georgia, Augusta, Georgia

THE FAMILY AND ALCOHOLISM

PRESENTLY A GOLDEN age is opening in the recognition of the relationship between alcoholism and the family. Many recent reviews and books have been published that attest to the growing interest in this field [1, 2, 27, 32, 36, 40, 50, 57, 60]. There is now recognition of the effect of the family on alcoholism to supplement earlier findings on the effect of alcoholism in the family.

The Effect of Alcoholism on the Family

Regardless of the family system, alcoholism is a major stress on individual members and the family system. Alcoholism is an economic drain on family resources, threatens job security, demands adjustive and adaptive responses from family members who do not know how to appropriately respond, and may interrupt normal family tasks, and cause conflict. In brief, alcoholism creates a series of escalating crises in family structure and function that may bring the family system to a system crisis [3, 11, 30, 37, 42, 49]. In addition to these psychological conse-

---

Edward Kaufman, MD, Associate Professor in Residence, Department of Psychiatry and Human Behavior, University of California, Irvine Medical Center, Orange, California.

E. Mansell Pattison, MD, Professor and Chairman, Department of Psychiatry, Medical College of Georgia, Augusta, Georgia.

quences, alcoholism creates chronic physical disease and sexual dysfunction; they in turn produce further marital conflict [41, 56].

The Effect of the Family on Alcoholism

A converse dynamic occurs, in that marital and family conflict may evoke, support, and maintain alcoholism as a symptom of family system dysfunction, as a coping mechanism to deal with family dysfunction, and as a consequence of dysfunctional family styles, rules, and patterns of alcohol use. In such a case, alcoholism is not the cause of family dysfunction, but the effect of family dysfunction [31].

Early studies focused on the personality structure of the husbands and wives, with the assumption that personality conflict was a basic dynamic [4, 14, 35]. Most focused on the male alcoholic and his nonalcoholic wife. It was often implied that the wife was neurotic and chose an alcoholic husband, or later that the wife became neurotic because of her husband's alcoholism. Or, perhaps even more misogynist was the view that the wife drove her husband to drink. In retrospect, these studies, which focused primarily on personality, were marred by selective biased samples, lack of comparative controls, and reductionistic interpretations of psychodynamics as psychopathology [15, 18, 19, 22, 24, 38, 43, 52, 54, 63]. In sum, the fable of the noxious wife is just that—a fable [39]. There is no validity to several earlier typologies of typical wives of alcoholics. Nor can one even conclude that wives of alcoholics are somehow specifically different from other wives [20, 51, 61].

A study by Bailey et al. [3] casts some light on the role of an alcoholic marriage in producing psychopathology in the spouse. They found that the incidence of wives' psychopathology was highest (65%) in those wives who were living with actively drinking alcoholics, 55% in wives of alcoholics separated or divorced for more than 6 months, 43% in wives living with alcoholic husbands who had been abstinent for 6 months or more, and 35% in controls. The same problem is contained in the study of men who marry women alcoholics. Although sparse, these reports often indicate significant psychopathology among these men—but better samples and comparative data may likewise demonstrate no specific type of male spouse of an alcoholic woman [12, 55].

A more fruitful approach has been the study of marital interactional dynamics, role perceptions, and marital patterns of expectation and sanctions about the use of alcohol. Couples with alcoholism appear to engage in neurotic interactional behavior similar to that in other neurotic marriages, which are both dissimilar from healthy marital interaction. The only consistent feature that differentiates alcoholic marriages from other neurotic marriages is the existence of a parent of one partner who is an alcoholic. Other trends in alcoholic marriages in contrast to other neurotic marriages include communication patterns that reflect a high level of conflict for control and dominance [5] and the alcoholic consistently avoiding responsibility compared to the spouse [5]. Basically, alcoholic marriages are not unique but rather neurotic marriages in which alcoholism is part of the neurotic interaction [7, 25, 26, 28, 29, 47, 50, 53].

The Family and Alcoholism as a System Problem

Recent family research has moved away from a focus on the marital partners toward a consideration of the family system, the families of origin, the consequent life style of children from alcoholic families, and the kin structures of the extended family system. This provides a much broader view of alcoholism as a family problem.

The first conclusion from experimental observations of family systems is that alcohol use in a family is not just an individual matter. The use of alcohol and the consequential behavior of drinking is dynamically related to events in the family system. Thus, the use of alcoholism is purposeful, adaptive, homeostatic, and meaningful. The problem of alcoholism is not just the consequences of drinking per se, but more importantly the system functions that drinking fills in the psychodynamics of the family system [6, 9, 17, 58, 59, 65]. Thus, alcoholism may properly be considered as a family systems problem.

The parents of adult alcoholics play an important role in infantilization of the alcoholic and may contribute to spouse conflict and disengagement. They have all too often been neglected in traditional family treatment of alcoholism. Thus the systems approach is extended to a larger consideration of the nuclear family embedded in generational and kinship systems. The problem of alcoholism runs in families across generations and extends into the kinship system.

Alcoholism and Children in the Family System

Much of the alcoholism family literature has focused primarily on the marital partners, while neglecting the roles and functions of children in the family, and the consequences of alcoholism for the children. Margaret Cork called them the forgotten children [16]. In the immediate situation of the alcoholic family, children are often the most severely victimized. They have growth and development problems, school and learning difficulties, develop emotional problems, and frequently exhibit significant behavior dysfunctions [13, 21, 23, 64]. Further, these children are often subject to gross neglect and child abuse [48]. Teenage children are not immune to these adverse consequences, even though they are often considered less vulnerable — perhaps a misperception [8, 34, 44]. Just as significant are the long-term adverse consequences on personality patterning, identity formation, and dysfunctional attitudes toward alcohol [10, 45, 46]. Thus, family intervention must truly consider the needs of the child and teenage members both in terms of short-range problems and longer term preventive concerns.

What has frequently been neglected is the involvement of the children as part of the family system that provokes and perpetuates alcoholism. Young children may encourage parental drinking to temporarily quiet violence or to release affection. Parents may drink because of their frustration in controlling adolescent acting out, particularly drug abuse. Children of all ages may provoke parental discord to avoid having limits set and consistently maintained.

TYPICAL FAMILY DYNAMICS

Like most symptoms of family dysfunction, alcoholism is a systems-maintaining and a systems-maintained device. Drinking may serve as a symptom or expression of stress created by conflicts within the family system. Excessive drinking usually occurs when family anxiety is high. Drinking stirs up higher anxiety in those dependent on the one who drinks. The anxiety causes everyone to do more of what they are already doing. Drinking to relieve anxiety and increased family anxiety in response to drinking can spiral into a crisis, lead to collapse, or establish a chronic pattern [9]. Drinking frequently triggers anger in the drinker and provocation in others, which then triggers further anger and provocation despite attempts by the alcoholic to absorb the anger with alcohol. Drinking contributes significantly to provocation, verbal abuse, and physical violence.

Triangulating family systems are prone to alcoholism. In such systems, conflict or distance between two parties is automatically displaced onto a third party (e.g., in-law, lover, therapist, child), issue, or substance (alcohol or drugs) [9]. This is in contrast to a threesome wherein each member can move freely with the other two.

Female alcoholics tend to marry male alcoholics, but male alcoholics usually do not marry female alcoholics. Despite different male and female alcoholism rates, marital patterns more likely reflect psychosocial role dynamics. Individuals tend to choose spouses with equal levels of ego strength and self-awareness but with opposite ways of dealing with stress [9]. Frequently opposites attract in male and female relationships, particularly obsessives and hysterics. In such relationships each person sees himself or herself as giving in to the other. The one who gives in the most becomes "deselfed" and is vulnerable to a drinking problem [9]. If it is the wife, she begins drinking during the day to help her through her chores, hiding it from her husband to be ready for ideal togetherness when he returns — until she passes out several times and the problem is recognized. If it is the husband, he becomes more and more burdened by his responsibility at work and to his wife and children and increases his social drinking. He drinks excessively at home but manages to prolong his functioning at work until this too eventually falls apart.

Bowen [9] has also observed another style of interaction in which the dominant partner becomes progressively involved in work, removing him or her from the family. This hyperfunctioning partner then begins to drink as an outlet for responsibilities.

Even after a pattern of alcoholism is established, these couples continue in a highly competitive relationship. The alcoholic repeatedly tries to control and avoid responsibility through subtle, passive-dependent techniques. The spouse tries to control by being forceful, active, blunt, and dominating. Neither ever clearly becomes dominant, but the fight continues indefinitely as both feel they are being dominated. The adherence to a competitive style blocks the possibility of mutually satisfactory ways of interacting and prevents the kind of risk-taking that leads to growth. One area where fighting frequently occurs is in blaming each other for the family's problems. This dual projection blinds the couple from seeing their respective roles in creating problems. They frequently fight endlessly about "who started it" and readily duplicate this position in therapy with the hope that the therapist will judge right and wrong. Drunkenness is an important stage in the communication problems of such couples. Communication with a drunk is frustrating and exasperating. The usual response is to let the drunk person set the rules, follows his or her lead, cease trying to communicate, and withdraw. Withdrawal involves long periods of silence and, in the long run, leads to escalation of negative feelings and distrust and, ultimately, to explosive expressions of anger.

Some individuals marry alcoholics or potential alcoholics to meet certain needs and preexisting traits of their own. These and others who are "normal" develop many personality changes in response to living with an alcoholic.

The alcoholic leaves the spouse starved for attention and affection. Early in the marriage, he or she expresses love through sex and material possessions. Spouses then withhold affection because it leads to sex, an act the alcoholic believes forgives all past transgressions, particularly drinking. As alcoholism progresses, the alcoholic becomes progressively unable to perfom sexually, and the marriage becomes asexual.

The alcoholic loses his or her parental role in areas other than sexual functioning. The male alcoholic readily gives up his role as a parent. Other roles, such as household chores and maintenance, are also rapidly abandoned and given over to others. The male's role as the breadwinner is the last to go, and job loss may be necessary before treatment is sought. These families develop a chronic atmosphere of silence and tension, and their children complain of a lack of fun and laughter.

Alcoholism breeds alcoholism and drug abuse in the children of these marriages. The nonalcoholic wife may encourage the older son to take over responsibilities abdicated by the father, placing the son in overt competition with the father in both behavior and drinking. Daughters in such families feel that the alcoholic father prefers them to the mother and that, if mother were more loving, father would not drink. They believe the ills of weak men can be cured by love and tend to marry alcoholics, and repeat this pattern in multiple marriages.

As nonalcoholic members take over full management of the family, the alcoholic is relegated to child status, which perpetuates drinking. Coalitions occur between the nonalcoholic spouse and children or in-laws, tending to further distance the alcoholic. Children are terrified of the violence so commonly seen in alcoholic families. School phobia may result from the child's desire to stay home to protect the parent(s) from harm. Alcoholic fathers are prone to abuse their children through violence, sexual seduction, or assault. Alcoholic mothers are more prone to abuse their children through neglect. The nonalcoholic spouse may neglect children through directing his or her attention to the alcoholic. Although not all alcoholics seriously abuse or neglect their children, the majority have difficulties in child-rearing. The emotional disturbance that characterizes alcoholic families leaves the children feeling rejected and unable to identify with either parent.

The patterns that develop in family members of the alcoholic have been labeled as the disease of "co-alcoholism." In the early phases of co-alcoholism, there is denial and rationalization with the hope that the alcohol-related behavior will improve. There is responsibility and guilt for the alcoholic's behavior, and some withdrawal. In the middle phases, there is hostility, disgust, pity, preoccupation with protectiveness, and shielding of the alcoholic. The co-alcoholic will drink with the alcoholic as a way of tolerating the alcoholic's behavior. In the advanced stages, the hostility, withdrawal, and suspiciousness become generalized to one's total environment. In the final stages of co-alcoholism, responsibility for and quarrelling with the alcoholic are all-encompassing. Outside interests decline, and needs to maintain the self are disregarded. Psychosomatic symptoms or drug and alcohol dependence may occur, and separation is threatened or demanded. Frequently, the alcoholic will become sufficiently motivated for treatment when the co-alcoholic reaches the detachment aspects of these final phases. The role of the co-alcoholic has also been termed as that of the "enabler," as the co-alcoholic is the one who enables the alcoholic to continue his or her behavior.

Thus, the spouse and family build up many defenses that create problems when and if the alcoholic gets sober. If the alcoholic stops drinking, the spouse no longer fights with him or her about drinking, but about whether drinking will be resumed, which paradoxically triggers resumption of drinking.

The alcoholic who is sober and doesn't want to be is still psychologically drunk and punishes everyone around because he or she expects and doesn't receive exceptional rewards for giving up alcohol.

The romance of sobriety wears off after a while, and the slightest stress will again trigger alcohol misuse. The grief work in giving up alcohol may last for months or years. During this period of prolonged grief and high, unfulfilled expectations, the recovering alcoholic is referred to as a "dry drunk." If the family system is not counseled during this phase of the cycle, and if the family does not learn new patterns of relating to each other to replace those developed during alcoholism, then the old system will draw the alcoholic and the family back to symptomatic consumption of alcohol.

What is seen most commonly is a family system where the nonalcoholic parent has made a cross-generational coalition with a child, generally of the opposite sex, which excludes, alienates, and infantilizes the alcoholic. Such coalitions are also common between the co-alcoholic and his or her own parents or a lover, or between the alcoholic and a lover (generally one who is the child of alcoholics). Thus, attention to familial relationships outside of the alcoholic-spouse diad are essential to understanding and changing the alcoholic as well as maintaining sobriety after it occurs.

THE FAMILY AS A DETERMINANT OF REHABILITATION

In keeping with the observations of alcoholism as a system problem, the attitudes, structure, and function of the family system has been shown to be perhaps the one most important variable in the successful outcome of alcoholism treatment. The alcoholic person enters treatment from a family system and returns to that family system. If the system is dysfunctional, it may vitiate any individual treatment gains, whereas, if the family changes or adapts more appropriate functions, it may sustain improvement and change in the alcoholic member [33, 62, 66]. A later chapter presents a system of classifying families with alcohol problems, a system that addresses the modification of treatment approaches and techniques necessary to deal with these different types of families.

REFERENCES

1. Ablon, J. Family structure and behavior in alcoholism: A review of the literature. In: *The Biology of Alcoholism: Social Pathology* (Vol. 4), Kissin, B. and Begleiter, H. (eds.). Plenum: New York, 1976.
2. Bailey, M. Alcoholism in marriage: A review of research and professional literature. *Q. J. Stud. Alcohol* 22:81–97, 1961.
3. Bailey, M. B., Haberman, P. W., and Alksne, H. Outcomes of alcoholic marriages: Endurance, termination, or recovery. *Q. J. Stud. Alcohol* 23:610–623, 1962.
4. Ballard, R. G. The interaction between marital conflict and alcoholism as seen through MMPIs of marriage partners. *Am. J. Orthopsychiatry* 29:528–546, 1959.
5. Becker, J. V., and Miller, P. M. Verbal and nonverbal marital interaction patterns of alcoholics and nonalcoholics. *J. Stud. Alcohol* 37:1616–1624, 1976.
6. Berenson, D. Alcohol and the family system. In: *Family Therapy: Theory and Practice*, Guerin, P. J. (ed.). Gardner Press: New York, 1976.
7. Billings, A. G., Kessler, M., Gomberg, C. A., and Weiner, S. Marital conflict resolution of alcoholic and nonalcoholic couples during drinking and nondrinking sessions. *J. Stud. Alcohol* 40:183–195, 1979.

8. Bosma, W. G. Alcoholism and teenagers. *Md. St. Med. J.* 24:62–68, 1975.

9. Bowen, M. Alcoholism as viewed through family systems theory and family psychotherapy. *Ann. N.Y. Acad. Sci.* 233:115–122, 1974.

10. Burk, E. D. Some contemporary issues in child development and the children of alcoholic parents. *Ann. N.Y. Acad. Sci.* 197:189–197, 1972.

11. Burton, G., and Kaplan, H. M. Marriage counseling with alcoholics and their spouses: II. The correlation of excessive drinking with family pathology and social deterioration. *Br. J. Addict.* 63:161–170, 1968.

12. Busch, H., Kormendy, E., and Feverlein, W. Partners of female alcoholics. *Br. J. Addict.* 68:179–184, 1973.

13. Chafetz, M. E., Blane, H. T., and Hill, M. J. Children of alcoholics: Observations in a child guidance clinic. *Q. J. Stud. Alcohol* 32:687–698, 1971.

14. Chassell, J. Family constellation in the etiology of essential alcoholism. *Psychiatry* 1:473–482, 1938.

15. Clifford, B. J. A study of wives of rehabilitated and unrehabilitated alcoholics. *Soc. Casework* 41:457–460, 1960.

16. Cork, M. R. *The Forgotten Children.* Addiction Research Foundation: Toronto, 1969.

17. Davis, D., Berenson, D., Steinglass, P., and Davis, S. The adaptive consequences of drinking. *Psychiatry* 37:209–215, 1974.

18. Deniker, P., Saugy, D., and Ropert, M. The alcoholic and his wife. *Comp. Psychiatry* 5:374–383, 1964.

19. Dinaburg, D., Click, I. D., and Feigenbaum, E. Marital therapy of women alcoholics. *J. Stud. Alcohol* 38:1247–1258, 1977.

20. Edwards, P., Harvey, C., and Whitehead, P. C. Wives of alcoholics: A critical review and analysis. *Q. J. Stud. Alcohol* 34:112–132, 1973.

21. El-Guebly, N., and Offord, D. R. The offspring of alcoholics: A critical review. *Am. J. Psychiatry* 134:357–365, 1977.

22. Fox, R. The alcoholic spouse. In: *Neurotic Interaction in Marriage*, Eisenstein, V. (ed.). Basic Books: New York, 1956.

23. Fox, R. Children in the alcoholic family. In: *Problems in Addiction: Alcohol and Drug Addiction*, Bier, W. C. (ed.). Fordham University Press: New York, 1962.

24. Futterman, S. Personality trends in wives of alcoholics. *J. Psychiat. Soc. Wk.* 23:37–41, 1953.

25. Gorad, S. L. Communicational styles and interaction of alcoholics and their wives. *Fam. Proc.* 10:475–489, 1971.

26. Gorad, S. L., McCourt, W. F., and Cobb, J. C. A communications approach to alcoholics and their wives. *Q. J. Stud. Alcohol* 32:651–668, 1971.

27. Hanson, K. J., and Estes, N. J. Dynamics of alcoholic families. In: *Alcoholism: Development, Consequences, and Intervention*, Estes, N. K. and Heinemann, M. E. (eds.). C. V. Mosby: St. Louis, 1977.

28. Hanson, P. G., Sands, P. M., and Sheldon, R. B. Patterns of communication in alcoholic marital couples. *Psychiat. Q.* 42:538–547, 1968.

29. Hersen, M., Miller, P., and Eisler, R. Interaction between alcoholics and their wives: A descriptive analysis of verbal and nonverbal behavior. *Q. J. Stud. Alcohol* 34:516–520, 1973.

30. Jackson, J. The adjustment of the family to the crisis of alcoholism. *Q. J. Stud. Alcohol* 15:562–586, 1954.

31. Jacob, T., Favorini, A., Meisel, S. S., and Anderson, C. M. The alcoholic's spouse, children, and family interaction: Substantive findings, and methodological issues. *J. Stud.*

Alcohol 39:1231–1251, 1978.

32. Janzen, C. Families in the treatment of alcoholism. *J. Stud. Alcohol* 38:114–130, 1976.

33. Kalashian, M. Working with the wives of alcoholics in an outpatient setting. *J. Marr. Fam.* 21:130–133, 1959.

34. Kammeier, M. L. Adolescents from families with and without alcoholism. *Q. J. Stud. Alcohol* 32:364–372, 1971.

35. Karlen, H. Alcoholism in conflicted marriages. *Am. J. Orthopsychiatry* 35:326, 1965.

36. Kaufman, E., and Kaufmann, P. *Family Therapy of Drug and Alcohol Abuse*. Gardner Press: New York, 1979.

37. Kephart, W. M. Drinking and marital disruption: A research note. *Q. J. Stud. Alcohol* 15:63–73, 1954.

38. Kogan, K. L., and Jackson, J. K. Role perceptions in wives of alcoholics and nonalcoholics. *Q. J. Stud. Alcohol* 24:627–632, 1963.

39. Kogan, K. L., and Jackson, J. K. Alcoholism: The fable of the noxious wife. *Ment. Hyg.* 49:428–453, 1965.

40. Krimmel, H. E. The alcoholic and his family. In: *Alcoholism: Progress in Research and Treatment*, Bourne, P. G. and Fox, R. (eds.). Academic Press: New York, 1973.

41. Lemere, F., Smith, J. W. Alcohol-induced sexual impotence. *Am. J. Psychiatry* 130:212–213, 1973.

42. Lemert, E. M. The occurrence and sequence of events in adjustment of families to alcoholism. *Q. J. Stud. Alcohol* 21:679–697, 1960.

43. MacDonald, D. Mental disorders in wives of alcoholics. *Q. J. Stud. Alcohol* 17:282–287, 1956.

44. McLachlan, J. F. C., Walderman, R. L., and Thomas, S. *A Study of Teenagers with Alcoholic Parents* Monograph No. 3. Donwood Institute: Toronto, 1973.

45. Mik, G. Sons of alcoholic fathers. *Br. J. Addict.* 65:305–315, 1970.

46. Miller, D., and Jang, M. Children of alcoholics: A 20-year longitudinal study. *Soc. Wk. Res.* 13:23–29, 1977.

47. Mitchell, H. E. The interrelatedness of alcoholism and family conflict. *Am. J. Orthopsychiatry* 24:547–559, 1968.

48. Olson, R. J. Index of suspicion: Screening for child abusers. *Am. J. Nurs.* 76:108–110, 1976.

49. Orford, J., Oppenheimer, E., Egert, S., and Hensman, C. The role of excessive drinking in alcoholism-complicated marriages: A study of stability and change over a one-year period. *Int. J. Addict.* 12:471–475, 1977.

50. Paolino, T. J., Jr., and McCrady, B. S. *The Alcoholic Marriage: Alternative Perspectives*. Grune & Stratton: New York, 1979.

51. Paolino, T. J., Jr., McCrady, B., Diamond, S., and Longaburgh, R. Psychological disturbances in spouses of alcoholics. *J. Stud. Alcohol* 37:1600–1608, 1976.

52. Price, G. A study of the wives of twenty alcoholics. *Q. J. Stud. Alcohol* 5:620–627, 1945.

53. Rae, J. B., and Drewery, J. Interpersonal patterns in alcoholic marriages. *Br. J. Psychiatry* 120:615–621, 1972.

54. Rae, J. B., and Forbes, A. R. Clinical and psychometric characteristics of wives of alcoholics. *Br. J. Psychiatry* 112:197–200, 1966.

55. Rimmer, J. Psychiatric illness in husbands of alcoholics. *Q. J. Stud. Alcohol* 35:281–283, 1974.

56. Schuckit, M. A. Sexual disturbance in the alcoholic woman. *Med. Aspects Hum. Sex.* 6:44–65, 1971.

57. Scott, E. M. *Struggles in an Alcoholic Family.* Charles C Thomas: Springfield, Ill., 1970.

58. Steinglass, P., Weiner, S., and Mendelson, J. H. A systems approach to alcoholism: A model and its clinical application. *Arch. Gen. Psychiatry* 24:401-408, 1971.

59. Steinglass, P., Weiner, S., and Mendelson, J. H. Interactional issues as determinants of alcoholism. *Am. J. Psychiatry* 128:275-280, 1971.

60. Steinglass, P. Experimenting with family treatment approaches to alcoholism, 1950-1975: A review. *Fam. Proc.* 15:97-123, 1976.

61. Tarter, R. Personality of wives of alcoholics. *J. Clin. Psychol.* 32:741-743, 1976.

62. Webb, N. L., Pratt, T. C., Linn, M. W., and Carmichael, J. S. Focus on the family as a factor in differential treatment outcomes. *Int. J. Addict.* 13:783-786, 1978.

63. Whalen, T. Wives of alcoholics: Four types observed in a family service agency. *Q. J. Stud. Alcohol* 14:632-638, 1953.

64. Wilson, C., and Orford, J. Children of alcoholics: Report of a preliminary study and comments on the literature. *J. Stud. Alcohol* 39:121-142, 1978.

65. Wolin, S., Steinglass, P., Sendroff, P., Davis, D. I., and Berenson, D. Marital interaction during experimental intoxication and the relationship to family history. In: *Alcohol Intoxication and Withdrawal,* Gross, M. (ed.). Plenum: New York, 1975.

66. Wright, K. D., and Scott, T. B. The relationship of wives' treatment to the drinking status of alcoholics. *J. Stud. Alcohol* 39:1577-1581, 1978.

53

BARBARA S. MCCRADY, PhD, Brown University and Butler Hospital,
Providence, Rhode Island

MARITAL DYSFUNCTION: ALCOHOLISM AND MARRIAGE

MARITAL DYSFUNCTION is often perceived as a natural concomitant to alcoholism and alcohol abuse. Many clinicians refer to the alcoholic marriage as a unique entity, with regularly occurring, identifiable characteristics. This chapter examines these two commonly held views about alcoholism and marriage, and highlights current issues in the field. The chapter is divided into three main sections: (1) statistical information about the incidence of marriage, marital dysfunction, and separation and divorce among alcoholics; (2) a review of the major theoretical approaches to understanding alcoholism and marriage; and (3) a discussion of current issues in the area.

STATISTICS

There are four major types of incidence figures of interest: (1) rates of marriage among alcoholics; (2) rates of separation and divorce among alcoholics; (3) rates of marital dysfunction among intact couples; and (4) figures on the relationship between marriage and the onset of alcohol abuse or alcoholism. A number of large-scale studies have compared rates of marriage among alcoholics to rates of marriage in a comparable age range of the general population. These studies (sum-

---

Barbara S. McCrady, PhD, Associate Professor, Section of Psychiatry and Human Behavior, Brown University and Butler Hospital, Providence, Rhode Island.

marized in Paolino et al. [34] suggest comparable marriage rates for alcoholics in outpatient clinics and private hospitals, but lower marriage rates for those alcoholics who are psychotic, public inebriates, or in public hospitals. None of these studies, however, analyzed data by sex or by age groups. Thus, as a group, it appears that the majority of alcoholics marry at the same rate as the general population.

In contrast to these fairly normative marriage rates, studies consistently find that alcoholics' separation and divorce rates are four to eight times as great as comparable rates in the general population. In contrast to the figures on marriage rates, the variability in separation and divorce is not clearly attributable to variations among treatment facilities. Studies also suggest that the rate of separation and divorce is even higher among alcoholic women than among alcoholic men. These statistics, taken as a whole, indirectly demonstrate the marked negative effects that alcoholism has on marital functioning. What is less clear, however, is how often alcoholic couples remain married, but still experience marked dysfunction. Few studies have directly addressed this question, but many authors have described disruptions in finances, decision making, and child-rearing practices, as well as incidents of domestic violence [15] in alcoholic families. Careful studies defining marital problems and surveying these across a wide population are still needed.

The final incidence and prevalence question about alcoholism and marriage is the relationship between marriage and the onset of and recovery from alcohol problems. Studies of alcoholic men [4, 15, 24] have shown that greater than half the couples studied married before the husband developed drinking problems. Furthermore, Polich et al.'s [36] data show the lowest rates of marriage and the highest divorce rates among alcoholics with severe problems 4 years after treatment. These data suggest that marital dysfunction may often contribute to the development of alcohol problems, and that continued heavy drinking after treatment is strongly related to further marital disruption.

MODELS OF ALCOHOLIC MARRIAGES

Models of alcoholism and alcoholic marriages developed in the last 50 years have gradually shifted in emphasis from a focus on the individual alcoholic and the individual spouse, each with their own separate psychological problems, to a focus on the marriage as an interactional system in which alcohol is a problem.

The Disturbed Personality Hypothesis

The disturbed personality hypothesis (DPH), a model of the wives of alcoholic men, was first introduced in the 1930s. Clinical reports (reviewed in Paolino and McCrady [33]) described these women as riddled by neurotic conflicts and ravaged by sexual fears, dependency conflicts, poorly controlled aggressive impulses, and a desire to dominate a weakened male. The DPH was derived from psychodynamic concepts of conflict, the unconscious, and defense mechanisms. Basically, these women were seen as fixated at a particular psychosexual stage, and, as adults, were seen as continuing to experience conscious and unconscious conflicts as a result of this early fixation. Marriage to an alcoholic or potential alcoholic was seen as a neurotic resolution of this conflict, but was at the same time a symptom of the underlying conflict. Some of these early authors saw an interactional component to these marriages, stating that alcoholic men also unconsciously marry these women to meet their own neurotic needs.

Since the DPH is a psychoanalytic hypothesis, it is extremely difficult to test, since it is impossible to directly measure unconscious processes. Rather, deductions must be derived about observable behaviors and reportable feelings. The relationship between the observables and the original hypothesis is not always obvious. However, several types of data are relevant to examining the validity of the DPH. These data sources have included (1) general measures of psychological disturbance, (2) interpersonal perception studies, and (3) dependency and dominance studies.

There are several reports of measured psychopathology of wives of alcoholics. Five independent studies using the Minnesota Multiphasic Personality Inventory (MMPI) or the Psychological Screening Inventory [23] have found scores of wives of alcoholics falling within the normal range [33]. Only one study [20] found evidence of disturbance in this group. These results do not support the view that wives of alcoholics generally are psychologically disturbed.

A second source of data pertinent to the DPH is interpersonal perception studies. These studies have involved wives' ratings of themselves and their alcoholic mates. The studies suggest that wives of alcoholics tend to see themselves as stereotypically feminine, and see themselves as having emotional problems whether or not their husbands are drinking [21, 22, 32]. However, two studies were unable to distinguish troubled alcoholic from troubled nonalcoholic couples [28] or wives of alcoholics from wives of nonalcoholics [20] using person perception techniques.

A third type of data relevant to the DPH are studies of dependency and dominance conflicts. Studies of these constructs have been plagued by poorly defined methodology, but several have found that alcoholic men tend to see their wives as more dominant then the wives see themselves [7, 8, 12, 28]. Only one study, which more carefully defined its terms [23], was unable to find dominance of the wife among alcoholic couples.

Taken as a whole, studies of the disturbed personality hypothesis provide conflicting results. The vast majority of the studies have not demonstrated a unique personality pattern among wives of alcoholics, and have not consistently demonstrated any generalized level of psychological disturbances among this group. Some studies do suggest a pattern of increased dominance among this group, but this is not a consistent finding. Also, if this dominance exists, it is not clear that the cause is based in personality traits; it may just as well be a necessary response to a situation in which the other mate is unable to participate in decision making or control of the family. This notion is discussed under "Sociological Stress Theory."

It should also be kept in mind that the DPH was a theory about wives of alcoholic men, proposed at a time in which traditional sex roles and role relationships were the norm. No similar theory about husbands of alcoholic women has ever been proposed, and in fact some writers have suggested that alcoholic women's problems are rooted in their husbands' lack of dominance in the relationship. It may be that the DPH is best seen as a social reaction to women who took on nontraditional roles, which was interpreted as psychopathology by traditional clinicians.

The Decompensation Hypothesis

The decompensation hypothesis (DH) is a corollary to the disturbed personality hypothesis. The DH states that, if an alcoholic man is able to successfully stop drinking, then his wife will decompensate. This decompensation is said to occur because marriage to an actively drinking alcoholic was thought to be a defense against unconscious psychological conflicts. Removal of this defense was thought to result in a disintegration of the woman's personality integration, with resultant severe psychological problems, such as a major depression or psychosis.

Many clinical reports have made this observation (reviewed by Paolino and McCrady [33]), and some investigators found relationships between husbands' cessation of drinking and wives' hospitalizations [25]. There are two major problems in considering the validity of the DH. First, the subjects of study have usually been women in treatment or couples in treatment. This certainly represents an atypical population, and says nothing about the fate of wives of alcoholics who recover without the wife's getting involved in treatment. The second problem with interpreting such clinical observations is the lack of consideration of alternative explanations. For example, if a spouse has had to overfunction for a number of years, and suddenly again has a mate on whom she can rely, she may then be able to attend to her own needs, conflicts, and problems, with the result looking like decompensation. An alternative explanation, offered by sociological researchers, is that the readjustment of roles and role definitions that accompanies recovery is difficult, and may result in a difficult period for both partners.

Sociological Stress Theory

With the introduction of sociological approaches to alcoholic marriages, the field began a transition from considering individual personality disturbances of alcoholics and wives of alcoholics, to considering the interrelatedness of alcoholism and the functioning of the marital unit. Joan Jackson is widely recognized as the pioneer in this approach to alcoholic marriages.

The central tenet of Jackson's [15] model is that marriage to an alcoholic is a stressful experience. This stress results in certain necessary role redefinitions as the family copes with a chronically dysfunctional and unpredictable member; this stress also results in painful feelings and disorganized behavior in family members as they cope with the stress. Jackson attempted to define stages that families went through in coping with a husband's alcoholism, and she also participated in an active basic research program to study the major components of her model.

Jackson identified family stages of adjustment to alcoholism by studying women who were active participants in Al-Anon. These women and their families probably were not representative of wives of alcoholics in general, since they had sought help, specifically chose a self-help approach, and wanted to participate in group discussions. Thus, what Jackson observed in these women may not be characteristic of wives of alcoholics in general, and there are no data to suggest whether or not her findings apply to husbands of female alcoholics.

Keeping these cautions in mind, seven family stages are described. The first stage, "attempts to deny the problem," is characterized by the spouse occasionally wondering about her husband's drinking, but allowing herself to be convinced that nothing is wrong. However, if the husband's drinking continues, Stage 2, "attempts to eliminate the problem," gradually emerges. At this stage, marital conflict increases, the wife protects her husband from the consequences of his drinking, and the wife and family attempt to control the alcoholic's drinking. Role definitions and expectations remain unchanged. In Stage 3, "disorganization," the wife loses hope, and chaos, anger, and fear predominate. The wife's behavior becomes inconsistent, and she no longer supports her husband's role in the family. However, alternate role definitions have not yet emerged. If this state continues, however, eventually Stage 4, "attempts to reorganize in spite of the problem," emerges. The wife takes over the role responsibilities of her husband, makes decisions, and controls the home. She also is less willing to cover up for her husband. The alcoholism may continue, but the family is a better functioning, better-organized unit. However, if the husband continues to drink, the stress continues, and the wife may decide to separate from her husband. Separation is the major characteristic of Stage 5, which is followed by Stage 6, "efforts to reorganize the family without the husband." The wife may feel extremely guilty about her decision.

If the husband stops drinking, Stage 7, "reorganization," may occur. This is also a stressful time for the family. Having the husband reassume a role in decision making and resuming his share of the responsibilities is hard for him to achieve. The wife, who has had to steel herself to live without this sharing and support, may feel apprehensive that her husband will resume problem drinking and let her down again, thus threatening the stability that she had been able to achieve.

Thus, while decompensation hypothesis proponents would see this anxiety as evidence for the wife's need for a weakened mate in order to survive, Jackson would argue that this is a normal, expected response to disruptions in role functioning in the family unit, and that this response is similar to that of other temporarily disrupted family units when the family is reunited.

A number of studies have supported the premise that wife disturbance is directly related to an alcoholic husband's drinking [15, 16, 17, 18]. However, few studies have found precisely the same stages in family organization that Jackson observed. Undoubtedly, Al-Anon women are a unique subset of wives of alcoholics [1, 2, 35].

Sociological stress theory made two major contributions to the understanding of alcoholism and marriage. First, the model clearly suggests that wives engage in a range of behaviors in response to drinking. Second, these behaviors were seen as coping behaviors, rather than as psychopathology. Jackson clearly introduced the field to a more humane view of the difficulties of living with an alcoholic. Her work can be criticized methodologically, and also for its omissions. She viewed alcoholism as a unique problem, and did not consider the continuum of alcohol problems. Thus, from her work, we learn nothing about the effects on the family of relatively mild drinking problems. She also did not study husbands of alcoholic women, thus perpetuating the myths that women do not have drinking problems, and that their husbands have no role in their wives' problems.

Systems Theory

While the 1940s to the 1960s focused on the individuals involved in an alcoholic marriage, in the 1970s the field began to shift toward considering the marital and family system as a unit. General systems theory–based models and social learning theory–based models have taken this more interactional approach to conceptualizing alcoholic marriages.

In the 1960s and early 1970s, general systems theorists began to examine alcoholic families. The main premise of their approach was that alcoholism is an integral component of the family's functioning. Thus, while an individual may have developed alcohol problems prior to his or her marriage, once the alcoholic enters a marriage, a new system develops. Each person in the family system has certain roles that he or she fulfills. The possible roles in a family are limitless, but an alcoholic family member may occupy the sick role in the family. The homeostatic balance in the family is believed to depend upon this role. Thus, if the alcoholic member stops drinking, the homeostasis of the family is threatened. Systems theorists would predict then that the actions of the family would be directed toward reachieving homeostasis, which could result in family efforts to help the person return to drinking, or could result in the development of sick behaviors in another family member. It is significant that this model and the decompensation hypothesis both predict that the spouse of an alcoholic could exhibit problem behaviors after the alcoholic stops drinking, but that the mechanism by which this occurs is quite different according to the two models. Since this is a very simplified description of systems theory, the reader is referred to Steinglass [38] for a more comprehensive description of these models.

Systems models are difficult to test, because most traditional research methods utilize linear, deductive hypothesis testing, while systems models involve complex patterns of interaction, rather than cause-effect relationships. Two main types of studies have been used to study general systems theory models of alcoholic marriages. The first methodology has involved complex observations of alcoholic families' interactions, using various ways of coding these interactions. The second approach has been to study communication patterns, by either using simulated interactional games or by coding samples of conversation.

Complex observations of the interactions of alcoholic families were pioneered by Steinglass and his colleagues at George Washington University. Observations of couples have revealed that alcoholic couples tend to have distinct and different styles of interaction that characterize their drinking and nondrinking interactions [39]. Since this research group is now focusing their work on whole family interactions, their current findings are beyond the scope of this chapter.

Communications studies have focused on two questions: (1) Is the alcoholic's communication pattern characterized by a responsibility-avoiding, indirect style; and, (2) Are there unique communication problems that characterize alcoholic couples? In examining the first question, Gorad et al. [11] developed an experimental game to measure direct responsibility-avoiding communication. They found that alcoholic couples tended to share and collaborate less than normal couples, and that the alcoholic men in the study used responsibility-avoiding modes of communication less than their wives did and less than normal control husbands. The study clearly supported a communications model of alcoholism. However, Rizzo [S. Rizzo, personal communication] was unable to replicate these findings, utilizing a similar experimental paradigm.

Other communication studies have tried to describe verbal communication patterns. Several studies have found a high frequency of hostile and/or coercive verbal interactions in alcoholic couples [3, 5]. Couples who are highest on hostile and coercive interactions prior to treatment have been found to have the poorest treatment outcomes [29, 31]. A paucity of effective communication skills have been noted, including a low rate of friendly acts [3], a low rate of cognitive acts [3], a low rate of relationship-relevant messages emitted by the alcoholic [19], a low rate of total verbal output, [3, 9], and a lack of intimate, positive exchanges [6]. Alcoholics have also been observed to increase the rate and amount of verbal output while drinking [3, 9], and to increase their assertive or aggressive responses [5]. One study has found no differences between male and female alcoholic couples on a number of communication measures [27]. As a whole these studies suggest that alcoholic couples interact in dysfunctional ways, although the exact pattern of these interactions may not be unique to alcoholic couples. Further, the changes in these patterns when drinking lend support to the systems hypothesis that alcohol serves positive functions in the family system.

Social Learning Theory

Social learning theory approaches also consider the positive role of alcohol in the marriage, by examining reinforcing consequences of drinking that maintain the drinking behavior. In general, social learning theorists view problem drinking as a learned behavior, which occurs in response to certain discriminable cues, and which is maintained both by positive reinforcement and avoidance of aversive consequences. A functional analysis (10) of the drinking behavior can be used to describe current conditions maintaining an abusive drinking pattern.

There are four components to a functional analysis of any behavior. "Antecedent stimuli" are discriminative stimuli that increase the probability of occurrence of the response. "Organismic variables" are internal responses to the external stimuli. These may include physiological responses, cognitions (including self-statements, expectancies, etc.), or emotional responses. The "response" can be described in terms of rate, frequency magnitude, pervasiveness, and form of the response. "Consequences," the final component in a behavioral chain, may be primarily positive, aversive, or neutral. In complex behaviors, such as alcoholism, a combination of discrete stimuli may sum to result in a complex discriminative stimulus for drinking. Similarly, since a number of different kinds of consequences occur after drinking behavior, the balance of these consequences probably affects the probability of reoccurrence of the behavior, rather than the occurrence of a single consequence [37].

Alcoholic couples are postulated to have poor communication and problem-solving skills. They engage in positive exchanges at a low rate, and evolve, over the years, a mode of interacting that involves attempts to control each other coercively, such as through threats or nagging. As the aversive situation escalates over the years, communication becomes more ambiguous, vague, and inconsistent. As a result of these poor communication skills and ineffective methods of control, a large backlog of problems accumulates. On these dimensions, alcoholic couples resemble other couples experiencing marital distress. The differences between alcoholic and other distressed couples are expressed later in the behavioral chain, in that in the former, drinking is a high-probability response to these marital antecedents, and may result in marital consequences that serve to maintain the drinking behavior. Thus, while antecedent variables and communication patterns may be similar across many types of distressed marriages, the organismic variables, responses, and consequences are quite different in alcoholic couples.

Several studies have found the above postulated relationship between interpersonal conflict and subsequent drinking behavior. For example, Hore [13, 14] examined the relationship between environmental stresses and relapses from abstinence in a small group of alcoholic men. He found that 100% of interpersonal stresses, defined as a quarrel with a spouse or lover, were associated with a drinking relapse within 2 weeks of the stress, suggesting a strong relationship between drinking behavior and relationship conflict. Marlatt and Gordon [26] report that 18% of relapses in a group of abstinent alcoholics were associated with interpersonal conflict, although they did not discriminate marital from other interpersonal situations. Communication studies of alcoholic couples, reviewed under "Systems Theory," also suggest many negative interactions that may cue drinking behavior.

To date, no one has studied organismic variables, which play a major role in the subsequent chain of events in which alcoholic couples engage. One can speculate that cognitions that follow a marital conflict may be retaliatory, or involve expectations of improved negotiation or arguing skills after the ingestion of alcohol. Or, the alcoholic's cognitions may revolve more around thoughts of hopelessness about the possibility of resolving these problems, followed by thoughts of escaping the unpleasant interaction by drinking.

Marital consequences of drinking are quite varied, and may serve to strongly reinforce the drinking response. One or both members of the couple may markedly change their behavior after drinking, resulting in positive exchanges not present during nondrinking interactions [39]. The alcoholic member of the couple may increase his or her assertive or aggressive responses, which might reinforce the drinking [5]. Alcoholics also seem to increase their rate and amount of verbal output while drinking, which also may be reinforcing to them in a marital relationship in which their verbal output is typically low [3, 9]. However, some studies have not noted these improvements in the alcoholic's marital communications while drinking, but rather have noted a decrease in relevant communications while drinking [5], and an increase in spouse, rather than alcoholic communications, while drinking [5].

In conclusion, there is good evidence that alcoholic marriages are characterized by marked conflict. The drinking response to the conflict distinguishes these marriages from other troubled marriages. This response often is inadvertently reinforced, but may also actually cue further marital conflict, which would then cue further drinking. Thus, the social learning model of alcoholic marriages has some strong empirical support, and also provides a model for understanding the repetitiveness of interactions in these couples.

CURRENT ISSUES AND CONCLUSIONS

The preceding sections of the chapter discuss the incidence of marriage and marital dysfunction among alcoholics, and evaluate five major theoretical models of alcoholism and marriage. Several conclusions can be drawn from this review. First, it is apparent that alcoholics frequently marry, but that marital disharmony and disruption are strongly associated with alcohol problems. Alcoholism also is often associated with certain dysfunctional patterns in marriages, such as changes in role definitions, a variety of poor communication skills, and repetitive interactions, which inadvertently contribute to maintaining the alcoholic's drinking. The traditional view that the spouse of an alcoholic is seriously disturbed and needs to be married to an impaired mate is probably of limited value in understanding interactions of alcoholic couples. Recognizing the role shifts required by the stress that the couple is experiencing, and recognizing the subtle ways in which the current interactions are continued, are two major components of understanding alcoholic couples. In particular, recognizing the circular cueing and reinforcement relationship between drinking and marital problems helps the clinician to unlock that relationship, rather than perceiving it as representing the true needs of the couple.

Two "meta" issues in the field require attention. First, is the concept of an "alcoholic marriage" a viable one? Second, are alcoholic marriages unique entities that must be considered discontinuously from the rest of the psychological and sociological research on marriage?

It may be that the concept of the alcoholic marriage has outlived its usefulness. To date, the data do not find patterns of interaction that characterize all or even the largest majority of subjects in studies. Findings are hard to replicate and vary greatly with sample characteristics. This variability reflects a number of factors. Most importantly, looking for the alcoholic marriage suggests that alcohol problems and alcoholism are a unitary phenomenon. The behaviors that accompany drinking vary dramatically with such variables as age, sex, ethnic background, learning history about alcohol, social support systems, drinking systems, length of drinking, religion, physical health, consequences of drinking, and so forth. To assume that all people who experience problems with alcohol will experience similar forms of marital interaction is simply fatuous. To continue to build models that describe and explain these marriages as a unitary group is an exercise in futility.

Similarly, many studies using as controls nonalcoholic couples who are either maritally troubled or psychiatrically troubled have found few differences between the alcoholic and troubled controls. Orford [30] argues eloquently in this regard that alcohol-troubled couples cannot be considered separately from other troubled couples, and that much of the general research on marital variables must be applied to this population. For example, the literatures on families experiencing various forms of stress and the effects of this stress on family roles show similarities to findings on alcoholic family-role assignments and their reactions to stress. As described in the social learning section, these findings are not surprising, since the choice of response, drinking, is different than other responses, but the antecedents and dysfunctional communications may be similar across many types of distressed groups.

Of necessity, the arguments here are brief. However, the point is clear. Alcoholic marriages are not unique. To understand them, and to develop effective treatments, a model is needed that facilitates assessing the unique patterns that exist within an individual couple. Social learning theory and general systems theory both provide models that provide such flexibility by providing a framework for assessing marital patterns, without providing a preset explanation of what those patterns will be. Further refinements for developing sophisticated assessment and interventions based on these models are currently being developed (e.g., in the labs of Steinglass and McCrady), and these results should further contribute to the ability to understand individuals' alcoholic marriages, rather than the alcoholic marriage.

REFERENCES

1. Bailey, M. B. Al-Anon family groups as an aid to wives of alcoholics. *Social Work* 10: 68-74, 1965.
2. Bailey, M. B. Psychophysiological impairment in wives of alcoholics as related to their husbands' drinking and sobriety. In: *Alcoholism: Behavioral Research, Therapeutic Approaches.* Fox, R. (ed.). New York: Springer, 1967.
3. Billings, A. G., Kessler, M., Gomberg, C. A., and Wiener, S. Marital conflict resolution of alcoholic and nonalcoholic couples during drinking and nondrinking sessions. *J. Stud. Alcohol* 40:183-196, 1979.
4. Clifford, B. J. A study of the wives of rehabilitated and unrehabilitated alcoholics. *Soc. Casework* 41:457-460, 1960.
5. Cvitković, J. F. *Alcohol Use and Communication Congruence in Alcoholic and Nonalcoholic Marriages* (Doctoral dissertation, University of Pittsburgh, 1979). Abstracted in: *J. Stud. Alcohol* 40:49, 1979, abst. 168.
6. Djukanović, B., Milosavčević, V., and Jovanovi, R. [The social life of alcoholics and their wives.] *Alkoholizam*, 16:67-75, 1976. Abstracted in: *J. Stud. Alcohol* 39:1699, 1978, abst. 1144.
7. Drewery, J., and Rae, J. B. A group comparison of alcoholic and nonalcoholic marriages using the interpersonal perception technique. *Br. J. Med. Psychol.* 115:287-300, 1969.
8. Duhamel, T. R. The interpersonal perceptions, interaction and marital adjustment of hospitalized alcoholic males and their wives. *Disser. Abst. Int.* 10B:6254, 1971.
9. Foy, D. W., Miller, P. M., and Eisler, R. M. *The Effects of Alcohol Consumption on the Marital Interactions of Chronic Alcoholics.* Paper presented at the meeting of the Association for the Advancement of Behavior Therapy, San Francisco, 1975.
10. Goldfried, M. R., and Sprafkin, J. N. Behavioral personality assessment. In: *University Programs Modular Studies,* Spence, J. T., Carlson, R. C., and Thibaut, J. (eds.). General Learning Press: Morristown, N.J., 1974.
11. Gorad, S. L., McCourt, W. F., and Cobb, J. C. A communications approach to alcoholism. *Q. J. Stud. Alcohol* 32:651-668, 1971.
12. Gynther, M. D., and Brilliant, P. J. Marital status, readmission to hospital, and intra-

personal and interpersonal perceptions of alcoholics. *Q. J. Stud. Alcohol* 28:52-58, 1967.

13. Hore, B. D. Factors in alcoholic relapse. *Br. J. Addict.* 66:89-96, 1971.

14. Hore, B. D. Life events and alcoholic relapse. *Br. J. Addict.* 66:83-88, 1971.

15. Jackson, J. K. The adjustment of the family to the crisis of alcoholism. *Q. J. Stud. Alcohol* 15:562-586, 1954.

16. Jackson, J. K. The adjustment of the family to alcoholism. *Marr. Family* 18:361-369, 1956.

17. Jackson, J. K. Family structure and alcoholism. *Ment. Hyg.* 43:403-406, 1959.

18. Jackson, J. K. Alcoholism and the family. In: *Society, Culture and Drinking Patterns*, Pittman, D. J. and Snyder, C. R. (eds.). Wiley: New York, 1962.

19. Klein, R. M. *Interaction Processes in Alcoholic and Nonalcoholic Marital Dyads*. (Doctoral dissertation, Washington University, 1979). Abstracted in: *J. Stud. Alcohol* 40:49, 1979, abst. 169.

20. Kogan, K. L., Fordyce, W. E., and Jackson, J. K. Personality disturbance in wives of alcoholics. *Q. J. Stud. Alcohol* 24(2):227-238, 1963.

21. Kogan, K. L., and Jackson, J. K. Role perception in wives of alcoholics and nonalcoholics. *Q. J. Stud. Alcohol* 24:627-639, 1963.

22. Kogan, K. L., and Jackson, J. K. Personality adjustment and childhood experiences. *J. Health Hum. Behav.* 5:50-54, 1964.

23. Lanyon, R. I. *Psychological Screening Inventory Manual*. Research Psychologists Press: New York, 1973.

24. Lemert, E. M. The occurrence and sequence of events in the adjustment of families to alcoholism. *Q. J. Stud. Alcohol* 21:679-697, 1960.

25. Macdonald, D. E. Mental disorders in wives of alcoholics. *Q. J. Stud. Alcohol* 17: 282-287, 1956.

26. Marlatt, G. A., and Gordon, J. *Determinants of Relapse: Implications for the Maintenance of Behavior Change*. Paper presented at the 10th International Conference on Behavior Modification, Branff, Alberta, Canada, March 1978.

27. McCrady, B. S., and Wiener, J. *Verbal and Non-Verbal Marital Interactions in Male and Female Alcoholics*. Paper presented at the Annual Meeting of the Association for the Advancement of Behavior Therapy, Chicago, November 1979.

28. Mitchell, H. E. Interpersonal perception theory applied to conflicted marriage in which alcoholism is and is not a problem. *Am. J. Orthopsychiatry* 29:547-559, 1959.

29. Moos, R. H., Bromet, E., Tsu, V., and Moos, B. Family characteristics and the outcome of treatment for alcoholism. *J. Stud. Alcohol* 40:78-88, 1979.

30. Orford, J. Alcoholism and marriage: The argument against specialism. *J. Stud. Alcohol* 36:1537-1563, 1975.

31. Orford, J., Oppenheimer, E., Egert, S., and Hensman, C. The role of excessive drinking in alcoholism-complicated marriages: A study of stability and change over a one-year period. *Int. J. Addict.* 12:471-495, 1977.

32. Orford, J., Oppenheimer, E., Egert, S., Hensman, C., and Guthrie, S. The cohesiveness of alcoholism-complicated marriages and its influence on treatment outcome. *Br. J. Psychiatry* 128:318-339, 1976.

33. Paolino, T. J., Jr., and McCrady, B. S. *The Alcoholic Marriage: Alternative Perspectives*. Grune & Stratton: New York, 1977.

34. Paolino, T. J., Jr., McCrady, B. S., and Diamond, S. Statistics on alcoholic marriages: An overview. *Int. J. Addict.* 13:1285-1293, 1978.

35. Pattison, E. M., Courlas, P. G., Patti, R., Mann, B., and Mullen, D. Diagnostic-therapeutic intake groups for wives of alcoholics. *Q. J. Stud. Alcohol* 26:605-616, 1965.

36. Polich, J. M., Armor, D. J., and Braiker, H. B. *The Course of Alcoholism: Four Years after Treatment*. Rand: Santa Monica, 1980.

37. Sobell, M. B., Sobell, L. C., and Sheahan, D. B. Functional analysis of drinking problems as an aid in developing individual treatment strategies. *Addict. Behav.* 1:127–132, 1976.

38. Steinglass, P. The conceptualization of marriage from a systems theory perspective. In: *Marriage and Marital Therapy* Paolino, T. J., Jr. and McCrady, B. S. (eds.). Brunner/Mazel: New York, 1978.

39. Steinglass, P., Davis, D. I., and Berenson, D. *In-Hospital Treatment of Alcoholic Couples*. Paper presented at the American Psychiatric Association 128th Annual Meeting, Anaheim, California, May 1975.

54

ISMET KARACAN, M-D, DSc(Med), Baylor College of Medicine
TERRY L. HANUSA, MD, Loyola University of Chicago

THE EFFECTS OF ALCOHOL RELATIVE TO SEXUAL DYSFUNCTION

IN *MACBETH*, SHAKESPEARE made one of the first clinical observations on sexual dysfunction and alcohol: "[Drink] provokes the desire, but it takes away the performance." The current state of knowledge is vaguely reminiscent of Shakespeare's observations 350 years ago. Physicians as well as laymen recognize that alcohol affects sexual performance—that with low doses, both sexes display increased overt behavior, while with increasing doses, men become less easily aroused and progressively less potent—but systematic research to support and elaborate such observations has been meager. An important obstacle to objective investigation has been the taboo against discussing sexual dysfunction, even in the medical community. However, the advent of the sexual revolution has encouraged more and more men and women to seek professional help for their sexual problems. In a parallel trend, the recognition of alcohol as a prevalent yet treatable illness has fostered the development of therapeutic programs for alcoholics who would have encountered only harsh social disapproval and ostracism a few decades ago. Promising methodologi-

---

Ismet Karacan, MD, DSc(Med), Professor of Psychiatry and Director, Sleep Disorders and Research Center, Baylor College of Medicine, and Associate Chief of Staff for Research, Veterans Administration Hospital, Houston, Texas.
Terry L. Hanusa, MD, Loyola University of Chicago, Stritch School of Medicine, Chicago, Illinois.

cal advances for the more precise measurement of sexual arousal are enabling the more rigorous study of the effects of alcohol on the sexual response and functioning of both men and women. In a review of available studies of these effects, this chapter considers the role of such instruments as the mercury strain gauge and the photoplethysmograph, suggests an objective means of diagnosing and treating impotence in male alcoholics, and evaluates the current state of the art.

THEORIES OF ALCOHOL AND SEXUAL MECHANISM INTERACTION

Blood Alcohol Level, Anxiety, and Performance

Low blood levels of alcohol have been associated historically with increased sexual desire in both men and women. According to Ewing [3], sexual behavior increases because ethanol primarily affects the nostral portion of the cerebrum, the mediator of the self-controlling and self-critical faculties. Alcohol relaxes these anxiety- or self-awareness–reducing functions of the brain and produces a sense of euphoria. Therefore, following alcohol ingestion in a social situation, sexual aggression by either sex can seem less threatening. At higher blood alcohol levels (BALs) having too much to drink can account for inadequate sexual performance. The implications are that at a low BAL, a reduction in guilt may lead to increased promiscuity, whereas at a higher BAL, the desire might be present, but diminished physiologic abilities impede performance.

Psychoanalytic View of Alcoholism

Abraham [1] proposes the psychoanalytic view that alcoholic behavior is secondary to homosexual traits. According to this theory, drinking is a means of dealing with repressed homosexual conflicts. At times, the disinhibitory effect of alcohol allows overt homosexual encounters to occur, but strong heterosexual socialization usually prohibits such encounters.

Biological Effects

Alcohol has measurable neurological, endocrinological, and biochemical effects on both men and women. A central nervous system (CNS) depressant, ethanol primarily acts on the reticular activating system [4]. Peripheral neuropathy secondary to alcoholism can disrupt the autonomic peripheral nerves, which regulate muscle control and relaxation as well as vascular functions. Pathological conditions of these nerves may lead to impotence in men and orgasmic dysfunction secondary to decreased sensory input in women. Endocrinological effects of ethanol on sexual functioning include gynecomastia and testicular atrophy in a higher percentage of alcoholics than in the general population; sometimes increased levels of prolactin and estrogen, which some but not all researchers associate with decreased libido [8]; and an increased incidence of diabetes mellitus leading to peripheral neuropathy. Biochemical effects on male alcoholics include difficulty obtaining and/or maintaining erections associated with disulfiram (Antabuse) use. Alcohol has also been reported to slow the motility of, and produce structural changes in, sperm cells of young men [15] and disturb the reproductive system in female alcoholics [17].

Environmental versus Physiological Effects and Alcohol Use

Concerning sexual behavior, there is considerable controversy as to which factors are more salient—the known physiological effects of alcohol or the acting out of sociopsychological characteristics given the right opportunity. Although even low BALs have been shown to influence sexual arousal, other studies have demonstrated that merely drinking nonalcoholic beverages believed to contain alcohol will significantly affect sexual behavior [19]. Is the alcohol itself an etiologic factor or merely a cue, a learned behavior, for sexual legitimacy? The popular conclusion is that both kinds of factors interact to produce variations in sexual behavior. For example, an anxiety-reducing or disinhibitory effect of alcohol might under certain circumstances compensate for its pharmacologically depressant impact on sexual arousal.

LIMITATIONS OF LABORATORY RESEARCH

Ethical considerations, which prohibit creating realistic human models of sexuality in the laboratory setting, have limited systematic research of associations between alcohol and sexual dysfunction. Therefore, despite evidence that naturally occurring sexual behavior is a complex function of physiological and sociopsychological factors, most studies rely on either subjective reports of past experiences or the use of sophisticated, artificial devices that measure physiological arousal. The former lack an objective index of physiological arousal, compromising internal validity, while the latter have not been established to represent all relevant parameters of naturally occurring sexual behavior, compromising external validity. Nevertheless, the use for the past 18 years of the mercury strain gauge transducer to measure nocturnal penile tumescence, and the more recent application of the vaginal photoplethysmograph to measure vaginal blood flow have yielded more objective results than previous subjective methods. The gauge detects the penile circumference changes that accompany erections, while the photoplethysmograph detects vaginal pulse pressure as an indicator of sexual excitement. The physiological and psychosocial effects of alcohol on sexuality in men and women are examined separately herein because of vast differences in their levels of methodological progress.

ALCOHOL AND SEXUAL DYSFUNCTION IN WOMEN

Sexual Response Correlated with Alcohol

Research in female sexual dysfunction has been severely limited until recently, when the development of the vaginal photoplethysmograph provided an objective measure of sexual inadequacy. In 1976, Wilson and Lawson [18] used this instrument to study sexual arousal, as reflected by increased vaginal pressure, in 16 female student social drinkers who denied having any medical or psychiatric disorders. Four levels of alcohol were administered and electromyogram (EMG) monitoring of muscle tension levels from the subject's forehead was undertaken as a supplementary measure of sexual arousal. Their data demonstrated a negative linear relationship between increased amounts of alcohol and vaginal pulse pressure. However, the psychosocial measures did not support the physiological data; neither the subjects' self-reports nor the Thematic Apperception Test showed a correlation between alcohol levels and sexual excitement.

Sexual Differences between Alcoholics and Nonalcoholics

Since sexual dysfunction is likely to be more pronounced in alcoholics than in social drinkers, other studies have compared sexual parameters in female alcoholics and nonalcoholics.

Reproductive disturbances. There is evidence that alcoholism disturbs the female reproductive system [17]. Of married or formerly married female alcoholics, 75% reported obstetrical or gynecological problems compared to 33% of married controls. Moreover, the onset of binge drinking has been correlated with a variety of reproductive abnormalities or normal changes such as menopause.

Sexual attitudes and behavior. Female alcoholics are typically considered sexually inadequate or promiscuous. Case reports indicate that they have few heterosexual encounters and little desire for such encounters. In Levine's study [9] of 16 female alcoholics, eight engaged in no heterosexual relations, five were promiscuous, and all denied orgasm. Sexual arousal was difficult when these women were not drinking, but when intoxicated, the promiscuous women were more likely to engage in intercourse than when sober.

Levine also observed the female alcoholics to be hostile toward, or frightened by, men. These attitudes often lead female alcoholics to seek homosexual encounters. In Beckman's comparison [2] of the effects of drinking on the sexual enjoyment and practices of female alcoholics and nonalcoholics, a higher percentage of alcoholics admitted to having homosexual relationships.

Beckman [2] further reported that while drinking, alcoholics were more likely to enjoy and engage in sexual intercourse as well as perform a wider range of sexual acts with a greater variety of partners than matched normal controls. The female alcoholics claimed to be less satisfied sexually than both alcoholic men and nonalcoholic women.

ALCOHOL AND SEXUAL DYSFUNCTION IN MEN

Effects on Sexual Performance

The complex interaction between physiological factors and learning in the development of sexual dysfunctions is better understood in men than in women, possibly because sexual functioning is more likely to be globally than selectively disturbed. Acute ingestion of large amounts of alcohol (a high BAL) or chronic abuse of alcohol can result in impotence (inhibited sexual excitement), defined by the American Psychiatric Association (APA) as the partial or complete failure to attain or maintain erection until completion of the sexual act. Whalley [16] found that 54% of 50 hospitalized alcoholics, compared to 28% of matched controls, reported erectile impotence. According to Masters and Johnson [10], "The second most frequent factor in the onset of secondary impotence [full erection was possible in the past] can be directly related to a specific incidence of acute ingestion of alcohol or to a pattern of excessive alcohol intake per se." Even one incident of alcohol-associated impotence can snowball into a habitual pattern in which impaired arousal becomes a learned response to drinking. This psychological impotence may also be exacerbated by organic involvement; however, if alcohol ingestion becomes chronic enough to irreparably damage certain neurological, endocrinological, and vascular functions. The mercury strain gauge has been used not only to measure the effects of alcohol on sexual arousal, but also to distinguish primarily organogenic from psychogenic impotence [6] in male alcohol abusers.

Blood alcohol level and impotence. Several researchers have used the mercury strain gauge to measure sexual response to highly arousing, explicit, erotic stimuli (e.g., films) under conditions of low, moderate, and high levels of alcohol intake. Rubin and Henson [13] studied 16 adult nonalcoholics, while Wilson et al. [20] monitored otherwise-healthy alcoholics. Findings in both populations corroborate clinical reports of alcohol-induced secondary impotence; large doses of alcohol generally depressed penile tumescence and rate of erection. Wilson et al. [20] found that most decremental effects of alcohol on tumescence occur in BALs beyond 40–50 mg/100 ml, but Rubin and Henson [13] noted that some erectile capacity — from 20% of maximum capacity to full erection — may remain even at levels as high as 106 to 156 mg/100 ml (100 mg/100 ml is a common legal intoxication level).

The results of both studies also dispell the popular belief that low to moderate levels of alcohol significantly increase sexual arousal. Rubin and Henson [13] found low to moderate amounts to have little or no effect on elicicted arousal in most subjects. However, when the lower levels did show an effect, mean erection was significantly decreased and suppression was not uniform across all parameters. Peak erection and latency to a criterion level of tumescence were only slightly affected, suggesting that lower BALs primarily affect maintenance of tumescence rather than degree of maximum erection or speed of arousal progression.

These studies support clinical findings that decremental effects of alcohol on sexual arousal in men may be selective rather than total unless alcoholism has continued long enough to produce impotence-relevant organic dysfunctions or chronic impotence has become a learned response to drinking.

Improved sexual performance. There have been some subjective reports of alcohol improving male sexual performance. Claims that alcohol use or abuse heightens sexual excitement may reflect an increase in the sensory threshold, prolonging erection so that the partner's probability of orgasm is enhanced [13]. In a study of 200 alcoholic men [3], alcohol intake relieved premature ejaculation in 23 of the 26 men suffering from this dysfunction. Unlike erectile impotence, however, neither premature ejaculation (recurrent absence of reasonable voluntary control of ejaculation) nor ejaculatory impotence (inability to ejaculate after a sufficient period of intercourse), are considered alcohol-related dysfunctions; in Whalley's study [16], the frequency of these two disorders was similar in alcoholics and matched controls.

SEXUAL ATTITUDES AND PSYCHOSOCIAL CHARACTERISTICS OF MALE ALCOHOLICS

Marriage and Sexual Satisfaction

In his comparative survey of the attitudes of 50 hospitalized alcoholic men and a matched group of nonalcoholic men, Whalley [16] discovered that the alcoholics lost their virginity at an earlier age and married at about the same age, but tended to choose a slightly older woman. More alcoholics believed their wives had been unfaithful and their marriages more often ended in separation. The alcoholics also felt less sexually satisfied overall than the nonalcoholics, which Whalley [16] attributed to their greater preferred frequency of sexual intercourse, reduced opportunities for intercourse, and possibly, more frequent erectile impotence.

Sexual Crime and Drinking

McClelland et al. [11]. proposed that recognition of his sexual assertiveness may be more important to the young alcoholic than sexual arousal, implying an association between drinking and a need for sexual power. This suggestion is compatible with Rada et al.'s findings [12] of a positive correlation between alcoholism and forcible rape, an act of violence often attributed to a need to demonstrate power over an unwilling and uncooperative victim. Approximately 50% of 77 convicted rapists were drinking when they committed the rape and over 33% of this group were alcoholics. Furthermore, the drinking rapists whose acts were classified as the most violent had significantly higher mean plasma testosterone levels than either other rapists or normal controls and alcoholic rapists had significantly higher plasma testosterone levels than the nonalcoholic rapists. These results are particularly interesting considering contradictory claims that testosterone levels are often decreased in alcoholics following alcohol ingestion. This study illustrates well the difficulty in separating psychological factors from physiological factors to determine the most salient cause of a particular alcohol-associated sexual disorder.

DIAGNOSIS AND TREATMENT OF ALCOHOL-ASSOCIATED IMPOTENCE

Alcohol Abuse and Nocturnal Penile Tumescence

Over the past 18 years, an objective diagnostic procedure has been developed — nocturnal penile tumescence (NPT) monitoring — for determining whether impotence is organogenic, psychogenic, or of mixed etiology. The clinical experience of Karacan and co-workers also supports Masters and Johnson's identification [10] of a wide range of organic disorders that often lead to impotence, including alcoholism. In a recent preliminary study [7] of alcohol abusers who presented at the Baylor Sleep Disorders and Research Center for treatment of impotence, 50% of them had clearly abnormal NPT, suggesting some degree of organic erectile impairment. It was concluded that chronic alcohol abuse may damage the physiological erectile mechanisms that normally allow maximum engorgement of the penis, although sufficient data to indicate whether the defects are primarily neural, vascular, or hormonal are not yet available. It is believed that such damage may account for impotence in at least half of alcoholics who present with this complaint.

Evaluation Procedure

A comprehensive clinical workup, including both physical examinations and psychological tests, is particularly critical considering (1) the evidence that NPT is more likely to be partially than totally impaired in alcoholism than in other organic disorders, such as diabetes mellitus [5], implicating impotence of mixed etiology; and (2) the numerous psychological associations between alcohol and sexual functioning held by the general public. Therefore, it is recommended that physicians refer all alcoholic patients complaining of impotence to a sleep disorders center for three consecutive nights of NPT monitoring and the supplementary examinations, including (1) a complete medical history; (2) careful examination of the external genitalia for structural defects; (3) measurement of penile arterial pressure, pulse volume, and temperature; (4) tests of autonomic nervous system function and bulbocavernosus-ischiocavernosus muscle activity; (5) hormone assays and drug screens; (6) psychiatric interviews and a better of psychological tests. Beyond the scope of this chapter, a detailed explanation of the NPT and other procedures is available elsewhere [6].

Differential Diagnosis and Treatment

Generally, NPT that is absent or significantly diminished compared to the normative data for the patient's age group designates a high probability of organic involvement. The psychological evaluation, which identifies mental deficiencies, emotional instability, and performance anxiety as positive indicators of psychological involvement, is designed for differential diagnosis independent of the NPT evaluation. The urologist collates the various examination results from the other evaluation team members and recommends a course of treatment. Depending on the final diagnosis, treatment may consist of, for example, implantation of an inflatable, penile prosthesis [14] or referral for behavioral or other appropriate sex therapy.

CONCLUSION

Any form of alcohol use or abuse can lead to a variety of sexual dysfunctions in men and women. Alcohol consumption certainly increases the frequency of these dysfunctions. However, no direct cause and effect relationship between the physiological effects of alcohol and sexual functioning can be drawn because the interaction between subjective personality and environmental factors influences physiological effects. Therefore, therapy for the sexually disturbed alcoholic is necessarily more complex than merely treating the sexual dysfunction. Although important diagnostic and treatment procedures have been developed, these modalities are still in their infancy.

REFERENCES

1. Abraham, K. The psychological relations between sexuality and alcoholism. *Int. J. Psychoanal.* 7:2-10, 1926.
2. Beckman, L. J. Reported effects of alcohol on the sexual feelings and behavior of women alcoholics and non-alcoholics. *J. Stud. Alcohol* 40:272-282, 1979.
3. Ewing, J. A. Alcohol, sex, and marriage. *Med. Aspects Hum. Sex.* 2:43-50, 1968.
4. Farkas, G. M., and Rosen, R. C. Effects of alcohol on elicited male sexual response. *J. Stud. Alcohol* 37:265-272, 1976.
5. Karacan, I., Salis, P. J., Ware, J. C., Dervent, B., Williams, R. L., Scott, F. B., Attia, S. L., and Beutler, L. E. Nocturnal penile tumescence and diagnosis in diabetic impotence. *Am. J. Psychiatry* 135:191-197, 1978.
6. Karacan, I., Salis, P. J., and Williams, R. L. The role of the sleep laboratory in the diagnosis and treatment of impotence. In: *Sleep Disorders: Diagnosis and Treatment*, Williams, R. L. and Karacan, I. (eds.). Wiley: New York, 1987.
7. Karacan, I., Snyder, S., Salis, P. J., Williams, R. L., and Derman, S. Sexual dysfunction in male alcoholics and its objective evaluation. In: *Phenomenology and Treatment of Alcoholism*, Fann, W. E., Karacan, I., Pokorny, A. P., and Williams, R. L. (eds.). Spectrum: New York, 1980.
8. Lemere, F., and Smith, J. W. Alcohol-induced sexual impotence. *Am. J. Psychiatry* 130:212-213, 1973.
9. Levine, J. The sexual adjustment of alcoholics: A clinical study of a selected sample. *Q. J. Stud. Alcohol* 16:675-680, 1955.
10. Masters, W. H., and Johnson, V. E. *Human Sexual Inadequacy*. Little, Brown: Boston, 1970.
11. McClelland, D. C., Davis, W. N., Kalin, R., and Wanner, E. *The Drinking Man*. Free Press: New York, 1972.
12. Rada, R. T., Laws, R. T., and Kellner, R. Plasma testosterone levels. *Psychosom. Med.* 38:257-268, 1976.
13. Rubin, H. B., and Henson, D. E. Effects of alcohol on male sexual responding. *Psychopharmacol.* 47:123-134, 1976.
14. Scott, B. F., Byrd, G. J., Karacan, I., Olsson, P., Beutler, L. E., and Attia, S. L. Erectile impotence treated with an implantable, inflatable prosthesis: Five years of clinical experience. *J.A.M.A.* 241:2609-2612, 1979.
15. Wallgren, H., and Barry, H. *Actions of Alcohol* (Vol. 1). Elsevier: Amsterdam, 1970.
16. Whalley, L. J. Sexual adjustment of male alcoholics. *Acta Psychiatr. Scand.* 58:281-298, 1978.
17. Wilsnack, S. C. Sex role identity in female alcoholism. *J. Abnorm. Psychol.* 82:253-261, 1973.

18. Wilson, G. T., and Lawson, D. M. Effects of alcohol on sexual arousal in women. *J. Abnorm. Psychol.* 85:489–497, 1976.

19. Wilson, G. T., and Lawson, D. M. Expectancies, alcohol and sexual arousal in women. *J. Abnorm. Psychol.* 87:358–367, 1978.

20. Wilson, G. T., Lawson, D. M., and Abrams, D. B. Effects of alcohol on sexual arousal in male alcoholics. *J. Abnorm. Psychol.* 87:609–616, 1978.

55

EDWARD KAUFMAN, MD, University of California, Irvine Medical Center, Orange, California

ALCOHOLISM AND THE USE OF OTHER DRUGS

THE USE AND ABUSE OF and dependence on other drugs by alcoholics is not a new phenomenon, nor is the similar abuse of and dependence on alcohol by drug misusers. However, increased utilization of combinations of alcohol and drugs was one of the outstanding social occurrences of the 1970s [25] and is continuing through the present decade.

This chapter examines four different aspects of this problem: (1) the abuse of drugs by alcoholics and problem drinkers; (2) the abuse of alcohol by drug abusers and dependents; (3) polydrug abuse that includes alcohol; (4) alcohol as a steppingstone to other drugs. The chapter concludes with a section on treatment implications when alcohol problems are complicated by those of other drugs.

EXTENT OF THE PROBLEM

The Abuse of Drugs by Alcoholics and Problem Drinkers

There are many factors that make the use of drugs by alcohol misusers of great concern. The obvious hazards of such combined abuse include overdose, coma, and death. The additive and synergistic effects of alcohol and sedative drugs also

---

Edward Kaufman, MD, Associate Professor in Residence, Department of Psychiatry and Human Behavior, University of California, Irvine Medical Center, Orange, California.

lead to traffic deaths and other accidents, as well as homicide and other crimes of violence [9].

In an excellent review of the literature from 1925 to 1972, Freed [17] noted that the percentage of drug abuse by alcoholics ranged from 5 to 52% and concluded that at least 20% of alcoholics used at least one other drug prone to dependence. As evidence of a recent increase in drug use by alcoholics, Rosenberger [32] noted that younger alcoholics tend to abuse multiple drugs (52%) much more frequently than older alcoholics (16%). Ashley et al. [3] also noted the greater use of drugs by alcoholics under 40 (more than one in three) as compared to those over 40 (less than one in five).

The media in the late 1970s described that the youth of America were giving up drugs and switching back to alcohol. Schnoll's [34] synthesis of the literature emphasized that this is not the case, but that what has occurred is an ever-increasing use of both alcohol and other drugs.

Another consistent trend is that illicit drug abuse is much higher in alcohol users who drank heavily than in light drinkers [39] (e.g., amphetamines, 20% vs. 0%; barbiturates, 18% vs. 2%; marijuana, 51% vs. 5%). There is also considerably higher use of drugs by incarcerated criminal alcoholics [9].

In a study of National Institute on Alcohol Abuse and Alcoholism-funded alcoholism treatment programs in 1975 [38], it was noted that 30 to 60% of all clients were using drugs in addition to alcohol at the time of admission, and about half of these were abusing these drugs. Most of these drugs were obtained by prescription from private physicians. This study also confirmed that the phenomenon was more common in those under age 30.

Personal reports by alcoholics tend to underreport drug use. However, when the urines of alcoholic inpatients are routinely monitored for drugs, the incidence of drug use is much higher (e.g., 38% by urinalysis as compared to 9% self-reporting), as determined by Chelton and Whisnant [10]. Dependence on drugs by alcoholics is obviously lower than use and in several studies cited by Carroll et al. [9], dependency ranged from 5 to 10%.

Since amphetamines cause an opposite neurophysiological response than alcohol, it would be expected that these drugs would be less frequently used by alcoholics than sedatives. Carroll et al. [9] found in several studies that the use of amphetamines by alcoholics ranged from 1 to 4%. Kipperman and Fine [26] found that alcoholics used amphetamines to help maintain a wakeful state so that they could consume additional alcohol. Alcoholics may use amphetamines to attempt to counteract impairment of psychomotor skills. However, this interaction is complicated, and the combination may frequently cause a decrease in performance [11]. In addition, combinations of alcohol and amphetamines may cause increased overactivity and excitability [11].

Women alcoholics, as separate from men, have not been studied with respect to drug abuse until quite recently. Corrigan [12] noted that 82% of women alcoholics have used other drugs in addition to alcohol. About half used other drugs while drinking. Of these, 42% used tranquilizers or sedatives, 24% sleeping pills, and 15% stimulants [12]. As with men, those who drank heavily and those under 30 ran a considerably higher risk of combining other drugs with alcohol.

Alcoholics are prone to substitute narcotics for alcohol when the former are readily available. Many alcoholics readily become dependent on codeine when prescribed by physicians in the same way that they do on sedatives and tranquilizers. In a study of 451 United States Army enlisted men after their return from Vietnam, Goodwin et al. [21] noted that prior to enlistment, nearly 50% were regular drinkers, 25% had drinking problems, and 4% were alcoholics. Problem drinking declined in Vietman (75% decreased their drinking) as opiate use rose (50% tried opiates and 20% were opiate dependent). After Vietnam, opiate use decreased (less than 2% were opiate dependent) and problem drinking again became ascendant as nearly 33% had drinking problems and 8% were alcoholic.

The abuse of drugs by alcoholics is quite variable according to age, ethnosocial variables, and availability. In the late 1960s, barbiturate abuse in alcoholics was common in the United States and Canada. In a study of 893 alcoholics in Toronto, 129 (15%) were also drug abusers, 89 (70%) of the latter group abusing barbiturates [16]. In Australia, where bromureides were freely available over-the-counter preparations in the 1960s, use of and dependence on these drugs were quite common [41]. A study of 1,006 patients attending an Australian alcoholism clinic showed that 87 were dependent on bromureides, 84 patients simultaneously misused alcohol, and three (who had stopped drinking) were consuming excessive amounts of bromureides instead of alcohol [41]. Mandrax (methaqualone and diphenhydramine) was abused in combination with alcohol in England in the 1960s and early 1970s [2]. This phenomenon of combining alcohol and methaqualone was also noted in America in the early 1970s by Inaba [23].

Wesson et al. [40] in their national study noted that approximately 11% of those individuals presenting for treatment at agencies specializing in alcoholism also had concomitant and significant amounts of nonopiate drug abuse. Ashley et al. [3] divided over 1,000 alcoholics in Toronto into two groups of 773 mixed (abnormal and excessive use of drugs) and 228 pure alcoholics, whose use of prescribed drugs did not reach excessive levels. Of pure alcoholics, 27% used tranquilizers and 8.9% barbiturates. Few used opiates (1.6%), other hypnotic sedatives (3.0%), amphetamines (1.0%), or antidepressants (2.3%). Mixed alcoholics normally used these drugs similarly: tranquilizers (16.2%), antidepressants (4.4%), barbiturates (4.0%), other hypnotic sedatives (3.1%), and opiates (2.2%). The pattern of abnormal use by the mixed group was different. Barbiturates were used abnormally by 60.5%, tranquilizers by 45.2%, opiates by 17.5%, amphetamines by 11.0%, other hypnotic sedatives by 8.3%, and antidepressants by 2.6%. This study implies that although abuse of prescription drugs is rampant in alcoholics, the majority can use these drugs "normally" without abusing them. This is in contrast to the author's own experience, which is that dependence-prone drugs of any kind cannot be prescribed for alcoholics in an outpatient setting without a high risk of abuse and dependency.

Even when alcoholics use these drugs at prescribed levels, this use may be highly problematic when the alcoholic is still drinking. The effects of alcohol and sedative drugs are either additive or synergistic. Thus many dangerous and devastating effects of alcohol are intensified by normal or prescribed use of these drugs. Such combinations lead to combined dependencies, more serious and difficult to treat withdrawal syndromes, increased overdoses, and traffic accidents. The popularities of alcohol and diazepam use lead to frequent unintentioned as well as to purposive combined use. Awareness of the problems of combinations of alcohol and drugs led the California Medical Association and Board of Medical Quality Assurance in January 1981 to issue a policy that stimulants, methaqualone, and schedule II barbiturates are not appropriate for patients with a history of alcoholism.

One of the unrecognized aspects of the problems of combining diazepam and alcohol was pointed out in a study by Bo et al. [8]. Of auto drivers who had been hospitalized following accidents 74 were compared with a control group who had not had an accident. Of those hospitalized, 41.8% retained alcohol in their blood, as did 1.5% of controls. Of injured drivers, 9.5% had diazepam in their blood as compared with 2.0% in the control group. Of the accident group, 10.8% had consumed both alcohol and diazepam as compared to none of the control group.

The Abuse of Alcohol by Drug Abusers and Dependents

Heroin addicts. Over the past decade there has been an increase in the use of alcohol by heroin addicts. The phenomenon itself is by no means a new one and the quantitative increase in alcohol use may simply be a direct result of the decreasing purity of available heroin. As increasingly pure heroin has returned to the street marketplace in certain locales, the increase in use of alcohol has leveled off, if not decreased.

The increasing tendency of many heroin addicts, particularly those who abuse multiple drugs, to abuse alcohol was noted by Richman [30]. Although alcohol and opiates do not potentiate each other, the combination is a frequent cause of death [11], as they do have an additive effect. In a group of narcotic-using decedents examined in New York City, more than 40% of those tested for blood or brain alcohol were positive. Half of these had blood alcohol levels (BALs) of over .10 [4]. The only factor differentiating a group of dead narcotic addicts from a control group was heavy alcohol use [4]. In support of indications of increasing alcohol use by narcotic addicts, Baden and Haberman [4] noted that narcotism plus alcoholism was the cause of death in 10% of narcotic-related deaths in the 1950s and had risen to 20% in 1972.

In Orange County, California in 1976, heroin and alcohol accounted for 40% of narcotic deaths and heroin plus drugs another 12%. Barr and Cohen [5] found the prevalence of drinkers who consumed large amounts among drug addicts to be 50.3%.

Methadone maintenance patients. One aspect of drinking by heroin addicts, which has been studied in depth, is drinking by these addicts when they participate in methadone maintenance treatment. Gearing [18] noted that 11% of such patients abuse alcohol. Kreek [27], however, estimates that 12% of methadone patients consume more than 12 oz of alcohol daily and 13% consume 4 to 12 oz daily. Gelb et al. [20], in a study of 101 methadone maintenance patients (MMPs) found that 12% consumed 3 oz or more of alcohol a day.

At LaLlave Methadone Maintenance Program in New Mexico [36], only 5% of patients had alcoholism on admission, whereas 25% of retained patients were alcoholic after 15 months and 34% after 4 years. At the Addiction Research and Treatment Corporation Methadone Maintenance Treatment Program (MMTP) in New York City [6], 32% of patients had evidence of alcohol intake by Breathalyzer, and an additional 15% refused testing. Curtis and Mike [15] found that 15 (8%) of 189 MMP had alcohol abuse without drug abuse, 61 (32%) drug abuse without alcohol abuse, and 22 (12%) both drug and alcohol abuse. Kreek [28] noted that 20% of long-term MMPs had chronic alcohol abuse prior to treatment but that after 3 or more years of chronic treatment an additional 5%, or 25% in all, were alcohol abusers. Stimmel et al. [37] noted that prevalence of alcohol abuse in MMPs varied from 10 to 40%, with some investigators noting that alcohol abuse increases by 100% after initiating a methadone maintenance program. Barr [5] found that 13.7% of 586 MMPs had high alcohol consumption and numerous problems from alcohol. However, 16.6% had high consumption with few or no problems. Alcohol abuse by MMPs is a major factor in contributing to the high incidence of liver damage in these patients [7, 20].

Gelb et al. [19] determined that in 68% of alcohol-abusing MMPs, regular alcohol abuse preceded narcotic use. Alcohol abuse began after entering a MMTP in 29% of alcohol-abusing MMPs. Gearing, in a study cited by Barr and Cohen [5], noted that previously reported alcohol problems tended to disappear in patients who remained on methadone maintenance for 4 or more years.

Thus there is no doubt that alcoholism is a serious problem among MMPs, particularly those who stay in treatment for several years and do not sustain meaningful intrapsychic as well as social and vocational changes. Much of the alcoholism that occurs existed prior to the MMTP, either preceding or concurrent with heroin dependence. However, when the basic adaption of a MMP does not change, then such individuals constantly seek alcohol and other drugs to achieve the euphoria, obliteration, or relaxation they experienced on heroin.

Alcoholism is such an integral part of the life cycle of heroin dependence that one must consider that some MMPs who become newly dependent on alcohol while on maintenance treatment would have become alcoholic even if they did not receive such treatment. Croughan et al. [13] studied a group of 200 narcotic addicts upon admission to the Clinical Research Center in Lexington, Kentucky and reinterviewed them 5 years later. They found that the proportion of subjects positive for alcoholism increased between two- and three-fold during the 5-year follow-up period.

The Polydrug Abuser

The term "polydrug" was introduced in the 1970s to describe the phenomenon of multiple abuse and dependence on a combination of drugs and alcohol [25]. As defined by the National Institute of Drug Abuse for funding purposes, the term came to mean drug abuse wherein the primary drug problem was not heroin, methadone, or alcohol. However, when Wesson et al. [40] studied polydrug abuse treatment programs in America, they found that the modal polydrug abuse pattern was that of an individual who uses nonopiates, alcohol, and narcotic drugs in various combinations. They found that of clients with substance abuse problems in traditional treatment agencies, the following percentages were polydrug abusers: alcohol treatment agencies, 13%; mixed substance abuse agencies, 40%; and mental health agencies, 71%. Alcohol use combined with nonopiate abuse constitutes 11% of alcohol treatment program intakes. Across their entire sample, alcohol and/or nonopiate abusers accounted for 21% of mixed-substance agency intakes.

The National Youth Polydrug Study [33] noted that alcohol was second only to marijuana as the substance most regularly used by youth in treatment for polydrug abuse (79.8% vs. 85.9%). However, weekly users of both marijuana and alcohol report having used an average of slightly more than three other substances on a regular weekly basis. Interestingly, regular users of marijuana and alcohol used fewer additional substances than the regular users of other types of drugs [33].

Other situations where polydrug abuse has been uncovered without clearly existing primary drug or alcohol problems is in hospital emergency rooms and psychiatric inpatient settings. Crowley et al. [14] found that over 33% of adults in a psychiatric hospital had drug and/or alcohol problems. They found that recent alcohol use was associated with the use of cocaine, sedative-hypnotics, and antianxiety drugs. Conversely, they also found that those who used antianxiety drugs heavily also used alcohol excessively. This is not a new problem. In 1941, Moore et al. [29] noted that among 475 patients first admitted to a mental hospital for drug psychosis, 38% were alcoholics or problem drinkers. Among 136 readmissions from the same group, 65% were alcoholics or problem drinkers. Among psychiatric inpatients in Sweden [1], excessive alcohol dependence was found in 24% of all patients, exclusive sedative-hypnotic dependence in 3%, and a combined alcohol-sedative dependence in 9%. All patients admitted to Toronto Hospital outpatient departments for drug misuse and overdose were studied over a 6-month period (24). Of 3,548 such patients, 1,125, or 31.7%, used alcohol in addition to one or more other drugs (usually benzodiazepines or barbiturates).

Alcohol as a Steppingstone to Other Drugs

The steppingstone hypothesis was controversially presented as a primary danger of marijuana in that it led to use of hard drugs, particularly heroin. A major refutation of this theory has been that alcohol is a more common precursor (and therefore steppingstone) to heroin dependence. Schut et al. [35] showed that 97 of 100 heroin addicts reported using alcohol prior to drugs. Rosen [31] similarly reported that alcohol was the first substance abused by 89% of 183 subjects. Greene [22], in a survey of 1,544 subjects, found that 94% of the regular users of heroin were at some point in time regular users of alcohol. He found that 72% of regular users of heroin first used alcohol on a regular basis. Greene's [22] study also noted that 65% of marijuana abusers also first used alcohol on a regular basis. It is proposed herein, however, that neither alcohol nor marijuana are truly steppingstones in that they seduce a nonpredisposed individual down the path to hard drugs. Rather, they are both very commonly used in society and are used and abused more frequently by those who eventually go on to hard drugs.

TREATMENT IMPLICATIONS

A major conclusion that must be drawn is that alcoholism is frequently complicated by abuse of and dependence on other substances. Thus, in every stage of the treatment of alcoholism, one must be aware of the strong possibility that other substances will be involved, either preceding, concomitant with, or following the alcoholism. Therefore, therapists must take detailed histories of specific drugs of abuse at intake. Concomitant drug abuse is a very important factor in detoxification programs for alcoholics. Pure alcoholics can be detoxified in 3 to 5 days. However, when long-acting sedative-hypnotics and minor tranquilizers complicate the picture, detoxification has to deal with a two-phase withdrawal process and may take up to several weeks.

The treatment of drug-abusing alcoholics requires knowledge of the pharmacology of these drugs as well as of the varying personality structures and coping mechanisms of such clients. The utilization of recovering pure alcoholics as therapists in alcohol rehabilitation programs is widespread and effective in dealing with similar alcoholics. However, such alcoholics may miss the mark in dealing with alcoholics with widespread drug abuse. This is more the case when that drug abuse is related to the illicit drug market and other aspects of the street scene. When dealing with these mixed populations, it is necessary to add to Alcoholics Anonymous such programs as Narcotics Anonymous and Pill Heads Anonymous. It is also quite helpful to employ recovering drug abusers who can identify with such patients as well as specifically confront their defenses.

Alcoholics who abuse multiple drugs tend to be sicker psychologically than those who do not [25]. Some of the alcoholics in this group are those with massive, overwhelming anxiety who desperately seek any substance to relieve their anxiety. Such patients may have self-medicating borderline syndromes or overt psychosis with alcohol and drugs and may need appropriate antipsychotic medication. Likewise, problem-drinking drug abusers are more deeply disturbed than those who do not drink [5]. This mixed drug and alcohol population has a higher incidence of depression and suicide, and these factors must be evaluated [5]. Antidepressant medications should be considered in this group [4], but they may be abused, particularly the sedating tricyclics.

In addition, whether the client is a drug-abusing alcoholic or a problem-drinking drug abuser, the prognosis is much poorer than with pure alcoholism or drug abuse. Therefore, programs that deal with such clients will require a more flexible approach, higher staff-client ratios, and more professional staffing. Such patients will also require longer stays in each programmatic phase, including hospitalization for detoxification, residential programming, halfway house participation and aftercare.

The mixed alcohol and drug-dependent patient is still another example of the need for an individualized treatment program. These programs must be geared to the unique needs of each client rather than putting all alcoholics into one group and attempting to sell them and the community that any single approach is the answer.

REFERENCES

1. Allgulander, C., and Borg, S. Sedative-hypnotic and alcohol dependence among psychiatric inpatients. *Br. J. Addict.* 73:123–125, 1978.
2. Any questions? *Br. Med. J.* 2:45, 1973.
3. Ashley, M. J., le Riche, W., Olin, J. S. et al. Mixed drug-abusing and pure alcoholics: A socio-medical comparison. *Br. J. Addict.* 73:19–34, 1978.
4. Baden, M. M., and Haberman, P. W. Drinking, drugs and death. *Int. J. Addict.* 9(6):761–775, 1974.
5. Barr, H. L., and Cohen, A. The problem drinking drug addict. In: *National Drug/Alcohol Collaborative Project: Issues in Multiple Substance Abuse*, Gardner, S. (ed.). Department of Health, Education and Welfare: Washington, D.C., 1980.
6. Barton, F. E., Bennett, M. J., and Clarke, W. M. *Approaching Alcohol Problems in a Methadone Maintenance Program.* Paper presented at the North American Congress on Alcohol and Drug Problems, December 1974.
7. Bihari, B. Alcoholism and methadone maintenance. *Am. J. Drug Alcohol Abuse* 1(1):78–87, 1974.
8. Bo, O., et al. Ethanol and diazepam as causative agents in road traffic accidents.

In: *Alcohol, Drugs and Traffic Safety*, Isrealstam, S. and Lambert, S. (eds.). Addiction Research Foundation: Toronto, 1975.

9. Carroll, J. F. X., Malloy, T. E., and Kendrick, F. M. Multiple substance abuse: A review of the literature. In: *National Drug/Alcohol Collaborative Project: Issues in Multiple Substance Abuse*, S. Gardner (ed.). Department of Health, Education and Welfare: Washington, D.C., 1980.

10. Chelton, G. L., and Whisnant, C. L. The combination of alcohol and drug intoxication. *South. Med. J.* 59:393, 1966.

11. Cohen, S. The effects of combined alcohol-drug abuse on human behavior. *Drug Abuse Alcoholism Rev.* 2(3):1-13, 1979.

12. Corrigan, E. M. *Alcoholic Women in Treatment*. Oxford: New York, 1980.

13. Croughan, J. L., Miller, J. P., Whitman, B. Y., and Schober, J. G. Alcoholism and alcohol dependence in narcotic addicts: A prospective study with a five-year follow-up. *Am. J. Drug Alcohol Abuse* 8(1), in press.

14. Crowley, T. J., et al. Drug and alcohol abuse among psychiatric admissions. *Arch. Gen. Psychiatry* 30:13-20, 1974.

15. Curtis, J. L., and Mike, V. Methadone maintenance measuring treatment outcome. *N.Y. St. J. Med.* 78(4):2177-2182, 1978.

16. Devenyi, P., and Wilson, M. Abuse of barbiturates in an alcoholic population. *Can. Med. Assoc. J.* 104:219-221, 1971.

17. Freed, E. X. Drug abuse by alcoholics: A review. *Int. J. Addict.* 8:451-473, 1973.

18. Gearing, F. R. Evaluation of methadone maintenance treatment program. In: *Methadone Maintenance*, Einstein, S. (ed.). Dekker: New York, 1971.

19. Gelb, A. M., Richman, B. L., and Onand, O. P. Quantitative and temporal relationships of alcohol use in narcotic addicts and methadone maintenance patients undergoing alcohol detoxification. *Am. J. Drug Alcohol Abuse* 5(2):191-198, 1978.

20. Gelb, A. M., Richman, B. L., and Deyser, N. P. Alcohol use in methadone maintenance clinics. *Am. J. Drug Alcohol Abuse* 6(3):367-373, 1979.

21. Goodwin, D. W., Davis, D. H., and Robins, L. N. Drinking amid abundant illicit drugs. *Arch. Gen. Psychiatry* 32:230-233, 1975.

22. Greene, B. T. Sequential use of drugs and alcohol: A reexamination of the stepping-stone hypothesis. *Am. J. Drug Alcohol Abuse* 7(1):83-99, 1980.

23. Inaba, D. S. Methaqualone abuse: Hiding out. *J.A.M.A.* 224:1505-1509, 1973.

24. Kaplan, H. L. Alcohol use by patients admitted to hospital emergency rooms før treatment of drug overdose and misuse. *J. Stud. Alcohol* 41(9):882-893, 1980.

25. Kaufman, E. Polydrug abuse or multidrug misuse: It's here to stay. *Br. J. Addict.* 72: 339-347, 1977.

26. Kipperman, A., and Fine, E. A. The combined use of alcohol and amphetamines. *Am. J. Psychiatry* 131(11):1277-1280, 1974.

27. Kreek, M. J. Physiologic implications of methadone treatment. In: *Proceedings of the Fifth National Conference on Methadone Treatment*. National Association for the Prevention of Addiction to Narcotics: New York, 1973.

28. Kreek, M. J. Medical complications in methadone patients. *Ann. N.Y. Acad. Sci.* 311:110-134, 1978.

29. Moore, M., Raymond, A. F., and Gray, M. C. Alcoholism and the use of drugs. *Q. J. Stud. Alcohol* 2:496-504, 1941.

30. Richman, A. Trends in the use of multiple drugs by narcotic addicts, 1972-1975. In: *Proceedings of Second National Drug Abuse Conference, New Orleans, Louisiana, April 4-7, 1975*. Dekker: New York, 1976.

31. Rosen, A., Ottenberg, D. J., and Barr, J. L. Patterns of previous use of alcohol in a

group of hospitalized drug addicts. *Drug Forum* 4(3):261-272, 1975.

32. Rosenberger, C. M. Young alcoholics. *Br. J. Psychiatry* 115:181-188, 1969.

33. Santo, Y., Farley, E. C., and Friedman, A. S. Highlights from the national youth polydrug study. In: *Drug Abuse Patterns among Young Polydrug Users and Urban Appalachian Youths.* Department of Health, Education and Welfare: Washington, D.C., 1980.

34. Schnoll, S. H. *Alcohol and Other Substance Abuse in Adolescents in Addiction Research and Treatment: Converging Trends.* Pergamon: New York, 1979.

35. Schut, J., File, K., and Wohlmuth, T. Alcohol use by narcotic addicts in methadone maintenance treatment. *Q. J. Stud. Alcohol* 34:1356-1359, 1973.

36. Scott, N. R., Winslow, W. W., and Gorman, D. C. Epidemiology of alcoholism in methadone maintenance patients. In: *Proceedings of the Fifth National Conference on Methadone Treatment.* National Association for the Prevention of Addiction to Narcotics. New York, 1973.

37. Stimmel, B., Cohen, M., and Hanbury, R. Alcoholism and polydrug abuse in persons in methadone maintenance. *Ann. N.Y. Acad. Sci.* 311:99-109, 1978.

38. Tuckfeld, B. S., McLeroy, K. R., Waterhouse, G. J., et al. *Multiple Drug Use among Persons with Alcohol-Related Problems.* Research Triangle Institute: Research Triangle Park, N.C., 1975.

39. Wechsler, H., and Thum, D. Teen-age drinking, drug use and social correlates. *Q. J. Stud. Alcohol* 34:1220-1227, 1973.

40. Wesson, D. R., Carlin, A. S., Adams, K. M., and Beschner, G. *Polydrug Abuse: The Results of a National Collaborative Study.* Academic Press: New York, 1978.

41. Wilkinson, P., Kornaczewski, A., Pankin, J. G., and Santamaria, J. N. Bromureide dependence in alcoholics. *Med. J. Australia* 2:479-482, 1971.

Section **VII**

Distinctive Treatment Populations

56

JOSEPH WESTERMEYER, MD, PhD University of Minnesota

ALCOHOLISM AND SERVICES FOR ETHNIC POPULATIONS

ETHNICITY DOES NOT have the same basis in reality as a rock, bird, or sound. Rather it is an abstraction applied to what people think, say, and do, especially as these phenomena vary from one group of people as distinct from another. Reseachers concerned with ethnic similarities and variation order their observations in such categories as beliefs, values, norms, attitudes, and customs.

To be sure, ethnic considerations are not entirely abstract. They do have bases in ordinary events and characteristics that can be observed among people everywhere. People can be divided into distinct ethnic groups on the basis of appearance (physiognomy, dress, hairstyle, ornamentation), language, religion, residence, birthplace or geographic origin, social organization, last name — although a particular group usually overlaps with other groups on any one of these characteristics. One is generally born into an ethnic group and remains in it for life (albeit with some limited in- and outmigration). Members views themselves as belonging to the group and having a primary loyalty to it. Marriage generally occurs within the group.

As a concept, ethnicity can expand or contract to fit the needs of the investigator. For example, one can think of all Chinese, or only Yunnanese Chinese, or Yunnanese emigrants in Southeast Asia, or Yunnanese merchants in the high-

---

Joseph Westermeyer, MD, PhD, Professor, Department of Psychiatry, University of Minnesota, Minneapolis, Minnesota.

lands of Southeast Asia. Further, ethnic characteristics of a group can change over time as they migrate, change class characteristics, profess other religions, or adopt new languages or names.

Since ethnicity is a concept applied to groups of people rather than to single persons, it is prone to abuse by way of stereotyping individuals. This is particularly true in applying sociocultural data in the clinical context with a single patient. Clinicians must perforce view the patient as a universe of one, at the same time not ignoring relevant sociocultural information.

DEMOGRAPHIC VARIATIONS

Social characteristics of alcoholic patients have been widely studied among various ethnic groups. In the United States, these groups have included white or Euro-Americans, black Americans, Native Americans, and Puerto Rican Americans. Similar observations have been made among aborigine and nonaborigine alcoholic patients in Australia.

Among black and Puerto Rican alcoholics, unskilled occupations have ranged from 50 to 75% — much higher than in Euro-American alcoholics at the same facilities [14, 25, 34]. Low occupational achievements were also found among alcoholic aborigines in Australia as compared to nonaborigines [6]. As one might expect, higher unemployment rates were generally found in these groups with unskilled occupations [14, 25]. Alcoholic Native Americans in two widely separated regions have been noted to have more unemployment [38] and less income [29] than other alcoholics.

In several studies black alcoholics [6, 14, 25, 29, 34, 36, 38, 49] have included many single and separated persons. By contrast, Euro-Americans and nonaborigine Australians have shown a relatively greater number of alcoholics currently married and living with a spouse [6, 29, 36, 38].

Educational achievement among alcoholics has shown more variability than the above factors. For example, black alcoholics have less average education than white alcoholics in one sample [34], but the same mean educational level in another sample [36]. In general, however, the groups with low occupational achievement, low married rates, and high unemployment also tended to have relatively less education [6, 29].

These demographic differences may influence the prognosis for alcoholism in various ethnic groups. Regular employment, skilled or white-collar occupations, and economic resources have generally been associated with greater improvement following treatment [8, 15, 22, 35]. Married patients and those living with a family persist in treatment longer and also have a better prognosis [8, 15, 35, 51]. (This has also been documented among drug abusers in England [9]. High arrest rates, also noted frequently among alcoholics from certain ethnic groups [6, 14, 29], have an adverse effect on treatment outcome [35]. As stated by one investigator, "Outcome is best predicted by what the patient brings to treatment, not what happens to him [or her] there" [32].

CLINICAL VARIATIONS

Many physiological signs of alcoholism have shown considerable similarity among alcoholics from different ethnic backgrounds [6, 14, 24, 38, 45]. Significant alcohol-related experiences also develop in about the same order among both Finnish and American alcoholics [27]. These plainly indicate certain ethnicity-free aspects of alcoholism.

Numerous differences exist as well. Average volumes of alcohol under 250 g a day were taken by white alcoholics in the United States [29] and Australia [13], with mean volumes of 250 to over 400 g among Native Americans [29] and aborigines [13]. In New York, Puerto Rican alcoholics drank more than black alcoholics on the average [14]. Higher daily volumes of alcohol were associated with time-limited or binge drinking, while lower volumes occurred among daily titer alcoholics. ("Titer" here refers to those who drink a regular amount throughout the day over a period of months of years.)

Medical complications differed according to type of drinking pattern. White alcoholics with more titer drinking were noted to have liver disease three times as often as black alcoholics who had more binge drinking, while the latter group had hallucinations three times more often [28]. This tendency for white alcoholics to have more hepatic and general medical complications and black alcoholics to have more seizures, hallucinations, and delerium tremens has been noted by others [10, 36]. Among Native American tribes, a group with daily controlled titer drinking experienced death from cirrhosis four times more often than another group with episodic binge drinking [18].

The pattern of blackouts among various ethnic groups presents more of a dilemma. Blackouts were reported much more often among Anglo-Catholics compared to French Catholics in Canada, although other indications of physiological dependence were similar [24]. Whites—drinking relatively less in volume—have consistently reported more blackouts than blacks [36, 37]. Yet, Puerto Rican males —drinking relatively higher volumes—reported more blackouts than black alcoholics, while the drinking-blackout relationship was the converse for females in both groups [14]. This erratic pattern suggests that blackouts may be strongly influenced by psychocultural factors as well as by pharmacological actions.

Rates of alcohol-related violence and criminality are also strongly influenced by ethnicity. Native Americans in Minnesota had more accidental and homicidal death, but less suicide as compared to the general population [45]. In a study from Arizona the ratios of police contact with alcohol-related problems ranged widely among four ethnic groups [4].

ACCESS TO TREATMENT

Availability of general medical care is affected by social class and by distance to the medical facility [17, 21]. These same factors also influence access to treatment for alcoholism [11, 47]. Since residence and class differences sometimes coexist with ethnic differences, access to care for alcoholism can vary widely among ethnic groups.

Identity differences between treatment staff and alcoholic patients can influence access to care. Black alcoholics consistently use treatment facilities run by white professionals less than do white alcoholics [20, 23, 37]. Hispanic alcoholics use such facilities even less than do white and black alcoholics [14, 26]. Withdrawal among some Native American alcoholics may be more severe because of the impediments to treatment in some times and places [38]. Familiarity, proximity, communication, and acceptance appear to account for these access problems. While white alcoholics in Georgia were often advised to go for alcoholism treatment, black alcoholics had to make a clear and definite request to obtain such assistance [20]. In a California program, there was notable mutual suspicion between the white staff and the Native American patients [29]. In a survey of attitudes toward alcoholism treatment in an Hispanic community, respondents "indicated a preference to have the clinic in the neighborhood" [26]. Aborigine alcoholics requiring readmission for alcoholism returned for treatment considerably less often than other alcoholics in Austrialia [6].

It is likely that ethnic attitudes and values also prevent access to treatment in some instances. Great stigma against alcoholism in Jewish communities may actually impede the recognition and referral for treatment [50]. Continued support for deviant drinking practices in some black American communities may serve the same purpose [20].

These access problems can be improved or resolved by a variety of methods. One such method is to provide easier geographic proximity. For example, when a New York alcoholism center moved into an area with more Hispanics, a greater number of Hispanic patients entered the facility [14]. Another method has been to include a greater number of indigenous ethnic people on the staff of the treatment facility, a solution that has been employed for Native American alcoholics in several areas [31]. A third approach is to design a treatment program that takes ethnic and ecological factors into account [16]. A Navaho program did this by using disulfiram (Antabuse) to overcome peer pressure favoring drinking and by working with local traders as resource persons [7]. A fourth method has been to demonstrate sensitivity regarding ethnic differences. This method has been used effectively with Native American alcoholics in the United States [38, 40] and has also been effective for expatriate Caucasian and Asian drug addicts by Asian staff in Asia [43, 48].

In some cases ethnic groups have the resources to care for their own members. This situation has been cited among Jewish communities in which rabbis, synagogues, and Jewish social agencies can aid the alcoholic [50]. The situation is more complex among ethnic groups with sparse populations or with limited resources. Political considerations become major factors in these contexts [46].

Lack of access can have serious consequences for many alcoholics. It has been suggested that black Americans in the South and Native Americans, in the North are more apt to go to jail, prison, and morgues or to remain actively drinking in the community as a result of limited access to remedial institutions [20, 41].

TREATMENT METHODS

Culture-Bound Treatments

Some treatments are specific to given cultural groups, due to factors such as belief, language, and ritual, and cannot be readily transferred from one culture to another. Consequently those from other ethnic groups do not integrate the treatment form into healing. Examples include the use of peyote, drumming, sand painting, and other traditional approaches among Native American people. Some of these approaches have been used among Native American people with some effectiveness against alcoholism [1, 5, 12]. (Traditional curing methods have similarly been employed for opium addiction in Asia [39].)

Diffusion of Treatment Technology

Such treatment approaches as disulfiram, Alcoholics Anonymous, detoxification, residential treatment, and outpatient care have proven acceptable to and effective for alcoholic patients from Caribbean Islanders [3], to black and white Georgians [19], to Navaho herders [30]. Active involvement by a physician in providing medical care favors entry into treatment [26] and persistence with treatment [33]. Some treatment methods may fit better with certain cultural factors, such as the prescribing of disulfiram in cultures where peer pressure strongly undermines attempts at abstinence [30].

Ethnic Bias in Treatment

Although bias in access to treatment does exist among some ethnic groups, most studies indicate that bias does not prevail in treatment itself. Among black and white alcoholics in a Georgia program, there was no favoritism in type of services rendered [19, 20]. In Austrialia, aborigines and other alcoholics had similar lengths of stay, with the elopement and "against advice" discharges being even lower among the aborigines [6].

Objective similarity in services and outcomes may not be the same as subjective experiences, however. For example, aborigine alcoholics returned for subsequent treatment much less often than expected [6]. (Among Asian narcotic addicts, those from ethnic minorities had as good an outcome from treatment as majority members, but complained bitterly about various aspects of their care [42].)

TREATMENT OUTCOME

Once treatment has been undertaken, ethnicity may not bias treatment outcome. In one comparison of black and white participants in a drinking-driving program, the outcomes at 6 months were similar. These two groups resembled each other regarding their drinking histories, types of alcohol-related problems, and performance while in treatment [2].

While the data are sparse, treatment programs with an ethnic emphasis may not fare any worse than other treatment programs, but neither do they achieve superior results. In a follow-up study of 83 alcoholics in a Native American program, 44% were improved—a good but not understanding percentage [31]. (A Buddhist program for opium addicts in Asia gave results on a 6- to 18-month follow-up much like that of a medically run program, although the mortality rate among elderly addicts in the former was much higher [42]. Further epidemiologic evaluation of these latter data suggested that certain community factors predicted outcome, while specific type of treatment was not as important [44].)

CONCLUSION

Class factors may masquerade as ethnic factors. Groups at a socioeconomic disadvantage in a society also come to alcoholism treatment as a disadvantage. They possess features inveighing against optimal outcomes (i.e., more are single, divorced, and separated; more are unskilled and unemployed; they have few material and social resources; there are more arrest records).

Ethnicity may influence the kind of alcohol-related problems that come to treatment. Cultures with predominantly titer drinking have more cirrhosis and other medical problems. Those having mostly a binge pattern demonstrate more seizures, hallucinations, delerium tremens, alcohol-related violence, arrests, and greater daily volumes of ethanol. Despite these two general trends, the overall course of alcohol dependence is remarkably similar among various cultures. Blackouts—a poorly defined entity—show considerable ethnic variation for reasons that are unclear.

Ethnic bias in treatment for alcoholism is most manifest in regard to access to treatment programs. Economically disadvantaged minorities are admitted to treatment less often than epidemiologic findings would warrant. Once engaged in treatment, however, they generally have full availability of services, they persist in treatment, and their outcome is comparable to that of others.

Ethnically oriented programs appear more effective in facilitating entry into treatment among socioeconomically disadvantaged groups. There are as yet no indications that these programs have outcome results superior to programs without an ethnic emphasis.

REFERENCES

1. Albaugh, B., and Anderson, P. Peyote in the treatment of alcoholism among American Indians. *Am. J. Psychiatry* 131:1247–1257, 1974.
2. Argeriou, M. Reaching problem-drinking blacks: The unheralded potential of the drinking driver programs. *Int. J. Addict.* 13:443–459, 1978.
3. Beaubrun, M. H. Treatment of alcoholism in Trinidad and Tobago, 1956–65. *Br. J. Psychiatry* 113:643–658, 1967.
4. Beigel, A., Hunter, E. J., Tamerin, J. S., Chapin, E. H., and Lowery, M. J. Planning for the development of comprehensive community alcoholism services: I. The prevalence survey. *Am. J. Psychiatry* 131:1112–1116, 1974.
5. Bergman, R. L. Navaho peyote use: Its apparent safety. *Am. J. Psychiatry* 128:695–699, 1971.
6. Chegwidden, M., and Flaherty, B. J. Aboriginal versus nonaboriginal alcoholics in an alcohol withdrawal unit. *Med. J. Austr.* 1:699–703, 1977.
7. Ferguson, F. N. A treatment program for Navaho alcoholics. *Q. J. Stud. Alcohol* 31:898–919, 1970.
8. Gerard, D. L., and Saenger, G. *Out-Patient Treatment of Alcoholism.* University of Toronto Press: Toronto, 1966.
9. Gossop, M. Drug dependence: A study of the relationship between motivational, cognitive, social and historical factors, and treatment variables. *J. Nerv. Ment. Dis.* 166:44–50, 1978.
10. Gross, M. M., Rosenblatt, S. M., Lewis, E., Chartoff, S., and Malenowski, B. Acute alcoholic psychoses and related syndromes: Psychosocial and clinical characteristics and their implications. *Br. J. Addict.* 67:15–31, 1972.
11. Hoffman, H. County characteristics and admission to state hospital for treatment of alcoholism and psychiatric disorders. *Psychol. Rep.* 35:1275–1277, 1974.
12. Jilek, W. G. Indian healing power: Indigenous therapeutic practices in the Pacific Northwest. *Psychiatr. Ann.* 4:13–21, 1974.

13. Kamien, M. Aborigines and alcohol intake: Effects and social implications in a rural community in western New South Wales. *Med. J. Austr.* 1:291-298, 1975.
14. Kane, G. *Inner City Alcoholism: An Ecological and Cross-Cultural Study.* Human Science Press: New York, 1981.
15. Kissin, B., Rosenblatt, S. M., and Machover, S. Prognostic factors in alcoholism. *Psychiatr. Res. Rep.* 24:22-43, 1968.
16. Klein, J. A., and Roberts, A. C. A residential alcoholism treatment program for American Indians. *Q. J. Stud. Alcohol* 34:860-868, 1973.
17. Kosa, J., Antonovsky, A., and Zola, I. K. *Poverty and Health.* Harvard University Press: Cambridge, Mass., 1969.
18. Kunitz, S. J., Levy, J. E., Odoroff, C. J., and Bollinger, J. The epidemiology of alcoholism in two southwestern Indian tribes. *Q. J. Stud. Alcohol* 32:706-720, 1971.
19. Lowe, G. D., and Alston, J. P. An analysis of racial differences in services to alcoholics in a southern clinic. *Hosp. Commun. Psychiatry* 24:547-551, 1973.
20. Lowe, G. D., and Hodges, H. E. Race and the treatment of alcoholism in a southern state. *Soc. Problems* 20:240-252, 1972.
21. Mellsop, G. W. The effect of distance in determining hospital admission rates. *Med. J. Austr.* 2:814-817, 1969.
22. Mindlin, D. F. The characteristics of alcoholics as related to prediction of therapeutic outcome. *Q. J. Stud. Alcohol* 20:604-619, 1959.
23. Nathan, P. E., Lipson, A. G., Vettraino, A. P., and Solomon, P. The social ecology of an urban clinic for alcoholism: Racial differences in treatment entry and outcome. *Int. J. Addict.* 3:55-63, 1968.
24. Negrete, J. C. Cultural influences on social performance of alcoholics: A comparative study study. *Q. J. Stud. Alcohol* 34:905-916, 1973.
25. Novick, L. F., Hudson, H., and German, E. In-hospital detoxification and rehabilitation of alcoholics in an inner city area. *Am. J. Public Health* 64:1089-1094, 1974.
26. Paine, H. J. Attitudes and patterns of alcohol use among Mexican Americans: Implications for service delivery. *J. Stud. Alcohol* 38:544-553, 1977.
27. Park, P., and Whitehead, P. C. Developmental sequence and dimensions of alcoholism. *Q. J. Stud. Alcohol* 34:887-904, 1973.
28. Rimmer, J., Pitts, F. N., Reich, T., and Winokur, G. Alcoholism: II. Sex, socioeconomic status, and race in two hospitalized samples. *Q. J. Stud. Alcohol* 39:942-952, 1971.
29. Royznho, V., and Ferguson, L. C. Admission characteristics of Indian and white alcoholic patients in a rural mental hospital. *Int. J. Addict.* 13:591-604, 1978.
30. Savard, R. J. Effects of disulfiram therapy in relationships within the Navaho drinking group. *Q. J. Stud. Alcohol* 29:909-916, 1968.
31. Shore, J. H., and Von Fumetti, B. Three alcohol programs for American Indians. *Am. J. Psychiatry* 128:1450-1454, 1972.
32. Smart, R. G. Do some alcoholics do better in some types of treatment than others? *Drug Alcohol Depend.* 3:65-75, 1978.
33. Smart, R. G., and Gray, G. Multiple predictors of dropout from alcoholism treatment. *Arch. Gen. Psychiatry* 35:363-367, 1978.
34. Strayer, R. A study of the Negro alcoholic. *Q. J. Stud. Alcohol* 22:111-123, 1961.
35. Trice, H. M., Roman, P. M., and Belasco, J. A. Selection for treatment: A predictive evaluation of an alcoholism treatment regimen. *Int. J. Addict.* 4:303-317, 1969.
36. Viamontes, J. A., and Powell, B. J. Demographic characteristics of black and white male alcoholics. *Int. J. Addict.* 9:489-494, 1974.
37. Vitols, M. M. Culture patterns of drinking in Negro and white alcoholics. *Dis. Nerv. Syst.* 29:391-394, 1968.

38. Westermeyer, J. Chippewa and majority alcoholism in Twin Cities: A comparison. *J. Nerv. Ment. Dis.* 155:322–327, 1972.
39. Westermeyer, J. Folk treatment for opium addiction in Laos. *Br. J. Addict.* 68:345–349, 1973.
40. Westermeyer, J. Clinical guidelines for cross-cultural treatment of chemical dependence. *Am. J. Drug Alcohol Abuse* 3:315–322, 1976.
41. Westermeyer, J. Use of a social indicator system to assess alcoholism among Indian people in Minnesota. *Am. J. Drug Alcohol Abuse* 3:447–456, 1976.
42. Westermeyer, J. Medical and nonmedical treatment for narcotic addicts: A comparative study from Asia. *J. Nerv. Ment. Dis.* 167:205–211, 1979.
43. Westermeyer, J., and Berger, L. J. "World traveler" addicts in Laos: I. Demographic and clinical description. *Am. J. Drug Alcohol Abuse* 4:479–493, 1977.
44. Westermeyer, J., and Bourne, P. Treatment outcome and the role of the community in narcotic addiction. *J. Nerv. Ment. Dis.* 166:51–58, 1978.
45. Westermeyer, J., and Brantner, J. Violent death and alcohol use among the Chippewa in Minnesota. *Minn. Med.* 55:749–752, 1972.
46. Westermeyer, J., and Hausman, W. Mental health consultation with government agencies: A comparison of two cases. *Soc. Psychiatry* 9:137–141, 1974.
47. Westermeyer, J., and Lang, G. Ethnic differences in use of alcoholism facilities. *Int. J. Addict.* 10:513–520, 1974.
48. Westermeyer, J., Soudaly, C., and Kaufman, E. An addiction treatment program in Laos: The first year's experience. *Drug Alcohol Depend.* 3:93–102, 1978.
49. Zimberg, S. Evaluation of alcoholism treatment in Harlem. *Q. J. Stud. Alcohol* 35:550–557, 1974.
50. Zimberg, S. Sociopsychiatric perspectives on Jewish alcohol abuse: Implications for the prevention of alcoholism. *Am. J. Drug Alcohol Abuse* 4:571–579, 1977.
51. Zwerling, I., and Clifford, B. J. Administrative and population considerations in outpatient clinics for the treatment of chronic alcoholism. *N.Y.S. J. Med.* 57:3869–3875, 1957.

57

SHARON C. WILSNACK, PhD, University of North Dakota
School of Medicine

ALCOHOL ABUSE AND ALCOHOLISM IN WOMEN

UNTIL RECENTLY, WOMEN drinkers received little attention in the literature on alcohol problems. Most clinical and experimental research involved only men, with findings then often assumed to apply equally well to women. In the past 5 to 10 years, however, there has been growing public concern about alcohol problems in women and an increase in research on these problems. Comprehensive reviews of recent research on women and alcohol are available elsewhere [15, 20, 25]. The purpose of the present, briefer review is to highlight major research findings concerning women's drinking and drinking problems; to summarize available data on gender differences in patterns, antecedents, and consequences of alcohol abuse and alcoholism; and to consider possible implications of recent research findings for the treatment and prevention of alcohol problems in women.

DRINKING AND DRINKING PROBLEMS IN WOMEN

Recent reports of dramatic increases in women's drinking and drinking problems receive relatively little support from available research data. Although the proportion of women who drink at least occasionally (i.e., those who are not total abstain-

---

Sharon C. Wilsnack, PhD, Associate Professor of Psychology, Department of Neuroscience, University of North Dakota School of Medicine, Grand Forks, North Dakota.

ers) increased fairly steadily from World War II until the mid 1960s, this proportion appears to have leveled off, at around 55 to 60%, in recent years [8, 18]. Despite the increase in women drinkers in the 1950s and 1960s, men at all ages and socioeconomic levels still consume more alcohol more frequently than do women. (Gender differences in quantity consumed per occasion are reduced somewhat when male-female differences in average weight and body fluid content are taken into account [18].)

Men also exceed women in rates of heavy drinking and drinking problems, with no marked changes in recent years. A 1979 national survey of adult drinking practices [8] classified 14% of men and 4% of women as heavy drinkers (averaging 1 oz or more of absolute alcohol a day). In the same survey, 20% of men drinkers and 10% of women drinkers reported experiencing one or more symptoms of alcohol dependence or loss of control during the past 12 months, while 9% of men drinkers and 5% of women drinkers reported one or more adverse social consequences (drinking-related problems at work, with family or friends, and others). Interestingly, among persons reporting very heavy levels of drinking (more than 120 drinks a month), women exceeded men in rates of adverse interpersonal consequences, perhaps suggesting a more negative social reaction to heavy drinking and drunkenness in women. It is possible that surveys have underestimated rates of drinking problems in women by neglecting certain problems that may be particularly common among women (e.g., drinking-related problems with children or with household responsibilities).

Although the evidence does not indicate marked changes in rates of drinking and drinking problems among women in general in recent decades, drinking does appear to have increased in certain population subgroups, most notably among female adolescents [33]. Public concern about increased drinking in women may be based in part on changes in these population subgroups. In addition, existing alcohol problems of women may be becoming more visible, as some of the traditional stigma surrounding women's alcohol abuse begins to weaken and women more readily acknowledge and seek help for their drinking-related problems.

GENDER DIFFERENCES IN ALCOHOLISM PATTERNS AND SYMPTOMS

Like studies of drinking and drinking problems in the general population, research on clinical samples has found differences between alcoholic men and alcoholic women. These include differences in the onset and course of alcoholism, alleged differences in extent of psychopathology among alcoholic men and women, and possible gender differences in the relationships of life stress and affective disorder to drinking.

Onset and Course of Alcoholism

Women alcoholics generally report a later age of onset of heavy drinking than men alcoholics. Men's earlier use and abuse of alcohol may occur because drinking in American society is associated more closely with masculine than with feminine roles and thus may have an early attraction for men that it does not have for women.

The fact that men and women alcoholics enter treatment at roughly the same age despite the women's later start is often cited as evidence that drinking problems progress more rapidly for women than men [1, 11]. However, similar ages at entrance into treatment do not necessarily mean that men's and women's alcohol problems are equally severe or have progressed equally as far. In fact, several studies have found that on admission women's alcohol problems on the average are less severe than those of men. Such findings may suggest that women enter treatment for alcoholism at an earlier stage than men, perhaps reflecting women's earlier loss of social support and/or general male-female differences in help-seeking behavior.

General Differences in Psychopathology

Many early clinical reports describe alcoholic women as more abnormal or pathological than alcoholic men. Data cited to support this belief have included alcoholic women's higher rates of marital instability, psychiatric treatment, suicide attempts, and marriage to alcoholic spouses. However, the interpretation of these data is unclear, as several reviews have noted [1, 10, 11]. For example, the reported difference in suicide attempts may simply reflect the higher incidence of suicide attempts among women in the general population, and/or the higher incidence of depressive disorders among women than men alcoholics (a discussion of which follows). In any case, it is difficult to separate indicators of greater "pathology," which may have preceded the development of drinking problems, from the social consequences of drinking, which may be more severe for women than for men.

Drinking and Life Stress

Although the evidence is not entirely consistent, a number of studies have found that women alcoholics are more likely than men alcoholics to report that the onset of their problem drinking was linked to a specific life crisis or stress [1, 11]. Frequently reported precipitants include marital problems, divorce or separation, death of a spouse or parent, obstetrical or gynecological problems, and children growing older and leaving home.

It is possible that life stress actually has a greater impact on women's drinking than on men's. However, it is also possible that if the social stigma of alcohol abuse is greater for women than for men [22], women may simply feel more ashamed and guilty about their drinking and thus feel more of a need to explain or rationalize it in terms of external life circumstances. A third possibility is that women are more sensitive in general to interpersonal relationships and crises and therefore more likely to remember and report life events that preceded their problem drinking. Several studies are currently underway that may permit a choice among these explanations. If life stress does play a greater role in women's drinking, this might suggest that women undergoing life crises or life transitions, such as recently divorced or widowed women, are at particularly high risk for alcohol abuse. Preventive interventions with such groups (e.g., alcohol education, support groups, or training in coping skills) might reduce these women's risk of turning to alcohol or other drugs to cope with their stressful life situations.

Affective Disorder and Alcoholism

A clinically important distinction has been made between those alcoholics who show evidence of affective disorder (particularly depression) prior to developing alcoholism or during periods of remission, those alcoholics whose drinking is part of a sociopathic life style, and those primary alcoholics who develop alcoholism in the absence of a preexisting psychiatric disorder [27]. Like rates of affective disorder and sociopathy in the general population, affective-disorder alcoholism appears to be more common among women than among men, while sociopathic alcoholism is more common among men than among women.

The fact that as many as 25 to 30% of alcoholic women may present a pattern of affective-disorder alcoholism underscores the importance of obtaining a careful clinical history of depressive symptoms and their temporal relationship to alcoholism symptoms. Follow-up studies suggest that affective-disorder alcoholic women have higher rates of suicide attempts but also better long-term outcomes than either sociopathic or primary alcoholic women.

ETIOLOGIC THEORIES AND RISK FACTORS

As in men, alcoholism in women represents a complex interaction of biological, psychological, and sociocultural influences. The following describes briefly several etiologic theories that give particular attention to the development of alcoholism in women, and summarizes data concerning biological and psychosocial factors that may affect women's specific risk for alcohol problems.

Genetic Factors

Although recent research supports a genetic predisposition to alcoholism, much of this research has involved only male subjects. For example, a widely cited study by Goodwin et al. found that young adult sons of alcoholics adopted early in life by nonalcoholic parents had higher alcoholism rates than adopted-out sons of nonalcoholics [14]. An attempt to replicate these findings with a small sample of daughters of alcoholics failed: adopted-out daughters of alcoholic parents did not differ from adopted-out daughters of nonalcoholic parents, although both groups showed increased risk for alcoholism relative to women in the general population [14].

Additional studies involving larger samples of women are needed before genetic influences are discounted or minimized for women. However, the limited available data on women suggest that early family disruption, such as adoption, childhood environmental influences (including parental modeling), and cultural sanctions against heavy drinking in women, may override genetic contributions to women's alcohol abuse and alcoholism.

Early Family Disruption

Like women with other psychiatric disorders, alcoholic women report high rates of family disruption in their early life experience. Disruptive events include loss of one or both parents through death, divorce, or separation, and psychiatric problems such as alcoholism or psychosis in parents or other close relatives. While alcoholic women and men both report higher rates of early family disruption than women and men in the general population, alcoholic women report even more experiences of this sort than alcoholic men [13].

As suggested earlier with regard to life stress, it is possible that women are more sensitive in general to changes in interpersonal relationships and therefore more likely than men to recall and report those interpersonal losses or disruptions they have experienced. However, it is also possible that women who experience early family disruption are actually more strongly affected than men and consequently more likely to develop alcoholism or other psychiatric disorders later in life. Disruption of important interpersonal relationships early in life may underlie the depression and low self-esteem often observed in alcoholic women and may produce lasting feelings of loss, sadness, and anger, which are important to address in counseling or psychotherapy with adult alcoholic women.

Psychodynamic Theories: Dependency, Power, and Low Self-Esteem

Psychodynamic theories of alcohol use and abuse emphasize psychological motivations for drinking and underlying conflicts that enhance psychological needs for the effects of alcohol. Two leading psychodynamic theories, the dependency theory and the power theory, are based primarily on research and clinical experience with men and may be somewhat less relevant to women's drinking behavior.

According to the dependency theory [4], drinking gratifies dependency needs (by producing feelings of warmth, sentimentality, and closeness to others) while allowing the drinker to maintain an outward appearance of independence and maturity. Men are believed to drink more than woman due to the greater social sanctions against overt expression of dependency needs by men. Women who drink heavily despite the greater social support for expression of female dependency are presumed to have unusually intense dependency needs and/or unusually limited chances for satisfying these needs.

A second psychodynamic theory proposes that drinking gratifies needs for feelings of personal power over others [24]. Because men traditionally have been socialized to be concerned about their personal power and are more likely than women to experience social demands to display power, they are thought to be more likely than women to desire the temporary feelings of power produced by alcohol. Like the dependency theory, the power theory originated largely from studies of men drinkers. Two studies of women drinkers [30] found that drinking reduced women's thoughts about power. In one study, social drinking also increased several traditionally feminine qualities of women's thoughts. These findings suggest that drinking may produce in both men and women psychological mental states consistent with traditional sex-role stereotypes and sex-role expectations, perhaps because drinkers of both genders interpret the nonspecific physiological effects of alcohol in ways that are shaped by their own sex-role training.

Resembling McClelland's power theory in some respects are models that explain women's drinking in terms of negative self-image and low self-esteem [3, 4]. Studies have found that alcoholic women have lower self-esteem than both nonalcoholic women and alcoholic men, although it is unclear whether low self-esteem preceded or only followed the women's alcohol abuse. While self-esteem models view drinking as temporarily increasing women's feelings of self-confidence and personal adequacy, one recent study [23] found that drinking decreased feelings of personal self-satisfaction in women social drinkers. Since expectations about the effects of alcohol are generally positive regardless of alcohol's actual effects, women with negative self-images may drink in hope of feeling better about themselves. If drinking then reduces their feelings of adequacy and self-esteem (because of social disapproval of women's drinking or for other reasons), a vicious circle may begin in which low self-esteem leads to increased drinking, which in turn lowers self-esteem still further.

Social Role Theories: Sex Roles and Sex-Role Conflicts

Recent studies suggest that conflicts surrounding traditional feminine roles may be more common among problem drinking and alcoholic women than among women in the general population. These conflicts have taken two major forms. In one form, the women experiences inconsistent sex-role attitudes and behaviors within her own personality, for example, overt expression of traditionally feminine attitudes and values by a woman whose actual behavior deviates from traditional feminine role expectations [2, 30]. A second form appears less frequently in the research literature but is often observed by clinicians. In this case the woman is not internally conflicted about her sex-role orientation but is in a social environment that demands sex-stereotyped behavior, for example, an assertive, independent woman whose significant others expect her to behave in traditionally feminine passive-dependent ways [26]. Results from a 1975 national survey may reflect either or both forms of sex-role conflict, or simply the stress of combining multiple roles: married women employed outside the home had higher rates of heavy and problem drinking than either unmarried employed women or married women not employed outside the home [18].

Drinking may result from sex-role conflicts in at least two ways: (1) by reducing or seeming to reduce tension, stress, and conflict related to sex-role performance; and (2) by symbolizing or expressing sex-role attitudes and values, such as the rejection of traditional feminine roles. In addition, traditional sex roles may affect drinking opportunities and exposure to drinking situations. Further research is needed to determine how prevalent sex-role–related reasons for drinking are among alcoholic and problem drinking women (one study [2] suggests that as many as 25% of alcoholic women may experience internal psychological sex-role conflicts) and how sex-role conflicts interact with other biological and psychosocial factors that increase women's risk for alcohol abuse.

Life Experience Risk Factors: Sexual Experience and Reproductive Disorders

As previously discussed, women alcoholics in a number of studies have been more likely than men alcoholics to report specific life events or crises as possible precipitants of their excessive drinking. Many of these events involve losses or transitions in areas of traditional feminine role performance (e.g., marital problems, divorce, separation, children leaving home, and others), although employment-related events may assume added importance as more women enter occupational roles outside the home.

Two specific types of life experience that may increase women's risk of alcohol abuse are sexual dysfunction and obstetrical and gynecological disorders. A recent review of clinical and epidemiological studies [31] found that samples of problem drinking and alcoholic women have rather consistently reported elevated rates of both sexual difficulties and reproductive disorders. For example, rates of sexual inhibition, reduced sexual responsiveness, and orgastic dysfunction in 13 samples of alcoholic women ranged from 28 to 100%. Although most studies lacked adequate nonalcoholic control or comparison groups, rates of sexual dysfunction reported by alcoholic women were higher than rates reported by nonalcoholic women in the few studies that did include control groups. In 16 studies, rates of gynecological and obstetrical disorders (including menstrual irregularities, hysterectomy, early menopause, infertility, spontaneous abortion, complications of labor and delivery, and stillbirths) were higher among alcoholic women than among women in the general population.

Most clinical studies of alcoholic women lack time-ordered data, making it difficult to separate sexual and reproductive problems that preceded and possibly contributed to women's alcohol abuse from those that resulted from excessive drinking. The clearest example of the second type of problem is the fetal alcohol syndrome and other fetal alcohol effects that result from heavy alcohol consumption during pregnancy (see Chapter 23 in this volume). In the few studies that attempted to time-order sexual and reproductive problems relative to the onset of heavy drinking, alcoholic women reported elevated rates of sexual and obstetrical-gynecological problems both before and after the onset of problem drinking. If replicated with stronger research designs (e.g., longitudinal studies), these findings may suggest a reciprocal relationship between sexual or reproductive dysfunction and excessive drinking, in which women's distress about sexual or reproductive problems contribute to heavy drinking, which in turn produces new or exacerbates existing sexual and reproductive difficulties. The findings would also be consistent with a causal pattern in which some third conditon contributes to both alcohol abuse and sexual or reproductive disorders (e.g., an as yet undiscovered biological predisposition, traumatic early sexual experiences, or chronic psychological or environmental stress).

Two additional sexual experiences that may affect women's risk for alcoholism are homosexuality and a history of sexual abuse. Although suffering from methodological limitations, several studies have reported higher rates of alcohol problems among lesbians and homosexual men than among heterosexual women and men in the general population, and higher rates of homosexuality among alcoholic women than among nonalcoholic women [31]. Among the factors that may place homosexual persons at increased risk for alcohol problems are heavy drinking norms within many gay communities, the prominent role of the gay bar as a social and recreational center, and the alienation and isolation experienced by homosexual persons as the result of social disapproval and rejection.

Sexual abuse and incest are rarely mentioned in the early literature on women alcoholics, probably because of the sensitive nature of the topics. Recently, however, researchers and particularly clinicians have paid increasing attention to these experiences and their possible relationships to women's drinking. Paternal alcohol dependence was present in 28% of father-daughter incest cases reported in a recent national study [19]. Since daughters of alcoholic fathers are at increased risk for alcoholism, these findings may imply above average rates of father-daughter incest in the childhood histories of alcoholic women. Unpublished data and anecdotal reports from treatment personnel support the impression that many alcoholic women have experienced incest or other sexual abuse as children and adolescents. One treatment director recently told the author that 85% of the alcoholic women entering his program reported, when asked, a history of incest or other sexual abuse. Better empirical data are needed to document such clinical impressions, and to determine the role of these traumatic sexual experiences as risk factors for both sexual dysfunction and alcohol abuse.

CONSEQUENCES OF ALCOHOLISM FOR WOMEN

Psychosocial consequences. Studies comparing the psychosocial consequences of alcoholism for women and men have generally found that men report more public, visible consequences such as driving while intoxicated and public intoxication arrests, financial difficulties, and work-related problems, while women report more marital and family disruption and possibly more negative psychological consequences, such as feelings of guilt, shame, an self-criticism [11, 12]. These differences follow traditional sex-role lines and may also reflect social class differences. Since many studies of alcoholic women have used middle-class and upper-middle-class samples, the emerging picture of the "typical" alcoholic woman (late onset of drinking, private as opposed to public consequences of drinking) may apply primarily to higher-status alcoholics. A smaller number of studies of alcoholic women of lower socioeconomic status indicate drinking patterns more similar to those of men, characterized by early onset of drinking, drinking in public, and more visible social consequences [12, 27].

Biomedical consequences. Some evidence suggests that women alcoholics are more likely than men alcoholics to develop and to die from liver disease, including alcoholic cirrhosis [17], although other studies have failed to find gender differences in either incidence or mortality of liver disorders [6]. Additional biomedical consequences of alcohol abuse in women are reviewed by Hill [17]. Deleterious effects of alcohol abuse on women's sexual and reproductive functioning, including fetal alcohol syndrome and fetal alcohol effects, are discussed earlier in this chapter and elsewhere in this volume.

Social reactions to women's drinking. Although the empirical evidence for these conclusions is mixed, a number of writers have suggested that social reactions to alcohol abuse differ depending on whether the drinker is a woman or a man. Specifically, society is said to judge women's alcohol problems, when acknowledged, more harshly than men's. At the same time, there is believed to be a greater effort by family, friends, and helping professionals to deny or cover up drinking problems when the drinker is a woman. Several writers have suggested that both parts of this paradox — the harsher social reaction to women's drinking problems and the greater effort to deny that the problems exist — arise because women's drunkenness and its feared consequences (including open expression of sexuality and neglect of home and family) seriously violate traditional stereotypes of acceptable feminine behavior and pose a threat to existing patterns of male-female relationships [12, 22, 26]. Additional research data on social attitudes toward drinking and drinking problems in women and men, and how these attitudes are expressed in action, may help clarify the degree to which a sexual double standard exists and the effects of such a double standard on the development of alcohol problems in women.

ALCOHOLISM TREATMENT IN WOMEN

Although research on the antecedents and consequences of alcohol abuse in women has increased in the past decade, empirical data concerning the effectiveness of treatment programs for women are still very limited. Much of the treatment literature consists of extrapolations from research on etiologic factors and clinical impressions and recommendations by treatment personnel who have worked with alcoholic women. One exception is a recent study of 150 alcoholic women in treatment that examined a variety of antecedents and consequences of alcoholism in addition to treatment outcome [9].

Despite the dearth of research data, some general themes can be identified in the recent literature on alcoholism treatment for women. These include issues related to the effectiveness of alcoholism treatment in women and to special treatment needs of alcoholic women.

Outcome of Alcoholism Treatment in Women

Two recent reviews [5, 6] have addressed the question of whether alcoholism treatment is any more or less effective for women than for men. The reviews found that most studies either do not distinguish between outcome rates for women and men or simply exclude women from their samples altogether, generally because of the small numbers of women involved. Of those studies that have compared women and men, most have found no differences in outcome rates [5]. This group includes a national sample of 122 women and 876 men [6] in which few gender differences were found in treatment outcome at a 30-month follow-up. Of studies that have reported gender differences, slightly more have reported better outcomes for men than for women.

A number of methodological problems may explain these inconsistent findings. Problems include lack of attention to subgroups of alcoholics (e.g., those with vs. those without preexisting affective disorders); lack of comparability of outcome criteria across studies; small sample sizes; inadequate follow-up intervals; and failure to take into account treatment type and amount, therapist characteristics, patient population characteristics (e.g., proportions of men and women), and admission characteristics (demographic characteristics, severity of alcoholism, etc.). An additional problem noted in several studies is a tendency to combine for purposes of data analysis small numbers of women with much larger numbers of men. Presenting findings from such studies as if they generalized to all alcoholic men and women is grossly misleading, since extremely small numbers of women were studied and no cross-gender comparisons were made.

Given these methodological problems, most writers agree that further studies that make global comparisons between heterogeneous samples of alcoholic women and men are unlikely to be useful. Instead, the most helpful information will result from well-designed studies, employing clearly defined outcome criteria, of the differential effectiveness of specific treatment modalities in specific subgroups of alcoholic women and men.

Treatment Needs of Alcoholic Women

If, as some studies suggest, alcoholism treatment is less effective for women than for men, this may reflect in part a failure of alcoholism treatment programs to consider possible gender differences in the antecedents and consequences of alcoholism and resulting differences in treatment needs of women and men alcoholics. Since many alcoholism treatment models have developed within populations that are primarily or exclusively male (e.g., Veterans Administration hospitals), such models may be more consistent with the characteristics and treatment needs of men than of women alcoholics.

Several recent reviews raise some issues that may be particularly important in the treatment of alcoholic women. As noted earlier, most of these treatment recommendations lack rigorous empirical support but are based instead on clinical experience and extrapolation from research on etiologic factors. The following discussion draws upon papers by Beckman [1], Braiker [6], Gomberg [10, 11], Tamerin [28], Trice and Beyer [29], and upon the author's own clinical observations.

Assessing alcoholic subtypes. The importance of distinguishing between women who develop alcoholism following one or more episodes of clinical depression and women whose alcoholism develops in the absence of depressive episodes is discussed earlier in this chapter. For nonpsychiatrist clinicians who suspect they are dealing with a woman of the first (affective disorder) type, psychiatric consultation may be helpful in determining (1) the presence and severity of current affective disorder, and (2) the potential usefulness of antidepressant medication (e.g., where depressive symptoms clearly preceded the onset of excessive drinking and are of the so-called endogenous type most likely to respond to antidepressants).

In addition to affective-disorder alcoholics, two other subtypes are alcoholic women whose drinking begins or increases following stressful life events and women who drink in response to sex-role related conflicts and stresses. Some research suggests that each of these subgroups may comprise as many as 25 to 30% of women alcoholics. Treatment for women in the first group should help the women resolve her feelings about the precipitating life crisis of life transition and find alternatives to alcohol or other drugs for coping with the crisis and associated stresses. Treatment for women in the second group should include attention to the woman's feelings about herself and her roles as a woman. Women's therapy and support groups may help such women identify social pressures to conform to traditional sex-role expectations, and may increase their acceptance of themselves as persons, independent of sex-role stereotypes. Several writiers have noted the need for alcoholism treatment personnel to be aware of their own expectations regarding women's and men's behavior so that they can avoid communicating and reinforcing rigid and constraining sex-role stereotypes.

Negative self-image and low self-esteem. Research studies discussed earlier have documented the negative self-image and low self-esteem observed by clinicians who treat alcoholic women [4]. Whether negative self-feelings preceded or followed the woman's excessive drinking, most writers agree that they need to be actively and directly addressed in treatment. Suggestions for helping the alcoholic woman begin to feel better about herself include providing a pleasant and attractive treatment environment, helping the woman restore her physical appearance, introducing her to recovering alcoholic women who can provide support and serve as positive role models, and offering various expressive and activity therapies that may enhance self-esteem, such as music and dance therapy, movement therapy, physical fitness, and sports. Because of the alcoholic woman's vulnerable self-esteem, a somewhat less confrontive and more supportive counseling approach may be indicated (especially early in treatment) than is often used with men.

Some writers believe that unexpressed anger is a major source of low self-esteem among alcoholic women. Psychotherapy that explores sources of anger and direct training in assertive behavior can help women identify, accept, and express appropriately the anger they experience. In cases where women's low self-esteem is primarily the result of destructive interpersonal relationships or living situations, direct environmental intervention is often necessary to provide an environment more supportive of the woman's self-image and recovery efforts. Active efforts to enhance self-esteem early in treatment may increase alcoholic women's sense of personal worth and as a result their motivation to change their drinking behavior. By strengthening personal incentives to stop drinking, such approaches may prove more effective than simply waiting for self-esteem to improve as a result of changes in drinking and associated problems.

Involvement of significant others. If interpersonal crises and losses are more likely to precipitate alcohol abuse in women than in men, it is possible that the involvement and support of significant others may play an even greater role in women's recovery from alcoholism than in men's. A number of clinicians, including Tamerin [28], feel that because alcoholic women so frequently report problems related to their marriages and children the treatment of choice for most is marital or family therapy.

Findings discussed earlier concerning the high incidence of sexual dysfunction among alcoholic women suggest that one specialized treatment modality available to alcoholic women and their partners should be sexual counseling or therapy. Clinicians working with alcoholic women should be comfortable discussing sexual experience and sexual problems and should be aware of well-qualified professionals to whom they can refer sexual difficulties that they themselves do not feel competent to treat.

Use of psychoactive medication. Since alcoholics as a group are at high risk for abuse of other drugs, caution is necessary in prescribing psychoactive medication to alcoholic women or men. This caution may be particularly important for women alcoholics, since women in general are more likely than men to be given physicians' prescriptions for a variety of psychotherapeutic medications and thus may be more at risk for multiple substance abuse [7]. Drugs for the treatment of major mental disorders, such as affective disorders or schizophrenia, should be distinguished from psychoactive drugs with a high potential for abuse (e.g., barbiturates, sedatives, and minor tranquilizers). Drugs of the former type may be appropriate and necessary for women whose alcoholism occurs in conjunction with major psychiatric disorders.

Therapist gender. Some treatment programs recommend routine assignment of women therapists to alcoholic women. Women therapists are assumed to have greater empathy with women clients and to be more helpful to clients in dealing with their feelings about themselves as women. In addition, having a woman therapist provides a positive female role model and may remove one crutch — traditional male-female role playing — used by some women to avoid confronting difficult therapeutic issues.

Few empirical data are available regarding advantages of women versus men therapists. One recent unpublished study [16] found that women alcoholics who had men as group psychotherapists increased in assertive behavior, while comparable clients who had women therapists decreased in anxiety; a large variety of other outcome variables showed no differences associated with therapist gender. Although women therapists may offer some advantages in general, individual therapist characteristics, including the therapist's own sex-role attitudes and behavior, may have a stronger effect on treatment outcome than the therapist's biological gender.

Gender composition of therapy groups. A related issue is whether women alcoholics have better outcomes in all-women therapy groups or in mixed groups with men. Some group therapists argue that in mixed groups women are more likely to engage in traditional feminine role behavior (e.g., nonassertive, sexualized relations with male group members) and less likely to develop new, more self-sufficient behavior patterns. Further, certain sensitive topics, such as marital or sexual difficulties, may be easier for women to discuss with other women than with men. On the other hand, women alcoholics frequently have important issues to work out in relation to men as well as women, and these might be best discussed and new behaviors practiced in a mixed-gender setting. Providing both same- and mixed-gender experiences may be more effective than either used alone. For example, all-women's groups might be offered early in treatment for initial female support and role modeling, followed by mixed-gender groups that either replace or supplement the women's groups. Women's groups with male and female coleaders also combine the advantages of female support with opportunities to discuss and practice new behaviors in relation to men.

Practical skills training and child care. Encouraging women to explore new roles and life styles is of little value if they lack the skills to make such changes. Several writers have observed that many alcoholic women, particularly those in traditional homemaker roles, need continued education and training in a variety of practical survival skills (e.g., vocational skills, financial management, life and career planning, parenting skills) in order to attain more satisfying personal and occupational roles following treatment.

Another practical issue neglected by many treatment programs is the need to provide child care for clients with children. Lack of child care is one of the most frequently reported barriers to treatment among alcoholic women, particularly those who are single parents. Staff of programs that provide child care, either at their own facilities or through cooperative arrangements with other agencies, believe that it reduces alcoholic women's ambivalence about entering treatment and their guilt about how drinking has affected their children. Providing child care also offers an opportunity for early identification and intervention in psychiatric and behavioral problems, for which children of alcoholic parents are at increased risk.

Self-help groups for women alcoholics. In addition to Alcoholics Anonymous and its affiliated groups, Al-Anon and Alateen, a new self-help group for women has developed in recent years. Women for Sobriety, founded by a recovering alcoholic woman, Dr. Jean Kirkpatrick, offers a recovery program designed to address special needs of alcoholic women, including a major focus on self-image and self-esteem. Women for Sobriety groups are currently available in many parts of the United States. They are intended to provide specialized support for recovering alcoholic women in addition to other treatment programs or self-help groups in which they may be involved. Details of the program are presented in Kirkpatrick [21].

PREVENTION OF ALCOHOL PROBLEMS IN WOMEN

If relatively few research data exist regarding treatment effectiveness or special treatment needs of alcoholic women, even less research attention has been given to strategies for preventing or minimizing alcohol problems in women. Although a number of prevention demonstration projects have been conducted in recent years, most of these have tested prevention models without reference to possible gender differences in prevention needs or program effectiveness.

Despite this general lack of attention to prevention programing for women, a few model prevention programs for women have been conducted. These include a national mass media campaign targeted at women conducted in 1982 by the National Institute on Alcohol Abuse and Alcoholism, a California public education campaign designed to reduce heavy drinking in pregnancy, a program designed to increase coping skills and decrease risks of alcohol abuse among recently divorced and separated women, and several programs that attempt to enhance natural community support systems for women at risk for alcohol problems. Most of these programs are described in recent publications of the National Clearinghouse for Alcohol Information, Rockville, Maryland. Outcome evaluations of several ongoing projects will provide the first empirical data on effectiveness of various types of prevention models within specified populations of women.

A recent review of alcohol problems prevention for women [32] suggests four priorities for future research: (1) careful evaluation of specific strategies for reducing specific alcohol-related problems in specific target groups of women; (2) research examining the strength of various social and cultural influences on women's drinking, including social norms, alcohol beverage advertising, media portrayals of alcohol, and drinking contexts; (3) evaluation of innovative prevention approaches for women in heavy drinking environments (e.g., wives of alcoholic men); and (4) increased attention to women as providers of prevention services. The review notes the need to develop strategies for preventing or minimizing not only problems women experience as a result of their own drinking (e.g., problems with work, family, friends, or health) but also problems women experience as a result of others' drinking, such as accidents, rape, or other physical abuse. Most of Wilsnack's review deals with primary prevention of alcohol problems, that is, attempts to prevent problems from developing in the first place. A second review [5] considers some possible approaches to secondary prevention (early identification and intervention), including methods for reaching "hidden" alcoholic women and for training community gatekeepers, such as physicians, attorneys, and law enforcement personnel, who deal with problem drinking and alcoholic women.

SUMMARY AND CONCLUSIONS

Despite many similarities between alcoholic men and alcoholic women, gender differences have been reported or suggested in certain antecedents and consequences of alcohol abuse and in treatment needs and responses. Further research comparing women and men alcoholics is clearly needed. Finding similarities between women and men in the development and consequences of alcoholism will allow accumulated research knowledge from studies of men to be applied to women as well. Finding differences will allow treatment and prevention programs to take into account more effectively special characteristics and special needs of both women and men.

If a major contribution of recent research on women and alcohol has been to demonstrate that women alcoholics differ from men alcoholics in some important ways, perhaps the major task of future research will be to examine similarities and differences among problem drinking and alcoholic women within various demographic and clinical subgroups. As noted earlier, most research to date has included primarily white, middle-aged, middle-class alcoholic women. Much less is known about women in other population subgroups (e.g., much younger or older women, working-class women and women of upper socioeconomic status, and ethnic minority women). Other subgroups for whom little information is available are employed women, including professional women and women in nontraditional occupations; lesbians; daughters of alcoholic parents; and women in military service. Further clinical and general population studies of women in these and other subgroups may allow treatment and prevention efforts to be targeted more precisely not only to the needs of women as a group but also to the special characteristics and needs of specific subgroups or women with or at risk for alcohol problems.

REFERENCES

1. Beckman, L. J. Women alcoholics: A review of social and psychological studies. *J. Stud. Alcohol* 36:797-824, 1975.
2. Beckman, L. J. Sex-role conflict in alcoholic women: Myth or reality. *J. Abnorm. Psychol.* 87:408-417, 1978.
3. Beckman, L. J. The self-esteem of alcoholic women. *J. Stud. Alcohol* 39:491-498, 1978.
4. Blane, H. T. *The Personality of the Alcoholic: Guises of Dependency.* Harper & Row: New York, 1968.
5. Blume, S. B. Researches on women and alcohol: Casefinding, diagnosis, treatment, and rehabilitation. In: *Alcoholism and Alcohol Abuse Among Women: Research Issues* (Research Monograph No. 1 of the National Institute on Alcohol Abuse and Alcoholism). United States Department of Health, Education and Welfare: Washington, D.C., 1980.
6. Braiker, H. B. The diagnosis and treatment of alcoholism in women. In: *Special Population Issues* (Alcohol and Health Monograph No. 4 of the National Institute on Alcohol Abuse and Alcoholism). United States Department of Health and Human Services: Washington, D.C. In press.
7. Celentano, D. D., McQueen, D. V., and Chee, E. Substance abuse by women: A review of the epidemiologic literature. *J. Chronic Dis.* 33:383-394, 1980.
8. Clark, W. B., and Midanik, L. Alcohol use and alcohol problems among U.S. adults. In: *Alcohol Consumption and Related Problems* (Alcohol and Health Monograph No. 1 of the National Institute on Alcohol Abuse and Alcoholism). United States Department of Health and Human Services: Washington, D.C. In press.
9. Corrigan, E. M. *Alcoholic Women in Treatment.* Oxford University Press: New York, 1980.
10. Gomberg, E. S. Women and alcoholism. In: *Women in Therapy,* Franks, V. and Burtle, V. (eds.). Brunner/Mazel: New York, 1974.
11. Gomberg, E. S. The female alcoholic. In: *Alcoholism: Interdisciplinary Approaches to an Enduring Problem,* Tarter, R. E. and Sugerman, A. A. (eds.). Addison-Wesley: Reading, Mass., 1976.
12. Gomberg, E. S. Problems with alcohol and other drugs. In: *Gender and Disordered Behavior,* Gomberg, E. S. and Franks, V. (eds.). Brunner/Mazel: New York, 1979.
13. Gomberg, E. S. Risk factors related to alcohol problems among women: Proneness

and vulnerability. In: *Alcoholism and Alcohol Abuse Among Women: Research Issues* (Research Monograph No. 1 of the National Institute on Alcohol Abuse and Alcoholism). United States Department of Health, Education and Welfare: Washington, D.C., 1980.

14. Goodwin, D. W., Schulsinger, F., Knop, J., Mednick, S., and Guze, S. B. Alcoholism and depression in adopted-out daughters of alcoholics. *Arch. Gen. Psychiatry* 34:751–755, 1977.

15. Greenblatt, M., and Schuckit, M. A. (eds.). *Alcoholism Problems in Women and Children.* Grune & Stratton: New York, 1976.

16. Guinle, M. P. *Program Modes and Counselor Sex in the Treatment of Female Alcoholics.* Doctoral dissertation, University of Mississippi, 1979.

17. Hill, S. Y. Biological consequences of alcohol for women. In: *Alcoholism and Alcohol Abuse Among Women: Research Issues* (Research Monograph No. 1 of the National Institute on Alcohol Abuse and Alcoholism). United States Department of Health, Education and Welfare: Washington, D.C., 1980.

18. Johnson, P., Armor, D. J., Polich, S., and Stambul, H. *U.S. Adult Drinking Practices: Time Trends, Social Correlates and Sex Roles* (Working note prepared for the National Institute on Alcohol Abuse and Alcoholism). Rand Corporation: Santa Monica, Calif., 1977.

19. Julian, V., Mohr, C., and Lapp, J. Father-daughter incest: A descriptive analysis. In: *Sexual Abuse of Children: Implications for Treatment,* Holder, W. M. (ed.). American Humane Association: Englewood, Colo., 1980.

20. Kalant, O. J. (ed.). *Research Advances in Alcohol and Drug Problems: Alcohol and Drug Problems in Women* (Vol. 5). Plenum: New York, 1980.

21. Kirkpatrick, J. *Turnabout: Help for a New Life.* Doubleday: New York, 1978.

22. Knupfer, G. Problems associated with drunkenness in women. In: *Special Population Issues* (Alcohol and Health Monograph No. 4 of the National Institute on Alcohol Abuse and Alcoholism). United States Department of Health and Human Services: Washington, D.C. In press.

23. Konovsky, M., and Wilsnack, S. C. Social drinking and self-esteem in married couples. *J. Stud. Alcohol,* in press.

24. McClelland, D. C., Davis, W. N., Kalin, R., and Wanner, E. *The Drinking Man: Alcohol and Human Motivation.* Free Press: New York, 1972.

25. National Institute on Alcohol Abuse and Alcoholism. *Alcoholism and Alcohol Abuse Among Women: Research Issues* (Research Monograph No. 1 of the National Institute on Alcohol Abuse and Alcoholism). United States Department of Health, Education and Welfare: Washington, D.C., 1980.

26. Sandmaier, M. *The Invisible Alcoholics: Women and Alcohol Abuse in America.* McGraw-Hill: New York, 1980.

27. Schuckit, M. A., and Morrissey, E. R. Alcoholism in women: Some clinical and social perspectives with an emphasis on possible subtypes. In: *Alcoholism Problems in Women and Children,* Greenblatt, M. and Schuckit, M. A. (eds.). Grune & Stratton: New York, 1976.

28. Tamerin, J. S. The psychotherapy of alcoholic women. In: *Practical Approaches to Alcoholism Psychotherapy,* Zimberg, S., Wallace, J., and Blume, S. B. (eds.). Plenum: New York, 1978.

29. Trice, H. M., and Beyer, J. M. Women employees and job-based alcoholism programs. *J. Drug Issues* 9:371–385, 1979.

30. Wilsnack, S. C. The impact of sex roles on women's alcohol use and abuse. In: *Alcoholism Problems in Women and Children,* Greenblatt, M. and Schuckit, M. A. (eds.). Grune & Stratton: New York, 1976.

31. Wilsnack, S. C. Alcohol, sexuality, and reproductive dysfunction in women. In:

Fetal Alcohol Syndrome: Human Studies (Vol. 11), Abel, E. L. (ed.). CRC Press: Boca Raton, Fla. In press.

32. Wilsnack, S. C. Prevention of alcohol problems in women. In: *Special Population Issues* (Alcohol and Health Monograph No. 4 of the National Institute on Alcohol Abuse and Alcoholism). United States Department of Health and Human Services: Washington, D.C. In press.

33. Wilsnack, S. C., and Wilsnack, R. W. Sex roles and adolescent drinking. In: *Youth, Alcohol, and Social Policy*, Blane, H. T. and Chafetz, M. E. (eds.). Plenum: New York, 1979.

58

JEFFREY M. BRANDSMA, PhD, Medical College of Georgia, Augusta, Georgia

E. MANSELL PATTISON, MD, Medical College of Georgia, Augusta, Georgia

HOMOSEXUALITY AND ALCOHOLISM

PEOPLE WITH A HOMO-erotic sexual preference become alcoholic, and are at high risk of doing so. However, it is now only of historical interest that some of the early psychoanalytic writers postulated a causal connection between homosexuality and the development of alcoholism. Karl Abraham's 1908 paper, which was influential in the early 1930s [1], postulated that alcoholics were struggling with latent homosexual wishes in line with Freud's theory of paranoia. Even then, however, there were many other competing theories in psychoanalysis, and today, although there are several different psychodynamic formulations of alcoholism [5, 9], homosexuality is not considered an etiologic variable. The prevailing zeitgeist in psychoanalysis is that alcoholism can occur in any type of character structure, and treatment must be oriented to current ego-coping styles.

Besides becoming theoretically irrelevant, no empirical evidence has shown homosexuality to directly cause alcoholism. Yet the correlation persists in the

---

Jeffrey M. Brandsma, PhD, Professor of Psychiatry, Medical College of Georgia, Augusta, Georgia.

E. Mansell Pattison, MD, Professor and Chairman, Department of Psychiatry, Medical College of Georgia, Augusta, Georgia.

minds of some clinicians. The correlation rests on the oft-noted fact that many alcoholics and homosexuals are troubled by passive-dependent character problems thought to stem from early childhood. Secondly, alcohol encourages regressions, and what often emerge in some form when drinking are homosexual fantasies or anxieties. Despite this, it is much less often that drinking leads to homosexual behavior, except by those who engage in a homosexual life style or are actively struggling with homosexuality.

THE INCIDENCE OF ALCOHOLISM AMONG HOMOSEXUALS

It can be stated that alcoholics do not have a higher incidence of homosexuality. These are independent conditions when causality is considered in this direction [13]. However, the question of whether the incidence of alcoholism among homosexuals is higher than in the larger population has been answered definitively in the affirmative. Homosexuals are more prone to alcoholism, particularly lesbians, and the extent has been called by some an epidemic.

Saghir and Robins [11] found homosexual men to be similar in alcohol problems when compared to the normal population, but homosexual women had a much greater degree of drinking problems. This confirmed Swanson et al.'s [4] findings about lesbians. Later studies [3, 7, 10, 16] have found both on the West Coast and in the Midwest that approximately 30% of the male homosexual population was in the later stages of alcoholism, this being much higher than in the population at large, which is estimated to be at 10 to 20%.

The explanation for this phenomenon is largely agreed upon and rests on the following reasons.

1. Homosexuality is defined as deviant in this society. Therefore, as a group, homosexuals are exposed to oppression from families and others, resulting in frustration, stress, anxiety, and alienation. Alcohol helps homosexuals cope with the internal distress caused by external social prejudice and their own shame, guilt, and so forth.

2. Sociologically speaking, if one is deviant in one characteristic, one is likely to be deviant in others, since one becomes inured to social condemnation and associates with deviant peers. Peer group attitudes will tend to tolerate more deviance. Risk factors that make one vulnerable to deviance (childhood deprivation, stormy adolescence, low self-esteem, problems of trust, heavy drinking in a family member) also contribute to alcoholism [8].

3. Socially legitimate socialization places for homosexuals are largely limited to bars or parties serving alcohol. The homosexual bars are the social nexus for

the gay community. The following quote is as true for males as it is for females:

> Bars for lesbians have taken on the characteristics and significance of the community center, the coffee break, family gatherings, clubs, societies, and a church picnic. . . . Lesbian women usually are forced to socialize in very limited environments . . . Traditionally, these environments are bars, and lesbian women look to them as places for meeting friends, finding partners, relating with peers, performing most other human social functions. Bars provide the atmosphere where "It is okay to be me, even if only for a few hours a week." [15, p. 4]

Empirically, Bell and Weinberg [4] found that 65 to 75% of homosexual men and 17% of homosexual women had cruised at bars. "Cruising" was defined as time spent looking for a sexual partner. Of those that did attend bars, the modal frequency was one to two times a week, with over 50% of the men and over 30% of the women doing this at least one, two, or more times a week. Only 20% said bars were not important in their cruising time, but 30% spent a third or more of their cruising time in bars. Fifield [7] found that 90% of her sample in Los Angeles spent 80% of their total social activity time (not just cruising) in bars or at parties that served alcohol. Her sample averaged 19 nights a month in these activities and consumed six drinks a night on the average. There is no doubt that bars are crucial not only for cruising, but also for other socialization activities.

4. Alcohol is a useful disinhibitor and antianxiety agent. This is important in meeting new friends, cruising, and for reducing anxiety about sexual performance. Thus it is that the homosexual life style and social context contribute to the use and abuse of alcohol.

TREATMENT OF HOMOSEXUAL ALCOHOLICS

The treatment of homosexual alcoholics is notably problematic. Fifield [7] found that only four of 46 agencies who treated alcoholics in a city with a large gay community attempted to make any outreach efforts toward homosexuals. Fewer than 25% of the agencies provided training for their staff in this area, and only 2% of the staff were gay.

These not-atypical conditions lead to problems throughout the treatment process.

For example, if sexual preference is known to be homosexual, a person can be denied treatment. Also, as homosexuals enter the treatment system they have to put up with hostility, inattention, snide remarks, and rejection from both support and treatment staff. On the other hand, many agencies do not identify them or respond specifically to them; this is usually a mistake as well.

Often homosexual persons are reluctant to seek treatment for alcoholism because many treaters misguidedly want to change their sexual preference or total life style. This is not a denial of alcoholism, but a fear of the deterioration of their social contacts or sexual performance.

Because of the life style, sexual problems are usually intertwined with alcoholism. It is difficult in treatment to separate problems and interventions because drinking is integral to the sexual life style. Many heterosexual therapists in effect attempt selective denial in this regard (ignoring the sexual part of alcoholism); this attempt often feeds into the denial problems inherent in alcoholism. On the other extreme, sexuality can be used as a distraction from alcohol issues.

And, finally, in patient-to-patient interactions, especially in groups, homosexuals experience ostracism from other alcoholics. This is true in straight Alcoholics Anonymous (AA) groups as well as other programs.

ATTEMPTS AT SOLUTION TO TREATMENT PROBLEMS

In the last decade, attempts have been made to deal with these problems.

First, alcoholism programs have made contact with the leaders of the homosexual community in large cities to let them know that they are welcome and to begin a necessary dialogue.

Second, educational efforts are being made to raise the consciousness of homosexuals through pamphlets, information services [6, 12, 17], and group discussions. More treatment personnel are being educated in the unique aspects of the homosexual life style and its impact on alcoholism; literature in this area seems to be increasing, and a special issue of the *Journal of Homosexuality* has recently been devoted to this topic [2].

Third, some concerned groups have advocated opening coffee houses rather than bars. Given the profitability of alcohol and the psychoactive effects compared to coffee, this alternative may be difficult to implement, but the attempt to expand social activities in nonalcoholic directions is an important one.

Fourth, where feasible, specially defined groups or distinct treatment tracks are provided. They can be provided through community treatment programs (nationwide there were an estimated 100 specialized programs in 1980) or in the self-help movement. In the latter, there are organizations such as Alcoholics Together (AT—largely in Los Angeles), Women for Sobriety, and the Gay Alcoholics Anonymous (GAA—an estimated 300 groups nationwide in 1980). GAA caused some controversy initially as to whether this separation is in violation of the spirit of AA versus an appropriate evolution and expansion of AA principles. The need seems to have tipped the scales in this controversy. Today in the GAA literature honesty and acceptance are emphasized, with no effort to change gayness, but rather to come to terms with alcoholism. The National Association of Gay Professionals (NAGAP) was formed in 1978 (204 West 20th Street, New York, New York 10011); they publish a newsletter and compile a relevant bibliography on homosexuality and alcoholism.

Finally, attempts are being made to understand and deal with both the original and nontraditional extended family systems that homosexuals come from and live in, as well as their important dyadic relationships. Strategically this usually involves bringing significant others into the treatment situation.

SUMMARY

In summary, homosexuals are at much higher risk of alcoholism because their social life style is almost invariably intertwined with alcohol. A broadened understanding of this social context and its risks needs to be better understood both by homosexuals and those who treat their alcoholism. Programs must differentiate to provide outreach and informed treatment strategies without attacking sexual preference or a person's total social life style. However, the treatment of a homosexual alcoholic cannot just focus on the alcoholism, but must attend to the social and psychological processes of interdigitation between homosexual life style and drinking behaviors. Effective treatment of the alcoholism will likely require appropriate review and some changes in the particular high-risk homosexual life style behavior that leads to alcohol abuse.

REFERENCES

1. Abraham, K. The psychological relations between sexuality and alcoholism. In: *Selected Papers*. Hogarth Press: London, 1927.
2. Alcoholism and homosexuality. *J. Homosex.* 7 (Whole no. 4), 1981.
3. Barr, R. F., Greeberg, H. P., and Dalton, M. S. Homosexuality and psychological adjustment. *Med. J. Australia* 1:187-189, 1974.
4. Bell, A. P., and Weinberg, M. S. *Homosexualities: A Study of Diversity among Men and Women*. Simon & Schuster: New York, 1978.
5. Blum, E. M. Psychoanalytic views of alcoholism: A review. *Q. J. Stud. Alcohol* 27 (2):259-299, 1966.
6. Christenson, S., Ihlenfeld, G., and Kinsolving, J. *Lesbians, Gay Men and Their Alcohol and Other Drug Use: Resources*. Wisconsin Cleaninghouse for Alcohol and Drug Information: 1980.
7. Fifield, L. *On My Way to Nowhere, Alienated, Isolated, Drunk: An Analysis of Gay Alcohol Abuse and an Evaluation of Alcoholism and Alcoholism Rehabilitation Services for the Los Angeles Gay Community*. Gay Community Services Center: Los Angeles, 1975.
8. Gomberg, E. S. Problems with alcohol and other drugs. In: *Gender and Disordered*

Behavior: Sex Differences in Psychopathology, Gomberg, E.S. and Franks, V. (eds.). Brunner/Mazel: New York, 1979.

9. Hartocollis, P., and Hartocollis, P. C. Alcoholism, borderline, and narcissistic disorders: A psychoanalytic overview. In: *Phenomenology and Treatment of Alcoholism*, Fann, W. E., Karacan, I, Pakorny, A. D., and Williams, R. L. (eds.). Spectrum: New York, 1980.

10. Lohrenz, L. J., Connelly, J. C., Coyne, L., and Spare, K. E. Alcohol problems in several midwestern homosexual communities. *J. Stud. Alcohol* 39(1):1959-1962, 1978.

11. Saghir, M. T., and Robins, E. *Male and Female Homosexuality: A Comprehensive Investigation*. Williams & Wilkins: Baltimore, 1973.

12. Schwartz, L. *Alcoholism in the Lesbian/Gay Community*. Do It Now Foundation: Phoenix, 1980.

13. Small, E. J., and Leach, B. Counseling homosexual alcoholics: Ten case histories. *J. Stud. Alcohol* 38:2077-2086, 1977.

14. Swanson, D. W., Loomis, S. D., Lukesh, R, Cronin, R, and Smith, J. A. Clinical features of the female homosexual patient: A comparison with the heterosexual patient. *J. Nerv. Ment. Dis.* 155:119-124, 1972.

15. Weathers, B. *Alcoholism and the Lesbian Community*. Gay Council on Drinking Behavior: Washington, D.C., 1976.

16. Weinberg, M. S., and Williams, C. J. *Male Homosexuals: Their Problems and Adaptations*. Oxford University Press: New York, 1974.

17. Ziebold, T. O., and Mongeon, J. E. *Ways to Gay Sobriety: Recovery Strategies for Homosexual Alcoholics in Recovery and Reconstruction*. Gay Council on Drinking Behavior: Washington, D.C., 1980.

59

JEROME F. X. CARROLL, PhD, Eagleville Hospital and Rehabilitation Center, Eagleville, Pennsylvania

SIDNEY H. SCHNOLL, MD, PhD, Northwestern University Medical School

MIXED DRUG AND ALCOHOL POPULATIONS

THERE ARE AT LEAST three situations in which treatment personnel may encounter patients who have mixed drug and alcohol problems. The largest and most clearly recognized mixed drug and alcohol populations are to be found in combined treatment programs, that is, substance abuse programs where both alcohol and drug dependent persons are treated together, in the same manner, at the same time, and with no distinction to their respective substance(s) of abuse.

The second situation pertains to polydrug programs. Unfortunately, due to lack of uniformity in the definition of the term "polydrug" [6], and a concomitant failure to carefully examine and document the role of alcohol in the evolution and maintenance of a polydrug substance abuse pattern, the extent and scope of mixed drug and alcohol populations are likely to be underestimated in some polydrug programs.

Studies such as that of the National Drug/Alcohol Collaborative Project (NDACP) and the National Youth Polydrug Study (NYPD) very clearly have dis-

---

Jerome F. X. Carroll, PhD, Director of Psychological Services, Eagleville Hospital and Rehabilitation Center, Eagleville, Pennsylvania.

Sidney H. Schnoll, MD, PhD, Northwestern Institute of Psychiatry, Northwestern University School of Medicine, Chicago, Illinois.

closed the significant role alcohol plays for most polydrug abusers, namely as a substitute for other substances of abuse or as a substance used to boost, balance, counteract, or sustain the effects of other substances of abuse [3, 11]. In addition, the substance abuse histories of the majority of polydrug abusers studied in the NDACP revealed that alcohol and marijuana were among the first substances abused by this population.

The third situation where mixed drug and alcohol populations may be found is in substance-specific treatment programs, that is, programs designed to treat only alcoholics or only drug addicts. Unfortunately, it is in these settings that the coexistence of alcohol and drug problems is most likely to go undetected and/or unreported. For a variety of reasons (e.g., funding sources that preclude the admission and treatment of other addictions, politics, prejudices, etc.), administrative and treatment staffs may be either inadequately trained and/or unwilling to inquire about or report the presence of substance abuse problems other than the one for which their respective programs were established and funded.

MULTIPLE SUBSTANCE ABUSE

Mounting evidence from a variety of studies [6, 12, 15], both in this country and abroad, clearly have documented a movement away from substance-specific patterns of abuse to patterns of multiple substance abuse (MSA). Many MSA patterns, moreover, are distinguished by the abuse of both alcohol and other drugs, either in sequence and/or as concurrent substances of abuse [6]. Obviously, MSA patterns present a considerable challenge to traditional substance-specific treatment (i.e., alcohol only or drug only), as well as the administrative, policy-making, and financial superstructures that support such programs.

This chapter focuses primarily on combined treatment, its underlying philosophy, its effectiveness, its challenges and advantages, and finally its implications for the substance abuse fields. For the most part, it reports on Eagleville Hospital and Rehabilitation Center's 12 years of experience with combined treatment.

Eagleville is a private, not-for-profit hospital devoted to treatment, training, and research in the field of alcoholism and drug dependency. Its combined treatment program was initiated in 1968. Two years earlier, Eagleville had converted from a tuberculosis sanatarium to an alcohol rehabilitation center. The decision to attempt a combined treatment program grew, in part, out of the demands of surrounding communities for help in meeting a mounting drug abuse problem. The discovery that many drug addicts also had past and current alcohol abuse problems and that substantial numbers of alcoholics had also abused drugs (most commonly prescription drugs such as barbiturates and minor tranquilizers) also facilitated this decision.

Eagleville is organized as a modified therapeutic community. Its treatment strategies are predicated upon an abstinence approach to substance abuse rehabilitation, although medications (e.g., psychotropics, Antabuse) are prescribed in the treatment process when and if the particular treatment needs of the patient require such assistance.

Since Eagleville accepts any and all varieties of substance abuse problems, the only restrictions the community exercises on admissions are that the substance abuser not be so emotionally disturbed and out of control (blatantly psychotic) or physically infirmed or disabled as to be unable to actively participate in the program. Multiply handicapped persons, those confined to wheel chairs, and even a paraplegic have been admitted to treatment at Eagleville.

Those entering the community do so voluntarily, although some are pressured to do so by family members, employers, and the courts. In fact, a small portion of residents are referred to Eagleville directly from prison as a condition of parole or probation. The clinical experience with these men and women has been at least as favorable as with those of the other residents.

The Eagleville treatment program addresses the whole person and involves a multidisciplinary team approach to rehabilitation. The inpatient program, which can accommodate 126 residents, lasts 45 days on the average; the actual length of stay for any resident is determined by his or her particular problems, dynamics, resources, and overall readiness for treatment in a lesser care facility. An additional 50 to 60 beds are available in a partial hospitalization, half-work and half-therapy program known as the Candidate Program. The Candidate Program lasts from 3 to 6 months, depending on the individual's rehabilitation needs.

THE GENERIC PERSPECTIVE

Eagleville's philosophy of therapy is generic, which means to say that the particular substance(s) of abuse is(are) less important than the underlying dynamics of the addictive process. The generic perspective grew out of the recognition that contemporary addictive patterns typically include the abuse of both alcohol and other drugs and the fact that addicted men and women, regardless of the substance(s) they may have abused, tend to present with etiologies, defenses, personality dynamics, psychopathologies, and treatment needs that are far more similar than they are dissimilar [4, 7]. For example, consider how frequently the following factors have been noted among both the alcoholic and the drug-dependent person: disruptive family background, with one or more family members also abusing a substance; excessive denial and rationalization; little or no self-esteem, coupled with considerable underlying guilt and feelings of inadequacy, as well as high levels of depression, anxiety, and fear; impaired physical health; inadequate social skills; poor sexual adjustment; and strained or broken relationships with spouse and children.

ADMISSION AND DIAGNOSTIC CRITERIA

Single Eagleville's combined treatment program does not preclude admitting any would-be resident on the basis of past or present substance(s) abused, staff has had to work with a great variety of substance abuse patterns. This has necessitated a process of continuing refinement of admission criteria and the diagnostic system.

Admission Criteria

Individuals who, at the time of admission, present with evidence of a current substance abuse problem or substance dependence problem are admitted for treatment, unless otherwise determined to be ineligible or unsuitable for admission to Eagleville. Individuals who have had serious substance abuse problems or substance dependence problems in the past, but who have been abstaining from substances during the last 12 months due to incarceration and/or hospitalization and/or treatment at another facility are also considered for admission.

Substance abuse is distinguished by the following four criteria: (1) nonexperimental involvement with or consumption of a substance for a period that exceeds 1 month (this involvement may be continuous or episodic); (2) evidence that this involvement has led to significant, negative, psychobiosocial consequences; (3) evidence of pathological patterns of use; and (4) psychological dependence.

Substance dependence is distinguished by the same four criteria, in addition to the following two criteria: (1) evidence of tolerance for the substance, or (2) evidence of withdrawal symptoms. The definitions of substance abuse and substance dependence are based on the criteria specified in DSM-III [25].

"Pathological patterns of use" pertains to the compulsive consumption of amounts that exceed the normal levels of use in this society (e.g., with alcohol, normal consumption may be defined as an average of under 3 oz/day and/or less than 5 oz on any drinking day); use of licit substances in a manner other than medically prescribed, especially in instances that indicate loss of control; use of an illicit substance with evidence of loss of control; use of a substance as a substitute for another abused substance; use of a substance to boost, balance, counteract, or sustain the effects of another abused substance; use of a substance to counteract bad feelings and tension; and the secretive use of a substance, especially when such usage is guilt-provoking.

Diagnostic Criteria

Diagnosis of substance abuse problems should address both the current problem (considered the last 12 months, when the person was at risk) and past problems. The course of all substance abuse patterns, both current and past, should also be described according to the following three categories: (1) continuous (more or less daily maladaptive use); (2) episodic (periods of abstinence interspaced between periods of continuous, maladaptive use and/or consumption; (3) in remission (previously exhibited maladaptive use that has not occurred during the last 12 months when the person was at risk (i.e., when the person was able to have ready access to the substance).

All residents admitted to Eagleville with a current and/or past substance abuse and/or substance dependence problem(s) are assigned both a current and past substance abuse and/or substance dependence diagnosis, according to the following classification scheme: A, A + D, D, D + A, and M. Each of these major diagnostic codes should also reflect the course that the pattern of abuse has followed, namely continuous, episodic, or in remission.

These diagnoses are assigned according to the following circumstances: "A" is assigned whenever the patient's substance abuse problem involves only alcohol, meaning no other drugs have ever been abused. Experimental use of a drug ("tried it a few times [10 or fewer episodes] to see what it was like") would not disallow a diagnosis of "A."

"A + D" is used whenever there is evidence of a current (last 12 months), primary alcohol abuse problem, coupled with either a current and/or past secondary drug problem. The secondary diagnosis of "D" in this instance, as is also the case with the primary diagnosis of "A," should include a description of the course of the abuse pattern.

"D" is assigned whenever the resident's substance abuse problem involves only the abuse of a drug(s) other than alcohol. The fact that someone drinks or drank nonabusively (see previous discussion of substance abuse) does not disallow the use of this diagnostic category.

"D + A" is used whenever there is evidence of a current (last 12 months), primary drug abuse problem, coupled with either a current and/or past secondary alcohol problem. Both the primary and secondary diagnoses also contain a description of the course of each abuse pattern.

"M" is the classification noted whenever the pattern of abuse indicates nearly equal degrees of maladaptive use of both alcohol and drugs.

DOES COMBINED TREATMENT WORK?

The Evidence

After carefully reviewing the literature on combined treatment [5], it can be concluded that very few empirical studies have been attempted to answer the question, "Does combined treatment work?" In fact, only three such studies were uncovered [1, 9, 24]. The Cole and Cole study [9] was based on the opinions of directors of programs, staff, and clients concerning the perceived effectiveness of combined treatment, and in that respect, it differs from the Aumack [1] and Veterans Administration [24] studies. The latter studies attempted to generate empirical data relating to treatment outcome criteria designed to indicate whether combined treatment was better than, equal to, or less effective than segregated or substance-specific treatment.

Experimental Results

The two empirical studies [1, 24] indicated that combined treatment produced more or less the same results as segregated or substance-specific treatment. Aumack did caution, however, that "residents (both alcoholics and drug-dependent persons) exposed to combined treatment conditions were less likely to abstain from using alcohol than those exposed to single treatment" [1]. He also cautioned regarding this finding that use was not equivalent to abuse. The Veterans Administration [24] study reported slightly more favorable outcomes for alcoholics in segregated treatment programs, with the qualifications that "near parity of yield" was noted for combined and segregated treatment programs.

The Cole and Cole study concluded that "no clear superiority can be attributed to either combined or separate treatment" [9, p. 11]. They did report, however, observing that more optimistic attitudes were held by staff and clients regarding the possibility of recovery in combined treatment programs. Older alcoholics, on the other hand, tended to hold more negative attitudes toward combined treatment. Such attitudes, in the opinion of the authors, could generally be overcome within a 6-month period of time.

Clinical Observations

A number of programs have attempted combined treatment. One program reporting a negative experience with combined treatment was that of the Silver Hill Foundation [16]. The Silver Hill program was an alcoholism program that provided detoxification, education, and personal counseling services to a patient population whose average age was 55. They instituted a crash program to accommodate 22 adolescent drug abusers. The experiment failed, seemingly due to inadequate preparation for and experience in dealing with youthful substance abusers, as well as considerable resistance on the part of some staff and the alcoholic patients to implementing a combined treatment program at Silver Hill.

On the other hand, several programs have written of their success with combined treatment [8, 13, 17, 18, 19]. Eagleville [17], for example, compared the type of discharge its residents received before (1966–68), during (1969–70), and after (1971–74) the inception of its combined treatment program (see Table 1). The originally reported data has been updated by including similar information for 1979. Note additional categories, namely A + D and D + A, have been added to reflect Eagleville's present diagnostic system.

Inspection of Table 1 clearly indicates that the rate of regular discharges (i.e., those successfully completing the inpatient phase of treatment) has remained relatively constant for alcoholics. Some increase in against medical advice (AMA)

Table 1
Type of Discharges Received by Percentage and Mean Number of Days Stay at Eagleville Hospital and Rehabilitation Center

Type of discharge	Alcohol Abusers 1966-68	1969-70	1971-74	Drug Abusers 1969-70	1971-74	A[a] $n=492$ (1979)	A + D[a] $n=321$ (1979)	D[a] $n=252$ (1979)	D + A[a] $n=236$ (1979)
Regular[b]	56	55	56	24	42	55.3	44.2	51.2	47.9
Against medical advice (AMA)	10	13	17	17	13	17.7	17.8	13.5	14.8
Absent without leave (AWOL)	21	16	14	29	21	8.9	13.4	14.7	13.6
Disciplinary[c]	6	3	6	19	21	3.4	10.3	8.7	11.4
Transfers or with consent	6	11	7	10	3	14.6	13.7	11.9	11.9
Incarcerated	—	—	—	—	—	0	.6	.4	.4
Mean days inpatient stay	41[d]	43	42	34	36	32.8	30.3	31.0	29.4

[a] See p. 000 for explanation.
[b] In 1979, phase completed.
[c] In 1979, broke hospital rules.
[d] For 1966 only.

discharges for alcoholics is noted (10% in 1968-69 vs. 17% in 1971-74 and in 1979); however, fewer absent without leaves occurred for alcoholics (21% in 1966-68 vs. 8.9% in 1979). On the other hand, combined treatment clearly has benefited Eagleville's drug abusers with respect to a number of categories (e.g., regular discharges, absent without leaves, and disciplinary discharges). Overall, it would appear that on the basis of type of discharge, combined treatment at Eagleville has resulted in gains for both alcoholics and drug abusers.

The reader will note a decrease in the mean number of inpatient stay days for alcoholics reflected in the 1979 figures. This change reflects the imposition of more stringent length of stay (LOS) requirements by the primary funding sources (Pennsylvania's medical assistance program) rather than any deterioration in Eagleville's capacity for holding and successfully treating alcohol-dependent residents.

Even where success was reported for combined treatment programs, a number of common problems were encountered in implementing combined treatment [17, 18, 19]. These problems dealt with preparing staff and the existing resident population to constructively accept and cope with the racial and age differences that typically emerge whenever a substance-specific program attempts to convert to a combined treatment program. Staff and resident prejudices concerning alcoholics and addicts were also cited as major obstacles that had to be surmounted.

In addition, when staff and residents felt forced to integrate and/or where very negative attitudes existed within the therapeutic system toward instituting a combined treatment program, from administrators to line staff to residents, serious problems were encountered. The same pertains to external systems that too may be resistant to combined treatment and can, as a result of this resistance, adversely affect the effectiveness of program's combined treatment effort.

What the research and clinical evidence seems to suggest is that alcoholics and addicts can be combined in a common treatment program with at least as much success as with substance-specific treatment. Whether any particular treatment program should attempt combined treatment or whether any particular substance abuser should be referred to a combined versus substance-specific program are questions that cannot be categorically answered as yes or no.

SPECIAL CONSIDERATIONS IN IMPLEMENTING COMBINED TREATMENT PROGRAMMING

Staffing Issues

No matter how well-planned any treatment program may be, the level of commitment and motivation of the staff to implement the program will often determine its ultimate success or failure. This is especially true of combined treatment programming.

In selecting staff for a combined treatment program, it is strongly recommended to obtain staff with experience in working with all types of addiction. Ideally, there should be a balance among staff with respect to alcohol and drug treatment experience. In addition, the composition of the staff should parallel the patient population with respect to such demographic variables as race, age, and sex. Having some recovered alcoholic and recovered drug-dependent staff is also strongly recommended when implementing combined treatment programs.

Creating an ambience of acceptance and enthusiasm for combined treatment is also very important. In some cases, this may necessitate surfacing and working through any resistance or negative feelings and attitudes that staff may hold toward working with the other addiction. (The same principle also holds for patients already in the program.) Helping staff to appreciate a generic perspective, the value of being able to work with all forms of addiction, especially with the growing numbers of multiple-substance abusers, career advancement opportunities, and job mobility will also facilitate implementation of a combined treatment program.

To do anything well requires quality preparation, and supervision. This is certainly true in the case of combined treatment programming. Where combined treatment efforts have faltered, staff were often pressed to do combined treatment with little or no preparation. This simply sets up a failure experience for everyone concerned. Having available trainers and supervisors experienced with combined treatment would significantly improve a program's chances of succeeding. If trainers and supervisors experienced with combined treatment are unavailable, then training and supervisors should at least be balanced with respect to alcohol and drug treatment experience.

IMPLEMENTING A WITHDRAWAL PROGRAM FOR MIXED DRUG AND ALCOHOL POPULATIONS

Whereas some aspects of withdrawal are of medical necessity specific to certain classes of drugs of abuse, the overall withdrawal process at Eagleville reflects the community's commitment to the generic perspective. Residents who are withdrawing, regardless of what substance(s) they may have abused, are integrated into the regular treatment program as rapidly as their withdrawal progress permits. This approach offers several advantages over free-standing detoxification programs.

1. Residents are able to utilize the entire range of services available at Eagleville instead of being restricted to one part of the program.
2. Residents become so involved in the regular treatment program that they have very little time to dwell on the discomfort of the withdrawal syndrome.
3. Residents more readily see the withdrawal phase of treatment as just one

component of the overall treatment process and are thus less likely to believe that treatment is finished when withdrawal is completed.

Integrating withdrawal into the treatment process also alters the expectations of the staff and in turn those of the resident. Instead of looking for the medical complications of withdrawal, the staff encourages full participation in all activities, unless directed otherwise by the physician.

At Eagleville, the withdrawing resident is monitored regularly by the physicians and nurses. Because Eagleville's program is built around an abstinence model of treatment, the medical staff gives the resident only enough medication to decrease the discomfort of withdrawal, and this typically is done for a limited period of time with decreasing dosages. The medicating process also is made easier by the active participation of the withdrawing resident in the program.

For patients in substance-specific programs, the withdrawal regime usually is not difficult, unless the resident has concealed or "forgotten" to report the abuse of other substances. However, in combined programs, patients could be taking any combination of drugs. It is, therefore, very important for the staff, especially the physicians, to understand the relationship between various groups of medications. For example, any drugs that demonstrate cross-tolerance and cross-dependence with one another have a similar mechanism for the development of dependence. It is, possible, therefore, to use a single medication to withdraw patients from one or more drugs in that class [22].

Table 2 lists all of the drugs in the depressant or sedative-hypnotic class. Withdrawing patients from any of these drugs can be performed safely with phenobarbital [21, 23]. Drugs that fall into the opiate class (Table 2), all display cross-tolerance and cross-dependence with methadone, which is the drug of choice for withdrawal. For patients dependent on stimulant drugs there are no specific drugs effective in treating the withdrawal syndrome.

When patients present with a mixed dependence that crosses drug classes, the treatment of choice is to place the patient on a medication that specifically blocks the withdrawal for each class of drug he or she has abused. Once stabilized, the patient should be withdrawn from one drug at a time. This tends to prolong the withdrawal process, but makes it easier for the patient.

As the use of increasing numbers of drugs continues, the treatment of withdrawal and other medical aspects of drug abuse becomes more complicated. For example, patients may report having taken various drugs that they bought on the street; however, what they received may have been quite different from what they intended to purchase [14, 22]. Thus it is possible that patients may be dependent on drugs they never knew they were taking, or they may become dependent, because they were unaware of the close relationship between two or more drugs they were taking.

Any program involved in combined treatment should have a member on the staff or a consultant who is familiar with this problem and the pharmacology of MSA.

Diagnosis

In combined treatment programs (and in substance-specific treatment programs), the taking of a complete and accurate substance abuse history is critical to the success of the program. Eagleville's diagnostic criteria have already been outlined. Patients with preliminary diagnoses of either alcohol only or drug only especially should be carefully screened for the possible abuse of the other substance category.

Staff should be aware that alcoholics will often minimize or "forget" having abused various prescription drugs or smoked marijuana, while addicts similarly often dismiss the significance of past and present misuse of alcohol.

Table 2
Drug Classifications by Substances Abused

Sedative-Hypnotics
  Alcohol
  Barbiturates: Seconal (secobarbital), Nembutal (pentobarbital), Amytal (amobarbital), Tuinal (secobarbital and amobarbital), Luminal (phenobarbital)
  Sleeping pills: Noctec (chloral and/or hydrate), Quaalude, Parest and Sopor (methaqualone), Placidyl (ethclorvynol), Doriden (glutethimide), Nodular (methyprylon), Dalmane (flurazepam)
  Minor tranquilizers and anxiolytics: Equanil and Miltown (meprobamate), Valium (diazepam), Librium (chlordiazepoxide), Serax (oxazepam), Ativan (lorazepam), Tranxene (clorazepate), Verstran (prazepam)

Opiates
  opium
  heroin (diacetylmorphine)
  morphine
  Dilaudid (hydromorphinone)
  Numorphan (oxymorphone)
  codeine
  Talwin (pentazocine)
  Dolophine (methadone)
  Darvon (propoxyphene)
  Demerol (meperidine)

Stimulants
  Benzedrine (amphetamine)
  Methedrine (methamphetamine)
  Dexedrine (dextroamphetamine)
  Preludin (phenmetrazine)
  Plegine (phendimetrazine)
  Ritalin (methylphenidate)
  cocaine

To facilitate the taking of a careful and thorough substance abuse history, some questions used at Eagleville are provided. Alcoholism counselors might supplement their normal questioning about drinking by asking such questions as

1. Have you ever taken any medication for problems associated with your drinking? If so, what medications did you use and for how long?
2. Did you ever use these medications in a manner different from that prescribed by your doctor (e.g., taking more than the prescribed amount and/or using them longer than your doctor had indicated)?
3. Did you ever use medication prescribed by a doctor for a relative or friend to help you calm your nerves or get to sleep at night?
4. Did you ever take any medication or pills just to see what it was like and how it would work?
5. Did you ever take any medication or pills just to enjoy the feeling they give you?
6. Did you ever take any medication or pills for some other nonmedical reason, and not because you needed it?
7. Have you ever taken medication or pills to help you get ready for some big event, or to help you accomplish something?
8. Have you ever taken any medication or pills before going out, so that you could enjoy yourself more with other people?
9. Did you ever take any medication or pills when drinking to get a better buzz or a different kind of high?
10. Did you ever take any medication or pills to help you counteract the effects of hangovers?
11. Did you ever use any medication or pills to help you overcome withdrawal symptoms when you couldn't drink and/or were trying to stop drinking?
12. Did you ever smoke any "grass"—marijuana? If so, how often and for how long? Did you ever smoke grass while you were drinking?

Drug abuse counselors similarly should inquire more carefully about alcohol abuse and the extent to which the patient continues to drink by asking questions such as

1. Do you still attend social gatherings or parties where you do some social drinking? If yes, what do you typically drink? How much? How often?
2. At these gatherings, do you typically make contacts with others who are using drugs or could supply them to you? Did you ever use drugs while attending such parties?
3. What did you typically use when you couldn't get your drug of choice? Did you ever use alcohol as a substitute? [If patient names marijuana, inquire whether it was used along with alcohol.]

4. Have you ever gotten high on drugs and alcohol? Was it a pleasant high?

5. Did you ever use alcohol to get a more mellow high or to help you withdraw from heroin or any other drug(s) of abuse?

Treatment

Basically, the rehabilitative sequence is the same in most substance abuse programs, whether combined treatment or substance-specific treatment: doing withdrawal; psychobiosocial evaluation and history taking; restoring physical health through proper diet, rest, and activities; providing addiction education; challenging defenses, facilitating catharsis, promoting insight, instilling hope, encouraging spiritual renewal, and facilitating the learning of new modes of coping with personal needs and social demands through individual and/or group therapy; developing adequate aftercare plans (e.g., participation in Alcoholics Anonymous (AA) and/or Narcotics Anonymous (NA); and assisting the individual to handle the separation from treatment (e.g., through ritualized discharge ceremonies wherein achievements are acknowledged and feelings about treatment and leaving are shared).

In February 1980, a generically oriented, sequential substance abuse treatment goal model was introduced at Eagleville by the first author to assist the staff in setting treatment priorities and documenting their services to residents and the impact of these services. The model, adapted from Egan's [10] model for systematic helping and interpersonal relating, defines a progression of goals that occur in two phases. The two phases and their associated goals are

Phase 1

　Detoxification and continuing detoxification
　Restore physical health (specify goal)
　Restore emotional stability (specify goal)
　Motivate for treatment (includes building trust, reducing denial, providing addiction education, and resolving values conflicts)
　Aftercare planning I (establish need for post-inpatient treatment/support

Phase 2

　Challenging destructive defenses
　Facilitate catharsis (specify) and develop insight
　Building self-esteem
　Aftercare planning II (developing specific alternatives for lesser care continuing treatment)
　Aftercare planning III (preparation for discharge and implementation of aftercare plan)

The progression inherent in the two phases with their respective goals implies that staff should assist the residents to achieve a minimally acceptable level of competence or functioning with respect to the goals in phase 1 before addressing phase 2 goals. On the other hand, certain phase 1 goals may be carried throughout the treatment process, as in the case of a continuing serious emotional or physical problem (e.g., high blood pressure, diabetes, cirrhosis, depression). One advantage of the model is that it more rapidly and clearly facilitates the identification of progress, blocking, or regression in the resident's rehabilitation.

Typically phase 1 goals are addressed during the first 10 to 12 days in treatment. The remaining time in treatment at Eagleville is directed primarily to the sequence of goals in phase 2. This model is equally well suited for alcoholics, heroin addicts, and multiple-substance abusers.

Heterogeneity

In providing treatment to mixed drug and alcohol populations, staff and patients alike will have to cope with greater levels of heterogeneity of age, race, sex, socioeconomic status, education, and values than would be found in substance-specific treatment programs. The greater heterogeneity to be found in a mixed substance abuser program may constitute a serious obstacle to treatment in some programs [16], while a stimulant for growth and therapeutic progress in others [17]. Which of the two outcomes a combined treatment program experiences will depend to a great extent on the attitudes of the staff and the patients toward mixing populations and the quantity and quality of training, education, and experience the staff has for dealing with the heterogeneity associated with such populations. In the hands of an experienced, well-trained and skilled clinician, such differences can provide unique opportunities for therapeutic growth and stimulation [2, 6, 17].

Aftercare

Aftercare considerations in combined treatment are again similar to those associated with substance-specific treatment. They center around people, places, and things, as well as providing for meeting the addicted persons' continuing physical, psychological, educational, vocational, social, family, and spiritual needs. These needs vary considerably from person to person within various groups of substance abusers, but less so across groups, especially when the entire socioeconomic spectrum of substance abusers within a particular group are considered.

With respect to resources, there very clearly are more AA chapters than NA chapters throughout the country. Similarly, communities are far more advanced in providing various supports to the recovering alcoholic than the recovering addict. To the extent that existing alcohol-oriented community resources are exclusionary in their response to recovering people who have abused drugs, aftercare planning becomes more difficult. However, outpatient clinics and the patients' families can be important factors in establishing a strong aftercare program and therefore may compensate for some of these difficulties.

IMPLICATIONS OF COMBINED TREATMENT FOR THE SUBSTANCE ABUSE FIELDS

As already noted, multiple-substance abuse, that is, the abuse of both alcohol and other drugs, either sequentially and/or concurrently, is the predominant pattern of substance abuse — especially among substance abusers below the age of 40. If this trend continues, as there is reason to believe it will, then the categorical split between alcohol and drug programming, treatment, prevention, and research will more and more prove to be a costly impediment to future progress.

In taking this position, the authors are not necessarily advocating that everyone convert from substance-specific to combined treatment, even though the evidence to date indicates that combined treatment is at least as effective as substance-specific treatment. The authors are advocating, however, adopting a generic perspective. This perspective recognizes the significance of multiple-substance abuse patterns and the need to educate and train staff how to cope effectively with all forms of addiction, no matter what substance may appear to be dominant at any given instance in the substance abuser's history of abuse. In this way, the overall effectiveness of treatment should improve whether in a combined treatment or substance-specific treatment setting.

In a similar vein, efforts to create an effective prevention program should also reflect a generic perspective. Youth are particularly likely to abuse both alcohol and other drugs. The goals of both the National Institute on Alcohol and Alcohol Abuse and the National Institute on Drug Abuse with respect to prevention are for all purposes identical. The approaches advocated by the two institutes, moreover, are also practically the same. A cooperative, integrated national prevention program would seem to be an obviously desirable goal.

Research too needs to be coordinated. It is totally unacceptable that data systems developed and maintained by NIDA and NIAAA remain incompatible. It is a basic axiom of research that if one fails to ask the right questions, the right answers cannot possibly be obtained. At a minimum, drug abuse–oriented research must carefully inquire about past and present alcohol abuse and vice versa.

Obviously, if substance abusers continue to abuse both alcohol and drugs, national planners and legislators must take this fact into account. Legislators and national planners must assume a generic perspective, lest limited resources be squandered in combatting substance abuse problems.

REFERENCES

1. Aumack, L. Evaluation of Eagleville's residential combined treatment program. In: *National Drug/Alcohol Collaborative Project (NDACP) Final Report* (NIDA Grant H81 DA 01113), Carroll, J. F. X. (ed.), National Institute on Drug Abuse: Rockville, Md., 1977.
2. Carroll, J. F. X. "Mental illness" and "disease": Outmoded concepts in alcohol and drug rehabilitation. *Commun. Men. Health J.* 11:418–429, 1975.
3. Carroll, J. F. X. (ed.). *National Drug/Alcohol Collaborative Project (NDACP) Final Report* (NIDA Grant H81 DA 01113). National Institute on Drug Abuse: Rockville, Md., 1977.
4. Carroll, J. F. X. Similarities and differences of personality and psychopathology between alcoholics and addicts. *Am. J. Drug Alcohol Abuse* 7:219–236, 1980.
5. Carroll, J. F. X., and Malloy, T. E. Combined treatment of alcohol and drug-dependent persons: A literature review and evaluation. *Am. J. Drug Alcohol Abuse* 4:343–364, 1977.
6. Carroll, J. F. X., Malloy, T. E., Hannigan, P. C., Santo, Y., and Kenrick, F. M. The meaning and evolution of the term "multiple-substance abuse." *Contemp. Drug Prob.* 6: 101–134, 1977.
7. Carroll, J. F. X., Malloy, T. E., Roscioli, D. L., and Godard, D. R. Personality similarities and differences in four diagnostic groups of women alcoholics and drug abusers. *J. Stud. Alcohol* 42:432–440, 1981.
8. Catanzaro, R. J. Combined treatment of alcoholics, drug abusers, and related problems in a "family residential center." *Drug Form* 2:203–212, 1973.
9. Cole, S. G., and Cole, E. A. *Assessment of Inpatient/Residential Combined Treatment for Alcohol and Drug Abuse Clients* (ADM 281-76-0024). National Institude on Drug Abuse and ADAMHA: Rockville, Md., 1977.
10. Egan, G. *The skilled helper: A model for systematic helping and interpersonal relating.* Brooks-Cole: Monterey, Calif., 1975.
11. Farley, E. C., Santo, Y., and Speck, D. W. Multiple drug-abuse patterns of youth in treatment. In: *Youth Drug Abuse*, Beschner, G. M. and Friedman, A. S. (eds.). Lexington: Lexington, Mass., 1979.
12. Gerston, A., Cohen, M. J., and Stimmel, B. Alcoholism, heroin dependency, and methadone maintenance: Alternatives and aids to conventional methods of therapy. *Am. J. Drug Alcohol Abuse* 4:517–531, 1977.
13. Heilman, R. O. *Evolution of a Combined Treatment Program in the Treatment of Drug Dependence.* Unpublished manuscript, 1974. (Available from Drug Dependency Program, Veterans Administration Hospital, 54th and 48th Avenues, S. Minneapolis, Minn., 55417).
14. Inaba, D., Way, E. L., Blum, K., and Schnoll, S. H. Pharmacological and toxicological perspectives of commonly abused drugs. *Med. Mono. Series* 1:(Whole No. 5), 1978.
15. Kaufman, E. Polydrug abuse or multidrug misuse: It's here to stay. *Br. J. Addict.* 72: 339–347, 1977.
16. Neuman, C. P., and Tamerin, J. S. The treatment of adult alcoholics and teenage drug addicts in one hospital: A comparison and critical appraisal of factors related to outcome. *Q. J. Stud. Alcohol* 32:82–93, 1971.
17. Ottenberg, D. J. Combined treatment of alcoholics and drug addicts: A progress report from Eagleville. *Contemp. Drug Prob.* 4:1–21, 1975.
18. Ottenberg, D. J. The reluctance to combine. *Am. J. Drug Alcohol Abuse* 4:279–291, 1977.

19. Ottenberg, D. J., and Rosen, A. Merging the treatment of drug addicts with an existing program for alcoholics. *Q. J. Stud. Alcohol* 32:94–103, 1971.

20. Schnoll, S. H. Pharmacological aspects of youth drug abuse. In: *Youth Drug Abuse: Problems, Issues and Treatment*, Beschner, G. M. and Friedman, A. S. (eds.). Lexington, Lexington, Mass., 1971.

21. Schnoll, S. H. Guidelines for the care of the drug abusing patient. *Hosp. Med.* 12 (10):85–97, 1976.

22. Schnoll, S. H. Alcohol and other substance abuse in adolescents. In: *Addiction Research and Treatment: Converging Trends*. Pergamon: New York, 1979.

23. Smith, D. E., and Wesson, D. R. A new method for treatment of barbiturate dependence. *J.A.M.A.* 213:294–295, 1970.

24. Veterans Administration. *Evaluation of the Pilot Alcohol and Drug Treatment (PADAT) Project*. Unpublished manuscript, 1977. (Available from Veterans Administration, Department of Medicine and Surgery, Washington, D.C. 20420).

25. Williams, J. B. W., (ed.). *Diagnostic and statistical manual of mental disorders, DSM-III* (3rd ed.). Washington, D.C.: American Psychiatric Association, 1980.

60

MATILDA M. RICE, MD, Nassau County Department of Drug and Alcohol Addiction, Nassau, New York

ALCOHOL USE AND ABUSE IN CHILDREN

THIS CHAPTER DEALS specifically with children who drink, exploring the multietiologic factors of alcohol abuse in children, the drinking pattern in different age groups, showing that drinking habits change with chronological age, together with motivation, psychodynamic interpretations, and children's attitudes toward alcohol.

The biopsychosocial complexity of alcoholism when it refers to children is even more difficult to understand and to explain than it is in the adult population.

The clinical findings herein are based on direct contact with 5,100 children, from grade three through grade 12, who were interviewed over a 1-year period of time in the schools by the staff of the Northeast Nassau Alcoholism Counseling services.

To support the clinical findings, the literature was searched and a recent increase in publications describing the effects of parental alcoholism on children was found. These children were studied from various psychological points of view, and the effects of parental alcoholism were found to be damaging to ego functions and processes of identification. Authors called these children "the forgotten children," "the hidden tragedy," "the neglected problem."

It was surprising to find very few studies dealing directly with children who drink. Children who drink do not necessarily come from alcoholic families; thus, this is a separate problem to be addressed.

Matilda M. Rice, MD, Nassau County Department of Drug and Alcoholic Addiction, Nassau, New York.

This subject provokes anxiety among researchers, clinicians, educators, and families alike. The selective inattention to this problem is consistent with similar patterns of avoidance of other topics involving children, too painful to be acknowledged, such as physical abuse, incest or other forms of sexual abuse, and suicide.

The extent of the problem is difficult to evaluate objectively because of the lack of prospective studies, lack of reliable and valid statistical data, and lack of a clear definition of alcohol abuse and addiction in children. The reported prevalence of alcohol abuse in children varies greatly with the population studied and the diagnositc criteria used.

Many studies use the diagnostic criteria for alcoholism in adults, while others use standards for mental illness in children, both fail in determining the presence or absence of specific clinical features charactristic to children who drink. Another difficulty is the fact that the problem is underreported for many reasons, among which are lack of recognition, lack of early diagnosis, and denial and resistance from families and professionals in close contact with children.

Direct interviews with children do not provide reliable statistical data since some youngsters might have a tendency to exaggerate to show off, or, on the contrary, to deny by simply defiance or in fear of punishment.

CONTRIBUTING FACTORS

The National Institute of Alcoholism and Alcohol Abuse estimated in 1978 that 1.1 million preteens and teens have serious drinking problems. Historically, the average or per capita alcohol consumption has increased steadily in most Western countries since World War II. There has not only been an increase in the population that uses alcohol, but also a rise in the proportion of heavy drinkers.

Concomitantly with the increased per capita consumption of alcohol there has been, in the last decades, an increased integration of drinking practices. Since drinking is seen as less deviant, it is considered less necessary to protect the so-called vulnerable groups (such as women and children) from its effects, and drinking becomes less role-specific. In the past, most drinking was carried out in all-male groups; integrated drinking practices become a family and a social affair.

In 1970-71, Wechsler and Thum [21] found that 32% of junior high boys and 23% of junior high girls, 61% of senior high boys and 59% of senior high girls were drinking heavily more than five times a month. In 1974 Wechsler studied 1,700 students in grades seven through 12 and found a higher proportion drinking heavily and more frequently, and he also noted that the proportion of girls drinking equals that of boys [22].

A national survey conducted in 1974 estimated that 90% of high school seniors and 60% of seventh graders used alcohol, with a high incidence of problem drinking.

Alcohol is perceived as a social beverage rather than a drug, is readily available at home, therefore frequently the exposure to alcohol is in the home with parents or other adults present. Drinking in children is seen as learned behavior, starting at home at an early age and moving outward into a peer-controlled environment later.

The first use of alcohol at an early age precedes the use of drugs, unlike in the past, when young people who began using street drugs at an early age would start using alcohol as young adults.

The lowering of the legal drinking age was a reaction to increased use of illicit drugs among young people, which raised the tolerance toward their use of alcohol as less deviant behavior.

The escalation of the drinking among children is thus more adequately understood when drinking is seen as a social act and is so perceived by the child who attempts to relate prematurely to the adult world as common adult behavior.

Davis et al. [3] suggest that the abuse of alcohol has adaptative consequences sufficiently reinforcing to serve in maintaining the habit of drinking regardless of the underlying causation. Drinking in young children is thought to serve this purpose of adaptation since children are in need of identification with adults and use alcohol as a shortcut to an adult role, trying to regain a feeling of omnipotence, self-definition, and mastery, since alcohol indeed supports all primary ego defense mechanisms.

The association between parental drinking and the probability of drinking by their children implies a basic continuity in expectations about drinking behavior from one generation to the next.

In this society the child is discouraged from playing roles reserved for adults, although children might be allowed at times to play these roles in anticipation of later achievement of adult status, as in the case of alcohol use and abuse.

It appears there is a multietiologic basis for drug and alcohol abuse. Many factors—such as genetical, hereditary, and prenatal influences, biochemical changes, together with behavior patterns, and familial influences—should be taken into consideration when studying the child who starts drinking at an early age.

Genetic studies completed by Goodwin et al. [7, 8] on adoptees who had been separated from their biological parents within the first 6 weeks of their lives and who had at least one parent with the hospital diagnosis of alcoholism show the possibility of a genetic transmission of the disease; the alcoholism rate in the probands was 4 times that of the control group. Recent studies on the role of prenatal influences, based on the knowledge that the alcohol penetrates both the placental barrier and the blood-brain barrier of the fetus, suggests the hypothesis of a physical dependency on alcohol in utero reactivated by moderate drinking in childhood.

Whether there are hereditary markers, prenatal influences or constitutional factors, the child still does not invent the idea of drinking; it is learned from parents first and then peers.

There is a growing social acceptance of intoxication as a means of having fun and an increase in the recreational use of drugs.

A study of the Youth Network Council indicates that the users of alcohol admitted that drinking and getting high is their way of having fun. Society at large, and the family as a nucleus of society, plays a very important role in promoting these attitudes among the younger generation.

The family is a system in which the change in the functioning of one family member is automatically followed by a compensatory change in another family member.

> Of all illnesses which affect family life none is more devastating than that of alcoholism. The steady sense of security, love, and warmth necessary for adequate development of children are so unpredictably present in such a home that a child has difficulty developing the trust and confidence in himself and others which he will need for successful living. Neither the alcoholic father nor the alcoholic mother can play adequately the role of parent, so that there are gross failures of identification in the growing child—a condition which can warp all his future relationships. Treatment must be directed toward overcoming the alcoholism in the parent, as well as helping the child to adjust to the difficult family situation. [6]

The following describes project activities that were part of a two-fold outreach and educational program, supported by the county and the school district.

ELEMENTARY GRADE CHILDREN

The children were interviewed in groups by grades and also offered individual interviews upon request. The children were very cooperative and interested, actively participating in all activities. Drinking was consistently found as having started at family reunions, birthday parties, and holidays, under the supervision and approval of the parents, as early as age 5. If some of the children became drunk, adults considered it funny. Generally, the children expressed a fear of displeasing their parents if they refused to drink; they felt that they were expected to drink as a sign of growing up, or showing that they were part of the family. They expressed a feeling of "must," or "have to"—some said they were afraid to say no to their parents. Many of the children did not even like the taste of alcohol, but they drank it to be like everybody else. It was found that 3% of second-grade children, 8% of third-grade children, 14% of fourth-grade children, and 22% of fifth-grade children had been drunk at least once and some experienced hangovers.

The general attitude toward alcoholics by this age group is one of disgust and scorn, as they consider alcoholics to be bums, consistent with the culturally defined stereotype of the alcoholic. They found it difficult to accept the concept of alcoholism as a disease or to admit that parents or persons they know might be alcoholics. Somehow the idea of drinking, even heavy drinking, had no connection with alcoholism.

As part of the program they were encouraged to write letters and over 1,000 letters were received. The letters showed that the children had serious knowledge of alcoholism, and they all had contacts with drinking people more than once. They expressed concern about members of the family, neighbors, or themselves. One 9-year-old girl wrote a sad letter saying that she hated alcohol because her babysitter's boyfriend died in a car accident while intoxicated and her babysitter cried a lot. Another little girl expressed concern about "irregular babies" after seeing a movie on the fetal alcohol syndrome. An 8-year-old boy described his uncle as "unshaved, dressed in old dirty clothes, does not comb his hair" and asked if it could be that his uncle was an alcoholic.

Educational materials were distributed, including cartoon books, pamphlets addressed to children, puzzles, and a questionnaire on drug and alcohol abuse devised especially for elementary children. A movie was shown that was a favorite about a goldfish who gets drunk. Nonjudgmental information was offered; emphasis was on alcoholism as a disease and the alcoholic as a sick person in need of help. The effects of alcohol on the body were discussed, with special focus on the growing child.

Drinking was considered to be a potential problem at this early age when:

1. The child enjoyed the feeling that the alcohol produced and was able to explain it well.

2. The child liked the taste of liquor so much that he or she would empty glasses after a party by drinking what was left at the bottom.

3. The child started lying about drinking, hiding or stealing drinks. For example, one extremely cute 8-year-old girl was emptying her grandmother's bottles of wine. The grandmother, a chronic alcoholic, was hiding bottles of red wine under the bed. The little girl would pour out half of the wine and replace it with cherry soda. She had been doing this since she was 6 years old, and nobody ever noticed.

4. The child is aware that alcohol reduces anxiety, improves sleep, improves relations with people, and improves hyperkinetic behavior.

In this age group very little drug abuse was found, although there was some glue sniffing or some pot smoking in fifth grade.

JUNIOR HIGH SCHOOL CHILDREN

Moving into junior high school, a very different motivation for drinking was found. These children were drinking outside the home, seeking peer approval and acceptance as part of a group. Generally they denied drinking because of peer pressure, saying that they drank because they liked to get high. The findings confirmed recent studies that drinking was not a response to tension, nor an expression of hostility toward authority.

The attitude of junior high children toward alcoholics differed dramatically from that of younger children. They perceived some alcoholics as successful businessmen, relatives, and/or favorite sports stars or actors, and they did not consider drinking as deviant behavior.

The common patterns of drinking were beer drinking on weekends, in empty parking lots, street corners, or parks. Drinking was not associated with any form of entertainment, such as music or dancing.

No differences were found between sexes, races, religions, or academic levels. Drinking seemed to be a very important part of their lives, sometimes the only way they were able to relate one to another. Surprisingly, children on the honor roll and the favorite school athletes were the heaviest drinkers, but they all felt that they were able to control the use of alcohol. None of the junior high school children interviewed expressed any problem in purchasing liquor without proof of age, or even drinking in bars.

All children were very cooperative with the study staff. A few lectures were given, and they were divided into small discussion groups. They did not consider alcoholism as a stigma and they did not consider themselves as having any problems. Drinking beer on the weekend was seen as a good way to socialize; however, they were concerned and asked many questions about driving while intoxicated.

The school administration expressed concern about heavy drinking on the premises, frequently finding empty beer bottles on the grounds and in the bathrooms.

Drinking in this age group was considered to be a problem with a poorer prognosis when the weekend and beer-, group-drinking pattern changed to:

1. Drinking every day
2. Drinking before school
3. Drinkng on school grounds
4. Drinking alone, at home, or in hiding
5. Replacing beer with hard liquors
6. Lowering of the level of functioning of the child, showing up as lower academic achievement, failing courses, or poor attendance.
7. Emerging antisocial behaviors — fights, violence, vandalism, or illegal acts.

HIGH SCHOOL CHILDREN

The high school students claimed boredom as their main reason for drinking: their feeling of apathy was almost universal and very penetrating. Statements such as, "There is nothing else to do," or "Everybody drinks" were not uncommon.

High school students denied peer pressure as a strong motive for drinking and they appeared to be self-centered, narcissistic, and defiant toward any form of authority. They did not perceive alcohol abuse, not even being drunk, as pathological behavior; on the contrary, they felt very strongly that no drinking was abnormal. The impression was that everybody in the high school drank more than occasionally, and staff were surprised at the large number of students who admitted having had blackouts.

The attitude toward alcohol had changed again, and this group perceived adults as having drinking problems, being disturbed and disturbing; the children showed scorn and disrespect for an adult drinking; at the same time they expressed sincere concern about younger children who drank too much.

The students frequently questioned the effects of alcohol on sexual performance, but they showed no interest in the problems of drinking and driving, unlike the junior high group, in spite of the fact that a majority of the high school students already had a driver's license.

In this group too, similar to the junior high group, a total convergence of sexes, socioeconomic status, and religion was found; but in the senior high school, unlike the junior high, school performance and overall functioning seemed to be greatly affected by alcohol use. Also, an increased association between heavy drinking and truancy or other types of antisocial behavior was found. There were a very high number of polydrug abusers, with many combinations of drugs used together with alcohol.

This study in the schools was consistent with national studies in showing the prevalence of heavy drinking among children. According to a 1978 survey by the New York State Division of Substance Abuse Services, 65.3% of Long Island high school students labeled themselves drinkers, and 12.1% considered themselves heavy drinkers (they drank more than 10 times in the previous 30 days).

The major social problems of juvenile delinquency, alcoholism, drug abuse, and suicide all have strikingly common correlates: low self-esteem, a sense of powerlessness, low interpersonal and social skills, poor academic or vocational performance, and poor family relationships [15].

There is an urgent need for more services for children, for diagnosis, prevention, and treatment. Schools can play a very important role by developing health curriculum programs in primary grades, by encouraging participation of preschoolers in alcohol education classes, and by using school-based social workers for identification of the problem and intervention when necessary. One such program is BABES (Beginning Alcohol Basic Education Studies), which has reached over 2,000 children in the metropolitan Detroit school area [15].

The identification of children at risk, the treatment of alcoholism in the family, educational programs, and more value-oriented strategies were found to be very useful tools in the prevention of alcoholism in children.

In reviewing the histories of adult patients at an alcoholism clinic, a correlation between an early onset and the severity of alcoholism was consistently found. Early detection, diagnosis, and treatment have both immediate and future good results.

Alcoholism is a treatable disease and the prevention of chronicity and life-long patterns of drinking are addressed most efficiently and with best results in childhood.

A few short case histories are presented in an attempt to illustrate the common findings of alcoholism in the family, dual addiction, school problems, earlier onset of problem drinking, and different patterns of abuse.

Case Examples

A 15-year-old white boy, a weekend drinker, drinks up to 36 cans of beer over a period of 48 hours. He also smokes marijuana. He was seen once in the emergency room after drinking a quart of Scotch in 2 hours. He is the oldest of three children, with both parents alcoholics. He started drinking at age 6, being encouraged by his father (who gets upset when the child smokes marijuana) in spite of his own blackouts from alcohol and liver damage. The boy has a long history of academic underachievement, with specific learning disabilities; he was left behind in second grade, and has attended special classes since.

A 14-year-old white girl was referred to the clinic by the school following a suicide attempt. The father is alcoholic. The mother is dominant, angry, overcontrolling, and uses Valium. The child is the eldest of three children; her younger brother, age 9, drinks beer occasionally. She started drinking at age 10 for symptomatic relief. She also uses Valium prescribed to her by a physician for anxiety and poor sleep. She is a heavy weekend drinker and uses hard liquor. After being unfairly punished by her mother, she drank a whole bottle of southern comfort and took 20 or more 10 mg Valiums, which she does not remember even taking. She was admitted to the intensive care unit semicomatose. When a therapist first saw her she admitted she was very depressed; she had a very low self-esteem and felt worthless and hopeless.

A 16-year-old black boy started drinking at age 9. He drank up to two quarts of beer or wine daily, had numerous blackouts, and became assaultive while intoxicated. He had twin sisters 1 year old. He dropped out of school in 11th grade because he was always a slow learner. Both parents were alcoholics. He already had several arrests for felony and petit and grand larceny. He smoked marijuana and took cocaine regularly.

A 14-year-old girl came to the clinic by herself because of depression and suicidal ideas. Both parents were alcoholics, and her father committed suicide 2 years earlier. She hated her mother and thought that her mother was responsible for her father's death. Sometimes she thought her mother actually killed her father. The girl drank six to 20 beers daily for symptomatic relief. She also took Valium (up to 100 mg daily) and Nembutals for sleep. She had severe anxiety attacks, felt spasms in her chest, became diaphoretic, and had migraine headaches. She drempt frequently about her father and said that when she was drunk she felt him close to her. She felt she was no longer able to cope with school and wanted to drop out.

A 16-year-old white girl, the youngest of three children, drank two six-packs of beer daily. On the weekend she drank beer and one bottle of Jack Daniels. She also smoked marijuana. She started drinking at about age 10. She came to the clinic following a suicide attempt by superficially cutting her wrists. This happened after she broke up with her boyfriend. She felt that he accused her of drinking too much, but this was not fair since he was drinking too. Her father was alcoholic. The mother was cold, domineering, and rejecting. She felt she was the black sheep of the family, that her father did not like her; he felt that all women were inferior. She said she tried all her life to act like a boy to gain his affection. She said that she felt all her life, and especially the past few years, a lot of pressure to achieve to prove to her father that women could be good too. She felt even more rejection from her father after she started dating. She was a junior in high school and her academic work did not suffer in spite of her heavy drinking.

A 16-year-old white boy, who was a hyperkinetic child, was diagnosed as moderately brain-damaged at age 6 and placed on Ritalin. He started drinking at around age 8 by emptying glasses after parties at home. Both parents were alcoholics. On a weekend he drank two quarts of vodka, one quart of Jack Daniels, and two six-packs of beer. He drank beer daily. He has a history of five suicide gestures, (the first one at age 10, the last one a few weeks before his admission to the hospital). He was seen in the hospital with a thigh-length cast after a car accident. He was hit by a car while walking intoxicated in the middle of traffic. He had been in jail three times for assaultive behavior when intoxicated. He dropped out of school on his 16th birthday and had no plans for the future.

REFERENCES

1. Bosina, W. G. H. Children of alcoholics: A hidden tragedy. *Md. State Med. J.* 21:34–46, 1972.
2. Cook, M. The forgotten children: A study of children with alcoholic parents. Canada Publishing: Ontario, 1949.
3. Davis, D., Benson, D. Steinglass, P., and Davis, S. The adaptive consequences of drinking. *Psychiatry* 37:299–315, 1974.
4. Demone, H., Jr. *Implications from Research on Adolescent Drinking.* Paper presented at the Alcohol Education Conference, Department of Health, Education and Welfare: Washington, D.C., 1966.
5. Demone, H., Jr. and Wechsler, H. Changing drinking patterns of adolescents since the 1960s. In: *Alcoholism Problems in Women and Children,* Greenblatt, M. and Schuckit, M. (eds.). Grune & Stratton: New York, 1976.
6. Fox, R. *The Effect of Alcoholism in Children.* Paper distributed by the National Council on Alcoholism: New York, 1979.
7. Goodwin, D., Schulsinger, F., and Hermansen, L. Alcohol problems in adoptees raised apart from alcoholic biological parents. *Arch. Gen. Psychiatry* 28:238–243, 1973.
8. Goodwin, D., Schulsinger, F., and Moller, N. Drinking problems in adopted and nonadopted sons of alcoholics. *Arch. Gen. Psychiatry* 31:146–149, 1974.
9. Guebaly, N., and Offord, D. The offspring of alcoholics: A critical review. *Am. J. Psychiatry* 134:4, 357–365, 1977.
10. Jessor, R., and Jessor, S. L. Adolescent development and the onset of drinking: A longitudinal study. *Q. J. Stud. Alcohol* 51:36–37, 1975.
11. MacKay, J. R. Clinical observations on adolescent problem drinkers. *Q. J. Stud. Alcohol* 22:124–134, 1961.
12. Maddox, G. L., and McCall, B. *Drinking among Teenagers.* Rutgers Center of Alcohol Studies: New Brunswick, N.J., 1964.
13. Miller, D., and Jang, M. Children of alcoholics: A 20-year longitudinal study. *Soc. Work Res.* 13:23–29, 1977.

14. Morrison, J., and Stewart, M. A family study of the hyperactive child. *Biol. Psychiatry* 3:189-195, 1971.

15. Nowlis, H. *Generic Prevention.* Keynote speech, National Association of Prevention Professionals 3rd annual meeting: Washington, D.C., 1980.

16. Partanen, J., Brunn, K., and Markenen, T. *Inheritance of Drinking Behavior.* Rutgers Center of Alcohol Studies: New Brunswick, N.J., 1964.

17. Pittman, D. J., and Synder, C. R. (eds.). *Society, Culture and Drinking Patterns.* Wiley: New York, 1962.

18. Rosenberg, G. M. Young alcoholics. *Br. J. Psychol.* 115:181-188, 1969.

19. Slobod, S. B. The children of alcoholics: A neglected problem. *Hosp. Community Psychiatry* 25:605-606, 1974.

20. Smart, R. G., and White, J. *Effects of Lowering the Legal Drinking Age upon High School Students.* Toronto Addiction Research Foundation: Toronto, 1972.

21. Wechsler, J., and Thum, D. Drug use among teenagers: Patterns of present and anticipated use. *Int. J. Addict.* 8:909-920, 1973.

22. Wechsler, J., and Thum, D. Teenage drinking, drug use and social correlates. *Q. J. Stud. Alcohol* 34:1220-1227, 1973.

23. Whitehead, P. C., and Ferrence, R. Women and children last: Implications of trends in consumption for women and young people. In: *Alcoholism Problems in Women and Children,* Greenblatt, M. and Schuckit, M. (eds.). Grune & Stratton: New York, 1976.

24. Willis, M. *Preschoolers Participate in Alcohol Education Classes.* National Clearinghouse for Alcohol Information of the National Institute on Alcohol Abuse and Alcoholism, Information and Feature Service N: 72, June 1980.

61

WILLIAM J. FILSTEAD, PhD, Lutheran Center for Substance Abuse, Park Ridge, Illinois

ADOLESCENCE AND ALCOHOL

Within the last decade adolescent misuse and abuse of alcohol has become a major social problem. Many segments of society have expressed concern about the consequences of this alcohol misuse and as a result an array of diversified efforts (treatment services, prevention programs, education materials, medical campaigns, school curriculums, etc.) have been mounted to respond to the direct and indirect manifestations of adolescent alcohol misuse [7].

In order to understand the magnitude and scope of this problem, it is necessary to identify some of the major conceptual and clinical assumptions that form the foundation for thinking about this problem. This chapter begins by exploring these assumptions and conceptual issues, reviewing the extent and scope of this problem as defined through various surveys of adolescent populations, identifying factors that influence the delivery of treatment services; it concludes with some observations as to what efforts need to be mounted to gain a better understanding of the issues associated with adolescents and alcohol use and misuse.

William J. Filstead, PhD, Lutheran Center for Substance Abuse and Parkside Medical Services Corporation, Lutheran General Medical Center, Park Ridge, Illinois.

KEY ASSUMPTIONS AND CONCEPTUAL CONSIDERATIONS

The Nature of the Phenomenon

Adolescence, like alcohol misuse, is a complex phenomenon. There are phases and stages to both realities that need to be assessed when approaching these conditions. In addressing the issue of adolescent alcohol use-misuse, one has to consciously be aware of the variability in the individual's stage of development and the consequences of alcohol misuse.

The age of the adolescent involved with alcohol is central to the clinical decisions that need to be made. It is an established fact that age, alcohol use, and negative consequences from misuse are highly correlated.

The Reality of Adolescence

Adolescence is a time of rapid change and development. These physiological and psychosocial changes affect and can be affected by alcohol use. The interactions between the personal and social changes of an adolescent and the use or misuse of alcohol can cloud clinical issues and developmental processes. Any program or service directed at this age group needs to be cognizant of these dynamics. A 13-year-old and a 17-year-old, while both being adolescents, are at significantly different junctures in their development.

Definitional Confusion

While it may be clear to some what problem drinking is, what one thinks is problematic. Terms such as teenage "alcoholism," "alcohol abuse," "problem drinking," and so forth add to the conceptual confusion and fail to distinguish among even the most general classes of drinking behavior [11].

Unfortunately, many professionals and the public at large tend to see these terms as synonymous, as representing the same type of behavior or clinical condition. They are not the same. The terms represent distinct facets of drinking behavior, each with its own set of consequences and considerations. Noting this and being consciously aware of these differences in drinking behavior is fundamental to the clinical approaches used with adolescents. The personal preference of this author is to talk about use and misuse. The notion of misuse can run the gamut of negative consequences. Such a concept also lessens the emotionalism associated with the previously identified terms.

Teenage Alcoholism

The etiology of alcoholism is not clearly established; consequently, the relationship between adolescent drinking and alcoholism is not clear [9]. This has led to an ongoing debate as to the existence of adolescent alcoholism. Are there teenage alcoholics?

While there is ample evidence concerning the psychological, social, and interpersonal disruptions encountered by adolescents who misuse alcohol, the physical consequences of misuse are minimal [4]. Even when there are physiological consequences, adolescents only rarely show physical dependence on alcohol [13].

According to strict medical criteria of increased tolerance and withdrawal symptoms there are cases of adolescents who experience these symptoms, but it is clearly far less than the suggested 6 million teenage alcoholics. A survey of the youth and alcohol literature by Blane and Hewitt [2] suggests that societal perceptions as to the nature and seriousness of adolescent use of alcohol has undergone a radical shift. Available data does not support a significant increase in the frequency of alcohol use, the magnitude or scope of the problem, nor the consequences that result from such use. It is the perception of these realities at this time that makes them real. If people define a situation as real, it is real in its consequences.

The model of adult alcoholism is generally applied to adolescents. Many questions have been raised about the appropriateness of this framework as it applies to adolescents. Clearly, many signs and symptoms of misuse are comparable between these two age groups, for example, negative consequences in various areas of life, preoccupation with drinking, continued use in spite of negative consequences, and so forth. Other signs or symptoms are not similar, including such conditions as the progressive nature of the disease, physiological dependency, major medical complications, and other chronic aspects of alcoholism.

More thought needs to be given to the utility of this adult alcoholism paradigm. While it provides a working model for evaluating and intervening with adolescents, these assets may be outweighed by the assumptions that underlie this model, assumptions that may impose on individuals issues or considerations that cannot be effectively addressed. For example, use or experimentation with alcohol or other substances may not necessarily result in continued use or misuse. Other factors are likely involved in the choices of use or nonuse. What these factors are and how they interface with the developmental processes of adolescence needs further investigation [10].

ETIOLOGY AND PREVALENCE OF ADOLESCENT ALCOHOL USE AND MISUSE

In general, the most popular concepts for explaining the development of adolescent use and/or misuse of alcohol can be classified into three general categories: the parental modeling theory [12], the peer pressure theory [5], and the personality theory [8]. There is much debate as to the relative strengths of these factors in the development of patterns of nonuse, use, or misuse. What clearly seems to be the case is that parents and peers have varying influence on adolescents, depending on the age of the adolescent. The respective influence of parents and peers is closely related to developmental issues as well as the specific influence of peers as role models and parents as providers of value systems. These two sets of influences shape and are shaped by the personality issues and dynamics that are part of the adolescent.

There is clearly the belief that adolescents use and misuse alcohol more than earlier generations of adolescents. While the validity of this perception may be questioned, policy makers and others have acted on the premise that it is true. These pronouncements are a major problem confronting anyone who is trying to comprehend this problem and what could or should be done about it.

A survey of the adolescence and alcohol literature by Blane and Hewitt [2] attempted to put in perspective these questions pertaining to prevalence of use and misuse, and problems associated with use.

1. Do individuals have their first drinking experience at an earlier age? For the time period 1941-75 the answer is No, although recently 1965-75 there has been a trend toward an earlier age of consumption.

2. Are more teenagers drinking now than in earlier generations? No.

3. Do girls and boys have comparable levels of drinking? No, not for the years 1941-75. Boys appear to drink earlier, are likely to drink regularly, and experience more problems due to their drinking than girls. However, recent data (that since 1975) indicate a change in this pattern. It now seems that there are few differences between girls and boys and their alcohol consumption. However, girls still tend to experiment and/or use other substances more than boys.

4. Are teenagers drinking more? Data are inconsistent and contradictory on this issue. There does appear to be a trend toward increased consumption levels due to an earlier age of initial experimentation as well as a decline in the use of other substances.

5. Do teenagers get more intoxicated and by implication are there more problems as a result of this intoxication? The survey data for 1941-75 indicate there were no changes in the rate of drunkenness or the consequences of this drunkenness.

Data examined by Blane and Hewitt as well as others suggest that over this time period there are very few changes in the level of alcohol consumption and its consequences. Yet public perceptions and impressions provide another perspective, one that clearly indicates this phenomenon of teenage alcohol use and misuse is a major social problem requiring a substantial and comprehensive educational and intervention effort on the part of public and private sectors.

Two principal difficulties associated with trying to monitor the prevalence and consequence of alcohol consumption, especially historically, are (1) changing social values and normative systems that redefine reality, and (2) definitional and measurement considerations attendant with the quantification of these matters. It is only a slight exaggeration to suggest there are as many definitions of alcohol abuse, consequences due to drinking, and the like, as there are surveys attempting to measure these concepts.

Elsewhere, this author has attempted to develop a scale to establish the degree of alcohol misuse among teenagers [6]. This 14-item Adolescent Alcohol Involvement Scale was developed through an examination of key discriminating questions on other such surveys and various reliability and validity work to establish its usefulness in identifying the level of alcohol use and/or misuse in adolescents. These questions probe the extent to which alcohol use affects three areas of adolescent life: psychological functioning, interpersonal relationships, and family life.

Total score cutoff points were established so that four conceptually distinct groupings of subjects could be made: (1) those who did not use alcohol or whose use was at a minimal level; (2) those who used alcohol but did not experience or display any problematic behavior associated with its use; (3) those who used alcohol and experienced problems and/or difficulties; and (4) those who used alcohol and experienced problems to the level and degree reported by adolescents who were being treated for alcoholism. In effect, this last group represents respondents who were using alcohol and experiencing problems like adolescent alcoholics.

Data from high school surveys using this instrument suggest that 5% of high school students are using alcohol similar to adolescents who are being treated for alcoholism; an additional 19% are using alcohol to a point where there are substantial changes in their lives and significant problems exist as a result of this pattern of use. Only 5% report not ever using alcohol, whereas the majority of students indicate use but without difficulties or problems (71%). In this last population the use of alcohol is generally infrequent.

TREATMENT INTERVENTION STRATEGIES

Given this situation of conceptual vagueness, definitional confusion, the questionable application of the adult alcoholism model to adolescents, and the prevalence and scope of this problem, the question of what treatment services and intervention programs are most needed must be addressed.

Alcoholism and its manifestation in individuals, while it may involve common elements, does have unique or individually specific nuances that need to be recognized. To suggest that all alcoholics could profit by a given course of treatment ignores the importance of assessing what treatment needs are most salient and which service or services could best address those needs. If this identification of individual treatment needs is central to the treatment of adults, then it is vital in approaching adolescents.

When offering treatment services for adolescents, there are three general issues that shape the process of evaluating the patient's clinical needs. First, physiological and psychological development issues must be addressed, such as, "Where is the individual relative to developmental considerations?" "What role, if any, do these developmental considerations play in the assessment of the person's clinical situation and needs vis-à-vis the pattern of alcohol use?"

Secondly, "What are the consequences of alcohol and/or substance use and misuse?" While there are some very practical ways to discuss alcohol misuse and its consequences on an individual's life, the implications of these labels (problem drinking, alcohol abuse, and the like) are less clear when applied to adolescents than to adults. For example, if a child continues to use alcohol in spite of negative consequences, one could suggest that such behavior indicates abuse or problems due to drinking. Whether or not it represents "loss of control," a term used to discuss an adult's inability to drink according to his or her intentions or not to drink because of adverse consequences, is a debatable issue.

Therefore, there are similar examples of drinking behavior, drinking despite negative consequences, disruptions in one's life, increased frequency and/or amount of use, and so forth that may or may not have the same clinical meaning for an adolescent as for an adult. However, it does appear that the earlier the age when use and/or experimentation begins, the greater the likelihood that one may become extensively involved with those substances and as a result be more likely to experience the negative consequences.

The third issue relates to the focus of the intervention and the strategies for responding to the clinical situation of the adolescent. Often alcohol misuse is central to the adolescent's clinical situation. However, while alcohol abuse may be a salient consideration, it could also be a mask for other personal or interpersonal difficulties that need to be directly and forceably addressed along with the alcohol misuse.

The extent to which alcohol misuse or other difficulties become the focus of treatment requires differential assessment on the part of therapist evaluating and treating the patient. One cannot assume what the primary focus of treatment should be. While this is true for any clinical encounter, it is especially so for adolescents involved with alcohol and other substances.

RANGE OF SERVICES

Any agency providing alcoholism services has to be aware that adolescents may require a range of inpatient, outpatient, and transitional living facilities. Rather than providing a standard package of services, the agency needs to establish sound clinical criteria by which decisions can be made as to what level of care is most appropriate for the adolescent's needs.

At the Lutheran Center for Substance Abuse, criteria has been developed for identifying the extent to which the adolescent has experienced impairment in a number of key clinical areas. Depending on the extent of the impairment, decisions are made as to what type of service would be most appropriate. These areas of assessment are

1. Onset of alcohol-substance abuse
2. Disruptions in life style and/or interpersonal relationships
3. Extent of dependency
4. Violent or aggressive behavior
5. Psychiatric condition
6. Willingness to address the problem
7. Family and/or social support system
8. Openness about pattern of misuse
9. Extent of polydrug dependency

Depending on the degree of impairment experienced in any of these areas, decisions are made as to the most appropriate treatment service. The levels of care available through the combined programs at Lutheran Center for Substance Abuse, a hospital-based treatment program, and Parkside Lodge of Mundelein (PLM), a residential, nonhospital-based treatment program, are

1. Intensive medical and/or psychiatric care
2. Hospital-based treatment
3. Nonhospital, residential-based treatment
4. Alternative living arrangements
5. Outpatient services of varying intensity and duration

The objective of these services is to maintain the individual in the level of care that is appropriate for the clinical condition, provide adolescents with as much freedom as can be tolerated, and accomplish the treatment in as effective and cost-efficient a manner as possible. This structure of services maintains an individual as close to the realities of his or her everyday social world as is feasible given the clinical needs of the individual.

FUTURE DIRECTIONS

While a considerable amount of information regarding adolescents and their use or misuse of alcohol is available, very little is known about key issues that shape this topical area. The following remarks suggest directions that may prove useful in pursuing in order to better understand the development, treatment, and recovery from problems associated with alcohol misuse.

1. There is a dearth of information about the ways in which knowledge is acquired and attitudes formed and shaped about alcohol and its place in social activities. How do young people learn about such matters?

2. It is important to understand the etiology of drinking behavior, including a focus on what factors tend to lead to a choice of drinking or not drinking. The factors and processes that lead to a decision to try alcohol, and the impact of these first drinking experiences on subsequent drinking patterns and practices, is critical to an understanding of appropriate and inappropriate alcohol-use patterns.

3. The relationship of age and the developmental issues that are prominent at these specific times needs to be better understood. Failure to control for such an important variable can have consequences on the type of programs being developed, the data collected through various research endeavors, and ultimately, the public policies that are formulated to address this societal concern.

4. Bacon has provided a provocative observation on the type of thinking that dominates the alcohol field.

> Our viewpoint for describing and evaluating what is called the conceptual confusion *in thinking* about "things in the field" relates to a "problem orientation" as contrasted with a "phenomenological" orientation.... This judgment may be characterized by the assertion that an intellectual art of any given field may be characterized as moving toward maturity as it applies itself primarily to phenomena of a given class rather than to the "problem" or "pathology" of that class. [1, p. 59-60]

He goes on to say, "The heavy emphasis on problems (however described) and the almost cavalier nonrecognition of the phenomena of alcohol, its use, attendant attitudes, and so forth, is striking" [1].

This situation, as described by Bacon, applies not only to treatment approaches but to prevention programs as well. In fact, the problem focus of most prevention programs may be a major impediment in the ability of these programs to have the types of impact they intend.

Much confusion has existed as to what to prevent among whom. Also, in some cases these prevention programs have been more or less intervention programs and therefore this topic has had its share of activities that are often multipurposed and even at cross-purposes with other so-named activities. The recent work described by Bloom and Snoddy [3] offers a conceptual framework that is aimed not at drinking behavior or drinking problems per se, but rather on emphasizing coping or skills-acquiring tasks that form a constellation of abilities that are brought to bear when the issue of alcohol is considered. Perhaps, as they suggest, embedding alcohol information as one component of a larger knowledge or value domain predicated on strengthening and enhancing one's psychosocial repertoire has potentially greater payoff than the sole focus approach that is applied in most alcohol prevention-education programs.

In general this chapter emphasizes the need to develop procedures and processes for capturing an understanding for what drinking and nondrinking decisions mean in adolescence and what consequences drinking behaviors during these phases of adolescence have, if any, for subsequent adult psychosocial development and drinking behaviors. What is keenly needed is research aimed at identifying what consequences drinking-related events (including nondrinking decisions), experiences, patterns, and attitudes during this period of life have on the development of adult alcoholism. Through such activities future research and treatment and/or prevention programs can be immeasurably improved. More clear thinking and fewer knee-jerk reactions need to be established as the mode of approach to use in developing policies, priorities, and programs within this complex and complicated area of adolescence and alcohol.

REFERENCES

1. Bacon, S. Concepts. In: *Alcohol and Alcohol Problems: New Thinking and New Directions*, Filstead, W., Rossi, J., and Keller, M. (eds.). Ballinger: Cambridge, Mass., 1976.

2. Blane, H., and Hewitt, L. *Alcohol and Youth: An Analysis of the Literature, 1960-1975* (Prepared for the National Institute of Alcohol Abuse and Alcoholism NIAAA Contract ADM-281-75-0026). National Information Service: Washington, D.C., 1977.

3. Bloom, G., and Snoddy, J. The child, the teacher, and the drinking society: A conceptual framework for alcohol education in the elementary school. In: *Alcohol and Alcohol Problems: New Thinking and New Directions*, Filstead, W., Rossi, J., and Keller, M. (eds.). Ballinger: Cambridge, Mass., 1976.

4. Gitlow, S. Alcoholism: A disease. In: *Alcoholism: Progress in Research and Treatment*, Bourne, O. and Fox, R. (eds.). Academic Press: New York, 1973.

5. Jessor, R., Collins, M., and Jessor, S. In becoming a drinker: Social-psychological aspects of an adolescent transition. *Ann. N. Y. Acad. Sci.* 197:199-213, 1972.

6. Mayer, J., and Filstead, W. The Adolescent Alcohol Involvement Scale: An instrument for measuring adolescent use and misuse of alcohol. *J. Stud. Alcohol* 40(3):291-300, 1979.

7. Mayer, J., and Filstead, W. *Adolescent and Alcohol*. Ballinger: Cambridge, Mass., 1980.

8. McClelland, D., Wenner, E., and Vannerman, R. Drinking in the wider context of restrained and unrestrained assertive thoughts and acts. In: *The Drinking Man: Alcohol and Human Motivation*, McClelland, D., Free Press: New York, 1971.

9. Murphree, H. Some possible origins of alcoholism. In: *Alcohol and Alcohol Problems: New Thinking and New Directions*, Filstead, W., Rossi, J., and Keller, M. (eds.). Ballinger: Cambridge, Mass., 1976.

10. Pandina, R., and White, H. Pattern of alcohol and drug use of adolescent students

and adolescents in treatment. *J. Stud. Alcohol* 42(5):441-456, 1981.

11. Rachal, J. Defining adolescent alcohol use: Measurement used and the results from a national study of junior and senior high school students. In: *Defining Adolescent Alcohol Use: Implications toward a Definition of Adolescent Alcoholism*, O'Gorman, P., Strinfield, S., and Smith, I. (eds.). National Council on Alcoholism: Washington, D.C., 1976.

12. Rachal, J., Williams, J., Brehm, M., Cavanaugh, B., Moore, R., and Eckerman, W. *A National Study of Adolescent Drinking Behavior, Attitudes, and Correlates*. Research Triangle Institute: Research Triangle Park, N.C., 1975.

13. Schonberg, S., and Litt, I. Medical treatment of the adolescent drug abuser: An opportunity for rehabilitative intervention. *Primary Care* 3:23-37, 1976.

62

GABE J. MALETTA, PhD, MD, Minneapolis Veterans Administration Medical Center, Minneapolis, Minnesota

ALCOHOLISM AND THE AGED

THE AREA OF ALCOHOL abuse among the elderly is a neglected but crucial one that is only now beginning to be realized and critically studied [23]. There is a widely held belief that alcohol abuse clearly declines with increasing age. This may, in fact, be a misconception. Alcoholism is a serious personal and social problem in the elderly, but as one peruses the literature it becomes clear that the specifics of this problem are elusive [2, 5].

On balance, ethanol usage seems to be more moderate among the elderly as compared to younger groups. However, the data from which this statement arises are open to several methodologic questions; in fact, the true incidence of ethanol usage among the elderly is probably underreported.

Many of the impairments seen in younger populations, those that bring them to the attention of society as a result of alcohol abuse (e.g., work absences, arrest for traffic and other violations, family problems involving police involvement, etc.) may not be extant in an older person's history. Younger individuals with alcohol problems come to the attention of employers, welfare workers, mental health centers, and so forth, while older alcoholics primarily come to the attention of medical hospitals, where a disease of the specific organ system rather than the whole patient is usually treated.

Gabe J. Maletta, PhD, MD, Director, Geriatric Research, Education and Clinical Center, Minneapolis Veterans Administration Medical Center, and Assistant Professor, Departments of Psychiatry and Neurology, University of Minnesota School of Medicine, Minneapolis, Minnesota.

Also, many elderly people have stopped driving, and most are not regularly employed. There may be difficulties regarding the true numbers of elderly who do have an alcohol problem due to what is thought by some to be an increasing use of denial in the elderly, which could cause marked underreporting of alcoholism on random surveys.

There seems to be a reluctance of clinicians, be they physicians, psychologists, social workers, or the like, concerning questioning elderly people about their drinking habits. This seems similar to the problems encountered when dealing with the sexual history of elderly individuals. Clinicians seem averse to delving into these particular emotion-laden and potentially embarrassing areas.

Another problem that could cause an underreporting of alcohol abuse by elderly patients is that the detrimental effects of chronic alcohol abuse on intellectual processes frequently are overlooked by clinicians and instead attributed to dementia, incorrectly considered by many to be a normal phenomenon of advancing age.

From a medical standpoint, alcoholism is detrimental to elderly patients for a variety of reasons. In fact, heavy use of alcohol in elderly individuals can be a serious health threat. For example, elderly patients commonly take a variety of medications, and it is well known that drug and alcohol interactions in these patients are particularly hazardous [17]. In older patients, whose metabolic and excretory functions are clearly compromised with advancing age, even modest amounts of alcohol consumption can impair cognitive functioning when compared to younger, more physiologically competent individuals.

Finally, identifying alcohol abuse as a unique problem in the elderly and attempting to separate the social consequences of alcohol from those related strictly to aging is very difficult.

THE PROBLEM OF ALCOHOL ABUSE IN THE ELDERLY

Extent

When considering the extent of the problem of alcoholism in the elderly, quantification becomes difficult. Overall, a review of the literature suggests that older people seem to drink less than younger ones; but even this statement is frequently followed by disclaimers, usually regarding the validity of the data gathered from the elderly.

One problem seems to be two differing sets of criteria regarding what is meant by alcoholism in young versus old individuals. In the young, a working definition of an alcoholic is an individual who has had one or more major life problems that can be directly related to alcohol (e.g., two or more nontraffic arrests; marital separation or divorce; evidence of health impairment; loss of a job, etc.). In the older alcohol abuser, many of these criteria are no longer valid, and parameters that would attempt to quantitatively measure the extent of the problem are difficult to develop, and even more difficult to try to relate with any relevance to the younger drinker.

Needless to say, there is much difference of opinion in the literature regarding the extent of alcohol problems in old age. It's clear that the exact incidence of alcoholism in elderly people is not really known. A recent review suggests that alcohol problems affect between 2 to 10% of the general elderly population in the United States (or up to 2.5 million people). Of the 4 to 5% of patients over 65 residing in nursing homes, as many as 50% are thought to have alcohol problems. Alcoholism may account for up to 12% of the male and 4% of the female admissions to inpatient psychiatric facilities, and is thought to occur even more frequently in outpatient facilities [4, 14].

There are two age peaks reported regarding alcohol abuse in the older age groups, one in the 45- to 54-year-age group (23 per 1,000), and another peak between ages 65 and 74 (21 per 1,000). There are even higher rates among widowers, elderly individuals in difficulty with the police, and patients with chronic medical problems—anywhere from 20 to 60% of elderly hospital admissions have concomitant alcohol problems, and the cause and effect relationship is not clear. Elderly widowers are the most vulnerable of population subgroups, with a rate of 105 per 1,000. Interestingly, this same group also has the highest suicide rate of all populations studied.

As stated earlier, on balance, people seem to reduce their alcohol consumption as they grow older, usually after age 50. There is no single reason noted for this reduction (if it is indeed valid, since for whatever reasons, elderly people may distort the facts and not report the true extent of their consumption).

In old age, drinking problems may be grouped into the following several categories, some unique, while some overlap with those mentioned for the younger drinker [13].

1. Untoward symptoms developed as a result of drinking (e.g., blackouts, memory loss, and uncontrolled tremor)
2. Psychological dependence, as well as health problems related to alcohol use
3. Problems with relatives, friends, or neighbors related to alcohol use
4. Problems with employment, finances, or other socioeconomic indicators as a result of alcohol use
5. Problems with law enforcement officials, including belligerence, secondary to alcohol use.

People are usually defined as problem drinkers if they exhibit more than one of the listed symptoms.

Since elderly individuals frequently hold fewer jobs, tend to drink alone, and have more health problems in general, it is frequently difficult to quantitate the number of older people who exhibit some of the listed problems. Also, many older individuals are never diagnosed as being alcohol abusers because they never become involved with agencies or care-providing systems set up to assist problem drinkers [22].

Financial pressures of the elderly may be one reason for the reported reduction in consumption levels; perhaps there is fear of exacerbating an already compromised health picture (which might involve cognitive dysfunction); or, there may even be fear of compromising a reputation that took a lifetime to develop. In any event, perspective is essential when considering the extent of the problem in the elderly. Even if alcohol abuse is less of a problem in the elderly than in younger individuals, it is, nevertheless, a serious one. Not only is there a disruption in the life of the older individual, but his or her family, friends, and community are also profoundly affected by this problem.

Demographics

When one reviews the studies concerning the demographics of alcohol use in the elderly, it becomes clear that few generalizations can be made since each of the samples, by necessity, comes from a very specific population or institutional setting. Cultural and ethnic specificity, as well as socioeconomic and even geographic variables, must be considered when attempting to make worthwhile general statements about the elderly problem drinker.

Mishara and Kastenbaum [13] have summarized studies of the proportion of elderly people seeking treatment for alcohol problems at various agencies. Their compilation demonstrates a great diversity; that is, for persons over age 60 admitted to institutions for alcohol-related disorders, the range is between 5 and 54% of admissions. This wide range is what is generally reported and undoubtedly refers back to the specificity and diversity of each subpopulation of elderly individuals studied.

If, instead, one looks at the percentage of all people who come to the attention of institutions and are treated for alcohol problems, then a fairly small proportion of those treated are over age 60. Mishara and Kastenbaum [13] suggest these findings may be due to four possible explanations:

1. A low incidence of alcohol-related problems among the elderly
2. Elderly people are not treated because of institutional prejudices ("ageism")
3. Elderly alcohol abusers do not seek treatment
4. Alcoholism may not be adequately diagnosed among elderly patients receiving treatment for other medical or psychiatric problems

The final possibility listed is a particularly important one. Frequently there are problems of alcohol abuse in elderly patients who are admitted to hospitals for other medical difficulties and these abuse problems are overlooked in the diagnostic workup of the presenting problem [9]. This idea is reinforced by the fact that, unlike younger alcoholics who are most frequently treated at state and county mental hospitals, 78% of older alcoholic patients are admitted for treatment to a general or Veterans Administration (VA) hospital, which may reflect the need for elderly alcoholics to be initially admitted to a hospital for treatment of a medical condition, with the alcoholism being discovered only later in the workup.

A long-term state-wide study regarding demographics by age of alcohol and other drug abusers reported some general observations about the older alcoholic in the state of Washington [16]. It must be emphasized again, however, that if one were to study the demographics of the elderly alcoholic in a large urban area like Cleveland, Detroit, or New York, rather than in the state of Washington, some very different specific data might be found. Nevertheless, the data reported in this study make some important general points concerning older drinkers.

1. Older alcoholics (age 60 and over) were more prevalent than older drug abusers (50 and over), even with the higher cutoff age for the cohort of drinkers.

2. The older alcoholic group had a higher proportion of males, Caucasians, and individuals with a lower educational level.

3. Older alcoholics seem to have an alcohol intake somewhat less than that of younger patients, approximately 5 days per week of active drinking at the rate of five drinks per drinking day. This is less than the data reported for younger patients, both in amount of alcohol and frequency of drinking.

4. The older alcoholic was more likely to be a voluntary patient, rather than one brought in for treatment by the system.

5. Older alcoholics who enter treatment are less likely than their younger counterparts to receive Antabuse. This may be because they frequently present with more medical problems than the younger alcoholic, and are probably felt to represent a higher risk patient in terms of Antabuse therapy, which is not a benign treatment.

6. Older patients appear to require a shorter period of time in treatment, and seem to have a slightly better prognosis than their younger counterparts. It should be pointed out here that treatment interventions for the elderly may be much more effective when delivered through facilities serving the aged (e.g., senior citizen programs, nursing homes, outpatient programs) rather than through programs dealing specifically with treatment for alcoholism (see Section IX, this volume). Undoubtedly, much education must be provided for these facilities before they would be useful for the elderly alcohol abuser. It should be noted that Alcoholics Anonymous (AA), although receptive to all ages, does not offer special programs for the elderly.

Causes

Obviously, no one cause for alcoholism in the elderly is known to exist at this time. However, there are a number of hypotheses attempting to relate the unique problems of the elderly with the specific problem of abusing drugs. This line of reasoning assumes that the problem of alcohol abuse began *de novo* in old age, although an earlier minor drinking problem might be theoretically exacerbated by problems associated with aging. Some of the more common causes of abuse are thought to be (1) feelings of uselessness and being forgotten; (2) feelings of dependency; (3) poverty; (4) reactions to alienation; (5) feelings of low status by society.

In fact, it has been suggested that alcohol abuse in the elderly is not so much a medical as it is a social problem [6]. Many problems occur in daily living (e.g., bereavement, loss of job status, isolation, loneliness, boredom, loss of physical prowess) and occur more frequently in older individuals. A particularly interesting theory is that concerning the sense of loss of life structure and subsequent feelings of self-worthlessness that may follow grown children leaving home. These feelings may then help lead the individual into the development of substance abuse.

It might be suggested that beginning to drink, or increasing a heretofore small drinking problem in old age, is an attempt to drown one's increasing life problems in alcohol. It is interesting to point out here that the highest suicide rate of any cohort studied is among elderly male widowers, although any direct relationships are merely speculation. Also, it must be remembered that abuse of alcohol intensifies somatic problems, and therefore loss of self-esteem, which tends to occur in older individuals in the first place.

However, even in the face of these many problems, it remains that a large majority of older people who experience some or all of these stresses never do develop into substance abusers. Therefore, although there is a clear association between many of these biopsychosocial hardships and growing old, and an association between growing old and abusing drugs, it must be emphasized that there are no good data directly linking these two observations. Another way of stating the same point is to note that the concomitance of life problems and substance abuse in the same elderly individual is no proof that one caused the other.

Even though researchers continue to point to the relationship between the problems of growing older and alcohol abuse, there are really few data that compare the characteristics of those older problematic drinkers with those older individuals who either drink socially or not at all. Also, and very importantly, there are no studies to date comparing older to younger individuals in terms of reasons for drinking.

From a psychotherapeutic viewpoint, it might be suggested that the belief that there is no other way for depressed old people to cope other than by means of alcohol may in fact be a countertransference problem based on the observer's perception of old age.

It would be helpful indeed to look beyond the problem drinking per se and the general statements about the problems encountered during aging and look instead at some of the maladaptive behavior patterns in individual elderly problem drinkers, patterns that may have led to this situation. For example, one might consider the well-known dependency and denial problems seen in some abusers, and look at these people in relation to developmental problems, as well as with their difficulty managing feelings and impairments (i.e., the self-care functions of an individual's ego). It may be that these particular maladaptive behavior patterns play a significant role in whether or not an elderly individual is predisposed to becoming an alcohol abuser. One might consider the threshold concept of neurophysiology here (i.e., two individuals may be primarily influenced by a long-term personality problem predisposing them to alcohol abuse). When life stresses associated with aging become prominent (physical decline, bereavement, retirement, etc.) the individual with a low threshold for tolerance will respond by abusing alcohol, while the individual with the higher threshold (which is never reached because the stress is not severe enough) does not. These possible relationships are indeed important areas to consider and to study.

Possible Subgroups

There is a general feeling among those interested in the area that elderly alcoholics may not be a homogeneous group. The clearest separation involves the question of whether the older ethanol abuser represents the younger alcoholic who just got older, or whether the problem springs *de novo* in old age; and, if that is the case, at what particular age it begins.

There is some evidence to indicate that anywhere from 5 to over 20% of elderly people who are problem drinkers began drinking after age 45. Gaitz and Baer [7] found that over 11% of 100 elderly persons studied began their heavy drinking after age 60, but most other studies reviewed suggest that in the populations studied, the percentage of drinking problems that begin over age 60 is fairly small. It appears the majority of actively drinking older alcoholics began having a problem in their 40 or 50s, and may not have began drinking regularly until that time.

Rosin and Glatt [15] studied older alcoholics in England, and suggested that elderly drinkers could be separated into two groups: those who began drinking early and continued into old age, and those who began drinking heavily at an older age. They suggested further that there were two types of factors integral to these drinking problems, primary and reactive. The most important primary factor was habitual, excessive drinking, related to psychological dysfunction of those individuals involved, including personalities exhibiting self-indulgence and egocentricity. Reactive, or environmental factors, included such things as bereavement, retirement, and loneliness.

Thus, the time of onset for a drinking problem in an elderly person may be dependent both upon the basic psychological makeup (life-long behavior pattern) of the individual, as well as the type and severity of environmental life stresses impinging on him or her during critical periods. This is another example of the combined nature versus nurture concept of etiology, which seems to characterize so many complex diseases.

It appears as though about half of those individuals who were alcoholics during their young adulthood years and who live to be over age 65 give up their drinking. This is accomplished either alone or with help from family or organizations like AA. The group that does continue to drink has much higher rates of alcohol-related health problems than those patients who previously had an early drinking problem but stopped drinking. These medical problems were chronic (e.g., cirrhosis, peptic ulcer) rather than acute in nature. Interestingly, the need to detoxify or to treat alcohol withdrawal in elderly alcoholics is much less frequent than when compared with younger drinkers.

It is useful to clarify the distinguishing characteristics observed between the elderly alcoholic who has been drinking heavily for many years and the individual who begins drinking heavily for the first time in old age as a reaction to perceived life stress. There are some striking contrasts between these two groups, which can be labeled "early onset" and "late onset." The most distinctive feature of the early-onset group, whose members have been drinking all their lives and have not died, is the exhibition of a social isolation and total lack of interpersonal relationships. These drinkers have become the stereotyped wino or skid row bum. It is important not to overgeneralize in this area since the elderly resident cohort contains relatively the fewest heavy drinkers in the skid row population. What is clear is that even though all residents are not heavy alcohol abusers, drinking problems usually antedate arrival on skid row, and almost all of the residents there are socially isolated [1]. For a comprehensive treatise on this area of alcohol-related psychopathology, Schuckit and Pastor [19] should be consulted.

It is noteworthy that this early-onset group of alcoholics, mostly men, have few if any momentos of their past (photographs, address books, personal records). They generally have no contact with family or friends, and frequently do not know the whereabouts of their spouse or children, or even if any grandchildren exist. They may not even own the clothes they are wearing, which may come from the Salvation Army, police officers, or the like. After discharge from the hospital, where they are usually admitted for malnourishment, exacerbation of chronic problems like peptic ulcers, chronic obstructive pulmonary disease, and frequently with varying degrees of cognitive impairment, they almost never return for any follow-up clinic appointments.

They could be considered as the dregs of society and should by all rights be the saddest of creatures. Paradoxically, many clinicians report varying remnants in many of these individuals of a clear-cut social charm. It is important to remember that it must require distinctive social skills for one to survive so long in a society that frowns on chronic, active alcoholics, besides having little use even for non-drinking elderly individuals. In these early-onset drinkers, their psychopathology must be considered important and the primary factors of Rosin and Glatt [15] would seem appropriate here.

In contrast, individuals in the second, or late-onset, group are represented by both sexes, and frequently were called social drinkers earlier in life; they may not have drunk alcohol at all. If there were some early periods of drinking, it was usually in response to some social stress, but it was never considered problematic. This late-onset group of elderly drinkers is thought to be larger than the aforementioned early-onset group. Alcohol becomes a serious problem late in life, perhaps as an attempt at coping with the disappointments associated with their aging. It is important to reiterate that the life circumstances of these individuals are often quite different from the circumstances of the young, and may be due to society's frequently callous handling of the elderly (e.g., forced retirement, poverty, and rejection). Rather than the psychopathology exhibited by the early-onset drinkers, a psychosocial causation, perhaps complicated by organic disease, is more appropriate with the late-onset drinkers. They may be thought of as responding to the reactive factors described by Rosin and Glatt [15].

Rather than exuding remnants of social charm like the first group, these late-onset drinkers are frequently depressed and even suicidal on admission to a hospital or an agency, and they may present as withdrawn and hostile. These are individuals who earlier in life had more affiliations and more occupational stresses than early-onset drinkers. They also were more likely, when possible, to live with their families throughout much of their lives.

These late-onset patients usually do much better with treatment than the early-onset group, and their prognosis is somewhat better. Psychotherapy, antidepressant pharmacotherapy, and frequently AA are helpful. AA provides a new social group where the individual can be subjected to a larger idea, and where serving as a sponsor may be beneficial toward providing a new sense of purpose, dignity, and self-esteem in helping others.

Alcohol Abuse and Organic Mental Disorders in the Elderly

There are two ways in which the impact of combining the concepts of alcohol abuse and organic mental disorders (OMD) in an elderly individual might be viewed. The most obvious has to do with the concept of correctly diagnosing disturbed behavior in an elderly individual, especially differentiating among chronic, irreversible dementing processes, acute, reversible deliria, and atypical depressions. Much has been written on this crucial subject in terms of insuring proper subsequent treatment, and the reader is referred to Maletta and Pirozzolo [11] for more information. It is sufficient in this context to point out that when evaluating an elderly patient, the clinician should be aware that a disoriented, disturbed older individual may in fact not be demented (and in need of a quick nursing home placement) but instead may be delirious secondary to a multitude of etiologies, including being drunk or withdrawing from alcohol. These signs of acute organicity should be viewed in the context of being temporary and reversible.

This section focuses on those patients where there is a combined problem of alcohol abuse and OMD, whether or not the cause of the disorder is directly related to the alcohol, or whether it is due to any of the other causes of OMD in the elderly [11]. There are both treatment and prognostic reasons that necessitate identifying OMD in elderly alcoholics. Those alcohol abusers with concomitant organicity are more likely to have serious medical problems than those without, even though there may be a similarity in ages of the two groups. It has also been suggested that those elderly alcoholics with OMD might have a less optimistic prognosis following treatment [19].

Gaitz and Baer [7] studied 100 consecutive admissions of elderly patients to a county hospital and reported the following data:

1. Forty-four people had alcoholism of some type.
2. For 36 of these patients, alcoholism was the principal diagnosis, whereas it was secondary for the other eight.
3. Of the alcoholic group, 27, or over 60%, also had concomitant organic mental disorders of some kind (although the specifics of the diagnosis were not clear).

In an attempt to clarify what influence the organicity may have had on the elderly alcoholics, those with combined alcoholism and OMD were compared in several categories to those alcoholics without OMD, and also to those nonalcoholic patients with OMD. Three areas demonstrated significant differences.

1. The alcoholic groups were younger and contained more males.
2. Compared to alcoholics without OMD, those with combined alcoholism and OMD were younger.
3. The alcoholic groups either lived alone, or their families tended to be negative or even rejecting, based on data from structured family interviews.

When followed for 3 subsequent years the nonalcoholic group with OMD had a nonstatistically significant higher mortality rate. However, the differences in age of the survivors and nonsurvivors were significant, and when taken into account, revealed that the alcoholics with OMD did indeed die at a younger age.

The mortality rate of the patients with alcoholism but without OMD was 12%, much less than either group with OMD. In all other categories this population resembled the group with alcoholism and OMD. Other data comparing alcoholics with OMD and those without OMD demonstrated that those with OMD reported less education, had fewer nontraffic police problems, fewer job problems, and a much higher rate of serious health problems unrelated to their cognitive dysfunction [3, 18].

In a patient with combined alcoholism and OMD, or even alcoholism with other concomitant medical problems, an accurate diagnosis and appropriate demographic follow-up and prognosis becomes extremely difficult. Studies that report very low percentages of alcoholism in elderly patients admitted to mental hospitals perhaps may be instead placing those individuals into the much more prevalent and acceptable diagnosis of OMD, with the concomitant alcoholism problem being overlooked and therefore unreported and untreated [20]. Simon and Neal [21] reported that among a sample of 534 admissions to a psychiatric screening hospital, over 50% of those elderly patients who drank to excess suffered from organic brain syndrome. The authors felt that since alcoholism problems were frequently present at the same time as other psychiatric conditions, including OMD, it was difficult to accurately determine a diagnosis of alcoholism in an elderly patient.

TREATMENT OF THE ELDERLY ALCOHOL ABUSER

There seems to be a prevailing attitude held by many that with elderly individuals it is useless to attempt to actively treat biopsychosocial problems, including those of alcohol abuse. It is as though when an individual reaches a certain point in life, the cost of being treated becomes greater than the benefit to be accrued. Although this view may indeed be considered valid in certain unique situations encountered infrequently in medicine, some in society place all who pass beyond that age of 65 into this category. It is somewhat the same regarding treatment for the elderly alcohol abuser, although in some quarters the position is taken that alcohol abuse is alcohol abuse no matter at what stage of life it appears, and should be vigorously treated by medical, psychosocial, or combined means.

When discussing medical treatment of alcohol abuse, one is usually discussing the use of medications to treat symptoms. In elderly alcoholics, the most common symptoms treated are anxiety and depression. Although there is little evidence in the literature for the efficacy of this approach, antianxiety and antidepressant agents are widely used in this population.

It should be noted that when using psychotropics, or for that matter, any drugs in the elderly, special precautions must be taken. Type, dose, and mode of administration of the drug; side effects; physiological ambience of the individual; existing disease processes; problems with homeostatic mechanisms; and other drugs taken concomitantly in terms of drug interactions must all be considered when prescribing for an older patient [10]. The elderly alcoholic, by virtue of his or her relatively poor health when compared to the nonalcoholic control, is especially susceptible to untoward, and potentially dangerous, drug effects. As mentioned earlier, the increase in number of medical problems frequently exhibited by the elderly alcoholic is the main reason given why some drugs that clearly cause untoward physiological effects (e.g., disulfiram) are used infrequently in older alcoholics.

When considering psychotherapeutic approaches with the elderly alcoholic, it is important to point out that old age is not a prohibition to effective psychotherapy [8]. It appears there would be a better prognosis for those elderly patients who began drinking *de novo* in late life, and whose problems may have been catalyzed by psychosocial events encountered during aging. These people are to be contrasted with the early-onset drinker, who is more likely to have psychopathologic problems, and thus might be less amenable to a psychotherapeutic approach.

The most effective treatment for elderly alcohol abusers must take into account the unique and distinctive psychosocial features that they and also their families manifest. It is well known that older alcoholics are frequently kept hidden by their families from public view, often until the patient becomes medically quite sick. Unfortunately, many elderly alcoholic abusers remain forever unidentified and therefore untreated [12].

When discussing treatment, prognosis must also be considered, and with the elderly there are relatively few outcome studies comparing them with younger alcohol abusers. In fact, it is difficult to determine a therapeutic success, since the criteria utilized are not always carefully specified. Mishara and Kastenbaum [13] suggest that at least three types of graduated success criteria could be considered; and further, the particular criterion invoked in an outcome study must be clearly specified. The three types of success criteria are

1. Total abstinence from alcohol
2. Abstinence with significant improvement in major domains of functioning as well
3. Significant overall improvement in functioning without giving up all use of alcoholic beverages

A major and crucial treatment issue regarding older problem drinkers is whether the patient should be treated solely for alcoholism, or whether a more comprehensive treatment view should be taken, with those events that were integral to the onset of the drinking problem (especially those in later life) are also attacked. Certainly the latter approach seems the most appropriate and probably eventually the more effective.

REFERENCES

1. Bahr, H., and Caplow, T. *Old Men Drunk and Sober.* New York University Press: New York, 1973.
2. Blose, I. L. The relationship of alcohol to aging and the elderly. *Alcoholism Clin. Exp. Res.* 2:17-21, 1978.
3. Blusewicz, M., Dustman, R., Schenkenberg, T., and Beck, E. Neuropsychological correlates of chronic alcoholism and aging. *J. Nerv. Ment. Dis.* 165:348-355, 1977.
4. Bozzetti, L. P., and MacMurray, J. P. Drug misuse among the elderly: A hidden menace. *Psychiatric Ann.* 7:95-107, 1977.
5. Chafetz, M. E. Alcoholism: An illness that demands recognition and treatment. *Geriatrics* 28:38, 1973.
6. Gaillard, A., and Perrin, P. Alcoholism in aged persons. *Rev. Alcohol.* 15:5-32, 1969.
7. Gaitz, C. M., and Baer, P. E. Characteristics of elderly patients with alcoholism. *Arch. Gen. Psychiatry* 24:372-378, 1971.

8. Kastenbaum, R. Psychotherapy with the older client. In: *Clinical Psychology and Aging*, Storandt, M., Siegler, I., and Elias, M. (eds.). Academic Press: New York, 1978.

9. Lennon, B. E., Rekosh, J. H., Patch, V. D., and Howe, L. P. Self-reports of drunkenness arrests. *Q. J. Stud. Alcohol* 31:90–96, 1970.

10. Maletta, G. J. Use of psychotropic drugs in the older patient. In: *The Aging Nervous System*, Maletta, G. and Pirozzolo, F. (eds.). Praeger: New York, 1980.

11. Maletta, G. J., and Pirozzolo, F. J. Assessment and treatment of behavioral disturbances in the geriatric patient. In: *Behavioral Assessment and Pharmacology*, Pirozzolo, F. and Maletta, G. (eds.). Praeger: New York, 1981.

12. Mayfield, D. G. Alcohol problems in the aging patient. In: *Drug Issues in Geropsychiatry*, Mayfield, D. G. (ed.). Williams & Wilkins: Baltimore, 1974.

13. Mishara, B., and Kastenbaum, R. Treatment of problem drinking among the elderly. In: *Alcohol and Old Age*, Mishara, B. and Kastenbaum, R. (eds.). Grune & Stratton: New York, 1980.

14. Pascarelli, E. F. Drug dependence: An age-old problem compounded by old age. *Geriatrics* 29:109–114, 1974.

15. Rosin, A., and Glatt, M. Alcohol excess in the elderly. *Q. J. Stud. Alcohol* 32:53–59, 1971.

16. Schukit, M. A. *An Overview of Alcohol and Drug Abuse Problems in the Elderly*. Testimony before the Subcommittee on Alcoholism and Narcotics, and Subcommittee on Aging, of the Senate Committee on Labor and Public Welfare, Washington, D.C., June 1976.

17. Schukit, M. A. Geriatric alcoholism and drug abuse. *Gerontologist* 17:168–174, 1977.

18. Schukit, M. A., and Miller, P. L. Alcoholism in elderly men: A survey of a general medical ward. *Ann. N.Y. Acad. Sci.* 273:558–571, 1976.

19. Schukit, M. A., and Pastor, P. A. Alcohol-related psychopathology in the aged. In: *Psychopathology of Aging*, Kaplan, O. J. (ed.). Academic Press: New York, 1979.

20. Simon, A., Epstein, L., and Reynolds, L. Alcoholism in the geriatric mentally ill. *Geriatrics* 23:125–131, 1968.

21. Simon, A., and Neal, M. Patterns of geriatric mental illness. In: *Process of Aging* (Vol. 1), Tibbitts, C. and Donahue, W. (eds.). Atherton Press: New York, 1963.

22. Williams, E. P. Alcoholism and problem drinking among older persons. In: *Alcohol and Problem Drinking among Older Persons*, Williams, E. (ed.). National Technical Information Service: Springfield, 1973.

23. Zimberg, S. The elderly alcoholic. *Gerontologist* 14:221–224, 1974.

Section VIII

Alcoholism Treatment Personnel

63

WILMA J. KNOX, PhD, Veterans Administration Medical Center, Biloxi, Mississippi

THE PROFESSIONALS: THE ISSUE OF ALCOHOLISM

WITHIN EACH PROFESSIONAL group are adherents to a disease concept of alcoholism. A brief description of their position is followed herein by results from large sample surveys of established professional groups relating to the disease concept, other definitions, and treatment of alcoholism. Differences among professional administrators concern staffing patterns and combining drug and alcohol programs. Younger professionals' viewpoints are considered briefly. Several examples of objective methods available to researchers are included.

Many professionals seem unaware that their definition of alcoholism has legal implications. The "Anglo-American legal tradition exempts from blame those whose behavior is determined by illness" [15]. If alcoholism is established in law as a disease, the alcoholic may be considered not guilty not only in instances of public drunkenness, but in crimes of many varieties [8].

Wilma J. Knox, PhD, Staff Psychologist, Veterans Administration Medical Center, Biloxi, Mississippi, and Associate Professor, University of Southern Mississippi, Hattiesburg, Mississippi.

THE DISEASE CONCEPT

Gitlow states the position of adherents to the disease concept with conviction and "question[s] the motives of those who would strip the alcoholic of his 'disease' label" [5, p. 6]. He points out that etiology is unknown in many diseases and claims "there is little question but that the history, symptoms, and signs of alcoholism form a recognizable pattern." Distribution is "easily discernable," and the complications of alcoholism are "commonplace." The therapeutic goal is abstinence; directive and confrontive psychotherapy is recommended, as is education about the disease and assistance from Alcoholics Anonymous (AA).

Gitlow considers the "disease" label necessary to obtain treatment resources for alcoholics with public approval and to fix responsibility for the care of alcoholics within medical and related health professions. He appeals to authority by listing national organizations (including the American Psychological Association) who "have now each and all officially pronounced alcoholism as a disease." When contacted, the American Psychological Association could not locate an official action to that effect and considered it "unlikely that the association would have taken a public stance in support of this one conceptual framework" [Mary Logan, Administrative Projects Assistant, American Psychological Association, personal communication].

PSYCHIATRISTS AND PSYCHOLOGISTS

Knox [10] surveyed 345 Veterans Administration (VA) psychiatrists and 480 VA psychologists, asking them to check all answers with which they agreed in defining alcoholism and its etiology, typical behavior, criteria for successful treatment, preferred treatment, and financial benefits. Other questions limited to one answer dealt with prognosis, motivation, site of care, and respondents' own attitudes toward working with alcoholics. Remarkably the two groups' answers were in significant agreement (using rank-order correlations) on all questions except two: Psychologists were more favorable toward various pension payments for alcoholics than psychiatrists, and the two groups differed in rank ordering behaviors typical of alcoholism.

Both groups rarely selected "disease" as a definition of alcoholism. In spite of directions to check as many statements as wished, "disease" was left blank approximately 66% of the time. Jailing for public drunkenness or jail terms and court probation for treatment had very few adherents and were essentially rejected. The groups were opposed to social drinking for alcoholics, placed little weight on verbal promises to stop drinking, and felt that prognosis for sobriety was poor.

More psychologists described alcoholism as a behavior problem than psychiatrists, but both groups selected that definition most frequently and also preferred symptom complex and escape mechanism to the disease concept. Psychologists and psychiatrists agreed that AA and group therapy were preferred treatments and that AA and neuropsychiatric hospitals were the appropriate agencies to handle most alcoholic problems. High motivation to stop drinking was considered necessary.

In spite of the groups' marked preference for hospital care, most would want to be personally involved only 25% or less of their working time. About 40% of each group were unwilling to undertake full-time work with alcoholics, but about 20% of each group would willingly do so. Six years later a study of 233 psychologists from this sample showed they held essentially the same attitudes toward drug abusers, with few exceptions. In the interim, however, the group became willing to devote more time to the treatment of alcoholics [11].

SOCIAL WORKERS AND NURSES

Social Workers

In a sample of 588 VA social workers surveyed in general medical settings and neuropsychiatric facilities, considerable agreement was found with VA psychologists and psychiatrists [8]. Exceptions included the social workers' endorsement of the disease definition of alcoholism, particularly those at general medical hospitals. The total group, however, selected multiple definitions and over 60% of the group selected escape mechanism, symptom complex, disease, and behavior problems. The social workers (particularly neuropsychiatric workers) were willing to devote more time to treating alcoholics and had more individuals (particularly males) who reacted positively to the prospect of full-time work with alcoholics.

Nurses

Lemos and Moran [13] included 128 registered nurses among 464 treatment personnel tested at one VA hospital. The Marcus Alcoholism Questionnaire indicated the nurses did accept the disease theory, as did most of the subgroups tested at that hospital. The nurses scored higher than small samples of other professional groups in considering alcohol to be highly addicting and an alcoholic to be unable to control his or her drinking. Sex, age, or experience working on an alcohol unit did not affect attitudes significantly.

ADMINISTRATIVE PERSONNEL

Seventy-one alcoholism coordinators in the Northeast were queried as part of a stratified sample to evaluate implementation of the alcoholism policy for Civil Service employees [17]. Despite support of the policy by hospital directors, coordinators lacked official time, staff help, and funds to carry out the policy. Medical facilities were available in 87% of the programs, however. Coordinators' staff size was directly related to case load, cases per 100 employees, use of policy procedures, and developing program resources through consultation with medical personnel, unions, affected supervisors, and community treatment resources.

Lambert and Cummins [12] surveyed attitudes toward merging drug and alcoholism services. They contacted 144 administrative directors of state programs for drug abuse and alcoholism. Directors of separate alcoholism programs were consistently least favorable toward six effects of combining programs, and directors of currently combined programs were most favorable. A survey of local alcohol treatment personnel revealed that group showed substantially greater opposition to integration of services than state-level administrators.

YOUNGER PROFESSIONALS

Psychology Graduate Students

Attitudes of 172 VA psychology trainees were assessed as part of a study about drug abuse [9]. They seemed to seek freedom of movement for alcoholics in treatment and endorsed outpatient treatment and open ward care within a psychiatric hospital. Grouping of alcoholics for treatment was recommended within a psychiatric hospital or through the use of a special hospital for this condition. The graduate students were willing to devote more personal working time to treatment of drug abusers; about 75% of the group selected 25% or below for alcoholics.

Psychiatric Residents

Coryell and Wetzel [2] surveyed 378 third-year psychiatric residents on effectiveness of six therapies for four diagnostic categories, including alcoholism. A significant association was noted between location of training and attitudes toward specific treatments regardless of the diagnostic category. Significant differences were found between attitudes toward specific treatments, treatments for specific diagnoses, and interaction between diagnoses and treatments. Group therapy was considered essential for alcoholics by the majority of residents; this treatment was preferred only for alcoholism. The residents were also positive toward milieu therapy, but less support was noted for individual therapy. Somatic therapy and vitamin therapy were essentially rejected.

Nursing School Graduates

Gurel and Spain [6] compared attitudes toward alcoholics using 24 nursing graduates from a Roman Catholic rural college and 29 nurses from an urban state university program. None of the selected nurses had as yet had special education or experience with alcoholics. In general, graduates of the rural religious school were more comfortable in working with alcoholics. Within this group, nurses who were not comfortable with alcoholics had less favorable attitudes toward alcoholism on the Marcus Alcoholism Questionnaire in comparison to their classmates or nurses from the nonreligious urban school.

RESEARCH TOOLS

Objective Tests of Attitudes

Few objective psychological tests have been developed or widely used to examine attitudes toward alcoholism. Marcus' Alcohol Questionnaire [13] was developed in Canada in 1963 through a factor analytic study. Several factors were related to the disease concept of alcoholism. Bell's Attitude toward Alcoholic Persons [1] was adapted from a scale designed for disabled persons. Tolar and Tamerin's Attitudes toward Alcoholism Scale was primarily concerned with etiology, but little data have been published beyond the original article. [16]. The primary function of the Knox questionnaire was to evaluate allegiance to the disease concept and other issues in an equitable fashion; the question has not been readily adaptable to other purposes.

Behavioral Indices

Behavioral indices rarely have been utilized in evaluating differences among professionals. Hanna [7] found that admission treatment recommendations at a psychiatric outpatient clinic interacted with problem drinking and subject characteristics. Problem drinkers that professional staff referred to the alcohol team labeled themselves as alcoholics, had alcohol mentioned in their records, or had already been diagnosed alcoholic.

Lowe and Alston [14] found no pattern of racial discrimination in delivery of services at an alcoholism clinic offering inpatient and outpatient treatment in the South. These authors were of the opinion that clinic philosophy and organizational structure were crucial to the clinic's performance. The philosophical emphasis was that of people relating to people and providing as much treatment as quickly as possible. Some traditional procedures were eliminated, such as establishing differential diagnoses, specifying prognoses, and denying treatment to poor candidates. The director and senior therapists (including psychiatrists) were part-time employees, did not dominate staff decisions, and did not support bureaucratic solutions.

Unasked Questions

In considering questionnaire responses of working professionals to the disease concept, it should be noted that the variable of years of education has been confronted with attitude. In addition, no specific comparison has been made of the relationship between adherence to the disease concept and willingness to work with alcoholics. The special problems of professional attitudes toward female or minority group alcoholics have not been explored.

Frequently issues have been examined in the literature that may be related to differences among professionals but the question of attitude was not examined per se. For example, in a hospital study over a period of 4 years Davis and Jones [3] found blacks were more likely to be diagnosed schizophrenic, whereas Caucasians were diagnosed alcoholic and depressed more frequently.

An inviting situation for a study of staff differences occurs when alcoholics who are not referred for treatment are located in a specific hospital setting. Those professionals who do not make referrals for alcohol treatment should provide an interesting contrast to alcohol treatment teams. Fink et al. [4] noted that two physicians in a group of 10 were three to five times more likely to recommend partial hospitalization in a university-affiliated psychiatric hospital. This study illustrates the importance of determining subjective biases of clinicians and points out the potential use of educational programs for non-patient-specific variables.

ACKNOWLEDGMENTS

The author wishes to acknowledge the support of the Medical Research Service of the Veterans Administration.

REFERENCES

1. Bell, A. H., Weingold, H. P., and Lachin, J. M. Measuring adjustment in patients disabled with alcoholism. *Q. J. Stud. Alcohol* 30:634–639, 1969.
2. Coryell, W., and Wetzel, J. D. Attitudes toward issues in psychiatry among third-year residents: A brief survey. *Am. J. Psychiatry* 135:732–735, 1978.

3. Davis, W. E., and Jones, M. H. Negro versus Caucasian psychological test performance revisited. *J. Cons. Clin. Psychol.* 42:675-679, 1974.

4. Fink, E. B., Heckerman, C. L., and McNeill, D. An examination of clinician bias in patient referrals to partial hospital settings. *Hosp. Commun. Psychiatry* 30:631-632, 1979.

5. Gitlow, L. E. Alcoholism: A disease. In: *Alcoholism Progress in Research and Treatment*, Bourne, P. G. and Fox, R. (eds.). Academic Press: New York, 1973.

6. Gurel, M., and Spain, M. D. Differences in attitudes toward alcoholism in graduates of two schools of nursing. *Psychol. Rep.* 41:1285-1286, 1977.

7. Hanna, E. Attitudes toward problem drinkers: A critical factor in treatment recommendations. *J. Stud. Alcohol* 39:98-109, 1978.

8. Knox, W. J. Attitudes of social workers and other professional groups toward alcoholism. *Q. J. Stud. Alcohol* 34:1270-1278, 1973.

9. Knox, W. J. Attitudes of psychology graduate students toward drug abuse. *Prof. Psychol.* 5:185-190, 1974.

10. Knox, W. J. Attitudes of psychiatrists and psychologists toward alcoholism. In: *Medicine, Law and Public Policy*, Kittrie, N. N., Hirsh, H. L., and Wegner, G. (eds.). AMS: New York, 1975.

11. Knox, W. J. Attitudes of psychologists toward drug abusers. *J. Clin. Psychol.* 32:179-188, 1976.

12. Lambert, M. D., and Cummins, M. J. Perception of state administrators toward combined alcoholism and drug abuse services. *Drug Alc. Depend.* 12:65-72, 1977.

13. Lemos, A. V., and Moran, J. Veterans Administration hospital staff attitudes toward alcoholism. *Drug. Alc. Depend.* 3:77-83, 1978.

14. Lowe, G. D., and Alston, J. P. Hospital structure and racial discrimination. *J. Alc. Drug. Educ.* 19:29-37, 1974.

15. Pastor, P. A. Mobilization in public drunkenness control: A comparison of legal and medical approaches. *Alc. Drug Abuse Instit. Tech. Publ.* 19:1-35, 1976.

16. Tolar, A., and Tamerin, J. S. The attitudes toward alcoholism instrument: A measure of attitudes toward alcoholics and the nature and causes of alcoholism. *Br. J. Addict.* 70:223-231, 1975.

17. Trice, H. M., Beyer, J. M., and Hunt, R. E. Evaluating implementation of a job-based alcoholism policy. *J. Stud. Alcohol* 39:448-465, 1978.

64

CHAIM M. ROSENBERG, MD, PhD, Boston University School of Medicine

THE PARAPROFESSIONALS IN ALCOHOLISM TREATMENT

IN 1788, THOMAS TROTTER presented his thesis on drunkenness for the degree of Doctor of Medicine at Edinburgh University. In 1804, Benjamin Rush, the American physician, published a paper on the same topic. These pioneer medical researchers described the increased dependence and withdrawal syndromes, as well as the changes in behavior, associated with chronic alcoholism. Unfortunately, the bulk of the medical community remained—and continues to remain—largely disinterested in alcoholism and in caring for those who have become addicted to this drug.

Until the beginning of the 19th century, the traditional belief stressed the virtues of alcoholic liquors. However, the rapid spread of habitual drunkenness gave rise to considerable public concern. In 1813, the Massachusetts Society for the Suppression of Intemperance was established, and soon the temperance movement spread throughout the United States as well as in Europe. This movement became linked with many of the religious and humanitarian movements of the time, including abolitionism and missionary work.

The temperance movement had the backing of the clergy, but was also spread by efforts of lay persons, many of whom were former alcoholics who had taken the pledge of abstinence. One such group was the Washington Total Abstinence Movement, which was founded in Baltimore in 1840 as a working-class drive

---

Chaim M. Rosenberg, MD, PhD, Associate Professor of Psychiatry, Boston University School of Medicine, Boston, Massachusetts.

against habitual drunkenness [3]. The members of this group pledged themselves to bring to their meetings friends who were drunkards or heavy drinkers. In this way, a fellowship of alcoholics was established in which members could discuss their drinking experience and share ways of conquering their dependence on alcohol.

With the spread of the temperance movement, a literature was developed aimed at combating the spread of alcoholism [8]. These "Temperance Tales" presented an image of the alcoholic as a social outcast and physically debilitated derelict. Alcohol was the demon that dragged a person from respectability and affluence into degradation and poverty. The alcoholic was seen as someone living in the shabbiest corners of human society, beyond the reach of medical practice, and fit only as an object of scorn or of charity.

The concept of alcohol as a condition that degrades, together with the belief that salvation comes through abstinence, are basic to the philosophy of Alcoholics Anonymous (AA). The founders of this lay movement were influenced by the ideas of the Oxford group—a nondenominational, evangelical movement—as well as by the writings of the psychoanalyst C. G. Jung [15]. Alcoholics Anonymous filled an enormous gap in services for the chronic alcoholic. While detoxification and the treatment of complications still took place in the hospital setting, ongoing care and follow-up were increasingly left to AA. In this way, an informal partnership developed between the official health care system and the AA fellowship of sober alcoholics.

The clear division of labor between the lay organizations and the generic health care system began to break down around 1970, mainly as a result of the national commitment to reduce the prevalence and incidence of alcoholism and alcohol-related problems. The establishment of the National Institute on Alcohol Abuse and Alcoholism (NIAAA), with a heavy inflow of federal dollars, brought into the treatment system large numbers of people who had no formal training in one or other of the health professions. In the early years of the 1970s, many of these paraprofessionals were former alcoholics who had, for many years, remained active members of AA. This was also a time of growth in the community psychiatry movement, where it was believed that indigenous workers, without formal educational credentials but trained in counseling skills, could effectively respond to the needs of the large numbers of mentally distressed people who would seek help in the mental health centers.

ALCOHOLISM COUNSELORS

For want of a better name, the title "alcoholism counselor" was proposed to describe this new member of the treatment team. Since this type of person had had no formal training, and had no defined position (in a field already occupied by physicians, psychologists, social workers, and nurses), pressures increased to establish training programs and to set standards of competency through some form of certification.

On August 30, 1974, Roy Littlejohn Associates submitted a proposal to the NIAAA for a national standard for alcoholism counselors [12]. Among the recommended requirements for certification were that the alcoholism counselor (1) have no history or evidence of alcohol or other drug misuse for at least 2 years immediately prior to certification; (2) have completed a training program in alcohol studies; (3) have 1 year of experience in alcoholism counseling; and (4) have some knowledge and skill in alcoholism counseling.

In the Littlejohn document, alcoholism counseling is described as a new profession, and an alcoholism counselor was "recognized as a key member of a prevention/treatment/rehabilitation team in programs where persons with alcohol problems receive help." These full-time, paid counselors were to gradually replace the voluntary workers who were members of lay organizations. They would be capable of undertaking a wide range of tasks, including intake, assistance in the development of a treatment plan, individual and group counseling, client evaluation, crisis intervention, working with families, outreach, case consultation, assisting in program development, education and prevention, and even program consultation.

A considerable stimulus for paraprofessional training was provided through grants from the NIAAA. This training was frequently undertaken under the sponsorship of a university but did not lead to academic credits. Increasingly, training is now being provided through community colleges, where the trainees can receive academic credits for their efforts. Those seeking training anticipate that it will help them to become certified as alcoholism counselors.

In February 1977, some 3 years after the Littlejohn proposal, a special Alcohol, Drug Abuse and Mental Health Administration (ADAMHA)/NIAAA planning panel issued its final report on alcoholism counselor credentialing. This became known as the Finger Report, so named after its chairman, Kenneth Finger, PhD, of the University of Florida at Gainesville. Credentialing of alcoholism counselors was seen to be necessary "to assure quality of care to alcoholic people, to obtain third-party payments, and to provide recognition to the counselors for their valuable services." Finger's committee recommended that a national credentialing organization for alcoholism counselors be established to provide recognition for the "newly emerging profession of alcoholism counseling."

The newly formed National Association of Alcoholism Counselors held its first national conference in 1976 with 50 persons in attendance. By 1977, the number had increased to 100, and the following year more than 300 were in attendance, including family and guests. A high point of the conference was an open AA meeting with nearly 500 people present, both from the conference itself and from the local community.

The National Association of Alcoholism Counselors is something of a hybrid organization. On the one hand is its insistence that alcoholism counseling is a profession that exists alongside other professional groups, such as physicians, social workers, and nurses. On the other hand, it still draws strength from its constituency of volunteer, sober alcoholics who are members of AA, as evidenced from its 12-point Code of Ethics, which begins with the affirmation to work toward recovery for the client and his or her family and ends with a pledge to "God, to my clients, and to my fellow man."

According to Finger's committee, there are approximately 3,000 alcoholism treatment centers in the United States, with a total of between 8,000 and 10,000 alcoholism counselors. Those who have worked in the alcoholism field over the past 10 years cannot but be aware of a gradual shift in the makeup of people who are called alcoholism paraprofessionals or alcoholism counselors. When this author and colleagues started to train paraprofessionals in 1971, the typical applicant was a 40-year-old male who had been addicted to alcohol and had gained sobriety through involvement with AA. This prototypical person had limited formal education beyond the high school level, and certainly no professional qualifications in one or other of the health professions. He was indeed a paraprofessional.

Gradually, however, a shift has taken place, partly because of the increase in the number of funded, full-time positions as alcoholism counselors and the increasing number of college graduates (at the Bachelor's or Master's level) who have been trained to do counseling. This upgrading of the counseling role makes the term "paraprofessional" less and less tenable.

CONFLICT IN THE FIELD

As Pattison [9] points out, alcoholism has long been recognized as one of the leading public health problems of the nation. This fact notwithstanding, professional schools continue to offer little formal training in chronic alcoholism and its treatment. Generations of young physicians and nurses have based their attitude toward the alcoholic on their experiences on the emergency flood and inpatient wards, where they meet the dirty, noisy, delapidated, skid row drunk. They do not know that most alcohol abusers continue to work and can often maintain an outward respectability. As a result, professionals have felt negatively toward alcoholics and, until recently, left this patient population to the paraprofessional. The recent trend to introduce alcoholism treatment into the mainstream of medical practice has brought some professionally trained people into the field. This has provoked concern and even friction between professionals and nonprofessionals. This discord arises from differences in values, identities, and motivation, as well as from a tendency for professionals to treat paraprofessionals as subordinates [6]. Kalb and Propper [7] noted that the nonprofessional working in the alcoholism field gains skills by direct observation of those already active in helping the alcoholic. He or she learns that salvation (cure) comes through adherence to the revealed truth. Questioning established dogma or entertaining alternative ideas is to be avoided. It has also been argued [14] that the support for these beliefs—as systematized in the philosophy of AA—is so powerful as to inhibit the development of scientifically based alcoholism research and treatment methods.

TREATMENT

It remains a fact that there is not yet a specific and effective treatment for alcoholism [5, 9]. What exists today is a wide assortment of approaches, including medication and behavior modification. However, some form of ongoing, talking therapy (psychotherapy, counseling, etc.) is generally the main method used to get alcoholics to give up alcohol and to alter their style of living. This state of affairs continues despite the lack of firm evidence that this treatment method is any more successful than simply telling the person that he or she is drinking too much and that drinking should stop.

THE ROLE OF THE PARAPROFESSIONAL

What, then, is the role of the paraprofessional whose principal clinical tool is counseling? It has been often stated that the attitude of care givers toward their patients has a significant impact on the outcome of treatment, and that the effects of treatment are determined by the quality of the relationship between therapist and patient. Failure in alcoholism treatment is said to be a self-fulfilling prophesy. A therapist who holds that alcoholics are poorly motivated and uninterested in getting better will have these views confirmed, while a therapist whose attitude is one of optimism will have a greater rate of success. Finally, it is believed that former alcoholics who become therapists are more successful at their task than therapists who have never had a drinking problem. Unfortunately, no proof for any of these beliefs exists. Neither can it be said that the length of training in counseling skills significantly affects treatment outcomes [1, 10, 11, 13]. These findings are not all that surprising, since the counseling process is one factor among many (and perhaps only a minor factor) that determines outcome. Other significant variables include the patient's education and economic level, social stability, and the degree to which coercion is used.

There have been a number of studies in which paraprofessionals have been employed in unusual, but potentially useful, ways. Bissonette [2] suggested that bartenders could play a valuable role as mental health "gate keepers." These people—with proper training—could discourage excessive drinking among their customers and refer them to treatment centers if their drinking seems to be getting out of control. Other groups with public visibility, such as the clergy, police, and hairdressers, could be similarly trained. Davis and Hagood [4] came up with an interesting idea of employing trained paraprofessional workers to help alcoholic mothers and their families in their homes. The paraprofessionals chosen for this work were selected on the basis of their experience with alcoholism, their ability to work with children and to manage a household, and their skills in relating with others. The paraprofessional was required to get to know the family and to make therapeutic contracts with each family member. The worker would visit the family at home, encourage the alcoholic to achieve sobriety, help out with household management, assist the family members in developing better communication with each other, and help the family to make better use of existing community services. Unfortunately, no means of comparison with other treatment programs was provided, but these authors suggested that their program was successful in meeting the stated goals.

THE PRESENT, THE FUTURE

Health care is now very big business. The cozy and direct treatment relationship between the general medical practitioner and the patient has been replaced by specialization. Other health care workers, such as nurses and social workers, are less and less willing to work in a hierarchical system, and are attempting to enforce the authority of their own guilds by seeking direct responsibility for patient care. In the mental health fields the professional disciplines of psychiatry, psychology, social work, and psychiatric nursing are all involved in offering psychotherapy.

With the availability of federal, state, and city monies, there has been a rapid expansion of alcoholism services. New programs have been established, not only in the traditional hospital and social service agencies, but also in new settings— such as detoxification centers, halfway houses, and rehabilitation programs. There were simply not enough trained workers available to fill all these new positions, and many paraprofessionals found employment in the alcoholism field. Recently, however, university-trained people with skills in counseling have begun to replace the paraprofessional. Without the ability to bill third-party payers directly, these workers must continue to depend on public money to ensure the continuity of their jobs.

It remains to be seen whether the Association of Alcoholism Counselors will develop into a body that can determine standards for certification that will be nationally recognized. Similarly, it remains to be seen whether the paraprofessional counselor will find a permanent place as a member of the alcoholism treatment community. It is probable that paraprofessionals—both inside and outside the generic health care system—will occupy a position comparable to that of the laboratory technician, case aide, or recreational worker. They will undertake tasks such as patient intake, counseling, referral, patient follow-up, and outreach work. In these roles they will require supervision from the professional staff. More complex tasks — such as the development of a treatment plan, patient evaluation, case consultation, program development, education and prevention, training, and program consultation — would remain the responsibility of those with a higher level of academic training and experience.

It is probable that the role of the paraprofessional or even the university-trained counselor is too limited and does not provide sufficient flexibility to deal with new research findings and changing approaches to care. Already, there has been considerable debate about the efficacy of psychological treatment in altering drinking behavior and modifying the life style of the alcoholic. Furthermore, the recent upsurge of interest into the biological aspects of alcoholism could well lead to a more effective medical response to alcoholism, in much the same way that tranquilizers changed the treatment of schizophrenia and lithium carbonate the treatment of affective disorders. The paraprofessional working in such lay organizations as AA will continue to play a significant role in assisting alcoholics. However, within the generic health care system, it is probable that a higher degree of training and sophistication will be needed to enable these workers to find and keep positions that provide for flexibility and offer opportunities for advancement and increased responsibility.

REFERENCES

1. Argeriou, M., and Manohar, V. Relative effectiveness of non-alcoholics and recovered alcoholics as counselors. *J. Stud. Alcohol* 39:793–700, 1978.
2. Bissonette, R. Bartender as mental health service gate keeper: A role analysis. *Community Ment. Health J.* 13:92–99, 1977.
3. Blumberg, L. M. The institutional phase of the Washington Total Temperance Movement. *J. Stud. Alcohol* 39:1591–1606, 1978.
4. Davis, T. S., and Hagood, L. A. In-home support for recovering alcoholic mothers and their families: The family rehabilitation coordinator project. *J. Stud. Alcohol* 40:313–317, 1979.
5. Edwards, G., Oxford, J., Egert, S., Guthrie, S., Hawker, A., Hensman, C., Mitcheson, M., Oppenheimer, E., and Taylor, C. Alcoholism: A controlled trial of "treatment" and "advice." *J. Stud. Alcohol* 38:1004–1031, 1977.
6. Freudenberger, H. J. The professional and the human services worker: Some solutions to problems they face in working together. *J. Drug Issues* 6:273–282, 1976.
7. Kalb, M., and Propper, M. S. The future of alcohology: Craft of science. *Am. J. Psychiatry* 133:641–645, 1976.
8. Lender, M. E., and Karnchanapee, K. R. "Temperance Tales": Antiliquor fiction and American attitudes toward alcoholics in the late 19th and early 20th centuries. *J. Stud. Alcohol* 38:1347–1370, 1977.
9. Pattison, E. M. Ten years of change in alcoholism treatment and delivery systems. *Am. J. Psychiatry* 134:261–266, 1977.

10. Rosenberg, C. M., Gerrein, J. R., Manohar, V., and Liftik, J. Evaluation of training of alcoholism counselors. *J. Stud. Alcohol* 37:1236–1246, 1976.

11. Rosenberg, C. M., Liftik, J., and Manohar, V. The impact of training on career mobility of alcoholism counselors: A follow-up study. *J. Stud. Alcohol* 39:1284–1289, 1978.

12. Roy Littlejohn Associates, Inc. *Proposed National Standard for Alcoholism Counselors—Final Report.* Submitted to National Institute on Alcohol Abuse and Alcoholism (Contract No.: ADM-41-74-0010), August 30, 1974.

13. Skuja, A. T., Schneidmuhl, A. M., and Mandell, W. Alcoholism counselor trainees: Some changes in job-related functioning following training. *J. Drug Educ.* 5:151–157, 1975.

14. Tournier, R. E. Alcoholics Anonymous as treatment and as ideology. *J. Stud. Alcohol* 40:230–239, 1979.

15. William, W. The society of Alcoholics Anonymous. *Am. J. Psychiatry* 106, 1949.

65

LECLAIR BISSELL, MD, CAC, Brown University

RECOVERED ALCOHOLIC COUNSELORS

THERE IS A BODY OF knowledge that can and should be obtained by anybody trying to counsel alcoholic people. One is not equipped to do this kind of counseling simply by virtue of being a trained mental health professional familiar with normal and abnormal development and psychodynamics.

There are many ways of gaining this knowledge. The recovered alcoholic has learned it experientially—he or she has been there. The recovered alcoholic counselor borrows from personal experience from what he or she has observed in an Alcoholics Anonymous (AA) group, and from the shared life experience of a great many other alcoholics, and brings all of this to the work situation.

ATTITUDES AND BELIEFS

Recovered alcoholics do not refer to themselves as "ex-alcoholics," prefering instead to call themselves either recovered alcoholics, arrested alcoholics, or, in some cases, recovering alcoholics—the latter in an attempt to express the philosophy

---

LeClair Bissell, MD, CAC, Clinical Associate Professor of Psychiatry and Human Behavior, Brown University, Providence, Rhode Island.

that recovery is an ongoing process and that no one ever stands still in terms of human growth. There is tremendous resistance to using the word "ex-alcoholic," which would imply a completely different concept of recovery from that which is understood by most AA members (i. e., that cure from alcoholism occurs in such a way as to permit a return to social drinking). Most AA members feel quite strongly that, although they can recover through total abstinence, they cannot safely go back to "normal" drinking.

This particular group of counselors, then, brings with them several fairly strong philosophical beliefs or biases. One is that alcoholism is a permanent condition, just as diabetes is a permanent condition, in spite of the fact that a diabetic may have normal blood sugar and normal urine when following a recommended diet or taking appropriate medication. They feel that total abstinence from alcohol must be a goal of treatment. Most also are extremely wary of other medication, particularly those drugs that are similar in their actions to alcohol, primarily the sedative-hypnotics, which would include sleeping pills, minor tranquilizers, and the like.

Unfortunately, this quite sensible attitude sometimes generalizes to all mood-changing drugs and causes problems if the recovered alcoholic counselor stubbornly resists the use of lithium or a major tranquilizer when these drugs are genuinely needed by a psychotic alcoholic patient. If the recovered alcoholic counselor is so rigid that he or she cannot move from the stance that all drugs are bad to that of some drugs are bad, conflicts may develop with other staff with whom he or she should be working as a member of a team.

The counselor is often mistrustful of professional people. Not only has he or she seen medication inappropriatly prescribed, but the counselor is well aware that professionals often fail to diagnose alcoholism or confront patients adequately about their drinking. The recovered alcoholic counselor's own illness very likely was mismanaged by physicians. He or she may thus lack the respect for and awe of professional people that other paraprofessionals frequently bring with them.

Recorded alcoholic counselors are usually members of AA. Criteria for their selection has been extremely varied. Some were hired after very short periods of sobriety and are not yet themselves stable enough to take responsibility for treating others. The more experienced treatment facilities usually do not hire a recovered alcoholic until that individual has been totally abstinent for at least 2 years; they will, in addition, insist that the individual demonstrate a reasonably balanced personal life style, one in which his or her own activity in AA is well integrated into work and social life [1]. A person who after some years of sobriety still attends AA seven nights a week has not yet learned to play, relates poorly to the opposite sex and to family, and has little interest in anything other than alcoholism. Such a person is scarcely an ideal candidate [4, 5].

TREATMENT STRENGTHS

What the recovered alcoholic counselor can do that no one else can do is to be a role model of successful recovery for a sick patient. If this is done well, if the recovered alcoholic counselor is attractive and makes living without alcohol an attractive prospect, there is every reason for a sick alcoholic to imitate that person. Part of the counselor's role model function is the ability during a counseling session to illustrate certain points from personal history. This does not mean that the session deteriorates into a monologue in which the counselor endlessly details his or her own story, but, rather, one in which the counselor uses his or her own experience with drinking to illustrate, confirm, and explain. This kind of sharing does alter the therapist-patient relationship and thus is different from what other mental health professionals do, particularly, if a therapist is trained to keep his or her own personal life entirely out of the transaction. Social distance in the treating setting is thus reduced.

As well as serving as a role model, the recovered alcoholic counselor usually knows the culture and language of AA and can introduce the patient to the AA group, often skillfully matching individuals.

The counselor who is also a recovered alcoholic understands through personal experience the denial part of the illness; he or she is also aware that since the alcoholic's perception is clouded by the effects of alcohol itself, these patients do not respond very well to the usual insight-oriented psychiatric interventions. In other words, waiting to ask the appropriate question so that the alcoholic will arrive at the appropriate conclusions and choose to go into treatment is unlikely to work. Successful treatment of the alcoholic requires that one be more directive than is usual. The recovered alcoholic counselor usually knows this from his or her own twelfth step experience and may be directive more readily than the professional trained to a more passive role.

CONTACTS WITH OTHER PROFESSIONS

There are in contact with other professions problems on both sides: an untrained alcoholism counselor tends to generalize from personal experience and to assume that all alcoholics are like him or her and the people in the local AA group. Such a counselor knows the disease of alcoholism but little about other illnessess. He or she does not know what or how much he or she does not know. This counselor is not trained to evaluate a suicidal patient automatically, nor able to recognize a psychotic. He or she is not a trained marriage counselor. The counselor, like anyone else, must be taught to know and recognize personal strengths and limitations and to know when to ask for help. Most counselors are quite willing to learn and to share what they know with others.

The mental health professional has a different body of information that may or may not be useful and may even be counterproductive, particularly if alcoholism is regarded only as symptom of something else—an approach that may set the professional to trying to find out what the real problem is in hopes that solving that will make the alcoholism go away. While this approach yields little success, all concerned must be alert to the fact that some people are both alcoholic and emotionally ill and, if this is the case, both problems must be addressed. The mental health professional sometimes assumes that only an alcoholic can understand an alcoholic, that somehow the recovered alcoholic counselor magically, by virtue of having been there, is a superior therapist or has secrets that others can not learn. This is untrue. Once it is recognized that there is a body of knowledge to be had about alcoholism, the professional can forget the mystique and learn to do much of what the recovered alcoholic counselor does. Each must learn from the other to form an effective team.

COMPETENCE

The issue of the level at which the counselor is competent must also be addressed. The arrested alcoholic counselor may be at his or her best in crisis intervention, in breaking down the denial of the alcoholic patient, in making sobriety seem not only possible but desirable, and in helping the person through the early phases of recovery so as to build in new habit patterns and a degree of comfort during change. This person may be superb when working as part of a multidisciplinary team. If the same person attempts to do private practice and to deal with a variety of other problems, required skills may be lacking.

Even within a multidisciplinary team, an individual now counseling a group of alcoholics who have been sober 1½ years will find that the nature of their concerns will have altered. They know better how to stay sober. Now they are concerned with the right job, realistic expectations of marriage, or dealing with children. This material is important and the recovered alcoholic counselor may or may not have the background to help.

An ideal relationship between the recovered alcoholic and other professionals should almost duplicate the relationship between the treatment facility and AA itself, in that ideally each should attempt to complement the other without either deferring to or competing with the other, so that each understands and acknowledges the other's area of expertise and uses it appropriately. Each knows about slightly different things, each is able to talk to the patient in entirely different ways, and to evaluate different areas. The alcoholic counselor is usually strongest in early confrontation, role modeling, denial breakdown, and the teaching of new habits of sobriety. The professional is usually strongest at evaluating whether or not there are other problems, physical or emotional, that might complicate the course of recovery, and to arrange for appropriate treatment for these additional problems when they are present. Also, the professional can always give something that the recovered alcoholic counselor cannot offer, and that is the endorsement of the authority figure as a member of an acknowledged profession. It is not uncommon to hear an alcoholic patient say, "My doctor never told me that," because, in fact, the doctor never did—and when only a lay person, the counselor, has provided information, that carries less clout. The counselor can well use appropriate professional backing. When the counselor and the professional share with each other their perceptions in a discussion of an individual client situation, they learn and borrow from each other's skills. Each becomes more competent.

COUNSELOR CREDENTIALING

Much has been done in an attempt to professionalize alcoholism counseling. Initially there was simple on-the-job training. Subsequently there were efforts to provide recovered alcoholic counselors with a credential earned after personal recovery. A Bachelor's level recovered alcoholic with a background in banking can enter a Master's degree program for a MSW or a Master's in counseling. Some schools have designed special Master's level programs in alcoholism. There still exists, however, the problem of the nondegreed counselor. Insisting on a degree does not really solve personnel problems, since many very effective people have relatively little formal education, particularly those in minority groups. It may well be unreasonable to expect of them certain verbal abilities or test-passing skills. Counselors can, and do, come from a variety of backgrounds. Some treatment facilities hire and train their own counselors and prefer this method. A great many will do some training on the job but will also insist that the person attend some of the summer schools of alcohol studies or specialized counselor training courses as well.

Some facilities will hire only the certified alcoholism counselor who has had training and experience elsewhere. Others have been known to hire people and put them to work with no training or experience whatsoever, even in virtually unsupervised settings.

Another group of treatment counselors, usually smaller in number, are not recovered alcoholics, but are instead members of Al-Anon (the family group similar to Alcoholics Anonymous), or those who have, without actual Al-Anon membership, been drawn to the field because of an alcohol problem in their own home, usually that of a parent, husband, or wife. Their own personal experience is then through a close significant person.

A recent influx into alcoholism counseling has brought two other groups of would-be counselors. One is the so-called ex-addict from a drug treatment background. These people are often active drinkers themselves, frequently problem drinkers, who have created a great deal of anxiety and resistance on the part of recovered alcoholics [5]. Another group consists of a variety of mental health professionals or those with counseling degrees, large numbers of whom are unable to find work because of an increasing supply of trained people while funds for human services are being reduced. These people are presenting themselves as alcoholism counselors with little particular interest or background in alcoholism, either academic or experiential, and they are often blissfully unaware that there is anything in particular to be learned.

Unfortunately, the attempt to develop a special credential for counselors has in some cases led to examinations based on paper and pencil tests, which present little challenge to a recent graduate skilled in handling multiple-choice questions but may prove difficult for people long out of school, and these tests often fail to determine competence. Testing efforts have been on a state-by-state basis. Many people have received credentials under a grandfather clause. Subsequently other credentialling procedures have been developed, usually employing a combination of written and oral examinations, in which the counselor is asked to show competence in the field. Some states have made reciprocity agreements with other states to accept each other's credentials.

In 1980, a federal contract was let to develop national criteria for alcoholism counselor credentialing. Many health professionals, the present author among them, have been examined and certified as alcoholism counselors and list this credential along with their MD, PhD, MSW or other degrees. This reflects a concern that health professionals recognize that they are not currently, simply by virtue of existing training, equipped to counsel alcoholic people. There is much that must be learned that is not routinely well taught in most professional schools today. Exactly how useful the current credentials may prove to be, or where and by whom they will be accepted, remains to be seen.

EMPLOYMENT SETTINGS

There are many hundreds of recovered alcoholic counselors working in a variety of settings. They are employed not only in health care and voluntary agencies, but they are also to be found in private practice and in union and industrial settings, frequently in employee assistance programs. For example, the *New York Times* has an alcoholism counselor, as does International Paper, Eastman Kodak, National Maritime Union, International Longshoreman's Association, and many others. These people are salaried on-site counselors who deal with alcohol problems as well as with a variety of other human problems that may interfere with job performance. Supervisors are taught to confront problem employees on the basis of work performance only, and then to refer the person for counseling, either to the medical or the personnel department, depending on the individual firm. The department receiving the referral determines what kind of problem it is, whether it is a simple indifference to the job, or whether the cause is a personal problem of some sort, which may or may not be alcoholism.

In the past, most industrial counselors have been men, but with the growing awareness of alcoholism in women more women are being hired, particularly by the larger firms who have more than one counselor.

Treatment centers usually attempt to have a variety of people on the counseling staff and to include women as well as representatives of different age groups and life styles, as well as those from diverse backgrounds, ethnic and otherwise.

PROBLEMS IN THE USE OF COUNSELORS

Power and financial considerations can cause conflict within treatment settings in that usually such facilities are so structured that high salaries and supervisory positions fall almost automatically, if not by law, to the degreed professional. It is not uncommon to find an extremely skillful and competent person working incredibly long hours and producing a highly skilled service while being paid ridiculously little money for it. Such considerations are receiving increasing attention in the field, as is the whole issue of counselor burn-out [3, 4, 5].

Since the counselor is using himself or herself and personal experience so very much in treatment, this may be among the reasons why burn-out and personal exhaustion occur after 2 or 3 years of doing treatment. People who were initially working with other alcoholics with tremendous energy and enthusiasm report that they became tired, unhappy, personally drained, and much less effective with their clients. The very personal involvement and identification that initially reassures the patient that he or she is understood and cared about may exact a toll from the helper. In addition, the recovered alcoholic counselor, by virtue of his or her own attendance at AA, is often faced with having patients join the same AA group where the counselor goes to maintain sobriety. Today's patient may be tomorrow's co-group member and a peer the day after. Many factors confuse and break down normal distancing. It may be that the professional who is trained to distance from the patient from the very beginning and to remain more dispassionate succeeds in protecting the self better.

Common in freestanding alcoholism treatment centers are a variety of "bridge people"—individuals who are both recovered alcoholics and trained professionals regardless of the order in which those experiences were obtained. They too do some counseling, while providing a link between differing vantage points held by the counselor and other professionals. Such an individual has credibility in both groups and can interpret each to the other. Within International Doctors in AA alone (a group now about 1,700 strong composed of doctoral-level people who are themselves AA members) there are well over 200 physicians who are now working full-time in alcoholism treatment. These men and women can bridge many cultural and communication gaps.

Recovered alcoholic counselors currently deliver extremely valuable service in many areas. Sometimes their skills are realistically valued and appropriately used. At other times they are simultaneously exploited and harshly criticized. Other professionals admire them, defer to them, compete with them, work smoothly with them, or seek to undermine them and the importance of what they can contribute. Desperately needed are professionals willing to make the effort to understand the recovered alcoholic's background, life experience, limitations, and the meaning of AA in his or her life.

REFERENCES

1. A.A. Guidelines. *Cooperating with Courts, A.S.A.P. and Similar Programs.* Author: New York.
2. King, B. L., Bissell, L., O'Brien, P. Alcoholics Anonymous, alcoholism counseling and social work treatment. *Health Soc. Work,* 4(4):182–198, 1979.
3. White, W. L. *A Systems Response to Staff Burn-Out.* IICS: Rockville, 1978.
4. White, W. L. *Incest in the Organizational Family: The Unspoken Issue in Staff and Program Burn-Out.* HCS: Rockville, Md., 1978.
5. White, W. L. *Relapse as a Phenomenon of Staff Burn-Out among Recovered Substance Abusers.* HCS: Rockville, Md., 1979.

Section IX

Alcoholism Treatment Facilities

66

EILEEN M. CORRIGAN, DSW, Rutgers–The State University

INFORMATION AND REFERRAL CENTERS

THE DESIGNATION OF "information and referral center" implies a formal organization with measurable goals and clear lines of authority. An information and referral center, however, does not exist as an entity. As yet, there is no clearly established network of such centers throughout the United States. Nationwide the current umbrella organizations for information and referral centers is either the United Way or AIRS (Alliance Information and Referral Service). The actual number of information and referral (I&R) centers is unknown. In addition, such services often are specialized (e.g., aging, alcohol), and it is these that are addressed in this chapter. For a time there seemed to be a groundswell of interest in such services and the development and expansion of treatment services and information centers was seen as complementary [8]. An interesting and useful description of the history and variability in these services can be found in an article by Long [11], wherein the primary function of these centers has been described as giving access to the wider network of treatment services.

Eileen M. Corrigan, DSW, Professor, Graduate School of Social Work, Rutgers–The State University, New Brunswick, New Jersey.

ALCOHOL INFORMATION AND REFERRAL CENTERS

Information and referral centers are viewed as an important component of a comprehensive alcoholism service. An alcoholism information and referral service can refer to either a hospital-based service, a National Council on Alcoholism affiliate, a local community council, an intergroup office of Alcoholics Anonymous, or a community-based program offering services. One such service offers information on Dial-A-Message [15]. Efforts to offer a 24-hour service are not always consistent; there also may be wide variability in staffing patterns within a given service, ranging from the paid employee, sometimes a professional, during daytime hours, to volunteers, possibly recovered alcoholics, during the evening.

The National Council on Alcoholism has more than 200 affiliates with alcoholism information centers nationwide. Most major treatment centers for alcoholics have such a service, as required to be recognized as a comprehensive treatment service. Yet contrary to the image of a fully functional program that matches need with the treatment services available in a community, such referral activities may often be marginal. Certainly little is written about alcoholism information and referral centers, as any search of the literature quickly demonstrates. Yet such a dearth in the literature is not peculiar to the specialized alcoholism center, but also applies to the more generic information and referral center. There are, however, frequent discussions of information and referral activities at national meetings where service concerns are addressed [10]. The effectiveness of a wide range of media activities employed to introduce problem drinkers and significant others in their lives to the available services is more frequently the focus in the literature.

Information and referral centers were specifically designated as reimbursable under Title XX of the Social Security Act. Yet, a recent report indicates most states limiting eligibility to a welfare-eligible population such as Aid to Dependent Families (ADC), Supplementary Security Income (SSI), and Medicaid recipients, rather than to the community at large [12].

Paths to Treatment

Schmidt et al. [14] have demonstrated a different referral path to treatment, one that is based on social class. For example, referrals by family members and friends occur with similar high frequency in all social classes, whereas physicians were more likely to refer patients in the highest social class. Feagins [6], in a similar vein, notes minorities and females also having a different referral network. In a comparison of sources of referral for blacks and nonblacks he cites fewer and different sources of referrals for blacks. Similar to this finding on blacks, Feagins also notes fewer referral sources for women. Others [3, 4, 7] have also cited a clear pattern of more frequent self-referrals by women.

The remaining chapter addresses the variables identified as important in effective referral and offers some recommendations for the future development of such centers.

FUNCTION OF INFORMATION AND REFERRAL CENTERS

The primary task of an information and referral center is to provide information and referral about community alcoholism services to those who seek help. Such a service is meant to be a careful fit between the needs of the person requiring treatment and the available community service [3]. It is now known that typical inquiry to an I&R center involves others calling about a problem drinker; it is immediately necessary to differentiate the problem drinker's readiness for treatment from the caller's wish for help. Thus, the staff of the I&R center needs to be sensitive and alert to both the caller's needs as well as those of the problem drinker. To focus only on the problem drinker may mean losing an opportunity for early intervention, even life-saving intervention, since the caller is a critical link to the problem drinker. It may be necessary to point the way to treatment for the caller, independent of any help recommended for the problem drinker, who may or may not be ready for such help.

Staffing

Once the preliminary assessment is made as to need it often sets the course for the appropriate referral. Skillful matching of individual need to service cannot be the work of the inexperienced or a casual staffing arrangement. Intensive training for new staff is often needed.

Since many of the information and referral centers primarily receive their initial request for information by telephone, it is clear that skilled professional counseling is most necessary at this critical time. Based on available information many of the I&R centers do not offer this level of staffing. In fact, according to Pattison [13], just the opposite may be true.

Users

Much of the literature relating to referrals consists of an analysis of the sources of referrals at the receiving treatment setting [7] rather than a detailing of the characteristics of the users of an I&R center. A description of the users of such services is critical to monitor who is reached, to assess trends, and to determine if targeted populations for service are being reached.

There is only one known study of an alcoholism I&R center, operated within a community council, that offers descriptive details of the users, and a follow-up of the outcomes of the referrals [3]. A precoded questionnaire, ready for data processing, was designed for use by the information and referral staff. The service information was usually that obtained by the staff but not recorded in any systematic fashion. The form was used with considerable success by up to 15 social workers in a busy metropolitan I&R center and enabled program planners to document service given as well as ultimate provide a means for designing a study to follow-up the service users [1, 3]. It was found that using such a form sensitized staff to review these items consistently with each caller. Also, it was possible to give a description of those who actually received a referral for treatment as well as describe the users of the service.

Women problem drinkers were more likely to call about themselves than to have someone inquire on their behalf. As shown in Table 1, slightly more than one in four of the problem drinkers calling for themselves were women, but fewer than one in five of the other calls were made on behalf of women. Almost a third of the callers were minority members, primarily black (23%), with a smaller percentage (7%) Hispano (mainly Puerto Rican). While this was generally representative of the population of New York City, where the study was conducted, it may not represent the distribution of problem drinkers in need of treatment. The bulk of the inquiries were made about problem drinkers under 50, with an average age of approximately 40 years. There were twice as many young self-callers (20-29 years); the older problem drinker (over 60) was more likely to be called about. The relatively high percentage of individuals who have had previous treatment seems consistent with what is known about the multiplicity of services used by problem drinkers. Primarily the relatives of problem drinkers used the service, mostly a spouse, the wife, and this accounted for 55% of the other callers.

EFFECTIVENESS OF REFERRALS

Results of Referrals

Considerable variability has been reported in the success of referrals. The study cited followed the users of an information and referral service from the point of referral to a time period some 30 days later [3]. A relatively good referral outcome is reported for this program, which was staffed by experienced social workers at a metropolitan community council. A better outcome was found for problem drinkers who made the initial inquiry in contrast to a call made by a significant other. Of the problem drinkers calling themselves, 68% sought treatment and 11% used a resource other than the one suggested. When someone else initiated the inquiry, 54% of the problem drinkers about whom they called did reach a resource, with even more, 19%, using a resource different than that recommended. Overall then, 60% of all problem drinkers for whom help was sought reached treatment following a referral. In contrast, Pattison [13] reports fewer than 20% of referrals for treatment as successful; no details about the background of the staff making these referrals is given, nor is information available about any differences that might exist between problem drinkers and significant other callers. Yet Pattison notes that more than 60% of the problem drinkers eventually sought treatment at an identified facility, presumably other than the one recommended by the alcoholism I&R centers. The similarity between the percentage ultimately reaching treatment in both reports is striking. Pattison, however, believes this raises serious question about the appropriate use of resources. His concern may be a variant of the question raised earlier about the appropriateness of the match between the needs of the problem drinker and the resources recommended.

Table 1
Characteristics of Alcoholism I&R Center Users

	Percentage of Alcoholic Self-Callers ($n = 150$)	Percentage of those Called-About ($n = 156$)
Sex[a]		
Male	73	82
Female	27	18
Ethnicity		
White	71	67
Black	23	23
Puerto Rican	5	9
Unknown	1	1
Age[a]		
20–29[b]	15	8
30–39	25	31
40–49	35	28
50–59	19	19
60+	6	14
Religion		
Catholic	59	59
Protestant	31	31
Jewish	3	3
Other	3	3
None	3	0
Unknown	1	4
Previous treatment	51	46

[a]Self-callers compared with those called-about; sex, $\chi^2 = 3.86$, 1 df, $p < .05$; age, $\chi^2 = 10.80$, 4 df, $p < .05$.
[b]Includes one self-caller and one significant other caller under age 20.

The Key Variables

Based on data accumulated in a number of studies, several components of an effective referral have been identified. Most important may be the relationship between the referral agent and the individual who is being referred. Demone [5], summarizing the results of several field experiments in the early 1960s, describes institutions in which alcoholism was believed to be a major problem but the proportion of individuals identified and referred was relatively low. The populations in these field experiments cannot be considered to represent a cross-section of the community in need of service, since they were admissions to an emergency room as well as residents of correctional institutions, one for women and the other for juveniles. Such settings do reflect where alcoholics can be found, but often are not, and where the success of referrals is reported to be low. Demone [5] cites a substantial improvement as a result of the field experiment: 65% of the experimental group but only 5% of the control group at the hospital emergency room reached treatment, with similar good results reported at the correctional facilities.

Intensive contact was thought by Demone to be the major factor in the improved referral picture for the experimental group. It is possible also that consistent, intensive contact with the same two professionals in the emergency room, a physician and social worker, from the time of entry into the emergency room through the referral process would complete the explanation for such a dramatic improvement in the outcome of referrals. Another component of service that should increase the likelihood of success was identified first in Kogan's study [9] of social work practice. A decidedly different and better outcome was found when the referral center contacted the receiving agency. Corrigan's study [3] gave further support to this finding. It is not known how much credence and attention has been given to this particular finding by those who are currently involved in I&R centers.

CONCLUSIONS

There is no Michelin guide rating the quality of the community services established to treat alcoholics, nor, for that matter, is there such a rating system in effect for any of the human service agencies. Information and referral centers can assume such a meaningful task but none are known to do so. When referrals are made relatively few individuals in need of help are aware of the competence of those providing the service; neither are they aware if the service offered by the treatment setting is sufficiently comprehensive. Word of mouth remains the future patient's most trustworthy guide to treatment, unless the referral is made by a competent, caring, knowledgeable professional or even a prior user of a service. The latter, however, may not have sufficient information to give informed advice. Information and referral centers are a tool for education, early identification, and making sense out of matching available services with the needs of problem drinkers. These centers also have the potential for reaching special population groups who are underserved. Their role in early case finding could be enormously effective and they most likely could also be a powerful force in prevention. Targeting special populations is seen as an appropriate function of I&R centers and the media is clearly an avenue that I&R centers can use to reach individuals in need of help [2]. Yet, unclear goals and standards for information and referral services persist. This is not likely to change unless regulations from a national agency guide the development of this neglected service broker.

REFERENCES

1. Corrigan, E. M. Linking the problem drinker with treatment. *Social Work* 17:54-61, 1972.
2. Corrigan, E. M. Mass media and the problem drinker. In: *Proceedings of the 3rd Annual Alcoholism Conference of the NIAAA*. National Institute on Alcohol Abuse and Alcoholism: Washington, D. C., 1973.
3. Corrigan, E. M. *Problem Drinkers Seeking Treatment* (Monograph 8). The Rutgers Center of Alcohol Studies: New Brunswick, N. J., 1974.
4. Corrigan, E. M. *Alcoholic Women in Treatment*. Oxford University Press: New York, 1980.
5. Demone, H. W., Jr. Experiments in referral to alcoholism clinics. *Q. J. Stud. Alcohol* 24:495-502, 1963.
6. Feagins, J. L. *Descriptive Study of Variance in Sources of Referral*. Doctoral Dissertation, University of Pittsburgh, 1974.
7. Hoffman, H., and Noem, A. V. Social background variables, referral sources and life events of male and female alcoholics. *Psychol. Rep.* 37:1087-1092, 1975.
8. Kahn, A. J., Grossman, L., Bandler, J., Clark, F., Galkin, F., and Greenwalt, K. *Neighborhood Information Centers: A Study and Some Proposals*. Columbia University School of Social Work: New York, 1966.
9. Kogan, L. The utilization of social work research. *Soc. Casework* 44:569-574, 1963.
10. Levinson, R. W. *Technology/Manpower: Information and Referral Roundtable*. Paper presented at the meeting of The National Conference on Social Welfare, Washington, D.C., 1976.
11. Long, N. Information and referral services: A short history and some recommendations. *Soc. Serv. Rev.* 47:49-62, 1973.
12. National Institute on Alcohol Abuse and Alcoholism, Division of Special Treatment and Rehabilitation. *Title XX of The Social Security Act in Relation to Social Services for Alcoholic Persons*. Author: Washington, D.C., 1979.
13. Pattison, E. M. Rehabilitation of the chronic alcoholic. In: *The Biology of Alcoholism: Clinical Pathology* (Vol. 3), Kissin, B. and Begleiter, H. (eds.). Plenum: New York, 1974.
14. Schmidt, W., Smart, R., and Moss, M. *Social Class and The Treatment of Alcoholism*. Toronto: University of Toronto Press, 1968.
15. Sinnett, E. R., and Hart, J. B. Temporal patterns of the use of non-prescribed drugs: Some behavioral correlates. *Percept. Mot. Skills* 47:332-334, 1978.

67

MARC GALANTER, MD, Albert Einstein College of Medicine, Bronx, New York
JACOB SPERBER, MD, Albert Einstein College of Medicine, Bronx, New York

GENERAL HOSPITALS IN THE ALCOHOLISM TREATMENT SYSTEM

GENERAL HOSPITAL ADmissions have for a long time included a significant proportion of alcoholics — at least 10% of admissions in most community settings, and as much as 50% in some public hospitals [14, 24]. Prior to the 1960s, however, the diagnosis of alcoholism in these admissions was most often not made; instead, the admitting diagnosis was narrowly limited to one or another of the medical sequelae of alcoholism, such as gastric ulcer or pancreatitis. This inattention of general hospitals to the alcoholism in their patients corresponded to widespread social prejudice against alcoholics and to a relative underdevelopment of specialized methods and systems of treatment for alcoholism. The administrative and medical staffs of general hospitals were not immune to this bias.

The alcoholism literature of the early 1960s reflects a nascent awareness of the magnitude of alcoholism in the general hospital patient population. The literature of the 1940s and 1950s paid little attention to the prevalence of alcoholism among medical patients. From 1960 to 1967, two such studies appeared [12, 16].

The past two decades have witnessed the establishment of a variety of profes-

---

Marc Galanter, MD, Associate Professor and Director, Division of Alcoholism and Drug Abuse, Department of Psychiatry, Albert Einstein College of Medicine, Bronx, New York.

Jacob Sperber, MD, Clinical Instructor and Outpatient Director, Division of Alcoholism and Drug Abuse, Department of Psychiatry, Albert Einstein College of Medicine, Bronx, New York.

sional and nonprofessional specialized treatment approaches for alcoholism, and the availability of such freestanding programs has increased the need for awareness and sophistication among general physicians in order to effect appropriate referrals.

In parallel to this growth of knowledge about and specialized facilities for the treatment of alcoholism, there has been a gradual and as yet incomplete relaxation of the resistance of general hospitals to recognize and address alcoholism in a systematic way. Chafetz's 1962 report of two innovative general hospital ward programs for alcoholics signaled the beginning of a generation of progress in the acceptance of alcoholism as a legitimate medical illness [3]. Two avenues of approach that have been successful in increasing the impact of general hospitals on the treatment of alcoholism have been education for hospital staff, and restructuring of the organizational relationships among specialized care units. The latter approach has been facilitated by conceptualizing the general hospital care unit as a component (subsystem) in the complex social system through which the alcoholic travels. Systematic attention to the relationships among medical care personnel, alcoholism care specialists, and the other social agencies and forces that impinge upon the course of a person's alcoholism can transform wastefully fragmented treatment into effective comprehensive care.

SCOPE OF THE PROBLEM

Large numbers of alcoholics are admitted to the medical and surgical wards of general hospitals. Many more could benefit from admission. Until the past decade, however, the majority came and went without being diagnosed as alcoholic and without being referred for appropriate aftercare. Even the care that was given was compromised by bias and ignorance.

Initial studies of the prevalence of alcoholism among general hospital admissions revealed that one in 10 admissions was directly related to alcohol abuse [12]. Some of these studies relied on chart review and predicted that direct patient research would yield higher rates of alcoholism. Barcha et al. [2] interviewed a series of admissions to all the adult wards of a general hospital and found that 21% of the men were active alcoholics or problem drinkers, with another 13% in remission. Of the women 6% were active alcoholics or problem drinkers, with another 1.5% in remission. Galanter reported that 21% of inpatients at a large city hospital in the Bronx were alcoholics, with three times greater prevalence among black and Hispanic patients compared to white patients [7]. The highest reported prevalence of alcoholism in a general hospital was found among the overwhelmingly impoverished ethnic minority population at Harlem Hospital, where 60% of the men and 34% of the women were found to be alcoholic [23]. In a report on the percentage of alcoholics in the population of a community general hospital, Moore found that 10% of the patients — 18% of the men and 5.5% of the women — were alcoholics, with an additional 3.5% questionably alcoholic [13].

These studies also revealed a consistent pattern of failure of physicians to diagnose alcoholism [2]. Moore's group found that the doctors of the patients they studied made an alcoholism diagnosis only 50% of the time [13]. An Australian review showed that Australian physicians in the 1960s were diagnosing less than one out of 10 cases of alcoholism admitted to general hospitals [20]. Another study revealed that well-trained physicians who could offer verbal knowledge about alcoholism nonetheless frequently failed to diagnose it, especially in the nonderelict population [22]. Alcoholism is missed more frequently in patients of higher socioeconomic position [12]. Wolf et al. [22] noted that "alcoholics who are in the less severe phases are likely not to be diagnosed or referred for treatment. This means that a substantial portion of the alcoholic population may not receive treatment at a time when therapy might have more beneficial consequences than in late-stage alcoholism" [22, p. 78].

Even when the diagnosis of alcoholism is made, many physicians do not plan for appropriate treatment. Abbott et al. [1] found that physicians failed to refer to alcoholism aftercare any of a sample of 16 patients hospitalized with acute pancreatitis. A definite history of alcoholism existed in 14 of the 16. When the hospital physicians were surveyed, many felt that alcoholism prevention programs did not work. Others reported that they did not know the mechanism of referral. Yet others felt that the patient bears the responsibility for seeking alcoholism treatment [1, p. 275].

Greater awareness of alcoholism as a common entity among general hospital patients can lead to earlier suspicion of related disorders among general hospital admissions. Alcoholics have higher incidences of peptic ulcer, cirrhosis, fatty liver, and pancreatitis [2]. In a review of 34 cases at a community hospital, alcoholic hepatitis was found to be the leading cause of fevers of unknown origin. Of the four cases attributed to alcoholic hepatitis, three initially gave no history of alcohol abuse, and none had stigmata of chronic liver disease on physical exam [10].

An additional problem in general hospitals that do make the diagnosis of alcoholism and refer alcoholics for treatment is the heterogeneity of the alcoholic population. Pattison et al. [18] demonstrated that different alcoholic populations need different treatments. They concluded, "A treatment facility should pay close attention to the characteristics of the population it seeks to serve. Commendable and useful treatment methods elsewhere may be inappropriate, redundant, or destructive for its population. Treatment philosophy and methods should be congruent with the anticipated population" [18]. Since the treatment needs of the alcoholic are heterogeneous and complex, the general hospital physician is likely to need the services of a consultant specialized in alcoholism treatment in order to effect optimal referrals for alcoholic patients.

ATTITUDES AND THE SEARCH FOR A SOLUTION

Many alcoholics in general hospitals do not receive correct alcoholism diagnoses and referrals because of negative medical staff attitudes. One general hospital study reported that physicians' attitudes toward inpatient alcoholism treatment ranged from supportive to hostile and oppositional: "Many physicians, in particular, felt that alcoholics should not be admitted to the hospital, and that public and insurance monies were being spent for coddling these individuals" [15, p. 424]. Similar negative attitudes toward the medical treatment of alcoholism were found among Australian physicians [20]. A study of 15 general hospital physicians found aversive attitudes toward alcoholics even though this group of doctors showed competent understanding of alcoholism in the abstract [22]. These last two studies found a link between aversive physician attitudes and the failure to refer patients for treatment. One also found that "physicians prefer a medical diagnosis to one that includes psychosocial dysfunction. . . . Thus, it rarely occurs that the physician views the alcoholic as a person with an illness that has certain physiological, psychological and social concomitants; the typical occurrence is rather the diagnosis of a particular physical or systems disorder in a person who also happens to be an alcoholic" [22, p. 79]. Thus the failure of psychosocial conceptualization also contributes to failure to refer for psychosocial treatment.

Two types of strategy to correct poor general hospital treatment of alcoholism are reported: (1) educational efforts to modify attitudes of staff in the existing hospital structure, and (2) modifications of hospital organization to include specialized alcoholism treatment within the general hospital.

Reports of educational interventions have appeared during the past decade. One study showed that a 3-day training seminar for nurses resulted in improved attitudes toward alcoholics and their treatment [19]. Another study showed that a specific, brief training program for medical personnel in a general hospital improved attitudes toward and knowledge about alcoholic patients [5]. The medical personnel in the study worked on a general hospital unit specialized in alcoholism treatment. The training was provided by personnel of a state mental hospital alcoholism unit. Jones and Novak [11] describe an extensive program of alcohol education for general hospital nurses and administrators at 31 Texas hospitals. They report uniformly significant amelioration of knowledge and attitude of trainees toward alcoholics. The program brought the educational personnel of each hospital to 2½-day training seminars, and trained them in the use of educational materials provided for use at each of the hospitals. These reports of brief educational seminars for the personnel of existing medical units do not address questions of long-term modification of staff behavior and of continuing education and support for sophisticated alcoholism care.

Significant long-term impact on general hospital care of alcoholics has been demonstrated in several reports of structural changes made in treatment systems [9]. In common to all of these projects was the integration of alcohol specialists into the structure of the general medical service, usually as consultants. The American Hospital Association supported a project at San Francisco's Mt. Zion Hospital in the 1950s in which a multidisciplinary team consulted on the treatment of all hospitalized alcoholics. The consultants assisted the medical staff in dealing with medical and behavioral management, as well as providing in-service training [3]. The study demonstrated improved treatment, including referral of a majority of the patients to aftercare.

In a second study Chafetz showed that designating specific psychiatric and social work consultants for alcoholics seen on an emergency ward powerfully increased follow-up care. Of those seen by the consultants, 65% subsequently attended a follow-up clinic, whereas only 5% of those not seen by the consultants went for aftercare [4].

An Australian study described the effect of establishing an alcoholic clinic in a general hospital in 1964. The clinic provided outpatient care, and patients requiring admission were admitted to a general medical service. The authors report that "with the development of the clinic there has been a gradual change in the attitudes of both medical and nursing staff within the hospital.... Increased knowledge of alcoholism and experience with these patients have produced a more sympathetic, understanding and hopeful atmosphere" [20, p. 162].

In a report of a program in which a newly established alcohol rehabilitation service began to admit alcoholics to general medical hospital beds, the project director found that on-ward personnel, nurses and aides, underwent modification of initial negative attitudes toward alcoholics after they had had the opportunity to witness therapeutic change in patients. This program specifically did not undertake extensive formal education programs to modify staff attitudes. Rather, it relied on the educational effects of exposure of staff to effective treatment, the presence of which was achieved by structural modification of the general wards and integration with a new system of psychosocial care [15].

The largest reported program of integration of medical and addiction services was the Hospital Referral Program of the Addiction Services Agency of New York City [8]. In 1975 referral teams in eight general hospitals provided consultation on 10,907 patients, of whom 3,525 were referred to treatment. Addiction and alcohol counselors provided in-hospital consultation to facilitate placement in long-term treatment for addicted and alcoholic patients who were seen for acute care. Of all the 1975 referrals, 56% were for alcoholism, and 81% of all referrals appeared at the treatment agency to which they were referred within 1 week of referral. Alcohol detoxification programs were completed by 83% of those placed. These data demonstrate the powerful effect of integrating alcoholism specialists into the general hospital setting. A detailed report on the operation of this program at one of the hospitals (Bronx Municipal Hospital Center) demonstrated how the availability of specialized addiction consultation facilitated not only referral for addiction treatment, but also the delivery of acute medical care in the hospital, the coordination of treatment planning, and the education of staff [6]. A follow-up report observed positive changes in the attitudes of hospital staff toward alcoholic patients [7].

The New York City program fell victim to budget cuts, but a subsequent report from the Bronx Municipal Hospital Center program proposed two other models for integration of acute medical and specialized alcoholism services: "The first would include the transfer of patients to the alcoholism ward prior to discharge from the medicine service, and the second would include active counseling on the medical wards with subsequent transfer to the ambulatory alcoholism program" [9]. The latter proposal requires more resources and provides a greater degree of structural integration between medical and alcoholism services.

A SYSTEM APPROACH

System theory examines the interactions among functionally related structures [21]. A system considered in isolation from forces in its environment is a closed system. An open system is one that interacts with external structures that may affect the inner functioning of the system as well. If the external structures impinging on a system are also conceived of as systems, then an open system constitutes a hierarchy of subsystems whose interactions may affect the inner functioning of each subsystem. In this way an open system model can serve as a good antidote to the distortions that arise from viewing an entity in isolation from its environment or larger context [6]. The traditional general hospital view of the alcoholic suffered from precisely this kind of distortion, because it sought to view each of the alcoholic's single organ systems (e.g., pancreatitis) as a closed system in isolation from the social, psychological, and even other medical aspects of the patient's alcoholism.

General system theory takes on certain characteristics when applied to human problems, and can be viewed as social system theory [17] that examines the interaction between biological, psychological, social, and economic entities. People become actors with actions in roles. They view each other with expectations based on role differentiations. They cluster in functional groups and organizations, which also interact in patterned ways.

Most general hospital medical care is delivered from an implicit, closed-system perspective [7]. Some medical conditions, such as appendicitis or a fractured bone, can be adequately assessed and treated in relative isolation from other forces impinging on the patient's life. The clinicians focus on the pathological organ so narrowly that they can often be heard referring to the patient as "an appendix" or "a hip." Such shorthand may offend the humanistic observer, but in fact the narrowly conceived treatment is usually adequate to heal the pathology. The patient is discharged from the system with relatively little consideration of other aspects of his or her existence.

The microbial theory of infection has forced the hospital system to adopt a limited, open-system perspective for certain infectious illnesses. Clinicians know that the entry of a case of gonorrhea or of tuberculosis into the hospital subsystem signals the existence of other, functionally related cases outside the hospital but within the patient's social system. Clinicians are expected to initiate interventions that affect persons outside the usual treatment subsystem, such as quarantine and case finding. Even this open-system view of the patient's infection limits itself to the patient's biological interactions outside the hospital subsystem, and takes little or no notice of psychological, cultural, or economic forces contributing to the entry or reentry of the patient into the hospital subsystem.

The studies reviewed demonstrate that the medical professions show great resistance to moving beyond limited models in their approach to alcoholics and other addicts in the general hospital. Medical staff are used to narrow assessment of biological symptoms and the application of specific treatment procedures. Pancreatitis in an alcoholic, for example, is treated biologically, and the subsiding of symptoms and abnormal laboratory values signals the time for discharge from the system. Alcoholism, with all of its complications, has significant etiologic sources in psychological, social, economic, as well as biological aspects of the patient's existence; treatment of an isolated organ system complication is, therefore, very unlikely to cure the complication, to say nothing of the alcoholism. At best, physicians with a narrow view of alcoholism sometimes refer alcoholic patients to alcohol psychosocial treatment systems at the time of discharge. Compliance with such referrals is predictably low, at least in part because the authority of the referrals is undermined by the low priority the referring doctor has placed on the psychosocial aspects of the alcoholism during the admission [6].

If a medical ward's personnel do not have regular contact with staff from the local alcoholism treatment facility then that medical ward can be viewed as functioning as a closed system. The staff of the medical ward can provide meaningful care for the patient's alcohol-related organ system complications only if they also initiate the correct psychosocial measures to address the underlying alcoholic behavior. And yet, because of their organizational isolation from agents of organizations expert in such measures the medical staff remain unsophisticated about the assessment of the psychosocial needs of alcoholics and unpracticed in skills needed to motivate compliance with referrals. Even if the medical staff receives brief training, with time their knowledge of local resources will become outdated and newly hired staff will not have been trained.

An open system approach poses the challenge of structural integration of the two subsystems. In human systems, this is directly achieved by defining roles for one actor who belongs to both subsystems. The general hospital programs reviewed that were most successful in effecting initiation of long-term, psychosocial treatment of alcoholics were those that achieved significant integration of the general hospital ward with specialized alcoholism treatment programs. Actors from a specialized alcoholism treatment subsystem were assigned consultation roles within the medical-surgical ward subsystem. The expansion of the ward subsystem to include these new actors with their new and more differentiated roles modified the medical staff's expectations of the patients, the illness, and of the alcoholism treatment system. With each new consultation the medical staff learned more about their open system relationships with other subsystems of the larger health care delivery system, and a more complete perspective on alcoholic patients and their treatment was established. Thus, a structural modification of the closed system that integrates it with other organizations introduces a regular flow of new information, values, and expectations into the medical care subsystem in a way which has constructive consequences far beyond providing referral services or staff education.

Application of system theory to alcoholism treatment in the general hospital demonstrates that a solution for a complex problem is best based on a perspective that takes into account all of the forces that contribute significantly to the problem. Specialized organizations, such as general hospitals, tend to ignore causal forces whose management is not within the scope of their specialization. System theory provides a useful perspective for designing optimal solutions for complex human problems like alcoholism.

REFERENCES

1. Abbott, J. A., Goldberg, G. A., and Becker, E. B. The role of a medical audit in assessing management of alcoholics with acute pancreatitis. *Q. J. Stud. Alcohol* 35:272–276, 1974.
2. Barcha, R., Stewart, M. A., and Guze, S. B. The prevalence of alcoholism among general hospital ward patients. *Am. J. Psychiatry* 125(5):681–684, 1968.
3. Chafetz, M. E., Blanc, H. T., and Abram, H. S. Establishing treatment relations with alcoholics. *J. Nerv. Ment. Dis.* 134:395–409, 1962.
4. Chafetz, M. E., Blanc, H. T., and Hill, M. J. *Frontiers of Alcoholism*. Science House: New York, 1970.
5. Distefano, M. K., Craig, S. H., Henderson, G. L., and Pryer, M. W. Effects of brief alcoholism training on general hospital personnel. *Psychol. Rep.* 37:1321–1322, 1975.
6. Galanter, M. D., Karasu, T. B., and Wilder, J. F. Alchol and drug abuse consultation in the general hospital: A systems approach. *Am. J. Psychiatry* 133(8):930–934, 1976.
7. Galanter, M. D., Karasu, T. B., and Wilder, J. F. Initiating alcoholism, treatment on medical services. In: *Currents in Alcoholism* (Vol. 1), Seixas, F. A. (ed.). Grune & Stratton: New York, 1977.
8. Galanter, M. D., Karasu, T. B., Wilder, J. F., Sexton, B., and Fried, A. Drug and alcohol referrals from the general hospital program: I. A multi-hospital program. In: *Proceedings of The National Drug Abuse Conference, Inc., New York, 1976: Critical Concerns in the Field of Drug Abuse*. Dekker: New York, 1978.
9. Galanter, M. D., Karasu, T. B., Wilder, J. F., Schubmehl, J., Adel, H. N., and Sofer,

S. C. Inpatient rehabilitation for the medically ill alcoholics. In: *Currents in Alcoholism* (Vol. 6), Galanter, M. (ed.). Grune & Stratton: New York, 1980.

10. Gleckman, R., Crowley, M., and Esposito, E. Fever of unknown origin: A view from the community hospital. *Am. J. Med. Sci.* 274(21):21-25, 1977.

11. Jones, R. L., and Novak, D. G. An alcohol education program for the general hospital: An experiment in Texas. *Ann. N.Y. Acad. Sci.* 273:442-452, 1976.

12. Kearney, T. R., Bonime, H. B., and Cassimatis, G. The impact of alcoholism on a community general hospital. *Commun. Ment. Health J.* 3(4):373-376, 1967.

13. Moore, R. A. The prevalence of alcoholism in a community general hospital. *Am. J. Psychiatry* 128(5):638-639, 1971.

14. Moore, R. A. Ten years of inpatient programs for alcoholic patients. *Am. J. Psychiatry* 134(5):542-546, 1977.

15. Nagy, B. R. Setting up a successful alcoholism treatment program in a hostile environment—a general hospital. *Ann. N.Y. Acad. Sci.* 273:420-426, 1976.

16. Nolan, J. P. Alcohol as a factor in the illness of university service patients. *Am. J. Med. Sci.* 2:135-142, 1965.

17. Parsons, T. *The Social System.* Free Press: Glencoe, Ill., 1951.

18. Pattison, E. M., Coe, R. C., and Doerr, H. O. Population variation among alcoholism treatment facilities. *Int. J. Addict.* 8(2):199-229, 1973.

19. Powell, B. J., Mueller, J. F., and Schwerdtfeger, T. Attitude changes of general hospital personnel following an alcoholism training program. *Psychol. Rep.* 34:461-462, 1974.

20. Rankin, J. G., Santamaria, J. N., and O'Day, D. M. Studies in alcoholism: 1. A general hospital medical clinic for the treatment of alcoholism. *Med. J. Australia* 17:157-162, 1967.

21. Van Bertalanffy, L. *General Systems Theory.* Braziller: New York, 1968.

22. Wolf, I., Chafetz, M. E., Blanc, H. T., and Hill, M. J. Social factors in the diagnosis of alcoholism. *Q. J. Stud. Alcohol* 26(1):72-79, 1965.

23. Zimberg, S., Lipscomb, H., and Davis, E. B. Sociopsychiatric treatment of alcoholism in a urban ghetto. *Am. J. Psychiatry* 127(12):1670-1674, 1971.

68

KIM A. KEELEY, MD, MSH, Kingsboro Psychiatric Center, Brooklyn, New York

EMERGENCY ROOM TREATMENT OF ALCOHOL ABUSE AND ALCOHOLISM

SUCCESSFUL EMERGENCY room treatment for alcoholism can provide an important boost toward sobriety. The physician and his or her colleagues can be sure that when they encounter an alcohol-dependent person in an emergency setting, something unusual is going on in the life of their patient. Alcoholics do not want to spend time in emergency rooms. Moreover, few of the patients who use alcohol before they get to the emergency room planned on arriving there in the first place.

Not all emergency patients who have been drinking can be classified as alcoholics. Most studies indicate a variety in consumption patterns among patients. Some are alcohol-dependent and have been so for a long time, while others have consumed an excess over a brief period and are temporarily rather than chronically intoxicated. A third group may or may not be intoxicated, but they have experienced a health complication associated with their alcohol consumption. In the medical literature, all of these patients usually are grouped together when emergency room treatment is discussed.

A special risk of morbidity seems to apply when alcohol use and drug abuse is associated with an emergency room visit. This is borne out by retrospective studies of chemical users who die suddenly in emergency room settings [6]. These groups

---

Kim A. Keeley, MD, MSH, Director for Inpatient Services, Kingsboro Psychiatric Center, and Clinical Associate Professor of Psychiatry, State University of New York Downstate Medical Center, Brooklyn, New York.

are more likely (50 vs. 28%) to have visited the emergency room within a 6-month period prior to death, compared to those with purely medical or surgical complaints and no evidence of alcohol or drug abuse.

In urban settings, alcohol use typically is detectable in up to 40% of emergency patients. Breathalyzer analysis of 6,266 consecutive Boston patients showed positive readings for 22% of the men and 11% of the women [12]. Unfortunately, diagnostic suspicion is sometimes low. Amdur [1] discovered only 136 alcoholic patients when he sifted through 9,933 consecutive emergency room records collected over 6 months in Chicago. Closer analysis often clarifies the facts. In Brooklyn, Solomon and his colleagues [10] interviewed 162 randomly selected patients using the Alcohol Abuse Scale, and 25% (41) were classifiable as alcoholics. Less than half (16 of 41) had the diagnosis entered on their hospital record; of these, only 6 out of 16 were referred for alcoholism treatment.

Alcohol Intoxication and Overdose

Intoxication and withdrawal are the two most common alcohol-related syndromes encountered in an emergency setting. Often they coexist. The fact that an overdose of alcohol can occur is not commonly recognized. American folklore has it that alcohol is a safe drug, with the most serious consequences being to fall asleep or at least to lose motor coordination. These consequences prevent overdose, it is suggested, because drinking behaviors cannot continue. Unfortunately, this scenario applies more often to the nontolerant individual and not to the alcoholic. The latter is able to tolerate high blood alcohol levels. For the alcohol-dependent person, loss of consciousness and even noticeable motor impairment may not occur until blood levels of .30% and higher are reached. Nontolerant individuals would find such levels life-threatening. Lethal coma has been associated with blood alcohol levels (BAL) as low as .35% [9] and .40% [5].

In emergency conditions the possibility that alcohol has been consumed along with one or more kinds of drugs further compounds the treatment task. Alcohol potentiates the central nervous system (CNS) depressant effects of barbiturates and benzodiazepines. It interacts with hallucinogens, marijuana, and stimulants by contributing to overall CNS toxicity.

For these reasons it is essential first to consider whether an alcohol overdose or withdrawal is present. Every patient will have a limited ability to function while under the influence, reflected by stupor or more complete loss of consciousness. Obtaining a BAL provides critical information on this point. Even when blood levels are in the .20 to .40% range, however, the clinician cannot know how high the level was or for how long it remained at a higher level. Carefully taking a history or reports from other observers can inform the clinician about these variables, yet in many cases this information will have a low reliability. Therefore, the clinician is advised to proceed as if significantly higher BALs have been in effect prior to emergency room admission.

At the same time an analysis of the urine for drugs of abuse should be conducted. These laboratory tests should be accompanied by standard precautions for maintaining the patient's airway and respiratory dynamics, fluid and electrolyte balance, and protection against pressure burns. It should not be assumed that the danger of respiratory depression is passed merely by admitting the alcoholic to an emergency ward.

Alcohol Withdrawal

For the alcohol-tolerant individual, acceptance for emergency treatment will often be associated with the onset of a withdrawal syndrome. In contrast to those patients who are stuporous or comatose because of an overdose of alcohol, the person with withdrawal symptoms frequently is tremulous and restless, agitated, perhaps assaultive or destructive, and usually irritable. Tactile and visual hallucinations are common, as is sweating and a cool skin temperature. Sometimes the stigmata of alcohol overdose are also present, such as pressure burns, cigarette stains, and clotted mucous or dried body fluids on the skin and clothing. Even the more affluent patient may show obvious inattention to grooming. These indications should be taken as signs of overdose and dependence rather than simple intoxication.

Alcohol withdrawal is often self-treated with beverage alcohol before the emergency room is consulted. Signs of intoxication may be present along with symptoms of withdrawal. Slurred speech, ataxia, nausea, and vomiting can obscure the withdrawal process. Care must be taken to discriminate between an intoxicated state that precedes obtundation versus the toxic phenomena that temporarily can be more dramatic than the early signs of withdrawal. The BAL can give a useful but not conclusive indication of which clinical problem is ascendant, since higher levels are suggestive of overdose.

Frequent monitoring of the clinical course is the best method for distinguishing between overdose and withdrawal complicated by intoxication. Progressive clouding of consciousness and diminished reactivity to stimuli should alert the physician to the possibility of an overdose. In such circumstances medications commonly used to treat withdrawal should not be prescribed. Instead, careful monitoring of the patient's vital functions should be continued until consciousness is regained. Routine care of the comatose patient may have to be instituted. Adequate preparation for the emergency treatment of alcoholism requires that a full range of resuscitation equipment be available along with physicians and other personnel who know how to prescribe and operate the equipment.

In most cases extreme measures will not be necessary if alcohol is the only drug to have been ingested. The typical case of mixed alcohol intoxication-withdrawal syndrome usually progresses within a few hours toward a clear-cut clinical picture of withdrawal. Coexisting medical problems and/or abuse of other drugs may interfere with this process, however. Withdrawal symptoms due to alcohol alone begin 6 to 24 hours after a major reduction in consumption. When untreated they generally persist for at least 48 to 96 hours. If emergency room admission occurs well after the withdrawal syndrome has begun, the possibility of delirium tremens is significantly increased. Delirium tremens (DTs) most commonly occurs 2 to 4 days after a dependent person ceases drinking.

Delirium Tremens

Along with an overdose of alcohol, delirium tremens is a life-threatening development, one that the emergency room therapist must work strenuously to avoid. The diagnosis of delirium tremens applies when several of the following are present simultaneously: confusion; disorientation to time, place, and/or person; delusions and ideas of reference; hallucinations; and wide mood swings over very short periods of time. Hallucinations are typically visual and/or tactile, although auditory hallucinations are sometimes reported in withdrawal states. When auditory hallucinations are a prominent feature and signs of withdrawal are minimal, alcoholic hallucinosis and alcohol idiosyncratic intoxication should be part of the differential diagnosis.

In addition to these disorders of mental functioning, delirium tremens involves a progression of behavioral impairment from motor restlessness toward outright tonic-clonic convulsions. Assessment of CNS reactivity will disclose hyperactive reflexes, enhanced sensitivity to noise and light, and sometimes, at later stages, cog-wheel rigidity. Grand mal seizures may occur infrequently as an early sign of serious withdrawal symptoms, especially when medical or surgical conditions have obscured the patient's alcohol dependence or the prodromal signs of withdrawal. Ordinarily, seizures occur on the second to fourth day after drinking stops and after several of the prodromata are seen. Tachycardia in alcohol withdrawal is not especially diagnostic, but hyperthermia is associated with the occurrence of delirium tremens. Furthermore, if the patient is disoriented and uncooperative, fever may be one of the few reliable signs of associated medical injury or illness. Lumbar puncture, chest and skull films, and a battery of blood chemistry tests may be required to clarify the etiology of the delirium. In the past delirium tremens has been reported to have a mortality rate about 15% [11]. In the contemporary United States it is unusual to see classic delirium tremens because the alcohol withdrawal syndrome is easy to treat and usually recognized before seizures have begun. No investigation of the current morbidity of delirium tremens has appeared in the literature recently, and the death rate is said to be 1% or lower [4].

A diagnosis of impending DTs or incipient DTs is sometimes used to indicate that withdrawal symptoms are severe but not classic DTs. Clinicians sometimes use these terms when they believe the likelihood of seizure activity is high but not yet manifest. Rum fits is another diagnosis sometimes used to indicate seizure activity related to alcohol withdrawal. The terms "alcohol withdrawal delirium" and "alcohol withdrawal" are suggested in the DSM-III [2] of the American Psychiatric Association. Seizures are considered possible occurrences with both diagnoses, the distinguishing feature being the presence of a delirium. The critical point for the clinician is that seizures and delirium can be ominous complications of alcohol withdrawal, regardless of how they are designated.

Drug-Free Treatment of Withdrawal

Some clinicians favor a drug-free treatment regimen when withdrawal symptoms are mild to moderate. While their assessment of symptom severity is a clinical judgment based on experience, they also select this treatment strategy knowing in advance that special rooms and staff are available where the patient can be monitored continuously. This technique is derived from observations that a kind of sensory deprivation occurs for the withdrawing alcoholic. Such a patient is usually disoriented to the normal cues and stimuli in the environment. When a supportive staff provides physical comfort, frequent verbal reassurance and orientation, they are surrounding the patient with familiar cues to counteract the dysphoria and confusion of the withdrawal state. The patient who is severely impaired is generally able to focus attention for a brief time on the interventions of the therapeutic team, which results in a temporary calming effect.

An advantage of this approach is that the patient recovers mental capacity without having to use yet another drug. This can be important once sobriety is achieved, because it avoids having to introduce and perhaps accustom the patient to a new array of pharmacologic effects. Subsequent treatment of alcoholism often depends on the patient's willingness to avoid the use of all drugs. For some, the commitment to abstinence is apt to deteriorate if the clinician who is requesting total abstinence has to acknowledge that drugs used in the emergency room, albeit not alcohol, contributed to the patient's sobriety. Since total abstinence is widely acknowledged to be a critical accomplishment for alcoholics, the emergency room physician should give serious thought to minimizing the use of drugs in treating alcohol withdrawal, especially when adequate resources are available to continue the supportive regimens that are initiated in the emergency room.

Whether or not drugs are used, treatment should include a complete physical examination to search for medical or surgical problems. Ordinarily an intravenous need not be installed unless fluid loss has been detected or reported. Furosemide has been recommended if overhydration requires therapy. Bed rest, adequate nutrition, and comfortable surroundings need to be arranged, along with an adequate amount of socialization appropriate to the circumstances. The patient who is awake should not be left unattended nor isolated from others. Responsiveness to cultural factors can also ensure a successful outcome. Spanish-speaking patients may be more comforted by Spanish-speaking staff. Minority-group patients sometimes are assisted more effectively by clinicians who are minority members. Recovered alcoholic staff often zero in on problems and anxieties effectively.

Magnesium and thiamine deficiency occur in some chronic alcoholics because of their inadequate diet. Thiamine is commonly administered in 100 mg doses intramuscularly for 3 days. Peripheral neuropathy and Wernicke's encephalopathy have been attributed to thiamine deficiency, especially in chronic alcoholics whose nutritional status is poor. Hypomagnesemia is thought to increase the likelihood of seizures during withdrawal, and a few practitioners urge administration of 50% magnesium sulfate solution, 2 cc intramuscularly every 4 to 6 hours, until the danger of seizures is passed. The efficacy of magnesium replacement therapy has not been consistently established, however. Use of magnesium is not considered necessary by many clinicians, including those who rely on antiseizure medications as the therapy of choice.

Drug Treatment of Withdrawal

Pharmacotherapy of alcohol withdrawal syndrome in contemporary medicine usually involves administration of a benzodiazepine. This family of compounds is safe over a wide dose range, although alcohol does potentiate their sedative action [3]. Chlordiazepoxide often is preferred over diazepam because it is less likely to depress or slow mental functioning. Its antianxiety is beneficial over the short and intermediate clinical course. After recovery, it has a reduced tendency to cause euphoria or other alterations of consciousness, which might appeal to a person who has been accustomed to using alcohol or drugs.

During an acute withdrawal characterized by severe symptoms, doses of chlordiazepoxide ranging as high as 50 to 100 mg intramuscularly or per os every hour or so may be necessary to reduce agitation and anxiety. Intramuscular doses of benzodiazepine are effective when care is given to choosing the site of injection, which should include muscle rather than fat. Between doses, careful and supportive nursing attention should be given. Once a satisfactory level of comfort is obtained, the frequency and amount of doses can be modified.

Ideally, medication is not prescribed in the emergency room, but after the patient arrives at an alcoholism detoxification unit. Sometimes this kind of referral is not possible. In a relatively uncomplicated situation where delirium tremens is not considered likely, a regimen of decreasing doses of chlordiazepoxide can be established over a 3- or 4-day period. Starting at 50 mg per os t.i.d. chlordiazepoxide is given 25 mg per os t.i.d. on the next day. On the third day, 10 mg per os t.i.d. is given, and then medication is discontinued. In a minority of cases, anxiety will subside only briefly, shortly to resume its intensity and threaten sobriety. Whether this is a sign of continued withdrawal or underlying psychiatric disturbance is not clear. In the interest of supporting efforts to stay sober, chlordiazepoxide or a similar minor tranquilizer may prove useful if given for a limited period. By this time, however, the emergency room physician ordinarily will have referred the patient elsewhere for follow-up care.

A wide variety of medications, most with sedative properties, have been recommended during the past years for the treatment of the alcohol abstinence syndrome. Paraldehyde once was favored because it is largely excreted by the lungs, bypassing the liver, which may be operating inefficiently due to prolonged contact with alcohol. However, paraldehyde can irritate the gastrointestinal tract, it is subject to degradation if not stored carefully, and some consider it hepatotoxic [7]. Meprobamate, barbiturates, hydroxyzine, other neuroleptics, including phenothiazines, and even ethanol itself have all been used with varying degrees of success or failure. The best course is for the clinician to become familiar with one medication or two, and to use them regularly. Gallant [5] favors oxazepam because, unlike chlordiazepam, it is not metabolized in great amounts by the liver. Chlordiazepam is currently the most commonly selected agent. Whatever benzodiazepine is prescribed, they are considered safe, with few side effects, and useful for alcohol withdrawal syndrome, whether mild or severe.

Treatment of Intoxication and Overdose

The clinician may be hard pressed to determine whether drug treatment is useful whenever the physical findings or laboratory values confirm that alcohol is still present in the blood. When intoxication is the dominant feature or if BALs range close to .10% or higher, the capacity that alcohol has to potentiate other drugs may pose unwanted difficulties in therapy [7]. Combined alcohol-drug use can prolong the excitement and agitation of intoxication, produce stupor and respiratory or circulatory distress, and obscure signs of an underlying medical disorder.

When signs of intoxication subside, the clinician can reasonably decide that the BAL is no longer rising. If signs of withdrawal appear, drug treatment is justifiable, although with the caveat that tolerant persons may go into withdrawal even when BALs are high. This may present difficulties in unduly potentiating the action of any drugs that are prescribed. Treatment need not be withheld if reasonable doses of a safe drug are used, and neurological and cardiovascular assessments should be performed before subsequent doses are administered.

Recent reports suggest that intravenous naloxone can reverse alcohol-induced coma [8]. Doses of 0.2 to 0.4 mg given once or several times (total cumulative doses of 3.5 μg/kg to 725 μg/kg are reported) have led to rapid improvement. However, this modality currently has not been tested widely, and its safety is not yet clinically established for simple intoxication. As an alternative, hemodialysis may be used for extremely high alcohol overdoses.

Psychiatric Complications

Psychiatric symptoms are important complications of alcohol intoxication and/or withdrawal states. Thought disorders and aggressive behaviors are common. Due to the disinhibitory action of alcohol, it is much more likely that these psychiatric problems are alcohol-induced and not indicative of what a person is like when sober. Less frequent but certainly not rare is the patient with a history of psychiatric disturbances who will use alcohol to assuage tensions and anxieties.

Psychiatric consultation is often necessary in all of these cases. Suicidal or homicidal urges, threatening and aggressive actions, delusions of persecution, and ideas of reference that remain fixed in spite of reassurance signify a dangerous potential that can neither be safely nor briefly treated in an emergency room setting. Neuroleptic therapy and psychiatric hospitalization may have to be considered. In these cases, the choice between benzodiazepines and stronger psychotropic medications can be a difficult one.

These complications require the emergency room staff to be conscious of their personal safety. Whether security guards or extra clinical staff are used to address the potentially assaultive patient, it should be understood by every staff member that restraining agitated patients sometimes will be necessary. Procedures to handle these situations should be worked out and practiced in advance. Often it is important to have as many staff as possible to join in confronting a difficult patient, since this sometimes convinces the patient that further acting out will be to no avail. It is also important to recognize the danger of initiating restraining actions, be they physical or pharmacologic, when there are too few staff available to complete the restraining process.

Alcohol Hallucinosis

A rare psychiatric complication of alcohol dependence, one that ordinarily does not involve major behavioral difficulties, is called "alcohol hallucinosis." The presence of unpleasant auditory hallucinations without concomitant delirium, confusion, or dementia, suggests this diagnosis. The hallucinations begin about 24 to 48 hours after ethanol intake is stopped. While auditory phenomena are the primary disturbances, visual and tactile hallucinations may also occur but not with the intensity noted during a typical withdrawal period. In some cases the auditory symptoms persist with varying intensity over an extended period of time. It is possible for the clinical distinction between alcoholic hallucinosis and schizophrenia to be difficult. The age of onset for the former is usually in the 30s or 40s, however, and the association with alcohol is also distinctive. Phenothiazines may be useful in the acute phases, but they have had only middling success in the long-term therapy of this illness.

Alcohol Idiosyncratic Intoxication

Formerly called "pathological intoxication," this is another psychiatric complication of alcohol use. Little attention is paid to this variant today, it appears, since it tends to overlap with straightforward problems of alcohol intoxication. Diagnosis rests on the presence of a dysphoric mental state and a history within the past hour or two of ingesting a small quantity of alcohol, such as one or two cocktails or a bottle or two of beer. There is no premorbid abnormality that identifies potential victims of this disorder. Symptoms are quite out of character, surprising in their intensity, and may include harmful and dangerous behaviors. Studies documenting this syndrome in large numbers have not been reported. These cases are treated the same way as when intoxication is due to ingestion of much larger amounts of alcohol. Diagnosis is made by taking a history about previous experiences with alcohol use, although amnesia for these events is often reported.

Electroencephalogram (EEG) changes suggestive of a temporal lobe disturbance may be involved, according to some authors. As with most episodes involving emotional changes, the differential diagnosis should include psychiatric disorders.

Acetaldehyde Reactions

Small amounts of alcohol also may not be tolerated well by a minority of patients from Asian and Eastern European backgrounds. Due to genetically deficient enzymatic systems enough acetaldehyde accumulates to produce vasodilatation and a reddish flush to the head and neck. Similar occurrences have been reported with patients using sulfonamide antidiabetic drugs. Abnormal behavioral responses to alcohol are not observed with these flush reactions.

A flush reaction is also common when alcohol is ingested by patients who are taking disulfiram. Disulfiram blocks the action of the enzyme aldehyde dehydrogenase, causing a buildup of circulating acetaldehyde. For those patients who choose to use it, the drug can have an important motivating effect on their desire to stay sober, since nausea occurs when alcohol and disulfiram are used together.

Sometimes accidently, and rarely because of purposeful drinking, more severe alcohol-disulfiram reactions may require immediate attention. Vasodilatation is produced with flushing, throbbing headache, palpitations, feverishness, sweating, lightheadedness, nausea, and vomiting. Hypotension may persist after an initial short-lived rise in blood pressure. If copious amounts of alcohol have been consumed, the ethanol-disulfiram reaction can lead to a life-threatening collapse of the cardiovascular system.

Ordinarily, smaller amounts of alcohol have been absorbed, sometimes inadvertently from such innocuous substances as salad dressing or dessert topping. In these cases, the alcohol-disulfiram reactions are not severe, despite their annoying characteristics. Antihistamines alleviate the symptoms, and Benadryl may be given in doses of 25 to 100 mg either per os or intravenously, depending on the severity of the syndrome. Some investigators have also indicated that intravenous vitamin C is useful, but no rationale has been proposed for this measure. Others have relieved symptoms with carbogen, a mixture of 95% oxygen and 5% carbon dioxide. Presumably this induces deeper respiration, which enhances the exhalation of alcohol.

Holding Units

For those patients who are too sick to leave the emergency room except via referral to another acute care resource, consideration should be given to admitting them to a holding unit. This is a quieter hospital area where intensive care is not given but patients can be treated and are observed when official hospital admission does not seem justified. Ordinarily it takes several hours for patients with moderately severe intoxication or withdrawal symptoms to reach a point where the physician can be sure that improvement is steady and progressive. Once that point is reached, the patient can be referred to the appropriate echelon of the alcoholism treatment system. Official admission to an acute care hospital bed might be avoided. An emergency room holding unit and a multimodal community treatment system can enhance the treatment of alcoholism as well as the level of satisfaction in providing that treatment.

ACKNOWLEDGMENTS

The editorial and bibliographic assistance of Joel Solomon, MD, State University of New York Downstate Medical Center, Jane Bemko, MLS, Baylor Medical College, and Virginia Rolett, MSLS, Project Cork Resource Center, Dartmouth Medical College, is gratefully acknowledged.

REFERENCES

1. Amdur, M. A. Alcohol-related problems in a general hospital emergency room. *Ill. Med. J.* 148:509, 1975.
2. American Psychiatric Association. *Diagnostic and Statistical Manual of Mental Disorders* (3rd ed.). Author: Washington, D.C., 1980.
3. Baldessarini, R. J. *Chemotherapy in Psychiatry.* Harvard University Press: Cambridge, 1977.
4. Cohen, S. *The Substance Abuse Problems.* Haworth Press: New York, 1981.
5. Gallant, D. M. Psychiatric aspects of alcohol intoxication, withdrawal, and organic brain syndromes. In: *Alcoholism and Clinical Psychiatry*, Solomon, J. (ed.). Plenum: New York. In press.
6. Keeley, K. A., and Kahn, P. A. Alcoholism and drug abuse in the emergency room. In: *Currents in Alcoholism*, Seixas, F. (ed.). Grune & Stratton: New York, 1977.
7. Knott, D. H., and Beard, J. D. Diagnosis and therapy of acute withdrawal from alcohol. In: *Acute Drug Abuse Emergencies*, Bourne, P. (ed.). Academic Press: New York, 1976.
8. Mackenzie, A. I. Naloxone in alcohol intoxication. *Lancet* March 31, 1979, p. 733–734.
9. Schukit, M. *Drug and Alcohol Abuse.* Plenum: New York, 1979.

10. Solomon, J., Vanga, N., Morgan, J. P., and Joseph, P. Emergency room physicians' recognition of alcohol misuse. *J. Stud. Alcohol* 41:583-586, 1980.

11. Victor, M. Treatment of alcohol intoxication and the withdrawal syndrome: A critical analysis of the use of drugs and other forms of therapy. In: *Acute Drug Abuse Emergencies*, Bourne, P. (ed.). Academic Press: New York, 1976.

12. Wechsler, H., Thum, D., Demone, H. W., Jr., and Dwinnell, J. Social characteristics and blood alcohol level: Measurements of subgroup differences. *Q. J. Stud. Alcohol* 33:132-147, 1972.

69

EARL X. FREED, PhD, Veterans Administration, Washington, D.C.

MENTAL HOSPITALS: HOSPITALIZATION AND TREATMENT OF THE ALCOHOLIC

MENTAL HOSPITALS HAVE long represented one of the most important interfaces between alcoholism and the field of mental health. Historically, mental health professionals were among the first to admit alcoholics to their facilities, namely, mental hospitals. This seeming acceptance of alcoholism as a form of mental illness may have proven a mixed blessing, both for the alcoholics themselves and for the field of alcoholism. On the one hand, it did create an asylum, a sheltering environment for persons unable to function in society; it afforded an opportunity for inpatient detoxification; it represented one of the first steps in what has become a successful movement to decriminalize alcoholism; and it conveyed the message that alcoholism was treatable and that a hopeful prognosis could be entertained for a disorder heretofore deemed incurable. Attitudinal training of staff and the focusing of multidisciplinary mental health approaches have been other benefits.

On the other hand, problems were created. These included and have not been limited to the traditionally long duration of psychiatric hospital treatment and the relative nonspecificity of psychiatric hospital treatment for alcoholism. Further, there has been the question of whether alcoholics and other psychiatric patients should be treated together on the same inpatient ward. In addition, psychiatric

---

Earl X. Freed, PhD, Deputy Assistant Chief Medical Director for Research and Development, Veterans Administration, Washington, D.C.

hospitalization has often resulted in institutionalization, which hampered efforts at effective reentry to society and fostered isolation of the alcoholic. Finally, placing alcoholism within the mental health purview may have discouraged experimentation with other models of care as well as attenuated research efforts with a basically biological orientation.

The Changing Role of the Psychiatric Hospital

There has been a long history of advocating the hospital as the primary site for the treatment of alcoholism because of the hospital's full range of resources. In recent years this trend has been reversed with the emphasis on outpatient, community, and other nonhospital settings. For example, one principle enumerated in the *Accreditation Manual for Alcoholism Programs* of the Joint Commission on Accreditation of Hospitals [9] is that the alcoholism program shall integrate its services with other community resources in the human service system and shall be responsive to community needs."

Impetus for this integration of services has come from the reduction in numbers of state and county psychiatric hospitals and the reduction in state psychiatric hospital populations. Thus, in 1976, there were 304 state and county psychiatric hospitals, 183 private psychiatric hospitals, and 24 neuropsychiatric hospitals in the Veterans Administration (VA) system [14]. Other trends have been the inclusion of psychiatric units in general hospitals, the recognition of alcoholism as an illness instead of a form of willful behavior, a generally more humanistic trend in the treatment and perception of the psychiatrically ill, a redefinition of the need for custodial and long-term psychiatric care, and deinstitutionalization of psychiatric patients [15]; that is, the current stress is on treatment rather than on the provision of domicile. What these developments portend for the future of alcoholism treatment vis-à-vis psychiatric hospitals remains to be seen, but a fair appraisal is that alternatives to psychiatric hospitalization will continue to be sought. Nevertheless, there are few options when commitment is required, and a recent report found that 17% of a random sample of 103 patients involuntarily committed to Maryland state psychiatric hospitals were intoxicated at the time of commitment; "they were not necessarily thought to be violent by the police or family bringing them to the hospital for commitment, yet there was a previous history of violence in over half the sample" [7].

A recent National Institute of Mental Health (NIMH) publication, *Psychiatric Services and the Changing Institutional Scene, 1950–1985* [13], notes that the percentage of first admissions with specific diagnoses of alcohol disorders increased from 9% in 1946 to 26% in 1972. The statement made in this publication about schizophrenia holds for alcoholism as well: "It cannot be emphasized too strongly that the number of new cases ... will continue to increase until research produces the knowledge needed to prevent its occurrence."

THE COURSE OF PSYCHIATRIC HOSPITALIZATION OF ALCOHOL-DEPENDENT PERSONS

Effective management of the hospitalized alcoholic may pose a host of problems, especially when alcoholism and other serious psychiatric disorders, such as schizophrenia or depression, coexist. Alcohol-dependent persons have been characterized as actively engaged in denial as a defense mechanism and as having acting-out tendencies with poor impulse control. These tendencies may manifest themselves in alcoholics' not entering treatment after an initial overture to do so, dropping out of treatment very early, or utilizing the psychiatric hospital on a revolving-door basis. Such alcoholic patients are never in treatment long enough for emotional benefits to accrue or for significant changes in their drinking behaviors to take place. It has been hypothesized that the alcoholic may interpret the reduction in physical discomfort experienced after detoxification as an indication of well-being, especially emotional well-being, and thus may leave the hospital too early and against medical advice [6].

The obverse has also been documented [5]. The dilemma of the alcoholic patient remaining in the psychiatric hospital may be that while hospitalized, his or her tenuous internalized controls are reinforced by the institutional regimen, routines, and external controls, none of which is available when the patient reenters the community. Further, positive effects of the hospital stay may be counteracted because of the milieu-dependent learning with little carry-over of benefits to the extra-hospital environment.

Guidelines for Admission of Persons with Alcohol Problems to Psychiatric Hospitals

Guidelines for admission of alcoholic patients to psychiatric hospitals have been offered recently. The American Medical Association [2] recommends:

> A patient should be admitted to an *acute psychiatric hospital or service* if, in addition to his wanting to prevent a serious drinking bout, he has a psychiatric condition severe enough to require acute psychiatric hospital care. This might include, but not be limited to a patient who (1) is overtly psychotic; (2) is so severely depressed that he is probably suicidal; (3) represents a serious management problem because he is extremely confused or has other behavioral difficulties that cannot be adequately managed on a medical or surgical service.

The Committee on Alcoholism and Drug Abuse of the Medical Society of the State of New York has cited similar criteria [8]:

> Possible admission to Psychiatric Department for an alcoholic who is (1) in a deteriorating mental or physical state; (2) in need of close medical, surgical or psychiatric

supervision; (3) psychotic, severely depressed and/or suicidal; (4) suffering from mental disease in which the alcoholism is secondary, and who is drinking; (5) exhibiting marked antisocial behavior, even though he is not intoxicated; (6) an apparently intoxicated individual and is confused, disoriented, and without a companion in whose care he can be put.

These criteria highlight the need for careful examination of patients and for identification of problems associated with alcoholism. There is some evidence that psychiatric disorders such as schizophrenia, mania, or depression may mask alcoholism or vice versa and that diagnoses may be missed.

In many psychiatric hospitals, the procedure is first to admit patients to triage or general admission wards and then to refer them to the specialized alcoholism treatment units that are selective in patient recruitment.

Discharge of the Alcoholic Patient from the Hospital

The *Manual on Alcoholism* [2] emphasizes what is known about other psychiatric patients — even on admission, discharge planning should begin with contingencies for aftercare: "As with any patient, the alcohol-dependent patient should be discharged from the hospital as soon as such discharge is medically indicated. In each instance, however, appropriate plans should be made prior to discharge for continuing aftercare at the hospital or by a private physician, or, as frequently will be required, for psychological and social rehabilitation by public and voluntary agencies" [2].

Discharge planning implies the attainment of treatment goals and outcomes. For the individual patient these may range from very specific outcomes to complex interactions of goals. For example, the Veterans Administration, a large health care system including 172 medical centers, has been a major treatment resource for veteran patients with alcohol-related problems and a major source of research data in the field of alcoholism. The Veterans Administration's goals for treatment of alcohol and drug-dependent patients reinforce the multifactorial and multidisciplinary aspects of alcoholism. Outcomes with medical, vocational, social, interpersonal, and quality-of-life factors are enumerated [4, p. 286]:

It is expected that upon completion of treatment, a patient will:

1. Not use drugs or alcohol in a manner that is illegal; that is damaging to physical health, family or job adjustment; or that threatens personal safety.
2. Be free of pain, illness, and disability to the extent reasonable to expect from currently available medical practice.
3. Be free of serious disorders of perception, cognition, mood and self-esteem.
4. Interact with people in a way that is not seriously stressful to the patient himself or to others.

5. Support himself in the community to the extent that age and physical health permit.

6. Manage his affairs in such a way that his immediate needs for food, clothing, shelter, transportation, and medical care are met in a responsible manner.

7. Not assault others, steal, drive while impaired by drugs or alcohol, or engage in other activities that endanger the public safety or welfare.

8. Obtain satisfaction from socially acceptable sources such as work, relationships with family and friends, and leisure time activities.

UTILIZATION OF PSYCHIATRIC HOSPITALS BY PERSONS WITH ALCOHOL PROBLEMS

Despite the recent emphasis upon community-based services, hospital-related services continue to be used excessively by alcoholics and alcohol abusers. In 1975, $8.40 billion was expended for all types of hospital care; this represents 66% of the total expenditure of $12.74 billion for alcohol-related health services [17].

Within the Veterans Administration during the period 1970-77, the proportion of patients discharged with a principal diagnosis of alcoholism increased from 7.7% to 10.8%, while the proportion of patients with a principal diagnosis of alcoholism on the biennial census day increased from 8.1% to 10.7%. Table 1 presents data from two VA reports [1, 16] on the proportion of defined alcoholics and problem drinkers in VA hospitals on four consecutive census dates.

It is noteworthy that almost 33% of all patients in VA psychiatric hospitals at

Table 1
Proportion by Censuses of Defined Alcoholics and Problem Drinkers in VA Hospitals

	1970	1973	1975	1977
All VA hospitals				
Defined alcoholics	15.1%	19.0%	17.4%	21.2%
Problem drinkers	5.1%	5.7%	5.1%	4.8%
Total hospital census	85,550	82,485	78,830	75,058
General hospitals				
Defined alcoholics	13.7%	17.6%	15.6%	19.6%
Problem drinkers	NA	4.9%	4.9%	4.6%
Total general hospital census	53,870	58,461	59,790	58,896
Psychiatric hospitals				
Defined alcoholics	17.5%	22.4%	22.9%	27.0%
Problem drinkers	NA	7.6%	5.8%	5.5%
Total psychiatric hospital census	31,680	24,024	19,040	16,161

the time of the 1977 census had problems identified with alcoholism. Another highlight of the 1977 VA census [16] dealing with alcoholism and psychiatric hospitals was that alcoholism prevalence among patients in VA medical centers "was consistently higher in psychiatric hospitals than in general hospitals regardless of affiliation or psychiatric residency. This relationship remained when the data from 12 designated general hospitals with large psychiatric components were aggregated with data from psychiatric hospitals. Approximately 62% of the defined alcoholics were under care for alcoholism on September 28, 1977, in the psychiatric hospitals" and 69.7% of the defined alcoholic patients had been admitted for alcoholism in psychiatric hospitals. Finally, 2.5% of patients in psychiatric hospitals had problems of alcoholism and other drug use.

A comprehensive report on psychiatric hospital utilization by alcoholics [12] indicated, in state and county mental hospitals, the ratio of male to female alcoholic admissions was almost six to one and about two to one in private mental hospitals. In the age groups from 35-44 and 45-64, alcohol disorders were the leading diagnoses for males admitted to state and county mental hospitals in 1970. Alcohol disorders were the second leading diagnoses for males, aged 25-34 and 65 and over, and for females aged 35-44 and 45-64.

TREATMENT OF ALCOHOLIC PATIENTS IN PSYCHIATRIC HOSPITALS

A 1970 national survey of private psychiatric hospitals [10] indicated that 9% of the respondent institutions refused admission to alcoholics, 8% had special bed units for alcoholics, and an additional 33% had special alcoholism treatment programs. Earlier, a national survey of state mental hospitals [11] found that 31% had special ward units for alcoholics and that an additional 20% had special alcoholism treatment programs. The report concluded that 88% of the hospitals used AA and that "group psychotherapy, drug therapy and individual psychotherapy were each used in over half. The estimated overall rate of improvement was 60% at discharge, 39% up to a year after discharge, and 33% for periods over a year after discharge. There was no significant difference between hospitals with special interest or units and those which accepted patients reluctantly."

A recurrent issue has been the question of whether or not to treat alcoholics separately from other psychiatric patients and, more recently, from drug addicts. The issue is still an open one with evidence on both sides [17]. In a sense, the justification for alcohol treatment programs separate from those of other patients in a psychiatric hospital would seem to hinge on identification of unique characteristics of the alcoholics or of unique treatment needs following detoxification. In fact, the treatment offered has been that generally available to all patients at the hospital.

The traditional treatment approaches for alcoholism in psychiatric hospitals seem to have been AA, didactic lectures, and individual and group psychotherapy. There have been recent trends to emphasize family therapy and behavior modification approaches. Occupational, recreational, industrial, and milieu therapies, as well as psychoactive medication and long stays in the mental hospital armamentarium, have also been employed. Rehabilitation counseling, deterrent drugs such as disulfiram, psychodrama and role-playing techniques, hypnosis, aversive conditioning methodologies, psychoanalysis, meditation, and even the use of hallucinogenic agents convey some notion of the range of therapeutic modalities that have been reported. In addition, innovative treatment approaches, initially related to psychiatric hospitals but later emerging in their own right as facilities appropriate for alcoholics, are night hospitals, day hospital programs, halfway houses, and domiciliaries.

The mental hospital treatment goal for alcoholics has invariably been total abstinence. Psychiatric hospital regimens usually preclude controlled or any kind of drinking by patients, most of whom may be taking psychoactive medication.

Treatment effectiveness has received substantial review [3, 17]. Baekeland et al. [3] state that "the fundamental questions in hospital treatment" are "(1) How effective is it? (2) How much of its reported effectiveness can be attributed to treatment and how much to the kind of patient treated? (3) Is any particular kind of pretreatment regimen better than any other? (4) Is hospital treatment better than outpatient treatment? (5) How necessary is posthospital outpatient follow-up treatment?" Their review of a number of studies revealed that about 41.5% of patients improved with hospitalization, but the attribution of improvement remains a difficult question. Others report success rates from 30 to 70% [17]. There seems to be no strong evidence favoring a prolonged inpatient treatment stay. The Health, Education and Welfare report [17] summarizes, "Few differences in effectiveness among treatment settings, types, and duration have been identified."

REFERENCES

1. *Alcoholism and Problem Drinking: 1970-1975. A Statistical Analysis of VA Hospital Patients* (Controller Monograph No. 5). Veterans Administration: Washington, D.C., 1977.
2. American Medical Association. *Manual on Alcoholism.* Author: Chicago, 1977.
3. Baekeland, F., Lundwall, L., and Kissin, B. Methods for the treatment of chronic alcoholism: A critical appraisal. In: *Research Advances in Alcohol and Drug Problems* (Vol. 2), Gibbins, R. J., Israel, Y., Kalant, H., Popham, R. E., Schmidt, W., and Smart, R. G. (eds.). Wiley: New York, 1975.
4. Baker, S. L., Jr., Lorei, T., McKnight, H. A., Jr., and Duvall, J. L. The Veterans Administration comparison study: Alcoholism and drug abuse—combined and conventional treatment settings. *Alcohol.: Clin. Exper. Res.* 1:285-291, 1977.
5. Freed, E. X. The dilemma of the alcoholic patient in a psychiatric hospital. *J. Psychiat. Nursing* 7:133-135, 1969.

6. Gibson, S., and Becker, J. Changes in alcoholics' self-reported depression. *Q. J. Stud. Alcohol* 34:829–836, 1973.

7. Ginzburg, H. M., and Rappeport, J. R. Alcoholics and involuntary commitments. In: *Currents in Alcoholism: Psychiatric, Psychological, Social and Epidemiological Studies* (Vol. 4), Seixas, F. A. (ed.). Grune & Stratton: New York, 1978.

8. *Guidelines for Admission of Alcoholics to Hospitals.* Christopher D. Smithers Foundation: New York, 1973.

9. Joint Commission on Accreditation of Hospitals. *Accreditation Manual for Alcoholism Programs.* Author: Chicago, 1974.

10. Moore, R. A. Alcoholism treatment in private psychiatric hospitals: A national survey. *Q. J. Stud. Alcohol* 32:1083–1085, 1971.

11. Moore, R. A., and Buchanan, T. K. State hospitals and alcoholism: A nationwide survey of treatment techniques and results. *Q. J. Stud. Alcohol* 27:459–468, 1966.

12. National Institute of Mental Health. *Utilization of Mental Health Facilities by Persons Diagnosed with Alcohol Disorders* (DHEW Publication No. HSM 73-9114). U.S. Government Printing Office: Washington, D.C., 1972.

13. National Institute of Mental Health. *Psychiatric Services and the Changing Institutional Scene, 1950–1985* (DHEW Publication No. ADM 77-433). U.S. Government Printing Office: Washington, D.C., 1977.

14. National Institute of Mental Health. *Staffing of Mental Health Facilities, United States, 1976* (DHEW Publication No. ADM 78-522). U.S. Government Printing Office: Washington, D.C., 1978.

15. National Institute of Mental Health. *Deinstitutionalization: An Analytic Review and Social Perspective* (DHEW Publication No. ADM 79-351). U.S. Government Printing Office: Washington, D.C., 1979.

16. *1977 Supplement to Alcoholism and Problem Drinking: 1970–1975. A Statistical Analysis of VA Hospital Patients* (Controller Monograph No. 8). Veterans Administration: Washington, D.C., 1978.

17. United States Department of Health, Education and Welfare. *Technical Report in Support of the Third Special Report to the U.S. Congress on Alcohol and Health from the Secretary of Health, Education, and Welfare* (DHEW Publication No. ADM 79-832). U.S. Government Printing Office: Washington, D.C., 1978.

70

ROBERT A. MOORE, MD, University of California, San Diego

THE INVOLVEMENT OF PRIVATE PSYCHIATRIC HOSPITALS IN ALCOHOLISM TREATMENT

PSYCHIATRY AND PSYCHIatric hospitals, like general medicine and general hospitals, were not noted for their early concern for the alcoholic patient. Withdrawal psychoses and organic brain damage were accepted as general responsibilities but the treatment of the causative disease all too often was not.

Early Involvement

There were pioneers in the psychiatric treatment of alcoholism, identified with private psychiatric hospitals, such as Knight [9], Menninger [10], and Strecher [21], who did much to encourage psychiatrists and their hospitals to get involved. The 1956 official recognition of alcoholism as a disease by the American Medical Association [2] gave a further impetus to physicians, including psychiatrists, to take responsibility for the treatment of alcoholism and to put pressure upon their hospitals to do likewise. With better reimbursement from private and government insurance, and with the phasing down of state hospitals and county hospitals, there occurred a significant movement of patients toward general hospital psychiatric units, private psychiatric hospitals, and specialized alcoholism hospitals [15].

Robert A. Moore, MD, Clinical Professor of Psychiatry, University of California, San Diego, School of Medicine, and Medical Director, Mesa Vista Hospital, San Diego, California.

Recent Involvement

A 1970 survey of the 128 private psychiatric hospitals then members of the National Association of Private Psychiatric Hospitals, with 71 responding [12], gave the first indication of the depth of psychiatric hospital involvement in alcoholism treatment. As Table 1 shows, most facilities accepted alcoholic patients, usually without limitations, though only 41% had established specialized programs or units for them. Of admissions 11% were alcoholic, although, undoubtedly, the number would be higher if those with other primary psychiatric diagnoses were also included. One sample facility, for example (whether it is representative or not is not known), found that 50% of male admissions and 22% of female admissions to a private psychiatric hospital fell within the alcoholism range of the Michigan Alcoholism Screening Test; however, only 76% of these men and 40% of these women were given a diagnosis of alcoholism, primary or secondary [13]. Interestingly, a National Institute of Mental Health (NIMH) survey showed 10% of admissions to private psychiatric hospitals were alcoholics in 1970, the same as a decade earlier. During the same period, as a point of contrast, the proportion of

Table 1
Comparison, by Percentage, of Surveys in 1970 and 1980 of Private Psychiatric Hospitals[a]

	1970 Census (n = 71)	1980 Census (n = 43)
Accept alcoholic patients	81	77
Accept alcoholics without limitations	68	74
Percentage of admissions	11	15
Special alcoholism units	8	—
Special alcoholism program	33	—
Program or unit	41	46
Staff attitudes toward alcoholic patients		
Enthusiastic	8	—
Accepting	88	61
Reluctant	3	39
Reasons for lack of therapeutic effectiveness[b]		
Lack of patient motivation	71	45
Lack of knowledge of etiology	31	7
Lack of knowledge of treatment	26	—
Lack of adequate follow-up	25	25
Inadequate program	11	—
Lack of family motivation	3	18
Lack of individualized treatment	—	5

[a]Based on compiled data [5, 12].
[b]The 1970 survey allowed multiple responses; the 1980 survey only one.

Veterans Administration hospital admissions who were alcoholic had increased four times, to 30% [19].

Current Involvement

During the decade of the 1970s, the quarterly *Journal of the National Association of Private Psychiatric Hospitals* published seven articles on alcoholism [3, 4, 7, 18, 22, 23, 27]. Of course, psychiatrists on the medical staffs of these hospitals, as well as other hospital staff professionals, published widely in the alcoholism literature elsewhere. However, this literature survey did not suggest a rapidly growing interest in alcoholism.

A 1980 survey of the present 181 member hospitals of the National Association of Private Psychiatric Hospitals (NAPPH) drew response from only 43 hospitals [5]. As was true of the 1970 survey and is shown in Table 1, most hospitals accepted alcoholic patients without limitations, although the proportion with specialized programs or units had not increased significantly. If these two surveys can be compared, considering the much smaller response to the second and with the questions not framed exactly the same, it appears that alcoholic patients have increased from 11% of all admissions to 15%, an increase of over a third. Perhaps even more significant is the jump of the proportion of staff whose attitude toward the treatment of alcoholic patients is reluctant, from 3 to 39%. Is this a result of alcoholics becoming more visible in the hospitals?

As a check on the current involvement of private psychiatric hospitals, a survey was made of the descriptions each hospital gave of its services in the Directory of Member Hospitals of NAPPH [16]. These findings (shown in Table 2) cannot be considered completely accurate either, since some hospitals may have written less about their services than they provide. Nevertheless, this survey corroborates the 1980 survey as to hospitals providing specialized programs or units — about half. Specialized units for alcoholics are more likely to be found in larger, nonprofit hospitals with intermediate lengths of stay and with open medical staffs. When specialized units and specialized programs without units are combined, the more likely hospital is larger, with a short length of stay, for profit, and having an open staff.

TREATMENT PROGRAMS

Hospital Treatment of Alcoholism

A report in the mid-1970s, reviewing the preceding 10 years' progress in inpatient programs, did not suggest any big change had occurred [14] and it is probable that no great change has occurred since then. The mainstay of programs is individual and group psychotherapy, alcoholism education, Alcoholics Anonymous, and

Table 2
Specialized Alcoholism Treatment Units and Programs, by Percentages, in Private Psychiatric Hospitals[a]

	Number of Respondents	Unit	Program	Program or unit
Size of hospital				
100 beds or more	72	24	32	56
Less than 100 beds	109	9	36	45
Length of stay[b]				
Under 30 days	97	15	40	55
30 days to 6 months	69	17	30	47
6 months or more	10	0	10	10
Ownership				
Proprietary	114	11	39	50
Nonprofit	67	21	25	46
Medical staff[b]				
Open	113	17	33	50
Closed	53	13	26	39
Combined	8	0	50	50
Total	181	15%	34%	49%

[a]Based on 1980 survey [16].
[b]Less than 181 because of inadequate information.

disulfiram treatment. Many programs add extras, such as conjoint and family therapy, transcendental meditation, biofeedback, and others. It is striking how little change there is in basic programs. It would be less troubling if this was a result of basic programs having demonstrated their efficacy. More probably, it reflects the dominance of craft over science that has held back the development of more effective treatments [8]. At least one author attributes this situation to Alcoholics Anonymous [24].

There is general agreement that psychiatric hospitalization is indicated when the patient has a psychiatric condition serious enough to require hospitalization irrespective of the diagnosis of alcoholism, including such conditions as psychosis, severe depression, delirium, and so forth [1]. It is also believed by many in the field that such hospitalization is also indicated to interrupt a destructive drinking pattern and/or to provide an intensive program to motivate a resistive patient [14].

The prevalence of other serious psychiatric disorders among alcoholic patients is not insignificant. Of 293 women in a detoxification center 14% had an affective disorder [20], 5% of alcoholics are estimated to be schizophrenic [25], and the suicide rate may be as high as 15% [6, 11, 26]. The 1980 survey of NAPPH hospitals [5] estimated that 55% of their alcoholic patients had a significant clinical depression, 8% a psychosis, 14% a borderline personality, and only 10% a well-integrated personality.

Treatment in Private Psychiatric Hospitals

Table 3 allows some comparison of preferred treatments in private psychiatric hospitals in 1970 [12] and in 1980 [5]. Removing occupational and recreational therapy from the 1970 survey (since they are standard for all programs), little change has occurred. In 1970, the order of treatment importance was individual and group psychotherapy (not divided), Alcoholics Anonymous, detoxification, disulfiram, and alcoholism counseling. In 1980, the order is group psychotherapy, Alcoholics Anonymous, detoxification, alcoholism education (not included in the 1970 survey), and alcoholism counseling. Disulfiram has dropped to ninth position. Marital and family therapy, not included in 1970, is now of sixth greatest importance. Thus, the surveys confirm the earlier observation that the core programs remain unchanged [14].

Table 1 allows a comparison of 1970 and 1980 reasons for lack of greater therapeutic effectiveness, though a different way of framing questions limits this comparison. In 1970, the biggest obstacles were lack of patient motivation, knowledge of etiology, and knowledge of treatment. In 1980, lack of patient motivation was again first, followed by lack of adequate follow-up (fourth in 1970) and lack of family motivation. Lack of knowledge of etiology and treatment is not empha-

**Table 3
Comparison of Preferred Treatment Approaches in Private Psychiatric Hospitals**[a]

	1970 Census ($n = 71$)	1980 Census ($n = 43$)
Group psychotherapy	97	1
Individual psychotherapy		7
Occupational therapy	95	
Recreation therapy	89	10
Alcoholics Anonymous	77	2
Detoxification	72	3
Disulfiram	71	9
Alcoholism counseling	66	5
Aversion therapy	17	13
Alcoholism education	—	4
Marital and family therapy	—	6
Diagnostic assessment	—	8
Informal peer interaction	—	11
Miscellaneous	—	12

[a] 1970 survey by percentages utilizing [12]; 1980 survey by rank order of most important [5].

sized in 1980; rather, the blame for lack of greater success is placed upon the patient and the family. Perhaps if more were known, if science had greater emphasis than craft, there would be less inclination to blame patients and families for treatment failures.

THE PRESENT AND FUTURE ROLE OF THE PRIVATE PSYCHIATRIC HOSPITAL

The Role of the Psychiatrist

Clearly, the role of the psychiatrist and the private psychiatric hospital are intertwined. If the role of either is diminished, the role of the other is equally diminished. Currently, the idea that psychiatrists have something special to offer in the continuum of services for the alcoholic patient is being seriously questioned. The psychiatrist finds himself or herself in a position of having to renegotiate his or her role with the public and other treatment providers [15]. As social model programs gain dominance, the medical model that includes the psychiatrist is threatened with loss of a position in the treatment system. Even within the medical profession itself, psychiatrists are under pressure from other physicians to give up their turf in the field of alcoholism. There is some agitation, for example, to have alcoholism classified among physical disorders rather than mental disorders [15] in the disbelief alcoholism is a mental disorder. Clearly, it is a mental disorder when alcoholism is recognized as a form of behavior under brain-mind control, whatever the complex of etiological factors that lead to the final common pathway.

In no way is this to say that alcoholism is the exclusive property of the psychiatrist. Rather, if the psychiatrist has prepared himself or herself to be an expert in the treatment of alcoholism, he or she is a valuable member of the treatment continuum. The psychiatrist does not automatically assume that mantle by completing psychiatric training; it is assumed by developing additional special skills and knowledge in such roles as the primary physician, psychotherapist, program director, program consultant, researcher, or teacher.

The Role of the Private Psychiatric Hospital

The question must be addressed whether the private psychiatric hospital has a role that differs from other hospitals, such as public hospitals, community mental health centers, general hospitals, and specialized alcoholism hospitals. With more adequate reimbursement plans, public hospitals and community mental health centers are required for a much smaller portion of the population, those not covered by some insurance plan. Most people are covered by insurance. The general hospital may be the preferred site of treatment for the alcoholic with serious, life-threatening physical illness. The alcoholism specialty hospital has the advantage of its focus not being obscured by other clinical problems, though it may provide a narrower spectrum of services and treatment approaches.

The private psychiatric hospital is available financially to the majority of the population despite discrimination in some insurance plans, such as Medicare and Medicaid. The private psychiatric hospital provides a wide range of treatment resources and plenty of space in which to utilize them. Staffing and equipment are available for most contingencies and an interdisciplinary team experienced in broad-scale treatment planning and diagnostic assessment is in place. The concept that alcoholism is a simple condition requiring a single standardized treatment plan is incorrect and a factor in the failure not to develop more effective treatment programs.

The data cited earlier about the high prevalence of serious psychiatric diagnoses existing in the alcoholic population points up a specific and unique role for the private psychiatric hospital. The otherwise mentally ill alcoholic cannot be properly treated in nonpsychiatric alcoholism treatment programs. Thus, the private psychiatric hospital becomes a specialized referral source for that proportion of alcoholic patients coming to all types of programs whose mental state makes them impossible to handle. There is growing experience that sicker alcoholics are being referred to private psychiatric hospitals.

The NAPPH Committee on Alcoholism developed a position paper in 1978 [17]. Conditions appropriate for a private psychiatric hospital were listed as follows:

1. Alcoholism occurring in conjunction with a major mental disorder requiring psychiatric hospital care
2. Alcoholism occurring in conjunction with serious medical and neurological complications requiring hospital care at the level provided in a psychiatric hospital
3. Alcoholism occurring in conjunction with a neurotic disorder or a characterological disorder best treated in a psychiatric hospital

A fourth group of patients were those who, after detoxification, have no significant medical or psychiatric illness. For these patients, nonpsychiatric hospital treatment should be adequate. It is necessary, however, to express a caveat: Will diagnostic assessment in nonpsychiatric programs be adequate to differentiate these four groups?

SUMMARY

Private psychiatric hospitals have been involved in the treatment of alcoholism for many years and members of their medical staffs have been pioneers in this field. Surveys of member hospitals of the National Association of Private Psychiatric Hospitals demonstrate no major changes between 1970 and 1980 although it would appear there has been a significant increase in the proportion of total admissions who are alcoholic. Treatment programs continue to have a basic program emphasizing group therapy, Alcoholics Anonymous, alcoholism education, and alcoholism counseling. The continued and future role of the private psychiatric hospital closely parallels the role renegotiated by the psychiatrist in this field. The private psychiatric hospital offers unique opportunities for sophisticated diagnostic assessment and treatment planning. By natural selection, it may become the resource for the alcoholic patient who is more severely impaired by other psychiatric disorders.

REFERENCES

1. American Medical Association. *Manual on Alcoholism.* Author: Chicago, 1977.
2. American Medical Association, Council on Mental Health, Committee on Alcoholism. Hospitalization of patients with alcoholism (Reports of officers). *J.A.M.A.* 162:750, 1956.
3. Connelly, J. C. Alcoholism: Clinical and research perspectives. *J. N.A.P.P.H.* 9:37–40, 1978.
4. Connelly, J. C. Current issues in the hospital treatment of alcoholism: The role of the alcoholism counsellor. *J. N.A.P.P.H.* 10:32–34, 1979.
5. Connelly, J. C., and Wilson, G. F. Unpublished data, 1980.
6. Goodwin, D. W. Alcohol in suicide and homicide. *Q. J. Stud. Alcohol* 34:144–156, 1973.
7. Horman, R. Alcoholism: A legislative prospective. *J. N.A.P.P.H.* 9:33–36, 1978.
8. Kalb, M., and Propper, M. S. The future of alcohology: Craft or science? *Am. J. Psychiatry* 133:641–645, 1976.
9. Knight, R. The dynamics and treatment of chronic alcohol addiction. *Bull. Menninger Clin.* 1:233–250, 1937.
10. Menninger, K. *Man Against Himself.* Harcourt, Brace: New York, 1938.
11. Miles, D. P. Conditions predisposing to suicide: A review. *J. Nerv. Men. Dis.* 164:231–246, 1977.
12. Moore, R. A. Alcoholism treatment in private psychiatric hospitals. *Q. J. Stud. Alcohol* 32:1083–1075, 1971.
13. Moore, R. A. The diagnosis of alcoholism in a psychiatric hospital: A trial of the Michigan Alcoholism Screening Test (MAST). *Am. J. Psychiatry* 128:1565–1569, 1972.
14. Moore, R. A. Ten years of inpatient programs for alcoholic patients. *Am. J. Psychiatry* 134:542–545, 1977.
15. Moore, R. A. The psychiatrist and the treatment of alcoholism. In: *Current Psychiatric Therapies* (Vol. 20), Masserman, J. H. (ed.). Grune & Stratton: New York. In press.
16. National Association of Private Psychiatric Hospitals. *Directory of Member Hospitals.* Author: Washington, D.C., 1980.
17. National Association of Private Psychiatric Hospitals, Task Force on Alcoholism. *Position Paper on Alcoholism.* Unpublished manuscript, 1979.
18. Neuman, C. P. Prognostic factors in the evaluation of addicted individuals. *J. N.A.P.P.H.* 3:12–16, 1971.

19. Redick, R. W. *Utilization of Psychiatric Facilities by Persons Diagnosed with Alcohol Disorders* (National Institute of Mental Health Statistics, Series B, Number 4; DHEW Publication 73-9114). U.S. Government Printing Office: Washington, D.C., 1973.

20. Schuckit, M. A., and Morrissey, E. R. Psychiatric problems in women admitted to an alcoholic detoxification center. *Am. J. Psychiatry* 136:611-617, 1979.

21. Strecher, E. A. Chronic alcoholism: A psychological survey. *Q. J. Stud. Alcohol* 2:12-17, 1941.

22. Stubblefield, R. L. Synopsis: Multidimensional problems of alcoholism. *J. N.A.P.P.H.* 9:31-32, 1978.

23. Taylor, I. J. The mask of alcoholism. *J. N.A.P.P.H.* 8:31-35, 1976.

24. Tournier, R. W. Alcoholics Anonymous as treatment and as idealogy. *J. Stud. Alcohol* 40:230-239, 1979.

25. Winokur, G., Reich, T., Rimmer, J., and Pitts, F. N. Diagnosis and familial psychiatric illness in 259 alcoholic probands: III. Alcoholism. *Arch. Gen. Psychiatry* 23:104-111, 1970.

26. Woodruff, R. A., Clayton, P. J., and Guze, S. B. Suicide attempts and psychiatric diagnosis. *Dis. Nerv. Sys.* 33:617-621, 1972.

27. Yoerg, R. The role of private psychiatric hospitals in providing alcoholism services. *J. N.A.P.P.H.* 4:9-13, 1972.

71

ROBERT F. STUCKEY, MD, Fair Oaks Hospital, Summit, New Jersey
JOSEPH S. HARRISON, MDiv, CAC, Fair Oaks Hospital, Summit, New Jersey

THE ALCOHOLISM REHABILITATION CENTER

THIS CHAPTER IS WRITTEN in the language characteristic of the rehabilitation center movement. The authors share the opinion predominant in rehabilitation centers that alcoholism is a separate, permanent, and distinct disorder with an essential or acquired biological basis. At this time, there is no biological solution for alcoholism. Thus, rehabilitation consists of methods and techniques used to effect a massive change in life style, from an old reward system using chemically induced highs, to a new one based on spiritual values and relationships. There is (1) a room with no exit, (2) emotional pain, (3) the removal of an old support system, and (4) the provision of a new one. A typical rehabilitation center is a residential therapeutic community of recovering alcoholics sharing experiences and feelings in a chemical-free environment. The average minimum stay is approximately 28 days.

Robert F. Stuckey, MD, Medical Director, Alcohol Rehabilitation Unit, Fair Oaks Hospital, and Fair Oaks–South, Summit, New Jersey.

Joseph S. Harrison, MDiv, CAC, Program Director, Alcohol Rehabilitation Unit, Fair Oaks Hospital, Summit, New Jersey.

HISTORICAL DEVELOPMENT

Modern rehabilitation from alcoholism began with the advent of Alcoholics Anonymous (AA) in the mid-1930s. This organization produced a subculture of recovered alcoholics who were of one voice in rejecting the prevailing view of alcoholism as a symptom of underlying psychological problems. From the beginning, they insisted that there was a permanent change in the alcoholic's biochemistry, and that abstinence was the only reasonable approach to recovery. They rejected both will power and insight as the essential force for change, and developed a group-oriented program that depended on power outside of the self. They depended on each other and on spiritual resources that could be collectively utilized. The latter was systematized into the 12 steps of recovery.

From the beginning of this movement through the 1950s and 1960s, the health care community resisted the AA philosophy and recovery rates remained low. As a result, there was continued rejection of the alcoholic by the mainstream of health care facilities. Thus, there emerged in the late 1940s numerous shared recovery centers. They were usually operated by a recovered person or a couple who had an outstanding following in the sober community. Many times these programs began in the homes of the leaders. As time passed, they began to boast of a recovery rate of over 60% (based on abstinence for 1 year). These programs were centered around the 12 steps of AA, as well as the written material sanctioned by AA.

Shared recovery programs tended to take on characteristics of the leader. They were oftentimes somewhat dictatorial, rigid, or excessively religious, depending upon the personality of the central figure. These programs were largely didactic and meditative in nature. They worked to develop a new life style based on the attitudes and philosophy of AA. For many years, these centers were the most available resource for the alcoholic and his or her family and were the backbone of the rehabilitation movement. By the 1960s, new capabilities in the area of mental health opened up new possibilities for recovery centers. These included the therapeutic communities for sociopaths begun by Maxwell Jones, the concept of roles from psychodrama, transactional analysis, and Gestalt therapy, and the concepts of system theory. All of these new therapeutic innovations began to emphasize the power of the group. Reality therapy and behavior therapy emphasized responsible behavior within the group context as a source of change. There developed greater reliance on lay leaders and less reliance on the physician. These therapies were practiced and systematized in the community mental health movement stimulated by President Kennedy in 1961. But in the mid-70s, the mental health movement and the AA community began to potentiate each other. This was catalyzed by the Joint Commission on Accreditation of Hospitals' accrediting process. Mental health professionals saw the group as the context of change and AA saw the group as the source of change.

As the rate of recoveries increased and the net of AA aftercare was in place throughout the United States, there arose in the 1970s medical-psychiatric treatment units that were attached to psychiatric hospitals or under the psychiatric or medical service of an acute care hospital. These units tended to be more professional. The programs reflected a union between psychiatry, psychology, general medicine, and social work. In most cases, a psychiatrist or internist was the primary therapist, with emphasis and therapy directed toward underlying conflicts and depression. Minor tranquilizers and other sedatives were often used as an adjunct therapy. AA meetings were usually available, but the degree of importance of these varied widely.

By the mid 1970s, this medical model and the shared recovery center mode of treatment began moving toward each other. The latter began using more medical services, adding detoxification units, and taking a serious interest in the physical and emotional wellbeing of their clients. They also became more professional in their counseling skills, moving from a guru style in which the leader was the fountain of recovery, to a therapeutic community style. Many of the medical-psychiatric models began to see the potency of the shared recovery units and added stronger AA components, modified their use of habit-forming medication, and employed a disease concept approach to treatment. In addition, the trained alcoholism counselor became the primary therapist. Today, most rehabilitation centers, regardless of their origins, are a blend of these historic movements.

ESSENTIAL COMPONENTS

There is ongoing growth and development of the typical rehabilitation program utilizing the following key ingredients:

1. Strong AA orientation
2. Skilled alcoholism counselors as primary therapists
3. Psychological testing and psychosocial evaluations
4. Medical and psychiatric support for coexisting problems
5. Therapists trained in systematized methods of treatment, including Gestalt, psychodrama, reality therapy, transactional analysis, behavior therapy, activity therapy, and stress management
6. Use of therapeutic community and crisis intervention
7. Systems therapy, especially with employers and later including a strong family component
8. Family- and peer-oriented aftercare

THE KEY TO REHABILITATION

Valliant [3] has described the rehabilitation process in terms of the well-known psychoanalytic mechanism of defense. He describes a combination of identification, reinforcement, sublimation, reaction formation, altruism, new love objects, and a substitute compulsion. This is a comprehensive and accurate view, but these authors prefer to use the language of rehabilitation. Tiebout [2] described the essential character structure of the alcoholic, no matter how well disguised, as a narcissistic egocentric core with feelings of omnipotence. Some summarize this character as a "defiant individuality." The present authors believe this character uniformly coexists with addiction whether as antecedent or stigmata.

Protecting the availability of chemically induced highs becomes the ultimate priority of the alcoholic and he or she must be omnipotent master of his or her fate at all costs. For protection of this identity the alcoholic develops a delusional level of denial, a genuine self-deception. He or she conceptualizes the problem, then, as lying outside the self and resists with primitive rage all efforts to break this denial.

The traditional psychotherapeutic techniques have relied on insight and intellect (mental processes more or less controllable) to effect change in the core character structure of the alcoholic. The alcoholic's wall of denial has successfully resisted all attempts at a resynthesis by this route.

AA and recovery centers, on the other hand, have sought to directly foster an emotional upheaval of the ego's center. William James, in his book *Varieties of Religious Experience,* coined this transformation as "ego deflation at depth" [1]. The mystics call it "being grounded" or "centered down."

Treatment centers utilizing recovered alcoholics and other professionals provide a carrot-and-stick motivation to the active alcoholic. He or she is offered the obvious hope and encouragement from the models of success presented. If possible, the support systems that have enabled his or her drinking are cut off. Unlike techniques of traditional therapies, the alcoholic is not encouraged to look within the self for strength. Rather, his or her sense of failure and pain are intensified by confrontation and life review. The recovered alcoholic therapists are not conned by tangential discussions of coexisting internal and external problems. The alcoholic is allowed no escape from the paradox that his or her drinking is the primary problem, that he or she must take responsibility for this, and yet within the self there lies no defense against the next drink. The alcoholic cannot drink and cannot quit drinking. He or she is pressured into hopelessness in himself or herself and the old support systems. An alcoholic's rage-charged denial is ineffective against a recovered therapist. The patient is asked to accept guidance, help, and control from a source outside himself or herself and is given no alternative.

In most cases he or she accepts this support from peers and their source of power, usually conceived as a loving God.

Pragmatically, it has been found that this surrender or turnaround brings the resynthesis of the ego from the core narcissism to an ego integrated with proper object relations. Patients describe it as feeling together or having peace of mind, but most importantly they note that with the loss of egocentricity is the desired loss of the compulsion to drink.

Many other changes of attitudes, feeling, and behavior often occur automatically and simultaneously with the surrender to predecessors, peers, and a higher power. These changes include loss of loneliness, guilt, shame, confusion, defensiveness, self-pity, resentment, grandiosity, manipulativeness, sociopathy, cynicism, depression, and despair. In place of these there develops openness, optimism, an ability to befriend others, and laughter.

To summarize the turnaround, alcoholics love to recover once they know they have absolutely no alternative.

Case Example

A.W. was a high-ranking police official from a large suburban area. He was sent by his city under strong job jeopardy to seek treatment. His wife was in the process of divorcing him and he was showing signs of deep depression. Initially, he felt that the only way he could recover was if his wife would return and he could have some guarantee that all would be well. Guarantees were not forthcoming. The spouse did agree to participate in the family program along with the children and postpone any permanent decision, pending his abstinence and recovery. His job was available only on the condition of following all aftercare plans, including abstinence. After several days of struggle and confrontation by a loving peer group, he stated, "I know I can't do it myself, and I want to get better regardless of what my family does," implying the breakthrough toward a turnaround. He accepted alcoholism as his problem and that he needed a support group. He then began to accept direction from others. An apartment was secured for him after discharge. Negotiations were made with the spouse and at a joint family conference, she reaffirmed her desire to live separately for the foreseeable future. A means of communication was established by agreement, and aftercare and AA commitments were clearly understood. The final phase of the turnaround was reached as he dropped his resentment of the changes and engaged in the guided commitments cheerfully. After a year of sober living, the family is reunited and quality of life and work much improved.

It must be emphasized that all these transformations are based on emotional upheaval and are short-lived if not integrated with intellect, insight behavior, priorities, values, and life style. Many hours of rehabilitation and years of AA aftercare are provided as a form of reinforcement and integration of this emotionally based change. There is also the magically effective reinforcer synonymous with the recovery subculture, that is, helping other alcoholics. This alone prevents return to core narcissism in many agnostic alcoholics.

THE FAMILY COMPONENT

It becomes apparent in treating the alcoholic that the family also suffers. Their involvement with the feelings and behavior of the alcoholic produce a loss of self-awareness and self-actualization. Some type of treatment is clearly indicated. Current programs for family members at Fair Oaks Hospital begin before or while the alcoholic is in rehabilitation and continue for a minimum of 3 months afterward. Many programs offer residential care.

Presently, families are seen as addicted to the alcoholic in much the same way the alcoholic is addicted to alcoholism. They have to be taught to find a new resource within themselves, to find a peer group, and to stop reacting to and attempting to control the alcoholic. Teaching them this type of healthy selfishness is the only way to interrupt their addiction and their enabling role in the abnormal system. Returning the rehabilitated alcoholic to an untreated family is to seriously lower the probability of recovery. Family programs combine didactic sessions and shared common experiences of recovery in group therapy centering around "here and now" feelings. Programs should provide a wide spectrum of opportunities for families to be copatients. Family members are slow to accept their own addiction and the coexisting denial of their inner-feeling world, although they progress faster than the toxic alcoholic once the denial is broken down. Family therapy in the area of addition is one of the current growing parameters of the rehabilitation movement. It remains largely a peer-oriented, separate track from the alcoholic rather than conjoint therapy.

EMPLOYER INVOLVEMENT

The greatest motivating force known in alcohol rehabilitation is job jeopardy. This is true not only for those entering treatment, but for those in continuing aftercare and later recovery. The patients at Fair Oaks Hospital have only a 20% relapse rate if the employer is involved, but they have a 40% relapse rate if they are secretive with their employer. A back-to-work conference with the employee assistance counselor (and, it is hoped, supervisor, shop steward, and occasionally the family) is the single most important hour in treatment in the experience of the authors. It secures the most effective commitment to abstinence and aftercare that can be facilitated.

In the work place, the alcoholic's supervisor and coworkers (often codrinkers) are as ambivalent with anger and guilt as are the family. Their anger and negative feelings are justifiable. Good rehabilitation must provide some resolution of these issues, or there is little chance of an improved work situation for either the alcoholic or coworker, even if the drinking ceases.

SOME KEY INGREDIENTS IN THE REHABILITATION PROCESS

Education

The term "disease concept" is taught to embrace the entire disorder, with its signs, symptoms, and progressive characteristics. It is a very necessary aspect of rehabilitation to provide the patient with an understandable concept of what has happened to him or her, and to also address the issue of its permanent nature and its inevitable progression toward destruction and death. Knowledge of the nature and consequences of the illness makes abstinence logical. It reduces the guilt, confusion, and self-doubts that have plagued the alcoholic who has never known why he or she was such a failure. The disease concept communicates hope in a way that no psychological theory can. It implies that only one part of the self is disabled and the healthy parts will thrive if the alcoholic separates himself or herself from alcohol and mind-altering drugs.

Education is also important for teaching the recovery language of the sober subculture. This allows the alcoholic to participate in its signs, symbols, values, priorities, and traditions. This facilitates comfortable entry into the community of AA.

Small Group Therapy

The authors believe that recovery is a team sport and loners rarely obtain sobriety. The heart of the rehabilitation process takes place in small groups. The group provides, through its love and support, a safe place for emotional openness that can be duplicated in the AA community. The weakness of one-to-one counseling is that self-disclosure remains a private affair, and the counselor becomes too central a figure. One of the hazards of leading a patient to a state of surrender of self-will is that the patient can become the easy prey of a charismatic leader. This has often happened in religious movements, and indeed was the downfall of the Oxford movement, from which AA sprang; it was disastrously documented in mass suicides in Guyana. Groups should emphasize here-and-now openness of all feelings and thoughts. They should also be characterized by self-disclosure of the leader and alternating confrontation and support from peers. The group is centered around the commitment to abstinence and the need for emotional dependence on other recovering people. It is hoped that a patient learns to never be alone with a painful emotion such as guilt and fear. He or she learns to identify these feelings, to communicate them, and then to replace them with an experience of support or intimacy. This tool is learned in treatment for lifelong availability, particularly in AA. Patients also come to experience that the wisdom of a combined peer group is most often superior to a single trained therapist.

Medical and Psychiatric Evaluation and Intervention

Because of the unique role accorded to the physician in this culture as an authoritarian voice in all matters of health, it is very important to have a physician who can support openly the philosophy of rehabilitation as it is outlined in this chapter.

Yet, there must be accurate diagnosis and treatment of coexisting mental illness. Many rehabilitation centers still deny the existence of primary emotional and mental problems among their patients. The results have been far too many suicides and psychotic episodes that could be successfully treated. The high rates of 2-year recovery advertised by rehabilitation centers is dependent upon careful diagnosis and treatment of coexisting medical and psychiatric disorders, yet emphasizing abstinence from habit-forming drugs.

Patients should have a reliable psychological screening evaluation. It may uncover serious psychopathology in about 20% of patients. In most cases, however, it only reassures the patient that he or she is not crazy, that any abnormal behavior was the result of the addiction. Psychological screening is, therefore, a useful tool to cut off routes of escape in rationalization. It keeps the alcoholic from hiding behind an unfounded suspicion of mental illness and forces him or her to accept the primary nature of the addictive disease. These screening devices can also assess the level of organicity or toxicity and aid in appropriate treatment planning.

Aftercare

Within the rehabilitative process, the three following steps must also be included:

1. The recovering person needs to learn new behavior.
2. New behavior needs to be practiced with fellow patients in a controlled environment.
3. Following the return to the community, there must be some means of evaluating new behavior.

Most treatment modalities have adequate training in new behavior and most have opportunities for practicing that new behavior in a controlled environment. However, successful rehabilitation must include some way to monitor early recovery. This is best accomplished in small groups of patients who have shared the same inpatient recovery experience. Centers who admit from a wide geographic area have greater trouble with this vital phase of treatment.

Formal aftercare should be a commitment and extend a minimum of 8 weeks after discharge. Many rehabilitation centers have extensive aftercare up to 2 years and others have patients return for week-long refresher periods during early sobriety. The debate about the length of formal aftercare revolves around developing an overreliance of the patient on the treatment center.

The backbone of true aftercare support, however, is AA. There was no epidemic of treatment centers until the AA support network was in place and effective throughout the country. Rehabilitation centers using AA aftercare uniformly report that better than 80% of their clients are not drinking at a point 2 years after treatment.

It is the authors' opinion that as new rehabilitation centers are opened and as existing ones are strengthened, they will continue to merge the best of AA and shared recovery systems with the best that is available from the scientific disciplines. The future holds promise for better diagnosis and treatment of coexisting mental and physical disorders and for the subclassification of alcoholism. Finally, it is the authors' belief that there is a growing acceptance of life style change as a path to recovery.

REFERENCES

1. James, W. *The Varieties of Religious Experience*. Longmans: London, 1912.
2. Tiebout, H. Alcoholics Anonymous: An experiment of nature. *Q. J. Stud. Alcohol* 22: 52–68, 1961.
3. Valliant, G. *Personal Lectures*. Papers presented at Northeastern Psychiatric Seminars, Boston, 1981.

72

JAMES W. SMITH, MD, Schick Shadel Hospital, Seattle, Washington

TREATMENT OF ALCOHOLISM IN AVERSION CONDITIONING HOSPITALS

THIS CHAPTER FOCUSES primarily on the techniques and outcomes of inpatient alcoholism treatment facilities using aversion conditioning as a major therapeutic modality. At the present there are 16 hospitals in the United States that meet this criterion, three Schick Shadel Hospitals and 13 Raleigh Hills Hospitals. Other hospitals also use aversion conditioning as part of their program.

AVERSION CONDITIONING

Aversion conditioning in general includes pairing a stimulus (e.g., the sight, smell, or taste of an alcoholic beverage) associated with an unwanted behavior e.g., drinking alcoholic beverages) with a noxious (aversive) stimulus (e.g., nausea or electric stimulus). This pairing is designed to associate the aversive stimulus with the formerly pleasant stimulus (sight, smell, and taste of alcoholic beverages) to such a degree that the unwanted behavior (drinking alcohol) is eliminated.

Agras [1] in commenting on behavior change methodologies notes that some unwanted behaviors can be reduced in frequency or completely eliminated, either by reinforcing competing adaptive behaviors or by using extinction procedures. At other times, as in the case of self-destructive behaviors, it is necessary to

---

James W. Smith, MD, Executive Director, Schick Shadel Hospital, Seattle, Washington.

bring behavior under control rapidly, which is not usually possible with reinforcement or extinction procedures. In such cases aversive procedures are applicable.

Three major paradigms for the use of aversive procedures are available. The first is that of classical conditioning, in which the aversive stimulus is paired with elements of the unwanted behavior (such as the sight or smell of an alcoholic beverage). The second is that of punishment, where the behavior (drinking alcoholic beverages) is followed by the aversive stimulus. The third procedure is avoidance training, in which the person avoids punishment by avoiding or rapidly discontinuing the unwanted behavior (e.g., by pushing away the glass of alcoholic beverage) before the aversive stimulus is given. In clinical practice, most treatment facilities that use aversive procedures employ a combination of these three paradigms.

History

Aversive conditioning is perhaps the oldest approach to abstinence-oriented alcoholism treatment. The ancient Romans placed spiders or other repellent objects in the bottom of the wine cup to be discovered by the drinker after draining the vessel. In more modern times Kantorovich [11] gave one of the first reports on the use of aversion conditioning using electrical stimulation.

In the United States, in 1935, Charles Shadel [16] founded the hospital system that still bears his name (now Schick Shadel Hospitals). He and Voegtlin [20] developed a pharmacologic aversion technique that still forms the basis of treatment at the Schick Shadel Hospitals and at the Raleigh Hills Hospitals. The first Shadel Hospital was founded in Seattle, Washington. In 1943, Shadel opened a second hospital in the Raleigh Hills section of Portland, Oregon. This was later sold and formed the basis of the present Raleigh Hills Hospital system.

Therapeutic Techniques

Although aversive conditioning was originally, and still is, a major factor in treatment, both hospital systems employ other therapeutic modalities as well. In order to show the similarities and differences more clearly each hospital program is discussed separately.

SCHICK SHADEL HOSPITAL TREATMENT

Emetine Aversion

In 1940 Voegtlin [20] first reported on the techniques in which emetine-induced nausea was paired with the sight, taste, and smell of a variety of alcoholic beverages (with emphasis placed on the patient's preferred beverage). Emphasis was also placed on the temporal relationship between the unconditioned stimulus (nausea) and the conditioned stimuli (sight, smell, and taste of alcoholic beverages). The value of a treatment is vitiated if drinking is delayed until after the onset of nausea [13]; the later situation would lead to backward conditioning, which Frank [6, 7] calls a most difficult form of conditioning to develop and a form easily extinguished. In fact, Elkins [3] suggested that backward conditioning, since it pairs alcohol with decreasing nausea, could actually increase the reward value of the alcohol.

The usual treatment session involves having the patient take nothing except clear liquids by mouth for 6 hours prior to treatment. This reduces the likelihood of aspiration of solid stomach contents during treatment. The patient, after receiving a full explanation of the treatment procedure, is taken to the treatment room, which is small in size and has shelves containing all types of alcoholic beverages along the walls. It also has cutouts of various liquor ads on the walls. The intent is to have the majority of the patient's visual stimuli associated with alcoholic beverages and visual cues for drinking. The patient is then seated in a comfortable chair with an attached large emesis basin. He receives an injection containing the emetic agent, emetine, (see Voegtlin [20] for details). The emetic effect begins in approximately 5 to 8 minutes. Prior to that time the patient is given two 10 oz glasses of warm water with a small amount of added salt. The water provides a volume of easily vomited material, while the salt content tends to counteract the excessive loss of electrolytes during the procedure. Shortly before the expected onset of nausea the nurse administering the treatment pours a drink of the patient's preferred alcoholic beverage and mixes it with an equal amount of warm water. The patient is then instructed to smell the beverage and to take a small mouthful, swish it around in the mouth to get the full flavor ot it, and then to spit it out into the basin. This "sniff, swish, and spit" phase is designed to insure that the patient has well-defined visual, olfactory, and gustatory sensations associated with the preferred beverage prior to the onset of the aversive stimulus of nausea. The nausea and vomiting ensue shortly thereafter and the procedure is altered to that of "sniff, swish, and swallow." The alcoholic beverage swallowed is shortly returned as emesis so that no significant amount of alcohol is retained to be absorbed, an event that would negate the treatment. After an intensive conditioning session in the treatment room lasting 20 to 30 minutes the patient is returned to the hospital room, where 30 minutes later another drink of alcoholic beverage is given containing an oral dose of emetine, which induces a slower acting residual nausea lasting up to 3 hours.

The average patient receives 5 aversion treatments encompassing approximately 15 hours of aversive conditioning during the initial 10-day intensive treatment phase. The treatments are usually administered on an alternate day basis with a pentothal interview administered on the nonaversion treatment day (e.g., day 1 aversion treatment, day 2 pentothal interview, day 3 aversion treatment, etc.).

Some patients develop adequate aversion in only three treatments, while others require six or more [17]. The medical staff determines the adequacy of aversion by the response of the patient in the treatment room and his or her own hospital room afterward as well as by questioning the patient under pentothal the following day (see below for details of the pentothal interview).

Although the patient's preferred beverages are emphasized in each treatment session, aversion does not generalize to all alcoholic beverages (e.g., if only bourbon whiskey was used for treatment the patient would have no aversion to Scotch). Therefore, the patient receives all types of alcoholic beverages sometime during the treatment process. Carbonated beverages are never mixed with the alcohol and ice is never added, as both are associated with appropriate nonalcohol-containing drinks. Also, both tend to diminish the sensations of odor and taste of the alcoholic beverage and are thus contraindicated during treatment. On the contrary, warm water is often mixed with the beverage to be conditioned against in order to bring out the odor and flavor more strongly.

Purpose

The purpose of aversion conditioning is two-fold. First, sufficient aversion must be developed so that the patient is granted a period of time free of active craving for alcohol, a period during which there is an opportunity to reorient his or her life in a way that does not contain alcohol. Second, the treatment tends to break down conditioned reflexes to drink. Most social drinkers going out to dinner may automatically call for a drink; for others playing poker automatically calls for a drink, and so forth. The alcoholic usually has these normal conditioned responses to take a drink and many more: getting angry may call for a drink, 5 o'clock may call for a drink, getting home from work may call for a drink, and the like. When adequate aversion is achieved, these past associations are no longer present. Descriptions of the treatment [17] emphasize that the experience is different from a hangover in that the aversive stimulus (nausea) is presented simultaneously with alcoholic beverages in order to achieve the counterconditioning. In contrast, the hangover occurs the morning after at a time too remote to develop a conditioned aversion. In fact, as Elkins [3] suggests, if alcohol is used to relieve the hangover the reward value of alcohol is enhanced and the person may be conditioned to take a drink by the hangover (instead of conditioned to avoid it).

These same descriptions [17] also emphasize that the treatment does not make it impossible to drink since one could deliberately break down even a high level of aversion by drinking an alcoholic beverage (even if much was later vomited) repeatedly until a significant amount had been retained and absorbed. The euphoriant effect of the absorbed alcohol would rapidly eliminate the conditioned aversion response so that the patient could once more drink without nausea. The procedure instead is intended to make it possible to not drink, that is, to eliminate the urges to consume alcohol and thus lead to a comfortable sobriety.

Since this type of pharmacologic aversion treatment is relatively physically demanding, not all patients are suitable candidates. Upon admission to the hospital each patient receives a comprehensive physical evaluation by the medical director. Upon detoxification of the patient [18] the medical director designs the treatment program based on the patient's physical condition and laboratory findings. The patients who are not candidates for emetine aversion therapy are assigned to faradic aversion therapy instead.

Faradic Aversion Therapy

Faradic (electrical stimulation) aversive therapy was instituted at Schick Shadel Hospital in 1970 because of the perceived need for a less physically strenuous aversive technique and because various studies [2, 9, 14, 22] indicated potential usefullness of this technique in alcoholism treatment. The patient is assigned to the faradic therapy modality only after the attending physician determines that he or she is either physically or emotionally unable to tolerate the emetine aversion procedure. The chemical aversion method is treatment of first choice because it has a long history of successful use at the hospital. In addition, Garcia and Ervin [8] showed that gustatory and olfactory stimuli are specifically and rapidly associated with visceral states (e.g., nausea); cutaneous stimuli (e.g., shock) are more rapidly and specifically associated with visual cues. Therefore, on theoretical grounds nausea should be a more effective aversive stimulus in eliminating alcohol consumption [10].

The faradic aversion technique also involves five individual treatment sessions. During each session a pair of electrodes is attached to the forearm of the dominant hand and placed approximately 2 in (0.05 dm) apart. The electrodes are attached to an electrostimulus machine capable of delivering 1 to 20 mA (AC) (constant current). The faradic therapist runs an ascending series of test stimuli to determine the level perceived as aversive by the patient on that particular day (there is a relatively wide variance between patients and within the same individual from day to day).

The treatment paradigm [10] consists of pairing an aversive level of electrostimulation with the sight, smell, and taste of alcoholic beverages. At the direction of the therapist (forced choice trial) the patient reaches for a bottle of an alcoholic beverage, pours some of it in a glass and tastes it without swallowing. Electrostimulus onset occurs randomly throughout the entire behavior continuum from reaching for the bottle through tasting the alcoholic beverage. The number of electrostimuli with each trial vary from one to eight.

An additional 10 free choice trials are designed so that the patient is negatively reinforced with removal of the aversive stimulus if he or she selects a nonalcoholic choice such as fruit juice.

The patient is instructed to not swallow alcohol at any time throughout the faradic session, and this behavior is closely monitored by the therapist to insure compliance. If the patient should swallow alcohol more than twice during the treatment (a rare occurrence) the session is terminated. A completed faradic aversion session lasts from 20 to 45 minutes, depending on selection speed of the individual patient. The total time of exposure to aversive conditioning is no more than 4 hours during the initial 10-day course of treatment.

Reinforcement Treatment

Both the emetine and faradic aversion method include two reinforcement conditioning sessions, the first at 30 days and the second at 90 days after the initial 10-day treatment.

Pentothal Interview

In the mid-1940s the technique of the pentothal interview was introduced into the Schick Shadel Hospital treatment program [19]. The patient receives five of these pentothal interviews in addition to five aversion treatments. He or she also receives one pentothal interview on each of the scheduled admissions for reinforcement treatment at 30 days and 90 days.

Although the procedure is generally referred to as a "pentothal interview" the medication used is a mixture of equal parts of sodium thiopental and sodium amytal diluted to a concentration of 0.3% in normal saline. This mixture is administered by slow intravenous drip at a rate that keeps the patient in a deeply sedated state just short of sleep. The interview is conducted in this state.

The average patient receives between 300 mg to 400 mg of each drug during the 20- to 40-minute interview. The amount given varies greatly depending on the size and tolerance of each individual. However, if administered in the manner described an overdosage is easily avoided. Although the patient is not taken to the deep level of sedation common to surgery, he or she is prepared for the treatment in much the same way as if it were presurgery. That is, a 5-hour fast is required and premedication with atropine is administered in dosages similar to those used preoperatively. At the conclusion of the interview the patient receives a small additional dose of the "pentothal," which deepens the sedation to the point where light sleep is attained.

The patient may sleep anywhere from 15 minutes to several hours after the interview. Many have the erroneous impression that the longer they sleep the better the treatment. However, since the drugs are metabolized relatively rapidly those patients who sleep for several hours are sleeping on their own for the majority of that time. Furthermore, the objective is not sleep but the attainment of a state of relaxation sufficient to enable the patient to talk freely and to bring out any emotional or environmental factors that may be contributing to the drinking problem. During the pentothal interview patients are less likely to block material that is in some way unpleasant to them. This facilitates obtaining information sufficient to make a psychiatric diagnosis in a relatively brief time (four or five interviews) instead of the weeks or months that are often required using conventional interviewing techniques [19]. Pentothal interviews should not be equated with intensive psychotherapy since they are intended only to facilitate the discussion of personal problems or situations that may contribute to drinking.

Treatment Adjuncts

In addition to the somewhat dramatic treatment elements of aversion conditioning and pentothal interviews, each patient participates in an educational program with lectures concerning the physiology of alcohol addiction, the physical and psychological effects of heavy drinking, and so forth. The emphasis is on the goal of achieving a life free from alcohol (and other drugs). Relaxation training techniques are also taught in order to provide a suitable drug-free method of dealing with tension. Each patient also participates in group and individual counseling sessions and has a psychiatric evaluation from the hospital consulting psychiatrist. The psychiatric evaluation is based largely on material obtained from the pentothal interviews. Patients found to have significant psychopathology (approximately 20%) are referred for appropriate care after completing their alcoholism treatment [19].

Aftercare

The hospital also maintains an organized Aftercare Department where an individualized aftercare plan is developed in consultation with the patient and (when possible) family and significant others. The aftercare counselor then makes any referrals agreed upon (e.g., AA, marriage counseling, vocational training, etc.) and maintains contact for up to 2 years posttreatment.

Results of Treatment

The first published report of the results of this treatment was a study by Voegtlin [20] in which he reported 64% of 538 patients remained abstinent for 4 years or longer. Subsequent studies have reported rather similar results [10, 12, 21].

A comparison of the emetine aversion treatment and faradic aversion treatment reported virtually identical abstinence rates for the two groups 2 years after treatment [10]. Two subsequent unpublished studies support this original observation [4, 5].

RALEIGH HILLS HOSPITAL

History

In 1942 a second Shadel Hospital was opened in the Raleigh Hills area in Portland, Oregon. The treatment methodology used at that hospital was the same as initially used at the Seattle Shadel Hospital [16, 20]. This hospital was later sold and eventually became the foundation for the Raleigh Hills Hospital system, which now contains 13 hospitals in 6 states.

Emetine Aversion

After detoxification and medical evaluation the typical patient is placed in the treatment room in which the windows are blacked out and the walls are set up as in a bar, with different forms of alcoholic beverages exhibited on the shelves around the patient. After the treatment nurse explains the treatment and its expected effects, the patient, as in Shadel's treatment paradigm, receives an intramuscular injection containing the emetic agent emetine. This is followed by drinking a glass of warm water and, near the onset of nausea, drinks of alcoholic beverages. The first treatment usually includes five or six drinks. The second treatment (on day 3, following a day of rest) involves a similar procedure except the number of drinks given is doubled from the first treatment. Patients usually receive five such treatments with a day of rest in between. By the fifth treatment they may receive as many as 20 drinks during the treatment session [23].

The patient is usually discharged at the end of a 10-day treatment program (postdetoxification) and returns for periodic reinforcement treatments. The single-day reinforcement session is usually a somewhat abbreviated session modeled on the fifth treatment. The length of time until the first reinforcement varies with the apparent conditioning of the patient, and the general consensus of the physician and other staff regarding the degree of conditioning, patient attitudes, and other prognostic factors. The first reinforcement treatment is usually at 1 to 2 weeks following initial discharge. Additional dates are tailored to the needs of the patient over the succeeding year. Each patient receives six such treatments but fewer or more may be given depending on the individual and the circumstances [23]. Upon discharge it is emphasized that patients are welcome to come to the hospital for reinforcement treatment or to simply stay overnight without further cost for the remainder of their life as long as they do not return to drinking alcohol. This policy is regarded as a safety mechanism to avoid relapse, since patients are made to feel welcome at any time they should experience an urge to drink [23].

Education and Counseling

Patients participate in informal group therapy. Psychiatric consultation is available on a selective basis and those requiring ongoing psychiatric therapy are referred to resources in their home areas. Each patient attends a round table session with the medical director that includes the medical aspects of alcohol addiction. A second round table is held by the staff psychologist, who deals with behavioral and psychological issues. A third roundtable is held with the counselor, who addresses issues related to attaining sobriety through the aversion method.

In addition to these educational sessions the treatment team (medical director, director of nurses, staff psychologist, alcoholism counselor, and aftercare coordinator) assesses the needs of the patient and develops an individualized treatment and aftercare plan. Appropriate referral is made for additional additional help (e.g., assertiveness training, marriage counseling, etc.) and the aftercare program is updated at the time of each reinforcement treatment. Emphasis is placed on the need for permanent abstinence. Family and significant others are encouraged to participate in the educational and treatment planning process.

Patients also receive meditation instruction and relaxation training using a biofeedback apparatus that monitors tension, the electromyogram (EMG). These procedures are undertaken in an attempt to give patients a suitable drug-free method of dealing with tension.

TREATMENT RESULTS

Wiens et al. [23] reported that 63% of 261 patients receiving emetine aversion reported they were abstinent from alcohol for the 1 year between treatment and follow-up. Other studies [15] show similar results.

ETHICAL CONSIDERATIONS

Aversion conditioning sometimes comes under attack as a treatment modality because it involves deliberately causing acute discomfort for the patient, an act that is repugnant to most people, particularly those in the helping professions. However, in alcoholism one must consider the alternative. Continued drinking or multiple relapses all too often lead to death or at least permanent disability as well as dissolution of family and other important social ties. To undertake a course of action (or inaction) that does not rescue the person from this potentially lethal situation is to hurt that person much more severely. As noted earlier [1] in cases of self-destructive behavior (such as alcoholism) the behavior should be brought under control as rapidly as possible, thus making aversion conditioning more suitable than other slower, though more pleasant, methods. The moral question seems to resolve itself down to, "Does the technique work? How long does it take compared to other methods?" There appears to be no way that discomfort of some sort can be avoided. The problem is primarily to determine which discomfort is most intense and/or more dangerous and which lasts longer. In short, the dilemma seems to be more of a bookkeeping problem than a moral problem.

Perhaps the most persuasive argument in favor of aversion procedures is that it is extremely rare for a patient to discontinue treatment. Despite the discomfort they are able to see in themselves the rapid loss of desire for alcohol and feel that the freedom from craving alcohol is worth the short period of discomfort.

CONCLUSIONS

Pharmacologic aversion conditioning using emetine-induced nausea as an aversive stimulus has been used since 1935 to treat alcoholism. There are currently 16 hospitals in the United States (16% of the private investor-owned alcoholism beds) using this therapy. All have permanent abstinence from alcoholic beverages as their major treatment goal and all report long-term abstinence rates of approximately 60%.

Three hospitals also use faradic (electrostimulus) aversion conditioning in patients that they consider unsuitable for pharmacologic aversive conditioning. They also report abstinence rates of approximately 60% using this treatment modality. These same three hospitals also use pentothal interviews as part of their therapeutic regimen.

All aversion conditioning hospitals employ adjunctive techniques of educational sessions, counseling, relaxation training, aftercare and follow-up reinforcement treatments, and referral to appropriate agencies after discharge.

REFERENCES

1. Agras, W. S. (ed.). *Behavior Modification: Principles and Clinical Applications.* Little, Brown: Boston, 1972.
2. Blake, B. G. A follow-up of alcoholics treated by behavioral therapy. *Behav. Res. Ther.* 5:89–94, 1967.

3. Elkins, R. L. *Aversion Therapy for Alcoholics: Chemical, Electrical or Imagery?* Paper presented at the meeting of the Southeastern Psychological Association, Miami Beach, April 1971.

4. Facts Consolidated. *A Research Study Conducted among Those Who Have Completed the Schick Treatment for the Control of Alcoholism through November 1975.* Author: Los Angeles, Calif., 1977.

5. Facts Consolidated. *A Research Study Conducted among Those Who Have Completed the Schick Treatment for the Control of Alcoholism During 1976.* Author: Los Angeles, Calif., 1978.

6. Franks, C. M. Behavior therapy: The principles of conditioning and the treatment of the alcoholic. *Q. J. Stud. Alcohol* 24:511, 1963.

7. Franks, C. M. Conditioning and conditioned aversion therapies in the treatment of the alcoholic. *Int. J. Addict.* 1:61, 1966.

8. Garcia, J., and Ervin, F. D. Gustatory-visceral and telereceptor-cutaneous conditioning: Adaptation internal and external milieus. *Commun. Behav. Biol.* 1(6):389–415, 1968.

9. Hsu, J. Electroconditioning therapy of alcoholics: A preliminary report. *Q. J. Stud. Alcohol* 26:449–459, 1965.

10. Jackson, T. R., and Smith, J. W. A comparison of two aversion treatment methods for alcoholism. *J. Stud. Alcohol* 39:187–191, 1978.

11. Kantorovich, N.V. [An attempt at curing alcoholism by associated reflexes.] *Nov. Reflek. Fiziol. Nero. Sis.* 3:436, 1929.

12. Lemere, F., Voegtlin, W. L., Broz, W. R., O'Hollaren, P. Conditioned reflex treatment of chronic alcoholism. *Northwest Med.* 41(3):88, 1942.

13. Lemere, F., and Voegtlin, W. L. An evaluation of the aversion treatment of alcoholism. *Q. J. Stud. Alcohol* 11:199, 1950.

14. Morosko, T. E., and Baer, P. E. Avoidance conditioning of alcoholics. In: *Control of Human Behaviors* (Vol. 2), Ulrick, R. E., Stachnick, T. and Mabry, J. (eds.). Scott, Foresman: Glenview, Ill., 1970.

15. Neubuerger, O. W., Matarazzo, J. D., Schmitz, R. E., Pratt, H. H. One-year follow-up of total abstinence in chronic alcoholic patients following emetic counterconditioning. *Alcoholism* 4(3):306–312, 1980.

16. Shadel, C. A. Aversion treatment of alcohol addiction. *Q. J. Stud. Alcohol* 5:216, 1940.

17. Smith, J. W. Conditioned reflex aversion treatment of alcoholism. *West. Med.* (Suppl. 3) 7(12):45–47, 1966.

18. Smith, J. W. Medical management of acute alcoholic intoxication. *G.P.* 38(6):89, 1968.

19. Smith, J. W., Lemere, F., and Dunn, R. B. Pentothal interviews in the treatment of alcoholism. *Psychosomatics* 12:330–331, 1971.

20. Voegtlin, W. L. The treatment of alcoholism by establishing a conditioned reflex. *Am. J. Med. Sci.* 99:802, 1940.

21. Voegtlin, W. L. Conditioned reflex therapy of chronic alcoholism: Ten years' experience with the method. *Rocky Mt. Med. J.* 44(10):807–812.

22. Vogler, R. E., Lunde, S. E., Johnson, G. R., Martin, P. L. Electronical aversion conditioning with chronic alcoholics. *J. Consult. Clin. Psychol.* 34:302–307, 1970.

23. Wiens, A. N., Montague, J. R., Manaugh, T. S., English, C. J. Pharmacological aversion counterconditioning to alcohol in a private hospital: One year follow-up. *J. Stud. Alcohol* 37:1320–1324, 1976.

73

JEFFREY M. BRANDSMA, PhD, Medical College of Georgia, Augusta, Georgia

RICHARD J. WELSH, MSW, University of Kentucky College of Medicine

ALCOHOLISM OUTPATIENT TREATMENT

STRICTLY SPEAKING, OUTpatient treatment of alcoholism is not a treatment. It is a situational context where treatment takes place, usually labeled as such in order to be contrasted with inpatient treatment. Historically inpatient treatment was often assumed to be the treatment of choice because alcohol problems only came to the attention of helpers when there were severe manifestations associated with intense or chronic alcohol abuse (i.e., heavy intoxication, addiction, or medical and psychiatric problems). Beyond this, many alcoholics at this stage of drinking were unable to interrupt their pattern of drinking or were too enmeshed in a problematic family context to begin effective treatment. Indeed, for the problems just mentioned, an inpatient setting with a higher degree of control and separation from the community is more desirable. Another advantage of inpatient treatment (although unfortunate) are the policies of payment by third parties for inpatient but not outpatient treatment, although this is changing [11]. The problems of alcoholism have a wide range of expression and inpatient treatment is not only not a prerequisite for success, it may be disadvantageous if the stay is extended for many days. It is also unfortunately true that alcoholics are not well treated by general hospitals; they are

---

Jeffrey M. Brandsma, PhD, Professor of Psychiatry, Medical College of Georgia, Augusta, Georgia.

Richard J. Welsh, MSW, Associate Professor of Clinical Social Work, University of Kentucky College of Medicine, Lexington, Kentucky.

often viewed as special problems who require too much attention, are unmotivated, and are not suitable for treatment [16].

The advantages for outpatient treatment are basically much lower economic and social cost. The patient being treated on an outpatient basis can expect a continued enmeshment in his or her community roles and benefit from community supports—job and family, to name the most important. Aside from the usual economic difficulties associated with alcoholism, the patient does not have to contend with the continually increasing cost burden of inpatient treatment, nor with the problems of institutionalization and dependency that occur to some extent with anyone, but particularly with alcoholics experiencing a hospital stay that lasts from 2 to 4 weeks. Outpatient treatment is inherently more flexible and accessible, thus giving it greater probability of being individualized. Thus it is simply more practical to treat alcoholism on an outpatient basis, and in fact, the major portion of most alcoholism treatment in this country is done in this way, using inpatient modalities as an adjunct.

CRITERIA

The criteria for outpatient treatment point to a modicum of social functioning as a basis for attempting to use this context. By this is meant that there would be no incapacitating medical or psychiatric problems, the postacute symptoms would be mild, the person would be capable of maintaining sobriety or controlling drinking to some extent, and less than maximal support would be required in order to maintain functioning. Appropriate candidates for outpatient treatment tend to have characteristics similar to persons who benefit from any psychological treatment. In the case of alcoholism literature, those characteristics are social intactness (married), higher socioeconomic class (education and occupation), motivation (fear or avoidance of consequences), a young age, and a low incidence of alcoholism in one's family history. Beyond this, alcoholics do better with counselors with whom they can form a good relationship and often these will be persons that tend to be dominant and can take charge when appropriate. As treatment continues there is a tendency for lower class patients to be given more medication and environmental intervention, higher class patients to be given more psychologically oriented treatments.

CONTEXTS

The contexts for outpatient treatment are basically four: (1) community mental health centers, (2) general hospital clinics, (3) free-standing alcoholism clinics, (4) and the office of a private practitioner. Although each context will offer similar types of services (to be iterated shortly), there are some differences to be noted. Community mental health centers have greater access to halfway houses, vocational rehabilitation services, and some psychiatric consultation. Hospital clinics have greater access to medical and psychiatric consultation, but may focus too much on physical problems and be less acceptable because of location, parking, and demands on space and time. Alcoholism clinics are oriented toward a person's drinking behavior, but may have little access to other resources. Practitioners are either therapists or doctors, with one more likely to ignore physical complications, the other the meaning of the symptoms psychologically; both tend to be narrow in their approach because their training was not necessarily relevant to the needs of the alcoholic.

An outpatient clinic offering traditional forms of psychotherapy is usually not satisfactory because an alcoholic typically needs more services than the modal clinic can provide—for example, detoxification and vocational help. The more services available, the better able a facility is to provide for the unique needs of each alcoholic. However, as services proliferate, the crucial issues of organization and coherence become more critical. Any alcohol program must be cognizant of its embeddedness in the local culture, to be aware of local attitudes, support systems (agencies), and helpers (clergy) in order to provide for continuity and coordination of the services available. Ideally services are not applied in a shotgun manner, but rather they are individualized and (it is hoped) have some theoretic coherence [13]. When these difficult issues are addressed, treatment effectiveness increases markedly.

TREATMENT GOALS

The goals of treatment depend largely on the theoretic view of alcoholism that is held, and often on the services available. Traditionally, the goal has been complete abstinence, and abstinence attainment was indicative of a successful outcome. Conventional wisdom held that the termination of drinking would have positive impact on all other areas of life functioning. Abstinence was based on the assumption that the "disease" could not be cured, but its course could be arrested by abstinence. This view is explicit in the philosophy of Alcoholics Anonymous (AA) and dominates the treatment practices of many organizations.

In the last decade, this consensus has been challenged by empirical studies that have evaluated other outcome criteria (and found the correlations to abstinence low), and by advocates of controlled drinking (i.e., a return to some form of nonproblematic, stabilized drinking). These advocates view alcoholism theoretically as learned behavior that can be unlearned, or as symptomatic either of an underlying personality disorder that itself needs treatment or of a familial dysfunction. Those who espouse a learning orientation opt for learning-based strategies of treatment (behavior modification); those who see alcoholism as symptomatic opt for problem solution or other forms of individual, group, or family psychotherapy. Many studies (over 70) have been collected to show that 5 to 15% of alcoholics can return to some pattern of attenuated drinking. Some have proposed using distinctive labels for differentiation (i.e., problem drinkers vs. alcoholics).

What is emerging out of the empirical studies and the controversy is a more explicit recognition that abstinence is only one of several possible treatment goals in the area of drinking behavior, and that other treatment goals in other important life areas are often as important to address for overall functioning of a person [12]. In terms of drinking behavior, a synthesis is emerging that most alcoholics should abstain (especially early in treatment), but some can, with effort, return to some form of drinking.

The abstinence goal is desirable if: (1) physical damage is occurring or likely to; (2) there are previous failures to learn controlled drinking; (3) there exists a belief in abstinence from experience or philosophy. Controlled drinking is desirable if: (1) a younger person is involved; (2) the person cannot accept the abstinence goal; (3) the person is motivated to persist in a program of treatment. The present authors support this synthesis and suggest that it be based on an assessment of the individual's developed tolerance physiologically, his or her personality organization psychologically, and negotiation with the patient.

In the past, the focus on abstinence has taken attention away from other important treatment goals. Now that abstinence is no longer enshrined, more realistic multiple and sequential treatment goals can be addressed with regard to specifying in the individual case which problems contribute to excessive drinking. Thus in treatment considerations, the alcoholic or problem drinker is now given status as a complex person embedded in a physiological, social, and psychological context, one who is engaging in a multidetermined behavior, overdrinking. Drinking behavior is both problematic in itself and probably symptomatic of overall life adjustment. Treatment must respond to the person and the variables that are controlling the problematic behavior.

MODAL TREATMENT

Because of the variability and diversity, it is inherently difficult to describe the modal treatment that occurs in outpatient settings. This chapter focuses upon the United States, but not upon detoxification programs, emergency care, day care, and halfway houses and quarter-way house programs. Of necessity, behavior modification must be mentioned, although it is covered in greater depth elsewhere in this volume. Certain treatments are not mentioned because they have not been shown to be effective and are no longer viable, including electric aversion, LSD, and multivitamins. Table 1 presents outpatient treatments in terms of what is modal in terms of frequency; various aspects of the table are then enlarged upon.

Medication usually involves sedative-hypnotics for withdrawal, then disulfram for motivation control. Disulfram alone, however, is not effective without a relationship with a therapist and a strict ritual of treatment—often with the spouse's involvement. If psychiatric symptoms persist, major tranquilizers or tricyclic antidepressants are the most popular treatments. Minor tranquilizers are not desirable because of the abuse potential in this population.

Treatment is usually more intense in terms of frequency in the initial stages. When stability of relatively sober functioning is achieved, frequency is reduced to one or two times each week, with allotment for emergencies. Follow-up is variable, but many centers begin lessening contacts in from 6 to 12 months after the initiation of treatment. Monthly visits or telephone calls in the period from 12 to 18 months are usual, with total treatment time from 2 to 24 months. Long-term follow-up in terms of minimal contact of an organized support system (e.g., group membership) seems to be crucial in terms of monitoring therapeutic benefits.

Group therapy is a very important treatment modality, but its forms are myriad. That it is so popular bespeaks its meeting of the dependency needs of the alcoholic as well as promoting a sense of universality rather than the social isola-

Table 1
Outpatient Treatment Elements

Basic Core	Generally Accepted	Specialized or Peripheral

Social history and drinking inventory
Supportive and Problem-solving counseling
Medication
	Group therapy
	Alcoholics Anonymous
	Al-Anon
	Alateen
	Broad spectrum cognitive behavioral therapies
	  Relaxation
	  Desensitization
	  Contracting
	  Role Playing
	  Covert sensitization
	  Rational-emotive therapy
	Psychotherapy
	  Couples and family therapy
	  Reality therapy
	  Transactional Analysis
	  Analytic psychotherapy
	Vocational counseling
	Follow-up visits
		Behavioral therapies
		  Biofeedback
		  Fee manipulation
		  Videotape modeling
		Outpatient detoxification
		Hypnosis
		Night hospital
		Telephone follow-up
		Home visits
		Recreational counseling

tion so often experienced by them. It is well known that AA meets in groups and has subgroup cells (the buddy system). Beyond this are often reported intake-orientation groups, didactic and pretherapy groups, interpersonal skills training (assertiveness, friendship), psychotherapy groups of various persuasions (usually involving some problem solving), and less frequently couples and relatives groups, employment and budget counseling groups, and even (very infrequently) marathon groups. The other forms of psychotherapy mentioned in Table 1 are currently popular. What evidence is available indicates that all are similarly effective if the person will stick with them for a minimum of five to 10 sessions [1].

The use of hypnosis is variable, but it is usually used as an adjunct to a behavior modification strategy such as relaxation or visualization; it has not been shown effective, nor is it much used to stop or control drinking by direct suggestion.

Aversion treatment runs the gamut from drug-induced vomiting, (in inpatient settings) to electric shock to the forearm, to covert sensitization where there is only visualization of aversive stimuli. Since there is evidence that electrical aversion is ineffective [10], the less intrusive, less physically painful procedures of covert sensitization are probably more popular and utilized. Biofeedback refers to programs that teach people to discriminate blood alcohol levels in order to control their intake of alcoholic beverages. Fee manipulation involves having a client pay a relatively large amount of money at the inception of treatment, with the proviso that he or she can earn it back if attendance or disulfram-taking behavior is consistent. Videotape modeling involves showing the alcoholic what he or she is like when drunk and/or also showing assertive or coping behaviors for problematic situations that could be modeled; the former type of videotape modeling is an inpatient strategy, the latter an outpatient one. In general broad spectrum behavioral packages of treatments created for empirical study are becoming unpackaged and used to deal with specific problems in individual patients.

OTHER ISSUES

Questions of whether treatment ideally should be on an inpatient or outpatient basis will ultimately depend on the individual being considered. The issue of outpatient or home detoxification is still moot, providing a mix of advantages and disadvantages. By and large, the vast majority of alcoholics (estimates range between 80 and 95%) do not need inpatient detoxification, but on the other hand 20 to 50% of those who begin outpatient detoxification will probably not complete it. Outpatient detoxification has been shown to be quite safe, but of course there should be medical and hospital back-up if unforeseen complications arise. In a few words, outpatient detoxification is safe and desirable, but attention to the dropout problem is needed (with everyday groups, coercion from the courts, etc.) [7].

The biggest inefficiency in outpatient treatment is the dropout rate, and it will remain a very large problem. However, inroads can be made with fee manipulation strategies or well-organized and well-administered coercion by the court system. The evidence is clear that coerced patients do as well or better when compared to voluntary clients, with the possible exception that AA does not seem to be a good treatment to be coerced into [4, 14, 15]. AA's buddy system, a subgrouping strategy, is another obvious way to deal with the problem of dropouts. This problem is crucial to address because evidence now indicates that if one attends a minimum amount of treatment, improvement can be expected [5]. Baekeland and Lundwall [2] have suggested seven ways to decrease the dropout rate:

1. Eliminate waiting lists and offer immediate entry.
2. Satisfy the patient's dependency needs by offering a wide range of ancillary services.
3. Offer a variety of treatment modalities to the patient.
4. Explain clearly to the patient the aims, scope, probable results, side effects, and duration of the treatment to which he or she is assigned.
5. Find out whether the patient has previously dropped out of therapy and if so explore the reasons thoroughly.
6. Maintain contact with significant others and enlist their help if necessary.
7. In more symptomatic patients, put a major emphasis on rapid symptom relief and do not withhold medication during initial treatment.

An important issue of controversy is the pervasiveness of AA in various treatment programs. For some, AA provides a philosophical and practical basis for all of treatment, including Al-Anon and Alateen as well as other treatments under the AA umbrella; for others AA is at best a peripheral adjunct offered only to a few. Thus there are three models of AA involvement — AA operates the program, AA collaborates in the program, or AA is irrelevant to a program. Each model can be used effectively, but if AA is emphasized, one must accept the goal of abstinence, the use of groups, a religious emphasis, and a disease concept of alcoholism — each at times applied with a high degree of rigidity. Although AA has proven exceedingly useful in many cases, these authors do not think it should be the basis for treatment or the only treatment offered. AA has done a great service historically, but has not been shown to be as effective as its proponents have claimed in recent years [3]. It is the opinion of the present authors that AA should be a part, but not the whole of alcoholism treatment. Closely related is the issue of using nonalcoholic paraprofessionals in the treatment of alcoholics. The experience of these authors, as well as that reported by others, would indicate that paraprofessionals should be included in the mix of treatments, as long as there is training and supervision [6, 19].

Still being debated is the efficacy of putting other substance abusers into treatment programs with alcohol abusers. This has seemed indicated because alcoholics often have myriad drug addictions. Programs that are combined have not found a decrement in overall effectiveness if a wide range of services are offered; the problems that often have to be addressed concern differing socioeconomic levels, life patterns, and values. In an era of budget cutting, combined treatment programs may become only an academic question since all substance abusers will likely be treated under one institutional umbrella in terms of psychological treatments. However, if physiochemical research turns up demonstrably different understandings of the dynamics of the various kinds of addiction, different kinds of treatments may be dictated.

Most outpatient facilities are dealing with a decrease in funding from their various sources, and this will necessitate new strategies of treatment delivery and prioritizing of essential services. One potentially useful model of cost-efficient and effective service is the use of imported therapists. In this kind of program, therapists from the community are trained to treat alcoholics in a supportive outpatient context on a part-time basis. This approach seems to provide benefits to therapists, patients, and agencies [4].

In closing, two groups should be mentioned that have not been well served by traditional outpatient facilities — or anybody else — namely, women and teenage alcoholics. Women tend to remain hidden, untouched by the services offered by their community; teens feel alienated from adult services. Both groups are often more affected by community denial of their being a problem ("She just keeps to herself," or "It's just a little youthful excess"). These two groups have different needs from adult male alcoholics and require different approaches. For example, drop-in centers and an information-prevention service for teens, and in some cases, a community outreach effort for women have proven useful.

When Gerard and Saenger [8] surveyed outpatient clinics, they found a wide variation in staffing, philosophy, and treatment goals. The same conditions exist today with even more variability. However, alcoholism and its treatment are seen in a more complex and sophisticated fashion today, and efforts are being made to match patients to treatments. While individualized treatment is both desirable and necessary, it is important that programs attain a coherent case management philosophy. It is hoped that the next decade will provide more clarity for the issues mentioned and a more efficient calculus of matching patients, therapists, and treatments.

REFERENCES

1. Armor, D. J., Polich, J. M., and Stambul, H. B. *Alcoholism and Treatment.* Wiley: New York, 1978.

2. Baekeland, F., and Lundwall, L. K. Dropping out of treatment: A critical review. *Psychol. Bull.* 82:738-783, 1975.

3. Baekeland, F., Lundwall, L. K., and Kissin, B. Methods for the treatment of chronic alcoholism: A critical appraisal. In: *Research Advances in Alcohol and Drug Problems* (Vol. 2), Israel, Y. (ed.). Wiley: New York, 1975.

4. Brandsma, J. M., Maultsby, M. C., and Welsh, R. J. *Outpatient Treatment of Alcoholism: A Review and Comparative Study.* University Park Press: Baltimore, 1980.

5. Emrick, C. D. A review of psychologically oriented treatment of alcoholism: II. The relative effectiveness of treatment versus no treatment. *J. Stud. Alcohol* 37:1055-1060, 1975.

6. Emrick, C. D., Lassen, C. L., and Edwards, M. T. Nonprofessional peers as therapeutic agents. In: *Effective Psychotherapy: A Handbook of Research*, Gurman, A. S. and Razin, A. M. (eds.). Pergamon: Elmsford, N.Y., 1977.

7. Feldman, D. J., Pattison, E. M., Sobell, L. C., Graham, T., and Sobell, M. Outpatient alcohol detoxification: Initial findings on 564 patients. *Am. J. Psychiatry* 132:4, 407-412, 1975.

8. Gerard, D. L., and Saenger, G. *Outpatient Treatment of Alcoholism: A Study of Outcome and its Determinants.* University of Toronto Press: Toronto, 1966.

9. Karlsruher, A. E. The nonprofessional as a psychotherapeutic agent: A review of the evidence pertaining to his effectiveness. *Am. J. Commun. Psychol.* 2:61-77, 1974.

10. Nathan, P. E., and Lipscomb, T. R. Behavior therapy and behavior modification in the treatment of alcoholism. In: *The Diagnosis and Treatment of Alcoholism*, Mendelson, J. H. and Mells, N. K. (eds.). McGraw-Hill: New York, 1979.

11. Noble, E. P. (ed.). *Third Special Report to the U.S. Congress on Alcohol and Health.* United States Department of Health, Education and Welfare: Bethesda, Md., 1978.

12. Pattison, E. M. Nonabstinent drinking goals in the treatment of alcoholics. In: *Research Advances in Alcohol and Drug Problems* (Vol. 3), Israel, Y. (ed.). Wiley: New York, 1976.

13. Pattison, E. M. The selection of treatment modalities for the alcoholic patient. In: *The Diagnosis and Treatment of Alcoholism*, Mendelson, J. H. and Mells, N. D. (eds.). McGraw-Hill: New York, 1979.

14. Rosenberg, C. M., and Liftik, J. Use of coercion in the outpatient treatment of alcoholism. *J. Stud. Alcohol* 37:58-65, 1976.

15. Smart, R. G. Employed alcoholics treated voluntarily and under constructive coercion: A follow-up study. *Q. J. Stud. Alcohol* 35:196-209, 1974.

16. Stein, L. I., Newton, J. R., and Bowman, R. S. Duration of hospitalization for alcoholics. *Arch. Gen. Psychiatry* 32:247-252, 1975.

74

GEORGE R. JACOBSON, PhD, De Paul Rehabilitation Hospital,
Milwaukee, Wisconsin

THE ROLE OF SHELTER FACILITIES IN THE TREATMENT OF ALCOHOLICS

AMONG THE INCREASING variety of new facilities and services that have recently become available to alcoholic persons, one of the oldest of such institutions—the shelter—continues to provide a unique and perhaps indispensable function in contemporary American society. Developing prior to modern concepts of alcoholism and the medical model of substance abuse, the establishment of shelters was seemingly motivated by an 18th and 19th century Christian sense of mission, humanitarianism, and charity. The evil influence of strong drink led men into a sinful and fallen way of life, and shelters provided a haven, out of harm's way and safe from temptation, wherein religion and spirituality could restore in them a sense of dignity while they sought sobriety. Flourishing during the period of Prohibition and the Depression, shelters served a segment of the population then scorned and despised in the United States, providing a refuge, a place of protection and safety, for many thousand of homeless and indigent men living on skid rows throughout the country.

Since the end of World War II and with the advent of contemporary scientific knowledge of alcoholism, shelters have continued their evolution in both princi-

---

George R. Jacobson, PhD, Director, Research and Training, De Paul Rehabilitation Hospital, Assistant Professor, Department of Psychiatry and Mental Health Sciences, Medical College of Wisconsin, and Clinical Associate Professor, Department of Psychology, University of Wisconsin–Milwaukee, Milwaukee, Wisconsin.

ples and practices. While still retaining a recognizable emphasis on the fundamental importance of man's spiritual well-being, and still serving a basically skid row clientele, shelters have become increasingly more businesslike in their operations while providing a greater variety of services. Physicians, psychologists, social workers, vocation and rehabilitation counselors, alcoholism counselors, and other professionals have joined the staffs of many of the larger and better-established shelters. Housing and recreational facilities, job training, meaningful work for reasonable pay, individual and group psychotherapy, and other services are offered in addition to the tradition of spiritual counseling and guidance.

The purpose of the remainder of this chapter is to provide readers a fuller definition and description of shelters and their purposes and programs, the populations they serve, the impact and outcomes of services, and a brief speculation on the future of shelters.

THE PRESENT NATURE OF SHELTERS

In certain aspects of philosophy, purpose, and function, shelters share some elements common to other agencies and facilities serving alcoholics, perhaps especially halfway houses. Both types of institutions are representative of social movements, are dedicated to sobriety as a way of life, and provide a group living experience for periods of time averaging 3 to 6 months. Donahue [4] and Rubbington [12] provide descriptions of halfway houses that clearly identify the role of such facilities in the rehabilitation of alcoholics. A key characteristic distinguishing halfway houses from shelters is the transitional living experience provided by the former, the implication that the resident is at a halfway mark or midpoint in the rehabilitation process, no longer in need of constant care but not yet ready to return to full and complete functioning. As Rubbington [11] points out, the halfway house first provides an immediate solution to the problem of being released from a hospital or a jail, offers social support to the resident, replaces dependency on alcohol and social agencies with dependency on the halfway house, then helps the resident to become self-reliant, finally returning the resident to the community as a relatively competent and functional adult.

Shelters, by contrast, imply no such time-limited transition period. Temporal aspects of sheltered environments may be quite brief — a haven to be sought for a week or two in the face of some crisis — or quite protracted — a sanctuary where one may remain, safe and protected, for years if necessary. Also, shelters tend to be more formally organized, more bureaucratized, more impersonal, often operated by off-site management, functioning according to principles of business and economics, and often having a strong element of Christian evangelism not typically found elsewhere. There are, of course, some small, independently operated shelters that tend to be responsive to a rather specialized clientele (e.g., battered women and their dependent children), but most shelters with which readers are likely to be familiar are those institutions operated by Christian missions (e.g., the Salvation Army) or municipal government (e.g., the Women's Emergency Shelter in Manhattan's Bowery). It is this group of facilities, and their primary clientele of chronically indigent and homeless men and women, which is the focus of this chapter.

Best known of such agencies are the Harbor Light and Men's Social Service Centers operated by the Salvation Army. Although services offered by the Salvation Army are available to persons with disabilities other than alcoholism, at least 80% of the clientele are known to have alcohol problems [10]. The philosophy and operating principles of these shelters are consistent across the country, and Katz [9] and Judge [8] describe them in nearly identical terms: "The primary function... is the rehabilitation and/or spiritual regeneration of unattached and homeless men. To men who are handicapped either mentally, morally, physically, socially, or spiritually, the center provides the opportunity to regain self-respect and acquire such moral and spiritual principles of conduct and habits of industry as to enable them to take their rightful place in society [13, p. 10]. According to Judge, the social service centers have "evolved from a very simple socialwork agency providing food, clothing, and shelter along with the time-honored program of spiritual evangelism, to a comprehensive rehabilitation effort which utilizes the newest treatment modalities in concert with traditional methods" [8, p. 462].

The evolution of shelters toward increasing professionalism and comprehensiveness of services is reflected in the results of Katz's survey of Salvation Army facilities 20 years ago. At that time there were 124 such shelter facilities, providing 10,388 beds, and recording over 57,000 admissions annually. Less than 10 years later there were 122 locations, a bed capacity of 11,192, and an admission rate of 69,632 men annually. These figures represent an 8% increase in capacity and a 22% growth in admissions. Katz's survey also revealed that more than 50% of the centers employed physicians, approximately 33% had full-time chaplains, nearly 15% of the centers had social workers, psychologists, and psychiatrists on staff, and only one facility provided vocational counseling. At all of the facilities spiritual counseling was provided, and nearly all (96%) provided regular medical care; 75% provided Bible study classes, and 50% provided regular Alcoholics Anonymous (AA) meetings on site. Lectures or educational films were offered by 40%; fewer than 33% provided group psychotherapy; fewer than 25% offered psychological testing; and approximately 10% provided individual psychotherapy.

For the year ending December 31, 1979 — the last period for which complete data are available — the utilization of health care professionals had increased at the social service centers (currently referred to as "adult rehabilitation centers"), alcoholism counselors had been added to the staffs, and women were being admitted to the Harbor Light facilities. According to two respondents [L. Caldwell of the Chicago office, and M. Verner of the New York office, July 28, 1981, personal communications] there were 112 social service centers providing 11,635 beds and recording 54,065 admissions for an average length of stay of 41 days and a total number of days of care in excess of 2.24 million. In addition, the Harbor Light facilities provided another 2,462 beds, admitted 167,238 men and 2,131 women, and provided 700,000 days of care.

A special, if not unique, feature of most shelters is of course, their religious and spiritual atmosphere, and perhaps the Salvation Army facilities best represent this characteristic, since each manager is an ordained minister. Thus the beneficiaries (as clients are called) are provided an extensive spiritual program including regular chapel services, Bible study, daily morning devotions, and individual spiritual counseling. Another significant feature of the social service centers is their emphasis on being self-sustaining business operations (in contrast to the Harbor Light units, which are supported in part by United Way funds, government grants, and other public and private funds). Typically the business is based on salvage, repair, and sale of donated goods solicited from the community. The labor necessary for much of this operation is provided by the beneficiaries, who are thus able to be at least partially self-supporting during their period of residence.

Beyond the spiritual and work-oriented aspects of the centers, medical, social, psychological, and recreational services are available. At some locations a wide range of amenities are offered, including bowling alleys, television and game rooms, laundromats, and reading rooms, in addition to the customary cafeteria, chapel, medical offices, and lecture rooms.

The nature of the programs is directed by a conceptual rationale in which alcoholism is viewed as a learned form of behavior arising out of complex interactions among personal, social, and cultural forces and leading to physiological changes and personality disturbances. Consequently, treatment is aimed at modification of underlying psychological processes, and changes in behavior, attitudes, opinions, and beliefs that support the basic pathology. To these ends, treatment is divided into five components. An initial intake process, aimed at determining the client's suitability to the progrm, and arranging for food, clothing, shelter, and immediate medical attention, is followed by a 30-day period of evaluation, adjustment, and probation. During this second phase of the program beneficiaries undergo further medical and psychosocial assessment, work assignments are made, spiritual and recreational participation is initiated, and attendance at lectures and AA meetings is begun. The third phase, which may last 2 to 4 months or more, is a period of specific treatment, which is developed at individual case conferences and may include group and/or individual psychotherapy, continuation of vocational, spiritual, and recreational activities, additional AA participation, and other functions. Preparation for return to the community is the focus of the next phase of the program, in which beneficiaries are assisted in locating permanent residences and employment upon completion of the program. In the final stage, separation, emphasis is on making the transition from a sheltered environment to the competitive labor market and independent living.

The central portion of the sheltered living experience, the focused treatment program of phase three, is formulated on the observation that alcoholic beneficiaries are usually men who lack ego strength, are deteriorated, have few inner resources, and are apparently loyal to a reference group that supports alcoholism as a life style. Through group pressure, individual contracts, didactic lectures, and by other means, the defensive structure of the beneficiary is disturbed, annoyed, and assaulted in order to destory the individual's assumedly unhealthy sense of personal identity and influence the client to assume the values, attitudes, and beliefs of the institution. A variety of rewards and punishments are applied to induce conformity to institutional norms. Beneficiaries are instructed in the faulty, blameworthy, and morally inferior aspects of their past behaviors and self-perceptions. A nuclear group, the Program Committee, comprised of long-term residents who are sober and actively working on their problems and who have demonstrated their sincerity, is trained to bring pressure to bear on newer beneficiaries to become honest and group-involved members of the sheltered community. In this context, simply minding one's own business is regarded as an undesirable form of behavior, and mutual concern and group responsibility are incorporated as part of the beneficiaries' new set of values.

Other similarly oriented shelter facilities exist in most larger American cities, particularly those with well-identified and geographically stable skid row areas. The characteristics of the Salvation Army's operations are viewed by the author as a prototype, however, because of their general visibility, the size of the chain, the relatively advanced state of their evolution, and the availability of public information. Other spiritual mission shelters do exist, of course, many of which provide only the basics of emergency food, clothing, and temporary housing, along with spiritual regeneration and humanitarian salvation. Halfway between the two ends of the shelter continuum, and perhaps among the most widely known of such agencies, is the Bowery Mission of New York, which celebrated its centennial in 1979. Staffed almost entirely by recovering alcoholics, it provides emergency food, clothing, and housing, some medical care, alcoholism education seminars, individual and group counseling, and Bible study groups and prayer meetings. Also located in New York's Bowery are two municipally supported facilities operated by the city's Department of Social Services. The Men's Shelter and the Women's Emergency Shelter provide food and temporary housing for transient, homeless, and unemployed men and women, a majority of whom report heavy drinking, and all of whom are without immediate sources of financial support. As public secular facilities rather than private religious-philanthropic agencies they do not have the spiritual orientation of the better known mission shelters.

CHARACTERISTICS OF THE CLIENTELE

Who are the men and women who use these urban metropolitan shelter facilities? That they are usually indigent and homeless has already been indicated. That most of them (i.e., approximately 80% according to Katz [9] have a history of drinking problems has also been established. Because many of them are apparently skid row inhabitants it may be redundant to go into great detail here (see Chapter 79), but some basic description may be useful. A survey of 52 women at the Women's Emergency Shelter in New York [6] revealed that 56% were white, 10% were foreign-born, 23% had never been married, and none were currently married, but 29% were divorced, 40% were separated or had been deserted, and 8% were widows. Religious affiliation was primarily Protestant (44%); 35% were Catholic, 7% were classified as "other," and 14% claimed no affiliation at all. The majority of the women (42%) were between the ages of 35 and 44; 14% were younger, 20% were 45 to 54 years old, 14% were 55 to 64 years old, and 10% were 65 or older. Most of the women (89%) had monthly incomes of less than $100; 10% had incomes of $100 to $500 a month, and 1% claimed incomes of more than $500 a month.

When asked to rate their own current drinking behavior, 32% of the women regarded themselves as drinking heavily, 31% rated themselves as moderate drinkers, and the remainder were light drinkers or abstainers. Administration of a standardized quantity-frequency index generally confirmed those self-perceptions. Relatively few of the women had ever consumed nonbeverage alcohol, and distilled spirits were preferred by a majority (38%) of the women. Drinking was most often a solitary activity, further removing the women from social contacts and suggesting that they are the most isolated and asocial of all skid row residents. The women rarely drank with male "bottle gangs" and were never observed drinking in groups with other women. Self-reports indicated that 19.2 years was the average age at the time of their first drink, and most women were 30 to 34 years old at the time of onset of heavy drinking.

When Bahr [1] interviewed 203 men living in two Salvation Army shelters, the Bowery Mission, the municipal Men's Shelter, and other housing facilities in that New York skid row area, he found that 36% of the men drank heavily (in agreement with figures of 33% and 36%, respectively, among men living in similar facilities in Chicago and Minneapolis), and another 14% reported having drunk heavily earlier in life. For most of the men, drinking heavily began prior to age 25. Bahr identified early- and late-onset heavy drinkers and determined that men in the first group discontinued family affiliations earlier, had higher rates of unemployment and lower status occupations, and had fewer voluntary social affiliations throughout life.

Comprehensive descriptions of male residents in Salvation Army shelter facilities have been provided by Katz [10] in San Francisco and Judge [8] in Chicago. Katz characterizes his two California samples as being part way between jailed alcoholics and alcoholics receiving outpatient treatment at public clinics, in terms of their level of social functioning and prognosis. His observation is not surprising in light of a report that 70% of his residents had been in jail at least once and a sizable minority had also been treated at outpatient clinics. Relatedly, his sample of residents show a normal distribution of IQs, and results of testing on the Minnesota Multiphasic Personality Inventory (MMPI) are "quite similar to [those] of other groups of alcoholics.... The men appear to have primarily character disorders, with a sprinkling of neuroses and psychoses" [8, p. 639].

In some ways the Chicago and San Francisco samples closely resemble each other, being nearly identical in age (44.6 and 45 years old) and similar in marital status (35% and 28% never married). But there are at least some apparent differences in other categories; for example, the California sample was composed of 55% high school graduates and 24% with some college education, whereas the mean years of education was 9.3 for the Illinois group.

In California most of the men were white, divorced (45%), and Protestant. Occupational skills were professional, managerial, or clerical (18%), skilled labor (28%), semiskilled (14%), and unskilled or service (29%). More than half of the men had lived in California for at least 10 years, 55% had been in some sort of institution during the 6 months prior to admission to the shelter, 56% had had no regular work during that same period, and half the group had received financial assistance during that same period, averaging $450 for the 6 months. The average man had a serious drinking problem of approximately 10 years duration, none had been abstinent for as much as 1 week during the 6 months prior to admission, and 6 months was the average duration of the longest period of abstinence since drinking had become a problem. Approximately 30% of the men had received some form of psychotherapy, and 44% had been active in AA.

Comparable data from the Salvation Army facility in Chicago indicates that 50% of the men had no occupational skills of any kind, and 10% usually worked in some food-service occupation. The most often reported trades were truck driver (10%) and painter (4%), and 10% of the sample had never held any job at all for more than a few weeks or months. Casual or spot labor was the usual employment for 52% of the men, and that had been their form of occupation for periods ranging between 2 and 10 years. More than 50% of the sheltered men had had 11 or more different jobs during their working lives, and 39% reported between 20 and hundreds of different jobs.

In a somewhat different vein, Bodine [2] found that among a sample of men at a Harbor Light facility in Los Angeles, 89% had experienced some recognizable crisis at the time of admission. And from the smaller urban community of Peoria, Illinois (1980 population, 125,591) Cumming [3] reports that 34% of the homeless men who "make the track" among the 55 social service agencies in and around the city spend at least part of their year in one or more of the local missions or shelters, but they have no contact with state psychiatric hospitals. By contrast, of those men whose "track" includes one visit to the state psychiatric hospital, only 5% have also been shelter residents during the same 2-year period. And among those men whose "track" included two or more psychiatric hospitalizations, none were shelter residents during the same 24 months. Related patterns of social service agency useage led Cumming to infer that, at least in that particular community, homeless men who use the shelters differ from those who use the psychiatric hospitals. On the other hand, Gunn [7] sees a good deal of similarity and overlap among the functions of shelters, jails, and psychiatric institutions.

Finally, comparisons of information provided by men who use a variety of shelters in Chicago, New York, Minneapolis, Syracuse, and Philadelphia suggest a relatively consistent picture of homeless, alienated, disaffiliated men, usually 45 years old or older, the vast majority of whom are not currently married but about half of whom had been married at least once. Most of them have had relatively little education, and of those currently working almost all are unskilled laborers. Very few of the men are physically healthy, at least 50% are currently and chronically alcoholic (although 15% to 20% of the residents are abstainers), many are chronically depressed, and others manifest schizoid characteristics.

OUTCOMES, CONFLICTS, ABUSES

Because of the homeless and indigent nature of most of the alcoholics who use shelters, and the disaffiliated and wandering life style of many such men, very little is known about the effects of the shelters on the lives of the residents, and even less substantive information is available regarding what becomes of the clients once they have left. For example, in one attempted follow-up study of shelter residents, fully 33% of the sample had disappeared without a trace within 1 year. On the other hand, when they can be located it is usually because they have been institutionalized in the course of "making a track," with resultant biases in outcome data.

With these problems in mind, then, it may be nonetheless instructive to review the data provided by Katz [10], Cumming [3], and Wiseman [14], and to comment on their observations. In Katz's studies of 293 and 503 Salvation Army alcoholic beneficiaries who were sought for follow-up 6 months after discharge from two California facilities, only 37% of the first group and 34% of the second group could be located and interviewed, thus reemphasizing the nomadic nature of the population. Among those who were interviewed, however, there appeared to have been a reduction of binge drinking during the follow-up period. More specifically, 25% of the respondents reported total abstinence during the follow-up period, 55% were abstinent for more than 3 months, 28% had not drunk for up to 3 months, and 17% reported no significant periods of abstinence at all. However, when asked to compare their drinking during the 6 months before and after their sheltered living, 32% reported no difference and the remainder reported some increase in duration of abstinence during the latter period (33% reported at least 12 weeks more abstinence after than before their sheltered living).

Regarding changes in employment patterns and earnings, 38% of the men reported having received nonsalaried financial assistance during the follow-up period, versus 50% during the 6 months prior to being at the shelters. Approximately 50% of the men reported increased earnings; the average income was $900 (versus $450 during the 6 months prior to admission), and 25% reported increases of at least $1,000. On the other hand, more than 50% of the respondents reported no vocational improvements since leaving the centers, and only 25% of the men reported an increase of 12 or more weeks of full-time employment since discharge. Only 15% of the respondents worked continuously during the entire follow-up period, and approximately 33% of them had done no regular full-time work at all.

Information regarding institutionalization is, of course, somewhat misleading because of sampling bias, but the overall trend toward decreased time spent in jail is encouraging. Moreover, 33% of the men stated that they had spent no time in any institution at all since leaving the centers, and another 33% reported at least some decrease in periods of institutionalization. Conversely, 18% of the respondents had spent half or more of the 6-month follow-up period in institutions.

Overall, results of having resided in a shelter are viewed as being generally favorable (with some qualifications, as discussed below), and many of the men were, in rather global terms, better off after than before shelter residence. Drinking behavior seems to show greater improvement than vocational patterns, and some of the men interviewed by Katz reported that they could remain abstinent only if they avoided regular employment. By quantifying his indices of changes in vocational behaviors among his two follow-up samples, Katz reported that 17% and 18% showed great improvement, 19% and 23% showed moderate improvement, and 65% and 59% were unimproved. Regarding drinking patterns, 27% and 21% were greatly improved, 21% and 27% moderately so, and 52% and 53% were not improved. Relatedly, 22% of the men appropriately tested at admission and follow-up showed increased symptoms of subjective distress or psychopathology, and 34% showed decreases.

On the basis of some serendipitous observations one might infer that men who can not be located may perhaps be better off than those who are trackable. Several months after completing his follow-up studies some of the men whom Katz [10] had been unable to locate earlier suddenly reappeared, requesting shelter again. Their self-reports suggested that they had been "on the average more successful than men who are located . . . [because it is] not so easy to locate those out in the community maintaining themselves or partially maintaining themselves" [10, p. 644].

Regardless of the sometimes questionable long-term outcome of sheltered experience, the temporary but immediate benefits are not generally disputed: disruption of destructive drinking patterns, medical attention, nutritious meals, improved personal hygiene and clean clothes, a safe place to sleep, and exposure to potentially beneficial religious, vocational, and recreational opportunities. If nothing more enduring than that were accomplished, shelters would continue to be valuable resources for the alienated and homeless persons who frequent them, as their role is far from being a nugatory one.

The nature and function of most contemporary shelters may unfortunately be inimical to better outcomes than those reported by Katz, for a variety of reasons. For one, improvement in terms of postdischarge outcome is intimately linked to length of stay, at least for Salvation Army beneficiaries. Specifically, when Katz [10] divided length of stay into periods of less than 1 month, 1 to 4 months, and 4 months or longer, the rates of no improvement for drinking behavior at follow-up were 74%, 45%, and 33%, respectively. Moderate improvement rates were, for the three lengths of stay respectively, 15%, 24%, and 25%, while great improvement was observed in 11%, 31%, and 42% of the follow-up respondents. But only 13% of the men had stayed 4 months or longer; 30% left the residences after less than 1 month, and 57% left between 1 and 4 months after admission.

Salvation Army facilities encourage neither very brief nor greatly protracted residence periods: one official considers 90 days a good length of stay, and a publication suggests 6 to 12 months. But most of the residents leave prematurely — nearly 33% were gone before the nuclear treatment aspects were even initiated — and "most men who leave prematurely do not show later improvement" [10, p. 643]. Whereas Salvation Army social service centers may not have been intended to be used as indefinite domiciles or sheltered workshops, nor as places of temporary shelter or short-term employment, they are not the former but they have become the latter. Officials are cognizant of reality, however, since "a sizable minority of the men are not offered any specific treatment, either because . . . their adjustment is too precarious to permit any tampering, or because they are so rigidly rejecting of any help offered. . . . Many of the men . . . leave prematurely, usually because of resumption of drinking" [10, pp. 330-331]. And, "Many of the clients coming to the centers . . . are not seeking psychotherapy and may not be seeking any kind of 'treatment.' Some of the men are certainly mainly interested in 'getting the creases out of their belly and putting a front on their back' " (i.e., obtaining food and clean clothing) [10, p. 645].

There is, then, a disparity between the goals and expectations of the staff for the clients, and of the clients for themselves, and therein lies the second major problem of shelter facilities. It has been repeatedly demonstrated that good therapeutic outcome is closely linked to the similarity of treatment goals held by therapist and patient, and this rule of thumb is frequently violated in shelter facilities. What are the expectations of the staffs and clients? According to one report, the staff wants clients who are well motivated for gaining insight and making personality changes, and views psychotherapy as the major agent of change. There appears to be a growing recognition that for each client there may be different paths to successful rehabilitation, and that insight may not always be a possible or necessary element, so perhaps some modifications in staff objectives are occurring. The emphasis on spiritual reawakening and constructive labor seems to remain largely unchanged.

But clients hold a different view, according to Wiseman's [14] study of men who make the loop of the shelters, missions, jails, and hospitals, and Cumming's [3] observations of men who "make the track." Wiseman points out that agents of social control see their own institutions as self-contained approaches to the rehabilitation of homeless alcoholics, and that the Christian missionaries believe they offer spiritual regeneration. The clients, however, see them as hypocritical businessmen who play the role of a savior while assigning the alcoholic the role of sinner, and then exploit the labor of the beneficiaries for profit. A vicious circle develops, as each institutionalization—each time they make the loop—renders clients less employable, and making the loop becomes increasingly more necessary, because these shelters and facilities are the only resources available for their survival. Consequently staffs of the institutions, seeing the same clients cycling through the system, become discouraged and cynical, and the clients react with apathy and hostility. As cycles on the loop continue, benefactors and beneficiaries see one another as exploiters and themselves as the exploited. The alcoholics are accused of abusing the system, and staffs are accused of taking advantage of the clients for purposes of continuing profit.

Cumming [3] takes a similar position, pointing out that missionaries who operate the shelters believe that if not for them many of the homeless alcoholics would die as a result of their drinking (and police and hospital personnel see themselves in that same way). The alcoholics hate the missions, according to Cumming, despite their dependence on them (or because of it) and see the missions as capitalistic business enterprises whose wealth has been accumulated through exploitation of skid row labor. Interestingly, the "mission stiffs," those alcoholics who take advantage of the shelters and go from mission to mission pretending to be converted, are viewed with disdain by their fellows. On the other hand, the homeless view themselves as providing jobs for health care and social service personnel just as they provide cheap labor for missions, shelters, and jails. The beneficiaries "wish that all these people would either leave them alone or give them what they want: medical care when they need it, and a clean, warm flop when their money runs out" [3, p. 501]. A further point of disparity and conflict between client and staff is the use of recovering alcoholics as counselors and therapists, since Cumming contends that the unreformed skid row men hate them.

The reality of benefactor-beneficiary conflict, and the possibility of exploitation of shelter residents, and the disparity of viewpoints of what constitutes appropriate objectives of rehabilitation, was pointedly demonstrated in California when a religious mission's shelter and a publicly funded clinic attempted to develop a cooperative program for skid row alcoholics [5]. The clinic was to provide counseling and the mission was to provide spiritual and vocational assistance, and the alcoholics had their choice of becoming clinic clients or shelter residents. The clinic began recruiting clients from outside skid row from the probation department, courts, hospitals, and other clinics, and inadvertently may have contributed to the skid row alcoholism problem by introducing people to the area who might not have otherwise arrived there on their own. The mission and the clinic disagreed over rehabilitation approaches, and eventually began to compete with each other for beneficiaries who appeared to be the best candidates. Alcoholism treatment was progressively neglected while control over recruitment of clients or residents became increasingly more important. Then, for political and economic rather than therapeutic reasons, the clinic instituted procedures that excluded the local population from the shelter. The authors [5] concluded that ill-defined problems and little agreement on how to conceptualize and treat alcoholism may plague treatment and social change efforts. Such turf issues and a strong motive for self-preservation among social service and health care agencies may indeed be a disservice, if not actually dangerous, to the alcoholic.

THE FUTURE OF SHELTERS

This author firmly believes in the value of shelters for the health, safety, and security of the homeless and indigent alcoholic, as well as for other alcoholic (and nonalcoholic) persons who may need a refuge during periods of crisis and change. He also sees a potentially beneficial effect in an opportunity for voluntary exposure to religious and spiritual experiences and voluntary participation in meaningful work. For some people, totally secular shelters, without an emphasis on labor, may be more beneficial, while for others a spiritual retreat and an opportunity for undisturbed meditation or reflection may be more useful. Although urban renewal may be displacing traditional skid rows, their missions, and their inhabitants, it is unlikely that comparable social engineering will ever produce a perfect society in which alcoholism or homelessness will cease to exist and all men and women will be competent in dealing with problems in living. Health care and social service agents, as well as managers, administrators, and governments, must recognize that alcoholics, like all people, have individual differences that must be respected, that differing alcoholisms exist, and not all will respond favorably to a single, universal formula.

Perhaps in the future one will see, in addition to the religious mission shelters, the development of secular, municipally funded shelters, where residents can work to maintain themselves and the facility if that is in their own best interest. Perhaps what is needed, in addition to urban shelters in the central city, are rural and pastoral shelters where troubled, and troubling, people can find personal restoration and simple dignity. Perhaps what is needed is a return to the original 18th and 19th century notion of the shelter, a refuge, a sanctuary, to be used in such a way, and for such a period of time, as best benefits each individual, with appropriate but not primary or undue consideration given to preservation of the institution itself. Indeed, in the future society may benefit from a restoration of the asylum, in the truest and best sense of the idea.

REFERENCES

1. Bahr, H. M. Lifetime affiliation patterns of early- and late-onset heavy drinkers on skid row. *Q. J. Stud. Alcohol* 30:645–656, 1969.
2. Bodine, R. J. *A Study of Crisis in a Residential Treatment Center for Alcoholics.* Doctoral dissertation, University of Southern California, 1974.
3. Cumming, E. Prisons, shelters, and homeless men. *Psychiatr. Q.* 48:496–504, 1974.
4. Donahue, J. A halfway house program for alcoholics. *Q. J. Stud. Alcohol* 32:468–472, 1971.
5. Fry, L. J., and Miller, J. Responding to skid row alcoholism: Self-defeating arrangements in an innovative treatment program. *Social Problems* 22:675–688, 1975.
6. Garrett, G. R., and Bahr, H. M. Women on skid row. *Q. J. Stud. Alcohol* 34:1228–1243, 1973.
7. Gunn, J. Prisons, shelters, and homeless men. *Psychiatr. Q.* 48:505–512, 1974.
8. Judge, J. J. Alcoholism treatment at the Salvation Army: A new men's social service center program. *Q. J. Stud. Alcohol* 32:462–467, 1971.
9. Katz, L. The Salvation Army men's social service center: I. Program. *Q. J. Stud. Alcohol* 25:324–332, 1964.
10. Katz, L. The Salvation Army men's social service center: II. Results. *Q. J. Stud. Alcohol* 27:636–647, 1966.
11. Rubbington, E. The future of the halfway house. *Q. J. Stud. Alcohol* 31:167–174, 1970.
12. Rubbington, E. The role of the halfway house in the rehabilitation of alcoholics. In: *Treatment and Rehabilitation of the Chronic Alcoholic,* Kissin, G. and Begleiter, H. (eds.). Plenum: New York, 1977.
13. *Salvation Army Men's Social Service Handbook.* Salvation Army: New York, 1970.
14. Wiseman, J. P. *Making the Loop: The Institutional Cycle of Alcoholism Rehabilitation.* Unpublished doctoral dissertation, University of California, Berkeley, 1968.

75

JIM ORFORD, PhD, University of Exeter, Exeter, Devon, England
RICHARD VELLEMAN, MSc, University of Exeter, Exeter, Devon, England

ALCOHOLISM HALFWAY HOUSES

THE TERM "HALFWAY house" implies a relatively small residential unit where people with problems will stay for a limited period of time. The unit is halfway between hospital or prison on the one hand and independent life in the community on the other; or, alternatively, halfway between a socially unstable and alienated existence on the one hand and integration within the community on the other. This definition clearly begs a number of questions about aims and goals, and these questions will be examined later.

In the United Kingdom the term "halfway house" is not in widespread use, and the generic term "hostel" is preferred. Use of the adjectives "small" and "therapeutic" to qualify the noun then become necessary to distinguish places which in the United States and Canada would be termed "halfway houses" from shorter stay establishments or those with a less serious rehabilitative intent. These questions of terminology are of far more than mere academic importance. Terms such as "therapeutic," and "rehabilitation" beg further questions, which should not be avoided, concerning programs and methods. In the world of institutions and small groups, halfway houses occupy an interesting but uncertain place. They raise

---

Jim Orford, PhD, Senior Lecturer in Clinical Psychology, University of Exeter, and Principal Clinical Psychologist, Exe Vale Hospital, Exeter, Devon, England.

Richard Velleman, MSc, Research Psychologist, University of Exeter, and Clinical Psychologist, Exe Vale Hospital, Exeter, Devon, England.

many issues that are of general significance for an understanding of residential establishments for health, social service, education, and correction. Sadly however, and this is true of so many topics within the field of alcohol and alcoholism studies, they have been discussed in isolation, without reference to the much wider and richer literature that exists on these related types of facility.

Recent Growth

A National Institute of Mental Health (NIMH) directory of 1972 [15] showed that 121 alcoholism halfway houses were established in the second half of the 1960s compared with 70, 41, and 11 in the preceding three quinquennia. By 1975 the NIMH was able to report 597 houses in the United States covering every state but one [16]. The country was in fact much better served, both overall and in coverage, with alcoholism halfway houses than with similar houses for the mentally ill (nearly three times as many of the former were reported). In his review, Rubington [26] considers 1,000 to be a conservative estimate of the total number of alcoholism houses in North America. Ogborne et al. [17] estimate around 50 such houses in Ontario and more than 150 in the whole of Canada.

Similar recent expansion has been evident on a smaller scale in the United Kingdom. The Federation of Alcoholic Rehabilitation Establishments (FARE) (a similar coordinating body exists in the United States in the form of the Association of Halfway House Alcoholism Programs—AHHAP—based in Minnesota) lists 63 hostels offering a total of 792 beds in 1979. All but a few have been established since 1960 and most since Department of Health funds were made available for starting such houses in 1973. The importance of demonstrating the effectiveness of such units is being forcibly underlined in Britain at the present time as this central government scheme is being terminated and local social service departments, financed partly by local taxes and under more severe pressure than ever to reduce spending, are often unwilling to take over funding.

VARIETIES OF HALFWAY HOUSES

It has been pointed out elsewhere, both with reference to residential accommodation in general [29] and alcoholism halfway houses in particular [23], that institutions vary in many ways and that a single stereotype can be misleading. The following are some of the sources of variation that have been described in the literature on alcoholism halfway houses.

Size

Twelve residents to an alcoholism halfway house is a common number: This is the median size of houses in the United Kingdom [8] and was the modal size of 23 houses studied in Florida in 1972 [12]. However, the variation in size in each of these samples was considerable: a range of four to 32 in the United Kingdom and seven to 53 in Florida. Differences of that magnitude must have major implications for organization. Multiple staff, some staff who are residential, rules and regulations, and a reduced chance of creating a homely atmosphere are all more likely as numbers increase.

Origins

Rubington [26] differentiates private, state, and church houses. Although he presents no evidence to support his claim, he believes private houses cater more to the white-collar resident and that they tend to suffer from the excessive degree of control vested in the manager. State houses, he believes, specialize in blue-collar residents and tend to be larger, with a more structured program. Finally, church houses concentrate particularly on skid row drinkers, are larger and more regimented. Otto and Orford [23] also noted differences in origins among houses in London, England. A number had their origins in a religious mission or society, and among this group were the larger and longest established houses. Others had their origins in modern, secular concerns with treatment or rehabilitation. Many had been set up as a result of the special interest of someone working in a specialist psychiatric treatment service, usually in conjunction with a voluntary body active in the residential social work field. Similar modern initiatives may be taken by councils on alcoholism or occasionally by university departments of psychology [32].

Staffing

Ratios of care staff to residents vary widely: from 1:3 to 1:18 [23] and 1:2.5 to 1:14 [12]. These differences undoubtedly reflect differences in philosophy as well as funding considerations. Hence some houses where the attempt is to create a homelike, democratic, nontreatment-oriented environment have fewer staff relative to resident numbers, and some of the smaller houses may be without any staff who are themselves living on the premises.

As is the case with hostels for the mentally ill [2, 25] staff sometimes have a relevant professional background such as probation, social work, clinical psychology, or nursing, but most do not. Whether or not this is a good thing is a matter for debate. Available evidence from related mental health fields suggests that nonprofessional workers make as effective treatment agents as do professionally trained workers [6]. Rather more important may be the related issues of the status of work in halfway houses, working conditions for staff, and staff dissatisfaction and turnover. These matters have received relatively little systematic attention. It is the experience of these authors that halfway house staff complain of isolation and lack of supervision sufficiently often for these matters to command greater attention. Such problems are not, of course, confined to alcoholism halfway houses.

A special feature of the alcohol problems field is the special influence of Alcoholics Anonymous (AA) and the role of former problem drinkers as halfway house staff. This appears to be a much stronger factor in North America, where approximately 60% of staff are recovering alcoholics [12, 16].

The Program

Such structural attributes as size, origins, and staffing are related to orientation and program content, although not, it could be argued, in the simple way that Rubington [26], for example, suggests. The most systematic comparison of halfway house programs has been reported by Ogborne et al. [20]. They find houses in Ontario, Canada differ most markedly in the factor of AA emphasis. Houses that require or strongly encourage attendance at AA meetings have a predominance of staff who endorse conservative and AA-oriented opinion statements. For example, such staff thought residents should be encouraged to go to church and that staff should represent the more conservative values of society; they believed as well that AA should be an indispensable component and that a recovered alcoholic was usually the best person to help another alcoholic. They also believed that staff and residents should be like one happy family, and that houses should be places where, first and foremost, residents are made to feel easy and at home. They were markedly more likely to report spending over 30 hours a week with halfway house residents. This latter finding is particularly important in view of Otto and Orford's [23] results at two English houses where time spent with residents was associated with residents' liking for staff and with favorable comments of residents about house atmosphere.

A second and related factor that Ogborne et al. [20] find to be correlated with AA orientation, although not perfectly, is the existence of a formal structured program of treatment activities organized by staff. Roughly one third of the houses they studied involved residents in such a program for more than 20 hours a week. Such houses were less likely to have an AA orientation than were others. In Britain, although examples of treatment-intensive houses exist (e.g., [32]), relatively few are of this kind. Otto and Orford [23] concluded that most hostels aim to influence their residents via the shared experience of communal group living in the context of a house that promotes certain specified drinking goals and certain general rehabilitation aims. Rubington [26] also describes the process in terms of milieu rather than technique, but places rather more emphasis upon the importance of identifying with staff and the development of commitment to their norms.

Authority Structure

As in hostels for the mentally ill [2] and in other types of residential facilities [29], alcoholism halfway houses differ markedly one from another in the degree of autonomy or decision-making power given to residents. Otto and Orford [23] found wide variation in practice. Houses varied from those that involved residents in all day-to-day decisions as well as some matters of policy making and discipline at one end of the spectrum, to those that reserved most decisions for staff and had rules for even such everyday matters as time of rising in the morning. Particularly discriminating were decisions concerning house membership. The more democratic houses made a special attempt to involve residents when a decision had to be made whether or not to discharge a fellow resident who had been drinking, and also in the choice of new residents. Observation of the process at two particular houses, however, suggested that even in such houses staff had by far the greater authority over these matters. Although the question of authority within a halfway house is one about which residents, staff, and policy makers all appear to feel most strongly, there is no convincing evidence that one style is more effective than the other overall. There is reason to believe from other work [31], however, that different residents may respond better to different types of regimes. This confirms the view that flexibility of approach is important in the rehabilitation of problem drinking. It may be impossible to provide flexibility over the matter of authority patterns within one establishment, however, and it follows that variety among houses as a whole is strongly to be encouraged.

The authors' observations of hostels in Britain suggests that on the whole they allow considerably more decision-making freedom to residents than do other types of establishments, such as the probation hostels described by Sinclair [28], or hostels for the mentally ill [2]. To take just one instance, influence over the selection of new residents is not infrequently denied even to care staff in such institutions, these decisions being made by an outside consultant or committee. Convincing evidence has been presented elsewhere [29] that staff autonomy is itself a crucial variable, with staff who have the greatest freedom to make decisions providing a higher quality of resident care than those whose fredom is more restricted. The physical separation of most halfway houses from larger institutions at least provides them with the scope for allowing considerable staff autonomy.

Another variable, discussed by Martin and Segal [12] and by Martin [11] is termed "staff expectation for client independence." This variable was assessed using a 40-item role expectations scale that examined the degree to which staff expected residents to, for example, have their own bank account, get a job, prepare dinner, and go on errands when asked by staff. Martin hypothesized that staff members would base their expectations of clients on client characteristics such as age, sex, drinking and work histories, and socioeconomic status, which might be thought to be indicative of outcome. Her investigation of 23 halfway houses in Florida, however, showed staff expectations to be largely uninfluenced by such characteristics, although staff did expect less independence from women, and once residents were working staff expected increasing independence as earnings rose. Martin concluded that expectations in general are set by the formal structure and philosophy of a unit, resulting in expectations in any one house remaining relatively inflexible in the face of different client types. If this is the case it may be a particular shortcoming, as resident needs and abilities surely vary considerably.

An interesting finding from Martin and Segal's analysis was that staff expectations correlated with numbers of staff and residents (greater expectations when numbers were smaller) and with the staff to resident ratio (higher expectations when there were relatively many staff compared to residents).

Bureaucracy and Atmosphere

Martin and Segal were interested in the correlation between aspects of bureaucratic organization in halfway houses and staff expectations for clients. None of the aspects studied were strongly related to staff expectations although one variable, complexity, was positively related to staff expectations when the sheer number of staff working in a house was controlled. There were two measures of complexity: the number of distinct occupational titles of all paid employees excepting clerical (horizontal complexity), and the number of supervisory levels in the hierarchical structure (vertical complexity). Unfortunately Martin and Segal [12] were unable to operationalize one aspect of bureaucracy, formalization (the extent to which rules, procedures, and roles are explicit and formal), which is probably the aspect that comes closest to the general public's conception of what bureaucracy is.

Martin's work on alcoholism halfway houses is important because of the links it forges with the much older and wider literature on organizations in general. Another recent attempt to make such links is Moos' work employing the concept of atmosphere and the Community-Oriented Programs Environment Scale (COPES), a scale described by Moos [13] that is similar to his Ward Atmosphere Scale (WAS) and one that has been used in a variety of treatment and rehabilitation settings. The scale is designed to measure 10 dimensions, three termed "relationship" dimensions (involvement, support, spontaneity), four "treatment program" dimensions (autonomy, practical orientation, personal problem orientation, anger and aggression), and three "system maintenance" dimensions (order and organization, program clarity, staff control). Yates [32] has reported the use of COPES in two houses set up as part of the Alcoholics Rehabilitation Research Group project in Birmingham, England. Both houses were treatment-oriented, employing personal skills training in their programs, but they contrasted on the question of whether controlled drinking was allowed as a long-term drinking goal. The house where this was allowed was described by residents as higher on personal problem orientation and on involvement, although the difference is just as likely to be attributable to staff and client differences as to differences in drinking goals. At both houses staff described greater autonomy than did the residents, and described less staff control and order and organization, a finding that is in keeping with Moos' work [13] using the WAS.

Rubington [27] examined what he called "institutional atmosphere" on a scale that he devised and completed himself during the course of participant observation in four halfway houses in the Boston area. He was concerned with testing his view that halfway houses work by creating an informal, homelike atmosphere in contrast to the institutional climates experienced by many of their residents elsewhere during periods in prison and in hospital, for example. His scale certainly appears to have discriminated clearly between the houses in his small sample. A high score was achieved if a house issued written rules, had many mandatory meetings, dish lists, detail lists, relatively many beds, many beds in a dormitory, many specialized rooms, bulletin boards, door control, lack of access to the kitchen, and if staff did not play cards, talk informally, eat meals, and attend outside AA meetings with residents. It may be argued that Rubington's scale confounds two variables — atmosphere and structure. Hence it should be possible to have a house with a structured program that is still relaxed and homelike, and an unstructured house that is more institutional. A larger sample might reveal these possible patterns.

Residents' Characteristics

Because halfway houses are in part a response to the need for accommodation it is only to be expected that the majority of halfway house residents will be homeless, either chronically or temporarily. In general residents are likely to be people who have lost, or who perhaps have never had as adults, stable roots in family, employment, and community [26]. A comparison of residents' characteristics data provided by Otto and Orford [23], Ogborne et al. [17], and from a halfway house in Devon, England by Velleman [30] bears out this expectation. The average resident has a long-standing drinking problem of approximately 15 years duration, and the majority have served prison terms, have worked less than half of the previous 12 months, and have spent most of that time living outside a stable family setting. The majority are unemployed and unmarried or separated from spouses at the time of entering the halfway house. These are important considerations as Costello's [4] meta analysis of alcoholism treatment studies has clearly shown. Being in employment and being married are two factors strongly predictive of overall success rates for study samples at follow-up.

Once again, however, it would be quite wrong to form a fixed stereotype of the alcoholism halfway house resident. Marked differences are to be found in the clientele of different halfway houses and these differences at least partly reflect differences in aim and in selection policy. There were evident differences of this type between the two houses studied intensively by Otto and Orford [23]. House A was intended, at least in part, as an aftercare facility for men who had received treatment in a psychiatric unit, while house B was intended for chronic drunkenness offenders. As a consequence, residents of house A had spent more time living recently with family or friends and less time sleeping outdoors or in cheap lodgings. In addition there were important historical differences. House A residents had had more education and were more likely to have had higher status jobs in the past. They also achieved higher scores on a scale of previous social stability devised by Otto and Orford to assess the degree to which residents had ever in their adult lives achieved a period of social stability.

Ogborne et al. [17] have shown the wide variation that exists in halfway houses in Ontario. Percentages married varied from 0 to 26%, living recently in own apartment or house 6 to 46%, jailed in the last year 12 to 56%, and having four or more skid row characteristics 0 to 52%. In Britain a recent Department of Health report [5] stressed that residential units do have a part to play in the care of problem drinkers who still have homes, families, and jobs, and that they can play a part in detoxification, in the provision of temporary relief separation for both client and family, in the provision of temporary accommodation, an alternative to hospital care, or in providing a transitional stay between hospital and a full return to social and family environment. The Birmingham project has shown how a deliberate policy can influence selection. In that case a determined treatment philosophy and an effort to recruit residents of better prognosis resulted in no fewer than 50% at one house and 30% at the other having been in stable residence in their own homes in the 3 months prior to admission [32].

There are some even more obvious client variables: for example, the mix of men and women, young and old, and those with drinking problems and those without. Although the majority of houses listed by FARE in Britain [8] and *Yearly Census Report* of the AHHAP [33] in the United States are for men only, an increasing number of houses cater to both sexes, and some are for women only. Whether this balance truly reflects needs is difficult to know. Women may certainly find it more difficult to find provision in their own area, and the Department of Health and Social Security report [5] makes particular mention of women with young children for whom few hostels make provision.

The age variable is one that frequently gives hostel organizers cause for concern. Those in need of provision range widely in age and different age groups may have different needs. Younger residents may have drinking problems complicated by other problems such as drug abuse and they may require a more intensive therapeutic milieu. The oldest residents, on the other hand, may need a refuge that can be a permanent home, where drinking is discouraged but where the occasional lapse is recognized as likely and not penalized by immediate discharge. Houses of the latter type are rare, although one has recently been opened in Devon, England. The fact that different houses cater to different parts of the age spectrum is again shown by Ogborne et al.'s [17] figures. Percentages of residents under 30 varied in their sample from 3 to 58%.

The rapid recent growth of specialist provision for men and women with drinking problems is itself an interesting phenomenon worthy of study. The majority of alcoholism halfway houses are fully specialist, requiring evidence of a drinking problem on admission. A minority, however, while making special provision for this group, accommodate people with other problems besides. For example, Otto and Orford [23] found two such houses among 11 that they surveyed in London.

THE OUTCOME FOLLOWING HALFWAY HOUSE RESIDENCE

Short-term Outcome

Length of stay. The concept of rehabilitation implied by the term "halfway house" suggests that residents should remain for long enough to absorb the socializing influence of the house and to acquire the personal and material resources necessary for more independent living. At the same time they should not outstay their welcome by using the house as a long-term home. Accordingly, many halfway house staffs regard a period of residence of a few months, often somewhere in the region of 3 to 9 months, as an ideal length of stay. Figures showing the actual length of stay of alcoholism halfway house residents show how infrequently this ideal is achieved.

The main problem is premature termination. Otto and Orford [23] in England and Ogborne et al. [17] in Canada both found that half of all new residents in a variety of houses had left within the first 4 to 7 weeks, and that only a minority (usually 10 to 33%) remain for 3 months or more. This finding is repeatedly reported from individual hostels [22, 30].

There is a further problem at the other end of the length of stay continuum. Of those residents who do remain, a considerable proportion turn out to have long-term needs for sheltered or semi-independent accommodation and support. This is a familiar problem in residential work and calls into question the halfway house philosophy of rehabilitation. As with hostels for the mentally ill [2], it is found that where policy allows, many residents remain in alcoholism hostels for 1 year or even 2 years or more. Where policy does not permit such lengths of stay alternative arrangements have to be made. In Britain it has certainly been the case that many councils on alcoholism and other voluntary bodies who have set up alcoholism hostels have within a few years recognized the need to set up longer term houses for a proportion of their clients.

Mode of leaving. A second major source of difficulty arises when examination is made of the proportions of residents who leave with and without approval of staff, sober or drinking, and with or without a stable residence in mind as destination. Otto and Orford [23] reported only 10 to 15% of residents in the two houses they studied leaving in a planned and orderly manner, with the full approval of staff. A large proportion of the remainder left after drinking, and others left after a dispute or disappeared without warning. A small number left in an orderly fashion but with the intention of resuming drinking. Ogborne et al. [17]

report only 22% of all residents in a sample of over 1,500 from 28 different halfway houses left with staff approval; 33% were asked to leave, most because of drinking, and another 34% left without being asked, half of this latter number not informing staff that they were going. Again, similar results are obtained elsewhere [22, 30, 32].

Reducing the rate of unsatisfactory terminations. Clearly these findings pose important questions. Either halfway houses are failing with a large percentage of their clients, or alternatively the halfway house rehabilitation model only fits the facts in a minority of cases. In so far as the first of these statement holds any truth, it becomes important to know how rates of premature and unsatisfactory departures can be reduced. Available figures do suggest that these rates vary within limits. Ogborne et al. [17] found rates of leaving with staff approval varied between 2 and 48%. Proportions of residents leaving within 1 month of arrival varied between 2 and 49%. Part of this variation undoubtedly can be attributed to client characteristics. Ogborne and Wiggins [19] show the skid row factor (use of nonbeverage alcohol, admission at any time to a detoxification center, time in jail within the last year, the number of times picked up for drunkenness in the last year, unstable accommodation) to be a significant determinant of premature leaving, and results presented in Ogborne et al.'s [17] report suggest the same factor may be an even more important determinant of leaving without staff approval.

However, even if the ideal of a stay of several months followed by departure with the approval of staff is accepted uncritically, there are findings that suggest that client characteristics are not the only influences. Ogborne and Wiggins [19] have themselves demonstrated the influence of the variable of program structure. Houses with a formal structured program of therapeutic events (20 or more hours a week), of which there were five, produced different lengths of stay data than did those houses without such a program, of which there were 10 in their sample. The difference was strongest for residents low on the skid row factor. Half of such residents in houses without a structured program had left by 6 or 7 weeks, whereas in houses with a formal program 15 or 16 weeks passed before half had left. There is a strong suggestion that men who are high on the skid row factor are influenced also. At 3 months 80 to 95% of these men had left as opposed to 70% from houses with formal treatment programs.

It has already been pointed out that wide variation exists in the authority structures, degrees of resident autonomy, and atmospheres to be found in halfway houses and Rubington [27] has recently reported a study that suggests that these matters may be more than purely incidental to the problem of short-term outcome. Among the four houses that he studied, the two with the lowest scores on his scale of institutional atmosphere produced the lowest rates of premature leaving and the highest rates of leaving abstinent. This is an important lead, although his sample is of course small and the matter may be far more complex. Wilbur et al.'s [31] work suggesting that some residents may prefer and do better in a more democratic atmosphere while others may prefer and do better in a more paternalistic climate; Otto and Orford's [23] finding that dissatisfaction with authority patterns was highest in the middle of the range of resident decision-making autonomy and was lowest at the extremes; and from the wider literature on residential care, Sinclair's [28] finding that the leadership qualities of wardens in probation hostels were confounded by the factor of disagreement between the warden and the matron over the exercise of authority all testify to the extreme complexity of these matters.

Finally, extra complexity is added by Otto and Orford's [23] close examination of two houses over a period of some months, and their analysis of data available from the same houses over a period of some years. They argued that houses do not remain the same from one period to another. Overall philosophy may remain relatively constant over a period of years, but climate oscillates in the way described by Rapoport [24] in a therapeutic community. Climate at any one time may depend particularly upon the leadership style of the staff member in charge, but is in addition a complex function of the mix of residents, their attitudes and expectations, and the emergence of leaders among them. Grygier's [9] work in Canadian correctional institutions should lead one to expect a complicated set of dynamics involving goodness of fit between staff and resident attitudes.

Long-term Outcome

The growing demand for objective evaluation of treatment and, in particular, the need to demonstrate cost-effectiveness are being felt in the alcoholism halfway house movement, as elsewhere. Present financial constraints add to the strength of these demands. Evidence for the long-term effectiveness of halfway houses is hard to come by. On the basis of their review, Ogborne and Smart concluded: "No study has been found which adequately shows halfway house treatment to be better than any other treatment or superior to no treatment at all [but] ... such a lack of support for the promise of halfway houses is due as much to the shortcomings of present studies as to the results which they present" [18, pp. 14, 16].

They found only two studies that came anywhere near to matching the criteria that they considered ideal for an evaluation study. Both have severe limitations. Myerson and Mayer [14] reported a 10-year follow-up of 100 men, 22% of whom were classified as successfully rehabilitated and 24% as partially rehabilitated. Unfortunately results cannot easily be attributed to the halfway house experience 10 years earlier because the report says little about what happened to the men in the intervening years, and in any case very scanty details were provided of the halfway house itself.

In the second study, reported by Blumberg et al. [3], as many clients as possible were followed up at least a year after random assignment between a halfway house and one of two varieties of individual counseling. Fewer of the halfway house group achieved at least 1 year's sobriety during the period of the study

(12.5% vs. 23.3% of the intensively counseled group), but a poor response rate at follow-up makes it difficult to draw conclusions from this study. In addition Blumberg et al.'s [3] account of the halfway house concerned makes it clear that the milieu created left a lot to be desired. If halfway house climates change from time to time, even within a single unit, it becomes clear that it is not sufficient to base evaluation upon one house sampled during one limited period of time.

Annis and Liban [1] have recently reported a 3-month follow-up of 35 men who had entered one of five halfway houses following detoxication in comparison with 35 men who received detoxication but did not enter a halfway house. The two groups were carefully matched on a number of characteristics. Members of the nonhalfway house group were more likely to be arrested for public drunkenness (37% vs. 6%), but were less likely to return to the detoxication center during the follow-up period (26% vs. 49%). The proportions experiencing one or other of these events during follow-up were very similar (halfway house group 51%, control group 46%).

The Need for Adequate Evaluation

One must conclude, as Ogborne and Smart [18] did, that attempts at evaluation to date are quite inadequate. The limitations are similar to those that beset most evaluation studies of alcoholism treatment in general. The position with regard to alcoholism halfway houses is worse since very little outcome research of any kind has been attempted.

A major shortcoming lies in the failure to adequately describe the treatment provided. Enough is known about variations both between halfway houses and within halfway houses over time to make it clear that the simple specification "halfway house" is inadequate as a description.

Choosing criteria for successful outcome also poses considerable problems. The limitations of total abstinence from alcohol as a main indication of successful outcome has been recognized in the wider alcoholism treatment literature but is only now beginning to be recognized in the alcoholism halfway house evaluation literature. Total abstinence for a period of 1 year or more is rare after any form of alcoholism treatment. For example, Dwoskin et al.'s [7] follow-up of 185 consecutive discharges from an alcoholism halfway house discovered seven ex-residents who had remained abstinent for 12 months or more, a further 23 who had remained abstinent since discharge less than 12 months previously, 31 who were lost to follow-up in the first 2 months following discharge, and 124 who were known to have taken a drink during the follow-up period.

Preliminary results from the University of Birmingham project on three houses [32] shows how inadequate any system of categorization is when it attempts to summarize an ex-resident's drinking over a period as long as a year or more after leaving a halfway house. That study categorized the predominant drinking pattern in each of four successive follow-up periods of 3 months each. The results show that it is rare for an ex-resident to maintain either abstinence or controlled drinking throughout the follow-up year but the number of people with three, two, or one successful drinking periods is considerable. Periods of controlled drinking were as common as periods of abstinence or near-abstinence, and were not much less frequent following residence in a house that encouraged the traditional aim of total abstinence in comparison with a house that supported some residents in their aim of controlled drinking.

There remains the question whether drinking should properly constitute the main outcome criterion at all, and the still more fundamental question of whether residence in a hostel or halfway house should be expected to produce long-term gains after residence is terminated. This expectation may imply an "illness needing treatment" model, which some would argue may be inappropriate. An alternative environmental circumstances model suggests that in-hostel success [23] is a sufficient criterion in itself, and that long-term success can only be expected if a person's environment continues to be one that supports stability.

ISSUES REQUIRING RESOLUTION

Halfway houses have established themselves as a major feature on the alcoholism treatment landscape. Trends suggest a likely increase rather than a decrease in the prevalence of drinking problems in the foreseeable future and despite attempts to intervene early it seems likely that there will continue to be a demand for residential care for a considerable proportion of those people with long-standing drinking problems. Despite the lack of evidence upon which to base a strong case for their success in terms of proportions of residents rehabilitated, alcoholic halfway houses evidently meet a need. Enough research has been done, however, to indicate quite strongly where some of the issues lie that must be resolved if halfway houses are to function more effectively than at present.

Continuity of Care

Both the report of the Department of Health [5] in Britain and the report of the task force on halfway houses in Canada [17] have stressed the way in which hostels could provide a base for a wider range of services that could meet the needs of a wider range of clients with drinking problems. These services include detoxication, the provision of temporary accommodation for either the problem drinker or family, a base for crisis intervention, an alternative site to hospitalization for relatively intensive treatment, as well as the provision of short- or long-term accommodation for the homeless.

Providing such a continuous range of services from one community base would both utilize this base to the full and force those responsible to achieve greater clarity of purpose. Lack of clarity, for example over ideal lengths of stay, over treatment programs, and over authority patterns within the establishment, was identified by Otto and Orford [23] as one of the major present shortcomings of hostels. Fundamental differences of opinion exist, both between and within projects, over whether houses should be transitional or nontransitional, treatment-oriented or homely in atmosphere, democratic or paternal. Different emphases are placed by different people upon the treatment or rehabilitation function on the one hand and the provision of accommodation on the other.

The low rate of successful short-term outcomes highlights the major shortcoming of alcoholism halfway houses as presently operated. For most residents the image of halfway house residence as a temporary stage in a smooth passage from illness and social instability to abstinence and social integration is largely myth. A minority conform to this pattern but for the remainder the myth may be damaging because it leads to false expectations and to a severe disjunction in the continuity of care at the point of leaving the hostel or halfway house [23]. Most residents leave drinking or without approval and relationships are usually severed at this point. In at least one study of a psychiatric halfway house it was shown that continued contact after residence led to a much more positive adjustment in the community [10].

Halfway houses must, as a matter of some urgency, find some way of overcoming these problems. Integration with other alcoholism services, both residential and nonresidential, should be a goal. Perhaps it should be an aim to achieve such integration that staff would be appointed, not to work solely in a halfway house, but as workers within a general service with an overview of the continuity of facilities through which clients move, not in most cases in a smooth and orderly fashion in one direction, but rather in varied and complex ways.

Part of the blame for this stereotyped conception of alcoholism rehabilitation can be laid at the door of rigidity over drinking goals. The halfway house movement has been slow to accept the possibility of goals other than abstinence. This is undoubtedly partly due to the residential context, which makes the handling of potentially uncontrolled drinking difficult. There have been a small number of attempts to operate houses with the aim of controlled drinking, notably Bon Accord house in Ontario [21] and Thornhurst in Wolverhamptom, England [32]. Outcome figures for the latter house are comparable to those for comparison abstinence houses. An important advantage of flexibility over drinking goals concerns the way in which residents leave the house. Yates' comparison of Thornhurst and an abstinence house revealed a substantially higher proportion of residents returning to the former house for visits after leaving. Whereas in the comparison house many departures were "abrupt and on poor terms," the greater flexibility over the issue of drinking at Thornhurst resulted in an "avoidance of the inevitable sense of rejection and failure which terminates the residence of the large proportion of cases dismissed for drinking."

CONCLUSION

In conclusion one must note the important part that alcoholism hostels or halfway houses have come to play in the range of available alcoholism services. In comparison with penal or other institutional provisions, or in contrast with the absence of proper provisions, they represent a humane and relatively economic alternative (although there has been no detailed cost-effectiveness analysis of halfway house provisions). Indeed, in Britain at least, it is possible to foresee that with the move toward forms of provision that are more in the community and less in a hospital setting coupled with the growth of voluntary councils on alcoholism, hostels may come to play a more central role than hitherto. There are, however, a number of fundamental problems to which solutions must be found, and to this end variety, further innovation, good evaluation research, and a reduction in staff isolation must be encouraged.

REFERENCES

1. Annis, H. M., and Liban, C. P. Follow-up study of male halfway house residents and matched nonresident controls. *J. Stud. Alcohol* 40:63–69, 1979.
2. Apte, R. Z. *Halfway Houses: A New Dilemma in Institutional Care* (Occasional papers on social administration, No. 27). Bell: London, 1968.
3. Blumberg, L., Shipley, T. E., and Shandler, I. W. *Skid Row and Its Alternatives: Research and Recommendations from Philadelphia.* Temple University Press: Philadelphia, 1973.
4. Costello, R. M. Alcoholism treatment effectiveness: Slicing the outcome variance pie. In: *Alcoholism Treatment in Transition*, Edwards, G. and Grant, M. (eds.). Croom and Helm: London, 1980.
5. Department of Health and Social Security. *The Pattern and Range of Services for Problem Drinkers* (Report by the Advisory Committee on Alcoholism. Her Majesty's Stationery Office: London, 1978.
6. Durlak, J. A. Comparative effectiveness of paraprofessional and professional helpers. *Psychol. Bull.* 86:310–316, 1979.
7. Dwoskin, J., Gordis, E., and Dorph, D. Life-table analysis of treatment outcome following 185 consecutive alcoholism halfway house discharges. *Alcoholism: Clin. Exp. Res.* 3:334–340, 1979.
8. Federation of Alcoholic Rehabilitation Establishments. *Position Paper: Alcoholism Hostels Supported by DHSS Circular 21/73.* Author: London, 1979.
9. Grygier, T. Measurement of treatment potential. In: *Varieties of Residential Experience*, Tizard, J., Sinclair, I., and Clarke, R. V. G. (eds.). Routledge and Kegan Paul: London, 1975.
10. Holman, T., and Shore, M. F. Halfway house and family involvement as related to community adjustment for ex-residents of a psychiatric halfway house. *J. Commun. Psychol.* 6:123–129, 1978.
11. Martin, P. Y. Clients' characteristics and the expectations of staff in halfway houses for alcoholics. *J. Stud. Alcohol* 40:211–221, 1979.

12. Martin, P. Y., and Segal, B. Bureaucracy, size, and staff expectations for client independence in halfway houses. *J. Health Soc. Behav.* 18:376-390, 1977.
13. Moos, R. H. *Evaluating Treatment Environments: A Social Ecological Approach.* Wiley: New York, 1974.
14. Myerson, D. J., and Mayer, J. Origins, treatment and destiny of skid row alcoholic men. *N. Engl. J. Med.* 275:419-425, 1966.
15. National Institute of Mental Health. *Directory of Halfway Houses for the Mentally Ill and Alcoholics.* Author: Rockville, Md., 1972.
16. National Institute of Mental Health. Halfway houses serving the mentally ill and alcoholics, United States, 1971-1973. *Mental Health Statistics Series A* (No. 9). Author: Rockville, Md., 1975.
17. Ogborne, A. C., Annis H. M., and Sanchez-Craig, M. *Report of the Task Force on Halfway Houses.* Addiction Research Foundation: Toronto, 1978.
18. Ogborne, A. C., and Smart, R. G. Halfway houses for skid row alcoholics: A search for empirical evaluation. *Substudy 632.* Addiction Research Foundation: Toronto, 1974.
19. Ogborne, A. C., and Wiggins, T. R. I. Person-programme interactions in halfway houses for problem drinkers. *Brit. J. Addict.*, in press.
20. Ogborne, A. C., Wiggins, T. R., and Shain, M. Variations in staff characteristics, programmes and recruitment practices among halfway houses for problem drinkers. *Brit. J. Addict.* 75:393-403, 1980.
21. Oki, G. Alcohol use by skid row alcoholics: 1. Drinking at Bon Accord. *Substudy 612.* Addiction Research Foundation: Toronto, 1974.
22. Orford, J., Hawker, A., and Nicholls, P. An investigation of an alcoholism rehabilitation halfway house: I. Types of client and modes of discharge. *Brit. J. Addict.* 69:213-224, 1974.
23. Otto, S., and Orford, J. *Not Quite Like Home: Small Hostels for Alcoholics and Others.* Wiley: Chichester, 1978.
24. Rapoport, R. M. *Community as Doctor: New Perspectives on a Therapeutic Community.* Tavistock: London, 1960.
25. Raush, W. L., and Raush, C. L. *The Halfway House Movement: A Search for Sanity.* Appleton-Century-Crofts: New York, 1968.
26. Rubington, E. The role of the halfway house in the rehabilitation of alcoholics. In: *The Biology of Alcoholism: Treatment and Rehabilitation of the Chronic Alcoholic* (Vol. 5), Kissin, B. and Begleiter, H. (eds.). Plenum: New York, 1977.
27. Rubington, E. Halfway houses and treatment outcomes: A relationship between institutional atmosphere and therapeutic effectiveness. *J. Stud. Alcohol* 40:419-427, 1979.
28. Sinclair, I. Hostels for probationers: A study of the aims, working and variations in effectiveness of male probation hostels, with special reference to the influence of the environment on delinquency. *Home Office Research Studies* (No. 6). Her Majesty's Stationery Office: London, 1971.
29. Tizard, J., Sinclair, I., and Clarke, R. V. G. (eds.). *Varieties of Residential Experience.* Routledge and Kegan Paul: London, 1975.
30. Velleman, R. *Arden House: An Intensive Study of One Alcoholism Hostel.* Unpublished MSc dissertation, University of Exeter, England, 1980.
31. Wilbur, B. M., Salkin, D., and Bimbaum, H. The response of tuberculous alcoholics to a therapeutic community. *Q. J. Stud. Alcohol* 27:620-635, 1966.
32. Yates, F. *An Evaluation Study of Two Residential Programmes For Alcoholics: Comparing Abstinent and Controlled Drinking Objectives.* Unpublished doctoral dissertation, University of Newcastle, England, 1979.
33. *Yearly Census Report.* Association of Halfway House Alcoholism Programs: Minneapolis, 1979.

76

HAROLD W. DEMONE, JR., PhD, Rutgers–The State University

COMMUNITY HUMAN SERVICE AGENCIES AND ALCOHOLISM

THE THEME IS NOW HUMAN services. Be it the Johnson County Regional Planning Commission, Iowa City, Iowa [6], or the President's Commission on Mental Health [12] the thrust to view categorical and specialized services as one part of the larger whole is consistent. In Johnson County substance abuse is viewed as one component of the county-wide human services as they press toward efficiency and effectiveness.

The President's Commission on Mental Health stresses the development of comprehensive, integrated systems of care, and coordinated health and mental health planning, including alcoholism, at all levels.

CONTRASTING VIEWS

In contrast, in the alcoholism field there seems to be three identifiable views. Those supporting the integrationist theme suggest strengthening the existing generic care-giving system by providing it with alcoholism specialists who will perform all or several roles: intraorganizational advocacy, training of other staff, and

---

Harold W. Demone, Jr., PhD, Dean, Graduate School of Social Work, Professor, Social Work, Sociology, and the Center for Alcohol Studies, Rutgers–The State University, New Brunswick, New Jersey.

support of staff, and specialized services as necessary. Thus integrationists prefer to enhance the health maintenance organization (HMO), family service agency, general hospital, community mental health center, family practitioner, local psychiatrist, clergyman, and the like. A second significant direction in alcoholism is led by those who suggest that they be given the money, responsibility, and respectibility, and be left alone. Extensive use of paraprofessionals and self-help is emphasized. Some of the members of this group acknowledge, albeit begrudgingly, that for third-party reimbursement they may need to be individually certified and organizationally accredited. However, they insist that this be on their own terms. A third thrust also has a separatist theme in that its advocates urge the development of a range of specialized alcoholism programs controlled by alcoholism technicians; however, they acknowledge the necessary interdependence with other components of the human services industry. Specifically they accept the reality of the acute medical care, criminal justice, and welfare systems, and the occasional needs of their clients for these services. They seek to forge links where the specialized alcoholism industry is at its weakest.

Why this strong separatist theme in a problem as endemic, long-standing, and complicated as alcoholism?

As a rough rule of thumb society can manage only one primary control mechanism at a time for problems about which there is no clear consensus about either etiology or intervention. Thus alcohol excesses, blessed and cursed, have suffered from simplistic solutions and, as with all simplistic solutions to complex problems, failure has generally been the customary result.

Thus in the early 1930s when this nation gave up its glorious experiment with a national constitutional prohibition of alcohol sales a series of alternative steps were taken. Science (Yale), self-help (Alcoholics Anonymous), citizens (the National Council on Alcoholism), and government (for a long time only state-supported programs—the federal presence was late in arrival) all took their first careful steps in the 1930s and early 1940s. The combination of science, self-help, citizens, and the government was a potentially powerful one but it was not without opposition and stigma at the worst, and lethargy at the best. Thus Alcoholics Anonymous (AA) featured anonymity to protect its members and most early state-sponsored alcoholism programs were developed as independent authorities. The traditional public and mental health state agencies did not want the negative association with alcoholism. The Center of Alcohol Studies at Yale grew slowly and was eventually forced out of Yale as an inappropriate activity for a university. Similarly the National Council on Alcoholism spluttered for several decades, as compared to many other voluntary health agencies. Not surprisingly, a free-standing independent spirit evolved and substantially influenced the development of the field. Thus in the 1980s it is still necessary to persuade many alcoholism specialists that it is in the interest of their clients to join the larger human services industry. Many still remain unconvinced, and are often hostile and suspicious. To many, it is still "we" and "they."

DEFINITION

What, then, are human services? Schulberg and Demone [14] define human services as:

> Human services is both a conceptual rubric for organizing etiological notions about the biopsychosocial distresses faced by persons as well as a comprehensive caregiving arrangement required to relieve any or all of these distresses. Central to the human services rubric is its emphasis on the following principles:
>
> 1. Human distress is often founded in social system deficiencies rather than physiological, metabolic, or intrapsychic disorders. Rather than focusing on diagnostic labels which obscure these social system elements, increased concern should be paid to the daily "problems of living" adversely affecting persons.
> 2. The helping activities of various care givers have many qualities which are common and integral to all of them. These qualities are often not dependent or related to the care givers' particular professional training. Competence is the critical variable, and often, it transends arbitrary distinctions of degree and discipline.
> 3. Accessibility of services often is as important as their quality to the client seeking appropriate help. Accessibility must be viewed not only in terms of physical convenience but also with regard to such characteristics as psychological comfort, compatible staff, and appropriate hours.
> 4. Systems of service properly integrated to insure continuity of care are more effective than single services functioning in isolation. A range of human problems is so broad that only in exceptional instances can a given organization fully meet a client's total needs.
> 5. Service providers are accountable to multiple constituencies, including the clients obtaining their services. Determinations of program effectiveness must include the consumers' perspective as well as those of clinicians, administrators, and resource providers.

Thus human services may be seen as a way to organize, to conceptualize, and as a means to deliver services.

COMPONENT CLASSIFICATION SYSTEMS

Another way to understand the linkages and inseparability of the many human services is to examine the various typologies that have been developed to classify the various components. The classic example is the model used by the King County Department of Budget and Program Planning, Seattle, Washington [8]. Human needs are separated into four dimensions or categories: physical, emotional, intellectual, and social. (Interestingly alcoholism is classified under the category of "physical." Drug abuse is classified under "emotional.") A more elaborate classification is used in the Brockton, Massachusetts Human Services Accountability System [11]. They include employment and training, food and nutrition, individual and family life, housing services, physical health, mental health, social development, and cultural enrichment.

The Council of State Governments [2] uses even another classification system. Thirteen client or target groups most frequently in need of human services are designated. Alcoholism is one of the 13. Services provided to these client groups are then classified into four levels of care: care provided in institutions, care provided in alternative living arrangements, care provided in offices and clinics, and care provided at home.

Tested in Dekalb County, Georgia [2], several suggested uses of the latter classification system evolved. Recommended were the establishment of more formal organizational relationships, the allocation of resources, program planning, recognition of the interrelationships between target groups, professional relationship definitions, and recognition of the role of the political sector and of special interest groups.

Another way to note the complexity of human services is to examine various planning efforts. The Council for Community Services in Providence, Rhode Island [1] reported in 1975 that there were an estimated 42 state plans in Rhode Island related to human services. They also found that planning activities within state agencies were poorly coordinated, fragmented, primarily short-range, and highly categorical. Alcoholism in this case shared these negative injunctions with all other substantive service areas. Alcoholism, too, needed coordinated, comprehensive, and integrated planning services according to the council.

Another way of looking at the holistic nature of the human service industry is to examine client needs. Hart and Stueland [4] in their 1977 study of 563 alcoholics, using cluster analysis, identified five homogeneous groups that could be characterized by needs for rehabilitation. There were needs for (1) economic self esteem; (2) emotional security; (3) physiological and family problems; (4) physiological and emotional and economic security; (5) family, social, and vocational self-actualization; and (6) economic and emotional security and physiological problems. However differentiated, it is clear that the resources necessary to cope with this complex set of rehabilitation needs are not to be found in abundance in any human service agency, including those specific to alcoholism.

ALCOHOLISM AND OTHER PROBLEMS

Whether it be traffic safety, homicide, homosexuality, poverty, or tuberculosis, the significantly high relation between alcohol problems and the other conditions has been noted time and time again in the literature. Problems are seldom exclusive. Failure to understand the nature of the gay culture in the United States will negatively impact on the treatment of the alcoholic homosexual. Similarly, effective treatment of the tuberculous alcoholic must integrate knowledge of both tuberculosis and alcoholism. Homicide, traffic safety, and poverty are also complicated by many influences.

The issues of civil rights and civil liberties have come to the fore of American consciousness since the end of World War II, highlighted by the United States Supreme Court decision, *Brown* v. *Board of Education,* in 1954. The *Wyatt* v. *Stickney* federal court care in Georgia in mental health is a natural successor to the *Brown* v. *Board of Education* decision. Both have been followed by countless other actions, either generalizing or making more specific the rights of minorities: racial, ethnic, and handicapped. Thus alcohologists and other specialists are once again linked inseparably to the larger social scene. Special alcoholism programs directed to Native Americans, Alaskans, Chicanos, Puerto Ricans, blacks, black females, youth, the elderly, and white females, among others, are receiving increasing attention. Some are motivated by mixed ideologies, public health and civil rights for one, others by civil rights alone. In any case the target group is not white, male, and middle-aged. For special alcoholism efforts to be successful, basic understandings will be found in the general research literature, not the alcoholism-specific literature.

Dealing with women by women who place alcohol problems in the context of a woman's total experience in society is a classic example of this complexity. As stated by Sandmaier [13], a growing number of recovering alcoholic women are discovering that their experiences with alcoholism and their experiences as women are inseparable.

Another recent theme in American life is the increasing attention being paid to the elderly. Simultaneously the alcoholism industry is also discovering aging. That there is some contradiction in the claims that alcoholics have substantially shorter lives than nonalcoholics and that the cohort of alcoholics over age 65 should therefore be relatively small does not deter the alcohol industry advocates. Whatever the dimensions of the problem (it is not yet clear) the alcoholic aged need the competence of several disciplines. To remove alcohol from the isolated and lonely senior may not always be constructive unless something of positive value can be done for their anomie. The data is clear in several respects. The elderly are more isolated. Their health needs are greater. Their economic resources are limited. Their drinking patterns are different than those of younger people.

One vexing interorganizational issue plaguing alcoholism is the tendency for many outsiders and increasing numbers of insiders to speak of substance abuse. Typical of these threats was the results of a September 1975 mail survey to the 50 states and 144 state administrators [10], directors of combined alcoholism–drug abuse single state agencies, directors of individual state agencies for both alcoholism and drugs, and various other state categories. Of the 100 respondents the directors of combined programs evaluate the integration of substance abuse programs most favorable and the directors of alcoholism-specific programs viewed mergers least favorably.

A 1975 publication [3] reviewing the first year of the newly merged Indiana Division on Alcoholism and Drug Abuse into a single Division of Addiction Services, State Department of Mental Health concludes on a favorable note. Despite problems, an improvement over separate divisions is reported; specifically cited as favorable results are talent cross-fertilization, reduced effort duplication, and certain philosophical gains as a result of recognition that alcohol is also a drug.

Another endemic issue true of both the generic system and the specialized system is the dual track nature of the American health care industry. One system is for paying clients and the other for nonpaying clients. The alcoholism industry suffers from the same problem. The solution to this issue, as to most organizational problems, will not be found in the alcoholism system but in the larger human services industry and in the general societal attitude about equity.

An almost classic example of the tension between the intergrationist and separatist occurred in the 1970s about alcoholism programs in industry. Should there be alcoholism programs or troubled-employees programs? That apparent innocuous question developed into the focus point of an, as yet, unresolved conflict. In fact, many of the proponents of the troubled-employee approach were also of an isolationist stripe. They supported troubled-employees programs as a pragmatic solution to closed industrial gates. If by using a more innocuous term they were allowed in to do their job with alcoholics, they were not particularly alarmed. They failed to reckon with some of their more ideological brethren and found themselves viewed as the enemy.

A report by Jones [7] in 1975 of the Kennecott Copper Corporation's programs of professional counseling and referral for their 8,000 employees and their 24,000 dependents is almost a model for the service integrationist. The company utilized 220 community-based service agencies in Salt Lake County. Participation was voluntary, confidential, and available 24 hours a day by a telephone answering service.

Another illustration of the essential interrelationship of the parts of the human services industry is found in examining the linkage requirements of alcohol detoxification units [9]. To be maximally successful, among many other requirements, such units must have: access to a general hospital; access to an adequate aftercare system; assurance of smooth patient flow within the treatment system; and effective liaison between the health care system and the criminal justice system.

Marc Hertzman [5], former National Institute of Alcohol Abuse and Alcoholism executive assistant to the director, in 1976 identified several main challenges confronting the institute. Specifically cited were (1) increased attention to prevention of alcoholism and drug abuse; (2) elimination of the insularity of professionals in the alcoholism field; (3) integration of alcoholism and drug abuse services for those of other health specialists to create a total community service system, and finally, (4) program planning that includes consideration of the needs of specific at-risk populations. Thus all of the challenges identified by Hertzmann required a comprehensive outlook in programs.

It is clear that the alcoholism industry needs a modeling and systems approach to enhance and stimulate a better understanding of the many problems facing it. The underlying premise is that problems and their solutions are not found alone. Static explanations of problems and solutions are rejected.

REFERENCES

1. Council for Community Services, Inc. *Program Profile: Community Planning and Development.* Author: Providence, R.I., 1975.
2. Council of State Governments. *Human Services: A Framework for Decision Making.* Author: Lexington, Ky., 1975.
3. Griglar, W. F. *Combining Alcohol and Drug Programs at the State and Community Levels.* Indiana State Department of Mental Health: Indianapolis, 1975.
4. Hart, L. S., and Stueland, D. Application of the multidimensional model of alcoholism: Differentiation of alcoholics by mode analysis. *J. Stud. Alcohol* 40:283–290, 1979.
5. Hertzman, M. NIAAA: Past, problems and progress. *Contemp. Drug Problems* 5:45–56, 1976.
6. Johnson County Regional Planning Commission. *Human Services Study: Report on Substance Abuse.* Author: Iowa City, Ia., 1977.
7. Jones, O. F. Insight: A program for troubled people. In: *Occupational Alcoholism Programs,* Williams, R. and Moffat, G. (eds.). Charles C Thomas: Springfield, Ill., 1975.
8. King County Department of Budget and Program Planning. *Human Services in King County: An Introduction for Decision Makers* (Vol. 1). Author: Seattle, 1975.
9. Knott, D., and Fink, R. Problems surrounding emergency care services for acute alcoholism. *Hosp. Community Psychiatry* 26:42–43, 1975.
10. Lambert, M. D., and Cummins, M. J. *Perceptions of State Administrators toward Combined Alcoholism and Drug Abuse Services.* Social Science Institute, Washington University: St. Louis, 1976.
11. Massachusetts League of Cities and Towns. *Report on Production: Human Service Accountability System.* Author: Boston, 1974.
12. President's Commission on Mental Health. *Report to the President* (Vol. 1). U.S. Government Printing Office: Washington, D.C., 1978.
13. Sandmaier, M. Women helping women: Opening the door to treatment. *Alcohol Health Res. World* 2:17–23, 1977.
14. Schulberg, H. C., and Demone, H. W., Jr. *Stimulating Services Reform.* Aspen Systems Corporation: Rockville, Md., 1978.

77

LARRY S. HART, PhD, Center for Behavioral Consultation, Madison, Wisconsin

MULTIDIMENSIONAL REHABILITATION OF THE ALCOHOLIC

THE LAST 15 YEARS HAVE shown clinicians and researchers giving significant attention to the belief that people with alcohol problems do represent a broad spectrum of patients with a variety of alcohol, medical, psychopathological, affective, social, and vocational problems [7, 36]. A series of studies indicated univariate statistics accounted for a significantly lower proportion of population variance found in people considered to be alcoholic [36]. Univariate (in contrast to multivariate) methods of rehabilitation program evaluation have been shown to disguise the nature of rehabilitation outcomes found among people with alcoholism [6]. The purpose of this chapter is to cite relevant studies that are applicable to the rehabilitation of alcoholics and to delineate the components of assessment procedures in rehabilitation programs with specification paid to the application of the multidimensional model of alcoholism.

Operationally, rehabilitation of people with alcoholism is an integration of dynamic and systematic procedures to maximize the individual's psychological functioning (i.e., emotional, social, vocational, and biopsychological functioning) as well as to obtain drinking behavior goals that are medically and psychiatrically indicated. Therefore rehabilitation, which historically was a service delivered to clients of the state-federal vocational rehabilitation system, is redefined as a clin-

---

Larry S. Hart, PhD, Licensed Psychologist and Director, Center for Behavioral Consultation, Madison, Wisconsin.

ical enterprise performed by health care and allied health care providers as primary care physicians, psychiatrists, psychologists, psychiatric nurses, and rehabilitation counselors. The thrust of rehabilitation is upon the clinician's methods, not on the member facility of the practitioner. Rehabilitation of the patient with alcoholism occurs in the state-federal vocational rehabilitation system, inpatient rehabilitation programs, outpatient treatment clinics, community mental health centers, and the primary care office or the private practice of the psychiatrist or psychologist. Given this orientation, the rehabilitation of alcoholics is the heartland of the multidimensional model of alcoholism.

THE INTERRELATIONSHIP OF REHABILITATION AND THE MULTIDIMENSIONAL MODEL OF ALCOHOLISM

Jellenick [17] proposed a developmental disease model of alcoholism as well as a typology of alcoholic types. Some practitioners incorporated the developmental model as gospel. However, clinical researchers counterproposed the belief that alcoholism is a developmental condition with only a single cure of abstinence, which was not supported by empirical data [8, 9, 36]. The distinction in studies between the alcoholic and nonalcoholic was evident in research [15, 28]. The unitary trait model, as representative of alcoholism as a developmental disease condition, failed to account for the population variance within a group of patients considered to be alcoholic [36].

The multidimensional model of alcoholism proposed that the condition was representative of a variety of alcoholic disorders or syndromes, neurotic styles, personality and affective disorders, and drinking behavior patterns, as well as symptomatology [4, 13, 14, 22, 30, 31, 36]. Clearly the alcoholic-nonalcoholic distinction is an oversimplification [30] and a barrier to successful treatment and rehabilitation.

On the level of personality, people with alcoholism have been differentiated [11, 21, 22, 33]. Lawlis and Rubin [18] differentiated subgroups of alcoholics who were clients of rehabilitation programs by Cattell's 16 Personality Factors (PF). In complement to personality functioning, patterns of rehabilitation needs (e.g., physiological, emotional, vocational, economic, social, family needs, etc.) have been generated by factor analysis and rotational methods [7]. That study produced four rehabilitation need patterns. A conservative researcher may argue that distinction among patterns of rehabilitation need is suggestive of underlying groups. Thus, in a preliminary study of rehabilitation need profiles, Hart [7] generated seven distinct profile groups that implicated the necessity for differential selection of rehabilitation services as well as treatment interventions to benefit these patients. In further support of distinct rehabilitation groups of patients with alcoholism, Hart and Stueland [8] differentiated alcoholics on measures of rehabilitation need, yielding five homogeneous groups of individuals. Thus, these studies established that on axes of personality, behavior, and rehabilitation, people with alcoholism could be repeatedly factored or clustered into homogeneous groups. Practitioners and clinically oriented researchers argued that differential assessment and treatment needed to be performed in order to maximize psychological and behavioral recovery from drinking disorders and to minimize residual effects, as well as to sustain treatment and rehabilitation gains. Better outcomes would most likely be realized with this type of intervention into the clinician's practice in addition to changes in program management.

RESEARCH RELEVANT TO THE REHABILITATION OF THE ALCOHOLIC

The core feature of the multidimensional model of alcoholism centers on specifying the composition of the patient population, given what types of treatments are administered, will yield what outcomes [23, 24]. The position of Paul [25] is similar on the evaluation of psychotherapy studies. The following further examines the classification area as it specifies subgroups of alcoholics; each suggests differential management.

Nerviano et al. [22] conducted a multivariate analysis of Minnesota Multiphasic Personality Inventory (MMPI) profiles of male alcoholics in an inpatient and outpatient setting. The Nerviano group's study generated five inpatient types and three outpatient types. These groups spanned diagnostic descriptors, including neurotic, personality disorder, psychotic, and affective disorders, concurrent with alcoholic disorders. This study supports the finding of the Weissman group [37], which noted that 66% of their alcoholics surveyed had at least one psychiatric disorder other than an alcoholic problem.

The Steer et al. [33] study is important. The Steer group conducted a multivariate study of blood alcohol levels, quantity-frequency indices of ingestion of ethanol, and personality measures from the Eysenck Personality Inventory. The study [33] extracted seven homogeneous groups that were differentiated on these variables and included racial, medication, and paternal drinking background. These authors further generated clinically and empirically supported differential treatment regimes for these types.

Hart and Stueland [11] successfully classified female alcoholics by Catell's 16 PF. Factor analysis of the 16 PF scores derived six personality types: (1) a passive-impulsive neurotic style, (2) an introverted obessive-compulsive neurotic style, (3) a paranoid style, (4) a schizoid style, (5) a trait disorder with psychopathology, and (6) an extraverted obsessive-compulsive neurotic style. This research demonstrated that a diagnosis of alcoholism based solely on aberrant drinking is insufficient because (1) the alcoholism is superimposed on varying types of neurotic style and personality disorder, and (2) such a diagnosis without further examination of personality would be a barrier to successful rehabilitation.

In a prior investigation of rehabilitation need profiles, Hart and Stueland [8] clustered alcoholic patients on the Human Service Scale (HSS) [27]. Their study differentiated five homogeneous groups on the basis of psychological need deprivation. These groups were typed as follows: (1) economic self-esteem; (2) emotional security, physiological, and family stability; (3) physiological, emotional security, and economic security; (4) family, social, and vocational self-actualization; and (5) economic security, emotional security, and physiological. Subsequent to the provision of rehabilitation services, these groups were shown to be differentiated on the psychological need variables, but not drinking behavior [9].

Aside from the psychological and personality variables, other indices have been consistently shown to differentiate patients with alcoholism, including background factors of drinking and current conditions [14], sociodemographic variables [10, 26, 29], social and environmental factors [34], and family factors [20]. These variables have been shown to effect rehabilitation outcomes as assessed via psychological variables, but not drinking behavior variables [9]. Thus, these studies have implicated the interrelationship and differential effects of social, behavioral, psychological, psychiatric, vocational, and medical variables that produce an impact on the adjustment of people with alcoholism in determining the treatment [3] and rehabilitation outcomes [9]. It is these variables that enter into the complete assessment of the alcoholic rehabilitation patient.

THE MULTIDIMENSIONAL MODEL OF REHABILITATION ASSESSMENT IN CLINICAL ALCOHOLISM

Rehabilitation assessment of the patient with alcoholism is a systematic procedure whereby the clinician or counselor gathers the necessary data to select differential interventions in the development of an individualized program for the patient. The assessment incorporates the utilization of structured procedures, psychometric test data, and the clinical interview to specify the patient's disorders and problems, which can be minimized and thus, specified therapeutic goals reached. The proposed model assumes a thorough medical examination of each patient and referral to a clinician or rehabilitation counselor with a MS degree, whose task is to coordinate the patient's rehabilitation program, based on the compilation of the presenting clinical picture. The components of the rehabilitation assessment are presented below.

Clinical interview. The clinical interview component is best conducted by a psychiatrist, licensed psychologist, or psychiatric nurse and incorporates a clinical assessment of the patient's complaints, medical difficulties, symptoms of neurological disorder, social and family situation, and affective disorder, as well as drinking behavior and recent vocational history.

Personality. The patient is instructed to self-administer a psychometric test that measures psychopathology (e.g., MMPI, 16 PF, etc.). The purpose of the assessment of personality is to obtain test data along this axis that the clinician may have otherwise found inaccessible or failed to pursue during interviewing. It also provides a statistical verification for the clinician's prediction of the patient's diagnosis.

Affective disorder. Based on the author's clinical experience and empirical data, the prevalence of affective disorders among alcoholic patients is significant [37]. In clinical practice, this author routinely employs the Schedule for Affective Disorders and Schizophrenia—Life Time version (SADS-L)[32]. The SADS-L is a structured inteview procedure shown to have demonstrated reliability and validity against statistical measures [2, 32]. The efficacy of concurrent diagnostic validity in structured psychiatric interviews has been demonstrated [12].

Drinking behavior. An assessment of the alcoholism variant or specification of drinking behavior disorder needs to be conducted. The Alcohol-Use Inventory (AUI), a factor analysis-derived instrument, has been developed and reported by Wanberg, et al. [35]. The AUI consists of 16 primary scales and five second-order dimensions, which together measure psychological, social, marital, and family factors affecting alcohol use. Scales assessing deterioration are provided. Evidence of the AUI's external, construct, predictive, and discriminant validity has been reported by the Wanberg group [35] and evidence of the AUI's criterion-oriented concurrent validity against the HSS has also been reported [34]. Additional assessment instruments have been reported by Jacobson [16].

Rehabilitation needs. The HSS is a factor analysis derived instrument that assesses psychological need satisfaction in seven areas: physiological, emotional security, economic security, family, social, and economic self-esteem, and vocational self-actualization. Reliability of the HSS has been reported by Reagles and Butler [27], and Hart and Stueland [6, 8]. Growick et al. [5] reported on the HSS' validity as measured by the method of contracted groups among alcoholics. The HSS data provide the clinician with a specification of the patient's problem areas. Identification of each problem area suggests an avenue for intervention.

Psychological testing of cerebral integrity. An intellectual assessment of adaptive ability may be appropriate due to reports of deficits of neuropsychological functions [19, 38]. These results have implicated that integrity of certain neuropsychological functions may be linked to successful participation in treatment as well as control, versus abstinence in the patient's ability to moderate drinking behavior.

Consequently these components of the multidimensional model of rehabilitation assessment in clinical alcoholism incorporate the total constellation of psychiatric and rehabilitation needs of the patient, and dovetail into the diagnostic summary of the DSM-III [1]. Once the clinical problems have been defined, the practitioner formulates the individualized rehabilitation program based on the specification of disorders, difficulties, and needs derived from the multidimensional assessment. This is the task of the rehabilitation effort—to select those interventions that will maximize each individual's recovery and return the patient to his or her highest level of functioning.

SUMMARY

In summary, the rehabilitation of the alcoholic patient is based on the specification of the variants of alcoholism, psychiatric disorders, and delineation of rehabilitation needs based on the comprehensive assessment. The treatment and rehabilitation effort is individualized, and promotes the recovery of the patient with an alcohol disorder. The selection of treatment modalities for the alcoholic patient is reported [24]. A multidimensional model of rehabilitation assessment in clinical alcoholism is presented, and the similarity to the DSM-III's multiaxial evaluation noted. It is recommended that practitioners and program managers make modifications of their assessment procedures to allow people with alcohol problems to benefit from the differential assessment and rehabilitation model proposed in this chapter.

ACKNOWLEDGMENTS

The author wishes to express his appreciation to Marian Aebly, Medical Staff Office, Clinical Science Center, University of Wisconsin Hospital and Clinics—Madison, for her editorial assistance on an earlier draft of this manuscript.

REFERENCES

1. American Psychiatric Association. *Diagnostic and Statistical Manual of Mental Disorders* 3rd ed. (DSM-III). Author: Washington, D.C., 1980.
2. Endicott, J., and Spitzer, R. L. A Diagnostic interview: The schedule for affective disorders and schizophrenia. *Arch. Gen. Psychiatry* 35:837–844, 1978.
3. Foster, F. M., Horn, J. L., and Wanberg, R. W. Dimensions of treatment outcome. *Q. J. Stud. Alcohol* 33:1079–1098, 1972.

4. Goldstein, S. G., and Linden, J. D. Multivariate classification of alcoholics by means of the MMPI. *J. Abnorm. Psychol.* 74:661-669, 1969.

5. Growick, B. S., Butler, A. J., and Sather, W. Validation of the Human Service Scale as a program evaluation tool. *Rehab. Counsel. Bull.* 22:347-351, 1979.

6. Hart, L. S. *Differentiation of Rehabilitation Needs and Outcomes in Alcoholics.* Unpublished doctoral dissertation, Univerity of Wisconsin, 1976.

7. Hart, L. S. Rehabilitation need patterns of men alcoholics. *J. Stud. Alcohol* 38:494-511, 1977.

8. Hart, L. S., and Stueland, D. An application of the multidimensional model of alcoholism: Differentiation of alcoholics by mode analysis. *J. Stud. Alcohol* 40:283-290, 1979.

9. Hart, L. S., and Stueland, D. S. An application of the multidimensional model of alcoholism to program effectiveness:Rehabilitation status and outcome. *J. Stud. Alcohol* 40:645-655, 1979.

10. Hart, L. S., and Stueland, D. S. Relationship of sociodemographic and drinking variables to differentiated subgroups of alcoholics. *Commun. Ment. Health J.* 15:47-59, 1979.

11. Hart, L. S., and Stueland, D. S. Classifying women alcoholics by Cattell's 16 PF. *J. Stud. Alcohol* 41:911-921, 1980.

12. Helzer, J. E., Clayton, P. J., Pambakian, R., and Woodruff, R. A. Concurrent diagnostic validity of a structural psychiatric interview. *Arch. Gen. Psychiatry* 35:849-853, 1978.

13. Horn, J. L., and Wanberg, R. W. Symptom patterns related to excessive use of alcohol. *Q. J. Stud. Alcohol* 30:35-58, 1969.

14. Horn, J. L. Wanberg, R. W., and Adams, G. Diagnosis of alcoholism: Factors of drinking background and current conditions in alcoholics. *Q. J. Stud. Alcohol* 35:147-175, 1974.

15. Hoyt, D. P., and Sedlacek, G. Differentiating alcoholics from normals and abnormals with the MMPI. *J. Clin. Psychol.* 14:69-74, 1958.

16. Jacobson, G. R. *The Alcoholisms: Detection, Assessment and Diagnosis.* Behavioral Publications:New York, 1976.

17. Jellinek, E. M. Phases of alcohol addiction. *Q. J. Stud. Alcohol* 13:673-678, 1952.

18. Lawlis, G. F., and Rubin, S. E. 16 PF study of personality patterns in alcoholics. *Q. J. Stud. Alcohol* 32:318-327, 1971.

19. Loberg, T. Alcohol misuse and neuropsychological deficits in men. *J. Stud. Alcohol* 41:119-127, 1980.

20. Moos, R. A., Bromet, E., Tsu, V., and Moos, B. Family characteristics and the outcome of treatment of alcoholism. *J. Stud. Alcohol* 40:78-88, 1979.

21. Nerviano, V. J. Common personality patterns among alcoholic males: A multivariate study. *J. Consult. Clin. Psychol.* 44:104-110, 1976.

22. Nerviano, V. J., McCarthy, D., and McCarthy, S. M. MMPI profile patterns of men alcoholics in two contracting settings. *J. Stud. Alcohol* 41:1143-1152, 1980.

23. Pattison, E. M. A critique of alcoholism treatment concepts with special reference to abstinence. *Q. J. Stud. Alcohol* 27:49-71, 1966.

24. Pattison, E. M. The selection of treatment modalities for the alcoholic patient. In: *The Diagnosis and Treatment of Alcoholism*, Mendelson, J. H. and Mello, N. R. (eds.). New York, McGraw-Hill: 1979.

25. Paul, G. L. Strategy of outcome research in psychotherapy. *J. Consult. Psychol.* 31:109-118, 1967.

26. Perkins, D. V., Cox, W. M., and Levy, L. A. Therapist recommendation of abstinence or controlled drinking as treatment goals. *J. Stud. Alcohol* 42:304-311, 1981.

27. Reagles, R. W., and Butler, A. J. The Human Service Scale: A new measure of rehabilitation clinics and program evaluation. *J. Rehab.* 42:34-38, 1976.

28. Rosen, A. C. A comparative study of alcoholics and psychiatric patients with the MMPI. *Q. J. Stud. Alcohol* 21:253–266, 1960.

29. Seelye, E. E. Relationship of sociodemographic status, psychiatric diagnosis and sex to outcome of alcoholism treatment. *J. Stud. Alcohol* 40:57–62, 1979.

30. Skinner, H. A. A multivariate evaluation of the MAST. *J. Stud. Alcohol* 40:831–844, 1979.

31. Skinner, H. A., Jackson, D. N., and Hoffman, H. Alcoholic personality types: Identification and correlates. *J. Abnorm. Psychol.* 83:658–666, 1974.

32. Spitzer, R. L., Endicott, J., and Robins, E. Research diagnostic criteria: Rationale and reliability. *Arch. Gen. Psychiatry* 35:773–782, 1978.

33. Steer, R. A., Fine, E. W., and Scoles, P. E. Classification of men arrested for driving while intoxicated and treatment implications:A cluster analytic study. *J. Stud. Alcohol* 40:222–229, 1979.

34. Stueland, D., and Hart, L. A canonical correlation analysis of the Alcohol-Use Inventory and Human Service Scale. *J. Behav. Med.* 2:275–283, 1979.

35. Wanberg, R. W., Horn, J. L., and Foster, F. M. A differential assessment model for alcoholism:The scales of the Alcohol-Use Inventory. *J. Stud. Alcohol* 33:512–543, 1977.

36. Wanberg, R. W., and Knapp, J. A multidimensional model for research and treatment of alcoholism. *Int. J. Addict.* 5:69–98, 1970.

37. Weissman, M. M., Myers, J. R., and Harding P. S. Prevalence and psychiatric heterogeneity of alcoholism in a United States urban community. *J. Stud. Alcohol* 41:672–681, 1980.

38. Wilkinson, D. A., and Carlen, P. L. Neuropsychological and neurological assessment of alcoholism. *J. Stud. Alcohol* 41:129–139, 1980.

78

DAVID J. PITTMAN, PhD, Washington University, St. Louis, Missouri

THE POLICE COURT SYSTEM AND THE PUBLIC INTOXICATION OFFENDER

THIS CHAPTER IS CONCERNED with the police court system in reference to the public intoxication offender in American society. Legal sanctions that impinge on public inebriates, the magnitude of the problem, the traditional role of the criminal justice system in processing public drunkenness violations, innovations in handling public inebriates including the social movement to decriminalize public drunkenness, and the future of the police court system are discussed.

PUBLIC DRUNKENNESS: A CRIMINAL OFFENSE

Historically in North America and Europe, public drunkenness has been treated as a criminal offense in almost every legal jurisdiction. Laws existed on national, state, and/or local levels prohibiting public displays of drunkenness. Although disorderliness was a prerequisite under some laws, the homeless, skid row inebriates faced repeated arrest for disorderly and nondisorderly drunkenness.

David J. Pittman, PhD, Chairman and Professor of Sociology, Washington University, St. Louis, Missouri.

Many individuals arrested for public drunkenness are alcoholics, but treatment for alcoholism is clearly not part of the criminal justice system's functions. The process of arresting inebriates, detaining them for a few hours or days and then rearresting them has been termed a "revolving door" process [9]. Some individuals have been arrested 100 to 200 times and have served 10 to 20 years in jail on short-term sentences, which in reality is life imprisonment on the installment plan. The high recidivism rates for public drunkenness clearly indicate the futility of the criminal justice system in dealing with the underlying sociomedical problems of public inebriates.

Chronic drunkenness offenders are a group of excessive drinkers who may or may not be alcoholics, but whose drinking has involved them in difficulties with the police, the courts, and the penal institutions. They are a group for whom the criminal sanctions have failed along with existent community resources for rehabilitation. Although some of these men (very seldom women) are confirmed alcoholics, others are individuals whose present use of alcohol is indicative of the prodromal phase of alcoholism; others are nonaddicted excessive drinkers who will never become alcoholics.

Over two decades ago the present author stated:

> A Treatment Center should be created for the reception of the chronic public inebriate. This means that they should be removed from the jails and penal institutions as the mentally ill in this country were removed from the jails during the last century. Given the present state of knowledge concerning alcoholism, the time is ripe now for such a change. The present system is not only inefficient in terms of the excessive cost of jailing an offender 30, 40, or 50 times, but is a direct negation of this society's humanitarian philosophy toward people who are beset by social, mental and physical problems. [9, pp. 141-142]

THE MAGNITUDE OF THE PROBLEM

The more intense the enforcement of laws, the greater the effect they have on the deviancy. For the public intoxication offender, the enforcement has been indeed intense. The President's Commission on Law Enforcement and Administration of Justice in its final report stated, "Two million arrests in 1965 — one of every three arrests in America — were for the offense of public drunkenness. The great volume of these arrests places an extremely heavy load on the operations of the criminal justice system, it burdens police, clogs lower criminal courts, and crowds penal institutions throughout the United States" [10, p. 233].

There were, however, variations from city to city in how severely the drunkenness statutes were enforced by the police. At one extreme were the practices in Atlanta and Washington, D.C., where the enforcement procedures were very strict: in Atlanta, in 1965, of a total of 92,965 arrests, 52.5% were for drunkenness;

in Washington, D.C., the corresponding figure for 86,464 arrests was 51.8% for drunkenness. At the permissive end was St. Louis, where the police were more tolerant and had a sociomedical orientation to alcoholism. There, in 1965, of all arrests (44,701), 5.5% were for drunkenness [7]. The change from a punitive to a sociomedical orientation toward chronic drunkenness offenders in the United States is discussed later in this chapter.

In 1978, the Federal Bureau of Investigation (FBI) estimated that there were 1,176,600 arrests for public drunkenness in the United States, which accounted for approximately 11% of all estimated arrests in that year [4]. After public drunkenness had been decriminalized (i.e., it was no longer a criminal offense) in a number of states, the percentage as well as the number of arrests for public drunkenness declined throughout the 1970s. For example, in 1970, 23% of the total arrests reported by the FBI were for public intoxication. This trend can be expected to continue throughout the 1980s. However, public drunkenness still remains a criminal offense in several populous states, such as California, Texas, and Pennsylvania; furthermore, in certain states that have decriminalized public drunkenness, although public inebriates cannot be legally arrested for drunkenness, they are booked by the police on related charges such as disorderly conduct, vagrancy, loitering, and the like.

Persons arrested and held for prosecution for public drunkenness are almost never represented by counsel and almost always found guilty. In 1969, reports to the FBI from 2,640 cities representing a population of 66,155,000 showed that 86.2% of all persons charged with public drunkenness were found guilty [3]. This suggests that offenders whose violations are alcohol-related frequently find themselves incarcerated.

Social policies directed against a particular deviancy affect some group members differently than others, resulting in a corresponding effect on the larger public. The very nature of public intoxication excludes most middle-class and upper-class alcoholics and excessive drinkers who typically drink in private or semiprivate surroundings. American sociocultural values and legal statutes do not severely condemn individuals for excessive drinking as long as they do not bother other persons. Thus public drunkenness laws mainly affect the lower class who drink in public and, in effect, these statutes are class laws. There is also evidence which tentatively suggests that, within the lower class, some persons feel the brunt of the law more than others [9].

THE TRADITIONAL POLICE COURT SYSTEM

The traditional police court system to handle public drunkenness cases rests in the first instance in the police officer's power to arrest individuals suspected of violating a legal statute. It would be simplistic to expect that all public inebriates are arrested by the police. Bittner's [2] classic article on police actions on skid row, which encompasses a significant number of the public drunkenness offenders, presents a cogent analysis of the dynamics of the interaction between public inebriates and police officers. According to Bittner, the law becomes a resource to the policeman and a means of keeping the peace. The policeman uses arrest, for example, as a way of resolving problems rather than as a means of solving a particular crime. Situations occur, consequently, where every witness to a street fracas is subjected to coercive measures and/or is arrested. While coercive measures may be a subconscious effort to educate those involved to the force of authority, arrest is an unmistakable misuse of the law to maintain a particular definition of peace. In both instances, the civil liberties of those attacked have been violated [2].

But these individuals' civil liberties are rarely the subject of much concern. Public drunkenness offenders arrested on skid row are, by society's definition, at the bottom of the social ladder; they have given up their right to be treated as human beings deserving of ordinary respect because of the stigma society has attached to them and their behavior. These skid row public inebriates appear to have accepted the fact that they will not receive the usual deference and demeanor expected by citizens from those connected with law enforcement and community social agencies.

After arrest, the inebriate is transported to the jail for processing, which may generally take one of two forms: (1) being booked for public drunkenness and held (in a jail cell, police lockup, or the drunk tank) for court action; or (2) held in protective custody at the jail with no formal charge recorded and released when sober. If formally charged, the drunkenness offender rarely is released on bail, given his or her economic status, before court appearance. Since public inebriates rarely plead innocent, their court appearance is generally the next day, when justice is administered by the local judge or magistrate on an assembly-line basis. Pleading guilty, the public inebriate, depending upon the philosophy of the judge and general policies in that jurisdiction, is either released with a warning not to become drunk again in public or sentenced to a period of time (always less than a year, as public drunkenness is a misdemeanor) in a short-term correctional institution, also referred to in the literature as a "workhouse," "county farm," "county jail," "stockade," and so forth. In this process, from arrest to incarceration, medical care is minimal, if even existent, for the individual, resulting in the occasional death of individuals from delirium tremens, suicide, head injuries, and the like. Moreover, little effort is made, if any, to treat the individual's sociomedical problems resulting from years of excessive drinking. This sketch only outlines the primitiveness and inhumaneness of the criminal approach to the public drunkenness offender.

INNOVATIONS IN HANDLING PUBLIC INEBRIATES

Since 1955, a social movement to alter traditional police and court procedures in handling public inebriates and to decriminalize the public drunkenness offense has occurred in Czechoslovakia, Poland, Sweden, Great Britain, Canada, the United States, and other countries.

Bold approaches to handling the problem of public drunkenness within a sociomedical context first occurred in the 1950s, interestingly enough in Eastern Europe—namely, Czechoslovakia and Poland—with the establishment of sobering-up stations or detoxification centers. These stations, instead of jails, were used to process drunkenness cases.

Sobering-up stations have become an integral part of the network of alcoholism services in Poland and Czechoslovakia. For example, in Warsaw any person found drunk on the street or lying in a doorway is taken by the police to the sobering-up station. The Warsaw station is a 150-bed facility on the grounds of the State Sanatorium for Mental Disorders, and is one of the 22 such sobering-up stations in the country established under the Anti-Alcoholism Act of 1959 to handle "drunk on street" cases. Thus, in Poland all major cities have facilities that allow the public drunkenness offender to be processed by the police through a sociomedical context instead of jail.

In Czechoslovakia, patients from the sobering-up station are referred to lectures on alcoholism and its effects (called "Sunday schools" since the lectures are held on Sunday). Generally when the individual appears a second or third time at the sobering-up station, a full-scale medical and social evaluation begins and a plan for therapeutic intervention is worked out, involving voluntary approaches at first. If the patient does not proceed with voluntary treatment, then compulsory treatment is begun.

The first efforts to remove the chronic drunkenness offender from the criminal justice system in the United States began in St. Louis in 1963, when the St. Louis Board of Police Commissioners instituted a major policy change in reference to intoxicated persons on the street. The St. Louis Metropolitan Police Department made it mandatory for the police to transport all arrested public inebriates to the emergency rooms of one of the two city hospitals for physical examination. This meant that routine physical evaluation was provided all arrested inebriates processed by the police; if these individuals were in need of medical care, they were to be hospitalized instead of being jailed. If medical care were deemed unnecessary, the intoxicated person was held until sober—not more than 20 hours—and released to the community.

St. Louis was one of the few American cities in which this innovation in handling of public intoxication cases occurred. It squarely placed the locus of responsibility for the alcoholic in the treatment sphere. However, the Board of Police Commissioners was dissatisfied that large numbers of alcoholics were not admitted to the hospitals for medical care. At times more than 90% of the examined public intoxicants were returned by the physicians to the police for processing [8].

Therefore, the St. Louis Metropolitan Police Department, in conjunction with Washington University's Social Science Institute and an order of Catholic nuns, the Sisters of St. Mary, established the first detoxification center in 1966 for persons arrested for public intoxication, partially funded by the Law Enforcement Assistance Administration of the Department of Justice. This procedure was adopted with the pragmatic goals to reduce police time necessary to process arrested inebriates and to remove these individuals from the local system of courts and correctional institutions [12]. The St. Louis Detoxification and Diagnostic Evaluation Center was the first systematic attempt in the Western Hemisphere to provide treatment instead of jail for the drunkenness offender at the time the police officer intervened by arresting the inebriate. The function of the police officer was to transport the individual to the detoxification center, at which point police responsibility ended.

The St. Louis Detoxification Center, because of its original success, became the model for the creation of hundreds of other centers throughout the United States as more cities and states changed their policies and laws in reference to arrested public inebriates.

As a consequence of the President's Commission on Law Enforcement and Administration of Justice's recommendation in 1967, that public drunkenness in itself should not be a criminal offense, the success of the sociomedical approach in St. Louis, Washington, D.C., and the Vera Institute of Justice's Manhattan Bowery Project, and the desire of not only officials in the criminal justice system but the help-giving professions to develop means to remove the public inebriates from the jails and courts, the Uniform Alcoholism and Intoxication Treatment Act (Uniform Act) was adopted by the National Conference of Commissioners on Uniform State Laws in August 1971. The Uniform Act was designed to provide the various states a legal framework within which to cope with public drunkenness specifically and alcoholism generally from a sociomedical point of view instead of a criminal justice perspective. The Uniform Act's general policy is that "alcoholics and intoxicated persons may not be subjected to criminal prosecution because of their consumption of alcoholic beverages but rather should be afforded a continuum of treatment in order that they may lead normal lives as productive members of society" [11, p, 5].

By 1981, 34 states, the District of Columbia, and the Virgin Islands had adopted either the Uniform Act or variations of it. However, decriminalization does not remove all the problems connected with public drunkenness. It is only the initial step in providing care for individuals who have been historically ignored by the health-providing professions.

As Aaronson, Dienes, and Musheno in a recent study [1] indicate, the removal of criminal sanctions for public drunkenness must be accompanied by (1) the acceptance by public health authorities that the chronic police case inebriate has the illness of alcoholism; (2) the existence of institutional means for processing public inebriates through noncriminal facilities such as detoxification centers, community mental health centers, and/or general hospitals; (3) the acknowledgment by the police in any community which decriminalizes that the above institutional options are available to their officers on the street; and (4) the actual use of these institutional options by the police in processing large numbers of public inebriates who are found in all American major metropolitan centers.

THE FUTURE OF THE POLICE COURT SYSTEM

This chapter has presented the fact that public inebriates, coming to the attention of the police and courts, cannot be adequately managed by them if traditional methods and resources are used. Most police departments have performed well the functions of recognizing public inebriates, taking them into custody and transporting them to municipal facilities. This should continue to be their response to public intoxication, except for one crucial change—the destination of the drunkenness offender [14].

Currently, many police departments operate under the revolving door routine of repeated token criminal prosecution and short-term jailing. No matter how well performed, these actions will never alleviate the problem of public intoxication. Instead, chronic inebriates should be channeled to a medical facility for (1) immediate intervention to combat the acute characteristics of the illness, namely, intoxication; (2) treatment of any associated diseases frequently found among such individuals; (3) psychiatric evaluation and treatment, where indicated; and (4) social rehabilitation (e.g., job training, family counseling, etc.), if needed.

The role of the police in this process would be the channeling of the inebriates to the proper therapeutic facility. Although management of the problem begins with the police, it is not suggested that their role be enlarged or extended into the realm of treatment. Rather, the police function should be clearly defined and limited to (1) recognition and transportation of public inebriates to appropriate medical facilities in noncriminal cases, and (2) recognition of alcohol-related behavior in criminal cases, request for early medical diagnosis, and inclusion of findings of alcoholism in prosecutive and presentence reports. To perform these limited functions well, the police need training at the recruit, supervisory, and management levels. But, after directing subjects to the proper facility, the responsibility should then be left to other agencies and professions to take charge, treat, and do what is possible to rehabilitate chronic drunkenness and other alcohol-related offenses. Such changes are necessary for the police to be relieved of the sense of frustration that is a manifestation of their uncertain open-ended role in the revolving door process.

Peter Hutt, commenting on the results of such actions, said, "At some future time, hopefully, the policemen who ordinarily spend much of their time sweeping the streets of drunken derelicts will be released from that unpleasant and unnecessary chore, in order that they can get back to the business of fighting serious crime" [6].

REFERENCES

1. Aaronson, D., Dienes, C., and Musheno, M. *Decriminalization of Public Drunkenness: Tracing the Implementation of a Public Policy*. U.S. Government Printing Office: Washington, D.C. In press.
2. Bittner, E. The police on skid row: A study of peace keeping. *Am. Soc. Rev.* 32:699–715, 1967.
3. Federal Bureau of Investigation. *Crime in the United States: Uniform Crime Reports — 1969*. U.S. Government Printing Office: Washington, D.C., 1970.
4. Federal Bureau of Investigation. *Crime in the United States: Uniform Crime Reports –1978*. U.S. Government Printing Office: Washington, D.C., 1979.
5. Gillespie, D., Strecher, V., David, R., and Pittman, D. (eds.). *Alcohol, Alcoholism, and Law Enforcement*. Social Science Institute, Washington University: St. Louis, 1969.
6. Hutt, P. The recent court decisions on alcoholism: A challenge to the North American Judges Association and its members. In: *President's Commission on Law Enforcement and Administration of Justice, Task Force Report: Drunkenness*. U.S. Government Printing Office: Washington, D.C., 1967.
7. Pittman, D. Public intoxication and the alcoholic offender in American society. In: *President's Commission on Law Enforcement and Administration of Justice, Task Force Report: Drunkenness*. U.S. Government Printing Office: Washington, D.C., 1967.
8. Pittman, D. Drugs, addiction, and crime. In: *Handbook of Criminology*, Glaser, D. (ed.). Rand McNally: Chicago, 1974.
9. Pittman, D., and Gordon, C. *Revolving Door: A Study of the Chronic Drunkenness Offender*. Free Press: Glencoe, Ill., 1958.
10. President's Commission on Law Enforcement and Administration of Justice. *The Challenge of Crime in a Free Society*. U.S. Government Printing Office: Washington, D.C., 1967.
11. *Uniform Alcoholism and Intoxication Treatment Act*. U.S. Government Printing Office: Washington, D.C., 1971.
12. Weber, J. Final evaluation report. In: *The St. Louis Detoxification and Diagnostic Evaluation Center* (Law Enforcement Assistance Administration, U.S. Department of Justice Grant 284 [S.093]). U.S. Government Printing Office: Washington, D.C., 1970.

79

JACQUELINE P. WISEMAN, PhD, University of California, San Diego

SKID ROW ALCOHOLICS: TREATMENT, SURVIVAL, AND ESCAPE

SKID ROW IS AN AREA found adjacent to the commercial and/or factory and warehouse sections of most major urban centers. It exists, both symbolically and actually, as one termination point in a career of male alcoholics. Although skid row alcoholics are thought to comprise only about 5% of the total number of persons with a drinking problem, the public nature of their drinking and their concentration in one area has caused them to receive attention out of proportion to their numbers. Not all persons residing on skid row are alcoholics, however. Unemployed and indigent workers, the elderly and disabled living on meager pensions, Social Security, or welfare, and, more recently, young drug users and other societal misfits can also be found there. However, it is thought that a majority of persons who live on skid row have a serious alcohol problem [7, 14, 15]. Certainly, these men are the most visible citizens of the area.

Women comprise much less than 10% of the population on skid row, according to estimates by Bahr [4]. They also arrive there by different routes than men. Many are former prostitutes who have gradually sunk economically as they lost youthful charms. While these women may drink heavily, they are not a part of the bar and street drinking culture of the men. This chapter, therefore, focuses upon the male skid row alcoholic.

Jacqueline P. Wiseman, PhD, Professor of Sociology, University of California, San Diego, San Diego, California.

The appearance and general culture of the skid row area has remained remarkably constant over the years. Early studies of skid row [1], as well as later investigations [2, 3, 7, 15] carry descriptions that are strikingly similar: rundown decaying buildings, littered sidewalks, cubicle hotel rooms, pawnshops and junk shops, cheap, greasy spoon restaurants, small grocery stores, employment agencies for day labor, storefront missions and helping agencies.

Likewise, while there may be changes in the types of people on the scene, there is little change in the activities of skid row alcoholics. The men can be seen standing in groups of three or four passing a bottle, sitting on the sidewalk, searching garbage cans for discarded food to eat or empty bottles to sell, laughing and talking in the bars, standing in line when liquor stores open early in the morning, or eventually lying unconscious in the doorway of a building.

Alcoholics living on skid row have lost most social anchorages. In many cases, they started drinking in their 20s [3] and gradually their families of orientation, their wives, children, employers, and friends gave up on them. Bahr [2] refers to these men as disaffiliated, having no network of personal relationships to turn to in case of need or trouble. Rubington [10] suggests that skid row residence actually replaces these helping relationships to some extent, and thus the area can be seen as a place that helps solve some of these men's dilemmas as well as create them. Certainly, a constellation of treatment centers, social agencies, and public shelters offering counseling and temporary sustinence and residence, plus a retinue of run-down commercial establishments, have grown up within skid row to service the indigent alcoholic population. Although the avowed purpose of all but the commercial establishments is to help these men stop drinking and get off skid row, this goal has not been achieved to any extent in any American city. Furthermore, there is some evidence, to be discussed, that the phenomenon that is skid row is perpetuated by a web of interlocking, symbiotic social arrangements that have varied but little over the years.

SKID ROW: CHANGING AND YET CONSTANT

The Area

The term "skid row" originated in Seattle when lumberjacks living together in one area of the city used the muddy streets to slide logs to the mills. Similar inner-metropolitan settlements received great growth impetus all over the United States when countless unskilled, unmarried men, discharged from the military at the close of the Civil War, roamed the country looking for adventure and a new life. This congregation of outsiders became increasingly segregated from the remainder of the city. Commercial establishments of the areas, such as bars and flop houses, offered prices these men could afford. There was acceptance by others of similar circumstances, acceptance that was found nowhere else in town by these men, given the state of their finances, their unkempt appearance, and their rough manners. This combination of surface camaraderie and very real social segregation, some self-imposed, apparently aided in fostering a tavern culture that encouraged continued heavy drinking.

Over the years, various attempts at urban renewal have focused on skid row as a structural entity, but the area and people have shown remarkable tenacity. The early urban renewal approaches were quite direct — a bulldozer was used to level several city blocks, and middle-class housing, offices, sports complexes, stores, or other more desirable buildings and tenants were moved in. The result was not as anticipated. Skid row inhabitants merely moved to other, similar areas in the city, and, followed by hotel and bar owners, gradually reestablished their enclaves in one or more such districts there [7].

More recent attempts at eradicating skid rows have included attacks on the problem of human rehabilitation as well as physical renewal of run-down buildings. However, various government agencies concerned with drying out alcoholics and treating their alcoholism and other health problems, as well as counseling them on employment and relocation, have failed to make an appreciable dent in the skid row population. Of course, these services often are more an attempt at cosmetics than an all-encompassing effort on the part of city administrations to reclaim skid row men. Usually underfunded and understaffed, the existence of these helping agencies allows cities to strike a humanitarian pose while simultaneously indicating concern for the problem of merchants who complain that skid row men are ruining their businesses by hastening the spread of urban blight. Thus, where skid rows may have an average population of 2,000 to 3,000, drying out facilities may be limited to five to 10 beds, halfway houses to 10 to 20 inhabitants at a time, and medical services to a doctor or nurses who comes once a week, aided by paraprofessionals [6, 15].

Composition of the Population

Early skid row populations were predominantly indigent white men, 45 years of age and older. Blacks, Chicanos, and other ethnic groups were not made welcome. (Some cities have, of course, developed special ethnic or racial enclaves within skid row or near neighborhoods of similar description. New York has a Black skid row population and Los Angeles has an American Indian concentration, for instance.) More recently, however, non-Caucasions, including newly arrived immigrants, legal and otherwise, have braved possible rejection from skid row regulars as the housing squeeze forces them into cheap hotels. Young drug users and dropouts from the hippie generation who have been unable to cope with so-called straight society are now invading these areas. The mentally ill are also finding their way to skid row now in larger numbers. Due to recent civil rights amendments to, and court interpretations of, commitment laws, they can no longer be forced into long-term hospitalization. Unable to get employment, and living marginally on welfare, they drift to skid row where housing is cheaper and where there is a certain acceptance of eccentricity.

Various cohorts of slumlords have provided housing in skid row areas. These people invest in firetrap buildings, subdivide them with chicken wire into cubicles just big enough for a cot, a chair, and a night stand, and thus rent the total square footage of the building at great profit and in obvious violation of public health codes [7]. Over the years, entrepreneurial white skid row hotel operators have been succeeded by entrepreneurial Chinese, Pakistani, Hindu, and Koreans. The same sort of ethnic turnover can be noted in the grocery stores, the cafes, and other commercial establishments catering to skid row trade.

Homeless, drinking men of skid row have also attracted Christian missions that have a short-range goal of offering badly needed emergency food and shelter to them, and a long-range goal of converting these men to Christianity and weaning them away from alcohol. This dual purpose often results in what cynical skid row denizens refer to as "mission stiffs singing for their supper" — being forced to listen to a sermon and to sing hymns to qualify for hot soup and lodging at the end of the evening.

Police are a small but continually important element in skid row. As noted by Bittner [5], they are utilized primarily as peace keepers. Their job is to prevent drunken fights before they can start, prevent men from passing out on a sidewalk or in a gutter when they could be in a hotel or mission. Using the authority of their uniforms, and an intimate knowledge of skid row inhabitants, they get the alcoholic men to move on. Failing that, the police — usually at the behest of merchants — do regular sweeps of the area with the patrol wagon, arresting men who look like they might be drunk, and cleaning up the streets in this way.

The personnel of helping agencies, either governmental or private, round out the population, although like the mission workers and the police and most storekeepers, they do not live in the area.

TREATMENT OF SKID ROW ALCOHOLICS

In addition to detoxification centers, storefront drop-in social centers offering counseling and group therapy, medical services, and some attempt at long-term therapy through established Alcoholics Anonymous (AA) groups, skid row men may be sent to city hospital emergency wards for short-term drying out when necessary. They may also be committed to mental hospitals for long-term therapy. In these latter institutions, they may take part in group therapy and a variety of other treatments currently in use, including some type of behavior modification, Antabuse, or AA meetings.

A part of the early history of skid row alcoholics was the so-called revolving door syndrome [8, 13]. Public inebriates would be arrested, taken to the drunk tank of the jail to dry out, perhaps spend a few days incarcerated, and then be released, only to reappear shortly thereafter in court after a subsequent arrest, to repeat the whole process again. More recently, after the unfavorable publicity given this process—both in terms of the extralegal arrest and sentencing practices, as well as the costliness and futility of short drunk-tank stays—some city administrators have attempted to offer therapy in the jail. Psychiatrists and social workers were hired to offer treatment (usually group therapy plus AA), and men would then be sentenced to treatment for 30, 60, 90, or 120 days. This latter approach does not have a much better record for rehabilitating skid row alcoholics than the earlier revolving door method. Of course, both failures may be the result of the fact that there does not exist at present any known treatment for alcoholism with a high or even modest success rate.

It has been suggested that the city could both save on costly hospitalization of alcoholics and still get these men off the streets—thus pleasing complaining merchants—if wet hotels were to be established that would house indigent men addicted to alcohol, thus allowing them to drink in the privacy of their homes like middle-class alcoholics. However, this approach has never been able to gain widespread support, primarily because it seemed to be asking taxpayers to support nonproductive alcoholics and thus, in effect, underwrite alcoholism.

SKID ROW ALCOHOLICS AS A COMMUNITY RESOURCE

Although most discussions of skid row and the alcoholics who live there focus on the high cost to the cities and state in which they reside, there are hidden benefits to their existence as well. In addition to being the customers of skid row commercial establishments, there is evidence that skid row alcoholics make up the bulk of clients in city and state alcoholism treatment facilities, such as detoxification wards, state mental hospitals with alcoholic treatment facilities, and city-operated halfway houses and shelters [15]; thus, it is no exaggeration to say that their existence provides jobs for professionals and paraprofessionals in this field.

Skid row alcoholics also provide low-cost or free labor to cities that use them for snow removal. Farmers use skid row alcoholics for low-cost stoop labor or hand-harvesting. Merchants use them for handbill distributing, on clean-up crews, and in other nonskilled, low paying capacities [15]. City jails use alcoholics to do yard maintenance outside the jail and to do clean-up tasks inside because they are unlikely to try to escape than other prisoners, and there is less concern if they do. Some skid row alcoholics in farming regions claim that they are forced to work on harvests as part of sheriffs' work crews.

Skid row alcoholics are to be found in almost every unskilled and semiskilled position available in mental hospitals that have an alcoholism rehabilitation program. They tend grounds, work in the kitchen, aid in indoor maintenance, and do menial work (such as emptying bedpans) around wards where more incapacitated mental patients are kept. Missions that operate second-hand stores use the labor of skid row alcoholics to pick up donations, reupholster furniture, clean appliances, sort clothing, and the other myriad chores of readying discarded merchandise for sale to the public. For this work, the men receive board and room and a small weekly gratuity.

Skid row can also be seen as functioning as an area that can absorb a deployment of police to handle its nuisance problems when these officers are not needed elsewhere. At the same time, patrolmen can be pulled out of skid row if necessary, since it is seldom the scene of a serious crime. Thus, the area can be used to both justify and maintain a certain level of police force in a city.

SURVIVAL ON SKID ROW

Alcoholics on skid row do not see heavy drinking as their most pressing problem. Rather, it gives them some surcease in the long-term relationship and employment problems they face, while offering both pleasure and fellowship. Skid row men perceive their immediate concerns to be those of survival: obtaining food, shelter, clothing, and some money for alcohol. Skid row offers opportunities for the penniless to achieve all of those things if they know how to work the system. Wallace [14] has pointed out that an important part of the socialization of a newcomer is for an old-timer to teach him skid row resources and survival tactics to make him streetwise.

For instance, food is available at the missions, at drop-in alcoholism treatment centers that offer coffee and doughnuts as an attraction, and through qualifying for welfare food stamps. Places to sleep when there is no money for a hotel room include mission dormitories, county shelters, and, further down the scale, bus stations, libraries, parked unlocked cars, packing boxes, vacant lots with protective foliage, and space under bridges. Clothing is available at missions and at thieves' markets, mentioned below. Money can be obtained from welfare, and from working at odd jobs. Persons who work a minimum number of days at jobs covered by unemployment compensation may collect that money for the alloted span. Other sources of cash include selling blood and selling hair. Small stolen items are peddled at floating "thieves' markets," which are open-air informal gatherings at which people who steal and people willing to buy stolen goods meet and deal. Selling merchandise coupons to unscrupulous grocers and begging on the streets are further ways of obtaining money. If a man can only get a small amount of money, he soon learns it can be pooled with the money of others to buy a bottle, which can be shared by all [9].

Wiseman [15] observed there is a good deal of evidence that both punitive and rehabilitative agencies, both city and state, are used, one after another, by skid row alcoholics as survival resources, rather than for the purposes for which they were intended. Skid row alcoholics refer to this practice as "making the loop." Thus, skid row men will get lodging and steady meals by going to jail for a time. They will be released, picked up again, and then sent to the emergency ward of the city hospital. From there they may go to a mental hospital that has an alcoholism program, where they again have free shelter and meals. Alternatively, the skid row alcoholics may go from jail to a mission where they will work in some aspect of the second-hand store operation (if the mission has one), or they may go to a city-operated shelter, and from there to a halfway house. In all of these facilities, they usually offer surface cooperation with the ongoing alcoholism rehabilitation program, but cynically go and buy a bottle almost immediately upon discharge.

ESCAPE FROM SKID ROW

Those skid row men who do manage to attain sobriety for a time find that their job skills, experience, and references are so dated that they have a difficult time getting any employment. Compounding hindrances are age and possession of jail and mental hospital records. While job hunting, the men are usually supported by welfare and placed in the least expensive housing welfare workers can find — skid row hotels. Thus, during the time they are making a discouraging round of employers, they are living in their old drinking milieu. With such a combination of hopelessness and temptation, it is not difficult to understand why they often give up and begin drinking again. Later, they skip the job-hunting period entirely and just return to drinking immediately upon discharge from a rehabilitative institution.

Aside from low-paying, unskilled jobs, only one avenue of employment seems notable. Skid row men who attain sobriety and manage to make a good impression on professionals in the field of alcoholism treatment are often hired as counselors or helpers at treatment facilities. Some men find a new career in this way, turning their skid row past into valuable job experience. Eventually, however, many of these men return to drinking, even after a fairly lengthy period of such employment [11, 12].

For a majority of alcoholic men, death seems to be the only certain release from a skid row life. Their health broken by heavy drinking, exposure to the elements, improper diet, and compounded by the inevitable results of aging, this group of men usually has one of the highest morbidity and mortality rates of any in the city.

REFERENCES

1. Anderson, N. *The Hobo*. University of Chicago Press: Chicago, 1923.
2. Bahr, H. M. *Skid Row: An Introduction to Disaffiliation*. Oxford University Press: New York, 1973.
3. Bahr, H., and Caplow, T. *Old Men Drunk and Sober*. New York University Press: New York, 1974.
4. Bahr, H. M., and Garrett, G. R. *Women Alone: The Disaffiliation of Urban Females*. Lexington Books: Lexington, Mass., 1976.
5. Bittner, E. The police on skid row: A study of peace keeping. *Am. Soc. Rev.* 32:699–715, 1961.
6. Blumberg, L., Shipley, T. E., Jr., and Shandler, I. W. *Skid Row and Its Alternatives*. Temple University Press: Philadelphia, 1973.
7. Bogue, D. J. *Skid Row in American Cities*. Community and Family Study Center, University of Chicago: Chicago, 1963.
8. Pittman, D. J., and Gordon, C. W. *Revolving Door: A Study of the Chronic Police Case Inebriate*. Free Press: Glencoe, Ill., 1958.
9. Rooney, J. F. Group processes among skid row winos: A reevaluation of the undersocialization hypothesis. *Q. J. Stud. Alcohol* 22:444–460, 1961.
10. Rubington, E. The chronic drunkenness offender. *Ann. Am. Acad. Pol. Soc. Sci.* 315:65–72, 1958.
11. Rubington, E. Grady "breaks out": A case study of an alcoholic's relapse. *Soc. Prob.* 11:372–380, 1963.
12. Rubington, E. Organizational strains and key roles. *Admin. Sci. Q.* 4:350–369, 1965.
13. Spradley, J. P. *You Owe Yourself a Drunk*. Little, Brown: Boston, 1970.
14. Wallace, S. E. *Skid Row as a Way of Life*. Bedminster Press: Totowa, N.J., 1965.
15. Wiseman, J. P. *Stations of the Lost: The Treatment of Skid Row Alcoholics*. University of Chicago Press: Chicago, 1979.

80

HARRISON M. TRICE, PhD, Cornell University
JANICE M. BEYER, PhD, State University of New York at Buffalo

JOB-BASED ALCOHOLISM PROGRAMS: MOTIVATING PROBLEM DRINKERS TO REHABILITATION

A MAJOR DIFFICULTY IN treating alcoholism is that those suffering from this disorder to not readily seek help, and are typically resistant to the efforts of others to help them. Thus, in order for outside agents to intervene successfully to halt the progress of the disorder, it is first necessary to somehow motivate alcoholics and problem drinkers to seek, or at least go along with, efforts aimed at rehabilitation. Job-based alcoholism programs incorporate a variety of strategies designed to overcome this difficulty, and to otherwise assist problem-drinking employees to rehabilitate themselves. Furthermore, job-based programs intervene at a stage in the disorder when the affected person is still a relatively productive member of society who has not yet been labeled deviant or ejected from all normal social roles. Thus, they offer great potential for reducing the social and personal costs associated with problem drinking and alcoholism.

The strategies of job-based alcoholism programs have evolved over time. Some military organizations and private employers began programs for their

---

Harrison M. Trice, PhD, Professor, New York State School of Industrial and Labor Relations, Cornell University, Ithaca, New York, and Research Consultant, The Christopher D. Smithers Foundation, Mill Neck, New York.

Janice M. Beyer, PhD, Professor, School of Management, State University of New York at Buffalo, Buffalo, New York.

employees during World War II. Soon after the war, 12 or so pioneer programs were begun in industry, and some unions were also active. These early attempts to help problem-drinking employees through their work places were rather direct translations of principles gleaned from Alcoholics Anonymous. The central idea was the necessity of hitting bottom before rehabilitation would be an attractive alternative to continued drinking, and the complementary notion of creating some way, via the job, to speed up the process of hitting bottom [59]. In 1962 Trice formalized an approach to systematically apply these principles to work situations and employer-employee relationships [13]. His initial statement [73] included the basic elements of current prevailing strategies that are outlined in this chapter. With this foundation, job-based policies and programs could be made more credible and attractive to employers and unions.

At the present time there are thousands of job-based alcoholism programs run by employers, unions, and occupational associations. Of course, refinements and adaptations to local circumstances are continuously being developed, and there has been some controversy about even the central elements of policy strategies [11]. But the great majority of job-based programs designed to deal primarily with alcoholism still rely heavily on the strategies and principles Trice set forth in 1962. Recently, however, an extension of this movement to deal with other types of personal problems has generated sufficient support around a somewhat different set of rationales, to be considered a separate movement.

This chapter presents and discusses the basic strategies underlying job-based alcoholism policies and their rationales, as well as focusing upon an important extension and enlargement of job-based alcoholism programs—the recent movement toward employee assistance programs, which are designed to intervene in a wide variety of personal problems besides alcoholism. Also, the complex issues involved in evaluating the results of job-based programs are presented, and reports upon progress that has been made in improving evaluation efforts are discussed.

INTERVENTION STRATEGIES UNDERLYING JOB–BASED ALCOHOLISM POLICIES

Basic Behavior and Principles

Most job-based alcoholism policies use the fact that job performance declines among developing alcoholics as the starting point for their intervention strategy. There is good evidence that performance deteriorates as problem drinking increases, regardless of occupation, status, or amount of supervision [8, 45, 74]. The central strategy of job-based programs is to use the deteriorating performance of alcoholic employees as a basis for constructive confrontation, in which supervisors and managers confront affected employees with evidence of their impaired performance and simultaneously offer support for rehabilitation, without any stigma attached.

Supervisors do not necessarily need to be able to connect the poor performance directly to alcohol abuse — even though they often have excellent reasons to do so. The strategy calls for supervisors to confront poor performers solely on the basis of deficiencies in performance, and then, in a constructive manner, tell them about the policy and its offer of nonpunitive, nonjudgmental, rehabilitative help. It is then up to the employee involved to decide whether to take advantage of the opportunity provided by the policy. Most policies provide that this confrontation strategy be continued for at least two or three sessions if performance does not return to acceptable levels. In the second or third session, an additional strategy is added, called "crisis precipitation," in which the supervisor warns the employee that continued poor performance will be subject to discipline — initially a temporary suspension, but eventually discharge. Most policies, however, urge that even crisis precipitation be carried out in a constructive context of positive offers of help, and that the availability of rehabilitative opportunities similar to those provided for other health problems be repeatedly emphasized.

Guiding these concrete supervisory actions is a specific written policy that has been adopted by management and promulgated to all levels of supervision and employees. Policies differ somewhat across employers, but they usually articulate certain common principles on which job-based intervention strategies are based: Alcoholism is a treatable health problem, not a moral weakness; it causes much suffering and poor performance; a constructive approach should be taken to the problem, avoiding self-abasement and emphasizing positive supports; employees can choose whatever method they wish to regain normal performance with the positive backing of the company; at the same time, the nature of the disorder may call for the creation of a crisis, and job conditions will be used to do this as constructively as possible; finally, every effort will be made to incorporate unions, if present, in devising and carrying out the overall strategy.

How Policy Strategies Use Social Controls

The strategies underlying job-based policies were developed to capitalize on social controls present in workplaces and in the employer-employee relationship [73]. By external social controls is meant the "ability of a social group of society to engage in self-regulation" [38, p. 85]. That is, the concept refers to group processes that are aimed overtly at maintaining basic order by discouraging individual deviance while encouraging conformity by means of sanctions, or rewards, directed at individual behavior [55].

Social controls are activated when the expectations assigned to any institutional role are unmet by individuals occupying those roles [35]. Most social controls emanate from the interactions that generate social groups, and thus are assumed to be present in some form and strength in practically all interactions between persons [31, 63].

Social controls are strengthened or weakened by supporting mechanisms. Three that are important for job-based policies are internalized values, social distance, and group membership. At the individual level, persons must hold internalized values that are to some degree compatible with the social values underlying particular social controls or attempted social controls will be evaded or resisted [89]. The ineffectiveness of legal sanctions against marijuana at the present time and against alcohol during prohibition illustrate this point very well.

Other support mechanisms occur at the group level. Feelings of social distance [72] arise within groups between those failing to meet the obligations of their roles and those who do. Some social distance must emerge in this way before group members are willing or able to activate social controls against nonconforming members. Also, social controls must be applied in a way that allows poor role performers to retain their membership and remain within the group so that the group can continue to exert some social control over these persons. If those who fail to perform role obligations are excluded and lose their status as group members, they move beyond the controls of the group.

Internalized values. The constructive confrontation strategy employs all of these support mechanisms to some degree, but the process by which this happens is somewhat more complex than the descriptions above suggest. The social controls activated within given employer-employee relationships depend upon more or less explicit expectations of adequate performance. Even though formal performance expectations may be determined externally to individual workers, the large majority of workers have internalized personal work values that recognize the appropriateness of employers' general expectations of adequate performance from them, thus converting these expectations into felt obligations. Job-based alcoholism policies call for confrontation and possible sanctions whenever work performance obligations are unmet consistently.

At the same time, the confrontation must be balanced by the constructive part of the strategy, which taps into another set of internalized values—a humanitarian, helping ethic that is prominent in modern society. According to the policy, the employer—and union, if one is present—pledges to perform the confrontation within an understanding and sympathetic framework, making efforts to be both considerate and helpful. Policies generally provide the same support for treatment of alcoholism as for other health problems; the status and job rights of the problem drinker are also maintained. In sum, the policy includes concerns both for employees' welfare and for task performance by combining compassion with pressures from role obligations. It thus uses two sets of internalized values that tend to occur in supervisor-subordinate relationships.

Social distance. The implementation of job-based alcoholism policies requires some social distance between supervisors and employees. The very existence of the policy symbolizes the role obligations of employees and the authority that resides in supervision to enforce those obligations. But its mere existence does not create the social distance implied by the authority relationship. One controlled study found that only after training had reduced favorable sentiments toward problem employees to create feelings of moderate social distance were supervisors willing to confront such employees [77]. Without such training, and especially in the absence of a policy, many supervisors tend to feel very friendly and close to subordinates, including problem-drinking ones, probably because their roles and behaviors are highly interdependent and lead to frequent interactions. Such feelings of closeness militate against taking action to confront a problem-drinking employee.

A relevant example of this difficulty is the differential use of an alcoholism policy by skill level in federal government agencies [79]. Supervisors who supervised employees with higher skills, or at managerial and professional levels, used the policy far less often than other supervisors. Often supervisors of more skilled employees do not differ appreciably in educational and occupational statuses, and belong to the same professional or occupational association as their subordinates. Frequently they derive their primary social status from the occupation, rather than their position in the managerial hierarchy. All of these factors tend to lower social distance between such supervisors and their subordinates, producing little or no use of alcoholism policies.

In short, common identities and perspectives work against exercising social controls over others because using social controls requires that differences be perceived by those doing the controlling between themselves and those being controlled [26]. Job-based policies provide guidelines for establishing such differences based upon widely accepted norms of job performance. By calling attention to differences between the behaviors of problem-drinking employees and the behaviors prescribed by accepted norms, the policy lowers social acceptance of the behaviors [80] and sets problem drinkers apart from coworkers and supervisors who are abiding by these norms. Thus, the looser the norms of the referent group, the more difficult it is to engender social distance by emphasizing work-role performance; conversely, the tighter the norms of performance are, the easier it is to engender social distance by emphasizing work-role performance.

Group membership. The third support mechanism—keeping problem-drinking employees within present work groups and job-related roles—is greatly facilitated by the constructive, employee-oriented part of the policy. Without a formal policy, problem drinkers in work settings are likely to be discharged when their behavior can no longer be tolerated. Often the discharge follows a long period of tolerating and absorbing grossly deviant behavior. By providing acceptance of alcoholism as a health problem that deserves the same assistance as other health problems, by assuring confidentiality, and by guaranteeing continued job security during and after rehabilitation, the policy strategy allows the problem drinker to assume the sick role with minimal stigma and with maximum social supports without leaving the social setting and roles within which social controls are operating.

This part of the strategy can fail in two ways: One possibility is that the problem drinker may be treated with intolerance by coworkers and superiors, excluded from social groups, and assigned a deviant status. To avoid this, the policy sets forth principles intended to promote understanding and tolerance of the disorder; if employees and managers have received training on the policy, and it has the backing of top management and unions, intolerant reactions are less likely.

A second possibility is that the problem drinker will leave the job, either voluntarily or involuntarily. Problem drinkers sometimes resign rather than face and admit their drinking problems. Also, some problem drinkers qualify for early retirement, and thus can leave the job without admitting their problem and yet be assured of an adequate income. Occasionally problem-drinking employees must be laid off as part of general cutbacks. Finally, problem drinkers may be discharged in accordance with policy prescriptions because of failure to regain acceptable job performance and to cooperate with rehabilitation efforts.

No matter how it occurs, loss of group membership has one great danger, which is that persons who have lost other social ties will gravitate to deviant subgroups who hold group norms incompatible with normalizing and thus their undesirable behavior continues [76]. When problem drinkers assume sustained and stable roles within such deviant subgroups, the power of other social groups and norms over them is greatly diluted. Thus, maintaining normal ongoing group memberships is an important force in achieving social control. This is why the policy strategy guarantees job security and present status, and defers discharge until repeated confrontations and offers of help have been unsuccessful.

Overview. In sum, behind the strategies of alcoholism policies lie powerful collective authority and societal influences that represent universalistic rather than particularistic pressures toward conformity in individual behavior. Supervisors in work settings can legitimately confront employees about unacceptable work performance. Studies of Orthodox Jews, Cantonese Chinese, and Italian Americans [83], as well as 17th-century New England Puritans [68], indicate that these subcultures had powerful social controls over the drinking behavior of individual members. Drinking occurred frequently in these societies, but when misuse of alcohol interfered with role obligations based on consensual norms, strong pressures were brought to bear on the deviant drinker. Recent data [25] indicate these social controls have remained stable among United States Jews despite acculturation and secularization. Other empirical support for the effectiveness of social controls over drinking comes from Horton's [33] cross-cultural study, from the studies of Lemert [42, 43, 44] among the Northwest Coast Indians and Polynesian societies, and from an analysis of drinking among the Baffin Island Eskimo [32].

In pluralistic American society, similar social pressures may be found only in work places, where formal expectations of performance [70] as well as informal pressures from fellow workers [4] define the lower limits of acceptable behavior.

Job-based policies capitalize on the powerful sanctions against role-damaging drinking that are available in work places in contrast to the relatively ineffectual external controls exerted by families, communities, or religions in modern America. American society has failed to produce clear norms and sanctions concerning alcohol use so that developing alcoholics never face consistent definitions and sanctions—a situation that produces weak internal controls [36]. This is less true of work places, where some clarity of norms surrounding expected behaviors still exists.

Constructive Confrontation and Psychodynamics of Alcoholism

The strategy of constructive confrontation is responsive to widely recognized psychodynamics that usually accompany alcoholism. These include (1) internal feelings of guilt and self-hatred for excessive drinking and associated behaviors; (2) defense mechanisms, especially denial and rationalization, that are activated to defend the ego from both internal and external criticisms; and (3) interpersonal tactics of manipulation and projection used to counter any attempts by others to stop the alcoholic from drinking.

The guilt and self-hatred of the alcoholic can be dampened by the very fact that constructive help is being offered by the employer, who thereby expresses concerns and indicates that the individual involved is a valued member of the organization. Also, by treating alcoholism as a health problem that qualifies for sick leave and other medical benefits, the stigma the alcoholic fears is reduced. Finally, the emphasis on rehabilitation embodied in the strategy implies faith that treatment can be successful, and that the alcoholic can eventually return to full status as a valued and respected member of society.

Denial and rationalization are countered in job-based programs primarily by emphasizing job performance. It is hard for alcoholics to deny and rationalize away the employer's legitimate right to expect adequate performance of assigned work tasks; also, the realities of the job itself confront drinking employees with demands that are difficult to reconcile with the impairments associated with heavy drinking. These realities are dramatized when the supervisor confronts the alcoholic with specific evidence of poor performance. If the initial confrontation does not overcome the denials and rationalizations, further realities are imposed that the alcoholic finds increasingly hard to ignore. Progressive discipline is applied, usually starting with a written warning, and then progressing through suspensions for increasingly longer periods of time, and leading finally to termination. The costs incurred by the alcoholic who is suspended without pay are hard to deny, as is the impending crisis of losing the job entirely.

Alcoholics are very good at manipulating others with whom they interact to provide further justifications for continued drinking. One way in which they may try to do this is to blame their drinking on overwhelming personal problems, trying to thus explain or excuse their behavior and also elicit sympathy. They may also project their own self-hatred and guilt onto others, claiming rejection by others as a reason for their drinking. These devices are hard to use in the work place, which is governed by norms of impersonality and emotional detachment. Supervisors who maintain some social distance from subordinates can successfully resist the alcoholic's attempts to elicit so much tolerance and sympathy that the confrontation part of the strategy is omitted or deferred. The formality of having a written policy, especially when top management and unions are known to be really behind it, also bolsters the resistance of supervisors to manipulation by the alcoholic employee. After all, applying formal policies appropriately is an important part of a supervisor's work.

Constructive Confrontation and Dynamics of Supervision

The strategies of job-based policies are also consistent with what is known about the dynamics of supervision and leadership. Constructive confrontation requires two different types of behavior from supervisors: (1) to pay attention to work performance and be willing to exercise sanctions against subordinates with unsatisfactory performance; and (2) to be willing to offer help to employees with a personal problem like alcoholism in a supportive way. Research has produced repeated evidence that supervisory behaviors tend to cluster into two categories that parallel these requirements: one task-oriented and concerned about productivity, and the other employee-oriented and concerned with social and emotional factors [18, 40, 67]. A central issue in research on general supervisory behaviors and also on implementation of job-based policies is to what degree most supervisors can successfully combine these two types of behavior. Other issues relevant to the role of supervisors in job-based policies include their reluctance to use the policy, and the tendency of counselors to bypass supervisors in a rush to treatment.

Dual styles of supervision. Recent work on leadership and supervision [14, 34, 85] has suggested that effective leaders must vary their behaviors to fit the particular demands of a given situation. Because being exclusively task-oriented or employee-oriented will not be effective in all situations, these writers argued, supervisors need to be able to blend or alternate these types of behaviors. The strategy of constructive confrontation, of course, calls for just this kind of duality.

Earlier findings [18, 40, 49, 67], however, suggested that most managers tend to exhibit predominantly one style or the other. If managers find one set of behaviors more natural or easy than the other, and follow their normal inclinations when using the constructive confrontation strategy, they will emphasize half of the strategy and neglect the half that does not fit their inclinations. When this happens, the intervention has lost some of its motivating force. Consequently, one important problem that job-based programs must address is training managers so they can practice this duality of behavior successfully. On the other hand, this means that supervisory training about job-based intervention strategies provides an excellent opportunity to train line managers how to be more generally effective by being concerned about both task performance and employee welfare.

Supervisory reluctance. Reports based on early research and practical experience observed the tendency of line managers to vacillate in applying constructive confrontation. Typically supervisors progressed through three stages of vacillation before reaching a decision to confront [75, 84]. Eventually, however, the accumulated instances of poor performance mounted up to produce willingness to use the policy.

Because constructive confrontation is the central strategy in job-based programs, and because the immediate supervisor of the alcoholic employee has the central role in carrying out the strategy, whether supervisors are able and willing to use the strategy is crucial to successful implementation of job-based programs. Practitioners often claim that supervisors just won't do it, citing the sort of supervisory delays and uncertainties already described. Less skeptical observers believe that dovetailing traditional supervisory training with a focus on problem-drinking employees — and other problem employees — can shorten the period of vacillation and accelerate use of the strategy, as was indicated by a carefully controlled evaluation of such training [77]. Another study showed that greater familiarity with an alcoholism policy and its strategy was associated with significantly greater use of the policy by supervisors [6].

Bypassing. Another danger to the basic strategy occurs when program counsellors or treatment practitioners bypass the supervisor and the whole strategy of constructive confrontation to get the employee into treatment as rapidly as possible. The relative benefits and risks of the "rush to treatment" is a controversial issue. On the other hand, those who conclude that psychodynamics of alcoholism require the use of confrontation believe that bypassing dilutes the motivational power of the basic strategy, leaving nothing but a referral process. On the other, those in favor of bypassing feel that the important thing is to get the employee into outside treatment and then rely largely upon its effectiveness. Various factors encourage bypassing: supervisory vacillation and reluctance, the eagerness of outside treatment people to intervene, and often the manipulative skills of alcoholics, who see an opportunity to avoid confrontation by temporarily going along with treatment. The chief risks of bypassing is that employees will not be genuinely motivated to rehabilitate themselves, and thus fail to cooperate fully or persist with treatment efforts.

EMPLOYEE-ASSISTANCE PROGRAMS AS A SOCIAL MOVEMENT

Emergence of the Movement

Widespread social changes have altered the composition of the work force and increased the incidence of some social problems, thus creating pressures to enlarge the scope of alcoholism policies. Joining forces already present, these new pressures have produced the rapid emergence of a full-blown social movement called employee assistance programs (EAPs) [81]. In a broad sense, EAPs expand the strategies underlying job-based alcoholism policies to incorporate other kinds of personal problems that can adversely affect job performance — for example, marital and parent-child problems, emotional disturbances, and financial problems. Although EAP policy statements tend to publicly disavow job-generated personal problems, and concentrate on those brought into the work place from outside, many programs have nevertheless been willing to try to encompass any personal problem. Like job-based alcoholism programs, practically all focus on the assumed relationship between such personal problems and impaired job performance and make the further assumption that relief from personal problems will improve performance. Finally many proclaim that alcoholism is their major personal problem. Recent reports [86] suggest that EAP programs are proliferating rapidly through industry in the United States.

The changing composition of the work force is one factor that has promoted the EAP movement: The near-flood of women into the labor force is perhaps the most prominent such factor. Women have brought to the work place their traditional openness about personal problems and their willingness to accept help [48]. Their presence may thus have provided encouragement for the EAP concept of expanding assistance to cover other personal problems.

Other social factors contributing to the popularity of EAPs include the increasing incidence of marital problems and divorce, of problems in rearing children — especially teenagers — of financial problems stemming from easy availability of credit, and of other drug substance use and abuse, especially marijuana, drugs that are new to work places and can also produce impairments.

Also, pressures growing out of experiences with traditional alcoholism policies played an important role in the emergence of the EAP movement. First, both unions and management tended to see the older programs as good ideas, but too narrow, and thus often pressed for programs that dealt with more than just alcoholism. Marital problems, financial difficulties, emotional problems, and health problems of various kinds so often accompany problem drinking and alcoholism as to be practically inseparable from the drinking behavior itself; alcoholism is a disorder with many facets. Second, reinforcing this sentiment was the need often expressed by those managing alcoholism programs for a euphemistic way to package their efforts in order to reduce stigma and promote willingness among alcohol abusers to participate. Third, the basic strategy pivoted on impaired performance — a condition that could arise from a myriad of factors other than alcoholism. Fourth, a wide range of treatment facilities and practitioners have been eager to sell their services to industry and other employers. Clearly, the demand for such services, and the income from them, would be greater if services were provided for a wide range of problems, and not just alcoholism. Fifth, social workers, educational counselors, and clergy sought to find jobs in business and industry as EAP counselors helped to accelerate growth of the movement [64]. Their interests meshed with long-standing ideologies of humanitarianism present in personnel administration [87] and created a receptivity for the EAP approach within many companies.

Similarities and Differences Compared to Alcoholism Programs

EAPs are direct descendants of alcoholism programs in important ways: Many insist that alcoholism represents a large portion in their intervention efforts. Although EAPs assign supervisors less of a key role, it is still an important one because poor performance is also used as the primary justification for EAPs. Also, the EAP movement has adopted an emphasis on union involvement that became prominent rather late in the alcoholism program movement.

Despite these commonalities, there are important differences between EAPs and programs defined as focusing on alcoholism. Job-based alcoholism programs tend to use a core set of principles and concepts that together constitute a recognizable common strategy. In contrast, the general EAP idea seems to mean different things to different people. No coherent strategy has yet emerged — except bits and pieces borrowed from the alcoholism strategy, combined with a general concern for helping employees with their personal problems by referring them to appropriate professional helpers.

The EAP movement has introduced new occupations that seek regular, paid employment with work organizations by claiming some degree of expertise in working with and helping employees with a wide variety of emotional and personal problems. Since the movement lacks a distinct strategy for intervention, these occupations tend to take on a professional mystique that does not rest so much on the social controls of the work place, as it does on counselors' particular skills, often termed "motivational counseling." In contrast, the constructive confrontation strategy was designed for use by regular line supervisors without the cost of professional counselors and with, at most, the help of part-time personnel who have had some specialized training. Even other line managers can adequately perform the alcoholism policy coordinator or facilitator role [6].

EAPs not only put less emphasis on the role of the supervisor, but also tend to sometimes be less enthusiastic about any use of discipline or crisis precipitation than alcoholism programs. At best those who have been prominent in the movement have advocated a bifurcation of the strategy by assigning confrontation and discipline, if necessary, to the supervisory role, while giving the counselor of the program the pleasanter role of providing support, services, and referral to treatment opportunities.

It is hard to see why most supervisors should embrace the unpleasant role they have been assigned in such EAPs. EAP advocates ignorant of the work place may make these assumptions because they have fallen for stereotypical portrayals of managers as so concerned with productivity as to be unconcerned with their relations with their subordinates. Phillips and Older [54] point out that supervisors are prone to experience difficult negative feelings about themselves as they progress through the four stages identified by Trice and Roman [84] in dealing with alcoholic employees. Supervisors also have feelings, and cannot be expected to voluntarily behave toward their workers in a solely punitive way. In fact, data from federal managers showed that no matter what stage of poor performance employees had reached in hypothetical situations, the majority of supervisors chose to counsel with the employees themselves, rather than refer them to the policy coordinator, or take a variety of other steps, including discipline [7].

Consistent with the widely divergent roles sometimes assigned to supervisors and counselors in EAPs is the tendency for some in the EAP movement to claim to be more professional, better trained to counsel and refer problem employees to outside facilities, less punitive, less judgmental, and more supportive than those staffing the older alcoholism programs. Often they express an almost total belief in the need for treatment, or counseling of some type, for nearly all personal problems that impair performance. This belief can lead naturally to an espousal of the rush to treatment syndrome, and a preference for self-referrals over supervisory referrals. But often the self-referral is a fiction designed to avoid any reference to sanctions. In many so-called self-referrals, the supervisor and employee have already discussed the problem, and the employee has more or less voluntarily agreed to seek help from the EAP counselor. Supervisors cooperate with the subterfuge to give the employee a break; EAP counselors cooperate because they are eager to get referrals and do counseling. Thus, the potential for social control available in the work setting is deliberately bypassed in an effort to be compassionate.

The limited experience and knowledge of many counselors with work place concerns may also inadvertently lead to neglect of the social controls available in the work setting by an inordinate emphasis on service delivery systems. Without deliberately attacking or attempting to replace the strategy, it is merely overlooked, and heavy emphasis is placed instead on concerns taken from the treatment milieu: "intake into the program," "counseling of the employee by program staff," "professional diagnoses and prescribed treatment," and "feedback from treatment agency" [17].

Ideological Themes

The majority of EAP practitioners appear to be a new occupational breed in the work place; social workers seem to predominate, with a heavy sprinkling of pastoral counselors, teachers, and nurses. All occupations generate ideologies that sustain their members in carrying out their occupational roles [5]. The occupations of EAP practitioners emphasize ideologies of compassion, humanitarianism, understanding, tolerance, and a general helping ethic—all of which can clash with parts of the strategy of constructive confrontation. These occupational ideologies also tend to reject the traditional national business ideology of laissez-faire, which emphasizes individual responsibility and thus may attribute personal problems to factors employees brought on themselves.

From the early days of the 20th century, other social movements have tried to influence the ways in which management maintained productivity and related to employees. Emerging at the turn of the century, industrial betterment or industrial welfare was a mixture of humanitarianism and pragmatic employer self-interest directed toward maintaining productivity. Proclaiming that employee happiness was a business asset, it espoused thrift clubs, recreational facilities, death-benefit funds, lunchrooms, and safety training [62]. Next, Taylorism attempted to set up highly rational, scientific ways to match job and worker in order to stimulate maximum productivity. In so doing, the Taylorites linked productivity to a careful matching of worker abilities to specific work tasks [7], not to some vague goodness that would emerge from a more benevolent work environment. Contrasting with the narrow rational orientation of scientific management, the human relations movement underscored the need for employees to be viewed as social creatures who were best understood as members of informal groups within which they obtain recognition and social acceptance, and develop norms of productivity. Human relations advocates believed that management must realize that workers were not isolated individuals, as the Taylorites believed, but members of natural groups that generated attitudes and feelings that could help or hinder productivity [3, 47]. Of more recent vintage, the job enrichment movement is the "process of analyzing job content to determine if jobs can be changed in such a way that individuals in those jobs will have more interesting, challenging tasks and greater responsibility; also more opportunities to experience achievement, recognition for that achievement, growth and development, and advancement to better jobs" [69, p. 89]. Thus, an attempt is made to increase worker productivity through organizational change. Closely akin to this thrust has been the quality of work life [12] and the organizational development movements [23], both of which advocate substantial alternation in the way work and authority are structured in order to increase satisfaction, reduce alienation, and humanize work.

Within this historical framework, the EAP movement can be seen as yet another effort to sell management a broad strategy for increasing productivity. The movement is, in effect, a pragmatic but compassionate attempt to improve performance—this time by setting up programs to help employees to deal with their personal problems; in the process, they will improve their work performance. The EAP movement differs from its forerunners in that it uses a populist kind of psychiatry to manage problems of living in order to sustain employees' performance and productivity.

But like the other movements, the assumed connection between the program and productivity is an illusive one in EAPs. Some argue that the quality of raw material, managerial controls, and economic adversity [21] or opportunities for feedback and reinforcement [53] may better explain the results obtained in the famous Hawthorne experiments than the humanitarian strategies that were discovered and introduced there. As is discussed in more detail elsewhere in this chapter, it is extremely difficult to prove that humanistic types of interventions actually produce predicted improvements in productivity.

Ideological Differences with Constructive Confrontation Strategies

Why did EAP practitioners who were new to the work place attempt to coopt the earlier alcoholism programs and replace the constructive confrontation strategy with humanistic counseling and treatment? One reason might have been the tendency of the helping professions, especially social workers, to place little emphasis upon motivation as a prerequisite for recovery from alcoholism [66], putting them in conflict with a strategy that has its major purpose the motivation of problem-drinking employees to seek treatment or otherwise regain acceptable performance. This low emphasis may, in turn, be reinforced by an unwillingness by social workers to accept the sick role as a legitimate description of alcoholics [9]. Also, the importance given to the counselor role in the EAP strategy may be a concrete expression of the efforts of an occupational network to justify and thus secure jobs for itself in the business world. However, EAP proponents have accepted the central rationale of job impairment and job performance, perhaps because this rationale has characterized all past social movements that have tried to influence business and industry. The appeal to performance is the only sure way to obtain entry for their efforts.

To a substantial degree, those espousing job-based alcoholism programs helped EAP proponents to coopt them. Constantly plagued by second-class status within the larger alcoholism movement, proponents of job-based alcoholism programs worked to broaden their base of support while maintaining the identity and integrity of the job-based movement. To achieve this, persons with backgrounds in treatment were widely encouraged to participate and support the strategy. To numerous observers the zeal and enthusiasm with which counseling-oriented groups were welcomed was an open invitation to coopt the widely publicized success enjoyed by alcoholism programs based on the constructive confrontation strategy. Soon the underlying ideological and occupational differences fragmented the job-based movement, as competing forces attempted to extend the early successes, but in ways that differed from the proven strategies [46, 52]. Debate over "broad-brush" strategies characterized the middle and late 1970s [57].

Not only is there ideological conflict between proponents of the job-based strategies focused on alcoholism and some proponents of EAP or broad-brush programs, there is also conflict within the EAP movement itself. In the absence of a generally accepted underlying strategy, EAP practitioners tend to differentiate themselves from each other, many claiming to have some unique technique or skill that makes theirs the most successful strategy. Currently the ideological conflicts continue in a myriad of subterranean maneuvers within informal groups, in the clash between competing coalitions within profressional associations and government agencies, and in ever-present searches for personal power and influence.

There can be little doubt that there is a real threat of demise for the confrontation strategy in these developments. Furthermore, much of the conflict within and between these groups serves no useful purpose, and actually threatens the hard-won credibility that the earlier job-based alcoholism programs were able to achieve by calling into question the successes of the earlier strategy, which had otherwise been widely accepted.

Internal Inconsistencies

An obvious and central question to ask of any intervention effort is what motivates people to seek and persist with treatment. Asking this question relative to the EAP movement uncovers basic inconsistencies in the approach, as promulgated by many of its practitioners. On the one hand, there is widespread emphasis upon self-referrals: "Voluntarism . . . is indicative of a successful EAP and should be a goal of such a program" [90, p. 43]. But this emphasis contradicts the importance given the role of the motivational counselor." If an employee is self-referred, the counselor did not motivate that employee to seek help or otherwise take action. Obviously self-referrals were motivated to seek help by other forces. In some cases their supervisors leaned on them for impaired performance that could not easily be ignored. In other cases, employees may have asked their supervisors' or fellow-workers' advice and were indirectly referred. Many observers agree that there is a high likelihood that the majority of self-referred clients actually come from supervision or union sources. Thus Smart sees the term "self-referral" as lumping together a sizeable number of motivations: "It is quite possible that a voluntary patient has been under coercion from his family, friends, and even his employer" [65, p. 208] before he sought treatment. And Heyman concluded from her data: "It is highly doubtful that an employee ever comes to an alcoholism program in industry on a truly voluntary basis [29, p. 907]. There are also concerns that being a self-referral can actually undermine therapeutic efforts. Rosenberg and Liftik [58] found that self-referrals had high dropout rates in a large outpatient clinic.

With cases who will not self-refer, "motivational counselors" alone are powerless for the simple reason that the reluctant employee will never come to them in the first place—unless supervision or others motivate in some way—a condition that makes them no longer self-referrals. There is, of course, abundant evidence that alcoholics are unlikely to self-refer, and it is not clear that persons with other types of problems do not also use denial, rationalization, and other such devices to avoid facing their problems. In the absence of a reliable operational definition of self-referral, the term seems to be a symbol used to justify the role of a functionary [50, 78] and to allay anxieties of management and labor by implying that something professional will be done about the problem.

Furthermore, if the major and most desirable function of EAP counselors is to accept self-referrals and then refer these persons to outside treatment resources, it is not clear why high levels of counseling skills are needed. The most that can be claimed is that the EAP counselor enhanced motivation already present to do something about the problem, and then later helped to sustain motivation to persist with treatment. Of course, the latter motivating function is shared with the treatment facility and its personnel.

Another inconsistency in the EAP approach occurs when problems are classified in single categories when most disorders with which programs deal — certainly alcoholism — are multifaceted. Instances of problem drinking may be classified as marital problems, when in fact they are both, and include other problems as well. Thus, the actual mix of problems in a given work setting can be severely distorted by the way problems are classified. Because human cognition abilities are limited, people tend to see what their frames of reference suggest they will find [15]. Occupational and other ideologies of counselors will therefore have important impacts on how they define the problems of a population of employees [5].

The general acceptance of the impaired performance criterion creates another inconsistency: It suggests the use of a confrontation strategy, but there is reluctance by many in the EAP movement to extend the strategy of constructive confrontation to other personal problems. Nevertheless, the obvious question remains: To what extent is the strategy appropriate for other problems? There are reasons to believe it has worked in alcoholism cases; why won't it work with other problem employees? Support for the feasibility of such an approach is provided by its similarity to the strategy used in reality therapy. This well-known psychotherapeutic approach focuses "on the present, and on behavior; the therapist guides the individual to enable him to see himself accurately, to face reality, to fulfill his own needs, without harming himself or others. The crux of the theory is personal responsibility for one's own behavior, which is equated with mental health" [24, p. 287]. Given this similarity, and the proven and remarkable success of constructive confrontation, it seems advisable to extend the strategy to emotional and personal problems that trouble employees. Because the strategy motivates alcoholics does not imply it should be reserved exclusively for them. On the contrary, why not assume it can be made broadly useful until strong evidence to the contrary is found? The risks of making such an assumption seem minimal.

EVALUATION OF JOB-BASED PROGRAMS

Program evaluation efforts fall into three overlapping categories: (1) the assessment of the extent to which a given program strategy has been implemented; (2) the evaluation of outcomes from the program; (3) the evaluation of the feedback of findings into the action program for its improvement.

Program Implementation

The need to evaluate policy implementation is obvious, but neglected. Clearly, the outcomes of strategy depend on how that strategy is implemented. The organizational processes that do this are unfamiliar to many action-oriented persons. Moreover, criteria for full, partial, or minimal implementation remain vague and difficult to measure. In popular terms, there are only two extremes: paper programs and fully implemented ones — both of which are crude stereotypes. So-called paper programs may actually be programs in the early stages of adoption and formalization by top management, while fully implemented ones may neglect important aspects of strategy.

Because of this inchoate state of the art in the assessment of implementation, a listing of indices into implementation may be useful. What follows is a first effort to establish such a list:

1. The extent to which an intervention strategy has been clearly formulated; the extent to which it incorporates inputs from major divisions, departments, and geographical locations and from affected unions; the extent to which it is written down and explicitly adopted as the intent of the organization by the policy-making levels of management; and the extent to which it has been formally issued.

2. The extent to which information about the policy has been diffused among potential users, there is support for the strategy among potential users, and adequate resources have been allocated to the program.

3. The degree to which unions, if present, are informed, supportive, and involved in implementing the program.

4. The extent to which specific adaptations have been made for particular relevant groups in the work force.

5. The extent of development of specific techniques for increasing implementation: for example, training for supervisors and shop stewards, devices to create awareness, selection and training of program personnel.

6. The extent to which specific steps have been taken to interface with treatment facilities, and liaison roles developed.

7. The frequency of actual uses of the program relative to estimated opportunities for use in that setting.

Studies of implementation are sparse and recent. Using many, but not all, of these indices, Beyer and Trice [6] conducted an evaluation of the implementation of an alcoholism policy for federal government employees. They collected data from a sample of 634 supervisors plus policy coordinators and installation heads working in a sample of 71 federal installations in the Northeast. Despite defects in implementation, 11% of supervisors reported 164 occasions to use the policy, or a prevalence rate for policy use of 3.3% [82]. It was found [82] that weaknesses in implementation included relatively low familiarity with the policy among managers, ambivalent installation directors, meager program resources, and lack of formally designated alcoholism policy coordinators. Schramm et al. [61] reported some of the same problems in implementation, especially in the absence of a policy coordinator. Googins [27] obtained data from two groups of first-line supervisors in a large public utility: 45 who had referred subordinates into the program, and 40 who had not. Many of his findings parallel those of Beyer and Trice, especially the importance of supervisors' familarity with the policy and correlations to its use. Also, Kurtz and Googins [41] reported that being part of informal networks led supervisors into a collective awareness of drinking problems, which augmented signs of deteriorating job performance and acted to move reluctant supervisors to use the policy.

Program Outcomes

Beginning relatively early in their development, job-based programs were evaluated in terms of outcomes. Early efforts used time-series (before-after) designs. Franco [20] set the pattern for numerous subsequent evaluative studies of this type when he compared indices of job maintenance, formal supervisory ratings of performance, and absenteeism 3 years before intervention with the same indices 4 years after treatment. His job maintenance index included a measure of treatment outcomes. He reported that 72% of those who stayed in treatment for 1 year maintained their jobs.

Asma et al. [2] used a time-series design to evaluate a constructive coercion approach 5 years before and 5 years after the intervention. They reported that the number of sick days dropped dramatically following treatment, and that 72% of the employees treated improved. Hilker [30] used a similar time-series approach and reported much the same results.

Some recent research included comparison groups. Smart [65] compared outcomes from cases under pressure from their employer with those who entered the program voluntarily. His design thus used nonrandom comparison groups. In one treatment center, confronted cases showed about the same rates of favorable outcomes as voluntary ones, and in a second center the voluntary ones showed slightly more improvement than confronted ones. It seems fair to assume that voluntary cases were initially more motivated toward rehabilitation than those in the coerced category, and thus the results indicated that the confrontation strategy was effective.

Alander and Campbell [1] attempted a control group that would be randomized, but actually used a comparison group made up of hourly employees who did not participate in the program but were known to have drug- or alcohol-related problems. Their report concluded that those in the program were very successful on various job-related criteria following intervention. Chopra et al. [10] concluded much the same thing when they compared outcomes for two groups of employed men. The group of 86 males who had been referred through a job-based program using constructive coercion showed definite, improved chances for a positive outcome compared to 121 volunteers.

Like Smart, Moberg [51] compared employees who were self-generated with others who were pressured by their employers. He also found that volunteers were more responsive to treatment. Schramm et al. [61], who also used self-referrals as comparison groups with similar results, pointed out that self-referrals also often perceive their jobs as at risk.

Heyman [28, 29] collected data on the subjective experiences of employees who had been in five job-based programs, and had experienced varying degrees of constructive confrontation. She reports a "significant relationship between constructive confrontation and improvement in work performance for those whose preprogram performance had deteriorated" [29, p. 78]. Two Canadian studies concluded much the same thing. Using a scale to assess the pressure exerted on alcoholics by important people in their lives, and a scale to detect the amount of concern about their behavior, Finlay [19] concluded that crisis-level anxiety was a major factor in making them accessible to treatment. Freeburg and Johnston [22] described a year-long follow-up study of 365 alcoholic clients, the large majority of whom had received confrontation from their employers about inadequate job performance. They found improvements on four dimensions of job performance rated by supervisors.

Other evaluative research suggests that the deterrent and preventive effects of constructive confrontation may be more important than its positive interactions with treatment. Schramm and DeFillippi [60] reported that constructive confrontation accounted for a greater proportion of improvement than did characteristics of treatment programs. This is consistent with the findings of Edwards et al. [15] that, by themselves, identification and strong advice to alter behavior achieved outcomes equal to lengthy and costly treatment.

An Assessment of Evaluation Studies

Evaluation studies yield remarkable success rates for job-based alcoholism programs and their central strategies. Successes are much greater than would be expected, especially compared to the results of evaluation studies done on interventions tried with other social problems. Weiss [88, p. 126] observed that "one of the most serious impediments to putting evaluation results to use is their dismaying tendency to show that the program has had little effect." Elison [16] demonstrated that negative results have emerged in the evaluation of programs on a wide variety of social problems. Jackson and Morgan [37, p. 62] concluded, referring to managerial innovations like sensitivity training and job enrichment: "The critical reviews of research in all these fields show that there is no scientific evidence to support the claims of the proponents of these methods." Yet repeatedly studies of job-based programs have reported not only success, but unusually high degrees of frequency. How can these atypical results be best explained?

First, it seems likely that these results may be fairly accurate. Taken together, the results of these studies approach triangulization of methods so often advocated [39]. Studies done on diverse populations, using a variety of comparison groups, using data from company records, self-reports, and supervisors, and using various time frames all show remarkably similar results.

However, other aspects of these studies cast reasonable doubts on this favorable assessment. Often they were done by persons closely associated with the specific programs, who were not professionally trained in evaluation research. Of course, job-based programs must be sold to skeptical and reluctant segments of the organizations; thus their proponents have strong motives for the program to look good.

One obvious way that outcome reports could be biased is that those cases most likely to succeed were screened out. Possible sources of such bias are difficult to either verify or refute, and include selectivity by line or staff persons; layoff, transfer, death, retirement, or discharge; exclusion of short-term employees; self-selection by denial and refusal; union interference in certain cases; and differences in the visibility and power of employees. Also, these studies uniformly failed to report any evidence about policy implementation. Were they fully implemented, sources of selectivity described above would probably be substantially reduced, which could bring into the program a wider variety of cases, including those less responsive than many currently in the programs. A recent attempt to assess the amount of selectivity in a long-standing alcoholism program uncovered relatively modest effects amounting to, at most, 10% of cases [81].

Another possible explanation of these remarkably favorable findings is that many of the outcome measures used are unrelated to job performance, which is the ultimate criterion used to justify the strategy. Absenteeism, for example, is not necessarily related to productivity or quality of work. Much the same could be said for such often-used criteria as visits to the medical department, sickness and accident benefits, or number of grievances, disciplinary cases, and workmen's compensation cases. These criteria may be more responsive to the intervention strategy than actual job performance.

At the other end of the intervention cycle, treatment alone may generate favorable outcomes, suggesting that job-based interventions had little effect. Robichaud et al. [56] gave 21 male industrial employees, all of whom had experienced at least one disciplinary suspension prior to the treatment, a routine, supervised ingestion of disulfiram. Absenteeism declined markedly; when treatment was discontinued it rose sharply. "This treatment-specific reversibility argues against the notion that the primary therapeutic element in employee alcoholism treatment is the motivational (threat) inherent in identification and referral by one's employer" [56, p. 620].

Feedback

The progress of EAPs so far is sufficiently encouraging to make it appropriate to consider future program improvements. This brings into focus the third, and final evaluation step: assessment of the feedback, and utilization of data about program implementation and outcomes. This would be an effort to discover to what extent evaluative research data had actually been effectively used to improve intervention efforts, and to improve outcomes. Job-based programs seemed to have progressed sufficiently to warrant an effort of this kind, but none have appeared in the literature thus far.

SUMMARY

The basic strategies underlying job-based alcoholism programs—constructive confrontation and crisis precipitation—are grounded in the principles of social science, and fit within a tradition of pragmatic humanitarianism that has been prominent in national management ideologies since the beginning of the century. Recent trends to extend this movement to encompass a wider range of personal problems were fueled by the multifaceted nature of alcoholism, the changing composition of the United States work force, and the increasing incidence of personal problems.

There is danger, however, that the aims of the EAP movement will not be realized because of ideological conflicts within the movement, and lack of appreciation of the constructive confrontation strategy by proponents whose occupational experience and training were centered in treatment. Since no generally accepted, coherent strategies have emerged in the EAP movement to replace constructive confrontation and crisis precipitation as motivators, the use of these proven strategies to deal with other personal problems among employees seems warranted.

No results are available from systematic research evaluating EAPs. Studies evaluating the implementation of job-based alcoholism programs have produced strikingly similar results, especially that supervisors' familiarity with policy provisions and their general awareness of drinking problems was associated with greater use of these policies. Evaluations of outcomes of alcoholism programs have yielded uniformly positive results. Although, taken individually, studies can be faulted on various methodological grounds, the consistency and magnitude of these positive results across studies is remarkable—especially since similar evaluations of outcomes of other interventions fail to produce similarly positive findings.

There are many reasons for optimism about the future of job-based programs. If the central strategies survive the current ideological ferment intact, and especially if implementation efforts improve, there is good reason to expect that these programs will help increasing numbers of alcoholics to rehabilitate themselves.

REFERENCES

1. Alander, R., and Campbell, T. *An Evaluation Study of an Alcohol and Drug Recovery Program*. Paper presented at Annual Meeting or Alcohol and Drug Problems Association, San Francisco, December 1974.
2. Asma, F., Eggert, R., and Hilker, R. Long-term experience with rehabilitation of alcoholic employees. *J. Occ. Med.* 13:581–585, 1971.
3. Bendix, R. *Work and Authority in Industry*. Wiley: New York, 1956.
4. Bensman, J., and Gerver, I. Crime and punishment in the factory. *Am. Sociol. Rev.* 28:588–598, 1963.
5. Beyer, J. Ideologies, values, and decision making in organizations. In: *Handbook of Organizational Design*, Nystrom, P., and Starbuck, W. (eds.). Oxford, England: Oxford University Press, 1980.
6. Beyer, J., and Trice, H. *Implementing Change: Alcoholism Policies in Work Organizations*. Free Press: New York, 1978.
7. Beyer, J., and Trice, H. *Supervisory Reluctance to Use Discipline with Problem-Drinking Employees* (Working paper 16, Program on Alcoholism and Occupational Health, New York State School of Industrial and Labor Relations). Cornell University: Ithaca, N.Y., 1980.
8. Cahalan, D., Cisin, I., and Crossley, H. *American Drinking Practices*. College and University Press: New Haven, Conn., 1969.
9. Chalfant, H., and Kurtz, R. Alcoholics and the sick role: Assessments by social workers. *J. Health Soc. Behav.* 12:66–72, 1971.
10. Chopra, K., Preston, D., and Gerson, L. The effect of constructive coercion on the rehabilitative process. *J. Occ. Med.* 21:749–752, 1979.
11. Cosper, R. Drinking as conformity: A critique of sociological literature on occupational differences in drinking. *J. Stud. Alcohol* 40:868–889, 1979.
12. Cummings, T., and Molloy, E. *Improving Productivity and the Quality of Work Life*. Praeger: New York, 1977.
13. Dancey, T. The constructive coercion technique in alcoholism and drug dependency programs. In: *Drug Abuse in Industry*, Scher, J. (ed.). Charles C Thomas: Springfield, Ill., 1973.
14. Downey, K., Sheridan, J. and Slocum, J. The path-goal theory of leadership: A longitudinal analysis. *Organ. Behav. Human Perfor.* 16:156–176, 1976.
15. Edwards, G., Orford, J., Egert, S., Guthrie, S., Hawkins, A., Hensman, C., Mitcheson, M., Oppenheimer, E., and Taylor, C. Alcoholism: A controlled trial of "Treatment" and "Advice." *J. Stud. Alcohol* 38:1004–1029, 1977.
16. Elison, J. Effectiveness of social action programs in health and welfare. In: *Assessing the Effectiveness of Child Health Services* (Report of the Fifty-sixth Ross Conference on Pediatric Research). Ross Laboratories: Columbus, Ohio, 1967.
17. Erfurt, J., and Foote, A. *Occupational Employee Assistance Programs for Substance Abuse and Mental Health Programs*. Institute of Labor and Industrial Relations: Ann Arbor, Mich., 1977.
18. Fiedler, F. *A Theory of Leadership Effectiveness*. McGraw-Hill: New York, 1967.

19. Finlay, D. Anxiety and the alcoholic. *Social Work* 17:29–34, 1972.

20. Franco, S. A company program for problem drinking: Ten years follow-up. *J. Occ. Med.* 2:157–162, 1960.

21. Frank, R., and Kaul, J. The Hawthorne experiments: First statistical interpretation. *Am. Sociol. Rev.* 43:623–643, 1978.

22. Freedburg, E., and Johnston, W. Changes in drinking behavior, employment status, and other life areas for employed alcoholics three, six, and twelve months after treatment. *J. Drug Issues* 9:523–534, 1979.

23. French, W., Bell, C., and Zawachki, R. *Organizational Development: Theory, Practice and Research.* Business Publications: Dallas, 1978.

24. Glasser, W., and Zunin, L. Reality therapy. In: *Current Psychotherapies*, R. Corsini (ed.). F. E. Peacock Publishers: Itasca, Ill., 1973.

25. Glassner, B., and Berg, B. How Jews avoid alcohol problems. *Am. Sociol. Rev.* 45:647–664, 1980.

26. Goffman, E. *Stigma.* Prentice-Hall: Englewood Cliffs, N.J., 1963.

27. Googins, B. *The Use and Implementation of Occupational Alcoholism Programs by Supervisors: An Analysis.* Unpublished doctoral dissertation, Florence Heller Graduate School for Advanced Studies in Social Welfare, Brandeis University, 1978.

28. Heyman, M. Referral to alcoholism programs in industry: Coercion, confrontation and choice. *J. Stud. Alcohol* 37:900–907, 1976.

29. Heyman, M. *Alcoholism Programs in Industry.* Publications Division, Rutgers Center for Alcohol Studies: New Brunswick, N.J., 1978.

30. Hilker, R., Asma, F., and Eggert, R. A company-sponsored alcoholic rehabilitation program: Ten years evaluation. *J. Occ. Med.* 14:769–772, 1972.

31. Homans, G. *The Human Group.* Harcourt Brace Jovanovich: New York, 1950.

32. Honigmann, J., and Honigmann, I. How Baffin Island Eskimo have learned to use alcohol. *Social Forces* 44:73–83, 1965.

33. Horton, D. The functions of alcoholism in primitive societies: A cross-cultural study. *Q. J. Stud. Alcohol* 4:199–320, 1943.

34. House, R. A path-goal theory of leader effectiveness. *Admin. Sci. Q.* 16:321–338, 1971.

35. Hughes, E. Institutions. In: *New Outline of the Principles of Sociology*, Lee, A. (ed.). Barnes and Noble: New York, 1946.

36. Inkeles, A. Society, social structure, and child socialization. In: *Socialization and Society*, Clausen, J. (ed.). Little, Brown: Boston, 1968.

37. Jackson, J., and Morgan, C. *Organization Theory.* Prentice-Hall: Englewood Cliffs, N.J., 1978.

38. Janowitz, M. Social control and sociological theory. *Am. J. Sociol.* 50:82–108, 1975.

39. Jick, T. J. Mixing Quantative and Qualitative Methods—Triangulation in Action. *Admin. Sci. Q.* 24:602–611, 1979.

40. Kahn, R., and Katz, D. Leadership practices in relation to productivity and morale. In: *Group Dynamics: Research and Theory* (2nd ed.) Cartwright, D. and Zander, A. (eds.). Row, Paterson: Elsford, N.Y., 1960.

41. Kurtz, N., and Goofins, B. *Supervisors' Perspectives of Occupational Alcoholism Programs.* Paper presented at the Annual Meeting of the Association of Labor-Management Administrators and Consultants on Alcoholism, Detroit, Michigan, 1979.

42. Lemert, E. *Alcohol and the Northwest Coast Indians* (University of California Publications in Culture and Society, no. 6). University of California Press: Berkeley, 1954.

43. Lemert, E. Forms and pathology of drinking in three Polynesian societies. *Am. Anthropologist* 66:361–374, 1964.

44. Lemert, E. M. *Human Deviance, Social Problems, and Social Control* (2nd ed.). Prentice-Hall: Englewood Cliffs, N.J.: 1972.

45. Manello, T. A., and Seaman, F. J. *Prevalence Costs, and Handling of Drinking Problems on Seven Railroads, Final Report*. University Research Corporation: Washington, D.C., 1979.

46. Mauss, A. *Social Problems as Social Movements*. J. B. Lippincott: New York, 1975.

47. Mayo, E. *The Human Problems of an Industrial Civilization*. Division of Research, Harvard Business School: Boston, 1946.

48. McClelland, D. C. *Power: The Inner Experience*. Irvington Publishers: New York, 1975.

49. McGregor, D. *The Human Side of Enterprise*. McGraw-Hill: New York, 1960.

50. Meyer, J., and Rowan, B. Institutionalized organization: Formal structure as myth and ceremony. *Am. J. Sociol.* 83:340–363, 1977.

51. Moberg, P. *A Follow-Up Study of Persons Referred for Inpatient Treatment from an Industrial Program*. Paper presented at Annual Meeting of Alcohol and Drug Problems Association, San Francisco, December 1974.

52. Oberschall, A. *Social Conflict and Social Movements*. Prentice-Hall: Englewood Cliffs, N.J., 1973.

53. Parsons, H. M. What happened at Hawthorne. *Science* 183:922–932, 1974.

54. Phillips, D., and Older, H. A model for counseling troubled supervisors. *Alcohol Health Res. World* 2:24–30, 1977.

55. Pitts, J. Social control: The concept. In: *International Encyclopedia of the Social Sciences* (Vol. 16), Sills, D. (ed.). Free Press: New York, 1968.

56. Robichaud, C., Strickler, D., Bigelow, G., and Liebson, I. Disulfiran maintenance employee alcoholism treatment: A three-phase evaluation. *Behav. Res. Ther.* 17:618–621, 1979.

57. Roman, P. The emphasis on alcoholism in employee assistance programming. *Labor-Manag. Alcoholism J.* 8:186–191, 1979.

58. Rosenberg, C., and Liftik, J. Use of coercion in the outpatient treatment of alcoholism. *J. Stud. Alcohol* 37:58–65, 1976.

59. Schonbrunn, M. *A History of Job-Based Programs During 1940–1955* (Working Paper 9). Cornell University, New York State School of Industrial and Labor Relations, Program on Alcoholism and Occupational Health: Ithaca, 1977.

60. Schramm, C., and DeFillippi, R. Characteristics of successful alcoholism treatment programs for American workers. *Br. J. Addict.* 70:271–275, 1975.

61. Schramm, C., Mandell, W., and Archer, J. *Workers Who Drink*. D. C. Heath: Lexington, Ky., 1978.

62. Shuey, E. *Factory People and Their Employers: How Their Relations are Made Pleasant and Profitable*. Lentilhon: New York, 1900.

63. Simmel, G. *[The Sociology of George Simmel.]* Trans., Kurt Wolff. Free press: Glencoe, Ill., 1950.

64. Skidmore, R., Balsam, D., and Jones, O. Social work practice in industry. *Social Work* 19:280–286, 1974.

65. Smart, R. Employed alcoholics treated voluntarily and under constructive coercion. *Q. J. Stud. Alcohol* 35:196–209, 1974.

66. Sterne, M., and Pittman, D. The concept of motivation: A source of institutional and professional blockage in the treatment of alcoholics. *Q. J. Stud. Alcohol* 26:41–57, 1965.

67. Stogdill, R., and Coons, A. *Leaders' Behavior: Its Description and Measurement* (Research Monograph No. 88). Ohio State University, Bureau of Business Research: Columbus, 1951.

68. Straus, R. Reconceptualizing social problems in the light of scholarly advances: Problem drinking and alcoholism. In *Social Policy and Sociology*, Demerath, N., Larsen, O. and Schuessler, K. (eds.). Academic Press: New York, 1975.

69. Tannehill, R. *Job Enrichment*. Dartnell: Chicago, 1974.

70. Tannenbaum, A., and Kavcic, B. *Hierarchy in Organizations*. Jossey-Bass: San Francisco, 1974.

71. Taylor, F. *The Principles of Scientific Management*. Harper & Row: New York, 1911.

72. Triandis, H. C. Exploratory factor analysis of the behavioral components of social attitudes. *J. Abnorm. Psych.* 68:420–430, 1964.

73. Trice, H. *Alcoholism in Industry: Modern Procedures*. Christopher D. Smithers Foundation: New York, 1962.

74. Trice, H. The job behavior of problem drinkers. In: *Society, Culture, and Drinking Patterns*, Pittman, D. and Snyder, C. (eds.). Wiley: New York, 1962.

75. Trice, H. Reactions of supervisors to emotionally disturbed employees. *J. Occ. Med.* 7:177–188, 1965.

76. Trice, H. *Alcoholism in America*. McGraw-Hill: New York, 1966.

77. Trice, H., and Belasco, J. Supervisory training about alcoholic and other problem employees. *Q. J. Stud. Alcohol* 29:382–399, 1968.

78. Trice, H., Belasco, H., and Alutto, J. Role of ceremonials in organizational behavior. *Indus. Labor Rel. Rev.* 23:40–51, 1969.

79. Trice, H., and Beyer, J. Differential use of an alcoholism policy in federal organizations by skill level. In: *Alcoholism and Its Treatment in Industry*, Schramm, C. (ed.). Johns Hopkins Press: Baltimore, 1977.

80. Trice, H., and Beyer, J. A sociological property of drugs: Differential acceptance of users of alcohol and other drugs among university undergraduates. *J. Stud. Alcohol* 38:102–115, 1977.

81. Trice, H., and Beyer, J. M. A Data-Based Examination of Selection-Bias in the Evaluation of a Job-Based Alcoholism Program. *Alcoholism: Clinical and Experimental Research* (Vol. 5). In press.

82. Trice, H., Beyer, J., and Hunt, R. Evaluating the implementation of a job-based alcoholism policy. *J. Stud. Alcohol* 39:448–465, 1978.

83. Trice, H. and Pittman, D. Social organization and alcoholism. *Social Problems* 5: 2944–307, 1958.

84. Trice, H., and Roman, P. *Spirits and Demons at Work: Alcohol and Other Drugs on the Job* (2nd ed.). New York State School of Industrial and Labor Relations: Ithaca, 1978.

85. Vroom, V., and Yetton, P. *Leadership and Decision-Making*. University of Pittsburgh Press: Pittsburgh, 1973.

86. *Wall Street Journal*. Firms Offer Employees a New Benefit: Help in Personal Problems, August 15, 1979.

87. Watson, T. *The Personnel Manager*. Routledge and Kegan Paul: London, 1977.

88. Weiss, C. *Evaluation Research*. Prentice-Hall: Englewood Cliffs, N.J., 1972.

89. Williams, R. *American Society*. Knopf: New York, 1970.

90. Wrich, J. *The Employee Assistance Program*. The Hazelden Foundation: Central City, Minn., 1974.

81

LUCINDA A. ALIBRANDI, PhD, University of Arizona

THE FELLOWSHIP OF ALCOHOLICS ANONYMOUS

IF YOU ASK A MEMBER OF Alcoholics Anonymous (AA) how he or she stays sober the reply will often be, "By working with others." The tradition of one drunk helping another came from the experience of AA's cofounder, Bill Wilson. In a letter to Dr. Carl Jung, he said, "In the wake of my spiritual experience there came a vision of a society of alcoholics. If each sufferer were to carry the news of the scientific hopelessness of alcoholism to each new prospect, he might be able to lay every newcomer wide open to a transforming spiritual experience. This concept proved to be the foundation of such success as AA has since achieved" [18].

SERVICE TO OTHERS

The importance of service to other alcoholics is heavily emphasized by the text, *Alcoholics Anonymous* [1]. Sharing in a fellowship of former drunks, now recovering, begins with AA's first step: "We admitted we were powerless over alcohol, that our lives had become unmanageable" [1, p. 59]. Thus begins a dramatic change for the newcomer who has been assailed by a series of helpers: spouses, parents, doctors, lawyers, judges, employers, friends—all exhorting him or her

---

Lucinda A. Alibrandi, PhD, Assistant Professor, Addiction Studies, University of Arizona, Tucson, Arizona.

with endless demands, orders, and/or sentences to do something. Instead of being told, "This is what you should do," the AA newcomer is invited to share in "what we have done." Many hear for the first time at an AA meeting, "I know how you feel," rather than, "How can you possibly feel that way?"

AA's unity is based on its singleness of purpose—helping the alcoholic, as expressed in the twelfth step of the AA program: "Having had a spiritual awakening as the result of these steps, we tried to carry this message to alcoholics, and to practice these principles in all our affairs" [1, p. 60], and in the fifth tradition: "Each group has but one primary purpose—to carry its message to the alcoholic who still suffers" [1, p. 564]. Alcoholics Anonymous thus offers "a concept of the alcoholic rather than an understanding of alcoholism" [10, p. 34].

Bateson [6] has described the twelfth step as that "which enjoins aid to other alcoholics as a necessary spiritual exercise without which the member is likely to relapse" [6, p. 333]. Madsen [11] called the twelfth step "the missionary step, the pledge to help other alcoholics onto the road to sobriety. . . . 'Twelfth-stepping' gives a sense of purpose and serves as a constant reminder to the alcoholic of 'where he's been'" [11, p. 183].

Maxwell [12] saw disillusionment and hope as the two major factors in the alcoholic's decision to seek help. The drunk eventually finds that attempts to solve problems with alcohol are as ineffectual as alcohol has become in solving his or her problems. Along with the conviction that drinking, once an asset, has become a liability, there is a second necessary condition "of hope, without which an active movement toward help is not conceivable" [12, p. 578]. This hope comes through seeing a member of AA, once a drunk, now a sober, functioning, recovering alcoholic. Maxwell called the living, breathing example of one for whom AA has worked one of its greatest strengths.

According to Bales [5], AA members are held together by the many things they have in common. The twelfth stepper or the sponsor shares with the newcomer past drinking experiences, as well as the following:

> An intimate knowledge of the places and people the compulsive drinker inevitably gets to know, a bag of tricks, ruses, rationalizations, and defenses which they have been forced to build up in the course of their compulsive drinking, an odyssey of adventures and misadventures too often ending in tragedy, and the sense of a common fate: They are all alcoholics to whom drinking has become so dangerous and unmanageable that they can only go on by living a life of complete abstinence. It is upon these things that their solidarity rests [5, p. 575].

GROUP PROCESS

Gellman [7] based his analysis of AA on Jerome Frank's five basic functions of a group in the therapeutic process: permissiveness, support, stimulation, verbalization, and reality testing. Permissiveness allows the once-rejected inebriate to become an accepted alcoholic member of AA. Guilt and anxiety gradually change into confidence in oneself and in AA. The degradation the alcoholic once suffered as a drunk becomes the dignity of an alcoholic. This acceptance within AA, as noted by Kurtz [10], is not necessarily reflected socially. "Most AA's cherish the irony of the realization that, except for those closest to them who were injured by their destructive drinking, modern American society more readily accepts them as occasionally drunk than as members of Alcoholics Anonymous" [10, 223].

Frank's second therapeutic function of a group, support, is offered to the alcoholic in AA in many ways. The alcoholic finds no judgment of what he or she has been, but empathy and understanding of what he or she can become. As one member said [13], "I recently realized the obvious: that somewhere I had discarded the conviction that I was destined always to remain what I had always seemed to be" [13, p. 119]. The new member is soon offered the opportunity to extend support to others. With only a few days of sobriety a newcomer finds someone worse off, and the alcoholic's self-confidence is greatly increased when he or she can be of assistance. "His own feelings of inferiority are modified as soon as the member helps another person achieve sobriety" [13, p. 137].

Stimulation and verbalization come to each member of AA as the group encourages self-expression through identification with the problems of others. As one member has said, no neurotic can resist the temptation of talking about oneself and one's problems when others are doing so. Verbalization is an important therapeutic tool for putting feelings into words in an effort to clarify them. Once feelings are verbalized, clarified, and identified as common to others, they can often be changed.

And, finally, reality testing is especially characteristics of the AA process:

> The alcoholic comes to AA wanting to learn how to stay sober. Absolutely no emphasis is placed on exploring the unconscious or examining the underlying causality of the drinking behavior. The concentration is on achieving sobriety and staying away from the first drink. The therapeutic efforts are directed at accomplishing this purpose, not primarily at unearthing trauma and motive. [13, p. 139].

Kessel [8], a French journalist, described the first golden rule of AA: "An alcoholic will listen to another alcoholic with more confidence than to anyone else, and the man who has come to his help is helping himself as well" [8, p. 134]. When Bill Wilson and Dr. Bob Smith joined together in their struggle with alcoholism they "undertook their task with boundless enthusiasm and devotion, because they were as deeply committed to it by their own need for safety as by their desire to help others" [8, p. 135]. As Kurtz [10] has noted, "The acknowledgment of essential need to receive from others does not lead within Alcoholics Anonymous to infinitely increasing need to receive, but rather begets the ability to give" [10, p. 224].

Madsen [11] emphasized that "birds of a feather flock together." He made an even stronger statement than Kessel about the AA belief "that no one can understand an alcoholic but another alcoholic" [11, p. 158]. After many painful experiences with the stigma of alcoholism the early members of AA came together and literally stumbled across the answer: It takes one to help one. Then began their effort to educate the public and thereby improve their condition.

This philosophy is enacted by what Madsen classified as a folk society, and every member of AA acts as a "folk-curer, one who administers therapy outside the formal disciplines of medicine" [11, p. 170]. The belief that only an alcoholic can help another alcoholic

> Parallels the many curing groups in primitive and folk societies where it is believed that to recover from a disease conveys the power to cure the disease.... The majority of AAs, however, see their gift as simply the ability to share their experience and knowledge. [11, p. 170].

> Following affiliation, most alcoholics, especially the high-bottom drunks, begin the long process of AA folk psychotherapy. Its goals are to allow the alcoholic to know himself, define responsible goals, simplify and integrate the jungle of conflicting values within him, and develop the precious quality of self-respect. [11, p. 174]

Even though the members of AA function as folk therapists, Madsen recognized the importance of the newcomer's active participation in the recovery process. AA is seen as merely a tool to aid in recovery, but the tool must be picked up and used. The alcoholic is ultimately responsible for his or her own recovery. An AA sponsor can say to a prospective member, "Just don't drink today." But the newcomer then makes the decision to follow the advice. Madsen quotes a favorite AA expression, "We will walk with you but we cannot walk for you" [11, p. 169].

Folk psychotherapy, according to Madsen, is often more effective than medicine and psychiatry because it treats the whole person. "Likewise, Alcoholics Anonymous has achieved a success in treating alcoholics that dwarfs the combined efforts of medicine, psychology, and psychiatry" [11, p. 170].

What Gellman called permissiveness and support, Madsen identified as acceptance. The newcomer to AA is accepted as is. As the newcomer realizes this total acceptance by the group, the process of beginning to accept oneself begins. "With self-acceptance comes confidence. With confidence comes that alcoholic dream of a sense of worth" [11, p. 176].

A survey of AA members was conducted by Silcott [14] to identify the most important aspects of the recovery program according to its members. Major emphasis was placed on helping others. Also stressed were the importance of the continuous availability of meetings, a high level of AA activity, and being of service. Each of these aspects of AA is closely related to working with others. Also considered important to recovery were surrender and ego deflation, self-deflation, identification with other alcoholics, dealing with anger and resentment, and the need to work on impatience, intolerance, resentfulness, and self-pity. The major implication of this study "is that a complete, multifunctional, permanently available program is necessary for the alcoholic" [14, p. 126].

ALCOHOLICS ANONYMOUS LITERATURE

The AA literature is a fertile source of information about the tools used to achieve sobriety and maintain it daily. The book *Alcoholics Anonymous* [1] recommends specific action for recovery from alcoholism. The first chapter is devoted to the story of AA's cofounder, Bill Wilson. Chapter 2, "There Is a Solution," advances the AA theory that alcoholism is an illness and suggests a "useful program for anyone concerned with a drinking problem" [1, p. 19]. The alcoholic is described as one who has "lost the power of choice in drink.... We are without defense against the first drink" [1, p. 24]. The solution involves "self-searching, the leveling of our pride, the confession of shortcomings.... The great fact is just this, and nothing less: That we have had deep and effective spiritual experiences which have revolutionized our whole attitude toward life, toward our fellows, and toward God's universe" [1, p. 25].

In Chapter 3 the first step in recovery is the need "to fully concede to our innermost selves that we were alcoholics.... The delusion that we are like other people, or presently may be, has to be smashed" [1, p. 30].

Succeeding chapters to the agnostic, discussing the twelve steps, emphasizing the importance of action, and working with others, detail the program of recovery in AA. Chapter 11 emphasizes that "our book is meant to be suggestive only. We realize we know only a little" [1, p. 164].

Further discussion and elaboration of the fellowship can be found in *Twelve Steps and Twelve Traditions* [17], *Alcoholics Anonymous Comes of Age* [2], *The AA Way of Life* [15], and numerous pamphlets and booklets put out by the AA central office in New York. *The AA Way of Life* is composed of several hundred excerpts from the AA literature. Each excerpt is indexed into twelve dimensions, including the importance of surrender, faith, honesty, gratitude, humility, and service; and the dangers of the need to control, fear, dishonesty, resentment, false pride, and self-obsession.

In an influential AA pamphlet available at most AA meetings, *A Member's-Eye View of Alcoholics Anonymous* [4], several unique aspects of the program are presented. This member sees the lack of dogmatism as one of the strongest and most therapeutic principles of AA. The "formless flexibility of AA's principles," which is interpreted in many different ways as by many different adherents, finally forces each alcoholic to "use only himself as a frame of reference for his actions, and this in turn means he must be willing to accept the consequences of those actions" [4]. With the acceptance of responsibility comes the first step toward maturity.

Shortly after coming into AA the alcoholic finds that he or she has been invited to share in a personal recovery and the recovery of others as well. The major symptom, problem drinking, is dealt with first. Then the newcomer begins to receive an intuitive understanding that is compassionate, but not indulgent. "The 'therapists' in AA already have their doctorates in the four fields where the alcoholic reigns supreme: phoniness, self-deception, evasion, and self-pity" [4]. Newcomers find it difficult to con a former con artist.

A fourth unique quality of the recovering alcoholic in AA is the alcoholic's "omnipresent, bottomless, enthusiastic willingness to talk about alcoholism—its ins and its outs, its whys and its wherefores, its becauses and begats.... His need for a drink is literally talked to death. It has always seemed exquisitely fitting to me that people who once used their moths to get sick now use them to get well" [4].

This member also points out the reversal of form taken by the AA education process. Heavy emphasis placed on letting go of old ideas. The newcomer is not asked to learn new ideas so much as to unlearn old, and often defeating ones. "One of the major objectives of AA therapy is to help the alcoholic finally recognize these ideas and become willing to relinquish his death grip on them" [4].

One final major difference between AA and most other therapy for the alcoholic lies in the way the recovery steps are presented, rather than what they contain [4]: "They are reports of action taken, rather than rules not to be broken under pain of drunkenness.... No member is ever told he *must* perform these steps." And, in most cases, the steps are presented to the newcomer by a member who has taken them personally. The AA member shares experiences more often than he or she gives advice.

In his address to the American Psychiatric Association and the Medical Society of New York, reprinted in an AA pamphlet [16], Bill Wilson discusses the essence of the principles of AA:

> Boiled down, these steps mean, simply:
> 1. admission of alcoholism
> 2. personality analysis and catharsis
> 3. adjustment of personal relations
> 4. dependence upon some Higher Power
> 5. working with other alcoholics

Wilson sees deflation at depth as a "cornerstone principle of AA," and two alcoholics talking about their alcoholism as "identification at depth, a second cardinal AA principle."

Bill Wilson believed that one of AA's great natural advantages was the personal experience of drinkers who have recovered. Wilson discovered in 1935 what Maxwell pointed out in 1962, "the flesh-and-blood example of a person for whom the program has worked" [12, p. 578] gives hope to the hopeless.

SPONSORSHIP AS FOLK THERAPY

In a remarkably history of Alcoholics Anonymous, Ernest Kurtz has distilled the essense of sponsorship:

> The antidote for the deep system of denial was *identification* marked by open and undemanding narration infused with profound honesty about personal weakness....

The process of identification was offered without any demand for reciprocity or for anything else. The sober alcoholic told his own story out of the conviction that such honesty was required only by and necessary only to his own sobriety. . . . The therapeutic power of this process of identification arose from the witness it gave, a witness to the healing potency of *the shared honesty of mutual vulnerability openly acknowledged.* [10, p. 61]

The structure underlying recovery was examined in an empirical investigation of AA sponsorship [3]. Sponsors were systematically asked how they help others to achieve and maintain sobriety. Each bit of advice given by a sponsor to a newcomer was viewed as a tool for sobriety.

AA activities were found to be semantically organized and to vary systematically over the time phases of the newcomers' sobriety. Suggestions given by the sponsor at 2 months or less of sobriety were both qualitatively and quantitatively different from suggestions given at later stages of sobriety. As the length of sobriety increased, there was a shift from specific tools for abstinence and morale-building to emphasis on self-change and spiritual growth. Many who have tried to understand the AA process have called it a mystery, but each member of AA knows intuitively the healing potency of "the personal vulnerability of his own trembling self" [9].

An important implication of this study is the vast source of information about recovery from alcoholism available from those who are recovering. Much research employs alcoholics who are in detoxification programs but have little capacity to maintain sobriety. Further investigation of those who have found a new way of life, of those who are emotionally and physically healthy, can add a new dimension to an understanding of the alcoholic.

REFERENCES

1. *Alcoholics Anonymous: The Story of How Many Thousands of Men and Women Have Recovered from Alcoholism* (new and revised ed.). Alcoholics Anonymous World Services: New York, 1955.

2. *Alcoholics Anonymous Comes of Age: A Brief History of AA.* Alcoholics Anonymous: New York, 1957.

3. Alibrandi, L. A. The folk psychotherapy of Alcoholics Anonymous. In: *Practical Approaches to Alcoholism Psychotherapy,* Zimberg, S., Wallace, J., and Blume, S. B. (eds.). Plenum: New York, 1978.

4. *A Member's-Eye View of Alcoholics Anonymous.* Alcoholics Anonymous World Services: New York, 1970.

5. Bales, R. F. The therapeutic role of Alcoholics anonymous as seen by a sociologist. In: *Society, Culture and Drinking Patterns,* Pittman, D. J. and Snyder, C. R. (eds.). Wiley: New York, 1962.

6. Bateson, G. *Steps to an Ecology of Mind.* Ballantine Books: New York, 1972.

7. Gellman, I. P. *The Sober Alcoholic: An Organizational Analysis of Alcoholics Anonymous.* College and University Press: New Haven, Conn., 1964.

8. Kessel, J. *The Road Back: A Report on Alcoholics Anonymous.* Knopf: New York, 1962.

9. Kopp, S. *If You Meet the Buddha on the Road, Kill Him! The Pilgrimage of Psychotherapy Patients.* Bantam: New York, 1972.

10. Kurtz, E. *Not God: A History of Alcoholics Anonymous.* Hazelden Educational Services: Garden City, Minn., 1979.

11. Madsen, W. *The American Alcoholic.* Charles C Thomas: Springfield, Ill., 1974.

12. Maxwell, M. A. Alcoholics Anonymous: An interpretation. In: *Society, Culture and Drinking Patterns,* Pittman, D. J. and Snyder, C. R. (eds.). Wiley: New York, 1962.

13. Only, M. *High: A Farewell to the Pain of Alcoholism.* Prentice-Hall: Englewood Cliffs, N.J., 1974.

14. Silcott, E. J. *The Correspondence between Alcoholics Anonymous and the Adaptive Capacities of Its Members.* University Microfilms: Ann Arbor, Mich., 1971.

15. *The AA Way of Life: A Reader by Bill.* Alcoholics Anonymous World Services: New York, 1967.

16. *Three Talks to Medical Societies by Bill W., Co-Founder of Alcoholics Anonymous.* Alcoholics Anonymous World Services: New York, 1973.

17. *Twelve Steps and Twelve Traditions.* Alcoholics Anonymous World Services: New York, 1952.

18. Wilson, B. Letter to Carl Jung. In: *The AA Grapevine.* The Alcoholics Anonymous Grapevine: New York, January 1963.

82

JOAN ABLON, PhD, University of California, San Francisco

SUPPORT SYSTEM DYNAMICS OF AL-ANON AND ALATEEN

AL-ANON FAMILY GROUPS constitute a highly effective nonprofessional therapeutic and educational resource for spouses, families, and friends of alcoholics. This chapter presents an overview of the Al-Anon program, a description of the Al-Anon meeting format, and an analysis of the dynamics of the Al-Anon process. The Alateen program, a youth component of Al-Anon, also is described.

The Al-Anon program began in the late 1940s when a group of spouses and relatives of members of Alcoholics Anonymous (AA) first came together to discuss the common problems they shared in living with an alcoholic. By 1954 Al-Anon became incorporated as a separate fellowship known as Al-Anon Family Group Headquarters. Al-Anon is not formally affiliated with AA; however, the two organizations share many elements of a common belief system, structured in large part by the use of the twelve steps of AA as a philosophical and operational guide. The two organizations frequently cooperate in holding joint meetings on local, regional, national, and international levels. Alateen groups for children of alcohlics are sponsored by Al-Anon members and are considered a component of the Al-Anon program.

There currently are more than 15,000 Al-Anon groups, including 2,300 Alateen groups, meeting in 80 countries throughout the world [2]. Services are provided (1) through groups in varied community settings, (2) in prisons, hospitals, and other institutions, and (3) for lone individuals in communities where no or-

---

Joan Ablon, PhD, Professor, Medical Anthropology Program, Departments of Epidemiology and International Health, and Psychiatry, School of Medicine, University of California, San Francisco, San Francisco, California.

ganized groups exist. The number of Al-Anon family groups has tripled during the last 10 years, reflecting the effectiveness of these mutual aid groups as a therapeutic modality specifically developed to meet the particular problems shared by their members. Despite the rapid burgeoning of Al-Anon groups throughout the country Al-Anon still has received much less attention from clinicians, community care givers, or the general public than has AA.

Families of alcoholics have sought aid from many public and private sources. Feelings of failure frequently have been mutual on the part of practitioners and clients alike. Wives of alcoholics often are labeled as highly defensive and resistant to introspection and change. Their problems often appear to be as severe as those of their alcoholic spouses. (It now is recognized that there is a large number of women alcoholics in the United States and that the husbands of these women share with wives of alcoholic males common problems or ones even more severe. Nonetheless, in the alcohol literature typically the help-seeking nonalcoholic spouses referred to are wives. Because the greatest majority of Al-Anon members also are wives of alcoholic males, for the purposes of this chapter members are referred to as wives or female companions of alcoholic husbands.) Many wives reluctantly have made the rounds of available professional treatment facilities and often state that treatment programs have neither helped them or mitigated the spouse's drinking—the latter often being their presenting goal. In contrast, most members of Al-Anon feel their participation in the organization has been a highly successful experience, saving their sanity and their very lives. The spouse's participation in Al-Anon is often a significant factor in motivating the alcoholic to seek aid for his drinking problem, although the Al-Anon program cautions against this expectation.

In contrast to the abundance of information available on AA, very little has appeared in the professional literature on Al-Anon or Alateen. Bailey [5, 6] and Ablon [1], who worked with wives of alcoholics and Al-Anon groups, have provided the most substantial information in the alcohol literature. Ablon [1] has presented a detailed account of meeting format and analysis of the program dynamics. The discussion presented here is based on participant observation activities in a variety of Al-Anon groups in a West Coast metropolitan area, in-depth interviews with Al-Anon members, and immersion in the Al-Anon headquarters literature all over an 8-year period.

AL-ANON MEETINGS

Al-Anon meetings typically are held in churches or, less frequently, in schools or hospital buildings. Meetings are held at morning, afternoon, and evening hours 7 days a week to meet the scheduling needs of members. In large metropolitan areas there may be meetings specifically for males, special age and language groups, homosexuals, for members where there is sobriety in the home, or for special study groups. Each ongoing group meets once weekly, but many members attend three or more meetings a week, and thus go or belong to many groups. Especially in times of crisis, members often have need to rely heavily on continous and intensive group support. This pattern of frequent attendance at meetings is similar to that maintained by many members of AA. In one large West Coast city there currently are 30 weekly Al-Anon meetings and two Alateen meetings, an increase of 100% over the past 3 years.

Attendance at any one meeting may range from five to 25 persons. In most groups, all of the members are wives or female companions of alcoholic males. The dearth of male members may reflect in part the fact that men are more likely to walk out of a marriage to an alcoholic without making heroic attempts to seek help [8], and also the reluctance of men to attend largely female-dominated meetings. It is clear, however, that members always make special efforts to welcome males who appear at meetings and urge them to come again. Al-Anon members represent all ages and socioeconomic statuses. While in the past married, white, middle-class women constituted the majority of members, today the diversity of ages and life styles represented is striking. Members are in many types of relationships to the alcoholic and in many cases younger women are household companions of the alcoholic, although not legally married to him. It is noteworthy that within this diversity the common problems shared by all create a unifying warmth of atmosphere not frequently found between generations and life styles today.

Members come to Al-Anon through many pathways — more commonly they hear of Al-Anon through newspaper or television exposure or word-of-mouth encouragement than through the referrals of mental health professionals. Most persons come to their first Al-Anon meeting when the cumulative problems in their household have become too much to bear. Some say they were on the verge of a nervous breakdown or that they were considering suicide. Indeed, it often is possible to spot new members by their obvious distress and depression, which contrasts with the cheerfulness and joking demeanor of the regular members. Universally, members remark on what a great relief it was finally to find others who shared their problems and understood them so well.

Most members characteristically experienced great difficulty in accepting the fact of alcoholism in their homes. They associated the term "alcoholism" with some distant skid row bum. Even when they acknowledged the problem as such, they usually did not seek help until motivated by a medical or economic crisis or by delinquent acting out on the part of children. Most regard all of their help-seeking activities before they discovered Al-Anon as unsuccessful.

Meeting Format

There is a set meeting format that is followed with little variance at all meetings. A rotating chairman opens the meeting with a moment of silence, and then all recite the Serenity Prayer: "God grant me the serenity to accept the things I cannot change, the courage to change the things I can, and the wisdom to know the difference." A warm and supportive introduction of purpose is read, followed by the twelve steps adapted from AA. These embody the operational philosophy of the Al-Anon program, which the individual must implement if she is to progress. Sometimes the twelve traditions — policy statements concerning the nature of Al-Anon and limiting the appropriate commitments or activities of individuals and groups — also are read aloud. In the introductory section of the meeting it is pointed out that the alcoholic and his actions will not be discussed during the meeting; the focus will be on the behavior and attitudes of the members themselves. In keeping with the tradition of anonymity, last names are never used and that which transpires in the meeting must not be repeated elsewhere. Newcomers are immediately called "members," and in fact all who attend, unless they are announced visitors, are considered members. This mode of welcoming tends to offer security for newcomers who are given an immediate message that they now belong to a caring community and are no longer alone in facing their fears and problems.

The speaker for the week's meeting introduces herself and gives a short talk on any subject she chooses. She might choose one of the twelve steps for examination, commenting on her personal difficulty in achieving the step or on how much the step has helped her. She might choose to talk on a specific subject such as gratitude, acceptance, criticism, or anger, or on some recent occurrence, and discuss her own experiences in relation to this. As another alternative, the speaker may read from the book of daily readings for members, entitled *One Day at a Time in Al-Anon*, and comment on the lesson of the reading. She then chairs an open discussion for the remainder of the meeting. The speaker usually tries to give every person a chance to talk before concluding the meeting. A request is made for a volunteer to be the speaker for the next week's meeting. The session closes with all joining hands to recite the Lord's Prayer. Meetings last approximately 1½ hours.

Following most meetings small groups of members stay on to informally discuss current problems and crises or exchange news. Some regularly lunch together or go out for coffee following meetings. Much of the social and emotional impact of the program for some members occurs in these informal groups through personal encouragement and the exchange of strategies for action.

THE DYNAMICS OF AL-ANON

The Al-Anon programs works through a combination of educational and operational principles that must be accepted by the member if she is to change her attitudes and behavior. These principles include a didactic lesson that is also basic to the philosophy of Alcoholics Anonymous — that alcoholism is a disease of the body and the mind, and not a moral fault or perverse whim of the alcoholic. The acceptance of the disease concept removes many burdens of hostility, guilt, and shame from the member.

There are in addition three operational principles or directives based on the twelve steps of AA that involve changes in attitudes and behavior and act as the philosophical guides necessary to "work the program." The first is "loving detachment" from the alcoholic. This is no doubt the basic principle on which the others must rest. The member must come to accept the fact that she cannot control the actions of any person but herself. If she modifies her own thinking and behavior, conditions around her will improve for her. She may not, however, place her motivating faith in the hope that changes in herself will necessarily change the behavior of the alcoholic. In many instances this will occur, but often it does not. The object is to make the member's own life more manageable and enjoyable.

The second principle that must be operationalized is the reestablishment or sometimes initial establishment of self-esteem and independence. Many middle-class older members continually comment that Al-Anon gave them their first opportunity for self-definition. They had throughout their lives perceived themselves as someone's daughter, wife, or mother, but never as a worthy individual in their own right. Al-Anon frequently is called a "selfish" program. A chief goal is for members to take their own personal inventories and work on self-improvement. Members soon come to take more pride in their appearance and take better care of their children and their homes than prior to joining. After a period of years of focused attention to the actions of the alcoholic, it is both a great relief and a pleasure to have the luxury of examining one's needs and even one's own faults.

The third principle is the necessity for reliance on a Higher Power. Entrenched patterns of negative thinking and doing make it very diffficult for the individual alone to implement the philosophy of Al-Anon. The acceptance and implementation of the twelve steps and the required change of perspective and behavior can be accomplished only through spiritual means—relying for strength on a Higher Power. For most members this higher power is God or Jesus. For some it is the collective social support of the Al-Anon group. A guide for simultaneous emotional acceptance and courageous action is the Serenity Prayer, which is ritually recited at the beginning of each meeting.

Advice and encouragement in Al-Anon is given lovingly. Members treat each other gently despite the humor and sarcasm they may display toward themselves and their former behavior or toward the alcoholic. Al-Anon basically is not an encounter group, nor does it focus on here and now relationships within the group. To the contrary, there is a minimum of direct personal confrontation or conflict among members. Each individual mentions only those issues that she cares to discuss. Although responses to these comments may be made directly, they are not made to criticize or denigrate the individual. In fact, responses are usually made because the respondent wants to share a contrasting point of view or strategy of action that she had found to be successful.

The essential dynamic of Al-Anon appears to be a candid sharing of experiences in terms of both reactions to and practical strategies for coping with common problems. This type of exposure to a smorgasbord of methods for dealing with similar situations enables participants to examine their own modes of operation and stimulates possibilities of new insights and approaches. For many, the accepting, nonthreatening atmosphere of Al-Anon is more conducive to introspection and subsequent changes in behavior than traditional therapy settings. Indeed, members are often very critical and bitter about experiences in professional treatment.

While clinicians maintain that wives of alcoholics are highly resistant to introspection and looking at their role in their family problems, the observations of this author [1] and those of Jackson [9] testify to wives repeatedly talking about their own sick and misguided, frantic, or often coercive and emotional behavior before entering the program. Many members utilize the Al-Anon philosophy for examing all areas of their life for once without blaming every difficulty on the alcoholic. Frequently members examine their relationships with their children and realize that these often inappropriately have become the target of the hostility and anger they harbored toward the alcoholic.

The pragmatic approach of the Al-Anon program is in keeping with casework procedure as suggested by a variety of therapists who have worked with wives of alcoholics. For instance Bailey [4, 6], Kellerman [10], and Estes [7] have pointed up to the need for initial ventilation, for education about alcoholism, for a reality-based examination of the wife's coping behavior in relation to all areas of her family life and relationships, and for the development of ego strength and self-esteem to allow her to proceed more rationally in dealing with major life decisions. Those therapists who insist on focusing first on deep-seated emotional problems of wives who come seeking immediate aid for urgent daily reality problems may indeed encounter the resistance well documented in the literature.

Al-Anon does not aggressively proselyte or seek out members and, in fact, is called a program of "attraction rather than promotion." However, members are expected to do twelfth step work (carrying the message to others) by taking turns answering the Al-Anon switchboard or giving short panel talks on personal experiences at churches, hospitals, or other community settings when requested. Carrying the message of Al-Anon is an important element of the program, and an Al-Anon maxim is, "You can't keep it unless you give it away."

AL-ANON AS A SUPPORTIVE COMMUNITY

The significance of the affective nature of the Al-Anon group meeting cannot be overestimated. The functional dynamics of the group operate within a warm, sharing, and emotionally supportive community. Despite differences in age, socioeconomic features, and life style, members have all experienced severe and often even violent, fearful problems common to households and relationships where there is alcohol abuse. This commonality constitutes a haven for those who felt their problems to be unique before they joined Al-Anon. It also allows them to observe successful role models who cope with problems they perceive to be even more serious than their own. The homogeneity of the group in this respect of shared experiences provides a nonthreatening arena that encourages comparison of coping strategies, introspection, and the possibilities of change. Members often point up the value of the membership being closed to alcoholics. In this supportive environment away from the alcoholic and the emotions his presence provokes, the member can ventilate her hostilities freely and then proceed more clearly to "working the program." Members are given telephone lists and urged to call other members at any hour of the day or night when they are in need of support. Some members have sponsors who introduce them to the group and coach them through early crises, but this is not as common a pattern as in Alcoholics Anonymous.

The culture of Al-Anon groups is remarkably stable from meeting to meeting. The most effective groups are those that have the most outspoken long-time members who embody most articulately the Al-Anon philosophy in their talks and their advice. The Al-Anon maxim "principles before personalities" well characterizes all of the groups this researcher has observed over often lengthy periods of time. In practice the Al-Anon tradition will not allow idiosyncratic domination by individual members who do not represent the philosophy. It is said that phonies do not last in Al-Anon. Within the context of this author's research experience with a number of other nonprofessional self-help groups, Al-Anon clearly presents the most task-oriented and self-lessly caring membership witnessed.

THE ALATEEN PROGRAM

Alateen is a fellowship for children, ages 12 through 20, of alcoholics. Alateen was started in 1957 by a small group of teenagers whose parents were members of AA and Al-Anon. Today there are several thousand Alateen groups that meet weekly. Al-Anon sponsors attend Alateen meetings but ordinarily do not participate in discussion. Alateen, like Al-Anon, bases its program on the twelve steps of Alcoholics Anonymous, and regards alcoholism as a family disease. Members often live in chaotic and disorganized home situations. In the supportive Alateen community, young people work out common feelings of anger, guilt, fear, and resentment relating to the alcohol problems in their homes, which may severely complicate the usual painful problems of adolescence. Alateen members strive to separate themselves from the alcoholic parent and his problems, and focus on taking responsibility for their own behavior and happiness. The Alateen program encourages the development of productive modes of coping, not only with alcohol-related family problems, but with concerns in all areas of life.

Although the young people who come to Alateen characteristically benefit greatly from participation, parents report that persuading children to come for their initial meetings is very difficult. Many children are fearful of the alcoholic's discovery of their attendance, and others are too enshrouded in shame or hostility to be able to easily share their feelings and experiences. The sponsorship of new members by experienced ones has been the primary successful mode of recruitment. Those young adults who were members of the Alateen program in their teenage years are quick to laud its positive influence in their lives.

FOR INFORMATION

Al-Anon and Alateen represent valuable community referral resources for professionals. For information about local meetings, interested parties may call the Alcoholics Anonymous telephone listing in almost any city in the United States. On request professionals and others seeking to learn about Al-Anon may visit open meetings. Most meetings display an array of pamphlets and books distributed by the Al-Anon Family Group Headquarters, Inc. This literature describes the Al-Anon and Alateen programs, and discusses alcoholism as a family disease, and typical problems and situations in the alcoholic family. These publications are clearly and positively written. They basically are oriented by a family systems model that stresses the interactional and holistic nature of family-related alcohol problems. As of this writing Al-Anon has seven hardcover books, one booklet for preteen children, more than 40 pamphlets, a monthly magazine, three bimonthly newsletters (one for Al-Anon, one for Alateen, and one for Loners) and several cartoon booklets. Al-Anon material is available in 17 languages as well as in Braille and on tape. Inquiries for basic information on Al-Anon and Alateen, a sample of pamphlets, and a publication sheet may be addressed to Al-Anon Family Group Headquarters, Inc., P.O. Box 182, Madison Square Station, New York, New York 10010.

ACKNOWLEDGMENTS

The research on which this paper is based was supported in part by National Institute of Alcoholism and Alcohol Abuse Grant 2 R01 AA 00180 and National Institute of Mental Health Grant MH-08375.

REFERENCES

1. Ablon, J. Al-Anon family groups: Impetus for learning and change through the presentation of alternatives. *Am. J. Psychother.* 28(1):30–45, 1974.
2. Al-Anon Family Group Headquarters, Inc. *Al-Anon Today* (Form PI-4). Author: New York, 1979.
3. Al-Anon Family Group Headquarters, Inc. *One Day at a Time in Al-Anon.* Author: New York, 1965.
4. Bailey, M. B. The family agency's role in treating the wife of an alcoholic. *Social Casework* 44:273–279, 1963.
5. Bailey, M. B. Al-Anon family groups as an aid to wives of alcoholics. *Social Work* 10: 68–74, 1965.
6. Bailey, M. B. *Alcoholism and family casework.* Community Council of Greater New York: New York, 1968.
7. Estes, N. J. Counseling the wife of an alcoholic spouse. In: *Alcoholism: Development, Consequences and Interventions,* Estes, N. J. and Heinemann, M. E. (eds.). C. V. Mosby: St. Louis, 1977.
8. Fox, R. The alcoholic spouse. In: *Neurotic Interaction in Marriage,* Eisenstein, V. W. (ed.). Basic Books: New York, 1956.
9. Jackson, J. K. Alcoholism and the family. *Ann. Am. Acad. Pol. Soc. Sci.* 315:90–98, 1958.
10. Kellerman, J. L. Pastoral counseling of wife and family. In: *Al-Anon Faces Alcoholism,* Al-Anon Family Group Headquarters, Inc. (eds.). Cornwall Press: New York, 1965.

Section X

Alcoholism Treatment Methods

83

SHELDON ZIMBERG, MD, Mount Sinai School of Medicine, New York, New York

PSYCHOTHERAPY IN THE TREATMENT OF ALCOHOLISM

THE MAJOR PROBLEM in the diagnosis and treatment of alcoholism by health care professionals has been the belief that alcoholics are not generally motivated for treatment and could not be successfully treated even if motivated. This profoundly held belief in medical schools and other professional schools is established by the observations that many alcoholics are repeatedly treated for the severe medical and/or social consequences of alcoholism. They are thought to be unwilling or unable to enter treatment programs for their alcoholism, even when such programs are readily available and accessible. These repeated observations have resulted in a feeling of therapeutic nihilism regarding alcoholism.

The unfortunate reality of this situation is that the appropriate and effective techniques for engaging alcoholics in treatment that often lead to their recovery are not taught or observed by students and practitioners in the health care fields. The largest and most successful of self-help groups, Alcoholics Anonymous (AA), has demonstrated that thousands of alcoholics worldwide can be successfully rehabilitated. Alcoholics Anonymous is a uniquely creative, leaderless organization that meets the psychological needs of alcoholics and provides a variety of verbal interventions that in a broad definition can be considered a form of peer psychotherapy. The addition of medical, psychiatric, psychological, and social

---

Sheldon Zimberg, MD, Associate Professor of Psychiatry, Mount Sinai School of Medicine, and Director of Psychiatry, Joint Diseases North General Hospital, New York, New York.

interventions applied with a sophisticated understanding of the disease of alcoholism and the needs of alcoholics can significantly improve upon the already impressive results of AA.

This chapter discusses the theory, principles, and techniques of alcoholism psychotherapy from a psychodynamic viewpoint and presents the therapeutic approaches that have been successful with many alcoholics.

PSYCHODYNAMICS OF ALCOHOLISM

It has generally been accepted that genetic, sociocultural, and psychological factors are significant in the etiology of alcoholism. Other chapters in this volume discuss the genetic and sociocultural factors.

The psychodynamic conflict that has been considered to be the major psychological contributing factor to alcoholism has been conflicts with dependency. Blum's [3] review of psychoanalytic theories of alcoholism suggests that oral fixation, with its resulting conflict with dependency, and such characteristics as narcissism, demanding behavior, passivity, and dependency are the major psychological conflicts in alcoholism.

There has been much evidence accumulated regarding the observations that alcoholics were exposed to rejection by one or both parents and were overprotected or forced to have premature responsibility as a child, resulting in the excessive development of unmet dependency needs. Blane [2], in his book, *The Personality of the Alcoholic: Guises of Dependency*, reviewed much of the literature in this area and presented material based on his extensive clinical experience with alcoholics to support this hypothesis.

The dependency needs of alcoholics are not overtly expressed, but are repressed when they are not under the influence of alcohol. When intoxicated, alcoholics appear to have passive and dependent traits and often are looking for someone to take care of them. When sober, alcoholics are in many cases driven, perfectionistic people with obsessive-compulsive personality traits and very punitive superegos. Angry feelings are repressed in sobriety, but become overt during intoxication. Alcoholics have difficult interpersonal relationships because they unconsciously demand too much attention and are often unable to express their emotions. It has been said that the superego is soluble in alcohol, so during intoxication many unconscious feelings are expressed. Alcoholics are often amnestic in regard to the personality and behavioral changes they experience when intoxicated, so they truly do not see themselves as other people see them.

The core psychological conflict experienced by many alcoholics is a basic loss of self-esteem and profound feelings of worthlessness and inadequacy. These feelings are denied and repressed and lead to unconscious needs to be nurtured. Since such a profound degree of dependent needs cannot be met in an adult, anxiety and compensatory needs for control, power, and achievement result. Alcoholics are competent people, often with strong and intact egos when they are not drinking. They have a strong need for success that causes them to strive to a point where their reach exceeds their grasp. Their failure to achieve compensatory success and nurturance leads to the development of anxiety. Alcohol tranquilizes this anxiety and creates pharmacologically induced feelings of power, omnipotence, and invulnerability. McClelland et al. [9] demonstrated experimentally with male alcoholics that alcohol produces fantasies and images of power, strength, and an enhanced self-esteem. In women alcoholics, Wilsnack [18] demonstrated that alcohol produces fantasies of increased womanliness.

When alcoholics wake up after a drinking episode, they experience guilt and despair because of their punitive superegos and they recognize that they have not achieved anything more than before they drank. Thus, feelings of worthlessness are intensified and the conflict continues in a vicious circle until the individual becomes physiologically addicted to alcohol and the withdrawal manifestations and craving lead to alcohol-seeking behavior independent of the psychological conflict.

Thus, alcohol as a pharmacologic agent provides an artificial feeling state of power, control, and enhanced self-esteem that cannot be achieved in reality. The alcoholic's use of alcohol to produce such omnipotent feelings at will feeds excessive narcissism and produces a grandiose self-image. This intensive need for grandiosity can be called "reactive grandiosity." The major defense mechanism supporting the need for grandiosity, the one that protects the alcoholic from the awareness of the self-destructive aspects of drinking, is denial. The denial and need for grandiosity are the crucial defenses that must be penetrated in order to engage the alcoholic in psychotherapy.

It should be noted, however, that this conflict with dependency can be seen in other psychopathological conditions. In addition to the psychological factor, other factors, including a genetic predisposition and sociocultural conditions that encourage the use of alcohol to deal with unpleasant feelings, are necessary factors in the etiology of alcoholism. In any individual one or more of these etiologic factors may predominate and lead to alcoholism. A variety of treatment approaches have been developed to treat alcoholism. This chapter deals with the verbally oriented therapies.

PSYCHOTHERAPEUTIC TECHNIQUES

Alcoholics Anonymous

Alcoholics Anonymous has been one of the most successful treatment approaches for alcoholism. It can be considered a form of psychotherapy since the basis of AA therapeutic impact is verbal interactions between recovered alcoholics and active alcoholics conducted in a structured milieu with a standardized approach.

Alcoholics Anonymous is successful because it implicitly understands the psychological conflicts and psychological needs of the alcoholic. It provides open meetings where all alcoholics are accepted, whether they are drinking or not, and meetings open to nonalcoholics as well. It provides closed meetings that are limited to alcoholics with roundtable discussions of how to achieve and maintain sobriety. Sponsors are available to any AA member who wishes individual counseling and support. Alcoholics Anonymous functions through the collective wisdom and experience of its members, with minimal organizational structure and no hierarchy. The guiding principles are 12 steps to recovery and 12 traditions. There is no scientific, medical, or psychological theory that serves as the basis for the folk psychotherapy of AA, and yet it works amazingly well. Alibrandi [1] analyzed the tools used by sponsors in their work with active alcoholics in the book, *Practical Approaches to Alcoholism Psychotherapy*.

Tiebout, [15] a psychoanalyst, described the process by which an alcoholic becomes involved in AA. The process occurs with (1) the need to hit bottom; (2) the need to be humble; (3) the need to surrender; and (4) the need for ego reduction. The first step occurs when the alcoholic reaches a point of such severe social or physical deterioration that he or she is willing to recognize he or she has a serious drinking problem. This step permits penetration of the denial. The second step involves the recognition that the alcoholic can no longer control drinking. The third step involves the alcoholic's willingness to accept help from the outside. The fourth step involves the reduction of the excessive narcissism that invests the alcoholic's ego, which has given rise to the feelings of grandiosity and omnipotence. Tiebout did not indicate, however, what happens to this excessive narcissism. Clearly, the narcissism is subliminated toward the goal of AA to rescue other alcoholics. Thus, the grandiosity becomes fulfilled and socially useful.

In addition to the sublimation of the narcissism AA provides for other very important psychological needs of alcoholics. It is a supportive, nonjudgmental, nonpunitive group of fellow sufferers who will accept the alcoholic unconditionally. It meets many of the alcoholic's unmet dependency needs and provides the nurturing and interpersonal gratification that alcoholics often cannot find in the real world.

The confessional aspects of AA meetings also provide an outlet for the punitive superego, although the speakers' stories are often laced with a good deal of humor and enjoyment. The basic message, however, is "Look how much I lost by drinking and how much I have now gained because of sobriety." This message and the 12 steps to recovery require the alcoholic to see the consequences of drinking, to expiate his or her guilt, and to go on to a happy and successful sobriety.

Thus, the successful development of AA was based on an intuitive understanding of the alcoholic's psychological conflict and needs. It has been a very useful approach for many alcoholics, but by no means for all alcoholics. Other psychotherapeutic approaches are often required to facilitate the recovery of alcoholics in addition to or instead of AA participation.

Individual Therapy

Many alcoholics require professional intervention in their treatment. Such interventions should include medical evaluation and detoxification, differential diagnosis of alcoholism and other serious psychiatric or drug-abuse disorders, consideration for Antabuse maintenance, and an ongoing psychotherapeutic relationship. Most psychiatrists, as well as other mental health professionals, know little about alcoholism psychotherapy and generally are unwilling to treat alcoholics. Psychoanalytic psychotherapy has not been successful because the use of uncovering techniques leads to the development of anxiety, which can be a trigger to drinking, and the physiological hold of the drug (alcohol) on addicted alcoholics cannot be reduced through the use of interpretation, development of insight, or cognitive processes.

Silber [12], in a series of papers on the modified psychoanalytical approach to the treatment of alcoholism, indicated some success with uncovering techniques along with the therapist's lending the alcoholic some of his or her own ego. In Silber's view, alcoholism is a symptom of underlying psychological conflict and can be modified by analyzing the transference and developmental conflicts of alcoholic patients. Moore [10] has also indicated the important role of transference and countertransference issues in the psychotherapeutic treatment of alcoholism. However, Tiebout's [16] and Fox's [7] work with alcoholics indicates the value of direct intervention as opposed to the passive stance of the analyst.

The psychotherapeutic approach practiced by the present author is based on Tiebout's model. In this approach it is first necessary to stop the drinking before psychotherapy can proceed. The patient is confronted with the fact that he or she is an alcoholic and is provided with the evidence supporting the diagnosis. The patient is told that the drinking must be removed first, before any effective therapy can be utilized to help the patient maintain sobriety in the face of his or her psychological and other problems. A contract based on this goal is initially established.

The patient who is actively drinking at the beginning of therapy is detoxified on an ambulatory or inpatient basis, encouraged to start Antabuse and attend AA meetings. Once the drinking has stopped and the external control of Antabuse is in place, the alcoholic can be helped to understand his or her need for achievement and success and the role alcohol played in the patient's life through directive psychotherapy. The alcoholic can be helped to find better ways of dealing with unpleasant feelings and learn to improve interpersonal relationships. The progress of psychotherapy through various stages of recovery is described later in this chapter.

The major requirement in this interventionist approach to individual psychotherapy is to eliminate the use of alcohol initially, as indicated. However, directive psychotherapy by its very nature requires intervention in other aspects of the alcoholic's life during the early stages of recovery. The art of alcoholism psychotherapy is learning what aspects of the alcoholic's life and defense mechanisms need intervention, at what point in time, and how the intervention should be accomplished. In addition, it is important that one recognizes there are many aspects of the alcoholic's life and defense mechanisms that should not be interpreted or intervened against; rather, they should be redirected or left alone. Such processes of intervention or nonintervention should be based on a complete understanding of the alcoholic's current life situation, family, developmental, and drinking history, and personality makeup. The closeness achieved in individual psychotherapy and the therapeutic alliance can facilitate this sophisticated knowledge of the alcoholic's needs, conflicts, and defenses and make interventions much more successful. This aspect of individual psychotherapy with alcoholics represents its major advantage over other forms of psychotherapy.

Wallace [17] described the preferred defense structure of the alcoholic. He indicated the defense mechanisms and personality characteristics of the alcoholic are as follows: denial; projection; all-or-none thinking; conflict minimization and avoidance; rationalization; self-centered selective attention; preference for nonanalytic modes of thinking and perceiving; passivity versus assertion; and obsessional focusing. Wallace described these defense mechanisms and characteristics in detail and indicated that the therapist should selectively reinforce and encourage these defenses in the service of the goal of abstinence. The therapist should not explore, confront, or interpret these defenses early in the therapeutic process, but should rather redirect them, just as the reactive grandiosity is sublimated by AA members. Therefore, considerable skill and experience is needed in the therapy of alcoholism, based on knowledge of the underlying psychological conflicts and needs of the alcoholic, the particular alcoholic's situation at a particular point in time, and the alcoholic's stage of recovery.

Group Psychotherapy

Group therapy is the most common form of psychotherapy applied to alcoholics. Some therapists believe that group psychotherapy is the treatment of choice.

There are distinct advantages of group as opposed to individual psychotherapy, but there are also disadvantages. Blume [4] presented a detailed discussion of the techniques of group therapy with alcoholics in *Practical Approaches to Alcoholism Psychotherapy*. There is also a chapter in the present volume on group psychotherapy.

Some of the advantages of group psychotherapy include the economy of using one therapist to treat 8 to 10 patients in a 1½-hour period, although record-keeping can be more time-consuming. Group therapy can be more time-efficient in regard to the therapist's time in that, when several group members miss their scheduled group meeting, the rest of the group can continue. Therefore, that the therapist can save appointment time is a distinct advantage of group therapy over individual therapy.

Another distinct advantage of group therapy relates to the psychological needs of the alcoholic. As indicated, dependent needs are the area of major psychological conflict. Therefore, support of one's peers and development of improved interpersonal relationships can be a strong psychological benefit of the group process. The group permits a sharing of experiences and feelings and it offers alcoholics a chance to understand that they are not unique in their problems with alcohol or in their problems with feelings.

A major disadvantage of group psychotherapy is the lack of the development of the sophisticated knowledge about the individual patient by the therapist that can permit targeted interventions. There is also a less intense transference developed. Therefore, much of the group therapy work is often superficial and concentrated on avoiding drinking, maintaining sobriety, and improving interpersonal relations. There is usually a significant dropout rate of patients so that most alcoholism groups are open-ended, adding new members as others leave. Such turnover of patients maintains the superficial quality of the therapy, and further diffuses the transference. Therefore, the influence of the therapist on the individual patient is less than in individual therapy. It is the group that offers the major influence on patients.

It is this author's view that institutional treatment of alcoholism is best provided in group therapy where there is more control on participation and attendance during the institutional stay. In outpatients, particularly where there are significant psychological problems coexisting with the alcoholism, individual therapy seems preferable, in conjunction with AA, where peer-group support and influence can be obtained.

Group psychotherapy is a very valuable technique with alcoholics. Its therapeutic effect is enhanced greatly when the therapist or cotherapist is a recovered alcoholic, so that identification with someone who has had active alcoholism and has recovered can be provided.

It should be pointed out that many alcoholics are, at least initially, unwilling to attend AA meetings or group therapy because of the denial that they are alcoholics, the belief that they are somehow different from other alcoholics, or because they are socially isolated. An initial period of individual psychotherapy can often be effective in reducing the denial and encouraging involvement in peer-related therapeutic activities.

Couples Therapy

The involvement of the spouse of an alcoholic can be crucial in the ultimate recovery of the patient. Spouses should be encouraged to attend Al-Anon, where they can learn about alcoholism and reduce their enabling behavior in relation to the alcoholics' drinking. The anger and frustration in the nonalcoholic partner of an alcoholic marriage can be enormous. Such partners require education and guidance about alcoholism and understanding of their role in the condition.

Couples therapy can be of value where alcoholism has been a major factor in marital problems. Opening up channels of communication and empathy can enhance the recovery of the alcoholic and reduce anger and frustration in the spouse. Impediments to the recovery of the alcoholic, carried out consciously or unconsciously by the spouse, can be explored and altered, thus improving the chances of long-term sobriety.

Psychotherapy of alcoholic women can be greatly enhanced by couples therapy, since the husband's lack of communication, understanding, support, and encouragement can be considered as a major causal factor in the wife's alcoholism. This observation was made by Tamerin [14] in his discussion of the psychotherapy of alcoholic women.

Couples therapy, whether used exclusively or as part of individual or group psychotherapy for the alcoholic spouse, can either improve marital relationships or lead to divorce when problems in the marriage aside from the alcoholism are found to be irreconcilable.

Family Therapy

It has been said that alcoholism is a family disorder. Alcoholism severely affects family relationships and functioning. It is particularly devastating on the children.

Recently family therapy approaches have been applied to families of alcoholics. The work of Dulfano [6] and Steinglass [13] has indicated the value of this approach to the treatment of alcoholism.

In family therapy, the family is seen as a system whose members represent units of the system. The interactions of a wife to her husband or a mother to a particular child represent subsystems. Various roles are assigned to individuals in a family and various transactional patterns are established among individuals and subsystems in a family.

Alcoholism in one member of the family severely disrupts family communications, transactional patterns, roles, and the functioning of individual family members and the entire family. In alcoholism family therapy the entire family is brought together to discuss its problems. By discussing the distortions in communication, roles, and relationships that exist in the family, the role of alcoholism in one family member is discerned as a major causal factor. Helping the family improve their interactions serves to improve family functioning and leads to sobriety in the alcoholic family member.

Although theoretically sound, family therapy approaches are limited by the relatively few experienced practitioners that exist who are knowledgeable about family therapy and alcoholism. Also, the alcoholic family member should have, in addition to family therapy, specific treatment for alcoholism, such as AA or Antabuse, since continued drinking during the early stages of family therapy may discourage continued family participation.

Family therapy can be useful in the treatment of alcoholism, but primarily as an adjunct to alcoholism-specific therapy, since for the alcoholic family members denial, compulsion to drink, physiological addiction, and psychological dependence on alcohol can often be too potent to be eliminated by discussions of family interactions alone. In addition, family therapy can be intensely guilt- and anxiety-provoking and this contributes to the alcoholic's need to escape by drinking. Carefully utilized family therapy by a knowledgeable and skilled clinician can, in addition to alcoholism-specific therapy, lead to a long-term sobriety and a marked improvement in the family situation.

Psychodrama

The techniques of psychodrama developed by Moreno [11] have been applied to alcoholics by Blume [5] and Fox [8]. Scenes are enacted by patients and others relating to actual experiences of the past and/or present, or fantasies about the future, leading to insights regarding one's feelings and the feelings of others. These insights are called "action insights." The action insights are often accompanied by the release of emotions, which serves as a therapeutic catharsis.

The use of psychodrama with alcoholics can permit the exploration of unpleasant feelings and relationships that have led to feelings of isolation and despair that were habitually dealt with by drinking. Alcoholics can learn to express their feelings on the psychodrama stage and learn how others react to them. They can also learn how others think and feel about them, thus opening a new horizon of awareness and understanding.

Psychodrama can be used in terms of role playing in situations of stress. Such role playing can help modify habitual reaction patterns, which often were triggers to drinking, into more acceptable and satisfying experiences leading to growth.

Psychodrama should not be used as the sole treatment for alcoholism but could be a very helpful and insight-providing adjunct to individual or group therapy. Psychodrama is of particular value in a residential setting as part of intensive multimodality therapy since these alcoholics will have established social relationships with each other as part of living together in the institution. Considerable training and experience with this approach is required, since very intense emotions and reactions are sometimes generated during psychodrama enactments.

PRINCIPLES OF ALCOHOLISM PSYCHOTHERAPY

There are certain principles of alcoholism psychotherapy that are the basis of all effective therapeutic approaches based on verbal interventions. These principles may not be articulated or even understood by the therapist (whether professional or lay) who engages in helping alcoholics achieve sobriety, but they can be observed to operate in all successful psychotherapeutic approaches, including AA.

The first principle involves the establishment of a contract with the alcoholic that abstinence is the goal of treatment, and that the initial efforts of treatment have to concentrate on eliminating drinking as the first step in the treatment process. The initial steps, therefore, include detoxification from alcohol in an ambulatory or inpatient basis and the maintenance of sobriety through external control by using Antabuse and/or the peer-group pressure of AA.

The second principle involves the recognition of the intensive transference that the alcoholic will establish with the therapist. This transference is characterized by a great deal of dependence as well as manipulative and testing behavior. Because of the alcoholic's previous experience of rejection, he or she will test the therapist's interest and concern repeatedly. The alcoholic will appear very dependent on the therapist, but will also resist interventions by the therapist because of his or her grandiosity. Alcoholics believe that they can control their drinking as well as all other aspects of their lives despite obvious evidence to the contrary. Therapists should not be put off by this ambivalent transference relationship, but should understand it as part of the psychological conflict experienced by the alcoholic.

The third principle of alcoholism psychotherapy is recognizing and understanding the countertransference that may develop in the therapist in response to provocative behavior and drinking in the patient. This behavior represents a form of testing carried out unconsciously by the alcoholic as a test of the therapist's continued interest. Therapists often react with frustration and anger to such behavior. However, it is essential to recognize that the therapist is not omnipotent in regard to the alcoholic's drinking. A therapist can only provide the tools to assist the alcoholic's own determination and effort to achieve sobriety. In a contest of needs between gratification of therapeutic success in the therapist and grandiose control in the alcoholic, the alcoholic will always win, even though it is a pyrrhic victory. Recognizing this reality of the therapeutic process, the therapist must impose limits on the drinking behavior of the patient if treatment is to continue. If the patient cannot meet these conditions, treatment should be discontinued with the option to return when the patient is willing and able to engage in efforts leading to sobriety.

The fourth principle involves the observation that alcoholism psychotherapy progresses through several stages leading to recovery. The first stage exists when the alcoholic enters therapy. He or she usually does not want to give up alcohol, but is receiving a great deal of external pressure from a spouse, an employer, or from the alcoholic's own physical health. The alcoholic acknowledges that he or she cannot drink, but in reality wants to find a way to drink safely. The attitude toward drinking and the denial of drinking as a serious problem have not changed. During this early stage the alcoholic must be provided with external control over the impulse to drink and helped through directive counseling to deal with his or her unpleasant feelings and life situation without resorting to alcohol. The early stage of psychotherapy is by its nature unstable since there has been no significant change in attitude about drinking or an ego reduction. This stage can result either in a return to drinking or, through counseling and/or AA involvement, to a more secure stage where the alcoholic has obtained a significant attitudinal change and learned to live without alcohol in the face of problems. This progression can take about 6 months to 1 year to accomplish and leads to the stage where the alcoholic will not drink.

The second stage is fairly stable, with a relatively firm set of internalized controls over the impulse to drink and with no longer a conscious conflict about whether to drink or not. At this stage the use of Antabuse as an external control can be considered for discontinuation. This is the stage that most successful AA members have achieved. They have no insight into their psychological problems but their reactive grandiosity has been sublimated in the ego-enhancing feelings of control over a previously uncontrollable problem. Active AA members have an addition outlet for this grandiosity in rescuing other alcoholics. This stage represents a reasonably good stage of recovery for most alcoholics.

The third stage involves the situation where the alcoholic does not have to drink. This stage can be achieved through the development of insight into the alcoholic's personality conflicts. The use of alcohol can be understood as a way of dealing with the individual's conflicts. It requires the use of psychoanalytically oriented psychotherapy and self-understanding. Not every alcoholic needs to achieve this stage of recovery or wants to engage in psychoanalytic therapy. However, the option for use of this approach after well-established sobriety should be a mutual decision of the patient and therapist.

The last stage of recovery is a theoretical one and can be called "I can return to social drinking." Very few alcoholics can achieve this stage, and presently it is impossible to predict which alcoholic might be capable of this stage. In this author's experience, alcoholics with alcoholism secondary to various effective illnesses, phobic-anxiety states, or schizophrenia have at times been able to return to social drinking when the underlying condition has been effectively treated. However, in primary alcoholics who have reached a level of physiological addiction to alcohol, rarely is it possible to return to social drinking. Therefore, since every alcoholic would initially like to be able to drink safely, it is unrealistic to hold out this goal to patients. It is quite possible to live in this society without alcohol and even be happy. This is the attitudinal change that recovery from alcoholism requires.

SUMMARY

This chapter presents the psychodynamics of alcoholism and describes various psychotherapeutic techniques and the principles underlying these techniques that have been utilized successfully with alcoholics. Recovery rates of 60 to 80% have been reported when such treatment approaches are effectively applied [19].

REFERENCES

1. Alibrandi, L. A. The folk psychotherapy of Alcoholics Anonymous. In: *Practical Approaches to Alcoholism Psychotherapy*, Zimberg, A., Wallace, J., and Blume, S. B. (eds.). Plenum: New York, 1978.
2. Blane, H. T. *The Personality of the Alcoholics: Guides of Dependency*. Harper & Row: New York, 1968.
3. Blum, E. M. Psychoanalytic views of alcoholism: A review. *Q. J. Stud. Alcohol* 27: 259–299, 1966.
4. Blume, S. B. Group psychotherapy in the treatment of alcoholism. In: *Practical Approaches to Alcoholism Psychotherapy*, Zimberg, S., Wallace, J., and Blume, S. B. (eds.). Plenum: New York, 1978.
5. Blume, S. B. Psychodrama and the treatment of alcoholism. In: *Practical Approaches to Alcoholism Psychotherapy*, Zimberg, S., Wallace, J., and Blume, S. B. (eds.). Plenum: New York, 1978.
6. Dulfano, C. Family therapy of alcoholism. In: *Practical Approaches to Alcoholism Psychotherapy*, Zimberg, S., Wallace, J., and Blume, S. B. (eds.). Plenum: New York, 1978.
7. Fox, R. Antabuse as an adjunct to psychotherapy in alcoholism. *N.Y.S. J. Med.* 58: 1540–1544, 1958.
8. Fox, R. A. Multidisciplinary approach to the treatment of alcoholism. *Am. J. Psychiatry* 123:769–778, 1967.
9. McClelland, D. C., Davis, W. N., Kalin, R., and Warner, E. *The Drinking Man*. Free Press: New York, 1972.
10. Moore, R. A. Some countertransference reactions in the treatment of alcoholism. *Psychiat. Digest* 26:35–43, 1965.
11. Moreno, J. L. Psychodrama. In: *Comprehensive Group Psychotherapy*, Kaplan, H. and Sadock, B. J. (eds.). Williams & Wilkins: Baltimore, 1972.
12. Silber, A. An addendum to the technique of psychotherapy with alcoholics. *J. Nerv. Ment. Dis.* 150:423–437, 1970.
13. Steinglass, P. Experimenting with family treatment approaches to alcoholism, 1950–1975: A review. *Family Process* 15:97–123, 1970.
14. Tamerin, J. S. The psychotherapy of alcoholic women. In: *Practical Approaches to Alcoholism Psychotherapy*, Zimberg, S., Wallace, J., and Blume, S. B. (eds.). Plenum: New York, 1978.
15. Tiebout, H. M. Alcoholics Anonymous—An experiment in nature. *Q.J. Stud. Alcohol* 22:52–68, 1961.
16. Tiebout, H. M. Intervention in psychotherapy. *Am. J. Psychoanal.* 33:1–6, 1962.
17. Wallace, J. Working with the preferred defense structure of the recovering alcoholic. In: *Practical Approaches to Alcoholism Psychotherapy*, Zimberg, S., Wallace, J., and Blume, S. B. (eds.). Plenum: New York, 1978.
18. Wilsnack, S. C. The impact of sex roles in women's alcohol use and abuse. In: *Alcoholism Problems in Women and Children*, Greenblatt, M. and Schuckit, M. A. (eds.). Grune & Stratton: New York, 1976.
19. Zimberg, S. Psychiatric office treatment of alcoholism. In: *Practical Approaches to Alcoholism Psychotherapy*, Zimberg, S., Wallace, J., and Blume, S. B. (eds.). Plenum: New York, 1978.

84

NICK KANAS, MD, University of California, San Francisco

ALCOHOLISM AND GROUP PSYCHOTHERAPY

IN THE PAST DECADE, evidence has mounted to support the idea that alcoholism is a disease with biological, psychological, and social causes and effects [14, 23, 24]. Consequently, treatment has focused on a multimodal, multidisciplinary approach in which causal factors are isolated and a treatment plan is made that is specific to a given patient's needs. One type of treatment that has been found to be especially useful for the psychological problems of many alcoholics is group psychotherapy.

The purpose of this chapter is to explore the value of group psychotherapy for alcoholic patients. The effectiveness of this treatment modality is first considered, both from an anecdotal and an experimental viewpoint. Psychological considerations are then discussed, with particular emphasis on psychodynamic issues and important group psychotherapy curative factors. This is followed by a discussion of therapeutic considerations, emphasizing both formal issues and important treatment nuances. Finally, other types of therapeutic group activities that have been found to be useful for alcoholics are considered.

Nick Kanas, MD, Assistant Professor of Psychiatry, University of California, San Francisco, School of Medicine, and Assistant Chief, Psychiatry Service, Veterans Administration Medical Center, San Francisco, California.

EFFECTIVENESS OF GROUP PSYCHOTHERAPY FOR ALCOHOLICS

Anecdotal Reports

The anecdotal literature has generally been enthusiastic regarding the effectiveness of group psychotherapy for alcoholics. Stein and Friedman have stated: "Group psychotherapy is, in most instances, the treatment of choice for the psychological problems of the alcoholic" [25, p. 652], and they estimate that 60 to 70% of patients in group psychotherapy improve versus 20 to 40% of patients receiving individual psychotherapy. Other anecdotal accounts [6, 12] have stated much the same thing, and alcoholics have been treated in a variety of therapy groups emphasizing different theoretical and technical principles, including psychoanalytic [11, 13, 15], assertiveness training [1, 2], Gestalt [5], psychodrama [3, 9, 27], transactional analysis [26], aversion therapy [18], and insight-oriented theoretical principles [28, 29, 30]. In one uncontrolled study evaluating the effectiveness of psychoanalytically oriented group psychotherapy in conjunction with Antabuse, Greenbaum [13] found that 80% of patients who were in twice-weekly group psychotherapy remained sober during the treatment period, as compared with 50% who were in weekly group psychotherapy.

Controlled Experimental Studies

Despite these anecdotal accounts, a review of the literature has revealed few well-controlled studies measuring the effects of group psychotherapy with alcoholics. The best controlled of these studies was performed by Ends and Page [7], who compared the effects of three types of group psychotherapy, based on learning theory, client-centered therapy, and psychoanalytic principles, with the effects of a discussion group (control condition) on 63 inpatient alcoholics. After 15 sessions, they found that significantly more client-centered and psychoanalytic patients showed improved self-concept than control patients, as measured by Q-sort ratings and a 1½-year follow-up. Furthermore, significantly fewer client-centered patients required readmission than controls. In a second study of client-centered group psychotherapy, Ends and Page [8] again found this modality to be superior to a control condition using a Q-sort and the Minnesota Multiphasic Personality Inventory (MMPI). They also found that doubling the number of sessions, from 15 to 30 in a 6-week period of time, resulted in both quantitative and qualitative improvement, particularly in the area of improved reintegration and consolidation of gain. In another controlled study, Mindlin and Belden [20] gave an attitude questionnaire to hospitalized alcoholics before and after entering group psychotherapy, an occupational therapy group, and a no group (control) condition. They found that group psychotherapy patients significantly improved over controls regarding motivation and attitude toward alcoholism. McGinnis [17] added group psychotherapy for some patients in his Alcoholics Anonymons–oriented inpatient program. After seven sessions, lasting 1½ hours each, he found that the group psychotherapy patients experienced significant improvement in the Barron Ego-Strength Scale as compared to control patients not receiving group psychotherapy. Miller et al. [19] compared the effects of a confrontational group psychotherapy condition with an electrical aversion condition and a control condition on 30 inpatient alcoholics. After 10 days, they found no significant differences between the three conditions regarding reduced alcohol consumption or improved attitudes toward drinking, as measured by a pre- and post- taste test assessment procedure. However, the abbreviated treatments, small sample sizes, and unusual method of assessing improvement cast some doubt on the practical relevance of this study. Finally, Yalom has written about a type of group psychotherapy that emphasizes an insight-oriented approach focusing on interactions between the members in the here and now [28, 29, 30]. In one recent study [30] he and his colleagues studied the effect of this type of group psychotherapy on 20 alcoholic and 17 neurotic outpatients who met on a weekly basis. Outcome measures included 9-point rating scales evaluating improvement in symptoms and attainment of therapeutic goals, and raters included patients, therapists, and independent judges. Yalom et al. [30] found significant improvement in both populations at 8 and 12 months of therapy. They also found no significant differences in improvement between the alcoholic and neurotic samples.

In summary, most of these studies found group psychotherapy to be of value for alcoholics. They thus tend to support the claims made in the anecdotal literature regarding the effectiveness of this treatment modality.

PSYCHOLOGICAL CONSIDERATIONS

Psychodynamic Issues

Although each alcoholic patient has a unique set of biological, psychological, and social causes leading to the drinking problem, there are certain psychological themes that are commonly found in many alcoholics, and it is clinically useful to describe them for purposes of setting up effective treatment strategies. In one review, Kissin [14] found that 70 to 80% of alcoholics who were given additional psychiatric diagnoses had a personality disorder and were generally antisocial, passive-aggressive, impulsive, or schizoid; 10 to 15% were diagnosed as neurotic, usually anxiety or obsessive-compulsive; and 10 to 15% had a psychosis, including schizophrenia or manic-depressive disorder. While many alcoholics are not given secondary psychiatric diagnoses, some of them still have neurotic or characterological traits that affect their progress in treatment.

Psychodynamically, many alcoholics are seen as being fixated at the oral level of development, which results in narcissistic, passive-dependent, and depressive personality traits, sometimes with compensatory independency. The narcissism may lead to episodes of rage when infantile needs are not gratified, prompting countertransference reactions from the therapist. Many have self-destructive tendencies, poor impulse control, and low frustration tolerance. Denial and projection are frequent defense mechanisms. Anxiety is common, and many alcoholics drink because of an inability to tolerate much anxiety. The superego may be harsh and rigid, leading to guilt and self-punitive behavior. In some cases, the parental structure includes an overindulgent or inconsistent mother and an absent, alcoholic father, and there seems to be a high incidence of early object loss.

Because of these tendencies, insight-oriented individual psychotherapy is difficult with alcoholics. Group psychotherapy offers an advantage in dealing with some of these difficulties. First, many authors have described how the alcoholic's narcissism, primitive object relationships, and poor frustration tolerance may lead him or her to develop a primitive transference relationship with a therapist that complicates the course of individual psychotherapy or causes the patient to leave treatment impulsively [11, 15, 22, 25]. However, the presence of other group members and the relative transparency of the therapist in a group psychotherapy model helps diminish the intensity of the transference. This makes it possible for many alcoholics to safely explore transference issues and to develop a therapeutic alliance that counters a tendency to leave therapy. Second, the massive denial found with many alcoholics causes them to tune out therapeutic interpretations or refuse to acknowledge their alcoholism. In group psychotherapy, the presence of other patients who have been there and who can challenge this denial helps the alcoholic become aware of the use of this primitive defense mechanism. In addition, by being supportive and helpful, the other group members encourage some gratification of narcissistic and dependency needs, which allows the alcoholic to feel safe enough to admit to and explore his or her addiction problem. Third, some alcoholics drink to help them cope with anxiety or poor impulse control. Since the individual therapeutic situation may transiently increase a patient's anxiety, the resulting emotional pain may be intolerable for many alcoholics and lead to impulsive reactions such as drinking, suicidal behavior, or a flight from therapy. In the group psychotherapy setting, support and anxiety-reducing techniques can be used to modulate the anxiety level and discourage behavioral acting out.

Need for Power

McClelland et al. [16] have argued that alcoholics are driven by a strong wish to feel more powerful, and that drinking allows them to feel and act stronger. This concept has received some experimental support using the Thematic Apperception Test [16]. The authors feel that groups such as Alcoholics Anonymous (AA) socialize and channel this power need by converting it into more acceptable behavior, such as being a sponsor for other alcoholics. Butts and Chotlos [4] found that alcoholics were more close-minded and dogmatic than nonalcoholics, as measured by Rokeach's Dogmatism Scale. They relate this high dogmatism to feelings of isolation, helplessness, and powerlessness.

Curative Factors in Alcoholic Groups

One way of exploring the effectiveness of group psychotherapy for alcoholics is to examine the basic curative factors that are found in many psychotherapy groups. Yalom [29] has developed a method of delineating and studying these curative factors. He constructed statements that described each of 12 curative factors that he believed a priori were important in group psychotherapy. He wrote each statement on an index card so as to produce 60 different statements, five describing each of the 12 curative factors. He then gave his 60 cards to 20 psychiatric outpatients who had completed an average of 16 months of outpatient group psychotherapy, and he had them Q-sort the statements according to how helpful each was regarding the patient's group psychotherapy experience. Based on the rank order of the statements, Yalom was able to construct a rank order of curative factors, as is shown in Table 1. As can be seen from this table, interpersonal input (or the feedback that patients received from the group members and the therapists as to how they interacted with other patients), catharsis, group cohesiveness (or the feeling of being accepted by other group members), and insight were felt to be the four most important curative factors, according to the patients' evaluation of their group psychotherapy experience.

Table 1
Group Psychotherapy Curative Factors Compared

Yalom[a]	Rank Order	Feeney and Dranger[a]
Interpersonal input	1	Catharsis
Catharsis	2	Insight
Group cohesiveness	3	Interpersonal input
Insight	4	Group cohesiveness
Interpersonal output	5	Instillation of hope
Existential factors	6	Existential factors
Universality	7	Interpersonal output
Instillation of hope	8	Universality
Altruism	9	Altruism
Family reenactment	10	Family reenactment
Guidance	11	Guidance
Identification	12	Identification

[a]Yalom's 1975 study used 20 psychiatric outpatients after approximately 64 hourly sessions (one a week for an average of 16 months).
[b]Feeney and Dranger's 1976 study used 20 alcoholic inpatients after approximately 34 hourly sessions (five a week for an average of 49 days).

Feeney and Dranger [10] gave Yalom's Q-sort to 20 inpatient alcoholics who participated in a 90-day rehabilitation program. These patients similarly rank ordered Yalom's statements after an average of 49 days in group psychotherapy, and based on their statements, a rank order of curative factors was constructed for this population, also shown in Table 1. Note that the first four curative factors in this population were identical to Yalom's outpatient psychiatric population. In both studies, identification with other patients or the therapists was judged to be least important.

The above similarities in rank orderings of curative factors are probably due to several factors. Both populations were in advanced stages of group psychotherapy and were measured after 30 group psychotherapy sessions, an important minimum number found by Ends and Page [8]. Second, both populations were treated with an insight-oriented, interactional, here-and-now approach, as outlined by Yalom [29], and this similar treatment bias may have affected the types of curative factors that were judged to be important. Finally, since most patients in both populations had personality disorders or neurotic difficulties, they would be expected to benefit from a treatment approach that focused on insight, catharsis, immediate interpersonal inputs, and the importance of belonging to a group.

THERAPEUTIC CONSIDERATIONS

Formal Issues

Most psychotherapy groups treating alcoholics meet from one to three times each week for 1 to 2 hours a session. The number of patients may vary from five to 12, with the optimum being seven or eight. Most alcoholic groups are homogeneous; that is, they are comprised of patients whose principal problem involves dealing with alcoholism. Patients should not be included who are unmotivated, severely sociopathic, or who suffer from a moderate to severe organic brain syndrome or a psychotic condition, as these patients can be very disruptive and interfere with effective group work. To be truly psychotherapeutic, the group should have at least one experienced therapist who is trained to interpret psychodynamic issues and is sensitive to interpersonal interactions in the here-and-now. In order to maximize awareness of group process and minimize the potential negative effects of countertransference, two therapists are more effective than one. New patients should be screened and oriented prior to entering the group, thus allowing the therapist to become aware of the appropriateness of the patient for a given group, and the patient to become aware of what to expect when he or she begins group participation.

Alcoholic groups should be flexible and supportive, and they should provide an atmosphere where the patient will feel safe and accepted. The focus should be on interpreting interpersonal interactions in the here and now and in relating these to important psychodynamic issues influencing the patient's alcoholism. Honesty and the expression of feeling should be encouraged. At times, the leader may need to impose some structure, such as using a psychodrama or anxiety-reducing technique (see below).

Early Stage of Treatment

In the first few weeks of treatment, the new alcoholic patient is usually concerned with the achievement and maintenance of sobriety. His or her focus is often on the physical sequelae of alcohol, and psychosocial issues are frequently denied. Therefore, the group should be supportive and accepting of the new member and should acknowledge his or her concerns over sobriety and the physical effects of alcoholism. A flexible approach may be necessary, such as gratifying narcissistic and dependency needs in order to keep the patient in therapy or calling a patient who misses a session to inquire into his or her well-being. The therapist should help the new patient verbalize his or her history to other members in the group and should encourage the expansion of feelings and interaction with other patients in the here-and-now. Through the use of consensual validation and feedback from other members, the therapist can also help the new patient work through the mechanism of denial. This must be done in a clear yet supportive way so that the new patient can tolerate the resultant anxiety and feel that the feedback is in his or her best interest. Where there are several new members in the group, a quasi cohesion may form whereby the therapist is excluded by a superficial camaraderie so as to prevent confrontation of important issues [21]. The therapist should be aware of this phenomenon and should deal with it as any other form of resistance.

As the effects of withdrawal recede, physical status improves, and denial mechanisms are worked through, most patients begin to consider important psychological and social sequelae of their drinking, such as loneliness, depression, poor interpersonal skills, marital problems, and unemployment. These important psychosocial sequelae should be dealt with in the group, both as to their psychotherapeutic implications as well as to their survival implications. Often, a feeling that one is not alone and is cared for by others in the group may improve a patient's loneliness and lowered self-esteem. Simply giving advice and encouragement may result in the patient moving into a halfway house or beginning to look for a job. Gradually, the patient becomes more self-confident and able to meet survival needs.

Later Stage of Treatment

After the first few weeks of treatment, when the patient's physical and psychosocial status is stabilized, the patient is ready for more intensive work regarding intrapsychic and interpersonal issues. Using observations in the here-and-now, the therapist may make comments on a given alcoholic's style of relating to other people. Psychodynamic interpretations may be made that encourage the expression of feelings and give insight into the causes of a patient's alcoholism. Although unconscious conflicts may be explored, only those directly related to a patient's drinking problem should be considered. In order to keep this focus, some modification in technique may be necessary, such as more active participation in the discussion by the therapist, avoidance of issues not felt to be relevant to the patient's drinking, and dilution of the transference. Despite these modifications, a high level of anxiety may result, which can be modulated by various anxiety-reducing techniques, such as structuring the group with an agenda, using a blackboard to explain dynamics, and video playback or written summaries of previous sessions [28]. Another useful technique is that of "making the rounds," whereby all patients are encouraged to give feedback on an issue of importance to the group. Gradually, the members will gain insight into various neurotic and characterological antecedents of their drinking behavior, with the hope that they will learn more effective ways of dealing with anxiety and relating to others.

A common phenomenon involving alcoholics in treatment is extragroup contact among the members [28]. This may become a problem if a subgroup forms that holds back information or attacks another member in the therapy group. The therapist should make it clear from the beginning that should such a subgroup develop, any relevant discussions that occur should be thoroughly addressed in the larger group. All potential new members should be warned of the dangers of subgrouping in any pregroup orientation they have with the therapist.

The Inebriated Patient

Alcoholics often act out conflicts and reduce anxiety by coming to the group session intoxicated. This is often followed by guilt on the part of the inebriate and produces ambivalence on the part of other group members. They feel frustrated and angry that the group work is being interrupted, while at the same time they feel guilty that they may somehow be responsible for the inebriate's slip. In addition, many group patients have a strong desire to support and aid the fallen member. The solution to this situation involves an open acknowledgment of the needs of both the inebriate and the other patients. If the inebriate is severely intoxicated, he or she will not be able to process feedback and may further disrupt group work. Consequently, the inebriate should be excused from the group that day, with a clear statement that he or she will be welcomed back next time, when sober. A call at home or support from other group members between the group sessions may be important to counter the inebriate's shame and encourage him or her to return. Concerning the feelings of the other patients in the group, the possible acting-out and anxiety-producing implications of the inebriate's drinking episode should be addressed. Responsibility for the drinking behavior should be placed on the person who did the drinking, not on other group members. The frustration, anger, and guilt felt by some group members, as well as possible rescue fantasies, should also be addressed in the group. A drinking episode is a major event in the life of a group of alcoholics, and its importance should be addressed and explored to the fullest extent possible.

OTHER THERAPEUTIC GROUPS

A number of group formats have been found therapeutic for alcoholics even though their primary goal is not insight into important intrapsychic and interpersonal issues. Nevertheless, important dynamic issues come up in these groups from time to time, and for this reason a brief description of some of them is outlined below.

Educational Groups

The purpose of educational groups is to provide information on a variety of issues involving alcoholism: causes, physical sequelae, familial impact, community resources, and so forth. These didactic activities are usually centered around a topic and utilize lectures, films, videotapes, or displays. They are usually followed by a discussion period that not only clarifies factual issues but considers misconceptions and emotional reactions patients have about themselves and their problem. Many alcoholics are cognitively misinformed about the medical, psychological, and social issues of alcoholism, and educational groups have been found useful in altering these misconceptions.

Activity Groups

Activity groups are usually organized around a specific type of activity, usually of a recreational or occupational nature; examples include sporting events, crafts, dance, and music. By encouraging nonalcoholic interactions, patients relearn social skills and become involved with other people in a sober context. In addition, they become familiar with community resources and learn to organize their life through initiating and carrying out the activity (e.g., planning a party or making a vase). Finally, a trained activity therapist can sometimes gain insight into important intrapsychic or interpersonal issues that may arise in the context of the activity; this insight may be passed on to the patient's therapist.

Community Meetings

Community meetings involving patients and staff have been found useful in many inpatient alcohol rehabilitation units where patient government and techniques of milieu therapy are practiced. These meetings often have an agenda and may be conducted by a patient who has been elected to lead the community. Typical agenda items may include passes, planning for future activities, presenting treatment plans, and discussing ward problems involving all members of the community, such as coping with a drinking patient. In performing this ward business, therapeutic issues arise that can be discussed then and there or in a later group or individual therapy session. These meetings also allow patients to confront the staff as a whole, thus tapping into patient fantasies and concerns.

Alcoholics Anonymous

Alcoholics Anonymous, and other related self-help groups such as Al-Anon and Alateen, aim at encouraging sobriety through reinforcement and submission to a higher power. Sober interactions are encouraged through meetings or AA-sponsored clubs or activities, thereby countering isolation and loneliness. For many alcoholics, the AA approach is quite effective and therapeutic.

Family Therapy

Family therapy represents a type of group therapeutic experience in which the participants are all members of the same family. Much has been written regarding the alcoholic family structure and the systems approach to dealing with this problem. In some cases, multiple family groups have been organized where different families can share common problems and concerns involving alcoholic members.

REFERENCES

1. Adinolfi, A. A., McCourt, W. F., and Geoghegan, S. Group assertiveness training for alcoholics. *J. Stud. Alcohol* 37(3):311–320, 1976.
2. Alberti, R. *Assertiveness: Innovations, Applications, Issues.* Impact Publications: San Luis Obispo, Calif., 1977.
3. Blume, S. Psychodrama and alcoholism. *Ann. N.Y. Acad. Sci.* 233:123–127, 1974.
4. Butts, S. V., and Chotlos, J. Closed-mindedness in alcoholics. *J. Stud. Alcohol* 35:906–910, 1974.
5. Cook, R. S. Alcoholic treatment: The group experience. *Ill. Med. J.* 139:514–518, 1971.
6. Doroff, D. R. Group psychotherapy in alcoholism. In: *The Biology of Alcoholism: Treatment and Rehabilitation of the Chronic Alcoholic* (Vol. 5), Kissin, B. and Begleiter, H. (eds.). Plenum: New York, 1977.
7. Ends, E. J., and Page, C. W. A study of three types of group psychotherapy with hospitalized male inebriates. *J. Stud. Alcohol* 18:267–277, 1957.
8. Ends, E. J., and Page, C. W. Group psychotherapy and concomitant psychological changes. *Psychol. Monogr.* 73(10):1–31, 1959.

9. Evseeff, G. S. Group psychotherapy in the state hospital. *Dis. Nerv. Syst.* 9:214-218, 1948.

10. Feeney, D. J., and Dranger, P. Alcoholics view group therapy: Process and goals. *J. Stud. Alcohol* 38(5):611-618, 1976.

11. Feibel, C. The archaic personality structure of alcoholics and its indications for group therapy. *Int. J. Group Psychother.* 10:39-45, 1960.

12. Fox, R. Groups psychotherapy with alcoholics. *Int. J. Group Psychother.* 12:56-63, 1962.

13. Greenbaum, H. Group psychotherapy with alcoholism in conjunction with Antabuse treatment. *Int. J. Group Psychother.* 4(30):30-45, 1954.

14. Kissin, B. Theory and practice in the treatment of alcoholism. In: *The Biology of Alcoholism: Treatment and Rehabilitation of the Chronic Alcoholic* (Vol. 5), Kissin, B. and Begleiter, H. (eds.). Plenum: New York, 1977.

15. Martensen-Larsen, O. Group psychotherapy with alcoholics in private practice. *Int. J. Group Psychother.* 6:28-37, 1956.

16. McClelland, D., Davis, N., Kalin, R., and Wanner, E. *The Drinking Man.* Free Press: New York, 1972.

17. McGinnis, C. A. The effect of group therapy on the ego-strength scale scores of alcoholic patients. *J. Clin. Psychol.* 19:346-347, 1963.

18. Miller, E. C., Dvorak, B. A., and Turner, D. W. A method of treating aversion to alcohol by reflex conditioning in a group setting. *J. Stud. Alcohol* 21:424-431, 1960.

19. Miller, P. M., Hersen, M., Eisler, R. M., and Hemphill, D. P. Electrical aversion therapy with alcoholics: An analogue study. *Behav. Res. Ther.* 11:491-497, 1973.

20. Mindlin, D. F., and Belden, E. Attitude changes with alcoholics in group therapy. *Calif. Ment. Health Res. Dig.* 3:102-103, 1965.

21. Mullan, H., and Sangiuliano, I. *Alcoholism: Group Psychotherapy and Rehabilitation.* Charles C Thomas: Springfield, Il., 1966.

22. Pfeffer, A. Z., Friedland, P., and Wortis, S. B. Group psychotherapy with alcoholics. *J. Stud. Alcohol* 10:198-216, 1949.

23. Secretary of Health, Education and Welfare. *First Special Report to the U.S. Congress on Alcohol and Health.* National Institute on Alcohol Abuse and Alcoholism: Washington, D.C., 1971.

24. Secretary of Health, Education and Welfare. *Alcohol and Health: New Knowledge.* National Institute on Alcohol Abuse and Alcoholism: Washington, D.C., 1974.

25. Stein, A., and Friedman, E. Group therapy with alcoholics. In: *Comprehensive Group Psychotherapy*, Kaplan, H. I. and Sadock, B. J. (eds.). Williams & Wilkins: Baltimore, 1971.

26. Steiner, C. *Games Alcoholics Play.* Ballatine Books: New York, 1972.

27. Weiner, H. An overview of the use of psychodrama and group psychotherapy in the treatment of alcoholism in the United States and abroad. *Group Psychother.* 19:159-165, 1966.

28. Yalom, I. D. Group therapy and alcoholism. *Ann. N.Y. Acad. Sci.* 233:85-103, 1974.

29. Yalom, I. D. *The Theory and Practice of Group Psychotherapy* (2nd ed.). Basic Books: New York, 1975.

30. Yalom, I. D., Bloch, S., Bond, G., Zimmerman, E., and Qualls, B. Alcoholics in interactional group therapy: An outcome study. *Arch. Gen. Psychiatry* 35:419-425, 1978.

85

EDWARD KAUFMAN, MD, University of California, Irvine Medical Center, Orange, California

E. MANSELL PATTISON, MD, Medical College of Georgia, Augusta, Georgia

FAMILY AND NETWORK THERAPY IN ALCOHOLISM

FAMILY THERAPY AND other system interventions have slowly emerged over the past decade as essential to the treatment of alcoholism. This has only occurred since the fields of alcoholism and family therapy have ended their disengagement from one another and permitted cross-fertilization. Many of the basic tenets of family therapy are applicable to alcoholism, but they can only be utilized if the therapist has a knowledge of alcoholics and their family systems. These systems are discussed elsewhere in this volume and will not be repeated. However, families with an alcoholic have been classified into four different types of family systems [5]. These systems relate directly to the type of family and system intervention that is necessary for successful treatment; they are (1) the functional family; (2) the neurotic enmeshed family; (3) the disintegrated family; (4) the absent family. These systems may occur sequentially in some families as the family passes through different phases of the alcoholic family life cycle; in other families they may represent the only system established.

Edward Kaufman, MD, Associate Professor in Residence, Department of Psychiatry and Human Behavior, University of California, Irvine Medical Center, Orange, California.

E. Mansell Pattison, MD, Professor and Chairman, Department of Psychiatry, Medical College of Georgia, Augusta, Georgia.

The Functional Family System

The functional family system (type 1) is apparently stabilized and happy. The parents maintain a loving spouse relationship with a relatively good sexual adjustment. They are successful as a parenting team; their children are well adjusted, and have good relationships with each other and with their peers. Drinking in the alcoholic partner does not evolve as a result of family stresses, but primarily from response to social strains and/or personal neurotic conflict. Excessive drinking is often outside the home, in binges, at parties, or at bedtime. Functional family systems usually exist in the early phases of alcoholism and frequently deteriorate.

Such families respond well to a focus on their response to the drinking behavior and to contracts that limit their responsibility for and responses to the drinking member. The alcoholic member may respond well to an aversive conditioning program or Antabuse. Reconstructive family therapy is resisted because the family system protects the working homeostatic adjustment.

The Neurotic, Enmeshed Family System

In neurotic, enmeshed families (type 2), drinking behavior interrupts normal family tasks, causes conflict, shifts roles, and demands adjustive and adaptive responses from family members who do not know how to appropriately respond. Drinking also triggers anger in the drinker despite attempts by the alcoholic to absorb the anger with alcohol. Alcoholism creates physical problems, most notably sexual impotence or dysfunction, which in turn produce further marital conflicts. In these families, excessive drinking occurs when family anxiety is high and the drinking stirs up higher anxiety in those dependent on the one who drinks.

Stresses in any single family member affect the entire family with urgency and immediacy. Communication is often not direct but through a third party. Likewise, conflicts are triangulated (projected) onto another family member. Everyone in the family feels guilty and responsible for each other, but particularly for the alcoholic and his or her drinking. The alcoholic abdicates parental roles. As nonalcoholic members take over management of the family, the alcoholic is relegated to child status, which perpetuates drinking. Coalitions occur between the nonalcoholic spouse and children or in-laws, which tends to further distance the alcoholic.

The patterns that develop in enmeshed family members of the alcoholic have been labeled as the "disease" of co-alcoholism. In the early phases of co-alcoholism, there is assumed responsibility and guilt for the alcoholic's behavior. In the middle phases, there is hostility, disgust, pity, preoccupation with protectiveness, and shielding of the alcoholic. The co-alcoholic will drink with the alcoholic as a way of tolerating his or her behavior. In the advanced stages, the hostility, withdrawal, and suspiciousness may be generalized to one's total environment. In the final stages of co-alcoholism, assumed responsibility and quarreling with the alcoholic are all-encompassing. Outside interests decline, and needs to maintain the self are disregarded. Psychosomatic symptoms or drug and alcohol abuse may occur in the spouse, and separation is threatened or demanded. Frequently, the alcoholic will become sufficiently motivated for treatment when the co-alcoholic reaches the detachment of this final phase.

These families respond to treatment approaches that involve and restructure the entire family system. Hospitalization of the drinking member may be necessary in order to involve the family in therapy. Alcoholics Anonymous (AA) for the alcoholic and Al-Anon and Alateen for the rest of the family may be necessary supportive adjuncts.

The Disintegrated Family System

The disintegrated family system (type 3) is frequently a later state of the neurotic, enmeshed system, although the functional system may also regress directly to a disintegrated system. There is a past history of reasonable life and family function, but at the point of entering treatment, the family system has collapsed. The family is separated and there may be no family contact. Alcoholics from such families must first learn to take responsibility for themselves and stop blaming spouse, family, friends, and employers. They often require 3 months or more of abstinence before vocational retraining and family reinvolvement can be initiated. The spouse and family should be contacted at this time and supportive counseling and/or Al-Anon recommended. If these measures are successful and the family wishes to explore reunion, family therapy can commence.

The Absent Family System

Although the absent family system (type 4) may be an end-stage of deterioration, the more frequent pattern is total loss of family of origin early in the drinking career. Alcoholics from this type of family have little or no family contacts, friends, social, or vocational relationships. Their significant others (such as board and care operators or "bottle gang" buddies) provide minimal social support. Their contacts with their family of origin may be renewed after months of sobriety, but usually contact with their prior families of procreation is impossible. If individual therapy and social-vocational rehabilitation is successful they may form new nuclear families. This is unusual, but does occur in younger alcoholics from this type of family system.

FAMILY THERAPY METHODS

In working with alcoholics and their families, the therapist is faced with a unique problem, that of wet and dry family systems. A "wet" system is one in which the alcoholic continues to drink problematically, while a "dry" system is one where active drinking is not a problem, but the family's problems may continue. Some therapists, particularly those who work in AA-oriented programs, will only work with dry systems. This should not be a precondition of treatment with family systems, however. A dry system is always preferable; however, it may be an unreasonable expectation for many families at the onset of treatment. In all families, the therapist should suggest measures to effect a dry state, at least temporarily, and in some instances the therapist should insist on these measures.

Achieving a Dry System

If the alcoholic is drinking so severely that he or she is unable to attend sessions without being under the influence and/or if functioning is severely impaired, then the first priority is to interrupt the pattern of drinking. Thus, the first goal is to persuade the family to pull together to initiate detoxification. A variety of family and network intervention techniques have recently been developed in which all members of the alcoholic's network confront him or her about the need for treatment. Detoxification may be done on an outpatient basis, but if the drinking is severe, immediate short-term hospitalization may be required. If the drinking is only moderately severe or intermittent, then the family should be offered alternatives to initiate a temporary alcohol-free state. These alternatives should include social detoxification centers, AA and Antabuse. Antabuse should not be given to another family member for daily distribution as this tends to reinforce the family's being locked into the alcoholic's drinking or not drinking. If the alcoholic refuses to initiate abstinence, then the therapist is stuck with working with the wet system.

Working with Wet Systems

Since the wet system is a reality, the therapist should have techniques available to work with such families. When a member arrives at a session intoxicated, the therapist should not deal directly with this problem. Rather, he or she should ask the sober spouse and family members to deal with the intoxicated person. This offers an excellent opportunity to observe how the family interacts during intoxication, which is one of the most critical phases of family system function. In subsequent sessions this behavior can be reexamined or videotapes of this behavior can be reviewed. In general, it is easier to ask the hyperfunctioning (sober) partner to change than the underfunctioning (alcoholic) one.

In working with wet systems it is critical that the therapist not maintain the illusion that problems are being resolved because the family is in therapy when, in fact, the problems are still being reinforced. Provision of support systems for the other family members may help reduce the emotional intensity fixated on the alcoholic (or therapist). Al-Anon is a valuable support system, as are significant others and social network systems of relatives and friends. Other supports, such as vocational training, jobs, social agencies, pastors, and attorneys, may be essential. Groups for responsible drinkers may be helpful to the alcoholic if he or she can keep drinking from becoming destructive.

The therapist can offer the family three choices as their only alternatives, as outlined by Berenson [1].

1. Keep doing exactly what you are doing.
2. Detach or emotionally distance yourselves from the alcoholic.
3. Separate or physically distance yourselves from the alcoholic.

Thus, the family is presented with three choices, each of which may seem impossible. The problem is resolved by choosing one of three courses of action and following through or by experiencing the helplessness and powerlessness of these situations being repeated and clarified. The therapist clarifies that these are the only options, and should not expect one to be adopted right away. The family then shares despair and hits bottom sufficiently to become responsible for themselves rather than continuing to try to change the alcoholic. When they do this, the alcoholic may get worse in order to get the family back into the entanglement. The therapist must prepare the family for this situation. If the family can say, "We prefer you not to kill yourself or us, but we are powerless to help you," it is unlikely that the alcoholic will kill himself or herself or someone else. These options then open the door to consider new family adaptations apart from whether the alcoholic is wet or dry [1].

Interventions with Different Family Systems

Different schools of family therapy tend to utilize different languages, techniques, or strategies. Few data exist to compare the efficacy of different family therapy methods, much less to compare them as they are applied to alcoholism. The integration of structural, systems, psychodynamic, and behavioral methods is stressed as suitable to individual therapist styles, work settings, and types of family alcoholism problems encountered. Therefore, some general principles for working with the four types of family systems are summarized.

In the functional family system (type 1) members have learned to function with a minimum of overt conflict, so that they avoid psychologically oriented interventions. Here family educative approaches are often helpful. Explanation of the medical effects of alcoholism and the medical complications of alcoholism may be the most useful initial entry into family participation. Such families will often then participate in educative-cognitive exploration of family roles and explicit and observable behavioral interaction. Exploration of implicit family rules and behavioral expectations can be followed by the development of family contracts and behavioral role practicing. Intensive family exploration of personal and interpersonal dynamics may not be necessary or may be resisted because the family system protects the working homeostatic adjustment. Many families will respond to the more cognitive and behavioral approaches.

In the neurotic, enmeshed family systems (type 2), many of the same initial approaches to family involvement and commitment as mentioned above may be necessary. However, much more active structural and psychodynamic work will have to be done in most cases. In these families, educative and behavioral methods may provide some initial relief, but will likely not impact the enmeshed, neurotic relationships. Here explicit family psychotherapy is usually required (discussion follows). Often, multiple generations and kinship systems are interlocked with the nuclear family dynamics, and the involvement of the larger social systems, where possible, will likely be helpful. In contrast to the functional family system, where work with the nuclear family is usually sufficient, work with just the nuclear family in the neurotic, enmeshed family system may often be insufficient. Further mechanisms for disengagement of the enmeshed nuclear family members are required. Here concomitant involvement with AA or Al-Anon may be very helpful, along with involvement of family members in more significant kinship, friendship, and community relationships.

In the disintegrated family system (type 3) the use of family intervention might seem irrelevant. However, many of these marriages and families have fallen apart only after severe alcoholic behavior. Further, there is often only pseudoindividuation of the alcoholic from marital, family, and kinship ties. These families usually cannot and will not reconstitute during the early phases of alcoholism rehabilitation. Thus, the initial and early stages of treatment should focus primarily on the individual alcoholic. However, potential ties to spouse, family, kin, and friends should be explored early in treatment, and some contact should be initiated. There should be neither explicit or implicit assumptions that such familial ties will be fully reconstituted. When sobriety and personal stability have been achieved over several months, more substantive family explorations can be initiated to reestablish parental roles and family and kinship relationships—still without reconstitution. These family definitional sessions can then serve as the springboard for either appropriate redefinition of separated roles or for reconciliated family structure. In either case, it is important for both the alcoholic and his or her family system to renegotiate new roles and relationships on the basis of his or her identity as a rehabilitated alcoholic. Some families may not wish reunion, but can achieve healthy separation. Families that do desire reunion must establish a new base for family relationships.

The absent family system (type 4) presents rather different problems. Here the issue is not reconstitution, but rather the development of new social networks, new social systems, and new life styles. Often alcoholics in such circumstances have little ability to form effective social relations and do best in partially institutionalized social support systems. However, some of these alcoholics do learn to participate in effective social systems over time in a graduated fashion, and may even build new functional families.

MODIFICATIONS OF FAMILY THERAPY FOR ALCOHOLISM

In adapting the techniques of family therapy to alcoholism it has been found that a synthesis of structural, systems, behavioral, and psychodynamic approaches is most helpful.

Structural Methods

The therapy begins with early joining maneuvers in which the therapist functions as a host and relates to the family and each member using the family's style, language, affects and rules [4]. Ultimately the therapist joins the family by understanding them and helping them change. Joining with the total family provides the therapeutic leverage necessary to change the family. Joining with individual family members or subsystems may be a powerful restructuring tool. Joining the entire family is much easier with the dry system, since it is very difficult to join with the drinking alcoholic in a therapeutic way.

In utilizing the structural method, a structural map is used as a fluid diagnostic tool that helps to focus the therapy. The genogram [2] is helpful as an information-gathering and synthesizing device. The restructuring techniques that have been adapted to the family treatment of alcoholics include the therapeutic contract, assigning tasks, utilizing the symptoms of the index patient (IP), paradox, interpretation, reenactment, marking boundaries, education and teaching, and the use of the total family network. Restructuring psychotherapy is used mainly for type 2 families. It may also be used with type 3 families after several months of sobriety have been achieved, as previously described.

The Therapeutic Contract

The therapeutic contract deals with establishing the terms, duration, and cost of therapy, as well as which members of the family and network should attend. With the alcoholic's family, the issue of drinking and how it will be dealt with should be made a part of the contract. The way a family should deal with drinking may vary according to the type of family and extent of drinking. At times, contingency contracting, in which each family member agrees to certain mutually satisfying behaviors, can be extremely helpful. The contract should focus on modifying the behavior of the identified patient before changing the behavior of other family members [3]. Changes can be suggested in other family members if they are reframed in the context of helping the identified patient. The contract should include an agreement to work on resolving disagreements. The family's involvement in AA and Al-Anon may also be a part of the contract, though such a commitment may be a later goal in therapy.

Assigning Tasks

Tasks may be assigned within the session or as homework. The best task is one that uses the presenting problem to make a structural change in the family [3]. It is preferable for a task to be accomplished in the session before tasks are given to be performed at home. A couple might be asked to speak to each other in the session while facing each other directly and without a child sitting between them. If this is successful, then the couple can be assigned to eat dinner in a restaurant without their children or eventually to take a vacation by themselves. When hostility has abated, closeness can be built by asking family members, particularly the family distancer, to plan a pleasant surprise for each other and not discuss it until the next session. The tasks should be compatible with the therapist's goals for restructuring the family at each given point in the therapy. Therapeutic homework assignments permit the therapist and the therapeutic work to live with the family until the next session. The therapist may also assign the direction of a task, have the family choose the specifics, and then reinforce their choice. A wife who is overinvolved with the amounts of alcohol her husband is consuming on a daily basis could be given the task of estimating how many drinks he has every day and writing it down without telling him. The husband can be asked to write down the actual amounts, so that they can be compared in a subsequent session. The discrepancies will demonstrate the futility of the wife's efforts and diminish her overinvolvement in his drinking. This task is also a paradoxical one, the nature of which is described below.

Utilizing the Symptom of the Identified Patient

The symptom of the identified patient or IP is especially critical. Thus, the first goal should be to influence the rest of the family to help the IP with the symptom [3]. If the symptom of some other family member is focused on before the IP's symptom is alleviated, the family may be unduly stressed and leave treatment.

The symptom may be exaggerated in order to emphasize the family's need to extrude it. Examples of this include encouraging a family to continue the "glories" of overindulging the infantilizing the alcoholic or asking a combative couple to fight for 1 hour daily. A symptom that is an externalized acting out of family conflicts can be prescribed to be performed within the family so that the family can deal with it (e.g., adolescent stealing, secret drinking).

The Paradox

The paradox [6] is a universal determinant of human behavior in which individuals do the opposite of what they feel they are being pushed to do. In recognition of the power of the paradox, paradoxical directives can be used to achieve change. Such tasks may appear absurd because they require families to do what they have been doing rather than requiring them to change because the latter is what everyone else has been demanding. If the family then follows the therapist and continues what they have been doing, then the therapist assumes power over the symptom. If the family continues to oppose the therapist, then they will reverse the symptom. If they comply with the therapist, then they can acknowledge their power over the symptom and have the power to change it. The paradox uses the principle of the double bind to change the symptom; it is an overt message that urges the family to obey the opposite covert message. The paradox challenges the use of symptoms to maintain distance from the basic conflict. The demand to own symptoms makes them volitional and personalizes the conflict. When properly delivered, the paradox leaves the family chafing at the bit to make desired changes.

Relabeling or reframing the symptom may also be very helpful, as when adolescent acting out is termed an attempt to bring disengaged or divorced parents together or to relieve parent-child responsibilities.

Interpretation

Interpretations can be extremely helpful if they are utilized without blaming, guilt induction, or dwelling on the hopelessness of long-standing, fixed patterns. The repetitive patterns and their derivatives are pointed out to the patient and family. The maladaptive aspects of these patterns on the family and on the alcoholic are pointed out and the family is given tasks to help them change these patterns immediately.

In using a psychodynamic approach, the therapist should avoid the role of the passive listener, which is ineffective with alcoholics as well as their families. Rather, the therapist should be involved with the family as a genuine human being who deals with the immediate moment of experience between himself or herself and the family. Nevertheless, it is felt that a family history of each family member is helpful in understanding the repetition of triangulating patterns from one generation to the next and that pointing out these recurring triangles is a way of changing them.

Reenactment

Patients usually direct their communications to the therapist. They should be required to talk to each other. They should be asked to enact transactional patterns rather than to describe them. The more a family is able to actualize [3, 4], the better the therapist's understanding of the time patterns in a family. Role playing and family sculpture are helpful ways to facilitate actualization of patterns (as well as to change them). Manipulating space (by changing seating or placing one member behind a one-way mirror) is a powerful tool for generating actualization. Working with the family when the alcoholic is inebriated creates a power reenactment of family interactions. The family should resolve still-unresolved conflicts in the sessions rather than talk about old disagreements. When a therapist finds himself or herself bored with a session, it is frequently because actualization (or change) is not occurring.

Marking Boundaries

Marking boundaries [4] is done by delineating individual and subsystem boundaries. Individuals should not answer for or feel for others, should be talked to and not about, and should listen to and acknowledge the communication of others. Individuals should not interrupt one another. Nonverbal checking and blocking of communications should also be observed and, when appropriate, pointed out and halted. Boundaries may be established temporarily by the therapist's placing himself or herself or furniture between subsystems. If successful, these boundaries should continue to be maintained outside of therapy.

The parental subsystem should be protected from intrusion by children as well as other adults in and outside the family. In order to strengthen the executive, parental system, sessions that exclude everyone else should be held. When individuals are deprived of a key role by a new boundary, one that did not previously exist in the family, they should be provided with a substitute role.

Education and Teaching

Giving the family knowledge about alcohol and alcoholism is almost always helpful, as described previously. The support and nurturance that a family can appropriately offer its members should be taught, understood, and encouraged. The therapist may have to assume executive functions as a model and then step back so the family can assume them. Families may be taught how to handle schools or social agencies, parents taught how to confirm each other or react differently to their children. Helpless family members can be taught to tap their potential in social and vocational areas.

Use of the Total Family Network

Other significant family members and social network members, including employers, housekeepers, siblings, aunts and uncles, neighbors, and friends, may be involved. Families who present as only two persons are very difficult to change. Couples groups or multiple family groups can provide some leverage by supplying other parental figures to such systems. Invariably there is another person (such as a boyfriend, sibling, aunt, or grandparent) who can be extremely helpful in changing family systems; that is, the triangle that led to the problem is reversed in order to achieve otherwise impossible structural changes. In the same manner, significant others, including employers and friends, can indeed become significant change agents in family systems.

SUMMARY

This chapter presents the intimate relationship of the problem of alcoholism to family systems. This relationship may be rather singular, as in the case of focal individual alcoholism in a stable and healthy family system, or it may be quite generalized, as in the case of multigenerational- and multikin-involved cases of alcoholism. Four descriptive types of family systems of alcoholism are presented. These are not definitive types, however; they are but illustrative of a broad spectrum of family involvements in alcoholism. The differential utilization of different types of family treatment interventions tailored to these different types of systems is described. Finally, alcoholism is viewed as a family systems problem, with therapeutic interventions framed as systems interventions. A treatment approach that synthesizes psychodynamic systems, structural and behavioral approaches, and specifically adapts these techniques to alcoholism is offered.

REFERENCES

1. Berenson, D. The therapist's relationship with couples with an alcoholic member. In: *Family Therapy of Drug and Alcohol Abuse*, Kaufman, E. and Kaufmann, P. (eds.). Gardner Press: New York, 1979.
2. Bowen, M. Theory in the practice of psychotherapy. In: *Family Therapy*, Guerin, P. (ed.). Gardner Press: New York, 1976.
3. Haley, J. *Problem Solving Therapy*. Jossey-Bass: San Francisco, 1977.
4. Minuchin, S. *Families and Family Therapy*. Harvard University Press: Cambridge, Mass., 1974.
5. Pattison, E. M., and Kaufman, E. Family therapy in the treatment of alcoholism. In: *Family Therapy and Major Psychopathology*, Lansky, M. (ed.). Grune & Stratton: New York, 1981.
6. Watzlawick, P., Weakland, J., and Fisch, R. *Change: Principles of Problem Formation and Problem Resolution*. Norton: New York, 1974.

86

JOHN A. EWING, MD, Center for Alcohol Studies, Chapel Hill, North Carolina

DISULFIRAM AND OTHER DETERRENT DRUGS

DISULFIRAM, BEST KNOWN in the United States under the trade name Antabuse, was reported by Hald and Jacobsen in 1948 to be a drug sensitizing the organism to ethyl alcohol [4]. While taking the drug for experimental purposes themselves, they accidentally discovered that they experienced unpleasant physiological responses when drinking beverage alcohol. When first introduced, the medication tended to be given in what today would be considered excessively high doses. This led to frequent adverse reactions that are rarely seen today. Also, early on many therapists felt that the patient should first be sensitized with the drug and then given alcohol as a means of convincing him or her as to the unpleasantness of the response should drinking occur. This technique is rarely, if ever, employed today. Instead, as will be shown, the patient's cooperation is enlisted and a convincing description of the disulfiram-ethanol reaction (DER) is given.

Mechanism

Disulfiram is an inhibitor of aldehyde dehydrogenase. Since acetaldehyde is the first metabolic breakdown product in the metabolism of alcohol, patients who have been treated with the drug experience acetaldehyde toxicity. The levels of

---

John A. Ewing, MD, Director, Center for Alcohol Studies, and Professor of Psychiatry, School of Medicine, University of North Carolina at Chapel Hill, Chapel Hill, North Carolina.

acetaldehyde that accumulate appear to be sufficient to lead to a chain of biochemical events such as the release of neurotransmitters, histamine, and prostaglandins. The clinical correlates are described below. The DER is not unlike the acetaldehyde toxicity seen in many Oriental subjects when they consume beverage alcohol [2].

Dosage

Most clinicians start patients on a loading dose of 500 mg daily for about 5 days. Thereafter, a daily dose of 250 mg is adequate. For some patients, such as a small woman, 125 mg may suffice. Antabuse tablets of the 500 mg size are scored into quarters and, therefore, this is a convenient dosage form to prescribe since the patient can then take one-half or one-quarter of a tablet.

Deterrence, Not Aversion

It is important to understand that as presently used, disulfiram is a deterrent drug. That is, the fear of a DER deters the patient from taking that first drink. Aversive therapy, described elsewhere in this handbook, involves a form of conditioning by associating the alcoholic beverage and some unpleasant state. Since today the patient is not exposed to the experience of a DER it is vital that he or she be fully compliant, informed, and anxious to be insured against the temptation of taking that first drink.

From time to time one hears anecdotes about wives who surreptitiously get their alcoholic husbands to ingest disulfiram. How they accomplish this is hard to understand since the medication is relatively insoluble. Allegedly, however, the husband concludes that he has become sensitive to alcohol since he always gets sick when he drinks it, and he then quits voluntarily. Physicians who are requested to collude in such a plan should refuse. Only patients who fully understand what they are taking, and why, should receive disulfiram therapy.

Disulfiram, by itself, is not a treatment for alcoholism but a means whereby the patient who accepts that he or she has the disease of alcoholism protects the self from impulsive drinking. Patients taking disulfiram should also be involved in other therapeutic programs. As long as they are taking the medication, it is important that they remain in the care of a physician. Family cooperation in the plan is essential.

The duration of disulfiram therapy will depend upon the progress made by the patient in other therapeutic programs. For example, many patients, with the help of Alcoholics Anonymous (AA), become secure in the conviction that they must avoid alcohol in any form, with this conviction becoming sufficient deterrence in itself. Other patients ask to be allowed to continue on the medication, using it almost like a talisman to provide protection. One young alcoholic physician calls disulfiram "my daily magic pill." He fully understands what would happen if he were to use alcohol; by invoking his daily magic he is free to go about his day's activities without falling back into alcoholic drinking patterns.

Some patients who accept disulfiram therapy and also go to meetings of AA report that fellow AA members criticize the use of this medication. Indeed, most physicians working with many alcoholics are familiar with the patient who stops the disulfiram under such criticism and then has an alcoholic relapse. This author prefers to warn patients in advance of the possibility of such criticism if they discuss their use of disulfiram unnecessarily. Patients in the early phases of recovery from alcoholism need all the help they can get and must understand this. However, some of the hard-line antidisulfiram attitudes among AA members seem to be softening.

One should assume that virtually all alcoholics are wishing that they could be normal drinkers, just as diabetics wish they could be normal dieters. Trying to drink normally is part of the history of the chronic alcoholic, who typically has many episodes of abstinence and relapse. Thus, even though the ideal candidate for disulfiram therapy will not expose himself or herself to the danger of a DER, one must not be surprised that a certain number of patients will. Indeed, it is only when such a patient takes a few sips of an alcoholic beverage that disulfiram is likely to prove more effective than a placebo. Most patients experiencing a DER will then stop drinking.

Indications

The primary indication for disulfiram therapy is, like that for AA, the desire to stop drinking. This presupposes that the patient has become convinced that he or she suffers from alcoholism, is not able to be a normal drinker, and therefore needs to choose abstinence. The more intelligent and cooperative the patient, the better the results will be.

Compliance

Even before the patient starts taking Antabuse the physician should explain that any time the therapy is discontinued (except following a planned conference involving the physician and other family members) it must be assumed that the patient, however unconsciously, is setting himself or herself up to start drinking some days, weeks, or months hence. Various possible scenarios should be discussed in advance. Thus, the patient who forgets one or more doses can be assured that he or she can start again as soon as the lapse is remembered, provided no drinking has occurred. This is discussed in the contract provided in Figure 1. Another standard excuse is that the patient was on a trip; the alcoholic should be warned always to carry the disulfiram with him or her. The issue of becoming

I, the undersigned, accept disulfiram (Antabuse®) therapy as a means of deterring myself from drinking alcoholic beverages. I recognize the dangers which are connected with drinking alcohol in any form, whether in beverages, cough mixtures, vitamin tonics or any other substance containing alcohol. I also realize that some other medications such as paraldehyde, metronidazole (Flagyl®) or phenytoin (Dilantin®) may cause problems. Therefore, any time a doctor is prescribing for me I will tell him that I am taking Antabuse so that he can avoid giving me any other drug that might cause a bad reaction.

I understand that the reaction which occurs if a person drinks after taking Antabuse is one involving much discomfort and sickness. This can include flushing of the face, sweating, throbbing in the head and neck, palpitations, breathing difficulty, nausea, vomiting, dizziness, blurring of vision and usually a significant fall in blood pressure. While fatalities are uncommon, death could occur in someone who drinks while taking Antabuse.

For these reasons, I will notify my family that I am taking this medication so that there will be no danger of my accidentally taking any alcohol. I will carry a card stating that I am on Antabuse. It will give recommendations for treatment of the reaction to alcohol should it occur. Should I forget to take a dose, I can safely take it as soon as I remember. However, I must never increase the dose unless my doctor advises it. If I experience any unusual and persisting feelings or symptoms, I will contact my doctor so that he can determine if they may be related to the medicine.

I fully understand that attempting to drink small amounts of alcohol while taking Antabuse is a dangerous method of trying to control excessive drinking. Not only are there potentially dangerous physical effects, but the long-term effect may be to provoke a significant degree of emotional depression.

I agree to inform Dr._____ in advance should I wish to stop taking the medication, so that this can be fully discussed and family members informed.

I understand that there is a possibility of a reaction which may last for many days (up to 14) after stopping Antabuse, should I take an alcoholic beverage thereafter. Should I want to commence taking Antabuse again, I have to wait until all alcohol is out of my system before doing so (usually 24 hours from the time of the last drink).

Name:_____

Date:_____

Witness:_____

Figure 1. Contract for Alcoholic Patients Taking Disulfiram

overconfident and believing that the medication is no longer required must also be discussed, as should special temptations, such as holidays, and celebrations, such as weddings.

Although metabolites of disulfiram can be detected in breath, blood, and urine, there is no simple office test that can confirm that a patient is taking the medication regularly and adequately. However, as explained, the ideal patient is taking the drug voluntarily to deter himself or herself from the temptation to drink.

Disulfiram under Coercion

A variety of special programs have successfully utilized disulfiram to help patients achieve sobriety or near-sobriety. Some have involved judges giving prisoners the option of taking disulfiram or serving time in jail. Some physicians and clinics and employee health services have used their authority to require patients to report for their dose of disulfiram five or more times a week. A similar approach may seem tempting for the family member who wishes to ban drinking by the alcoholic. Unfortunately, such people rarely have the dispassionate interest of the judge or the clinic nurse and emotional consequences tend to ensue.

Where the alcoholic is accepting disulfiram therapy and living with a spouse this author always recommends that the medication be taken very ostentatiously so that the spouse receives daily reassurance that drinking relapses are not likely to occur. The ideal arrangement is for the medication to be on the breakfast or dinner table and for the patient to take it very openly, without verbal comment, while the spouse is at the table.

Contracting

This author has found disulfiram therapy much more successful since, many years ago, introducing a written contract. This is discussed with the patient, and with other family members when possible, at length before the medication is started. Any physician or clinic can prepare a suitable contract, which should be signed and put in the chart. Both the patient and spouse should have copies to take with them. A suitable contract is published as Figure 1 and can be photocopied. All details of the contract should be gone over by the physician with the patient. This contract refers to the fact that the patient will carry an Antabuse card. These are obtainable from sales representatives of Ayerst Laboratories in the United States. On one side of the card the patient's name, address, and phone number are listed, along with those of the physician. It mentions emergency measures to counteract a DER. The other side of the card states, "I am on ANTABUSE (disulfiram) therapy. If I am disoriented, too ill to give a history, or unconscious, I may be having a serious Antabuse (disulfiram)-alcohol reaction. **Do not administer alcohol, paraldehyde, or any mixture with an alcohol content."**

Going over the details of this card and the contract can be crucial to the successful and effective use of the deterrent drug. Once the patient accepts the plan of disulfiram therapy and takes the prescription that has been written, this author is in the habit of providing the first dose, to be taken right there in the office. This is the best way to get the patient started and to cope with any initial doubts or second thoughts. On many occasions, after the patient has swallowed that first disulfiram tablet, he or she has been heard to say that the feeling is one of a sense of relief. The relief refers, of course, to the awareness that now he or she is unlikely to get involved in a drinking episode and to experience all the complications with which the alcoholic is so familiar.

Contraindications

The foregoing should make it clear that a primary contraindication is when the patient is not yet ready to contemplate a life without alcohol or is intellectually incapable of understanding the use of a deterrent drug. Young patients with a heavy history of impulse-ridden behavior generally do not do very well with a deterrent drug. While a history of schizophrenia is not an absolute contraindication, there is a possibility that disulfiram will more easily precipitate a psychotic reaction in such people. This may be due to the fact that disulfiram is a dopamine beta-hydroxylase inhibitor [7].

Severe myocardial disease may be a contraindication but one has to keep in mind the danger of the alternative, which is continued heavy alcoholic drinking. The same could be said of liver disease. However, liver function tests should certainly be on record so that they can be followed and the disulfiram stopped if there is evidence of worsening rather than improvement.

Pregnancy is an absolute contraindication in this author's opinion, since the safety of disulfiram in pregnancy has not been demonstrated. The alcoholic woman who is taking disulfiram should also be taking precautions against becoming pregnant. The alcoholic who is already pregnant should be helped to find sobriety using methods other than disulfiram.

There are some drugs alluded to in the contract that may cause problems with disulfiram. The administration of metronidazole (Flagyl) with disulfiram has led to psychotic reactions. Patients taking other drugs, such as isoniazid, phenytoin, and anticoagulants, may require smaller doses when on disulfiram. This is the reason that it is vital to emphasize to the patient, when discussing the contract, that all other physicians prescribing treatment must know about the disulfiram.

The importance of avoiding alcoholic beverages extends to medications containing alcohol. Men should be warned about aftershave lotions containing alcohol. The same would be true for alcohol skin rubs. The skin itself does not absorb alcohol, but alcohol vapor can be absorbed through the lungs.

Adverse Reactions

Dr. Ruth Fox, first medical director of the U.S. National Council on Alcoholism, was the first physician to use disulfiram in the United States. She was aware of the fact that complications occurred in as many as 10% of patients when 2 g a day was the accepted dose. However, after using it for 20 years and with over 3,000 patients at the modern dose level she commented that she had seen remarkably few side effects [3]. This was also the experience of others in giving disulfiram to healthy young men [10]. Thus, some of the complaints of alcoholic patients taking disulfiram may well represent their early difficulties in adjusting to life without alcohol.

Probably the most common initial reaction is that of mild drowsiness or lethargy. Indeed, some patients sleep better when they take their dose in the evenings. Complaints of headaches are sometimes voiced and, if these are severe, may justify a reduction in the total dosage. Disulfiram administration in the early days or weeks is sometimes associated with some degree of impotence in men, but continued complaints are rare if the patient is given appropriate assurance. The alternative of continued heavy drinking is more likely to be associated with sexual problems. Some patients complain of a metallic taste in their mouth and occasionally a spouse will comment about bad breath.

The adverse reactions most likely to require discontinuance of the drug are neuritis, psychoses, and hepatitis. Disulfiram neuritis is usually a peripheral neuropathy but the literature contains one or two cases of optic neuritis. Disulfiram psychosis usually presents as delirium, delirium with affective or paranoid features, or as acute manic, schizophrenic, or depressive syndromes without delirium [5]. Hepatitis is rare.

Some patients, on initiating disulfiram therapy, experience skin reactions that usually respond satisfactorily to administration of antihistamines.

Complications

The most frequent complication is undoubtedly that of the reaction to ethanol to be described below. As indicated, disulfiram may interfere with the metabolism of other drugs, such as phenytoin, isoniazid, warfarin, and metronidazole. Should formaldehyde or trichlorehtylene be inhaled, the presence of disulfiram will increase the toxicity.

Disulfiram-Ethanol Reactions

Ideally, the DER is to be avoided. Nevertheless, it can occur accidentally, due to lack of judgment, because of giving in to impulse and as a suicide attempt. Although hundreds of thousands of patients have taken millions of doses of disulfiram over more than 30 years, the literature contains only about 20 deaths. However, the DER does call for medical intervention in most cases.

The patient may experience flushing of the skin, particularly on the face. A throbbing headache is common. Respiratory distress and hyperventilation can be followed by respiratory depression. Complaints of pain in the chest can simulate a myocardial infarction and the patient may be aware of palpitations and be suffering from arrhythmias. Typically the blood pressure falls, there is sweating and sometimes nausea and vomiting. The patient may complain of apprehensive feelings, weakness, and dizziness and can display confusion. Severe reactions can go on to heart failure, unconsciousness, convulsions, and death.

Treatment is basically that of the treatment of shock, including the administration of oxygen. Ephedrine can be administered to maintain blood pressure. Ascorbic acid appears to give considerable relief when administered in an intravenous dose of 1 g. However, if the patient does benefit from ascorbic acid, for example in the emergency room of a hospital, continued observation is essential since the signs and symptoms of DER can recur within an hour or two. Further administration of ascorbic acid is indicated then.

If the patient is vomiting and can get rid of any alcohol remaining in the stomach this is bound to be beneficial since this will mean less acetaldehyde buildup. In some instances gastric lavage may be indicated. The experimental use of a drug that inhibits the liver metabolism of ethanol (4-methylpyrazole) has indicated that it will counteract a DER [6]. However, this drug is not yet available for administration to humans in the United States.

The Absent Disulfiram-Ethanol Reaction

From time to time one hears of the patient who allegedly ingests disulfiram but goes on drinking. In the first place, it is important to realize that a mere dose or two is not likely to sensitize the patient to ethanol at once. Second is the question of compliance. Some patients are remarkably adept at appearing to swallow disulfiram while keeping the tablet in the mouth for later disposal. Indeed, some of the clinics involved in coercive programs discussed above are in the habit of crushing the tablets and giving them as a liquid suspension.

Other forms of noncompliance can also occur. One family doctor watched a patient apparently swallow disulfiram regularly without developing any alcohol sensitivity. The patient was a die maker who had learned to make tablets that resembled disulfiram out of aspirin. The patient's cunning was only discovered when the doctor tasted a tablet.

Some patients allegedly have been able to avoid much in the way of a DER by loading themselves with huge doses (10 g or more) of ascorbic acid before consuming alcohol.

Anecdotes exist concerning patients who allegedly have successively less and less severe DERs as they go on drinking. There is some scientific evidence to support this [9] and of course reaching higher levels of ethanol intoxication will provide a degree of anesthesia to lessen the impact of the DER itself. These examples simply serve to emphasize that disulfiram is a drug that should be taken voluntarily and with full compliance in order to avoid the temptation of the first drink.

Nonoral Disulfiram

In the United States, disulfiram is only available in the oral form. However, in some countries physicians have experimented with disulfiram in injectable or depot forms. In the case of the latter, sterile tablets are implanted under the skin. The results suggest that it is unlikely that this form of disulfiram administration will be introduced in the United States. Sterile abscesses may form and the tablets are sometimes extruded. Moreover, significant blood levels do not appear to be maintained. Where success has been claimed it is primarily due to the fear of a reaction. Thus, implanted patients told that they would remain sensitive for 6 months will often wait 6 months before trying to start drinking again.

Other Sensitizing Drugs and Substances

Citrated calcium carbimide is available in Canada and some other parts of the world as Temposil. It, too, leads to an acetaldehyde-poisoning reaction.

Some, but not all, people who are taking metronadizole (Flagyl) have some kind of sensitivity reaction when they drink alcoholic beverages. This is not a reliable enough complication to justify the use of metronadizole as a deterrent drug, however. Recent reports indicate that a disulfiramlike reaction can occur on consuming alcohol for several days after treatment with moxalactam, cefamandole, or cefoperazone [1].

Some substances used in industry are also able to interfere with the metabolism of alcohol, such as dimethylformamide [8]. Sensitivity reactions have also been described in subjects who drink alcohol after eating the coprinus (inky cap) mushroom [8].

At the present time, disulfiram is the only approved drug available in the United States for helping patients to be afraid to drink.

REFERENCES

1. Buening, M. K., Wold, J. S., Israel, K. S., and Kammer, R. B. Disulfiramlike reaction to β-lactams. *J.A.M.A.* 245:2027, 1981.

2. Ewing, J. A., Rouse, B. A., and Pellizzari, E. D. Alcohol sensitivity and ethnic background. *Am. J. Psychiatry* 131:206–210, 1974.

3. Fox, R. Disulfiram-alcohol side effects. *J.A.M.A.* 204:179–180, 1968.

4. Hald, J., and Jacobsen, E. A drug sensitising the organism to ethyl alcohol. *Lancet* 255:1001–1004, 1948.

5. Liddon, S. C., and Satran, R. Disulfiram (Antabuse) psychosis. *Am. J. Psychiatry* 123:1284–1289, 1967.

6. Lindros, K. O., Stowell, A., Pikkarainen, P., and Salaspuro, M. Treatment of the disulfiram (Antabuse)-alcohol reaction by 4-methylpyrazole. *Alc. Clin. Exp. Res.*, 5:159, 1981.

7. Major, L. F., Lerner, P., Ballenger, J. C., Brown, G. L., Goodwin, F. K., and Lovenberg, W. Dopamine-β-hydroxylase in the cerebrospinal fluid: Relationship to disulfiram-induced psychosis. *Biol. Psychiatry* 14:337–344, 1979.

8. Myers, R. D., and Ewing, J. A. Aversive factors in alcohol drinking in humans and animals. *Pharmac. Biochem. Behav.* 13(Suppl. 1):269–277, 1980.

9. Peachey, J. E., Zilm, D. H., and Cappell, H. Burning off the Antabuse: Fact or fiction? *Lancet* 1(8226):943–944, 1981.

10. Silver, D. F., Ewing, J. A., Rouse, B. A., and Mueller, R. A. Responses to disulfiram in healthy young men: A double-blind study. *J. Stud. Alcohol* 40:1003–1013, 1979.

87

JOEL SOLOMON, MD, State University of New York Downstate Medical
Center, Brooklyn, New York

THE ROLE OF DRUG THERAPIES IN THE CONTEXT OF ALCOHOLISM

THE USE OF PSYCHOACTIVE medication for the treatment of the chronic phase of alcoholism has been the subject of research, speculation, and controversy for many years. Although there have been many studies that purport to demonstrate the effectiveness of psychoactive medication in this patient population, methodological problems in most of these studies prevent any general conclusions from being drawn. Viamontes in 1972 [36] reviewed 89 British and American studies that attempted to evaluate the effectiveness of psychotropic medication in the rehabilitation of chronic alcoholics, and found the majority of these studies to be uncontrolled and representing the clinical impressions of the investigators rather than objectively valid, research-based evaluations. He concluded that no drug has been proven better than placebos in the treatment of chronic alcoholics. Similar conclusions were also drawn in earlier reviews by Ditman [10] and Benor and Ditman [3].

These conclusions should not imply that there are no alcoholics who can be helped by the use of psychoactive medication. Quite the contrary, there are alcoholics who suffer a variety of specific psychiatric disorders for which psychoactive medication is clearly indicated [34]. In these, as in any other psychiatric patients, medication is often indicated and should be prescribed judiciously and monitored

---

Joel Solomon, MD, Clinical Associate Professor, and Director, Division of Alcoholism and Drug Dependence, State University of New York Downstate Medical Center, Brooklyn, New York.

closely, particularly if the patient continues to drink. The use of medication in these patients has been demonstrated to be effective if (1) the patient's psychiatric condition is carefully diagnosed, and (2) treatment with psychoactive medication is based upon this diagnosis [21]. On the other hand, the evidence implies that as a routine aspect of treatment for alcoholic patients, psychoactive medication appears to be generally ineffective and, in most cases, probably harmful.

The absence of a clear-cut approach to use of psychotropic medication in the alcoholic is due to many factors. One of the major stumbling blocks has been a lack of attention paid to the diagnosis of psychiatric problems. Too often medication is prescribed under the assumption that it is being used to treat a patient's alcoholism, when in reality it may be controlling psychiatric symptoms. The converse also occurs when medication is withheld in an alcoholic who may also be psychiatrically impaired, under the assumption that psychotropic medication is ineffective in the treatment of alcoholics. (Treatment of the psychiatrically impaired is covered in Section VI.) This chapter addresses the use of medication in long-term treatment of the nonpsychiatrically impaired alcoholic.

A wide range of medications have at various times purported to be effective in the treatment of alcoholism, and although some continue to be used, evidence regarding their effectiveness remains scanty. There are, additionally, a number of potential hazards that should also be considered when prescribing any medication to a recovering alcoholic patient.

1. Alcoholic patients stimulate a variety of negative attitudes in physicians, which may subsequently affect the way they are treated [6]. To prescribe medication and think that the patient's alcoholism is being treated is illusory and often a means for the physician to deal with his or her own negative attitude. Medication alone is no treatment for alcoholism.

2. The alcoholic patient has often relied on drugs as an attempt to solve a variety of life problems. The prescription of medication continues to reinforce the attitude of chemical problem solving, often at the expense of developing new skills or strengthening old ones.

3. The prescription of medication may give the alcoholic the sense that the alcoholism is being treated, rendering therapy, Alcoholics Anonymous, or other treatment unnecessary. Medication, particularly among patients in whom denial and rationalization are active and strong, can seriously undermine the treatment of alcoholism.

4. The possibility of a slip is always present, and the risk of potentiating the effects of alcohol with other central nervous system depressants should be a consideration.

5. Risk of abuse of and dependency on a variety of psychoactive medication should be of real concern to the prescribing physician. To substitute one dependency for another can in no way be construed as treatment, and is invariably countertherapeutic.

6. Psychoactive medication often has side effects to which the alcoholic may be particularly sensitive. Development of these side effects may seriously undermine the physician's credibility with the patient and damage one of the essentials of treatment, the relationship.

7. The alcoholic may be unreliable about dosage and the times medication is to be taken, particularly if he or she is drinking. Compliance in this group of patients is notoriously poor.

8. If psychoactive medication is prescribed, indications for its prescription should be very clear. The prescribing physician must differentiate between treatment of alcoholism and treatment of its complications.

9. Members of AA often have strongly negative attitudes concerning the prescription of medication, particularly tranquilizers. If the prescription of these drugs risks putting patients in conflict with their AA group, this might be yet another mitigating factor against prescribing medication.

ANTIANXIETY AGENTS, MINOR TRANQUILIZERS, SEDATIVE-HYPNOTICS

The most heated aspect of the controversy surrounding medication is in the use of antianxiety agents, minor tranquilizers, and sedative-hypnotics in the long-term treatment of alcoholism. There is little question that these drugs are effective to treat acute withdrawal syndrome, reduction of anxiety, and induction of sleep. As a result, their use in the treatment of alcoholism has been based upon the hypothesis that alcoholics are anxious and have a variety of sleep disturbances that either lead to or contribute to their drinking. It follows that if these symptoms were relieved, the alcoholic would no longer have a need to drink.

The other side of the argument is that to substitute another drug for alcohol is merely to cross-addict the alcoholic but to do nothing to alter patterns of coping behavior that may have led to or propagated the alcoholism.

The final question, however, remains: Is there any real role for these medications in the long-term treatment of alcoholism? This controversy is based not only on theoretical grounds, but on rather practical ones as well, considering that over 65% of physicians polled via questionnaire used some form of tranquilizer in treating their alcoholic patients [16].

In Viamontes' review paper [36], if one looks only at the 43 studies that evaluate this class of drugs, there were 27 positive and five negative results in the uncontrolled studies, and no positive and 11 negative results in the controlled group. It is particularly striking that among the controlled studies, none showed benefit.

Most of the early studies cited in the literature are based upon the short-term (6 weeks or less) effects of drugs, and some of them do demonstrate improvement at least for the immediate postwithdrawal period [15, 27]. Bowman and Thirmann

[4] compared chlordiazepoxide, oxazepam, and a placebo in a 6-week double-blind trial, and found the three drugs essentially equally effective and better than the placebo as measured by symptomatic improvement and a physicians' global rating scale. Studies such as this, although interesting from the perspective of symptom relief during the early stages of treatment, reveal little concerning the long-term treatment of alcoholism. There is, in fact, some evidence that the total reduction of anxiety during the early phase of treatment can actually be detrimental to the achievement and maintenance of abstinence. Shaffer et al. [32] described a study in which chlordiazepoxide, as might be expected, was significantly more effective than a placebo in reducing anxiety and craving for alcohol. While on weekend passes, however, more patients on chlordiazepoxide drank or failed to return to the patient unit than those on the placebo who, although they craved alcohol, were able to remain abstinent. Patients on chlordiazepoxide, on the other hand, described themselves as feeling so good that they no longer felt alcoholism was a problem, and thus began drinking. Hoff [15], however, found that his group of patients treated with chlordiazepoxide showed a significant improvement and willingness to explore personal problems over a control group. Unfortunately, his control group received no placebo medication, which represents a major methodological problem. The question is clearly not a simple one.

Kissin [21] also felt that there are indeed some alcoholics who can benefit from the use of these medications, particularly during the early phases of treatment. This conclusion was based upon the studies of Kissin [21], Ditman [10], and Rosenberg [31], which demonstrated that the use of chlordiazepoxide, although not necessarily effective as a specific treatment, did keep alcoholic patients engaged in treatment. For example, in Rosenberg's study [31], during the first 20-week follow-up period, the chlordiazepoxide group (as compared to the disulfiram, multivitamin, or no medication group), had the highest retention rate. Of perhaps more importance was their finding that after this initial period, differences between groups were lost.

Baekeland and Lundwall [1], in reviewing the literature, also found anxiety and depression among the characteristics of those alcoholics who dropped out of treatment, and when these patients were given chlordiazepoxide or oxazepam they were less likely to drop out than nonmedication groups or patients on other medications. Among the conclusions drawn from this extensive review is that there will be a group of patients with symptoms that strongly contribute to dropping out of treatment. In this group of patients, major emphasis should be placed on rapid symptom relief, and medication should not be withheld where it might be of assistance. Consequently, remaining in treatment appears to be related to improvement [12].

Kissin has been one of the most vocal proponents for the careful use of medication. He has conducted several large studies that report better rates of improvement in patients who were treated with chlordiazepoxide than either other drugs or placebo. The rationale for the use of medication was described as follows:

In the alcoholic in whom significant physical dependence has developed, persistent withdrawal symptomatology characterized by tremulousness, anxiety, depression, and insomnia, may persist for periods of up to 6 months or more after the cessation of drinking. This symptom complex, which the alcoholic knows can be at least temporarily relieved by alcohol, acts as a consistent reinforcement, both physical and psychological, to the underlying predisposing pathology which drove him to drink in the first place. Accordingly, it would seem rational and experimental evidence tends to support this view that to the extent that one can help to control this withdrawal symptomatology, one can help the alcoholic achieve and maintain sobriety. [20]

Fabre et al. [11], in an open study, lent support to this position in finding that Triazolam, a benzodiazepine, was highly effective in reducing symptoms of insomnia and anxiety in a group of alcoholics during the early stages of recovery. The authors, however, acknowledge that double-blind studies are clearly needed, as well as long-term follow-up, before any general conclusions can be drawn. Ditman [10] also concluded that drugs may have some value, although limited, in the symptomatic treatment of alcoholics, but there was no evidence to support their use in the treatment of alcoholism generally. The role of the symptoms of the protracted period of abstinence in contributing to relapse should not be minimized. Begleiter and Porjesz [2] have recently described a subacute withdrawal syndrome involving central nervous system (CNS) alterations that persist for long periods of time subsequent to administration and removal of ethanol. If this syndrome does indeed contribute to relapse, understanding how this happens would obviously be of great importance. Related to this would be the role of medication in treating this specific syndrome, and thereby reducing the risk of relapse, if relapse, at least in some patients, were in some way based on a treatable protracted abstinence syndrome.

In addition to the absence of carefully controlled long-term studies, sedative-hypnotic and tranquilizing medication also has specific problems associated with it. For example, there are some recent animal studies that indicate that diazepam acts to increase the tendency to self-administer alcohol in a free-choice situation. Several control groups did not manifest this behavior [8].

There is also some evidence that although sedative-hypnotics are effective in relieving insomnia, tolerance develops and rebound insomnia ensues with regular use [18].

The question, however, remains unanswered: Are there any alcoholic patients who might benefit from the judicious use of antianxiety medication during the rehabilitation phase of treatment? The evidence is clear that these drugs are not a routine treatment for alcoholism. There are no conclusive studies demonstrating that alcoholics as a group can benefit in any way from the use of these drugs in routine, long-term treatment. It appears, however, that there may be a highly select, small group of alcoholics in whom anxiety acts as a major inhibition to treatment and a cause of relapse. Although there are no long-term, controlled studies that demonstrate the effectiveness of medication in these patients, clinicians are well aware of their existence. These are patients in whom a small amount of medication will relieve enough anxiety to allow treatment to proceed, but will not totally obliterate discomfort and thereby eliminate the motivation to continue treatment.

Unfortunately, there have been no studies that specifically look at the effect of medication in these particular patients. Most, if not all, studies conducted in this area have examined groups of patients without consideration for specific patient characteristics. The only attempt at identifying a subgroup of patients was Kissin's study [21], which found that if the level of anxiety was used as a criterion for treatment with chlordiazepoxide, patients receiving medication did significantly better. Clearly, more studies of this kind need replication in a placebo-controlled, double-blind model.

The choice of specific tranquilizing agent should be of some concern when treating the alcoholic. Based on efficacy and safety, the benzodiazepines would be the drugs of choice. Concerning the specific benzodiazepines, oxazepan and lorazepan are both rapidly metabolized to inactive metabolites after repeated use, and less frequently cause drowsiness due to accumulation of the drug. Hepatic function may also be a consideration when prescribing, since these two drugs are not metabolized by the liver.

ANTIDEPRESSANTS

Literature on alcoholism and affective disorders has been reviewed in many places and from many perspectives. Conclusions generally drawn from most of these studies are that alcoholics are frequently depressed, and their depressions seem similar to those seen in primary affective disorders [13]. This depression, seen so often in alcoholics, has been the justification for prescribing antidepressant medication. Unfortunately, the issue remains unclear. For example, if the alcoholism were an attempt to medicate a depression, one might expect that antidepressant medication, by relieving the depression, would also render the underlying need to drink unnecessarily.

On the other hand, if depression were the result rather than the cause of the alcoholism, one would expect little relief of either depression or alcoholism from treatment with antidepressant medication, but rather lifting of depression if alcohol consumption were stopped. This issue of alcohol-induced depression is particularly important, especially if treatment is to be based upon it. Mayfield and Montgomery [25] described a depressive syndrome of chronic intoxication manifested by profound depression following moderately extended periods of intoxication. Tamarin and Mendelson [35] also found "prolonged drinking led to progressive depression, guilt, and psychic pain." These conclusions were reached in a controlled setting where chronic intoxication was found to have a depressive effect upon the subject with rapid relief of symptoms barely recalled when the drinking ceased. Obviously, antidepressant medication would be of little value in these alcohol-induced depressions, which probably represent the majority of depressions in alcoholics seen in clinical practice.

In Viamontes' [36] review of the literature, he cited 16 studies that evaluated the use of antidepressants in alcoholics. Once again, the results are striking. Of the uncontrolled studies, there were seven successes and two failures. Of the controlled studies, no successes and seven failures.

Ditman [10] described a double-blind study in which 116 alcoholic outpatients were treated with imipramine and 79 with a placebo. Although the study was a short one, at the end of 3 weeks there was no significant difference in rapid dropout rate. In another study by Ditman [9], there was no difference in abstinence rate after 6 months between a group of patients on amitriptyline and a group taking a placebo. Others have been equally unimpressd by the effect of antidepressants in the treatment of alcoholism. For example, in a double-blind evaluative study of amitriptyline there was no superiority of this drug over a placebo found in either maintenance in treatment or promotion of abstinence [7].

Kissin and Gross [22] reported on several studies in which a variety of drugs and combinations were compared. Among their findings was that imipramine alone was less effective than a placebo in treating alcoholics. However, they also found that chlordiazepoxide plus imipramine was more effective than either drug alone or a placebo.

Antidepressants clearly have no place in the routine treatment of alcoholism. However, if the alcoholic is indeed suffering from a primary affective disorder that is clinically apparent once the patient becomes abstinent, then antidepressant medication would be indicated as with any other depressed patient.

Several authors have explored the combined use of minor tranquilizers and antidepressant medication. Kissin and Gross [22] reviewed many of these studies, which were largely uncontrolled and with a wide range of improvement rates that made it difficult to draw any general conclusions.

In addition to its role in the treatment of depression, imipramine has been described as an effective agent in the treatment of panic disorder [23]. A recent report by Quitkin and Rabkin [29] described several neurotic disorders, including panic, that were seen in alcoholic patients and successfully treated with imipramine. Once again, careful evaluation of the primary disorder before institution of medication is essential.

LITHIUM

In 1949, Cade [5] published the first account of lithium being used in the treatment of mania. It has, subsequently, become the treatment of choice in manic depressive illness, and has been tried in a variety of other behavioral disorders, including alcoholism.

Among the earliest reports of successful use of lithium in an alcoholic population was that of Kline et al. [24], who found that relapse among a group of chronic and periodic alcoholics was significantly reduced during the time these patients were maintained on lithium. Alleviation of depression did not appear to be the primary factor contributing to improvement of the alcoholism, since both the lithium and control groups showed significant improvement in depression.

Other studies [26] have also shown lithium to be effective in reducing drinking and its resultant morbidity in depressed alcoholics. They also found that patients treated with a placebo, rather than lithium, had significantly greater alcohol-related morbidity if they were depressed. This evidence would support the hypothesis that depression, at least in some alcoholics, can be an important factor in the persistence of drinking behavior, and that lithium can help to reduce both the depression as well as the drinking.

A subsequent report by Reynolds et al. [30] described a prospective double-blind, placebo-controlled study of 1 year's duration, which showed lithium to have a powerful influence in reducing drinking and alcohol-induced incapacity in depressed alcoholics.

These, as well as other studies, indicate that lithium may indeed be an effective treatment in a specific subgroup of depressed alcoholics. There is little evidence, however, that lithium is an effective treatment for alcoholism when depression is not present. Although some animal studies indicate that lithium may decrease voluntary alcohol consumption in rats [14], the evidence for this in humans is scanty.

A recent report by Judd et al. [17] attempted to explore this phenomenon. They concluded that lithium may exert an effect upon the alcohol experience by specifically attenuating the alcohol-induced high and craving. They also found this effect to be pronounced in alcoholics who have had a major depressive illness, but were not clinically depressed at the time of the study. Their results would neither confirm nor refute the conclusion of Merry et al. [26] that improvement in depression is the mechanism by which lithium modifies the drinking behavior of alcoholics.

Thus, lithium may indeed be an effective treatment for alcoholism found in a subgroup of patients with a primary affective disorder, and perhaps by some other mechanism may reduce the high and craving for alcohol, although more controlled and reproducible studies are necessary before this assumption can be justified. At this point, however, there is no evidence to justify the use of lithium in routine treatment of alcoholism.

MAJOR TRANQUILIZERS

Major tranquilizers have been used in the treatment of both the withdrawal and recovery phase of alcoholism with little indication as to benefit. Ditman [10], in reviewing studies done on phenothiazines, notes that among controlled trials there was no evidence that any of these drugs were of assistance in long-term treatment of alcoholism.

If major tranquilizers have any place in treating alcoholic patients, it is among those who may also be suffering from schizophrenia. However, the interaction between these two conditions is far from clear. Kesselman et al. [19] have recently outlined the pharmacologic treatment of this group of patients with a combined diagnosis that would include both a major and a minor tranquilizer, at least during the acute and subacute phases. The problem with the phenothiazines, as with so many other drugs in the treatment of alcoholism, is that they have been used in too indiscriminate a fashion; on the other hand, if patients are carefully selected, these drugs may prove useful. Kissin [20] was a particularly strong proponent of using patient characteristics to determine treatment. He emphasized the importance of psychiatric diagnosis and specific treatment, including medication, based upon that diagnosis. Other than in certain psychiatric instances, major tranquilizers have no place in the treatment of alcoholism per se.

Lysergic Acid Diethylamide

Lysergic acid diethylamide (LSD) is one of the many therapeutic drugs that has generated a great deal of enthusiasm based upon several uncontrolled studies.

Smart and Storm [32] critically reviewed the studies that purported to demonstrate LSD as a useful adjunct to treatment, and found the majority of these studies to be characterized by inadequate controls, few consistently applied pretreatment and posttreatment criteria, and poor follow-up. They concluded that there is no solid evidence available that showed LSD to be effective in the treatment of alcoholism.

LSD has all but fallen by the wayside as a treatment for alcoholism. Its use has been summarized by Mottin:

> The recent reports reveal the usual support from occasional uncontrolled studies, and the rate controlled study with negative results; the balance of controlled studies continue to challenge any support of a pharmacological effect. The assumption that a single overwhelmingly transcendental experience might benefit the alcoholic has not been disproved so much as has simply the assumption that an active drug contributes uniquely to such treatment. [28]

CONCLUSION

There appear to be few, if any, controlled studies that indicate that the use of any medication prevents relapse among chronic alcoholics who are in remission. On the other hand, there is no evidence that withholding medication has a more positive result than prescribing medication.

The difficulty, at least in part, lies in the lack of controlled studies that confirm the value of medication among alcoholics. Perhaps of even more importance would be delineating specific subgroups of alcoholic populations in whom appropriate medication might be effective. Lacking conclusive evidence, clinicians will have to use their best judgment, realizing the shortcomings and problems associated with the use of medication in alcoholics, and understanding that the vast majority should be treated without the use of psychoactive drugs.

REFERENCES

1. Baekeland, F., and Lundwall, L. Engaging the alcoholic in treatment and keeping him there. In: *The Biology of Alcoholism*, Kissin, B. and Begleiter, H. (eds.). Plenum: New York, 1977.

2. Begleiter, H., and Porjesz, B. Persistence of a "subacute withdrawal syndrome" following chronic ethanol intake. *Drug Alcohol Depen.* 4:353-357, 1979.

3. Benor, D., and Ditman, K. S. Tranquilizers in the management of alcoholics: A review of the literature to 1964. *J. Clin. Pharmacol.* 7:17-25, 1967.

4. Bowman, E. H., and Thimann, J. Treatment of alcoholism in the subacute stage. *Dis. Nerv. Sys.* 27:342-346, 1966.

5. Cade, J. F. Lithium salts in the treatment of psychotic excitement. *Med. J. Aust.* 2:349-352, 1949.

6. Chappel, J. N., and Schnoll, S. H. Physician attitudes: Effect on the treatment of chemically dependent patients. *J.A.M.A.* 237:2318-2319, 1977.

7. Charnoff, S. Long-term treatment of alcoholism with amitriptyline and emylcamate: A double-blind evaluation. *Q. J. Stud. Alcohol* 28:289-294, 1967.

8. Deutsch, J. A., and Walton, N. Y. Diazepam maintenance of alcohol preference during alcohol withdrawal. *Science* 198:307-309, 1977.

9. Ditman, K. S. Evaluation of drugs in the treatment of alcoholics. *Q. J. Stud. Alcohol* 22(Suppl.):107-116, 1961.

10. Ditman, K. S. Review and evaluation of current drug therapies in alcoholism. *Psychosom. Med.* 28:667-677, 1966.

11. Fabre, L. F., Gainey, A., Kemple, S., McLendon, D. M., and Metzler, C. M. Pilot open-label study of triazolam in the treatment of insomnia following alcohol withdrawal. *J. Stud. Alcohol* 38:2188-2192, 1977.

12. Gerard, D. L., and Saenger, G. *Outpatient Treatment of Alcoholism.* University of Toronto Press: Toronto, 1966.

13. Gibson, S., and Becker, J. Alcoholism and depression. *Q. J. Stud. Alcohol* 34:400-408, 1973.

14. Ho, A. K. S., and Tsai, C. S. Lithium and alcohol preference and withdrawal. *Ann. N.Y. Acad. Sci.* 273:371-377, 1976.

15. Hoff, E. C. The use of pharmacological adjuncts in the psychotherapy of alcoholics. *Q. J. Stud. Alcohol* (Supp 1)22:138-150, 1961.

16. Jones, R. W., and Helrich, A. R. Treatment of alcoholism by physicians in private practice. *Q. J. Stud. Alcohol* 33:117-131, 1972.

17. Judd, L. L., Hubbard, B., Janowsky, D. S., et al. Lithium carbonate and ethanol-induced "highs" in normal subjects. *Arch. Gen. Psychiatry* 34:463-467, 1977.

18. Kales, A., Bixler, E. D., Tan, T. L., and Scharf, M. B. Chronic hypnotic drug use, ineffectiveness, drug-withdrawal insomnia, and dependence. *J.A.M.A.* 227:513, 1974.

19. Kesselman, M., Solomon, J., Beaudett, M., and Thornton, B. Alcoholism and schizophrenia. In: *Alcoholism and Clinical Psychiatry*, Solomon, J. (ed.). Plenum: New York. In press.

20. Kissin, B. Medical management of the alcoholic patient. In: *Biology of Alcoholism* (Vol. 5), Kissin, B. and Begleiter, H. (eds.). Plenum: New York, 1977.

21. Kissin, B. Patient characteristics and treatment specificity in alcoholism: Recent advances in the study of alcoholism. *Ex. Med.* Series No. 407:110-122, 1977.

22. Kissin, B., and Gross, M. M. Drug therapy in alcoholism. *Am. J. Psychiatry* 125:69-79, 1968.

23. Klein, D. F., and Fink, M. Psychiatric reaction patterns to imipramine. *Am. J. Psychiatry* 119:432-438, 1962.

24. Kline, N. S., Wren, J. C., Cooper, T. B., et al. Evaluation of lithium therapy in chronic and periodic alcoholism. *Am. J. Med. Sci.* 268:15-22, 1974.

25. Mayfield, D. G., and Montgomery, D. Alcoholism, alcohol intoxication and suicide attempts. *Arch. Gen. Psychiatry* 27(3):349-353, 1972.

26. Merry, J., Reynolds, C. M., Bailey, J., and Cooper, A. Prophylactic treatment of alcoholism by lithium carbonate. *Lancet* 2:481-482, 1976.

27. Mitchell, E. H. Rehabilitation of the alcoholic. *Q. J. Stud. Alcohol (Supp. 1)* 22:93-100, 1961.

28. Mottin, J. L. Dry-induced attenuation of alcohol consumption. *Q. J. Stud. Alcohol* 34:444-472, 1973.

29. Quitkin, F., and Rabkin, J. G. Hidden psychiatric diagnosis in the alcoholic. In: *Alcoholism and Clinical Psychiatry*, Solomon, J. (ed.). Plenum: New York. In press.

30. Reynolds, C. M., Merry, J., and Coppen, A. Prophylactic treatment of alcoholism by lithium carbonate: An initial report. *Alcoholism: Clin. Exp. Res.* 1:109, 1977.

31. Rosenberg, C. M. Drug maintenance in the outpatient treatment of chronic alcoholism. *Arch. Gen. Psychiatry* 30:373-377, 1974.

32. Shaffer, J. W., Freinek, W. R., Wolf, S., et al. A controlled evaluation of chlordiazepoxide (Librium) in the treatment of convalescing alcoholics. *J. Nerv. Ment. Dis.* 137:494-507, 1963.

33. Smart, R. G., and Storm, T. The efficacy of LSD in the treatment of alcoholism. *Q. J. Stud. Alcohol* 25:333-338, 1964.

34. Solomon, J. Psychiatric characteristics of alcoholics. In: *The Biology of Alcoholism* (Vol. 7), Kissin, B. and Begleiter, H. (eds.). Plenum: New York. In press.

35. Tamerin, J. S., and Mendelson, J. H. The psychodynamics of chronic inebriation: Observations of alcoholics during the process of drinking in an experimental group setting. *Am. J. Psychiatry* 125:886-899, 1969.

36. Viamontes, J. A. Review of drug effectiveness in the treatment of alcoholism. *Am. J. Psychiatry* 128:1570-1571, 1972.

88

OVIDE F. POMERLEAU, PhD, University of Connecticut School of Medicine, Farmington, Connecticut

CURRENT BEHAVIORAL THERAPIES IN THE TREATMENT OF ALCOHOLISM

CURRENT BEHAVIORAL treatment of problem drinking and alcoholism is based on operant conditioning and social learning concepts. In this framework excessive drinking is seen as a behavior that is under the control of antecedent stimuli and consequent events (reinforcers), and the task of remediation and therapy is thus one of modifying or managing various environmental events to engender abstinence or reduced drinking and to improve social functioning [17]. The behavioral point of view has led to a more critical examination of many of the current assumptions and practices in the treatment of alcohol problems: Among the concepts that have been brought into question, mainly because of lack of scientific support, have been the disease model (particularly when applied indiscriminantly over the entire spectrum of alcohol abuse) and universal mandatory abstinence as the sole goal of treatment [14, 26]. Behavioral methodology has also helped raise standards in patient assessment and program evaluation; among the chief recommendations are (1) the establishment of pretreatment baseline measures, (2) assessment of function in several life areas, (3) prolonged posttreatment follow-up, and (4) corroboration of self-reports through informants as well as by objective measures [29].

The present chapter reviews some of the recent developments in the behavioral treatment of problem drinking and alcoholism. Three groups of techniques are differentiated: those in a context in which the object of therapy is (1) abstinence or (2) moderation or (3) those in which the emphasis is on preventing relapse. While the present survey is, of necessity, selective and makes no claim to being comprehensive, the procedures described are representative of what behavior modification therapy has to offer.

TECHNIQUES FOR ABSTINENCE

Aversive Conditioning

Punishment of drinking behavior and the pairing of sights, smells, and tastes associated with drinking with aversive stimuli in Pavlovian conditioning are the oldest of the behavioral techniques—a tradition that started more than 50 years ago with the apparent success of the Soviet physician N. V. Kantorovich in treating alcoholics. Despite the fact that current behavioral practice deemphasizes aversive procedures, the association between the two remains strong among nonbehaviorists.

Although initial reports on electrical aversive conditioning were quite encouraging, present better-controlled studies have failed to support the early claims. For example, Hedberg and Campbell [10] compared shock avoidance with behavioral procedures using positive reinforcement and found it to have the highest dropout rate and to be the least effective. Similar findings have been reported by Miller et al. [21] in which 30 chronic alcoholics were randomly assigned to a procedure in which they received 500 trials of escape training over 10 days. Painful dermal shocks were paired with sips of alcohol; the shock could be terminated by spitting out the alcohol. There were two control groups—one in which a shock of low intensity was paired with sips of alcohol and one in which group confrontation therapy was provided—in an attempt to partition out attention placebo and expectancy factors. No statistically significant differences were found among the three procedures in posttreatment alcohol consumption using an analogue taste test or in attitudes toward drinking. The data were interpreted as suggesting that subject selection, therapeutic instructions, and expectancy may be more important in producing a favorable outcome than aversive conditioning per se. In another recent study, Vogler, Compton, and Weissbach [33] found that short-term positive changes in drinking rate observed across different treatment groups could not be attributed to any single component of their treatment package, including electrical aversion. Finally, Wilson et al. [35] found no support for the widespread presumption that dermal shock establishes a conditioned aversion to ethanol—*ad libitum* drinking (in a laboratory test where consumption was neither encouraged nor discouraged) remained unchanged following conditioning.

The current status of chemical aversion using nausea-inducing substances such as emetine is less clear. The procedure first developed by Voegtlin in 1940 continues to be used: An emetine-pilocarpine-ephedrine mixture is administered intravenously; at the earliest sign of nausea the patient is given a drink of preferred beverage to smell and to taste, with additional drinks given over a 30-minute to 1-hour period as nausea and vomiting persist; booster sessions are given to patients whenever they feel a return of the urge to drink. Of over 4,000 patients treated in the first 13 years at Shadel Hospital, 44% remained totally abstinent from 2 to 13 years [12]. Similar results have been reported in a recent study by Wiens et al. [34] at Raleigh Hills Hospital, with 63% of 261 alcoholic patients treated remaining abstinent at 1 year. In an attempt to explain why these techniques are not in wider use, Nathan and Goldman [24] observed that patients who choose such treatment not only have to be highly motivated to use such an approach to overcome their problem but they may also be the ones who have more to lose by continued excessive drinking, in that they tend to come from a higher socioeconomic group. Moreover, Nathan and Goldman point out that chemical aversion is only one component of treatment in Shadel and Raleigh Hills Hospitals; the potential benefits of rehabilitation, personal counseling, family therapy, Alcoholics Anonymous, and a warm, supportive milieu cannot be ignored.

Contingency Management in the Hospital Setting

Over the past 10 years, a variety of innovative therapeutic interventions based on operant conditioning concepts have been explored at Baltimore city hospitals. For example, hospital employees were referred to treatment in response to work decrements and absenteeism caused by excessive drinking. Treatment involved being given the opportunity to work, contingent on taking Antabuse; failure to report to the hospital's alcoholism clinic on a given day resulted in no work for that day and thus, no pay. For the 21 employees who were treated in this program, absenteeism dropped significantly, from 9.8% prior to treatment to 1.7% during treatment [27]. When the Antabuse requirement was eliminated, absenteeism went back up to 6.7%, suggesting that the contingency, rather than identification or threat by the employer, was the effective component of therapy. The study also points out that the maintenance of treatment benefits cannot simply be left to chance but requires long-term contingencies and management. In a similar approach with 20 problem drinkers, monetary deposits were returned contingent on taking Antabuse at a clinic over a prescribed period of time (a minimum of 3 months); complete abstinence for 2 months was obtained in

95% of the patients and for 6 months in 40% [3]. The same techniques were also used with 25 heroin addicts who were alcoholics: Patients who received methadone contingent upon ingesting Antabuse spent significantly fewer days drinking and had fewer drug-related arrests than did patients who received methadone whether or not they took Antabuse [13].

In related work, Griffiths et al. [9] have demonstrated that chronic alcoholic inpatients will voluntarily moderate their alcohol intake when reinforcement is contingent on doing so and punishment or loss of reinforcement is contingent on not doing so; among the reinforcers and punishers used have been enriched versus impoverished living environments, weekend passes, special ward privileges versus no passes and limited privileges, and usual socialization privileges versus brief periods of interpersonal isolation. As a whole, the work of these investigators shows that the behavior of even hard-core addicts can be modified as long as contingencies can be provided so that reinforcement for continued sobriety is greater than that for alcohol consumption.

Fixed Interval Drinking Decisions

Behavioral clinicians have been critical of the position that holds that drinking is simply a symptom of a disease, a symptom that must be given up as a precondition of therapy. The behavioral perspective is that environmental events that contribute to problem drinking and the consequences that maintain it need to be modified in the individual patient to make effective changes. From this point of view, the typical inpatient rehabilitation environment is seen as artificial and not representative of the world in which alcohol is available — the environment in which the alcohol abuser must learn to function more effectively and not to drink. Gottheil and his associates at the Coatesville Veterans Administration Medical Center have examined an important facet of the alcoholic's world — the opportunity to drink — in the context of an otherwise standard inpatient rehabilitation environment. Alcoholics in the Fixed Interval Drinking Decision (FIDD) program could choose to drink 1 or 2 oz of 80 proof ethanol by reporting to the nursing station at the appointed hour; the alcohol was given in a medicine cup, in a neutral fashion. A maximum of 26 oz could be consumed each day over a 5-day staff workweek. Rehabilitation consisted of group and individual therapy as well as Alcoholics Anonymous (AA) and educational seminars. In an important sense, the FIDD environment constituted a learning situation in which patients could find out for themselves whether or not they could function while continuing to drink (i.e., whether or not they could become social drinkers). Among the interesting early results was the finding that 33% of patients abstained completely while on the FIDD schedule and another 33% began drinking but stopped [7]; in response to a questionnaire, patients stated that drinking straight ethanol, limited to one drink an hour in the absence of a context of socializing, gave little pleasure and often made them feel worse. In subsequent reports, Gottheil's group indicated that the subjective discomfort of those who drank during the FIDD program increased during hospitalization, whereas the discomfort of those who abstained decreased [1].

A follow-up of 415 patients at 6, 12, and 24 months [8] showed that FIDD abstainers had significantly fewer drinking problems at each follow-up period than drinkers. The percentage of patients who were abstinent during the entire 6-month follow-up period was 18.5%; 8% abstained the entire 24-month period. The percentage of patients reporting abstinence for the last 30 days of a given follow-up period increased as a function of time and the percentage drinking on no more than 15 of the last 30 days without intoxication remained constant. Grouping abstinence and drinking without intoxication as "doing well," the proportion of patients in the improved category stayed around 50% over the 24-month follow-up period. Clinically, the program seems to have been as, or more, beneficial than standard hospital rehabilitation for similar patients. While FIDD research did not carry out direct experimental manipulation of the variables that control drinking, providing drinking opportunities and tracking the results has led to a number of useful observations about the decision to drink. The research lends further support to the position that emphasizes the importance of psychological and environmental factors in alcohol abuse. It is interesting to note that, defining relapse as reported intoxication following treatment, there was no difference in the frequency of subsequent relapse when abstainers (during treatment or follow-up) were compared with drinkers who moderated, anticipating subsequent work in which the explicit goal of treatment was the inculcation of a moderate pattern of drinking (controlled drinking).

TECHNIQUES FOR MODERATION

Blood Alcohol Level Discrimination

In the blood alcohol level (BAL) discrimination procedure of Lovibond and Caddy [15] at the University of New South Wales, alcoholics were taught to discriminate different intoxication levels using a breath-alcohol measurement device for feedback; subsequently, the alcoholics received dermal shock contingent on exceeding designated BALs to train them to be able to restrict drinking to moderate levels. In a recent study that extended the original observations, Caddy and Lovibond [5] assigned 60 alcoholics to BAL discrimination training plus aversive conditioning, BAL training alone, or aversive conditioning alone; follow-up evaluations 6 to 12 months after therapy indicated significant improvement (abstinence or sharply reduced drinking) for 76% of the group receiving BAL training plus aversive conditioning, compared with 65% for the group receiving BAL training alone, and 50% for the group receiving aversive conditioning alone. While these preliminary results were encouraging, the experiments, as such, did not constitute proof that alcoholics were actually discriminating BAL from internal cues once the external feedback was removed.

Research by Nathan and his associates at Rutgers University attempted to resolve the issue by studying the processes by which alcoholics and non-alcoholics inform themselves about level of intoxication [23]. Initial studies demonstrated that nonalcoholic college studenst could acquire and maintain accurate BAL discrimination, whether provided by internal (physiological or affective concommitants of drinking) or external (number and strength of drinks consumed) cues. Subsequent studies established that, unlike nonalcoholics, alcoholics were not able to learn to discriminate BAL effectively on the basis of internal feelings and sensations, although they could discriminate BAL by referring to external cues. Nathan and his associates went on to test the hypothesis that alcoholics may have a fundamental deficit in the ability to discriminate blood alcohol on the basis of internal cues, because shifting levels of tolerance experienced during previous heavy drinking episodes might cause discrete sets of internal cues to become associated with many BALs, not just one (as in the case of the social drinker). Nathan found that groups of nonalcoholics differing in drinking pattern or in family history of alcoholism did not differ in ultimate BAL-estimation accuracy following internal cue training; however, using standing steadiness before and after consuming alcohol as a measure of tolerance, low-tolerant subjects (those whose body sway, sober vs. drunk, differed markedly) were found to be significantly more accurate than high-tolerant subjects. While these studies did not confirm expectations for the new therapeutic procedure for inculcating moderation, research on the technique has led to a better understanding of intoxication in alcoholics and has provided theoretical support for programs that utilize external feedback training in the treatment of alcoholism.

Individualized Behavior Therapy for Alcoholics

Among the best-known, multicomponent programs with the explicit goal of training alcoholics to drink moderately is the individualized behavior therapy for alcoholics study conducted by the Sobells at Patton State Hospital [31, 32]. In their project, 70 alcoholic volunteers in a state hospital were put in one of four treatment groups: patients were assigned to controlled drinking status if they requested it and if there were no contraindications; otherwise, they were assigned to abstinence. Patients who qualified for controlled drinking were assigned randomly to behavioral treatment with moderation as a goal or to traditional treatment with abstinence as a goal; patients who qualified for abstinence were assigned randomly to behavioral treatment with abstinence as a goal or to traditional treatment with abstinence as a goal. Behavioral treatment consisted of 17 sessions in a simulated bar or living room, with videotaped self-confrontations and dermal shock for inappropriate drinking during practice drinking sessions. Traditional treatment relied on group therapy, chemotherapy, physiotherapy, and attending AA sessions. Treatment time was similar for all groups and an intensive follow-up (involving contracts every 3 to 4 weeks) was carried out over a 2-year period.

Outcome results at the 2-year follow-up were analyzed according to an elaborate scheme that included general emotional adjustment, vocational satisfaction, status of driver's license, residential status, and stability, as well as drinking disposition. Experimental groups using behavior modification (with either controlled drinking or abstinence as the goal of treatment) functioned significantly better with respect to overall social adjustment and drinking disposition than did traditional control groups; of all the groups, the controlled drinking group functioned best on the several indicators, including number of days abstinent. When abstinent days and controlled drinking days were combined under the heading "functioning well," the percentages of patients functioning well 80% or more of the time were as follows: 79% functioning well in the behavioral moderation group versus 22% in its traditional control group; 54% functioning well in the behavioral abstinence group versus 21% in its traditional control group. An independent 3rd-year outcome evaluation using rigorous methodological standards has confirmed the original observations [4]. While the inability to make direct comparisons of abstinence with controlled drinking as a goal represents a serious limitation of the original investigation, the Patton study, taken in the context of related research, has established the relevance of individualized treatment goals for alcoholics [30]. Though the experimental demonstration of sustained moderate drinking was first carried out with state hospital gamma alcoholics, subsequent work has extended these concepts to problem drinkers at an earlier stage of difficulty.

Multicomponent Therapy for Middle-Income Problem Drinkers

Pomerleau and his associates at the University of Pennsylvania [25] have developed an integrated treatment sequence using self-management techniques for middle-income problem drinkers. Treatment was provided on an outpatient basis, with weekly sessions over 3 months and five additional sessions at increasing intervals over 9 months. In addition to paying a fee for service on a sliding scale based on income, participants were asked for a commitment fee of up to $300. The fee was prepaid and could be earned back in its entirety by (1) keeping daily records of alcohol consumed or of craving (refunds based on completeness of records, not content), (2) coming to treatment with no detectable breath-alcohol, (3) carrying out selected nondrinking activities as corroborated by a monitor, and (4) attending follow-up. If the participant dropped out, all fees were forfeited. Treatment emphasized moderate drinking as the goal of therapy, but, if further use of alcohol was medically contraindicated, a similar approach was used to inculcate abstinence. Among the techniques used, besides record keeping and contingency management, were quotas for daily drinking, social reinforcement for moderation or abstinence, and behavior therapy for depression, tension, or nonassertiveness. Thirty-two participants were assigned randomly to either behavioral treatment or traditional treatment groups, led by experienced therapists. Traditional treatment was conducted over the same number of sessions as behavioral treatment and emphasized abstinence rather than moderation. Therapy consisted of confronting denial of problem drinking, social support for nondrinking, and psychotherapy for depression, anxiety, or inadequate socialization. Fees, set on a sliding scale, were paid each session.

Participants reduced their alcohol consumption significantly in both treatment programs. Behavioral participants reduced alcohol consumption significantly during therapy, whereas traditional participants reduced alcohol consumption significantly prior to therapy. Significantly more traditional participants (43%) dropped out of therapy than did behavioral (11%) participants. At the first anniversary point, 72% of behavioral participants were classified as improved (6% abstinent; 66% drinking a median of 35% of baseline rate) compared with 50% of traditional participants (14% abstinent; 36% drinking a median of 40% of baseline rate). The data suggested that the effects of traditional therapy were mixed, helping those participants who were receptive, driving out those who were not; moreover, reduced consumption seemed to be more the result of compliance with initial therapist demands (made during the screening period) than the effect of denial confrontation in subsequent therapy. The favorable effects of behavioral treatment occurred during therapy, consistent with reports for similar applications in the contingency management literature.

These encouraging findings for middle-income problem drinkers are corroborated by a study of a similar population by Miller [22]: 78% of subjects treated using self-control techniques were found improved at a 1-year follow-up, compared with 70% of subjects treated using aversive conditioning and 54% of subjects treated with a composite procedure; posttreatment drinking was approximately 33% of pretreatment levels, the same as in Pomerleau's study [25]. A recent report on 70 socially stable problem drinkers by Sanchez-Craig [28] provides an important replication and extension of the original findings for controlled drinking, as it is the first study in which the only difference in therapy for randomly assigned subjects is the goal of treatment—abstinence or moderation. Preliminary findings indicate that patients assigned to controlled drinking consumed significantly less than those assigned to abstinence during the first 3 weeks of treatment (a time during which both groups were expected to abstain); moreover, patients assigned to controlled drinking continued to be more successful than those assigned to abstinence during the remainder of therapy. Sanchez-Craig suggests that more frequent drinking in the abstinence group may reflect the unacceptability of such a goal for this particular population and it may also represent a difficulty inherent to an either/or rule in which a slip from abstinence is not cognitively differentiated from total relapse. A follow-up study is currently being conducted to see if these trends persist. While the subject characteristics that constitute the best prognosis for controlled drinking have yet to be determined precisely, the weight of current evidence suggests that moderation cannot now be arbitrarily excluded as a goal of therapy, particularly in a nonaddicted, socially stable population.

TECHNIQUES FOR SUSTAINING IMPROVEMENT

Contingency Management in the Community and Family

The community reinforcement procedure developed by Hunt and Azrin [11] at Anna State Hospital is based on social learning theory. The program contains four separate components designed to provide satisfactions that will continue to interfere with drinking: (1) placement in steady and remunerative employment, (2) marital and family counseling to increase involvement and pleasure in family activity, (3) social clubs to provide support for nondrinking during free time, and (4) enhancement of activities such as hobbies and formal recreation to provide alternatives to drinking. Results from the program have been extremely favorable, with the treated group significantly reduced on such indicators as time spent drinking, time unemployed, time away from home, and time institutionalized, when compared with a matched control group. A recent revision of the program [2] attempted to deal with some of the limitations of the original procedure; thus, temporary lapses into problem drinking (slips) in response to job loss or some short-term impulse were handled by incorporating Antabuse into the treatment program, adding special procedures to motivate and train patients to use the drug. Additionally, the program was modified to include procedures that taught the patient to identify and handle situations that were known to lead to excessive drinking, or feelings that constituted danger signals, as well as providing regular status reports to the counselor concerning these events. Finally, to make therapy more efficient, demands on the counselor for assistance in nonalcohol-related problems were shifted to nonprofessional buddies in the client's neighborhood, and counseling was performed in a group setting. Results for 20 men admitted to Anna State Hospital for alcoholism indicated that matched controls exposed to the standard hospital procedure drank 27 times more often than community reinforcement patients, were institutionalized 100 times as much, and were absent from their homes nine times as much. Moreover, while the original community reinforcement treatment program required 50 hours for the average patient, the modified procedure required only 30 hours. Treatment benefits were not transient and were sustained over a 2-year follow-up.

Further corroboration for the community reinforcement approach is provided by studies by Hedberg and Campbell at Schick Shadel Hospital and McGrady and associates at Butler Hospital. In a well-controlled study, Hedberg and Campbell [10] randomly assigned 49 alcoholic outpatients to behavioral family counseling, systematic desensitization, covert sensitization, or aversive shock. Program data showed behavioral family counseling to be the most effective procedure in a 6-month follow-up, and aversive shock, the least effective. McCrady et al. [19] assigned 33 persons hospitalized for alcoholic problems to one of three groups: (1) joint hospitalization followed by couples and/or individual outpatient therapy for both spouses; (2) couples and/or individual outpatient therapy without joint admission; and (3) individual inpatient and outpatient treatment alone. In evaluations 6 to 8 weeks and 6 to 8 months after hospital discharge, all groups showed significant decreases in the number of reported marital problems, depression, anxiety, and other psychological symptoms, as well as decreased impairment from use of alcohol. The two groups receiving couples and/or individual therapy showed significant decreases in quantity of alcohol consumed; the group receiving inpatient and outpatient therapy alone did not. An interesting implication from this preliminary study is that, from the point of view of cost, joint or individual hospitalization seems to be less effective in reducing alcohol consumption than couples therapy. On the whole, while the success of the community-family reinforcement approach is impressive, considerable work still remains to be done to isolate the essential treatment components in order to increase the efficiency of the procedure; unless this is done, dissemination of these techniques to nonresearch funded, fee-for-service programs will be difficult.

Programmed Relapse and the Abstinence Violation Effect

Marlatt and his associates at the University of Washington have explored the problem of maintenance of treatment benefits from the perspective of cognitive behavior therapy. In a recent review on the determinants of recidivism, Marlatt and Gordon [18] noted that a high percentage (90%) of those who relapse following alcoholism treatment in their program had continued drinking following the first drink in the initial slip. They postulated a series of cognitive steps, each constituting a point at which relapse prevention techniques might be applied to good effect: For example, in setting an all-or-nothing goal, such as total abstinence, the individual experiences a sense of personal control over the designated behavior in low-risk situations. On the other hand, high-risk situations may be experienced as beyond personal control (e.g., turning down a drink offered by a drinking buddy or resisting drinking when feeling intensely angry or depressed). If the individual can execute an effective coping response (e.g., assertion or carrying out a rehearsed alternative behavior), the probability of relapse in the high-risk situation may decrease significantly and the perception of control is regained. If the coping response is not carried out, and if the person has expectancies that consumption of the alcohol will provide certain benefits (e.g., "I won't feel so nervous," or, "I'll stop trembling and feel better"), the stage is set for a full-blown relapse. Additionally, if the requirement of abstinence is seen in absolutistic terms, then, once that first drink is taken, the rule is broken and all control is surrendered—the "abstinence violation effect." Among the intervention procedures suggested by Marlatt [17] are (1) behavioral assessment to identify potential high-risk situations and to recognize those minidecisions (apparently irrelevant decisions, AIDs) that precede a relapse; (2) relapse rehearsal (modeling, role playing, etc.); (3) cognitive restructuring concerning expectations, to stop the second drink should the first be taken; and (4) in some cases, actually staging a programmed relapse, in which the therapist controls the setting and events associated with resumption of drinking and allows the patient to learn that he or she determines the outcome, not the alcohol.

These ideas are empirically based and have been tested in treatment research. Marlatt [16] had observed that the types of relapse situations reported following therapy in his aversive conditioning program were: (1) frustration and inability to express anger (29%); (2) inability to resist social pressure to drink (23%); (3) intrapersonal negative emotional states (10%); (4) inability to resist intrapersonal temptation to drink (21%); (5) other (17%). A subsequent study [6] was conducted to provide specific training in the above categories; the focus was on how not to drink. Forty inpatient alcoholics were assigned to a skills-training group, a discussion group, or to standard hospital treatment alone. On a verbal role-playing measure of responses to situations associated with drinking and relapse, the skills-training group demonstrated a significant performance improvement over control groups. A 1-year posttreatment follow-up validated the analogue test: Skills training decreased the duration and severity of relapse episodes. While it remains to be demonstrated that self-reported reasons for drinking and relapse (attribution) cause the behavior in question, the fact that alcoholics given skills training drank less, were employed more, and attended aftercare more regularly is promising. The cognitive intervention strategies suggested by Marlatt clearly warrant further exploration, especially in the context of multimodal treatment programs.

CONCLUSION

Recent trents in behavioral treatment are quite encouraging, in particular the development of comprehensive multimodal programs making specific provision for sustaining improvement. While the methodological strengths of the behavioral approach and the assiduousness of its adherents should help it continue to generate increasingly effective programs, an important shortcoming should be noted. Though a few seminal studies, such as those on the objective measurement of alcoholics' drinking by Mello and Mendelson [20], have influenced some of the treatment practices described in this chapter, the incorporation of basic research findings into therapeutic application has left much to be desired. In some cases, treatment has been consistent with an empirically derived general model of human behavior; in other cases, innovations have been based on trial and error. What remains to be accomplished is the development of a rational therapy for problem drinking and alcoholism — one that is derived from a scientific understanding of the behavior, physiology, and biochemistry of excessive ethanol consumption.

ACKNOWLEDGMENTS

Preparation of this chapter was facilitated by National Institute on Alcoholism and Alcohol Abuse Center Grant No. 1 P 50 AA 03510-03.

REFERENCES

1. Alterman, A., Gottheil, E., and Crawford, M. Mood changes in an alcoholism treatment program based on drinking decisions. *Am. J. Psychiatry* 132:1032–1037, 1975.

2. Azrin, N. H. Improvements in the community reinforcement approach to alcoholism. *Behav. Res. Ther.* 14:339–348, 1976.

3. Bigelow, G., Strickler, D., Liebson, I., and Griffiths, R. Maintaining disulfiram ingestion among outpatient alcoholics: A security-deposit contingency contracting procedure. *Behav. Res. Ther.* 14:378–381, 1976.

4. Caddy, G. R., Addington, H. J., and Perkins, D. Individualized behavior therapy for alcoholics: A third-year independent double-blind follow-up. *Behav. Res. Ther.* 16:345–362, 1978.

5. Caddy, G., and Lovibond, S. Self-regulation and discriminated aversive conditioning in the modification of alcoholics' drinking behavior. *Behav. Ther.* 7:223–230, 1976.

6. Chaney, E. F., O'Leary, M., and Marlatt, G. A. Skill training with alcoholics. *J. Consult. Clin. Psychol.* 46:1092–1104, 1978.

7. Gottheil, E., Murphy, B., Skoloda, T., and Corbett, L. Fixed interval drinking decisions: II. Drinking and discomfort in 25 alcoholics. *Q. J. Stud. Alcohol* 33:325–340, 1972.

8. Gottheil, E., Thornton, C., Skoloda, T., and Alterman, A. Follow-up study of alcoholics at 6, 12, and 24 months. In: *Currents in Alcoholism*, (Vol. 6), Galanter, M. (ed.). Grune & Stratton: New York, 1979.

9. Griffiths, R., Bigelow, G., and Liebson, I. Relationship of social factors to ethanol self-administration in alcoholics. In: *Alcoholism: New Directions in Behavioral Research and Treatment*, Nathan, P. E., Marlatt, G. A., and Loberg, T. (eds.). Plenum: New York, 1978.

10. Hedberg, A., and Campbell, L. A comparison of four behavioral treatments of alcoholism. *J. Behav. Ther. Exper. Psychiatry* 5:251-256, 1974.

11. Hunt, G. M., and Azrin, N. H. The community-reinforcement approach to alcoholism. *Behav. Res. Ther.* 11:91-104, 1973.

12. Lemere, F., and Voegtlin, W. An evaluation of the aversive treatment of alcoholism. *Q. J. Stud. Alcohol* 11:199-204, 1950.

13. Liebson, I., Tommasello, A., and Bigelow, G. A behavioral treatment of alcoholic methadone patients. *Ann. Intern. Med.* 89:342-344, 1978.

14. Lloyd, R. W., and Salzberg, S. C. Controlled social drinking: An alternative to abstinence as a treatment goal for some alcohol abusers. *Psychol. Bull.* 82:815-842, 1975.

15. Lovibond, S., and Caddy, G. Discriminated aversive control in the moderation of alcoholics' drinking behavior. *Behav. Res. Ther.* 1:437-444, 1970.

16. Marlatt, G. A. Craving for alcohol, loss of control, and relapse: A cognitive behavioral analysis. In: *Alcoholism: New Directions in Behavioral Research and Treatment*, Nathan, P. E., Marlatt, G. A., and Loberg, T. (eds.). Plenum: New York, 1978.

17. Marlatt, G. A. Alcohol use and problem drinking: A cognitive behavioral analysis. In: *Cognitive-Behavioral Interventions: Therapy, Research, and Procedures*, Kendall, P. C. and Hollon, S. D. (eds.). Academic Press: New York, 1979.

18. Marlatt, G. A., and Gordon, J. R. Determinants of relapse: Implications for the maintenance of behavior change. In: *Behavioral Medicine: Changing Health Life Styles*, Davidson, P. (ed.). Brunner/Mazel: New York, 1979.

19. McCrady, B., Paolino, T., Longabough, R., and Rossi, J. Effect of joint hospital and admission and couples treatment for hospitalized alcoholics: A pilot study. *Addict. Behav.* 4:155-165, 1979.

20. Mello, N. K., and Mendelson, J. H. A quantitative analysis of drinking patterns in alcoholics. *Arch. Gen. Psychiatry* 25:527-539, 1971.

21. Miller, P., Hersen, M., Eisler, R., and Hemphill, D. Electrical aversion therapy with alcoholics: An analogue study. *Behav. Res. Ther.* 11:491-497, 1973.

22. Miller, W. R. Behavioral treatment for problem drinkers: A comparative outcome study of three controlled drinking therapies. *J. Consult. Clin. Psychol.* 46:74-86, 1978.

23. Nathan, P. E. Studies in blood alcohol level discrimination. In: *Alcoholism: New directions in Behavioral Research and Treatment*, Nathan, P. E., Marlatt, G. A., and Loberg, T. (eds.). Plenum: New York, 1978.

24. Nathan, P. E., and Goldman, M. S. Problem drinking and alcoholism. In: *Behavioral Medicine: Theory and Practice*, Pomerleau, O. F. and Brady, J. P. (eds.). Williams & Wilkins: Baltimore, 1979.

25. Pomerleau, O. F., Pertschuk, M., Adkins, D., and Brady, J. P. A comparison of behavioral and traditional treatment for middle-income problem drinkers. *J. Behav. Med.* 1:187-200, 1978.

26. Pomerleau, O. F., Pertschuk, M., and Stinnett, J. A. A critical examination of some current assumptions in the treatment of alcoholism. *J. Stud. Alcohol* 37:849-867, 1976.

27. Robichaud, C., Strickler, D., Bigelow, G., and Liebson, I. Disulfiram maintenance employee alcoholism treatment: A three-phase evaluation. *Behav. Res. Ther.* 17:618-621, 1979.

28. Sanchez-Craig, M. Random assignment to abstinence or controlled drinking in a cognitive-behavioral program: Short-term effects on drinking behavior. *Addict. Behav.* 5:35-39, 1980.

29. Sobell, L. C., Sobell, M. B., and Ward, E. (eds.). *Evaluating Alcohol and Drug Abuse Treatment Effectiveness: Recent Advances*. Pergamon: New York, 1980.

30. Sobell, M. B. Goals in the treatment of alcohol problems. *Am. J. Alcohol Abuse* 5:283-291, 1978.

31. Sobell, M. B., and Sobell, L. C. Individualized behavior therapy for alcoholics. *Behav. Ther.* 4:49-72, 1973.

32. Sobell, M. B., and Sobell, L. C. Second-year treatment outcome of alcoholics treated by individualized behavior therapy: Results. *Behav. Res. Ther.* 14:195-215, 1976.

33. Vogler, R. E., Compton, J., and Weissbach, T. Integrated behavior change techniques for alcoholics. *J. Consult. Clin. Psychol.* 43:233-243, 1975.

34. Wiens, A., Montague, J., Manaugh, T., and English, C. Pharmacological aversive conditioning to alcohol in a private hospital: One year follow-up. *J. Stud. Alcohol* 37:1320-1324, 1976.

35. Wilson, G. T., Leaf, R., and Nathan, P. E. The aversive control of excessive drinking by chronic alcoholics in the laboratory setting. *J. Appl. Behav. Anal.* 8:13-26, 1975.

89

ARMANDO R. FAVAZZA, MD, University of Missouri–Columbia
School of Medicine

THE ALCOHOL WITHDRAWAL SYNDROME AND MEDICAL DETOXIFICATION

ALCOHOL "DETOXIFI-cation" refers to "treatment intended to rid the organism of alcohol and to promote recovery from its effects," while alcohol "detoxication" refers to "the condition of recovery from the effects of alcohol in the organism" [5]. Despite these differences, the terms are used interchangeably by clinicians.

No adequate treatment currently exists that actively rids an organism of alcohol. Clinicians have attempted to treat acute alcohol intoxication with such agents as amantadine, amino acids, cortisone, epinephrine, fructose, glucose, insulin, sucrose, thyroid extract, and vitamins. Although intravenous fructose infusion enjoys some popularity, a recent study failed to demonstrate its effectiveness [6]. This treatment has its dangers; since the administration of fructose may increase serum levels of uric acid and of lactate, it may precipitate attacks of gout, and may cause lactic acidosis in patients with hepatic failure.

The acutely intoxicated person who comes to the attention of a physician should receive a physical examination, and a blood ethanol level should be obtained. If there is any cause to suspect multiple drug use then a drug screen should be ordered, even though the laboratory results may not be ready for several hours.

Armando R. Favazza, MD, Professor and Chief, Section of General Psychiatry, University of Missouri–Columbia School of Medicine, Columbia, Missouri.

It is quite difficult to determine the presence or absence of an underlying psychiatric disorder in an intoxicated person. Information should be obtained from any person who accompanied the patient and from the patient's family, with special attention to depression and suicidal tendencies. A check should be made to see if the patient has a medical chart. In uncomplicated cases no specific medical treatment may be needed. Ideally the patient should be in a sheltered environment until the acute phase of intoxication passes. Detoxification centers exist in some communities. Rarely, such patients may need to use the sheltered environment of a hospital ward for a day or less. Not infrequently a great deal of ingenuity is required to find an appropriate place for patients to dry out. Sometimes the patient's friends or family can be called upon, as may selected social agencies. Attempts should be made to have all patients return for an outpatient medical-psychiatric evaluation once they have become sober.

Although the vast majority of acutely intoxicated patients recover rapidly, severe medical problems may complicate the clinical course. Fatal respiratory depression may occur in acutely intoxicated persons; a blood ethanol level of 5,000 mg/l will result in death for 50% of patients. If coma is present in a patient whose ethanol level is less than 4,000 mg/l then it is likely that other serious medical problems are involved, such as liver failure, pancreatitis, hypoglycemia, and drug abuse. Patients in alcoholic coma may need artificial respiratory support as well as correction of acid-base, electrolyte, sugar, blood volume, and temperature abnormalities [7]. Analeptics such as caffeine and picrotoxin should not be used. Hemodialysis or peritoneal dialysis, although rarely used for acute intoxication, might be considered in patients when (1) high ethanol blood levels and severe acidosis are present, (2) ethanol blood levels are greater than 6,000 mg/l, or when (3) dialysable drugs were ingested along with alcohol.

CHARACTERISTICS OF PATIENTS IN NEED OF DETOXIFICATION

A study of 260 consecutive patients in Los Angeles who were in need of alcohol detoxification revealed the following (patients with obviously serious disorders such as jaundice, gastrointestinal hemorrhage, or fractures were not included) [1]:

1. The average age of both male and female patients was 46 years. Most had been heavy drinkers for more than 10 years.
2. Tremor, found in 81% of the patients, was the most common admission symptom. Other nervous system symptoms included blackouts (73%), headaches (49%), and hallucinations (45%). About 50% of the patients had such gastrointestinal symptoms as vomiting, diarrhea, and abdominal pain.
3. A total of 74% of the patients had participated previously in Alcoholics

Anonymous (AA) programs, 56% had a family history of alcoholism, and 38% had used disulfiram in the past.

4. On physical examination systolic hypertension (140 mm Hg) was found in 34% of patients, tachycardia (100 beats per minute) in 43%, and fever (100° F) in 1.4%.

5. Of the patients examined 29% had 0.0 blood ethanol levels, while 17% had blood ethanol levels of more than 300 mgs. The presence of tremor did not correlate with blood ethanol level, but the incidence of hallucinations increased as the ethanol level diminished.

6. Some abnormal laboratory value was found in 90% of patients. Anemia was present in 32% of patients; 19% had leukopenia, while 13.5% had leukocytosis. A major electrolyte abnormality, hypokalemia, was present in 33% of patients. Tests of liver function revealed an elevation of serum gamma glutamyl transpeptidase (SGGT) in 77%, and of alkaline phosphatase in 40% of patients.

The percentages of the various characteristics roughly agree with those found in comparable studies. Even after screening for obvious surgical and medical pathology, the overwhelming majority of detoxification patients will be found to have multiple organ dysfunctions, many of which may require therapeutic intervention.

ALCOHOL WITHDRAWAL SYNDROME

Syndromes of mild withdrawal include irritability, sleeplessness, and tremor. Symptoms of severe withdrawal (delirium tremens) include marked tremulousness, sweating, hallucinations (predominantly visual), seizures, and delirium (labile affect, and impaired orientation, memory, intellectual functions, and judgment). Increased catecholamine production as a result of the stress of withdrawal may result in tachycardia and low-grade fever. Although mild withdrawal symptoms typically appear several hours after withdrawal, while severe symptoms typically appear 48 to 60 hours after withdrawal, there is great overlap and variation in their clinical manifestation [7]. Frequently withdrawal symptoms may appear following trauma, infections (such as pneumonia), or gastritis. Patients with concurrent medical and surgical problems are at high risk for the development of delirium tremens.

MEDICAL MANAGEMENT OF ALCOHOL WITHDRAWAL SYNDROME

Patients with mild withdrawal symptoms can be treated effectively with oral minor tranquilizers (such as chlordiazepoxide 100-300 mg daily), multivitamins, a good diet, and observation in a relatively quiet environment. The presence of severe withdrawal symptoms is indication of a potentially fatal physiological process. Management of such patients involves the following:

1. Environment. Hospitalization is necessary. Because these patients are overly sensitive to all stimuli they should be placed in quiet, single or double rooms. Mechanical restraints should not be used. Patients with full-blown delirium tremens may require around-the-clock nursing care for several days.

2. Medication. By a wide margin the most favored medications used by clinicians are the benzodiazepines [2]. The benzodiazepines are effective, relatively free of side effects, easy to administer, and well accepted by patients [3]. Although all the benzodiazepines appear to be equally effective, intravenous diazepam and oral chlordiazepoxide are commonly used. In theory there may be some advantage in using oxazepam because it has a half-life of only 8 hours, and accumulation of it or of its active metabolites is minimal. The benzodiapepines should not be injected intramuscularly because of their incomplete and unpredictable absorption.

Intravenous diazepam (2.5 mg/min) or chlordiazepoxide (12.5 mg/min) can be used initially. Once the patient is calm, oral chlordiazepoxide 50-100 mg every 4 to 8 hours can be used. In a typical patient the dose can be reduced by about 25% daily (e.g., 400 mg on day 1, 300 mg on day 2, etc). Patients exhibiting an elevation of temperature and/or a rapidly rising pulse rate may need higher doses. When giving large amounts of these medications it is necessary to observe the patient closely and to monitor the dosage at least daily because of possible toxicity to the central nervous system as manifested by respiratory depression, ataxia, and confusion. Since the benzodiazepines may be addictive when administered in moderate doses for several weeks, it is best to have the patient drug-free or on the lowest amount of medication needed at the termination of the detoxification stage of treatment.

Many other medications are relatively effective in treating the severe alcohol withdrawal syndrome, but each is problematic in some way and none is superior overall to the benzodiazepines. Paraldehyde is hepatotoxic and can be administered only as a foul-smelling liquid. It may result in proctitis if given rectally. Intramuscular injection (10-15 cc) is painful. Phenothiazines are associated with such side effects as lowering of the seizure threshold, hypotension, and frightening extrapyramidal reactions. Haloperidol is a potent major tranquilizer with a high incidence of extrapyramidal side effects; it is best reserved for the treatment of persistent alcoholic hallucinosis. Ethanol should not be used as a therapeutic agent except in the unlikely event that no other medications are available. It does not make much sense to administer ethanol since it is the toxic agent that underlies the pathological process. At no time should alcohol be linked with therapeusis, especially since alcoholics frequently search for rationalizations to continue their drinking. Propranolol, a beta-blocking agent, is contraindicated for patients who have asthma, cardiomyopathy, chronic obstructive respiratory disease with bronchospasm, and diabetes requiring insulin (conditions frequently found in alcoholics). Estimated blood levels of the drug are unreliable in patients with low serum albumin and with impaired liver function and blood flow [8]. Antihistamines such as hydroxyzine can produce marked anticholinergic side effects; furthermore, the tachycardia, confusion, delirium, and hallucinations associated with high doses may complicate the clinical evaluation of patients with delirium tremens. Lithium carbonate is a dangerous drug. The difference between a therapeutic and a toxic blood level is very small, and it is relatively easy to induce such side effects as ataxia, tremor, convulsions, and lethal coma. Barbiturates are highly addictive and, in high doses, are linked to respiratory depression. Chlormethiazole appears to be a relatively safe and effective drug, but it is not available in the United States.

The medical treatment of "rum fits," (a grand mal type of convulsion) associated with the severe withdrawal syndrome is controversial [4, 9]. Patients with a history of epilepsy or of prior seizures during withdrawal, and patients who develop several grand mal type of withdrawal seizures, should be treated with anticonvulsant medication. Diazepam is an effective anticonvulsant as well as an excellent drug for other symptoms of withdrawal. It should be administered intravenously in order to achieve therapeutic anticonvulsant blood levels. Because of its safety and multiple therapeutic effects intravenous diazepam is a better initial drug to use than intravenous phenytoin. Once intravenous diazepam has been given the patient should receive oral benzodiazepine medication. In addition, oral phenytoin (100 mg three times daily) may be administered for 1 to 2 weeks. The presence of focal seizures or status epilepticus may indicate an underlying epileptic disorder requiring neurological consultation. Although an increasing number of clinicians do not feel that any special medication is necessary for patients who have one or even several abstinence convulsions, most physicians continue to treat such patients with anticonvulsants. Once a decision has been made to treat a patient with anticonvulsant medication, then the initial dose should be given intravenously. The administration of oral medication alone will prove ineffective since it may take several days to reach a therapeutic blood level. Since the majority of seizures occur with the first two days of withdrawal, the prophylactic use of oral phenytoin is questionable.

Although vitamin deficiencies are not directly implicated in the pathophysiology of the withdrawal syndrome, patients undergoing detoxification usually are given multivitamins, especially large doses of thiamine (10–100 mg intramuscularly, or in an intravenous infusion). Since many alcoholics do have varying degrees of vitamin deficiencies and since multivitamins in moderate doses are safe, inexpensive, and possibly helpful, there is no compelling reason not to give them in patients undergoing detoxification. Specific vitamin replacement is mandatory for patients with illnesses such as scurvy, beriberi, pellagra, megaloblastic anemia, and Wernicke-Korsakoff syndrome. Among the most common signs and symptoms of vitamin deficiencies found in alcoholics are glossitis, progressive weakness and muscle wasting, paresthesias, ataxia, and opthalmoplegias such as horizontal mystagmus, paralysis of lateral conjugate gaze, and bilateral weakness of the external recti muscles.

Fluid and electrolyte disturbances are often present in patients undergoing the severe alcohol withdrawal syndrome. Each patient must be evaluated individually; there is no common pattern of disturbance. Thus, some patients may be overhydrated, while others are dehydrated. Severe dehydration should be regarded as a medical emergency. Adequate hydration will decrease the morbidity and mortality associated with delirium tremens and is essential to proper treatment.

Hypokalemia, a condition associated with loss of gastrointestinal secretions, should be suspected in patients with prolonged vomiting and/or diarrhea. Hypokalemia may also result from use of diuretics. Hypokalemia may result in weakness and electrocardiographic changes; serious arrhythmias may be precipitated in digitalized patients. Severe hypokalemia may lead to respiratory insufficiency and is life threatening. A recent study found that hypokalemia may precede the onset of delirium tremens [10]. Daily serum potassium levels were obtained from 37 chronic alcoholics when alcohol was withdrawn during hospitalization. All the patients had normal potassium levels at admission. Eleven patients who did not develop severe withdrawal symptoms had normal, unchanged potassium levels. Of patients who developed delirium tremens 26 demonstrated decreasing potassium levels and eventual hypokalemia. Serum potassium levels rose slowly during the period of delirium and then rapidly increased to normal levels at the end of the episode. Changes in potassium levels were not associated with changes in serum electrolyte or acid-base balance. Administration of potassium in moderate doses during the delirious episode had no effect on serum potassium levels. The findings of this study may result in diagnostic and therapeutic approaches to delirium tremens, but they first need to be replicated in further investigations.

Although hypomagnesemia has been implicated in the pathophysiology of delirium tremens by some investigators, its role, if any, is unclear. Patients with marked hypomagnesemia, providing renal function is relatively intact, may be treated with intravenously administered magnesium sulfate (2 g) on the first day of withdrawal [9]. Magnesium should not be prescribed routinely, nor should it be used in place of other, less toxic medications for treatment of withdrawal seizures.

Although mild metabolic alkalosis secondary to prolonged vomiting may be found, severe acid-base imbalances typically are not associated with delirium tremens. If such imbalances are present, then other causes, such as lung disease, renal failure, diabetic ketoacidosis, and ethylene glycol or methyl alcohol poisoning should be suspected.

It is often difficult to evaluate hematological findings during withdrawal. Erythropoiesis, for example, may be depressed in folate-deficient chronic alcoholics. When alcohol is withdrawn and a normal diet started, then reticulocytosis may occur. This phenomenon may create a diagnostic dilemma since reticulocytosis is often associated with hemolysis or bleeding. Alcohol withdrawal may, in some patients, be associated with temporary high platelet and low hemoglobin levels.

The overall medical evaluation of alcoholics goes beyond the scope of this chapter. Suffice it to note that since many patients undergoing detoxification have a history of chronic alcoholism they need to have a thorough medical examination with special attention given to the acute problems of head trauma, internal bleeding, hepatic failure, and infection. Because heavy alcohol use may suppress granulocyte production, bacterial infection may result in leukopenia rather than the usually found leukocytosis.

CONCLUSION

While there is no adequate treatment available for acute alcohol intoxication, it is possible to detoxify patients with the alcohol withdrawal syndrome effectively. Because many such patients are chronic alcohol abusers they should receive a thorough medical examination or, at the least, should be screened for medical-surgical problems. Patients with mild alcohol withdrawal symptoms may be treated on an outpatient basis with oral benzodiazepine medication. Patients with severe withdrawal symptoms should be hospitalized and placed in a quiet environment. Fluid and electrolyte imbalances should be corrected. The medications of choice for detoxification are the benzodiazipines in high doses. Intravenously administered diazepam is the medication of choice for the prevention and treatment of withdrawal seizures. Even patients without evidence of a vitamin deficiency are customarily given multivitamins and a large amount of thiamine.

REFERENCES

1. Craig, J. R., and Mosier, W. M. clinical and laboratory findings on admission to an alcohol detoxification service. *Int. J. Addict.* 13(8):1207–1215, 1978.
2. Favazza, A., and Martin, P. Chemotherapy of delirium tremens. *A. J. Psychiatry* 131:1031–1033, 1974.
3. Greenblatt, D. J., and Shader, R. I. *Benzodiazepines in Clinical Practice.* Raven Press: New York, 1974.
4. Josephson, G. W., and Sabatier, H. S. Rational management of alcohol withdrawal seizures. *South. Med. J.* 71:1095–1097, 1978.
5. Keller, M., and McCormick, M. *A Dictionary of Words about Alcohol.* Rutgers Center of Alcohol Studies: New Brunswick, N.J., 1968.

6. Levy, R., Elo, T., and Hanenson, I. B. Intravenous fructose treatment of acute alcohol intoxication. *Arch. Intern. Med.* 137:1175–1177, 1977.

7. Sellers, E. M., and Kalaut, H. Alcohol detoxication and withdrawal. *N. Eng. J. Med.* 294(14):757–762, 1976.

8. Sellers, E. M., Silm, D. H., and Degani, N. C. Comparative efficacy of propranolol and chlordiazepoxide in alcohol withdrawal. *J. Stud. Alcohol* 38(11):2096–2108, 1977.

9. Thompson, W. L. Management of alcohol withdrawal syndromes. *Arch. Intern. Med.* 138:278–283, 1978.

10. Wadstein, J., and Skude, G. Does hypokalaemia precede delirium tremens? *Lancet* 549–550, September 1978.

90

DAVID J. HUBERTY, MSW, Central Minnesota Mental Health Center,
St. Cloud, Minnesota

JAMES C. BRANDON, Northern Pines Mental Health Center,
Brainerd, Minnesota

NONMEDICAL ALCOHOL DETOXIFICATION

TRADITIONALLY, HEALTH care has been equated with medical care—implying a physician diagnosing and treating a patient's illness, disease, or physical complications. In more recent years, an interdisciplinary team of health care professionals has been utilized with increasing acceptance. The emotional and social components of even the most medicalized illnesses, such as cancer, diabetes, heart disease, and stroke have been recognized as legitimate areas for psychosocial-family intervention and treatment [2]. Likewise, the emotional, social, and physical interrelated components of alcoholism and drug dependency (chemical dependency) are increasingly recognized as requiring a multidisciplinary team approach to achieve any maximum benefit for the chemically dependent patient. Of course, the alcoholic for years has received a multidisciplinary segmented approach to his or her condition by police (in jail), in the doctor's office, in the welfare department waiting room, "counseling" with the bartender, and embarrassed spouse in tears,

---

David J. Huberty, MSW, Coordinator of Detoxification Services, Central Minnesota Mental Health Center, St. Cloud, Minnesota.

James C. Brandon, Chemical Dependency Family Therapist, Northern Pines Mental Health Center, Brainerd, Minnesota.

or in the minister's office. The results of this segmented approach are that the alcoholic patient ends up on the late stages of alcoholism, back in the hospital with pancreatitis, cirrhosis, or with sufficient brain damage to result in lengthy hospitalization at a public or state institution.

HOSPITAL EMERGENCY ROOMS AND ALCOHOLICS

Hospital emergency rooms are filled day and night with more serious kinds of medical problems than the intoxicated patient usually represents. Acute and oftentimes critical medical emergencies require the total physical and emotional energies of a full emergency room staff. The drunk patient who is only in need of detoxification, evaluation, and appropriate referral sources is only in the way in a busy emergency room and is often left to wait while other more emergent medical problems are being taken care of. While waiting for his or her blood pressure to be checked, the boisterous, obnoxious, very drunk patient in the emergency room becomes an irritant to the staff and other patients. This alcoholic not only prevents other patients from receiving first-class emergency treatment, but the alcoholic is often actually denied the most appropriate primary treatment for alcoholism when intoxication is treated in a hospital emergency room. Even when the emergency room is well staffed and well trained to treat the alcoholic patient, the bureaucracy, bright lights, shiny floors, uniforms, and otherwise serile atmosphere of the emergency room frequently leaves the intoxicated patient alienated and inadvertently pushed away from the health care system. For the 5% of the alcoholic population who are unemployed and of a skid row image, intervention in the emergency room is very strictly medical. For the 95% of the hidden alcoholics described by Shropshire [5] who are employed, educated, successful, well dressed, have health insurance, and in general, have social and family characteristics similar to the staff treating them, the state of intoxication or a doctor-patient discussion of some recent binge is too often viewed as a situational event rather than as a progressive disease state.

DETOXIFICATION CENTERS—AN EMERGENCY ROOM FOR THE ALCOHOLIC

Failure to utilize a crisis intervention team approach with alcoholic patients may simply reflect a lack of immediate availability of such trained personnel to physicians and to hospital emergency rooms. To fill this vacuum in health care delivery, many states have encouraged detoxification centers. By 1980, 34 states had added legal impetus by decriminalizing public drunkedness, following the Uniform Alcoholism and Intoxication Treatment Act drafted in 1971 by the National Conference of Commissions on Uniform State Laws. Some states, such as Minnesota, went so far as to mandate such facilities by directing each Mental health Area Board to develop a nonmedical or "subacute detoxification program," which was defined by statute as "a social rehabilitation facility established for the purpose of facilitating access into care and rehabilitation by detoxifying and evaluating the person and providing entrance into the continuum of care specifically for alcoholism and drug abuse. Such facilities shall be under medical supervision and shall have available services of a licensed physician for medical emergencies" [3]. Many detoxification centers are modeled after successful experimental detoxification programs in Toronto, Canada by the Addiction Research Foundation and other forerunners, such as the first detoxification center in North American in St. Louis in 1966. The crisis intervention approach provides entry or reentry into a continuum of care in which the individual may receive a total range of services necessary for rehabilitation, growth, and reentry into family and society.

Once referred by a medical doctor, emergency room staff, police, or a self-admission, nonmedical detoxification centers are uniquely equipped to continue the alcoholism or drug dependency evaluation and to further intervene with trained chemical dependency counselors. Many have around-the-clock nursing staff, medical (physician) back-up, and available psychological and psychiatric consultation. An average of 3 to 5 days in detoxification center is a typical amount of time to perform an assessment or diagnosis of early-stage, middle-stage, or late-stage alcoholism. This time also permits the bringing together of spouses, children, parents, employers, and anyone else who may be able to penetrate the defense system of denial, alibis, and grandiose promises that the alcoholic uses which have been so convincing to his or her family. Physicians, hospital staff, or family counselors taking less time are not likely to uncover the very private kinds of emotional and family problems that the alcoholic is desperately trying to keep secret.

In referring an intoxicated patient to a detoxification or receiving center, the technique of the referral may be critical. Seasoned doctors, nurses, and police officers have learned not to ask, "Do you want to go to the detox center?" More effective is a firm but caring, "You need to go and I want you to go there because I care about your health and what is happening to you. What is more, I will take you there or I will make immediate arrangements to have you taken there. Since I have already set it up, are you willing to go there under these conditions?" When not feeling threatened or afraid the alcoholic patient is frequently willing to do what he or she does not want to do, either because the alcoholic is passive and compliant or because he or she, in fact, has been waiting to be coaxed or pushed to get help. Admission is a healthy crisis that precipitates family involvement. Detoxification centers should emphasize a family approach in order to uncover problems that may be going on at home.

The purpose of most detoxification programs is four-fold: (1) to detoxify and facilitate withdrawal from mood-altering chemicals; (2) to evaluate the individual's present and/or potential chemical dependency; (3) to intervene in this progressive illness with pressure from family members, employers, nurses, and counselors; and (4) to refer the client to other appropriate inpatient or outpatient treatment facilities and/or Alcoholics Anonymous (AA) whenever such need is evident.

The Detoxification Process

Immediately upon admission in many facilities, a nursing assessment is begun. Vital signs are monitored and a drinking and drug history is obtained from the patient and from family members whenever possible with a look to both prescribed and illicit medications. The health history should include checking for hypertension, diabetes, seizures, and other medical complications whose symptoms may be masked by the state of intoxication or confused with alcoholism symptoms. With around-the-clock nursing staff and physician back-up (even telephone consultation) appropriate maintenance medications are continued and withdrawal medications prescribed (i.e., Valium, Librium) when vital signs indicate such a need in response to the physician's standing orders.

Important in the detoxification process is that being "undrunk" should not be confused with being fully detoxified; complete detoxification implies an average of 72 hours of good eating and sleeping, alleviation of anxiety and depression, and for some, additional sufficient time to insure medical safety in regard to barbiturate and other drug withdrawal. Back-up medical services are provided for referral of patients to acute hospital admission in cases of emergency health problems as illustrated in the following case.

Case Example

A 73-year-old male brought to the detoxification center by state troopers had first been observed driving erratically and later striking a parked car. Once apprehended, the officer noted an odor of alcohol, incoherent speech, and staggered gait. Upon admission, blood pressure was 200/110, pulse was 100, and body movement indicated a weakness on the left side rather than overall body sluggishness. An immediate nursing decision was made to transport him to the small town's hosptial emergency room as a possible stroke victim. The following morning, the physician on duty at the emergency room informed the detoxification center staff that the patient did, in fact, suffer a stroke and his family had confirmed that the patient did have a couple of drinks that day because "he had not been feeling well." The family further verified that this patient's drinking had never caused any problems in the past.

Less than 10 years ago, weaving drivers running into parked cars with an odor of alcohol were simply jailed!

One medical indicator of the success of detoxification centers in one state is that since the advent of such centers in 1972, incidents of delirium tremens have virtually been eliminated in Minnesota [7].

The Evaluation Process

Alcoholism both conceals itself and reveals itself in several ways: While Weinberg [6] has suggested several key techniques for uncovering psychological and behavioral symptoms, the authors' focus on three symptoms commonly misunderstood by patients and their families as well as professionals: (1) loss of control, (2) blackouts, and (3) preoccupation.

The loss of control misconception is that a mysterious and magical, uncontrolled, perhaps daily drinking binge will automatically result after one beer or shot for the alcoholic. The phenomenon of loss of control does not mean a patient will always get drunk once drinking starts, but rather that the alcoholic cannot accurately predict beforehand when he or she will or will not drink to intoxication once drinking starts. Documented loss of control usually includes initial successful control over several weeks or months in response to a change in drinking patterns with an eventual return to the original problem drinking pattern. The fact of initial success in controlling drinking further entrenches the patient's denial system that "I am not alcoholic because I have regained control."

Blackouts are often misinterpreted as "passing out." On the other hand, they may be accurately understood as alcohol-induced amnesia and memory loss, but accepted as somewhat normal or commonplace. While blackouts alone are not sufficient diagnostic criteria, increasing frequency of blackouts for a given patient is an extremely important diagnostic indicator.

Preoccupation with alcohol may best be illustrated through Heilman's [1] discussion of the urge characteristic of chemical dependency: Here chemical dependency is viewed as an overwhelming recurrent urge to repeat the experience of intoxication (or getting high) — a loss of choice. The strength of this urge achieves primacy in a person's psychology as a need that recurrently demands fulfillment. This urge becomes autonomous through conditioning so that it needs no external or internal stimulation — it can trigger itself.

Within detoxification centers, an evaluation or diagnostic component is provided by chemical dependency counselors in conjunction with nursing staff. Family members are included whenever possible as they most frequently have the data that is desperately needed in order to make an accurate diagnosis. The alcoholic has the same information: However, the alcoholic has channeled his or her attempts to control drinking, the fact of blackouts, his or her preoccupation, and other symptoms into such a well-integrated defense system of denial and grandiose and unconscious delusions that this filtered information is useless because of its subjective distortions.

At times it is necessary to negotiate the diagnosis with the patient in order to slowly bring him or her along to a realization of how serious the drinking actually is.

Case Example

A 29-year-old divorced male, complaining of headaches, agreed to enter a detoxification center with encouragement from a friend. The patient appeared to be only moderately intoxicated. He had a bandage over his right temple and eccymotic periorbital areas bilaterally. Blood pressure was 130/90, pulse 100, temperature 98, and respiration 18 and of good quality. The patient had in his possession a discharge slip, dated 2 days prior, indicating he had received emergency room treatment for a skull fracture with recommendation for rest and elevation of head. The patient had the following medications with him, all current and accurately labeled: Ampicillin 500 mg b.i.d., Darvocet N 100 p.r.n., and Ativan 1 mg t.i.d. and two at bedtime. The friend was unable to provide much information; he stated that the patient had just returned to this area seeking employment. It was determined, at this point, to transport the client to an acute medical facility.

Sixty days later, this patient was readmitted to the detoxification center by the local police, as he had been reported drunk and disorderly in a local restaurant. Upon admission, the patient was extremely intoxicated, displaying wide mood swings varying from screaming and kicking to sitting in the corner and crying. At admission, blood pressure was 118/86; pulse was 92. Four hours later, blood pressure was 120/90, pulse 100. Eight hours after admission, blood pressure was 130/90, and pulse of 110 was noted. Twelve hours after admission, blood pressure rose to 140/100, with a pulse of 112. The patient at this point, was seen by the alcoholism counselor. The patient appeared extremely anxious; hand tremors were noted when he lit his cigarette. The patient was very receptive to talking about his drinking pattern. He stated he had no recollection of being admitted and the last thing he remembered was drinking at a local bar. He stated tht he had been successfully treated for heroin addiction 2 years earlier while in the military. He stated that in recent months, however, he had been drinking quite heavily and it seemed to be causing increasing problems. A diagnostic evaluation was conducted and it was determined that the patient was in chronic middle-stage alcoholism and primary inpatient treatment was indicated. The patient was encouraged to think about this and an appointment was made to discuss this further prior to discharge.

Forty-eight hours after admission, the patient was seen again by the alcoholism counselor. The patient stated he felt much better and after much thougth realized he had a serious drinking problem but would like the opportunity to quit on his own. While the counselor acknowledged the patient's sincerity, he doubted his ability and yet encouraged the patient to try on his own. The counselor asked the patient what he would be willing to do if trying on his own failed to work out. The patient stated: "I really haven't thought about that because I don't have any doubts that I can do it, but I guess I would go to [residential] treatment if I get drunk again." This agreement was written down in contract form and signed by the patient and counselor. The patient was discharged after 72 hours and encouraged to return if he ever felt the need.

Fourteen days after discharge, this patient voluntarily admitted himself to the detoxification center moderately intoxicated. He stated he had been dry for 2 weeks and decided that he could handle a couple of beers. However, he felt he was again losing control and wanted to stay in the detoxification center to stop himself before he got worse.

The following morning, this patient was confronted by the alcoholism counselor along with the RN as to his prior commitment of going to treatment if he could not "do it on his own." The patient agreed that he had lost control and was unable to stop on his own and agreed to enter a primary treatment center for treatment of his alcoholism.

The Intervention Process

In professional frustration therapists silently scream to themselves, "Can't the patients see what's happening to themselves and their families?" Of course, the fact is that no, they cannot see what they are doing and this is precisely the problem. Alcoholism has been called the disease that tells the patients that they do not have a disease!

Intervention is the process whereby the family (spouse, children ages 4 and up, in-laws, parents) and other concerned persons—friends, employer, minister, bowling team members—all present to the alcoholic a panoramic view of the very real problems drinking is causing. They mirror the alcoholic's behavior in an office or home setting during a session that is planned in advance with family and friends coached in presenting their concern. The confrontation must be firm yet not blaming. The information reported must be factual and not judgmental. The alcoholic needs to know the people involved are truly concerned and that they have a highly specific plan and timetable for recovery. Such a plan communicates hope for change in a person who has felt hopeless to change, since he or she had secretly tried and failed to change several times before.

Detoxification centers lend themselves well to this intervention process.

1. The presence of a patient in the detoxification center is usually a crisis in itself or is a result of a crisis. The patient's psychological defenses (denial, rationalization, projection) are down and not operating well.

2. There are sufficient controls over the patient to ensure that the intervention session can actually take place. He or she is a captive audience and does not have the choice of not showing up for the confrontation session.

3. Detoxification centers have specialized in developing a wide variety of resource contacts to begin a program of recovery (i.e., hospital alcohol treatment programs, drug treatment centers, mental health centers, outpatient alcoholism counselors, psychiatrists, ministers, and AA meeting schedules).

Case Example

Joseph, age 54, was brought to the detoxification center with the assistance of his 26-year-old son. The following day his wife and 9 children, ages 8–31, showed up for an evaluation and intervention session. The counselor had no prior data on his problem drinking other than the fact of his admission. Using the 25-question Michigan Alcoholism Screening Test [4], which samples and weighs classical symptoms such as blackouts, loss of control, hiding bottles, arguments, solitary drinking, use as medication for sleep or relief of tension, the counselor asked that any or all family members respond with whatever information they had in order to form a consensus. Several family members had different examples of different problems that they had not shared with each other because they thought the example and incident seemed insignificant by itself. By the ninth question, the 8- and 12-year-old daughters were in tears. The counselor asked Joseph how he felt to see his daughters crying; he replied, "This is enough—I'll go wherever you want [to treatment]." Because of the as yet tremendous tension within Joe, each child was asked by the counselor to walk past him to the doorway and stop and say to their father, "I love you and thank you." With the first child, Joe cried and they hugged; that scene repeated itself with the following eight children. When Joe's wife came, he stared at her angrily and said, "Just get out of here."

Later, much of the tension between Joseph and his wife was alleviated in the hospital treatment program and he maintained sobriety at 6-month follow-up.

The Referral Process

Referrals from detoxification centers are frequently made to residential treatment programs for the treatment of alcoholism and chemical dependency. These referrals would include those to private hospitals, free-standing residential treatment centers, Veterans Administration hospitals with alcohol treatment units, or to state hospital chemical dependency treatment programs. However, because timing is critical, such referrals are most often backed up with direct transportation to treatment so that the patient does not have the time or opportunity to change his or her mind between discharge from the detoxification center and admission to the treatment program. A vital technique in the referral process is to not let the alcoholic patient slip through the cracks of a referral by allowing him or her to make it to the hospital independently. If the patient is in need of primary treatment for alcoholism, a day or two at home will usually result in an immediate return of the denial and grandiose defense system, whereby the alcoholic says, "I have a problem, but now I can take care of it on my own."

If inpatient treatment is not necessary, outpatient referrals may be made to chemical dependency counselors, psychologists, social workers at mental health centers, family service agencies, private therapists experienced in alcoholism counseling, and, of course, to AA. Patients are also referred back to their private physician for follow-up services as well as to private phsychiatrists for additional evaluation and psychiatric consultation when needed. Being most familiar with the variety of alcoholism treatment resources, detoxification centers are uniquely qualified to assist a patient in finding the most appropriate chemical dependency resource within a given community's continuum of care.

Case Example

Suzanne, 27, was brought to the detoxification center by the sheriff's department after she was found passed out in the street. She was heavily intoxicated, tearful, and fearful, demanding that she be released in order to take care of her 18-month-old son. The deputy informed the detoxification staff that the son had been placed in emergency protective custody by the county social service offices.

Upon admission, vital signs were within normal range and she admitted drinking until she passed out. She denied blackouts, minimized the frequency of her drinking episodes, and stated that the physical symptoms of nausea and vomiting were her only problems with drinking. The patient was found to be in good physical condition and her withdrawal was uneventful.

The day following admission, the alcoholism counselor contacted the county social service department regarding the custody of her child. It was reported that the patient's landlord had been concerned about the child for the past 2 months and had reported that concern to the welfare department. The patient was reported to have been on numerous binges and had, on occasion, left the child unattended. The social service office also stated that the patient had medical assistance insurance and if it were determined that she were alcoholic and in need of treatment, funds would be available for inpatient residential treatment.

During the diagnostic interview, the patient denied that alcohol was causing her any problems and claimed that the episode that brought her to detoxification treatment was simply caused by drinking too much at a party and this was the first time it had ever happened. The patient, at this time, was confronted with the information about her child and the reports from her landlord. The patient burst into tears and said that she had been unable to control her drinking for more than a year, but was afraid to get help for herself because somebody might take away her child if they knew she was an alcoholic.

During her 4-day stay at the detoxification center, the county social worker visited her with her baby. With firm but caring confrontation, Suzanne began to realize that only her not getting help would prevent her from keeping her child. Arrangements were made to place the child in a temporary foster home and the patient was referred and transportation provided to a residential, hospital-based inpatient treatment program.

SUMMARY

Because detoxification centers were a new concept in health care delivery in the early 1970s and are generally not hospital-based, few physicians and emergency room nurses have become familiar with detoxification centers as viable resources. Directors of detoxification centers need to court the medical profession in order to develop familiar and smooth working relationships. However, experience, time, and tradition will tend to achieve this. Detoxification centers have dared to provide medical care delivery for the alcoholic patient in the 1970s but will predictably earn increased physician and hospital respect and cooperation in the next decade, all leading to a community-team approach of earlier recognition, diagnosis, family intervention, and treatment.

REFERENCES

1. Heilman, R. Common denominators: Dynamics of drug dependency. In: *Proceedings of the 7th Annual Eagleville Conference*, Ottenberg, D. and Carpey, E. (eds.). Alcohol, Drug Abuse, and Mental Health Administration: Rockville, Md., 1974.
2. Huberty, D. Adapting to illness through family groups. *Int. J. Psychiatry Med.* 5:231–242, 1974.
3. *Minnesota Laws*, C. 892, Sec. 1, 1971.
4. Selzer, M. L. The Michigan Alcoholism Screening Test: The quest for a new diagnostic instrument. *Am. J. Psychiatry* 127(12):1653–1658, 1971.

5. Shropshire, R. The hidden faces of alcoholism. *Geriatrics* 30:99–102, 1975.
6. Weinberg, J. Interviewing techniques for diagnosing alcoholism. *Am. Fam. Physician* 9:107–115, 1974.
7. Wrich, J. *Report to the Minnesota Chemical Dependency Association.* Paper presented at the annual meeting, January 1977.

Section XI

Organization and Evaluation of Alcoholism Treatment Systems

91

E. MANSELL PATTISON, MD, Medical College of Georgia, Augusta, Georgia

A SYSTEMS APPROACH TO ALCOHOLISM TREATMENT

THE ORGANIZATION OF treatment systems and the selection of treatment methods for alcoholism has advanced significantly in the past decade [74]. In part this has been due to the recognition of alcoholism as a multivariate syndrome that requires a variety of intervention methods, and in part to the reflection of an attempt to match specific treatment methods to the specific needs of the individual alcoholic [72, 73, 76, 77].

This chapter reviews some of the conceptual and methodological issues involved in constructing a systems model of alcoholism treatment. First, methodological approaches to a systems analysis of alcoholism treatment are examined. Second, current issues in selection and matching of treatment to the patient are surveyed. Third, a systems model within which to organize the various components of treatment is set forth, which discusses treatment components presented in other chapters.

METHODS OF ANALYSIS OF TREATMENT

Consideration of treatment several decades ago generally focused on the selection of the best treatment available for all persons who were diagnosed as alcoholic. In the ensuing years it has become evident that there is no one best treatment,

---

E. Mansell Pattison, MD, Professor and Chairman, Department of Psychiatry, Medical College of Georgia, Augusta, Georgia.

that different types of alcoholism syndromes require different treatment interventions, and that there is no one specific diagnosis of alcoholism. Rather one must address systems of alcoholic treatment. This requires the development of a panorama of diagnostic, selection, and evaluation methods appropriate to each element of a comprehensive system of treatment. Methodological strategies are considered toward this end.

First, the vast majority of diagnostic alcoholism instruments are based on the binary decision concept. Such diagnostic instruments may be useful for certain epidemiologic survey purposes, or for screening and initial triage decisions. However, all such binary decision diagnostic methods fail to provide an adequate methodology for differential selection of treatment [45, 65].

A second strategy has been the use of multivariate analyses of personality variables to construct predictive typologies for treatment prescription and outcome prediction [19, 21, 59, 70]. Similar typologies have been derived for sociodemographic variables [40, 41]. These typologies do describe meaningful clinical subtypes of alcoholics, and may have some predictive value. However, they focus on limited sets of preexistent exogenous client variables, and they fail to provide measures of interaction with endogenous treatment variables.

A third strategy is just the reverse of the aforementioned; it uses simple correlational or complex multivariate analyses of treatment variables, yet does not account for preexistent background variables, or their interaction with treatment variables [2, 4].

A recent review by Gibbs and Flanagan [36] failed to reveal any consistent or even consensual data on prognostic indicators of alcoholism treatment outcome, much less prediction for treatment methods. The problems with both types of studies noted are both clinical, and methodological. The clinical problem is that most of these studies are based on populations at one alcoholism facility, thus, immediately skewing the predictability of any typology as well as its generalizability. Potent typologies must encompass a broad spectrum of variations of the alcoholism syndrome. The methodological problem is that such studies generate predictive measures derived from individual differences, ignoring the joint and interactive effects of different variables, or producing higher level abstract data that is difficult to interpret back in clinical terms.

A fourth strategy is the use of multivariate scales to assess background and current status variables, which in turn can generate typologies. The work of Marlatt [54] and of Wanberg et al. [101] are distinctive in this area. This strategy can sample numerous populations and assess multiple background variables and degrees of disability in various current life functions associated with alcoholism. However, the application of these sophisticated methods is somewhat limited by a linear analysis of treatment processes, which precludes statistical analysis of the interactional effects of exogenous and endogenous variables.

This leads one to a fifth strategy, which this author considers the most promising methodology, termed "causal pathway analysis." The exemplary work of Moos and of Costello is pioneering in alcoholism. In brief, data sets are accumulated for each major block of variables in the treatment sequence. Empirical typologies can be derived for subpopulations of alcoholics entering any given treatment system. Subsequent analysis of the interaction of block variables for each typology can then be conducted in relation to treatment variable blocks and discrete outcome variables. In this manner, one can determine the extent to which preexistent variables in each typology interact with and influence the effect of various treatment variables. Further, one can separate the indirect (interactional) effects that combine to influence outcome from direct (noninteractional) effects on outcome. Finally, one can determine different pathways of direct and indirect influence on specific outcome variables. In a pictorial sense, it is as though one were taking a moving picture of a similar group of people walking through a sequence of treatment scenarios, and by the end of the film one can now observe how the different outcomes were the result of the interaction between different types of people and specific treatment experiences. This begins to approximate a research methodology for differential treatment. However, it is, at the same time, a limited method for clinical differential diagnosis and treatment selection.

Some of the preliminary findings from the Costello research are of great interest [18]. For example, preexistent psychosocial variables do not exert a direct effect on treatment outcome, but rather have an indirect influence through the current status and disabilities of the alcoholic, or the treatment difficulty measure (TDS). In turn, the TDS directly interacts with treatment participation and with treatment outcome. Clinically, this suggests the importance of evaluation of current status and disabilities, rather than a major focus on the past history, in making differential treatment recommendations. However, since the prior development of psychosocial competence indicates potential for treatment change, it cannot be ignored. Thus, initial differential diagnosis must assess both current level of dysfunction and potential for improvement based on prior competency attainment.

Costello also found that aftercare participation significantly influenced treatment outcome, which calls attention to the importance of both the active treatment period and the aftercare treatment period in a sequential model of rehabilitation.

Finally, Costello found that simple direct links between pretreatment status and outcome status on discrete variables were potent. That is, despite many complex interactional effects, the most potent predictor on specific outcome variables was pretreatment status on the same variable. Thus, vocational status at entry was the most potent predictor of posttreatment vocational function, marital interaction at entry was the best predictor of marital interaction at follow-up, and so forth. Again, in clinical perspective, this finding suggests the value of discrete assessments of specific areas for specific treatment intervention, but it also may generally indicate what levels of rehabilitation can reasonably be set as goals for treatment.

The work of Moos and his colleagues has focused more on the interactional issues [8, 9, 10, 11, 60, 62]. They found that their typologies account for only 13% of the outcome variance, although the typologies correlate 0.44 and 0.52 with outcome. Thus, the conceptual simplicity of their typologies leads to significant decrement in predictive utility. Clinically, this highlights the importance of using typologies only for general guidelines in treatment selection, which must then be clinically individualized.

Pursuing the interactions, the Moos group found that although both social background and intake symptoms are relatively strong predictors of outcome, most of the total effect of the intake symptoms were directly on outcome, whereas the social background variables acted indirectly upon treatment participation. The effect of unique program treatment variables on outcome, up to 33%, was almost as strong as that of patient variables. But more importantly, most of the explained outcome variance (23-40%) is shared by interaction between patient and treatment variables. Or, 28 to 72% of the patient variable effects are shared in interaction with treatment variables. Alcohol consumption and behavior patterns at outcome were most directly influenced by treatment variables, but other variables, such as marital function and occupational function, were directly related to intake status. Yet, program selection, program perceptions, and program participation were most strongly influenced by social background, rather than intake symptoms. In summary, this work suggests that social background variables influence the choice of treatment programs and treatment participation, while disability status at intake is directly linked to level of rehabilitation at outcome. Treatment experience significantly influences outcome per se, but that effect is strongly influenced by interaction with patient variables.

In sum, this author finds these two sets of studies strongly indicative of the value of differential diagnosis and differential treatment selection, which can produce more precise treatment outcomes on specific variables.

SELECTION AND MATCHING OF TREATMENT

Some scientists who acknowledge and accept the multivariate syndrome model have questioned the utility of treatment selection, because of sparse research evidence, even going so far as to suggest to clinicians that the cheapest and simplest treatment be offered indiscriminately to all.

Examples of skepticism about differential treatment are shaded in their degrees of doubt. Armor et al. [1], in their national survey of National Institute on Alcohol Abuse and Alcoholism-supported programs, found little evidence for the differential effectiveness of treatment modalities, although significant improvement was produced by most; the same was reported by Emrick [28] for psychological methods of treatment. Both concluded there was little evidence to support differential treatment efforts. In a different vein, Edwards et al. [26] reported that patients who were seen diagnostically and received no treatment did as well at follow-up evaluation as a control group who received active treatment. This report was taken by some to indicate that treatment might well be just ineffectual — thus, differential diagnosis and treatment would be considered superfluous. Two other recent studies on untreated alcoholics also report similar improvement, but found that the areas of improvement varied considerably from treated alcoholics [44, 98]. Nonetheless, these data lend weight to skepticism about differential treatment. Ogborne [66] recently reviewed patient characteristics as predictors of treatment outcome. He found that patient characteristics were so dominant a variable, that he wondered if different treatments made much difference. He concluded, "But what is by no means clear is whether or not different patients are more or less likely to remain with or be helped by different treatment modalities. The literature provides only limited evidence relevant to this issue and the results are inconclusive." More critical was a study by Levinson and Sereny [50], which compared an intensive structured treatment experience with a generic unstructured treatment approach, which was equally effective. He, therefore, questioned the value of the effort and the expense of more specific treatment methodologies. Finally, Stinson et al. [95] recently compared four systems of care and found no differences between intensive selective treatment and generic low input approaches. They conclude, "No particular system of care demonstrated superior effectiveness.... The study was unsuccessful in delineating a rationale for differentially assigning particular patients to any particular treatment approach."

Thus, although the concept of treatment selection has been widely accepted, there are many caveats about the application thereof.

The essence of the selection problem is to optimize treatment effectiveness by matching the characteristics of patients with the most appropriate treatment facilities, those that will provide the most appropriate treatment methods, administered by the most appropriate personnel. Thus, one seeks to match clientele by facility by treatment by personnel. One may ask, "What evidence is there that matching occurs, what evidence is there of mismatching, and what evidence is there of the consequences thereof?"

First, one must consider the evidence for matching processes. The most clearcut data come from an analysis of types of alcoholics who enter different treatment facilities. Comparisons of the clientele of skid row facilities, halfway houses, hospitals, and outpatient clinics reveal striking homogeneity of each within-group clientele, and major between-group differences [8, 9, 10, 11, 23, 29, 46, 78, 79]. This data suggests a covert social process of linking, in which different types of alcoholics seek out a facility congruent with their alcoholism pattern or life style.

This process is highlighted in studies of the same type of facility, but with differences in programs and personnel, which in turn offer the image of differences. Again, one finds different types of alcoholics attracted to different kinds of hospitals [25], halfway houses [69], and outpatient clinics [35]. And finally, one must note the reverse, where apparent facility differences reflect the same covert social program process. In this case, skid row facilities of jail, clinic, and mission, all superficially different, offer the same social shelter to identical skid row clientele [103].

A second set of evidence is negative in content. These are studies that demonstrate that treatment personnel ignore the spectrum of problems associated with alcoholism, and ignore individual goals, needs, and expectations of clientele. Two studies found that although program personnel acknowledged the existence of emotional, social, vocational, and physical rehabilitation problems, they focused solely on emotional problems and treatment thereof [27, 81]. Another study of 10 different facilities reported that the personnel in each program did not offer consistent treatment in accord with program intent, but provided idiosyncratic treatment based on personal proclivity [38]. Two recent studies found that treatment staff ignored client needs and expectations and made no attempt to offer treatment based on client needs [39, 55]. And finally, in a major monograph report, Schmidt et al. [88] report an elegant study of a treatment program where differential diagnosis for treatment was made at admission, but when the alcoholic clientele entered the actual treatment program the needs assessments were ignored, and the alcoholics were treated in accord with generic social class biases. These negative data raise the question of treatment efficacy when treatment is not being directed to even identified major areas of disability.

Part of the problem is the legacy of the folk science unitary model of alcoholism, which assumed that abstinence was the major and primary goal of treatment, and its corollary, that if abstinence were achieved then the person was rehabilitated. Thus, specific program efforts aimed at intervention and rehabilitation in the spheres of emotional, social, vocational, and physical function were often ignored as irrelevant. Thus, there is neither differential diagnosis of disabilities in each sphere of function, nor differential treatment intervention directed to each area of disability, nor recognition and assessment of possible treatment gains in each area of disability. Just on the face validity of clinical logic, it does not seem plausible that treatment efficacy can be optimized by generic, global, diffuse, and nonspecific treatment of such singularly different dimensions of change as drinking behavior, psychological function, social interaction, physical function, and vocational competency. Pattison et al. [80] have extensively explicated data that demonstrate the low outcome covariance between changes in drinking, emotional, social, vocational, and physical function. Similarly, Stein and Bowman [94] and Bowman et al. [7] have found that drinking measures per se have a low correlation with social behavior. A good example of the issue is provided by Lowe and Thomas [52], who evaluated treatment outcome on three variables. In their follow-up population, 70% had achieved vocational rehabilitation, 62% psychosocial-behavioral rehabilitation, and 34% abstinence.

Third, what evidence suggests that matching is effective or makes a difference? In a review of the generic characteristics of treatment programs and methods, Costello [15, 16] found that the more specific and individualized treatment programs had lower dropouts and higher success rates. In a different vein, Kissin et al. [49] found that successful participants in drug, milieu, and psychotherapy treatment had significantly different personality and social patterns. Trice et al. [97] similarly reported different social and psychological patterns for successful Alcoholics Anonymous (AA) affiliaters versus psychotherapy attenders. Vannicelli [99] reported higher satisfaction in treatment where the patient chose the specific contract content for treatment. In matching patients by level of conceptual capacity, McLachlan [56] reported that when patients were matched to both therapy and aftercare environments 77% recovered, when matched to either aftercare or therapy environments alone 61% and 65% recovered, and when mismatched to both therapy and aftercare only 38% recovered. Two studies by Pattison et al. [78, 79] evaluated the relationship between treatment facility programs and methods and patterns of treatment outcome. They found substantial evidence that matching does affect outcome. A similar clinical correlation of matching is reported by Kern et al. [46]. More elegant multivariate statistical analysis studies have separated the effects of patient variables from treatment variables. Although patient variables do account for major portions of outcome variance, the direct effects of treatment variables, apart from patient effects, account for up to 30% of outcome variance [22, 90]. Finney and Moos [33] have reported matching processes similar to Pattison et al. [78], although they found considerably more "looseness" in natural matching. Further, they confirm the major contribution of treatment variables to outcome variance, but were unable to find specific correlations with specific treatments.

In sum, the face validity of the matching concept appears sound. There are scattered empirical studies that support both the existence of social matching processes and the efficacy of treatment matching. From a clinical point of view, the value of matching is supported, but there is only modest research demonstration of the efficacy of matching in available rigorous studies.

A PATHWAY MODEL OF THE TREATMENT SYSTEM

It is easy to assume that differential diagnosis and differential treatment selection means one decision. However, this author proposes that there are a series of differential decisions that must be made throughout the sequence of the system of rehabilitation. Figure 1 presents a systems model of the sequence of movement

Figure 1. Phases of the Treatment System

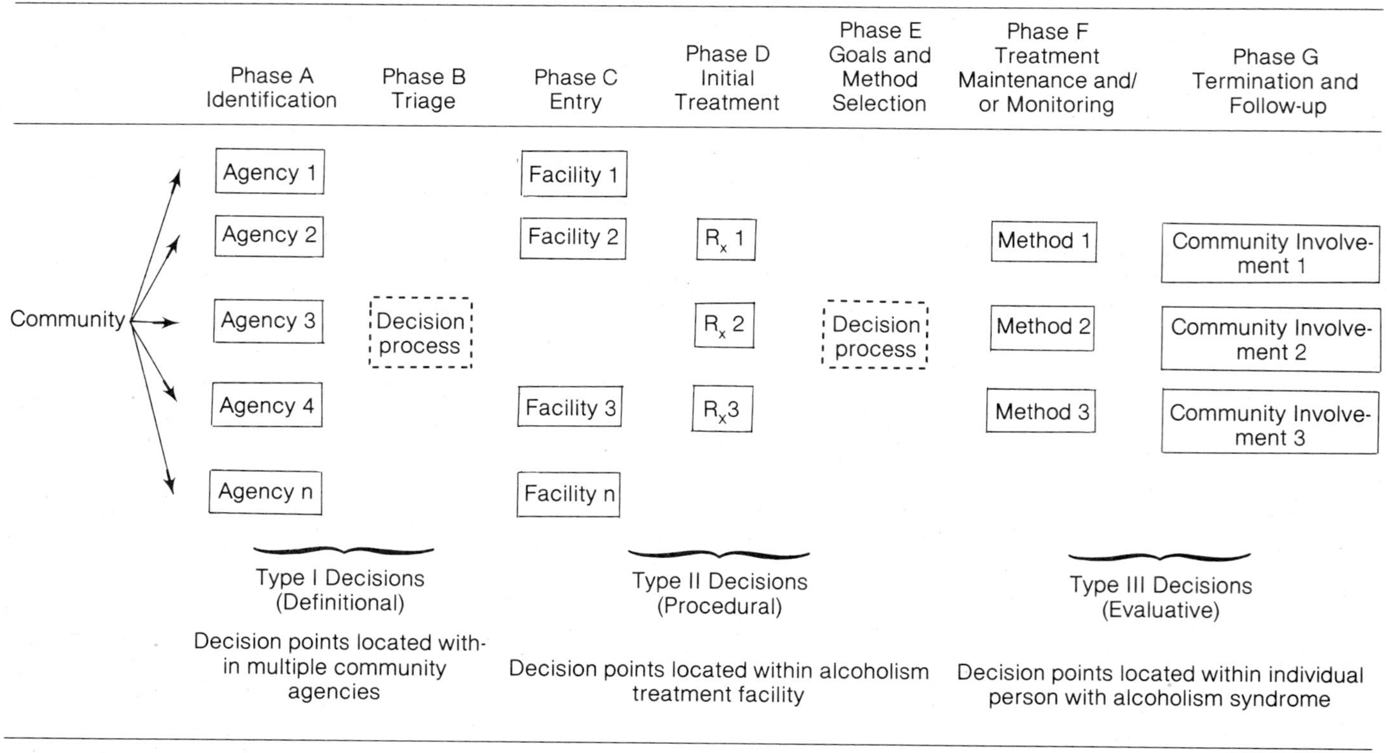

Phase A Identification	Phase B Triage	Phase C Entry	Phase D Initial Treatment	Phase E Goals and Method Selection	Phase F Treatment Maintenance and/ or Monitoring	Phase G Termination and Follow-up
Agency 1		Facility 1				Community Involvement 1
Agency 2		Facility 2	$R_x 1$		Method 1	
Agency 3	Decision process		$R_x 2$	Decision process	Method 2	Community Involvement 2
Agency 4		Facility 3	$R_x 3$		Method 3	
Agency n		Facility n				Community Involvement 3

Type I Decisions (Definitional)

Decision points located within multiple community agencies

Type II Decisions (Procedural)

Decision points located within alcoholism treatment facility

Type III Decisions (Evaluative)

Decision points located within individual person with alcoholism syndrome

Community

through different facilities and stages of rehabilitation. In each phase there are decisions to be made. In consonance with the terminology of causal pathway analysis, each of these phases is considered as a block that contains a set of variables. This author is deliberately setting out a clinical model of the pathways of treatment here, so that what variables exist in which blocks in the sequence can be more firmly established. This is important clinically, and just as important for further methodological application of causal pathway analysis. For, as Magoon has commented,

> A different and more profound weakness is the lack of good description of the modeled situation; many path analysts simply do not spend sufficient time carefully examining the phenomena they model statistically. Good applications of path analysis will often have to await the patient accumulation of case study data, longitudinal studies, and ethnographic accounts in order to be reasonably useful as statistical accounts of the whole interrelated phenomenon. [53]

The systems model is based upon the assumption of alcoholism as a multivariate syndrome, in which one may use typological categories as a means of reducing the complexity of alcoholism to paradigm types that in turn can be fit into a flow through a treatment system [43].

Miller [57] has recently pointed out that the utility of diagnosis of alcoholism as a syndrome lies in the description of consistently intercorrelated sets of signs and symptoms with predictive implications for etiology, prognosis, treatment, and prevention. There are several major issues imbedded in this perspective.

First, a simple binary diagnostic decision as to whether the person does or does not have the syndrome is inadequate for the utilization of syndrome diagnosis. As Miller [57] comments, "A large amount of information is lost when the data regarding various aspects of the problem are reduced to a binary nomenclature. Certainly this reduction cannot improve our prediction of such complex events as treatment outcome."

Second, a syndrome does not imply that there is just one pattern of signs and symptoms in the syndrome; rather, there may be various combinations of patterns of signs and symptoms that represent subsets of the syndrome.

Third, different sign and symptom sets may have different predictive utility, depending upon whether one attempts to predict etiology, treatment, outcome, or prevention. Thus no one set of intercorrelated items may be usefully predictive for all dependent variables.

Fourth, the collation of items in a syndrome diagnosis from a research perspective is a statistical maneuver. The clinical application of such derived typologies must be done with care. The problem is as noted by Finney and Moos, [33], "It should be kept in mind that their main strength and weakness are two sides of the same coin: a simplification of reality. A typology may allow efficient assignment of patients to general methods of treatment. Treatment programs will have to remain flexible, however, to be responsive to individual differences that inevitably obtain among persons within types." Thus a syndrome diagnosis can, it is hoped, provide the clinician with a general life style categorization within which to place a patient, one that will generate guidelines for treatment; however, individuation to a much finer degree must be implemented at the clinical level [34].

With these assumptions in mind, one can now consider in some detail the various types and sequences of decisions to be made throughout the pathway model of a treatment system, as shown in Figure 1.

The treatment of the alcoholic is not a single event, or a single set of events, but rather is a process that involves a series of decision points throughout an entire community system [17, 20]. Thus this author views selection of treatment in both longitudinal and cross-sectional perspective. The alcoholic person enters this system through multiple community ports, proceeds through the treatment system, and reenters the community. As a heuristic device seven phases of treatment have been identified, each of which involves treatment selection decisions. However, it must be emphasized that there are three types of decision processes involved [75, 76].

Type I decisions are definitional. These decisions involve criterion for denoting a person as alcoholic, defining a need for treatment, and deciding where, when, and how to make a referral.

Phase A is that of community identification, which occurs in various agencies of entry throughout the community. Note that not all possible candidates for definition as alcoholic may be so denoted. Or, if defined as alcoholic, a person may not be defined as in need of treatment, or even yet may not be considered for referral. These decision processes may in a given agency entry port result in actual definition of only high-risk or low-risk cases for referral.

Phase B is a triage, or the process of referral from the entry port agency to a treatment facility. Decision processes involve how and when to refer the alcoholic and where to refer. Again there are potential and real-life discrepancies. The triage process may be desultory or definitive. Alcoholics may be triaged indiscriminately to all facilities or selectively to only one facility.

Next are type II decisions, where are procedural. Here the decision process revolves around general clinical operations that will effectively promote facility entry and induction into the general treatment program; select immediate interventions required to meet physical, social, and psychological crises of the patient; and finally proceed to individual assessment for ongoing definitive treatment method selection.

Phase C is the entry process. The procedural decisions involve methods to reduce personal anxiety, isolation, and alienation of the alcoholic, resolve denial and rationalization, provide initial hope and positive expectation, and provide socialization into the treatment milieu. It should be noted that these are generic operations, although their application will vary somewhat with each individual entry.

Phase D involves initial treatment. Again the procedural decisions do not involve definitive treatment, but address general treatment problems presented by the alcoholic patient. One might consider these treatment interventions for complications of the current life style, but not for treatment of the alcoholism. Here one is concerned with immediate problems of detoxification, medical complications of chronic alcohol use, immediate disabling psychological symptoms, such as ambient anxiety and/or depression, transitory neuropsychological impairment, lack of clothes, food, or shelter, or social crises with the immediate family, legal or social agencies.

Phase E involves the selection of goals and methods for definitive treatment of the alcoholic person on an ongoing basis. This includes evaluation of degrees of deficit and potential for change in specific target areas of behavior. This may involve the selection of multiple interventions in the areas of drinking behavior per se, psychological function, social behavior, vocational function, and physical dysfunction.

Finally, there are type III decisions, which are evaluative. Here one is concerned with decisions that evolve from ongoing and regular review of the patient's progress toward specific treatment goals, appropriate utilization of specific treatment procedures, and individual progress toward treatment termination based on goal attainment. This is followed by evaluation of individual plans for community reentry and planned reinvolvement in community life.

Phase F is that of treatment maintenance and monitoring. Evaluation decisions involve review and assessment of treatment involvement, treatment participation, and goal attainment.

Phase G involves termination and follow-up. This covers evaluation of maximum treatment benefit, remaining functional deficits, suitable levels of community function, and assessment of appropriate community methods for community reentry.

In summary, the model of system flow described identifies decision points at each stage of the treatment process. It should be noted that the decision points in type I (definitional) are located externally in multiple community agencies. These types of decisions are most generic. The type II decisions (procedural) are located within each alcoholism treatment facility. While these decisions are generic in terms of program operation, they must be modified to meet individual variation in presenting conditions. These decisions lead in phase E to specific individualized treatment plans. Type III decisions (evaluative) are points located within each individual and are the most specific of the treatment decisions.

BLOCK VARIABLES

As indicated, treatment selection proceeds from the most general treatment decisions in the community to the most specific decisions with each alcoholic. Yet each decision point does not exist in isolation, but is imbedded in the prior decision processes and their consequences. It is therefore inadequate to simply evaluate the effect of a specific treatment decision in terms of the immediate consequence, since decision outcomes are influenced considerably by prior variables and events in the pathway of treatment. The possible significance of these variables in the pathway of treatment can be illustrated by consideration of the variable sets, which exist in "blocks" at each phase of treatment, as illustrated in Figure 2.

Psychological background. Variables in block 1 include age, sex, ethnicity, vocational skills and competence, education, and marital and social history. Taken together they comprise a level of psychosocial competence.

Social and family interaction. This block (2) involves the current level of social function and interaction with spouse, family relatives, and significant others in the community. It includes the alcoholic's social standing, degree of social deviancy, and the extent of social support for treatment or social support for continued alcoholism. These factors influence entry into treatment, program participation, aftercare participation, and ultimate treatment outcome [60, 61, 62, 68, 86, 91, 102, 104].

Perceptual and attitudinal sets. Block 3 includes the similarities and differences of the alcoholic and significant others about the definition of the alcoholism, need for treatment, motivation for change, perceived needs, and perceived goals [42].

Drinking patterns. Block 4 involves measures of consumption [47, 51]; the severity of the consequences of drinking behavior; the meaning, involvement, and investment in drinking [37]; and possible assessment of the stage of development of the alcoholic process [63, 64, 93].

Signs and symptoms of disability. This block (5) involves the degree of dysfunction and loss of competence due to alcoholism. It includes physical disabilities; neuropsychological disabilities, which may limit the degree of program participation, and may or may not be reversible [6, 96]; vocational disabilities; and social and/or family disabilities.

Treatment potential. The treatment potential (block 6) is derived from data in blocks 1 through 5. An alcoholic who is a good risk, with many assets and few disabilities, might respond equally well to a variety of treatments; whereas an alcoholic who is a poor risk (like the skid row stereotype, with few assets and many liabilities) might respond poorly to any treatment intervention. Between these extremes are probably different types of alcoholics who vary in their prognosis for improvement in specific areas of disability.

Identification. Identification (block 7) includes definitions of who is alcoholic, information imparted, attitudes and expectations generated, social constraints on entry (probation, jail, divorce, treatment fees), and the context of identification (social, legal, medical).

Several recent studies have reemphasized the difficulty in linking the alcohol-

Figure 2. Block Variables in the Treatment System

	1 Psychological Background	2 Social and Family Interaction	3 Perceptual and Attitudinal Sets	4 Drinking Patterns	5 Signs and Symptoms of Disability	6 Treatment Potential
Set I: Preexistent blocks						
Set II: Pretreatment blocks	7 Differential Identification	8 Triage Diagnosis	9 Entry Assessment	10 Initial Treatment Diagnosis		
Set III: Treatment blocks	11 Patient Treatment Selection	12 Personnel Treatment Selection	13 Content of Treatment Selection	14 Treatment Assessment	15 Aftercare Assessment	
Set IV: Outcome block	16 Differential Outcome Assessment					

ic from the identification agency to the treatment agency [14]. This process may skew the type of alcoholic who enters treatment, or the degree to which a good match is obtained so that the alcoholic actually enters a suitable treatment program.

Triage. Variables in block 8 (triage) include criteria for referral, method of referral, mechanisms of referral, participation of the index alcoholic in the referral process, availability of referral resources, and degree of objective and subjective suitability and acceptance of referral.

This is a critical phase, for most dropouts occur right here. This is undesirable, of course, from a clinical standpoint, and certainly biases predictive research efforts. Baekeland and Lundwall [3] report that dropouts from inpatient programs range from 13 to 40%, and in outpatient programs from 52 to 75%. Patient motivation, attitudes, expectations, and perceptions of the program become initial variables [61, 84]. In addition, the social climate of the program is an immediate, determining variable [9].

Entry assessment. Entry assessment (block 9) includes prior negative treatment experience, self-expectations and perceptions, significant other expectations and perceptions, social climate, waiting time for entry, degree of immediate support and reduction of anxiety, degree of immediate symptom relief, provision of necessary immediate life support (food, clothes, shelter), degree of entry mechanics, such as paperwork and financial evaluation, and participation of significant others in the entry phase. Immediate physical assessment in terms of need for detoxification, immediate major physical impairments, and maintenance of daily life patterns are paramount [31]. Reports indicate the importance of providing socialization with other clientele, immediate involvement of the family and significant others, and the provision of education about alcoholism and information about further treatment alternatives.

Initial treatment diagnosis. Variables in block 10 include needs for medical, welfare, and social intervention, degree of socialization, involvement of family and significant others, and methods and mechanisms for transition into intermediate phases of treatment.

Patient treatment selection. In block 11 are (1) individual expectations and goals of treatment [12, 67]; (2) the degree of patient participation in the evaluation and selection of treatment alternatives [30, 100]; and (3) the interaction of patients with other patients, which provides a specific gestalt of treatment experience [85].

Personnel treatment selection. Block 12 (personnel treatment selection) includes the attitudes, values, and interests of treatment personnel; their levels of training and competency; congruency and collaboration between team personnel; and congruency and interaction between treatment personnel and the patient [71].

Content of treatment selection. Specific types of treatment is the first variable in block 13; the second is that of more generic aspects of treatment implementation, including frequency, intensity, levels of interaction; the third variable is that of singularity of treatment or combinations of treatments; the fourth is the variable of who is involved in the treatment process (e.g., individual, marital, family, peer, and social network members of the treatment process [9, 10, 11].

Treatment assessment. Block 14 (treatment assessment) variables include the degree of patient participation in selection of methods and goals, the congruence of methods and goals with prior status and potential for change, the methods and mechanisms of assessment, and the degree of feedback utilization of such clinical assessment [5].

Aftercare assessment. Aftercare assessment variables (block 15) include linkage to the treatment program, methods and mechanisms of transition, linkages between clients, linkages to family, significant others, and community social network, and level of participation and significant other response. This has been a neglected dimension until recently in the sequence of treatment. But recent evaluative studies provide modest support for the value of aftercare programs [13, 24, 48, 82, 83, 87, 99]. Perhaps more important is the issue of community reentry and the reinvolvement of the alcoholic in community life and structure with family, significant others, and community relations, which have been shown to be significant factors in subsequent outcome [8, 32, 89].

Differential outcome assessment. The first set of variables in block 16 (differential outcome asessment) concerns biases in sampling, as outlined by Miller et al. [58]. A second set is that of different sources of information that can provide convergent validity of outcome measures, as indicated by Sobell and Sobell [92]. A third set of variables is associated with the location of and cooperation of subjects. Moos and Bliss [60] found that difficult to locate and uncooperative subjects were generally in the poor outcome category.

SUMMARY

The selection of treatment for alcoholics has been described in terms of a system flow model. There is no single treatment decision, but rather a series of treatment decisions as the patient proceeds through the system of treatment. Evaluation of the effectiveness of treatment methods and treatment selection decisions is embedded in the complex of variables associated with the entire system of treatment. These variables are briefly set forth in 16 blocks of variables throughout the treatment system.

Finally, one must distinguish between the research process and the clinical process. Obviously this author has set forth an immensely complicated decision system. For the clinician a much more simplified operational schemata must be developed. Further, a highly rigorous individualized assessment process may not be clinically necessary. In fact, one must explore in much detail the limits of specificity of treatment. On the other hand, this analysis may illustrate the pitfalls of treatment selection and evaluation that are observed from only one point along the pathway of treatment.

REFERENCES

1. Armor, D. J., Johnson, P., and Stambul, H. *Alcoholism and Treatment*. Rand Corporation: Santa Monica, 1976.
2. Baekeland, F. Evaluation of treatment methods in chronic alcoholism. In: *The Biology of Alcoholism* (Vol. 5), Kissin, B. and Begleiter, H. (eds.). Plenum: New York, 1977.
3. Baekeland, F., and Lundwall, L. K. Engaging the alcoholic in treatment and keeping him there. In: *The Biology of Alcoholism* (Vol. 5), Kissin, B. and Begleiter, H. (eds.). Plenum: New York, 1977.
4. Baekeland, F., Lundwall, L. K., and Kissin, B. Methods for the treatment of chronic alcoholism: A critical appraisal. In: *Research Advances in Alcohol and Drug Problems* Israel, Y. (ed.). Wiley: New York, 1975.
5. Bean, K. L., and Karasievich, G. O. Psychological test results at three stages of inpatient alcoholism treatment. *J. Stud. Alcohol* 36:838–852, 1975.
6. Berglund, M., Leijonquist, H., and Horlea, M. Prognostic significance and reversibility of cerebral dysfunction in alcoholism. *J. Stud. Alcohol* 38:1761–1770, 1977.
7. Bowman, R. S., Stein, L. I., and Newton, J. R. Measurement and interpretation of drinking behavior. *J. Stud. Alcohol* 36:1154–1172, 1975.
8. Bromet, E., and Moos, R. H. Environmental resources and the posttreatment functioning of alcoholic patients. *J. Health Soc. Behav.* 18:326–338, 1977.
9. Bromet, E., Moos, R. H., and Bliss, F. The social climate of alcoholism treatment programs. *Arch. Gen. Psychiatry* 33:910–916, 1976.
10. Bromet, E., Moos, R. H., Bliss, F., and Wuthman, C. Treatment experiences of alcoholic patients: An analysis of five residential treatment programs. *Int. J. Addict.* 12:953–958, 1977.
11. Bromet, E., Moos, R. H., Bliss, F., and Wuthman, C. Posttreatment functioning of alcoholic patients: Its relation to treatment participation. *J. Consult. Clin. Psychol.* 45:829–842, 1977.
12. Canter, F. M. Treatment participation related to hospitalization goals of patients and their families. *Psychiatr. Q.* 46:81–87, 1972.
13. Chavpil, M., Hymes, H., and Delmastro, D. Outpatient aftercare as a factor in treatment outcome: A pilot study. *J. Stud. Alcohol* 39:540–544, 1978.
14. Corrigan, E. M. Linking the problem dinker with treatment. *Soc. Work* 17:54–60, 1972.
15. Costello, R. M. Alcoholism treatment and evaluation: I. In search of methods. *Int. J. Addict.* 10:251–275, 1975.
16. Costello, R. M. Alcoholism treatment and evaluation: II. Collation of two-year follow-up studies. *Int. J. Addict.* 10:857–868, 1975.
17. Costello, R. M. Programming alcoholism treatment: Historical trends. In: *Alcoholism and Drug Dependence*, Madden, J. S., Walker, R., and Kenyon, W. H. (eds.). Plenum: New York, 1977.

18. Costello, R. M. Evaluation of posthospital adjustment: Path analysis of causal chains. *Eval. Health Prof.* 1:83-93, 1978.
19. Costello, R. M., Biever, P., and Baillargen, J. G. Alcoholism treatment programming: Historical trends and modern approaches. *Alcoholism Clin. Exp.* 4:311-318, 1978.
20. Costello, R. M., Giffen, M. B., Schneider, S. L., Edington, P. W., and Maunders, K. B. Comprehensive alcohol treatment planning, implementation, and evaluation. *Int. J. Addict.* 11:553-570, 1976.
21. Costello, R. M., Lawlis, G. F., Manders, K. R., and Celistino, J. F. Empirical derivation of a partial personality typology of alcoholism. *J. Stud. Alcohol* 39:1258-1266, 1978.
22. Cronkite, R. C., and Moos, R. H. Evaluating alcoholism treatment programs: An integrated approach. *J. Consult. Clin. Psychol.* 46:1105-1119, 1978.
23. Dalahaye, S. An analysis of clients using alcoholism agencies in a community service. In: *Alcoholism and Drug Dependence*, Madden, J. S., Walker, R., and Kenyon, W. H. (eds.). Plenum: New York, 1977.
24. Dubourg, G. O. Aftercare for alcoholics: A follow-up study. *Br. J. Addict.* 64:155-163, 1969.
25. Edwards, G., Kyle, E., and Nicholls, P. Alcoholics admitted to four hospitals in England. *Q. J. Stud. Alcohol* 35:499-522, 1974.
26. Edwards, G., Orford, J., Egert, S., Gutherie, S., Hawker, A., Hensman, L., Mitcheson, M., Oppenheimer, E., and Taylor, C. Alcoholism: A controlled trial of "treatment" and "advice." *J. Stud. Alcohol* 38:1004-1031, 1977.
27. Einstein, S., Solfson, E., and Gecht, P. What matters in treatment: Relevant variables in alcoholism. *Int. J. Addict.* 5:295-307, 1970.
28. Emrick, C. D. A review of psychologically oriented treatment of alcoholism: II. The relative effectiveness of different treatment approaches and the effectiveness of treatment versus no treatment. *J. Stud. Alcohol* 36:88-108, 1975.
29. English, G. E., and Curtin, M. E. Personality differences in patients at three different alcoholism treatment agencies. *J. Stud. Alcohol* 36:52-68, 1975.
30. Ewing, J. A. Matching therapy and patients: The cafeteria plan. *Br. J. Addict.* 72:13-18, 1977.
31. Feldman, D. J., Pattison, E. M., Sobell, L. C., Graham, T., and Sobell, M. B. Outpatient alcohol detoxification: Initial findings on 564 patients. *Am. J. Psychiatry* 132:407-412, 1975.
32. Finlay, D. G. Effect of role network pressures on the alcoholic's approach to treatment. *Soc. Work* 11:71-77, 1966.
33. Finney, J. A., and Moos, R. H. Treatment and outcome for empirical subtypes of alcoholic patients. *J. Consult. Clin. Psychol.* 47:25-38, 1979.
34. Garitano, W. A., and Ronall, R. E. Concepts of life style in the treatment of alcoholism. *Int. J. Addict.* 9:585-592, 1974.
35. Gerard, D. L., and Saenger, G. *Outpatient Treatment of Alcoholism*. University of Toronto Press: Toronto, 1966.
36. Gibbs, L., and Flanagan, J. Prognostic indicators of alcoholic treatment outcome. *Int. J. Addict.* 12:1097-1111, 1977.
37. Gillies, M. C., Aharan, C., Smart, R. G., and Shain, M. The alcoholic involvement scale: A method of measuring change in alcoholics. *J. Alcoholism* 10:142-148, 1975.
38. Hadley, P. A., and Hadley, R. G. Treatment practices and philosophies in rehabilitation facilities for alcoholics. *Proceed. Am. Psychol. Assoc.* 80:779-780, 1972.
39. Hague, W. H., Donovan, D. M., and O'Leary, M. R. Personality characteristics related to treatment decisions among inpatient alcoholics: A nonrelationship. *J. Clin. Psychol.* 32:476-479, 1976.

40. Hart, L. S., and Stueland, D. An application of the multidimensional model of alcoholism: Differentiation of alcoholics by mode analysis. *J. Stud. Alcohol* 40:283-290, 1979.

41. Hart, L. S., and Stueland, D. Relationships of sociodemographic and drinking variables to differentiated subgroups of alcoholics. *Commun. Ment. Health J.* 5:47-57, 1979.

42. Henry, J. D., and Zastowny, J. R. Perceptual differences in alcoholics and significant others. *Alcohol Health Res. World* 3:36-39, 1978.

43. Horn, J. L. Comments on the many faces of alcoholism. In: *Alcoholism: New Directions in Behavioral Research and Treatment*, Nathan, P. E., Marlatt, G. A., and Lorgerg, T. (eds.). Plenum: New York, 1978.

44. Imber, S., Schultz, E., Funderbuck, F., Allen, R., and Flamer, R. The fate of untreated alcoholics. *J. Nerv. Ment. Dis.* 162:230-274, 1976.

45. Jacobson, G. R. *The Alcoholisms: Detection, Diagnosis, and Assessment*. Human Sciences Press: New York, 1976.

46. Kern, J. C., Schmelter, W., and Fanelli, M. A comparison of three alcoholism treatment populations. *J. Stud. Alcohol* 39:785-792, 1978.

47. Khavari, K. A., and Farber, P. D. A profile instrument for the quantification an assessment of alcohol consumption: The Khavari Alcohol Test. *J. Stud. Alcohol* 39:1525-1539, 1978.

48. Kirk, S. A., and Masi, J. Aftercare for alcoholics: Services of community mental health centers. *J. Stud. Alcohol* 39:545-547, 1978.

49. Kissin, B., Platz, A., and Su, W. Social and psychological factors in the treatment of chronic alcoholism. *J. Psychiatr. Res.* 8:13-27, 1968.

50. Levinson, T., and Sereny, G. An experimental evaluation of "insight therapy" for the chronic alcoholic. *Can. Psychiatr. Assoc.* 14:143-146, 1969.

51. Little, R. E., Schultz, F. A., and Mandell, W. Describing alcohol consumption: A comparison of three methods and a new approach. *J. Stud. Alcohol* 38:554-562, 1977.

52. Lowe, W. C., and Thomas, S. D. Assessing alcoholism treatment effectiveness: A comparison of three evaluative measures. *J. Stud. Alcohol* 37:883-889, 1976.

53. Magoon, A. J. Path analysis and evaluation models. *Eval. Health Prof.* 1:94-99, 1978.

54. Marlatt, G. A. The drinking profile: A questionnaire for the behavioral assessment of alcoholism. In: *Behavior Therapy Assessment: Diagnosis, Design, and Evaluation*, Mash, E. J. and Terdahl, L. G. (eds.). Springer: New York, 1975.

55. Martin, P. Y. Client characteristics and the expectations of staff in halfway houses for alcoholics. *J. Stud. Alcohol* 40:211-221, 1979.

56. McLachlan, J. F. C. Therapy strategies: Personality, orientation, and recovery from alcoholism. *Can. Psychiatr. Assoc. J.* 19:25-30, 1974.

57. Miller, W. R. Alcoholism scales and objective assessment methods: A review. *Psychol. Bull.* 83:649-674, 1976.

58. Miller, B. A., Pokorny, A. D., Valles, J., and Cleveland, S. E. Biased sampling in alcoholism treatment research. *Q. J. Stud. Alcohol* 31:97-107, 1970.

59. Mogar, R., Wilson, W., and Helm, S. Personality subtypes of male and female alcoholic patients. *Int. J. Addict.* 5:99-113, 1970.

60. Moos, R. H., and Bliss, G. Difficulties of follow-up and alcoholism treatment outcome. *Stud. Alcohol* 39:473-490, 1978.

61. Moos, R. H., and Bromet, E. Relation of patient attributes to perception of treatment environment. *J. Consult. Clin. Psychol.* 46:350-351, 1976.

62. Moos, R. H., Bromet, E., Tsu, V., and Moos, B. Family characteristics of the outcome of treatment for alcoholics. *J. Stud. Alcohol* 40:78-88, 1979.

63. Mulford, H. A. Stages in the alcoholic process: Toward a cumulative, nonsequen-

tial index. *J. Stud. Alcohol* 38:563-583, 1977.

64. Mulford, H. A. Treating alcoholism versus accelerating the natural recovery process: A cost-benefit comparison. *J. Stud. Alcohol* 40:505-583, 1979.

65. Neuringer, C., and Clopton, J. R. The use of psychological tests for the study and identification, prediction, and treatment of alcoholics. In: *Empirical Studies of Alcoholism*, Foldstein, G. and Neuringer, C. (eds.). Ballinger: Cambridge, Mass., 1976.

66. Ogborne, A. C. patient characteristics as predictors of treatment outcome for alcohol and drug abuse. In: *Research Advances in Alcohol and Drug Problems* (Vol. 4), Israel, Y. (ed.). Plenum: New York, 1978.

67. O'Leary, M. R., Rohsenow, D. F., and Chaney, E. F. The use of multivariate personality strategies in predicting attrition from alcoholism treatment. *J. Clin. Psychiatry* 40: 190-193, 1979.

68. Orford, J., Oppenheiner, E., Egert, S., Hensman, D., and Gutherie, S. The cohesiveness of alcoholism-related marriages and its influence on treatment outcome. *Br. J. Psychiatry* 128:318-339, 1976.

69. Otto, S., and Orford, J. *Not Quite Like Home: Small Hostels for Alcoholics and Others*. Wiley: New York, 1978.

70. Partington, J. T., and Johnson, F. G. Personality types among alcoholics. *Q. J. Stud. Alcohol* 30:21-34, 1969.

71. Pattison, E. M. A differential view of manpower resources. In: *The Paraprofessional in the Treatment of Alcoholicsm*, Staub, G. E. and Kent, L. M. (eds.). Thomas: Springfield, Ill., 1973.

72. Pattison, E. M. Rehabilitation of the chronic alcoholic. In: *The Biology of Alcoholism* (Vol. 3), Kissin, B. and Begleiter, H. (eds.). Plenum: New York, 1974.

73. Pattison, E. M. A conceptual approach to alcoholism treatment goals. *Addict. Behav.* 1:177-192, 1976.

74. Pattison, E. M. Ten years of change in alcoholism treatment and delivery systems. *Am. J. Psychiatry* 134:261-266, 1977.

75. Pattison, E. M. The Jack Donovan Memorial Lecture, 1978: Differential approaches to multiple problems associated with alcoholism. *Contemp. Drug Problems* 9:265-309, 1978.

76. Pattison, E. M. The selection of treatment modalities for the alcoholic patient. In: *The Diagnosis and Treatment of Alcoholism*, Mandelson, J. H. and Mello, N. K. (eds.). McGraw-Hill: New York, 1979.

77. Pattison, E. M. Differential treatment of alcoholism. In: *Phenomenology and Treatment of Alcoholism*, Fann, W. E. (ed.). Spectrum: New York, 1980.

78. Pattison, E. M., Coe, R., and Doerr, H. O. Population variation among alcoholism treatment agencies: *Int. J. Addict.* 8:199-299, 1973.

79. Pattison, E. M., Coe, R., and Rhodes, E. J. Evaluation of alcoholism treatment: Comparison of three facilities. *Arch. Gen. Psychiatry* 20:478-488, 1969.

80. Pattison, E. M., Sobell, M. B., and Sobell, L. C. *Emerging Concepts of Alcohol Dependence*. Springer: New York, 1977.

81. Pemper, K. Dimensions of change in the improving alcoholic. *Int. J. Addict.* 11: 641-649, 1976.

82. Pittman, D. J., and Tate, R. L. A comparison of two treatment programs for alcoholics. *Q. J. Stud. Alcohol* 30:888-899, 1969.

83. Pokorny, A. D., Miller, B. A., Kanas, T., and Valles, J. Effectiveness of extended aftercare in the treatment of alcoholics. *Q. J. Stud. Alcohol* 34:435-443, 1973.

84. Pratt, R., Linn, M., Carmichael, J., and Webb, N. The alcoholic's perception of the ward as a predictor of aftercare attendance. *J. Clin. Psychol.* 33:915-918, 1977.

85. Price, R. H., and Curlee-Salisbury, J. Patient-treatment interaction among alcoholics. *J. Stud. Alcohol* 36:659–669, 1975.

86. Rae, J. B. The influence of wives in the treatment outcome of alcoholics: A follow-up study at two years. *Br. J. Psychiatry* 120:601–613, 1972.

87. Sands, P. M., and Hanson, P. G. Psychotherapeutic groups for alcoholics and relatives in an outpatient setting. *Int. J. Group Psychother.* 121:22–33, 1976.

88. Schmidt, W., Smart, R. G., and Moss, M. K. *Social Class and the Treatment of Alcoholism*. University of Toronto Press: Toronto, 1968.

89. Simpson, W. M., and Webber, P. W. A field program in the treatment of alcoholism. *Hospit. Commun. Psychiatry* 22:170–173, 1971.

90. Smart, R. G., and Gray, G. Multiple predictors of dropouts from alcoholism treatment. *Arch. Gen. Psychiatry* 35:363–367, 1978.

91. Smith, C. G. Marital influences on treatment outcome in alcoholics. *J. Ir. Med. Assoc.* 60:433–434, 1967.

92. Sobell, L. C., and Sobell, M. B. Convergent validity: An approach to increasing confidence in treatment outcome conclusions with alcohol and drug abuse. In: *Evaluating Alcohol and Drug Abuse Treatment Effectiveness: Recent Advances*, Sobell, L. C., Sobell, M. B., and Eard, E. (eds.). Pergamon: New York, 1978.

93. Stallings, D. L., and Oncken, G. R. A relative change index in evaluating alcoholism treatment outcome. *J. Stud. Alcohol* 38:457–464, 1977.

94. Stein, L. I., and Bowman, R. S. Reasons for drinking: Relationship to social functioning and drinking behavior. In: *Currents in Alcoholism* (Vol. 2), Seixas, F. A. (ed.). Grune & Stratton: New York, 1977.

95. Stinson, D. J., Smith, W. G., Amidjaya, I., and Kaplan, J. M. Systems of care and treatment outcome for alcoholic patients. *Arch. Gen. Psychiatry* 36:535–539, 1979.

96. Tarter, R. E. Neuropsychological investigations of alcoholism. In: *Emprical Studies of Alcoholism*, Goldstein, G. and Neuringer, C. (eds.). Ballinger: Cambridge, Mass., 1976.

97. Trice, H. M., Roman, P. M., and Belasco, J. A. Selection for treatment: A predictive evaluation of an alcoholism treatment regime. *Int. J. Addict.* 4:303–317, 1969.

98. Tuchfeld, B. S., Simuel, J. B., Schmitt, M. L., Ries, J. L., Kay, D. L., and Waterhouse, G. J. *Changes in Patterns of Alcohol Abuse without the Aid of Formal Treatment: An Exploratory Study of Former Problem Drinkers* (Final report to NIAAA). Research Triangle Institute: Research Triangle Park, N.C., 1976.

99. Vannicelli, M. Impact of aftercare in the treatment of alcoholics. *J. Stud. Alcohol* 39:1875–1886, 1978.

100. Vannicelli, M. Treatment contracts in an inpatient alcoholism treatment setting. *J. Stud. Alcohol* 40:457–471, 1979.

101. Wanberg, K. W., Horn, J. L., and Foster, F. M. A differential assessment model for alcoholism: The scales of the alcohol use inventory. *J. Stud. Alcohol* 38:512–543, 1977.

102. Webb, N. L., Pratt, T. C., Linn, M. W., and Carmichael, J. S. Focus on the family as a factor in differential treatment outcomes. *Int. J. Addict.* 13:783–796, 1978.

103. Wiseman, J. P. *Stations of the Lost: The Treatment of Skid Row Alcoholism*. Prentice-Hall: Englewood Cliffs, N.J., 1970.

104. Wright, K. D., and Scott, T. B. The relationship of wives' treatment to the drinking status of alcholics. *J. Stud. Alcohol* 39:1577–1581, 1978.

92

ALLAN BEIGEL, MD, University of Arizona College of Medicine
BARBARA REED HARTMANN, PhD, University of Arizona College of Medicine

COMMUNITY EPIDEMIOLOGY AND TREATMENT PLANNING

ALCOHOLISM TREATMENT services are ideally viewed as an integral and integrated dimension of a locally developed comprehensive community behavioral or public health system with emphasis on continuity of care for consumers. The pattern of services to be provided should be determined on the basis of identified epidemiologic principles and delivered within the sociocultural fabric of the specific community.

To develop an effective and appropriate community-oriented intervention strategy the framework for planning treatment services must continually derive its knowledge base from information regarding the prevalence and incidence of alcohol usage within the locale. This especially holds true for alcoholism services, since no clear distinction between appropriate use and misuse of ethanol exists. As one reviews the relevant literature concerning drinking practices, the stereotype of the inebriate as a social reprobate is replaced by an awareness that the eth-

---

Allan Beigel, MD, Professor of Psychiatry, University of Arizona College of Medicine, and Director, Southern Arizona Mental Health Center, Tucson, Arizona.

Barbara Reed Hartmann, PhD, Assistant Professor, University of Arizona College of Medicine, Department of Family and Community Medicine, Tucson, Arizona.

anol-misusing population in a community is both large and diverse. Moreover, community perception of the drinker varies along particular dimensions not necessarily predictable from the literature.

Although there are legislative constraints that limit the scope of total community behavioral health system involvement, each community subsystem should assemble the kinds and levels of care that the evidence suggests can most productively create opportunities for effective clinical interventions.

The planning and policy development aspects of providing community-specific alcoholism services present significant challenges to local agency executives, administrators, consumers, and other decision makers. Collectively, these personnel need to address the highly complex problems that will ultimately determine the shape of the operational system of available resources.

Within behavioral health, relatively recent legislation has returned the obligation for planning to the jurisdiction of local communities. This dramatic change has occurred because of the belief that more efficient, coordinated, and (it is hoped) effective treatment services than have existed in the past can be developed if derived from a local planning base.

The contemporary philosophy of locale-specific service delivery is to increase the level of health and well-being of the community as a unified whole. In recognition of the many stresses created by a highly urbanized technological society, with its problematic pace and consequent tensions of living, sociotherapeutic efforts have been directed toward development of programs that will intervene in the evolution of behavioral health casualties.

It is critical to understand that personal beliefs in the arena of treatment planning are frequently contradictory and may vary between communities and often within a community. Dissension may exist both in the conception of individual and collective responsibility for human well-being as well as among the diverse perceptions of the social and political mechanisms available for use in achieving and maintaining such well-being.

In a broad sense, discussions of these issues closely approximate the public opinion central to a community's political and historical development; the resulting treatment services often reflect these guiding ethics. Within this caveat that the planning and delivery of community-specific alcoholism treatment services should be intimately related to the total pattern of considerations that give rise to the need and demand for such services, this chapter presents a review of some of the methodologies of epidemiologic investigation of alcoholism with their accompanying assets and liabilities. Secondly, a generic orientation to the types of decisions required for planning in terms of community epidemiology is offered. This is followed by discussion of two projects: (1) a low-cost prevalence study, and (2) a community attitude awareness study, both conducted within a specific community and subsequently used to operationalize the goal of developing locale-specific alcoholism programming.

EPIDEMIOLOGIC INVESTIGATION OF ALCOHOLISM

Ideally, epidemiologic inquiry considers several elements that, when provisionally stated, form a scientific hypothesis that can then be tested. These elements include (1) description of the population at risk, (2) cause, (3) expected effect, (4) amount of the cause needed to produce the effect, and (5) period of time between exposure to the cause and observation of the effect.

In behavioral health epidemiology, including alcoholism, however, a complete hypothesis following these criteria is rarely achieved. The reason for this deficiency is the overall fragility of the scientific bases for those theoretical constructs that attempt to explain who, when, where, and perhaps why some persons experience behavioral dysfunction. The social correlates of behavioral problems and their etiologic significance have not been sufficiently specified, although the search for such answers has been active at least since Hippocrates. And, depending upon the prevailing attitudes in the society at the time, perspectives concerning the relationship between the social milieu and the health and well-being of the members will change to reflect these attitudes.

The movement in the 20th century from the conceptual basis of evolutionary and adaptational forces to explain behavioral illness to the more recent general systems theory with its focus on ecology serves as an example of perspective change in behavioral health epidemiology. Currently, the nuclear problem for specifying incidence and prevalence of alcoholism is inherent in the methodological constraints above. Nevertheless, although the answers for the set of facts needed for a complete epidemiologic inquiry are still partial, investigators and planners in the alcoholism field have been able to operationalize the knowledge already accumulated.

To develop a community epidemiology of alcoholism, one must provide statements corresponding to each of the five elements listed above. The forthcoming hypothesis would then be stated and the results tested and analyzed [4]. Completing this process could amount to developing an epidemiologically sound, locale-specific theory of alcoholism causation. Such a theory would address questions such as, What constitutes alcoholism? What is the incidence of alcoholism in the particular locale? In what way is alcoholism a problem for the community? For the individual? What kind of community response may best deal with alcoholism?

Methodology

Many researchers [3, 4, 5, 6, 11] have investigated the incidence (rate of appearance of new cases) and prevalence (rate of existence of cases) of alcoholism. There are four epidemiologic methodologies ordinarily used either alone or in combination. These approaches, based upon their source of information, include (1) the social indicators, or *ex post facto* method, (2) the key informant method, (3) the number in treatment method, and (4) the community survey [8].

An "indicator" is a class, set, or group of potentially observable phenomena that appears to be empirically related in some measure to a specific variable (i.e., conceptual domain). The social indicators method is a secondary analysis that collects easily obtained population statistics that have been hypothesized as related to alcoholism. There are two primary sources for this data: (1) past research findings, and (2) information banks, including research centers and governmental agencies. Statistics such as the number of driving while intoxicated (DWI) arrests, the incidence of cirrhosis of the liver, per capita consumption of alcohol beverages, and other indicators form the data base. There have been numerous research studies using this approach since these data tend to be routinely gathered across society in natural settings, appear highly reliable, and are easily and unobtrusively collected. Additionally, findings from these studies provide information that cannot be obtained through experimental research to yield a comprehensive estimate of the level of the problem.

An example of epidemiologic inquiry using social indicators as the method base is that of Jellinek [6, 7]. Since it was not possible to conduct a survey to determine the actual number of alcoholics in the country, he tried to answer the question by positing a relationship between reported deaths caused by cirrhosis and alcoholism in heavy drinkers. An equation specifying this relationship was then derived from the data. There has been much activity in the research based on Jellinek's work and findings, as well as a multitude of studies offering other social indicators as a means for determining the incidence and prevalence of alcoholism.

Key informants are persons who, by virtue of their role, are presumed knowledgeable concerning the problem in question. Upon solicitation, these experts offer their beliefs relating to the issue. These opinions may then be used as an analytic tool by the researcher, under certain limited conditions [9], and often can unveil the socially hidden or unexpected population of problem drinkers. Generally, findings derived solely from informants are not used per se, but rather interpreted in association with data generated by other methods.

Epidemiologic inquiry using the number of persons in treatment is based upon the hypothesis that certain facts about those persons diagnosed as problem drinkers who have already entered a treatment setting will assist in developing understanding of those who are alcoholic, but have not sought services or have not been identified during treatment for other problems. Demographic and other specific information is collected from the patients' case histories or from some secondary document (e.g., monthly or annual reports of treatment activity). Studies using this data base have also employed standardized structured or unstructured interviews with patients, former patients, and/or their families. Results have then been compiled with respect to the research questions [11].

The fourth method, the community survey, derives its data from a standardized questionnaire and/or interview of a sample of the population in the locale [12]. The composition of the sample must meet certain established criteria to be appropriate for scientific inquiry [8]. The interviewer presents the questions to the respondents, whose replies are subsequently tabulated and analyzed [10]. The advantages of a community survey include breadth of scope of both information gathered and population studies, as well as an extremely high level of accuracy of information collected. A competently designed and sophisticated community survey usually proves to provide a remarkably solid planning base.

The particular method of inquiry one chooses will depend upon what one wants to find out. However, validity and reliability in all methods is contingent upon a clear statement of the major question that the epidemiologic research poses and some preliminary findings that lead to the question. An explication of what is to be done and for what purpose is required. There must also be a definition of terms to foster consensual understanding of the qualitative aspects of the research: what is stated about which population using what tools. A most important goal of any epidemiologically scientific investigation is that the results be generalizable to the total population.

In each of the methods given above, there is some aspect that, given the current state of the art, prevents total realization of this goal. With the social indicators method, there can be variability in the amount of detail and the level of accuracy of the base data as well as a lack of uniformity in the available indicators used as variables. There is also a general inability to randomize the data as well as to control the independent variable. The much greater difficulty, though, is the risk of erroneous interpretation of the findings. This arises in part from the overall complexity of defining causal relationships in behavioral science.

Key informants may not necessarily know the data upon which their opinion is based. However, even inaccurate reports may still be valuable insofar as it may be equally important in behavioral health research to discover what has been missed entirely, misunderstood, or misperceived. There is usually an extremely low response rate to solicitation unless these persons are polled via personal contact, which frequently is not possible due to time, financial, or other constraints.

Case history data reflects the situations only of those who have entered organized treatment systems and have received a diagnosis of alcoholism. This group is not necessarily sufficiently representative of the particular population in question to serve as a base for epidemiologic decision making, leaving room for error in any attempt to make relevant assertions about the total community. Variations ranging from the lack of uniformity in the diagnostic process to differences in utilization rates among treatment providers contribute to the inadequacies of this approach.

Community surveys tend to miss (as respondents) transients and others who will eventually utilize the treatment system. There is difficulty in achieving representative response samples, adequate and valid instrument development, and correctly completed protocols. Additionally, a high monetary cost and a significant period of time are required to prepare for and to finish the task. Finally, in those communities lacking funds for this purpose, surveys may be precluded as a resource for treatment services planning.

A GENERIC FRAMEWORK FOR TREATMENT SERVICE PLANNING DECISIONS

There are four basic dimensions involved in planning treatment services within a community. Initially, the fundamental questions of a politicized economy (namely, who will get what) sets the process in motion. Arriving at an answer to this question is an extremely complex undertaking and underscores the local planner's responsibility to identify and act in consideration of the community's traditions, values, and existing institutions, as well as within the mandates of relevant federal and state legislation. This community-level orientation to the planning and organization of services results in variability by locale in both the character and structure of the human services system. The dominant values and traditional roles of the community will to a great extent govern the organization of the system. For example, most behavioral health systems involve private organizations, both profit and nonprofit, as well as public agencies. How these agencies will relate to each other in terms of what services are provided to whom, and in what manner, depends upon the goals and traditions of the individual community.

The second dimension of decision making in the planning process addresses the types of services to be furnished and the distribution of funds. Additionally, eligibility for services and the planning for the total range of components is accomplished. As with the first dimension, frequently there is legislation directing the choices available. Such directives may address issues surrounding provision of services to an entire population as a matter of right versus provision of services to a select group only. In general, this second level of planning determines the nature and the quality of the system, because it is here that concerns derived from local and external forces shaping the community environment, needs assessments, existing community resources, and the inclusion of both consumer and provider participation in the planning process impact.

The range of complexities of planning for alcoholism services becomes quite evident within the third dimension, which determines the method of delivering the services. There are three key factors that operate: financing, technology, and organizational design.

Financial factors include all sources of funding, from appropriation to service delivery and collections, ordinarily involving such elements as fee for services, third-party payers, or other client revenue, as well as nonclient origins, such as public funding and donations. The specific funding patterns for alcoholism services clearly impact upon the size, the operation, and the stability of the services.

Technological factors include the skills and knowledge of the providers in addition to the equipment necessary to deliver the services to consumers. Within this aspect of planning especially, cooperation and collaboration between specialist providers and planners is critical. Concerns about the continually changing technology in association with those related to quality assurance and provider responsiveness are well-recognized consumer interests.

In conjunction with the decisions involving technological issues are those that address the organizational arrangements for optimal service delivery. Location of services within the population area must be studied. Further, considerations of service functions performed, areas of specialization, target clientele, and actual client pathways through the system in terms of both direct services and necessary secondary support activities must be identified and analyzed.

The final dimension of planning for alcoholism services involves the actual delivery setting and characteristics of its services, such as accessibility, availability, quality, cost, continuity, and accountability. Relevant concerns also include location and quality of land sites; design, financing and construction of buildings; staffing pattern and positions; and specific budgetary allocation.

Overall, the task of planning for community alcoholism services is amenable to careful analysis and successful completion despite the inherent difficulties generally related to human services planning.

COMMUNITY EPIDEMIOLOGY: PIMA COUNTY, ARIZONA

To demonstrate the value of developing a community-specific epidemiologic approach to planning for treatment services, the following description of two phases of a community planning effort is provided [1, 2].

The first phase involved a community prevalence survey. Most previous prevalence research had been completed as part of comprehensive projects surveying drinking practices. These usually involved extremely high costs and lengthy periods of investigation. Moreover, the majority of this work was not undertaken for purposes of treatment planning.

The prevalence survey was conducted by a cadre of nine community planning aides whose primary purpose was the implementation of an initiation and development grant awarded to the Pima County Health Department by the National Institute on Alcohol Abuse and Alcoholism. The survey itself attempted to identify visible problem drinkers as well as to estimate the number of nonvisible problem drinkers.

Identification of overt problem drinkers was accomplished through contact with every community agency expected to have served problem drinkers in the previous 2 years and the subsequent gathering of demographic information concerning these persons. Data pertaining to the census tract of residence, race, age, sex, marital status, usual employment, and annual income was collected. Other useful information was not uniformly available. Approximately 200 agencies were contacted: criminal justice agencies, public health agencies, welfare agencies, social agencies, religious agencies, mental health agencies, hospitals, and other human service providers.

Identification of nonvisible problem drinkers was attempted by a letter requesting data mailed to key informants — in this instance, clergy and physicians.

By identifying the visible problem drinker population, the results provided sufficient data upon which the initial programming decisions of the comprehensive treatment system were based. Analysis of the data showed that among visible problem drinkers, 91% were males. The agencies having contact with the highest number of problem drinkers were from the law enforcement system. A delineation of the percentage of overt problem drinkers by socioeconomic status as well as by ethnic identity was made. Also, the age range for peak agency contact was determined by ethnic group. Additionally, the contact rate for males of different ethnic identities was described by the provider agency.

Discussion of these findings was directed to demonstrating the viability of using prevalence survey findings to guide the decision making within the planning process. The finding that the vast majority of problem drinkers were reported by law enforcement agencies led to the development of liaisons between these agencies and the community planning task force as well as to the development of emergency detoxification services whereby visible problem drinkers would be admitted to the treatment system rather than to the criminal justice system. The Arizona statute removing public inebriation from the criminal code, while providing for alternative local alcoholism reception centers, in part resulted from the findings of this prevalence survey.

Other findings, such as the high agency contact rate of minorities, held implications for planning staffing patterns and outreach efforts. Actual geographical location of specific services (such as emergency detoxification) was suggested. The greatest number (40%) of visible problem drinkers were shown to reside in the then-existing Model Cities neighborhood. This finding not only helped bring about development of a nonmedical detoxification center within this area, but also assisted in establishing a liaison with the Model Cities project for a planning and services provision.

The second phase of the Pima County epidemiologic planning activity for the development of comprehensive alcoholism services undertook to assess community awareness and attitudes [2]. Key questions were developed and pretested before answers were sought through a statistical random sampling. These data provided a core of information around which relevant services would be built. The specific questions to be answered were part of a larger door-to-door health survey and the responses were grouped to provide knowledge on each of these five areas: (1) How does the community as a whole and each of its four major ethnic groups (Anglo, black, Native American, Mexican-American) rate the seriousness of alcoholism as compared to other major public health problems? (2) What are the drinking practices of the population as a whole? (3) How aware are members of each of the four major ethnic groups of currently existing community alcoholism services? (4) To what extent do the members of the community recognize and acknowledge drinking problems in themselves and/or others and where would these individuals turn for help with such a problem? and (5) How is the alcoholic perceived by the community as a whole and by members of each of the various ethnic groups?

The survey questionnaire was administered to one or more persons from 1,975 households. The three initial questions requested rank ordering of six health problems, whether any of the members of the family experienced any of these illnesses, and if so which ones. The remainder of the survey requested information on drinking (12 questions) and demographics (10 questions).

Results patterned rather surprisingly in some instances and it was in these unexpected findings that the value of researching the knowledge of the community becomes most evident. For example, in the rank ordering of health problems, "drug problems" was ranked as the most serious health problem, followed by cancer, alcoholism, cardiac problems, arthritis, and mental illness. The tabulation for each ethnic group showed that Native Americans rated alcoholism as most serious. Blacks and Mexican-Americans rated alcoholism second, while Anglos regarded alcoholism as fourth in seriousness. Findings about drinking practices seem rather interesting in that the abstinence rate was 26.5%, mid-range between the rates reported for similar communities from other prevalence surveys. Of those who reported having consumed some alcohol in the week prior to the survey, 16% reported daily drinking, and of those only 33% characterized themselves as drinking fairly heavily or heavily. The fact that 66% of the population of heavy drinkers did not consider themselves to have a problem suggested a valuable direction for community consultation and education programs.

Community knowledge of existing alcoholism services showed an overall lack of awareness. Although Alcoholics Anonymous was highly recognized among Anglos (less so among the other ethnic groups), other specialized services for alcoholism experienced less recognition than general medical facilities and services. These findings showed a pattern of community need for increased knowledge as to existing programs.

Additionally, findings related to the community's perception of the alcoholic person pointed to the fact that the preponderance of minority respondents reported problem drinking to be related to a lack of willpower rather than to illness.

Also, in regard to the community awareness of problem drinkers, the results showed that a significant proportion of persons having drinking problems did not utilize such services, thereby remaining nonvisible.

Overall, this second phase of the Pima County community survey suggested that in view of the ethnic differences in attitudes toward alcoholism and the awareness of existing resources, the most effective approach to developing services would be through individualized and culture-specific education and treatment programs.

SUMMARY

This chapter enumerates four basic dimensions involved in community planning for treatment services. This framework organizes the findings of epidemiologic inquiry in a particular geographical area and provides a concrete and prioritized direction for community-specific treatment services development. Finally, discussion of a two-phase community planning effort has served to demonstrate the applicability of the approach and the overall practicality of developing the community system of services within a locale-specific model of alcoholism.

REFERENCES

1. Beigel, A. E., Hunter, E. J., Tamerin, J. S., Chapin, E. H., and Lowery, M. J. Planning for the development of comprehensive community alcoholism services: I. The prevalence survey. *Am. J. Psychiatry* 131(10):1112–1116, 1974.
2. Beigel, A., McCabe, T. R., Tamerin, J. S., Lowery, M. J., Chapin, E.H., and Hunter, E. J. Planning for the development of comprehensive alcoholism services: II. Assessing community awareness and attitudes. *Am. J. Psychiatry* 131(10):1116–1121, 1974.
3. Cahalan, D., and Cisin, D. H. American drinking practices: Summary of findings from a national probability sample: I. Extent of drinking by population subgroups. *Q. J. Stud. Alcohol* 29:130–152, 1968.
4. Edwards, G. Epidemiology as applied to alcoholism: A review and examination of purposes. *Q. J. Stud. Alcohol* 34:28–56, 1973.
5. Hagnell, O., and Tunving, K. Prevalence and nature of alcoholism in a total population. *Soc. Psychiatry* 7:190–201, 1972.
6. Jellinek, E. M. *The Disease Concept of Alcoholism.* College and University Press: New Haven, Conn., 1960.
7. Jellinek, E. M., and Keeler, M. Rates of alcoholism in the United States of America, 1940–1948. *Q. J. Stud. Alcohol* 13:49–59, 1952.
8. Kerlinger, F. N. *Foundations of Behavioral Research* (2nd ed.). Holt, Rinehart & Winston: New York, 1973.
9. Lipscomb, W. R. Survey measurements of the prevalence of alcoholism. *Arch. Gen. Psychiatry* 15:455–461, 1966.

10. Mulford, H. A., and Wilson, R. W. *Identifying Problem Drinkers in a Household Survey: A Description of Field Procedures and Analytical Techniques Designed to Measure the Prevalence of Alcoholism* (Series W, No. 16). U.S. National Center for Health Statistics: Washington, D.C., 1966.

11. Tamayo, M. B., and Feldman, D. J. Incidence of alcoholism in hospital patients. *Soc. Work* 20(2):89–91, 1975.

12. Warheit, G., Bell, R., and Schwab, J. *Planning for Change: Need Assessment Approaches.* National Institute of Mental Health: Rockville, Md., 1969.

93

RUDOLF H. MOOS, PhD, Stanford University and Veterans Administration Medical Center, Palo Alto, California

RUTH C. CRONKITE, PhD, Stanford University and Veterans Administration Medical Center, Palo Alto, California

JOHN W. FINNEY, PhD, Stanford University and Veterans Administration Medical Center, Palo Alto, California

A CONCEPTUAL FRAMEWORK FOR ALCOHOLISM TREATMENT EVALUATION

IN SPITE OF EXTENSIVE research aimed at evaluating the treatment of alcoholism, very little is known still about the factors that contribute to or mediate successful outcome. Evaluations of treatment programs invariably find that patient characteristics and treatment factors combined explain only a small proportion of the variation in posttreatment functioning. As a case in point, Polich et al. [35] accounted for only 4.2% of the variance in long-term abstinence and 9.2% in drinking problems with a combination of patient- and treatment-related factors, even though they studied patients

---

Rudolf H. Moos, PhD, Social Ecology Laboratory, and Professor, Department of Psychiatry and Behavioral Sciences, Stanford University, Stanford, California, and Veterans Administration Medical Center, Palo Alto, California.

Ruth C. Cronkite, PhD, Social Ecology Laboratory, Department of Psychiatry and Behavioral Sciences, Stanford University, Stanford, California, and Veterans Administration Medical Center, Palo Alto, California.

John W. Finney, PhD, Social Ecology Laboratory, Department of Psychiatry and Behavioral Sciences, Stanford University, Stanford, California, and Veterans Administration Medical Center, Palo Alto, California.

drawn from a heterogeneous set of treatment programs. Such findings reflect a conceptual crisis in treatment outcome research and highlight the need for a paradigm shift in evaluations of alcoholism programs. In essence, the traditional patient input—"black box" treatment—outcome paradigm must be changed by (1) placing more emphasis on formative evaluation, that is, on the process and implementation of treatment, and (2) exploring the factors that intervene between treatment and follow-up.

To address these issues, an integrated conceptual framework is presented herein, one that encompasses sociodemographic and intake-functioning factors, characteristics of treatment programs and patients' treatment experiences, and posttreatment factors that intervene between the end of the treatment and the evaluation of follow-up functioning. Most studies have focused on the relationship between patient factors and treatment outcome, and only a few have considered the effects of both patient characteristics and treatment variations on outcome [1, 7, 13, 35]. Recently, however, it has become apparent that (1) treatments often are only partially implemented [32] and (2) posttreatment factors can account for increments in outcome variation that are almost equal to the portions of variance explained by background characteristics and intake functioning alone [14, 18]. Such findings underscore the need for a broad process-oriented conceptual framework to guide the formulation of future studies of alcoholism treatment outcome.

The conceptual framework shown in Figure 1 outlines the processes through which treatment outcome is shaped by six sets of factors: (1) sociodemographic factors (2) pretreatment symptoms and functioning levels, (3) treatment experiences, (4) life stressors, (5) the patient's coping responses to such stressors, and (6) environmental resources, such as the supportive aspects of a patient's family and work settings. The first two are patient-related pretreatment factors, the effects of which are often contrasted with the third set of treatment-related variables. The remaining three are extra- or posttreatment factors. To illustrate the conceptual framework, each of these sets of factors is discussed and their relationships to one another and to posttreatment functioning explored. The implications of the framework for clarifying some recurrent issues that arise in evaluating treatment programs are then considered.

THE PRETREATMENT DOMAINS

Sociodemographic Factors

Such indices as gender, age, marital status, ethnicity, and socioeconomic status (especially educational and occupational level) have been studied extensively in relation to alcohol abuse. Among individuals who enter treatment programs, for example, a higher than expected proportion are men; Catholic or liberal Protes-

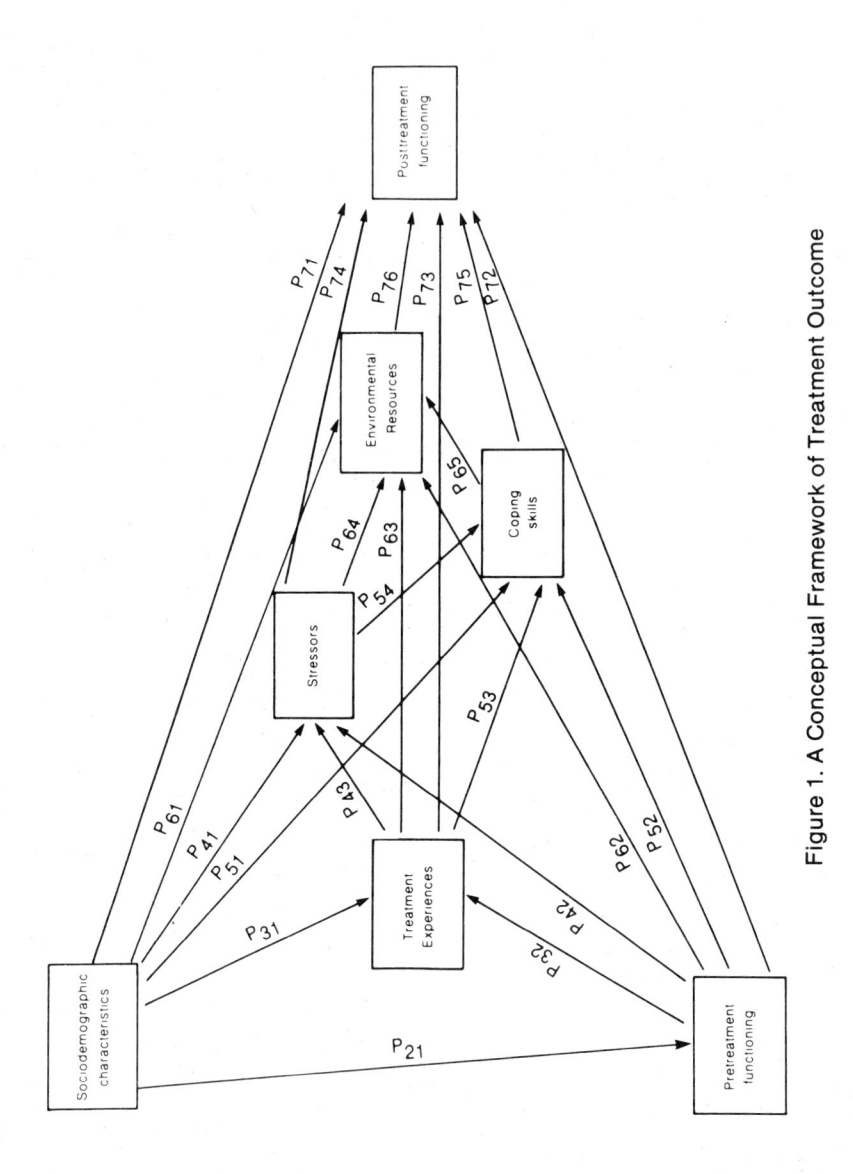

Figure 1. A Conceptual Framework of Treatment Outcome

tant; black, Spanish-American, or Native American; separated or divorced; from southern regions; and below the median income and occupational prestige levels. Region, ethnicity, religion, and gender are associated with strong sociocultural norms regarding drinking customs and sanctions, while factors such as marital and socioeconomic status reflect an individual's current social stability.

Although individuals entering treatment can be distinguished to some extent from the general population and its subset of problem drinkers, they nevertheless exhibit a wide range of sociodemographic characteristics that are related to the type and severity of alcohol abuse and associated indices of psychological and social functioning (as illustrated by path P_{21} in Figure 1). In general, alcohol consumption is lower and associated symptoms less severe among well-educated patients of high socioeconomic status. Female alcoholics consume less alcohol and are more likely to drink alone or at home, while their male counterparts more often drink with friends or in bars. For male patients, being married is related to better intake functioning, but such a marital status difference is negligible among female patients [4].

Sociodemographic characteristics are also important predictors of posttreatment functioning (as shown by path P_{71} in Figure 1). For instance, higher socioeconomic status and social stability are associated with better treatment outcome [1, 30]. Being married is related to better posttreatment functioning among male patients, although not among female patients [15]. Such findings suggest that sociodemographic characteristics are indicators of the personal assets that patients have when entering treatment, and that such assets in turn are associated with better prognosis.

Pretreatment Symptoms and Functioning

Most often patient functioning variables are assessed at entry into an alcoholism program so that they can be used as baselines against which to evaluate posttreatment functioning or treatment outcome. Therefore, both pre- and posttreatment functioning variables are considered in this section.

Individuals who abuse alcohol differ in drinking behavior as well as in their social, psychological, and occupational functioning. For example, one patient at intake may have a history of intense but infrequent binges, while another indicates a pattern of heavy daily drinking. Other distinctions among patients include perceived functions of alcohol use (to reduce tension, to be sociable), the context of drinking (alone at home, at a bar), social functioning (number of friends, involvement in community organizations), and symptoms of depression. Although there is some homogeneity of patient populations in specific programs, different subtypes of patients have been identified within programs [16], indicating that there may be substantial individual differences among the persons treated at a facility.

Just as abusive drinking is the primary presenting problem of alcoholic patients, abstinence or reduction of alcohol consumption is the primary treatment outcome measure. Recognition of the multiple problems exhibited by patients at intake, however, has led to a multidimensional orientation toward posttreatment functioning [22]. At a minimum, the following domains should be assessed: (1) drinking behavior, (2) physical conditions, (3) social relationships, (4) psychological functioning, and (5) occupational performance. Ideally, a standard core set of measures should be used, but the number of dimensions or variables within domains and the variety of measurement techniques available suggest that it may take some time to develop consensus among researchers.

Although there is a direct relationship between patients' functioning at intake and their treatment outcome (as noted by path P_{72} in Figure 1), the initial assessment of patients should not be guided solely by the projected measurement of outcome variables. As suggested by the model, other important questions focus on patient pretreatment functioning. For example, what patient characteristics influence treatment selection or attrition within programs (path P_{32})? To what extent is patients' initial functioning related to the occurrence of subsequent stressful life events (path P_{42})? Such issues need to be considered at the initiation of an evaluation study in order to develop appropriate measures of patient characteristics.

THE TREATMENT DOMAIN

Ironically, while the intervention program lies at the heart of any study of treatment, it often is an undifferentiated "black box" in evaluations of alcoholism programs. This point was stressed by Crawford and Chalupsky [11] who, after examining the reports of 40 program evaluations, concluded that "typically no observation or measures are taken during treatment. This cloak enveloping treatment processes effectively masks any possibility of identifying treatment correlates and differences within an institution, across therapists, over time within a given setting, etc." [11, p. 72].

Lack of attention to treatment variables reflects the summative nature of most evaluations of alcoholism programs. The question addressed in such studies is, "Are the persons receiving the treatment package functioning better at follow-up, on average, in comparison to (1) their pretreatment functioning (most common comparison); (2) persons receiving some other treatment package; (3) persons receiving less treatment; or (4) persons receiving no formal treatment (least common comparison)?" The summative model implies that if the answer to this question is yes, the program should be continued or expanded, while if the answer is no, the program should be terminated [9].

The summative approach, although popular (perhaps because of its simplicity), has at least two serious drawbacks. First, a policy maker or administrator usually is not in a position to kill a program on the basis of a negative evaluation; rather, an attempt most often will be made to correct a deficient program. Second, a summative evaluation provides no information as to why a program or treatment package is effective or ineffective. In contrast, formative evaluations are oriented toward program improvement and focus on the implementation and process of treatment. Consequently, they are much more likely to provide information that will be useful to policy makers, program administrators, service providers, and researchers.

Parameters of Treatment

Formative evaluations illuminate "black box" programs by assessing various parameters of treatment. While treatment variables can be classified in a number of ways, it is useful to distinguish treatment experiences as to type (inpatient, outpatient, aftercare), modality (pharmacologi, psychodynamic, behavioral), specific therapeutic component within modality (individual vs. group psychodynamic therapy sessions), duration (length of stay in a residential program), amount (number of therapy sessions, number of times Antabuse is administered), quality (empathy expressed by a counselor, supportiveness of a hospital environment), and staff characteristics (professional or paraprofessional, experienced or inexperienced). An eighth dimension is that of intensity (ratio of amount to duration).

Multifaceted assessment that examines within- as well as between-program variations in treatment affords the opportunity to explore issues that usually receive only scant attention in summative evaluations. These issues include (1) treatment implementation, (2) relationships between patient characteristics and treatment experiences, and (3) relationships between treatment experiences and treatment outcome.

Treatment Implementation

Examination of treatment implementation, or what Suchman [39] referred to as the evaluation of effort, focuses on "the quantity and quality of treatment activity that takes place" [39, p. 61]. While expenditure of effort is no guarantee of treatment effectiveness, it would seem to be a crucial prerequisite in most instances. In this regard, monitoring treatment activity and quality is a form of "manipulation check" that can prevent the summative evaluation of a nonexistent program (for a dramatic example, see [32, pp. 149–150], or one that was only partially implemented. Such monitoring allows for a shift in focus to the following kinds of questions: "Do patients in a program with an enriched aftercare service actually receive more aftercare?" "Are former alcohol abusers who serve as paraprofessional peer counselors more empathic than professionally trained therapists?" "Does a therapeutic community provide more cohesion, support, and autonomy than conventional hospital treatment?"

With respect to the assessment of program activity, the present authors used data on duration of treatment and three therapeutic component measures (therapy sessions, films and lectures on alcoholism, and Alcoholics Anonymous meetings) to provide information on the relative intensity of treatment within three residential alcoholism programs. Lack of intensity of treatment emerged as one plausible reason why length of stay was not related to outcome in one program [17].

Information on the quality of an alcoholism treatment program can be obtained from an assessment of its social climate. The Community-Oriented Programs Environment Scale (COPES) was used to evaluate the social environments of residential alcoholism programs [6]. The COPES Form R (real) allows patients and staff to describe their program on 10 dimensions that represent three underlying domains. The involvement, support, and spontaneity subscales measure the relationship domain, whereas the autonomy, practical orientation, personal problem orientation, and anger and aggression subscales measure the primary therapeutic goals of programs (that is, the treatment program or goal-orientation domain). The last three subscales—order and organization, program clarity, and staff control—measure the extent to which the program functions in an orderly, organized, clear, and coherent manner (the system maintenance domain).

Figure 2 shows the COPES profiles for patients from a public hospital alcoholism unit and from a Salvation Army Center (for more details see [6]). Although the patients in these two programs were similar in background characteristics and the severity of their alcohol problems, they saw the treatment environments of their programs as quite different. The public hospital program placed only average or slightly above average emphasis (relative to normative data) on the relationship dimensions of support and spontaneity, and below average emphasis on the program dimension of practical planning for release and functioning in the community. Its relatively loose organizational structure is reflected in its low-to-average emphasis on the system maintenance dimensions. In contrast, the Salvation Army Center provided more encouragement for patients and staff to interact with and be supportive of one another. Its strongest emphasis in the treatment domain was on practical planning for release, which was exemplified by the training school housed at the facility and the importance placed on working while in the program. Finally, the program was well organized and clear in its expectations for patients.

Form I (ideal) of the COPES, which allows program members to describe their preferred program climate, provides information on staff and patient goals and values. Form I can be used in conjunction with Form R to identify areas of program satisfaction as well as areas in which change is desired. Feedback of COPES data on discrepancies between staff and patient perceptions, between program and normative data, and bewteen actual and preferred environmental profiles provides a framework with which the interested parties can articulate their concerns about the treatment environment. With this information (which may include an item-by-item analysis of discrepancies), program staff can institute changes that are

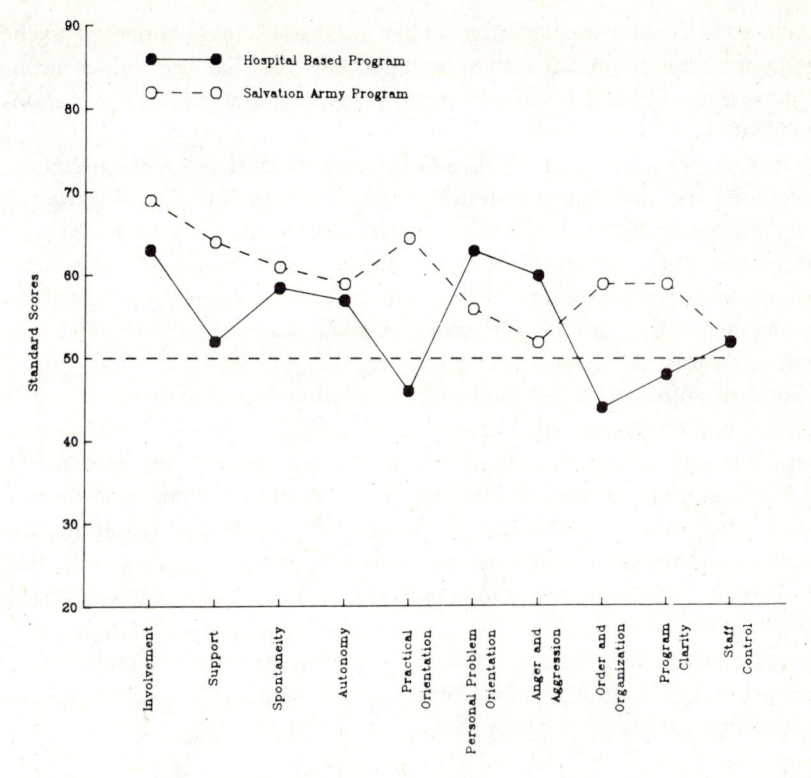

Figure 2. Community-Oriented Programs Environment Scale Profiles for Hospital-Based and Salvation Army Programs

consistent with an underlying treatment ideology. At a later point, the social climate of the program can be reassessed to determine the degree to which program changes have produced the desired impact. Such an assessment-change-reassessment cycle is the essence of formative program evaluation (see [26, 27] for examples).

Relationships between Patient Characteristics and Treatment Experiences

Alcoholism treatment usually is not provided to individuals on a random basis. Various personal and social factors (such as beliefs about the effectiveness of different types of treatment, physical and psychological functioning at intake, cost considerations and socially structured referrals) combine to determine program selection and admission. Such selection processes produce systematic relationships between patients' demographic and symptom characteristics and treatment programs (paths P_{31} and P_{32} in Figure 1). For instance, Bromet and et al. [7] found that clients in a milieu-oriented program that emphasized insight-oriented psychotherapy were better educated, more stable socially, and had less serious alcohol problems than clients in a Salvation Army program that emphasized vocational rehabilitation.

Once in a program, individuals may also receive differential treatment as a result of self-selection and/or staff-determined allocation. In comparing what appeared to be self-selection into treatment activities, Cronkite and Moos [15] found that female patients attended more lectures and films than did male patients. With respect to staff-determined allocation, one commonly held view (not always implemented) is that patients with more severe impairment should receive more intensive treatment.

Similarly, different patient demographic and symptom characteristics may be related to participation in aftercare (usually outpatient group therapy) following inpatient treatment. Pokorny et al. [34] observed that persons with better marital and work histories and fewer severe symptoms of alcohol dependence were more likely to attend aftercare therapy sessions. Cronkite and Moos [15] found that unmarried women and married men were more likely to participate in outpatient follow-up visits than married women or unmarried men. Factors accounting for such differential participation rates may include the reliance by staff on certain patient background characteristics for making differential recommendations for aftercare, and how strongly a patient's spouse or significant other encourages aftercare treatment.

Relationships between Treatment Experiences and Outcome

Only a few studies have examined the effects of specific therapeutic components of residential alcoholism treatment on patient posttreatment functioning (path P_{73} in Figure 1). There is some evidence that the use of disulfiram is associated with positive outcomes (i.e., lower rate of rehospitalization and more frequent abstinence). Patients who perceived their treatment environments more positively (that is, higher in involvement, support, personal problem orientation, and program clarity) were found to be functioning better in several areas at a 6-month follow-up [13]. However, Gillies et al. [19] found no relationship between 30 treatment variables and outcome in either of two inpatient alcoholism facilities. Research on the effects of outpatient therapy sessions and aftercare visits also has yielded mixed results (see Finney et al. [17] for a review of some relevant work).

Since most of these studies simply correlated treatment measures and outcome indices, they may have confounded the effect on outcome of patient characteristics and treatment experiences. Some researchers (such as Bromet et al. [7] and Polich et al. [35]) have attempted to estimate the impact of treatment after statistically adjusting for the effects of patient factors on treatment selection and outcome. This form of statistical adjustment has at least two drawbacks; discussion of these issues follows the description of the conceptual framework.

THE POSTTREATMENT DOMAINS

Many researchers have speculated that such factors as life change events, coping responses, and environmental resources may be important influences on a patient's adjustment following treatment, but only a few have examined their relationships to outcome or their relationships to each other and to pretreatment and treatment variables.

Stressful Life Events

Stressful life events (such as separation or divorce, death of a family member, moving to a new area) have been implicated as important factors in the exacerbation of a wide range of psychiatric disorders. Since problem drinkers often feel that consuming alcohol provides relief from stress, the occurrence of high-risk situations may contribute to relapse episodes among alcoholic patients (path P_{74} in Figure 1). Some studies have reported an association between life events or stressful situations and relapse among persons treated for alcoholism [23], while others have observed that patients who experience more negative life events show poorer treatment outcome [18].

While stressors may affect outcome, the likelihood of their occurrence is affected by patient background (path P_{41}) and treatment-related factors (path P_{43}). For instance, patients of higher socioeconomic status tend to experience fewer stressful life events than do patients of lower status. Moreover, treatment may reduce the likelihood of subsequent stressful events. For example, short-term abstinence that is facilitated by treatment can eliminate the possibility of certain types of stressful events (such as legal problems due to driving while intoxicated), or a patient's improved functioning can reduce the likelihood of a marital separation, which in turn serves to maintain remission. Stressful life events can play an important mediating role between pretreatment, treatment, and posttreatment variables.

Coping Responses

The coping responses available to a patient to adapt to a stressful life event or an aversive posttreatment environment are important for understanding the recovery process (path P_{75} in Figure 1) and also may be shaped by treatment (path P_{53}). Moreover, coping skills can influence the quality of a patient's environmental resources (path P_{65}), which in turn can affect outcome (path P_{76}).

Different coping styles such as active behavioral approaches (trying to find out more about the situation, talking with a spouse or other relative), active cognitive approaches or mental preparation (considering alternatives, drawing on past experiences), and avoidance or tension reduction (trying not to worry, taking anger out on another person) can serve to facilitate or hinder the recovery process.

More specifically, certain coping responses, such as avoidance and emotion-focused approaches, have been associated with relapse among alcoholic patients [14], while the reliance on active behavioral and cognitive approaches has been related to improved functioning among other populations [33]. The use of a single coping method, regardless of its general efficacy, may be less effective than the ability to draw on a broad range of coping skills. The success of coping may depend not only on the way in which an individual responds to stress, but also on the number and timing of coping responses the person utilizes.

In addition to affecting outcome and other posttreatment experiences, coping skills may mediate the effect of patient characteristics on posttreatment functioning. Patients who have a higher sociodemographic status and less severe intake symptoms are more likely to use a broader array of coping behaviors and to have the skills to deal more effectively with stressful situations (paths P_{51} and P_{52} in Figure 1). Treatment may also affect outcome by helping patients improve their coping skills (paths P_{53} and P_{75} in Figure 1). For example, better outcome was reported among alcoholic patients who participated in role playing aimed at the development of problem-solving skills and appropriate adaptive responses to stressful situations than among patients who did not receive such training [10]. More generally, treatment may help patients develop effective alternatives to drinking as a way of coping with stress. Appropriate coping behaviors may improve interactions among family members or friends (path P_{65}), and thus help to maintain improved posttreatment functioning (path P_{76}).

Environmental Resources

The types of environmental resources most commonly available to an alcoholic patient include family and marital resources, resources in the work setting, and community support networks. These sets of variables have been examined in terms of (1) their presence or absence, and (2) if present, the quality of social environment they provide for patients. In general, such environmental resources may be influenced by stressful life events (loss of employment may affect family functioning; path P_{64} in Figure 1), and, in turn, may influence an alcoholic patient's posttreatment functioning (path P_{76} in Figure 1). The quality of environmental resources also vary with a patient's background characteristics and pretreatment functioning (paths P_{61} and P_{62}). Individuals who enter treatment with less severe symptoms and higher education, and who are employed or married, are more likely to return to supportive home, work, and community settings than those who are more disadvantaged at intake.

Family and marital resources. While married patients tend to show more favorable posttreatment adjustment than single, separated, or divorced patients, such a dichotomous marital status distinction does not take into account the variability in treatment outcome among married patients. For example, a wife is likely to be a positive force in facilitating the recovery process among male patients while married women are more likely to report poor marital relations and to have husbands who drink heavily and encourage them to drink [29].

The two family environment factors most commonly associated with positive treatment outcome are high levels of cohesion and support and low levels of control [31]. An active recreational orientation (participating in sports and other social and recreational activities) and a moral, religious emphasis are also related to positive posttreatment functioning [5, 18]. These findings indicate that the quality of the family environment is important for understanding variations in treatment outcome among patients returning to family settings.

Work environment. In the same way that the family environment can affect treatment outcome, stable employment and the quality of the work environment can influence posttreatment functioning. Although there is little research relating the work environment to prognosis of alcoholic patients, there is evidence that, for patients not living in family settings, more involvement and cohesion among fellow employees, higher levels of support from supervisors and managers, and more emphasis on task orientation, clarity, innovation, and physical comfort are related to better outcome of treatment for alcoholism [5]. The differential effect of the work environment on unmarried versus married patients may be due to the "buffer" effect of family settings; that is, spouses and other family members may cushion the impact of an adverse work environment or contribute to an emotional detachment from the work setting.

Community support networks. Although marital and family support systems are the most common, additional environmental resources may be available to patients. These include a variety of community support networks, ranging from informal care givers such as friends, neighbors, and clergy, to organized voluntary service groups such as religious organizations, employment services, legal aid societies, and mutual self-help groups (AA). In addition to turning to conventional professionally run health and welfare agencies, patients may seek out these informal sources for advice and support to help them mobilize their psychological resources for handling stressful situations, gaining mastery of their environments, and so on.

ISSUES IN TREATMENT EVALUATION

Having presented a framework that organizes some of the key sets of variables involved in the treatment and outcome of alcoholism, serveral issues are now considered that may be clarified by shifting to process-oriented evaluations conducted within the broad conceptual framework developed here.

Treatment selection and assignment. The paths linking a patient's sociodemographic characteristics and intake symptoms to treatment underscore the importance of issues related to staff bias in treatment allocation and inappropriate patient decision making in treatment selection. One salient issue is whether patients who manifest more severe drinking problems and/or psychosocial deficits receive more intensive treatment than those with less severe symptoms. While some clinicians believe that more impaired clients should receive more treatment, the inverse may actually hold. This can occur if certain clients (such as those with higher sociodemographic status or less severe symptoms) are perceived by staff as having more potential for improvement, and/or if such patients are motivated to participate more actively and thus structure more intensive treatment regimens for themselves. By focusing on the link between pretreatment patient factors and treatment experiences, researchers can better understand biased treatment selection and allocation processes.

Assessing posttreatment functioning. There are a number of issues with respect to the measurement of outcome variables (for example, the desirability of cumulative assessment, such as the number of weeks worked during the follow-up interval, and the need to determine the validity of self-report measures of drinking behavior). One issue is emphasized here — the timing of outcome assessment — an issue that is crucial to the expanded process-oriented model of evaluation research. In summative evaluations, it makes sense to schedule the measurement of outcome at a temporally distant point after program participation since the major question addressed is, "Does the program work in some ultimate sense?" Given the focus on posttreatment factors, however, it is apparent that "to ask what effects the program has on variable Y, when Y is a long-term, remote variable subject to dozens of other influences, is to invite a negative report" [12, p. 409].

In contrast, if treatment outcome variables were assessed at program termination and at several later points, it might be possible to identify which immediate treatment effects were diluted (or, less likely, amplified) by patients' posttreatment experiences. A program component might be effective in improving a patient's psychological functioning within the protective confines of a residential alcoholism program, but totally ineffective in preparing the patient to cope adequately with the inevitable stresses of everyday life. Similarly, a multipoint assessment of outcome variables might enable an evaluator to identify lagged or sleeper effects. Training in certain coping skills, for instance, could lead to long-term improvement even though it has no immediate beneficial impact during treatment.

Estimating treatment effects. The confounding of pretreatment patient characterisitcs with treatment selection and/or assignment makes it difficult to accurately gauge the impact of treatment. When researchers have attempted to control for the effects of patient characteristics, the most common procedure has been to enter patient characteristics and then treatment variables in a regression predicting posttreatment functioning. Such an asymmetric approach attributes the shared variance (that is, the explained variance in posttreatment functioning that can be accounted for by either patient characteristics or treatment variables) to the set that is entered first (i.e., patient factors), thus underestimating treatment effects. This systematic underestimation of treatment impact can be avoided by performing path analyses in which the direct effects of patient characteristics on outcome are separated from their indirect effects via treatment variables, or by partitioning the variance in treatment outcome into those components that are unique to and shared by patient and treatment variables [13].

Although path analysis or partitioning the explained variance may give a clearer picture of the relative effects of patient- and treatment-related variables, various adjustment procedures (like matching and linear regression techniques) may still provide biased estimates of treatment effects. In fact, two plausible statistical procedures in some instances gave different estimates of treatment component and treatment duration effects when applied to the same data [17]. In order to generate unbiased estimates of treatment impact, one needs to ensure a correspondence between the statistical analysis (with its underlying model) and the processes of treatment selection-allocation that produces systematic treatment variations across patients [36].

In practice, imposing control over the selection process may be a less onerous undertaking than trying to assess selection determinants or searching for adjustment techniques that yield unbiased estimates of treatment effects. Control over treatment selection does not necessarily imply random assignment, however, at least in the sense of each patient having an equal probability of being assigned to each treatment or control condition. If, for example, ethical considerations suggested that severely impaired individuals should receive more treatment, a researcher could implement such treatment goals, accurately model the process of treatment allocation, and in turn obtain unbiased estimates of treatment effects.

Patient dropout. The conceptual model presented herein could also be used to better understand the factors that contribute to high patient dropout rates, which average over 25% for inpatient programs and over 60% for outpatient programs. With respect to patient characteristics, Baekeland and Lundwall [3] concluded that individuals who drop out of inpatient programs tend to be more passive-aggressive and psychopathic, more prone to deny hostility and interpersonal problems, and more likely to depend on alcohol for relief from psychological distress than persons who remain in treatment. More recently, Smart and Gray [38] found that treatment variables were also important predictors of dropout. Patients who remained in treatment were those who more often had one type of therapy (such as group) as opposed to a mixture of therapies, had received medications, and had either a physician or nurse as their primary therapist. The extent to which treatment variables are causally related to dropout is important, since they may be altered more readily than many patient attributes.

The conceptual framework presented illustrates that extratreatment factors, such as the quality of a patient's family or work setting, may also account for some of the variation in length of stay. In making their decisions, patients undoubtedly weigh the perceived costs and benefits of dropping out versus remaining in treatment. Knowledge of patients' extratreatment environmental circumstances would allow researchers to better model patients' decision-making processes and perhaps to identify those individuals for whom early treatment termination does not imply a poor prognosis.

Interrelationships among domains. The conceptual framework presented here suggests a shift in focus toward the interrelationships among the sets of factors involved in the treatment and recovery process. The model allows for detailed tracing of patient and treatment effects and highlights potentially important interaction effects.

1. *Tracing patient- and treatment-related effects.* The paths in the model suggest that patient characteristics have indirect as well as direct effects on treatment outcome. In an attempt to estimate such a model [14], it was found that a substantial portion of the total effect of patient background characteristics on treatment outcome was indirect, or mediated by treatment and posttreatment factors. For instance, patients with higher sociodemographic status were more likely to participate actively in treatment and to return to less stressful life situations after treatment. Thus, patient background variables may reflect not only what the alcoholic brings to treatment in terms of personal resources, but also what environmental resources or stressors the patient will return to after treatment.

Similarly, the conceptual framework may further an understanding of the way in which treatment effects may be filtered through posttreatment factors. Although Cronkite and Moos [14] found that the direct effect of treatment on outcome was weak, they observed that its total effect was more substantial and could be traced to its cumulative indirect effects via posttreatment factors. Specifically, treatment was linked to reduced stressors and more effective coping responses, which in turn were associated with improved posttreatment functioning.

These findings suggest that treatment may be more effective when oriented toward patients' posttreatment life circumstances. The benefits to be derived from such an approach were indicated in an evaluation of a community reinforcement program that emphasized rearranging marital, occupational, and community resources [2]. More specifically, the experimental program consisted of conventional hospital treatment, plus special marital, family, and job counseling, access to job search services, an active program-related social club, and a daily self-report monitoring system. Patients in the community reinforcement program experienced greater success than a matched control group of individuals who received only standard hospital treatment.

2. *Patient-treatment interactions.* For decades, an appealing idea in the alcoholism field has been that of matching subgroups of patients with different treatment regimens in order to maximize outcome. Although the notion of patient-treatment interaction effects has great intuitive appeal, it has not received much empirical attention. Conceptual frameworks that highlight the interconnections of predictors of treatment outcome may help researchers to identify interaction effects, or to assess the extent to which a matching program is implemented and is successful.

Only a few studies on alcoholic patients have isolated significant interaction effects [20]. In the authors' own research, it was found that male patients responded more positively to group therapy than did women, while female patients received more benefit from lectures and films on alcoholism than did men [15]. In contrast, no significant patient-treatment interaction effects were found in several other studies [37, 16]. One reason for the failure to identify many instances of patient-treatment interactions may be that crudely measured variables have been used to classify both patients and treatments. The demographic characteristics of patients (such as gender, age, socioeconomic status) that typically have been examined, at best serve only as proxy measures for more relevant constructs. When McLachlan [25] used the theoretically relevant variable of cognitive complexity to differentiate among patients, he was successful in detecting an interaction with treatment modalities.

A natural extension for interaction studies suggested by the model is to utilize information about a patient's posttreatment environmental resources and stressors. Two young unmarried men without severe dependence symptoms may respond differently to an abstinence-oriented program depending on the extent to which they subsequently encounter social pressure to drink [35]. Similarly, an abstinence-oriented program may be less successful than a program whose treatment goals include controlled drinking for women who are married to a spouse who drinks heavily. Programs that match patients to differential treatments might be more successful, then, if such posttreatment influences were considered.

Reciprocal effects. The conceptual framework presented here is one of many that could be formulated and estimated. There are several ways in which it might be modified to incorporate additional predictors of outcome or alternative interrelationships among various sets of variables. Since the direction of causal relationships in alcoholism research is often ambiguous, one extension might be to modify the model to include reciprocal effects, such as the mutual effects of patient posttreatment functioning and environmental resources. Or, when focusing on the outcome of treatment for married patients, the inclusion of spouse-related variables might prove fruitful for understanding the functioning of both individuals.

CONCLUSIONS

The typical summative evaluation of an alcoholism program finds little if any effect of treatment. Such results leave the program administrator and evaluator in an unenviable position, since they provide little information as to why the program failed or how a more effective program might be formulated. A two-pronged paradigm shift in alcoholism treatment evaluations — increased focus on treatment implementation and treatment process and exploration of post- or extratreatment factors—in conjunction with the conceptual framework developed here can help to isolate sources of program failure and decay in treatment gains and to formulate program reorientation strategies.

By examining data on specific program components such as group therapy, Antabuse administration, and films and/or lectures on alcoholism, the evaluator can determine if the program was implemented adequately. If the intended treatment was in fact delivered, the relationships between specific treatment components and (especially immediate) outcomes can be explored, and the program reoriented to concentrate its resources on those components that are associated with better outcome. No example of such a formative evaluation process was located in the alcoholism literature; however, in the field of education, process-product research has been used to identify specific teacher behaviors that are related to desired student outcomes. In some instances, teachers have been trained to use these apparently effective behaviors, and their positive effects on student achievement have been demonstrated in evaluations using traditional experimental research designs [8].

Information about extratreatment factors can also help to identify obstacles to the maintenance of program gains and suggest strategies for program reformulation. The value of focusing on such factors has been shown in recent investigations of the posttreatment environmental precipitants of relapse episodes [23, 24]. Most relapses seem to occur as a result of exposure to high-risk situations, such as being confronted with social pressure to drink or dilemmas that generate feelings of frustration and anger. Recognizing that high-risk situations inevitably occur and influence the recovery process, researchers have also begun to focus on the identification of more effective coping behaviors for dealing with such situations. Specifically, Litman et al. [21] found that patients who did not relapse adopted a multiplicity of cognitive coping styles and possessed a flexibility that enabled them to cope with a variety of difficult situations. These findings suggest important foci for future treatment efforts.

The relationships between extratreatment factors and client functioning is being pursued by other researchers in the alcoholism field. Mulford [28], for instance, has argued that, at any point, an individual may be located at one of several cumulative, nonsequential stages in an alcoholism process and in a separate recovery process. Mulford's conceptualization of the recovery process is consistent with the framework formulated herein in that treatment is viewed as only one of many factors that contribute to recovery. Community resources and other natural forces are seen as playing an important role, although the influence of any one factor is thought to be relatively weak.

These considerations underscore the need for researchers to explore treatment processes in greater detail and to focus on extratreatment factors. The inherently formative evaluation framework developed here affords the opportunity for greater insight into treatment processes, better understanding of the extratreatment factors that contribute to recovery and relapse, and an enriched data base with which to develop more effective treatment programs oriented toward patients' normal life situations.

ACKNOWLEDGMENTS

Preparation of the manuscript was supported by NIAAA Grant AA02863 and Veterans Administration medical research funds.

REFERENCES

1. Armor, D. J., Polich, J. M., and Stambul, H. B. *Alcoholism and Treatment.* Wiley: New York, 1978.
2. Azrin, N. H. Improvements in the community-reinforcement approach to alcoholism. *Behav. Res. Ther.* 14:339-348, 1976.
3. Baekeland, F., and Lundwall, L. Dropping out of treatment: A critical review. *Psychol. Bull.* 82:738-783, 1975.
4. Bromet, E., and Moos, R. H. Sex and marital status in relation to the characteristics of alcoholics. *J. Stud. Alcohol* 37:1302-1312, 1976.
5. Bromet, E., and Moos, R. H. Environmental resources and the posttreatment functioning of alcoholic patients. *J. Health Soc. Behav.* 18:326-338, 1977.
6. Bromet, E., Moos, R. H., and Bliss, F. The social climate of alcoholism treatment programs. *Arch. Gen. Psychiatry* 33:910-916, 1976.
7. Bromet, E., Moos, R. H., Bliss, F., and Wuthmann, C. The posttreatment functioning of alcoholic patients: Its relation to program participation. *J. Consult. Clin. Psychol.* 45: 829-842, 1977.
8. Brophy, J. E. Teacher behavior and its effects. *J. Educ. Psychol.* 71:733-750, 1979.
9. Bryk, A. S. Evaluating program impact: A time to cast away stones, a time to gather stones together. *New Dir. Prog. Eval.* 1:31-58, 1978.
10. Chaney, E. F., O'Leary, M. R., and Marlatt, G. A. Skill training with alcoholics. *J. Consult. Clin. Psychol.* 46:1092-1104, 1978.
11. Crawford, J. J., and Chalupsky, A. B. The reported evaluation of alcoholism treatments, 1968-1971: A methodological review. *Addict. Behav.* 2:63-74, 1977.
12. Cronbach, L. J. *Designing Educational Evaluations.* Stanford Evaluation Consortium: Stanford, Calif., 1978.
13. Cronkite, R. C., and Moos, R. H. Evaluating alcoholism treatment programs: An integrated approach. *J. Consult. Clin. Psychol.* 46:1105-1119, 1978.
14. Cronkite, R. C., and Moos, R. H. Determinants of the posttreatment functioning of alcoholic patients: A conceptual framework. *J. Consult. Clin. Psychol.* 48:305-316, 1980.
15. Cronkite, R. C., and Moos, R. H. Sex and marital status in relation to the treatment and outcome of alcoholic patients. *Sex Roles,* in press.
16. Finney, J. W., and Moos, R. H. Treatment and outcome for empirical subtypes of alcoholic patients. *J. Consult. Clin. Psychol.* 47:25-38, 1979.
17. Finney, J. W., Moos, R. H., and Chan, D. A. Length of stay and program component

effects in the treatment of alcoholism: A comparison of two techniques for process analyses. *J. Consult. Clin. Psychol.* 49:120–131, 1981.

18. Finney, J. W., Moos, R. H., and Mewborn, C. R. Posttreatment experiences and treatment outcome of alcoholic patients six months and two years after hospitalization. *J. Consult. Clin. Psychol.* 48:17–29, 1980.

19. Gillies, M., Lavertz, S. G., Smart, R. G., and Aharan, C. H. Outcomes in treated alcoholics: Patient and treatment characteristics in a one-year follow-up. *J. Alcohol.* 9:125–134, 1974.

20. Kissin, B., Platz, A., and Su, W. H. Social and psychological factors in the treatment of chronic alcoholism. *J. Psychiatr. Res.* 8:13–27, 1970.

21. Litman, G., Eiser, J. R., Rawson, N., and Oppenheim, A. Differences in relapse precipitants and coping behavior between alcoholic relapsers and survivors. *Behav. Res. Ther.* 17:89–94, 1979.

22. Maisto, S., and McCollam, J. The use of multiple measures of life health to assess alcohol treatment outcome: A review and critique. In: *Evaluating Alcohol and Drug Abuse Treatment Effectiveness: Recent Advances*, Sobell, L. C., Sobell, M. B., and Ward, E. (eds.). Pergamon: New York: 1979.

23. Marlatt, G. A. Craving for alcohol, loss of control, and relapse: A cognitive behavior analysis. In: *Alcoholism: New Directions in Behavioral Research and Treatment*, Nathan, P. E., Marlatt, G. A., and Loberg, J. (eds.). Plenum: New York, 1977.

24. Marlatt, G. A., and Gordon, J. Determinants of relapse: Implications for the maintenance of behavior change. In: *Behavioral Medicine: Changing Health Life Styles*, Davidson, P. (ed.). Brunner/Mazel: New york, 1979.

25. McLachlan, J. Therapy strategies, personality orientation, and recovery from alcoholism. *Can. Psychiatr. Assoc. J.* 19:25–30, 1974.

26. Moos, R. *Evaluating Treatment Environments: A Social-Ecological Approach*. Wiley: New York, 1974.

27. Moos, R. Improving social settings by social climate measurement and feedback. In: *Social and Psychological Research in Community Settings*, Munoz, R., Snowden, L., and Kelly, J. (eds.). Jossey-Bass: San Francisco, 1979.

28. Mulford, H. A. Stages in the alcoholic process: Toward a cumulative nonsequential index. *J. Stud. Alcohol* 38:563–583, 1977.

29. Mulford, H. A. Women and men problem drinkers. *J. Stud. Alcohol* 38:1624–1639, 1977.

30. Ogborne, A. C. Patient characteristics as predictors of treatment outcome for alcohol and drug abusers. In: *Research Advances in Alcohol and Drug Problems* (Vol. 4), Israel, Y., Glaser, F. B., Kalant, H., Papham, R. E., Schmidt, W., and Smart, R. G. (eds.). Plenum: New York, 1978.

31. Orford, J., and Edwards, W. *Alcoholism: A Comparison of Treatment Advice with a Study of the Influence of Marriage*. Oxford University Press: Oxford, England, 1977.

32. Patton, M. Q. *Utilization-Focused Evaluation*. Sage: Beverly Hills, 1978.

33. Pearlin, S. I., and Schooler, C. The structure of coping. *J. Health Soc. Behav.* 19:2–21, 1978.

34. Pokorny, A. D., Miller, B. A., Kanas, T., and Valles, J. Effectiveness of extended aftercare in the treatment of alcoholism. *Q. J. Stud. Alcohol* 34:435–443, 1973.

35. Polich, J. M., Armor, D. J., and Braiker, H. B. *The Course of Alcoholism: Four Years After Treatment*. New York: Wiley, 1981.

36. Reichardt, C. S. The statistical analysis of data from nonequivalent group designs. In: *Quasi Experimentation: Design and Analysis Issues for Field Settings*, Cook, T. D. and Campbell, D. T. (eds.). Rand McNally: Chicago, 1979.

37. Smart, R. Do some alcoholics do better in some types of treatment than others? *Drug Alcohol Depend.* 3:65–75, 1978.

38. Smart, R., and Gray, G. Multiple predictors of dropout from alcoholism treatment. *Arch. Gen. Psychiatry* 35:363–367, 1978.

39. Suchman, E. A. *Evaluative Research: Principles and Practice in Public Service and Social Action Programs.* Russell Sage Foundation: New York, 1967.

94

LINDA C. SOBELL, PhD, Addiction Research Foundation, Toronto, Canada

MARK B. SOBELL, PhD, Addiction Research Foundation, Toronto, Canada

TED D. NIRENBERG, PhD, Sea Pines Behavioral Institute, Hilton Head Island, South Carolina

DIFFERENTIAL TREATMENT PLANNING FOR ALCOHOL ABUSERS

TREATMENT PLANNING is a critical process in the treatment of individuals with alcohol problems. The treatment plan reflects the conceptual structure of the ongoing treatment process — the goals of treatment and the strategies to be used to achieve those goals. It also (1) meaningfully organizes clinical data, (2) gives overall direction to the treatment process, and (3) provides a framework for evaluating treatment progress. In essence, the treatment plan is a blueprint for treatment.

The sine qua non of differential treatment planning is the recognition that each client is unique, not only in terms of descriptive characteristics, but in terms of needs, choice of treatment strategies, and expected outcomes. Each client

---

Linda C. Sobell, PhD, Clinical Institute, Addiction Research Foundation, and University of Toronto, Toronto, Canada.

Mark B. Sobell, PhD, Clinical Institute, Addiction Research Foundation, and University of Toronto, Toronto, Canada.

Ted D. Nirenberg, PhD, Sea Pines Behavioral Institute, Hilton Head Island, South Carolina, and Georgia Southern University, Statesboro, Georgia.

enters treatment with a different set of past experiences, abilities, strengths, and dysfunctions. These factors should be carefully considered and incorporated into the treatment plan when appropriate.

Although many clinicians recognize the importance of and have been using treatment plans when treating alcohol abusers, little has been written on this topic. Thus, the goal of this chapter is to describe the process of differential treatment planning—identifying, developing, and evaluating treatment goals and strategies for individual clients.

TREATMENT PLANNING

Treatment planning is a process by which treatment goals are determined and strategies for achieving the goals are formulated. Goals are developed based on an assessment of the client's life health functioning and are intended to ameliorate specific problems or areas of dysfunction for the client. In some ways, the treatment goals constitute an inverse profile of the client's assessed dysfunctions or problems (treatment needs). For example, if increased communication and satisfaction within the marriage is a treatment goal, then the inverse of this goal, marital discord, is obviously a problem.

Treatment plans usually contain both long-term and short-term goals. Long-term goals, developed and agreed upon by the therapist and client, represent the aim and ultimate purpose of therapy. However, long-term goals often take considerable time and effort to achieve and, thus, are frequently partitioned into several short-term goals defining more immediate treatment objectives. Short-term goals are usually incremental, proximal objectives that relate in a stepwise progression to a long-term goal. Short-term goals allow progress to be evaluated more frequently, and they provide more opportunities to reinforce clients for behavior changes. Finally, for all goals specific treatment strategies are carefully and operationally delineated. This chapter includes several examples of actual treatment plans describing long- and short-term goals and their respective treatment strategies.

Since a treatment plan frequently requires updating and revision, treatment planning is best conceptualized as a dynamic rather than a static process. Treatment planning is a continuous process since (1) some needs and problems are not always apparent early in treatment, (2) some problems identified early in treatment may initially be too difficult for a client to deal with and progress must await the resolution of other problems, (3) some problems may take longer than others to remediate, and (4) during treatment new problems can arise that demand immediate therapeutic consideration and intervention. Also, progress toward some goals may be directly related to progress toward other goals. For example, a person who feels lonely may desire more social relationships but may lack adequate social skills. Until those skills are acquired, the goal of increased social relationships is likely to be elusive.

In most cases the client plays a substantial role in all phases of treatment planning. In the early stages the client provides information about his or her life functioning (e.g., alcohol and other problems, available strengths and resources, goals). Initially, the therapist uses this information to assess the client's functioning, and then develops a treatment plan with the client. Client involvement in treatment planning is essential since (1) it provides critical information about the desirability, feasibility, and ease with which various treatment strategies are or can be implemented, and (2) it sets the stage for active client participation in treatment.

ASSESSMENT, A PRECURSOR TO TREATMENT PLANNING

A thorough assessment of an individual with a drinking problem is a difficult task. Not only are many and varied factors frequently antecedent to the drinking, but the drinking itself can have multiple consequences. Thus, cause and effect relationships are sometimes difficult to ascertain. Moreover, cues indicating the presence of alcohol problems are often diverse and may not, in isolation, appear related to drinking behavior. A comprehensive assessment of the client's overall life health, therefore, is an essential percursor to treatment planning.

In most assessment processes the therapist, to some extent, is greatly dependent on the client's self-reports — what the client says or perceives about himself or herself. Generally, it has been concluded that one can have confidence in alcohol abusers' self-reports of drinking and related behaviors when the individuals are interviewed in a clinical setting and when they are alcohol-free [4]. Since valuable information can also be gleaned from sources other than the client and since some small proportion of self-reports may be invalid, it is best to base assessments on a convergence of evidence. Primary sources of information can include (1) the client's self-reports; (2) interviews with significant others, especially those involved directly (e.g., spouse, children) or indirectly (e.g., employer, probation officer) in the treatment process; (3) the therapist's observations of the client during the assessment process; (4) clinical and other official records (e.g., arrest, hospitalization); (5) physical and mental health indices at the time of the initial assessment (e.g., liver functioning, cognitive functioning). Since some incidence of error is probably intrinsic to all measures, a convergent validity criterion seeking mutual corroboration among several assessment measures can increase the therapist's confidence in the overall assessment.

Treatment needs and problems need to be operationalized, and when possible, the assessment should include objective measurement of the behaviors under study (e.g., How many days a week is the client absent from work as a result of drinking? How much and when does the client drink? How many situations does the client avoid because he or she would have to interact with others?). Vague and ambiguous terms, such as "become more independent" or "become less anxious" fail to adequately specify the exact nature of the problem. If problems are operationally defined, however, treatment can be facilitated. For example, as a generic goal, "to become more independent" could refer to many things. It might relate to becoming more responsible for one's own financial obligations and not depending on others for transportation. If so, the treatment plan might include having the client maintain a financial ledger, pay all bills on time, refinance or consolidate debts, save money toward the purchase of a used car, and so on. If, however, independence means becoming more assertive vis-à-vis resisting unjustified demands and requests from others, then the course of treatment would probably include assertiveness training. If needs and problems are operationally defined, such ambiguities can be avoided, and the treatment aims and directions will be clarified for both the client and therapist.

IDENTIFYING TREATMENT NEEDS

A detailed assessment of the client's past and present use of alcohol is essential for identifying treatment needs. Clients should be asked about (1) the specific quantities of alcohol they consume on a regular basis; (2) their drinking patterns (e.g., more on weekends than weekdays, only in the evenings); (3) where and with whom they most often drink; and (4) the circumstances that are antecedent to their drinking (e.g., boredom, anger, negative self-statements). Indicants of tolerance and dependence should also be elicited (e.g., the most alcohol ever consumed in one 24-hour period; highest recorded blood alcohol concentration; history of alcohol withdrawal symptoms; past or present indications of acute or chronic liver dysfunction such as abnormal enzyme levels; and any health problems associated with drinking, such as ulcers, gastritis, pancreatitis, gout, memory loss).

A detailed assessment of drinking behavior delineates essential information to be used when considering certain treatment strategies. For example, clients who have never experienced more than a few days of abstinence or whose present environment is extremely conducive to excessive drinking (e.g., all their friends drink heavily) might find it very difficult to abstain from alcohol, and consequently, their compliance with other aspects of treatment may be jeopardized. Thus, it is important to evaluate the difficulty that the clients might initially encounter as they attempt to refrain from problem drinking while in treatment. In certain cases, short-term use of an antialcohol drug (i.e., disulfiram) may demonstrate to the client that he or she can function adequately without alcohol.

Short-term enforced abstinence periods also give the therapist an opportunity to observe and evaluate the client when he or she is not under the influence of alcohol. The assessment of drinking behavior can also reveal whether or not a client's present environment is a high-risk one for problem drinking (e.g., drinking occurs on the job; most of one's weekend social activities involve drinking; all of one's friends drink heavily; the primary social activity is meeting with friends at the neighborhood tavern). Such information is important in the formulation of treatment strategies. While the environment cannot always be changed (e.g., it may not be feasible to change jobs to a setting where little or no drinking occurs), clients can be made aware of those aspects of the environment that appear to involve a high risk for problem drinking.

While a drinking problem is essential to the diagnosis of an alcohol disorder, by no means is drinking the only problem in the lives of most alcohol abusers. Whether drinking is used to deal with life problems, causes life problems, or both, most alcohol abusers can identify other major life problems (e.g., physical, psychological, vocational, social, recreational, interpersonal, familial, financial, legal, environmental). The development of a treatment plan, therefore, requires a careful assessment of other areas of life health, besides drinking.

Thus, as with drinking behavior, an in-depth and multifaceted assessment of the client's overall life functioning is a prerequisite to the development of a differential treatment plan. Consider, for example, a client who reports serious work-related problems. First, the nature of the vocational difficulties need to be evaluated—specifically (1) Does the client possess the necessary vocational skills for the job? (2) Are problems outside the work environment contributing to the job problems? (3) Is there a physical health problem? (4) Might the problem be resolved by more assertive behaviour, such as having the client talk with his or her employer? (5) Does the client have an accurate perception of his or her abilities and opportunities for job advancement? A clear and precise understanding of the nature of the problem is critical to the development of a meaningful treatment plan.

Inaccurate or incomplete assessments can lead the therapist and client to decide upon inefficient or inappropriate treatment strategies. Consider the following example. An individual complains of being continually passed over for job promotion, saying that he is qualified and has received excellent performance evaluations in the last year, but that his supervisor does not like him. During the assessment the therapist notes that the client is meek and timid in interactions with others. The client has also stated that he feels his lack of assertiveness is a significant impediment to job advancement. If one were to proceed from this limited data base, a treatment plan might be developed that involves the acquisition of social skills—training the client to be more assertive and forceful in interactions with his employer. However, if the desired promotion involves a job having supervisory responsibilities and the client lacks relevant experience or training, then he might have an inaccurate perception of his own skills and abilities. Given the latter information, simple acquisition of social skills is not likely to help this client, whereas participating in a training program about supervising others might enhance his chances for future advancement.

During the assessment process and prior to the development of treatment strategies, consideration should also be given to extraneous factors that may influence treatment efforts. Usually these factors delimit the treatment approach or lengthen the period of treatment. For instance, if a client is coerced into treatment, consideration must be given to how cooperative the client will be. While coercion is not necessarily a restrictive factor, it certainly must be addressed early in treatment. Other factors, such as organic brain damage, physical impediments, psychiatric problems, polydrug use, and the client's family environment must also be considered in the development of a treatment plan.

DEVELOPING TREATMENT GOALS AND STRATEGIES

All treatment goals and strategies need to be clearly operationalized, and when possible, worded positively (e.g., "learn to deal with anger more assertively" as opposed to "stop losing one's temper," and "maintain increased periods of abstinence" as opposed to "do not get drunk"). Positively stated goals more often provide direction for constructive behavior change.

Since drinking is usually not an individual's sole problem, and since alcohol abuse often pervades many aspects of a person's life, treatment will usually focus on multiple areas of life functioning. When treatment is multimodal, the treatment goals will need to be prioritized according to the following concerns: first, which problems are more acute or most in need of immediate attention? and second, in what ways can goals and strategies be logically ordered? For instance, stable living arrangements should probably be found for chronic alcoholics before instituting social or vocational skills training. Similarly, it might be important to develop a strategy to enable a client to maintain more than a few days of abstinence (e.g., hospitalization; short-term use of disulfiram) before proceeding with other aspects of treatment (e.g., couples therapy or vocational training). Conversely, in some cases drinking may be unlikely to cease unless other changes occur first (e.g., changing residences to a nondrinking environment such as a halfway house).

When considering whether goals are achievable, attention should be given to available time and resources as well as the client's present level of functioning. In many cases, especially with low-functioning or uncooperative clients, it may be necessary to initially to set minimally demanding and easily accomplished goals (e.g., arriving at appointments on time, attending a class, calling a bill collector, calling friends and inviting them for dinner). In fact, since many long-term goals often require a significant investment of effort from clients (e.g., financial stability, job retraining, marital harmony), the principle of shaping can be used to shape progress toward more demanding goals. In such cases, the long-term target behavior is gradually changed through reinforcement of successive, readily achievable behavior changes (i.e., a series of small steps toward the ultimate goal). The process of using short-term goals and strategies to achieve long-term, more difficult goals is illustrated in the following two examples.

Example 1

Long-term goal: Nonproblem level of alcohol consumption.
A. Phase I. Enforced abstinence (short-term goal—STG)
   1. Written contract specifying the use of disulfiram for 60 days (Strategy—S)
   2. Daily self-administered disulfiram (S)
   3. Functional analysis of alcohol consumption and related behaviors (S)
      a. Self-monitoring of cravings for alcohol and their situational determinants via written daily logs (S)
      b. In-session role playing of typical drinking situations; developing effective alcohol refusal skills via assertiveness training (i.e., role playing, modeling, in vivo practice, and therapeutic instruction) (S)
   4. Blood test to assess liver function (S)
B. Phase II. Self-imposed abstinence (STG)
   1. Written contract specifying no drinking for 30 days (S)
   2. Continued functional analysis of alcohol consumption and related behaviors (S)
   3. In-session role playing of typical drinking situations and drink refusal skills (S)
C. Phase III. Nonproblem drinking (STG)
   1. Written contract specifying drinking limits for 60 days (S)
   2. Self-monitoring of alcohol consumption, cravings, and their situational determinants via written daily logs (S)
   3. Modification of the topography of the client's drinking responses (e.g., decrease tendency to gulp drinks, the need to finish all drinks, drinking alone) (S)
   4. Introduction and encouragement of the use of portable breath alcohol testers when considering whether to drive after drinking (S)
D. Phase IV. Follow-up and evaluation (STG)
   1. Gradually increase the interval between treatment sessions (e.g., from weekly to biweekly) to decrease dependence on treatment (S)
   2. Biweekly telephone contacts for 6 months to obtain self-reported information on client's drinking behavior (S)
   3. Early intervention if the drinking pattern is suggestive of problem drinking (S)

4. Collateral verification of the client's reports of drinking (S)
5. Assure availability of phone contacts or additional treatment if problems develop (S)

Example 2

Long-term goal: Career evaluation and advancement.
A. Phase I. Evaluation of interests, potential, and feasibility of pursuing another career (STG)
   1. Administration of Strong Vocational Interest Test (S)
   2. Vocational counseling at the Veterans Administration (VA) Center (S)
   3. Career planning and counseling at a local state college (S)
   4. Checking with employer about feasibility of taking a course during work hours (S)
   5. Pursuing VA educational benefits (S)
B. Phase II. Enroll and perform satisfactorily in a technical training program at a state college (the appropriateness of the program to be determined in Phase I) (STG)
   1. Attend all classes (S)
   2. Complete all class assignments on time (S)
   3. Set aside a specific amount of time each week to study (S)
   4. Pass all courses with at least a grade of C (S)
   5. After 1 year, client will evaluate his or her status and satisfaction with the program with the college's career counseling staff (S)
C. Phase III. Complete 2-year training program (STG)
   1. Decrease work from full-time to part-time to complete the training program sooner (S)
   2. Get a part-time job on weekends to supplement income (S)
   3. Attend all classes, complete all assignments promptly, and set aside a specific period of time to study (S)

In these and other cases, shaping is specifically designed to reinforce successful incremental approximations to the achievement of the long-term goal. The clinical significance of shaping is that in many cases, since little environmental (extratreatment) reinforcement is received for working toward long-term goals or change (e.g., taking a course of 2 years to obtain a degree that qualifies one for a particular trade or occupation), the use of shaping gives clients a structure by which to self-reinforce. In other words, short-term goals allow clients to experience more immediate and relevant success in behavior change.

Some goals are not readily amenable to the principle of shaping, but nevertheless can be expressed as multiple stepwise progressive interventions that allow clients to recognize demonstrable progress toward the long-term goal. As an example, the case of a low-income client with a $2,000 indebtedness is offered.

While one obvious goal for this individual is financial stability, it is unrealistic to believe the debt can be paid off in a short time. However, as illustrated in the following example, such a long-term goal can be partitioned into several short-term progressive goals.

Example 3

Long-term goal: Financial stability and independence.
A. Prior to each therapy session, pay all bills due each week and handle other related financial matters (e.g., respond to past-due notices from credit companies, call creditors) (STG)
   1. Keep a monthly financial ledger book of all bills and their due dates as well as the amount paid and the new balance owing (S)
   2. At each therapy session, review all bills paid; if bills are unpaid the client is to write out checks at the end of the therapy session and mail the payments immediately thereafter (S)
B. For income tax purposes pay child support by check or money order (STG)
C. Balance check book once a month (STG)
D. Cancel Master Charge credit card (STG)
E. Work overtime to pay off outstanding debts more quickly (STG)
F. Use next year's income tax return to pay off additional bills, especially those where interest accrues on the unpaid balance (STG)
G. Stop making long distance telephone calls; have telephone disconnected until back telephone bill is paid (STG)
H. Open a savings account and set aside $25 per month; this money is to be used for personal positive reinforcement (e.g., dinner at a restaurant, clothes, etc.) each time a major bill is completely paid (STG)

Sobell and Sobell [3] have noted that different treatment strategies necessitate different costs for clients, depending on their life styles, values, and resources. Consequently, a distinction should be made between "effective" and "effective and least restrictive" treatments. An effective treatment is one that helps a client achieve goals and has a high probability of maintaining those accomplishments in the future. An effective and least restrictive treatment is one that requires the least total change in the client's life style. For example, an effective treatment for alcohol abuse may require the client to forever avoid situations where others are drinking (e.g., not going to parties, restaurants, bars). On the other hand, an effective and least restrictive treatment may involve learning to say no to offers of alcohol in drinking situations. Similarly, if one works where a large number of the employees drink, either during or after work, changing jobs to a situation where drinking on the job does not occur might be effective, but if the same job benefits (e.g., loss of pay, rank, retirement) cannot be obtained, then this strategy may be quite costly.

A final but crucial aspect of treatment planning concerns developing strategies for dealing with future problems. Although future problems cannot be specifically addressed until they arise, consideration can be given to the general idea of recognizing and dealing with new problems in the future. For instance, the need for early interventions can be stressed should unexpected or difficult problems arise. With drinking behavior, a serious relapse may be avoided if the client can identify the onset of abusive drinking. In essence, the therapist discusses with the client the likelihood that problems will arise in the future, and stresses that the critical factor is in how those problems are managed. Such a focus often characterizes the final stages of the treatment process.

MONITORING TREATMENT PROGRESS

Multiple short-term goals provide numerous opportunities for (1) increasing the client's awareness of behavior change, (2) demonstrating to the client that he or she can successfully change behavior, (3) rewarding the client within the therapeutic setting for appropriate change, and (4) providing the therapist and client with continuous feedback relating to progress (positive and negative) toward the long-term goals. Also, if a client is having difficulty making particular changes, an early intervention can occur and reasons for lack of progress can be carefully probed and the treatment plan modified accordingly.

Clearly, people are continually impacted by their environment, and such is the case when people are in treatment. Consequently, therapists need to be aware of significant events (positive and negative) that occur in their clients' lives, especially as these events enhance or detract from the ongoing treatment. Since unexpected and new factors (e.g., job promotion, death in the family, loss of one's job) can drastically affect a client's functioning while in treatment, new goals and strategies will have to be formulated as situations arise. In this regard, evaluation of treatment progress must also examine how well a client resolves new problems that arise during treatment. Attending to changes that the client makes in the natural environment can also provide the therapist with evidence of the client's ability to function independently of treatment and to generalize the skills learned in therapy to the extratreatment environment.

For several reasons, clients are more likely to be dependent on therapy early in treatment than at later stages. Often clients enter treatment as the result of a crisis and a self-identified need for help. The confidential and self-disclosing nature of therapy gives the therapeutic relationship special significance; the client can share accomplishments and personal difficulties with the therapist without fear of further disclosure. However, while a dependence on the therapeutic relationship may be encouraged in the early stages of therapy, as treatment continues it is important to encourage and reinforce the client for self-sufficiency.

Developing specific treatment goals aimed at increasing the client's self-sufficiency is important, since the client cannot continue in treatment forever. Furthermore, the critical evaluation of treatment efficacy is whether gains made in treatment are maintained and generalize to the extratreatment environment [1, 2]. One way of developing a client's self-sufficiency outside of therapy is to structure the treatment goals so that the client sees himself or herself as gaining an investment in the environment (e.g., employment, meaningful relations with others, economic security). If positive environmental gains have been made, then the idea of losing those gains might become a factor that can support the client's continued successful functioning, and the environment, rather than the therapist, can provide positive feedback to the client.

The principle of shaping can also be used to facilitate the termination of treatment. If a client is compliant with treatment and is making progress, then the therapeutic relationship is probably of some value to the client or, in other words, positively reinforcing for the client. At this point two important questions arise: first, will terminating the relationship engender difficulties for the client? and second, can the client function adequately without further treatment? Without empirical evidence, answers to these questions simply reflect clinical judgment. However, one way of diminishing the reward value of the therapeutic relationship without impairing client functioning is to gradually terminate treatment—sessions should be scheduled to occur with lesser frequency (e.g., sessions changed from weekly to biweekly in frequency). Then, if no problems develop, sessions can be further extended to every 4 to 6 weeks, and so on, until therapy plays little, if any, role in the client's life. Shaping clients out of treatment also allows for resumption of more frequent scheduling should problems arise, as well as providing a performance-based criterion for ending treatment.

SUMMARY

Treatment planning is not a new concept, but little has been written on the topic. What has been lacking in the literature is a format for systematically developing, organizing, and evaluating treatment. This chapter attempts to present one way that treatment plans can be conceptualized and used in both clinical and research settings. Four major aspects of treatment planning are stressed: (1) client involvement in treatment planning is essential to the development of a meaningful and useful treatment plan; (2) treatment planning is a continuous process that provides guidance and direction for the therapist and client; (3) partitioning long-term goals into multiple short-term goals is a way of building in early successes, providing evidence of change, and enhancing client motivation for making further changes; and (4) by operationalizing goals and strategies, they become more amenable to measurement and evaluation, as well as focusing attention on the ultimate purpose of therapy—to achieve behavior change.

REFERENCES

1. Kazdin, A. E., and Wilson, G. T. *Evaluation of Behavior Therapy: Issues, Evidence and Research Strategies.* Ballinger: Cambridge, Mass., 1978.
2. Keeley, S. M., Shemberg, K. M., and Carbonell, J. Operant clinical intervention: Behavior management or beyond? Where are the data? *Behav. Ther.* 7:292-305, 1976.
3. Sobell, L. C., and Sobell, M. B. Alcohol problems. In: *Behavioral Approaches to Medical Treatment*, Williams, R. B. and Gentry, W. D. (eds.). Ballinger: Cambridge, Mass., 1977.
4. Sobell, L. C., and Sobell, M. B. Alcohol treatment outcome methodology. In: *Prevention, Intervention and Treatment: Concerns and Models* (National Institute on Alcohol Abuse and Alcoholism Alcohol and Health Monograph No. 3). National Institute on Alcohol Abuse and Alcoholism: Washington, D.C. In press.

95

CHAD D. EMRICK, PhD, Veterans Administration Medical Center, Denver, Colorado

EVALUATION OF ALCOHOLISM PSYCHOTHERAPY METHODS

THIS CHAPTER FOCUSES on major findings of a review of the English literature in which some form of psychologically oriented treatment of alcohol abuse was evaluated. All studies published from 1952-71 were included in the review except (1) those not evaluating psychological treatment, but rather strictly medical or biochemical treatment or treatment by incarceration; (2) those evaluating treatment not for alcohol abuse but for alcohol intoxication, alcoholic psychoses, or alcohol-related diseases; (3) those reporting outcome only for a few patients to exemplify various kinds of treatment responses; and (4) those following up a sample in which some but less than 50% of the patients received some type of psychologically oriented treatment [8]. Studies published from 1972-73 were added to the review for analysis of change rates of formally treated patients relative to change rates of abusers having no formal treatment [9].

Investigation into the area of relative treatment effectiveness (i.e., determining if any one treatment approach is more effective than a comparison approach) included additional (some unpublished) literature from 1972-81 [11]. In the review of this area, all possible studies were obtained that randomly assigned pa-

---

Chad D. Emrick, PhD, Psychologist, Veterans Administration Medical Center, Mental Health and Behavioral Sciences, and Assistant Clinical Professor in Psychiatry, University of Colorado, Health Sciences Center, Denver, Colorado.

tients to two or more psychologically oriented treatments or evaluated sequential groups for whom the order of experimental interventions was counterbalanced. This body of research was screened for all outcome differences significant at the .05 level or better, using two-tailed tests. Two-tailed tests were used since the operating hypothesis of this investigation was that no treatment outcome differences would be observed. In studies where just some groups were randomly assigned, only the results for those groups were considered. Some studies were excluded because allocation of patients to groups was not clearly random, randomization was admittedly broken for all groups involved, or patients were found to be similar or comparable on certain characteristics rather than being randomly assigned. In this area of investigation, studies pertaining to evaluation of predominantly biological-medical treatments and behavior therapy interventions are not given direct attention (unlike [11]) because other chapters in this volume deal with these areas. However, data from these studies are at times included in the analyses of issues that are addressed in the chapter (e.g., relative effectiveness of different amounts of treatment and different strategies for involving patients in treatment).

When specific results and the methods used to obtain them were reported, the former were checked wherever possible for accuracy, the latter for appropriateness. Greater weight regarding relative treatment effects was given to those long-term differences found more than 6 months after the start of treatment or after the termination of intensive therapy, depending on the evaluation procedure used by the investigators. In a previous work, Emrick [9] considered as long-term differences only those found more than 6 months after termination of all treatment by at least 50% of patients in all comparison groups. The definition of long-term effects adopted for this analysis more accurately reflects the reality of treatment. As Edwards et al. [6, p. 1019] have stated, "For many patients it would be artificial and against normal clinical practice to suppose that the treatment process is abruptly terminated after a certain number of months, or at the moment of inpatient discharge."

Three points are to be made about the general nature of the studies used in all aspects of the review. First, a staggering array of treatment approaches was evaluated—ranging from multimodal packages to group hypnotherapy to individual insight-oriented psychotherapy. These programs and components were applied for short and long terms, in inpatient, outpatient, and halfway house settings, in prisons and in industries. Second, those treated had only two commonalities: They were adults and they were in contact with treatment agents who labeled them and responded to them as alcohol abusers. This reflects the fact that "alcohol abuse" can be defined as "a label attached to a drinking pattern defined as deviant by the social control institutions" [4]. Third, those evaluated are a biased sample of alcohol abusers in that they represent only those who come into contact with treatment agents. There is some evidence that this subgroup has, on the whole, more serious drinking and related problems than those who do not have formal treatment [5].

RESULTS

Drinking Outcome Rates

Gross rates. One of several questions asked of the literature is "What percentage of treated alcohol abusers improve in drinking behavior?" Data on drinking outcome following treatment were placed in one of nine carefully defined categories [8]. Outcome rates were based on figures that excluded patients who had dropped out of treatment rapidly (i.e., before five outpatient visits or 2 weeks of inpatient or residential treatment) as well as those who could not be contacted at follow-up or who were dead or institutionalized for reasons not directly related to alcohol (e.g., unrelated physical illness or accident). Pooled data from 265 studies indicated that about 33% of alcohol abusers were totally abstinent during follow-up periods of varying lengths, about 50% were drinking without problems, about 66% were improved in drinking behavior to at least some minimal extent, about 33% were unimproved, and about 5% were drinking more during follow-up than before treatment. These results suggest that people with alcohol problems have a good chance of improving in drinking behavior when they become involved in formal alcohol abuse treatment. Given that patients were found to fit each of nine drinking outcome categories, another implication is that treatment does not lead to just one of two drinking outcome statuses, namely abstinence or no change. Rather, patients experience a range of outcomes, including reducing drinking to a nonproblem level, drinking with problems but less frequently or intensely than before treatment, and drinking more after than before treatment.

Rates by follow-up time. Gross drinking outcome rates are informative yet they mask a lot of variance in treatments, patients, therapists, research design quality, and reporting quality. To uncover some of these sources of variance other questions were asked of the literature. One concerned the effects of length of follow-up time on drinking outcome rates. The categorized drinking outcome data from 260 studies [7, 10] were allocated into one of four groups, depending on the time the data were collected in relation to treatment. These four groups were (1) during the initial active phase of treatment, (2) during aftercare treatment, (3) less than 6 months after the termination of all formal treatment contact, and (4) more than 6 months after the termination of all formal therapy. When data were collected while patients were in active treatment, the abstinence rates found averaged around 50%. Average abstinence rates dropped to about 33% when the data were collected during aftercare treatment. When patients had terminated all treatment contacts, whether for more or less than 6 months, the abstinence rates dropped still further, averaging about 20%. With regard to the rate of overall improvement (a category that includes even minimal reduction in alcohol abuse), the average figures remained fairly constant over the four periods. Apparently many patients who do not remain totally abstinent as they move away from active treatment are at least able to abuse alcohol less than before treatment. This analysis of the data suggests that the likelihood of an alcohol abuse patient being abstinent depends, in part, on the stage of his or her involvement in treatment, but being at least somewhat improved in drinking is not affected by the stage of treatment. The fact that abstinence rates dropped automatically as data collection moved from intensive treatment through aftercare and into posttreatment suggests that patients on the whole may benefit from prolonged treatment. Perhaps routine treatment efforts are too brief to afford patients the opportunity to establish solid alternatives to alcohol abuse in the face of stimuli that have become cues for drinking.

Amount of Treatment

General literature. Another question asked of the literature is whether alcohol abusers who have formal treatment are, on the whole, functioning better than those who have no or at most minimal exposure to treatment. Analysis of data from 384 outcome studies plus reports of changes in drinking behavior for untreated alcohol abusers [9] indicated that 14% of abusers who received no or at most minimal treatment were abstinent during follow-up evaluations of at least 6 months duration. For treated abusers who had been followed up 6 months or more after termination of all treatment, the abstinence rate was 28%. While this difference in favor of treated abusers was statistically significant ($p < .001$), it was not sizable enough to be of practical significance. On the other hand, the figures that represented any amount of drinking behavior improvement, no matter how small (i.e., total improvement scores) showed a statistically significant difference in favor of treated abusers that was also of practical significance. While 42% of non- or minimally treated abusers were at least somewhat improved, 63% of the treated patients were so improved ($p < .001$). These results need to be interpreted cautiously because the data for non- or minimally treated patients were drawn from just a handful of studies that were of variable research quality. Also, comparisons of no versus minimal treatment did not control for the patient characteristic variable through random assignment. The findings suggest that alcohol abusers are, in a practical sense, as likely to be abstinent for 6 months or more with no or minimal treatment as they are to be abstinent 6 months or more after treatment. However, more than minimal treatment may increase an abuser's chances of reducing his or her drinking problem to at least some extent for 6 months or more after treatment. These findings are consistent with those of the analysis of different follow-up lengths in suggesting the instability of total abstinence as an outcome status once treatment is terminated as well as the durability of at least some improvement in drinking as a posttreatment adjustment.

Clinical trials. To assess further the question of whether more treatment is better than less, randomized trials published from 1952–81 were reviewed for differences in outcome between groups of patients receiving varying intensities, amounts, or durations of treatment. This approach has considerable advantage over a review of the general literature because it controls for a powerful determinant of outcome, namely, patient characterizing variables, with the result that any observed differences may be more clearly traceable to differences in treatment amounts.

NO DIFFERENCES. The weight of data from randomized trials is strongly in favor of no differential effects for varying amounts of treatment. In all, 17 of 24 studies found absolutely no differences on a wide variety of measures, which typically included some measure of drinking behavior. Patient groups varied across these studies. For example, they ranged in social class from mostly lower class groups to mostly middle-class and above patients. Also, groups varied on marital status, ranging from studies where only a small fraction of patients were married to those where 100% were married. What follows are examples of the follow-up times and amounts of treatment that were compared in the studies*: (1) at 3 months after admission, a mean of 9.31 days of inpatient detoxification versus a mean of 30.45 inpatient days including detoxification; (2) at 1 year after discharge, 6 weeks of regular psychiatrically oriented inpatient treatment versus 6 weeks of inpatient treatment during which all formal aspects of the program were discontinued; (3) at more than 2 years after termination of therapy, a mean of 10 outpatient disulfiram treatment sessions versus a mean of 32 sessions, which included group psychotherapy in addition to disulfiram; (4) at 1 year after intake, with an initial assessment and counseling session, a mean of 5.2 days of inpatient treatment and 4.7 hours of contact with a social worker and no contact with a psychiatrist versus an initial assessment plus counseling session plus a mean of 23.9 inpatient days, a mean of 18.3 hours of contact with a social worker and a mean of 9.7 outpatient visits with a psychiatrist; and (5) at the end of treatment and 3, 12, and 24 months after termination, reading a self-help manual plus keeping written records of drinking behavior versus 10 weeks of outpatient treatment focused on learning self-control of drinking behavior or 10 weeks of such outpatient treatment that also included relaxation training.

DIFFERENCES. Only three studies found outcome differences during a follow-up of 6 months or less, while six studies observed differences at more than

---

*A complete list of references for the clinical trials can be obtained by writing the author.

6 months (two studies observed differences in both evaluation periods). As an example of short-term differences, Harris and Walter [13] found that outcome at 6 months after intake for patients who had an average of 10.9 outpatient visits plus monthly face-to-face evaluation interviews surpassed outcome for patients who had either an average of 5.9 outpatient visits plus a telephone or mail contact upon failure to continue with treatment or a mean of 4.8 visits plus no further contact other than 6 months after intake. The group receiving the longer treatment plus more intensive evaluation of progress had fewer days when more than six standard drinks were consumed, fewer residential moves, and less time spent in jail or in a hospital. No differences were observed for other measures (e.g., arrests, total abstinence from alcohol). The alcohol abusers in this study were, as a group, fairly socially disintegrated. Of the 65 patients, only 29.2% were employed and 32.3% were married.

An example of long-term differences is found in Stinson et al. [26]. At 18 months after treatment admission, 4 to 6 weeks of intensive inpatient treatment with a mean of 3.79 hours of professional treatment a day versus 4 to 6 weeks of peer-oriented treatment with a mean of 1.26 hours a day of professional treatment resulted in no outcome differences except that the peer-oriented patients were better in drinking behavior as assessed by the Goal Attainment Scale method. While this difference may have been a chance finding because of the large number of outcome comparisons made, the results at least indicate that intensive treatment was no more efficacious than peer-oriented treatment.

DISCUSSION. The evidence from 24 clinical trials strongly supports brief, simple, nonintensive treatment when nondifferentially applied to alcohol abusers. Only four studies found differences for varying amounts and intensities of inpatient treatment. In one case, the differences were uninterpretable and in another, the difference favored less intense treatment. In the two studies where differences were found to favor a greater length of inpatient or residential treatment [21, 22, 27] the long-term beneficial effects were limited to those of social stability for the more heavily treated groups. The majority of patients in these studies appear to have suffered from social disruption and the longer inpatient-residential stay seems to have stabilized them. These findings should not, however, be taken to support longer hospital stays for socially disintegrated patients, because treatment of social instability can be accomplished much less expensively in nonhospital, residential settings. In fact, in the Wanberg et al. [27] study, patients who were provided extra care were treated outside the hospital in a therapeutic community. Further qualifying these findings is that fact that in Pittman and Tate's [21, 22] case, the extra amount of hospital stay was confounded with aftercare treatment and, therefore, the stabilizing effects may have been derived, at least in part, from such treatment. Also, Pittman and Tate's findings may not be generalizable beyond their sample. Boggs (1967), in a study very similar to that of Pittman and Tate's, in which apparently similarly socially disintegrated patients were used, failed to find any difference in outcome at a median of 13.2 months after inpatient discharge.

With respect to amount of initial outpatient treatment, the evidence again tends to support very brief intervention. Only one study found a relationship between the amount of such treatment and outcome [13]. In this study of fairly socially disintegrated patients, the amount of initial treatment was confounded with amount of follow-up evaluation. Patients who had the most treatment were the only ones who received monthly face-to-face evaluation interviews, plus less frequent checks on blood levels and telephone interviews with collaterals. Such assertive evaluation efforts may have been experienced as active aftercare and thus the study may be seen more as supporting the effectiveness of greater amounts of aftercare treatment than as supportive of greater amounts of initial outpatient treatment. Consistent with this possibility, Caddy and Addington [3] found that, with respect to bringing about improvement in drinking behavior for socially stable patients 1 year after inpatient discharge, eight sessions of behaviorally oriented aftercare treatment were superior to four sessions of such treatment. Also, Budenz and Heitzinger [2] found that two degrees of active aftercare led to better drinking outcome at 12-month follow-up than did nonintensive, evaluation-only contacts. Additionally, the group receiving the greater amount of active aftercare was better at 12 months on several nondrinking variables than were those receiving less or no active aftercare. Contrary to these data in support of greater amounts of outpatient aftercare treatment, Caddy and Addington's study did not find differential effects for larger versus smaller amounts of disease-oriented aftercare treatment or for such aftercare treatment versus no aftercare or evaluation-only posttreatment contacts. Apparently only some types of aftercare interventions are rendered more effective when applied more intensively or extensively.

In summary, data from the clinical trials literature suggests that, in general, alcohol abusers should be treated with brief, simple, and nonintense interventions. However, there is some evidence that prolonged residential treatment and active outpatient aftercare or evaluation efforts may help stabilize socially deteriorated patients. Also, some active aftercare treatment efforts may be of benefit to socially intact patients. In any event, a large amount of inpatient or outpatient treatment for the random, socially integrated patient is not supported by the clinical trials literature nor is a large amount of hospital or initial outpatient treatment for the random socially deteriorated patient.

The final word is not yet written regarding the beneficial effects of greater amounts of treatment. None of the studies reviewed actually evaluated long-term treatment. The largest amount of treatment studied was 3½ months of inpatient-residential care. Therapy that is provided over a period of several years with the goal of changing character structure has not yet been tested against briefer therapies. The paucity of differential effects in the studies reviewed may be a function largely of the brevity of the treatments being compared. This is a researchable issue. Another possible explanation for the large number of studies that failed to reject the null hypothesis is that sample size was often small. In over half the studies (i.e, 13) sample size was less than 30 for each group. In such studies there is considerable danger of committing a type II error. With larger samples, some of the strategies compared might have shown differential effects. In only six studies did the sample size exceed 100 for one or more groups. Of interest is the finding that studies showing differences for varying amounts of inpatient-residential treatment had sample sizes of 30 or better, whereas those reporting difference for varying amounts of outpatient-aftercare treatment had small samples ($n < 30$). Perhaps the differential effects for outpatient-aftercare treatment are more robust than are those for inpatient-residential treatment.

The most compelling reason for not resting with the findings of this review is that only five of the 24 clinical trials took into account different types of patients in their analyses of the data (i.e., they analyzed either prospectively or retrospectively interactions between specific types of patients and different amounts of treatment). Perhaps certain patients may need greater amounts of some types of treatments, while other patients may benefit from greater amounts of another approach. A 2-year follow-up of married, male patients studied by Edwards et al. [6]—item 4 under "No Differences"—provides an intriguing example in support of this consideration.

Orford et al. [18] reported that gamma alcoholics (those high in physiological dependence on alcohol) were significantly better off if they had had intensive treatment versus brief counselling. Of those having brief counselling, none had a good treatment outcome adjustment at 2-year follow-up, while 69% of those who had intensive treatment were rated as having a good outcome ($p < .005$, Fisher-Yates test of significance in 2 × 2 contingency tables). Nongamma types, on the other hand, did not respond better to intensive treatment. In fact, this group, of whom 84% were not highly physiologically dependent on alcohol, demonstrated a nonsignificant trend in favor of brief counselling (46% of the group had a good outcome with brief counselling vs. 29% with a good outcome with intensive treatment). Abstinence was the goal of treatment in this study, a goal that may be particularly suitable for highly physiologically dependent abusers. Thus, gamma abusers benefited from greater amounts of this treatment approach whereas those who were generally not highly physiologically dependent did not. If anything, the latter may have been less well off with larger amounts of abstinence-oriented treatment. Perhaps such patients would be better responders to treatment oriented to a nonproblem-drinking goal.

In any event, until the day more information is obtained about which types of patients can benefit from what amounts of which types of treatments, the question of relative effectiveness of different amounts of treatment can receive only the limited response given in this review. Until that day, treatment efforts should be kept to a minimum, in the interest of saving limited financial and human resources, except for perhaps some types of active aftercare treatment for patients in general, and nonhospital, residential treatment for socially deteriorated abusers.

Treatment Involvement Techniques

Building on the hypothesis that treatment is at least helpful in reducing the severity of alcohol problems, the literature was searched for evidence regarding effective approaches for engaging alcohol abusers in treatment. A review of randomized trials from 1952–81 found several approaches that were more effective than comparison strategies in getting patients involved in treatment (e.g., staying in treatment longer, staying until completion of a time-limited treatment, requesting treatment): audiotape feedback of outpatient group counseling sessions (vs. feedback of individual sessions), no videotape playback of drinking sessions while in inpatient treatment (vs. 5 and 30 minutes of playback without counseling), contingent shocking of drinking behavior while in outpatient treatment (vs. noncontingent shocking), contingent shocking of drinking behavior while in inpatient treatment (vs. noncontingent shocking or no shocking while attached to electrical aversion equipment), special assistance from a social worker during 2 to 4 weeks of outpatient evaluation (vs. no special assistance), compulsory outpatient treatment for state penitentiary parolees (vs. voluntary treatment), taped relaxation therapy while in inpatient treatment (vs. no relaxation treatment), disulfiram as an adjunct to inpatient milieu treatment (vs. milieu therapy only), twice a week outpatient treatment including disulfiram (vs. once a week treatment with or without disulfiram or twice a week treatment without disulfiram), chlordiazepoxide (Librium) (vs. placebo or vitamins), chlordiazepoxide (vs. diazepam, Valium), a combination of meprobamate and promazine hydrochloride (Prozine) (vs. placebo), three sessions of videotape training on how to benefit from psychotherapy (vs. standard alcohol education films), telephone calls to outpatients upon rapidly dropping out of treatment (vs. impersonal letters), personal letters with or without return envelopes to outpatients who rapidly dropped out of treatment (vs. no contact with dropouts), viewing videotapes of patients having long-term successes (vs. no videotapes), 1g of cannabis plus alcohol education and counseling at each outpatient visit (vs. only counseling and education), a letter during detoxification offering outpatient treatment upon discharge (vs. no letter), being followed by a professional in an outpatient clinic after meeting that professional in a hospital emergency room (vs. being referred to the clinic by a medical resident in the emergency room), and insight-oriented outpatient therapy or outpatient rational behavior therapy (vs. Alcoholics Anonymous — AA). These data suggest that treatment involvement can be enhanced by (1) reducing anxiety through such means as tranquilizers, relaxation training, and cannabis; (2) giving attention and support in the form of frequent meetings, personal attention or special assistance from a care giver, group counseling, personal letters, telephone calls, continuity of care; (3) modeling how to benefit from treatment through videotapes; and (4) establishing an avoidance paradigm using such strategies as disulfiram and compulsory treatment with severe consequences for failure to cooperate with therapy. Obversely, alcohol abusers can be driven away from treatment by employing such aversive techniques as noncontingent or sham electrical aversive conditioning and videotape playback of drunken comportment without counseling. Those techniques that research has demonstrated to be relatively effective in engaging alcohol abusers in treatment should be utilized to get patients into the most effective interventions. Those procedures that drive patients away from psychotherapy should be avoided. (See [9] for a dicussion of iatrogenic treatment effects on alcohol abusers.)

Locus of Treatment

A review of the clinical trials literature found four studies that dealt with the variable of locus of treatment. For socially deteriorated patients, inpatient treatment appears to offer the opportunity for more comprehensive medical treatment than does outpatient therapy, yet no differences in posttreatment functioning have been demonstrated across the outpatient-inpatient split. For more socially integrated patients, the evidence tends to support less restriction over more. While one study found short-term differences in favor of hospital treatment (vs. in-community therapy), two other studies found long-term differences against 24-hour hospital treatment and in favor of either outpatient therapy or daycare treatment. Perhaps less restrictive treatment supports the coping abilities of relatively socially intact patients with the result that their level of functioning remains better over the long haul. Further clinical trials are recommended to assess this possibility.

Traditional Outpatient Psychotherapy

No differential treatment effects were observed comparing psychotherapy (vs. hypnosis), group therapy alone (vs. group therapy plus disulfiram or disulfiram alone), psychiatrically oriented clinic treatment (vs. AA), psychotherapy plus pharmacologic therapy (vs. pharmacologic therapy alone), insight therapy (vs. systematic desensitization or covert sensitization), individual counseling and psychotherapy (vs. systematic desensitization), traditional group therapy (vs. behaviorally oriented group therapy), and traditional outpatient treatment for drinking-driving offenders (vs. power motivation training treatment).

Differential effects were found in just three studies. In one study of drinking-driving offenders, traditional abstinence-oriented group treatment was found to be less effective on drinking and nondrinking variables than were behaviorally oriented therapy groups oriented toward the goal of nonproblem drinking. In another, a structured experientially oriented group that was added to multifaceted outpatient treatment was less effective on nondrinking outcome measures than was an assertiveness training group. In the third study, traditional insight-oriented therapy (mostly individual) was found to be superior to AA contacts with respect to economic and legal indices at the end of treatment and with regard to employment status at 6-month follow-up. Although other significant differences may have occurred for insight-treated patients versus those treated with AA and other methods, incomplete reporting prevents a clear determination of this possibility.

What few differential effects have been observed for traditional outpatient psychotherapy techniques tend to suggest that such approaches are, in some cases, less effective than are behaviorally oriented strategies. However, only two studies have reported such findings and in both the data were collected shortly after the end of treatment. Also, the type of approach was confounded with the goal of treatment in one of the projects. Furthermore, as noted at the beginning of this section, other clinical trials have failed to find differences between traditional treatment and behaviorally oriented approaches. Certainly more clinical trials are needed before drawing any firm impressions regarding the relative effectiveness of traditional outpatient interventions.

Nature of Admission (Compulsory vs. Voluntary)

Only four clinical trials have contributed data to the issue of compulsory versus voluntary admission for alcohol abusers. The findings suggest that compulsory outpatient treatment for chronic municipal court offenders is no more effective than voluntary outpatient therapy or no treatment. The lack of positive findings appears to be due, in part, to inadequate strength of the negative consequences for failure to comply with treatment. A combination of enforced inpatient treatment followed by outpatient work may, on the other hand, be more effective than voluntary outpatient care. This may be a function, at least partially, of the medical attention given the municipal court offender during the inpatient stay. For patients who face a severe penalty for not complying with treatment (e.g., state prison parolees who face a prolonged imprisonment for failure to remain in treatment), compulsory outpatient treatment may be more effective than voluntary outpatient treatment.

Mode of Treatment

Group versus individual. Only one clinical trial allowed for assessment of the relative effectiveness of group therapy versus individual therapy. In that project, group therapy was found to be more effective in keeping patients in treatment. In the absence of any more data, nothing can be stated as to the relative effectiveness of group therapy as a treatment mode. This absence of data is surprising in the face of the widespread assumption among helpers that group therapy is a particularly appropriate mode of treatment for many alcohol abusers.

Marital versus individual. Only three clinical trials assessed the relative effectiveness of traditional marital therapy versus individual treatment. No differences were found, but in each case samples were quite small, numbering fewer than 20 patients in each group compared. In one of the studies [16] traditional marital therapy was also compared with a behaviorally oriented marital therapy approach. Data collected at the end of treatment show the behaviorally oriented intervention to be superior to traditional marital therapy, as well as to individual therapy, on measures of marital adjustment and marital interactions. This study is not yet complete. Follow-up data are being collected to see if these differences are stable over a year after treatment.

Because of the small number of studies involved and their limited size, no conclusions can be drawn about the relative effectiveness of traditional marital versus individual therapy. This is clearly an area in need of further investigation.

Differential Diagnosis and Treatment Planning

Earlier in this chapter, the need to identify specific patient-treatment interactions was noted. The search for a particular treatment approach that is most effective for all patients (a search that many of the researchers who contributed data to this review appear to have engaged in) fails to consider that different individuals will respond in various ways to whatever approaches are offered. Until it is known which patients respond best to what interventions, treatment efforts will, this author believes, continue to be of limited effectiveness. Unfortunately, today there is only a modicum of knowledge regarding systematic ways to diagnose patients differentially and to assign them to the most appropriate treatment interventions. This final section reports on some of the promising findings in pursuit of such knowledge—those of Skinner [25], McLachlan [14], Reynolds et al. [24], and Polich et al. [23]. Pertinent data from Orford et al. [18] have already been described.

Skinner [25] factor-analyzed the Alcohol-Use Inventory and identified four major syndromes of alcohol abuse. The first factor, Alcohol Dependence, should be helpful in differentially assigning patients to nonproblem-drinking versus abstinence drinking outcome goals. Patients scoring low on this factor may be appropriate candidates for the nonproblem-drinking goal. Factor II, Perceived Benefits from Drinking, measures anxiety symptoms related to use of alcohol and might prove helpful in differentially assigning patients to relaxation, social skills, or stress management training. Factor III, Marital Discord, may be useful in assessing the interactions of marital or other close relationship problems with the alcohol abuse problem. Patients who score high on this dimension might be suitable for communication skills training or other types of marital therapy interventions. Factor IV, Polydrug Use, might be used to identify those who need special medical attention for problems related to drug abuse and who need interventions designed to alter the life style of polydrug abusers.

McLachlan [14] evaluated the drinking outcome status of 94 patients 12 to 16 months after treatment. These patients had been detoxified and then given 26 hours of group therapy by one of five therapists during 3 weeks of inpatient care. These groups varied on the amount of structure provided by the therapists. Following hospital discharge, patients who lived in the city where the hospital was located received active aftercare in the form of weekly group meetings and weekly telephone or face-to-face contacts with a volunteer. Patients who lived outside the city had much less structure to their aftercare, receiving only letters from the volunteer. McLachlan hypothesized that certain patients (those scoring high on a measure of interpersonal development—conceptual level) would respond best to less structured groups and aftercare treatment. Others (those scoring low on conceptual level) would be better responders to more structured groups and aftercare. Post hoc analysis of the data supported McLachlan's hypothesis. When high conceptual level patients received more nondirective groups and also had little structure to their aftercare (i.e., they received only letters from the volunteer), they were more often classified as recovered with respect to drinking behavior than were similar patients who had more structured groups and active aftercare. The reverse was the case with low conceptual level patients. These patients had the best outcome when they received both structured groups and structured aftercare. For all patients combined, McLachlan found a recovered rate of 77% for those who were matched in their need for structure for both group therapy and aftercare treatment, yet he observed a mere 38% recovery rate for those who were mismatched in both areas.

In a double-blind prospective study, Reynolds et al. [24] randomly assigned alcohol abusers to lithium or placebo tablets. Patients were designated as either depressed or nondepressed depending on their score on a standard measure of depression (Beck Depression Inventory). During a mean of about 10 months of treatment, patients who were designated as depressed responded significantly better to lithium than to the placebo. Nondepressed patients, on the other hand, did no better on lithium than on the placebo. Depressed patients on lithium drank a mean of just 1 day during treatment compared to placebo-treated depressed patients who drank a mean of 48 days ($p < .01$). Also, only a third of lithium-treated depressed patients drank alcohol at all, whereas 100% of the placebo-treated depressed patients did ($p < .025$).

Finally, Polich et al. [23] conducted a 4-year follow-up study of patients treated in alcoholism treatment centers funded by the National Institute on Alcohol Abuse and Alcoholism. Earlier (at 18 months after admission) these patients had been followed up and classified as being either abstinent or drinking without problems. The stability between the two evaluation times of these two types of drinking outcome was found to interact with three patient characteristics at intake. For those who were under the age of 40, unmarried, and low in psychological and physical dependence on alcohol at intake drinking without problems at 18 months was a far more stable adjustment than was being abstinent. At 4-year follow-up, 32% of the abstainers had relapsed into problem drinking, whereas only 3% of the nonproblem drinkers had relapsed. For those who were, at intake, 40 or over, married, and high in psychological and physical dependence on alcohol, the stability of drinking outcome statuses was dramatically reversed. Abstainers had only a 4% relapse rate from 18 months to 4 years, while the nonproblem drinkers had a 50% relapse rate! These data suggest that some patients do much better being totally abstinent after treatment while others are much better off learning to drink without problems.

Studies such as these will enable therapists to develop differential treatment strategies based on assessment of each patient's need for structure, depression level, degree of psychological and physiological dependence on alcohol, quality of marital interaction, use of drugs other than alcohol, age, and so forth. This level of assessment activity should improve significantly the effectiveness in treating alcohol abusers.

CONCLUSION

The salient findings of this review of studies, which evaluated various aspects of alcohol abuse treatment, are

1. People with alcohol problems have a good chance of improving in drinking behavior when they become involved in formal alcohol abuse treatment.

2. Patients experience a range of drinking outcomes, not just total abstinence or no change.

3. Abstinence appears to be an unstable response to treatment, whereas the condition of having at least some improvement in drinking behavior seems to be a more durable response to therapeutic intervention.

4. A large amount of inpatient or initial outpatient treatment is not recommended for the random, socially integrated patient, and therapy offered outside a 24-hour hospital setting may be better than in-hospital treatment for such patients.

5. A large amount of hospital or initial outpatient treatment is not recommended for the random, socially deteriorated patient. The only apparent benefit of 24-hour hospital treatment versus outpatient therapy for this type of patient is the provision of a more comprehensive medical treatment of physical problems

that are related to alcohol abuse; otherwise, the random, socially deteriorated patient can be treated outside the 24-hour *hospital* setting without compromising effectiveness.

6. Perhaps some types of active aftercare should be provided for patients in general, and prolonged residential, nonhospital treatment should be considered for the socially deteriorated patient.

7. Some strategies seem to be relatively effective in getting patients involved in treatment. Generally they involve reducing anxiety, giving attention and support, modeling how to benefit from treatment, and establishing strong avoidance paradigms. Some strategies seem to drive people away from treatment.

8. No firm impression can be derived regarding the effectiveness of traditional outpatient psychotherapy approaches versus comparison outpatient interventions, although behaviorally oriented treatments may be more efficacious in some cases.

9. Compulsory treatment may be more effective than voluntary treatment, but only if the consequences for failure to comply with treatment are severely aversive.

10. No impressions can be drawn regarding the relative effectiveness of marital or group therapy versus individual treatment.

These statements are not intended to be pronouncements of solid fact. There are too many limitations in the data to warrant that. In some areas of analysis, very few studies were available. Sample size was often small. Many patients no doubt did not comply with treatment and they may have thereby distorted actual treatment effects. In the clinical trials, randomization was in all probability not strictly adhered to in many (most?) cases and there were numerous other methodological flaws in many of the studies. Also, the types of interventions studied have been weighted in the direction of what researchers are interested in and may therefore not be representative of the bulk of routine treatment provided in the field. With these and other limitations, the findings of this review should be read more for their heuristic value than for marking the way along an unquestioned road in providing treatment.

Further research should be directed toward refinement of those approaches that appear generally to be more effective than comparison methods (see, in addition to the data in this chapter, an excellent review of alcohol abuse treatment outcome studies by Miller and Hester [15]). Also, more research toward further identification of optimal patient-treatment interactions is warranted [19, 20].

In line with the latter endeavor, efforts have been made toward discovering general prognostic indicators among patient characteristics, but this work has been disappointing [12, 17].

More fruitful may be attempts to isolate patient characteristics that are specific indicators (i.e., indicators that interact in certain ways with some treatments and differently with others). The potential productiveness of such attempts is exemplified in this chapter by findings from several research efforts. If substantiated by further research, findings such as these can give treatment personnel guidelines for delivering individualized, and therefore potentially more effective, treatment.

While in pursuit of efficacious treatments, helpers need to keep in mind that, just as with any attempt to help people, alcohol abuse treatment may harm some patients. Further investigation is needed to identify those types of treatments that might be harmful to patients with specific characteristics. For example, as indicated by data in the Polich et al. [23] and Orford et al. [18] studies, certain patients may be harmed by striving toward total abstinence, while others may suffer deleterious effects from efforts to drink without problems.

An impressive array of evaluative research has been done in the alcohol abuse treatment field toward finding the most beneficial treatment approaches. It is hoped that efforts will be continued toward advancement of the knowledge of those methods that have the best chance of helping each individual alcohol abuser and the least chance of harming him or her.

ACKNOWLEDGMENTS

The author wishes to express his gratitude to Mr. Charles G. Allen, MA, Denver Veterans Administration Medical Center, who played a vital role in the preparation of this chapter.

REFERENCES

1. Boggs, S. L. Measures of treatment outcome for alcoholics: A model of analysis. In: Pittman, D. J. (ed.), *Alcoholism*. New York: Harper & Row, 1967.
2. Budenz, D., and Heitzinger, R. *Alcoholism Alternatives Follow-up Project A164-01 77032: Final Report*. Unpublished manuscript, Madison General Hospital, Madison, Wisconsin, 1979.
3. Caddy, G. R., and Addington, H. J., Jr. *An Evaluation of Behavioral Innoculation and Other Approaches in Reducing Alcoholic Relapse*. Paper presented at the 15th annual convention of the Association for the Advancement of Behavior Therapy, Toronto, November, 1981.
4. Cahn, S. *The Treatment of Alcoholics: An Evaluative Study*. Oxford University Press: New York, 1970.
5. Chafetz, M. E., Blane, H. T., and Hill, M. J. (eds.). *Frontiers of Alcoholism*. Science House: New York, 1970.
6. Edwards, G., Orford, J., Egert, S., Guthrie, S., Hawker, A., Hensman, C., Mitch-

eson, M., Oppenheimer, E., and Taylor, C. Alcoholism: A controlled trial of "treatment" and "advice." *Q. J. Stud. Alcohol* 38:1004-1031, 1977.

7. Emrick, C. D. *Psychological Treatment of Alcoholism: An Analytic Review.* Unpublished doctoral dissertation, Columbia University, 1973.

8. Emrick, C. D. A review of psychologically oriented treatment of alcoholism: I. The use and interrelationships of outcome criteria and drinking behavior following treatment. *Q. J. Stud. Alcohol* 35:523-549, 1974.

9. Emrick, C. D. A review of psychologically oriented treatment of alcoholism: II. The relative effectiveness of different treatment approaches and the relative effectiveness of treatment versus no treatment. *Q. J. Stud. Alcohol* 36:88-108, 1975.

10. Emrick, C. D. Psychological treatment of alcoholism: Eleven major conclusions based on an extensive review of the outcome literature with an emphasis on getting away from technology and back to the basics of treatment. *Proceedings of a Workshop on Alcoholism for Mental Health Professionals.* Division on Alcoholism, Department of Public Institutions: Lincoln, Nebraska, 1976.

11. Emrick, C. D. Perspectives in clinical research: Relative effectiveness of alcohol abuse treatment. *Family Commun. Health* 2:71-88, 1979.

12. Gibbs, L., and Flanagan, J. Prognostic indicators of alcoholism treatment outcome. *Int. J. Addict.* 12:1097-1147, 1977.

13. Harris, R. N., and Walter, J. *Outcome, Reliability and Validity Issues of Alcoholism Follow-up.* Paper presented at the 27th annual meeting of the Alcohol and Drug Problems Association of North America, New Orleans, September 1976.

14. McLachlan, J. F. C. Therapy strategies, personality orientation and recovery from alcoholism. *Can. Psychiatr. Assoc. J.* 19:25-30, 1974.

15. Miller, W. R., and Hester, R. K. Treating the problem drinker: Modern approaches. In: *The Addictive Behaviors: Treatment of Alcoholism, Drug Abuse, Smoking, and Obesity,* Miller, W. R. (ed.). Pergamon: New York, 1980.

16. O'Farrell, T. J., and Cutter, H. S. G. Evaluating behavioral marital therapy for alcoholics: Procedures and preliminary results. In: *Essentials of Behavioral Treatments for Families,* Hamerlynck, L. A. (ed.). Brunner/Mazel: New York. In press.

17. Ogborne, A. G. Patient characteristics as predictors of treatment outcomes for alcohol and drug abusers. In: *Research Advances in Alcohol and Drug Problems* (Vol. 4), Israel, Y., Glaser, F. B., Kalant, H., Popham, R. E., Schmidt, W. and Smart, R. G. (eds.). Plenum: New York, 1978.

18. Orford, J., Oppenheimer, E., and Edwards, G. Abstinence or control: The outcome for excessive drinkers two years after consultation. *Behav. Res. Ther.* 14:409-418, 1976.

19. Pattison, E. M., Coe, R., and Doerr, H. O. Population variation among alcoholism treatment facilities. *Int. J. Addict.* 8:199-229, 1973.

20. Pattison, E. M., Coe, R., and Rhodes, R. J. Evaluation of alcoholism treatment: A comparison of three facilities. *Arch. Gen. Psychiatry* 20:478-488, 1969.

21. Pittman, D. J., and Tate, R. L. A comparison of two treatment programs for alcoholics. *Q. J. Stud. Alcohol* 30:888-889, 1969.

22. Pittman, D. J., and Tate, R. L. A comparison of two treatment programs for alcoholics. *Int. J. Soc. Psychiatry* 18:183-193, 1972.

23. Polich, J. M., Armor, D. J., and Braiker, H. B. Patterns of alcoholism over four years. *Q. J. Stud. Alcohol* 41:397-416, 1980.

24. Reynolds, C. M., Merry, J., and Coppen, A. Prophylactic treatment of alcoholism by lithium carbonate: An initial report. *Alcoholism: Clin. Exp. Res.* 1:109-111, 1977.

25. Skinner, H. A. Primary syndromes of alcohol abuse: Their measurement and correlates *Br. J. Addict.* 76:63-76, 1981.

26. Stinson, D. J., Smith, W. G., Amidjaya, I., and Kaplan, J. M. Systems of care and treatment outcomes for alcoholic patients. *Arch. Gen. Psychiatry* 36:535-539, 1979.

27. Wanberg, K. W., Fairchild, D., and Bonn, E. M. *Evaluation of an Extended-Residential Therapeutic-Community Program for Severe and Chronic Alcoholism.* Unpublished manuscript, Fort Logan Mental Health Center, Denver, 1978.

96

GLENN R. CADDY, PhD, Nova University, Ft. Lauderdale, Florida

EVALUATION OF BEHAVIORAL METHODS IN THE STUDY OF ALCOHOLISM

TEN YEARS AGO THE TASK of evaluating alcoholism therapies in general, and the behavioral approaches in particular, was far less complex and far more suspect than it is today. In recent years, however, an increasing number of behaviorally oriented clinicians have been drawn to the study of alcohol abuse and its treatment, and this attraction has brought significant increases both in the scope of the behaviorally oriented procedures that have been employed to treat alcohol abuse and in the methodological sophistication of the evaluation studies that have been conducted following such treatment. Further, as behaviorally oriented clinicians have broadened their theoretical assumptions regarding the dynamics of behavioral disorders, and as the significance of cognitive phemonena has become more widely recognized, behaviorally oriented researchers and clinicians have been responsible for the emergence of both multivariate theoretical models of alcohol dependence and multivariate treatment strategies [19, 96]. Interestingly, it has been only since the emergence of these multivariate behaviorally based treatment strategies that comprehensive and scientifically sophisticated multiple measurement outcome evaluation studies have been conducted.

The aforestated notwithstanding, it is still necessary to impose some caveat re-

---

Glenn R. Caddy, PhD, Professor and Director of Clinical Training, Nova University, Ft. Lauderdale, Florida.

garding the interpretation of virtually all treatment evaluation research findings. This is so because it is difficult, if not impossible, to conduct truly scientifically convincing comparisons of therapeutic techniques. Franks [39] reflected on this issue when he noted the problems of random selection of subjects and of the setting up of triple-blind procedures. He considered such problems insurmountable. Despite these difficulties, progress toward greater scientific integrity in treatment evaluation research is continuing and valuable scientifically tolerable comparative treatment research is now being reported in areas that include alcohol dependency.

CHEMICAL AVERSION THERAPIES

Virtually all the behaviorally oriented studies reported in the alcoholism treatment literature prior to 1970 involved either the introduction of specific laboratory-based conditioning procedures as a component in an otherwise nonbehavioral treatment program or alternately, they involved the use of one or occasionally two behaviorally based techniques as part of a "narrow band" treatment endeavor. The first scientifically credible alcoholism treatment follow-up studies to include a behavioral component were conducted by Voegtlin and his associates at the Shadel Hospital in Seattle. Over a period of more than ten years, these investigators followed over 4,000 subjects who had been treated using emetine aversion in a classical conditioning paradigm within a program that included an array of other abstinence-oriented therapies, all of which were provided together with a very strong expectation of positive treatment outcome.

Voegtlin and his colleagues reported the rate of abstinence in their subjects to range from 44% in those subjects who remained abstinent from the time of their first treatment [62] to 70% for those subjects who experienced some relapse during the first year but who, following further treatment, returned to abstinence [120]. Overall abstinence rates of around 60% were reported as typical of the Shadel program at the first posttreatment year, with about 38% maintaining abstinence for as long as 5 years [63, 119, 122, 123]. It should be noted, however, that these investigators made no attempt to determine the spontaneous remission rate likely to be found in similar populations of what were clearly highly motivated and generally well-to-do patients. Thus, it is not possible to evaluate the extent to which any single treatment component employed at Shadel contributed to the overall recovery of the patients treated within that program.

In a similar noncontrolled study with a similar patient population, Wiens et al. [127] reported a 63% abstinence rate at the end of a 12-month follow-up period, at which time 92% of 261 patients had been evaluated. On the other hand, Neubuerger et al. [93] reported the results of a study virtually identical to that offered by Wiens et al. [127]. In this second research program, data from two similar but separate treated populations of 275 and 290 patients produced abstinence rates of 33 and 43%, respectively (allowing for one slip, these same figures were 39 and 50%, respectively). Given the similarity of the Wiens and the Neubuerger treatment programs, it is tempting and probably appropriate to relate the substantially lower abstinence rates found by Neubuerger et al. to characteristics of their patients for, by and large, their subjects were significantly less stable maritally and vocationally and they drank greater quantities than the subjects studied by Wiens et al. Certainly, the earlier experiences at Shadel indicated the importance of patient characteristics as factors related to successful treatment. Lemere and Voegtlin [62], in fact, had reported that when 100 charity cases were treated with conditioned reflex therapy, the results were disappointing.

While still other investigators employing chemical aversive conditioning procedures have reported treatment successes of around 50 to 60% based on criteria of abstinence [72, 117], Wallerstein [126] reported an improvement rate of only 24% in his emetine conditioning group during a 3- to 24-month follow-up period. Similarly, Quinn and Kerr [102] reported that only one of their 15 alcoholic subjects who completed 50 conditioning sessions remained abstinent despite the fact that both group and individual therapy were provided concurrently [101].

Recognizing the limitations of the traditional chemical aversive conditioning approaches to alcoholism treatment, yet arguing for the need to combat the intrinsic positive reinforcement that alcohol consumption provides the alcohol abuser, Lovibond [64] reported on a pilot study involving the development of alcohol aversion induced by motion sickness. In this work, the subject was rotated in a chair until vestibular stimulation induced nausea, at which time the chair was halted and the subject asked to take a small quantity of alcohol. Thereafter, the sequence was repeated until the nauseous state was heightened again, at which time further alcohol was administered. Lovibond [S. H. Lovibond, 1980, personal communication] has been able to induce conditioned nausea with this sequence and has precipitated a response in some of his subjects characteristic of taste aversion learning. Unfortunately, this work is at a very early stage of development and no clinical outcome data are yet available for examination.

Taking the weight of the evidence into account, it appears that when chemically based aversive conditioning procedures are employed as part of a package including standard yet highly structured adjunctive treatments with patients whose prognoses are particularly favorable, an impressive percentage benefit from such interventions. It must be noted that to date, however, none of the chemical aversive conditioning studies reporting favorable results has provided a credible scientific analysis of the unique contribution played by aversive conditioning to the overall outcome of patients undergoing such treatment. The only study that did attempt to measure the efficacy of emetine aversion alone [126] suggested that the technique had little to recommend it when administered independent of additional procedures. From the vantage point of hindsight, of course, such a finding appears eminently reasonable, especially when it is recognized that there is very little evidence to support the theoretical assumptions regarding the classical conditioning of nausea on which the chemical aversive procedures were based.

ELECTRICAL AVERSION TECHNIQUES

Electrical aversion techniques have long been seen to offer certain technical advantages over chemical aversion procedures. These advantages include greater control of the parameters of the aversive experience as well as greater feasibility for providing repeated conditioning trials within each session [40, 103]. Of course, electrical aversion also offers (in certain respects) a less unpleasant consequence for both patient and therapist following the administration of the therapeutic procedure than is true in the case of chemical aversion procedures.

The earliest study employing electrical aversion to suppress drinking behavior was reported by Kantorovich in 1929 [57]. In this research, 20 subjects were assigned to an electric shock conditioning sequence with a further 10 subjects being assigned (apparently not randomly) to a hypnotherapy or medication control condition. The results indicated an outcome favoring the conditioning procedure, but with only five of the 17 experimental group subjects who developed a stable conditioned response remaining abstinent 3 months following treatment, these differences hardly demonstrated the efficacy of the experimental procedures.

Subsequently, a variety of uncontrolled group and single case studies employing various shock-related learning paradigms with differing subject samples and differing adjunctive methodologies also have reflected uncertain support for electrical aversive procedures, with abstinence rates ranging from zero to about 60% [16, 17, 27, 53, 71, 77]. Several more recent and somewhat methodologically more sophisticated comparative treatment studies, however, have provided some support for the use of electrical aversive therapy [42, 48], yet such support has not been general [34, 68].

In an attempt to examine the differential treatment responsiveness of alcoholics to various shock procedures, Marlatt [66] randomly assigned inpatient subjects to one of four conditions employing either a punishment, escape, or avoidance paradigm, or a noncontingent punishment procedure. In addition, a further randomly assigned comparison group received only the standard hospital treatment. Based on a criterion of either abstinence or improvement at 3 months posttreatment, no significant between-group differences were noted. Overall, 21% of the entire study population was abstinent, with an additional 64% rated as improved. Interestingly, however, and this is consistent with other research findings, the punishment paradigm group showed the greatest percentage reduction in alcohol consumption (94%) with the escape, avoidance, noncontingent, and control group subjects showing reductions of 69%, 65%, 23%, and 42%, respectively (see also [28]). Marlatt also observed another interesting finding; namely, aversive shock procedures appear to produce a relatively high rate of nonabstinent yet improved cases even when the treatment goal has been abstinence. This observation also has been noted in other electrical aversion studies wherein the percentage of cases reporting moderate alcohol use has, on occasion, exceeded the percentage of abstinent outcomes [12, 42].

Lovibond and Caddy [65] introduced a variation of electrical aversive counterconditioning as part of a broad-spectrum behavioral treatment program. This procedure, known as discriminated aversive conditioning, employed an electric shock-based punishment paradigm that was administered contingent upon blood alcohol concentrations exceeding 0.065%. Lovibond and Caddy randomly assigned 31 alcoholic subjects to the experimental procedure and 13 subjects to an additional noncontingent shock control condition. At the 12-month follow-up, these authors reported 21 of the 28 experimental subjects who completed the study to be completely successful, with an additional three cases improved. In the control condition, a particularly high dropout rate (8 of 13) neither permitted nor required the application of statistical procedures to evaluate the differential treatment effects. In a subsequent study, Caddy and Lovibond [22] conducted a components analysis of their previously developed program. In this second study, 60 alcoholic subjects completed treatment following random assignment to one of three treatment groups: an aversion plus self-regulation group, which was identical to the original procedure; a self-regulation group, which was identical to the original program but excluded the use of shock; and an aversion group that was similar to the original procedure but omitted the self-regulatory procedure. The results immediately after treatment showed subjects in the aversion plus self-regulation group to be progressing best, with 85% making some gains and 65% in the highest success category. The self-regulation group demonstrated similar though less striking improvement and the aversion-only condition showed the least improvement, with only 20% of subjects in the highest success category and 55% showing some improvement. Six months after treatment, the aversion plus self-regulation group continued to show greatest improvement due to a heavy loading (45%) of subjects in the top success category. The self-regulation group again showed intermediate improvement, with subjects in the aversion-only group again considerably less improved. Only 37 patients had completed 12 post-treatment months at the time of the publication, yet the trends apparent in the earlier data were maintained at this time, also. The removal of the shock aversion component from the entire package resulted in a modest decline in overall improvement (60% vs. 80% improvement at the 6 month and 65% vs. 76% at the 12 month posttreatment). There also was a trend noted in these data for the subjects in the self-regulation group to perform better than subjects in the aversion group based on a criterion of relapse, though this trend did not prove statistically significant.

In a somewhat similar study, Vogler et al. [124] found that the results from their broad spectrum program, which included electrical aversion, were somewhat superior (though in most cases not significantly so), to the results they reported for a group that received alcohol education and behavioral counseling only. A subsequent, and again similar, study by this group [125], but this time employing a sample of nonalcoholic problem drinkers, concluded that subjects in the group receiving electrical aversion showed no greater improvement than did subjects in two other groups who received similar broad-spectrum behavioral programming but without the aversion therapy (see also [82, 83]).

Overall, the data suggest that when electrical aversion is used as part of a multifaceted treatment program, the aversion component appears to contribute, though in some instances minimally, to the success rates achieved. In the absence of adjunctive procedures, however, as Hedberg and Campbell's [50] study indicates, the electrical aversive conditioning procedures do not result in favorable treatment outcomes. Clinical experience with individual cases suggests that electrical aversive procedures occasionally produce quite profound effects. For example, one female patient in the Lovibond and Caddy [65] study reported feeling absolutely devastated by the entire shock experience, which, nevertheless, she considered to be particularly important. It was not the shock per se that produced this extreme reaction. Rather, she was devastated because she had allowed herself to develop such a serious drinking problem that she chose to subject herself to aversion therapy in order to shock herself out of her previous complacency. For this patient, the aversive procedures contributed to her motivation to change and at the same time helped her reduce her desire to drink alcohol. It seems, in fact, that the outcome expressed in this case is not an atypical reaction from a person who is determined to benefit from exposure to electrical aversive conditioning. Whereas investigators conducting the early electrical aversion studies assumed that such procedures led to peripheral suppression of drinking by inducing a competing anxiety response via classical conditioning, the more recent work suggests that electrical aversion, in particular when used in a punishment paradigm, results in a reduction in the incentive motivation to drink [65, 103] or impacts upon more general cognitively related therapeutic factors [48, 78]. These changes in the cognitive structures of alcohol-abusing patients undergoing aversion therapy have yet to be studied.

COVERT SENSITIZATION

When applied to alcoholism, covert sensitization involves the imaginal development of a set of aversive scenes, usually nausea- and emesis-related, which then are paired with images of the act of drinking [23, 24, 25]. On both theoretical and practical grounds, covert sensitization offers advantages over chemical and electrical aversion procedures. It permits the patient and the therapist to adjust the topography of the aversive imagery to the specifics of the patient's drinking behavior; it allows direct (imaginal) association between the aversive image, the behavior, and the environment associated with the drinking; it is sufficiently mobile that it can be employed independently by the patient when he or she feels tempted to drink; and it is less unpleasant than the other aversive approaches to alcoholism therapy.

Given such advantages, it is somewhat surprising that covert sensitization studies have been reported so sparingly in the alcoholism literature. In the few case studies that have employed covert sensitization, the short-term results have been encouraging [3, 107]. Uncontrolled studies using larger sample sizes have reported more variable results, yet here too results have been positive irrespective of the context provided by adjunctive procedures. Miller [73], for example, employed covert sensitization (hypnotic aversion) and reported an 83% abstinence rate at a mean of 9 months posttreatment for 24 alcoholics. Anant [4], on the other hand, provided covert sensitization therapy alone and reported that all of the 25 alcoholic subjects who completed his program maintained abstinence for periods ranging from 8 to 15 months. Unfortunately, these promising results were not maintained at a subsequent follow-up [5].

The most impressive uncontrolled investigation of covert sensitization to date has been reported by Elkins and Murdock [37], who provided covert sensitization therapy to 24 alcoholics as part of their inpatient treatment. As well as administering the covert sensitization procedures, Elkins also monitored his subjects' autonomic reactivity and he related these autonomic indices to subjective reports of the development of nausea. By combining data from these two sources, Elkins reported success at discriminating those subjects who developed conditioned nausea (those who became nauseauous to alcohol images), from those subjects who were able to induce nausea on demand only when imagining nausea. Elkins and Murdock [37] reported that 22 of their 24 alcoholic subjects were able to develop demand nausea and of these, 15 were able to develop significant conditioned nausea. Follow-up on Elkins' subjects indicated that those who achieved only demand nausea remained abstinent for a mean of 3.7 months posttreatment. Those who developed conditioned nausea, however, sustained abstinence for a mean of 14.9 months. Subsequently, Elkins [36] has reported that 30.8% of his conditioned nausea, however, sustained abstinence for a mean of 14.9 months. Subsequently, Elkins [36] has reported that 3.08% of his conditioned nausea subjects maintained abstinence for periods ranging from 5 to 62 months. None of his demand nausea subjects, however, was abstinent at the time of the second follow-up. Interestingly, when Elkins evaluated his treatment outcome in terms of restricted drinking criteria, 88% of his conditioned nausea subjects and 83% of those who reached only the demand nausea stage wwere drinking without difficulties.

There also exists a small number of controlled studies that have evaluated covert sensitization in relation to one of a number of comparison procedures. Ashem and Donner [7], for example, compared alcoholic subjects assigned to a covert sensitization procedure to subjects assigned to a waiting list–control sequence and reported that 40% of the 15 subjects who received covert sensitization were abstinent at 6 months posttreatment, whereas none of the 8 control subjects maintained abstinence. In yet another example, Hedberg and Campbell [5] compared covert sensitization, electrical aversion, systematic desensitization, and a behavioral family therapy program. The results from this work indicated that 9 of the 14 abstinence-seeking subjects assigned to the covert sensitization procedure met an abstinent or improved criterion at 6 months posttreatment and the one subject who chose a restricted drinking outcome also attained his goal. This 67% success outcome showed the covert sensitization alone procedure to be less effective than the behavior family therapy and systematic desensitization procedures, both of which met the success criteria on 87% of cases. Covert sensitization was seen to produce favorable outcome, however, when compared with the electrical aversion procedure (25% improved) employed by these investigators (see also [98]).

Overall, while the available data are inadequate to permit any definitive conclusions regarding the long-term efficacy of the covert sensitization approach, the research that is available indicates that when employed in the absence of other procedures, covert sensitization appears to offer some short-term benefit in relation to no treatment. In general, however, the technique has not been shown to offer significant advantages over other active treatment procedures, nor is it clear the extent to which covert sensitization contributes to overall treatment outcome when the technique is employed as simply one component in a multifaceted treatment program. Perhaps those subjects who establish a conditioned nausea reaction to alcohol during covert sensitization therapy and who work to maintain the conditioned response subsequently may benefit significantly from the application of the technique, but more research will be required before this possibility can be confirmed.

SOCIAL SKILLS TRAINING

Social skills training and, in particular, assertiveness training have received increasing attention in the behavioral literature over the past 10 years. This attention has not missed the alcoholism field, where Miller and Eisler [76] have noted that alcoholics commonly fail to show more behavioral indications of assertiveness when compared with nonalcoholics even though they may describe themselves as assertive, and where increased assertiveness scores have been correlated with better pretreatment adjustment [115]. A relatively large number of behavioral treatment programs, especially those investigating multifaceted strategies, have included assertiveness training, marital skills training, and other social skills training components, in order to minimize the possibility of the alcoholic experiencing the sort of serious interpersonal conflicts that commonly are associated with relapse [65, 75, 87, 111, 124]. None of these studies, however, has employed a design that permitted the teasing out of the possible contribution to the overall outcome of the social skills training components.

McClelland [69] reported the outcome of a study in which 52 alcoholic inpatients received power motivation training (see also [32]), designed to help them to achieve more socially acceptable methods of expressing personal power than is possible through alcohol use. At 12 months posttreatment, 50% of the subjects who underwent the experimental procedure were successful, whereas only 28% of those who received the standard hospital treatment were functioning in this category (see also [70]). In another study reporting results over a 1-year period, Chaney et al. [26] compared alcoholics who, in addition to receiving standard inpatient care, were assigned randomly to either (1) a short-term social skills training group including assertiveness training, interpersonal skills training, and relaxation training; (2) a discussion group that stressed dealing with feelings such as anxiety and anger, which inhibit assertiveness; or (3) a control group that received only the standard hospital program. At follow-up, subjects in the social skills training group scored significantly lower than subjects in either of the other two groups on indices that included total number of drinks consumed, total number of intoxicated days, and average length of each drinking episode. Chaney et al. [26] also examined an array of treatment data that they had gathered from each of their subjects to establish predictors of treatment outcome. Analyses of these data indicated that the measure of "latency until assertive responding" was equal to or superior in outcome predictability to any of the other highly predictive drinking history and demograhpic measures (see also [50]).

Against such findings, however, is the evidence from Intagliata's [55] controlled study in which alcoholic subjects were assigned randomly to either a problem-solving skills training plus standard inpatient program or the standard hospital procedure alone. Intagliata reported that despite marginal benefits found in favor of subjects in the experimental group at the end of a 30-day posthospital period, only 14 of the 22 experimental subjects had made practical use of their problem-solving skills and "it was evident that subjects had already forgotten significant portions of the training material" [55, p. 496].

Thus, while the available evidence, and it is again sparse, argues for social skills training as a component in the treatment of alcoholics, it is unclear whether social skills training is likely to be of benefit to all those who develop serious alcohol problems or whether its efficacy is limited to certain alcoholic individuals. At this stage, it seems reasonable to argue that social skills training is of general value in the treatment of the earlier stage problem drinker [118] and also that the technique is likely to have special value in the treatment of those alcohol-related negative assertion responses for which Foy et al. [38], have developed drink refusal training. Irrespective of the specific social skills training provided, however, it would seem likely that patients undergoing such training may need additional and continued training on an outpatient basis to maximize the prospects of the maintenance of the gains made during the primary training phase.

PROGRESSIVE RELAXATION AND SYSTEMATIC DESENSITIZATION

Progressive relaxation training [56] has been used frequently over the past decade as an increasingly common adjunctive component in the treatment of alcoholism. Systematic desensitization [128], on the other hand, which is both a more complex procedure and one with a more specific application, has been used more rarely in alcoholism therapy. Typically, when relaxation training procedures are used, the aim is to provide the patient with a mechanism for dealing with stress that previously may have provoked the desire to drink. Relaxation procedures also are used commonly to facilitate sleep in those alcohol-abusing patients for whom sleep is difficult and who often induce sleep with alcohol. Systematic desensitization, however, is used to help the patient deal with specific environmental factors (such as certain feared situations) that typically have provoked anxiety. Other procedures of a similar genera, like electromyographic biofeedback and transcendental meditation, also have been adapted for use in the treatment of alcohol abusers, though these procedures have been employed only rarely. The very few studies that have reported using these latter techniques (transendental meditation in particular), have contained serious methodological flaws, thus making their findings generally uninterpretable (see the reviews by Aron & Aron [6] and Benson [11], and also the hypnosis treatment research by Edwards and Guthrie [35] and Smith-Moorehouse [108]).

Blake [16, 17] reported treatment results at 1 year for alcoholic subjects who had received either relaxation training plus electrical aversion or electrical aversion alone. These results reflected a nonsignificant advantage in support of the combined procedure. Similar minor advantages in favor of relaxation training were reported by Freedberg and Johnston [41]. In this study, 80 alcoholic subjects were assigned randomly either to receive or not receive relaxation training that was a component in a 3-week residential program. At 12 months posttreatment, the relaxation subjects were found to be functioning slightly better on a variety of life functioning measures, although no significant between-group differences on drinking behavior were noted. Miller et al. [89] also reported that problem drinker subjects benefited when relaxation training was added to outpatient-administered behavioral self-control training. These investigators reported success rates (based on abstinence plus restricted drinking criteria) of 40% for their behavioral self-control subjects alone and 75% and 79%, respectively, for those subjects who received behavioral self-control training plus individually administered relaxation, and behavioral self-control training plus group administered relaxation training.

Still other investigators have conducted research with alcoholics using electromyographic biofeedback to facilitate relaxation [113, 114] or have explored relaxation training contrasted with meditation or a quiet rest control condition [94, 95]. These investigators demonstrated that their subjects were capable of learning to reduce muscle potential ratings, heart rate activity, and subjective reports of anxiety. None of these studies, however, evaluated the consequences of such learning on subsequent changes in life functioning or those drinking variables that must be influenced if successful treatment outcome is to be reported.

Turning now to the systematic desensitization literature, Kraft and Al-Issa [59, 60] and Kraft [58] have reported the application of systematic desensitization as the sole treatment for alcoholic patients, the diagnosis for whom seriously implicated social anxiety. (In each instance, systematic desensitization was directed to reducing the anxiety that had been interfering with the social functioning of these patients.) At 12 to 40 months posttreatment, all 8 subjects studied by Kraft [58] were reported to be restricting their drinking without difficulty. Subsequently, Kraft [T. Kraft, 1971, personal communication] has reported similar success with 7 of 9 selected alcoholic patients treated with systematic desensitization.

Other noncontrolled research also has reported on the value of systematic desensitization in the treatment of alcoholism. Hodgson and Rankin [52] reported a case in which they employed an in vivo systematic desensitization procedure requiring daily priming doses of vodka followed by a monitoring sequence that focused on the subject's desire to drink. This procedure led to a gradual extinction on both anxiety and drinking desire measures as well as contributing to significant reduction in alcohol consumption at a 6-month follow-up. Somewhat similarly, Pickens et al. [97] have reported success in an alcoholic patient for whom stimulus-facing procedures were introduced to reduce the salience of cues that previously had elicited the desire to drink. Further, and along these same lines, Hall [46, 47] developed the concept of abstinence phobia and advocated the use of systematic desensitization in order to deal with the fear that (she argues) comes from the inability of many alcoholics to cope with sobriety.

In the only controlled comparative assessment of systematic desensitization to appear in the alcoholism literature to date, Hedberg and Campbell [50] compared behavioral family counseling, electrical aversion, covert sensitization, and systematic desensitization. These investigators reported success rates (defined in terms of abstinence or much improvement), at 6 months posttreatment for their subjects undergoing systematic desensitization to be 90% in the 10 cases for whom abstinence was the treatment goal (with 60% abstinent) and 80% for those five subjects who sought only to restrict their drinking. These success rates were virtually identical to those achieved by the subjects who underwent behavioral family counseling. Subjects in both these groups were found to be functioning in a superior fashion to those in the two aversion groups.

Overall, it seems that, despite limited data and a lack of adequately controlled research, for at least some alcohol-abusing individuals, relaxation training and systematic desensitization procedures do offer benefit over no treatment or other treatment not including such procedures. It would appear likely that both procedures would be of value as components available within a multifaceted treatment program, but again, there is little reason to believe that these components would be seen as valuable for all alcoholics. More data are needed to determine the extent of the likely contribution of both these procedures to overall treatment effectiveness.

OPERANT METHODS AND CONTINGENCY CONTRACTING

Operant treatment procedures are so named because they modify drinking responses by manipulating the consequences of those responses. One of the earliest operant approaches to the management of alcohol abuse was reported in a case study by Sulzer [116]. Sulzer evaluated his patient as being particularly concerned that continued drunkenness would lose him the companionship of two friends who were moderate drinkers. Thus, under the direction of the therapist it was agreed by all that the patient and his friends would meet daily for a few drinks, but if the patient ordered or drank hard liquor the friends would leave immediately. It was agreed also that further social interaction would occur in the homes of all three participants, but an abstinence requirement was applied in this instance. While Sulzer provides no follow-up data from which the gauge the overall impact of this procedure, he does indicate that his procedure proved effective.

There have been several major research programs that have allowed inpatient alcoholics access to alcohol in order to investigate the extent to which certain environmental contingencies effect alcoholics' drinking practices. The first of these programs was conducted by Cohen and her colleagues at the Baltimore City Hospital [13, 29, 30]. The other major research program of this type is the Fixed Interval Drinking Decisions Program developed by Gotthiel and his colleagues at the Coatesville Veterans Administration Hospital [2, 43, 44, 45].

The work of the Baltimore group and that of others [33, 91, 92] has demonstrated convincingly, at least under laboratory conditions, that the drinking practices of alcoholics can be brought under environmental control. Somewhat paradoxically, Bigelow et al. [14] demonstrated that even subsequent access to alcohol may be used as a reinforcing consequence following restricted drinking by alcoholics. These investigators noted that not one of their five inpatient subjects drank above the 8 oz a day criterion when alcohol from a subsequent day was made contingent upon not exceeding this predetermined amount. In contrast, when no contingencies were attached to their drinking, all five subjects drank to extreme intoxication. In a somewhat similar vein, Gottheil et al. [43, 44] used a contingency approach to study the hypothesized inability of alcoholics to abstain and/or to resist the desire to drink. Data from the Coatesville program do not support these hypotheses.

Miller et al. [79] reported on a single subject operant treatment designed to examine the effectiveness of contingent reinforcement for reduced blood alcohol concentration readings. These investigators employed random breath-testing to monitor alcohol usage, with the data being collected twice weekly both in the subject's home and at the subject's place of employment. Zero blood alcohol concentration readings were reinforced with hospital commissary coupons. Contingent reinforcement, noncontingent reinforcement, and nonreinforcement strategies were all employed with this one subject. Results of the study indicated that the contingent reinforcement sequence was much more effective than either of the two other procedures in reducing drinking in this subject.

The use of contingency contracting in the treatment of alcoholism also has focused on components outside of the actual act of drinking. Bigelow et al. [15] employed contracting in a study with 20 alcoholic subjects who agreed to take disulfiram for 3 months. The contingencies in this study provided for a forfeiture by each subject of a portion of his security deposit if he failed to report for his medication prior to beginning work. While the study did not involve a control condition, the results proved most impressive, with subjects taking their medication on 95.6% of over 2,000 patient workdays (see also [74]).

Perhaps the most interesting of all the operant techniques is the community reinforcement approach developed by Hunt and Azrin [54]. This work is particularly important because the study extended the operant findings observed in the laboratory setting to the natural environment. Hunt and Azrin assigned 16 inpatient alcoholic subjects to two matched and essentially equal groups. The subjects in the experimental group received community reinforcement counseling along with the standard hospital treatment. Subjects in the control condition received standard hospital care, which was comprised of milieu therapy, information about alcohol-related health risks, and counseling regarding interpersonal problems associated with continued drinking. Participation in Alcoholics Anonymous (AA) also was available. The community reinforcement counseling, on the other hand, involved direct modification of the subjects' interpersonal and environmental support systems. An experienced behavioral clinician aided in the setting of specific goals for each patient and helped each find employment and improvement in familial relationships. This clinician also aided in the structuring of reinforcing social activities for each subject. This effort, which began in the hospital, continued throughout a 6-month aftercare phase, during which time frequent home visits were made in order to help the subjects strengthen the reinforcement value of naturally occurring reinforcers. At the 6-month follow-up, it was found that subjects in the experimental group had spent significantly less time drinking, unemployed, and away from home (or institutionalized) than had subjects in the control condition.

While data from operant paradigm studies such as reported herein suggests that it is possible to modify the alcoholic's environment or influence the rewards that he or she derives from the environment, it also is clear that it is difficult to influence dramatically the alcoholic's drinking practices in the natural environment. Researchers are still a long way from being able to specify and arrange all the relevant variables, and to control precisely the behavioral consequences for the drinker and those around him or her in such a way as to provide patients with long-term stability in a sober and reinforcing life style. Finally, it must be stated that despite the generally positive results that have been reported by investigators employing operant methodologies, the number of controlled studies addressing these issues continues to be extremely limited.

BEHAVIORAL SELF-CONTROL TRAINING AND COGNITIVE THERAPIES

Behavioral self-control training has emerged in the behavior therapy literature largely as a consequence of the growing recognition of the role that cognitive processes and structures play in all behavior change. As far as the alcoholism literature is concerned, the most important contribution that behavioral self-control training has made is in the area of the restricted drinking research. Lovibond and Caddy [65] were among the first investigators to employ behavioral self-control training as a major component in the treatment of alcoholism. As noted earlier, these investigators also undertook an analysis of the unique role of each of their major treatment components. Caddy and Lovibond [22] found that at the end of a 12-month follow-up, a comprehensive behavioral self-control program produced greater improvement in alcoholic subjects than did an aversion therapy component without behavioral self-control training (64% vs. 50%). The most impressive results, however, were shown by those subjects assigned to the original combined aversion therapy and behavioral self-control training program (77% success). Other investigators also have included behavioral self-control training within their multifaceted inpatient or outpatient programs. Typically, these programs also have explored a restricted drinking treatment goal. Little attempt has been made in these studies, however, to tease out the relative contributions to the overall treatment outcome made by the behavioral self-control components [105, 106, 110, 111, 124, 125].

W. R. Miller and his colleagues [49, 81, 82, 83, 86] reported the development of a comprehensive behavioral self-control package that included (1) determining the appropriate limits for alcohol consumption via an educational approach combined with specific blood alcohol concentration discrimination training, (2) self-monitoring of alcohol consumption, (3) rate control training, designed to alter the topography of the drinking behavior, (4) self-reinforcement to encourage ongoing progress, (5) functional analyses of drinking behaviors with training in stimulus control techniques, and (6) alternatives training, designed to teach coping skills to be used in situations where alcohol previously had been used. Miller [81] compared the results of this package with two alternative approaches, an electrical aversive conditioning procedures, and a multifaceted program incorporating techniques derived from Lovibond and Caddy [65] and Sobell and Sobell [110]. Miller reported no significant between-group differences during the course of a 12-month follow-up. The author noted, however, that the alternative treatment procedures consumed far more therapist time than the more economical behavioral self-control procedure. In a second study, Miller et al. [84] compared two different approaches to behavioral self-control training: a bibliotherapy (minimal therapist contact) condition, and a paraprofessional therapist-administered self-control training program involving 10 weekly sessions. Again, no significant differences were found between these two conditions although in this study the follow-up period was only 3 months (see also [87, 88]). Finally, in the most recent report from this group, Miller et al. [89] report a comparison between bibliotherapy with a behavioral self-control orientation and two more extensive broad-spectrum behavior therapies. These authors report in a preliminary analysis, done at 6 months following treatment, that no statistically significant differences between their groups emerged. And, as was true of Miller's other studies, about 70% of the subjects assigned to the behavioral self-control training program made significant improvement.

Using a program similar to Miller's, Alden [1] also reported success rates in her problem drinking subjects of about 70%. Alden, however, did find significant differences between her enriched multifaceted program and her standard behavioral self-control package (see also [100]).

Despite the relatively impressive results reported in these various studies, evaluating overall the unique contribution made by behavioral self-control training in any of these studies is difficult, for none of them has incorporated a design involving random assignment of subjects to a no treatment control condition. Caddy [20] currently is conducting an aftercare evaluation study that includes a no treatment control condition that will address the relative effectiveness of both behavioral self-control training and, more generally, cognitive behavior therapy as applied in the prevention of alcoholic relapse. Unfortunately, at the present time, the data from this study are not available for presentation.

Given the relative lack of research in this area at this time, it is not clear whether the impressive results reported in the behavioral self-control literature are a function of the more mechanical aspects of behavioral self-control training, like self-monitoring, or whether the potency of these techniques lies in their more basic cognitive components, which act on individuals' belief systems regarding alcohol use and the extent to which one sees oneself as capable of overcoming the difficulties that have emerged with drinking [8]. Alternately, the positive effects reported may be a consequence of the interaction between these two general areas. Irrespective of the primary locus of these positive effects, however, what is particularly striking about the behavioral self-control approach is the extent to which even those alcohol abusers who have been exposed to the traditional perspectives of alcoholism find themselves easily drawn to the learning perspectives that are communicated along with behavioral self-control training and the cognitive strategies generally. If such attraction proves to be more than simply a reflection of enthusiasm for a new approach or the demand characteristics associated with certain unique interviewing situations, it would seem highly likely that behavioral self-control training presented within a learning-based multivariate framework will prove most valuable in treatment generally and especially so in prevention and/or early intervention programs.

Turning now to an examination of the more broad cognitive-behavioral approaches to alcoholism treatment, one is faced with a paucity of evaluation studies in the cognitive behavior therapy literature generally, and in the alcoholism literature in particular. Sanchez-Craig [104, 105, 106] has described methods for teaching coping that include cognitive restructuring and the covert rehearsal of adaptive behaviors, and Marlatt [67] has proposed a method of alcoholic relapse prevention based on a cognitive behavior therapy orientation. To date, however, the only controlled investigation to have been conducted addressing the efficacy of cognitive behavior therapy approaches in relation to other approaches in the alcoholism literature has been conducted by Brandsma et al. [18]. These investigators compared the outcome of 104 alcoholic subjects who were randomly assigned to and completed either a rational behavior therapy group, an insight therapy group, an AA attendance group, or a no treatment control condition (a total of 197 subjects initially began the study). The results at 12 months posttreatment indicated that subjects in all three treatment groups had improved relative to subjects in the control condition and that subjects receiving the rational behavior therapy sequence, whether provided by a professional or a paraprofessional, were as successful as those insight therapy patients who received their therapy from a highly experienced professional. Subjects in both these therapy groups also showed lower dropout rates and slightly better success rates than those subjects assigned to the AA condition, although these comparisons, with the exception of the differential dropout rate, typically failed to prove statistically significant by the 12 month posttreatment.

The promising results from cognitive behavior therapy approaches to the treatment of alcoholism must be interpreted cautiously because very few such studies have been conducted. Nevertheless, the successes of cognitive behavior therapy outside of the alcoholism literature, yet focused on problems that are commonly experienced by alcohol abusers (see, for example, Beck's [9, 10] work on depression), portend favorably for their employment more widely in the treatment of alcoholism.

BROAD-SPECTRUM BEHAVIORAL APPROACHES

While much of the earlier work in behaviorally based therapeutics was conducted from a narrow-band perspective that focused on a limited segment of behavior, present-day behavioral clinicians generally have been moving toward a far more comprehensive view of the dynamics of clinical problems. With this movement has come the development of broad-spectrum approches. While at least some of the earlier work in the alcoholism literature was advantageously conducted within a multifaceted treatment framework, this work overall was not behaviorally based. Today, with the emergence of the multivariate perspectives of alcohol abuse and dependence, there has evolved a greater recognition of the complexity of addictive behavior and this increasing recognition also has broadened greatly the focus in alcoholism treatment.

This does not mean, of course, that present-day multitreatment intervention programs that claim to confront the full range of drinking problems necessarily offer broad-spectrum programming. The most basic difference between a multicomponent treatment approach and the broad-spectrum approach is that in the former case, the patient is subjected to a variety of often questionably integrated therapeutic elements, each designed to provide something. The broad-spectrum approach, on the other hand, focuses not on what the treatment service can provide the patient, but what an assessment determines the patient to really need [61]. It is a therapy based on an integrated systems approach to the unique dynamics of the individual case. Within the alcoholism literature those treatment programs that have been based on a multimodal model typically have conceptualized alcoholism in a multivariate framework. The vast majority of such treatment programs also have provided therapy with flexible drinking-related goals (that is, therapy in which restrictive drinking was not excluded).

While many of the procedures reviewed elsewhere in this chapter have appeared to be narrow-band in nature, in some instances some of these procedures have been examined out of context, for they have been evaluated as if they were administered as independent components, whereas, at least sometimes, they have been employed within broad-spectrum treatment research programs (see, for example, the components in the studies of Caddy and Lovibond [22], Miller et al. [80], Pomerleau et al. [99], and Vogler et al. [124]).

One particularly important study not addressed elsewhere in this chapter, but illustrating well an early attempt at broad-spectrum programming, is the study by Sobell and Sobell [111]. These investigators (see also Mills et al. [90]) developed a research treatment program conducted with inpatient alcoholics at Patton State Hospital. In this study, subjects assigned to the experimental group received individualized behavior therapy during a semistructured 17-session treatment sequence that included everything from assertiveness training to videotaped self-confrontation of drunken comportment. Control subjects, on the other hand, received only the standard hospital care (limited group therapy). In addition, both experimental and control group subjects were given the opportunity, within certain limits, to select either an abstinent drinking goal or a controlled drinking goal. Thereafter, in what comes close to a blueprint for high-quality treatment outcome evaluation research, one of the investigators traced 69 of their original 70 subjects during an exhaustive 2-year follow-up. Assessments at 6 and 12 months, based on criteria including social stability, interpersonal functioning, vocational and physical health, and drinking practices, showed the experimental subjects to be functioning significantly better than control subjects irrespective of the drinking goal operating in the groups to which they had been assigned [110]. A 2nd-year follow-up found that the individualized behavior therapy subjects treated with a controlled drinking goal functioned significantly better than their respective control subjects. Differences between the behavior therapy subjects treated with an abstinence goal and their control subjects did not retain statistical significance during the 2nd-year follow-up [112]. A subsequent study employing a double-blind design [21] with 49 of the original Patton subjects provided independent evidence indicating that during the 3rd year posttreatment subjects in the two individualized behavior therapy groups continued to function better than subjects in the two conventional hospital treatment groups.

Comparing the broad-spectrum behavioral treatment programs with simpler drinking-focused methods reported in the alcoholism literature, one is impressed by the high quality of the research associated with the evaluation of the broad-spectrum strategies. Miller and Hester [85] reviewed 19 such studies and reported 15 to include control or comparison groups typically involving random assignment of subjects and employing quantifiable assessment procedures with specified outcome criteria. Further, in 14 of these studies, more than 90% of the subjects were located at the longest follow-up interval and in 18 of these studies, client self-reports were checked against corroborative data sources.

It is reasonably clear that the data comparing broad-spectrum behavioral approaches with nonbehavioral programs, typically, though not always, containing a less intensive therapeutic experience, provide strong support in favor of the broad-spectrum approaches. When behavioral self-control training is compared to the more comprehensive broad-spectrum programming, however, the relative advantage of broad-spectrum programming noted in the previous comparison seems to be lessened significantly and the advantages of the more expensive programming become uncertain. Some investigators have found broad-spectrum programming to offer no significant advantages over behavioral self-control training [82, 83, 125], whereas other investigators have noted significant differences in favor of the broad-spectrum strategies [1, 22]. Under such circumstances it has been suggested by Miller and Hester [85] that the more extensive broad-spectrum approaches cannot be justified for all clients from a cost-effectiveness viewpoint. It is the position of the present author that Miller's conclusion, even if ultimately correct, is premature, for truly adequate testing of the comparison between these two behavioral approaches has only just begun.

BEHAVIORAL TREATMENT IN PERSPECTIVE

Examining the trends in the application of behavioral approaches to the treatment of alcoholism, one is struck by the extent to which the literature of the 1970s reflects the change from narrow-band, single-component behavioral therapies to the more broad-spectrum endeavors. Simplistic and generally inadequately conceptualized behaviorally influenced treatment programs have begun to give way to truly integrated behavioral programs based on multivariate perspective and emphasizing patients' unique clinical histories and present dynamics. These trends are far more obvious in the clinical research literature, however, than in community treatment programs, where a lack of clinical sophistication and a marked degree of resistance to the behavioral perspective characterizes many alcoholism treatment operations. In fact, even in the more costly multifaceted inpatient treatment facilities that serve alcoholic populations, the provision of behavioral components beyond relaxation and assertiveness training represents the exception rather than the therapeutic rule. Further, even when such services are rendered, they are rarely integrated to form a truly broad-spectrum model of care. Such an effort simply is beyond the experience of most alcoholism treatment personnel at the present time.

The other major trend that has emerged in the alcoholism treatment literature, largely as a consequence of the development of behaviorally based programming, has involved the appearance of increasingly sophisticated and scientifically credible treatment outcome evaluation research efforts [109]. While as late as 1971 the median effort expended in conducting credible treatment outcome evaluation studies was seen to be unacceptable [31], by 1975 this picture had changed appreciably, with high-quality research designs and methodologies appearing commonly, if not consistently, in the behaviorally based alcoholism treatment literature.

Paradoxically, however, the more researchers move toward high-quality treatment outcome evaluation programming and the more integrated behaviorally based alcoholism treatment programs are developed, the more impossible it is recognized to be to tease out the unique contribution made by each of the components within overall treatment programming. The difficulties that follow random assignment or matched pairing of subjects to various treatment conditions (each probably differing in therapeutic credibility) and the difficulties associated with comparing treatment efficacy across extremely diverse subject populations are difficulties that have not retreated simply because a more scientific stance has been adopted regarding the task of treatment outcome evaluation. Similarly, it is now no less difficult than previously to evaluate the meaning of differing rates of overall success in many of the current comparative treatment outcome studies. Even when statistical significance is achieved following such comparisons, it still is necessary to examine the effects reported on the individual subjects who compose the various treatment groups before one can appreciate the impact of the group-based statistics.

The emergence of the multivariate perspective and broad-spectrum behavioral programming has led to the belief that maximal therapeutic advantage can be achieved only when the unique needs of the patient are met by equally unique and responsive therapeutic planning. This means that future attempts to evaluate broad-spectrum behavioral approaches to alcoholism treatment will provide even greater challenge to the clinical researcher, for no longer will it be possible to employ a research design that requires the random assignment of subjects to one of several highly structured and static treatment sequences. Rather, it will be necessary to evaluate the outcome of therapy against a background of constant change, both in the subject and in the therapy. While no doubt such work will be more complicated, surely also it will closer approximate the provision of sophisticated treatment services in the real world. Hence, it will permit a more valid index of what really can be achieved when individualized behaviorally based therapy is applied in the treatment of alcoholic people.

CONCLUSIONS

The following assertions are offered as reasonable conclusions regarding the efficacy and significance of the various behavioral treatment elements and approaches that are examined in this chapter.

1. Both from a theoretical and pragmatic perspective, the continued general use of either chemical or electrical aversive therapies for the treatment of alcoholism cannot be justified at this time. In certain cases, however, limited electrical aversive procedures may be used valuably with other therapies designed to influence cognitions regarding the importance of drinking and the concept of control. The real issue here is whether or not the end justifies the means.

2. While covert sensitization has been shown to provide short-term benefits in relation to no treatment, by itself the technique has not been shown to offer advantages over a number of other therapeutic procedures. This does not imply that covert sensitization offers only minor advantages when employed as one element in a multifaceted treatment program. It is likely, in fact, that the technique may offer an advantage to some highly motivated patients who could use it to aid them to reduce their incentive motivation to drink, especially in high-risk situations. Nevertheless, more research with covert sensitization is required to address its potential value as a component in broad-spectrum programming.

3. Social skills training procedures have found consistent support in the alcoholism treatment literature. These techniques would appear to offer advantage particularly in the treatment of many problem drinkers in an early stage. The evidence suggests that a rather intensive program of social skills training may be required by many alcohol abusers (and their families) and that ongoing assistance in this regard may be necessary to ensure the everyday use of these procedures.

4. When used in concert with other therapeutic components, relaxation training has been shown to offer advantage to a wide range of alcohol-abusing

individuals. Here again, however, while such a technique may be used with great benefit by the devotee, many patients fail to continue its use following treatment. Systematic desensitization does not appear directly relevant to the treatment of most alcohol-abusing individuals. Meditation procedures and biofeedback training have been seldom used and generally poorly evaluated as therapeutic components directed toward alcoholism.

5. Operant procedures have been shown to be influential in regulating the drinking practices of alcohol-abusing individuals both in the laboratory and without. When these procedures have been used in the community with the involvement of family and other potent external reinforcers they have proved valuable, but also extremely labor-intensive.

6. Behavioral self-control training has produced consistent and impressive results in the treatment of alcoholism. Most of the work using these procedures has been done with subjects who are not unduly physiologically or psychologically depleted, however, and so it is not clear just how influential such training is when compared more widely with other behavioral treatment approaches to alcoholism.

7. Broad-spectrum behavior therapy holds the promise for making the greatest overall contribution to the treatment of alcoholism of all the behavioral approaches, for it provides for the prescription of any and all of the aforementioned procedures to the individual case. Given the cost of such truly individualized behavior therapy, however, it will be necessary to develop the approach with special attention to cost-benefit analyses.

Despite the significance of the progress made in the behavioral treatment of alcoholism, much more high-quality evaluative research is needed before professionals can feel confident in assertions regarding the relative merits of each of the various therapeutic elements examined in this chapter. Nevertheless, behaviorally oriented investigators from several different disciplines are continuing to move with increasing sophistication to address the questions of which therapeutic procedures under which conditions most benefit which types of patients. Such a movement encourages the view that over the next decade behavior therapy will continue to increase its contribution to the alcoholism treatment field in terms of both its increasing clinical sophistication and its developing treatment evaluation technology.

REFERENCES

1. Alden, L. Evaluation of a preventive self-management programme for problem drinkers. *Can. J. Behav. Sci.* 10:258–263, 1978.
2. Alterman, A. I., Gottheil, E., Skoloda, T. E., and Grasberger, J. C. Social modification of drinking by alcoholics. *Q. J. Stud. Alcohol* 35:917–924, 1974.

3. Anant, S. S. The treatment of alcoholics by a verbal aversion technique. *Manas: J. Sci. Psychol.* 13:79-86, 1966.

4. Anant, S. S. A note on the treatment of alcoholics by a verbal aversion technique. *Can. Psychol.* 8:19-22, 1967.

5. Anant, S. S. Treatment of alcoholics and drug addicts by verbal aversion techniques. *Int. J. Addict.* 3:381-388, 1968.

6. Aron, A., and Aron, E. N. The transcendental meditation's effect on addictive behavior. *Addict. Behav.* 5:3-12, 1980.

7. Ashem, B., and Donner, L. Covert sensitization with alcoholics: A controlled replication. *Behav. Res. Ther.* 6:7-12, 1968.

8. Bandura, A. Self-efficacy: Toward a unifying theory of behavior change. *Psychol. Rev.* 84:191-215, 1977.

9. Beck, A. T. *Depression: Causes and Treatment.* University of Pennsylvania Press: Philadelphia, 1972.

10. Beck, A. T. *Cognitive Therapy and the Emotional Disorders.* International Universities Press: New York, 1976.

11. Benson, H. Decreased alcohol intake associated with the practice of meditation: A retrospective investigation. *Ann. N.Y. Acad. Sci.* 233:174-177, 1974.

12. Bhakta, M. Clinical application of behavior therapy in the treatment of alcoholism. *J. Alcohol.* 6:75-83, 1971.

13. Bigelow, G., Cohen, H., Liebson, I., and Faillace, L. A. Abstinence or moderation? Choice by alcoholics. *Behav. Res. Ther.* 10:209-214, 1972.

14. Bigelow, G., Liebson, I., and Lawrence, C. *Prevention of Alcohol Abuse by Reinforcement of Incompatible Behavior.* Paper presented at the Seventh Annual Convention of the Association for the Advancement of Behavior Therapy, Miami Beach, December 1973.

15. Bigelow, G., Strickler, D., Liebson, I., and Griffiths, R. R. Maintaining disulfiram ingestion among outpatient alcoholics: A security deposit contingency contracting procedure. *Behav. Res. Ther.* 14:378-381, 1976.

16. Blake, B. G. The application of behavior therapy to the treatment of alcoholism. *Behav. Res. Ther.* 3:75-85, 1965.

17. Blake, B. G. A follow-up of alcoholics treated by behaviour therapy. *Behav. Res. Ther.* 5:89-94, 1967.

18. Brandsma, J. M., Maultsby, M. C., and Welsh, R. J. *The Outpatient Treatment of Alcoholism: A Review and Comparative Study.* University Park Press: Baltimore, 1980.

19. Caddy, G. R. Toward a multivariate analysis of alcohol abuse. In: *Alcoholism: New Directions in Behavioral Research and Treatment,* Nathan, P. E., Marlatt, G. A., and Loberg, T. (eds.). Plenum: New York, 1978.

20. Caddy, G. R. *Preventing Alcoholic Relapse: A Comparison of Aftercare Procedures.* Paper presented at the American Psychological Association Annual Convention, New York, 1979.

21. Caddy, G. R., Addington, H. J., and Perkins, D. Individualized behavior therapy for alcoholics: A third-year independent double-blind follow-up. *Behav. Res. Ther.* 16:345-362, 1978.

22. Caddy, G. R., and Lovibond, S. H. Self-regulation and discriminated aversive conditioning in the modification of alcoholics' drinking behavior. *Behav. Ther.* 7:223-230, 1976.

23. Cautela, J. R. Treatment of compulsive behavior by covert desensitization. *Psychol. Rep.* 16:33-41, 1966.

24. Cautela, J. R. Covert sensitization. *Psychol. Rep.* 20:459-468, 1967.

25. Cautela, J. R. The treatment of alcoholism by covert sensitization. *Psychother.: Theory, Res. Prac.* 7:86-90, 1970.
26. Chaney, E. F., O'Leary, M. R., and Marlatt, G. A. *Skill Training with Alcoholics.* Unpublished manuscript, University of Washington School of Medicine, Seattle, 1978.
27. Ciminero, A. R., Doleys, D. M., and Davidson, R. S. Free-operant avoidance of alcohol. *J. Behav. Ther. Exp. Psychiatry* 6:242-245, 1975.
28. Claeson, L. E., and Malm, U. Electro-aversion therapy of chronic alcoholism. *Behav. Res. Ther.* 11:663-665, 1973.
29. Cohen, M., Liebson, I. A., and Faillace, L. A. A technique for establishing controlled drinking in chronic alcoholics. *Dis. Nerv. Sys.* 33:46-49, 1972.
30. Cohen, M., Liebson, I. A., Faillace, L. A., and Allen, R. P. Moderate drinking by chronic alcoholics. *J. Nerv. Ment. Dis.* 153:434-444, 1971.
31. Crawford, J. J., and Chalupsky, A. B. The reported evaluation of alcoholism treatments, 1968-1971: A methodological review. *Addict. Behav.* 2:63-74, 1977.
32. Cutter, H. S. G., McClelland, D. C., Boyatzis, R. E., and Blancy, D. D. *The Effectiveness of Power Motivation Training for Rehabilitating Alcoholics.* McBer: Boston, 1975.
33. Cutter, H. S. G., Schwab, E. L., and Nathan, P. E. Effects of alcohol on its utility for alcoholics. *Q. J. Stud. Alcohol* 30:369-378, 1970.
34. Devenyi, P., and Sereny, G. Aversion treatment with electro-conditioning for alcoholism. *Br. J. Addict.* 65:289-292, 1970.
35. Edwards, G., and Guthrie, S. A comparison of inpatient and outpatient treatment of alcohol dependence. *Lancet* 1:467-468, 1966.
36. Elkins, R. L. Covert sensitization treatment of alcoholism: Contributions of successful conditioning to subsequent abstinence maintenance. *Addict. Behav.* 5:67-69, 1980.
37. Elkins, R. L., and Murdock, R. P. The contribution of successful conditioning to abstinence maintenance following covert sensitization (verbal aversion) treatment of alcoholism. *IRCS Med. Sci.: Psychol. Psychiatry: Soc. Occ. Med.* 5:167, 1977.
38. Foy, D. W., Miller, P. M., Eisler, R. M., and O'Toole, D. H. Social skills training to teach alcoholics to refuse drinks effectively. *J. Stud. Alcohol* 37:1340-1345, 1976.
39. Franks, C. M. Behavior therapy: The principles of conditioning and the treatment of the alcoholic. *Q. J. Stud. Alcohol* 24:511-529, 1963.
40. Franks, C. M. Alcoholism. In: *Symptoms of Psychopathology: A Handbook,* Costello, C. G. (ed.). Wiley: New York, 1970.
41. Freedberg, E. J., and Johnston, W. *Changes in Drinking Behavior, Employment Status and Other Life Areas for Employed Alcoholic Clients Three, Six, and Twelve Months after Treatment* (Substudy 977). Addition Research Foundation: Toronto, 1978.
42. Glover, J. H., and McCue, P. A. Electrical aversion therapy with alcoholics: A comparative follow-up study. *Br. J. Psychiatry* 130:279-286, 1977.
43. Gottheil, E., Corbett, L. O., Grasberger, J. C., and Cornelison, F. S., Jr. Treating the alcoholic in the presence of alcohol. *Am. J. Psychiatry* 128:475-480, 1971.
44. Gottheil, E., Corbett, L. O., Grasberger, J. C., and Cornelison, F. S., Jr. Fixed interval drinking decisions: I. A research and treatment model. *Q. J. Stud. Alcohol* 33:311-324, 1972.
45. Gottheil, E., Murphy, B. F., Skoloda, T. E., and Corbett, L. O. Fixed interval drinking decisions: II. Drinking and discomfort in 25 alcoholics. *Q. J. Stud. Alcohol* 33:325-340, 1972.
46. Hall, S. M. The abstinence phobia. In: *Behavioral Analysis and Treatment of Substance Abuse* (NIDA Research Monograph 25, DHEW Publication No. 017-024-00939-3) Krasnegor, N. (ed.). U.S. Government Printing Office: Washington, D.C., 1979.

47. Hall, S. M. The abstinence phobias: Links between substance abuse and anxiety. *J. Consult. Clin. Psychol.*, in press.

48. Hallam, R., Rachman, S., and Falkowski, W. Subjective, attitudinal and physiological effects of electrical aversion therapy. *Behav. Res. Ther.* 10:1-13, 1972.

49. Hamburg, S. R., Miller, W. R., and Rozynko, V. *Understanding Alcoholism and Problem Drinking.* Social Change Associates: Half Moon Bay, Calif., 1977.

50. Hedberg, A. G., and Campbell, L., III. A comparison of four behavioral treatments of alcoholism. *J. Behav. Ther. Exp. Psychiatry* 5:251-256, 1974.

51. Hersen, M., Eisler, R. M., and Miller, P. M. Historical perspectives in behavior modification: Introductory comments. In: *Progress in Behavior Modification*, Hersen, M., Eisler, R. M., and Miller, P. M. (eds.). Academic Press: New York, 1975.

52. Hodgson, R. J., and Rankin, H. J. Modification of excessive drinking by cue exposure. *Behav. Res. Ther.* 14:305-307, 1976.

53. Hsu, J. J. Electroconditioning therapy of alcoholics: A preliminary report. *Q. J. Stud. Alcohol* 26:449-459, 1965.

54. Hunt, G. M., and Azrin, N. H. A community reinforcement approach to alcoholism. *Behav. Res. Therapy* 11:91-104, 1973.

55. Intagliata, J. C. Increasing the interpersonal problem-solving skills of an alcoholic population. *J. Consult. Clin. Psychol.* 46:489-498, 1978.

56. Jacobson, E. *Progressive Relaxation.* University of Chicago Press: Chicago, 1938.

57. Kantorovich, N. V. An attempt of curing alcoholism by associated reflexes. *Nov. Refleksol. Fiziol. Nerv. Sis.* 3:436-445, 1929.

58. Kraft, T. Alcoholism treated by systematic desensitization: A follow-up of eight cases. *J. Royal Coll. Gen. Prac.* 18:336-340, 1969.

59. Kraft, T., and Al-Issa, I. Alcoholism treated with desensitization: A case study. *Behav. Res. Ther.* 5:69-70, 1967.

60. Kraft, T., and Al-Issa, I. Desensitization and the treatment of alcoholic addiction. *Br. J. Addict.* 63:19-23, 1968.

61. Lazarus, A. A. *Multimodal Behavior Therapy.* Springer: New York, 1976.

62. Lemere, F., and Voegtlin, W. L. An evaluation of the aversion treatment of alcoholism. *Q. J. Stud. Alcohol* 11:199-204, 1950.

63. Lemere, F., Voegtlin, W. L., Broz, W. R., O'Hollaren, P., and Tupper, W. E. The conditioned reflex treatment of chronic alcoholism: VIII. A review of six years' experience with this treatment of 1,526 patients. *J.A.M.A.* 120:269-270, 1942.

64. Lovibond, S. H. Behavioral control of excessive drinking. In: *Progress in Behavior Modification* (Vol. 5), Hersen, M., Eisler, R. M., and Miller, P. M. (eds.). Academic Press: New York, 1977.

65. Lovibond, S. H., and Caddy, G. Discriminated aversive control in the moderation of alcoholics' drinking behavior. *Behav. Ther.* 1:437-444, 1970.

66. Marlatt, G. A. *A Comparison of Aversive Conditioning Procedures in the Treatment of Alcoholism.* Paper presented at the Western Psychological Association Meeting, Anaheim, Calif., April 1973.

67. Marlatt, G. A. Craving for alcohol, loss of control, and relapse: A cognitive-behavioral analysis. In: *Alcoholism: New Directions in Behavioral Research and Treatment*, Plenum: New York, 1978.

68. McCance, C., and McCance, P. F. Alcoholism in northeast Scotland: Its treatment and outcome. *Br. J. Psychiatry* 115:189-198, 1969.

69. McClelland, D. C. Drinking as a response to power needs in man. *Psychopharmacol. Bull.* 10(4):5-6, 1974.

70. McClelland, D. C. The impact of power motivation training on alcoholics. *J. Stud. Alcohol* 38:142-144, 1977.

71. McGuire, R. J., and Vallence, M. Aversion therapy by electric shock: A simple technique. In: *Conditioning Techniques in Clinical Practice and Research*, Springer: New York, 1964.

72. Miller, E. C., Dvorak, A., and Turner, D. W. A method of creating aversion to alcohol by reflex conditioning in a group setting. *Q. J. Stud. Alcohol* 21:424-431, 1960.

73. Miller, M. M. Treatment of chronic alcoholism by hypnotic aversion. *J.A.M.A.* 171:1492-1495, 1959.

74. Miller, P. M. A behavioral intervention program for chronic public drunkenness offenders. *Arch. Gen. Psychiatry* 32:915-918, 1975.

75. Miller, P. M. Alternative skills training in alcoholism treatment. In: *Alcoholism: New Direction in Behavioral Research and Treatment*, Nathan, P. E., Marlatt, G. A., and Loberg, T. (eds.). Plenum: New York, 1978.

76. Miller, P. M., and Eisler, R. M. Assertive behavior of alcoholics: A descriptive analysis. *Behav. Ther.* 8:146-149, 1977.

77. Miller, P. M., and Hersen, M. Quantitative changes in alcohol consumption as a function of electrical aversive conditioning. *J. Clin. Psychol.* 28:590-593, 1972.

78. Miller, P. M., Hersen, M., Eisler, R. M., and Hemphill, D. P. Electrical aversion with alcoholics: An analogue study. *Behav. Res. Ther.* 11:491-497, 1973.

79. Miller, P. M., Hersen, M., Eisler, R. M., and Watts, J. G. Contingent reinforcement of lowered blood alcohol levels in an outpatient chronic alcoholic. *Behav. Res. Ther.* 12:261-263, 1974.

80. Miller, P. M., Stanford, A. G., and Hemphill, D. P. A comprehensive social learning approach to alcoholism treatment. *Soc. Casework* 55:279-284, 1974.

81. Miller, W. R. Behavioral self-control training in the treatment of problem drinkers. In: *Behavioral Self-Management: Strategies, Techniques and Outcomes*, Stuart, R. B. (ed.). Brunner/Mazel: New York, 1977.

82. Miller, W. R. Behavioral treatment of problem drinkers: A comparative outcome study of three controlled drinking therapies. *J. Consult. Clin. Psychol.* 46:74-86, 1978.

83. Miller, W. R. *Effectiveness of Non-Prescription Therapies for Problem Drinkers*. Paper presented at the Annual Meeting of the American Psychological Association, Toronto, Canada, August 1978.

84. Miller, W. R., Gribskov, C. J., and Mortell, R. L. Effectiveness of a self-control manual for problem drinkers with and without therapist contact. *Int. J. Addict.*, in press.

85. Miller, W. R., and Hester, R. K. Treating the problem drinker: Modern approaches. In: *The Addictive Behaviors: Treatment of Alcoholism, Drug Abuse, Smoking, and Obesity*, Miller, W. R. (ed.). Pergamon Press: Oxford, 1980.

86. Miller, W. R., and Munoz, R. F. *How to Control Your Drinking*. Prentice-Hall: Englewood Cliffs, N.J., 1976.

87. Miller, W. R., Pechacek, T. F., and Hamburg, S. Group behavior therapy for problem drinkers. *Int. J. Addict.* 16:827-837, 1981.

88. Miller, W. R., and Taylor, C. A. Relative effectiveness of bibliotherapy, individual and group self-control training in the treatment of problem drinkers. *Addict. Behav.* 5:13-24, 1980.

89. Miller, W. R., Taylor, C. A., and West, J. B. Focused versus broad-spectrum behavior therapy for problem drinkers. *J. Consult. Clin. Psychol.* 48:590-601, 1980.

90. Mills, K. C., Sobell, M. B., and Schaefer, H. H. Training social drinking as an alternative to abstinence for alcoholics. *Behav. Ther.* 2:18-27, 1971.

91. Nathan, P. E., and O'Brien, J. S. An experimental analysis of the behavior of alcoholics during prolonged experimental drinking. *Behav. Ther.* 2:455-476, 1971.

92. Nathan, P. E., Titler, N. A., Lowenstein, L. M., Solomon, P., and Rossi, A. M. Behavioral analysis of chronic alcoholism. *Arch. Gen. Psychiatry* 22:419-430, 1970.

93. Neubuerger, O. W., Matarazzo, J. D., Schmitz, R. E., and Pratt, H. H. One-year follow-up of total abstinence in chronic alcoholic patients following emetic counterconditioning. *Alcoholism: Clin. Exp. Res.* 22:306-312, 1980.

94. Parker, J. C., Gilbert, G. S., and Thoreson, R. W. Anxiety management in alcoholics: A study of generalized effects of relaxation techniques. *Addict. Behav.* 3:123-127, 1978.

95. Parker, J. C., Gilbert, G. S., and Thoreson, R. W. Reduction of autonomic arousal in alcoholics: A comparison of relaxation and meditation techniques. *J. Consult. Clin. Psychol.* 46:879-886, 1978.

96. Pattison, E. M., Sobell, M. B., and Sobell, L. C. *Emerging Concepts of Alcohol Dependence.* Springer: New York, 1977.

97. Pickens, R., Bigelow, G., and Griffiths, R. An experimental approach to treating chronic alcoholism: A case study and one-year follow-up. *Behav. Res. Ther.* 11:321-325, 1973.

98. Piorkowski, G. K., and Mann, E. T. Issues in treatment efficacy research with alcoholics. *Percep. Mot. Skills* 41:695-700, 1975.

99. Pomerleau, O. F., Pertshuck, M., Adkins, D., and Brady, J. P. A comparison of behavioral and traditional treatment for middle-income problem drinkers. *J. Behav. Med.* 1:187-200, 1978.

100. Pomerleau, O. F., Pertshuck, M., Adkins, D., and d'Aquili, E. Treatment for middle-income problem drinkers. In: *Alcoholism: New Directions in Behavioral Research and Treatment*, Nathan, P. E., Marlatt, G. A., and Loberg, T. (eds.). Plenum: New York, 1978.

101. Quinn, J. T., and Henbest, R. Partial failure of generalization in alcoholics following aversion therapy. *Q. J. Stud. Alcohol* 28:70-75, 1967.

102. Quinn, J. T., and Kerr, W. S. The treatment of poor prognosis in alcoholics by prolonged apomorphine aversion therapy. *J. Ir. Med. Assoc.* 53:50-54, 1963.

103. Rachman, S., and Teasdale, J. *Aversion Therapy and Behaviour Disorders.* Routledge and Kegan Paul: London, 1969.

104. Sanchez-Craig, B. M. A self-control strategy for drinking tendencies. *Ontario Psychol.* 7:25-29, 1975.

105. Sanchez-Craig, B. M. Cognitive and behavioral coping strategies in the reappraisal of stressful social situations. *J. Counsel. Psychol.* 23:7-12, 1976.

106. Sanchez-Craig, M. *Reappraisal Therapy: A Self-Control Strategy for Abstinence and Controlled Drinking.* Paper presented at the Taos International Conference on Treatment of Addictive Behaviors, Taos, New Mexico, February 1979.

107. Smith, R. E., and Gregory, P. B. Covert sensitization by induced anxiety in the treatment of an alcoholic. *J. Behav. Ther. Exp. Psychiatry* 7:31-33, 1976.

108. Smith-Moorehouse, P. M. Hypnosis in the treatment of alcoholism. *Br. J. Addict.* 64:47-55, 1969.

109. Sobell, L. C. Alcohol treatment outcome evaluation: Contributions from behavioral research. In: *Alcoholism: New Directions in Behavioral Research and Treatment*, Nathan, P. E., Marlatt, G. A., and Loberg, T. (eds.). Plenum: New York, 1978.

110. Sobell, M. B., and Sobell, L. C. Alcoholics treated by individualized behavior therapy: One-year treatment outcome. *Behav. Res. Ther.* 11:599-618, 1973.

111. Sobell, M. B., and Sobell, L. C. Individualized behavior therapy for alcoholics. *Behav. Ther.* 4:49-72, 1973.

112. Sobell, M. B., and Sobell, L. C. Second-year treatment outcome of alcoholics treated by individualized behavior therapy: Results. *Behav. Res. Ther.* 14:195-215, 1976.

113. Steffen, J. J. Electromyographically induced relaxation in the treatment of chronic alcohol abuse. *J. Consult. Clin. Psychol.* 43:275, 1975.

114. Steffen, J. J., Nathan, P. E., and Taylor, H. A. Tension-reducing effects of alcohol: Further evidence and some methodological considerations. *J. Abnorm. Psychol.* 83: 542–547, 1974.

115. Sturgis, E. T., Calhoun, K. S., and Best, C. L. Correlates of assertive behavior in alcoholics. *Addict. Behav.* 4:193–197, 1979.

116. Sulzer, E. S. Behavioral modification in adult psychiatric patients. In: *Case Studies in Behavior Modification*, Ullmann, L. P. and Krasner, L. (eds.). Holt, Rinehart & Winston: New York, 1965.

117. Thimann, J. Conditioned reflex treatment of alcoholism: I. Its rationale and technique. *N. Eng. J. Med.* 241:368–370, 1949.

118. Van Hasselt, V. B., Hersen, M., and Milliones, J. Social skills training for alcoholics and drug addicts: A review. *Addict. Behav.* 3:221–233, 1978.

119. Voegtlin, W. L. The treatment of alcoholism by establishing a conditioned reflex. *Am. J. Med. Sci.* 199:802–810, 1940.

120. Voegtlin, W. L., and Broz, W. R. The conditioned reflex treatment of chronic alcoholism: X. An analysis of 3,125 admissions over a period of 10½ years. *Ann. Intern. Med.* 30:580–597, 1949.

121. Voegtlin, W. L., and Lemere, F. The treatment of alcohol addiction: A review of the literature. *Q. J. Stud. Alcohol* 2:717–803, 1942.

122. Voegtlin, W. L., Lemere, F., Broz, W. R., and O'Hollaren, P. Conditioned reflex therapy for chronic alcoholics: IV. A preliminary report on the value of reinforcement. *Q. J. Stud. Alcohol* 2:505–511, 1941.

123. Voegtlin, W. L., Lemere, F., Broz, W. R., and O'Hollaren, P. Conditioned reflex therapy of alcoholic addiction: VI. Follow-up report of 1,042 cases. *Am. J. Med. Sci.* 203: 525–528, 1942.

124. Vogler, R. E., Compton, J. V., and Weissbach, T. A. Integrated behavior change techniques for alcoholics. *J. Consult. Clin. Psychol.* 43:233–243, 1975.

125. Vogler, R. E., Weissbach, T. A., Compton, J. V., and Martin, G. T. Integrated behavior change techniques for problem drinkers in the community. *J. Consult. Clin. Psychol.* 45:267–279, 1977.

126. Wallerstein, R. S. *Hospital Treatment of Alcoholics.* Basic Books: New York, 1957.

127. Wiens, A. N., Montague, J. R., Manaugh, T. S., and English, C. J. Pharmacologic aversive counterconditioning to alcohol in a private hospital: One-year follow-up. *J. Stud. Alcohol* 37:1320–1324, 1976.

128. Wolpe, J. *Psychotherapy by Reciprocal Inhibition.* Stanford University Press: Stanford, Calif., 1958.

97

RAYMOND M. COSTELLO, PhD, The University of Texas Health Science Center at San Antonio

EVALUATION OF ALCOHOLISM TREATMENT PROGRAMS

A POPULAR ESTIMATE OF the prevalence of alcoholism is 7%. In addition, the number of people estimated to be affected somehow by contact with alcohol abusers is three to five for each alcoholic. Thus, in the United States, some 15 million people might be alcoholic, and they may implicate another 45 to 75 million in their disorder. These figures represent 30 to 40% of the American population.

The sequelae of alcoholism are not only medical or physical symptoms, but also psychological, spiritual, social, vocational, and legal problems in living. In socioeconomic terms, the cost of the disorder to society may be greater than that of any other public health problem.

In response to the vast numbers of alcoholics and to the vast cost of associated problems, the National Institute of Alcohol Abuse and Alcoholism (NIAAA) was created in the United States to coordinate the federal governments' attempt at amelioration through research, public education, and treatment. Although the inaugural year marking the beginning of the coordinated federal effort was about 1970, a mere decade later, in 1980, the demand for accountability caused programs to be shut down for want of demonstrated effectiveness. The programs of immediate concern are those described by the NIAAA as "comprehensive alcohol

---

Raymond M. Costello, PhD, Associate Professor of Psychiatry (Psychology), The University of Texas Health Science Center at San Antonio, and Assistant Director, Alcohol Treatment Unit, Audie Murphy Memorial Veterans Administration Hospital, San Antonio, Texas.

treatment programs"—comprehensive in the sense of providing direct and indirect services, short-term and long-term care, designed to influence behavioral, medical, psychological, and social events.

Evaluation is crucial to continued growth and development, yet the methodologies and logistics of evaluation research, especially in massive public health programs, or comprehensive care programs, are developmentally primitive. The purpose of this chapter is to contribute to the development of evaluation methodologies by integrating into historical perspective observations from alcoholism treatment program evaluations reported over the past 30 years. The sources for review are 80 reports that have been referenced in two recent publications [3, 6]. The standards of the Joint Commission on Accreditation of Hospitals (JCAH) [17] provides the organizational framework of the review.

DEFINITION OF TREATMENT PROGRAM

"Program" implies agenda or outline, a series of events to be followed sequentially. "Clinical program," or "treatment," refers to a complex of component interventions into the lives of affected individuals or cases. The complex is organized to provide a continuum of care in multiple settings, which vary considerably in terms of restrictiveness and administrative cost. The JCAH manual defines a complex of six clinical component interventions: outreach, emergency services, inpatient, intermediate, outpatient, and aftercare.

Outreach. The outreach component of clinical interventions facilitates identification (within a target population) of persons and their families who have problems related to the use of alcohol, facilitates procurement of alcoholism services, and alerts all public private human service agencies who serve the same target population to the importance of early identification and easy access to the service delivery system [17, p. 59].

Emergency services. The clinical component that provides 24-hour availability of the following services to all persons and their families with problems related to alcohol use and abuse is that of emergency services: (1) immediate medical evaluation and care, (2) supervision of persons by properly trained staff until they are no longer incapacitated by the effects of alcohol, (3) evaluation of medical, psychological, and social needs, leading to the development of a plan for continuing care, and (4) effective transportation services [17, p. 35].

Inpatient. The inpatient clinical component provides 24-hour supervised care under the direction of a physician in a hospital or other suitably equipped medical setting designed for the diagnosis and/or treatment of medical and/or psychiatric illnesses derived from or associated with alcohol abuse and/or alcoholism [17, p. 41].

Intermediate. The intermediate component facilitates the rehabilitation of the alcoholic person by placing him or her in an organized therapeutic environment in which he or she may receive diagnostic services, counseling, vocational rehabilitation and/or work therapy, while benefiting from the support that a full or partial residential setting can provide [17, p. 47].

Outpatient. The outpatient clinical component provides a variety of diagnostic and primary alcoholism treatment services on both a scheduled basis and nonscheduled basis in a nonresidential setting to alcoholic persons and their families whose physical and emotional status allows them to function in their usual environment [17, p. 53].

Aftercare. The aftercare clinical component provides care to patients who have progressed sufficiently through emergency, inpatient, intermediate, and/or outpatient services to a point in their recovery where they will benefit from a level of continued contact that will support and increase the gains made to date in the treatment process [17, p. 63].

Aftercare Component

The JCAH manual states that aftercare is an essential component necessary but not sufficient to constitute a program. Any one or more of the remaining five components, when added to aftercare, qualifies the program for a JCAH review. Thus, treatment program complexes can range from a minimum combination of two components to a maximum of all six components.

Although aftercare is required by JCAH as essential to a program, it is difficult to determine from the manual what types of services constitute aftercare. The guiding principle and standard 7.2.5.2 suggest that the care is not primary; that is, that such care is provided to cases after they have progressed through other forms of treatment. Thus a follow-up, follow-through, reinforcement, or booster system to make more probable the maintenance of therapeutic gains made elsewhere in the system is implied. Aftercare may be provided directly by program personnel or indirectly by other agencies subsequent to negotiation with the patient, or with the patient and family, and proper referral. All steps in this process must be documented, linked with prior treatment goals, and monitored by trained personnel. By design, potential relapses or loss of prior gains are detected early and prompt reinstitution of appropriate primary care forestalls a preventable recycling or resetting of the recovery process to the zero point.

In the earliest reports in the series [11, 18] a process of care consistent with the spirit of aftercare was evident. These two reports focused on the contribution of disulfiram to long-term outcome. Both investigative groups maintained that the recovery process was slow and arduous and that some sort of treatment contact sustained over a long-term period increased the probability of success. The former group was more sophisticated programmatically than the latter. Although Moore and Drury [18] had reasonable suggestions about how to begin treatment, they had few suggestions about how to maintain gains with difficult cases. Failure to persevere was attributed to preexisting psychopathology, that is, instability of character. Epstein and Guild [11], on the other hand, recommended aggressive intervention to maintain long-term contact. They recommended that the case must first be stabilized before introducing Antabuse. This stabilization was best accomplished in a hospital setting where proper medical care could be instituted and the patient begun on a normalized sleep and dietary schedule. Following this a rudimentary but careful process analysis of the impediments to recovery was described. Prescriptions for psychosocial interventions at the point of contact with these impediments were offered to assure long-term contact. Psychiatric diagnostic jargon was operationalized into behavioral referents to identify crisis points or roadblocks to recovery, and was not reified into immutable motive forces. In this regard, Moore and Drury might say that cyclothymics were not good treatment risks, but Epstein and Guild would suggest that cyclothymics might have a tendency to feel guilty and as if they had let down the treatment staff, and it was at this point that a crisis was at hand that required an aggressive response from the aftercare team.

By 1955 not only was the term "aftercare" used worldwide, some went so far as to consider aftercare the standard upon which successful treatment was based [13]. Three distinct stages of treatment were recognized by Glatt. The first stage, considered preliminary, consisted primarily of medical-physical interventions. The second stage was long-term psychosocial rehabilitation. The third stage, aftercare, was considered crucial in that its absence would severely limit whatever chances for success were generated by the prior two stages of care.

Sometime during the ensuing 15 years, however, the commitment to aftercare began to wear thin and investigators began to publish reports that questioned if "energetic aftercare" contributed more to outcome than did mere assurance that services would be readily accessible in time of need [9]. Dubourg [9] concluded that research was needed to determine how aftercare might be designed more effectively. He considered that aftercare might be incidental to outcome rather than crucial because of two salient observations: (1) many cases recover successfully following treatment without the aid of energetic aftercare; and (2) many cases who relapse do so in spite of attempts to institute aftercare.

Of the 80 studies used as sources for this review, 39, or nearly 50% reported aftercare services or were considered to have had such services, even if not labeled as such. Thus, only 50%, assuming at least one other treatment component, would have qualified as a JCAH program. The nature and extent of aftercare services varied widely. Some programs were energetic in initiating contact, were active in seeing that contact was maintained throughout primary care, and were monitoring closely that gains made during treatment were not lost because of a dispassionate objectivity on the part of program personnel [16]. Other programs simply informed their cases that various treatment services were available should they wish to make use of them.

A recent report attempted to evaluate the contribution of "aggressive follow-through" to long-term outcome, that is, 1 to 3 years after initial contact [4]. This term is somewhat more inclusive than the term "energetic aftercare," but can be used synonymously. In this report, the contribution to outcome variance of patient characteristics, program characteristics, and aftercare, in a sample of 29 published studies, was described statistically using a multiple regression technique called "path analysis." Aftercare was found to have a standardized effect as large as that of active treatment, and in addition was found to enhance indirectly the effect of treatment by two to three times its direct effect. These effects were statistically independent of patient characteristics. In a complementary evaluation utilizing all 80 source studies [6] a nearly perfect rank-order correlation was found between average success rate and percentage of studies reporting aftercare (i.e., follow-through) within five classes of outcome. Of 24 studies classified as "best outcome" (45% overall success) 19 (79%) were rated as having an energetic aftercare component. Eight of 13 (61%) studies with "good outcome" (34% overall success), 9 of 17 (53%) studies with "intermediate outcome" (30% overall success), 0 of 14 (0%) studies with "poor outcome" (19% overall success), and 1 of 12 (8%) studies with "poorest outcome" (12% overall success) were credited with an aftercare component.

Although Dubourg's invitation to more and better research regarding the design, implementation, delivery, and evaluation of aftercare components is well advised, the current best conclusion that seems to be supported by the preponderance of available evidence is that aftercare is essential to treatment programming. Glatt's comment might be paraphrased that aftercare is the standard upon which a treatment program must first be evaluated. If aftercare is indeed an important link to long-term success, then measurement of the adequacy of the component will provide indirectly a projective measure of long-term outcome.

Future studies may bear in mind that aftercare is not a primary care modality, and that its goal is to maintain gains made elsewhere. This necessitates that gains have actually been made and measured; otherwise there is no criterion to which aftercare can be directed. The proper dependent measure is then an "erosion of gain" criterion that reflects the influence of various aftercare modalities to retard loss of gain over time. This is similar to a concept of chemical half-life, as the index of interest could be defined as "primary gain half-life"—the length of time required before loss of one-half of the gain made in primary treatment, repeated for each source of gain. Aftercare could be compared against no aftercare, or various forms of aftercare could be compared.

The point of emphasis of this discussion is that a proper experimental model with relevant and valid outcome criteria must be selected before adequate evaluation of the component can proceed.

Inpatient, Intermediate Components

The JCAH distinction between intermediate and inpatient components is facilitated when the residential care is provided in a nonhospital setting, or when the hospital-based program is staffed primarily by nonpsychiatric professionals.

When, however, the hospital unit is staffed by psychological, medical, and vocational specialists, the distinction is less clear. Historically, 64 of 80 (80%) reports were generated from hospital-inpatient units [6] and three others drew volunteer cases from inpatient units for additional specialized treatment. It appeared that 61 reports were generated from inpatient-intermediate units; 6 reports were generated from inpatient-only units; and one other report was generated from an intermediate-only unit. Thus, 67 (84%) of these reports made inpatient services available to their clients, and 62 (78%) reported the availability of an intermediate care component.

The JCAH manual defines "inpatient care" as care designed for medical supervision of diagnosis and treatment of illnesses associated with alcohol abuse. The manual defines "intermediate care" as rehabilitative and work-oriented efforts. The intended distinction is obvious. The usual course of program evaluation, however, has been to blur what should be very sharp distinctions between these two components. The trend to minimize the importance of inpatient care is evident as early as 1955 by Glatt's reference to this type of care as "no more than preliminary . . . in the treatment of alcoholism" [13, p. 1318]. Subsequently, long-term outcome, on varous dimensions but primarily on alcohol use, has been the preferred criterion upon which to evaluate the merit of therapeutic programs, including inpatient components. Yet, inpatient components should be evaluated on the merit of their ability (1) to make accurate diagnosis of medical or psychiatric illnesses derived from or associated with alcohol abuse; and (2) to treat effectively these illnesses. Thus, accurate medical-psychiatric symptom description, followed by amelioration or control achieved quickly after admission, followed by effective referral to appropriate modalities of long-term care, should be the standards of quality inpatient care. As this care is ordinarily considered to be preliminary, however, seldom can a program evaluation find publication if it is addressed only to these criteria. Thus, inpatient care has been evaluated on the same dimensions as has intermediate care. This anomolous state of affairs has resulted in a British editorial [10] that asks for a response to the following question: "Leave out detoxification and leave out questions of underlying or concomitant physiological illness, and who then can quote a reference or two which proves that the investment in these [inpatient] units is basically justified? Given the expense, the boot is on that foot" [10, p. 2]. Thus, the editorial asks that the very criteria that could prove the effectiveness of inpatient care are those that should not be used in the evaluation. Evaluation specialists, clinicians, and administrators must work together to sharpen the distinction between these types of care and to develop operational evaluative criteria that fit appropriately the type of care being administered.

As early as 1953, certain observations were discovered, observations that have been rediscovered repeatedly. Wexberg [21] reported on the development of an outpatient alcoholism treatment clinic designed as a cost-effective interface with the criminal justice system. Three findings of this demonstration project have stood the test of time: (1) alcoholics are an extremely heterogeneous group with regard to many biopsychosocial dimensions, including alcoholism severity; (2) outpatient modalities of care are utilized by an extremely limited subgroup of alcohol abusers; and (3) medical and residential units are essential for comprehensive care. Further, Gallant et al. [12] concluded that although long-term outcome may not have been influenced in chronic, revolving-door alcoholics by inpatient treatment, serious physical problems were diagnosed in a large percentage of cases (44%) and these problems may have gone undetected or inadequately treated had the cases not been admitted to an inpatient unit. Finally, Willems et al. [22] reported two findings that appear commonly: (1) social stability of clients interacts with length of inpatient treatment to effect long-term outcome (i.e., socially maladjusted cases derive more benefit from long-stay inpatient treatment than from short-stay, and socially adjusted cases do as well in short-stay as in long-stay units); and (2) intensive, specialized, group-oriented treatment produces better results than inpatient treatment of a nonspecific type even if of longer duration.

These findings bear upon the distinction between inpatient and intermediate components. The intermediate component is designed to produce long-term effects, whereas the inpatient component is not. Those intermediate components that emphasize intensive, group-oriented, specialized treatment of the therapeutic community seem to be even more effective than intermediate components that do not, irrespective of the availability of inpatient care [6].

The points of emphasis in this section are that (1) the distinction between inpatient and intermediate components is crucial to adequate evaluation; (2) inpatient components must be supervised by medical specialists and must direct evaluation efforts to description and control of acute, symptomatic criteria; (3) intermediate components are not necessarily and probably should not be hospital-based (in light of both treatment philosophy and cost considerations) and must direct evaluation efforts to long-term rehabilitation criteria.

Emergency Services Component

The JCAH manual defines emergency services specifically in medical terms; thus, this component is not synonymous with generic crisis intervention. Standard 2.1.7 specifies a triage process to determine level of urgency and assignment to appropriate services. Standard 2.5 specifies appropriate medical evaluation and treatment of acute disorders, and supervision of medically ill persons by trained medical staff. Both 24-hour telephone and transportation services are also required to facilitate appropriate case management and follow-through referral. As acute alcohol intoxication is considered an acute medical illness qualifying for care under this component, recent reports evaluating detoxification centers could be considered in this section.

None of the 80 source studies reported specifically the availability of emergency services and the evaluation of these services, yet 67 reported inpatient hospital-based care. Thus, by inference 84% of the source studies might have separated, both conceptually and practically, these two modes of care for purposes of appropriate evaluation. The distinction between short-term and long-term outcome goals drawn between inpatient and intermediate components is relevant in this discussion also. The emergency services component is designed for appropriate medical evaluation and treatment of acute medical illnesses associated with alcoholism, primarily (but not limited to) acute alcohol intoxication. Thus, the standard of proof of effectiveness is much different than that for long-term care components.

In Canada, however, an attempt has been made to evaluate detoxification programs basically by reference to standards more appropriate for intermediate care, that is, long-term outcome [1]. As expected, in a series of studies, Annis and her colleagues were not able to demonstrate that merely sobering-up an alcoholic accomplished much more than sobering-up. She went on to recommend that outcome standards other than long-term outcome (i.e., humanitarian and custodial concerns) be utilized to evaluate outcome.

The Canadian experience probably generalizes to other countries and so merits summarizing. The design of the Ontario detoxication centers specified a two-phase service delivery system. Phase I initiated rehabilitation in a warm, caring environment as opposed to police drunk tanks. Phase II inovlved referral to social welfare and health facilities, including, in particular, specialized halfway houses. The report did not suggest that the phase I process was actually evaluated. There was no description of the range and severity of presenting symptoms, length of stay, medical, social, or psychological complications, nor degree of reduction of presenting symptomatology. There was also no description of counseling with the client to determine current mental status, and what attitude, understanding, motivation, or intention existed regarding present circumstances. Thus, there is no data upon which to decide how well rehabilitation was initiated. The detoxication team had a number of dispositional resources to which to refer, yet it is not clear what guidelines were used to direct referrals. Thus, no evaluation can be made of the appropriateness of either the assessment system or of the referral system. This situation is also evident in a very recent report [14], which attempted to describe statistically those criterial guidelines used by the staff of one detoxication center for referrals to a long-term program. The attempt was not successful and the authors concluded that such referral is not a systematic process.

The Annis report did include data on phase II of the project. Two outcome criteria, referrals accepted by cases to other agencies, and confirmed arrivals of referred cases to these agencies were used. The various detoxication centers ranged in rates of accepted referrals from 20 to 50%. No explanation for this marked range was given. Less than 10% of all referrals followed through by making at least one contact with the dispositional resource. More than half of this 10% dropped out after the initial visit, and two-thirds dropped out after two visits. Clearly, retention in treatment was a problem, yet retention is a crucial variable for program evaluation. Perhaps this is why JCAH requires both a 24-hour telephone system and a 24-hour transportation system for the emergency services component, and why aftercare is required to define a program.

The point of emphasis of this discussion, once again, is that clarity of objectives and relevance of outcome criteria are crucial to appropriate evaluation. Although Annis and her colleagues may have concluded that detoxication centers contribute little to rehabilitation, that conclusion is warranted only in the context of the evaluation scheme in which it was generated. Specification of more appropriate objectives with performance criteria tailored to those objectives may result in a more optimistic conclusion.

Outpatient Component

Outpatient care is by definition nonresidential care. A diagnostic phase is required to determine that cases possess sufficient coping resources to warrant a nonresidential disposition. The treatment phase is not defined by the JCAH manual in precise terms, so that any intervention administered in a nonresidential setting qualifies as outpatient care. Historically, however, the distinction between outpatient as a primary care modality and outpatient as an aftercare modality has not always been clarified. Only 32 of the 80 source studies (40%) reported the availability of an outpatient component. Of these 32, 22 studies reported an inpatient and/or intermediate component (16 with aftercare) and 10 studies reported an outpatient-only component (3 with aftercare). This suggests that evaluation reports are more frequently generated by programs with an inpatient and/or intermediate component. Of the 16 studies reporting outpatient and aftercare components in addition to inpatient and/or intermediate components it was usually unclear when the outpatient component was a primary care modality. Of the 3 studies with outpatient-only and aftercare components, the point at which primary outpatient care became aftercare was also unclear. As outpatient treatment wound down it appeared to blend imperceptibly into an aftercare modality wherein maintenance of earlier treatment gains was the primary objective. Even in those 13 studies without aftercare it was not clear that outpatient was utilized exclusively as a primary care modality. In this respect, it is essential that treatment objectives be specified, yet in most instances it appeared that cases were assigned to outpatient components either because this modality followed sequentially other types of care, because cases refused other types of care, because no other type of care was available, or because cases were considered to possess sufficient resources so that they could handle not being placed into a more restrictive environment. Thus, assignment to outpatient care is frequently by default. It is the rare program that assigns patients to outpatient care because clinically this is considered to be the most appropriate mode of care at the time. Likewise, the criteria for reentry into other components is usually not clear. Clinically, decisions are made on a daily basis whether treatment is working, and presumably proper referral or transfer decisions are made. Yet this continuous process of care generally has not been documented carefully in the source literature. Especially in those studies reporting an outpatient-only modality, when treatment begins to go awry it ordinarily results in loss of the case. Effort criteria to assess course of outpatient treatment and reassignment to more appropriate modes of care are, for the most part, missing from the literature. The obvious exception to this rule is blatant intoxication, which frequently results in a quick referral to a detoxication center to begin the process anew. The missing link in this process is an adequate analysis of the precipitants of relapse. Some investigators have begun to look at this area [15], but the link to proper evaluation of the care being delivered has not been made. Hore has reported, for example, that disruptions in emotional relationships with significant others, imminent changes in work or residence, or failing health are prime events leading to relapse. Yet the documentation and subsequent reporting of how these critical situations were managed by the treatment team are not available. Thus, evaluative decisions regarding the quality or adequacy of care must be postponed. Such decisions, however, must be made before the effectiveness of the mode of treatment in question can be determined. Historically, the evaluation cart has been before the service horse.

Outreach Component

The JCAH manual allows that outreach, although not a primary care modality, could qualify as sufficient to define a program if combined with aftercare. Although none of the 80 source studies reported specifically such a component, each had to contend with a question fundamental to the operation and evaluation of an outreach component. "Outreach" is a process of identification of persons in need of (or appropriate for) various alcohol-care services, knowledge of what services are available and where they can be located, and enabling persons to enter and accept the service delivery system [17, p. 77]. The issue of assessment is crucial to design, delivery, and evaluation of care, yet, historically, this issue has been and continues to be debated. Generally, the issue is phrased, "Who is an alcoholic?" More precisely the question involves the appropriate matching of the presenting picture (i.e., medical symptoms, psychodynamics, social resources) with treatment resources.

Numerous attempts have been made to develop a set of diagnostic criteria that result in an unequivocal dichotomous decision regarding presence or absence of alcoholism. These attempts have ranged from the complicated multitract, multilevel system of the National Council on Alcoholism [8] to a very simple eight-item checklist [20]. Although interest in making this simple discrimination may be waning, it highlights an important problem. That is, that alcoholism treatment services are delivered to a range of cases only some of whom would qualify for the diagnosis of alcoholism. It may be important, from an evaluation perspective, to assess if various components of care differ in effectiveness when evaluated with regard to case diagnosis. Evaluation of a detoxication center with regard to the short-term outcome of reduction of symptoms associated with acute intoxication should be accomplished without regard to the status of the case as alcoholic (although detoxication may prove in fact to be more difficult in alcoholics). The evaluation of performance of the detoxication center with regard to a follow-through criterion of completed referral to a long-term treatment alternative, however, would seem to turn on case diagnosis. For example, Annis [1] reported that 90% of the detoxication cases did not result in a referral, and that 10% did. Yet neither group was subdivided further by diagnostic class (or by some other variable related to diagnosis). If a substantial number of the 90% did not warrant additional care in the categorical alcoholism treatment system, a different denominator would be required to assess the adequacy of the link between the detoxication center and other program elements. Likewise, if a substantial number of the 10% were referred inappropriately, subsequent case retention rates may have been calculated inappropriately.

The enter and accept element is as essential to evaluation of the outreach component (as it is to any other component) as is the identification element. This requires a periodic examination along the lines of the Annis report. Percentage (of cases identified appropriately) accepting and percentage completing referral to appropriate dispositional resources are important performance criteria.

Management

The JCAH manual requires that each alcohol treatment program have a management system that will exercise general direction over and establish policies concerning the operation of the program [17, p. 9]. Specifically, the management component should assure that the dignity of all patients is enhanced and that their rights as human beings are protected; that proper program planning is documented; that proper fiscal management is followed; that an acceptable treatment environment is maintained; that personnel are monitored properly; and that the program is evaluated with regard to certain guidelines. Each of these six mandates is subject to evaluative scrutiny.

EVALUATION STRATEGIES

The most common evaluative strategy, irrespective of which component or combination of components is evaluated, has followed the experimental model. Numerous variations on the basic model occur repeatedly in the source literature. The most common approach has been the single group, post test-only design [7]. One group receives the treatment and outcome measurements are recorded at some interval after treatment. This approach and the one-shot case study, one group pretest-posttest, and the static group comparison are all actually preexperimental designs [2]. When a control group is added, with or without pretesting, or when the experimental group serves as its own control, the design is more appropriately referred to as experimental. The problem with use of any of these designs, of course, is that the fundamental assumptions of randomization (of people to treatments or treatments to time) and experimental control of extraneous variables cannot be met with any degree of rigor. At best, if this model is to be followed, a quasi-experimental approach is more appropriate.

Federal health legislation in the United States has mandated concurrent implementation of a quality assurance strategy as well as the more common program evaluation strategies in monitoring accountability [23]. Importantly, quality assurance activities are organized to assure adequacy and inappropriateness of care and to control costs by preventing overutilization [23, p. 412]. They rely on methods that focus on specific service plans and service transactions, thus minimizing the focus on data aggregation. The core evaluation processes of quality assurance involve an admissions certification and a continued stay review. Simply, "Does the case warrant the treatment in question?" and, assuming that the treatment in question is being delivered adequately, "Does the case warrant the continuation of such care?" In a previous section, it is suggested that the cart of program evaluation historically has been placed before the horse of quality assurance. Perhaps the next few years will see this situation remedied by a shift in evaluative focus away from an inappropriate experimental, research model to a process of care model. Evaluative questions can be asked with more precision and data collected in such a way that answers will be less equivocal. The problems associated with the experimental approach, at least as it has been utilized thus far, have been summarized as follows:

> We ... suggest that too much is being made of the studies which claim more scientific rigor by using multiple group pretest-posttest designs. ... Selection bias is an ubiquitous phenomenon influencing even these studies; use of volunteers only, imposition of exclusionary criteria; unequal or nonuniform exposure to treatment; and differential follow-up case retention rates pose serious interpretive problems. ... Experimental demand characteristics and nonorthogonality of dependent units ... [are] problemmatic. Put simply, if multiple groups are treated simultaneously in the same geographical location, the dependent units are not orthogonal. The clients can talk with one another, compare notes, develop expectancies, feel mistreated, or be treated as extraspecial. The experimenters can contribute to this confounding by giving special attention to their research subjects, perhaps simply by spending more time with those undergoing the preferred experimental treatment. It would be an interesting experimental challenge to randomly assign randomly selected subjects to multiple treatment groups; when the staff for each treatment were equally well trained, competent and energetic; when the subjects were blind to the fact that they were in an experiment with multiple treatments; when the subjects did not interact with one another across treatments, and within a treatment only when such interaction was an integral characteristic of the treatment; and when the different programs had equivalent follow-up resources. ... Statistical regression artifacts would also have to be avoided as the multiple comparison groups could not differ at present on impor-

tant, programmatically relevant variables . . . [to avoid] the "recurrent problem of packaging underadjusted selection differences as though they were treatment effects." [5, pp. 229-230]

The matter of appropriate evaluative criteria merits brief reiteration. The previous discussion should make it apparent that different outcome criteria will be required to affect the most meaningful evaluation of the various components. This point of emphasis is not novel to the alcoholism literature [19], but when made in the context of the proper definition of what constitutes a program, and in the context of the new evaluation methodology of quality assurance, the point assumes even added importance. Long-term versus short-term goals and objectives, symptom control versus behavioral development, and identification versus amelioration are all issues for evaluation requiring answers tailored to the treatment components or evaluation problems at hand.

REFERENCES

1. Annis, H. M. The detoxification alternative to the handling of public inebriates: The Ontario experience. *J. Stud. Alcohol* 40(3):196-210, 1979.
2. Campbell, D. T., and Stanley, J. C. *Experimental and Quasi-Experimental Designs for Research.* Rand McNally: Chicago, 1963.
3. Costello, R. M. Alcoholism treatment and evaluation: In search of methods. *Int. J. Addict.* 10(2):251-275, 1975.
4. Costello, R. M. Alcoholism treatment effectiveness: Slicing the outcome variance pie. In: *Alcoholism Treatment in Transition,* Edwards, G. and Grant, M. (eds.). Croom Helm: London, 1980.
5. Costello, R. M., Baillargeon, J. G., Biever, P., and Bennett, R. Therapeutic community treatment for alcohol abusers: A one-year multivariate outcome evaluation. *Int. J. Addict.* 15(2):215-232, 1980.
6. Costello, R. M., Biever, P., and Baillargeon, J. G. Alcoholism treatment programming: Historical trends and modern approaches. *Alcoholism: Clin. Exp. Res.* 1(4):311-318, 1977.
7. Crawford, J. J., and Chalupsky, A. B. The reported evaluation of alcoholism treatments, 1968-1971: A methodological review. *Addict. Behav.* 2:63-74, 1977.
8. Criteria Committee, National Council on Alcoholism. Criteria for the diagnosis of alcoholism. *Am. J. Psychiatry* 129:127-135, 1972.
9. Dubourge, G. O. Aftercare for alcoholics—A follow-up study. *B. J. Addict.* 64:155-163, 1969.
10. Edwards, G. Inpatient treatment of alcoholism. *Br. J. Addict.* 74(1):1-2, 1979.
11. Epstein, N., and Guild, J. Further clinical evaluation of tetraethylthinram disulfide in the treatment of alcoholism. *Q. J. Stud. Alcohol* 12:366-380, 1951.
12. Gallant, D. W., Bishop, M. P., Mouledoux, A., Faulkner, M. A., Brisolara, A., and Swanson, W. A. The revolving-door alcoholic: An impasse in the treatment of chronic alcoholics. *Arch. Gen. Psychiatry* 28:633-635, 1973.
13. Glatt, M. M. Treatment centre for alcoholics in a mental hospital. *Lancet* 265:1318-1320, 1955.

14. Holland, R., Evenson, R. C., and Izadi, B. Characteristics of detoxication patients referred to alcoholism treatment programs. *J. Stud. Alcohol* 40(9):914–916, 1979.

15. Hore, B. D. Life events and alcoholic relapse. *Br. J. Addict.* 66:83–88, 1971.

16. Jensen, S. E. A treatment program for alcoholics in a mental hospital. *Q. J. Stud. Alcohol (Suppl. 1)* 3:315–320, 1962.

17. Joint Commission on Accreditation of Hospitals. *Accreditation Manual for Alcoholism Programs.* Chicago: Author, 1974.

18. Moore, J. N. P., and Drury, M. O'C. Antabuse in management of chronic alcoholism. *Lancet* 261:1059–1061, 1951.

19. Pattison, E. M. A critique of alcoholism treatment concepts with special reference to abstinence. *Q. J. Stud. Alcohol* 27:49–71, 1966.

20. Reich, T., Robins, L. N., Woodruff, R. A., Taibleson, M., Rich, C., and Cunningham, L. Computer-assisted derivation of a screening interview for alcoholism. *Arch. Gen. Psychiatry* 32:847–852, 1975.

21. Wexberg. L. E. The outpatient treatment of alcoholism in the District of Columbia. *Q. J. Stud. Alcohol* 14:514–524, 1953.

22. Willems, P. J. A., Letemendia, F. J. J., and Arroyave, F. Two-year follow-up study comparing short- with long-stay inpatient treatment of alcoholics. *Br. J. Psychiatry* 122:637–648, 1973.

23. Woy, J. R., Lund, D. A., and Attkisson, C. C. Quality assurance in human service program evaluation. In: *Evaluation of Human Service Programs,* Attkisson, C. C., Hargreaves, W. A., Horowitz, M. J., and Sorenson, J. E. (eds.). Academic Press: New York, 1978.

98

MARVIN D. FEIT, PhD, University of Tennessee

MANAGEMENT AND ADMINISTRATION OF ALCOHOLISM PROGRAMS

THIS CHAPTER PRESENTS an understandable and practical model for clarifying the different foci and tasks of managing and administering alcohol programs. A major problem hindering the development of such a model has been the interchangeable use of program management and clinical management, implying that they mean the same thing. As they have quite different meaning, greater administrative effectiveness and the development of competent administration in the alcohol field can be made possible as the distinction between program management and clinical management is clarified.

Most existing organizational literature in the alcohol field that does focus on management is usually program-specific and therefore has limitations in understanding the requirements and broader issues of managing alcohol programs. For example, Schramm [7] described the development of an employee assistance program in industry, leaving readers to make their own connections to other settings. Other literature is usually not accessible or appropriate for administrators. Individual efforts to consolidate the expanding management literature have not been successful and the literature remains fragmented [1]. Thus, the complexities of

---

Marvin D. Feit, PhD, Associate Professor, University of Tennessee School of Social Work, and Assistant Clinical Professor, Department of Psychiatry, University of Tennessee Center for the Health Sciences, Memphis, Tennessee.

contemporary administration of alcohol programs are rarely discussed in the literature in an integrated, comprehensive, and helpful manner.

One central issue in competent management is how the concept is perceived. Management is too often viewed, discussed, and written about in general terms, such that it has become a vague and unitary concept. Efforts to understand what "management" means have not been particularly helpful because the methodologies of studies have not partialized the different managerial tasks, responsibilities, and skills required of staff and managers at all organizational levels. An objective of this chapter is to achieve this task by addressing management in the terms described.

THE USE AND MEANING OF MANAGEMENT

It is important to understand different usage of "management" in reference to the management and administration of alcohol programs. The preponderance of literature concentrates on clinical management or on managing treatment programs for alcoholics. In this context, the focus is on issues central to the development and implementation of clinical components directly affecting client services. This focus is limited in that it omits major administrative and business activities needed to support the clinical components. On the other hand, program management is much broader in scope and deals with issues central to managing organizations in which clinical components are designed to treat alcoholics. Program management is management from a total program or organizational perspective, where each administrative problem is viewed as it affects all aspects of an organization. In this perspective, management of clinical programs is a subset of overall program management.

This distinction between managing programs and management of clinical treatment does not by definition mean assigning administrative matters only to persons holding managerial positions. Indeed, management activities are required at all organizational levels and, therefore, are a part of every worker's job responsibility; it is the emphasis and focus of management responsibility that differs according to level. Thus, the purpose in this chapter is to identify the different types of managerial tasks and skills required of each category of worker, so that management as a concept becomes more understandable and practical.

Two additional points need to be mentioned. In this chapter, the terms "administrator" and "manager" are used interchangeably. Job labels are less important than the recognition and understanding of the broad spectrum of function, task, responsibility, and skill required of workers at all organizational levels. Workers are responsible for the operation of their agency, and every organizational position carries some administrative responsibility. Second, many of the identified administrative responsibilities may not necessarily be unique to alcohol management. However, their identification and understanding must come first. Then the chance for applying top management strategies successfully to many of the distinct situations in this field, such as client confidentiality, the collusion between treatment, health, and criminal justice personnel, the schism between two national funding sources as it affects the development and allocation of local program funds through single state agencies, the continuing confusion between rehabilitation and legal enforcement as a primary national policy thrust, and so forth, can be immeasureably improved.

DIFFERENT MANAGEMENT ACTIVITIES BY ORGANIZATIONAL POSITION

This discussion illustrates and describes what management in alcohol programs is about at various organizational levels. Table 1 is intended to clarify the distinctions in management tasks, responsibilities, and needed knowledge in relation to organizational position so as to provide a sound, rational basis for effective instruction in the uniqueness of alcohol program management. More importantly, by illustrating the many requirements of program management, attention can be given to this glaring deficiency in the comprehensive picture of managing alcohol programs.

The chart reflects a fact that in alcohol programs treatment and administration are the two major orientations. Imposed on these two orientations are the jobs held by individuals, usually arranged in an hierarchical structure. Thus, one would expect to find clinicians on one side of an orientation continuum and the executive director and high-level administrators on the other side. Between these positions lie a host of other key organization positions, such as clinical supervisors, and those who manage work groups, such as the director of clinical practice, the medical director, the residential center director, or the director of social services. In effect, the chart indicates that each organizational position can be placed in one of the four specified categories.

Clinical Management

While the positions obviously differ across each category in Table 1, each position possesses certain managerial activities. For example, a clinician has to perform certain administrative tasks in addition to providing direct treatment, tasks such as writing client progress notes, preparing client summaries, making decisions regarding which cases need greater or lesser intervention, evaluating one's own practice, seeking ways to improve interpersonal skills, and so forth. These administrative aspects of a clinician's job are listed in Table 1 in the first category.

As one moves to a position of supervisor of clinical workers or a unit supervisor

Table 1
Distinguishing between Program Management and Clinical Management by Different Managerial Requirements, Organizational Position, and Primary Orientation

Management Responsibility	Managerial Task Requirements	Organizational Position	Primary Orientation
Clinical	writing client progress notes agency reports preparing client summaries evaluating one's own practice seeking ways to improve interpersonal skills case management attending meetings	Direct service personnel (clinician, intake worker, outreach worker, counselor, recreation worker, pharmacist)	Treatment
Clinical	evaluate worker performance help workers with their cases supervise workers provide educational experiences for staff hold staff meetings prepare unit reports identify gaps in services help design and implement new services or modify existing services communicate administrative and policy changes organize group data based on single cases	Unit supervisors (nursing supervisor, counseling supervisor)	Treatment
Clinical	direct and coordinate work units make decisions about services offered monitor activities of interdepartmental work groups prepare reports participate in management team meetings evaluate services help set service objectives supervise unit heads evaluate unit head performance help prepare internal forms design and implement a treatment system develop budget and/or unit cost data	Department directors (medical director, director of nursing, director of social service, director of research and evaluation)	Administration
Program	provide overall program leadership manage multidiscipline work units accountable for fiscal matters responsible for legal or contractual matters secure funds maintain program policies	Administrators (deputy director, executive director)	Administration

Table 1 *(continued)*

Management Responsibility	Managerial Task Requirements	Organizational Position	Primary Orientation
	design an internal management and control system		
	design and implement a planning process		
	insure proper evaluation strategies		
	lease or purchase of equipment		
	monitor the effectiveness of treatment		
	work with various community groups		
	work with board of directors		
	meet external reporting requirements		
	deal with the public and the media		
	prepare reports		
	hold staff meetings		

the job itself naturally changes, and so does the nature of administrative responsibility and related tasks. For example, one must now evaluate worker performance, help workers manage their cases, supervise the activities of workers, hold staff meetings, prepare reports about the activities of a group of workers as well as noting unusual individual performances, call attention to gaps in service, help design and implement new services or modify existing services, and communicate administrative and policy changes to staff. These are tasks that clearly need not be addressed when working directly with clients.

It is important to recognize some unique aspects of people in these positions. First, these supervisors tend to primarily reflect an interest and concern with treatment. They supervise a group of clinical personnel and, indeed, are likely themselves to have emerged from such a position. Third, many new tasks face them for which they are often ill prepared. Fourth, they must now assess, evaluate, and translate individual concerns to group data and vice versa. It is these last aspects of the job that are often a source of much difficulty.

As a supervisor, the concept of group and application of group skills become an additional and a prominent factor in how well one does a job. For example, one must understand how small groups operate, how labor is divided among the workers, how to supervise and motivate different types of workers, and how to group data based on single cases so that decisions often involving policy considerations and affecting several workers can be made. In summary, a supervisor of a clinical work unit has started the transition from a direct service provider to thinking administratively about direct service, yet retains a strong treatment orientation.

A major and distinct shift in orientation occurs in the third management category when one is a director of a department. In this situation, the primary orientation and identification is administrative, with these people directing and supervising clinical supervisors. They are one level further removed from direct service and much closer to top management. Also, they are usually members of an executive's immediate management team and view organizational issues accordingly.

Department directors are expected to assume greater administrative and managerial responsibility, accountability, authority, and to provide leadership and direction to their subordinates. Hence, their managerial tasks differ but continue, in large measure, to be a natural progression of administrative promotion. While expected to continue with the administrative tasks previously described, their assignments take on added importance. For example, the type of administrative matters might include making decisions about the kind of services provided by their respective departments, the monitoring of activities by the various interdepartmental work groups, developing plans to evaluate clinical services, being responsible for setting service objectives, designing and implementing a treatment system, and developing a unit cost financial accountability system. These activities are administrative in orientation.

In summary, there are three management categories that together constitute the management of clinical programs. In each category three basic areas are covered: the primary orientation of workers, the typical job held by persons in each category, and a listing and clarification of the major administrative requirements that go along with each job. This sorting of administrative requirements and relating them to organizational position illustrates the complexity of clinical management and provides the basis for understanding the inherent difficulty in teaching management as a unitary concept. At the same time it lays the foundation for clarifying what program management is all about.

Program Management

The fourth category, therefore, brings together in a cohesive manner what managers of alcoholism programs do, what they are expected to know, and provides a picture of administrative responsibility not ordinarily illustrated in texts. This category is typified most by program administrators, executives (i.e., those directly responsible and most accountable for the entire program). These people are normally responsible to a board of directors or a similar group, and their job consists of relating to a variety of community or constituent groups as well as providing program direction and maintaining internal control.

This category is where the distinction between managing alcoholism programs and managing clinical programs is most evident. An administrator must be concerned with the increasing accountability requirements and complexities of managing alcoholism programs demanded by both funding agencies and the public, and understanding the application of new technologies that may have only an apparently indirect bearing on clinical practice. Indeed, as requirements and knowledge increase in an extremely wide range of administrative areas, more pressure is placed on managers to understand treatment itself and how it is related to the growth of administrative job responsibilities. A possible source of this pressure, particularly as it centers on administrative competence, is important to illustrate.

Administrative practice has changed drastically in a little more than a decade [2, 8]. Administrative competence requires extensive knowledge in an extremely wide range of areas and the ability to apply that knowledge to decision-making action [3, 5]. For example, competence must continually be demonstrated in the processes of internal management, fiscal management, contract development and monitoring, evaluation research, program planning, program development, policy development, treatment modalities, personnel policies, information systems, affirmative action, interorganizational relations, staff development and training, physical design, space requirements, consultation, interdisciplinary collaboration, and working with people representing the broader community (the board, politicians, funders, community groups). Superficial knowledge is inadequate; each area requires a depth of knowledge and understanding rarely required in the administration of alcoholism programs. While not necessary that one become an expert in each area or do everything, a certain level of in-depth sophistication is required to ask even simple questions or, more importantly, to ask questions that are answerable, particularly to such nonclinical staff as accountants, bookkeepers, evaluators, planners, and other specialists.

The concern for treatment in this explosion of administrative knowledge may appear to have been overlooked. There is a certain risk for this situation to occur, and it is one that administrators and those who teach administration must guard against. In essence, in the necessary rush to acquire technical competence one must never lose sight of the program's relationship to human need and client service. One can be seduced quite easily into designing elaborate and technically exquisite information systems or program plans, while not consciously addressing the key question of how they will affect staff and client service. Treatment issues must continue to be a necessary and integral part of the administrative knowledge base [1], as this volume so vividly documents, but with the tremendous amount of new material needed to be learned to survive in the political and funding arena, it is easy to understand a commonly held perception that to study management and administration is to forget about clients.

Administrators learn that a major part of their job lies in being a buffer between agency needs and public demands. This is a constant source of stress and often not resolvable. One example of this problem is in planning issues such as continuity of care and service integration. While these goals may be worthwhile, the issue is that their attainment in alcohol programming is beyond administrative control. Federal and state planners and evaluators simply hold administrators accountable to the goals, and do not become involved in the organizational clashes, political realities, and effects on the client population (i.e., the real world of administrators) [6]. Yet having to respond to both groups is a constant and continual source of stress for administrators.

The increased technical competencies required of present-day administrators is clearly one of the major differences separating those who manage clinical programs from those who manage organizations that offer clinical programs. In a sense, the usual evolution or progression up the management ladder, apparent in the first three categories described, does not easily occur at the administrator level. First, as has been noted, the technical knowledge required for program management is extensive and complicated. There is much to learn that is new and very different from the knowledge needed for managing treatment programs. Basically, none of the other three categories have tasks that adequately prepare administrators for effective program management. Second, the type of management style needed, the manner of dealing with people at this level, and the types of decisions that must be made are also very different.

Some examples explain these two points. In the technical arena an administrator is often faced with problems requiring legal advice, establishing and maintaining billing systems, maintaining a cash flow, deciding whether to purchase or rent equipment, understanding the purpose, conduct, and use of a financial or program audit, allocating resources across diverse work units, having constant access to vital control information, developing and maintaining a network of people external to the organization who can be relied upon for all kinds of support, and taking corrective management action when indicated to keep the organization solvent, among many other situations. While one can never teach or train personnel for these and other contingencies, as new knowledge must be applied on the job to be most effective, it is now possible to provide administrators with basic knowledge for understanding the technical aspects of financial management, evaluation strategies, designing information systems, personnel development, and as Hairston [4] notes, for obtaining data reflecting an organization's position on given issues. But the other three administrative and managerial categories do not adequately prepare one for top management. The learning needs of program management must therefore come from another source.

One is also not well prepared to deal with the types of decisions to be made nor with certain human problems at the top management level. Obviously, supervising employees, insuring that people do their jobs, evaluating worker performance, leading staff meetings, and setting goals and objectives are some of the familiar and transferable tasks previously learned. There are, however, some very important differences.

One such difference lies in the power ascribed to the executive-level positions. An administrator has the responsibility and the authority to make major decisions and is held accountable by all groups (employees, board, clients, interested community groups, regulatory and funding agencies). A decision scrutinized by all these parties inevitably insures high visibility and an inherent probability of criticism by one or more of these groups. An administrator must be prepared for such occurrences.

Another difference is the arena in which decisions must be made. Program administration requires the ability to manage situations where conflict is common. At this level, one must continually negotiate the differences between professional groups and treatment ideologies, between professionals and nonprofessionals, between external pressure groups and internal work groups, between service organizations, and between all components of an organization, including maintenance and clerical personnel, in such normal organizational functions as allocating resources, evaluating programs, selecting services to be offered or cut back, determining program objectives, and distributing the work. Nowhere in managing clinical programs does one deal with these common problems on a regular basis where organizational decisions are routinely required.

Problems posed by program administration are numerous, complex, and often the result of a series of related subproblems. Thus, problems defined at the administrative level are not always the way they appear, as a problem is usually the culmination of a series of smaller and related problems at other organizational levels, which have percolated to top management. Management of these problems involves an analysis of how the problem came to the attention of top management and, in turn, decisions impacting downward must reflect the relative importance of the problem and any related problems of the affected workers. For example, a decision to proceed with program evaluation at the management level requires an understanding of the different problems likely to emerge at all worker levels. As there is an inherent strain in the researcher-practitoner relationship [9], administrators must learn how to minimize potential negative effects arising from their interaction throughout all levels of the organization. Such an approach requires a thoughtful and carefully planned series of related activities targeted at the concerns of workers within the organization.

CONCLUSION

This chapter calls attention to program management and administration as distinguished from managing clinical programs. A typology is presented that identifies the typical jobs performed, their relevant management tasks and concerns, and the knowledge base needed at various organizaional levels. The first three categories incorporate the requirements for managing clinical programs, but do not adequately address the extensiveness of program management. The partialization of management in the four categories should make it abundantly clear that management is an understandable concept practiced by workers at all organizational levels. Moreover, the attention given to partialization makes supervision and training of personnel in this area potentially more effective, as one can target management programs to the needs of specific types of personnel.

In addition, it should be quite clear that program management and administration requires specialized knowledge, skills, and personal resources not normally developed in the usual promotional system in the organizational hierarchy. While certain aspects of top management can be developed at midlevel management positions, program administration is quite distinct, more complicated, and requires different experiential opportunities and learning experiences. The alcoholism field must recognize the distinctness of program management and direct attention to the development of its own administrative competency. Then will it be able to provide for its own direction and leadership, and compete more effectively for funds and the public trust.

REFERENCES

1. Feit, M. D. *Management and Administration of Drug Alcohol Programs*. Charles C Thomas: Springfield, Ill., 1979.
2. Gates, B. *Social Program Administration: The Implementation of Social Policy*. Prentice-Hall: Englewood Cliffs, N.J., 1980.
3. Gross, M., and Jablonsky, S. *Principles of Accounting and Financial Reporting for Nonprofit Organizations*. Wiley: New York, 1979.
4. Hairston, C. F. The nominal group technique in organizational research. *Social Work Res. Abstr.* 15:12–17, 1979.
5. Holosko, M. J., and Feit, M. D. *Workbook for Internal Management*. University of Tennessee Office of Continuing Social Work Education: Knoxville, 1981.
6. Matlins, S. M. Planning: A personal view and some practical considerations. *Ann. Am. Acad. Pol. Soc. Sci.* 417:47, 1975.
7. Schramm, C. J. Development of a successful alcoholism facility. In: *Alcoholism and Its Treatment in Industry*, Schramm, C. J. (ed.). Johns Hopkins: Baltimore, 1977.
8. Slavin, S. (ed.). *Social Administration: The Management of the Social Services*. Haworth Press: New York, 1978.
9. Weiss, C. H. *Evaluation Research*. Prentice-Hall: Englewood Cliffs, N.J., 1972.

EPILOGUE

THE FIELD OF ALCOHOLISM is progressing rapidly. The field is expanding in territory, in sophistication of research, in the detailed depth of inquiry, in the breadth of clinical experience. A mere 20 years ago, both clinical and research interest in alcoholism was in the doldrums. Today, as the contents of this book shows, alcoholism has become a clinical and research "growth industry." Therefore, in this epilogue, we briefly cast a critical eye back on the state of the field as reflected in the material in this book and anticipate important developments for the next decade.

First, the field of alcoholism has obviously burst beyond the boundaries of the clinical problem of "alcoholism" per se. It is the major public health significance of alcohol use that emphasizes the need for alcohol studies. Alcohol is probably the most important drug in our culture. But alcoholism is only one dimension of alcohol studies. The biology of alcohol in human biophysiological systems is an important basic science for the clinical science of alcoholism therapeusis. At the same time, a basic social science of alcohol use and alcohol abuse is emerging, albeit more slowly. We see many social aspects of alcohol use and alcohol abuse that can be neither analyzed nor attacked from the perspective of clinical alcoholism. Thus, it is more precise and accurate to state that the field of alcoholism has been transformed into the field of "alcohol studies." Such a field is comprised of the biology of alcohol, the psychology of alcohol effects, the sociocultural analysis of alcohol use and abuse, and a biopsychosocial clinical science of alcoholism. We anticipate that these distinctive subfields of alcohol studies can and should be identified more clearly, so that "alcohol problems" can be addressed as specific problems of biological, social, or clinical relevance.

Second, with increasing specialization of research, we anticipate an exacerbation of the already existing problem of communication among specialists and specialty fields. We recognize the necessity for technical language and internal precision. At the same time, there is the danger of the development of idiosyncratic assumptions, the pursuit of preciousness of detail with the loss of relevance, and the temptation of reductionistic explanation in terms of one's own field of expertise. The field of alcohol studies has yet to achieve much theoretical or conceptual cohesion that would promote synergistic research. Concept and theory building is an important task before us.

Third, there is a widening gap between the researcher in the laboratory and the clinician in the street. There is an inherent difference in approach between the researcher and the clinician. The researcher must ask tough-minded questions and carefully assay the evidence at hand. The answers provided by research are always tentative. On the other hand, the clinician must act; he or she must make decisions based on limited evidence within limited time. He or she must be decisive. These differences are clearly exemplified in the contrast between the research chapters and the clinical chapters of this book. The research evidence questions much of the current conventional clinical wisdom. Yet the "soft" clinical impressions and the recommendations reflect important experience and the face validity of observation. We suggest that both approaches are meritorious and complement each other. The task before us is to reduce the assumptive disparities between researcher and clinician. The researcher needs to appreciate the limits of experimental design lest the conclusions lead to skeptical nihilism, while the clinician needs to appreciate the limits of personal observation and experience that leads to ideological dogmatism. In the biomedical arena, the multiskilled clinician-researcher has been a successful model, which would well be emulated in the psychosocial arena.

Fourth, the evidence and opinion presented in this volume support and promote a revised definition of alcoholism as a multivariate syndrome. The concept of "alcoholism" has been under vigorous debate for two decades. In numerous chapters we find empirical evidence that clarifies assumptions rather than appealing to polemics. The underlying concepts of alcoholism are important if we proceed further in the development of effective diagnostic tests and measures. We view the current status of a definition of alcoholism as in flux. We would caution against premature closure. We need to pursue operational clarity of definitions of use, abuse, misuse, dependence, and alcoholism. At the same time we need further technical development of diagnostic methodologies for different research and clinical purposes.

Fifth, we note the rapid proliferation of basic biological research on alcohol. This area is moving so rapidly that no brief assessment is tenable. Currently, the state of these investigations are explorations into new territories of cellular and subcellular mechanisms. At the same time, there are promising new directions in the comparative study of alcohol with other addictive drugs that hold promise for finding common metabolic substrates for the general process of physiological tolerance and dependence common to all drugs of abuse.

Sixth, the section on medical aspects of alcoholism reflects major biomedical advances in our understanding of the physical complications of alcohol use. Old medical syndromes are refined and new syndromes and complications have been uncovered. Surely the medical complications of alcoholism are protean. Nevertheless, they reflect end-stage complications in chronic severe alcohol consumption. What is not clear are the physical/medical consequences and complications of different levels of alcohol consumption, with different frequencies, at different life stages. That is, we do not have a clear clinical picture of the dose-effect consequences of alcohol use and the risk levels for physical health involved. Thus we need appropriate clinical epidemiological studies of the various physical health risk factors related to alcohol consumption patterns.

Seventh, despite the fact that the medical complications of alcohol are recognized in health care systems, we are still faced with the widespread problem of nondiagnosis, misdiagnosis, and delayed diagnosis of the clinical behavioral problem of alcoholism, however we construe that diagnosis. The medical complications of alcoholism are identified, but the alcoholic is not diagnosed. That is, the medical complications are treated, but the alcoholism per se is left untreated. This reflects a major health system problem of identification and triage for the problem of alcoholism.

Eighth, the section on psychiatric aspects of alcoholism reflects a major advance in the differentiation of alcoholism as a clinical syndrome from other psychiatric diagnoses and syndromes. This is a salutary distinction for both research and clinical purposes. At the same time, new research reveals important interactional patterns between specific psychiatric syndromes and different types of alcohol problems. Further research on differential diagnosis is most important if we are to advance toward specificity of treatment and the treatment of combined psychiatric/alcohol syndromes of illness.

Ninth, the section on social aspects presents new empirical data on reformulation of the social behaviors associated with different patterns of alcohol use, misuse, and abuse. This is an area that has suffered from a lack of competent research and of substantial research support. But the materials presented offer vistas on the significance of these lines of inquiry. Most importantly, this material emphasizes the necessity to broaden our alcohol studies beyond the medical and clinical arenas. Conversely, this genre of social science studies contributes a major corrective to conventional clinical thinking that might reduce all problems of alcohol use to merely alcoholism.

Tenth, the social science section, the treatment facilities section, and the materials on treatment organization raise important issues about social and health system structure and function. To date, problems of alcohol have been separated from other social and clinical problems. Separate alcohol service systems have been erected. The pertinent materials in this book raise searching questions about the dysfunction of constructing isolated alcoholism service systems. Alcohol-related problems cross the boundaries of legal, welfare, health, and political systems. In historical perspective, we believe it has been necessary and valuable to promote alcoholism service systems as a separate entity. At the same time, we have evidence to demonstrate the confusion, inefficiency, and contradictory consequences of a separate system. Therefore, we see a major challenge to health and social system organizers to address new organizational systems for the delivery of alcohol-related services.

Eleventh, the sections on treatment methods, treatment personnel, and treatment facilities illustrate the fragmented status of the treatment field. Ideological factors still influence specific and general aspects of treatment. We do not believe that the evidence supports the prospect for one type or method of treatment, nor will any one facility afford all the resources for all types of necessary alcohol-related interventions. We view the last section of the book on treatment systems as only a modest initial proposal toward a necessary integration and synthesis of treatment.

Finally, although we have attempted to be comprehensive, we have not been exhaustive. The topic list in alcohol studies grows daily, as witness the regular literature citation sections of the *Journal of Alcohol Studies*. We do not believe it feasible to attempt to compile books that can contain all pertinent aspects of alcohol studies. Rather, we believe that there will be an increasing need for synthesis and integration of pertinent and relevant data that contribute to the growth of the field of alcohol studies as a whole. It is our hope that this volume makes a substantial contribution in this direction.

E. Mansell Pattison, MD
Edward Kaufman, MD

INDEX

Abstinence, 560
Acetaldehyde, 86, 142, 228
Acetaldehyde reactions, 845
Administration, 1211
Adolescents, 759, 769, 892, 987
   Youth Network Council, 762
Adrenal cortex, 315
Aftercare, 873, 880, 1199
Aged, the 779
Alcohol-disulfiram reaction. See Disulfiram-ethanol reaction (DER)
Alcoholics Anonymous. See Self-help groups
Alcoholism counselors, 804, 832
   See also Counselors
Alcoholism outpatient treatment, 885
Alcoholism rehabilitation center, 865
Alcohol metabolism, 83
Alcohol withdrawal, 47, 147, 177, 356, 601, 749, 838, 839
   alcohol idiosyncratic intoxication, 844
   delirium tremens, 147, 151, 840
   detoxification, 669
   early minor withdrawal, 151
   hallucinosis, 638, 844
   late major withdrawal, 151
   protracted alcohol withdrawal reaction, 152
   "rum fits," 1072
   trauma, 1074
Amino acids, 95, 251
Anesthesia, 343, 350
Antabuse. See Drugs
Appetite, 256
Arousal, 256
Association of Halfway House Alcoholism Programs (AHHAP), 908
Attitudes, 795, 802, 831
Autonomic nervous system, 199, 201
Autonomic peripheral nerves, 687
Aversion conditioning hospitals, 874

Aversion therapies, 563
   aversion conditioning, 854, 874, 1055
   chemical aversion conditioning, 1056, 1171
   electrical aversive conditioning, 1055, 1173
   emetine aversion, 875
   faradic aversion therapy, 878

Beginning Alcohol Basic Education Studies (BABES), 765
Behavioral theories and therapies
   behavioral psychology, 560, 1170, 1183
   behavioral therapies, 889, 1054, 1140
   behavior analysis, 540
   behavior modification, 651, 854
      See also Cognition
   broad-spectrum behavioral approaches, 1185
   classical conditioning, 562
   cognitive social learning, 560, 569
   contingency contracting, 1181
   contingency management, 1056, 1062
   covert sensitization, 1175
   Hullian learning theory, 565
   operant learning, 566–568, 1054
   progressive relaxation, 1179
   role theory, 723
   social learning, 1054
   social skills training, 1177
   systematic desensitization, 1179
Biologically active substances. See Vitamins, minerals, hormones, enzymes, and related biologically active substances
Biological tests
   amylase test, 236
   computed tomography, 168
   dexamethasone suppression test (DST), 312, 315
   liver biopsy test, 229
   liver enzymes test, 229
   neuropsychological testing, 169
   radionuclide scanning test, 229

1226 Index

Biological tests *(continued)*
  Sudan III test, 237
    See also Blood alcohol levels (BAL) and consumption measurements
Blood, 281
Blood alcohol levels (BAL) and consumption measurements
  blood alcohol concentration, 355, 390, 395
  blood alcohol level (BAL), 313, 687, 688, 690–691, 838
  blood alcohol level discrimination, 64, 1058
  QFV measurements, 72
  urine alcohol concentrations (UAC), 386
Bone marrow, 283
Brain-neurotransmitter receptor effector coupling effects, 107
Breathalyzer, 65
  See also Blood alcohol levels (BAL) and consumption measurements

Calorie, 257
Cardiac function, 335
Cardiac lipids, 334
Cardiac metabolism, 334
Cardiac morphology, 335
Cardiovascular system, 332
Central nervous system, 304
Cerebral blood flow, 169
Children, 529, 530, 663, 665, 673, 759, 772
  See also Marriage and family; Reproduction; Women
Christian missions, 896
Cigarette smoking, 264, 276, 308, 352
Cognition, 544, 1183
Cognitive behavioral therapies, 889
Community, 1062, 1182
  community human service agencies, 821, 894, 923, 994, 1076, 1114
  community mental health centers, 886
  community resource, 898
  environmental resources, 1130
Confabulation, 173
Cough, 325
Counselors, 1078
  counselor credentialing, 814
  paraprofessionals, 802, 810
  recovered alcoholic counselors, 810
Criminal and legal issues
  crime, sexual, 692
  crime, violent, 383, 389, 429, 647, 938
  criminal behavior, 411, 697
  criminal intent, 407
  criminality, 383, 429, 583, 647, 923, 926, 938
  criminal responsibility, 406
  Jackie C. Parker v. *The State of Maryland,* 412
  legal issues, 4, 287, 406, 795, 938, 1077
  legal prohibition, 437, 459
  police court system, 938
  Powell v. *Texas,* 412
  Robinson v. *California,* 410

Definitions and concepts of alcoholism, 17, 31, 40, 358, 367, 369, 443, 453, 459, 483, 492, 529, 769, 795, 875, 887, 925, 965, 1140, 1197, 1198
  abstinence violation effect (AVE), 574
  acquisition of drinking behavior, 569
  addiction, 9
  alcoholism syndrome, 3
  classification, 607
  cognitive-behavioral model, 573
  disease, 409
  drinking problems, 430
  high-risk drinking, 575
  multivariate alcoholism syndrome, 22
  risk population, 426
Dependence
  physical dependence, 9
  psychic dependence, 9
Detoxification, 889, 1068, 1069, 1076, 1204
  detoxification center, 859, 942
Diagnosis of alcoholism, 4, 31, 35, 40, 55, 64, 147, 435, 483, 520, 618, 640–641, 648, 693, 745, 779, 795, 830, 875, 887, 925, 1068, 1080, 1097, 1140, 1197
  binary diagnosis, 12
  differential diagnosis, 1163
  Diagnostic and Statistical Manual of the American Psychiatric Association (DSM-III), 19, 40, 632, 935
  Jellinek classification, 17
  multiple substance abuse, 743
  multivariate diagnosis, 13
  multivariate syndrome, 1089
  National Council on Alcoholism Diagnostic Criteria (NCA classification), 19
  primary alcoholic, 584
  secondary alcoholic, 584
  World Health Organization classification, 18
Dial-A-Message, 822
Diet, 1070
Digestion, 256
Disulfiram. *See* Drugs
Disulfiram-ethanol reaction (DER), 845, 1033, 1039
Divorce. *See* Marriage and family
Driving. *See* Highway and traffic
Dropout rate, 936
Drugs, 696, 761, 780
  amphetamines, 697, 698
  antianxiety agents, 1045
  antidepressants, 698, 1045
  antihistamines, 158
  barbiturates, 159
  benzodiazepines, 158, 159, 697, 849, 1071
  beta-blockers, 161
  bromureides, 698
  calcium carbimide, 1041
  chlormethiazole, 161
  deterrent drugs, 1033
  diazepam, 699
  disulfiram, 305, 308, 854, 860, 1033, 1045
  drug classifications, 752
  drug therapy, 652, 889, 1043
  ethylene glycol, 363
  haloperidol, 1071
  heroin, 699
  hormonal therapy, 323
  lithium, 162, 624, 1049, 1072
  lysergic acid diethylamide (LSD), 1051
  major tranquilizers, 1050
  marijuana, 697, 702
  methadone, 700
  methaqualone, 699
  minor tranquilizers, 1045, 1070
  multivitamins, 1070
  naloxone, 843
  narcotics, 698
  neuroleptic drugs, 641
  neuropharmacologic agents, 118
  opiates, 698
  paraldehyde, 162, 1071
  pharmacotherapy, 156, 842
  phenothiazines, 162
  phenytoin, 164
  polydrugs, 701
  propranolol, 363, 1214
  psychotropic drugs, 789
  sedatives and hypnotics, 697, 698, 1045

Index 1227

tranquilizers, 698

Economics, 415, 506, 886
  advertising, 421
  alcohol consumption, 415
  alcohol control, 415, 422–423
  econometric studies, 417
  "price elasticity," 416
  production and trade, 420
  taxation, 423
Education, 402, 436, 462, 468, 473, 762, 860, 871, 1031, 1109
Emergency room, 837, 1077
Emergency services, 1198, 1203
Emotion, 545
Enzymes. *See* Vitamins, minerals, hormones, enzymes, and related biologically active substances
Epidemiology and demography, 426, 441, 472, 505, 533, 656, 673–674, 710, 737, 760–762, 771, 780–782, 829, 852, 898–901, 947, 1109–1111, 1197
  community epidemiology, 1109
  community surveys, 1113
  drug and alcohol populations, 742
  high-risk groups, 460
  Jellinek formula, 445, 1112
  population surveys, 449
  prevalence rates, 1197
  sociodemography, 1121
Esophagus, 247
Evaluation, 918, 972, 1120, 1197

Factor analytic approach, 525
Federation of Alcoholic Rehabilitation Establishments (FARE), 908
Female alcoholics, 586
  See also Marriage and family; Women
Female reproduction, 296
Feminine hair pattern, 277
Fetal alcohol syndrome, 302
Fetus, 301
Fixed-interval drinking decisions, 1181
Follow-up, 889
Free-standing alcoholism clinics, 887

Gastrointestinal tract, 225, 245
Gay Alcoholics Anonymous. *See* Self-help groups
General hospitals, 828, 886
Genetics, 135, 623, 632, 638, 721, 761

Halfway houses, 854, 895, 907
Hematopoietic system, 281
Hemostasis, 289
Hepatotoxicity, 226
Highway and traffic
  automobile accidents, 343
  driving, 780
  highway safety, 395
  National Highway Safety Administration (NHISA), 478
  traffic safety, 779, 926
Holding units, 846
Homosexual, 690, 736
Hormones. *See* Vitamins, minerals, hormones, enzymes, and related biologically active substances
Hospitalization, 345
Hospitals, 782, 828, 848, 885, 1077, 1197
Hospital treatment, 858
"Hostel," 907
Hypnosis, 889

Infectious diseases, 263

Information, 402, 468, 474, 487, 762
  Alliance Information and Referral Service (AIRS), 821
  information and referral centers, 821
Intestinal absorption, 251
Intoxication, 838

Joint Commission on Accreditation of Hospitals, 1198

Korsakoff's Syndrome, 59
  See also Wernicke-Korsakoff Syndrome

Legal. *See* Criminal and legal issues
Leydig cell, 295, 320
Liver dysfunction, 196, 225, 326

Macrocytosis, 281
Male gonads and hormones, 294
Malnutrition, 225
Marriage and family
  divorce, 535
  family, 136, 530, 638, 663, 673, 718, 722, 759, 779, 870, 885, 987, 1022, 1062
  family history, 659
  marital and family therapy, 860
  marriage, 663, 673, 691, 759, 987
Maternal-placental-fetal system, 303
Measurement, 72
Medical illnesses
  abdominal pain, 347
  alcoholic cardiomyopathy, 336
  alcoholic coma, 1069
  alcoholic polyneuropathy, 194
  anhidrosis, 199
  anorexia, 256
  aspiration pneumonia, 266, 327
  bacterial peritonitis, 271
  bacterial pneumonia, 328
  beriberi, 1072
  bone disease, 260
  brain damage, 551
  bronchiectasis, 325
  cancer, 101, 349
  carcinoma, 329
  cardiac arrythmias, 201, 338
  cardiomyopathy, 260
  central pontive myelinosis, 174
  cerebral vascular accident, 340
  chronic neuropsychiatric disorders, 167
  chronic pancreatic insufficiency, 229
  cirrhosis, 226, 230, 830
  coronary artery disease, 338
  deficiency amblyopia, 175
  diabetes mellitus, 229
  dysphagia, 201
  dysphonia, 201
  episodic sleep disorders, 190
  facial dysmorphology, 302
  facial edema, 276
  fat emboli, 221
  fatty liver, 229
  fetal malformations, 297
  focal compressive neuropathies, 199
  fractures, 215, 345
  gastrointestinal bleeding, 247, 348
  gastrointestinal malabsorption, 196
  glossitis, 277
  gynecomastia, 277, 318
  head injury, 344
  hematologic disorders, 1073
  hemolytic anemia, 287
  hemophilus influenzae pneumonia, 267
  hepatic disease, 177
  hepatic encephalopathies, 175

Index

Medical illnesses (continued)
  hepatitis, 229
  hyperestrogenism, 314
  hyperlipemia, 221
  hypersomnolence, 189
  hypertension, 340, 362
  hypoandrogenism, 314
  hypogonadism, 320
  hypokalemia, 1073
  hypomagnesemia, 1073
  hypothermia, 199
  infection, 326
  infectious disorders, 1074
  infertility, 247
  insomnia, 188
  intestinal injury, 345
  Klebsiella pneumonia, 268
  Legionnaire's disease, 269
  limb compression syndrome, 217
  lung abscess, 266, 328
  malabsorption syndrome, 256
  Mallory-Weiss Syndrome, 247
  malnutrition, 255
  Marchiafava-Bignamini disease, 175
  megaloblastic anemia, 285, 1072
  megaloblastosis, 283
  menstrual disorder, 297
  metabolic alkalosis, 1073
  miscarriages, 297
  myopathy, 204
  neurological abnormality, 302
  nontraumatic idiopathic osteonecrosis of the femoral head, 219
  nutritional deficiency, 177, 195
  orthopedic problems (extremities), 344
  orthostatic hypotension, 199
  osteopenia, 218
  pancreatic ascites, 239
  pancreatitis, 231, 830
  pellegra, 174, 257, 258, 278, 1072
  peptic ulcer, 830
  peripheral neuropathy, 194
  pigmentation, 276
  Pneumococcal pneumonia, 265
  porphyria cutanea tarda, 279
  pruritus, 277
  pseudocysts, 239
  pulmonary hypertension, 329
  pulmonary tuberculosis, 269
  respiratory depression, 1069
  rosacea, 276
  scurvy, 257, 258, 1072
  seizures, 163, 176
  serum amylase, 348
  sideroblastic anemia, 286
  sideroblasts, 284
  skin disorders, 275
  skin flushing, 276
  spider nevi, 277
  steatorrhea, 249
  thiamine deficiency, 173
  tuberculosis, 329
  tuberculosis peritonitis, 272
  ulcero-osteolytic neuropathy, 278
  vitamin deficiencies, 195, 1072
  Wernicke-Korsakoff Syndrome, 59, 167
  "wine sores," 349
  zinc deficiency, 279
Membrane-receptor effects, 106
Mental hospitals, 831, 848
Methanol, 363
Mineral metabolism, 334
Minerals. See Vitamins, minerals, hormones, enzymes, and related biologically active substances
Motivation, 763
Mucociliary stream, 325
Muscle, 204, 260, 1073

National Association of Alcoholism Counselors, 804
Neuronal membranes, 148
Neurotransmitters, 91
Nicotine, 305
Nocturnal penile tumescence (NPT), 692
Nonalcoholic, 525
Nucleic acid metabolism, 98
Nutrition, 210, 249, 264, 305, 979, 1070

Outcome, 853, 901, 969, 980, 1120
  outcome, women, 727
Outpatient, 1205
Overdose, 838

Pancreas, 225, 231
Pentothal interview, 879
Perception, 542
Perinatal effects, 100
Peripheral and autonomic nervous system, 194
Peripheral circulation, 339
Personality, 371, 383, 500, 522–523, 581, 583, 585, 600, 649, 697, 1000
Phagocytosis, 325
Pharmacokinetics, 141
Pharmacology, 354
Pregnant uterus, 298
President's Commission on Law Enforcement and Administration of Justice, 939–940
Prevention, 307, 403, 415, 436, 454–455, 458, 468, 483, 491, 776, 1109
  Anstil's Law of Safe Drinking, 485
  healthy drinking, 483
  normal drinking, 374
  women (prevention), 731
Private practitioner's office, 886
Private psychiatric hospitals, 849, 856
Professionals, 795, 834
Prohibition, 464
Protein metabolism, 98
Psychiatric diagnoses
  affective disorder, 586, 618, 721
    bipolar, 619
    unipolar, 620
  alcoholic dementia, 167
  anxiety, 590, 639, 687, 1014
  borderline syndrome, 591, 628
  character disorders, 607
  depression, 584, 586, 618, 636, 655
  "depression spectrum disease," 587
  Feighner criteria, 649
  hyperactive child syndrome, 648
  mood disorder, 618
  narcissistic character, 610, 632
  neuroses, 630
  neurotic behavior, 581, 598
  oral character traits, 610
  organic mental disorders, 787
  passive-dependent, 612
  presenile dementia, 362
  psychopathology, 581, 786
  psychosis, 629
  psychosomatic diseases, 609
  schizophrenia, 629, 636
  sociopathy, 390, 583, 584, 594, 647
  suicide, 59, 655
Psychiatric hospital, 848
Psychological tests and measurements

Index

Adolescent Alcohol Involvement Scale, 773
Alcadd Test, 58
Alcohol Abuse Scale, 838
Alcohol-Use Inventory (AUI), 934
American Law Institute (ALI) tests, 407
Attitude Toward Alcoholic Persons Scale, 799
Barron Ego-Strength Scale, 1013
Breathalyzer tests, 65
Brief Michigan Alcohol Screening Test (BMAST), 21
Buss-Durkee Inventory, 59
Cattell's 16 PF, 932
causal pathway analysis, 1091
Chassell Inventory, 523
Clinical Institute Withdrawal Assessment for Alcohol (CIWA-A), 155
Community-Oriented Programs Environment Scale (COPES), 1126
consumption measures, 72
Definition of Alcohol Scale, 58
Dogmatism Scale, 1015
Edwards Personal Preference Schedule, 521
Eysenck Personality Inventory, 57, 521, 932
Fixed Interval Drinking Decision (FIDD) test, 1057
Halstead-Reitan Battery (HRB), 169
Human Service Scale (HSS), 933
Iowa Alcoholic Stages Index, 443
MacAndrews Alcoholism Scale, 58, 585
Marcus' Alcohol Questionnaire, 799
Michigan Alcoholism Screening Test (MAST), 58, 857
Minnesota Multiphasic Personality Inventory (MMPI), 56, 57–58, 519, 584–585, 639, 675, 932, 980
MODCRIT II test, 21
multivariate scales, 1090
neuropsychological measures, 105, 550
personality research form, 521
projective tests, 520
psychological screening inventory, 675
psychological testing, 55, 517
psychometric tests, 521
Q-sort, 980, 1016
Quantity Frequency-Variability Index, 58
See also Blood alcohol levels (BAL) and consumption measurements
Rorschach Inkblot Test, 519
Schedule for Affective Disorders and Schizophrenia—Life Time Version (SADS-L), 934
Sixteen Personality Factor Questionnaire, 524. *See also* Psychological tests and measurements, Cattell's 16 PF
Spare Time Activity Questionnaire, 56
Synonym Learning Test, 56, 57
ten-question drinking history, 308
Thematic Apperception Test, 1014
Total Severity Assessment Scale of Withdrawal, 154
Wechsler Adult Intelligence Scale (WAIS), 169
Wisconsin Card Sorting Test, 169
Psychophysiology, 554
Psychosocial, 790
Psychotherapy and psychodynamics
activity groups, 1019
affect, 608, 633
regulation, 590
aggression, 383
alexithymia, 614
anger, 602
anhedonia, 615
community meetings, 1019
countertransference, 598, 1016
couples therapy, 1005
denial, 1014
dependency, 722
didactic lectures, 854
education groups, 1019
ego-ideal, 592
ego structures, 589
family therapy, 854, 1006, 1020, 1022
group psychotherapy, 1004, 1011
group therapy, 871, 889, 958, 980, 987
guilt, 601
hyposymbolization, 614
individual and group psychotherapy, 854
individual therapy, 1003
influence of expectancies, 570
instinctual drives, 581
interpretation, 1030
issues of perceived control and self-efficacy, 572
marking boundaries, 1031
motivation, 547, 999
network therapy, 1022
obsessive, 600
obsessive-compulsive, 1000
outpatient psychotherapy, 1161
paradox, 1029
psychodrama, 1007
psychodynamics, 960, 1000
psychotherapeutic, 784
psychotherapy, 889, 999, 1152
reenactment, 1030
regression, 593, 602
self-care, 589
self-esteem, 1000
self-structures, 591
social skill deficits, 571
structural methods, 1028
superego, 608, 1000
support systems, 987, 1022
therapeutic contract, 1017, 1028
transferrence, 599
unconscious symbolic meaning of alcohol, 582
verbal therapy, 651
wet systems, 1018, 1025–1026
Public drunkenness, 938
Public intoxication, 938

Recovered alcoholic counselors. *See* Self-help groups
Referral, 822, 994, 1083
rehabilitation, 868, 930
reinforcement, 549
Reproduction, 293, 689, 724
Respiratory system, 263, 325
Revolving door syndrome, 938, 950
See also Skid Row
Role theory and labeling
labeling roles, 6
role theory, 376
social labeling, 372

Salvation Army, 896, 899
Self-care, 614
Self-help groups
Al-Anon, 891, 987
Alateen, 891, 987
Alcoholics Anonymous, 435, 702, 739, 796, 802, 810, 854, 860, 866, 889, 891, 955, 979, 987, 999, 1001, 1020
Alcoholics Together (AT), 739
Gay Alcoholics Anonymous, 739
Narcotics Anonymous, 702
Pill Heads Anonymous, 702
Sexual dysfunction, 686
Sexuality, 724
Shelter facilities, 894

1230 Index

Skeletal system, 215
Skid Row, 657, 894, 903, 946
Skin, 260
Sleep, 180
Small intestine, 249
Sobering-up stations, 942
Social drinkers, 66
Social learning theory, 680
Social service centers, 896
Sociocultural
  culture, 503, 510
  deviance, 370
  ethnicity, 141, 426, 657, 658–660, 698, 709, 829, 959, 1109, 1117
  morality, 491, 494
  social cost, 886
  social functioning, 886
  social perceptions, 493
  social policy, 490, 956
  social problems, 765, 784, 923
  sociocultural variants, 426, 441, 458, 1109
  sociology, 369
Spermatogenesis, 294
Stomach, 247
Stress, 720, 787, 1129
Surgery, 215, 240, 343, 345
Systems theory, 678, 698, 833, 1022

Thyroid function, 316
Tolerance, 47, 69, 88, 359
  craving, 560, 563
  cross tolerance, 359
  habituation, 9
  loss of control, 560
Trauma, 343
Treatment, 713, 742, 867, 1089, 1152
  amount, 1155
  assessment, 933
  behavioral assessment and treatment, 561
  block variables, 1099
  differential treatment, 1140
  drinking outcome rates, 1154
  pathway model, 1095
  treatment involvement, 1160
  treatment outcome, 880
  treatment planning, 1163

Urine flow, 322

Vitamins, minerals, hormones, enzymes, and related biologically active substances
  acetaldehyde dehydrogenase, 86
  acetylcholine, 94
  alcohol dehydrogenase (ADH), 85, 246, 294, 363
  aldehyde dehydrogenase, 363, 1033
  amino acids, 95, 251
  ascorbic acid, 261
  calcium, 210, 211, 253
  carbohydrates, 250
  corticosteroid-binding globulin, 315
  creatine phosphokinase, 212
  cyclic nucleotides, 97, 109
  disaccharidases, 250
  dopamine, 94
  D-xylose, 252
  endocrine disturbances, 311
  endorphins, 96
  enkephalins, 96
  enzymes, 85
    intestinal transport, enzymes involved in, 251
    microsomal, 251
    muscle, 208
    testicular, 296
  estradiol, 321
  estrogen, 321
  folate, 252, 256, 258–259, 285, 288
  folic acid, 264
  hormones
    antidiuretic (ADH), 298
    follicle-stimulating (FSH), 295
    growth (GH), 295, 317
    luteinizing (LH), 295
    thyroid-stimulating (TSH), 295
  human chorionic gonadotropin (HCG), 295, 320
  hypothalamic-pituitary-adrenocortical activity (HYPAC), 311
  immunoglobulins, 265
  iron, 253, 261, 287
  lipids, 250
  magnesium, 206, 259, 261
  magnesium, 206, 259, 261
  male gonads and hormones, 294
  morphinelike alkaloids, 87
  Na$^+$, K$^+$-ATPase, 91, 209
  norepinephrine, 92
  oxytocin, 298
  peptides, 96
  peptidyl opiates, 114
  phosphorus, 205
  potassium, 207
  prolactin (PRL), 295, 318
  proteins, 98, 261
  pyridoxine, 208, 259
  serotonin, 94
  sex steroid-binding globulin, 321
  sex steroids, 319
  testicular steroidogenesis, 296
  testosterone, 295
  tetrahydroisoquinolines (TIQs), 111
  thiamine, 195, 256, 352, 1072
  T-lymphocytes, 285
  transferrin, 261
  vasopressin, 322
  vitamins
    A, 261, 294
    B, 256
    B$_6$, 261
    B$_{12}$, 253, 261, 264, 286
    D, 253
  zinc, 256, 259, 261, 294
Voluntary intoxication, 407

Water diuresis, 322
Water and sodium transport, 251
Wernicke-Korsakoff Syndrome (WKS), 168, 171–174, 257–258, 1072
Women, 650, 656, 673, 686, 689, 718, 825, 892, 899, 987
  See also Children; Marriage and family; Reproduction
Work and industry
  employee-assistance programs, 962
  employer, 870
  industry, 1211
  jobs, 954
  work, 779
World Health Organization (WHO), 410